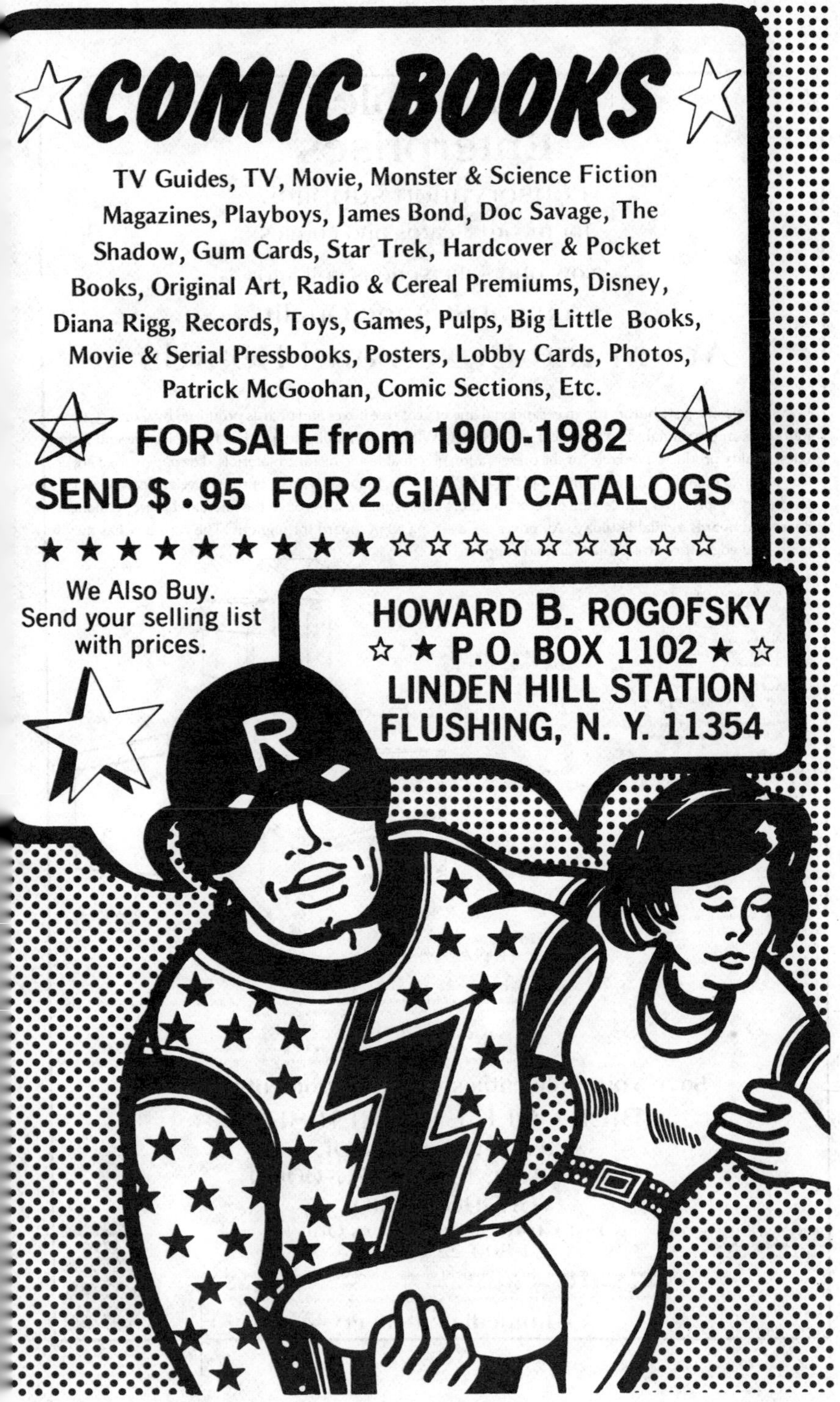

The Comic Book PRICE GUIDE™ 1982-1983

12th Edition

BOOKS FROM 1900—PRESENT INCLUDED

CATALOGUE & EVALUATION GUIDE—ILLUSTRATED

By

Robert M. Overstreet

SPECIAL CONTRIBUTORS TO THIS EDITION

Jerry DeFuccio, Tim Hessee, Ernst W. Gerber, & Dr. Richard D. Smith

SPECIAL ADVISORS TO THIS EDITION

****Bruce Hamilton *Hugh O'Kennon *Ron Pussell *Herb McCaulla***

****Dave Smith *John Snyder *Terry Stroud *Jon Warren***

Published and distributed to the collectors market by Overstreet Publications, Inc., 780 Hunt Cliff Dr. N.W., Cleveland, TN 37311.

Distributed to the book trade by Crown Publishers, Inc., One Park Avenue, New York, N.Y. 10016.

ISBN: 0-517-543494
ISSN: 0730-2916

12th Edition

TABLE OF CONTENTS

ACKNOWLEDGEMENTS

Larry Bigman (Frazetta-Williamson data); Glenn Bray (Kurtzman data); Cat Yronwode (Spirit data); Richard Olson (LOA data); Gary Carter (DC data); J. B. Clifford Jr. (E. C. data); Gary Coddington (Superman data); Wilt Conine (Fawcett data); Dr. S. M. Davidson (Cupples & Leon data); Al Dellinges (Kubert data); Kim Weston (Disney and Barks data); Kevin Hancer (Tarzan data); Charles Heffelfinger and Jim Ivey (March of Comics listing); Grant Irwin (Quality data); Fred Nardelli (Frazetta data); Mike Nolan (MLJ, Timely, Nedor data); George Olshevsky (Timely data); Richard Kravitz (Kelly data); Frank Scigliano (Little Lulu data); Gene Seger (Buck Rogers data); Rick Sloane (Archie data); David R. Smith, Archivist, Walt Disney Productions (Disney data); Don and Maggie Thompson (Four Color listing); Mike Tiefenbacher, Jerry Sinkovec, and Richard Yudkin (Atlas and National data); Tom Bocci (Classic Comics data); Raymond True (Classic Comics data); Greg Robertson (National data); Jim Vadeboncoeur Jr. (Williamson and Atlas data); Andrew Zerbe and Gary Behymer (M. E. data); Ron Pussell (Seduction and Parade of Pleasure data).

My appreciation must also be extended to Dan Hering, L. B. Cole, John Snyder, Steve Geppi, Bruce Hamilton, Jon Warren, Bob Cook, and Philip Levine who loaned material for photographing and especially to Hugh and Louise O'Kennon who again spent a weekend helping me photograph their stock. Special acknowledgement is also given to Ron Pussell, Scott Pell, David Stallman, James Kovacs, Tom Struck, Garth Wood, Jerry Sinkovec, Mike Tiefenbacher and Philip Levine for submitting an unusual amount of corrective data; to Dr. Richard Olson for rewriting grading definitions; to Larry Breed for his suggestions on re-organizing the introductory section; to Jim Sands for re-organizing the Classics section; to Terry Stroud, Hugh O'Kennon, Jon Warren, Dave Smith, John Knight, Rod Dyke, John Snyder, Roy Bonario, Gary Carter, Bill Cole, Rick Sloane, Jerry Wiest, Herb McCaulla, Steve Geppi, Joe Ferrara, & Ron Pussell, (pricing); to Tom Inge for his "Chronology of the American Comic Book;" to Jerry DeFuccio for his exclusive feature on Norman Mingo; to Norman Mingo for his outstanding cover art; to Tim Hessee for his article on "Pop Hollinger;" to L. B. Cole, E. B. Boatner, Carl and Gare Barks, and Jerry DeFuccio for their counsel and help; to Bill Spicer and Zetta DeVoe (Western Publishing Co.) for their contribution of data; and especially to Bill for his kind permission to reprint portions of his and Jerry Bails' **America's Four Color Pastime**; to Robert Crestohl for his statistical compilation; and to Walter Presswood and Dave Noah for their help in editing this volume.

I will always be indebted to Jerry Bails, Landon Chesney, and Larry Bigman whose advice and concern have helped in making **The Comic Book Price Guide** a reality; to my wife, Martha, for her encouragement and help in putting this reference work together; and to everyone who placed ads in this edition.

Acknowledgement is also due to the following people who have so generously contributed much needed data for this edition:

Lawrence Abbott
Perry Albert
Frank J. Alexander, Jr.
Jeffrey Allen
Jim Allen
Glenn Anzalone
Alfred Arruda
Bob Barrett
Robert Beerbohm
Jon Bennett
Dan Bernstein
Andre' Blaylock
Lee Boyett
Mike Brandon
Larry Breed
Steve & Janis Brewster
Chris Brown
Dave Browne
Peter Browne
Jeff Brubaker
John L. Bryant, Jr.
Fred L. Buza
Errett Callahan
Phillip B. Carpenter
Jim Carper
Jeff Carr
Barry A. Carter
Tony Ciccarello
Richard T. Clark
Dr. Alton B. Coalter, Jr.
Joe Cogliano II
Elwood Collier
Rich Collofello
Pat Comissiong
Jon A. Cornell
Robert Cowden

Dan Crawford
Phil Crowson
Lee H. DeBroff
Norman Delindis
Joe Desris
Michael Dice
David Dison
Gary Dunaier
Rick Durell
Byron Erickson
Bruce Ernst
George Evans
John & Jason Evans
Jon Reed Evans
Bob Farrington
Alan Fonseca
Andy Freedman
Jim Furfferi
Dana Gabbard
Steve Gans
John Garbarino
Derek Gardner
Paul Gilbert
Ken Gordon
Max Gottfried
Leonard P. Gray
Mike Grecco
Jack H. Green
Wallace I. Green
Todd Greenberg
Scott Gunter
Terry Hamilton
Dave Harazim
David G. Harper
Stephen B. Harrell
Wallace Harrington
Marty Hay
Steve Haynie
Charles Heffelfinger
Jerry Helms
Peter R. Herstedt
Roger Hill
Jason Hoelscher
Robert Ianno
Paul Jacobson
Scott Jehlik
Dennis Jellum
Mark Johnson
Terry Julian
Stephen B. Keisman
Mark Kirkpatrick

Richard Kiscaden
David L. Klees
Joe Koopmans
Steve Lambey
Robert Lipps
Peter MacDonald
Scott MacKenzie
Jack Mallette
Dominick Mandarino
Ruben Marcelo
Greg Marcopoulos
Edward R. Marcus
Marlen L. Martin
Wayne Mathieu
Michael McCarthy
Jack McGonigle
John McLaughlin
Chris Melancon
Jeff Melius
Jonathan A. Merrill
Joseph Metz
W. T. (Butch) Michaelson
Paul Mickelson
Wayne Mills
Ron Misenhimer
Ken Mitchell
Daniel Moak
Pete Morisi
Bill Morse
Alan Mullins
Wayne Mullins
Arthur Murphy
Patrick O'Connor
A. E. Oestreich, M.D.
Dick Olsen
Jackie Olson
Christopher Orlando
Levi N. Parry
Kenny Partridge
Stephen C. Passarelli
Scott Pell
Clarke M. Peterson
Dennis Petilli
Paul R. Petterson
Michael Allen Pincus
Dave Pinkerton
Ward Prentice
David Puckett
Hec Rambla
Michael Redman

David Reid
Michael Rhode
Robert M. Ricci
Farrell Riley
Mike Robertson
Douglas V. Rose
Tom Ruzza
J. R. Sams
Tony Santangelo
Joe Sarno
Warren F. Scadina
Derek Schlum
William K. Schoch
Steven Scholten
James A. Schut
Randall W. Scott
Daniel Searfoss
Michael Richard Seher
Rickey Shanklin
Kurt Shaw
Danny Sizemore
Scott Smith
Ben Stathart
Jason Stenklyft
Dan Stevenson
Roger Stewart
Chris Strear
Klaus Strzyz
George M. Suarez
William Sumlin III
Ed Summer
Steve Sundahl
Steven Swenson
Jim Thomas
Joseph A. Thompson
Sue Thompson
Douglas S. Thorson
Greg Vander Houwen
Bernie Velleman
Mike Wahl
Alan Walker
Jeff Walker
Curt Watrouse
Jay Wells
Kip Williams
John Wilson
Stan Wong
Dan Wright
R. Yudkin
Mark Zimmerman

PREFACE

Comic book values listed in this reference work were recorded from convention sales, dealers' lists, adzines, and by special contact with dealers and collectors from coast to coast. Prices paid for rare comics vary considerably from one locale to another. We have attempted to list a realistic average between the lowest and highest range observed. The reader should keep in mind that the prices listed only reflect the market just prior to publication. Any new trends that have developed since the preparation of this book would not be shown.

The values listed are reports, not estimates. Each new edition of the guide is actually an average report of sales that occurred during the year; not an estimate of what we feel the books will be bringing next year. Even though many prices listed will remain current throughout the year, the wise user of this book would keep abreast of current market trends to get the fullest potential out of his invested dollar.

By the same token, many of the scarcer books are seldom offered for sale in top condition. This makes it difficult to arrive at a realistic market value. Some of the issues in this category are: Action No. 1, All-American No. 16, Batman No. 1, Black and White No. 20, Captain America No. 1, Captain Marvel No. 1, Detective No. 27, Double Action No. 1, the No-Number Feature Books, Green Giant No. 1, March of Comics No. 4, Marvel No. 1, More Fun No. 52, Motion Picture Funnies Weekly No. 1, Silver Streak No. 6, Superman No. 1, Tough Kid Squad No. 1, Whiz No. 2 (No. 1), Wonder No. 1, Amazing Man No. 5, and Wow No. 1.

Some rare comics were published in a complete black and white format; i.e., All-New No. 15, Blood Is the Harvest, Boy Explorers No. 2, Eerie No. 1, Flash Gordon No. 5, If the Devil Would Talk, Is This Tomorrow, and Stuntman No. 3. As we have learned in the case of Eerie No. 1, the collector or investor in these books would be well advised to give due consideration to the possibility of counterfeits before investing large sums of money.

This book is the most comprehensive listing of comic books ever attempted. Comic book titles, dates of first and last issues, publishing companies, origin and special issues are listed when known.

The Guide will be listing only American comic books due to space limitation. Some variations of the regular comic book format will be listed. These basically include those pre-1933 comic strip reprint books with varying size—usually with cardboard covers, but sometimes with hardback. As forerunners of the modern comic book format, they deserve to be listed despite their obvious differences in presentation. Other books that will be listed are giveaway comics—but only those that contain known characters, work by known artists, or those of special interest.

All titles are listed as if they were one word, ignoring spaces, hyphens and apostrophes. Page counts listed will always include covers.

IMPORTANT. Prices listed in this book are in U. S. currency and are for your reference only. This book is not a dealer's price list, although some dealers may base their prices on the values listed. The true value of any comic book is what you are willing to pay. Prices listed herein are an indication of what collectors (not dealers) would probably pay. For one reason or another, these collectors might want certain books badly, or else need specific issues to complete their runs and so are willing to pay more. Dealers are not in a position to pay the full prices listed, but work on a percentage depending largely on the amount of investment required and the quality of material offered. Usually they will pay from 20 to 70 percent of the list price depending on how long it will take them to sell the collection after making the investment; the higher the demand and better the condition, the more the percentage. Most dealers are faced with expenses such as advertising, travel, telephone and mailing, plus convention costs. These costs all go in before the books are sold. The high demand books usually sell right away but there are many other titles that are difficult to sell due to low demand. Sometimes a dealer will have cost tied up in this type of material for several years before finally moving it. Remember, his position is that of handling, demand and overhead. Most dealers are victims of these economics.

We have invested in a printing computer which has completely changed the format and look of this book. The computer will speed up the editing process, give us a higher degree of accuracy, and help keep printing costs down. Each year thousands of new facts are edited into the main body of The Guide, increasing its size and cost to produce. Printing costs are always going up, so the computer will allow more data per page and will in time prove to be a savings for us all.

Everyone connected with the publication of this book advocates the collecting of comic books for fun and pleasure, as well as for nostalgia, art, and cultural values. Second to this is investment, which, if wisely placed in the best quality books (condition and contents considered), will yield dividends over the long term. The publisher of this reference work is a collector and has no comic books for sale.

TERMINOLOGY

Many of the following terms and abbreviations are used in this book and are explained here:

a—Story art; **a(i)**—Story art inks; **a(p)**—Story art pencils; **a(r)**—Story art reprint.

B&W—Black and white art.

Bondage cover—Usually denotes a female in bondage.

c—Cover art; **c(i)**—Cover inks; **c(p)**—Cover pencils; **c(r)**—Cover reprint.

Cameo—When a character appears briefly in one or two panels.

Colorist—Artist that applies color to the pen and ink art.

Con—A Convention or public gathering of fans.

Drug mention story—Story in which drugs play a minor role; i.e., cops vs. smugglers, dealers, etc.

Drug propaganda story—Where comic makes an editorial stand about drug abuse.

Drug use story—Shows the actual use of drugs: shooting, taking a trip, harmful effects, etc.

Debut—The first time that a character appears anywhere.

Fanzine—An amateur fan publication.

First app.—Same as debut.

Flashback—When a previous story is being recalled.

G. A.—Golden Age (1930s—1950s).

Headlight—Protruding breasts.

i—Art inks.

Infinity cover—Shows a scene that repeats itself to infinity.

Inker—Artist that does the inking.

Intro—Same as debut.

JLA—Justice League of America.

JSA—Justice Society of America.

Logo—The title of a strip or comic book as it appears on the cover or title page.

nd—No date.

nn—No number.

N. Y. Legis. Comm.—New York Legislative Committee to Study the Publication of Comics (1951).
Origin—When the story of the character's creation is given.
p—Art pencils.
Penciler—Artist that does the pencils.
POP—**Parade of Pleasure,** book about the censorship of comics.
R or r—Reprint.
Rare—10 to 20 copies estimated to exist.
S. A.—Silver Age (1956—Present).
Scarce—20 to 100 copies estimated to exist.
Silver proof—A black & white actual size print on thick glossy paper given to the colorist to indicate colors to the engraver.
S&K—Simon and Kirby (artists).
SOTI—**Seduction of the Innocent,** book about the censorship of comics.
Splash panel—A large panel that usually appears at the front of a comic story.
Very rare—1 to 10 copies estimated to exist.
X-over—When one character crosses over into another's strip.
Zine—See Fanzine.

After No. 9 Guide went to press, we began getting letters and phone calls about some new way that Marvel was coding its comics. As the year progressed, more and more inquiries were being made. With fandom's and Marvel's interest at heart we made a trip to Marvel to discuss this matter with them. It seems that all comics going directly to the comic shops have to be coded differently, as they are sold on a no-return basis while newsstand comics are not. Marvel held a special meeting with many of the major dealers at the San Diego convention to discuss this subject. Most dealers did not voice strong complaints against the special coding. Both printed versions are first original printings. The emblem on the cover is the only difference. The Price Guide did not detect any price differences between the two versions, so we have no intention of listing a difference at the present time.

Direct Sales (Comic Shops)

Newsstand

Direct Sales (Comic Shops) Overseas

Newsstand Overseas

Many of the better artists are pointed out. When more than one artist worked on a story, their names are separated by a (/). The first name did the pencil drawings and the second did the inks. When two or more artists work on a story, only the most prominent will be noted in some cases. There has been some confusion in past editions as to which artists to list and which to leave out. We wish all good artists could be listed, but due to space limitation, only the most popular can. The following list of artists are considered to be either the most collected in the comic field or are historically significant and should be pointed out. Artists designated below with an (*) indicate that only their most noted work will be listed. The rest will eventually have all their work shown as the information becomes available. This list could change from year to year as new artists come into prominence.

Adams, Neal
*Alcala, Alfredo
Aparo, Jim
*Austin, Terry
Baker, Matt
Barks, Carl
Beck, C. C.
Brunner, Frank
*Buckler, Rich
*Buscema, John
Byrne, John
*Check, Sid
Cole, Jack
Cole, L. B.
Craig, Johnny
Crandall, Reed
Davis, Jack
Disbrow, Jayson
Ditko, Steve
Eisner, Will
*Elder, Bill
Evans, George
Everett, Bill
Feldstein, Al
Fine, Lou
Foster, Harold
Fox, Matt
Frazetta, Frank
Golden, Michael
Gottfredson, Floyd
*Guardineer, Fred
*Heath, Russ
Howard, Wayne
Ingels, Graham
Jones, Jeff
Kamen, Jack
*Kane, Gil
Kelly, Walt
Kinstler, E. R.
Kirby, Jack
Krenkel, Roy
Krigstein, Bernie
*Kubert, Joe
Kurtzman, Harvey
Manning, Russ
*Meskin, Mort
Miller, Frank
Moreira, Ruben
*Morisi, Pete
*Nasser, Mike
*Newton, Don
Nostrand, Howard
Orlando, Joe
Pakula, Mac (Toth inspired)
*Palais, Rudy
*Perez, George
Raboy, Mac
Raymond, Alex
Ravielli, Louis
*Redondo, Nestor
Rogers, Marshall
Schomburg, Alex
Siegel & Shuster
Simon & Kirby (S&K)
Smith, Barry
Stanley, John
Starlin, Jim
Steranko, Jim
Torres, Angelo
Toth, Alex
Tuska, George
Ward, Bill
Williamson, Al
Wolverton, Basil
Wood, Wallace
Wrightson, Bernie

The following abbreviations are used with the cover reproductions throughout the book for copyright credit purposes. The companies they represent are listed here:

ACE—Ace Periodicals
ACG—American Comics Group
AJAX—Ajax-Farrell
AP—Archie Publications
ATLAS—Atlas Comics (see below)
AVON—Avon Periodicals
BP—Better Publications
C & L—Cupples & Leon
CC—Charlton Comics
CEN—Centaur Publications
CCG—Columbia Comics Group
CG—Catechetical Guild
CHES—Harry 'A' Chesler
CLDS—Classic Det. Stories
DC—DC Comics, Inc.
DELL—Dell Publishing Co.
DMP—David McKay Publishing
DS—D. S. Publishing Co.
EAS—Eastern Color Printing Co.
EC—E. C. Comics
ENWIL—Enwil Associates
EP—Elliott Publications
ERB—Edgar Rice Burroughs
FAW—Fawcett Publications
FF—Famous Funnies
FH—Fiction House Magazines
FOX—Fox Features Syndicate
GIL—Gilberton
GK—Gold Key
GP—Great Publications
HARV—Harvey Publications
HILL—Hillman Periodicals
HOKE—Holyoke Publishing Co.
KING—King Features Syndicate
LEV—Lev Gleason Publications
MCG—Marvel Comics Group
ME—Magazine Enterprises
MLJ—MLJ Magazines
NOVP—Novelty Press
PG—Premier Group
PINE—Pines
PMI—Parents' Magazine Institute
PRIZE—Prize Publications
QUA—Quality Comics Group
REAL—Realistic Comics
RH—Rural Home
S & S—Street and Smith Publishers
SKY—Skywald Publications
STAR—Star Publications
STD—Standard Comics
STJ—St. John Publishing Co.
SUPR—Superior Comics
TC—Tower Comics
TM—Trojan Magazines
TOBY—Toby Press
UFS—United Features Syndicate
VITL—Vital Publications
WDP—Walt Disney Publications
WEST—Western Publishing Co.
WHIT—Whitman Publishing Co.
WHW—William H. Wise
WMG—William M. Gaines (E. C.)
WP—Warren Publishing Co.
YM—Youthful Magazines
Z-D—Ziff-Davis Publishing Co.

ATLAS COMICS. The following list of publishers all printed **Atlas** comics and are coded throughout the book. The **Atlas Globe** insignia first appeared in November 1951 and lasted until September 1957 after which Marvel took over.

ATLAS Publishers' Abbreviation Codes:

ACI—Animirth Comics, Inc.
AMI—Atlas Magazines, Inc.
ANC—Atlas News Co., Inc.
BPC—Bard Publishing Corp.
BFP—Broadcast Features Pubs.
CCC—Comic Combine Corp.
CDS—Current Detective Stories
CFI—Crime Files, Inc.
CmPI—Comedy Publications, Inc.
CmPS—Complete Photo Story
CnPC—Cornell Publishing Corp.
CPC—Chipiden Publishing Corp.
CPI—Crime Publications, Inc.
CPS—Canam Publishing Sales Corp.
CSI—Classics Syndicate, Inc.
EPI—Emgee Publications, Inc.
FPI—Foto Parade, Inc.
GPI—Gem Publishing, Inc.
HPC—Hercules Publishing Corp.
IPS—Interstate Publishing Corp.
JPI—Jaygee Publications, Inc.
LMC—Leading Magazine Corp.
MALE—Male Publishing Corp.
MAP—Miss America Publishing Corp.
MCI—Marvel Comics, Inc.
MgPC—Margood Publishing Corp.
MjMC—Marjean Magazine Corp.

MMC—Mutual Magazine Corp.	**PPI**—Postal Publications, Inc.	**TCI**—Timely Comics, Inc.
MPC—Medalion Publishing Corp.	**PrPI**—Prime Publications, Inc.	**20 CC**—20th Century Comics Corp.
MPI—Manvis Publications, Inc.	**RCM**—Red Circle Magazines, Inc.	**USA**—U.S.A. Publications, Inc.
NPI—Newsstand Publications, Inc.	**SAI**—Sports Actions, Inc.	**VPI**—Vista Publications, Inc.
NPP—Non-Pareil Publishing Corp.	**SnPC**—Snap Publishing Co.	**WFP**—Western Fiction Publishing
OCI—Official Comics, Inc.	**SPC**—Select Publishing Co.	**WPI**—Warwick Publications, Inc.
OMC—Official Magazine Corp.	**SPI**—Sphere Publications, Inc.	**ZPC**—Zenith Publishing Co., Inc.
OPI—Olympia Publications, Inc.		

YOUR INFORMATION IS NEEDED: In order to make future Guides more accurate and complete, we are interested in any relevant information or facts that you might have. **Relevant and significant data includes:**

Works by the artists named elsewhere. **Caution:** Most artists did not sign their work and many were imitated by others. When submitting this data, advise whether the work was signed or not. In many cases, it takes an expert to identify certain artists—so extreme caution should be observed in submitting this data.

Drug issues—especially pre-code issues dealing specifically in drugs actually being used or being propagandized.
Pre-code bondage covers and panels.
Suggestive covers and panels.
Stories with excess of blood, gore, violence, torture, or mutilation.
Issues mentioned by Wertham and others in **Seduction**, **Parade**...
Transvestite issues.
Origin issues.
First and last appearances of strips or characters.
Title continuity information.
Beginning and ending numbers of runs.
Atomic bomb, Christmas, Flag and infinity covers.
Appearances by famous people (Beatles, Nixon, Presley, Wertham, etc.).
Swipes.

To record something in the Guide, **documented** facts are needed. Please send a photo copy of indicia or page in question if possible.

Non-relevent data—Most giveaway comics will not be listed. Literally thousands of titles came out, many of which have educational themes. We will only list significant collectible giveaways such as March of Comics, Disney items, communist books (but not civil defense educational comics), and books that contain illustrated stories by top artists or top collected characters.

Good Luck and Happy Hunting...

Robert M. Overstreet

Advertise in the Guide

is book reaches more serious comic collectors than any other publication and has proven results due to its world-wide circulation and use. Your ad will pull all year long until the w edition comes out.

splay Ad space is sold in full, half, fourth, and eighth page sizes. Ad rates are set in the early l prior to each edition's release. Write at that time for rates (between Oct.—Dec.).

PRINTED SIZES

FULL PAGE—8" long x 5" wide. HALF PAGE—4" long x 5" wide. FOURTH PAGE—4" long x 2½" wide. EIGHTH PAGE—2" long x 2½" wide. CLASSIFIED ADS will be retyped and reduced about one-half. No artwork permitted. Rate is based on your 4" typed line. DISPLAY CLASSIFIED ADS: The use of borders or bold face type or cuts or other decorations change your classified ad to display—rates same as regular display.

NOTE: Submit your ad on white paper in a proportionate version of the actual printed size. All full —Quarter page advertisers will receive a complimentary copy of the Guide. The NEW Guide will be professionally done throughout...so to reflect a consistently high quality from cover to cover, we must ask that all ads be neatly and professionally done. Full payment must be sent with all ads. All but classified ads will be run as is.

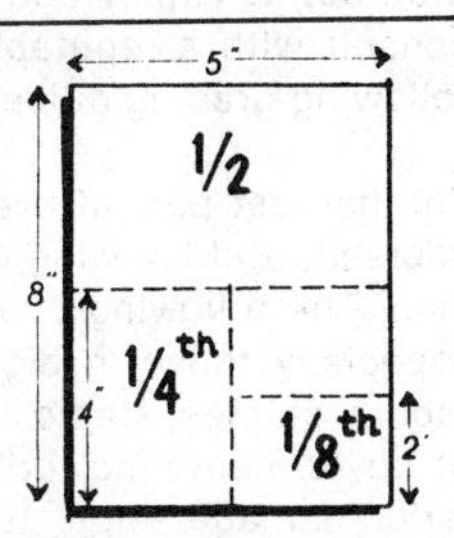

AD DEADLINE - COLOR—Nov. 15th
AD DEADLINE-Black & White—Jan. 15th

Overstreet Publications, Inc.
780 Hunt Cliff Dr. N.W.
Cleveland, Tennessee 37311

The PRICE GUIDE has become the STANDARD REFERENCE WORK in the field and is distributed to thousands of comic collectors throughout the world. Don't miss this opportunity to advertise in the Guide.

NOTICE: All advertisements are accepted and placed in the Price Guide in good faith. However, we cannot be held responsible for any losses incurred in your dealings with the advertisers. If, after receiving legitimate complaints, and there is sufficient evidence to warrant such action, these advertisers will be dropped from future editions.

SPECIAL NOTICE

If copyrighted characters are planned for your ad, the following must be done: Send a copy of your ad layout (including characters) to the company(s) or copyright owner(s) involved requesting permission for their use. A copy of this permission must be sent to us with your ad. DC Comics and Marvel Comics have indicated that you will have no problem getting permission, so if you must use their characters. . . write for the permission. For DC, write: Public Relations, DC Comics, Inc., 75 Rockefeller Plaza, N. Y., N. Y. 10019. For Marvel, write: Marvel Comics, c/o Mike Fredrich, 575 Madison Ave., N. Y., N. Y. 10022. Other companies such as Disney could be more of a problem. At any rate, we cannot accept any ads with copyrighted characters without a copy of the permission.

GRADING COMIC BOOKS

Before a comic book's true value can be assessed, its condition or state of preservation must be determined. In most comic books, especially in the rarer issues, the better the condition, the more desirable the book. The scarcer first and/or origin issues in PRISTINE MINT condition will bring several times the price of the same book in POOR condition. The grading of a comic book is done by simply looking at the book and describing its condition, which may range from absolutely perfect newsstand condition (PRISTINE MINT) to extremely worn, dirty, and torn (POOR). Numerous variables influence the evaluation of a comic's condition and **all** must be considered in the final evaluation. More important characteristics include tears, missing pieces, wrinkles, stains, yellowing, brittleness, tape repairs, water marks, spine roll, writing, and cover lustre. The significance of each of these will be described more fully in the grading scale definitions. As grading is the most subjective aspect of determining a comic's value, it is very important that the grader must be careful and not allow wishful thinking to influence what the eyes see. It is also very important to realize that older comics in above MINT condition are extremely scarce and are rarely advertised for sale; most of the nicer comics advertised range from VERY FINE to NEAR MINT. To the novice, grading will appear difficult at first, but as experience is gained, accuracy will improve. Whenever in doubt, consult with a reputable dealer or experienced collector in your area. The following grading guide is given to aid the panelologist.

GRADING DEFINITIONS

The hardest part of evaluating a comic is being honest and objective with yourself, and knowing what characteristics to look for in making your decision. The following characteristics should be checked in evaluating books, especially those in higher grades: degree of cover lustre, degree of color fading, staples, staple areas, spine condition, top and bottom of spine, edges of cover, centering, brittleness, browning/yellowing, flatness, tightness, interior damage, tape, tears, folds, water marks, color flaking, and general cleanliness.

VERY IMPORTANT: A book must be graded in its entirety; not by just the cover alone. A book in any of the grades listed must be in its **ORIGINAL** unrestored condition. Restored books must be graded as such; i.e., a restored book grading Fine might only be worth the same as a Very Good copy in its unrestored state. The value of an extensively restored book tends to usually be halfway between the value of its original state and the condition it appears to be after restoration. Examine books very closely for repairing before purchase. Major things to look for are: bleaching, trimming, interior spine and tear reinforcement, gluing, restapling, and recoloring. Dealers should state that a book has been restored and not expect to get as much as a book unrestored in that condition would bring. **Note:** Cleaning, stain removal, rolled spine removal, staple replacement, etc., if professionally done, would not be considered restoration as long as the printed condition of the comic has not been changed. After examining these characteristics a comic may be assigned to one of the following grades:

PRISTINE MINT (PM): File copies; absolutely perfect in every way, regardless of age. The cover has full lustre, is crisp, and shows no imperfections of any sort. The cover and all pages are extra white and fresh; the spine is tight, flat, and clean; not even the slightest blemish can be detected around staples, along spine, at corners or edges. Arrival dates pencilled on the cover are acceptable. As comics must be truly perfect to be graded PM, they are obviously extremely scarce even on the newsstand. Books prior to 1964 in this grade bring 20 to 50 per cent more.

MINT (M): Like new or newsstand condition, as above, but with very slight loss of lustre, or a slight off-centered cover, or a minor printing error. Could have pencilled arrival dates, slight color fading, and white to extra white cover and pages. Any defects noticeable would be very minor and attributable to the cutting, folding and stapling process.

NEAR MINT (NM): Almost perfect; tight spine, flat and clean; just enough minor defects of wear noticeable with close inspection to keep it out of the MINT category; i.e., a small flake of color missing at a staple, corner or edge, or slight discoloration on inside cover or pages; near perfect cover gloss retained.

VERY FINE (VF): Slight wear beginning to show; possibly a small wrinkle or crease at staples or where cover has been opened a few times; still clean and flat with most of cover gloss retained.

FINE (FN): Tight cover with some wear, but still relatively flat, clean and shiny with no subscription crease, writing on cover, yellowed margins or tape repairs. Stress lines around staples and along spine beginning to show; minor color flaking possible at spine, staples, edges or corners.

VERY GOOD (vg): Obviously a read copy with original printing lustre and gloss almost gone; some discoloration, but not soiled; some signs of wear and minor markings, but none that deface the cover; usually needs slight repair around staples and along spine which could be rolled; cover could have a minor tear or crease where a corner was folded under or a loose centerfold; no chunks missing, tape or brown pages.

GOOD (g): An average used copy complete with both covers and no panels missing; slightly soiled or marked with possible creases, minor tears or splits, rolled spine and small color flaking, but perfectly sound and legible. A well-read copy, but perfectly acceptable with no chunks missing, tape or brown pages.

FAIR (f): Very heavily read and soiled, but complete with possibly a small chunk out of cover; tears needing repairs and multiple folds and wrinkles likely; damaged by the elements, but completely sound and legible, bringing 50-70% of good price.

POOR (p): Damaged; heavily weathered; soiled; or otherwise unsuited for collection purposes.

COVERLESS (c): Coverless comics turn up frequently, are hard to sell and in many cases are almost worthless. It takes ingenuity and luck to get a good price; e.g., color xerox covers will increase the salability. A cover of an expensive book is scarcer and worth more.

IMPORTANT: Comics in all grades with fresh extra white pages usually bring more. Books with defects such as pages or panels missing, coupons cut, torn or taped covers and pages, brown or brittle pages, restapled, taped spines, pages or covers, water-marked, printing defects, rusted staples, stained, holed, or other imperfections that distract from the original beauty, are worth less than if free of these defects.

Many of the early strip reprint comics were printed in hardback with dust jackets. Books with dust jackets are worth more. The value can increase from 20 to 50 per cent depending on the rarity of book. Usually, the earlier the book, the greater the percentage. Unless noted, prices listed are without dust jackets. The condition of the dust jacket should be graded independently of the book itself.

STORAGE AND PRESERVATION OF COMIC BOOKS

By Ernst W. Gerber, P.E., Richard D. Smith, PhD, P.E., and other consultants (See editor's note)

Price Guide's Position: *The author of this article refers specifically to and recommends the use of Mylar* Type D polyester film products. However,* ***The Comic Book Price Guide*** *does not wish to endorse any particular brandname. As Mr. Gerber states, all references to Mylar* should be interpreted as meaning uncoated Mylar* Type "D" by Dupont Company or equivalent material such as Melinex* Type "O" or "516" by ICI Corp. or Scotchpar* by 3M Company.*

PREFACE: (by Ernst Gerber)

Comic books and many other popular collectibles are perishable; they will sooner or later deteriorate and die. I'm certain many of you have seen old comic books that were brown, brittle, and even falling apart. This sad ultimate fact scares many collectors and investors away from massing large expensive collections, for fear of loosing their investment.

Well, let's set the record straight once and for all! There is **no** reason to be scared, upset, or worried. Everything in this world deteriorates. You've seen beat up, worn out, five year old cars, but look at the value of well maintained 50 year old cars! You've seen 10 year old homes on their last legs, but also 300 year old Victorian homes worth a gold mine. The list of comparisons is endless. The fact in every case is that properly maintained, stored, and preserved, virtually anything including comics can be made to last many generations.

The problem has been that for the last 30 years nobody knew, or for that matter, cared about preserving comic books. However, during the last five years a virtual revolution has now produced an accute awareness of comic preservation. We're happy that we've been able to play a small part in that revolution. Many thanks go to the progressive attitude of the **Price Guide** editor in bringing the information to the collectors.

Now armed with this information about preservation techniques and storage devices, collectors should have renewed confidence that their investments can be made to last indefinitely. It is only the **lack** of information that should scare collectors!

It is our purpose to bring this information to you as clearly and simply as possible. We could write 200 pages of technical mumbo-jumbo about long chemical equations to impress you, but we'd rather talk plainly and get the point across. We're going to try not to repeat the information given in the last two years' **Guide** articles, so if you haven't yet read the other information, we'll provide them free of charge. Please send two (2) first class stamps and your re-

**Registered trademark by company as noted in article.*

quest to: Ernst W. Gerber, Guide Article, P. O. Box E, Center Lovell, ME 04016.

This year we've requested article contributions from various international experts in the field of archival storage and preservation. The response was overwhelming; too many to publish this year alone. The information contained in this article originates from hundreds of published sources. Most agree on the pertinent facts. This year we will include an excellent synopsis by world renowned preservation expert Dr. Richard D. Smith. After his summary, I will add specific detailed information in some areas of heightened interest that collectors have requested in the past year.

Interested readers should send us their suggestion for information they would like to see in next year's **Guide**. We will try to have your questions answered by additional expert guest contributions.

With that long winded preface I wish to remind all that only lack of knowledge should scare you away from our most favorite pastime and valuable investment—the collecting of comic books.

A SUMMARY FOR COLLECTORS (by Dr. Richard D. Smith)

INTRODUCTION

The long term preservation of comic books is a challenge that boggles the imagination. On one hand, how do you protect a low cost, relatively fragile product like comic books, made for temporary use from unstable materials against natural aging and deterioration? On the other hand, each comic book is unique because its condition has been modified by its particular use and storage history. Moreover, the components of comic books, e.g., papers, inks, coatings, etc., vary not only from publisher to publisher but also with changes in manufacturing techniques and availability of raw materials.

Consequently, this discussion will limit itself to general truths and preservation techniques that collectors can apply. There will be no discussion of techniques requiring conservatorial skill or the treatment of comic books with special problems. Even so, the treatments being recommended, though generally safe, can cause damage and due care must be exercised. Specific instructions should be obtained from experienced persons or manufacturers, and followed. The viewpoints expressed represent a consensus of the knowhow held by scientists and conservators.

The perspective taken is that (1) every use or handling and all treatments cause damage to the comic book and (2) each use or treatment must bring benefit that far outweighs the damage it causes.

CAUSES OF DETERIORATION

A comic book is normally made from a newsprint paper whose fiber furnish consists of 75 to 80 percent ground wood and 20 to 25 percent unbleached kraft fibers. It is probably held together with wire staples, printed with three to four different inks, and has a cover which may or may not have a varnished coating.

The groundwood fibers in newsprint are produced mechanically by holding debarked logs against mill stones revolving in a stream of water. The fibers are chemically identical to the original wood except for the changes caused by being torn apart and flushed with water. Their natural pH ranges from four to five just like wood itself. (pH of 5 is 100 times as acid as neutral pH of 7). The kraft fibers are chemically separated but not bleached to remove lignin. They provide the handling strength required to print the finished paper, and cut and bind it into a comic book. The finished comic book is very similar to wood itself, but not so permanent, because the paper fibers have been separated and they and the lignin surrounding them are accessible to chemical reactions.

Even though scientists don't understand all of the chemical reactions that occur during aging, the major causes of paper deterioration are known and identified as: (a) acid, (b) oxidative, (c) photochemical, (d) biological attacks, and (e) physical damage from use and storage.

The primary causes of comic book deterioration are acid and oxidative attack. The hydrolysis of cellulose, accelerated by acids, produces the embrittled paper books so common in research libraries in precisely the same way it embrittles comic books. Oxidative attack, though chemically more complex, involves oxygen from air and leads to discolored, more acid paper. The extreme reactivity of lignin, a major component in groundwood and unbleached fiber papers, may make oxidative attack the most serious cause of deterioration in comic books. The effect is cyclic because oxidative reactions produce acids which accelerate the rate of discoloration and embrittlement.

Fungus attack, more destructive than insect or rodent attack, occurs naturally during the warm, humid tropical conditions we enjoy in Summer. Further chemical attack occurs when light, particularly ultra-violet light, impinges on paper. This radiant energy initiates complicated oxidative and reduction reactions which cause newsprint papers to yellow. Ordinary wear is acceptable, if and only if, the benefit from use and handling outweigh the damage caused.

TECHNIQUES OF PRESERVATION

The life of comic books can be greatly extended by applying practical techniques to protect them against light, oxygen, acid attack and bad storage conditions. The following suggestions are listed in order of convenience for collectors to apply rather than in terms of their potential for reducing the rate of deterioration.

(a) **Keep away from ultra-violet light.** Lignin is very sensitive to ultra-violet light. (Most ordinary light contains ultra-violet light.) Near ultra-violet light is about 1,000 times more destructive than near infra-red light. Minimum light levels and ultra-violet filters, e.g., especially compounded acrylic (plexiglass) sheets, should be used for exhibitions and displays.

(b) **Seal out oxygen.** Storage in white sulfite envelopes is better than nothing, but the use of uncoated special archival polyester (Mylar*) envelopes is preferable. Polyvinyl chloride (PVC) envelopes should not be used because they exude plasticizers which are destructive. The use of other plastics should be evaluated on a case by case basis because certain compounds in common plastics can be destructive.

If stored in ordinary brown or white corrugated cartons, comics should be further protected by lining with appropriate archival acid-free materials. Far more preferable is storage in acid-free alkaline buffered archival quality boxes composed of strong, well purified, chemical wood fibers.

Storage in steel or wooden files is also desirable (raw wooden surfaces must be specially sealed with polyurethane varnish and let dry 30 days before use). If yhour collection value merits, consideration should be given to slowly bleeding nitrogen gas into the file to reduce the quantity of oxygen present (and provide very dry storage conditions).

(c) **Keep cool.** The rate at which paper deteriorates doubles each time the temperature increases 10° F. For example, the rate of deterioration at 85° F. is eight times faster than the rate at 55° F.

(d) **Keep dry.** Comic books should be stored in as dry a condition as possible. Fungus attack occurs at relative humidities above 65% R.H. Iron staples rust above 30% R.H. Comic books in good condition will not be seriously weakened by low relative humidities. All papers, including newsprint, regain almost 100 percent of their "before dried" strength in a few minutes at ordinary relative humidities.

(e) **Deacidify.** Deacidification, i.e., neutralization of existing acids and impregnation of an alkaline buffer to prevent re-acidification in the future, is essential to extend comic book life and reduce color changes. Only deacidification agents containing magnesium are recommended because magnesium offers the added merits of protecting lignin and reducing the rate of oxidative attack.

Aqueous deacidification involves dismantling the comic book and soaking the leaves one by one in a water bath of magnesium bicarbonate. The cost of raw materials is low but labor costs are high, and conservatorial know-how is necessary to avoid damaging weak, water-wetted paper. A side benefit is considerable quantities of colored deterioration products are washed from paper during immersion. Aqueous deacidification will slightly change the surface and dimensions of paper and eliminate the possibility of proving mint condition.

The nonaqueous approach, originated during research at the University of Chicago and marketed by Wei T'o Associates, uses expensive materials but involves low labor cost. There is no necessity to dismantle the comic book for treatment, the procedure is fast, and conservatorial skills are not required. The primary disadvantage of nonaqueous deacidification is colored deterioration-products are not removed because the high cost of the solution forces practitioners into efficient application techniques, e.g., spraying, brushing, or dipping. Both of these deacidification techniques deposit the same chemicals and provide long-term protection.

The vapor phase deacidification technique using cyclohexylamine carbonate (VPD) is not recommended because it in contrast to the preceding two methods, is not permanent, causes initially a mild browning reaction analogous to the browning of freshly cut apples, is incapable of deacidifying highly acidic paper, and introduces chemicals, which if they react with sulfates or nitrates (introduced by air pollution) will produce acids. These comments represent the consensus among scientists, but some respected conservators have a different opinion and continue to recommend VPD.

SUMMARY

The long term preservation of an ephemeral paper product like comic books, though difficult, can be obtained by collectors at a reasonable cost if sensible procedures are followed. Theoretically, a collector should deacidify his collection prior to vacuum drying and storing it in an inert atmosphere, in a Mylar* envelope, and in a time vault at as cold a temperature as possible. Practically, the collector should apply as many of the above preservation techniques as his pocket book allows and the uniqueness of his collection justify.

We thank Dr. Smith for his expert contribution to the field of comic book preservation. We will now discuss in greater detail a few topics of heightened interest.

PLASTIC BAGS

The ancient popular inexpensive method most used to store comics is "stick it in a plastic bag." So thousands of dealers sell vinyl, PVC, polyethylene, polypropylene, cellophane, etc. To a "**tee**," all guarantee that their product is non-migratory, non-volatile, non-additives, non-dangerous, non-PVC, non-plasticizers, non-etc. But that is **non**-sense.

All plastics are derivatives of chemical reactions, **all** of which contain some of the following: plasticizers, surface coatings, slip additives, reprocessed polymers, U.V. inhibitors, antioxidants, antiozonites, capability to degrade by oxidation, and acid-hydrolysis.

These can and will detrimentally effect your collections—thousands already have learned the hard way, with sacrificed documents and collectibles. As a temporary measure only, virgin polyethylene plastic bags are acceptable, but not the right way.

The Library of Congress Preservation Department learned the right way ten years ago. Their "choice of polyester film for conservation use is the result of its being one of the most stable and inert of the many different kinds of (plastic) films now available. . ."

The trade name for polyester film is Mylar* by Dupont, Melinex* by ICI Corporation, and Scotchpar* by 3M Company. However, since pure polyester film (Mylar* type D uncoated) is virtually impossible to heat seal by conventional methods, many firms sell "Mylar sleeves" or "heat sealable Mylar," which is many times **not** Mylar* at all, or at least Mylar* coated with a variety of volatile plastics to promote heat or pressure seal-ability, thus defeating the entire purpose of using the Mylar* in the first place. Collectors should be cautious; not all is as may appear. From personal experiences, a number of advertised Mylar* samples from firms were turned over to Dupont for testing and found **not** to be even remotely related to polyester film.

If in doubt regarding the type of material you have purchased, send us a sample for testing with a self-addressed stamped envelope.

Since there are many variations that can be added to Mylar*, the Library of Congress specifically requires that "polyester film used for conservation purposes must be entirely free of plasticizers, U.V. inhibitors, colored dyes, impregnants, and surface coatings, and meet Government specifications L-P 00679 and L-P 3779."

Uncoated Mylar* type D meets this requirement as does Melinex type "O." From discussions with a variety of experts, Mylar* type D or equal is most often specified by archival users. Other acceptable films such as Melinex* or Scotchpar* may be obtained if meeting equal specification as Mylar* D. It is up to the individual user to decide their relative merits; this user joins the majority of professionals in preferring the use of Mylar* D. Thus in the interests of brevity rather than each time giving the full specification of the polyester film, nor each time listing the three alternatives, when I refer to Mylar*, I mean uncoated Mylar* type D or **equal**.

To illustrate the significant differences between Mylar* and other commonly used plastics we've prepared the following graph showing relative quantities and qualities:

Polyethylene, vinyls, other common plastics (white bar)	Archival Quality Mylar* D (black bar)
Resistance to diffusion of gases like oxygen, CO2, sulfur dioxide, etc.	350 x greater than Polyethylene
Permanence, no noticeable change in storage.	2 years compared to more than 1000 years
Resistance to moisture, insect attack, fungus, mold, mildew, dust.	Fair compared to Excellent
Resistance to acids, ketones, oils, greases, solvents, and other harmful agents.	Fair compared to Excellent
Strength, creep resistance.	10 x Polyethylene; 1/3 the strength of steel
Containing plasticizers, slip additives, surface coatings, U. V. inhibitors, antioxidants, acid hydrolysis.	Potentially dangerous to Collectibles

CARDBOARD BOXES AND BACKING BOARD

We discussed this topic in detail in the last **Price Guide**; a brief synopsis:

(1). Never use any cardboard unless specifically identified as acid-free and manufactured of virgin wood cellulose, not reprocessed pulp cardboard.

(2). Always be certain that the acid-free board or boxes you buy specify a minimum pH (recommended 8.0 to 10.3), and most importantly, a specified percentage of alkaline reserve (3 percent minimum). Without it, acid-free is very temporary.

(3). Highly acidic corrugated cardboard boxes should not be used for the storage of comic books unless protected by Mylar*.

RESTORATION

The physical restoration of a comic book is a sensitive subject since there are two distinct schools of thought. (a) The changing, restoring, repairing of the natural condition of an artifact or collectible reduces its intrinsic as well as market value, and should never be done under any circumstances. (As in the field of coin collecting). (b) The upgrading of the condition of a comic book enhances its appearance and thus its value. (As with antique cars and furniture).

A recommendation in this article would make at least half of the school upset. So let it suffice to recommend each collector should carefully review the market value of restored comics prior to investing in that artform; then if you decide on restoration, select a reputable and **experienced** firm to do the work. Under no circumstances should you do any restoration work yourself, especially with tape repairs, for they will surely reduce the value of your comics.

CHEMICAL PRESERVATION

We have recently become aware of new chemical treatments which can effectively and safely extend the life of comic books, as well as whiten yellowing and browning comics. If interested in this topic, perhaps it can be discussed in detail in the next **Guide**. In the interim, do caution; household bleaches will whiten pages of comics, but only temporarily, and will increase the comic book acidity levels and further reduce their longevity. Beware of artificially whitened comic books; you're not getting what you paid for.

RECOMMENDATIONS

We've prepared a graph to approximately illustrate how a comic book ages under average conditions. Do note that the earlier you care for your books, the longer they'll last. Effects of aging cannot be reversed—only slow-

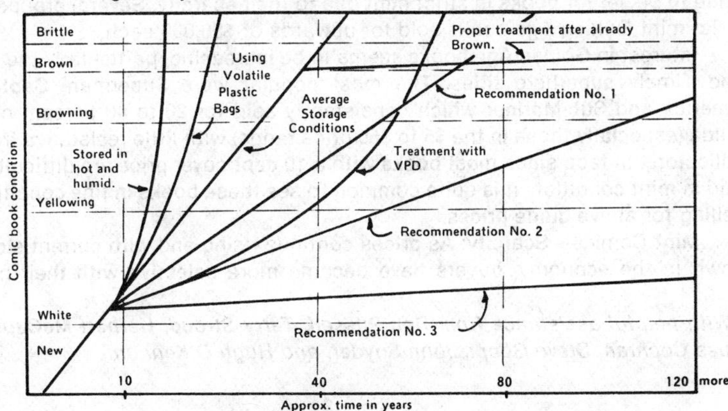

ed down. In the graph, the example ten year old comic is treated with a number of possible conditions and the approximated results are shown. Obviously the flatter the graph line, the longer the comic will live.

Each collector should choose the cost/benefit effectiveness for what he wants out of his collection and how he wishes to preserve its condition and consequent value.

(1). The cheapest answer is: Keep cool, dry, and dark. Short term storage in polyethylene bags is O.K.

(2). The moderate answer is: Store in Mylar* envelopes with or without acid-free cardboard inserts. Keep cool, dry, and dark.

(3). The most effective and expensive answer is: Chemically deacidify as recommended by Dr. Smith. Protect in Mylar*. Keep cool, dry, and dark.

Editor's Note:

Ernst W. Gerber is a registered professional engineer who has spent the last 5 years in research and development of archival quality storage techniques, equipment and supplies for collectors. As well as providing the **Guide** with information and articles, he has prepared articles and columns for a number of other publications.

Dr. Richard D. Smith, a registered professional engineer has 17 years experience in paper conservation, particularly deacidification. He has contributed research papers to books and other publications as well as several patents. He presently teaches at the Graduate School, University of Chicago and is employed by Wei T'o Associates, Inc.

Mr. Gerber has consulted many sources in the preparation of this article for the **Guide**, too many to list here. Any interested parties who wish to receive a copy of the full bibliography to this article should send $2.00 plus a self-addressed, stamped envelope to Mr. Gerber; he will provide sources and a lifetime reading list.

1981 MARKET REPORT

by Bob Overstreet,[1]

As the economy continued to slow during the year, collectors became more and more selective in their purchases. This led to an overall restricted growth in the comic book market. Books in less than fine condition were available in most titles selling at and below 1981 guide. However, demand for top condition prior to 1960 still exceeds current supply. Record prices continue to be set for books in strict mint due to their scarcity. Several groups of strict mint Golden Age books sold for upwards of $80,000 each.

Interest in Golden Age books seems to be increasing, particularly the DC and Timely superhero titles. The most popular were Superman, Captain America and Sub-Mariner which consistantly sold for 20 to 40 percent over guide (especially those in the $5 to $50 price range) with little resistance from collectors. In fact, since most books with a 10 cent cover price are difficult to find in mint condition, it is quite common to see these books in fine condition selling for above guide prices.

Mint Comics—Scarcity: As prices continue rising and with current slowdown in the economy, buyers have become more selective with their pur-

[1] *With helpful assistance from Ron Pussell, Terry Stroud, Herbert McCaulla, Russ Cochran, Steve Geppi, John Snyder, and Hugh O'Kennon.*

chases in general. These two factors along with high interest rates have affected all investment fields including collectibles. Buyers look for the finest items or the best deal. In comic collecting, this is expressed in increased demand for top condition books. Top condition books (VF or better) have disappeared in collections faster than the market could replace them. The greatest strain was placed on mint books (comics that are the sam the same as brand new books placed on the stands today).

The market's ability to sell mint comics is obviously related to the existing supply. Since by 1965 comic collecting and dealing had begun on a national level, most issues published after this time exist in great supply. On these books, demand plays a greater role than supply on what they sell for. The older an item is, the scarcer it becomes in mint condition. The following current **estimates** of number of copies that exist in mint condition (with a few minor exceptions[2]) are offered for your information:

Prior to 1942: 0-5 copies; 1942-1945: 5-15 copies; 1946-1949: 20-35 copies; 1950-1954: 10-25 copies (lower print runs); 1955-1958: 15-75 copies; 1959-1964: 75-500 copies.

Mile High and similar comics: Several years ago a large collection of Golden Age comics was discovered in the high country of Colorado. A local dealer investigated the lead and purchased this collection of approximately 22,000 comics. Almost every key Golden Age book was present. What made this collection so unique was the unbelievable state of condition of the books. They all had snow-white pages and most copies were unread with perfect cover gloss and brilliant colors. Over the past few years, this collection more than any other has greatly influenced or otherwise revolutionized grading standards. These comics were in the same condition as brand new comics on the stands today in every respect. Due to the sheer quantity of this collection, you can imagine the impact on the market as they were spread around. However, other collections much smaller in size have been discovered that are equal in quality to the Mile High books. One came out of the San Francisco area, and Cosmic Aeroplane Books turned up a beautiful collection in recent years which have now been liquidated into the market. The following are a few examples of prices brought during the year for books of Mile High quality: All-American No. 16—$2,000; Amazing Man No. 5—$1,500; More Fun No. 52 and No. 53—$6,000; Whiz No. 1—$8,000; Target No. 1—$1,200; All-Star No. 3—$1,600; Sensation No. 1—$1,000; Mighty Mouse No. 1—$125; Victory No. 1—$600; Mystic No. 1—$1,800; Human Torch No. 1—$2,000; Daring Mystery No. 1—$2,100; Flash No. 1—$2,150; Detective No. 33—$2,100; Batman No. 5—$400; Police No. 1—$1,000; Military No. 6—$210; Superman No. 26—$350; All-American No. 65—$68; Fight No. 48—$35; and Rangers No. 63—$24.

Other books that sold in 1981 are as follows: Superman No. 1 VF—$7,500; Action No. 1 VF-NM—$12,000; Double Action—$5,500; Amazing Fantasy No. 15 M—$1,000; Tales of Suspense No. 39—$350; Miss Fury No. 1 M—$600; Blue Ribbon No. 1 M—$300; Fantastic No. 1 M—$310; Weird No. 1 M—$270; Walt Disney Comics & Stories No. 1 F—$1,200; Wonder No. 1 F—$350; Jungle No. 143 M—$22; Wambi No. 3 M—$40; Rocket No. 3 M—$125; Blackhawk No. 60 NM—$35; Superman No. 76 VF—$185; and All-Star No. 57 VF—$185.

While books in high grade have always brought record prices for reasons mentioned previously, this is not true on the lower grade books. During the year, as the recession deepened, the available dollars to purchase books

[2] *Warehouse finds of a specific title or publisher occasionally occur (i.e., Poughkeepsie Dells and Gold Keys, Harveys, Firestone giveaways, etc.) which may significantly alter the estimates.*

declined. The lesser the condition, the more resistance was felt. Fine or better condition for the most part sold well, but VG or less met more and more resistance as the year progressed. Over the years there has been mistrust in the way many dealers grade books in VG or less. In ordering through the mail, most collectors will gamble when buying a book graded fine or better, as they feel that it must be a pretty nice book to receive that grade. But as the grade drops, the more mistrust there is from the buyer. Resistance to buy the lower grades, due to this tendency of over-grading in the market, has in itself contributed to the recent drop in prices. So in order to sell these lower grade books and be competitive, many dealers had to reduce prices. After all, since the condition wasn't attractive, the price had to be. These current market conditions have forced wider spreads between good and mint which is reflected in this edition. In most all cases, good has dropped while mint has gone up. The comic book market seems to be following patterns set in the coin and stamp fields years ago when, in those markets prices began to spread between the various grades as more and more lower grade items entered the market.

Due to the recent over-availability of books in the lower grades, the market has adjusted itself with reduced prices to meet the demand level. It would be worth pointing out here that this over-supply in lower grades of Golden Age books might be just a temporary condition since fewer and fewer collections are turning up. The wider spreads on fine and mint books should make the lower grades look a lot more attractive to prospective buyers. The adjusted prices should see many of these lower grades disappearing from the market—especially books in VG which, if graded accurately, is a very collectible condition. Some Golden Age books are scarce in any condition. These books should show price increases in all grades as they become identified and known in the market place, especially those with white pages.

The wider spreads developing in the market also makes grading that much more critical. Now, more than ever, accurate grading in buying and selling books can make the difference between profit and loss, especially since the dollar amounts between grades are much larger now.

Because of the more critical nature of properly grading books, the grading definitions in the front of this Price Guide have been updated. Standards for a mint book have been lowered slightly as very slight blemishes are present on all mint books due to the fact that comic books are not a high quality product. Slight blemishes do occur as they are being stapled, folded and trimmed. It has also been pointed out that books with extra-white pages usually bring a premium price in most grades and are becoming more and more sought after.

Inspired by recent films, Golden Age superhero titles sold very well, as mentioned earlier. Action, Superman, World's Finest, Detective, Batman, Adventure, Wonder Woman, Sensation, and All-Star were the most favorite. Timelys also were in high demand, especially war year issues, with Captain America and Venus by Everett at the top of the list. Centaur Publications' books showed a large growth such as Amazing Man, Amazing Mystery Funnies, Keen Detective Funnies, The Arrow, Funny Pages, Star Comics, Fantoman, etc., as well as renewed interest in Fawcett, Quality, MLJ, Nedor and Fox. DCs continued to be the hottest selling Golden Age title. Bondage covers from the Golden Age period have begun to be referenced to further illustrate some of the cross-over effect from pulps and earlier predecessors of comics.

The hot selling Centaurs were produced by the Lloyd Jacquet shop managed by Bill Everett. This shop created the characters and produced the books for several publishers in the 1939-41 period. These books, which contain art by Everett, Burgos, Gustavson, Tarpe Mills, Jack Cole, Wolverton and others, have become highly collectible. Some of the titles this shop produced were: Marvel Mystery, Daring Comics, Silver Streak, Daredevil, Target, Heroic, Blue Bolt, Victory, Green Giant, and Colossus.

Sales slowed for good girl art comics, crime comics, Avons, and special artist issues of the 1950s, but horror and crime books with bondage, spanking, mutilation, and otherwise grotesque scenes sold well. Mysterious Adventures is one good example. A.C.G. titles such as Forbidden Worlds, Adventures into the Unknown, Unknown Worlds, Herbie, etc. sold well and remained hard to get in condition. Ditko art books by Charlton showed good demand. DCs from the 1950-1960 period sold rapidly while Marvel Atlas titles showed little growth.

Many western titles again sold well, especially those with movie still covers or name cowboy titles such as Fawcett's Monte Hale, Hopalong Cassidy, Gene Autry, Lash Larue, etc., and Dell's Roy Rogers, Gene Autry, and The Lone Ranger. John Wayne comics continued to show a huge demand as well as all T.V. western books.

E.C.s, Ducks, and Little Lulus showed steady growth and seem to be blue chip items as their values keep inching up over the years. 3-D comics are up and the "craze" might be returning with the renewed interest in the movie industry as well as T.V.

Dell and Gold Key science fiction, fantasy and T.V. titles (due in part to their scarcity compared to Marvels and DCs) and other science fiction titles from the 1950s and 1960s were sought after. Planet Comics of the 1940s and early 1950s were very hot sellers. Dealers can't keep them in stock.

Interest in the reprint comics of the 1930s and 1940s picked up. Tip Top, Popular, Ace, King, Sparkler, and Super showed the strongest demand. These 1930s books in top condition seem to be drying up fast.

Love comics showed little increase but sold fairly well in condition. Drug books, **Seduction** and **Parade of Pleasure** issues have peaked. Katy Keene, Scribbly, Sugar and Spike, and Fox and the Crow were selling well at above guide prices. March of Comics remained hard to get. All movie books gained in popularity. Dell and Gold Key movie comics, Fawcett Movie Comics, Motion Picture Comics, Famous Stars, and Movie Comics were among the most popular. Harvey funny comics remained strong with other funny types staying the same.

Jim Sands spent all summer revamping the Classics section of the Price Guide. We feel the new format will be much easier to understand and should encourage more dealers and collectors to get involved with them. The demand for Classics seems to increase every year, especially for the original early issues. Thanks, Jim, for the good work!

Publicity of our hobby by radio, newspapers and T.V. persisted throughout the year. Terry Stroud appeared on the Merv Griffin show, treating the public with first looks at some rare comic books. Television continued to show interest as their scriptors included comic collections in several plots on some of the shows aired during the year. The Greatest American Hero has been a hit. Even the show's theme song got into the Top 20. One comic dealer traded and Action No. 1 for an antique car while another traded an antique car for an Action No. 1.

It seems that in spite of all the publicity comic collecting has received over the years, there are still people that haven't heard about it. For instance, last April a stamp company who advertised old stamps for sale in comics back in the late 1930s and 1940s, cleaned their files. The manager ordered that the 150 or so early Golden Age comics be purged from the files and shredded. An enlightened employee, while passing through the room, noticed the comics being shredded. Unfortunately, he only salvaged two or three books which he sold to a local comic shop for a handsome profit.

The biggest change in the recent comic market for 1981 was the price increase from 40 cents to 50 cents to 60 cents. Due to this, back issues of superhero titles are usually priced at a minimum of 75 cents. If it is a popular title (X-Men, New Teen Titans, Daredevil, etc.), it is priced as much as $1.50 for last month's issue.

While interest in the old 10 cents comics was increasing, most titles from 1964 to 1976 were slowing in sales with only a few exceptions. One theory offered for this slowdown in recent comics is that the prices increased too rapidly and became too high for books that are relatively common, especially compared to books from the 1950s or earlier. Exceptions were No. 1 issues, first appearances, special artist issues and other key books. Titles that did sell well were: Amazing Spider-Man Nos. 5-30, 90-122; Avengers Nos. 1-20, 57-up; X-Men Nos. 1-20, 49-up; and Conan which sold steadily at 1980 and over 1981 guide prices. (The upcoming Conan movie might have influenced this renewed interest.) X-Men sold well due in part to the popularity of the New X-Men. The Avengers were hot, also.

The hot sellers for 1981 were the more recent books in contrast to the earlier Silver Age titles. The New Teen Titans, followed closely by Miller Daredevil issues (Nos. 158-161, 163-up), are the current hot titles, and the prices on these books are going up rapidly. Good story line and unique art style caught the eyes of collectors on these books. Following closely behind in sales were X-Men, Avengers, Warlord, Moon Knight (especially appearances in Werewolf by Night), Micronauts, Rom, Spectacular Spider-Man No. 27 and No. 28, and all Byrne and Miller art issues.

While mint books continue to bring premium prices and spreads from good to fine keep increasing, books in fine condition, due to their scarcity, will probably be selling more and more towards the mint side. The current market indicates spreads of 1:3:5 or 6 which has been reflected in this edition. As books in the different grades either become more plentiful or dry up, the above spreads will change.

Original Art: Barks paintings continued to be in demand during the year with seven of the large paintings selling in the $20,000 to $30,000 range. A Barks pencil sketch for one of the paintings brought $880. A 9"x12" Barks duck painting sold for $4,600. A Disney Sleeping Beauty movie cel background watercolor brought $1,600. Two Snow White watercolor backgrounds sold for $3,000 and $4,000. Pogo Sunday page originals sold in the $800-$1,500 range depending on quality. An exceptional 1935 Flash Gordon full Sunday page original brought $7,000. Prince Valiant full Sunday pages sold for $800-$1,200 from the 1950s and $1,500-$3,500 from the 1930s and 1940s. An above average Foster Tarzan Sunday from 1934 brought $2,100. A Mickey Mouse daily from 1930, exceptional, sold for $4,000. Hogarth's Tarzan sold for $475 for a below average page to $1,800 for a choice one. A Frazetta "White Indian" comic book page from Durango Kid brought $1,070. A Felix the Cat Sunday from 1932 sold for $400. A Krazy Kat Sunday from 1925 brought $1,102; an Alley Oop daily from 1938, $125. A Johnny Comet Sunday page from 1952 brought $850, and a Frazetta Captain Comet comic book page sold for $1,375.

E.C. original art continued to show a lot of interest and sold well at all the Cochran auctions during the year. A few examples are: cover to Weird Science No. 21—$1,943; Wood story "EC Confidential"—$1,350; Graham Ingels horror—$1,065; Kurtzman "Jivaro Death"—$990; Feldstein "Cosmic Ray Bomb Explosion"—$883; cover to Tales From the Crypt No. 32—$665; Williamson story "50 Girls 50"—$4,428; early Craig story "Mutiny"—$440; Kamen story "Surprise Package"—$350; cover to Weird Fantasy No. 13—$1,070; Wood story "Mars Is Heaven"—$2,300; Davis story "Gas-tly Prospects"—$800; and Williamson story "Snap Ending"—$1,730.

INVESTOR'S DATA

The following tables compiled by Robert Crestohl denote the rate of appreciation of the top 50 Golden Age titles and the top 20 Silver Age titles over the past 11 years (1971-1981) since the first Price Guide was published. The retail value for a complete mint run of each title in 1981 is compared to its value in 1980 and 1971. By dividing the 1981 value by the 1980 or 1971 value, one can calculate the rate of appreciation of each title over the past year or past 11 years.

For example, a complete mint run of Action Comics retailed at $37,440 in 1981 and $2354 in 1971. From these figures it is calculated that every $100 investment in this title in 1971 would be worth $1590.48 in 1981. However, the rate of increase would be less for Fine and much less for Good over the same period.

The place in rank is given for each title by year, with its corresponding value. These tables can be very useful in forecasting trends in the market place. For instance, the investor might want to know which title is yielding the best dividend from one year to the next, or one might just be interested in seeing how the popularity of titles changes from year to year.

Superman overtook Donald Duck for the number five spot this past year. Batman was up 33 percent from 1980 and All-Star Comics increased 34.7 percent, but the really big gainers were in recent titles with X-Men jumping a huge 94 percent and Richie Rich moving up 46 percent. Little Lulu entered into the top 50 while Feature Books dropped out.

The following tables are meant as a guide to the investor and it is hoped that they might aid him in choosing titles in which to invest. However, it should be pointed out that trends may change at any time and that some titles can develop into real comers from a presently dormant state. In the long run, if the investor sticks to the titles that are appreciating steadily each year, he shouldn't go very far wrong.

As has been pointed out before, most titles that are appreciating the slowest are still increasing much faster than economic inflationary values during the same period.

TOP 50 TITLES
TOP 50 TITLES & RATE OF INCREASE OVER 1971 GUIDE VALUES

Title	1981 Guide Rank & Value		1980 Guide Rank & Value		1971 Guide Rank & Value		1981 Guide Value for Ea. $100 In 1971
Action Comics	1	$37440	1	$30548	6	$2354	$1590.48
Marvel Mystery Comics	2	34140	2	29649	4	2584	1321.21
Detective Comics	3	30688	3	24416	3	2747	1117.15
More Fun Comics	4	23661	4	18914	2	2816	840.23
Superman	5	22088	6	17162	12	1460	1512.88
Donald Duck	6	20844	5	18266	49	604	3450.99
Adventure Comics	7	19528	9	15408	1	3066	636.92
Walt Disney's C & S	8	19342	7	16856	11	1487	1300.74
Whiz Comics	9	18760	8	15970	13	1357	1382.46
Captain America	10	15707	10	13964	17	1303	1205.45
Batman	11	$12806	12	$9664	19	$1246	$1027.77
All Star Comics	12	12145	13	9015	9	1657	732.95
Police Comics	13	10023	16	7773	27	903	1109.97
All American Comics	14	9908	17	7655	23	1189	833.31
Mickey Mouse Magazine	15	9903	11	9729	18	1252	790.97
Flash Comics	16	9750	15	7783	14	1344	725.45
Planet Comics	17	9550	21	6621	48	613	1557.91
Captain Marvel Advs.	18	9241	14	7886	26	1009	915.86
Worlds Fair & Finest	19	8536	19	6840	30	841	1014.98
Dick Tracy	20	8356	22	6564	24	1116	748.75

Title	1981 Guide Rank & Value		1980 Guide Rank & Value		1971 Guide Rank & Value		1981 Guide Value for Ea. $100 In 1971
Motion Pic. Funnies Wkly.	21	$7500	18	$7500	—	N/A	N/A
Master Comics	22	$7415	20	$6626	25	$1021	$726.25
Human Torch	23	6991	24	5835	42	632	1106.17
Jumbo Comics	24	6482	25	5627	16	1320	491.06
Submariner	25	6400	26	5168	50	601	1064.89
Famous Funnies	26	6354	23	6150	7	2343	271.19
Pep Comics	27	6021	27	4787	28	880	684.20
Sensation Comics	28	5834	30	4659	38	681	856.68
Classics Comics	29	5742	29	4718	—	N/A	N/A
Star Spangled Comics	30	5731	28	4758	32	830	690.48
Wonder Woman	31	$5444	32	$4488	62	$537	$1013.78
Wow Comics	32	5282	31	4607	53	574	920.21
Hit Comics	33	4906	33	4149	64	523	938.05
Silver Streak Comics	34	4906	35	4081	82	394	1245.18
Superboy	35	4804	47	3432	91	360	1334.44
National Comics	36	4711	40	3681	39	676	696.89
Showcase	37	4604	44	3555	—	280	1644.29
Daredevil	38	4456	36	4016	41	639	697.34
Green Lantern Comics	39	4395	50	3360	83	390	1126.92
King Comics	40	4323	34	4112	5	2490	173.61
Crack Comics	41	$4273	46	$3495	48	$613	$697.06
Daring Mystery Comics	42	4220	38	3722	—	220	1918.18
Military Comics	43	4220	37	3759	65	520	811.54
Fantastic Four	44	4208	43	3570	—	254	1656.69
Smash Comics	45	4140	49	3398	31	833	497.00
Tip Top Comics	46	4100	48	3404	8	2088	196.36
Mystic Comics	47	4080	41	3585	95	340	1200.00
Little Lulu	48	4035	—	3122	—	219	1842.47
U.S.A. Comics	49	4030	42	3580	87	365	1104.11
Jungle Comics	50	3975	39	3692	29	861	461.67

TOP 20 TITLES (SILVER AGE—PRESENT)
TOP 20 TITLES & RATE OF INCREASE OVER 1971 VALUES

Title	1981 Guide Rank & Value		1980 Guide Rank & Value		1971 Guide Rank & Value		1981 Guide Value for Ea. $100 In 1971
Showcase	1	$4604	2	$3555	1	$280	$1644.29
Fantastic Four	2	4208	1	3570	2	254	1656.69
Amazing Spiderman	3	3466	3	3011	6	155	2236.13
Flash	4	2976	4	2544	7	142	2095.77
The Brave & the Bold	5	2632	5	2028	3	184	1430.43
T.T.A. & The Incredible Hulk	6	2360	6	1929	5	163	1447.85
Richie Rich	7	1934	8	1326	—	N/A	N/A
J.I.M. & Thor	8	1556	7	1413	10	123	1265.04
*Avengers	9	1450	12	1082	—	61	2377.05
*Green Lantern	10	1416	10	1163	14	96	1475.00
Advs. of the Big Boy	11	$1396	9	$1258	—	N/A	N/A
Jimmy Olsen	12	1389	11	1138	4	$170	$817.06
Challengers of the Unknown	13	1372	14	1020	8	140	980.00
Justice League	14	1318	13	1054	13	99	1331.31
*X-Men	15	1302	18	671	—	41	3175.61
Sugar and Spike	16	1183	17	801	—	46	2571.74
Lois Lane	17	1045	15	978	11	108	967.59
T.O.S. & Capt. America	18	986	16	977	15	83	1187.95
*Daredevil	19	614	20	504	—	51	1203.92
Strange Tales	20	592	19	588	12	100	592.00

To qualify for the TOP TWENTY SILVER AGE TITLES, the title must have begun no earlier than 1955. In the case of Tales of Suspense, Tales to Astonish, Journey Into Mystery, and Strange Tales, since the superheroes are the main interest, those sets are computed from where superheroes first appear.

** Year-end hot titles to watch in 1982; all Miller and Byrne art issues; New Teen Titans.*

The following table shows the rate of increase of the 50 most valuable single books and the 20 most valuable Silver Age books over the past two years. Comparisons can be made in the same way as in the previous table of the Top 50 titles. Ranking in most cases is relative since so many books fall under the same value. These books are listed alphabetically within the same value.

50 MOST VALUABLE BOOKS

Issue	1981 Guide Rank	1981 Guide Value	1980 Guide Rank	1980 Guide Value
Marvel Comics No. 1	1	$14000	1	$12000
Action Comics No. 1	2	11500	2	9200
Motion Picture Funnies Wkly. No. 1	3	7500	3	7500
Superman No. 1	4	7000	4	5600
Whiz Comics No. 1	5	6500	6	5000
Detective Comics No. 27	6	6000	5	5200
Double Action Comics No. 2	7	4500	10	3000
Batman No. 1	8	4000	12	2800
Captain America No. 1	9	3600	7	3000
Captain Marvel Adventures No. 1	10	3600	8	3000
More Fun Comics No. 52	11	$3500	11	$2800
Wow Comics No. 1	12	3500	9	3000
Walt Disney's C & S No. 1	13	2800	13	2500
More Fun Comics No. 53	14	2500	17	2000
Action Comics No. 2	15	2400	14	2100
Donald Duck Tells About Kites SCE	16	2400	15	2100
All American Comics No. 16	17	2000	33	1200
Marvel Mystery Comics No. 2	18	2000	16	2000
Donald Duck Four Color No. 9	19	2000	21	1800
Donald Duck March of Comics No. 4	20	2000	23	1800
Donald Duck Tells About Kites PGE	21	$2000	22	$1800
Boy Explorers No. 2	22	2000	18	2000
Action Comics No. 3	23	1800	26	1500
Marvel Mystery Comics No. 5	24	1800	19	1800
Red Raven Comics No. 1	25	1800	20	1800
Detective Comics No. 28	26	1700	25	1500
Superman No. 2	27	1600	28	1400
Whiz Comics No. 2	28	1600	27	1500
Human Torch No. 1	29	1500	32	1200
Action Comics No. 5	30	1500	31	1350
Detective Comics No. 1	31	$1500	42	$1050
Dick Tracy Feature Book	32	1500	32	1200
Mickey Mouse Four Color No. 16	33	1500	30	1400
All Star Comics No. 3	34	1400	—	900
Donald Duck Black & White No. 16	35	1400	29	1400
Donald Duck Four Color No. 29	36	1400	38	1200
Donald Duck March of Comics No. 20	37	1400	37	1200
Captain America No. 2	38	1300	34	1200
Action Comics No. 4	39	1200	43	1050
Detective Comics No. 33	40	1200	41	1050
Marvel Mystery Comics No. 3	41	$1200	35	$1200
Submariner No. 1	42	1200	—	950
Donald Duck Four Color No. 4	43	1200	36	1200
Flash Comics No. 1	44	1200	47	1000
Silver Streak Comics No. 6	45	1200	50	1000
Tales of Terror Annual No. 1	46	1200	50	1000
Daring Mystery Comics No. 1	47	1150	40	1100
Action Comics No. 7	48	1100	—	900
Action Comics No. 10	49	1100	—	900
Fantastic Four No. 1	50	1100	44	1000

20 MOST VALUABLE BOOKS (SILVER AGE)

Issue	1981 Guide Rank	1981 Guide Value	1980 Guide Rank	1980 Guide Value
Fantastic Four No. 1	1	$1100	1	$1000
Amazing Fantasy No. 15	2	1000	2	900
Showcase No. 4	3	1000	3	875
Amazing Spiderman No. 1	4	600	5	600

Issue	1981 Guide Rank	1981 Guide Value	1980 Guide Rank	1980 Guide Value
Incredible Hulk No. 1	5	600	6	480
If the Devil Would Talk	6	600	4	825
Journey Into Mystery No. 83	7	420	7	360
Fantastic Four No. 2	8	400	8	360
Richie Rich No. 1	9	375	17	240
Adventures of the Big Boy No. 1	10	350	9	300
Adventure Comics No. 247	11	$320	10	$270
Brave & the Bold No. 1	12	320	15	240
Showcase No. 1	13	320	16	240
Showcase No. 8	14	320	19	240
Avengers No. 1	15	300	11	240
Detective Comics No. 225	16	300	20	225
Fantastic Four No. 3	17	300	18	240
Jimmy Olsen No. 1	18	300	13	240
Tales to Astonish No. 27	19	300	12	240
Flash Comics No. 105	20	275	14	240

The following table lists the really hot titles over the past year. From one year to another, this list can change drastically.

HOT TITLES & RATE OF INCREASE 1981 GUIDE OVER 1980 GUIDE

Golden Age

Amazing-Man	70%
Scribbly	59%
Green Giant	56%
Planet Comics	44%
Superboy	40%
Mystery in Space	38%
All Star Comics	35%
Sugar & Spike	35%
Batman	33%
Target 1-30	33%
Green Lantern Comics	31%
Circus	29%
Superman	29%
Police Comics	29%
All American Comics	29%
Little Lulu	29%
National Comics	28%
Adventure Comics	27%
Dick Tracy	27%
Detective Comics	26%
Pep Comics	26%
More Fun Comics	25%
Flash	25%
World's Fair & Finest	25%
Submariner	25%
Sensation Comics	25%

Silver Age

X-Men	94%
Sugar & Spike	48%
Richie Rich	46%
Challengers of the Unknown	35%
Avengers	34%
The Brave & the Bold	30%
Showcase	30%

Recent

Spectacular Spider-Man	1400%
New Teen Titans No. 1-6	1319%
Daredevil No. 158-170	1041%
Moon Knight No. 1-3	200%
Warlord No. 1-38	115%
Iron Fist	83%
Teen Titans	76%
Rom No. 1-14	51%
The Defenders No. 1-90	42%
Micronauts No. 1-25	31%

COMICS WITH LITTLE IF ANY VALUE

There exists in the comic book market, as in all other collector's markets, items, usually of recent origin, that have relatively little if any value. Why even mention it? We wouldn't, except for one thing—this is where you could probably take your worst beating, investment-wise. Since these books are listed by dealers in such profusion, at prices which will vary up to 500 per cent from one dealer's price list to another, determining a realistic "market" value is almost impossible. And since the same books are listed repeatedly, list after list, month after month, it is difficult to determine whether or not these books are selling. In some cases, it is doubtful that they are even being collected. Most dealers must get a minimum price for their books; otherwise, it would not be profitable to handle. This will sometimes force a value on an otherwise valueless item. Since new comics are now priced at 60 cents or more each, most dealers who handle them get a minimum price of at least 75 cents. This is the **available** price to obtain a **reading** copy. However, this is not what dealers will pay to restock. Since many of these books are not yet collector's items, their salvage value would be very low. You may not get more than 5 cents to 10 cents per copy selling them back to a dealer. This type of material, from an investment point of view, would be of maximum risk since the salvage value is so low. For this reason, recent comics should be bought for enjoyment as reading copies and if they go up in value, consider it a bonus. On the other hand, you might buy a vastly over-priced golden-age comic and still expect to recover your loss after a reasonable passage of time. This, unfortunately, is not true of so many titles that we are put in a rather awkward position of listing.

THE PRICE GUIDE'S POSITION: We don't want to leave a title out just because it is presently valueless. And at the same time, we don't want to presume to "establish" what is collectible and what isn't. The passage of time and a change in collectors' interests can make almost any comic potentially valuable. Some books, by virtue of their age, will someday obtain a value as a cultural or historical curiosity. Therefore, we feel that all books, regardless of the demand for them, should be listed.

Since speculation in the comic book market began around 1964, most all titles since that time have been saved and are in plentiful supply. These books have been included for your information and can be found listed throughout The Guide with values assigned (under $1.00). The collector would be well advised to compare prices between several dealers' lists before ordering this type of material.

COLLECTING FOREIGN COMICS AND AMERICAN REPRINTS

One extremely interesting source of comics or early vintage—one which does not necessarily have to be expensive—is the foreign market. Many American strips, from both newspapers and magazines, are reprinted abroad (both in English and in other languages) months and even years after they appear in the states. By working out trade agreements with foreign collectors, one can obtain, for practically the cover price, substantial runs of a number of newspaper strips and reprints of American comic books dating back five, ten, or occasionally even twenty or more years. These reprints are often in black and white, and sometimes the reproduction is poor, but this is not always the case. In any event, this is a source of material that every serious collector should look into.

Once the collector discovers comics published in foreign lands, he often becomes fascinated with the original strips produced in these countries. Many are excellent, and have a broader range of appeal than those of American comic books.

CANADIAN REPRINTS

EC's: by J. B. Clifford

Several EC titles were published in Canada by Superior Comics from 1949 to at least 1953. Canadian editions of the following EC titles are known: (Pre-Trend) *Saddle Romances, Moon Girl, A Moon A Girl. . . Romance, Modern Love, Saddle Justice;* (New-Trend) *Crypt of Terror—Tales From the Crypt, Haunt of Fear, Vault of Horror, Weird Science, Weird Fantasy, Two-Fisted Tales, Frontline Combat,* and *Mad. Crime SuspenStories* was also published in Canada under the title *Weird SuspenStories* (Nos. 1-3 known). No reprints of *Shock SuspenStories* by Superior are known, nor have any "New Direction" reprints ever been reported. No reprints later than January 1954 are known. Canadian reprints sometimes exchanged cover and contents with adjacent numbers (e.g., a *Frontline Combat* 12 with a *Frontline Combat* No. 11 cover). They are distinguished both in cover and contents. As the interior pages are always reprinted poorly, these comics are of less value (about ½) than the U.S. editions; they were printed from asbestos plates made from the original plates. On some reprints, the Superior seal replaces the EC seal. Superior publishers took over Dynamic in 1947.

Dells: by Ronald J. Ard

Canadian editions of Dell comics, and presumably other lines, began in March-April, 1948 and lasted until February-March, 1951. They were a response to the great Canadian dollar crisis of 1947. Intensive development of the post-war Canadian economy was financed almost entirely by American capital. This massive import or money reached such a level that Canada was in danger of having grossly disproportionate balance of payments which could drive it into technical bankruptcy in the midst of the biggest boom in its history. The Canadian government responded by banning a long list of imports. Almost 500 separate items were involved. Alas, the consumers of approximately 499 of them were politically more formidable than the consumers of comic books.

Dell responded by publishing its titles in Canada, through an arrangement with Wilson Publishing Company of Toronto. This company had not existed for a number of years and it is reasonable to assume that its sole business was the production and distribution of Dell titles in Canada. There is no doubt that they had a captive market. If you check the publication data on the U. S. editions of the period you will see the sentence "Not for sale in Canada." Canada was thus the only area of the Free World in those days technically beyond the reach of the American comic book industry.

We do not know whether French editions existed of the Dell titles put out by Wilson. The English editions were available nationwide. They were priced at 10 cents and were all 36 pages in length, at a time when their American parents were 52 pages. The covers were made of coarser paper, similar to that used in the Dell Four Color series in 1946 and 1947 and were abandoned as the more glossy cover paper became more economical. There was also a time lag of from six to eight weeks between, say, the date an American comic appeared and the date that the Canadian edition appeared.

Many Dell covers had seasonal themes and by the time the Canadian edition came out (two months later) the season was over. Wilson solved this problem by switching covers around so that the appropriate season would be reflected when the books hit the stands. Most Dell titles were published in Canada during this period including the popular Atom Bomb giveaway, *Walt Disney Comics and Stories* and the *Donald Duck* and *Mickey Mouse* Four Color one-shots. The quality of the Duck one-shots is equal to that of their American counterparts and generally bring about 30 percent less.

By 1951 the Korean War had so stimulated Canadian exports that the

COLLECTION PROTECTION T.M.

"Mylar* Snugs", all made from Heavyweight 4 mil thick uncoated totally inert archival quality Mylar*Type D.
Mylar* Snugs should be used to protect your most prized collectibles. They are the finest and most permanent protection available anywhere.

100% Free Sample

Beware: There are imitations that look like Mylar, but may not be.

For those who have yet to compare our quality products with "others", we offer 100% free samples. (Limit one #58 to a customer.)
We are proud of the products we ourselves developed, patented, and manufactured over the past five years.
When buying polyester, Mylar, sleeves, envelopes, bags, or Snugs at stores, conventions or from friends be sure to know exactly what you're buying!
To identify our Snugs, look for:
1. Our trademark double die-cut flaps with double curvature to allow for easy opening & safe entry of collectibles.
2. Our trademark double flaps that can be conveniently (if so desired) folded over each other.
3. The super strong edge seal that is made after the flaps are cut rather than before in order to prevent seam splitting. Test for test, our patent pending process has 5 times the strength of any other!
4. Our Snugs are recognized worldwide by archivists, museums, and libraries as the finest product of its kind available anywhere!

When in doubt of what
products to buy; try our
free samples and then
join the rest - buying
THE BEST

Mylar*D, 4 mil Snugs™ (All with flaps unless otherwise noted)

Catalog No.	Item/Description	Size (inches)	Price per 10	(lbs)	Price per 50	(lbs)	Price per 200	(lbs)	Price per 1000	(lbs)
58	Comic, Regular Fits Comics from late 60's to present	7 1/4 x 10 1/2	6.25	(1)	15.00	(2)	52.50	(7)	246.00	(35)
61	Comic, Silver Gold Fits Comics from mid 40's to 1970	7 3/4 x 10 1/2	7.50	(1)	18.25	(2)	63.75	(7)	276.00	(35)
62	Comic, Super Gold Fits larger Comics of early 40's	8 1/4 x 10 1/2	7.75	(1)	19.50	(2)	69.75	(8)	318.75	(39)
66B	Comic, 3-ring Binder Series Fits most Comic books	8 x 10 3/4	8.25	(1)	20.00	(2)	69.00	(8)	319.00	(40)
63	Magazine Size	8 7/8 x 11 3/4	8.00	(1)	21.75	(2)	72.75	(9)	327.00	(44)
63B	Magazine Size, Binder Series	9 x 12	10.75	(1)	28.75	(3)	95.50	(9)	440.00	(46)
20	Coins, Stamps (No Flap)	2 1/4 x 2 1/2	2.75	(1)	7.00	(1)	25.25	(3)	110.00	(15)
21	Baseball Cards	2 1/2 x 3 1/2	3.75	(1)	9.50	(1)	30.75	(3)	144.00	(15)
24	Baseball Cards, Slides	3 x 4	3.75	(1)	9.75	(1)	31.50	(3)	148.00	(15)
25	Postcards, Money	3 3/4 x 5 3/4	5.25	(1)	13.50	(1)	43.25	(3)	198.00	(18)
27	Photos, Negatives, Cards	4 1/4 x 6	5.50	(1)	14.50	(1)	46.25	(4)	224.00	(20)
28	Photos, Negatives	5 1/4 x 7 1/4	5.75	(1)	15.25	(1)	50.50	(5)	225.00	(23)
56	Digests, TV Guide, Paperbacks	6 1/4 x 8 1/4	6.25	(1)	16.50	(2)	54.00	(6)	249.00	(28)
45	45 rpm Records, 7" Discs	7 1/4 x 7 1/4	5.50	(1)	14.50	(2)	49.00	(6)	225.00	(25)
53	Fits 8 1/2 x 11" Sheets	8 3/4 x 11 1/4	9.00	(1)	23.75	(2)	75.50	(8)	355.00	(40)
54	Fits 8 1/2 x 14" Sheets (legal)	8 3/4 x 14 1/4	10.25	(1)	27.00	(3)	91.25	(8)	415.00	(44)
67B	3-ring Binder Series (for 8 1/2 x 11)	9 x 11 1/4	9.75	(1)	25.75	(3)	85.00	(9)	395.00	(46)
64	Sheet Music	9 1/2 x 12 1/4	10.75	(1)	28.75	(3)	42.75	(10)	440.00	(50)
65	Life, Photo, Treasury	11 1/2 x 14 1/2	14.00	(2)	36.75	(4)	122.50	(15)	555.00	(75)
69	Portfolio	11 1/2 x 17 1/2	16.25	(2)	43.25	(5)	144.00	(19)	660.00	(90)
70	Tabloid	12 1/2 x 18 1/2	18.00	(2)	47.50	(5)	162.00	(21)	725.00	(99)
33	33 rpm LP Records, Albums	13 x 13	11.25	(1)	29.75	(3)	99.50	(10)	475.00	(50)
75	Newspapers, Original Art	18 x 24	30.50	(3)	107.50	(8)	345.00	(31)		

Custom Size, inquire

78	Sample Kit - one of Nos. 58, 61, 62, 66, & 63	3.50 each
79	Sample Kit - one of 20 different sizes	11.75 each

*Trademark of Dupont Co.
Mellinex by ICI Corp. may be used if equivalent in specification to Mylar D.

New!! Major Technilogical Breakthrough!

Another original development by our Engineering Department

Mylite™ Protective Envelopes

Lightweight, super strong, totally inert, permanently safe, made form 100% pure archival quality Mylar Type D (same material as our Snugs, only of thinner material.)

Now at last, an inexpensive answer to safe permanent storage and preservation of your more common collectibles. (**Mylar® Snugs** still the Best for your Best.) At last a permanent substitute for cheap, non-permanent poly bags and volatile vinyl sleeves!!!

The thinner Mylar® material allows for easy folding of the single flap, as historically done with Poly Bags. The Mylites™ are form fitting and can be used for paperback books and other bulkier items.

100% FREE SAMPLE

We know you're curious to see this new product so we'll send you a free sample when you send us a Self-Addressed (20¢) Stamped envelope.

Mylites, Lightweight Mylar®D Envelopes (All with flap)

Catalog No.	Item/Description	Size (inches)	Price per 100	(lbs.)	Price per 400	(lbs)	Price per 1000	(lbs)
158	Comic Regular Fits Comics in 1970's to Present	6 7/8 x 10 3/8	$ 9.50	(1)	32.75	(3)	69.00	(6)
161	Comic, Silver/Gold Fits Comics in 1950's & 60's	7 1/2 x 10 1/2	9.75	(1)	33.00	(3)	69.50	(6)
162	Comic, Large Gold Fits Comics in 1940's	7 7/8 x 10 1/2	10.50	(1)	36.25	(3)	76.25	(7)
163S	Small Magazine	8 5/8 x 11 1/4	14.00	(1)	48.50	(3)	101.75	(7)
163L	Large Magazine	8 7/8 x 11 3/4	14.50	(1)	50.00	(3)	105.25	(7)
124	Baseball Cards	2 7/8 x 4	6.50	(1)	19.50	(1)	40.00	(3)
127	Photos, Postcards	4 1/8 x 5 3/4	7.00	(1)	23.25	(2)	49.00	(5)
128	Photos, Small Paperback	5 3/8 x 7 5/8	8.00	(1)	27.50	(2)	58.00	(5)
156	Paperback, Digest, TV Guide	6 1/4 x 8 1/4	9.00	(1)	31.00	(2)	65.00	(5)
145	45 rpm Record Sleeves	7 3/8 x 7 3/8	9.25	(1)	32.00	(2)	67.00	(6)
153	Fits 8 1/2 x 11 Standard Sheets	8 3/4 x 11 1/4	14.00	(1)	47.50	(3)	99.00	(7)
164	Sheet Music	9 1/4 x 12 1/4	15.00	(1)	51.00	(3)	107.50	(7)
165S	Treasury Edition	10 1/2 x 14 1/2	19.00	(1)	65.25	(4)	137.00	(9)
165L	Photos, Lobby Card	11 1/2 x 14 1/2	19.50	(1)	67.25	(5)	141.50	(11)
133	Record Album	12 3/4 x 12 3/4	19.50	(1)	66.50	(5)	139.50	(12)
178	Super 78 Record Sleeves	10 1/4 x 10 1/4	13.50	(1)	47.00	(3)	98.00	(7)
Custom Sizes or Larger Quantities, please inquire								
179	Sample Kit - 10 different sizes	3.00 each						

Comments

Len Yokoyama, Hawaii
"Here I am with another order for your great products. Once again thanks for the outstanding service and quality items."

Ron Hickman, Pennsylvania
"Hurry- since one more day without being bagged in the "Snugs" is another day of aging. I want my collection to remain ageless."

Gary Springer, California
"Your acid-free comic boxes are the best I have seen in 12 years of collecting comics." Thanks for a fantastic product, your friend, Gary."

Wilson Fong, California
"Thanks for an excellent line of products and service."

Stephen D. Carmean, Virginia
"I wanted to offer you my congratulations & heartfelt thanks that there are still top-notch professionals in the business such as yourself."

Peter McCarthy, Massachusetts
"When people want to evaluate their comics, they think of the Overstreet price guide, and when people want to store their comics, they think of Gerber storage products."

Richardo Alejandro, California
"I can't get over the excellence of your "Snugs", which by the way are the best thing on the market today."

Jerry Woody, Alabama
"Storage of my collection is easier than ever and I can rest easy now knowing my collection will be safe from harmfull outside substances for years to come."

Herb Johnson, Massachusetts
"The storage boxes were of excellent quality and your service was very fast."

Gary Wolozy, Ohio
"Keep up the good work!"

Martha Taylor, Tennessee
"Thank you for providing an affordable and safe means of storing a smaller collection."

COLLECTION PROTECTION T.M.

ACID-FREE BOXES T.M.

Acid-Free Boxes

Acid Free Boxes

All of our Acid Free Boxes are made from Solid (not cheap corrugated) Acid Free (minimum ph of 8.5) 3% Alkaline Buffered Cardboard, made from virgin wood cellulose. All are white interior, steel blue exteriors.

Beware: Ordinary Corrugated Storage Boxes are not recommended for storage of your collectibles. The acid environment may migrate and damage your valued collectibles.

Box #16, 17, & 18 are shipped folded flat and are easily assembled.

All other boxes are shipped fully assembled with metal reinforced edges.

Catalog No.	Item/Description	Size (inches)	Price per 5	(lbs)	Price per 20	(lbs)
16	Silver/Gold Age Comics (100 Comics) Large, 70 mil Solid Cardboard	8 1/4 x 11 1/2 x 11 1/2	$ 18.50	(10)	59.75	(40)
17	Current Size Comics (180 Comics) Large, 70 mil Solid Cardboard	7 1/4 x 11 x 11	18.00	(10)	59.00	(40)
18	General Purpose & Magazines Large, 70 mil Solid Cardboard	9 x 12 x 12	19.25	(13)	63.50	(48)
10	Flip Top, metal reinforced edges Fits most Comic sizes	7 1/2 x 4 1/2 x 11	16.50	(5)	52.50	(25)
12	Comic Case, metal reinforced edges Fits most Comic sizes	9 x 3 x 3	9.75	(4)	31.25	(20)
14	Drop Front Shelf Box Fits most Comic & Magazine sizes	12 x 9 x 3	16.00	(5)	51.25	(25)
19	Shoe Box Style, metal reinforced For Cards, Photos, misc.	4 x 6 x 12	14.50	(5)	46.75	(25)

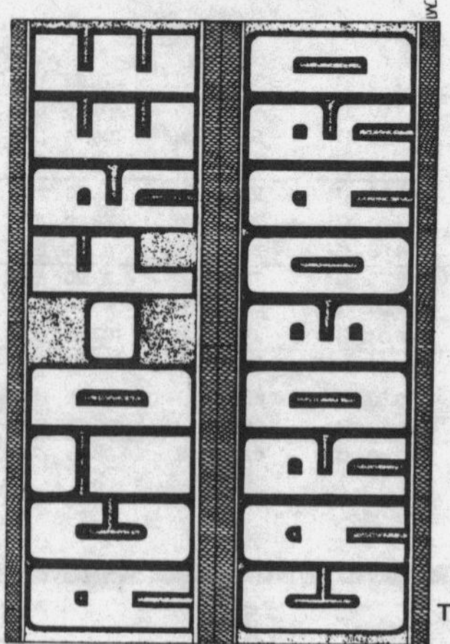

Acid-Free Cardboard (All min. ph 8.5 + 3 % Alkaline Buffer Added)

Acid Free Cardboard

The safest possible backing or barrier board or inserts with your collectibles. All boards are made from virgin wood cellulose fibers with a minimum ph of 8.5 (non-acid) plus an added 3% alkaline buffered reserve. Has been tested (accelerated aged) to maintain alkalinity for up to 400 years!

Warning: 98% of most common cardboard are not acid free with alkaline buffers. Beware of imposters. Our board has been used for years by archives and museums throughout the world.

Note: The 20-mil is Thinner and nice as comic inserts to add rigidity to bags. The Heavyweight 50 and 70 mil board is thicker and nice where more rigidity is required, expecially when storing comics without **Mylar** bags.

Catalog No.	Item/Description	Size (inches)	Price per 50	(lbs)	Price per 200	(lbs)	Price per 1000	(lbs)
34	20 mil Tan Gold Age	7 1/2 x 10 1/2	9.00	(3)	29.25	(12)	125.00	(58)
35	20 mil Tan Regular Size	6 7/8 x 10 3/8	8.50	(3)	27.75	(12)	119.50	(55)
37	Heavyweight Grey/White Gold Age Size	7 3/8 x 10 1/2	11.00	(7)	35.00	(27)	148.75	(135)
38	Heavyweight Grey/White Regular Comic Size	6 3/4 x 10 3/8	10.50	(7)	33.75	(25)	143.50	(125)
39	Heavyweight Grey/White Super Gold Size	7 3/4 x 10 9/16	13.00	(9)	41.75	(33)	177.50	(160)
40	Heavyweight Grey/White Magazine Size	8 1/2 x 11 5/8	15.00	(10)	48.00	(40)	198.00	(195)

We accept VISA, MasterCard — send no. & date

COLLECTION PROTECTION T.M.

MODULAR ARCHIVAL STORAGE CABINETS T.M.

Modular Archival Storage Cabinets (M.A.S.C.)T.M.

M.A.S.C.'s are:

- Another new original development by our Engineering Staff.
- Custom designed & manufactured at our Maine Division, home of beautiful Maine white pine.
- A new concept in safe storage as a handsome furniture display.
- The only furniture quality storage units in the world designed specifically for archival protection of collectibles.
- Fully Modular; begin with one unit plus base and have your storage units grow with your collections - safely.

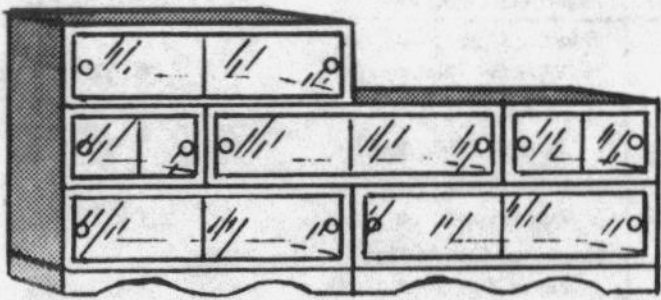

Our M.A.S.C.'s feature:

- Kiln Dried Main White Pine (1" plank)
- Furniture quality Rabbit routed corners.
- Counter sunk full plywood back.
- Special Ultra Violet reflective clear sliding doors. (See your collection safe.)
- Stained & finished interior with safe Polyurethane varnish (optional).
- Can be locked with sliding door locks (optional)
- Handsome decorative routed front trim.
- No fake wood, or plastic trim - all real 100% natural grain wood. (When is the last time you saw real wood Cabinets)

Dealers Comic Boxes

The permanent Comic Storage Box, 8"x 11"x24" length. Made from Kiln Dried Pine. Similar to construction of M.A.S.C. cabinets. Sliding solid plywood, it can easily be secured.

At last a permanent, safe, attractive, and indestructible storage container. Optional handles included (but not attached).

call our Toll Free Number to get on our FREE Mailing List.

Learn about special sales as they occur

1-800-343-9100

Catalog No.	Item/Description	Nominal Size		Price Each	(lbs)
93	Base Unit	12 x 24 x 3	$	9.75	(2)
94	11 1/2" High Full MASC For Comic Book & Magazine storage	10 x 24 x 11 1/2		19.75	(7)
95	11 1/2" High 1/2 MASC For Comic Book & Magazine storage	10 x 12 x 11 1/2		16.50	(4)
A	Option, Add removable shelf for smaller collectibles		Add	4.50	(1)
B	Option, Stain & add polyurethane		Add	5.00	
Note:	Custom sizes to fit modular scheme are available, request quotes				
88	Dealers' Comic Boxes Made from kiln dried pine, sliding solid cover	8 x 11 x 24		19.95	(10)

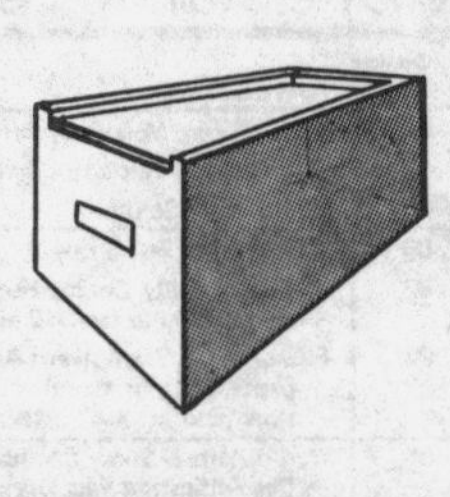

R. Wayne Richardson, Tennessee
"I continue to use and appreciate your fine products! The quality is top-notch."

Craig Leavitt, California
"I am now exclusively using your products to store and display my "Katy Keene Gems..." thank you for making them look so beautiful as well as safe..."

Harry Kleinman, California
"Your #33 Snugs work great to protect my animation drawings. Also makes them look real nice!"

Jeff Jarvis, Arizona
"I am very impressed with the quality of your bags. They are the best comic preservers I have ever seen. The glass shiney finish makes my comic inside look like a million bucks."

James Fahy, California
"I've ordered from you before, and was very pleased. Keep up the good work!...and the good product!!!!"

Bob Duyckinch, Jr., New Jersey
"I am very pleased with the 3 ring Mylar Snugs I received from you. They are fantastic and have made my collection look 100% better. My only problem is I didn't order enough the first time!"

Richard L. Martines, Hawaii
"After all for my best comics why not the best protection..."

Pat Toone, Illinois
"This is my 2nd order and I am pleased to say I think your products are the best one can buy. Thank you for your efforts in comic book protection."

Mike Wileman, Kansas
"I order with confidence, having dealt with you before. I have found nothing to compare with your products! Keep up the good work!"

John J. Miezejewski, Oklahoma
"I'm impressed! Snugs are superb and have made poly obsolete as far as my collection is concerned."

ORDER FORM

Note: Blank sheet of paper may also be used.

Your Name ______________________

Address ______________________

City ____________ State ______ Zip ______

COLLECTION PROTECTION T.M.

call our Toll Free Number to get on our FREE Mailing List.

Learn about special sales as they occur.

1-800-343-9100

Ordering Information:

Send: 1. Check
2. Money Order
3. VISA or M.C. number
& expiration date.

We accept VISA / master charge — send no. & date

To:
E. GERBER PRODUCTS, INC.
P.O. Box E
Center Lovell, ME 04016

Telephone Orders:

Call our Toll Free number 1-800-343-9100 to order or 1-207-925-1800 for information.
1. charge to VISA or M.C.
2. Request C.O.D. shipment;
You must have a listed phone number (to verify residence). $3.00 extra charge.

	Item Description Catalog Number	Unit Price	Total Price	Ship Weight
	Total Shipping Weight		**	
	5% Tax (Maine Residents)			
	Handling & Shipping Cost (from chart)			
	Total Amount			

Shipping:

Most orders are shipped via U.P.S., try to include street address. Shipping Costs are additional to prices listed. Total your order shipping weight and pick total Shipping and Handling costs from chart, add to Total Price.

Total Shipping Weight (lbs)	Your Zip Code Starts With 0, 1, or 2	3,4,5, or 6	7, 8, or 9	All Foreign Countries
0 – 5	$ 3.00	3.75	4.50	8.50
6 – 12	4.25	5.75	6.75	15.75
13 – 20	5.75	8.75	10.25	24.50
21 – 28	7.00	11.25	13.25	33.00
29 – 36	8.25	13.50	16.25	42.00
37 – 50	10.50	18.00	21.50	57.00

Above 50 lbs., add together additional amounts (example: 60 lbs. in Zip 1 would be 10.50 + 4.25.)

(Note: Costs subject to change depending on UPS rate increases)

Distributors

Minn. St. Paul Comics, St. Paul
Shinder's Read More, Minneapolis
Illinois Nostalgia Shop, Chicago
Heartland Comics, Galesburg
Book Stop, Cahokia
Glenwood Distributors, Collinsville
Family Book Exchange, Springfield
Starpost Enterprises, DeSoto
Missouri Book Gallery, Florissant
Rock Bottom Books, Columbia
Duckburg Books & Comics, Springfield
Kansas Prairie Dog Comics, Wichita
Nebraska Dragons Lair, Omaha
Trade-a-Tape, Lincoln
Oklahoma Bonney's, Norman
Texas Roy's & Millie's Books, Wichita
Dallas Gold & Silver Exchange, Dallas
The Remember When Shops, Dallas
Camelot, Houston
Maine Marstons', Presque Isle
Colorado Henry Gossage, Denver
Ten Little Indians Comic & Scifi Shop, Aurora
Security Book & Coin, Security

Penn. Eide's Comix SF Records, Pittsburgh
Beer Cans, Pittsburgh
Mike's Hobbies & Crafts, Johnstown
Book Bazaar, Northeast
American Comic Investor, Warrington
Comic Vault, Philadelphia
The Used Book Store, Kutztown
Delaware Xanadu, Wilmington
Virginia Benders, Hampton
Book Niche & Capital Comics Ctr. Alexandria
S. F. & Comic Book Shop, Annandale
The Hollinger Corporation, Arlington
Wash., D.C. Spring Gallery, Washington, D.C.
Maryland Barbarian Bookshop, Wheaton
Redbeard's Book Den, Silver Spring
Mindbridge Ltd., Baltimore
N. Carolina The Book Rack, Gastonia
Susan Cagle, Asheville
Heroes Aren't Hard To Find, Charlotte
Super Giant Books, Asheville
S. Carolina Doorway to Fantasy, N. Charleston
Book Exchange, Hanhan
Wisconsin BeeGee's Book Exchange, Brown Deer

Arizona Marty Hay, Spingerville
Utah Cosmic Aeroplane, Salt Lake City
Nevada Stella Enterprises, Sparks
California Golden Apple, Los Angeles
Scott Rosenberg, Beverly Hills
The Comic Shop, San Leandro
Hi De Ho Comic & Fantasy, Santa Monica
The Comic Gallery, San Diego
Comic Books Vol. III, Hawaiian Garden
Geoffrey's Graphic Books, Gardena
Fantasy Illustrated, Garden Grove
Fantasy Imprints, Poway
Comics & Fantasy, Santee
Book Harbor, Fullerton
Redbeard's Book Den, Newport Beach
Andromeda Bookshop, Santa Barbara
Alpha Omega Comics, Fresno
Quake Comics, Livermore
The Best of Two Worlds, Berkeley
Comic & Comix, Berkeley
Common Ground, Berkeley
Gary F. Wood, Berkeley
Brian's Books, Santa Clara
Comic Detectives, Sebastopol
Yesterday's Records and Books, Davis
The Comic Exchange (2 Stores), San Fran
Al's Comic Shop, Stockton
The Penny Ranch, Chico
Hawaii Parker Books, Pearl City
Comics Hawaii, Mililani Town
Aldamar World of Comics, Honolulu
David Oshiro, Waiange
Oregon Future Dreams, Portland
Wash. Golden Age Collectables, Seattle
Wally's Book & Comic Exchange, Kirkland

restrictions on comic book importation, which in any case were an offense against free trade principle, could be lifted without danger of economic collapse. Since this time Dell, as well as other companies, have been shipping direct into Canada.

HOW TO START COLLECTING

Most collectors of comic books begin by buying new issues in mint condition directly off the newsstand. (Subscription copies are, as a rule, folded and, hence, unsuited for collecting purposes.) Each week new comics appear on the stands that are destined to become true collectors items. The trick is to locate a store that carries a complete line of comics. In several localities this may be difficult. Most panelologists frequent several magazine stands in order not to miss something they want. Even then, it pays to keep in close contact with collectors in other areas. Sooner or later, nearly every collector has to rely upon a friend in Fandom to obtain for him an item that is unavailable locally.

Before you buy any comic to add to your collection, you should carefully inspect its condition. Unlike stamps and coins, defective comics are generally not highly prized. The cover should be properly cut and printed. Remember that every blemish or sign of wear depreciates the beauty and value of your comics.

The serious panelologist usually purchases extra copies of popular titles. He may trade these multiples for items unavailable locally (for example, foreign comics), or he may store the multiples for resale at some future date. Such speculation is, of course, a gamble, but unless collecting trends change radically in the future, the value of certain comics in mint condition should appreciate greatly, as new generations of readers become interested in collecting.

COLLECTING BACK ISSUES

In addition to current issues, most panelologists want to locate back issues. Some energetic collectors have had great success in running down large hoards of rare comics in their home towns. Occasionally, rare items can be located through agencies that collect old papers and magazines, such as the Salvation Army. The lucky collector can often buy these items for much less than their current market value. Placing advertisements in trade journals, newspapers, etc., can also produce good results. However, don't be discouraged if you are neither energetic nor lucky. Most panelologists build their collections slowly but systematically by placing mail orders with dealers and other collectors.

Comics of early vintage are extremely expensive if they are purchased through a regular dealer or collector, and unless you have unlimited funds to invest in your hobby, you will find it necessary to restrict your collecting in certain ways. However you define your collection, you should be careful to set your goals well within your means.

PROPER HANDLING OF COMIC BOOKS

Before picking up an old rare comic book, caution should be exercised to handle it properly. Old comic books are very fragile and can be easily damaged. Because of this, many dealers hesitate to let customers personally handle their rare comics. They would prefer to remove the comic from its bag and show it to the customer themselves. In this way, if the book is damaged, it would be the dealer's responsibility—not the customer's. Remember, the slightest crease or chip could render an otherwise Mint book to Near Mint or even Very Fine. The following steps are provided to aid the novice in the proper handling of comic books: 1. Remove the comic from its protective sleeve or bag very carefully. 2. Gently lay the comic (un-opened) in the palm of your hand so that it will stay relatively flat and secure. 3. You can now leaf through the book by carefully rolling or flipping the pages with the thumb and forefinger of your other hand. Caution: Be sure the book always remains relatively flat or slightly rolled. Avoid creating stress points on the covers with your fingers and be particularly cautious in bending covers back too far on Mint books. 4. After examining the book, carefully insert it back into the bag or protective sleeve. Watch corners and edges for folds or tears as you replace the book.

HOW TO SELL YOUR COMICS

If you have a collection of comics for sale, large or small, the following steps should be taken. (1) Make a detailed list of the books for sale, being careful to grade them accurately, showing any noticeable defects; i.e., torn or missing pages, centerfolds, etc. (2) Decide whether to sell or trade wholesale to a dealer all in one lump or to go through the long laborious process of advertising and selling piece by piece to collectors. Both have their advantages and disadvantages.

In selling to dealers, you will get the best price by letting everything go at once—the good with the bad—all for one price. Simply select names either from ads in this book or from some of the adzines mentioned below. Send them your list and ask for bids. The bids received will vary depending on the demand, rarity and condition of the books you have. The more in demand, and better the condition, the higher the bids will be.

On the other hand, you could become a "dealer" and sell the books yourself. Order a copy of one or more of the adzines. Take note how most dealers lay out their ads. Type up your ad copy, carefully pricing each book (using the Guide as a reference). Send finished ad copy with payment to adzine editor to be run. You will find that certain books will sell at once while others will not sell at all. The ad will probably have to be retyped, remaining books repriced, and run again. Price books according to how fast you want them to move. If you try to get top dollar, expect a much longer period of time. Otherwise, the better deal you give the collector, the faster they will move. Remember, in being your own dealer, you will have overhead expenses in postage, mailing supplies and advertising cost. Some books might even be returned for refund due to misgrading, etc.

In selling all at once to a dealer, you get instant cash, immediate profit, and eliminate the long process of running several ads to dispose of the books; but if you have patience, and a small amount of business sense, you could realize more profit selling them directly to collectors yourself.

WHERE TO BUY AND SELL

Throughout this book you will find the advertisements of many reputable dealers who sell back-issue comics magazines. If you are an inexperienced collector, be sure to compare prices before you buy. Never send large sums of cash through the mail. Send money orders or checks for your personal protection. Beware of bargains, as the items advertised sometimes do not exist, but are only a fraud to get your money.

The Price Guide is indebted to everyone who placed ads in this volume, whose support has helped in curbing printing costs. Your mentioning this book when dealing with the advertisers would be greatly appreciated.

THE BUYERS GUIDE
DYNAPUBS, 15800 Rt. 84 North
East Moline, IL 61244

COLLECTOR'S DELIGHT
P. O. Box 11021
San Diego, CA 92111

The Price Guide highly recommends the above adzines, which are full of ads buying and selling comics, pulps, radio tapes, premiums, toys and other related items. You can also place ads to buy or sell your comics in the above publications.

COMIC BOOK MAIL ORDER SERVICES

The following offer a mail order service on new comic books. Write for rates and details:

BILL COLE, P. O. Box 60, Wollaston, MA 02170 (Disney Comics)

DELTA - T COMICS, 11407 55 Avenue, Edmonton, Alberta, Canada T6H 0X3

DOUG SULIPA'S COMIC WORLD, 315 Ellice Ave., Winnipeg, Man., Canada R3B 1X7

FOUR COLOR DREAMS COMIC SERVICE, 9 St. Catherine Drive, St. Peters, MO 63376

FRIENDLY FRANK'S COMICS, 1025 North Vigo, Gary, IN 46403

PRESIDENTIAL COMIC BOOK SERVICE, P. O. Box 41, Scarsdale, NY 10583

SEA GATE DISTRIBUTORS, INC., 6514 20th Avenue, Brooklyn, NY 11204

STYX COMIC SERVICE, P. O. Box 3791, Winnipeg, Manitoba, Canada R2W 3R6

COMIC BOOK CONVENTIONS

As is the case with most other aspects of comic collecting, comic book conventions, or cons as they are referred to, were originally conceived as the comic-book counterpart to science-fiction fandom conventions. There were many attempts to form successful national cons prior to the time of the first one that materialized, but they were all stillborn. It is interesting that after only three relatively organized years of existence, the first comic con was held. Of course, its magnitude was nowhere near as large as most established cons held today.

What is a comic con? As might be expected, there are comic books to be found at these gatherings. Dealers, collectors, fans, whatever they call themselves can be found trading, selling, and buying the adventures of their favorite characters for hours on end. Additionally if at all possible, cons have guests of honor, usually professionals in the field of comic art, either writers, artists, or editors. The committees put together panels for the con attendees where the assembled pros talk about certain areas of comics, most of the time fielding questions from the assembled audience. At cons one can usually find displays of various and sundry things, usually original art. There might be radio listening rooms; there is most certainly a daily showing of different movies, usually science-fiction or horror type. Of course there is always the chance to get together with friends at cons and just talk about comics; one also has a good opportunity to make new friends who have similar interests and with whom one can correspond after the con.

It is difficult to describe accurately what goes on at a con. The best way to find out is to go to one or more if you can.

The addresses below are those currently available for conventions upcoming in 1981. Unfortunately, addresses for certain major conventions are unavailable as this list is being compiled. Once again, the best way to keep abreast of conventions is through the various adzines. Please remember when writing for convention information to include a self-addressed, stamped envelope for reply. Most conventions are non-profit, so they appreciate the help. Here is the list:

COMIC BOOK CONVENTIONS FOR 1982

ALL AMERICAN COMIC CON—c/o Old Weird Heralds, 6804 N.E. Broadway, Portland, OR 97213. Phone (503) 254-4942, evenings 287-3106.

ATLANTA FANTASY FAIR—c/o Harley Anton, P. O. Box 14262 S. E. Station, Baton Rouge, LA 70898. Aug. 13-15, 1982. Atlanta Biltmore Hotel.

BAYCON 8—Salvador Dichiera, P. O. Box 3931, San Francisco, CA 94119.

CHICAGO COMICON—Larry Charet, 1219-A West Devon Ave., Chicago, IL 60660. Phone (312) 274-1832.

CHICAGO-MONTHLY MINI CON—Write Larry Charet, 1219-A West Devon Ave., Chicago, IL 60660.

COLLECTORS' MEET (Burlington, Mass.)—R. C. Gesner, 8 Belmont St., Lowell, MA 01851.

COLORADO COMIC ART CONVENTION—P. O. Box 10741, Edgemont Branch, Golden, CO 80401.

COMIC CON III—c/o Scott Blacksher, 10473 Aphonia, El Paso, TX 79924. (915) 821-2617. July 16-18, 1982.

CREATION CON—159 W. 33rd St., Suite 908, New York, NY 10001. Phone (212) 594-7850. Holds major conventions in the following cities: Atlanta, Boston, Cincinnati, Cleveland, Detroit, London, Los Angeles, Philadelphia, Rochester, San Francisco, and Washington, D.C. Write or call for details.

DELAWARE VALLEY COMICART CONSORTIUM—Box 62, Maple Shade, NJ 08052. Attn: Frederick Marcus.

FANTACON—Tom Skultan, Veronica Cahill, Fantaco Ent. Inc., 21 Central Ave., Albany, NY 12210.

HOLLYWOOD COMIC BOOK & SCIENCE FICTION CONVENTION—Bruce Schwartz, 921 N. Gardner, Apt. 9, Los Angeles, CA 90046.

HOUSTON CON '82—P. O. Box 713, Stafford, TX 77477-0713, June 18-20, 1982

ITHACON VII, Ithaca, NY—Bill Turner, 1043 Auburn Rd., Groton, NY 13073.

MAPLECON V—P. O. Box 2912 Station D, Ottawa, Ontario, Canada K1P 5W9.

MID-OHIO CON, Roger A. Price c/o March of Dimes, 1090 Lexington Ave., Mansfield, Ohio 44907, Nov. 13, 1982 at Quality Inn Park Place, Mansfield, Ohio.

MINNEAPOLIS COMIC CONVENTION—Box 3221 Traffic Station, Minneapolis, MN 55403.

MOBILE COMIC ART AND SCIENCE FICTION FESTIVAL (2nd Annual), Howard Johnson's Motor Lodge, 3132 Government Blvd. For information: Steve Barrington, P.O. Box 2522, Mobile, AL 36652, (205) 457-1925.

NEW YORK COMIC ART CONVENTION '82—Phil Seuling, 6514 20th Ave., Brooklyn, NY 12204.

NEWCON '82—Don Phelps, P. O. Box 85, Cohasset, MA 02025.

ORLANDO CON '82—409 N. Semoran, Orlando, FL 32807.

PHOENIX, AZ. Fans of comics, gum cards, movies and other collectables meet at COLLECTORS' MARKETPLACE to swap, buy and sell. Quality Inn West, Sunday, Sept. 27, 10AM to 4PM. Information: 838-3629.

PITTCON '82—Ben Pondexter, 827 Anaheim St., Pittsburgh, PA 15219.

ROVACON 7—P. O. Box 117, Salem, VA 24153.

SAN DIEGO COMIC-CON—Box 17066, San Diego, CA 92117. Aug., 1982.

SKYCON 2, Dennis W. Howard, Super Giant Books, 38 Wall St., Asheville, NC 28801, May 1982.

SUFFOLK COUNTY COMIC BOOK AND BASEBALL CARD NOSTALGIA SHOW, Smithtown, N.Y., for information call Dennis (516) 724-7422.

SUPER-CON COMIC BOOK CONVENTIONS, Howard Johnson's Motor Lodge, 2 George St., Pawtucket, R.I., hours-10am to 5pm, 1982 dates: Jan 31, March 21, May 23, July 25, Sept 26 & Nov 7.

SUPERSTARS EXPO '82—Philip Hecht, 372 E. 17th St., Brooklyn, NY 11226.

WIZARDS NOSTALGIA CON IV—Hobbitt's Fantasy Shoppe Ltd., 10046 - 106 St., Edmonton, Alberta, Canada T5J 1C9.

COMIC BOOK CLUBS

ALABAMA—The Mobile Panelology Assoc., P.O. Box 2522, Mobile, AL 36652. Meets 1st Monday each month at 2301 Airport Blvd., Mobile, AL, 6:30pm to 9:30pm.

ARIZONA—Collectors' Marketplace, Phoenix, AZ. Meets last Sunday each month at Quality Inn West. Write: Visions, Box 28283, Tempe, AZ 85282, phone (602) 838-3629.

ARKANSAS—Little Rock Comic Club, c/o 7509 Cantrell No. 103, Little Rock, AR 72207. Meets every third Monday 7 p.m.

CALIFORNIA—The Comics Heroines Fan Club, Steve Johnson, P. O. Box 1329, Campbell, CA 95008.

CONNECTICUT—Equinox, c/o Kevin O'Neill, 11 Karen Ave., Stratford, CT 06497. (Produces its own fanzine "Equinox" where members contribute art and stories.)

FLORIDA—West Florida Comic Book Club, Troy Waters, 2275 Scenic Hwy., Apt. 110, Pensacola, FL 32503. (Monthly newsletter-zine)

KENTUCKY—A U.S. & Canadian Club, Dean Webb, 301 Chestnut Ave., Apt. 4, Berea, KY 40403. Annual dues—$3.00, includes newsletter.

MAINE—Maine Comics Club, Joe Veilleux, 63 North Main, Pittsfield, Maine 04967.

MASSACHUSETTS—Mad—The Mad Freaks Club, Ben Rosenberg, 109 Warren St., Newton Centre, MA 02159.

MINNESOTA—Minnesota Comics & Fantasy Assn., Box 3221 Traffic Station, Minneapolis, MN 55403. Puts on quarterly conventions and has informal gatherings.

NEW JERSEY—Comic Club of Maplewood, P. O. Box 65, Maplewood, NJ 07040.

NEW YORK—Destiny, Brian Friedman, 9202 Ave. M., Brooklyn, N.Y. 11236, fee $2.00; bi-monthly newsletter.

Little Lulu Fan Club, Norman F. Hale, 110 Bank St., Apt. 2H, New York, NY 10014.

OKLAHOMA—Oklahoma Alliance of Fandom, P.O. Box 18858, Oklahoma City, OK 73154, annual dues $7.00.

PENNSYLVANIA—Pittsburgh Comix Club, Ben Pondexter, 827 Anaheim St., Pittsburgh, PA 15219.

Comic Collectors of Western Pennsylvania, Kurt Shaw, 4 Elco Dr., Coraopolis, PA 15108.

The Erie Comic Book Club, c/o Mike Sopp, 438 W 32, Erie, PA 16508.

Marvel Mania, Stuart Schanbacher, 2708 E. Ontario St., Philadelphia, PA 19134.

TEXAS—Texas International Comic Book Club, Stuart Robertson, 514 Huntington Dr., Lewisville, TX 75067.

UTAH—The Great Salt Lake Comics, Clifford Kemple, 4085 West 3275 South, Salt Lake City, UT 84120.

CANADA—The International Comic Collector's Club, P. O. Box 11366 Station H, Nepean, Ontario, Canada K2H 5Z0. (Publishes a quarterly bulletin.) Annual dues—$10.00 year.

ENGLAND—The Association of Comics Enthusiasts, Denis Gifford, 80 Silverdale, Sydenham, London SE26 England.

Note: Anyone wanting their clubs listed in next year's guide, please send information.

THE HISTORY OF COMICS FANDOM

At this time it is possible to discern two distinct and largely unrelated movements in the history of Comics Fandom. The first of these movements began about 1953 as a response to the then-popular, trend-setting EC lines of comics. The first true comics fanzines of this movement were short-lived. Bhob Stewart's EC FAN BULLETIN was a hectographed newsletter that ran two issues about six months apart; and Jimmy Taurasi's FANTASY COMICS, a newsletter devoted to all science-fiction comics of the period, was a monthly that ran for about six months. These were followed by other newsletters, such as Mike May's EC FAN JOURNAL, and George Jennings' EC WORLD PRESS. EC fanzines of a wider and more critical scope appeared somewhat later. Two of the finest were POTRZEBIE, the product of a number of fans, and Ron Parker's HOOHAH. Gauging from the response that POTRZEBIE received from a plug in an EC letter column, Ted White estimated the average age of EC fans to lie in the range of 9 to 13, while many EC fans were in their mid-teens. This fact was taken as discouraging to many of the faneds, who had hoped to reach an older audience. Consequently, many of them gave up their efforts in behalf of Comics Fandom, especially with the demise of the EC groups, and turned their attention to science-fiction fandom with its longer tradition and older membership. While the flourish of fan activity in response to the EC comics was certainly noteworthy, it is fair to say that it never developed into a full-fledged, independent, and self-sustaining movement.

The second comics fan movement began in 1960. It was largely a response to (though it later became a stimulus for) the Second Heroic Age of Comics. Most fan historians date the Second Heroic Age from the appearance of the new FLASH comics magazine (numbered 105 and dated February 1959). The letter departments of Julius Schwartz (editor at National Periodicals), and later those of Stan Lee (Marvel Group) and Bill Harris (Gold Key) were most influential in bringing comics readers into Fandom. Beyond question, it was the reappearance of the costumed hero that sparked the comics fan movement of the sixties. Sparks were lit among some science-fiction fans first, when experienced fan writers, who were part of an established tradition, produced the first in a series of articles on the comics of the forties—ALL IN COLOR FOR A DIME. The series was introduced in XERO No. 1 (September 1960), a general fanzine for science-fiction fandom edited and published by Dick Lupoff.

Meanwhile, outside science-fiction fandom, Jerry Bails and Roy Thomas, two strictly comics fans of long-standing, conceived the first true comics fanzine in response to the Second Heroic Age. The fanzine, ALTER EGO, appeared in March 1961. The first several issues were widely circulated among comics fans, and were to influence profoundly the comics fan movement to follow. Unlike the earlier EC fan movement, this new movement attracted many fans in their twenties and thirties. A number of these older fans had been active collectors for years but had been largely unknown to each other. Joined by scores of new, younger fans, this group formed the nucleus of a new movement that is still growing and shows every indication of being self-sustaining. Although it has borrowed a few of the more appropriate terms coined by science-fiction fans, Comics Fandom of the Sixties was an independent if fledging movement, without, in most cases, the advantages and disadvantages of a longer tradition. What Comics Fandom did derive from science-fiction fandom it did so thanks largely to the fanzines produced by so-called double fans. The most notable of this type is COMIC ART, edited and published by Don and Maggie Thompson.

HOW TO SELECT FANZINES

In the early 1960s, only a few comic fanzines were being published. A fan could easily afford to subscribe to them all. Today, the situation has radically changed, and it has become something of a problem to decide which fanzines to order.

Fanzines are not all of equal quality or general interest. Even different issues of the same fanzine may vary significantly. To locate issues that will be of interest to you, learn to look for the names of outstanding amateur artists, writers, and editors, and consult fanzine review columns. Although you may not always agree with the judgements of the reviewers, you will find these reviews to be a valuable source of information about the content and quality of the current fanzines.

When ordering a fanzine, remember that print runs are small and the issue you may want may be out of print (OP). Ordinarily in this case, you will receive the next issue. Because of irregular publishing schedules that nearly all fanzines must, of necessity, observe, allow up to 90 days or more for your copy to reach you. It is common courtesy when addressing an inquiry to an ama-publisher to enclose a self-addressed, stamped envelope.

FAN PUBLICATIONS OF INTEREST

NOTE: We must be notified each year for listing to be included due to changes of address, etc.

THE ADAMA JOURNAL—Silver Unicorn Graphics, P.O. Box 7000-822, Redondo Beach, CA 90277; zine for TV series "Battlestar Galactica."

AFTA—Bill-Dale Marcinko, RPO 5009, CN 5063, Rutgers University, New Brunswick, NJ 08903.

BEM—Martin Lock, 3 Marlow Court, Britannia Square, Worcester WR1 3DP England.

CARTOON—The Cartoon Museum, Jim Ivey, 561 Obispo Ave., Orlando, FL 32807.

THE CLASSICS READER—W. J. Briggs, P. O. Box 1191, Station 'Q', Toronto, Ontario, Canada M4T 2P4.

COLLECTOR'S DREAM MAGAZINE—P. O. Box 127, Station T, Toronto, Ontario, Canada M6B 3Z9.

COLLECTOR'S PARADISE—Jay White, P.O. Box 3658, Cranston, R.I. 02910, covers several collectible fields.

COMIC BOOKS AS AN INVESTMENT—Comics & Comix, 2461 Telegraph Ave., Berkeley, CA 94704.

COMIC INFORMER—J.R. Riley, 3131 W. Alabama, Suite 301, Houston, TX, 77098; articles, new comics news, ads, etc.

THE COMIC PRESS—Russell Condello, 34 Burt Street, Rochester, NY 14609. (Articles about Silver Age Comics.)

THE COMIC READER—Street Enterprises, P. O. Box 255, Menomonee Falls, WI 53051. (Gives advance information on all new comics being published.)

THE COMICS JOURNAL—P. O. Box 292, Riverdale, MD 10840.

COMICS NEWSLINE—Frank Verzyl, P.O. Box 711, Lindenhurst, NY 11757. Gives advance info on all new comics published.

THE COMIC TIMES—305 Broadway, New York, NY 10007. (Gives advance info on new comics, movie reviews, etc.)

COMIXINE—Howard Stangroom, 10 Geneva Dr., Redcar, Cleveland T510 1JP, England.

THE COMPLETE EC LIBRARY—Russ Cochran, P. O. Box 437, West Plains, MO 65775. (A must for all EC collectors. Reprinting of the complete EC line is planned. Write for details.)

THE DUCKBURG TIMES—Dana & Frank Gabbard, 400 Valley View, Selah, WA 98942. (A quarterly fanzine for Barks and Disney fans.) (Subscriptions: $5 for 4 issues)

DYNAZINE—Eric Scalzi, 8 Palmer Dr., Canton, MA 02021. (No. 6—$1 PP, No. 7—75 cents PP).

ELFQUEST—2 Reno Rd., Poughkeepsie, NY 12603. (Fantasy comic publ.)

ERB-dom—Camille Cazedussus Jr., Rt. 2, Box 119, Clinton, LA 70722.

EXCALIBUR ENT.—507 5th Ave., New York, NY 10017. (Publishing adzines Manhunter & Shade.)

FANTASY TRADER—Gez Kelly, 34 Heworth Hall Dr., York Y03 0AQ England. (A monthly comics adzine with news and articles.)

FANTASY UNLIMITED—Alan Austin, 47 Hesperus Crescent, Millwall, London E14 9A8, England.

FAWCETT COLLECTORS OF AMERICA NEWSLETTER—Bernie McCarty, 1124 Abbot Lane, Park Forest South, IL 60466.

FULL CIRCLE COMIX—Jeff Cooke, 764 Lyman Ave., Muskegon, MI 49441.

FUTURE GOLD—Geoffrey Schutt, 4146 Marlaine Dr., Toledo, Ohio 43606. (Investors newsletter).

GRAPHIC STORY MAGAZINE—Bill Spicer, 329 North Ave. 66, Los Angeles, CA 90042.

THE GRAPHIC TIMES—David Johnson, 25 Cowles St., Apt. 42. Bridgeport, CT 06607; 6 issue sub.—$2.50.

GRATIS—36 Ivy Green Acres, Scarborough, Ontario, Canada M1G 2Z3.

THE HEROINES SHOWCASE—Steven Johnson, P.O. Box 1329, Campbell, CA 95008. Quarterly publ. about the comics heroines.

ICE CUBE—Greg Kokko, editor, Suite 210, 1800 Baseline Rd., Ottawa, Ont., Canada K2C 3N1. ($1.50 pp.)

KATY KEENE NEWSLETTER—QUARTERLY—Craig Leavitt, 1125 11th St., Modesto, CA 95354. ($12 yr.)

THE LOA READER—Rich Olson, Dept. of Psychology, Univ. New Orleans, New Orleans, LA 70122.

LOLLAPALOOSA—Mitch O'Connell, 5453 N. Lakewood, Chicago, IL 60640. (Published annually; focuses on comic art.)

MAD FREAKS USA—Ben Rosenberg, 109 Warren St., Newton Centre, MA 02159; newsletter for Mad Magazine freaks.

THE MARVEL COMICS INDEX—P. O. Box 127, Station T, Toronto, Ontario, Canada M6B 3Z9.

MEMORY LANE—BI-MONTHLY, P.O. Box 1627, Lubbock, TX 79408; covers film, radio, TV, music & comics.

MINDOT, THE ANIMATION QUARTERLY, 3112 Holmes Ave. South, Minneapolis, MN 55408. ($6 for 4 ishs.)

NEAR MINT—Al Dellinges, P.O. Box 34158, San Francisco, CA 94134; contains articles on comics, art and old movies.

OVR COMICS—1114 Devons Rd., London, England.

PHANTACEA—Jim McPherson, 1749 Collingwood St., Vancouver, B. C., Canada V6R 3K2.

THE RBCC—10885 Angola Rd., San Diego, CA 92126.

SPACE ACADEMY NEWSLETTER—Joe Sarno, P. O. Box 302, Des Plaines, IL. 60017.

STRIP SCENE—Carl Horak, Remuda Publ., 6312 Crowchild Trail S.W., Calgary, Alberta, Canada T3E SR5. Ph (403) 242-8532. (For strip collectors.)

THE SPIRIT CHECKLIST—Cat Yronwode, P. O. Box 86, Willow Springs, MO 65793.

TETRAGRAMMATON FRAGMENTS!!—Chris Rock, P. O. Box 14, West Plains, MO 65775. (UFO newsletter—send 50 cents for sample copy.)

THE UNICORN HUNTERS GUIDEBOOK—Silver Unicorn Graphics, P.O. Box 7000-822, Redondo Beach, CA 90277; a publication for unicorn aficionados.

VISIONS—Lamar Waldron, 335 Terrydale Dr., Marietta, GA 30067.

WORLD OF ELZON—K. C. Comics Group, 216B Sherbrook St., Winnipeg, Manitoba, Canada R3C 2B6. (Science Fiction/Fantasy Comic Magazine).

COLLECTING STRIPS

Collecting newspaper comic strips is somewhat different than collecting magazines, although it can be equally satisfying.

Obviously, most strip collectors begin by clipping strips from their local paper, but many soon branch out to strips carried in out-of-town papers. Naturally this can become more expensive and it is often frustrating, because it is easy to miss editions of out-of-town papers. Consequently, most strip collectors work out trade agreements with collectors in other cities in order to get an uninterrupted supply of the strips they want. This usually necessitates saving local strips to be used for trade purposes only.

Back issues of strips dating back several decades are also available from time to time from dealers. The prices per panel vary greatly depending on the age, condition, and demand for the strip. When the original strips are unavailable, it is sometimes possible to get photostatic copies from collectors, libraries, or newspaper morgues.

COLLECTING ORIGINAL ART

In addition to magazines and strips, some enthusiasts also collect the original art for the comics. These black and white, inked drawings are usually done on illustration paper at about 30 per cent up (i.e., 30 per cent larger than the original printed panels). Because original art is a one-of-a-kind article, it is highly prized and often difficult to obtain.

Interest in original comic art has increased tremendously in the past several years. Many companies now return the originals to the artists who have in turn offered them for sale, usually at cons but sometimes through agents and dealers. As with any other area of collecting, rarity and demand governs value. Although the masters' works bring fine art prices, most art is available at moderate prices. Comic strips are the most popular facet with collectors, followed by comic book art. Once scarce, current and older comic book art has surfaced within the last few years. In 1974 several original painted covers of vintage comic books and coloring books turned up from Dell, Gold Key, Whitman, and Classic Comics.

The following are sources for original art:

Tony Dispoto
Comic Art Showcase
P. O. Box 425
Lodi, NJ 07644

Artman
Bruce Bergstrom
1620 Valley St.
Fort Lee, NJ 07024

Fantasm
Andy Kamm
406 W. Marion St.
Lititz, PA 17543

Russ Cochran
P. O. Box 437
West Plains, MO 65775

The Cartoon Carnival
408 Bickmore Dr.
Wallingford, PA 19086

Steve Herrington
30 W. 70th St.
New York, NY 10023

The Cartoon Museum
Jim Ivey
509 N. Semoran
Orlando, FL 32807

Museum Graphics
Jerome K. Muller
Box 743
Costa Mesa, CA 92627

A Chronology of the Development of THE AMERICAN COMIC BOOK

By
M. Thomas Inge*

Precursors: The facsimile newspaper strip reprint collections constitute the earliest "comic books." The first of these was a collection of Richard Outcault's **Yellow Kid** from the Hearst **New York American** in March 1897. Commercial and promotional reprint collections, usually in cardboard covers, appeared through the 1920s and featured such newspaper strips as **Mutt and Jeff, Foxy Grandpa, Buster Brown,** and **Barney Google**. During 1922 a reprint magazine, **Comic Monthly**, appeared with each issue devoted to a separate strip, and in 1929 George Delacorte published 13 issues of **The Funnies** in tabloid format with original comic pages in color, becoming the first four-color comic newsstand publication.

**With the invaluable assistance of Bill Blackbeard and helpful suggestions and comments by William M. Gaines, Bob Overstreet, Hames Ware, Don and Maggie Thompson, Jerry Bails, and Ron Goulart, to all of whom the compiler is grateful.*

1933: The Ledger syndicate published a small broadside of their Sunday comics on 7" by 9" plates. Employees of Eastern Color Printing Company in New York, sales manager Harry I. Wildenberg and salesman Max C. Gaines, saw it and figured that two such plates would fit a tabloid page, which would produce a book about 7½" x 10" when folded. Thus 10,000 copies of **Funnies on Parade**, containing 32 pages of Sunday newspaper reprints, was published for Proctor and Gamble to be given away as premiums. Some of the strips included were: **Joe Palooka, Mutt and Jeff, Hairbreadth Harry,** and **Reg'lar Fellas**. M. C. Gaines was very impressed with this book and convinced Eastern Color that he could sell a lot of them to such big advertisers as Milk-O-Malt, Wheatena, Kinney Shoe Stores, and others to be used as premiums and radio give-aways. So, Eastern Color printed **Famous Funnies: A Carnival of Comics**, and then **Century of Comics**, both as before, containing Sunday newspaper reprints. Mr. Gaines sold these books in quantities of 100,000 to 250,000.

1934: The give-away comics were so successful that Mr. Gaines believed that youngsters would buy comic books for ten cents like the "Big Little Books" coming out at that time. So, early in 1934, Eastern Color ran off 35,000 copies of **Famous Funnies, Series 1**, 64 pages of reprints for Dell Publishing Company to be sold for ten cents in chain stores. Selling out promptly on the stands, Eastern Color, in May 1934, issued **Famous Funnies** No. 1 (dated July 1934) which became, with issue No. 2 in July, the first monthly comic magazine. The title continued for over 20 years through 218 issues, reaching a circulation peak of nearly one million copies. At the same time, Mr. Gaines went to the sponsors of Percy Crosby's **Skippy**, who was on the radio, and convinced them to put out a Skippy book, advertise it on the air, and give away a free copy to anyone who bought a tube of Phillip's toothpaste. Thus 500,000 copies of **Skippy's Own Book of Comics** was run off and distributed through drug stores everywhere. This was the first four-color comic book of reprints devoted to a single character.

1935: Major Malcolm Wheeler-Nicholson's National Periodical Publications issued in February a tabloid-sized comic publication called **New Fun**, which became **More Fun** after the sixth issue and converted to the normal comic-book size after issue eight. **More Fun** was the first comic book of a standard size to publish original material and continued publication until 1949. **Mickey Mouse Magazine** began in the summer, to become **Walt Disney's Comics and Stories** in 1940, and combined original material with reprinted newspaper strips in most issues.

1936: In the wake of the success of **Famous Funnies**, other publishers, in conjunction with the major newspaper strip syndicates, inaugurated more reprint comic books: **Popular Comics** (News-Tribune, February), **Tip Top Comics** (United Features, April), **King Comics** (King Features, April), and **The Funnies** (new series, NEA, October). Four issues of **Wow Comics**, from David McKay and Henle Publications, appeared, edited by S. M. Iger and including early art by Will Eisner, Bob Kane, and Alex Raymond.

1937: The first non-reprint comic book devoted to a single theme (although single-theme pulp magazines had included comic strips earlier) was **Detective Comics**, an offshoot of **More Fun**, which began in March to continue to the present. The book's initials, "D.C.," have long served to refer to National Periodical Publications, which was purchased from Major Nicholson by Harry Donenfeld late this year.

1938: "D.C." copped a lion's share of the comic book market with the publication of **Action Comics** No. 1 in June which contained the first appearance of Superman by writer Jerry Siegel and artist Joe Shuster, a discovery of Max C. Gaines. The "man of steel" inaugurated the "Golden Era" in comic book history. Fiction House, a pulp publisher, entered the comic book field in September with **Jumbo Comics**, featuring Sheena, Queen of the Jungle, and appearing in over-sized format for the first eight issues.

1939: The continued success of "D.C." was assured in May with the publication of **Detective Comics** No. 27 containing the first episode of Batman by artist Bob Kane and writer Bill Finger. **Superman Comics** appeared in the summer. Also, during the summer, a black and white premium comic titled **Motion Picture Funnies Weekly** was published to be given away at motion picture theatres. The plan was to issue it weekly and to have continued stories so that the kids would come back week after week not to miss an episode. Four issues were planned but only one came out. This book contains the first appearance and origin of the Sub-Mariner by Bill Everett (8 pages) which was later reprinted in **Marvel Comics**. In November, the first issue of **Marvel Comics** came out, featuring the Human Torch by Carl Burgos and the Sub-Mariner reprint with color added.

1940: The April issue of **Detective Comics** No. 38 introduced Robin the Boy Wonder as a sidekick to Batman, thus establishing the "Dynamic Duo" and a major precedent for later costume heroes who would also have boy companions. **Batman Comics** began in the spring. Over 60 different comic book titles were being issued, including **Whiz Comics** begun in February by Fawcett Publications. A creation of writer Bill Parker and artist C. C. Beck, **Whiz's** Captain Marvel was the only superhero ever to surpass Superman in comic book sales. Drawing on their own popular pulp magazine heroes, Street and Smith Publications introduced **Shadow Comics** in March and **Doc Savage Comics** in May. A second trend was established with the summer appearance of the first issue of **All-Star Comics**, which brought several superheroes together in one story and in its third issue that winter would announce the establishment of the Justice Society of America.

1941: Wonder Woman was introduced in the spring issue of **All-Star Comics** No. 8, the creation of psychologist William Moulton Marston and artist Harry Peter. **Captain Marvel Adventures** began this year. By the end of 1941, over 160 titles were being published, including **Captain America** by Jack Kirby and Joe Simon, **Police Comics** with Jack Cole's Plastic Man and later Will Eisner's Spirit, **Military Comics** with Blackhawk by Eisner and Charles Cuidera, **Daredevil Comics** with the original character by Charles Biro, **Air Fighters** with Airboy also by Biro, and **Looney Tunes & Merrie Melodies** with Porky Pig, Bugs Bunny, and Elmer Fudd, reportedly created by Bob Clampett for the Leon Schlesinger Productions animated films and drawn for the comics by Chase Craig. Also, Albert Kanter's Gilberton Company initiated the **Classics Illustrated** series with **The Three Musketeers**.

1942: Crime Does Not Pay by editor Charles Biro and publisher Lev Gleason, devoted to factual accounts of criminals' lives, began a different trend in realistic crime stories. **Wonder Woman** appeared in the summer. John Goldwater's character Archie, drawn by Bob Montana, first published in **Pep Comics**, was given his own magazine **Archie Comics**, which has remained popular over 35 years. The first issue of **Animal Comics** contained Walt Kelly's "Albert Takes the Cake," featuring the new character of Pogo. In mid-1942, the undated Dell Four Color title, No. 9, **Donald Duck Finds Pirate Gold**, appeared with art by Carl Barks and Jack Hannah. Barks, also featured in **Walt Disney's Comics and Stories**, remained the most popular delineator of Donald Duck and later introduced his greatest creation, Uncle Scrooge, in **Christmas on Bear Mountain** (Dell Four Color No. 178).

1945: The first issue of **Real Screen Comics** introduced the Fox and the Crow by James F. Davis, and John Stanley began drawing the **Little Lulu** comic book based on a popular feature in the **Saturday Evening Post** by Marjorie Henderson Buell from 1935 to 1944. Bill Woggon's Katy Keene appears in issue No. 5 of **Wilbur Comics** to be followed by appearances in **Laugh, Pep, Suzie** and her own comic book in 1950.

1950: The son of Max C. Gaines, William M. Gaines, who earlier had inherited his father's firm Educational Comics (later Entertaining Comics), began publication of a series of well-written and masterfully drawn titles which would establish a "New Trend" in comics magazines: **Crypt of Terror** (later **Tales from the Crypt**, April), **The Vault of Horror** (April), **The Haunt of Fear** (May), **Weird Science** (May), **Weird Fantasy** (May), **Crime SuspenStories** (October), and **Two-Fisted Tales** (November), the latter stunningly edited by Harvey Kurtzman.

1952: In October "E.C." published the first number of **Mad** under Kurtzman's creative editorship.

1953: All Fawcett titles featuring Captain Marvel were ceased after many years of litigation in the courts during which National Periodical Publications claimed that the super-hero was an infringement on the copyrighted Superman.

1954: The appearance of Fredric Wertham's book **Seduction of the Innocent** in the spring was the culmination of a continuing war against comic books fought by those who believed they corrupted youth and debased culture. The U. S. Senate Subcommittee on Juvenile Delinquency investigated comic books and in response the major publishers banded together in October to create the Comics Code Authority and adopted, in their own words, "the most stringent code in existence for any communications media."

1955: In an effort to avoid the Code, "E.C." launched a "New Direction" series of titles, such as **Impact, Valor, Aces High, Extra, M.D.,** and **Psychoanalysis**, none of which lasted beyond the year. **Mad** was changed into a larger magazine format with issue No. 24 in July to escape the Comics Code entirely.

1956: Beginning with the Flash in **Showcase** No. 4, Julius Schwartz began a popular revival of "D.C." superheroes which would lead to the "Silver Age" in comic book history.

1960: After several efforts at new satire magazines (**Trump** and **Humbug**), Harvey Kurtzman, no longer with Gaines, issued in August the first number of another abortive effort, **Help!**, where the early work of underground cartoonists Jay Lynch, Skip Williamson, Gilbert Shelton, and Robert Crumb appeared.

1961: Stan Lee edited in November the first **Fantastic Four**, featuring Mr. Fantastic, the Human Torch, the Thing, and the Invisible Girl, and inaugurated an enormously popular line of titles from Marvel Comics featuring a more contemporary style of superhero.

1962: Lee introduced **The Amazing Spider-Man** in August, with art by Steve Ditko, **The Hulk** in May and **Thor** in August, the last two produced by Dick Ayers and Jack Kirby.

1965: James Warren issued **Creepy**, a larger black and white comic book, outside Comics Code's control, which emulated the "E.C." horror comic line. Warren's **Eerie** began in September and **Vampirella** in September 1969.

1967: Robert Crumb's **Zap** No. 1 appeared, the first popular underground comic book.

1970: Editor Roy Thomas at Marvel begins **Conan the Barbarian** based on fiction by Robert E. Howard with art by Barry Smith.

1972: The Swamp Thing by Berni Wrightson begins in November from "D.C."

1973: In February, "D.C." revived the original Captain Marvel with new art by C. C. Beck and reprints in the first issue of **Shazam** and in October **The Shadow** with scripts by Denny O'Neil and art by Mike Kaluta.

1974: "D.C." began publication in the spring of a series of over-sized facsimile reprints of the most valued comic books of the past under the general title of "Famous First Editions," beginning with a reprint of **Action** No. 1 and including afterwards **Detective Comics** No. 27, **Sensation Comics** No. 1, **Whiz Comics** No. 2, **Batman** No. 1, **Wonder Woman** No. 1, **All-Star Comics** No. 3, and **Flash Comics** No. 1.

1975: In the first collaborative effort between the two major comic book publishers of the previous decade, Marvel and "D.C." produced together an over-sized comic-book version of **MGM's Marvelous Wizard of Oz** in the fall, and then the following year in an unprecedented cross-over produced **Superman vs. the Amazing Spider-Man**, written by Gerry Conway, drawn by Ross Andru, and inked by Dick Giordano.

1976: Frank Brunner's Howard the Duck, who had appeared earlier in Marvel's **Fear** and **Man-Thing**, was given his own book in January, which because of distribution problems became an over-night collector's item. After decades of litigation, Jerry Siegel and Joe Shuster were given financial recompense and recognition by National Periodical Publications for their creation of Superman, after several friends of the team made a public issue of the case.

1977: Stan Lee's **Spider-Man** was given a second birth, fifteen years after his first, through a highly successful newspaper comic strip, which began syndication on January 3 with art by John Romita. This invasion of the comic strip by comic book characters continued with the appearance on June 6 of Marvel's **Howard the Duck**, with story by Steve Gerber and visuals by Gene Colan. In an unusually successful collaborative effort, Marvel began publication of the comic book adaption of the George Lucas film **Star Wars**, with script by Roy Thomas and art by Howard Chaykin, at least three months before the film was released nationally on May 25. The demand was so great that all six issues of **Star Wars** were reprinted at least seven times, and the installments were reprinted in two volumes of an over-sized Marvel Special Edition and a single paperback volume for the book trade.

1978: In an effort to halt declining sales, Warner Communications drastically cut back on the number of "D.C." titles and overhauled its distribution process in June. The interest of the visual media in comic book characters reached a new high with the Hulk, Spider-Man, and Doctor Strange, the subjects of television shows; with various projects begun to produce film versions of Flash Gordon, Dick Tracy, Popeye, Conan, The Phantom, and Buck Rogers; and with the movement reaching an outlandish peak of publicity with the release of 'Superman' in December. Two significant applications of the comic book format to traditional fiction appeared this year: **A Contract with God and Other Tenement Stories** by Will Eisner and **The Silver Surfer** by Stan Lee and Jack Kirby.

A flashback of Norman Mingo and Alfred E. Neuman planning some new mischief, rendered by Jack Rickard especially for this article. Mingo regarded Rickard as his natural successor for the continuance of Alfred E. paintings on **MAD** covers. © E.C. Publications, Inc.

NORMAN MINGO AND ALFRED
The World's Greatest Facelift

by Jerry De Fuccio

Mingo proudly displaying paperbacks that grace his cover art.
Paperbacks © E.C. Publications, Inc.

Beyond a doubt, one of the best known faces of the 20th Century is that of the freckled and unworriable kid named Alfred E. Neuman. Indeed, his fame is so far-reaching and assured it will probably outlast that of Paul Newman, Edwin Newman and maybe even Cardinal Newman. Disregarding for a moment what this may say about the current state of our civilization and culture, one thing is clear—Alfred E. Neuman owes much of his world-wide renown to one man—Norman Mingo, a dapper artist with a military bearing who never went near a comic book or a humor magazine until he was past sixty. At an age when most citizens are looking forward to tacking senior onto their title and settling down to golf, knitting, Social Security and Florida, Norman Mingo embarked on an entirely new career. A career that was to make him and his work known to several generations of delighted readers who fell under the spell of an irreverent publication called **MAD**.

Mingo's maiden cover for **MAD**, which gave the world the very first painted portrait of our Alfred, was for the 30th issue, dated December, 1956. That was an election year and we'd come up with the idea of pushing our gap-toothed mascot-to-be as a write-in candidate for president. His competition for the Chief of State job consisted of Dwight D. Eisenhower and Adlai Stevenson. Ike finished first, Adlai ran second and Alfred trailed in somewhere after that. While he didn't make it into the Oval Office, he did manage to capture the attention of a goodly part of the world's population. It wasn't long after Norman began doing impressive covers, as I recall, that a French newspaper listed the three most readily recognizable American faces as Eisenhower, Marilyn Monroe, and Alfred E. Neuman. And not necessarily in that order.

I knew Norman Mingo from the time he painted his first **MAD** cover through the day he turned out his last Alfred E. Neuman—the one you see gracing **this** cover of **The Comic Book Price Guide** No. 12. We were friends for over two decades and I looked on him as sort of an ideal uncle. We shared several of kindly Bill Gaines' generous jaunts to the more exotic parts of the globe—the storied annual **MAD** trips that Gaines spent a full year planning for the relaxation and unwinding of his faithful editors, artists and writers. I remember especially the time in Mexico City, when our dining room hostess asked Norman why he didn't bring along his boy, too. She meant, of course, Alfred E. Neuman. Norman joined me for lunch on many of the occasions when he delivered a finished cover to **MAD** and didn't have to hurry back to Tarrytown. We were often joined by the irreplaceable **MAD** art director, John Putnam. Both Norman and John, elder statesmen of **MAD**, were partial to slow eating and ample conversation, which was all right with me. Any one would be fascinated at the way Putnam rearranged the meat, potatoes and vegetables on his plate, conceiving an entirely new layout other than that provided by the kitchen. Norman would say that John actually copy-cast his peas and carrots in equal lines; no widows.

Ah, John Francis Putnam is another **MAD** legend but I'd like to talk about Norman Mingo's work now—about the man himself and what he did before he came into the **MAD** offices and about the effect he had on the life and times of Alfred E. Neuman. . .and vice versa.

MAD Magazine wasn't that old when Norman climbed aboard. It had only graduated from being a comic book, six issues before he did his first, and definitive for all time, portrait of our immortal mascot. As is true with most great events of history, there are several versions of how Alfred E. Neuman came into being and how Norman Mingo got the job of being the official **MAD** court painter. The account that comes closest to matching my own memories is the one Al Feldstein crystallized recently. "The character, which later became our beloved Alfred E. Neuman, was first used by Bernie Shir-Cliff on the cover of the first Ballantine reprint paperback, **The MAD Reader**," Al told me. "Harvey Kurtzman, who was the editor of **MAD** at the time, then began to use this crude 'idiot' face in the magazine, which had recently turned from 'comic' to the current 'slick' format with issue No. 24. It was used as part of the cover border and sporadically in the magazine. When I took over **MAD** from Harvey, I finished up issue No. 28, did issue No. 29 and then decided that the 'Me Worry?' character that had been included in the cover border and inside the magazine under various names (i.e., Mel Haney, Melvin Cowznofsky, etc.), should become our featured trademark. After all, **Playboy** had the rabbit and **Esquire** had Esky the fat dirty old man. However, the portrait of the 'Me Worry?' kid that we'd been using was from an old print that had been around for years. It was in black and white, very crude, and lacked detail and charm. What I wanted was a full-color, humanized rendition of this face, and I wanted it infused with personality and impish lovable character."

The above crude "idiot" face, given to Mingo inspired the portrait of the "Me Worry?" kid.

Nobody on the then far-from-vast staff seemed quite suited to undertake the job Al had in mind. Finally, he decided to place an ad in The New York Times, looking for a portrait artist and/or illustrator who could do covers in the future and especially this assignment of painting the definitive "Me Worry?" kid. Feldstein, a man of uncanny instincts and determinations, simply adds, "Norman Mingo answered the ad."

The day that Norman came to call on Al Feldstein and Bill Gaines was the one when he was answering not one Times ad, but two. "In 1953, after many years of successful free-lancing in the New York advertising art market, I tried to go into silk screening," Norman later recalled. "My studio turned out great work but lost money. Financially the project wiped me out. So I answered two ads from the classified section of the New York Times. This was in 1956. First I went to Dancer, Fitzgerald, Sample, Inc., a Madison Avenue ad agency, and on the same day, visited **MAD**, down on Lafayette Street.'' He got both jobs.

Everybody at **MAD** was impressed with the portfolio of samples Norman showed them. Years later, he mentioned that they were entries in a World War II art competition, which he had **lost**. Anyway, Al decided to give him an assignment on the spot. ''In the back of my mind was the idea that we would run our 'Me Worry?' kid for President, as **MAD**'s write-in candidate. I instructed Norman as to what I

Alfred E. Neuman Presidential campaign button. © E.C. Publications, Inc.

While working for Dancer, Fitzgerald, Sample ad agency in the mid 1950s, Mingo painted the above ad for General Foods. © General Foods.

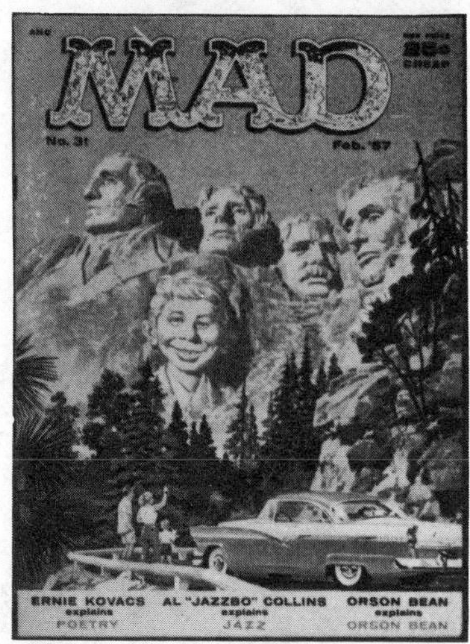

MAD No. 31—Mount Rushmore cover by Mingo. © E.C. Publications, Inc.

wanted in the way of 'look' for the kid, Norman did the job, and this definitive portrait set Alfred's look once and for all. Every artist since has had to follow this portrait exactly. There could be no deviation. The face lost something when it was changed in the slightest way."

Over in the art bullpen of the DFS agency Norman drew for such accounts as General Foods, Falstaff Beer, and the U.S. Army my Recruiting. In the moonlight hours he turned out color portraits of Alfred E. Neuman, working mostly in combination of water colors and acrylics. "However, the advertising work demanded more and more time and won out." Norman stepped down and Frank Kelly Freas, who copped awards for his science-fiction paintings year after year, took over the cover chores for a time.

After seven years with Dancer, Fitzgerald, Sample, the agency virtually retired Norman. **MAD** art director John Putnam got wind of it and called him in 1963. Norman came home to **MAD**. He did for Alfred E. Neuman what Leonardo DaVinci had done for the Mona Lisa—created an image that would endure. But Leonardo only painted the lady once, sitting there and smiling. Norman gave us the impish kid in a multitude of settings and poses. He painted him running for President, decked out as Uncle Sam, as Robin's replacement to a horrified Batman, as a hardhat, a fiddler on the roof, a member of the Godfather's wedding party, as both sides of the Generation Gap, as an organ grinder for King Kong, as Rosemary's Baby, as Barbra Streisand, and even as one of the sculptured heads at Mount Rushmore. One cover idea required a composition of Alfred as an innovative delivery boy for a pizza parlor, wheeling the bare and steaming delicacy out of the store like a hoop. This was one rare instance when Norman used a "live model." He had a giant pizza leaning against his easel for a few days. Finally, when the painting was finished, he simply disposed of it. John Putnam cagily suggested he should have had it bronzed and sold to the highest bidder at Seuling's next comic convention.

So, now we know something about what Norman had been up to from that fateful day in 1956 when he first encountered Feldstein, Gaines, and the rest of the Usual Gang of Idiots at **MAD**. But where had he been all those

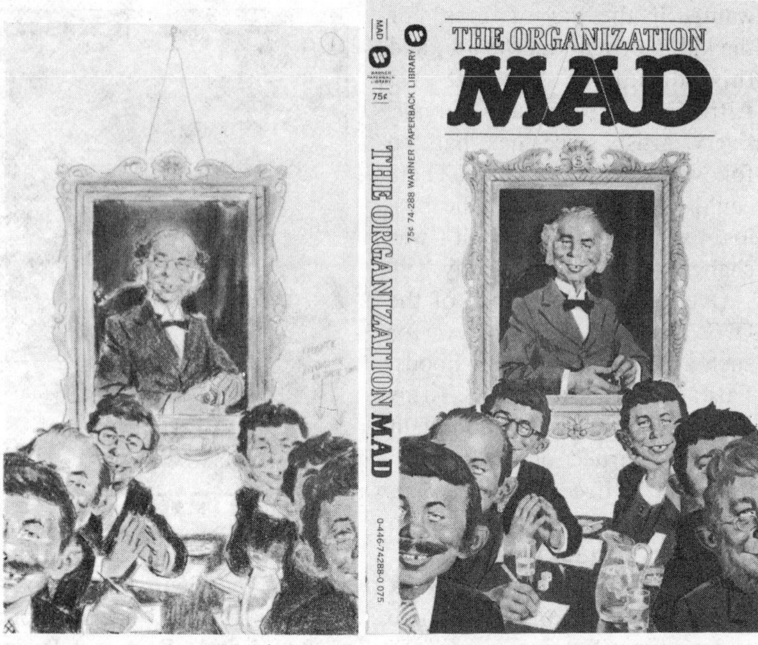

Mingo preliminary sketch and finished cover for **The Organization MAD** paperback. © E.C. Publications, Inc.

MAD preliminary sketch by Mingo. © E.C. Publications, Inc.

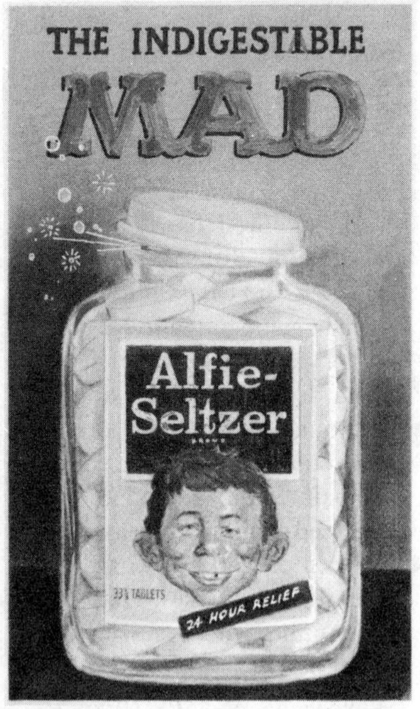

Mingo preliminary sketch for **The Indigestible MAD** paperback. © E.C.

years prior to that and what had he been doing? Well, Norman Theodore Mingo was born on January 20, 1896 in Chicago, Illinois. I think one of the reasons he was able to identify so well with **MAD**'s devilish Alfred E. Neuman was that he was somewhat of a self-styled bad boy himself up until the time he hit his early teens; a mischief-making kid who had frequent run-ins with the petty tyrants who dominate a child's world. Norman also tangled with his rather straight-laced father, John Oliver Mingo, whom he liked to describe as being "straight out of Dickens." John Oliver, a hard-working $25 a week mail-carrier, occasionally beat his young son, so I assume Norman didn't have any of Dickens' kindly old gentlemen in mind when he made that comparison.

Norman's first brush with illustration was a vicarious one and came about when he got a job selling that profusely illustrated slick magazine, **The Saturday Evening Post**. A budding entrepreneur, he not only peddled the magazines himself, but also used his home as the shape-up headquarters for several of the other local kids who sold the **Post**. His father didn't care for the ever-present bundles of pulp that filled up his easy chair and the front parlor. Young Norman's gentle mother, Cora, tried to mediate the frequent confrontations between boy and husband. More than once Norman threatened to leave home. It was an idle threat because the Mingo homestead continued to be his main distribution center. He must have been about 11 or 12 at the time and downright persuasive and enterprising.

Drawing seems to have come into his life early on. "I was interested in art as a kid," he told an interviewer, "and entered and won contests for art materials and a course in art from the Scranton School correspondence course. During high school I worked for Hart, Schaffner & Marx drawing model cards. I was so successful with my art I dropped out of high school and worked for a year full time." Norman went back to school, and by doing extra work, was able to graduate with his class in 1914. Even though he was a fullfledged professional now, Norman still did art work for the Parker Annual, his high school year book.

"World War I interrupted my art career and I served three years in the Navy. I'd been a standby sailor at the Chicago Yacht Club and the Navy put me in training at Great Lakes. I used my art to make drawings of all the moving parts of different pieces of machinery and as a result got commissioned. I spent six months aboard the USS Neptune in the Atlantic." The Neptune's sister ship, the USS Cyclops, went down in the Bermuda Triangle in March, 1918 with a full complement of 300 men. Still one of the great mysteries of the sea.

After leaving the service, Norman devoted himself to serious study at the Academy of Fine

At Chicago's famous Country Clubs

—see this Willys-Knight Great Six Roadster that has won such world-wide popularity

FISK BALLOON
FISK BALLOON
The dignified simplicity of the English Tudor Clubhouse of the famous Olympia Fields Country Club fits admirably in its attractive landscape setting. Here golf is carried to its zenith—with four wonderful courses laid out over hundreds of naturally beautiful acres of rolling ground.

MODERN engineering is rapidly making this Willys-Knight Great Six the fastest selling car of its class.

In Chicago sales are growing with leaps and bounds.

Everywhere throughout the city . . . at the leading country clubs, prominent hotels, exclusive sporting events . . . you will find this famous car in ever-increasing numbers.

Willys-Knight Great Six Roadster

$1850

Other Great Six prices: Touring, 5-Pass., $1750; Touring, 7-Pass., $1950; Coupe, $2195; Sedan, 5-Pass., $2295; Sedan, 7-Pass., $2495 The new Willys Finance Plan means less money down, smaller monthly payments and the lowest credit-cost in the industry. All prices f. o. b. factory. We reserve the right to change prices and specifications without notice.
Willys-Overland, Inc., Toledo, Ohio

This car will actually do over 70 honest miles per hour . . . with all of the tremendous reserve power that this implies.

It accelerates like lightning . . . climbs the steepest hills with effortless ease.

One of the many car ads rendered by Mingo during the roaring twenties.

"The 1920s were the great years for advertising art." Here, above and at left, are shown two examples of the hundreds of magazine ads prepared by Mingo during this period.

Arts in Chicago. The Windy City was a hotbed of cartoonists and illustrators in those heady years after World War I, being home base for the likes of Sidney Smith, Harold Gray, Garrett Price, Billy De Beck, Chester Gould, Matt and Benton Clark, and Hal Foster, to name but a few who flourished in the '20s. "The 1920s were the great years for advertising art," Norman once recalled. "I organized and was president of the art studio Mingo, Brink & Jipson, Inc. from 1923 to 1931. We had headquarters in the Wrigley Building in Chicago and offices in Detroit, Cleveland and Toledo. I'll never forget our first month's gross billing was $35,000 for artwork produced." Among the accounts providing such impressive billing were Studebaker, Packard, Willys-Overland, Old English Floor Wax, Cliquot Club beverages and Lysol. The studio turned out hundreds of slick magazine ads, many of which found their way into the pages of **The Saturday Evening Post**, the same magazine Norman sold door to door just a few years earlier. He had made a considerable leap forward.

For a spell in the late '20s one of Norman's employees was a young man named Charles Clarence Beck. Beck, now better known for his marvelous work on the original Captain Marvel, told me this about his stint in the Chicago studio. "I worked for Mingo in 1929 in Chicago. We took photos of cars and cut down their height, stretched their length and pushed their wheels up inside their fenders. Most of the time I cleaned palettes and spittoons and worked the switchboard. I got $10 a week. Times were rough—the Depression had just started." I find it interesting, in light of Beck's early art experiences, that the cover he did for the very first issue of **Whiz Comics** shows Captain Marvel tossing an automobile into a

IN MINGO'S CHICAGO ADVERTISING STUDIO YOUNG C.C.BECK LEARNED THAT REALISM IS SELDOM WANTED IN ART

The versatile Mingo also painted movie posters. The above example is from 1939.

brick wall.

The Depression hit Mingo's studio hard. He decided there was nothing left in Chicago and so the studio was closed and he left for New York. He was married now, son Ted being born in 1929. Dana was born in 1935. Settling in Scarsdale, Norman began an assault on the commercial markets at New York City. Fairly soon he got work on the Lucky Strike account, doing portraits of the celebrities who lent themselves to testimonial ads for the cigarettes. During the 1930s, in addition to a variety of advertising work, Norman also turned out double page illustrations for Hearst's Sunday supplement **The American Weekly**. That meant he was rubbing shoulders, in print anyway, with the likes of Willy Pogany and Virgil Finlay. The versatile future godfather of Alfred E. Neuman was equally at home doing complex exploded views of trains and roundhouses for the Atlantic Coastline Railroad and turning out politely sexy pinups for Mennen After Shave. Those who know Norman for the many clods he painted to grace **MAD** covers will be surprised to see that he was capable of giving Varga and Petty a run for their money. Dana Mingo seems to think he filled in for one of them once.

The pinups probably led to his doing movie posters as well, ranging from **Beau Geste**, the Gary Cooper version of 1939, to Marilyn Monroe's 1953 **Gentlemen Prefer Blondes**. Norman also managed to conquer the

Mingo easily proves his ability at pinup art with this movie poster. Only the girls are by him. © 20th Century-Fox

world of paper dolls for an outfit called Merrill Publishing. He did cut-out books with lustrous covers bearing the mini-portraits of such stars as Bette Davis, Sonja Henie, Rita Hayworth, Deanna Durbin, Alice Faye, and Mickey Rooney. Mickey Rooney? Norman kept busy throughout the 1930s and 1940s with an amazing range of commercial art jobs. In the early 1950s came that ill-fated silk screen business. As son Dana recalls, Norman's silk screened banners and display pieces were beautiful to behold but his business acumen came nowhere near matching his artistic abilities. The whole operation folded and Norman was desolate and depleted for months thereafter. Only an eventual spiritual rebirth prompted him to try again. He started reading the want ads. Fortunately for all of us, he noticed that classified that **MAD** had inserted. It was June, 1956, and Albert B. Feldstein had said to John Putnam, "John, I want to do **something** with this face—flesh it out as a viable portrait of a real kid."

Although he was a quietly humorous man, very perceptive of the follies of the world around him, Norman was not an idea man. "I could experiment with ideas until the cows came home and still be rejected, so I'm grateful that I didn't have to wrestle with the gag ideas." I was thinking back, while writing this piece, to all the cover ideas sessions I sat in on in my years with **MAD**. These intellectual wrestling matches were sort of like fraternal gatherings of the inner staff. While no two were exactly alike, they did follow a pattern. Al Feldstein would be there, along with Nick Meglin, Lenny Brenner, John Putnam and myself. Skylarking and high spirits were encouraged by Al, until he'd say, "O.K., close the door." Then, two folders of cover ideas were brought out; old ideas, mostly relics from the stone age of **MAD**, or maybe I should say rock age, since many dealt with Presley and the Beatles. After Al passed these venerable notions around, asking, "See anything here?" we turned to the folder of new ideas. By comparison, the new ones all seemed, initially at least, to be gems. Al would exclude himself from the early voting, though he'd smile wryly when it turned out that each of the others of us had voted for a different idea. Eventually we'd swing over to second choices and not-so-bads, that being the only way we could arrive at anything resembling agreement. Of course, if we were going to kid a current movie, things were easier. Alfred would replace Michael Pollard for a **Bonnie and Clyde** spoof; he'd replace Tatum O'Neil when we kidded **Paper Moon**. On our **Poseidon Adventure** cover, by the way, all you saw of our mascot was his telltale sneakers poking up through a Poseidon life preserver. That token appearance was enough to prompt an all-time high of three million copies sold.

Once the cover idea was agreed on, Al Feldstein would sketch it out quickly, southpaw, on regular typewriter size paper. That would be turned over to Norman and he would work up a rough in pastels. Once he got his okay he'd go to work on the finish.

"I don't work steadily on a cover," he explained once. "First I allow a couple of days just to think about the gag and gather a certain tension as the deadline

Fred Astaire as Neuman dancing with Barrie Chase. The Neuman mask is by John Chambers who also designed masks for the movie *Planet of the Apes*. Photo courtesy of NBC-TV Network.

draws nearer. I'll delay until I have to get the picture done and then I work very quickly.''

Norman rendered Alfred in every conceivable, and a few inconceivable, situations for over two decades. The kids of the kids who'd loved his first **MAD** covers came along to enjoy his work. Norman Mingo died on May 8, 1980 at the age of 84, leaving behind more credits than three or four average artists.

Sometimes, Norman and I would discuss the multitude of Alfreds he had painted to date. Would he, I asked, call them a flock, a pack, a rabble of Alfreds? Since Alfred was so self-assured and self-satisfied, but still did whatever Norman wanted him to do, then he'd prefer to say he had done a **bliss** of Alfreds.

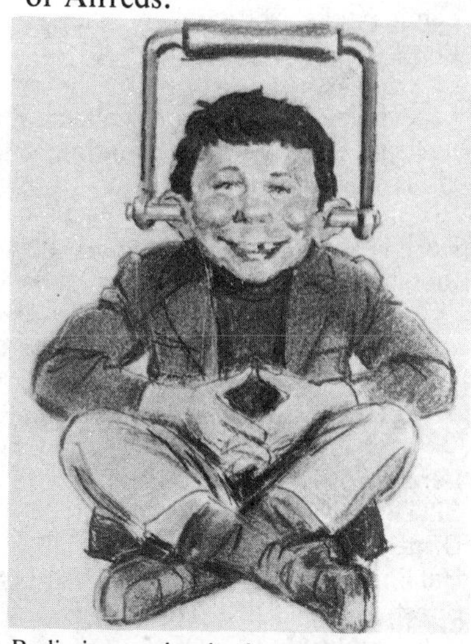

Preliminary sketch for **Portable Mad** paperback by Mingo. © E.C.

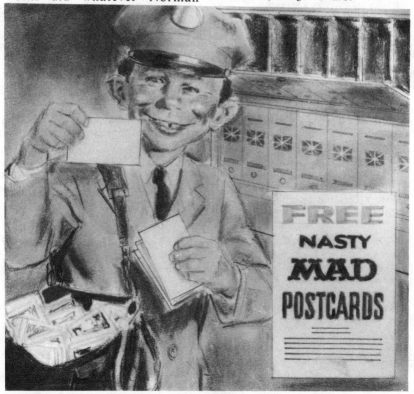

Mingo preliminary sketch for **MAD** Magazine. © E.C. Publications, Inc.

REWARD! WANTED TO BUY! TOP PRICES PAID!

Most of the collectors and dealers who advertise in this Price Guide are after your ol comic books. Not me. I enjoy comic books, but collecting old comic books is not m thing.

I specialize in the area of collecting the **original drawings** of certain specifi newspaper strip artists, paintings and drawings by certain illustrators, and certai kinds of Disneyana.

Here is a list of my specific wants. Since they are very specific, I **do** pay more fo them!

WANTED: TOP PRICES PAID!!

Original pen and ink drawings of newspaper comic strips by:

Percy Crosby (SKIPPY)
Bill DeBeck (BARNEY GOOGLE)
Disney Studio staff artists
Hal Foster (TARZAN, PRINCE VALIANT)
Chester Gould (DICK TRACY)
V.T. Hamlin (ALLEY OOP)
George Herriman (KRAZY KAT)
Burne Hogarth (TARZAN)
Walt Kelly (POGO)
Frank King (GASOLINE ALLEY)
George McManus (BRINGING UP FATHER)
Clifford McBride (NAPOLEON)
Alex Raymond (SECRET AGENT X-9, JUNGLE JIM, and FLASH GORDON)
E.C. Segar (POPEYE)
Cliff Sterrett (POLLY AND HER PALS)

Original paintings and drawings by:

J. Allen St. John, Carl Barks, Frank Frazetta, and Disney Studio staff artists.

Disneyana:

Pre-1955 Disney Studio animation drawings, studies, concept drawings, storyboar drawings, background paintings, and painted cels. There are a top want, absolutel top prices paid for choice originals.

Toys, especially tin wind-ups, dolls, bisque figurines, games, etc., which involv either Disney characters or comic strip characters, mostly pre-1955. This include Disney ceramic figurines, lamps, cookie jars, watches, jewelry, and other earl Disneyana.

These are my **top wants**, and I guarantee to pay the **highest prices** for these items which are in excellent, collectable condition.

For my offers, write or phone:

Russ Cochran Box 469 West Plains, MO 65775
417-256-2226

Russ Cochran Presents

THE COMPLETE  LIBRARY

Hee, Hee!! Yep, Kiddies, it's **me**, your hostess of horror from the **Haunt of Fear**, the Old Witch!! I'm here to tell you, in case you didn't already know, that 'way back in 1950-1955 there was a small comic book publishing company known as "EC" which published a line of comic books which have never been equalled (before or since) in quality of artwork and writing. The stories, written by Al Feldstein and Harvey Kurtzman, and the artwork by such comic art masters as Wally Wood, Al Williamson, Johnny Craig, Graham Ingels, Jack Davis, and many others, will please you . . . I guarantee it!

And now, my old buddy Russ Cochran is republishing the entire line of EC comics in a complete library of hardcover books! The complete runs of **WEIRD SCIENCE, TALES FROM THE CRYPT, TWO-FISTED TALES, WEIRD FANTASY,** and **SHOCK SUSPENSTORIES** have already been published, with the rest of the titles scheduled to appear over the next two to three years. For complete information on **THE COMPLETE EC LIBRARY**, write to the publisher. Do it today! You won't be sorry!! 'Bye, now!!

Russ Cochran **Box 469** **West Plains, MO 65775**

NEW DIMENSIONS

The BIGGEST & THE BEST
IN COMICS
and COMIC
RELATED
MATERIAL

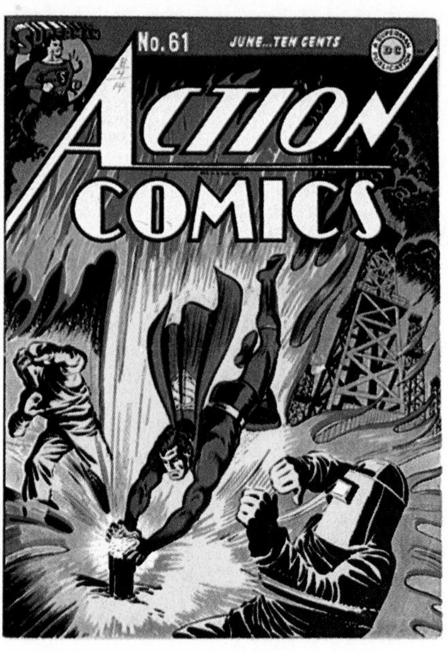

Action Comics No. 61, 1943. © DC

Adventure Comics No. 247, 1958. First Legion of Super-Heroes app. © DC

The Adventures of Bob Hope No. 9, 1951. © DC

All-American Comics No. 1, 1939. © DC

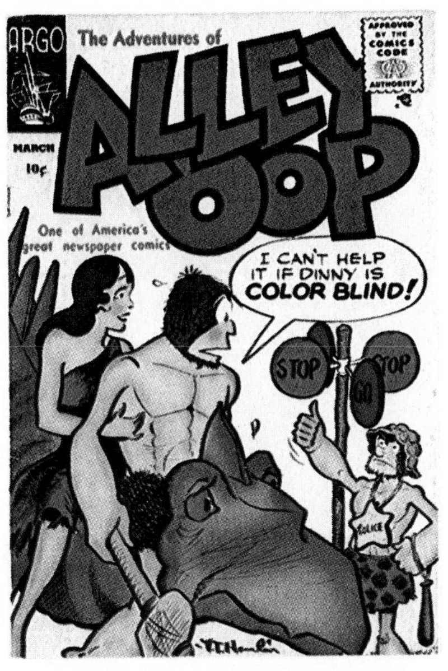

Alley Oop No. 3, 1956. © NEA Service

All-Flash No. 2, 1941. © DC

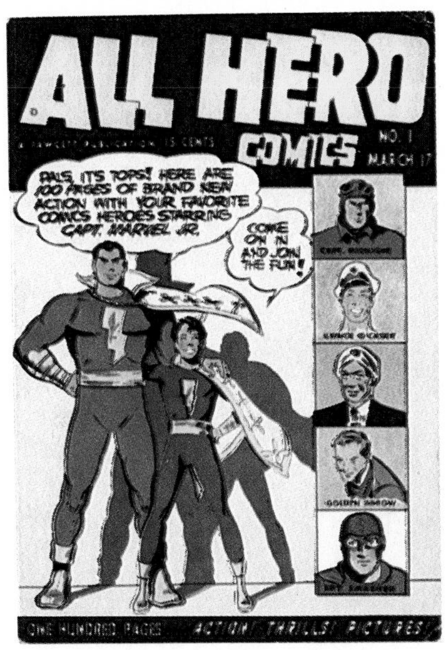

All Hero Comics No. 1, 1943. © Faw

All Select Comics No. 2, 1943. Cover by Alex Schomburg. © MCG

All Star Comics No. 12, 1942. © DC

All Winners No. 8, 1942. Schomburg cover art. © MCG

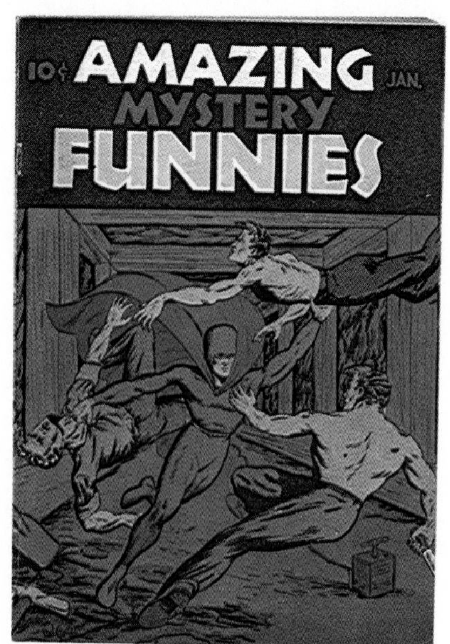

Amazing Mystery Funnies V3No. 1, 1940 © Cen

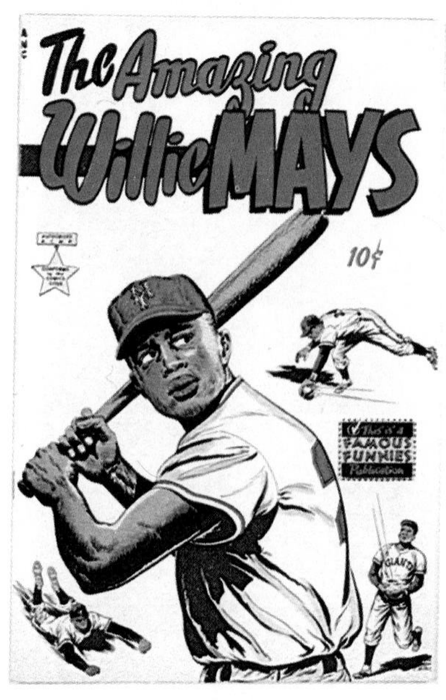

The Amazing Willie Mays, 1954. © FF

Animal Comics No. 5, 1943. Contains Pogo by Walt Kelly. © Oskar Lebeck

The Arrow No. 1, 1940. © Cen

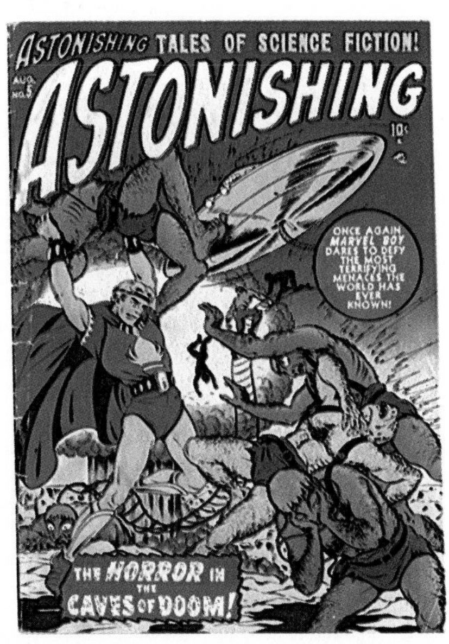

Astonishing No. 5, 1951. Marvel Boy app. © MCG

Authentic Police Cases No. 6, 1948. Matt Baker cover; used in **SOTI**. © Stj

Best of the West No. 1, 1951. © ME

The Blue Beetle No. 1, 1939. © Fox

Blue Bolt No. 3, 1940. © Funnies, Inc.

Boy Commandos No. 2, 1943. Cover by Simon & Kirby. © DC

Boys' Ranch No. 4, 1951. Simon & Kirby cover/art. © Harv

Buccaneers No. 27, 1951. Cover and inside art by Reed Crandall. © Qua

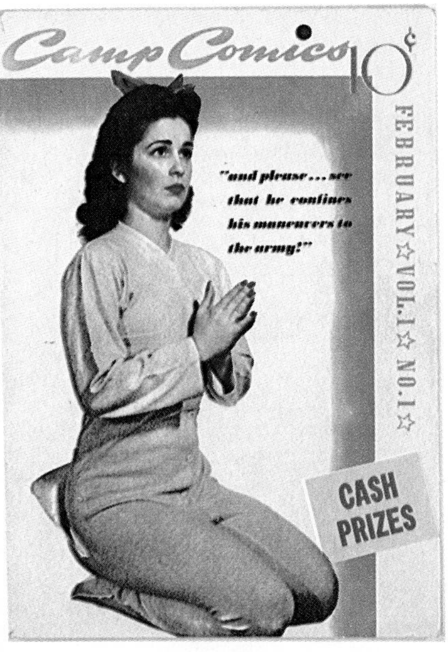

Camp Comics No. 1, 1942. © Whit

Captain Battle Jr. No. 1, 1943. © Lev

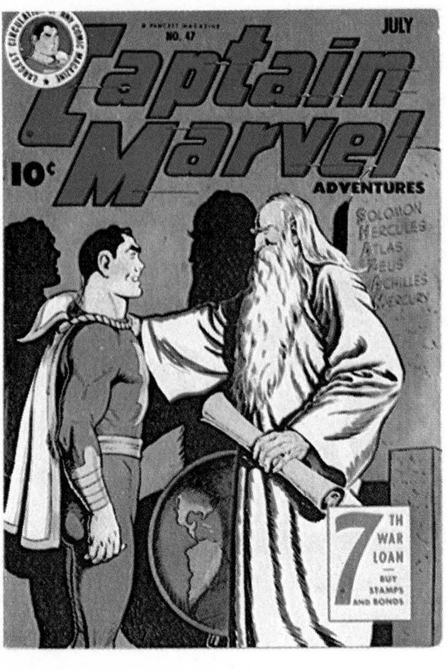

Captain Marvel Adventures No. 47, 1945. © Faw

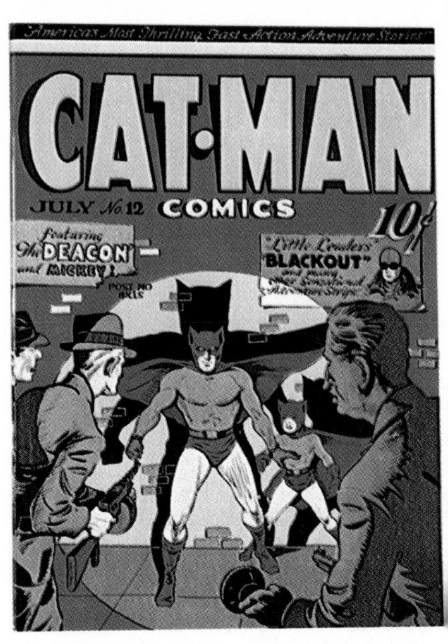

Cat-Man Comics No. 12, 1942. © Hoke

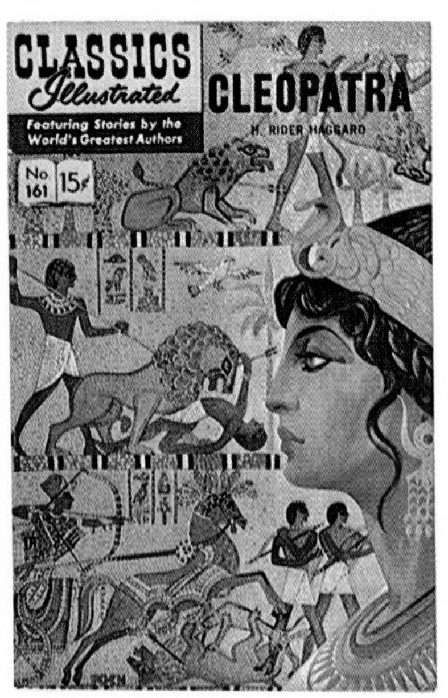

Classics Illustrated No. 161, 1964. © Gil

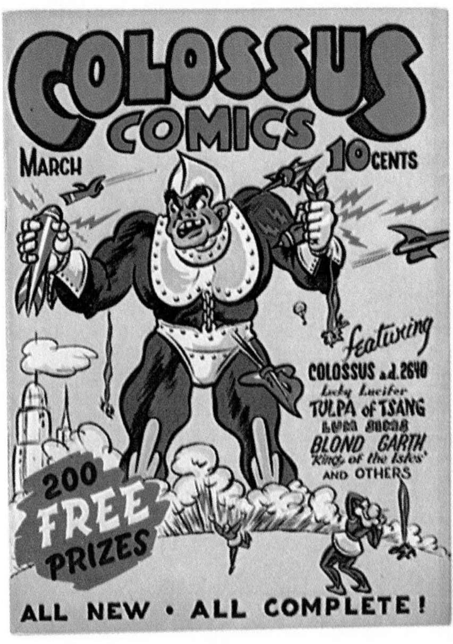

Colossus Comics No. 1, 1940. © Sun Publ.

Complete Mystery No. 3, 1948. © MCG

Crack Comics No. 18, 1941. Contains The Black Condor by Lou Fine. © Qua

Crackajack Funnies No. 1, 1938. © Whit

Crash Comics No. 3, 1940. © Tem Publ.

Dagar Desert Hawk No. 14, 1948. © Fox

Daredevil Comics No. 2, 1941. © Lev

Daring Comics No. 9, 1944. Schomburg cover art. © MCG

Dark Mysteries No. 2, 1951. © Master Comics

Detective Comics No. 54, 1941. © DC

Dick Tracy Black and White No. 8, 1939.
© Chicago Tribune-N.Y. News Syndicate

Eerie No. 2, 1951. Wally Wood cover art.
© Avon

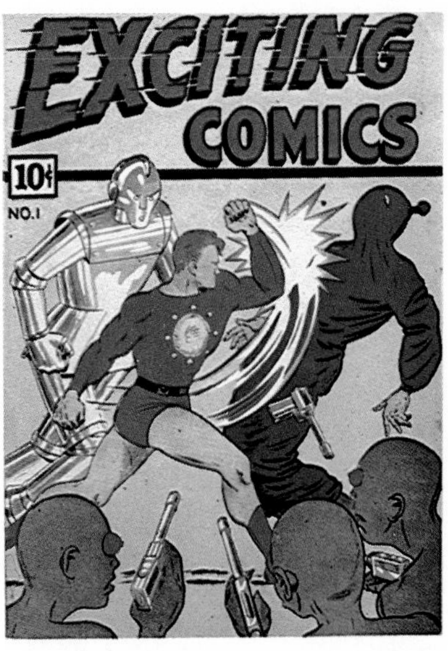

Exciting Comics No. 1, 1940. © BP

L.E.Cole
JOIN THE PARADE TO...

THANKS FOR MAKING

THE #1 COMIC OF 1981

WINNER OF THE
1980

EAGLE
AWARDS

FROM THE NEW DC

New York City, New York

SUPERSNIPE COMIC BOOK AND ART CATALOG
Profusely Illustrated $1.00

COMIC
SHOWCASE
DEATH
MARSHALL/81

NOW DOING MAIL ORDER! SEND US YOUR WANT LISTS (S*A*S*E REQUIRED)

ACTION COMICS No. 1
ALL–SELECT COMICS No. 1
ALL STAR COMICS No. 1
ALL WINNERS COMICS No. 1
BATMAN No. 1
DONALD DUCK (1st. appearance)
FANTASTIC FOUR No. 1
HUMAN TORCH No. 1
SPIDERMAN No. 1
SUPERMAN No. 1
WALT DISNEY COMICS & STORIES No. 1

Sleuthing done dirt cheap!

Can't find that number one (or origin issue)? Then why not try me?

Yes, I have **all** of the **No. 1** issues shown above & other **hard-to-find** comics especially those much sought after **early Marvels** (there are always available in stock a near complete set of all Marvel titles).

And besides this I also have the following:

(A) **WALT DISNEY** comics - all titles: Mickey Mouse, Donald Duck, Uncle Scrooge, Firestone & other Giveaways & Disney Collectibles: pop-ups, figures, games, Disney posters etc., etc.,

(B) **DC COMICS** (Golden Age, Silver Age up to the present- the **old** Flash, Green Lantern, Superman, Batman, as well as newer super-heroes of the 70's).

(C) **GOLDEN AGE & SILVER AGE** comics- these include Quality, Timely, Fox, Avon, Fiction House, Fawcetts, Motion Picture Comics, Dell, Westerns, Funny Animal Comics, Classics, etc.

(D) **MAD** comics - Panic, Humbug, Trump, Help & Horror, Crime & **EC** comics.

(E) Hundreds of **BIG LITTLE BOOKS**- all titles at **LESS** than catalog prices. Also available- the **original** Cupples & Leon comic "books".

(F) Rare **PULPS**- science fiction & pulp hero titles; **ARKHAM HOUSE** books

(G) **ORIGINAL ART**- including **Carl Barks** (Uncle Scrooge artist); Winsor McCay (**Little Nemo** artist); George Herriman (**Krazy Kat** artist) & other fine classic as well as modern artists.

(H) **SUNDAY COMIC PAGES** . Just about every major & minor comic strip character from the early **1900's** to the **1950's.** Strips include: **Little Nemo, Krazy Kat, Mickey Mouse, Donald Duck, Popeye, Tarzan, Flash Gordon, Prince Valiant, Terry & The Pirates, Dick Tracy, Superman. Pogo** & many, many more too numerous to list here.

I also **BUY & TRADE**, so let me know what you have. For my latest **GIANT 1982** catalog- "Number One Plus", write to the address below enclosing $1.00 in cash (or stamps). Hurry now or you could miss out on getting that issue you've been looking for!

SPECIAL – SPECIAL: MOVIE SALE

A ONCE IN A LIFE-TIME OFFER! Huge Catalog listing hundreds and hundreds of rare (and **ORIGINAL**) movie posters, lobby cards, autographed photos from the 1930's to the 1970's. You'll find your favorite movie stars as: Bogart, Gable, Garbo, Garland, Laurel & Hardy, Presley, Disney Titles & many, many more. Wide selection from B-Westerns, Horror, Science-Fiction, Comedy, Musicals, Etc. Act **NOW** to receive my **"1982 MOVIE CATALOG"**

(**NOTE**: Those wishing to receive **ONLY** the Movie Catalog **MUST** enclose .50 cents & a self-addressed stamped envelope. Want lists also welcomed. If you wish to receive **BOTH** the Comic & the Movie catalog, **send $1.50**)

write: **HAL VERB**
P.O. BOX 1815
SAN FRANCISCO, CA. 94101

OUR SPECIALTIES . . .

BUYING OUT STORES

GOT A FEW HUNDRED THOUSAND BOOKS? A **MILLION** BOOKS? WE ARE LOOKING FOR **LARGE LOTS** OF COMICS AND RELATED MATERIALS (Sci-Fi, Games, Cards, Records, etc. etc.). WE LOVE **WAREHOUSES, PUBLISHER'S REMAINDERS, STORE STOCKS,** LARGE COLLECTIONS, ETC. ETC. SMALLER STOCKS & COLLECTIONS APPRECIATED AS WELL.

THE MORE, THE MERRIER
Will Fly, Swim, Skateboard
Anywhere in the World

SUPPLYING DEALERS & INVESTORS

STOCKING NEW STORES

SELLING COMICS WHOLESALE IS OUR SPECIALTY. WE HAVE BEEN SUPPLYING DEALERS IN THE U.S. & ABROAD FOR YEARS. OUR LISTS INCLUDE BACK-ISSUE LISTINGS, LOTS, COLLECTIONS, ETC. **OPENING A STORE? LOOKING FOR INVENTORY?** WE HAVE PROVIDED THE INITIAL STOCKS FOR A DOZEN STORES OPENING IN THE LAST YEAR. **SEND FOR FREE WHOLESALE LISTS.**

BUYING & SELLING BLUE CHIP

OUR HUGE INVENTORY & WORLD-WIDE REACH ENABLES US TO BUY HIGH SELL LOW. COLLECTORS: **WE SEND OUT MORE GOLD & SILVER AGE LISTS THAN ANYONE:** MONTHLY, BI-MONTHLY, EVEN WEEKLY.

©

JOSEPH & PETER KOCH
241 W. 97th ST, 12K
NEW YORK, N.Y. 10025
212-834-0398

SAVE 20% THE NICE WAY

SAVINGS ON NEW COMICS IS JUST THE BEGINNING WHEN YOU BECOME A

NEW ISSUE

CLUB EXPRESS MEMBER!

Designed with the collector's very special needs in mind, Lone Star's NICE service (New Issue Club Express) offers you the kind of service, selection and savings unheard of until now. Subscribe to as many or as few titles as you like and receive a 20% discount on all new issues. Subscribe to 10 or more titles and receive NICE's Extended Discount — a 20% discount on anything and everything in Lone Star's big 16 page illustrated catalog; back issue comics, comic bags, storage boxes, gum cards, SF and fantasy games, portfolios, paperbacks, art books, special publications and much more. NICE service means you need never again pay full price for anything!

Terms are simple: You pay exact postage plus a $1.00 service charge on each shipment. That's all!

When you become a NICE Subscriber, you can look forward to all the following benefits on top of your 20% savings:

- You can start or stop a title at any time, order just a single issue or order multiples of the same issue. And you can get those hard-to-find direct sale titles, too.
- You'll never miss an issue. That's a GUARANTEE!
- We're FAST. Orders shipped by United Parcel insured. One or two day service to Mid-America. Delivery to either coast in 3 to 5 days shipping time. Our comics reach many areas well ahead of newsstand distribution.
- Specially designed shipping boxes protect even the smallest order. And an interior plastic wrapper adds still more protection.
- With each shipment, you receive a full and easy to understand statement plus a convenient reply form that includes a duplicate copy for your records.
- Monthly bonus offers include popular new publications at half price and comics autographed by your favorite comic writer or artist!
- Each month, you'll receive the NICE NEWSLETTER — 4 big pages of Marvel news, 4 DC news pages, plus Lone Star's own late-breaking news section. And there's more! Up-to-date listing of new publications at 20% discount, subscribers' letter column, previews of unpublished comic pages, pinups by leading comic artists — 16 to 20 pages of excitement every month!

JOINING THE NEW ISSUE CLUB EXPRESS IS AS SIMPLE AS . . .

Tell us what titles you want started and quantities desired. Be sure to give starting numbers or cover dates. Monthly and bi-weekly (every two weeks) shipping frequencies are available. Other special instructions? Just tell us what you want. Your first advance payment should total enough to cover two months worth of material. Payment may be made by cash, check, money order, Master Card or Visa. Send instructions and payment to:

LONE STAR
COMICS & SCIENCE FICTION

NICE SERVICE
511-PG East Abram
Arlington, Texas 76010
Phone (817) 265-0491

SAVE!

20%

ON

- NEW COMICS
  INCLUDING HARD-TO-FIND DIRECT-SALE TITLES!
- MAGAZINES
- PAPERBACKS
- COLLECTORS COMICS
- SF & FANTASY GAMES
- BAGS & BOXES
- ART BOOKS
- PORTFOLIOS
- AND MORE!

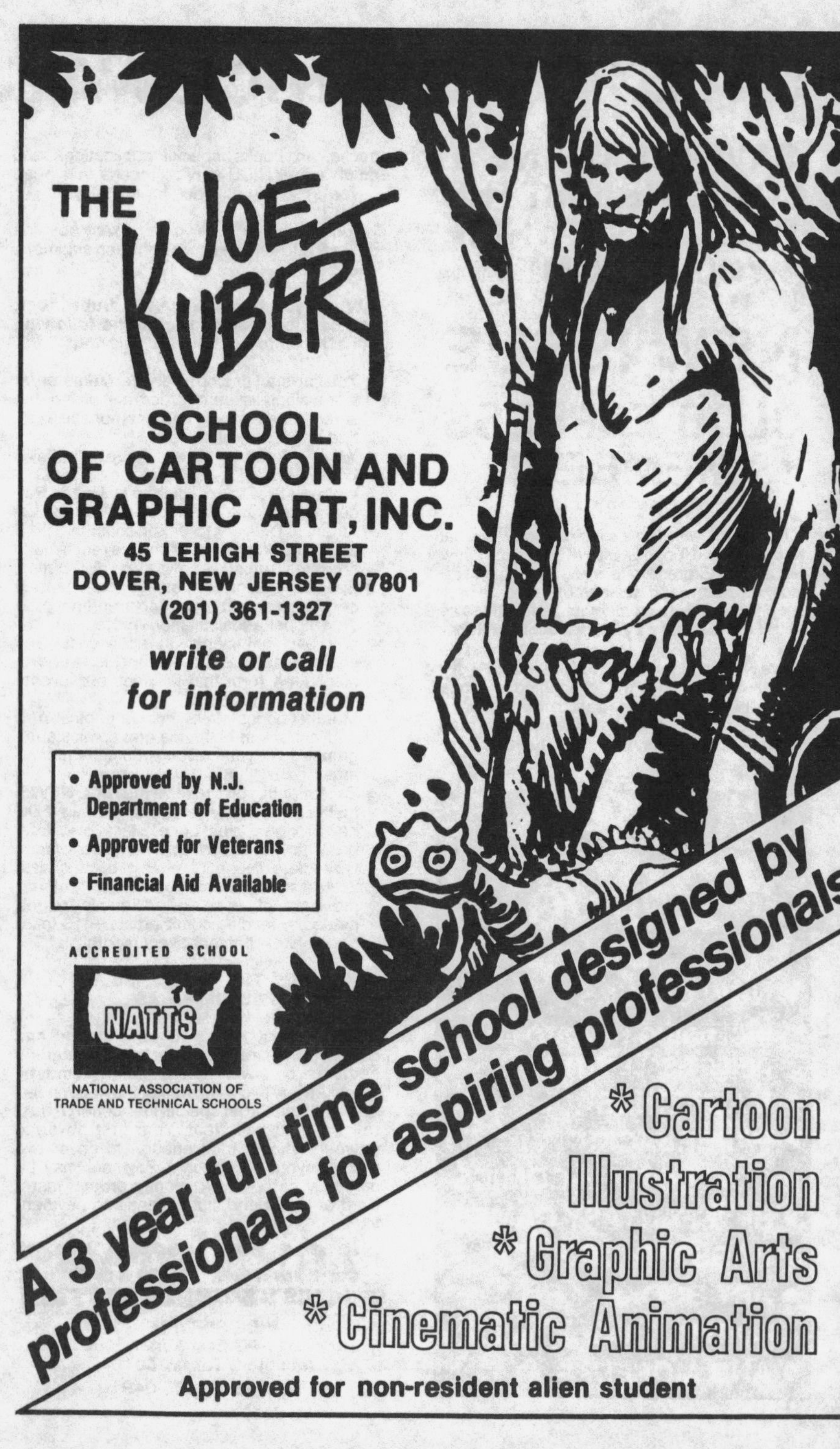
THE JOE KUBERT
SCHOOL
OF CARTOON AND
GRAPHIC ART, INC.
45 LEHIGH STREET
DOVER, NEW JERSEY 07801
(201) 361-1327
write or call
for information
• Approved by N.J. Department of Education
• Approved for Veterans
• Financial Aid Available
ACCREDITED SCHOOL
NATTS
NATIONAL ASSOCIATION OF
TRADE AND TECHNICAL SCHOOLS
A 3 year full time school designed by
professionals for aspiring professionals
* Cartoon
Illustration
* Graphic Arts
* Cinematic Animation
Approved for non-resident alien student

MARVEL COMICS GROUP
THE UNCANNY
X-MEN
116
DEC
DEATH TO THOSE WHO VIOLATE THE LAND AND LAWS OF THE SUN-GOD!
IRON FIST
MARVEL COMICS GROUP
30¢
15
SEPT
IRON FIST
IN FINAL BATTLE AGAINST THE X-MEN!
KUNG FU ACTION IN THE MIGHTY MARVEL MANNER!
MARVEL COMICS GROUP
16
SEPT
EDGAR RICE BURROUGHS'
JOHN CARTER, WARLORD
JOHN CARTER IS DEAD!
521 WHITE HORSE PIKE
OAKLYN N.J. 08107
PHONE 609·858·3877
mgr. FREDERICK MARCUS
STORE HRS. 1 to 9 tues–sat
OUR SIXTH YEAR
132 SOUTH 20 th ST.
PHILADELPHIA PA
ph 215 963 0788·19103
mgr. MIKE FERRERO
HRS. 1 to 6 mon–sat
Superman & Batman are registered trademarks of DC Comics Inc. & are © 1982 DC Comics Inc.—Used with permission.
MARVEL * D:C * WARREN
ECLISPE * DELL * CANADIAN
UNDERGROUNDS * FANZINES
ART BOOKS * STARLOG
HEAVY METAL * PLASTIC BAGS
MYLAR PAGES * ORIGINAL ART
2966 KENSINGTON AVE
PHILADELPHIA PA 19134
PHONE 215 423 3876
mgr. STEVE ANGERT
HRS. 10 to 6 mon–sat
ONE WEEK ENGA
1 TON
SUN-FIRE!
with ken sall

send one dollar (refundable with first order) to:

WSA
1057

SAMUEL FRAZER
Box 144
Old Bethpage, N.Y. 11804

(516) MY 4-4835

for catalog number 13

TOP PRICES PAID FOR YOUR COMICS

Let me know what you have to sell.

Completely Updated and Revised for 1982!
FANDOM DIRECTORY
FANDOM DIRECTORY 1979
FANDOM DIRECTORY 1980
FANDOM DIRECTORY 1981
From its beautiful full color cover to its listings of over 9000 names, addresses, and telephone numbers of fans eagerly waiting to hear from you, the 1982 Fandom Directory is a whole new experience.
If you're a dealer or publisher, or simply a fan or collector, whether you're interested in comics, SF, Star Trek, films, or whatever, you cannot afford to be without this valuable reference work.
You'll find friends and new customers from all around the world in the pages of the 1982 Fandom Directory, with nearly 400 pages jam-packed with information including indexes to fan clubs, fanzines, and fan gatherings from around the world.
Prize-winning fan fiction and illustrations also fill over 40 pages with sheer delight for the fannish at heart.
Our 4th Big Year!
FANDOM DIRECTORY 1982
COVERING: Comics, Pulps, Science Fiction, Fantasy, Star Trek, Old Time Radio, Film, Gum Card, and related Fandoms!
FANDOM COMPUTER SERVICES
Harry A. Hopkins
P.O. Box 4278
Norton AFB, Ca 92409
IN ADDITION to our mountain of regular features, this year we have featured major articles by Richard and Wendi Pini on their popular series ELFQUEST, and a real shocker (!) "Science Fiction in Eastern Europe" by R. P. Jasinski of Szczecin, Poland.
Order Form
Quantity Item Price Enclosed
1982 Fandom Directory . $7.95
1981 Fandom Directory . 3.95
1980 Fandom Directory . 3.95
Mid-Year '79 Directory . . 2.95
Shipping ($2.50 Overseas) $1.25
TOTAL. . . .
NAME
Address
City State Zip
FREE
YOU TOO CAN BE LISTED FREE OF CHARGE IN THE FANDOM DIRECTORY
FREE
The FANDOM DIRECTORY is an annual publication issued each March which lists THOUSANDS of fans like yourself. If YOU are a collector, fan, dealer, publisher, artist, convention organizer, or just an interested party whose interests include science fiction, comics, pulps, paperbacks, artwork, Star Trek, Star Wars, wargaming, gum cards, films, or related memorabilia, including posters, fanzines, artzines, etc., then YOU are entitled to be listed FREE OF CHARGE in the FANDOM DIRECTORY. Just fill out the data form below and mail it in. What could be simpler?!
DATA FORM
STATUS (Limit...5)
LOOK
INTERESTS (Limit... 10)
LOOK
Check One: New ( ) Update ( )
( ) FAN
( ) COLLECTOR
( ) DEALER
( ) EDITOR
( ) WRITER
( ) ARTIST
( ) PUBLISHER
( ) STORE
( ) ZINE
( ) CLUB
( ) CON CHAIRMAN
( ) CONVENTION
( ) MANUFACTURER
( ) SUB SERVICE
( ) Comics
( ) Pulps
( ) BLBs
( ) Books
( ) Paperbacks
( ) Original Art
( ) Posters
( ) Portfolios
( ) Fanzines
( ) Artzines
( ) Films
( ) Movie Matter
( ) Radio
( ) S F
( ) Star Trek
( ) Star Wars
( ) ERB
( ) Lovecraft
( ) Gum Cards
( ) Beer Cans
( ) Wargames
( ) Television
( ) Video Tape
( ) Comic Strips
( ) APAs
( ) Good Girl Art
( ) Horror
( ) Plastic Bags
( ) Records
( ) Undergrounds
( ) Marvel
( ) DC
( ) EC
( ) Gold Key
( ) Westerns
( ) Carl Barks
( ) Funny Animal
( ) Golden Age
( ) Silver Age
( ) Super Heroes
( ) Sword & Sorcery
( ) Animation
( ) Asimov
( ) Bradbury
( ) Computers
( ) D&D
( ) Special Effects
( ) Darkover
( ) Ellison
( ) Fantasy
( ) Heinlein
( ) Premiums
( ) Science
( ) Other... (Specify)
NAME
ADDRESS
CITY STATE ZIP TELEPHONE ( )

XANADU
COMICS AND COLLECTABLES INC.
THE MYSTERIOUS
MR. XANADU
INVITES YOU TO RECIEVE OUR 1982 DC/MARVEL CATALOG. SEND $1.50 IN CHECKS, M.O. OR STAMPS.*
XANADU SPECIALIZES IN
3-D COMICS · 50'S SPIRIT · FANZINES
UNDERGROUNDS
PLEASE CALL OR SEND A WANT LIST WITH A S.A.S.E.!
2 WEST FIFTH STREET
WILMINGTON DE. 19801
302 - 652 - 5098
*FREE "MR. XANADU" BUTTON FOR FIRST 250 ORDERS. AD EXPIRES 1-31-83
A REGULAR TBG ADVERTISER
HORROR COMICS
WEIRD TALES
BLACK MAGIC
ADVENTURES INTO TERROR
GHOST TALES
MYSTIC STORIES
STRANGE TALES
WITCH'S TALES
NIGHTMARE STORIES
DICK AYERS '81
©1982 XANADU C+C, INC.

NORTH TEXAS FINEST!

NEW & USED COMICS
WE BUY COLLECTIONS — TOP PRICES PAID!

Now — Two Locations Offering You:

STAR TREK * STAR WARS * OLD RADIO SHOWS
NEW & USED COMICS * MOVIE POSTERS * STILLS * LOBBIES
S-F PAPERBACKS & HARDBACKS * PULPS * GAMES
FANZINES & MAGAZINES * FANTASY & S-F POSTERS * FILMS
ART PORTFOLIOS * BEATLES * BUTTONS * ROCKY HORROR

LARRY HERNDON'S

REMEMBER WHEN

2431 Valwood Parkway
Dallas, Texas 75234
(214) 243-3439

581 W. Campbell #119
Richardson, Texas 75080
(214) 690-0374

Hours: Noon 'til 7:00
Sunday: 1:00 'til 5:00 — Closed Tuesday

SEND 25¢ FOR OUR EXCITING NEW CATALOG!

DINOSAUR BOXES & BAGS

SO TOUGH —MAKES ALL OTHERS EXTINCT!

COMIC BOXES
(8" x 27" x 11")

1 Box ----	$2.50 ea.
5 Boxes --	2.25 ea.
10 Boxes --	2.00 ea.
15 Boxes --	1.80 ea.

MAGAZINE BOXES
(9" x 15" x 11 3/4")

1 Box ----	$2.25 ea.
5 Boxes --	2.00 ea.
10 Boxes --	1.85 ea.
15 Boxes --	1.65 ea.

GUM CARD BOXES
(15" long)

1 Box ----	$1.25 ea.
5 Boxes --	1.00 ea.
10 Boxes --	.75 ea.
15 Boxes --	.65 ea.

All boxes are white cardboard, require no tape or staples, and have snug deep lids. Comic and magazine boxes have four layer ends with handhold shields.

PARTITIONS

1 - 5 -- $1.00 ea.
6 - 15 - .90 ea.

Holds up your comics in partially filled box. Adjusts to fit 3/4,½ or ¼ of box.

3-MIL PLASTICS BAGS

	Regular	Golden Age	Magazine
100 Bags	2.75	3.50	3.75
500 Bags	13.00	15.50	18.50
1000 Bags	23.50	28.50	31.25

Larger quantity pricing available.

GUM CARDS

Large selection of movie and TV shows. Available in sets, boxes or individually.
Send SASE for list

OLD TIME RADIO ON CASSETTE

Send large SASE for list.

All orders sent COD plus shipping the same day received.
Prices subject to change without notice.

TRADE & SAVE BOOKS

P.O. Box 640, Dept.A
Duncanville, Texas 75116
(214) 298-4276

REPRINTS

UDEY I (Stamped reprint) imited supply of this first rint of the Goudey series cards including Ruth, Gehrig, Hornsby . . . $ 25.00
UDEY II (Laminated for a ever mint appearance) cludes 3 Ruths, Gehrig, bb— 32 cards . . . . . . $ 8.00
UDEY III — 32 cards luding Williams, DiMaggio th . . . . $ 5.00
Y BALL I — 42 reprints the 1941 series . . . . $ 5.00
YBALL II — 42 more rints including 10 tinted ds from 1940 . . . . . $ 5.00
POSTAGE AND HANDLING (P & H)

EXHIBIT (Hall of Famers)
$ 4.00 plus postage & handling

s 32 card set features all Hall of ne players. Issued in late 1980, s is the second set released by new owners of the Exhibit ply Co., who have been issuing ds since the 1920's. Included are h, Cobb, Mantle, DiMaggio, liams, Foxx and 26 more.

TRY DEN'S COLLECTORS DEN

Plastic Card Protecting Pages
Largest Selection in Hobby!
16 Different Sizes

FINEST QUALITY PLASTIC SHEETS
ATURING
NON-MIGRATING PLASTIC IN ALL SHEETS
PLASTIC THAT DOES NOT STICK TOGETHER
STIFFNESS TO PREVENT CARD CURLING
NTELLIGENT DESIGN
RESISTANCE TO CRACKING
FULL COVERAGE OF CARDS, PHOTOS & POSTCARDS

OSTAGE & HANDLING SCHEDULE (P & H)
$ .01 to $ 20.00 add $ 2.00
$ 20.01 to $ 30.00 add $ 2.50
Over $ 30.00 add $ 3.00

MARYLAND RESIDENTS ADD 5% TAX
CANADIAN ORDERS — BOOKS ONLY
ANADIAN BOOK ORDERS ADD 25% postage
ders outside contiguous U.S.A. add 25% more
U.S. FUNDS ONLY

SEND $ 1.00 for DEN'S BIG 48-PAGE CATALOGUE
CATALOGUE WILL BE SENT FREE WITH ORDER

DEN'S COLLECTORS DEN
Dept. WW
P.O. BOX 606, LAUREL, MD 20707

THE SPORT AMERICANA FOOTBALL HOCKEY, BASKETBALL & BOXING CARD PRICE GUIDE
$ 8.95 plus postage & handling
NEW 2nd Edition — All Prices Revised

The latest edition of "THE FOOTBALL CARD PRICE GUIDE" contains all Topps, Fleer, Bowman, Philly Gum, Leaf, Kellogg, Kahn's, O-Pee-Chee and other significant American and Canadian football card issues plus all significant hockey, basketball, and boxing card issues — some dating to the 19th Century. Tens of thousands of prices, eight pages in full color, typical card for each set pictured front and back, history of sports cards, condition guide, and other special features are included.

THE SPORT AMERICANA PRICE GUIDE to the NON-SPORTS CARDS
$ 8.95 plus postage & handling
ALL NEW FIRST EDITION
AT LAST— A CURRENT & ACCURATE NON-SPORTS CARD PRICE GUIDE

The all new non-sports card price guide by Sport Americana is the finest book on American non-sports card ever produced. 19th Century cards through DALLAS and SUPERMAN II bubble gum cards are included. A must for non-sports collectors.

- Thousands of Prices
- Over 2000 Illustrations
- Eight Pages in FULL COLOR
- Over 500 Sets Checklisted
- Includes 19th Century Cards
- Descriptive Narratives for each Set
- Over 325 Pages in Lenght
- Wrappers Illustrated and Priced
- Stickers & Puzzle Cards Included

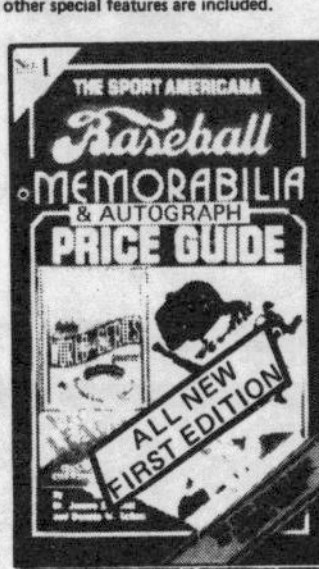

THE SPORT AMERICANA BASEBALL MEMORABILIA & AUTOGRAPH PRICE GUIDE
$ 8.95 plus postage and handling
THE ONE EVERYONE HAS AWAITED

The Baseball Memorabilia Price Guide has taken over a year to produce. Now you can find the current values for your programs, yearbooks, press pins, souvenirs, pins and coins, baseball statues, Exhibit or arcade cards, baseball envelopes, bubble gum paper inserts, magazines, autographed balls, photos and cards, and much, more more.

BALL HOLDERS
$ 2.50 plus postage & handling

House your favorite baseball or that special autographed ball in this attractive and functional gold-based holder.

COMPLETE MINT CARD SETS
number of cards in set= ( )

BASEBALL
1982 TOPPS (792) . . . . $ 21.00
1982 FLEER (660) . . . . $ 15.00
1982 DONRUSS (660) . . . . . . $ 15.00
1981 TOPPS (726) . . . . $ 22.00
1981 FLEER (660) . . . . $ 18.00
1981 DONRUSS (605) . . . . . . $ 18.00
1981 COKE (132) . . . . $ 15.00
1981 Topps Home Team- 5x7 Photos
Dodgers—Angels (18) . . . $ 5.00
White Sox—Cubs (18) . . . $ 5.00
Yankees—Mets (18) . . . . . $ 5.00
Rangers—Astros (12) . . . . $ 3.50
1981 Topps National Superstar
Photos — 5x7 Photos . . . . $ 5.00
1981 Topps Scratch-offs (108) . $ 8.00
1981 Topps Stickers (262) . . . $ 25.00
1980 TOPPS (726) . . . . $ 24.00
1980 Topps 5x7 Photos (60) . . $ 12.00
1978 TOPPS (726) . . . . $ 30.00
1977 Topps Cloth (73) . . . . . . $ 25.00
1976 KELLOGG (54 of 57) . . . $ 7.00
1975 HOSTESS (6 panels of 3) . $ 7.50
1973 KELLOGG 2-D (54) . . . . $ 40.00

FOOTBALL
1981 TOPPS (528) . . . . $ 17.00
1980 TOPPS (528) . . . . $ 19.00
1980 Topps 5x7 Photos (30) . . . $ 6.00
1975 FLEER Hall of Fame (84) $ 7.50
1970 KELLOGG (60) . . . . $ 16.00

ADD POSTAGE AND HANDLING (P & H) TO ALL ITEMS

1982 SPORT AMERICANA BASEBALL CARD PRICE GUIDE
$ 9.95 plus postage & handling
THE BOOK THAT MADE THE HOBBY FAMOUS
ALL NEW 4th EDITION
Includes 1982 TOPPS, FLEER, DONRUSS

- All Topps, Bowman, Fleer, Goudey, Play Ball, Kellogg, Donruss, Post Cereal, Leaf, Hostess, Red Man, O-Pee-Chee, and hundreds of other T cards, E cards, Regionals and Canadian issues
- Typical card for each set pictured both front and back
- 16 pages in full color
- Over 150,000 prices-All revised for 1982
- 500 pages in length
- Special section on pre-1900 cards
- History of baseball cards, condition guide, year in review, special articles
- THE ORIGINAL AND RECOGNIZED AUTHORITATIVE PRICE GUIDE

WHEN COLLECTORS SPEAK OF "THE" PRICE GUIDE, THIS BOOK IS THE ONE THEY MEAN

SUPER STAR SET

45 Card Set of All Superstars

- NO commons
- NO stiffs
- NO benchwarmers
- NO has-beens
- NO have-nots
- NO reprint set

4 different poses of
- Mickey Mantle
- Willie Mays
- Hank Aaron
- Ted Williams
- Joe Dimaggio
- Babe Ruth
- Lou Gehrig
- Sandy Koufax
- Bob Clemente

$3.50

1981 DALLAS COWBOY CHEERLEADERS
$ 6.00 plus postage and handling

The card above is number 11 in the set of 30. Would you really rather look at Mickey Mantle or George Brett than what is above? The cards are actual 5 x 7 photos of high quality — similar to the Superstar Photo series of baseball and football players issued by Topps over the last two years.

1937 DIAMOND STARS PRODUCED by SPORT AMERICANA
$ 3.00 (includes wrapper)

NEW

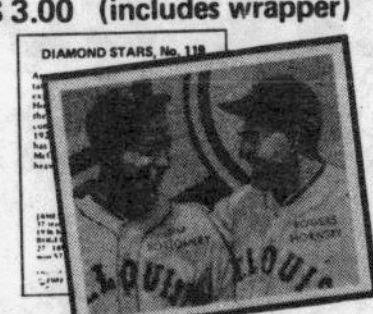

THE FULL COLOR 1937 DIAMOND STARS
Set includes:

109— Benny Frey
110— Pete Fox
111— Phil Cavaretta
112— Goose Goslin
113— Mel Harder
114— Roger Cramer
115— Gene Moore
116— Rip Collins
117— Linus Frey
118— Lefty Gomez
119— Jim Bottomley Rogers Hornsby
120— Lon Warneke

This set was originally scheduled for release by the National Chicle Co. in 1937 — but, it was never released. This is not a reprint set.

1982 BASEBALL COLLECTOR'S EDITION

A BASEBALL CARD ALBUM, SPECIALLY DESIGNED FOR 1982, WITH YOUR OWN NAME IN GOLD LETTERS ON THE FRONT, HIGHLIGHTS THIS COLLECTORS EDITION COMBINATION. ALSO INCLUDED ARE A COMPLETE SET OF 792 TOPPS 1982 BASEBALL CARDS AND 44 CLEAR PLASTIC CARD HOLDER SHEETS, WHICH ARE ENOUGH FOR THE ENTIRE SET.

ONLY $ 36.00

COMBINATION ALBUM/TOPPS BASEBALL CARD SET/SET OF 44 STYLE 9 PLASTIC SHEETS	$ 36.00 PPD
PERSONALIZED ALBUM	$ 8.00 PPD
TOPPS 1982 BASEBALL CARD SET	$ 21.00 PPD
SET OF 44 STYLE 9 PLASTIC SHEETS	$ 11.00 PPD

PERSONALIZE THE ALBUM(S) WITH THE NAME(S):

YOUR NAME (PLEASE PRINT)
ADDRESS

MAKE CHECK OR MONEY ORDER PAYABLE TO:
DEN'S COLLECTORS DEN
Dept. WW
P.O.BOX 606, LAUREL, MD 20707
U.S. FUNDS ONLY
TOPPS
MD RESIDENTS ADD 5% SALES TAX

ADD POSTAGE AND HANDLING (P & H) TO ALL ITEMS NOT MARKED POSTPAID

Investors Corporation of America

AVERY B. KLEIN, PRESIDENT

3386 CHALFANT ROAD — DEPT. PG-12

SHAKER HEIGHTS, OHIO 44120

—

216-921-7679

3-MIL COMIC, MAGAZINE & RECORD BAGS

Protect your comics, magazines, paperbacks and records with heavy-duty 3-MIL protective polyethylene bags. **THESE BAGS ARE MADE OF THE FINEST VIRGIN, HIGH-CLARITY, INERT POLYETHYLENE FILM AVAILABLE.** Samples available if you send a large (#10) self-addressed stamped envelope with 4 ounces (currently 71¢) of postage on it. (Canadians send 75¢ in coin.) These prices reflect a 5% price increase effective April 1, 1981. Unfortunately, due to the volatile price changes in the polyethylene area, these prices are subject to change.

OHIO RESIDENTS PLEASE ADD 6½% OHIO SALES TAX

REGULAR BAGS
(Also fits 45 rpm records)
(7 1/8" x 10 1/2" with 2" flap)
OR
NARROW REGULAR BAGS
(Fits new and recent comics)
(6 7/8" x 10 1/2" with 2" flap)

		U.S.*	Foreign
100	for	$ 5.25	$ 8.50
300	for	11.80	17.25
500	for	17.85	25.25
1,000	for	32.00	42.50
2,000	for	63.50	84.50
3,000	for	95.00	126.50
4,000	for	125.50	167.50
5,000	for	156.50	209.00
6,000	for	186.00	249.00

SILVER AGE BAGS
(7 1/2" x 10 1/2" with 2" flap)
OR
GOLDEN AGE BAGS
(7 7/8" x 10 1/2" with 2" flap)

		U.S.*	Foreign
100	for	$ 5.50	$ 9.25
300	for	14.00	19.25
500	for	20.00	27.25
1,000	for	34.00	45.75
2,000	for	67.00	90.00
3,000	for	100.00	135.00
4,000	for	131.00	178.00
5,000	for	163.00	221.00

MAGAZINE BAGS
(8 3/4" x 11 1/4" with 2" flap)

		U.S.*	Foreign
100	for	$ 5.75	$ 9.50
300	for	15.75	23.00
500	for	23.00	31.50
1,000	for	36.75	50.50
2,000	for	72.50	100.00
3,000	for	108.00	149.00
4,000	for	142.00	196.00
5,000	for	175.00	244.00

33 RPM RECORD BAGS
(12 3/4" x 12 3/4" with no flap)

		U.S.*	Foreign
50	for	$ 6.30	$ 9.50
100	for	10.50	14.75
300	for	25.00	32.50
500	for	36.75	47.25
1,000	for	65.00	84.00
2,000	for	129.00	166.00
3,000	for	189.00	244.00
4,000	for	248.00	324.00

PAPERBACK BOOK BAGS
(5" x 10" with no flap)

		U.S.*	Foreign
100	for	$ 4.25	$ 7.35
300	for	11.00	14.75
500	for	15.75	20.50
1,000	for	24.25	30.50
2,000	for	47.25	60.00
3,000	for	69.00	88.00
4,000	for	90.00	116.00
5,000	for	110.00	142.00

*U.S. prices are for Continental U.S. only. ALASKA, HAWAII, PUERTO RICO, etc., APO & FPO must add 75¢ per 100 bags for higher parcel post and insurance charges.

COMIC STORAGE BOXES

✓300 POUND TEST CORRUGATED WHITE CARDBOARD
✓30" LONG x 8" WIDE x 11" DEEP WITH 3" WIDE WHITE TOP
✓HOLDS UP TO 350 COMICS! !
✓COMES COMPLETE FOR EASY ASSEMBLY

THESE ARE THE LARGEST, STRONGEST COMIC STORAGE BOXES AVAILABLE!

PRICES

Quantity	Continental U.S.	Foreign
1 to 5	$5.00 each	$7.35each
6 to 10	$4.25 each	$6.30each
11 to 15	$4.00 each	$6.00 each
16 to 20	$3.75 each	$5.75 each
20 or more	$3.50 each	$5.50 each

MOST ORDERS ARE SHIPPED VIA U.P.S. PLEASE INCLUDE STREET ADDRESS & TELEPHONE.

OHIO RESIDENTS PLEASE ADD 6½% OHIO SALES TAX

Foreign prices are higher due to much higher postage charges.
4% Service Charge for Charge Card Sales

OVERSTOCK
81 PRICES OR LESS
ealer Inquires Welcomed
Satisfaction Guaranteed

LL COMICS MINT
10% Discount
(On orders over $100.)

Conan

1 .... $55.00
2 .... 24.00
3 .... 36.00
4,5 .... 20.00
6-10 ...... 12.00
11-15 .... 9.00
16-24 .... 6.00
25 .... 4.50
26-30 .... 2.10
31-36 .... 1.50
37 .... 4.50
38-50 .... 1.50
51-60 .... 1.20
61-87 .... .80

Howard The Duck

1 .... 12.00
2 .... 5.00
3 .... 2.50
4,5 .... 1.80
6-9 .... 1.50
10-15 ...... 1.20

Kamandi

1 .... 2.40
2-5 .... 1.80
6-10 .... 1.50
11-20 ...... 1.20

Star Trek (TV, GK)

22-30 .... 4.00
31,39 .... 2.25
45 .... 1.00

#1 Comics-All Mint

Adv. on Planet of Apes .. 1.50
Black Magic .... .80
Cat 3.75
Champions 3.60
Combat Kelley .... .80
Deadly Hands Kung-Fu .. 4.50
Famous 1st Ed. (Action #1) 5.50
Famous 1st Ed. (Detective #27) 4.00
Human Torch 1.50
Inhumans 2.70
Invaders 6.00
Iron Fist 4.50
Isis .... .80
J.I.M. 1.20
Kazar 1.50
Kazar (Giant) 1.50
Kobra 1.00
Kull 6.00
Man Thing 7.50
Marvel Tales 25.00
Marvel Team Up 14.00
Marvel Two In One 7.00
Marvel Chillers 1.00
Marvel Presents 1.50
Marvel Treasury (Giant) Spiderman 4.50
Red Sonja 1.80
Sandman .... .80
Secret Origin 2.10

#1 Comics-All Mint

Shadow 1.80
Shazam .... .80
Six Million Dollar Man .. 1.50
Spidy Super Stories ... 1.20
Stalker 1.50
Star Fire 1.50
Super Friends .... .80
Super Girl 3.00
Super Villian Team Up .. 2.25
Swamp Thing 6.00
Tor .... .80
2001 Space Odessy 1.20
Warlock 6.00
Weird Worlds 2.25
Werewolf By Night 3.00

(Add $3.00/order for postage on all above comics)

Satisfaction Quaranteed
Golden & Silver Age

Batman 1 (F) $1750.00
Batman 2 (F) 500.00
Batman 4 (F) 250.00
Amazing Fant, 15 (G) . 600.00
Avengers 1 (F) 300.00
Avengers 2 (F) 70.00
Avengers 3,4 (F) 50.00
Avengers 5 (F) 18.00
Daredevil 1 (F) 60.00
Daredevil 2 (F) 30.00
Daredevil 3 (F) 20.00
Daredevil 4,5 (F) 12.00
Fantastic-4 1 (F) ... 700.00
Four Color 147 (F) .. 175.00
Four Color 256 (F) ... 80.00
Four Color 263 (F) ... 80.00
Four Color 282 (VG) .. 70.00
Green Lantern 1 (F+) . 150.00
J.I.M. 83 (F) 240.00
Silver Surfer 1 (NM) .. 50.00
Silver Surfer 2 (NM) .. 20.00
Silver Surfer 3 (NM) .. 16.00
Silver Surfer 4 (NM) .. 25.00
Silver Surfer 5-7 (NM) . 12.00
Silver Surfer 8-10 (NM) 10.00
Silver Surfer 11-18 (NM) 6.00
Spiderman 1 (NM) ... 650.00
Spiderman 1 (F+) ... 600.00
Uncle Scrooge 1 (NM) . 370.00
Uncle Scrooge 1 (F+) . 250.00
Weird Sci 22 (VG) 80.00
Weird Fant 17 (VG) ... 120.00

88 Classic Ill. all originally 15 cents, no repeats, all fine or better $400.00

COOK'S COLLECTORS COMICS
Ivan Cook
1810 Edgecliff Cove
Carrollton, Texas 75006
Phone (214) 242-0094

Send 25 Cents for Catalog

COMICS • SCIENCE FICTION • FANTASY
Bought and Sold

707 Pacific Avenue, Santa Cruz, CA 95060
(408) 426-0158

COMICS • BASEBALL CARDS • ROCK & ROLL
JUNE 12 & 13, 1982
CHARLOTTE, N.C.
CALL OR WRITE FOR INFORMATION
HEROES AREN'T HARD TO FIND
1502 CENTRAL AVE. CHARLOTTE, N.C. 28205
704-375-7462

BRIGHTON—NOSTRAND BOOKS

COMICS - HUGE SELECTION - COMICS

		Postage
Old Comic Catalog	$1.50	.50
Comic Bags	$3.50	1.00
New Comics (per 100)	$20.00	3.00

Pulps — Playboys — Life — Geographs

BRIGHTON—NOSTRAND BOOKS
276 BRIGHTON BEACH AVENUE
BROOKLYN, NEW YORK 11235
Phone (212) 891-2849

LAND of ooH's & aH's COMICS

WELCOME

NEW
&
OLD
COMICS
INVESTMENT
MAGAZINES
PORTFOLIOS
&
ORIGINAL
ART

17179 A
BROOKHURST
FOUNTAIN
VALLEY
CALIFORNIA
92708

TEL. (714)
963-3591
ASK FOR
JOHN

ALFREDO ALCALA 82

JIM SANDS

For Fast, Fair, Buy and Sell (All Issues Wanted) Ship for My Immediate Check. Buying/Selling Nationally Since 1972.

— My Wants: Original Classics Art, Especially H.C. Kiefer.

Try My New Venture:

A Classics Critique

Three Issues Yearly: $8. The "Critique" is packed with Info, Articles, Want Lists, Letters, Polls, and More. Plan to Attend the First Classics Con, October 81, Albany, NY. SASE Required. 885-A Nevada Oval, Plattsburgh AFB, NY 12903.

H. SHELTON DRUM
1502 Central Avenue
Charlotte, NC 28205
704-375-7462
HEROES CONVENTION '82, JUNE 12th-13th

"WE SPECIALIZE IN MAIL ORDER!"

SHINDER'S READ MORE

MINNESOTA'S LARGEST COMICS RETAILER

SUNDAY, JANUARY 10, 1982

BOOKS
Movie
POSTERS

SHINDERS

SHINDER'S • 628 HENNEPIN AVENUE
MINNEAPOLIS, MN. 55403
Call: (612) 333-3628
OPEN: 6:30AM - 1AM, 365 DAYS A YEAR!
Look for our ads in the Buyer's Guide!!

DISCOUNTS TO 55%
COMIC BOOKS • MAGAZINES
MARVEL
DC
MASS MARKET
PAPERBACKS • MAGAZINES
ALTERNATIVE PUBLISHERS
NO
MINIMUM PER TITLE
D & D
UNDERGROUNDS
GLENWOOD
DISTRIBUTORS INC
124 Vandalia Collinsville, IL. 62234
618/345/1027
FAST
CONSISTENT SERVICE
PORTFOLIOS
ACCURATE
BOOKKEEPING
PRICE GUIDES
DIRECT SHIPPING
FROM OUR WAREHOUSE
FOR OUR FREE MONTHLY CATALOG

INTRODUCING...

HIGH-ENERGY

...some of fandom's younger talent.

HIGH-ENERGY...a new magazine created and produced by a small group of dedicated high-school students! Each thick, 8 by 10, AD-FREE issue contains a variety of short stories and is printed on high-quality slick paper. And the price is only $2.00 per copy! So if you're curious, and would like a refreshing change of pace, just send your orders to:

HIGH-ENERGY
2488 Trenton Dr.
San Bruno, CA 94066

·WAR · HORROR · FANTASY · SCIENCE FICTION·

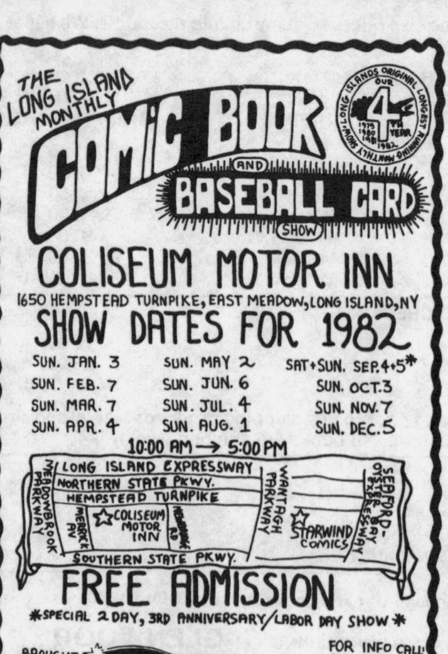

GALACTIC ENTERPRISES

FANTASY • SCIENCE FICTION • HORROR • GOTHIC MYSTERY

18 CRAIN HIGHWAY
GLEN BURNIE, MARYLAND

PHONE (301) 760-9538
OPEN SIX DAYS A WEEK

CONVENIENT TO 695, RITCHIE HIGHWAY AND BALTIMORE-ANNAPOLIS PIKE

MONDAY THROUGH FRIDAY 9 A.M. – 9 P.M.
SATURDAY 9 A.M. – 6 P.M.

10% OFF COMIC RESERVATION SERVICE • LARGEST SELECTION OF SF VIDEO TAPES
FANTASY GAMES • COMICS • SF BOOKS • SEND $1 FOR SF OR VIDEO CATALOG

GEPPI'S SUBSCRIPTION SERVICE

612½ Edmondson Avenue
Baltimore, MD 21228

A MINIMUM MONTHLY ORDER OF 10 BOOKS

PLAN A • 10-29 Order Shipped Monthly—Exact UPS Charges
PLAN B • 30-59 Order Shipped Monthly—We Pay Shipping
PLAN C • 30-59 Order Shipped Bi-Weekly—½ Exact UPS Charges
PLAN D • 30-59 Order Shipped Weekly—Exact UPS Charges
PLAN E • 60 or More Order Shipped Bi-Weekly—We Pay Shipping
PLAN F • 60 or More Order Shipped Weekly—½ Exact UPS Charges

A $10.00 SECURITY DEPOSIT will establish instant credit for your account. Thereafter your shipments will be invoiced upon delivery for your remittance. Your next shipment will be released upon receipt of payment for the previous shipment. Your $10.00 security deposit will be refunded or credited if subscription service is stopped.

WHY ORDER FROM US?

- Order 480 books over a twelve month period and receive a free 1983 Overstreet Price Guide
- One free plastic bag for each book shipped
- 10% discount on comics in 8-page back issue ad
- Complete selection of Whitmans, Harveys, DCs, Marvels, Pacifics, Archies, Fanzines
- Fast, accurate, and dependable service
- 8 years of service to the Baltimore/Washington/Virginia areas
- 4 stores to serve you better
- A Master Card/Visa plan that saves time

SPECULATORS: You Can Buy Large Quantities of Any Issue at Wholesale Rates! Inquire!

HOW TO ORDER:

Just check off each title and how many of that title you buy on a regular basis, as this will be considered a standing order. Count total number of books you will receive each month and mark that in box. Then select delivery plan you want to use and check off. Send check or money order for $10.00 with order form to Geppi's Subscription Service.

Changes in your order will be made upon written notification only.

(See Order Form Next Page)

Geppi's Subscription Service (continued)

MARVEL COMICS
__Avengers
__Capt. America
__Conan
__Daredevil
__Dazzler
__Defenders
__Dr. Strange
__Fantastic Four
__Ghost Rider
__G. I. Joe
__Incredible Hulk
__Iron Man
__Kazar
__King Conan
__Marvel Fanfare
__Marvel Tales
__Marvel Team-up
__Marvel 2 in 1
__Master Kung Fu
__Micronauts
__Moon Knight
__Peter Parker
__Powerman
__Rom
__Spider-Man
__Spider-Woman
__Star Wars
__Team America
__Thor
__What If. . . ?
__X-Men
__Dennis/Menace
__Any Marvel #1
__Any One Shot
__Mini Series
__Dennis Digest

DC COMICS
__Action
__All Star Squad
__Arak
__Batman
__Brave & Bold
__Camelot 3000
__Capt. Carrot
__Dark Force
__DC Comics Pres.
__Detective
__Firestorm
__Flash
__G. I. Combat
__Green Lantern
__House of Mystery
__Jonah Hex
__JLA
__Legion
__Pandura Pan
__Sgt. Rock
__Superboy
__Superman
__Superman Family
__Swamp Thing
__Teen Titans
__Unknown Soldier
__Warlord
__Weird War
__Wonder Woman
__World's Finest
__Adventure Digest
__Best of DC Digest
__Any DC #1
__Any One Shot
__Mini Series

MAGAZINES
__Amazing Cinema
__Amazing Heroes
__Adventure Illust.
__Artforms
__Barks Collector
__Cerebus
__Chronicles
__Cinemagic
__Cinefantastique
__Cinefex
__Comic Feature
__Comic Journal
__Comic Reader
__Comic Scene
__Crazy
__Creepy
__Dr. Who
__Duckburg Times
__Eclipse
__Eerie
__Elf Quest
__Enterprise Incid.
__Epic
__Famous Monsters
__Fangoria
__Fantastic Exploits
__Fantastic Films
__Fantasy Empire
__Fantasy Illust.
__Fantasy Modeling
__First Kingdom
__Future Gold
__Galaxia
__Hembeck
__Justice Machine
__L O C
__Marvel Album
__Marvel Bizzarre Ad
__Marvel/DC Team-Up
__Marvel Index
__Marvel Super Spec.
__MediaScene Prevue
__Nexus
__Panels
__Questar
__RBCC
__Rook

MAGAZINES (Cont'd.)
__Sal Q Portfolio
__Savage Sword
__Spirit
__Starburst
__Starlog
__Treasury Edition
__Vampirella

PACIFIC COMICS
__Starslayer
__Capt. Victory
__Ms. Mystic

ARCHIE COMICS
__If All
____
____
____
____
____
____
____
____

GOLD KEY COMICS
__If All
____
____
____
____
____
____
____
____

HARVEY COMICS
__If All
____
____
____
____
____
____
____

ANY SPEC BOOKS WANTED PLEASE LIST
____
____
____
____
____
____
____
____

Give Your Name **Clearly**: ______________________________
Address: ______________________________
City: ______________ St. ________ Zip ________
Ph. Work ______________ Home ______________

Total Books ☐

Plan A ☐
Plan B ☐
Plan C ☐
Plan D ☐
Plan E ☐
Plan F ☐

GEPPI'S COMIC WORLD—(Page 3)

Chamber of Darkness

4 (Smith; Conan try out)	$18.00

Champions

1	$6.00
2-5	2.50
6-10,16,17	2.00
11-15 (Byrne)	5.00

Conan

1	$75.00
2	35.00
3	50.00
4,5	28.00
6-10	20.00
11-13	15.00
14,15 (Elric)	18.00
16-22	11.00
23,24 (Red Sonja)	13.00
25	7.50
26-30	6.00
31-36,38-40,43-45,49	4.50
37 (Adams)	7.50
41,42,46-48,50,57	3.00
51-56,60	2.50
58,59 (1st Belit)	3.60
61-70	2.25
71-80	2.00
81-90	1.50
91-99	1.25
100 (Belit dies)	2.50
101-114,116-120	1.25
115	2.00
121-130	1.00
131-Present	.75
King Size #1 (Smith)	10.00
Annual #2	4.00
Annual #3	2.50
Annual #4,5	2.00
Annual #6	1.50
Giant Size #1	6.00
Giant Size #2	4.50
Giant Size #3-5	3.00

Creatures on the Loose

10 (1st King Kull)	$16.00

Daredevil

1-3	(Inquire)
4,5	$28.00
6-10	18.00
11,12,14-20	8.00
13	9.00
21-30	6.00
31-40	4.50
41-49,53	3.50
50-52 (Smith)	4.50
54-60	3.00
61-80	2.75
81-90	2.50
91-99	2.25
100,105	3.00
101-104,106-110	2.00
111-130	1.75
131-140	1.50
141-150	1.25
151-157	1.00
158-160 (Miller)	Inquire
161-165	7.50
166-170	5.00
171-180	3.00
181	5.00
182 (All Miller)	3.00
Giant Size #1	2.50
Special #1	5.00
Special #2,3	2.50
Special #4	2.00

Dazzler

1	$3.00
2	2.00
3-5	1.50
6-15	1.00
16-Present	.75

Defenders

1	$20.00
2 (Silver Surfer)	12.00
3-5	7.50
6-10	6.00
11-20	4.50
21-30	3.50
31-40	3.00
41-50	2.50
51-60	2.25
61-70	2.00
71-80	1.50
81-90	1.25
91-99	1.00
100	2.00
101-Present	.75
King Size #1	4.00
Giant Size #1	3.50
Giant Size #2,3	2.50
Giant Size #4,5	2.00

Devil Dinosaur

1	$1.50
2-9	1.00

Doc Savage

1	$2.50
2-8	1.25
Giant Size #1	1.50

Dr. Strange

169	$7.50
170-183	4.00
1 (Brunner)	7.50
2 (Brunner)	3.50
3-5	2.50
6-10	2.25
11-22	1.00
23-26 (Starlin)	2.25
27-40	1.50
41-48	1.25
49-55	1.50
56-Present (Rogers)	1.00
Annual #1	2.00
Giant Size #1 (Russell)	3.00

Dragonslayer

1,2	$1.50

Fantastic Four

1-25	(Inquire)
26-30	$29.00
31-40	18.00
41-47	12.00
48 (1st Silver Surfer)	30.00
49,50 (Silver Surfer)	15.00
51-60	10.00
61-65,68-70	7.50
66,67 (1st Warlock)	9.00
71,73,75,78-80	5.00
72,74,76,77 (S.Surfer)	6.50
81-90	4.00
91-99	3.50
100	12.00
101-111,113-120	3.00
112 (Hulk vs. Thing)	3.50
121-123 (Silver Surfer)	4.00
124-127,129-149	2.50
128	4.00
150 (Quick Silver weds)	3.00
151-154,158-160	2.25
155-157 (Silver Surfer)	3.00
161-180	2.00
181-199	1.50
200	2.50
201-208,219	1.25
209-218,220,221 (Byrne)	2.50
222-231	1.00
232-236 (Byrne)	3.00
237-Present (All Byrne)	1.50
Special #1	40.00
Special #2	25.00
Special #3	15.00
Special #4	7.50
Special #5	5.00
Special #6	3.50
Special #7-10	2.50
Special #11,12	2.00
Special #13-15	1.50
Giant Size #2-4	3.50
Giant Size #5,6	2.25

Fantasy Masterpieces Vo. 1

1	$3.00
2	2.75
3	3.00
4-6	2.50
7-11	2.00

Fantasy Masterpieces Vo. 2

1	$3.00
2-5	2.00
6,7	1.50
8-14	1.25

Fear

19 (1st HTD)	$15.00

Ghost Rider (1973)

1	$9.00
2-5	4.00
6-10	2.50
11-19	2.00
20 (Byrne)	2.50
21-30	1.75
31-34,36-40	1.50
35 (Starlin)	1.75
41-50	1.25
51-60	1.00
61-Present	.75

Godzilla

1	$1.50
2-24	.90

Howard the Duck

1	$10.00
2	6.00
3	3.50
4,5	2.00
6-10	1.75
11-20	1.50
21-31	1.25
Annual #1	1.50

Hulk

1-6	(Inquire)
102	$15.00
103-110	7.00
111-120	4.00
121-130	3.50
131-140	3.00
141 (1st Doc Samson)	3.50
142-150	2.50
151-176,179	2.25
177,178 (Warlock)	6.00
180 (1st Wolverine)	15.00
181 (Wolverine)	20.00
182 (Wolverine)	10.00
183-199	2.00
200	2.50
201-220	1.50
221-240	1.25
241-249,251-260	1.00
250	1.50
261-270	1.00
271-Present	.75
Giant Size #1	2.50
Special #1	7.50
Special #2	4.25
Special #3	3.50
Annual #4,5	3.00
Annual #6,8	2.00
Annual #7 (Byrne)	3.00
Annual #9,10	1.25

Human Fly

1	$2.00
2-10	1.25
11-19	1.00

Human Torch

1	$5.00
2-8	2.00

Inhumans

1	$3.00
2-5	1.50
6-12	1.25

Invaders

1	$7.00
2	3.50
3-5	2.50
6-11	2.25
12-19,29	2.00
20 (Rep. Sub-Mariner)	3.00
21-28	1.50
30-40	1.25
41 Giant Size	2.00
Giant Size #1	5.00
Annual #1	2.50

Iron Fist (All Byrne)

1	$15.00
2-14	4.00
15 (New X-Men)	15.00

Iron Man

1	$40.00
2	18.00
3-5	9.00
6-10	6.00
11-20	4.00
21-40,53,69	3.50
41-46,48-50	3.00
47 (Smith, Orig.)	7.50
51,52,54,57-60	2.50
55,56 (Starlin)	4.50
61-68,70	2.25
71-80	2.00
81-99	1.75
100 (Starlin-c)	5.00
101-117	1.50
118 (Byrne)	3.00
119,120,123-128 (Alcohol)	2.10
121,122,129,130	1.50
131-140	1.25
141-149	1.00
150	1.50
151-Present	.75
Giant Size #1	2.50
Special #1	5.00
Special #2	2.50
Annual #3,4	2.00

Iron Man & Submariner

1	$7.50

John Carter

1	$2.50
2-5,11	2.00
6-10	1.50
12-28	1.25

Kazar (1971)

1	$3.00
2,3	2.50

Kazar (1974)

1	$3.00
2-10	2.00
11-20	1.25

Kazar The Savage

1	$2.50
2-9	1.00
10-Direct Sale only	1.50
11-Present (D.S.O.)	1.00

King Conan

1	$3.00
2-5	1.50
6-Present	1.25

Kull

1	$9.00
2,3	5.00
4,5	4.00
6-10	3.50
11-15 (Ploog)	2.50
16-29	1.50

Logan's Run

1	$2.50
2-7	1.50

Luke Cage (Power Man)

1	$7.50
2-10	3.00
11-20	2.50
21-30	2.25
31-40	2.00
41-47	1.75
48-50 (Byrne)	3.00

51-56,58-60	1.50
57 (X-Men)	6.00
61-70	1.25
71-80	1.00
81-Present	.75
Giant Size #1	2.00
Annual #1	1.50

Machine Man

1	$1.50
2-5	1.25
6-19	1.00

Man-Thing Vo. 1

1 (HTD)	$10.00
2-4	4.50
5	3.50
6-11	2.50
12-20	2.00
21,22	1.50
Giant Size #1	2.50
Giant Size #2,3	2.00
Giant Size #4	12.00
Giant Size #5	10.00

Man-Thing Vo. 2

1	$1.50
2-8	1.00

Man From Atlantis

1	$2.00
2-8	1.25

Marvel Classics

1	$3.00
2,3	2.50
4-10	2.25
11-20	2.00
21-30	1.50
31-36	1.25

Marvel Feature (1971)

1 (Defenders)	$15.00
2,3 (Defenders)	9.00
4	2.50
5-8	2.00
9,10	1.50
11,12 (Thing)	2.00

Marvel Feature (1975)

1 (Red Sonja)	$3.00
2-5	2.00
6-8	1.50

Marvel Premiere

1 (Warlock)	$7.50
2	4.50
3 (Dr. Strange)	6.00
4 (Smith)	6.00
5-7,9,10	3.00
8 (Starlin)	3.00
11-14,16-20	2.25
15 (Orig. Iron Fist)	6.00
21-24	2.50
25 (Byrne)	5.00
26-30	2.00
31-35,38-40	1.50
36,37 (3-D Man Orig.)	2.50
41-49	1.25
50	2.00
51-56,61	1.00
57-60 (Dr. Who)	1.50

Marvel Spotlight Vo. 1

1,2	$4.50
3,4	2.50
5 (Ghost Rider Orig.)	7.50
6-8	3.00
9-12	2.25
13-20	1.50
21-27	1.25
28,29 (Moon Knight)	2.40
30,31,33	1.00
32 (Spider-Woman)	3.50

Marvel Spotlight Vo. 2

1	$1.50
2-10	1.00

Marvel Team-Up

1	$16.00
2,3	8.00
4 (X-Men)	10.00
5	5.00
6-10	4.50
11-20	3.00
21-30	2.50
31-40	2.25
41-52	2.00
53 (Byrne X-Men)	9.00
54,55 (Byrne)	4.50
56-58	1.80
59-70,79 (Byrne)	3.50
71-78,80	1.50
81-90	1.25
91-99	1.00
100 (Byrne & Miller)	3.00
101-Present	.75
Annual #1 (New X-Men)	10.00
Annual #2 (Starlin)	2.50
Annual #3,4	1.50

Marvel Two-In-One

1	$9.00
2-5	5.00
6-10	3.00
11-20	2.50
21-30	2.25
31-40	2.00
41,42,44-49	1.50
43,50,53-55 (Byrne)	2.40
51 (Miller)	5.00
52 (Moon Knight)	2.00
56-60	1.50
61-70	1.25
71-74,76-80	1.00
75	1.50
81-Present	.75
Annual #1	2.50
Annual #2	7.00
Annual #3,4	1.50
Annual #5,6	1.25

Master of Kung Fu

15	$7.50
16,17	4.50
18-20,24	3.50
21-23,25-30	3.00
31-40	2.50
41-50	2.25
51-70	2.00
71-90	1.50
91-99	1.25
100	1.50
101-110	1.00
111-Present	.75
Giant Size #1	2.50
Giant Size #2	2.00
Annual #1	2.50

Micronauts

1 (Golden)	$7.50
2-5 (Golden)	3.50
6-10	3.00
11-20	2.50
21-30	2.00
31-37	1.50
38 (Direct Sale only)	3.00
39-Present (D.S.O.)	1.50
Annual #1	2.50
Annual #2	2.00
Annual #3	1.25

Moon Knight

1	$2.50
2-5	2.00
6-10	1.50
11-14	1.25
15 (1st Direct Sale)	3.00
16-Present (D.S.O.)	2.00

Ms. Marvel

1	$3.00
2 (Orig.)	2.50
3-5	2.00
6-10	1.50
11-23	1.00

Nick Fury, Agent (1968)

1	$9.00
2,3	6.00
4,5	4.50
6,7	4.00
8-11,13-15	2.50

12 (Smith)	4.00
16-18	2.00

Nick Fury & His Agents (1973)

1	$2.00
2-5	1.00

Not Brand Echh

1	$7.50
2-4	4.50
5 (Forbush Orig.)	3.50
6-8	3.50
9-13	2.50

Nova

1	$6.00
2,3	3.50
4	2.50
5-10	2.00
11-20	1.50
21-25	1.25

Omega

1	$2.00
2-10	1.50

Peter Parker

1	$4.50
2-5	3.00
6-10	2.50
11-20	2.00
21-26,29,30	1.75
27,28 (Miller DD)	(Inquire)
31-40	1.50
41-49	1.25
50	1.50
51-60	1.00
61-Present	.75
Annual #1	2.00
Annual #2	1.25
Annual #3	1.00

Planet of the Apes (Mag.)

1	$2.50
2-11	1.50

Raiders Of The Lost Ark

1	$3.00
2,3	2.00

Red Sonja

1	$3.00
2-5	2.50
6-10	2.00
11-15	1.50

Red Wolf

1	$2.00
2-9	1.00

Rom

1	$3.00
2-5	2.50
6-10	2.00

11-17	1.50
18 (X-Men)	2.50
19-24	1.00
25 (Giant)	1.50
26-Present	.75

Savage She-Hulk

1	$2.50
2-5	2.00
6-10	1.50
11-20	1.25
21-24	1.00
25 (Giant)	1.50

Sgt. Fury

1	(Inquire)
2	$35.00
3-5	15.00
6-10	10.00
11-20	6.00
21-30	3.00
31-40	2.50
41-50	2.25
51-70	2.00
71-90	1.75
91-99	1.50
100	2.00
101-120	1.25
121-140	1.00
141-167	.75
Annual #1	4.00
Annual #2	2.00

Shanna, She Devil

1	$2.00
2-5	1.50

Sho-Gun Warriors

1	$3.00
2-5	2.50
6-10	2.00
11-20	1.50
21-25	1.00

Silver Surfer

1	$60.00
2	30.00
3	24.00
4 (low dist.)	45.00
5-7	20.00
8-10	15.00
11-18	12.00

Skull the Slayer

1	$2.00
2-8	1.00

Son of Satan

1	$2.50
2-8	1.50

Spider-Man

1-10	(Inquire)
11-13,15	$45.00
14 (Green Goblin)	54.00
16-19	30.00
20	32.00
21-25	15.00
26-30	12.00
31-38	10.00
39,40 (Green Goblin)	9.00
41-50	7.50
51-60	5.00
61-80	4.00
81-89	3.50
90 (Death Capt. Stacy)	4.50
91-93,95,99	3.00
94 (Orig. retold)	5.00
96-98 (Drug issues)	10.00
100 (Anniversary)	12.00
101 (1st Morbius)	7.50
102 (Orig. Morbius)	7.50
103-112,115-120	3.00
113,114 (Starlin)	4.00
121 (G. Stacy dies)	15.00
122 (G. Goblin dies)	15.00
123-140	2.50
141-150	2.25
151-160	2.00
161,162 (X-Men)	5.00
163-170	1.75
171-180	1.50
181-188,191-199	1.25
189,190 (Byrne)	3.00
200	3.00
201-220	1.00
221-Present	.75
Annual #1	30.00
Annual #2	15.00
Special #3,4	7.50
Special #5-8	4.50
King Size #9	3.00
Annual #10	3.00
Annual #11,12	2.50
Annual #13 (Byrne)	3.50
Annual #14,15 (Miller)	2.50
Giant Size #1	3.50
Giant Size #2	2.50
Giant Size #3-6	2.00

Spider-Woman

1	$2.50
2-5	2.00
6-10	1.75
11-20	1.50
21-30	1.25
31-37,39,40	1.00
38 (X-Men)	2.00
41-Present	.75

Spidey Super Stories

1	$2.00
2-10	1.75
11-30	1.50
31-40	1.25
41-50	1.00
51-Present	.75

Star Trek

1	$2.00
2,3	1.75
4-10	1.50
11-17	1.00

Star Wars

1	$12.00
2,3	6.00
4	7.50
5,6	4.50
7-10	3.50
11-20	3.00
21-30	2.50
31-38	2.00
39 (Empire)	3.00
40-44,50	2.00
45-49	1.00
51-Present	.75

Strange Tales

1-105	(Inquire)
106-109	$20.00
110 (Intro. Dr. Strange)	65.00
111	20.00
112,113	10.00
114	14.00
115 (Orig. Dr. Strange)	25.00
116-120	7.50
121-129	4.50
130 (Beatles cameo)	9.00
131-134	3.50
135 (Orig. N. Fury)	7.50
136-147,149-158	4.00
148 (Orig. Ancient One)	4.00
159 (Steranko)	4.00
160-168	3.00
169-177	1.25
178 (Warlock/Starlin)	7.00
179-181 (Starlin)	4.50
182-188	1.00
Annual #1,2	35.00

Sub-Mariner

1	$18.00
2	7.00
3-5	4.00
6-10,14	3.50
11-13,15-20	3.00
21-34,37,39,40	2.50
35,36,38	3.00
41-58,60	2.00
59,61	3.00
62-72	1.50
Special #1	3.00
Special #2	2.00

Super-Villain Team-Up

1	$3.00
2-5	2.00
6-14	1.50
Giant Size #1,2	2.00

Tales of Suspense

1-41	(Inquire)
42-45	$27.50
46-48	15.00
49-51,53	9.00
52 (1st Black Widow)	12.00
54-56	7.50
57 (Orig. Hawkeye)	8.00
58 (Capt. Amer. begins)	8.00
59,63	6.00
60-62,64-99	3.00

Tales to Astonish

1-36	(Inquire)
37-40	$27.50
41-43	14.00
44 (1st & Orig. Wasp)	16.00
45-48,50	12.00
49 (Antman/Gnt.-Man)	14.00
51-60	7.00
61-70	4.50
71-80	3.00
81-91	2.50
92,93 (Silver Surfer)	6.00
94-99	2.00
100,101	4.50

Tales to Astonish (New)

1	$2.00
2-10	1.50
11-14	1.00

Tarzan

1	$2.00
2-10	1.50
11-20	1.25
21-29	1.00
Annual #1	2.00
Annual #2,3	1.50

Thor

83-90	(Inquire)
91,92,94-96,98-100	$25.00
93,97	30.00
101,103,104,110	12.00
102,105-109	17.50
111,113-125	7.50
112 (Thor vs. Hulk)	12.00
126 (1st Thor title)	6.00
127-140	5.00
141-147,150-157	3.00
148,149 (Orig/Bl. Bolt)	4.50
158 (Reprint Orig.)	4.00
159-164,167-179	2.50
165,166 (Warlock)	4.50
180,181 (Adams)	4.00
182-192,194-199	2.25
193 (Silver Surfer)	5.00
200	4.00
201-220	2.00
221-240	1.75
241-250	1.50
251-270	1.25
271-299	1.00
300	2.50
301-Present	.75
Annual #1	14.00
Annual #2	4.00
Annual #3,4	3.00
Annual #5	2.00
Annual #6,7	1.50
Annual #8,9	1.25
Giant Size #1	2.00

Tomb of Dracula

1	$10.00
2-5	5.00
6-9	3.00
10 (1st Blade)	3.50
11-21	2.50
22-30	2.00
31-40	1.50
41-50	1.25
51-69	1.00
70 (Giant)	1.50

2001 A Space Odyssey

1	$1.50
2-10	1.00

Warlock

1	$7.50
2,3	4.50
4-8	3.00
9-15 (Starlin)	4.00

Werewolf By Night

1	$4.50
2-10	2.50
11-20	2.00
21-30	1.50
31,34-43	1.25
32 (1st/Orig. M. Knight)	5.00
33 (Moon Knight)	4.50
Giant Size #2,3	2.00

What If?

1	$6.00
2-5	3.50
6-12	2.50
13 (Conan)	3.00

14-20	2.00
21-26,28-30	1.50
27 (Phoenix Lives)	3.50
31-Present	1.25

X-Men

1-10	(Inquire)
11,13-20	$10.00
12	12.00
21-27,29,30	7.50
28 (1st Banshee)	10.00
31-40	4.00
41-49,52	3.00
50,51 (Steranko)	10.00
53 (Smith)	12.00
54,55 (Smith-c)	6.00
56-63,65 (Adams)	13.00
64,66	4.00
67-80	3.50
81-93	3.00
94 (New X-Men)	65.00
95	40.00
96-99	25.00
100	30.00
101 (1st Phoenix)	30.00
102-107,109,110	15.00
108 (Byrne begins)	25.00
111-115	12.00
116-120	10.00
121-125	7.50
126-129	6.00
130 (Dazzler)	7.50
131-136	5.00
137 (Phoenix Suicide)	9.00
138 (Cyclops quits)	4.00
139-143	3.00
144-149	1.50
150 (Giant)	2.00
151-Present	1.25
Giant Size #1	65.00
Giant Size #2	12.00
Special #1	10.00
Special #2	7.50
Annual #3	5.00
Annual #4	3.00
Annual #5	2.50

MAGAZINES

Epic Illustrated

1	$5.00
2-5	3.00
6-Present	2.50

Marvel Comics Super Special

1 (Kiss)	$7.50
2 (Conan)	5.00
3 (Close Encounters)	3.50
4-6	3.00
8 (Battlestar)	5.00
9 (Conan)	4.00
10 (Starlord)	4.00
11 (Shadow Realm)	5.00
12,13 (Shadow Realm)	4.50
14,15,17	3.00
16 (Empire Strikes)	4.00
18 (Raiders Lost Ark)	3.50
19,20	3.00
21-Present	2.50

Marvel Preview

1 (Adams)	$5.00
2	4.00
3	3.00
4 (Star Lord Orig.)	7.50
5,6 (Sherlock Holmes)	4.00
7-9	2.50
10 (Starlin/Byrne)	10.00
11 (Star Lord/Starlin)	9.00
12,13	2.50
14,15 (Star Lord/Starlin)	4.00
16-20,22,23	2.50
21 (Moon Knight	3.00
24 (Paradox)	3.50

Bizarre Adventures

25-28	$3.00
29-Present	2.50

Rampaging Hulk

1	$6.00
2 (X-Men)	4.50
3-10	3.50
11 (Moon Knight)	4.00
12,15,17,18,20 (M. Knight)	3.50
13,14,16,19	3.00
21-27	2.50

Savage Sword

1 (Smith, Adams)	$18.00
2 (Adams)	10.00
3,4	7.50
5-10	6.00
11-13,15	5.00
14(Adams), 16,17	7.50
18-30	4.00
31-40	3.50
41-50	3.00
51-60	2.50
61-70	2.25
71-Present	2.00

DC Comics

All Star Squadron

1	$2.00
2-5	1.50
6-10	1.00
11-Present	.75

Arak

1	$2.00
2-5	1.50
6-10	1.00
11-Present	.75

DC Comics Presents

1	$4.00
2-10	3.00
11-20	2.50
21-25	1.50
26	15.00
27-Present	.75

Madame Xanadu

1	2.00

Teen Titans, New

1	$15.00
2	7.50
3-5	6.00
6-10	4.00
11-15	3.00
16-Present	1.50

Warlord

1	9.00
2-5	4.50
6-10	3.00
11-20	2.50
21-30	2.00
31-40	1.50
41-47,49	1.25
48 (Arak/Insert)	2.00
50 (Anniversary Issue)	1.50
51-Present	1.00

3 MIL PLASTIC BAGS

	W/Order over $9.50	W/Out Plus Postage
COMIC SIZE	100/$3.75	100/$4.75
	1000/$30.00	1000/$36.00
GOLDEN AGE	100/$4.25	100/$5.25
	1000/$33.00	1000/$39.00
MAGAZINE SIZE	100/$4.75	100/$5.75
	1000/$36.00	1000/$42.00
COMIC BOX	1/$4.00	
	10/$30.00	10/$40.00

GRAPHITTI
60 Gayley Ave • Los Angeles, CA 90024
Hours: 11 — 7 • Monday — Saturday
Phone (213) 824-3656
The West Coast's most outrageous comic book and fantasy art emporium is now open in Westwood Village, adjacent to the UCLA campus. We carry a complete selection of comic books from 1933-present (golden age, EC, special artists, Disney, complete Marvel and DC groups, etc.); rare pulp magazines; big little books; vintage paperback books; movie posters and magazines of all varieties (1920s — present); limited edition graphics/ fantasy artprints; original comic book and fantasy artworks—it's all here!!!
The GRAPHITTI catalog will be available in July for $1. It features all the items we have available and is heavily photo-illustrated!
We are always interested in purchasing collections and outstanding individual pieces. We will not be outbid for high quality material!
FASTNER/LARSON 1979

MIDWEST'S LARGEST "TOTAL COMIC STORE" FEATURING GOLDEN AGE INVENTORY OF FINEST QUALITY... A QUARTER MILLION DC AND MARVEL COMICS ~ SILVER AGE TO DATE! AND MORE
WARRIOR'S HOT LINE 612 222 3366
ST. PAUL COMIC
176 W. 7th.
St. Paul, Minnesota
55103
SEND FOR THE WARRIOR'S
PRICE LIST AND UPDATE ON SPECIAL SALES!

HERE ARE TWO MORE DEFINITIVE BOOKS AVAILABLE FROM OVERSTREET PUBLICATIONS, EACH IN A CLASS OF ITS OWN!

The Paperback Price Guide™ by Kevin Hancer is crammed with information and is published annually.

The Complete Guide to American Pocket Watches™ by Cooksey Shugart is the only book of its kind and is published annually.

HERE'S WHAT YOU GET

- Lists most **paperbacks** from 1939 to 1959 — with many **digests** included
- Current **market trends** and **prices** are reflected
- Over 900 illos in **Full Color** and black & White
- Over 16,000 entries
- **Full Color Cover** by Fastner/Larson

Softback $9.95ppd.
Hardback $14.95ppd.

Paperbacks are rapidly becoming a prime collectible. Get in on the ground floor in this **Exciting New Field** and order today!

- Lists American **pocket watches** alphabetically by company.
- Over **600 illustrations** in **color** & Black & White
- Gives **history** and tells how a watch works
- 332 pages packed with information
- **Gold marks** identified

Softback $9.95 ppd.

Pocket watches are a long established prime collectible and this book will tell you everything you need to know about this exciting field. **Order your copy today!**

DEALERS—Write for quantity discounts.

The Complete Guide to American Pocket Watches™ is a comprehensive price guide to American pocket watches all in **one handy volume!** This book includes all manufacturers and is profusely illustrated. A **must** for easy identification of your watches.

The Paperback Price Guide™, profusely illustrated, lists most books published in the 1939-1959 period with selected listings into the 1960s.

Send all Orders to:

OVERSTREET PUBLICATIONS, INC.
780 Hunt Cliff Dr. NW
Cleveland, TN 37311

(615)472-4135

THE POP HOLLINGER STORY

The First Comic Book Collector/Dealer

By
Tim Hessee

Pop Hollinger in the IGA store marking magazines.

While browsing through a dealer's Golden Age comic books or looking at a friend's collection, have you come across comics from the 1940s or 1950s with brown paper tape on the spine and inside edges of the cover, restapled and possibly trimmed, and wondered who did it and why? This is the story of the man responsible—Pop Hollinger. Pop received two college degrees before World War I, earned four patents from the U. S. Government, and started an old comic book shop in the late 1930s. His story begins 96 years ago.

Harvey T. Hollinger was born during the last days of the Old West in Chapman, Kansas, on October 13, 1886. He was six when the Dalton Gang was butchered in Coffeyville, Kansas, a hundred miles south of Chapman, during their last bank robbery attempt; ten when Henry Ford's first cars rolled off a Detroit assembly line; 17 when the Wright brothers flew at Kitty Hawk. After high school, many of his classmates returned to the family farm, but not Pop. He left his parents' farm and bought two of those newfangled gadgets—a Harley-Davidson motorcycle and a photography camera. He biked around the Midwest earning money for gas and food selling photos he took of local people and communities. Life on the road was tough and Pop acquired much useful experience from the school of hard knocks. Having the motorcycle break down on a lonely country road was a quick teacher in the art of mechanics.

The words "maverick" and "rugged individualist" applied to Pop.

In 1908, tiring of the vagabond life, Pop married and in the same year enrolled at McPherson College in McPherson, Kansas. At the turn of the century, college was not necessary for many occupations. To teach in most public schools, a high school diploma was all that was needed, and few people continued their formal education. While in college, Pop played football and basketball. To help defray expenses, he and his wife Marie managed a boarding house and took in laundry. In 1912, Pop graduated with a degree in liberal arts. While completing his masters, he taught high school woodworking and shop.

In 1914, Pop and his family moved to Concordia, a North Central Kansa farm community of 8,000, to accept the position of teacher of applied sciences in the public high school. At the height of the Great Depression in 1933, Pop, now 47 years old, retired from his teaching job to become self-employed running a service station. He operated a second-hand store as a sideline in the basement under Glenn Cook's food store. From furniture and appliances to books and magazines, Pop sold anything people brought into his shop.

Pocket Books had started issuing 25 cent paperback editions of best-selling hardbacks in 1939. They caught on quickly with the public as a cheap means of reading current novels. Comic books had also just started to hit their stride with original material being created to help satisfy the demand. Used pulps, paperbacks, magazines, and comic books were consistent good sellers for Pop. In the late 1930s with his parental responsibilities completed, as his children were all grown and married, Pop sold his service station and made the transition from dealing part-time in second-hand merchandise to dealing full-time in used comic books and other periodicals.

Always an innovator, Pop used several ways to expand his comic book business. By 1940, he had enough stock to wholesale comic books to various businesses from cafes to food stores. Pop soon had 15 to 20 outlets all over North Central Kansas. At one time, he had five stores selling used comic books in Corcordia, compared to only three Concordia stores selling new comics. During this period, he started a mail order comic book club where, for 20 cents or 30 cents a week, a person could receive five or ten comics, respectively. Pop published a comic book catalogue in 1942. His ads for it stated: "Old or used comic books are worth money. We pay from 1¢ to $1.00 each for certain old comics....Be among the first in your community to collect old comics." In this same ad, Pop claimed to "carry a large assortment of every comic book published." He offered a "free hospital reading service for any patient in any hospital in U.S.A." This service was

JOIN OUR

Comic Book Club

GET YOUR CHOICE

of any Comic published the rest of this year and all of next year at less than

HALF PRICE

AND BETTER YET, YOU

PAY BY THE WEEK

MAILED ANYWHERE IN U.S.A.

The 50ct Club permits you to receive 5 Comic Books weekly for 20cts. (Plus tax)	The $1.00 Club permits you to receive 10 Comic Books weekly for 30cts. (Plus tax)

Just select your favorite, group or kinds of Comic Books you like best and arrange for the Club Subscription by mail -- then pay weekly as you read -- no other cost.

Send us the name of the Newsstand Dealer in your home town -- he will make arrangements for your club.

HOLLINGERS
HOBBY COLLECTORS
Concordia, Kansas

Reference: First National Bank, Concordia, Kansas

Old or Used Comic Books are

WORTH MONEY

We pay from 1¢ to $1.00 each for certain old comics.

What have you? Send for catalog list.

We buy any Comic Book

There are over 75 issues worth $1.00 each---100 worth 50 cts. a copy---250 at 25 cts. each---325 at 10 cts. and over 500 different issues worth 5 cts. a copy.

This catalog list together with all information will be sent to any address for 25 cts. Just paste or fasten a quarter into a piece of cardboard and mail it to us—Please PRINT your name and address. Be among the first in your community to collect old COMICS.

HOLLINGERS
HOBBY COLLECTORS
Concordia, Kansas

Reference: First National Bank, Concordia, Kansas

JOIN OUR COMIC BOOK CLUB

Examples of ads placed by Hollinger in the early 1940s.

available to shut-ins and recovering wounded military personnel. The advertising inserts that Pop placed in his comic books generated mail order business from across the country. He corresponded with and sold comics to several adult collectors from Iowa to North Carolina in the 1940s and 1950s. At least one collector made several trips over the years from Iowa to visit Pop's comic book shop.

At this time Pop made another decision. First issues and excess stock would be stashed away for the future. Remembering this was 1942, one's imagination cannot do justice to the quantity and quality of the comics Pop had. In 1968, he told me that among the many thousands of comic books he put away, there were 200 untaped **Roy Rogers** No. 1. This was an exception, however, as Pop usually put back just three or four of every first issue. Why Pop felt comic books would be collectible in the future can only be guessed. Children came in requesting back issues of their favorite comic. Most people treated comic books like newspapers and magazines: they threw them away. His ads generated interest in back-issue comic books from several adult collectors across the country. Noting all this and since he had enough storage space and more comic books than he knew what to do with, Pop evidently came to the conclusion that saving the excess books would not be a bad idea.

World War II was at its height in 1942. With most of Concordia's men from 18 to 40 years old in the service, there was a local shortage of manpower.

Women, older men, and children helped out with many working more than one job. Pop, in his mid-50s, volunteered to work where he could be most useful. He was asked to teach part-time in various high schools in the Concordia area. He did so and worked in his store in the evenings and on weekends.

Pop soon found out comic books did not wear well under constant buying, selling, and trading. Also, insects loved to munch on pulp paper in a damp basement. An elaborate system was devised for taking the staples out, treating the comic book with chemicals to keep insects at bay, applying brown paper tape to the spine and inside edges of the cover, restapling the comic book and, finally, pressing it flat using a press of his own design that exerted several hundred pounds of pressure. Pop treated several dozen comics at a time, the whole process taking four to five days. He referred to these as "rebuilt" comics.

After Pop's wife Marie died in 1946, he slept, ate, and lived in his store, much to the chagrin of his children. Pop partitioned off a section and installed a bed and hot plate. His children tried to persuade him to do otherwise, but he would not listen. Pop sold his house and lived a bachelor's life.

Pop stored his excess stock of comic books in boxes stacked from floor to ceiling. The comics from the early 1940s were generally in the lower boxes with the later issues in the upper ones. In 1951 it rained all spring. The flood stage of the Republican

FREE

"Hospital Reading Service"

FOR ANY PATIENT IN ANY HOSPITAL IN U. S. A.

Their choice of Comic Books will be delivered by mail postpaid to their room--no cost to them--just write us--for yourself or your friends--military or otherwise--no restrictions.

"SHUT INS" CORDIALLY OFFERED THIS SERVICE FREE

We carry a large assortment of every Comic Book Published

HOLLINGERS
HOBBY COLLECTORS
Concordia, Kansas
Reference; First National Bank, Concordia, Kansas

WE BUY USED COMIC BOOKS

THIS BOOK IS

Rebuilt --- Medicated

AND

Has Exchange Value

WRITE US

We buy

USED COMIC BOOKS

from one pound up to a ton

(WE PAY TRANSPORTATION)

HOLLINGERS
HOBBY COLLECTORS
Concordia, Kansas
Reference: First National Bank, Concordia, Kansas

JOIN OUR COMIC BOOK CLUB

Examples of ads placed by Hollinger in the early 1940s.

River was reached that June. The river's winding course brought it one mile north of Concordia. The central business district was inundated, including Pop's basement. After the water receded, Pop surveyed the carnage. The majority of his comic books were destroyed. With a few exceptions, everything prior to 1949 was lost. Pop hauled several truckloads of ruined comics to his son-in-law's farm and dumped them in a landfill. Those comic books from the early 1940s, including the 200 **Roy Rogers** No. 1, were gone forever. Undaunted, Pop, now 64, rebuilt his business and was able to continue servicing most of his wholesale accounts. His business, however, never fully recovered its pre-flood level.

In 1954, the nationwide cry of alarm concerning comic books spurred by Dr. Wertham and the Senate investigation caused a major recession throughout the comic book industry. Each passing month fewer new comic books were distributed, as some publishers went out of business and others cut back on the number of titles they published. Around the Concordia area some stores stopped selling new comic books altogether. This further encroached on Pop's comic store business. Since he was over 65 now, Pop opted for semi-retirement and opened his comic book shop only on Saturdays.

By the mid-1960s, Pop, in his late 70s, had set a slower pace for himself. During the weekdays he "rebuilt" comic books, hung out at the local pool hall playing rummy at a dollar a game, serviced his remaining wholesale accounts, worked on woodworking projects, or more often than not went fishing. On a lazy creek bank with the fishing slow and the sun warm, Pop would sometimes nod off. Finding it hard to catch a fish while asleep, he built a device to wake himself up. He attached it to his fishing line. A fish would bite, draw the line taut, trigger an alarm, and wake Pop. He built several for friends with a similar problem. Sundays he usually spent with his daughters and grandchildren eating dinner and enjoying their company.

I first became aware of Pop Hollinger on a Wednesday in the summer of 1965 when I was 12. Noting I was fascinated with comic books, my father, who traded comic books at Pop's store when he was a kid, told me about Pop. This was certainly good news. I promptly rode my bike downtown, found Cook's food store, and descended the stairwell. A ragged old comic book poster in a window proclaimed, "Superman sold here." The sign on the door said, "Hollinger's—Saturday 9-5." Stacks of old comic books were visible through the window of the door, and Saturday was three days away!

That Saturday morning I met Pop. He was sitting in a chair, hands behind his head, feet propped on a box, wearing a grey work shirt and pants. I never saw Pop in any other outfit. He was grey-haired, portly, almost toothless, with a receding hairline, a craggy nose, and rheumy eyes. Pop called me "Bud" as he did everyone except women, and he called them "Girlie." I cannot remember him ever using my given name. His ground rules were quickly learned: trade two for one, five cents each, or seven cents if the comic book was "rebuilt." With new comics now 12 cents, Pop figured the time he spent on the taped ones made them worth more. This was the beginning of a weekly relationship lasting six years.

The atmosphere of Pop's store was as much a part of it as the comic books he sold. On my first visit, I came into his shop out of bright sunlight to find myself standing in apparent darkness. The musty smell of age and mildew was my first sensory experience. Pop's comic books reeked of it. I came to love that pungent odor, and the "rebuilt" comics of Pop's still retain that smell today after 12 years. Looking straight ahead from the doorway, racks of comic books from knee to eye level became visible to me against the back wall. To the left of the comic book racks were the paperbacks; to the right, magazines. On the left of the doorway were Pop's desk, counter, comic book press, and work area where Pop kept his account books and "rebuilt" his comics. In front of the counter was Pop's chair. On the right of the doorway sat a potbelly wood stove and a rack of comics for which Pop had recently traded. In the center of his store stood a bench saw which Pop used in his woodworking. Pop made all the shelving for his shop and comic book outlets. His store was small—only about 20 feet wide and 30 feet long. The floor was unvarnished wood stained grey with the accumulation of dust, wear, and age. In back of his counter and desk was an empty room. Pop was in the process of moving into it before I met him and during the entire six years I frequented his store. It soon became a standing joke. Pop never did finish moving.

Pop's doorway was a time portal to the past. I could leave 1965 and enter the 1940s with one step. Pop's furnishings, from his wood stove to his comic book racks, were unchanged since he started his business 25 years before. The dust I stirred while browsing through Pop's comic book racks must have been the same dust my

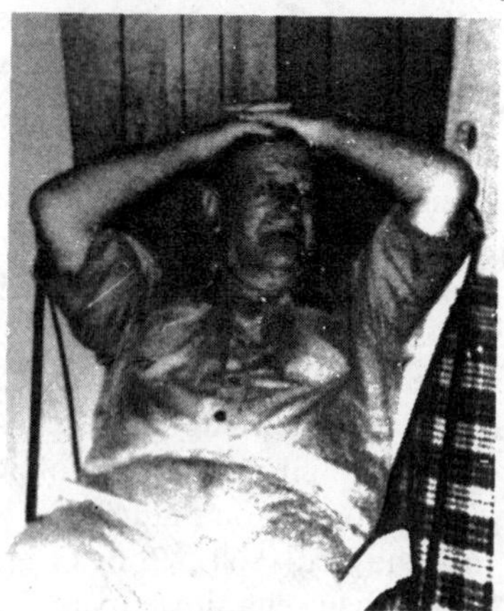

Photo of "Pop" taken by his friend Glenn Cook in 1968.

father stirred when he was 12. The accumulation of time changed almost everything in Concordia except Pop Hollinger's comic book store.

Walking into his basement, I usually found him in a familiar position, lounging in his chair, chewing tobacco or smoking a Pall Mall, and shooting the breeze with regular customers. Men he had known for years dropped by with armfuls of paperbacks and left with just as many. Old fishing buddies stopped in to let Pop know of the big one he missed out on that morning. Kids brought in comic books for trade, many of them purchased at stores selling Pop's taped comics. The advertising inserts he placed in most of his comic books constantly generated new business. Sometimes former customers dropped by to introduce their children to Pop or sell some old "rebuilt" comic books they found gathering dust in the attic. Almost every Saturday, Glenn Cook took time off from his store and dropped down to exchange fish stories or talk shop. In the winter the warmth of Pop's wood stove greeted patrons. In the summer a roving fan provided air circulation in the usually cool but damp basement.

As the old cliche goes, Pop had forgotten more than I knew about comic books. I had never seen a comic older than the 1960s and was ignorant of anything besides the current DC and Marvel superheroes. Pop introduced me to the Justice Society of America via an old **All Star** comic book. I was awed by a sense of wonder and a feeling of growing excitement. Who was this Hourman, Dr. Fate, Dr. Mid-nite, and Johnny Thunder? I could identify Wonder Woman and Hawkman, but the Flash and Green Lantern wore unfamiliar costumes, and the Atom was recognizable in name only. Yet I was reading a DC comic book advertising **Superman** and **Batman** comics! What had happened during the preceding 17 years? Thanks to Pop I acquired **Justice League of America** No. 21 and No. 22 which reintroduced the Justice Society and explained a lot of my dilemma. Pop was a walking encyclopedia of comic book history. He enlightened me on what Four-Color comics were and how Dell numbered them; how comic books started as newspaper strip reprints and progressed to original material; how the comics code came about and the collapse of the majority of comic book publishers; how DC and Dell benefited from the code at the expense of other comic book companies; what EC comics were and their progression into **Mad** magazine; and other fascinating information.

Of course, Saturdays at Pop's was the focal point of my early teen years. The anticipatory excitement started to rise from the pit of my stomach Friday evening. Would this Saturday be the one Pop brought out from his storeroom a box of comics he had stashed away years before? I would awake early Saturday morning, make the rounds of the drug stores and supermarkets selling new comic books and the ones selling Pop's "rebuilt" comics, and descend the stairwell of Pop's store promptly at nine a.m. After browsing Pop's comic book racks looking for any new additions, he and I would shoot the breeze. Over the years he told me about his comic book "rebuilding" process, the patents he had earned, the history behind his store, and introduced me to new gadgets he was working on. About once a month Pop would ask me to bring out a box of comic books from his storeroom. As I thumbed through them, my excitement rose with each discovery. Usually many good DC, Quality, Fawcett, EC, and Atlas titles turned up. Out of a box containing around 500 comic books, I would find 30 to 50 books to buy. Looking back and considering that all the comic books were from the late 1940s through the 1950s, I wonder today what I passed up all those years ago.

In 1966 I wrote to a guy whose letter was published in **Spider-Man**. From this contact I discovered the **Rocket's Blast -Comic Collector** and comic fandom. On a Saturday soon after, Pop, knowing I never traded any of the comic books I bought, asked me, "What do you do with all your comics?" I replied, "I keep what I want and trade or sell the rest to other collectors." A copy of the **RB-CC** was in Pop's hands the next Saturday. A few months later Pop said, "I have some comic books I want you to sell for me." He pulled out a stack from his desk drawer, all taped. **Walt Disney's Comics and Stories** No. 1, **All Winners** No. 1, **All Select** No. 1, **All Flash** No. 1, **Green Lama** No. 1, **All Hero** No. 1, and **Young Allies** No. 1 were some of them. They represented a treasure trove of classic Golden Age comic books that I had only read about, never hoped to see, and have not seen since. I sold them all for $150, a reasonable price at the time. The **Walt Disney's Comics and Stories** No. 1 pictured in **The Comic Book Price Guide** from 1972-1976 is this very one.

By 1971 Pop had been in the comic book business 32 years. This would be his last year for, in the spring, a fire occurred in the attic of Cook's food store. The insurance man told Glenn Cook that he was lucky in that if the fire had started in the basement among all the comic books, the entire building would have been lost. In order for the insurance policy to continue, the insurance man said Pop's comic books would have to go. Pop closed his shop shortly thereafter. He spent his retirement years fishing and continued with his woodworking. He continued to live in the basement under Cook's food store until 1976 when he moved to St. Ann's Nursing Home. At the age of 90, Pop Hollinger died on March 6, 1977.

Glenn Cook, recalling his almost 40 year relationship with Pop, told me, "Pop and I were real pals. We did much fishing together. We both liked fishing at night. One cloudy night we got lost and had trouble even finding the car! Pop had me climbing trees to see if I could find any lights so we could follow our way out. This was one night we did not get home until the wee hours of the morning. Pop always had a project of some kind going. During one Christmas season he and I made a Christmas tree holder so the trees would stand up while on display in front of my store. It folded up for easy storage. We traveled from town to town selling several of them. He had many friends and students of years back who often came to see him. He was good-natured, always agreeable, and very well thought of around Concordia. We had many funny experiences. He was such a jolly guy and a pleasure to be with.'' A cynical person might take these positive recollections with a grain of salt, but if Pop had a negative side, he kept it to himself. I never saw him in bad temper or heard him speak derogatorily of anyone during the 12 years I knew him.

During his life, Pop was awarded four patents for his creative and original thinking: the first one in 1916, the last one when he was in his 80s. The first patent concerned a problem Pop encountered while teaching high school woodworking. His students needed something besides the small desks they had to work on designs of projects they made prior to constructing them. Pop came up with a practical drawing board support and sold it to many schools and businesses. His other patents were for a tray dispenser unit used in supermarket meat departments, a tape dispenser for same, and a cabinet file for student records.

Pop Hollinger collected and stored thousands of comic books in the 1940s, knowing there would be a collector's market for them one day. He assured himself a certain amount of immortality with thousands of comic books in many private collections bearing his trademark: brown paper tape on the spine and inside edges of the cover. I think of Pop everytime I see one.

My thanks to the following people, without whose help and consideration this article would have been most incomplete: Mrs. Glenn Buoy, Mrs. Marlene Cunningham, Mr. Glenn W. Cook, Mr. Paul E. Montgomery, and Mrs. Marilyn Hessee.

DIRECTORY OF COMIC AND NOSTALGIA SHOPS

This is a current up-to-date list, but is not all-inclusive. We cannot assume any responsibility in your dealings with them. This list is provided for your information only. When planning your trips, it would be advisable to make appointments in advance. To get your shop included in the next edition, write for rates. Items stocked by these shops are listed just after the telephone numbers and are coded as follows:

(a) Golden Age comics
(b) Silver Age comics
(c) New comics, magazines
(d) Pulps
(e) Paperbacks
(f) Big Little Books
(g) Magazines (old)
(h) Books (old)
(i) Movie posters, lobby cards
(j) Original art
(k) Toys (old)
(l) Records (old)
(m) Gum trading cards
(n) Underground comics
(o) Old radio show tapes

ALABAMA:

Old South Comic Service & Dist.
1635 High St.
Montgomery, AL 36104
PH:(205)272-9592(a-c,e,g-j,m,n)

White's Book Store
110 E. St. N.
Talladega, AL 35160
PH:(205) 362-9614
(a,b,d,e,g,h,m,o)

ARIZONA:

Solar City Comics
P. O. Box 2634
Mesa, AZ 85204
PH:(602) 969-5367 (a-c)

Darcy's Discoveries
Greyhound Park and Swap
3801 E. Washington, Bldg.A-11
Phoenix, AZ 85034
PH:(602)877-2293(a,b,d,g,i,k,m)

A Little Bookstore
4117 N. 3rd Ave.
Phoenix, AZ 85013
PH:(602) 277-0757 (a-c,e,h,l)

The One Book Shop
708 S. Forest Avenue
Tempe, AZ 85281
PH:(602) 967-3551 (a-c,e,g-j,n)

The Comic Corner
5031 E. Fifth St.
Tucson, AZ 85711
PH:(602) 326-2677 (b,c,e,)

Fantasy Comics
2745 North Campbell
Tucson, AZ 85719
PH:(602) 325-9790 (a-c)

ARKANSAS:

Rock Bottom Used Book Shop
418 W. Dickson St.
Fayetteville, AR 72701
PH:(501) 521-2917 (a-h)

Trader-Back's
Used Books and Comics
7509 Cantrell, No. 103
Little Rock, AR 72207
PH:(501) 663-5773 (a-h)

CALIFORNIA:

Comics & Comix
2461 Telegraph
Berkeley, CA 94704
PH:(415)845-4091 (a-c,e,h,j-l,n)

Kings
2521 Durant Ave.
Berkeley, CA 94704
PH:(415) 548-1040 (b,m,n)

Comics & Comix
6135 Sunrise
Citrus Heights, CA 95610
PH:(916)969-0717 (a-c,e,h,j-l,n)

California Comic Book Co.
1853 Market St.
Concord, CA 94520
PH:(415) 680-7789 (a-c)

California Comics
1024 N. Citrus Ave.
Covina, CA 91722
PH:(213) 967-8838 (a-c,g,n)

Comics & Fantasies III
10070 So. DeAnza Blvd.
Cupertino, CA 95014
PH:(408) 446-3561 (a-c,g,m,n)

The Comic Enterprise
P. O. Box 897 (Mail order only)
Desert Hot Springs, CA 92240
PH:(714) 251-1304 (b,c,e)

Don's Comic & Record Shop
7168 Regional Street
Dublin, CA 94566
PH:(415) 829-6533 (a-c,f,l)

Land of ooH's & aH's
17179-A Brookhurst
Fountain Valley, CA 92708
PH:(714)963-3591 (a-c,e-g,i,j,m)

Alpha-Omega Comic & Trading Card Co.
2373 E. Shaw Ave.
Fresno, CA 93710
PH:(209) 221-6500 (a-e,g,i,m,n)

The Comic Syndrome
4540 E. Tulare
Fresno, CA 93702
PH:(209) 251-0888 (a-c,g,i,k,m)

Comic World
725 E. Olive Ave.
Fresno, CA 93728
PH:(209) 233-1282 (b-e,g,i,m)

Wonderland Comics
418 N. Blackstone
Fresno, CA 93701
PH:(209) 268-3950 (a-c,e,g-i,l-n)

Book Harbor
201 N. Harbor Blvd.
Fullerton, CA 92632
PH:(714) 738-1941 (a-c,e,h)

Latos Brothers—Fantasy Galore
106 N. Harbor
Fullerton, CA 92632
PH:(714) 738-3698
(a-d,f,g,i,j,m,o)

Fantasy Illustrated
12531 Harbor Blvd.
Garden Grove, CA 92640
PH:(714) 537-0087 (a-f,h,m)

The Compleat Paperbacker
15711 E. Amar Rd.
La Puente, CA 91744
PH:(213) 330-0400 (a-e,g,h,n)

Another World Book & Comic Shop
1615 Colorado Blvd.
Los Angeles, CA 90041
PH:(213) 255-1841 (a-c,e,i)

Golden Apple Comics & Records
7753 Melrose Ave.
Los Angeles, CA 90046
PH:(213) 658-6047 (a-c,g,j,l-n)

Graphitti
960 Gayley Ave.
Los Angeles, CA 90024
PH:(213) 824-3656

House of Animation
459 N. Sweetzer Ave.
Los Angeles, CA 90048
PH:(213) 653-0681 (j)

Millbrae Comics & Baseball Cards
1705 El Camino Real
Millbrae, CA 94030
(a,b,g,i,j,l,m)

The Book Sail
1186 N. Tustin Ave.
Orange, CA 92667
PH:(714) 997-9511 (a-j)

Comics & Comix
515 Cowper
Palo Alto, CA 94301
PH:(415)328-8100 (a-c,e,h,j-l,n)

Movie Memories Poster Shop
340 University Ave.
Palo Alto, CA 94301
PH:(415) 328-6265 (g,i,m)

Fantasy Imprints
14231 Garden Rd. #7
Poway, CA 92064
PH:(714) 748-4950 (a-c,e,g,h,n)

Comics & Comix
1110 K St. Mall
Sacramento, CA 95814
PH:(916)442-5142 (a-c,e,h,j-l,n)

The Comic Gallery
5011 Cass St.
San Diego, CA 92109
PH:(714)483-4853 (a-c,g,m,n)

Comic Kingdom
1629 University Ave.
San Diego, CA 92103
PH:(714)291-1515 (a-c,e,g,h,j,n)

Golden State Comics
4688 Boundary St.
San Diego, CA 92116
PH:(714) 283-3666 (b,c,e,g,m)

House of Comics
840 Broadway
San Diego, CA 92101
PH:(714) 234-5992 (a-c,e,m)

Amazing Adventures
3800 Noriega
San Francisco, CA 94122
PH:(415)661-1344(a-c,e,g,j,k,m)

Comics & Comix
700 Lombard
San Francisco, CA 94133
PH:(415)982-3511 (a-c,e,h,j-l,n)

Comics & Comix
650 Irving
San Francisco, CA 94134
PH:(415)665-5888 (a-c,e,h,j-l,n)

Gary's Corner Bookstore
1051 So. San Gabriel Blvd.
San Gabriel, CA 91776
PH:(213) 285-7575 (b,c,e,m)

Comic and Card Empire
388 N. Capitol Ave.
Capitol Shopping Center
San Jose, CA 95133
PH:(408) 258-2286 (b,c,m)

Comic and Card Empire
1451 Foxworthy Ave.
Foxworthy Shopping Center
San Jose, CA 95118
PH:(408) 264-2273 (b,c,m)

Comic Collector Shop
73 E. San Fernando
San Jose, CA 95113
PH:(408) 287-2254 (a-g,l,n)

Comics & Fantasies I
496 W. San Carlos
San Jose, CA 95110
PH:(408) 298-7980 (a-c,g,i,n)

Comics & Fantasies II
1375 Blossom Hill Rd.
San Jose, CA 95123
PH:(408) 448-3756 (a-c,g,n)

The Comic Shop
16049 E. 14th St.
San Leandro, CA 94578
PH:(415) 278-9545 (a,b,c,g)

Record King
1134 Fourth St.
San Rafael, CA 94901
PH:(415) 456-6161 (a-c,l,m)

Brian's Books
3225 Cabrillo Ave.
Santa Clara, CA 95051
PH:(408) 985-7481 (a-c,e-h,m,n)

Comicscene
5075 Stevens Creek Blvd.
Santa Clara, CA 95051
PH:(408) 243-5280
(b,c,e,g,h,m,p)

Atlantis Fantasyworld
707 Pacific Ave.
Santa Cruz, CA 95060
PH:(408) 426-0158 (a-c,i,j,m,n)

Markgraf's Comics
113 W. Church St.
Santa Maria, CA 93454
PH:(805) 925-7193 (b,c,e,g,i,m)

Hi De Ho Comics & Fantasy
1413 Fifth Street
Santa Monica, CA 90401
PH:(213) 394-2820
(a-d,f,g,i,j,m,n)

Comics and Fantasy
9315 Mission Gorge Rd.
Santee, CA 92071
PH:(714) 448-4538 (a-c,e,g-m)

American Comic Book Co.
12206 Ventura Blvd.
Studio City, CA 91604
PH:(213) 763-8330 (a-g,j,n)

The Fantasy Castle
18734 Ventura Blvd.
Tarzana, CA 91356
PH:(213) 345-9227 (a-e,g-j,o)

Passport Comic Shop
13247 Victory Blvd.
Van Nuys, CA 91401
PH:(213) 985-0555 (a-c,g,n)

Ralph's Comic Corner
294 E. Main St. (Inside)
Ventura, CA 93001
PH:(805) 653-2732 (a-c,e,m,n)

Imagination World
1304 W. Walnut Ave.
Visalia, CA 93277
PH:(209) 732-3020 (b,c,g,i,m,o)

Don's Comic & Record Shop
2678 N. Main St.
Walnut Creek, CA 94596
PH:(415) 933-1234 (a-c,f,l)

COLORADO:

Leasures Treasures
2801 W. Colorado Ave.
Colorado Springs, CO 80904
PH:(303)635-8539(a,b,d-i,k-m,p)

Capitol Hill Books
304 East Colfax
Denver, CO 80203
PH:(303)837-0700(b,c,e,g-i,m,n)

Dimensional Travelers Comics
Weekend Mall - 185 S. Sheridan
Denver, CO 80226
PH:(303) 232-6255 (b,c,e)

Security Book Exchange
Fountain Valley Shopping Ctr.
5644 S. Hwy. 85/87 Store No.6
Security, CO 80911
PH:(303) 390-6071 (a-e)

CONNECTICUT:

Space Travelers
116 Olivia Street
Derby, CT 06418
PH:(203) 734-6400
(a-c,e,g,h,j,m,n)

The Bookie
116 Burnside Ave.
East Hartford, CT 06108
PH:(203) 289-1208 (a-h,j)

Mostly Books
A Moondance Comic Outlet
222 Main Street
Farmington, CT 06032
PH:(203) 677-7134 (c,e)

Yesterday . . . and Today
215 Bank Street
New London, CT 06320
PH:(203) 442-1001 (a-c,f-i,l,m)

F+S Comics & Fantasy Shop
54 Bank Street
New Milford, CT 06776
PH:(203)355-3426(a-c,e-g,j,m,n)

DELAWARE:

Xanadu Comics & Collectables
2 West Fifth St.
Wilmington, DE 19801
PH:(302) 652-5098 (a-d,j,m,n)

FLORIDA:

The Book Gallery
1150 N. Main St.
Gainesville, FL 32601
PH:(904) 378-9117 (b,c,e,g,h)

The Time Machine
2635 N.W. 13th Street
Gainesville, FL 32601
PH:(904) 378-8794 (a-e,g,i,l,m)

Starship
5802 Stirling Road
Hollywood, FL 33021
PH:(305) 987-2258 (b,c,e,g,i,n)

Phil's Comic Shoppe
496 N.W. 69 Ave.
Atlantic Plaza
Margate, FL 33063
PH:(305) 974-8914 (a-c)

A&M Comics and Books
6650 Bird Rd.
Miami, FL 33155
PH:(305) 665-4167 (a-j,l-n)

A&M Comics and Books
1226 N .E. 163 St.
North Miami Beach, FL 33162
PH:(305) 945-1597 (a-j,l-n)

Sunshine Comics
6370 Bird Road
S. Miami, FL 33155
PH:(305) 667-8287 (b,c,e,i)

Enterprise 1701
1206 E. Colonial Dr.
Orlando, FL 32803
PH:(305) 896-1701 (b,c,e,g)

Haslam's Book Store, Inc.
2025 Central Avenue
St. Petersburg, FL 33713
PH:(813) 822-8616 (a-f,h)

Mediascopic Memorabilia
5646 Swift Rd.
Sarasota, FL 33581
PH:(813) 921-4577 (a-c,g,h,l)

The Book Shelf
211 East Oakland Ave.
Tallahassee, FL 32301
PH:(904) 224-2694 (a-c,e,g,h,n)

The Fandom Zone
1708 W. Kennedy Blvd.
Tampa, FL 33606
PH:(813) 254-1390 (a-c,e,j,n)

GEORGIA:

Collectors World Comic Shop
411 N. Glenwood Ave.
Dalton, GA 30720
PH:(404) 226-1769 (b,c,e,g,m,n)

The Paper Chase
112 E. Ponce de Leon
Decatur, GA 30030
PH:(404)378-6654 (a-c,e,g,i,j,m)

Fischer's Book Store
4029 Jonesboro Rd.
Forest Park, GA 30050
PH:(404) 361-2665 (a-c,e)

Fischer's Book Store
6569 Riverdale Rd.
Riverdale, GA 30274
PH:(404) 997-7323 (a-c,e,i,j,l)

HAWAII:

Aldamar World of Comics
409 N. King St.
Honolulu, HI 96817
PH:(808) 533-1333 (b,c,e,g,h,n)

IDAHO:

King's Komix Kastle
1706 N. 18th St.
Boise, ID 83702 (Appointments)
PH:(208) 343-7142 (a-h,m,n)

King's Komix Kastle
2560 Leadville
Boise, ID (No mail this address)
PH:(208) 343-7055 (a-h,m,n)

ILLINOIS:

Trackside Hobbies
101 Eighth Street
Cairo, IL 62914
PH:(618) 734-0125 (a,b,k,m)

The Book Nook
501 N. Neil St.
Champaign, IL 61820
PH:(217) 356-4773 (a-c,e-g)

The Comic Kingdom
3905 W. Lawrence Ave.
Chicago, IL 60625
PH:(312) 588-8455 (a-c,m)

Grand Bookstore
532 N. Clark St.
Chicago, IL 60610
PH:(312) 329-9396 (a-c,e,g-i,l-n)

More Fun Comics, Inc.
13741 Leyden Ave.
Chicago, IL 60627
PH:(312) 264-5347 (a-j,l,m)

Sherlock's Bookshop
2620 North Halsted Street
Chicago, IL 60614
PH:(312) 935-1664 (a-c,f,g,j)

Yesterday
1143 W. Addison St.
Chicago, IL 60613
PH:(312) 248-8087 (a,b,d-i,k,l)

Moondog's Comics
139 W. Prospect Ave.
Mt. Prospect, IL 60056
PH:(312) 398-6060 (a-c,f,m)

Town Square Antiques
102 E. Elm
Nashville, IL 62263
PH:(618) 327-4142 (a-c,k)

Carol's Paperback Book Exchange
110 W. State
O'Fallon, IL 62269
PH:(618) 632-5914 (c,e)

Moondog's Comics
1403 W. Schaumburg Rd.
Schaumburg, IL 60194
PH:(312) 529-6060 (a-c,f,m)

Family Book Exch. & Game Shop
2665 S. 10th
Springfield, IL 62703
PH:(217) 753-9211 (a-e,g-j,o)

B.J.'s Comic Corner
260 N. Ardmore Ave.
Villa Park, IL 60181
PH:(312) 834-0383 (a-m)

INDIANA:

The Bookstack
112 W. Lexington Ave.
Elkhart, IN 46516
PH:(219) 293-3815 (a,b,d,e,h)

Broadway Comic Book & Baseball Card Shop
2423 Broadway
Fort Wayne, IN 46807
PH:(219)744-1456(a-c,e-i,m,n,p)

The Comic Carnival & Nostalgia Emporium
6265 N. Carrollton Ave.
Indianapolis, IN 46220
PH:(317) 253-8882 (a-g,i,j,m)

John's Comic Closet
4610 East 10th St.
Indianapolis, IN 46201
PH:(317) 357-6611
(b,c,e,g,i,j,m,n)

Paula's Naptown Comics
4608 E. Michigan St.
Indianapolis, IN 46201
PH:(317) 359-0226 (a-c,g,n)

IOWA:

Quad City Coin Co.
318 Brady St., P.O.Box 184
Davenport, IA 52801
PH:(319) 322-5275 (a-c,g,m,n,p)

Comiclogue
2306 University
Des Moines, IA 50311
PH:(515) 279-9006 (a-c,g,j,m,n)

Comic World & Things
1626 Central Ave.
Dubuque, IA 52001
PH:(319) 556-9308 (a-g,m,n)

Oak Leaf Stamps & Comics
938A North Federal
Mason City, IA 50401
PH:(515) 424-0333 (a-j,m)

KANSAS:

Treasure Chest
1124 Moro
Manhattan, KS 66502
PH:(913)537-2344(a,b,d-i,k-m,p)

Comics & Fantasys
1402 West 17th
Topeka, KS 66604
PH:(913) 232-3429 (a-c,e,f,i,n)

Air Capital Comics
2515 E. Lincoln
Wichita, KS 67211
PH:(316) 681-0219 (a-p)

Prairie Dog Comics
615 Country Acres
Wichita, KS 67212
PH:(316) 722-6316 (b,c,e,m,n)

The Shadow's Sanctum
416 E. Harry
Wichita, KS 67211
PH:(316) 263-2270 (b-e,i)

KENTUCKY:

Book World
6704 Dixie Hwy.
Florence, KY 41042
PH:(606) 371-9562 (a-f,l-n)

The Great Escape
2433 Bardstown Road
Louisville, KY 40205
PH:(502) 456-2216 (a-e,l,m)

LOUISIANA:

Book Swap, Inc.
5050 W. Esplande Ave.
Metairie, LA 70002
PH:(504) 889-2665 (a-c,e)

The Book Shoppe
949 Avenue "F"
Westwego, LA 70094
PH:(504) 340-9864 (a-c,e,g)

MAINE:

Northwoods Funnies
Rt. 201, Main St.
Bingham, ME 04920
PH:(207) 672-4888 (a,b,d-h,n)

MARYLAND:

Comic Book Kingdom
4307 Harford Road
Baltimore, MD 21214
PH:(301) 426-4529 (a-c,f-h,m)

Geppi's Comic World
612½ Edmondson Ave.
Baltimore, MD 21228
PH:(301) 788-8222 (a-c,f)

Geppi's Comic World
Harbor Place
Upper Level, Light St. Pavilion
301 Light St.
Baltimore, MD 21202
PH:(301) 547-0910 (a-c,f)

Mindbridge, Ltd.
Merritt Park Shopping Ctr.
1786 Merritt Blvd.
Baltimore, MD 21222
PH:(301) 284-7880 (a-k,m,n)

The Magic Page
7416 Laurel-Bowie Rd. (Rte.197)
Bowie, MD 20715
PH:(301) 262-4735 (a-c,e)

Alternate Worlds
9924 York Road
Cockeysville, MD 21030
PH:(301) 667-0440 (a-c,g)

Galactic Enterprises
18 Crain Highway
Glen Burnie, MD 21061
PH:(301) 760-9538 (b,c,e,g-m)

Geppi's Comic World
8305 Fenton St.
Silver Spring, MD 20910
PH:(301) 588-2545 (a-c,e,f)

The Barbarian Book Shop
11254 Triangle Lane
Wheaton, MD 20902
PH:(301) 946-4184 (a-h)

MASSACHUSETTS:

Moondance Comics
Two stores opening shortly in western Mass. Call our Vermont store for details: (802) 257-7600
(a-c,e,g,i-k,m,n)

The Million Year Picnic
99 Mt. Auburn St.
Cambridge, MA 02138
PH:(617) 492-6763 (a-p)

Framingham Collectors Haven
169 Concord Street
Framingham, MA 01701
PH:(617) 879-0900 (b,c,m)

That's Entertainment
66 Hollis St. (Rte. 126)
Framingham, MA 01701
PH:(617) 872-2317 (a-c,f,k-m)

The Cheese Box
A Moondance Comic Outlet
32 Chapman Street
Greenfield, MA 01301
PH:(413) 774-5086 (c)

Saturday Matinee (Appointments)
237 Plymouth St.
Holbrook, MA 02343
PH:(617) 767-1295 (a,b,g,m)

Hollywood East Comic Shop
44 Billings Rd.
North Quincy, MA 02171
PH:(617) 773-9317 (a-c,g,m)

Bill Cole (Appointment only)
121 Liberty St.
South Quincy, MA 02169
PH:(617) 963-5510 (a,b)

Fabulous Fiction Book Store
587 Park Ave.
Worcester, MA 01603
PH:(617) 754-8826 (a-c,f,o)

That's Entertainment
151 Chandler Street
Worcester, MA 01609
PH:(617) 755-4207 (a-c,f,k-m)

MICHIGAN:

Curious Book Shop
307 E. Grand River
East Lansing, MI 48823
PH:(517) 332-0112 (a-k,m-p)

Doug Haines (appointment only)
1750 Woodside Drive
East Lansing, MI 48823
PH:(517) 351-6571 (a)

Argos Book Shop
1405 Robinson Rd.
Grand Rapids, MI 49506
PH:(616) 454-0111 (a-h,m,n)

The Collector's Corner
2 Jefferson at Fulton
Grand Rapids, MI 49503
PH:(616) 458-2803 (a-g,i-n,p)

K & P Coins, Comics
2618 Kibby Rd.
Jackson, MI 49203
PH:(517) 788-8498 (a,b,f,j,m)

The Book Exchange
2002 E. Michigan Ave.
Lansing, MI 48912
PH:(517) 485-0416
(a-c,e,f,i-k,m,n)

Classic Movie & Comic Center
19047 Middlebelt Rd.
Livonia, MI 48152
PH:(313) 476-1254 (a-g,i,l-n)

Painted Pony Comic Shop
218 S. Hamilton
Saginaw, MI 48602
PH:(517) 792-6602 (a-c,f,m)

The Reading Place
9724 Round Lake Rd.
Vermontville, MI 49096
PH:(517) 566-8510 (a-c,e,f,m)

The Book Stop
1160 Chicago Drive S.W.
Wyoming, MI 49509
PH:(616)245-0090 (a-c,e,g,j,n)

MINNESOTA:

Comic City—Minnesota Collective
3151 Hennepin Ave. S.
Minneapolis, MN 55408
PH:(612) 823-4445 (a-c,f,m,n,p)

Shinder's Read More Book Store
628 Hennepin Ave.
Minneapolis, MN 55403
PH:(612) 333-3628
(a-c,e,g,i,m,n)

Midway Book Store
1579 University Ave.
St. Paul, MN 55104
PH:(612) 644-7605 (a-h,n)

Shinder's Book & News
429 Wabasha St.
St. Paul, MN 55102
PH:(612) 227-0899
(a-c,e,g,i,m,n)

MISSISSIPPI:

Star Store Comics & Records
3913 Northview Dr.
Jackson, MS 39206
PH:(601) 981-9910 (a-j,l-n,p)

MISSOURI:

The Paperback Rack
126 E. 69 Highway
Claycomo, MO 64119
PH:(816) 452-7478 (a,b,d-h,n)

Rock Bottom Books & Comics
21-A N. 9th St.
Columbia, MO 65201
PH:(314) 443-0113 (a-c,e,g,h)

Book Gallery
#50 Grandview Plaza
Florissant, MO 63033
PH:(314) 921-4374 (c,e)

Bob's Comic Book World
107½ East Argonne
Kirkwood, MO 63122
PH:(314) 966-2343 (a-c)

The Book Rack
300 W. Olive
Springfield, MO 65806
PH:(417) 865-4945 (b-e,h,i,o)

Duckburg Books & Comics
607 East Madison
Springfield, MO 65806
PH:(417) 865-6487 (a-c,e,f,n,o)

MONTANA:

The Book Exchange
Holiday Village Shopping Ctr.
Missoula, MT 59801
PH:(406) 728-6342 (a,b,e,g,h,)

NEBRASKA:

The Dragon's Lair
8316 Blondo St.
Omaha, NE 68134
PH:(402) 399-9141 (a-c,e,i,n)

Star Realm
10801 ''Q'' St.
Omaha, NE 68137
PH:(402) 331-4844 (c,e,i,j,m)

NEVADA:

Friendly Neighborhood Comic Book Store
3981 West Charleston
Las Vegas, NV 89102
PH:(702) 878-8381 (a-j)

Stella Enterprises
126 ''B'' Street
Sparks, NV 89432
PH:(702) 359-7812 (a-c,j,m)

NEW HAMPSHIRE:

James F. Payette
P. O. Box 750
Bethlehem, NH 03574
PH:(603) 869-2020 (a,b,d-h,n)

Ixtlan Bookstore
A Moondance Comic Outlet
26 Washington Street
Keene, NH 03431
PH:(603) 357-3468 (c,e)

NEW JERSEY:

Eldorado
1400 N. Kings Hwy.
Cherry Hill, NJ 08034
PH:(609) 795-7557 (a-c,g,j,m)

Collector's Center
729 Edgar Road
Elizabeth, NJ 07202
PH:(201) 355-7942 (a-c,m,n)

Sparkle City East
8 Girard Rd.
Glassboro, NJ 08028
PH:(609) 881-8753 (a-g,i,j,l,m,n)

Quality Comics II
US#1 Flea Market
New Brunswick, NJ
(a-i,k,m,n)

Comicrypt II
521 White Horse Pike
Oaklyn, NJ 08107
PH:(609) 858-3877
(a-e,g,h,j,m,n)

Passaic Book Center
594 Main Ave.
Passaic, NJ 07055
PH:(201) 778-6646 (a-h)

Mr. Collector
311 Union Ave.
Paterson, NJ 07502
PH:(201) 595-0781 (c,g,m)

Quality Comics
14 Division St.
Somerville, NJ
(a-i,k,m,n)

NEW MEXICO:

Don's Paperback Books
1013 San Mateo S.E.
Albuquerque, NM 87108
PH:(505) 268-0520 (a-g)

Mic-onauts Book Store
415 W. 7th
Clovis, NM 88101
PH:(505) 763-4617 (b,c,e,g,h-j)

NEW YORK:

John S. Iavarone
7 Forest Ave.
Albany, NY 12208
PH:(518) 489-4508 (a-c,k,n)

The Incredible Pulp
786 Merrick Rd.
Baldwin, NY 11510
PH:(516) 223-0856 (a-c,f,g,i,m)

Comic Heaven
1670-d Sunrise Highway
Bay Shore, NY 11706
PH:(516) 665-4342 (a-c,e,g,i,j)

Brain Damage Comics
1289 Prospect Avenue
Brooklyn, NY 11218
PH:(212) 438-1335 (a-c,e,m)

Pinocchio Discounts
1814 McDonald Ave.
Brooklyn, NY 11223
PH:(212) 645-2573 (a-c,g,m)

World of Fantasy
737 L.I. Ave. (near D.P. Ave.)
Deer Park, NY 11729
PH:(516) 586-4071 (a-g,m-o)

Forest Hills Discount Books
63-56 108th St.
Forest Hills, NY 11375
PH:(212) 897-6100 (b,c,e,m)

Bush's Hobbies
414 Hawkins Ave.
Lake Ronkonkoma, NY 11779
PH:(516) 981-0253 (a,b,m)

Starwind Comics for Collectors
2900 Hempstead Tpk., Rm. 114
Levittown, NY 11756
PH:(516) 796-0679 (b,c,d,m)

Batcave
120 W. 3rd St.
New York, NY 10012
PH:(212) 674-8474 (b,c,e,g,l)

Funny Business
251 West 94th St.
New York, NY 10025
PH:(212) 222-2927 (a-d,g,l,n)

General Lee Fun
99 MacDougal St.
New York, NY 10012
PH:(212) 473-3039 (a-m,p)

Jerry Ohlinger's Movie Material Store, Inc.
120 W. 3rd St.
New York, NY 10012
PH:(212) 674-8474 (i)

Supersnipe Comic Book Euphorium
1617 Second Ave.
New York, NY 10028
PH:(212) 879-9628 (a-c,g,h,j,n)

West Side Comics
107 West 86th St.
New York, NY 10025
PH:(212) 724-0432 (a-c,j,n)

M & M Comics
Off B'way Mall, 48 Burd St.
Nyack, NY 10960
PH:(914)358-3335(a-d,f,g,j,m,n)

Empire Comics
1559 Mt. Hope Ave.
Rochester, NY 14620
PH:(716) 442-0371 (a-g,m)

Empire Comics
621 Titus Ave.
Rochester, NY 14617
PH:(716) 342-4250 (a-g,m)

Empire Comics
572 Stone Rd.
Rochester, NY 14616
PH:(716) 663-6877 (a-g,m)

Bill Townsend
138 Woodhaven Drive
Scotia, NY 12302
PH:(518) 399-0657 (a-c,g)

AAA Comics
51-4 Mansion Ave.
Staten Island, NY 10308
PH:(212) 356-4312 (a-c,m,n)

Dream Days Book Shop
110 Montgomery St.
Syracuse, NY 13202
PH:(315) 475-3995 (a-d,f,n)

NORTH CAROLINA:

Super Giant Books
38 Wall St.
Asheville, NC 28801
PH:(704) 254-2103 (a-c,e,h,j)

Alpha Book Center
North Park Mall
101 Eastway Dr.
Charlotte, NC 28213
PH:(704)597-0432 (b,c,e,g,h,l-n)

Heroes Aren't Hard to Find
1502 Central Ave.
Charlotte, NC 28205
PH:(704) 375-7462 (b,c,g,i,j,l,m)

The Nostalgia News Stand
919 Dickinson Ave.
Greenville, NC 27834
PH:(919) 758-6909 (b,c,e,g,l,n)

Tales Resold
1001 Whitaker Mill Road
Raleigh, NC 27608
PH:(919) 833-4383 (a-c,e,j)

NORTH DAKOTA:

Book Nook
320 Reeves Drive
Grand Forks, ND 58201
PH:(701) 772-3649 (b,c,e,g,n)

OHIO:

Comics, Cards and Collectables
533 Market Ave. North
Canton, OH 44702
PH:(216) 456-8907 (a-c,e-g,m)

Phantasy Emporium
117 Calhoun St.
Cincinnati, OH 45219
PH:(513) 281-0606 (a-h,j,m,n)

Cleveland Comic Book Co.
5437 Pearl Rd.
Cleveland, OH 44129
PH:(216) 842-2896 (a-j,m)

Bookie Parlor
2920 Wayne Ave.
Dayton, OH 45420
PH:(513) 256-6806 (a-c,e-h,j,m)

Brad's Bookshelf
54 N. Sandusky St.
Delaware, OH 43015
PH:(614) 393-5359 (a,b,d-f)

Comic Closet
16650 Chagrin Blvd.
Shaker Heights, OH 44120
PH:(216) 921-7677 (b,c,e)

The Comic Shop
5255 Hill Ave.
Toledo, OH 43615
PH:(419) 531-6097 (a-c,e-g,m,n)

The Funnie Farm Bookstore
328 N. Dixie Drive
Airline Shopping Center
Vandalia, OH 45377
PH:(513) 898-2794 (a-c,e,g,m,n)

OKLAHOMA:

Mind Over Matter
1015 N.W. 43rd
Oklahoma City, OK 73118
PH:(405) 524-7427
(a-c,e,g,i-k,m,n)

New World Comics & Science Fiction
3905 North Ann Arbor
Oklahoma City, OK 73122
PH:(405) 495-5311 (a-e,g-j,m)

The Comic Empire of Tulsa
3122 S. Mingo
Tulsa, OK 74145
PH:(918) 664-5808 (b,c,e-g,i,n)

OREGON:

Pegasus Books
12 N.W. Greenwood Ave.
Bend, OR 97701
PH:(503) 388-4588 (a-c,e,i,m)

Emerald City Comics
770 East 13th
Eugene, OR 97401
PH:(503) 345-2568 (a-e,g,l,n)

Armchair "Family" Bookstore
3205 S.E. Milwaukie Ave.
Portland, OR 97202
PH:(503) 236-0270 (a,b,d-h,m,n)

Book Rack
16441 S.E. Powell
Portland, OR 97236
PH:(503) 667-9669 (a-c,e)

Future Dreams
1800 East Burnside
Portland, OR 97214
PH:(503) 231-8311 (b-e,j)

Serendipity Corner
1401 S.E. Division
Portland, OR 97202
PH:(503) 233-9884 (a,b,d-f,h)

Rackafratz Comics
1193 Lancaster Dr. N.E.
Salem, OR 97301
PH:(503)371-1320 (a-c,e-g,i-n,p)

PENNSYLVANIA:

Fantasm - Records & Comics
Barr's Antique World (Sat.,Sun.)
Rt. 272 & Exit 21, PA Turnpike
Between Denver&Adamstown, Pa.
PH:(717) 626-2447 (b,j-l)

Trade-A-Book
906 Parade St.
Erie, PA 16503
PH:(814) 455-8500 (a,b,d,h)

The Comic Store
Park City Mkt.(No Mail Order)
Lancaster, PA 17603
PH:(717) 626-4660
(a-c,e,f,i,j,m,p)

Comic Universe
605 MacDade Blvd.
Milmont Park, PA 19033
PH:(215) 461-7960 (a-g,j,m)

Paperback Trader III
Whitpain Shopping Center
1502 DeKalb Pike
Norristown, PA 19401
PH:(215) 279-8855 (a-c,e,g)

Comic Investments & Cards for Collectors
8110 Bustleton Ave.
Philadelphia, PA 19152
PH:(215)725-7705 (a-c,f,g,j,m,n)

Comic Investments & Cards for Collectors
1435 Snyder Ave.
Philadelphia, PA 19145
PH:(215)468-8006 (a-c,f,g,j,m,n)

Comicrypt III
2966 Kensington Ave.
Philadelphia, PA 19134
PH:(215) 423-3876 (a,c,g)

The Comic Vault
7598-A Rear Haverford Ave.
Philadelphia, PA 19151
PH:(215) 473-6333 (a-j,l-n)

The Comic Vault
6390 Castor Ave. (at Levick)
Philadelphia, PA 19149
PH:(215) 289-2141 (a-j,l-n)

Fat Jack's Comicrypt
132 S. 20th St.
Philadelphia, PA 19103
PH:(215)963-0788 (a-c,g,i,j,n)

Record Rendezvous
134 So. 20th St.
Philadelphia, PA 19103
PH:(215) 561-7340 (a-e,g,j,l)

Eide's Comix, SF & Records
11 Federal St. (no mail order)
Pittsburgh, PA 15212
PH:(412) 231-3666 (a-j,l-n)

Book Swap
110 S. Fraser Street
State College, PA 16801
PH:(814) 234-6005 (a-n,p)

RHODE ISLAND:

Iron Horse Comics & Collectibles
834 Hope Street
Providence, RI 02906
PH:(401) 521-9343 (a-c,e,f,m,n)

The Super Universe II
72 The Arcade
Weybosset St.
Providence, RI 02903
PH:(401) 331-5637 (a-c,i,n)

SOUTH CAROLINA:

Book Exchange
1219 Savannah Hwy.
Charleston, SC 29407
PH:(803) 556-5051

Book Exchange
Berkley Sq. Shopping Ctr.
Goose Creek, SC 29445
PH:(803) 797-5500

Galaxy Book Store
5650 N. Rhett
N. Charleston, SC 29406
PH:(803) 554-4422 (a-c,j,n)

A Step Beyond
Heritage Square, Hwy. 78
(Located in the Exchange Center)
Summerville, SC 29483
PH:(803) 871-5500 (b,c,e,g,j,n)

SOUTH DAKOTA:

Lester's Pawnshop & Bookstore
On East Rice Street
Sioux Falls, SD 57101
PH:(605) 332-2121 (a-h)

TENNESSEE:

Rarities (Appointment Only)
3201 Wood Ave.
Chattanooga, TN 37406
PH:(615) 624-0568 (a-e,l)

White Book Shop
Rossville Blvd. Flea Market
at I-24
Chattanooga, TN 37408
PH:(404) 820-1449 (a-g)

Memphis Comics & Records
665 So. Highland
Memphis, TN 38111
PH:(901) 452-9376 (a-j,l-n,p)

Book Rack
Rivergate Plaza, Two Mile Pk.
Nashville, TN 37075
PH:(615) 859-9814 (a,b,e)

The Great Escape
1925 Broadway
Nashville, TN 37203
PH:(615) 327-0646 (a-i,l-n)

TEXAS:

Lone Star Comics & Science Fiction
511 East Abram Street
Arlington, TX 76010
PH:(817) 265-0491 (b-e,g-i,m)

Austin Books, Inc.
5002 N. Lamar
Austin, TX 78751
PH:(512) 454-4197 (a-e,h-j,n)

Big D Books, Comics, Games, and Fabulosities
1516 Centerville
Dallas, TX 75228
PH:(214) 328-0130 (a-i,l,m,o)

Lone Star Comics & Science Fiction
7738 Forest Lane
Dallas, TX 75230
PH:(214) 373-0934 (b-e,g-i,m)

Remember When
2431 Valwood Parkway
Dallas, TX 75234
PH:(214) 243-3439 (a-e,g-j,m,o)

Border Comics
3812 Devore Ct.
El Paso, TX 79904
PH:(915) 755-2136 (a-c,j,n)

Fantastic Worlds BookStore
Westridge Shop.Ctr. Breezeway
4816-A Camp Bowie Blvd.
Fort Worth, TX 76107
PH:(817) 731-6222 (a-c,e,g-i,n)

B&D Trophy Shop
4402-B N. Shepherd
Houston, TX 77018
PH:(713)694-8436 (a-c,e,g-i,l,m)

Roy's Memory Shop
2001 S.W. Freeway
Houston, TX 77098
PH:(713) 529-1387 (a-f,i,l,o)

Third Planet Books & Records
2339 Bissonnet
Houston, TX 77005
PH:(713) 528-1067 (a-g,i,l,n)

Remember When
581 W. Campbell, #119
Richardson, TX 75080
PH:(214) 690-0374 (a-e,g-j,m,o)

Books Unlimited
2914 E. Southcross Blvd.
San Antonio, TX 78223
PH:(512) 534-7525 (b,c,e,g,h)

Comic Quest
3911 Eisenhauer Rd.
San Antonio, TX 78218
PH:(512) 653-6588 (b,c,e,j)

The Dungeon Book & Comic Store
3600 Fredericksburg Rd. 126E
San Antonio, TX 78201
PH:(512) 732-2272 (b,c,e,g,h)

VERMONT:

Moondance Comics
8 High Street - Rear
In the Harmony Parking Lot
Brattleboro, VT 05301
PH:(802) 257-7600
(a-c,e,g,i-k,m,n)

VIRGINIA:

Book Niche & Capital Comics Ctr.
2008 Mt. Vernon Ave.
Alexandria, VA 22301
PH:(703) 548-3466
(a-c,e-h,m,n,p)

Geppi's Crystal City Comics
1755 Jefferson Davis Hwy.
Crystal City
Arlington, VA 22202
PH:(703) 521-4618 (a-c,f)

Zeno's Books
1112 Sparrow Road
Chesapeake, VA 23325
PH:(804) 420-2344 (a-j,m-o)

Hole in the Wall Books
905 West Broad St.
Falls Church, VA 22046
PH:(703) 536-2511 (a-e,g,h,j,l,n)

Marie's Books and Things
1709 Princess Anne St.
Fredericksburg, VA 22401
PH:(703)373-5196(a-c,e,f,h,i,l)

Bender's
17 E. Mellen St.
Hampton, VA 23663
PH:(804) 723-3741 (a-j,m-o)

Joe's Books and Things
8452 Centreville Road
Manassas Park, VA 22111
PH:(703) 361-4335 (a-h,j,l,m)

B & D Buyer Service
Rt. 2, Box 331
Moneta, VA 24121
PH:(703) 345-9639 (a-c,e,g)

Bruce's Books and Things
3910 Hull Street
Richmond, VA 23224
PH:(804) 233-1649 (a-h,j,l,m)

Nostalgia Plus
5610 Patterson Ave.
Richmond, VA 23226
PH:(804) 282-5532 (a-c,j,m,n)

Magic City Comics & Collectables
1924 Brookfield Dr.
Roanoke, VA 24018
PH:(703) 774-1957 (c-e,g-n,p)

The Trilogy Shop
5767 Princess Anne Rd.
Virginia Beach, VA 23462
PH:(804) 490-2205 (a-c,e,m)

Doug's Books and Things
13943 Jefferson Davis Hwy.
Woodbridge, VA 22193
PH:(703) 494-5733 (a-f,j,l,m)

WASHINGTON:

Kelley's Comic Shop
1316 Elm Street
Clarkston, WA 99403
PH:(509).758-2814 (b,c,e,l)

Wally's Book & Comic Exchange
128 Park Lane
Kirkland, WA 98033
PH:(206) 822-7333
(a-c,e,f,h,j,m,n)

The Comic Character
Seattle Underground Antique Mall
114 Alaskan Way S.
Seattle, WA 98104
PH:(206) 622-8868 (b,f-k,m)

Gemini Book Exchange
9614 16th Avenue S.W.
Seattle, WA 98106
PH:(206)762-5543 (c,e,n)

Golden Age Collectables
1501 Pike Place Market
401 Lower Level
Seattle, WA 98101
PH:(206)622-9799 (a-d,f,i,j,n,o)

Zanadu Comics/Paperback Exchange
209 Union
Seattle, WA 98101
PH:(206) 624-7250 (b,c,e,j,m,n)

Stamp Centre
7319 Greenwood Ave. N.
Seattle, WA 98103
PH:(206) 782-1167 (a-c,g,n)

The Book Exchange
University City East
E. 10812 Sprague
Spokane, WA 99206
(a-c,e,g,h)

The Comic Rack
South 14 Monroe
Spokane, WA 99204
PH:(509)747-4477 (a-c,e,f,i,m,n)

Collectors Nook
213 North ''I'' St.
Tacoma, WA 98403
PH:(206) 272-9828 (a,b,d-h,j-o)

WISCONSIN:

Capital City Comics
1910 Monroe St.
Madison, WI 53711
PH:(608) 251-8445 (a-h,j,m,n)

20th Century Books
2501 University Ave.
Madison, WI 53705
PH:(608)231-2916 (b-e,h,n)

Time Traveler Bookstore
7143 West Burleigh
Milwaukee, WI 53210
PH:(414) 442-0203 (a-h,k,m,p)

CANADA:

BRITISH COLUMBIA:

Ted's Paperback
269 Leon Ave.
Kelowna, B.C., Can. V1Y 6J1
PH:(604) 763-1258 (a-c,e,h,l)

Golden Age Collectables
742 Columbia
New Westminster, B. C.,
Canada V3M 1B4
PH:(604) 522-7636 (a-d,f,i,j,n,o)

Collectors' Books & Comics
3626 W. 16th Ave.
Vancouver, B.C., Can. V6R 3C4
PH:(604) 224-6212 (a,b,d-h,m,n)

The Comic Shop
2089 West 4th Ave.
Vancouver, B.C., Can. V6J 1N3
PH:(604) 738-8122 (a-k,m-o)

Golden Age Collectables
830 Granville St.
Vancouver, B.C., Can. V3Z 1K3
PH:(604) 683-2819 (a-d,f,i,j,n,o)

MANITOBA:

Calvin Slobodian
859 Fourth Ave.
Rivers, Man., Can. R0K 1X0
PH:(204) 328-7846 (a,b,d,j)

Comic World
389 Portage Ave.
Winnipeg, Man., Can. R3B 2C5
PH:(204) 943-1968 (a-c,e-h,l,m)

ONTARIO:

The Comic Book Collector
616 Dundas Street
London, Ont., Can. N5W 2Y8
PH:(519) 433-6004 (a-c)

Fantasy World Comics & Cards
169 Adelaide St. N.
London, Ont., Can. N6B 3G9
PH:(519) 433-2771 (a-e,g,h,m)

Comics Unlimited
8 Keewatin Ave.
Toronto, Ont., Can. M4P 1Z8
PH:(416) 489-1473 (b,c,g,m)

Queen's Comics & Memorabilia
1962 Queen St. East
Toronto, Ont., Can. M4L 1H8
PH:(416) 698-8757 (a-g,i,l,m)

Ken Mitchell (Appointment Only)
710 Conacher Drive
Willowdale, Ont., Can. M2M 3N6
PH:(416) 222-5808 (a,b,f,g)

QUEBEC:

Les Livres Comiques du Capitaine Quebec
5108 Decarie
Montreal, Que., Can. H3X 2H9
PH:(514)487-0970(a-c,e,g,i,m,n)

ENGLAND:

Comic Showcase
15 Catherine Street
London WC2, England
PH: 01 379 3345 (a-c,j)

Forbidden Planet
23, Denmark Street
London WC2H 8NN, England
PH: 01 836 4179 (a-c,e,g-j,n)

FRANCE:

Trismegiste
4 rue Frederic Sauton
75005 Paris-France
PH: (1) 633.91.94 (c,f,h,j)

Abbott & Costello #28, © STJ

Aces High #4, © WMG

Action Comics #1, © DC

The correct title listing for each comic book can be determined by consulting the indicia (publication data) on the beginning interior pages of the comic. The official title is determined by those words of the title in capital letters only, and not by what is on the cover.

Titles are listed in this book as if they were one word, ignoring spaces, hyphens, and apostrophes, to make finding titles easier.

A-1 (See A-One)

ABBIE AN' SLATS (. . . With Becky No. 1-4) (See Fight for Love, Treasury of Comics, & United Comics)
1940; March, 1948 - No. 4, Aug, 1948 (Reprints)
United Features Syndicate

	Good	Fine	Mint
Single Series 25, 28 ('40)	8.00	24.00	48.00
1 (1948)	4.00	12.00	24.00
2-4: 3 reprints from Sparkler No. 68-72	2.50	7.50	15.00

ABBOTT AND COSTELLO (. . . Comics)
Feb, 1948 - No. 40, 1956 (Mort Drucker art in most issues)
St. John Publishing Co.

	Good	Fine	Mint
1	9.00	25.00	50.00
2	5.00	14.00	28.00
3-9 (No.8, 8/49)	3.50	10.00	20.00
10-Son of Sinbad story by Kubert (new)	7.00	20.00	40.00
11-20	1.50	4.00	8.00
21-30: 28 r-No. 8	1.20	3.50	7.00
31-40	1.00	3.00	6.00
3-D No. 1 (11/53)	8.00	24.00	48.00

ABBOTT AND COSTELLO (TV)
Feb, 1968 - No. 22, Aug, 1971 (Hanna-Barbera)
Charlton Comics

	Good	Fine	Mint
1	.50	1.50	3.00
2-10		.50	1.00
11-22		.30	.60

ABC (See America's Best TV Comics)

ABRAHAM LINCOLN LIFE STORY
1958 (25 cents)
Dell Publishing Co.

	Good	Fine	Mint
1	2.00	5.00	10.00

ABSENT-MINDED PROFESSOR, THE (See 4-Color Comics No. 1199)

ACE COMICS
April, 1937 - No. 151, Oct-Nov, 1949
David McKay Publications

	Good	Fine	Mint
1-Jungle Jim by Alex Raymond, Krazy Kat begin	70.00	200.00	400.00
2	20.00	60.00	125.00
3-5	14.00	40.00	80.00
6-10	10.00	28.00	55.00
11-The Phantom begins(In brown costume, 2/38)	17.00	50.00	100.00
12-20	8.00	24.00	48.00
21-25,27-30	6.00	18.00	36.00
26-Origin Prince Valiant	35.00	100.00	200.00
31-40: 37-Krazy Kat ends	5.00	15.00	30.00
41-60	4.00	12.00	24.00
61-90	3.50	10.00	20.00
91-100	3.00	8.00	16.00
101-127	2.00	6.00	12.00
128-Brick Bradford begins	1.75	5.00	10.00
129-133	1.75	5.00	10.00
134-Last Prince Valiant	1.75	5.00	10.00
135-The Lone Ranger begins	1.75	5.00	10.00
136-151	1.75	5.00	10.00

ACE KELLY (See Tops Comics)

ACES HIGH
Mar-Apr, 1955 - No. 5, Nov-Dec, 1955
E.C. Comics

	Good	Fine	Mint
1-Not approved by code	8.00	24.00	45.00
2-5	6.00	16.00	32.00

NOTE: *All have stories by* **Davis, Evans, Krigstein,** *and* **Wood**; **Evans** *c-1-5.*

ACTION ADVENTURE (War) (Formerly Real Adventure)
June, 1955 - No. 4, Oct, 1955
Gillmore Magazines

	Good	Fine	Mint
V1No.2-4	.85	2.50	5.00

ACTION COMICS
June, 1938 - Present
National Periodical Publ./Detective Comics/DC

	Good	Fine	Mint
1-Origin & 1st app. Superman by Siegel & Shuster, Marco Polo, Tex Thompson, Pep Morgan, Chuck Dawson & Scoop Scanlon; intro. Zatara; reprinted in Famous 1st Edition. Superman story missing 4 pgs. which were included when reprinted in Superman No. 1. Used in **POP**, pg. 86	2300.00	6500.00	13,500.00
(Prices vary widely on this book)			
1(1976)-Giveaway; paper cover, 16pgs. in color; reprints complete Superman story from No. 1 ('38)	.70	2.00	4.00
2	600.00	1450.00	3000.00
3 (Scarce)	425.00	1050.00	2200.00
4	300.00	725.00	1500.00
5 (Rare)	375.00	900.00	1900.00
6-1st app. Jimmy Olsen (called office boy)	250.00	625.00	1300.00
7,10-Superman covers	260.00	700.00	1500.00
8,9	175.00	525.00	1100.00
11,12,14: 14-Clip Carson begins, ends No. 41	90.00	250.00	525.00
13-Superman cover; last Scoop Scanlon	110.00	315.00	650.00
15-Superman cover	100.00	280.00	600.00
16	70.00	190.00	400.00
17-Superman cover; last Marco Polo	75.00	210.00	450.00
18-Origin 3 Aces	50.00	140.00	300.00
19,20-Superman covers; 'S' left off Superman's chest-No. 20	60.00	175.00	400.00
21,22,24,25	40.00	110.00	240.00
23-1st app. Luthor & Black Pirate; Black Pirate by Moldoff	45.00	135.00	300.00
26-30	25.00	75.00	160.00
31,32	20.00	60.00	135.00
33-Origin Mr. America	24.00	70.00	150.00
34-40: 37-Origin Congo Bill. 40-Intro Star Spangled Kid & Stripsey	20.00	60.00	135.00
41	19.00	55.00	120.00
42-Origin Vigilante; Bob Daley becomes Fatman; Black Pirate ends; not in No. 41	22.00	65.00	140.00
43-50: 45-Intro. Stuff	19.00	55.00	120.00
51-1st app. The Prankster	14.00	40.00	80.00
52-Fatman & Mr. America become the Ameri-commandos; origin Vigilante retold	17.00	50.00	100.00
53-60: 56-Last Fatman. 58-Kubert Vigilante begins, ends No. 70	14.00	40.00	80.00
61-63,65-70: 63-Last 3 Aces.	12.00	36.00	72.00
64-Intro Toyman	14.00	40.00	80.00
71-79: 74-Last Mr. America	10.00	30.00	60.00
80-Third app. Mr. Mxyztplk(5-6/45)	17.00	50.00	100.00
81,82,84-90	10.00	30.00	60.00
83-Intro Hocus & Pocus	11.00	32.00	64.00
91-99: 93-X-Mas-c. 99-1st small logo(7/46)	8.00	24.00	48.00
100	14.00	40.00	80.00
101-Nuclear explosion-c	10.00	30.00	60.00
102-120	9.00	25.00	50.00
121-126,128-140: 135,136,138-Zatara by Kubert	7.00	21.00	42.00
127-Vigilante by Kubert; Tommy Tomorrow begins	14.00	40.00	80.00

Action Comics #19, © DC

Action Comics #59, © DC

Action Comics #82, © DC

ACTION COMICS (continued)	Good	Fine	Mint
141-160: 156-Lois Lane as Super Woman	8.00	22.00	44.00
161-167,169-175,177-180	6.00	16.00	32.00
168,176-Used in **POP**, pg. 90	7.00	20.00	40.00
181-199: 191-Intro. Janu in Congo Bill. 198-Last Vigilante	5.50	16.00	32.00
200-Last pre-code ish	6.00	18.00	36.00
201-220	4.00	12.00	24.00
221-240: 224-1st Golden Gorilla story	3.50	10.00	20.00
241,243-251: 248-Congo Bill becomes Congorilla. 251-Last Tommy Tomorrow	2.50	7.50	15.00
242-Origin & 1st app. Brainiac (7/58); 1st mention of Shrunken City of Kandor	7.00	20.00	40.00
252-Origin & 1st app. Supergirl and Metallo (5/59)	25.00	75.00	150.00
253-2nd app. Supergirl	2.50	7.50	15.00
254-1st meeting of Bizarro & Superman	3.50	10.50	21.00
255-1st Bizarro Lois & both Bizarros leave Earth to make Bizarro World	3.00	8.00	16.00
256-260: 259-Red Kryptonite used	2.00	6.00	12.00
261-1st X-Kryptonite which gave Superman his powers; last Congorilla in Action; origin Streaky The Super Cat	2.00	6.00	12.00
262-266,268-270	2.00	5.00	10.00
267(8/60)-3rd Legion app; 1st app. Chameleon Boy, Colossal Boy, & Invisible Kid	15.00	45.00	90.00
271-275,277-282: 280-Congorilla app.	1.50	4.00	8.00
276(5/61)-6th Legion app; 1st app. Brainiac 5, Phantom Girl, Triplicate Girl, Bouncing Boy, Sun Boy, & Shrinking Violet; Supergirl joins Legion	5.00	15.00	30.00
283(12/61)-Legion of Super-Villains app.	2.00	5.00	10.00
284(1/62)-Mon-el app.	2.00	5.00	10.00
285(2/62)-12th Legion app; Brainiac 5 cameo; Supergirl's existance revealed to world	2.00	5.00	10.00
286(2/62)-Legion of Super Villains app.	1.50	4.00	8.00
287(4/62)-14th Legion app.(cameo)	1.50	4.00	8.00
288-Mon-el app.	1.50	4.00	8.00
289(6/62)-16th Legion app.(Adult); Lightning Man & Saturn Woman's marriage 1st revealed	1.50	4.00	8.00
290(7/62)-17th Legion app; Phantom Girl app.	1.50	4.00	8.00
291,294-299: 297-Mon-el app; 298-Legion app.	1.00	3.00	6.00
292-Superhorse app.	1.00	3.00	6.00
293-Origin Comet(Superhorse)	2.00	5.00	10.00
300	1.20	3.50	7.00
301-303,305-308,310-320: 306-Brainiac 5, Mon-el app. 307-Saturn Girl app. 319-Shrinking Violet app.	.85	2.50	5.00
304-Origin & 1st app. Black Flame	1.00	3.00	6.00

	Good	Fine	Mint
309-Legion app.	1.00	3.00	6.00
321-340: 334-Giant G-20 (origin Supergirl), Legion-r. 336-Origin Akvar(Flamebird). 340-Origin, 1st app. Parasite	.55	1.60	3.20
(80 Pg. Giant G-20)	1.00	3.00	6.00
341-360: 347-Gnt. Supergirl G-33. 360-Gnt. Supergirl G-45; Legion-r	.40	1.20	2.40
(80 Pg. Giant G-33, G-45)	.75	2.25	4.50
361-380: 365-Legion app. 373-Giant Supergirl G-57; Legion-r. 376-Last Supergirl in Action. 377-Legion begins	.35	1.00	2.00
(80 Pg. Giant G-57)	.50	1.50	3.00
381-402: 392-Last Legion in Action. Saturn Girl gets new costume. 393-402-All Superman issues	.25	.75	1.50
403-420: 403-1st 52pg. ish; last-No. 413. 411-Origin Eclipso-(r) 413-Last 25 cent ish; Metamorpho begins; ends No. 418. 419-Intro. Human Target		.50	1.00
421-Intro Capt. Strong		.40	.80
422-424: 422 & 423-Origin Human Target; Green Arrow app. in No. 421,424		.40	.80
425-Adams-a; Atom begins	.50	1.40	2.80
426-436,438-442,444-448,450		.40	.80
437,443-100pg. Giants	.35	1.00	2.00
449-68pg. ish; Kirby Green Arrow-r	.20	.60	1.20
451-460: 454-Last Atom. 458-Last Green Arrow		.40	.80
461-486: 484-Earth II Superman weds Lois Lane		.40	.80
487(44 pgs.)-1st app. Microwave Man; origin Atom retold		.40	.80
488,489(44 pgs.): 488-Air Wave app. 489-Atom app.		.40	.80
490-499		.30	.60
500-Infinity-c; Superman life story; $1.00 size; 68 pgs., shows Legion statues in museum	.40	.75	1.50
501-508,510-518		.30	.60
509-Starlin-a		.40	.80
U.S. Navy Giveaway No. 1 (1944)-Regular comic format	17.00	50.00	100.00
. . . Special Edition No. 2 (1944)-U.S. Navy Giveaway; 68 pgs.; regular comic format	17.00	50.00	100.00
Wheaties Giveaway (1946, 32 pgs., 6½x8¼'', nn)-Vigilante story based on movie serial. NOTE: *All copies were taped to Wheaties boxes and never found in fine or mint condition.*	15.00	45.00	90.00

NOTE: ***Supergirl's*** *origin in 262, 280, 285, 291, 305, 309.* ***Adams*** *c-356, 358, 359, 361-64, 366, 367, 370-74, 377-79i, 398-400, 402, 404-06, 419p, 466, 468, 473i, 485.* ***Anderson*** *a-389, 393i, 395-428i, 430-433i, 443r, 485r; c-396p, 397p, 419i.* ***Buckler*** *a-447; c-483, 486.* ***Infantino*** *c-396, 397; a-419, 437, 443r.* ***Bob Kane's*** *Clip*

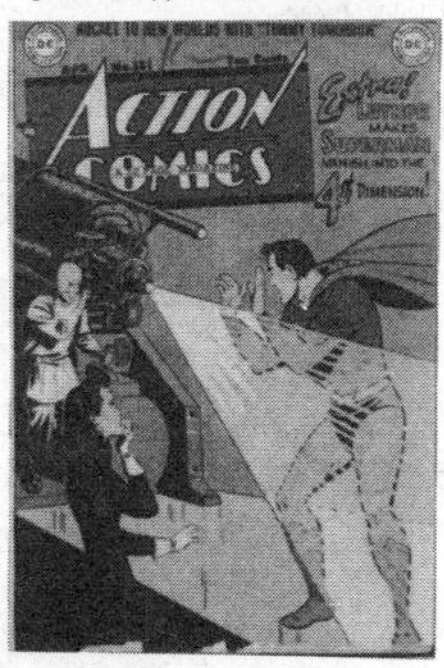

Action Comics #131, © DC

Action Comics #267, © DC

Action Comics #500, © DC

Adventure Comics #70, © DC

Adventure Comics #218, © DC

Adventure Comics #282, © DC

ACTION COMICS (continued)
Carson-14-41. ***Lopez*** *c-475, 484, 487, 488, 494.* ***Meskin*** *a-42-121(most).* ***Schaffenberger*** *a-474-76, 486; c-474, 476.* ***Staton*** *a-525, 526.* ***Toth*** *a-406, 407, 413.* ***Tuska*** *a-486p.*

ACTUAL CONFESSIONS (Formerly Love Adventures)
No. 13, October, 1952 - No. 14, December, 1952
Atlas Comics (MPI)

	Good	Fine	Mint
13,14	.85	2.50	5.00

ACTUAL ROMANCES
October, 1949 - No. 2, 1949 (52 pgs.)
Marvel Comics (IPS)

1	2.00	5.00	10.00
2	.85	2.50	5.00

ADAM AND EVE
1975, 1978 (35-49 cents)
Spire Christian Comics (Fleming H. Revell Co.)

By Al Hartley		.40	.80

ADAM-12 (TV)
Dec, 1973 - No. 10, Feb, 1976
Gold Key

1	.55	1.60	3.20
2-10	.30	.80	1.60

ADDAMS FAMILY (TV)
Oct, 1974 - No. 3, Apr, 1975 (Hanna-Barbera)
Gold Key

1-3	.35	1.00	2.00

ADLAI STEVENSON
December, 1966
Dell Publishing Co.

12-007-612-Life story; photo-c	2.00	6.00	12.00

ADULT TALES OF TERROR ILL. (See Terror Ill.)

ADVENTURE BOUND (See 4-Color Comics No. 239)

ADVENTURE COMICS (Formerly New Adventure)
No. 32, Nov, 1938 - Present
National Periodical Publications/DC Comics

	Good	Fine	Mint
32-39: 32-Anchors Aweigh (ends No. 52), Barry O'Neil (ends No. 60, not in No. 33), Captain Desmo (ends No. 47), Dale Daring (ends No. 57), Federal Men (ends No. 70), The Golden Dragon (ends No. 36), Rusty & His Pals (ends No. 52) by Bob Kane, Todd Hunter (ends No. 38) and Tom Brent (ends No. 39) begin; 39-Jack Wood begins, ends No. 42.	10.00	30.00	60.00
40-Intro. & 1st app. The Sandman. Socko Strong begins, ends No. 54	120.00	350.00	750.00
41-Drug mention story	35.00	100.00	210.00
42-47: 47-Steve Conrad Adventurer begins, ends No. 76	27.00	70.00	140.00
48-Intro. & 1st app. The Hourman by Bernard Baily	120.00	350.00	750.00
49,50	27.00	70.00	140.00
51-60: 53-Intro. Jimmy "Minuteman" Martin & the Minutemen of America in Hourman; ends No. 78. 58-Paul Kirk Manhunter begins, ends No. 72	20.00	60.00	120.00
61-Intro. & 1st app. Starman by Jack Burnley	95.00	275.00	600.00
62-65,68	27.00	70.00	140.00
66-Origin Shining Knight	35.00	100.00	210.00
67-Origin The Mist	27.00	70.00	140.00
69-Intro. Sandy the Golden Boy (Sandman's sidekick); Sandman dons new costume	30.00	85.00	180.00
70-Last Federal Men	27.00	70.00	140.00
71-Jimmy Martin becomes costume aide to the Hourman	27.00	70.00	140.00
72-1st Simon & Kirby Sandman	75.00	225.00	550.00
73-Origin Manhunter by Simon & Kirby; begin new series	120.00	350.00	750.00
74-Thorndyke replaces Jimmy, Hourman's assistant	35.00	100.00	225.00
75,76	35.00	100.00	225.00
77-Origin Genius Jones; Mist story	35.00	100.00	225.00
78-80-Last Simon & Kirby Manhunter & Burnley Starman	35.00	100.00	225.00
81-90: 83-Last Hourman. 84-Mike Gibbs begins, ends No. 102	22.00	65.00	140.00
91-Last Simon & Kirby Sandman	19.00	55.00	120.00
92-99,101,102-Last Starman, Sandman, & Genius Jones. Most-S&K-c. 92-Last Manhunter	14.00	40.00	80.00
100	17.00	50.00	100.00
103-Aquaman, Green Arrow, Johnny Quick, Superboy begin; 1st small logo (4/46)	30.00	90.00	200.00
104	17.00	50.00	100.00
105-110	14.00	40.00	80.00
111-120: 113-X-Mas-c	10.00	30.00	60.00
121-127,129,130	8.00	24.00	48.00
128-1st meeting Superboy-Lois Lane	8.00	24.00	48.00
131-140: 132-Shining Knight 1st return to King Arthur time; origin aide Sir Butch	7.00	20.00	40.00
141,143-149	6.00	18.00	36.00
142-Origin Shining Knight & Johnny Quick retold	7.00	20.00	40.00
150,151,153,155,157,159,161,163-All have 6-pg. Shining Knight stories by Frank Frazetta. 159-Origin Johnny Quick	17.00	50.00	100.00
152,154,156,158,160,162,164-166-Last Shining Knight	9.00	18.00	36.00
167-180	5.00	15.00	30.00
181-188,190-199	4.00	12.00	24.00
189-B&W and color illo in **POP**	6.00	18.00	36.00
200	5.50	16.00	32.00
201-208: 207-Last Johnny Quick (not in 205). 208-Last Pre-code ish.	4.00	12.00	24.00
209,211-220	3.50	10.00	20.00
210-1st app. Krypto	14.00	40.00	80.00
221-246,248,249	3.00	8.00	16.00
247(4/58)-1st Legion of Super Heroes app.; 1st app. Cosmic Boy, Lightning Lad, & Saturn Girl(origin)	70.00	180.00	400.00
250-255: All Kirby Green Arrow. 253-1st meeting Superboy-Robin. 255-Intro. Red Kryptonite in Superboy (used in No. 252 but with no effect)	4.00	12.00	24.00
256-Origin Green Arrow by Kirby	5.00	15.00	30.00
257-259	4.00	12.00	24.00
260-Origin & 1st app. Silver-Age Aquaman	5.00	15.00	30.00
261-266,268,270: 262-Origin Speedy in Green Arrow. 270-Congorilla begins, ends No. 281,283.	3.50	10.00	20.00
267(12/59)-2nd Legion of Super Heroes	22.00	65.00	135.00
269-Intro. Aqualad; last Green Arrow (not in No. 206)	5.00	14.00	28.00
271-280: 275-Origin Superman-Batman team retold (see World's Finest No. 94). 276-Intro Sunboy. 279-Intro. White Kryptonite in Superboy. 280-1st meeting Superboy-Lori Lemaris	2.50	7.50	15.00
281,284,287-289: 281-Last Congorilla. 284-Last Aquaman in Adv. 287,288-Intro. Dev-Em, the Knave from Krypton.	2.00	6.00	12.00
282(3/61)-5th Legion app; intro & origin Star Boy	5.00	15.00	30.00
283-Intro. The Phantom Zone	2.75	8.00	16.00
285-1st Bizarro World story (ends No. 299) in Adv. (See Action No. 255)	3.00	9.00	18.00
286-1st Bizarro Mxyzptlk	2.50	7.00	14.00
290(11/61)-8th Legion app; origin Sunboy in Legion	5.00	14.00	28.00
291,292,295-298	2.00	5.00	10.00
293(2/62)-13th Legion app; Mon-el & Legion Super Pets (intro & origin) app.	3.50	10.00	20.00

ADVENTURE COMICS (continued) **Good Fine Mint**

294-1st Bizarro M. Monroe, Pres. Kennedy 2.00 5.00 10.00

299(8/62)-1st Gold Kryptonite 2.00 5.00 10.00

300-Legion series begins; Mon-el leaves Phantom Zone(temporarily), joins Legion 10.00 30.00 60.00

301-Origin Bouncing Boy 4.00 12.00 24.00

302-305: 303-1st app. Matter Eater Lad. 304-Death of Lightning Lad in Legion 3.50 10.00 20.00

306-310: 306-Intro. Legion of Substitute Heroes. 307-Intro. Element Lad in Legion. 308-1st app. Lightning Lass in Legion 2.50 7.50 15.00

311-320: 312-Lightning Lad back in Legion. 315-Last new Superboy story; Colossal Boy app. 316-Origins & powers of Legion given. 317-Intro. Dream Girl in Legion; Lightning Lass becomes Light Lass; Hall of Fame series begins. 320-Dev-Em 2nd app. 2.00 5.00 10.00

321-Intro Time Trapper 1.50 4.00 8.00

322-326,328-340: 329-Intro Legion of Super Bizarros. 340-Intro Computo in Legion 1.00 3.00 6.00

327-Intro Timber Wolf in Legion 1.20 3.50 7.00

341-Triplicate Girl becomes Duo Damsel .85 2.50 5.00

342-344,347,350 .80 2.40 4.80

345-Last Hall of Fame; returns in 356,371 .80 2.40 4.80

346-1st app. Karate Kid, Princess Projectra, Ferro Lad, & Nemesis Kid 1.20 3.50 7.00

348-Origin Sunboy & intro Dr. Regulus in Legion 1.00 3.00 6.00

349-Intro Universo & Rond Vidar 1.00 3.00 6.00

351-1st app. White Witch 1.00 3.00 6.00

352,356-360 .70 2.00 4.00

353-Death of Ferro Lad in Legion .85 2.50 5.00

354(3/67)-Shadow Lass, Chemical King, Reflecto & Quantum Queen app. only as statues .85 2.50 5.00

355(4/67)-Insect Queen joins Legion .85 2.50 5.00

361-364,366,368-370: 369-Intro Mordru in Legion .70 2.00 4.00

365-Intro Shadow Lass .85 2.50 5.00

367-New Legion headquarters .70 2.00 4.00

371-Intro. Chemical King .85 2.50 5.00

372-Timber Wolf & Chemical King join .70 2.00 4.00

373,374,376-380: Last Legion in Adv. .55 1.60 3.20

375-Intro Quantum Queen .85 2.50 5.00

381-400: 381-Supergirl begins. 390-Giant Supergirl G-69. 399-Unpubbed G.A. Black Canary story .40 1.20 2.40

(80 Pg. Giant G-69) .60 1.80 3.60

401-410: 403-Giant Legion ish G-81; 409-52pg. ish begins; ends No. 420 .35 1.00 1.80

(68 Pg. Giant G-81) .60 1.80 3.60

411-416: 412-Animal Man origin reprint/Str. Adv. No. 180. 413-Hawkman by Kubert; G.A. Robotman reprint/Detective 178; Zatanna begins, ends No. 421. 416-100pg. Giant Supergirl DC-10 feat. Black Canary, Wonder Woman, Phantom Lady (Police), Girl of 1000 Gimmicks .50 1.00

(Giant DC-10) .30 .80 1.60

417-Morrow Vigilante; Frazetta Shining Knight r-/Adv. No. 161 .30 .80 1.60

418-Black Canary by Toth(r); unpubbed G.A. Dr. Mid-Nite story .40 .80

419-Black Canary by Toth & Zatanna story(r) .40 .80

420-424: Last Supergirl in Adv. .30 .60

425-New look, content change to adventure; Toth-a, origin Capt. Fear .40 1.20 2.40

426,427-Last Vigilante .30 .60

428-430: Black Orchid in all; Dr. 13 app.-No. 428 .40 .80

431-Spectre revived, ends No. 440; Toth-a .30 .60

432-439: 438-Unpubbed 7 Soldiers of Victory begins, ends No. 443 .30 .60

440-New Spectre origin .30 .60

441-458: 441-452-Aquaman app. 445-447-The Creeper app. 449-451-Martian Manhunter app. 449-Intro Marauder. 453-458-Superboy app; intro Mighty Girl No. 453. 457,458-Eclipso app. .30 .60

459-462($1.00 size, 68pgs.): 459-Flash, Deadman, Wonder Woman, Gr. Lantern, New Gods begin; Elongated Man story. 460-New Gods, Gr. Lantern end; Aquaman begins. 461-Justice Society begins; ends 466; death Earth II Batman (also No. 462). .50 1.00

463-Most copies printed without indicia; only a few thousand were printed w/indicia after mistake was found. .50 1.00

464-466: 464-Wonder Woman ends. 465-drug mentions (2). 466-Flash, Deadman, Aquaman end; last 68 pg. ish. .50 1.00

467-Starman, Plasticman begin .30 .60

468,471-478,480-489 .30 .60

469,470-Origin Starman .30 .60

479-Dial 'H' For Hero begins, ends 490 .30 .60

NOTE: *Legion app.-267, 282, 290, 293. Vigilante app.-420, 426, 427.* ***Adams*** *c-365-369, 371-373, 375-379, 381-383.* ***Anderson*** *a-383i, 453i.* ***Aparo*** *a-426, 427, 431-433, 434i, 435, 436, 437i, 438i, 459-461, 464; c-431-452, 459, 461, 462, 464-466, 468, 469(part).* ***Buckler*** *c-455.* ***Chaykin*** *a-438.* ***Cockrum*** *a-467.* ***Ditko*** *a-467-479p.* ***Giordano*** *c-409.* ***Grell*** *a-435-447.* ***Guardineer*** *c-45.* ***Infantino*** *a-399, 411, 416, 479-485, 487, 488; c-479-482-p.* ***Kaluta*** *c-425.* ***G. Kane*** *a-425.* ***Kirby*** *a-250-256.* ***Kubert*** *a-413.* ***Lopez*** *a-442,462, 463, 465, 466; c-463.* ***Meskin*** *a-81.* ***Moldoff*** *c-49.* ***Morrow*** *a-413-415, 422.* ***Nasser*** *a-449-451, 466.* ***Newton*** *a-459-461, 464-466.* ***Nino*** *a-425-427, 429, 432, 433.* ***Orlando*** *a-457p, 458p.* ***Simon/Kirby*** *c-73-97, 101, 102.* ***Starlin*** *c-471.* ***Staton*** *a-445-447i, 456-478p; c-458, 461(back).*

ADVENTURE COMICS
No date (Early 1940's) Paper cover, 32 pgs.
IGA

Two different issues; Super-Mystery reprints from 1941 10.00 30.00 60.00

ADVENTURE INTO FEAR
1951
Superior Publ. Ltd.

1 3.50 10.00 20.00

ADVENTURE INTO MYSTERY
May, 1956 - No. 8, July, 1957
Atlas Comics (OPI No. 1-7/BFP No. 8)

1-Everett-c 3.00 9.00 18.00

2,3,6,8: 3-Everett-c 1.50 4.00 8.00

4-Williamson-a, 4 pgs. 4.00 12.00 24.00

5-Everett-c/a, Orlando-a 1.50 4.50 9.00

7-Torres-a 2.00 6.00 12.00

ADVENTURE IS MY CAREER
1945 (36 pgs.)
U.S. Coast Guard Academy/Street & Smith

nn-Simon-a 3.50 10.00 20.00

ADVENTURES (No. 2 Spectacular. . . on cover)
11/49 - No. 2, 2/50 (No. 1 . . IN Romance on cover)
St. John Publishing Co. (Slightly large size)

1(Scarce); Bolle, Starr-a(2) 5.00 15.00 30.00

2(Scarce)-Slave Girl; China Bombshell app.; Bolle, L. Starr-a; (slightly large size) 10.00 30.00 60.00

ADVENTURES FOR BOYS
December, 1954
Bailey Enterprises

Comics, text, & photos 1.50 4.00 8.00

ADVENTURES IN DISNEYLAND (Giveaway)
1955 (12 pgs.) (Dist. by Richfield Oil)
Walt Disney Productions

Adventure Comics #346, © DC

Adventure Comics #425, © DC

Adv. Into Mystery #1, © MCG

Advs. In 3-D #2, © HARV

Advs. Into The Unknown #17, © ACG

Advs. Of Bob Hope #9, © DC

ADVS. IN DISNEYLAND (continued)	Good	Fine	Mint
	3.00	8.00	16.00

ADVENTURES IN PARADISE (See 4-Color No. 1301)

ADVENTURES IN ROMANCE (See Adventures)

ADVENTURES IN SCIENCE (See Classics Special)

ADVENTURES IN 3-D
Nov, 1953 - No. 2, Jan, 1954
Harvey Publications

1-Nostrand, Powell-a, 2-Powell-a	8.00	24.00	48.00

ADVENTURES INTO DARKNESS
No. 5, Aug, 1952 - No. 14, 1954
Better-Standard Publications/Visual Editions

5,7	2.00	6.00	12.00
6-Tuska, Katz-a	2.50	7.00	14.00
8-Toth-a(2)	3.00	8.00	16.00
9-10,14	1.50	4.00	8.00
11-Jack Katz-a	2.00	6.00	12.00
12-lingerie panels	1.50	4.50	9.00
13-Cannibalism story cited by T. E. Murphy articles	3.00	8.00	16.00

NOTE: ***Fawcette*** *a-13.* ***Sekowsky*** *a-11, 13(2).*

ADVENTURES INTO TERROR (Formerly Joker)
No. 43, Nov, 1950 - No. 31, May, 1954
Marvel/Atlas Comics (CDS/ACI)

43	3.50	10.00	20.00
44	3.00	9.00	18.00
3,4	2.00	6.00	12.00
5-Wolverton-c panel/Mystic No. 6	3.00	9.00	18.00
6,8	2.00	5.00	10.00
7-Wolverton-a "Where Monsters Dwell", 6 pgs.; Tuska-c	14.00	40.00	80.00
9,10,12-Krigstein-a	2.50	7.50	15.00
11,13-20	1.50	4.00	8.00
21-24,26-31	1.00	3.00	6.00
25-Matt Fox-a	2.00	6.00	12.00

NOTE: ***Colan*** *a-3, 5, 24, 25, 29; c-27.* ***Everett*** *c-13, 21, 25.* ***G. Kane*** *a-7.* ***Don Rico*** *a-4, 5.* ***Heath*** *a-4, 5, 24; c-9.* ***Sekowsky*** *a-3*

ADVENTURES INTO THE UNKNOWN
Fall, 1948 - No. 174, Aug, 1967 (No. 1-33, 52 pgs.)
American Comics Group
(1st continuous series horror comic)

1-Guardineer-a; adapt. of 'Castle of Otranto' by Horace Walpole	14.00	40.00	80.00
2,4,5	5.50	16.00	32.00
3-Feldstein-a, 9 pgs.	8.00	24.00	48.00
6-10	3.50	8.00	16.00
11-16,18-20	2.00	6.00	12.00
17-Story based on movie 'The Thing'	3.00	8.00	16.00
21-26,28-30: 25-A.C.G. staff app.	2.00	5.00	10.00
27-Williamson/Krenkle-a, 8 pgs.	12.00	35.00	70.00
31-50	1.50	4.00	8.00
51-59 (3-D effect)	3.00	8.00	16.00
60-Woodesque-a by Landau	1.00	3.00	6.00
61-Last pre-code ish	.85	2.50	5.00
62-90	.50	1.50	3.00
91,95,96(No. 95 on inside),107,116-All contain Williamson-a	2.50	7.00	14.00
92-94,97-106,108,110,111,113-115,117-127	.40	1.20	2.40
109,112-Whitney painted-c	.40	1.20	2.40
128-Williamson-a(r) from Forbidden Worlds No. 63	.85	2.25	4.50
129-150	.25	.75	1.40
151-153: 153-Magic Agent app.		.50	1.00
154-Nemesis series begins (origin), ends No. 170	.40	1.20	2.40
155-167,169-174: 157-Magic Agent app.	.30	.80	2.40
168-Ditko-a	.40	1.20	2.40

NOTE: *"Spirit of Frankenstein" series in 5, 6, 8-10, 12, 16.* ***Buscema*** *a-100, 106, 108-110, 158.* ***Craig*** *a-11, 152, 160.* ***Goode*** *a-45, 47, 60.* ***Landau*** *a-59-63.*

ADVENTURES INTO WEIRD WORLDS
Jan, 1952 - No. 30, June, 1954
Marvel/Atlas Comics (ACI)

1-Heath, Tuska-a	3.50	10.00	20.00
2	2.50	7.00	14.00
3-9: 7-Tongue ripped out	2.00	5.00	10.00
10-Krigstein, Everett-a	3.00	8.00	16.00
11,13,14,16-20	1.50	4.00	8.00
12,15-Tuska-a	1.50	4.50	9.00
21-23,25,26,28-30: 22-Bondage-c	1.50	4.00	6.00
24-Shows man holding hypo and splitting in two	3.00	8.00	16.00
27-Matt Fox end of world story-a; severed head cover	2.00	6.00	12.00

NOTE: ***Everett*** *c-6-8, 10, 12, 13, 18-20, 22, 24; a-25.* ***Heath*** *a-25.* ***Rico*** *a-13.* ***Maneely*** *a-3, 22; c-3, 27.* ***Robinson*** *a-13.*

ADVENTURES IN WONDERLAND
April, 1955 - No. 5, Feb, 1956 (Jr. Readers Guild)
Lev Gleason Publications

1-Maurer-a	1.50	4.50	9.00
2-4	1.00	3.00	6.00
5-Christmas issue	1.20	3.50	7.00

ADVENTURES OF ALAN LADD, THE (See Alan Ladd)

ADVENTURES OF ALICE
1945 (Also see Alice in Wonderland & . . at Monkey Island)
Pentagon Publishing Co./Civil Service

1	2.50	7.50	15.00
2-Through the Magic Looking Glass	2.00	6.00	12.00

ADVENTURES OF BOB HOPE, THE
Feb-Mar, 1950 - No. 109, Feb-Mar, 1968
National Periodical Publications

1	10.00	30.00	60.00
2	5.00	14.00	28.00
3-10	3.00	8.00	16.00
11-20	2.00	5.00	10.00
21-50	.85	2.50	5.00
51-93,95-105: 103-Infantino-a	.50	1.50	3.00
94-Aquaman cameo	.70	2.00	4.00
106-109-Adams c/a	1.50	4.00	8.00

NOTE: *Kitty Karr of Hollywood in No. 17-20,28. Liz in No. 26. Miss Beverly Hills of Hollywood in No. 7, 10, 13, 14. Miss Melody Lane of Broadway in No. 15. Rusty in No. 23, 25. Tommy in No. 24. No 2nd feature in No. 2-4, 6, 8, 11, 12, 28-on.*

ADVENTURES OF DEAN MARTIN & JERRY LEWIS, THE
(The Adventures of Jerry Lewis No. 41 on)
July-Aug, 1952 - No. 40, Oct, 1957
National Periodical Publications

1	10.00	30.00	60.00
2	5.00	14.00	28.00
3-10	3.00	8.00	16.00
11-20	2.00	5.00	10.00
21-30	1.00	3.00	6.00
31-40	.85	2.50	5.00

ADVENTURES OF G. I. JOE
1969 (3¼"x7")
Giveaways

1-Danger of the Depths. 2-Flying Space Adventure. 3-Secret Mission to Spy Island. 4-White Tiger Hunt. 5-Fantastic Free Fall. 6-Eight Ropes of Danger. 7-Capture of the Pygmy Gorilla. 8-Hidden Missle Discovery. 9-Space Walk Mystery. 10-Fight for Survival. 11-

ADVS. OF G.I. JOE (continued)

	Good	Fine	Mint
The Sharks' Surprise. 12-Secret of the Mummy's Tomb. each....		.30	.60

ADVENTURES OF HOMER COBB, THE
September, 1947 (Oversized)
Say/Bart Prod. (Canadian)

	Good	Fine	Mint
1-(Scarce)-Feldstein-a	15.00	45.00	90.00

ADVENTURES OF HOMER GHOST
June, 1957 - No. 2, August, 1957
Atlas Comics

	Good	Fine	Mint
V1No.1, V1No. 2	.80	2.40	4.80

ADVENTURES OF JERRY LEWIS, THE (Advs. of Dean Martin & Jerry Lewis No. 1-40)(See Super DC Giant)
No. 41, Nov, 1957 - No. 124, May-June, 1971
National Periodical Publications

	Good	Fine	Mint
41-60	.80	2.40	4.80
61-80: 68,74-Photo-c	.50	1.50	3.00
81-91,93-96,98-100	.35	1.00	2.00
92-Superman cameo	.50	1.50	3.00
97-Batman/Robin x-over	.50	1.50	3.00
101-104-Adams c/a; 102-Beatles app.	1.50	4.00	8.00
105-Superman x-over	.50	1.50	3.00
106-111,113-116	.30	.80	1.60
112-Flash x-over	.40	1.20	2.40
117-Wonder Woman x-over	.40	1.20	2.40
118-124		.50	1.00

ADVENTURES OF MANUEL PACIFICO, TUNA FISHERMAN, THE
1951 (Giveaway) (16 pgs. in color)
Breast O' Chicken Giveaway (Frieda-Bart Hind)

	Good	Fine	Mint
1-4	3.50	10.00	20.00

ADVENTURES OF MIGHTY MOUSE (Mighty Mouse Advs. No. 1)
No. 2, Jan, 1952 - No. 18, May, 1955
St. John Publishing Co.

	Good	Fine	Mint
2-5	3.00	8.00	16.00
6-18	2.00	5.00	10.00

ADVENTURES OF MIGHTY MOUSE (2nd Series)
(Two No. 144's; formerly Paul Terry's Comics; No. 129-137 have no No.'s)(Becomes Mighty Mouse No. 161 on)
No. 126, Aug, 1955 - No. 160, Oct, 1963
St. John/Pines/Dell/Gold Key

	Good	Fine	Mint
126(8/55), 127(10/55), 128(11/55)-St. John	1.00	3.00	6.00
nn(129, 4/56)-144(8/59)-Pines	1.00	3.00	6.00
144(10-12/59)-155(7-9/62) Dell	.85	2.50	5.00
156(10/62)-160(10/63) Gold Key	.85	2.50	5.00

NOTE: *Early issues titled "Paul Terry's Adventures of ...."*

ADVENTURES OF MIGHTY MOUSE (Formerly Mighty Mouse)
No. 166, Mar, 1979 - No. 172, Dec, 1979
Gold Key

	Good	Fine	Mint
166-172; 167,68,70,72-No reprint		.50	1.00

ADVENTURES OF MR. FROG & MISS MOUSE (See Dell Jr. Treasury No. 4)

ADVENTURES OF OZZIE AND HARRIET, THE (Radio)
Oct-Nov, 1949 - No. 5, June-July, 1950
National Periodical Publications

	Good	Fine	Mint
1	7.00	20.00	40.00
2-5	4.00	12.00	24.00

ADVENTURES OF PATORUZU
Aug, 1946 - Winter, 1946
Green Publishing Co.

	Good	Fine	Mint
nn's-Contains Animal Crackers reprints	.70	2.00	4.00

ADVENTURES OF PINKY LEE, THE (TV)
July, 1955 - No. 5, Nov, 1955
Atlas Comics

	Good	Fine	Mint
1	5.00	14.00	28.00
2-5	3.50	10.00	20.00

ADVENTURES OF PIPSQUEAK, THE (Formerly Pat the Brat)
No. 35, Nov, 1959 - No. 39, July, 1960
Archie Publications (Radio Comics)

	Good	Fine	Mint
35-39	.85	2.50	5.00

ADVENTURES OF PUSSYCAT, THE (Magazine)
Oct, 1968 (B&W reprints from men's magazines)
Marvel Comics Group

	Good	Fine	Mint
1-(Scarce)-Ward, Everett, Wood-a; Everett-c	7.00	20.00	40.00

ADVENTURES OF QUAKE & QUISP, THE (See Quaker Oats "Plenty of Glutton")

ADVENTURES OF REX THE WONDER DOG, THE (Rex. . No. 1)
Jan-Feb, 1952 - No. 45, May-Jun, 1959; No. 46, Nov-Dec, 1959
National Periodical Publications

	Good	Fine	Mint
1-(Scarce)-Toth-a	24.00	70.00	140.00
2	8.00	24.00	48.00
3-Toth-a	10.00	30.00	60.00
4,5	5.50	16.00	32.00
6-10	4.00	12.00	24.00
11-20	3.00	8.00	16.00
21-46	2.00	5.00	10.00

NOTE: ***Infantino, Gil Kane*** *art in most issues.*

ADVENTURES OF ROBIN HOOD, THE (Formerly Robin Hood)
No. 8, Nov, 1957 (Based on Richard Green TV Show)
Magazine Enterprises (Sussex Publ. Co.)

	Good	Fine	Mint
8	1.00	3.00	6.00

ADVENTURES OF ROBIN HOOD, THE
March, 1974 - No. 7, Jan, 1975 (Disney Cartoon)
Gold Key

	Good	Fine	Mint
1(90291-403)-Part-r of $1.50 editions	.50	1.50	3.00
2-7	.35	1.00	2.00

ADVENTURES OF SLIM AND SPUD, THE
1924 (3¾"x9¾")(104 pg. B&W strip reprints)
Prairie Farmer Publ. Co.

	Good	Fine	Mint
	5.00	14.00	28.00

ADVENTURES OF THE BIG BOY
1956 - Present (Giveaway)(East & West editions of early issues)
Timely Comics/Webs Adv. Corp./Illus. Features

	Good	Fine	Mint
1-Everett-a	70.00	200.00	400.00
2-Everett-a	35.00	100.00	200.00
3-5-Everett-a	17.00	50.00	100.00
6,7,9,10	5.50	16.00	32.00
8-Everett-a	14.00	40.00	80.00
11-20	2.50	7.50	15.00
21-30	1.50	4.00	8.00
31-50	.70	2.00	4.00
51-100	.35	1.00	2.00
101-150		.50	1.00
151-240		.20	.40
1-20 ('76-'79,Paragon Prod.)		.10	.20
Summer, 1959 ish, large size	3.50	10.00	20.00

ADVENTURES OF THE DETECTIVE
No date (1930's) 36 pgs.; 9½x12"; B&W (paper cover)
Humor Publ. Co.

	Good	Fine	Mint
Not reprints; Ace King by Martin Nadle	5.00	14.00	28.00

ADVENTURES OF THE DOVER BOYS

Advs. Of Jerry Lewis #45, © DC

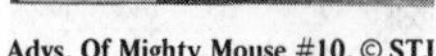
Advs. Of Mighty Mouse #10, © STJ

Advs. Of Rex The Wonder Dog #3, © DC

Advs. Of The Fly #29, © AP

Airboy Comics V3#7, © HILL

Air Fighters V2#8, © HILL

ADVS. OF THE DOVER BOYS (continued)
September, 1950 - No. 2, 1950 (No month given)
Archie Comics (Close-up)

	Good	Fine	Mint
1,2	1.50	4.00	8.00

ADVENTURES OF THE FLY (The Fly, No. 2; Flyman No. 32-39)
Aug, 1959 - No. 30, Oct, 1964; No. 31, May, 1965
Archie Publications

	Good	Fine	Mint
1-Shield app.; origin The Fly by S&K	10.00	30.00	60.00
2-Williamson, S&K, Powell-a	7.00	20.00	40.00
3-Origin retold; Davis-a	5.50	16.00	32.00
4-Adams-a(p)(1 panel); S&K-c; Shield x-over	4.00	12.00	24.00
5-10: 7-Black Hood app. 8,9-Shield x-over. 9-1st app. Cat Girl. 10-Black Hood app.	1.00	3.00	6.00
11-13,15-20: 20-Origin Flygirl retold	.70	2.00	4.00
14-Intro. & origin Fly Girl	.80	2.40	4.80
21-30: 23-Jaguar cameo. 30-Comet x-over in Fly Girl	.50	1.50	3.00
31-Black Hood, Shield, Comet app.	.50	1.50	3.00

ADVENTURES OF THE JAGUAR, THE
Sept, 1961 - No. 15, Nov, 1963
Archie Publications (Radio Comics)

	Good	Fine	Mint
1-Origin Jaguar	3.50	10.00	20.00
2,3	2.00	5.00	10.00
4,5-Catgirl app.	1.00	3.00	6.00
6-10: 6-Catgirl app.	.70	2.00	4.00
11-15: 13,14-Catgirl, Black Hood app. in both	.50	1.50	3.00

ADVENTURES OF TINKER BELL (See 4-Color No. 982)

ADVENTURES OF TOM SAWYER (See Dell Jr. Treasury No. 10)

ADVENTURES OF YOUNG DR. MASTERS, THE
Aug, 1964 - No. 2, Nov, 1964
Archie Comics (Radio Comics)

	Good	Fine	Mint
1,2	.50	1.50	3.00

ADVENTURES ON THE PLANET OF THE APES
Oct, 1975 - No. 11, Dec, 1976
Marvel Comics Group

	Good	Fine	Mint
1-Reprints from Planet of the Apes in color; Starlin-c	.35	1.00	2.00
2-11		.50	1.00

NOTE: ***Alcala*** *a-10r, 11r.* ***Nasser*** *c-7.* ***Ploog*** *a-1-9.* ***Starlin*** *c-6.*

ADVENTURES WITH SANTA CLAUS
No date (early 50's) (24 pgs.; 9¾x6¾''; paper cover) (Giveaway)
Promotional Publ. Co. (Murphy's Store)

	Good	Fine	Mint
Contains 8 pgs. ads	3.00	9.00	18.00
16 page version	3.00	9.00	18.00

AFRICA
1955
Magazine Enterprises

	Good	Fine	Mint
1(A-1 No. 137)-Cave Girl & Thun'da; Powell-c/a(4)	7.00	20.00	40.00

AFRICAN LION (See 4-Color No. 665)

AFTER DARK
May, 1955 - No. 8, Sept, 1955
Sterling Comics

	Good	Fine	Mint
6-8-Sekowsky-a in all	1.50	4.00	8.00

AGGIE MACK
Jan, 1948 - No. 8, Aug, 1949
Four Star Comics Corp.

	Good	Fine	Mint
1-Feldstein-a, ''Johnny Prep''	6.00	18.00	36.00
2,3-Kamen-c	3.50	10.00	20.00
4-Feldstein ''Johnny Prep''; Kamen-c	5.00	14.00	28.00
5-8-Kamen c/a	3.50	10.00	20.00

AGGIE MACK (See 4-Color Comics No. 1335)

AIN'T IT A GRAND & GLORIOUS FEELING?
1922 (52 pgs.; 9x9¾''; stiff cardboard cover)
Whitman Publishing Co.

	Good	Fine	Mint
1921 daily strip-r; B&W with color-c; Briggs-a	7.00	20.00	40.00

AIR ACE (Bill Barnes No. 1-12)
V2No. 1, Jan, 1944 - V3No. 8(No. 20), Feb-Mar, 1947
Street & Smith Publications

	Good	Fine	Mint
V2No.1-12	2.00	6.00	12.00
V3No.1-6,8: No. 8-Powell-c	1.50	4.00	8.00
V3No.7-Powell bondage-c	3.00	8.00	16.00
V4No.1-8	.85	2.50	5.00
V5No.1-7	.70	2.00	4.00
V5No.8-Powell-a	1.20	3.50	7.00

AIRBOY COMICS (Airfighters No. 1-22)
V2No.11, Dec, 1945 - V10No.4, May, 1953 (No V3No.3)
Hillman Periodicals

	Good	Fine	Mint
V2No.11,12-Valkyrie in No. 12	5.50	16.00	32.00
V3No.1,2(no No. 3)	5.00	14.00	28.00
4-The Heap app. in Skywolf	3.50	10.00	20.00
5-8: 6-Valkyrie app;	3.50	10.00	20.00
9,11: 9-Origin The Heap	3.50	10.00	20.00
10-Kirby-a	4.00	12.00	24.00
12-Skywolf & Airboy x-over; Valkyrie app.	5.00	14.00	28.00
V4No.1-Iron Lady app.	3.50	10.00	20.00
2-Rackman begins	2.00	6.00	12.00
3,12	2.00	6.00	12.00
4-Simon & Kirby-c	3.00	8.00	16.00
5-11-All S&K-a	4.00	12.00	24.00
V5No.1-9: 4-Infantino Heap. 8-Bondage-c	2.00	5.00	10.00
10,11: 10-Origin The Heap	2.00	5.00	10.00
12-Krigstein-a(p)	2.50	7.00	14.00
V6No.1-12: 6,8-Origin The Heap	2.00	5.00	10.00
V7No.1-12: 8,10-Origin The Heap	2.00	5.00	10.00
V8No.1-3,5-12	1.20	3.50	7.00
4-Krigstein-a	2.50	7.00	14.00
V9No.1-6,8-12: 2-Valkyrie app.	1.20	3.50	7.00
7-One pg. Frazetta ad	2.00	5.00	10.00
V10No.1-4	1.20	3.50	7.00

NOTE: ***Bolle*** *a-V4No.12.* ***McWilliams*** *a-V3No.7.* ***Powell*** *a-V7No.3, V8No.1, 6.* ***Starr*** *a-V5No.1, 12.* ***Dick Wood*** *a-V4No.12.*

AIR FIGHTERS COMICS (Airboy No. 23, V2No.11 on)
Nov, 1941; No. 2, Nov, 1942 - V2No.10, Fall, 1945
Hillman Periodicals

	Good	Fine	Mint
V1No.1-(Produced by Funnies, Inc.); Black Commander only app.	50.00	140.00	280.00
2(11/42)-(Produced by Quality artists & Biro for Hillman); Origin Airboy & Iron Ace; Black Angel, Flying Dutchman & Skywolf begin; 1st Valkyrie app.?; Fuji-a; Biro c/a	75.00	190.00	380.00
3-Origin The Heap & Skywolf	30.00	90.00	180.00
4	22.00	65.00	130.00
5,6	15.00	45.00	90.00
7-12	13.00	38.00	75.00
V2No.1-9: 2-Skywolf by Giunta; Flying Dutchman by Fuji; Valkyrie app. 5-Flag-c. 7-Valkyrie app.	11.00	33.00	66.00
10-Origin The Heap & Skywolf	11.00	33.00	66.00

AIR FORCES (See American Air Forces)

AIR WAR STORIES
Sept-Nov, 1964 - No. 8, Aug, 1966
Dell Publishing Co.

	Good	Fine	Mint
1-Glanzman c/a begins	.70	2.00	4.00
2-8	.35	1.00	2.00

ALADDIN (See Dell Jr. Treasury No. 2)

ALAN LADD (Adventures of . . .)
Oct-Nov, 1949 - No. 9, Feb-Mar, 1951
National Periodical Publications

	Good	Fine	Mint
1	7.00	20.00	40.00
2-9	4.00	12.00	24.00

ALARMING ADVENTURES
Oct, 1962 - No. 3, Feb, 1963
Harvey Publications

	Good	Fine	Mint
1-Williamson/Crandall, Powell(2)-a; Severin-c	2.00	6.00	12.00
2,3-Williamson/Crandall, Powell-a	1.50	4.00	8.00

ALARMING TALES
Sept, 1957 - No. 6, July, 1958
Harvey Publications (Western Tales)

	Good	Fine	Mint
1-Kirby c/a(4)	3.50	10.00	20.00
2-Kirby-a(4)	3.50	10.00	20.00
3,4-Kirby-a	3.00	8.00	16.00
5-Kirby/Williamson-a	3.00	8.00	16.00
6-Torres-a	3.00	8.00	16.00

ALBERTO (See The Crusaders)

ALBERT THE ALLIGATOR & POGO POSSUM (See 4-Color Comics No. 105, 148)

ALBUM OF CRIME
1949 (132 pages)
Fox Features Syndicate

nn-See Fox Giants. Contents can vary and determines price.

ALBUM OF LOVE
1949 (132 pages)
Hero Books (Fox)

nn-See Fox Giants. Contents can vary and determines price.

AL CAPP'S DOGPATCH (Also see Mammy Yokum)
No. 71, June, 1949 - No. 4, Dec, 1949
Toby Press

	Good	Fine	Mint
71(No.1)-Reprints from Tip Top No. 112-114	3.50	10.00	20.00
2-4: 4-Reprints from Little Abner No. 73	3.00	8.00	16.00

AL CAPP'S SHMOO (See Oxydol-Dreft)
July, 1949 - No. 5, April, 1950 (None by Al Capp)
Toby Press

	Good	Fine	Mint
1	8.00	24.00	48.00
2,4,5	5.00	15.00	30.00
3-Sci-fi trip to moon	6.00	18.00	36.00

AL CAPP'S WOLF GAL
1952
Toby Press

	Good	Fine	Mint
1,2-Edited-r from Li'l Abner No. 63,64	7.00	20.00	40.00

ALEXANDER THE GREAT (See 4-Color No. 688)

ALGIE
Dec, 1953 - No. 3, 1954
Timor Publ. Co.

	Good	Fine	Mint
1	.85	2.50	5.00
2,3	.55	1.60	3.20
Super Reprint 15	.35	1.00	2.00

ALICE (New Advs. in Wonderland)
1952
Ziff-Davis Publ. Co.

	Good	Fine	Mint
10-Spanking-c; Berg-a	4.00	12.00	24.00
11-Dave Berg-a	2.00	5.00	10.00
2-Dave Berg-a	1.50	4.00	8.00

ALICE AT MONKEY ISLAND (See The Advs. of Alice)
No. 3, 1946
Pentagon Publ. Co. (Civil Service)

	Good	Fine	Mint
3	3.00	8.00	16.00

ALICE IN BLUNDERLAND
1952 (No cover, 16 pages in color)
Industrial Services

	Good	Fine	Mint
nn-Facts about big government waste and inefficiency	10.00	30.00	60.00

ALICE IN WONDERLAND (See Advs. of Alice, 4-Color No. 331,341, Dell Jr. Treasury No. 1, Movie Comics, Single Series No. 24, Walt Disney Showcase No. 22, and World's Greatest Stories)

ALICE IN WONDERLAND
1965
Western Printing Company

	Good	Fine	Mint
. . . Meets Santa Claus(1950's), no date, 16 pages	3.00	8.00	16.00
Rexall Giveaway(1965, 16 pgs., 5x7¼") Western Printing (TV-Hanna-Barbera)	2.00	6.00	12.00
Wonder Bakery Giveaway(16 pgs. color, no No., no date) (Continental Baking Co.)	2.00	6.00	12.00

ALICE IN WONDERLAND MEETS SANTA
nd (16 pgs., 6-5/8x9-11/16", paper cover)
No publisher (Giveaway)

	Good	Fine	Mint
	10.00	30.00	60.00

ALIENS, THE (Captain Johner and . . .)
Sept-Dec, 1967
Gold Key

	Good	Fine	Mint
1-Reprints from Magnus No. 1,3,4,6-10, all by Russ Manning	.70	2.00	4.00

ALL-AMERICAN COMICS (. . . Western No. 103-126, . . . Men of War No. 127 on)
April, 1939 - No. 102, Oct, 1948
National Periodical Publications/All-American

	Good	Fine	Mint
1-Hop Harrigan, Scribbly, Toonerville Folks, Ben Webster, Spot Savage, Mutt & Jeff, Red White & Blue, Adv. in the Unknown, Tippie, Reg'lar Fellars, Skippy, Bobby Thatcher, Mystery Men of Mars, Daiseybelle, & Wiley of West Point begin	60.00	150.00	300.00
2-Ripley's Believe It or Not begins, ends No. 24	30.00	85.00	170.00
3-5: 5-The American Way begins, ends No. 10	19.00	55.00	110.00
6,7: 6-Last Spot Savage. 7-Last Bobby Thatcher	14.00	40.00	80.00
8-The Ultra Man begins	22.00	65.00	130.00
9,10	17.00	50.00	100.00
11-15: 12-Last Toonerville Folks. 13-Popsicle Pete begins, ends No. 26,28. 15-Last Tippie & Reg'lar Fellars	12.00	36.00	72.00
16-Origin & 1st app. Green Lantern (Rare). Inspired by Aladdin's Lamp; the hero was originally named Alan Ladd but was changed to Green Lantern due to appearance of movie star Alan Ladd; Solomon Grundy app.	400.00	1200.00	2600.00
(Prices vary widely on this book)			
17-(Scarce)	90.00	270.00	550.00
18	60.00	180.00	370.00
19-Origin & 1st app. The Atom; Last Ultra Man	85.00	250.00	520.00
20-Atom dons costume; Hunkle becomes the Red Tornado; Rescue on Mars begins, ends No. 25	50.00	150.00	310.00
21-23: 21-Last Wiley of West Point & Skippy. 23-Last Daiseybelle; 3 Idiots begin, end No. 82	40.00	120.00	240.00
24-Sisty & Dinky become the Cyclone Kids; Ben Webster ends	40.00	120.00	240.00

Al Capp's Shmoo # 2, © TOBY

All-American Comics #1, © DC

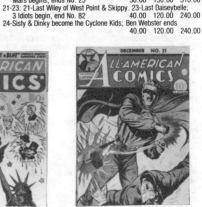

All-American Comics #21, © DC

All-American Comics #27, © DC

All-Famous Crime #8, © STAR

All-Flash #19, © DC

ALL AMERICAN COMICS (continued) — **Good** **Fine** **Mint**

25-Origin & 1st app. Dr. Mid-Nite; Hop Harrigan becomes Guardian Angel; last Adventure in the Unknown 60.00 175.00 360.00
26-Origin & 1st app. Sargon, the Sorcerer 45.00 125.00 260.00
27-Intro. Doiby Dickles, Green Lantern's sidekick 45.00 125.00 260.00
28-(No.28 on cover, No.27 on inside) Hop Harrigan gives up costumed identity) 24.00 70.00 140.00
29,30 24.00 70.00 140.00
31-40: 35-Doiby learns Green Lantern's i. d. 17.00 50.00 100.00
41-50: 50-Sargon ends 15.00 45.00 90.00
51-60 13.00 38.00 76.00
61-Origin Solomon Grundy 35.00 85.00 180.00
62-70: 70-Kubert Sargon 10.00 30.00 60.00
71-Last Red White & Blue 8.00 24.00 48.00
72-Black Pirate begins (not in No. 74-82); last Atom 8.00 24.00 48.00
73-80: 73-Winky, Blinky & Noddy begins, ends No. 82 8.00 24.00 48.00
81-88,90: 90-Origin Icicle 8.00 24.00 48.00
89-Origin Harlequin 10.00 30.00 60.00
91-99-Last Hop Harrigan 9.00 26.00 52.00
100-1st app. Johnny Thunder by Alex Toth 17.00 50.00 100.00
101-Last Mutt & Jeff 11.00 32.00 64.00
102-Last Green Lantern, Black Pirate & Dr. Mid-Nite 11.00 32.00 64.00

NOTE: *No Atom in 47,62-69.* ***Kinstler*** *Black Pirate-89.* ***Moldoff*** *c-16-23.* ***Toth*** *a-88, 92, 96, 98-102; c-92, 96-102.*

ALL-AMERICAN MEN OF WAR (Previously All-American Western)
No. 127, Aug-Sept, 1952 - No. 117, Sept-Oct, 1966
National Periodical Publications

127 (1952) 8.00 24.00 48.00
128 (1952) 7.00 20.00 40.00
2(12-1/'52-53)-5 5.50 16.00 32.00
6-10 4.00 12.00 24.00
11-20 3.00 8.00 16.00
21-28 2.00 6.00 12.00
29,30,32-Wood-a 3.50 10.00 20.00
31,33-50 2.00 5.00 10.00
51-70: 67-1st Gunner & Sarge by Andru 1.50 4.00 8.00
71-80 1.00 3.00 6.00
81-100: 82-Johnny Cloud begins, ends No. 111,114,115 .55 1.60 3.20
101-117: 112-Balloon Buster series begins, ends No. 114,116 115-Johnny Cloud app. .35 1.00 2.00

NOTE: ***Drucker*** *a-65,74.* ***Infantino*** *a-8.* ***Krigstein*** *a-128('52), 2, 3, 5.* ***Kirby*** *a-29.* ***Kubert*** *a-36, 38, 41, 43, 47, 49, 50, 52, 53, 55, 56, 60, 63, 65, 69, 71-73, 103; c-41. Tank Killer in 69, 71, 76 by* ***Kubert.***

ALL-AMERICAN SPORTS
October, 1967
Charlton Comics

1 .30 .60

ALL-AMERICAN WESTERN (Formerly All-American Comics; Becomes All-American Men of War)
Nov, 1948 - No. 126, June-July, 1952
National Periodical Publications

103-110-Johnny Thunder continues by Toth 4.00 12.00 24.00
111-126-All Toth-a 3.00 9.00 18.00

NOTE: ***Kubert*** *a-103-105, 107, 111, 112(1 pg.), 113-116, 121.* ***Kurtzman*** *1 pg.-112(Pot-Shot Pete).*

ALL COMICS
1945
Chicago Nite Life News

1 2.50 7.00 15.00

ALL DETERGENT COMICS
1979 (32 pages) (40 cents)
All Detergent (Giveaway with purchase) — **Good** **Fine** **Mint**

nn-Spiderman (origin); r-/Annual 2 .50 1.50 3.00

ALLEY OOP (See 4-Color No. 3 and Super Book No. 9)

ALLEY OOP
1947 - No. 18, Oct, 1949
Standard Comics

1 9.00 25.00 50.00
2-5 7.00 20.00 40.00
6-18: 17,18-Schomburg-c 6.00 16.00 32.00

ALLEY OOP
Nov, 1955 - No. 3, March, 1956 (Newspaper reprints)
Argo Publ.

1 5.00 14.00 28.00
2,3 3.50 10.00 20.00

ALLEY OOP
12-1/62-63; 9-11/63; 1965
Dell Publishing Co.

1,2(1963) 3.00 9.00 18.00
1,2(1965) 2.00 6.00 12.00

ALL-FAMOUS CRIME
1949 - No. 10, Nov, 1951
Star Publications

1 3.50 10.00 20.00
2,3,5 2.50 7.50 15.00
4-Drug mention story 3.00 9.00 18.00
6-8,10 2.00 6.00 12.00
9-Used in **SOTI**, illo-''The wish to hurt or kill couples in lovers' lanes is not uncommon perversion;'' L. B. Cole-c/a(r)/Law-Crime No. 3 7.00 21.00 42.00

NOTE: *All have* ***L. B. Cole*** *covers.*

ALL FAMOUS CRIME STORIES
1949 (132 pages)
Fox Features Syndicate

nn-See Fox Giants. Contents can vary and determines price.

ALL-FAMOUS POLICE CASES
Oct, 1951 - No. 16, Sept, 1954
Star Publications

1 3.50 10.00 20.00
2-6 2.50 7.50 15.00
7-Kubert-a 3.00 9.00 18.00
8-Marijuana story 3.00 9.00 18.00
9-16 2.50 7.50 15.00

NOTE: ***L. B. Cole*** *c-all; a-15, 1pg.* ***Hollingsworth*** *a-15.*

ALL-FLASH
Summer, 1941 - No. 32, Dec-Jan, 1947-48
National Periodical Publications/All-American

1-Origin The Flash retold by E. E. Hibbard 85.00 260.00 540.00
2 40.00 115.00 225.00
3,4 35.00 80.00 160.00
5-Winky, Blinky & Noddy begins, ends No. 32 22.00 65.00 130.00
6-10 17.00 50.00 105.00
11-13: 12-Origin The Thinker. 13-The King app. 14.00 40.00 80.00
14-Green Lantern cameo 17.00 50.00 100.00
15-20: 18-Mutt & Jeff begins, ends No. 22 11.00 32.00 64.00
21-31 10.00 30.00 60.00
32-Origin The Fiddler; 1st app. Star Sapphire; bondage-c 14.00 40.00 80.00

NOTE: *Book length stories in 2-13,16.*

ALL FOR LOVE

ALL FOR LOVE (continued)
Apr-May, 1957 - V3No.4, Dec-Jan, 1959-60
Prize Publications

	Good	Fine	Mint
V1No.1	1.50	4.00	8.00
2-6	.85	2.50	5.00
V2No.1-6	.55	1.60	3.20
V3No.1-4: 2-Powell-a	.35	1.00	2.00

ALL FUNNY COMICS
Winter, 1943-44 - No. 23, May-June, 1948
National Periodical Publications (Detective)

1-Genius Jones begins; Bailey-a	7.00	20.00	40.00
2	3.50	10.00	20.00
3-12,15-Genius Jones app.	2.50	7.00	14.00
13,14,17-23	2.00	5.00	10.00
16-DC Super Heroes app; Last Genius Jones	3.50	10.00	20.00

ALL GOOD (. . . Comics)
1944 (132 pgs.); Spring, 1946 (36 pgs.)
R. W. Boigt Publ. (1944)/Fox Features Syndicate

1(1944)-The Bouncer, Purple Tigress, Puppeteer, & The Green Mask; Infinity-c	5.00	14.00	28.00
1(1946)-Joy Family, Dick Transom, Rick Evans, One Round Hogan	2.50	7.50	15.00

ALL GOOD
Oct, 1949 (260 pages) (50 cents)
St. John Publishing Co.

(8 St. John comics bound together)	20.00	60.00	135.00

NOTE: *Also see Li'l Audrey Yearbook & Treasury of Comics*

ALL GREAT
1944; 1945 (132 pgs.); 1946 (36 pgs.)
Fox Features Syndicate

1944-Capt. Jack Terry, Rick Evans, Jaguar Man	5.00	15.00	30.00
1945-Green Mask, Bouncer, Puppeteer, Rick Evans, Rocket Kelly	5.00	15.00	30.00
1(1946)-Crazy House, Bertie Benson Boy Detective, Gussie the Gob	2.00	6.00	12.00

ALL GREAT (Dagar, Desert Hawk No. 14 on)
No. 14, Oct, 1947 - No. 13, Dec, 1947
Fox Features Syndicate

14-Brenda Starr-r	9.00	25.00	50.00
13-Origin Dagar, Desert Hawk; Brenda Starr (all-r); Kamen-c	10.00	30.00	60.00

ALL-GREAT CONFESSIONS
1949 (132 pages)
Fox Features Syndicate

nn-See Fox Giants. Contents vary and determines price.

ALL GREAT CRIME STORIES
1949 (132 pages)
Fox Features Syndicate

nn-See Fox Giants. Contents vary and determines price.

ALL GREAT JUNGLE ADVENTURES
1949 (132 pages)
Fox Features Syndicate

nn-See Fox Giants. Contents vary and determines price.

ALL HERO COMICS
March, 1943 (100 pgs.) (Cardboard cover)
Fawcett Publications

1-Captain Marvel Jr., Capt. Midnight, Golden Arrow, Ibis the Invincible, Spy Smasher, & Lance O'Casey	40.00	120.00	240.00

ALL HUMOR COMICS
Spring, 1946 - No. 17, December, 1949
Quality Comics Group

	Good	Fine	Mint
1	2.00	6.00	12.00
2-9	1.20	3.50	7.00
10-17	.85	2.50	5.00

ALL LOVE (. . . Romances No. 26)(Formerly Ernie)
No. 26, May, 1949 - No. 32, May, 1950
Ace Periodicals (Current Books)

26(No. 1)-Ernie app.	1.20	3.50	7.00
27-L. B. Cole-a	2.50	7.00	14.00
28-32	.85	2.50	5.00

ALL-NEGRO COMICS
June, 1947 (15 cents)
All-Negro Comics

1 (Rare)	60.00	180.00	400.00

NOTE: *Seldom found in fine or mint condition; many copies are brown.*

ALL-NEW COLLECTORS' EDITION (Formerly Limited Collectors' Ed.)
Jan, 1978 - Present (No. 54-58: 76 pgs.)
DC Comics, Inc.

C-53-Rudolph the Red-Nosed Reindeer	.35	1.00	2.00
C-54-Superman Vs. Wonder Woman	.40	1.20	2.40
C-55-Superboy & the Legion of Super-Heroes; Grell c/a	.70	2.00	4.00
C-56-Superman Vs. Muhammad Ali: story & wraparound Adams-c	.50	1.50	3.00
C-58-Superman Vs. Shazam; Buckler c/a(p)	.35	1.00	2.00
C-60-Rudolph's Summer Fun(8/78)	.35	1.00	2.00
C-62-Superman the Movie (68 pgs.; 1979) plus story	.30	.90	1.80
C-63-Superman & His Incredible Fortress of Solitude(9/81)	.30	.90	1.80
C-64-Superman II(9/81); Orlando-a; photo-c/insides	.30	.90	1.80

ALL-NEW COMICS (. . . Short Stories No. 1-3)
Jan, 1943 - No. 14, Nov, 1946; No. 15, Mar-Apr, 1947
Harvey Publications

1-Steve Case, Crime Rover, Johnny Rebel, Kayo Kane, The Echo, Night Hawk, Ray O'Light, Detective Shane begin; Red Blazer on cover only; Sultan-a	20.00	60.00	125.00
2-Origin Scarlet Phantom	12.00	36.00	72.00
3	10.00	30.00	60.00
4,5	9.50	28.00	56.00
6-The Boy Heroes & Red Blazer (text story) begin, end No. 12; Black Cat app.; intro. Sparky in Red Blazer	9.50	28.00	56.00
7-Kubert, Powell-a; Black Cat & Zebra app.	10.00	30.00	60.00
8-Shock Gibson app.; Kubert, Powell-a; Schomburg bondage-c	10.00	30.00	60.00
9-Black Cat app.; Kubert-a	10.00	30.00	60.00
10-The Zebra app.; Kubert-a(3)	9.50	28.00	56.00
11-Girl Commandos app.	9.00	25.00	50.00
12-Kubert-a	9.00	25.00	50.00
13-Stuntman by Simon & Kirby; Green Hornet, Joe Palooka, Flying Fool app.	10.00	30.00	60.00
14-The Green Hornet & The Man in Black Called Fate by Powell, Joe Palooka app.	8.00	22.00	44.00

15-(Rare)-Small size (5½x8½''; B&W; 32 pgs.). Distributed to mail subscribers only. Black Cat and Joe Palooka app.
(Sold in San Francisco in 1976 for $500.00)

NOTE: *Also see Boy Explorers No. 2, Flash Gordon No. 5, and Stuntman No. 3.* ***Powell*** *a-11.* ***Schomburg*** *c-11.*

ALL-OUT WAR
Sept-Oct, 1979 - No. 6, Aug, 1980 ($1.00)
DC Comics, Inc.

1-The Viking Commando(origin), Force Three(origin), & Black

All Love #29, © ACE

All-New Comics #7, © HARV

All-Out War #1, © DC

All-Select Comics #9, © MCG

All Star Comics #25, © DC

All-Star Squadron #1, © DC

ALL-OUT WAR (continued) — Good / Fine / Mint

Eagle Squadron begin; Kubert-c .50 1.00
2-6 .50 1:00

ALL PICTURE ADVENTURE MAGAZINE
Oct, 1952 - No. 2, Nov, 1952 (100 pg. Giants)
St. John Publishing Co.

1-War comics 5.50 16.00 32.00
2-Horror-crime comics 7.00 20.00 40.00

NOTE: *Above books contain three St. John comics rebound; variations possible.* ***Baker*** *art known in both.*

ALL PICTURE ALL TRUE LOVE STORY
October, 1952 (100 pages)
St. John Publishing Co.

1-Canteen Kate by Matt Baker 12.00 36.00 72.00

ALL-PICTURE COMEDY CARNIVAL
October, 1952 (100 pages)
St. John Publishing Co.

1-(4 rebound comics)-Contents can vary; Baker-a 10.00 30.00 60.00

ALL REAL CONFESSION MAGAZINE
No. 3, Mar, 1949 - No. 4, Apr, 1949 (132 pages)
Hero Books (Fox)

nn(1949),3,4-See Fox Giants. Contents can vary and determines price.

ALL ROMANCES (Mr. Risk No. 7 on)
Aug, 1949 - No. 6, June, 1950
A. A. Wyn (Ace Periodicals)

1 1.50 4.50 9.00
2-6 .85 2.50 5.00

ALL-SELECT COMICS (Blonde Phantom No. 12 on)
Fall, 1943 - No. 11, Fall, 1946
Timely Comics (Daring Comics)

1-Capt. America, Human Torch, Sub-Mariner begin; Black Widow app. 100.00 300.00 600.00
2-Red Skull app. 40.00 120.00 240.00
3-The Whizzer begins 30.00 80.00 160.00
4,5-Last Sub-Mariner 20.00 60.00 120.00
6-The Destroyer app. 17.00 50.00 100.00
7-9: 8-No Whizzer 17.00 50.00 100.00
10-The Destroyer & Sub-Mariner app.; last Capt. America & Human Torch issue 17.00 50.00 100.00
11-1st app. Blonde Phantom; Miss America app. 30.00 80.00 160.00

NOTE: ***Schomburg*** *c-2,4,9,10.*

ALL SPORTS COMICS
Oct-Nov, 1948 - No. 4, Apr-May, 1949 (52 pages)
Hillman Periodicals

1 2.50 7.50 15.00
2-Krigstein-a(p) 2.50 7.50 15.00
3,4 2.00 5.00 10.00

ALL STAR COMICS (. . . Western No. 58 on)
Summer, 1940 - No. 57, Feb-Mar, 1951; No. 58, Jan-Feb, 1976 - No. 74, Sept-Oct, 1978
National Periodical Publ./All-American/DC Comics

1-The Flash(No.1 by Harry Lampert), Hawkman(by Shelly), Hourman, The Sandman, The Spectre, Biff Bronson, Red White & Blue begin; Ultra Man's only app. 200.00 600.00 1300.00
2-Green Lantern, Johnny Thunder begin 110.00 325.00 670.00
3-Origin Justice Society of America; Dr. Fate & The Atom begin, Red Tornado cameo; last Red White & Blue; reprinted in Famous First Edition 300.00 800.00 1700.00
4 100.00 290.00 600.00
5-Intro. & 1st app. Shiera Sanders as Hawkgirl 85.00 250.00 520.00

Good / Fine / Mint

6-Johnny Thunder joins JSA 65.00 190.00 400.00
7-Batman, Superman, Flash cameo; last Hourman; Doiby Dickles app. 65.00 190.00 400.00
8-Origin & 1st app. Wonder Woman(added as 8pgs. making book 76pgs.;origin cont'd in Sensation No. 1); Dr. Fate dons new helmet; Dr.Mid-Nite, Hop Harrigan text stories & Starman begin; Shiera app.; Hop Harrigan JSA guest 130.00 380.00 800.00
9-Shiera app. 65.00 190.00 400.00
10-Flash, Green Lantern cameo, Sandman new costume 65.00 190.00 400.00
11-Wonder Woman begins; Spectre cameo; Shiera app. 60.00 170.00 360.00
12-Wonder Woman becomes JSA Secretary 55.00 160.00 340.00
13-15: Sandman w/Sandy in No. 14 & 15; 15-Origin Brain Wave; Shiera app. 50.00 150.00 310.00
16-19: 19-Sandman w/Sandy 40.00 120.00 250.00
20-Dr. Fate & Sandman cameo 40.00 120.00 250.00
21-Spectre & Atom cameo; Dr. Fate by Kubert; Dr. Fate, Sandman end 35.00 100.00 210.00
22,23: 22-Last Hop Harrigan. 23-Origin Psycho Pirate; last Spectre & Starman 35.00 100.00 210.00
24-Flash & Green Lantern cameo; Mr. Terrific only app.; Wildcat, JSA guest; Kubert Hawkman begins 35.00 100.00 210.00
25-27: 25-The Flash & Green Lantern start again. 27-Wildcat, JSA guest 30.00 85.00 180.00
28-30 25.00 75.00 160.00
31,32 25.00 75.00 160.00
33-Solomon Grundy, Hawkman, Doiby Dickles app. 45.00 125.00 260.00
34,35-Johnny Thunder cameo in both 25.00 75.00 160.00
36-Batman & Superman JSA guests 55.00 160.00 330.00
37-Johnny Thunder cameo; origin Injustice Society; last Kubert Hawkman 25.00 75.00 160.00
38-Black Canary begins; JSA Death issue 22.00 85.00 180.00
39,40: 39-Last Johnny Thunder 20.00 60.00 135.00
41-Black Canary joins JSA; Injustice Society app. 19.00 55.00 120.00
42-Atom & the Hawkman don new costume 19.00 55.00 120.00
43-49 19.00 55.00 120.00
50-Frazetta art, 3 pgs. 25.00 75.00 160.00
51-56 19.00 55.00 120.00
57-Kubert-a, 6 pgs. (Scarce) 25.00 75.00 160.00
58('76)-Flash, Hawkman, Dr. Mid-Nite, Wildcat, Dr. Fate, Green Lantern, Star Spangled Kid, Robin & Power Girl app. .30 .80 1.60
59-74 .30 .60

NOTE: *No Atom-27, 36; no Dr. Fate-13; no Flash-8, 9, 11-23; no Green Lantern-9, 18. no Johnny Thunder-5, 36; no Wonder Woman-9, 10, 23.* ***Buckler*** *c-63, 66.* ***Burnley*** *Starman-8-13.* ***Kubert*** *Hawkman-24-30, 33-37.* ***Moldoff*** *Hawkman-3-23.* ***Simon &Kirby*** *Sandman-14-17, 19.* ***Staton*** *a-66-74p; c-71-74.* ***Wood*** *a-58-65; c-63, 64.*

ALL-STAR SQUADRON
Sept, 1981 - Present
DC Comics

1-Original Atom, Hawkman, & Dr. Mid-Nite .45 .90
2-Robotman, Plastic Man, Hawkman, The Atom, Johnny Quick, & Liberty Belle; Kubert-c .45 .90
3,4 .30 .60

NOTE: ***Buckler*** *a(p)-1-4; c(p)-3,4.*

ALL-STAR STORY OF THE DODGERS, THE
April, 1979 (Full Color) ($1.00)
Stadium Communications

1 .50 1.00

ALL STAR WESTERN (All Star No. 1-57)
Apr-May, 1951 - No. 119, June-July, 1961
National Periodical Publications

58-Trigger Twins begin, end No. 116 6.00 18.00 36.00

ALL STAR WESTERN (continued)

	Good	Fine	Mint
59-66: 59-Bondage-c. 61-Toth-a, 2pgs.	3.00	9.00	18.00
67-Johnny Thunder begins; Gil Kane-a	4.00	11.00	22.00
68-80	2.00	5.00	10.00
81-98	1.50	4.50	9.00
99-Frazetta-a r-from Jimmy Wakely No. 4	4.00	11.00	22.00
100	3.00	8.00	12.00
101-107,109-116,118,119	1.50	4.50	9.00
108-Origin Johnny Thunder	2.50	7.00	14.00
117-Origin Super Chief	2.00	6.00	12.00

NOTE: ***Infantino*** *art in most issues. Madame app.-No. 117-119.*

ALL STAR WESTERN (Weird Western Tales No. 12 on)
Aug-Sept, 1970 - No. 11, Apr-May, 1972
National Periodical Publications

	Good	Fine	Mint
1-Reprints; Infantino-a	.35	1.00	2.00
2-Outlaw begins; El Diablo by Morrow begins	.30	.80	1.60
3-8: 3-Origin El Diablo. 5-Last Outlaw ish. 6-Billy the Kid begins, ends No. 8	.30	.80	1.60
9-Frazetta-a, 3pgs.(r)	.50	1.50	3.00
10-Jonah Hex begins	1.50	4.00	8.00
11	.50	1.50	3.00

NOTE: ***Adams*** *c-1-5;* ***Aparo*** *a-5.* ***Morrow*** *a-2-4, 10, 11. No. 7-11 have 52 pages.*

ALL SURPRISE
Fall, 1943 - No. 12, Winter, 1946-47
Timely/Marvel (CPC)

	Good	Fine	Mint
1-Super Rabbit & Gandy & Sourpuss	3.50	7.00	14.00
2-10,12	2.50	5.00	10.00
11-Kurtzman ''Pigtales'' art	6.00	12.00	24.00

ALL TEEN (Formerly All Winners; Teen No. 21 on)
No. 20, January, 1947
Marvel Comics (WFP)

	Good	Fine	Mint
20	2.00	4.00	8.00

ALL-TIME ROMANCE
1955
Ajax/Farrell Publications

	Good	Fine	Mint
22	1.25	2.50	5.00

ALL TIME SPORTS COMICS
Oct-Nov, 1948 - No. 7, Oct-Nov, 1949
Hillman Periodicals

	Good	Fine	Mint
1	2.50	5.00	10.00
2-7	1.75	3.50	7.00

ALL TOP
1944 (132 pages)
William H. Wise Co.

	Good	Fine	Mint
Capt. V, Merciless the Sorceress, Red Robbins, One Round Hogan, Mike the M.P., Snooky, Pussy Katnip app.	6.00	12.00	24.00

ALL TOP COMICS (My Experience No. 19 on)
1945 - No. 18, Mar, 1949; 1957 - 1959
Fox Features Synd./Green Publ./Norlen Mag.

	Good	Fine	Mint
1-Cosmo Cat & Flash Rabbit begin	3.50	7.00	14.00
2-7: 5-Drug mention story	2.00	4.00	8.00
8-Blue Beetle, Phantom Lady, & Rulah, Jungle Goddess begin (11/47); Kamen-c	40.00	95.00	185.00
9-Kamen-c	25.00	65.00	125.00
10-Kamen bondage-c	25.00	65.00	125.00
11-13	20.00	45.00	95.00
14-No Blue Beetle; used in **SOTI**, illo-''Corpses of colored people strung up by their wrists.''	25.00	65.00	125.00
15-17: 15-No Blue Beetle	20.00	45.00	95.00
18-Dagar, Jo-Jo app; no Phantom Lady or Blue Beetle	15.00	36.00	75.00
6(1957-Green Publ.)-Patoruzu the Indian; Cosmo Cat on cover only	.70	2.00	4.00
6(1958-Literary Ent.)-Muggy Doo; Cosmo Cat on cover only	.70	2.00	4.00
6(1959-Norlen)-Atomic Mouse; Cosmo Cat on cover only	.70	2.00	4.00
6(1959)-Little Eva	.70	2.00	4.00
6(Cornell)-Supermouse on cover, No. 6(Cornell)	.70	2.00	4.00

NOTE: *Jo-Jo by* ***Kamen****-12,18.*

ALL TRUE ALL PICTURE POLICE CASES
Oct, 1952 - No. 2, Nov, 1952 (100 pages)
St. John Publishing Co.

	Good	Fine	Mint
1-Three rebound St. John crime comics	10.00	30.00	60.00
2-Three comics rebound	8.00	24.00	48.00

NOTE: *Contents may vary.*

ALL-TRUE CRIME (. . . Cases No. 26-35; formerly Official True Crime Cases)
No. 26, Feb, 1948 - No. 52, Sept, 1952
Marvel/Atlas Comics(LMC/OCI No. 27/CFI No. 28,29)

	Good	Fine	Mint
26(No. 1)	2.50	7.50	15.00
27(4/48)-Electric chair cover	2.00	6.00	12.00
28-41,43-48,50-52	1.00	3.00	6.00
42-Krigstein-a	2.50	7.00	14.00
49-Used in **POP**, Pg. 79; Krigstein-a	3.00	9.00	18.00

NOTE: ***Robinson*** *a-47.*

ALL-TRUE DETECTIVE CASES (Kit Carson No. 5 on)
Feb-Mar, 1954 - No. 4, Aug-Sept, 1954
Avon Periodicals

	Good	Fine	Mint
1	6.00	18.00	36.00
2,3	3.00	9.00	18.00
4-Wood(?), Kamen-a	6.00	18.00	36.00
nn(100 pgs.)-7 pg. Kubert-a, Kinstler back-c	15.00	30.00	60.00

ALL TRUE ROMANCE (. . . Illustrated No. 3)
Mar, 1951 - No. 34, Mar, 1958; No. 4, Nov, 1957
Artful Publ. No. 1-3/Harwell(Comic Media)/Ajax-Farrell(Excellent Publ.)/Four Star Comic Corp.

	Good	Fine	Mint
1 (3/51)	4.00	12.00	24.00
2,3(12/51)-No. 5	3.00	8.00	16.00
6-Wood-a, 9 pgs. (exceptional)	6.00	18.00	36.00
7-10	2.00	6.00	12.00
11-13,15,17-20	1.50	4.00	8.00
14-Marijuana story	2.50	7.00	14.00
16-Heroin drug story	2.50	7.00	14.00
21-27,29-34	1.20	3.50	7.00
28-L. B. Cole, Disbrow-a	2.50	7.00	14.00
4(Farrell, 1957)	.50	1.50	3.00

ALL WESTERN WINNERS (Formerly All Winners; becomes Western Winners with No. 5)
No. 2, Winter, 1948-49 - No. 4, April, 1949
Marvel Comics(CDS)

	Good	Fine	Mint
2-Origin Black Rider, Kid Colt, & Two-Gun Kid	6.00	18.00	36.00
3,4	4.00	12.00	24.00

ALL WINNERS COMICS (All Teen No. 20; Official True Crime Cases No. 22 on; No. 1 advertised as All Aces)
Summer, 1941 - No. 19, Summer, 1946; No. 21, Winter, 1946-47 (no No. 20) (No. 21 continued from Young Allies No. 20)
Timely/Marvel Comics (USA, Young Allies, Inc.)

	Good	Fine	Mint
1-The Angel & Black Marvel only app.; Capt. America by Simon & Kirby, Human Torch & Sub-Mariner begin	200.00	600.00	1200.00
2-The Destroyer & The Whizzer begin; Simon & Kirby Captain America	80.00	240.00	500.00

All Star Western #80, © DC

All Top Comics #6, © FOX

All Winners Comics #1, © MCG

All Winners Comics #5, © MCG

All Your Comics, 1944, © FOX

Amazing Adventures V2#1, © MCG

ALL WINNERS COMICS (continued)

	Good	Fine	Mint
3,4	60.00	180.00	400.00
5,6: 6-The Black Avenger only app.; no Whizzer story	40.00	120.00	280.00
7-10	30.00	90.00	220.00
11-18: 12-Last Destroyer; no Whizzer story; no Human Torch No. 14-16	20.00	60.00	130.00
19-(Scarce)-1st app. & origin All Winners Squad	40.00	120.00	260.00
21-(Scarce)-All Winners Squad, Miss America app.	35.00	110.00	240.00

NOTE: ***Everett*** *Sub-Mariner-1, 3, 4;* ***Burgos*** *Torch-1, 3, 4.* ***Schomburg*** *c-12, 14.*

(2nd Series - August, 1948)
(Becomes All Western Winners with No. 2)

	Good	Fine	Mint
1-The Blonde Phantom, Capt. America, Human Torch, & Sub-Mariner app.	30.00	90.00	200.00

ALL YOUR COMICS
1944 (132 pages); Spring, 1946 (36 pages)
Fox Features Syndicate (R. W. Boight)

	Good	Fine	Mint
1-(1944)-The Puppeteer, Red Robbins, & Merciless app.	5.00	14.00	28.00
1-(1946)-Red Robbins, Merciless the Sorcerer app.	3.00	9.00	18.00

ALMANAC OF CRIME
1948 (148 pages)
Fox Features Syndicate

nn-Contain 4 rebound Fox titles. See Fox Giants. Contents can vary and determines price.

	Good	Fine	Mint
1	30.00	60.00	120.00

ALONG THE FIRING LINE WITH ROGER BEAN
1916 (Hardcover, B&W) (6x17'') (66 pages)
Chas. B. Jackson

	Good	Fine	Mint
3-by Chic Jackson (1915 daily strips)	5.00	15.00	30.00

AL OF FBI (See Little Al of the FBI)

ALPHONSE & GASTON & LEON
1903 (15x10'' Sunday strip reprints in color)
Hearst's New York American & Journal

	Good	Fine	Mint
by Fred Opper	17.00	50.00	100.00

ALVIN (TV) (See 4-Color Comics No. 1042)
Oct-Dec, 1962 - No. 28, Oct, 1973
Dell Publishing Co.

	Good	Fine	Mint
12-021-212	.50	1.50	3.00
2-28	.30	.80	1.60
Alvin For President (10/64)		.40	.80
. . . & His Pals in Merry Christmas with Clyde Crashcup & Leonardo 1(02-120-402)-12-2/64, reprinted in 1966 (12-023-604)	.30	.80	1.60

ALPHA AND OMEGA
1978 (49 cents)
Spire Christian Comics (Fleming H. Revell)

	Good	Fine	Mint
		.40	.80

AMAZING ADULT FANTASY (Amazing Adventures No. 1-6; Amazing Fantasy No. 15)
No. 7, Dec, 1961 - No. 14, July, 1962
Marvel Comics Group (AMI)

	Good	Fine	Mint
7	5.00	14.00	28.00
8-14: All Ditko-a	4.00	12.00	24.00

AMAZING ADVENTURE FUNNIES (Fantoman No. 2 on)
June, 1940 - No. 2, Sept. 1940
Centaur Publications

	Good	Fine	Mint
1-The Fantom of the Fair by Gustavson, The Arrow, Skyrocket Steele From the Year X by Everett - All reprints from Amazing Mystery Funnies & Funny Pages; Burgos-a	40.00	120.00	260.00
2-Reprints. This issue came out after Fantoman No. 2	25.00	70.00	150.00

Note: ***Burgos*** *a-1(2).* ***Everett*** *a-1(2).* ***Gustavson*** *a-1(5), 2.*

AMAZING ADVENTURES
1950 - No. 6, Fall, 1952
Ziff-Davis Publ. Co.

1950 (no month given) (8½x11'') (8 pgs.) Has the front & back cover plus Schomburg story used in Amazing Advs. No. 1 (possibly a pre-publication proof)

	Good	Fine	Mint
Estimated value. . . .			140.00
1-Wood, Schomburg, Anderson, Whitney-a	25.00	70.00	100.00
2-5-Anderson-a. 3-Starr-a	5.00	15.00	30.00
6-Krigstein-a	8.00	24.00	48.00

AMAZING ADVENTURES (Amazing Adult Fantasy No. 7)
June, 1961 - No. 6, Nov, 1961
Marvel Comics Group (AMI)

	Good	Fine	Mint
1-Origin Dr. Droom (1st Marvel-Age Superhero) by Kirby; Ditko & Kirby-a in all; Kirby c-1-6	9.00	25.00	50.00
2	5.00	14.00	28.00
3-6: Last Dr. Droom	3.50	10.00	20.00

AMAZING ADVENTURES
Aug, 1970 - No. 39, Nov, 1976
Marvel Comics Group

	Good	Fine	Mint
1-Inhumans by Kirby & Black Widow begin	.50	1.50	3.00
2-4: Last Kirby Inhumans	.35	1.00	2.00
5-8-Adams-a; 8-Last Black Widow	.70	2.00	4.00
9,10: 10-Last Inhumans (origin-r by Kirby)	.30	.80	1.60
11-new Beast begins(Origin), ends No.17; X-Men cameo	.35	1.00	2.00
12-14		.60	1.20
15-17-Starlin-c. 17-Starlin-a(p), 2pgs; origin Beast-r		.60	1.20
18-War of the Worlds begins; 1st app. Killraven; Adams-a	.60	1.80	3.60
19-26		.40	.80
27-Starlin-c		.50	1.00
28-39: 34-Death of Hawk		.30	.60

NOTE: ***Adams*** *c-6-8, a-18p.* ***Chaykin*** *a-18p, 19.* ***Ditko*** *a-24r, 27-37, 39.* ***Everett*** *inks-3-5, 9.* ***Ploog*** *a-12i.* ***Craig Russell*** *a-27-37, 39.*

AMAZING ADVENTURES
December, 1979 - No. 14, January, 1981
Marvel Comics Group

	Good	Fine	Mint
V2No.1: r-/X-Men No. 1,38; Kirby-a		.30	.60
2-14: 7,8-Origin Iceman		.30	.60

NOTE: ***Byrne*** *c-6p, 9p.* ***Kirby*** *a-6r, 9r, 10r; c-6, 7, 9.* ***Tuska*** *a-7-9.*

AMAZING ADVENTURES OF CAPTAIN CARVEL AND HIS CARVEL CRUSADERS, THE (See Carvel Comics)

AMAZING CHAN & THE CHAN CLAN, THE (TV)
May, 1973 - No. 4, Feb, 1974 (Hanna-Barbera)
Gold Key

	Good	Fine	Mint
1-4		.40	.80

AMAZING COMICS (Complete No. 2)
Fall, 1944
Timely Comics

	Good	Fine	Mint
1-The Destroyer, The Whizzer, The Young Allies, Sergeant Dix	40.00	90.00	200.00

AMAZING DETECTIVE CASES (Formerly Suspense No. 2?)
No. 3, Nov, 1950 - No. 14, Sept, 1952
Marvel/Atlas Comics (CCC)

	Good	Fine	Mint
3	2.00	5.00	10.00
4-6	1.50	4.00	8.00
7-11,14	1.00	3.00	6.00
12-Krigstein-a	2.50	7.00	14.00

AMAZING DETECTIVE CASES (continued) Good Fine Mint
13-Everett-a, 4 pgs. 2.00 5.00 10.00

AMAZING FANTASY (. . . Adult Fantasy No. 7-14; Amazing Adventures No. 1-6)
No. 15, Sept., 1962(on 1st pg.)
Marvel Comics Group (AMI)

15-Origin & 1st app. of Spider-Man by Ditko; Kirby/Ditko-c
170.00 500.00 1000.00

AMAZING GHOST STORIES (Formerly Nightmare)
No. 14, Oct, 1954 - No. 16, Feb, 1955
St. John Publishing Co.

14-Pit & the Pendulum story by Kinstler; Baker-c
5.00 14.00 28.00
15-Reprints Weird Thrillers No. 5; Baker-c, Powell-a
3.00 9.00 18.00
16-Kubert reprints of Weird Thrillers No. 4; Baker-c; Roussos, Tuska, Kinstler-a 4.00 11.00 22.00

AMAZING-MAN COMICS (Formerly Motion Pic. Funnies Wkly?)
No. 5, Sept, 1939 - No. 27, Feb, 1942
Centaur Publications

5(No.1)(Rare)-Origin A-Man the Amazing Man by Bill Everett; The Cat-Man by Tarpe Mills (also No. 8), Mighty Man, Minimidget & sidekick Ritty, & The Iron Skull by Burgos begins
120.00 360.00 800.00
6-Origin The Amazing Man retold; The Shark begins; Ivy Menace by Tarpe Mills app. 50.00 150.00 325.00
7-Magician From Mars begins; ends No.11 35.00 100.00 225.00
8-11: 11-Zardi, the Eternal Man begins; ends No. 16; Amazing Man dons costume; last Everett issue 24.00 70.00 160.00
12,13 20.00 60.00 130.00
14-Dr. Hypno begins; no Zardi or Magician From Mars; Reed Kincaid story 17.00 50.00 100.00
15-20 12.00 36.00 72.00
21-TNT Todd app. 12.00 36.00 72.00
22-Dash Darnell, the Human Meteor & The Voice app; last Iron Skull & Shark. 12.00 36.00 72.00
23-Intro. Tommy the Amazing Kid; The Marksman only app.
12.00 36.00 72.00
24,27: 24-King of Darkness, Nightshade, & Blue Lady begin; end No. 26 12.00 36.00 72.00
25,26 (Scarce)-Meteor Martin by Wolverton in both; 26-Electric Ray app. 40.00 120.00 250.00
NOTE: ***Everett** a-5-11; c-5-11. **Giunta** a-7-10. **Gustavson** a-6. **Simon** a-10.*

AMAZING MYSTERIES (Formerly Sub-Mariner No. 31)
No. 32, May, 1949 - No. 35, Jan, 1950
Marvel Comics (CCC)

32-The Witness app. 6.00 18.00 36.00
33-35 2.00 6.00 12.00

AMAZING MYSTERY FUNNIES
Aug, 1938 - V3No.8, Sept, 1940 (No. 24)
Centaur Publications

V1No.1-Everett-c(1st); Dick Kent Adv. story; Skyrocket Steele in the Year X on cover only 55.00 160.00 340.00
2-Everett 1st-a(Skyrocket Steele) 30.00 90.00 180.00
3 17.00 50.00 110.00
3(No. 4, 12/38)-nn on cover, No. 3 on inside
11.00 32.00 75.00
V2No.1-3 10.00 30.00 65.00
4-Dan Hastings begins; ends No. 5 10.00 30.00 65.00
5,6: Last Skyrocket Steele 10.00 30.00 65.00
7 (Rare)-Intro. The Fantom of the Fair; Everett, Gustavson, Burgos-a 60.00 180.00 380.00
8-Origin & 1st app. Speed Centaur 22.00 65.00 140.00
9-11: 11-Self portrait and biog. of Everett
11.00 32.00 75.00

Good Fine Mint
12 (Scarce)-Wolverton Space Patrol-a (12/39)
40.00 115.00 240.00
V3No.1(No. 17)-Intro. Bullet (1/40) 11.00 32.00 75.00
18,19,21-24-All have Space Patrol by Wolverton
27.00 80.00 170.00
20 10.00 30.00 65.00
Note: ***Burgos** a-V2No.3-9. **Eisner** a-V1No.2, 3. **Everett** a-V1No.2, 3, V2No.1-7; c-VlNo.1-4, V2No.1-6(most). **Guardineer** a-V2No.4. **Gustavson** a-V2No.4, 7, 12, 19, 20; c-V2No.7, 9, V3No.1. **McWilliams** a-V2No.9. **Tarpe Mills** a-V2No.4-6, 9-12, V3No.1. **Frank Thomas** c-V2No.11.*

AMAZING SAINTS
1974 (39 cents)
Logos International

True story of Phil Saint .20 .40

AMAZING SPIDER-MAN, THE (See All Detergent Comics, Amazing Fantasy, Aurora, Giant Comics to Color, Marvel Treasury Ed., Spectacular . . . , Spidey Super Stories, and Superman Vs. . . .)

AMAZING SPIDER-MAN, THE
March, 1963 - Present
Marvel Comics Group

1-Retells origin by Steve Ditko; F.F. x-over; intro. John Jameson & The Chameleon; Kirby-c 120.00 300.00 640.00
1-Reprint from the Golden Record Comic set .85 2.50 5.00
with record. . . . 1.00 3.00 6.00
2-Intro. the Vulture & The Terrible Tinkerer
42.00 125.00 250.00
3-Human Torch cameo; intro. & 1st app. Doc Octopus
22.00 65.00 140.00
4-Origin & 1st app. The Sandman; Intro. Betty Brant & Liz Allen
19.00 55.00 120.00
5,6: 5-Dr. Doom app. 6-1st app. Lizard 15.00 45.00 90.00
7-10: 8-Fantastic 4 app. 9-1st app. Electro (origin). 10-1st app. Big Man & Enforcers 11.00 32.00 70.00
11-13,15: 11-1st app. Bennett Brant. 13-1st app. Mysterio. 15-Intro. Kraven the Hunter 7.50 22.00 50.00
14-Intro. Green Goblin; Hulk x-over 10.00 28.00 60.00
16-19: 18-Fant.-4 app; 19-Intro. Ned Leeds 4.50 13.00 28.00
20-Intro & origin The Scorpion; 1st app. Spencer Smythe
5.00 15.00 32.00
21-30: 26-1st app. Crime Master. 28-Origin & 1st app. Molten Man
2.00 6.00 12.00
31-38: 31-Intro. Harry Osborn, Gwen Stacy & Prof. Warren. 36-1st app. Looter. 37-Intro. Norman Osborn. 38-Last Ditko issue
1.50 4.50 9.00
39,40-Green Goblin in both; origin No. 40 1.50 4.50 9.00
41-50: 42-1st app. Rhino & Mary Jane Watson. 46-Intro. Shocker. 50-Intro. Kingpin 1.20 3.50 7.00
51-60: 52-Intro. Joe Robertson. 56-Intro. Capt. George Stacy. 59-Intro. Brainwasher .90 2.60 5.20
61-80: 67-Intro. Randy Robertson. 73-Intro. Silvermane. 78-Intro. Prowler .70 2.00 4.00
81-89: 83-Intro. Schemer & Vanessa(Kingpin's wife).
.60 1.80 3.60
90-Death of Capt. Stacey .80 2.40 4.80
91-93,95,99: 93-Intro. Arthur Stacy .60 1.80 3.60
94-Origin retold .70 2.00 4.00
96-98-Drug books not approved by CCA 1.50 4.50 9.00
100-Anniversary issue 2.00 6.00 12.00
101-Intro. Morbius 1.20 3.50 7.00
102-Origin Morbius (52 pgs.) 1.20 3.50 7.00
103-112: 108-Intro. Sha-Shen. 110-Intro. Gibbon
.50 1.50 3.00
113,114-Starlin in part; 113-Intro. Hammerhead
.60 1.80 3.60
115-118 .50 1.50 3.00
119,120 .60 1.80 3.60
121-Death of Gwen Stacy (reprinted in Marvel Tales No. 98)

Amazing-Man Comics #24, © CEN

Amaz. Mystery Funnies #2, © CEN

Amazing Spider-Man #14, © MCG

Amazing Spider-Man #181, © MCG

American Air Forces #6, © WHW

America's Best Comics #24, © BP

AMAZING SPIDER-MAN (continued) **Good Fine Mint**

3.50 10.00 20.00

122-Death of Green Goblin 3.50 10.00 20.00

123-140: 124-Intro. Man Wolf, origin-No. 125. 129-1st app. The Punisher. 134-Intro. Tarantula. 139-Intro. Grizzly. 140-Intro. Glory Grant .35 1.00 2.00

141-160,163-170: 143-Intro. Cyclone. 167 1st app. Will O' The Wisp .30 .90 1.80

161,162-Nightcrawler app. from New X-Men. 161-Wolverine & Colossus cameo .50 1.50 3.00

171-181: 171-Nova app. 181-Origin retold; gives life history of Spider-Man .50 1.00

182-188: 187-Starlin-a .50 1.00

189,190-Byrne-a(p) .35 1.00 2.00

191-199,201,202,204,205,207-220: 194-1st Black Cat. .40 .80

200 .40 1.20 2.40

203-2nd Dazzler app. .40 1.20 2.40

206-Byrne-a(p) .25 .75 1.50

221-230: 226,227-Black Cat returns. 228-Juggernaut app. .30 .60

Annual 1 (1964)-Intro. Sinister Six 5.00 15.00 30.00

Annual 2 2.00 6.00 12.00

Special 3,4 1.20 3.50 7.00

Special 5-8 (12/71) .70 2.00 4.00

King Size 9 ('73)-Green Goblin app. .35 1.00 2.00

Annual 10(6/76)-Old Human Fly app. .35 1.00 2.00

Annual 11(9/77), 12(8/78) .30 .80 1.60

Annual 13(11/79)-Byrne-a .35 1.00 2.00

Annual 14(12/80): Miller a(p), 40pgs. .35 1.00 2.00

Annual 15(1981)-Miller c/a(p) .35 1.00 2.00

Giant-Size 1(7/74) .50 1.50 3.00

Giant-Size 2(10/74) .30 .80 1.60

Giant-Size 3(1/75), 4(4/75), 5(7/75), 6(9/75) .30 .80 1.60

Aim Toothpaste giveaway(36pgs., reg. size)-Green Goblin app. .50 1.50 3.00

Giveaway-Acme & Dingo Children's Boots(1980)-Spider-Man & Spider-Woman app. .50 1.00

Giveaway-Esquire & Eye Magazines(2/69)-Miniature-Still attached 2.00 5.00 10.00

. . . vs. the Prodigy Giveaway, 16 pgs. in color ('76)-5x6½''-Sex education; (1 million printed) 35 cents each .25 .50

NOTE: ***Austin** a-Annual No. 13i. **Byrne** a-189p, 190p, 206p, Annual 3r, 6r, 7r, 13p; Giant Size 1r, 3-5r; c-189. **Ditko** a-1-38, Annual 1, 2. **Kirby** a-8. **Miller** c-218. **Mooney** a-(i)-173, 189, 190, 193, 196-200. **Pollard** a-193-195p, 197p; c-187, 190. **Simonson** c-222. **Starlin** a-187p.*

AMAZING WILLIE MAYS, THE
No date (Aug, 1954?)
Famous Funnies Publ.

nn(Scarce) 17.00 50.00 100.00

AMBUSH (See 4-Color Comics No. 314)

AMERICA IN ACTION
1942; Winter, 1945 (36 pages)
Dell(Imp. Publ. Co.)/Mayflower House Publ.

1942-Dell-(68 pages) 3.50 10.00 20.00

1(1945)-Has 3 adaptations from American history; Kiefer, Schrotter & Webb-a 3.50 10.00 20.00

AMERICA MENACED!
1950 (Paper cover)
Vital Publications

Anti-communism
estimated value. . . . 250.00

AMERICAN COMICS
1940's
Theatre Giveaways (Liberty Theatre, Grand Rapids, Mich. known)

Many possible combinations. ''Golden Age'' superhero comics with new cover added and given away at theaters. Following known: Superman No. 59, Capt. Marvel No. 20, Capt. Marvel Jr. No. 5, Action No. 33, Whiz No. 39. Value would vary with book and should be 70-80 percent of the original.

AMERICAN AIR FORCES (See A-1 Comics)
1944 - 1945; 1951 - 1954
William H. Wise(Flying Cadet Publ. Co./Hasan(No.1)/Life's Romances/Magazine Ent. No. 5 on) **Good Fine Mint**

1-Article by Zack Mosley, creator of Smilin' Jack 3.00 8.00 16.00

2-4 1.50 4.50 9.00

NOTE: *All part comic, part magazine. Art by **Whitney, Chas. Quinlan, H. C. Kiefer,** and **Tony Dipreta.***

5(A-1 45),6(A-1 54),7(A-1 58),8(A-1 65),9(A-1 67),10(A-1 74), 11(A-1 79),12(A-1 91) 1.50 4.00 8.00

NOTE: ***Powell** a-5-12.*

AMERICAN GRAPHICS
No. 1, 1954; No. 2, 1957 (25 cents)
Henry Stewart

1-The Maid of the Mist, The Last of the Eries (Indian Legends of Niagara) (Sold at Niagara Falls) 2.00 5.00 10.00

2-Victory at Niagara & Laura Secord (Heroine of the War of 1812) 1.50 4.00 8.00

AMERICAN INDIAN, THE (See Picture Progress)

AMERICAN LIBRARY
1944 (68 pages) (15 cents, B&W, text & pictures)
David McKay Publications

3-6: 3-Look to the Mountain. 4-Case of the Crooked Candle (Perry Mason). 5-Duel in the Sun. 6-Wingate's Raiders 3.50 10.00 20.00

NOTE: *Also see Guadalcanal Diary & Thirty Seconds Over Tokyo (part of series?).*

AMERICA'S BEST COMICS
Feb, 1942 - No. 31, July, 1949
Nedor/Better/Standard Publications

1-The Woman in Red, Black Terror, Captain Future, Doc Strange, The Liberator, & Don Davis, Secret Ace begin 35.00 90.00 160.00

2-Origin The American Eagle; The Woman in Red ends 15.00 45.00 90.00

3-Pyroman begins 12.00 36.00 72.00

4 11.00 32.00 64.00

5-Last Captain Future-not in No. 4; Lone Eagle app. 9.00 26.00 52.00

6,7: 6-American Crusader app. 7.00 20.00 40.00

8-Last Liberator 5.50 16.00 32.00

9-The Fighting Yank begins; The Ghost app. 5.50 16.00 32.00

10-13,15-20: 10-Flag-c. 18-Bondage-c 5.00 14.00 28.00

14-Last American Eagle 5.00 14.00 28.00

21,24: 21-Infinity-c 4.00 12.00 24.00

22-Capt. Future app. 4.00 12.00 24.00

23-Miss Masque begins; last Doc Strange 6.00 18.00 36.00

25-Last Fighting Yank; Sea Eagle app. 5.50 16.00 32.00

26-The Phantom Detective & The Silver Knight app.; Frazetta text illo & some panels in Miss Masque 7.00 20.00 40.00

27,28-Commando Cubs app.; Doc Strange in No. 27; Tuska Bl. Terror No. 28 5.50 16.00 32.00

29-Last Pyroman 5.50 16.00 32.00

30,31 5.50 16.00 32.00

NOTE: *American Eagle not in 3, 8, 9, 13. Fighting Yank not in 10, 12. Liberator not in 2, 6, 7. Pyroman not in 9, 11, 14-16, 23, 25-27. **Schomburg (Xela)** c-12-14, 23-31.*

AMERICA'S BEST TV COMICS
1967 (Produced by Marvel Comics)
American Broadcasting Company

AMERICA'S BEST TV COMICS (continued)

	Good	Fine	Mint
1-Spider-Man, Fantastic Four, Casper, King Kong, George of the Jungle, Journey to the Center of the Earth app. (Promotes new TV cartoon show)	.85	2.50	5.00

AMERICA'S BIGGEST COMICS BOOK
1944 (196 pages) (One Shot)
Better Publications

	Good	Fine	Mint
1-The Grim Reaper, The Silver Knight, Zudo, the Jungle Boy, Commando Cubs, Thunderhoof app.	8.00	24.00	50.00

AMERICA'S FUNNIEST COMICS
1941 (80 pages) (15 cents)
William H. Wise

	Good	Fine	Mint
nn(No.1), 2	3.00	8.00	16.00

AMERICA'S GREATEST COMICS
1941 - No. 8, Summer, 1943 (100 pgs.) (Soft cardboard covers)
Fawcett Publications

	Good	Fine	Mint
1-Bulletman, Spy Smasher, Capt. Marvel, Minute Man & Mr. Scarlet begin; Mac Raboy-c	75.00	200.00	440.00
2	35.00	100.00	220.00
3	24.00	70.00	150.00
4-Commando Yank begins; Golden Arrow, Ibis the Invincible & Spy Smasher cameo in Captain Marvel	19.00	55.00	120.00
5	19.00	55.00	120.00
6	12.00	36.00	80.00
7-Balbo the Boy Magician app.; Captain Marvel, Bulletman cameo in Mr. Scarlet	12.00	36.00	80.00
8-Capt. Marvel Jr. & Golden Arrow app.; Spy Smasher x-over in Capt. Midnight; no Minute Man or Commando Yank	12.00	36.00	80.00

AMERICA'S SWEETHEART SUNNY (See Sunny)

ANARCHO DICTATOR OF DEATH (See Comics Novel)

ANCHORS ANDREWS (The Saltwater Daffy)
Jan, 1953 - No. 4, July, 1953 (Anchors the Saltwater. . . No. 4)
St. John Publishing Co.

	Good	Fine	Mint
1-Canteen Kate by Matt Baker, 9 pgs.	5.50	16.00	32.00
2-4	1.50	4.50	9.00

ANDY & WOODY (See March of Comics No. 40,55,76)

ANDY BURNETT (See 4-Color Comics No. 865)

ANDY COMICS (Formerly Scream Comics)
No. 20, June, 1948 - No. 21, Aug?, 1948
Current Publications

	Good	Fine	Mint
20,21-Archie-type comic	.85	2.50	5.00

ANDY DEVINE WESTERN
Dec, 1950 - 1952
Fawcett Publications

	Good	Fine	Mint
1	7.00	20.00	40.00
2-10	3.50	10.00	20.00

ANDY GRIFFITH (See 4-Color No. 1252,1341)

ANDY HARDY COMICS (See Movie Comics No. 3, Fiction House)
1952 - No. 6, Sept-Nov, 1954
Dell Publishing Co.

	Good	Fine	Mint
4-Color 389	1.00	3.00	6.00
4-Color 447,480,515	.70	2.00	4.00
5,6	.60	1.80	3.60
. . . & the New Automatic Gas Clothes Dryer ('52, 16 pgs., 5x7¼'') Bendix Giveaway	2.00	5.00	10.00

ANDY PANDA
1943 - Nov-Jan, 1962 (Walter Lantz)
Dell Publishing Co.

	Good	Fine	Mint
4-Color 25('43)	15.00	45.00	90.00
4-Color 54('44)	10.00	28.00	56.00
4-Color 85('45)	5.50	16.00	32.00
4-Color 130('46),154,198	3.00	8.00	16.00
4-Color 216,240,258,280,297	1.50	4.50	9.00
4-Color 326,345,358	1.00	3.00	6.00
4-Color 383,409	.70	2.00	4.00
16-30	.45	1.25	2.50
31-56	.35	1.00	2.00

(See March of Comics No. 5,22,79, & Super Book No. 4,15,27.)

ANDY PANDA
Aug, 1973 - No. 23, Jan, 1978 (Walter Lantz)
Gold Key

	Good	Fine	Mint
1-Reprints		.40	.80
2-10-All reprints		.20	.40
11-23: 15,17-19,22-Reprints		.15	.30

ANGEL
Aug, 1954 - No. 16, Nov-Jan, 1958-59
Dell Publishing Co.

	Good	Fine	Mint
4-Color 576(8/54)	.55	1.60	3.20
2(5-7/55) - 16	.35	1.00	2.00

ANGEL AND THE APE (Meet Angel No. 7) (See Limited Collector's Edition C-34 & Showcase No. 77)
Nov-Dec, 1968 - No. 6, Sept-Oct, 1969
National Periodical Publications

	Good	Fine	Mint
1-Not Wood-a	.25	.70	1.40
2-6-Wood-a in all	.30	.80	1.60

ANGELIC ANGELINA
1909 (11½x17''; 30 pgs.; 2 colors)
Cupples & Leon Company

	Good	Fine	Mint
By Munson Paddock	7.00	20.00	40.00

ANGEL OF LIGHT, THE (See The Crusaders)

ANIMAL ADVENTURES
Dec, 1953 - No. 3, Feb, 1954
Accepted Publications

	Good	Fine	Mint
1-3	.70	2.00	4.00

ANIMAL ANTICS (Movie Town. . . No. 24 on)
Mar-Apr, 1946 - No. 23, Nov-Dec, 1949
National Periodical Publications

	Good	Fine	Mint
1-Raccoon Kids begins	5.50	16.00	32.00
2-10	3.00	8.00	16.00
11-23: 14-Post-a	2.00	5.00	10.00

ANIMAL COMICS
1942 - No. 30, Dec-Jan, 1947-48
Dell Publishing Co.

	Good	Fine	Mint
1-1st Pogo app. by Walt Kelly (Dan Noonan art in most issues)	130.00	320.00	640.00
2-Uncle Wiggily begins	55.00	130.00	260.00
3,5	35.00	90.00	180.00
4,6,7-No Pogo	17.00	50.00	100.00
8-10	20.00	60.00	120.00
11-15	14.00	40.00	80.00
16-20	8.00	24.00	48.00
21-30: 25-30-''Jigger'' by John Stanley	6.00	18.00	36.00

NOTE: ***Dan Noonan*** *a-18-30.* ***Gollub*** *art in most later issues.*

ANIMAL CRACKERS (Also see Advs. of Patoruzu)
1946 - No. 31, July, 1950; 1959
Green Publ. Co./Norlen/Fox Feat.(Hero Books)

	Good	Fine	Mint
1-Super Cat begins	1.50	4.00	8.00
2-31	.70	2.00	4.00
31(Fox)-Formerly My Love Secret	.85	2.50	5.00
9(1959-Norlen)	.40	1.20	2.40
nn, no date, no publ.	.40	1.20	2.40

America's Best TV Comics #1, © MCG

Animal Adventures #2, © Accepted

Animal Comics #3, © DELL

Animal Fables #1, © WMG

Anthro #6, © DC

A-1 #21, © ME

ANIMAL FABLES
July-Aug, 1946 - No. 7, Nov-Dec, 1947
E. C. Comics

	Good	Fine	Mint
1	15.00	43.00	86.00
2-6	9.00	25.00	50.00
7-Origin Moon Girl	27.00	80.00	160.00

ANIMAL FAIR (Fawcett's . . .)
March, 1946 - No. 11, Feb, 1947
Fawcett Publications

	Good	Fine	Mint
1	2.50	7.00	14.00
2-6	1.20	3.50	7.00
7-11	1.00	3.00	6.00

ANIMAL FUN
1953
Premier Magazines

	Good	Fine	Mint
1-(3-D)	7.00	20.00	40.00

ANIMAL WORLD, THE (See 4-Color Comics No. 713)

ANIMATED COMICS
No date given (Summer, 1947?)
E. C. Comics

	Good	Fine	Mint
1 (Rare)	50.00	120.00	240.00

ANIMATED FUNNY COMIC TUNES (See Funny Tunes)

ANIMATED MOVIE-TUNES (Also see Movie Tunes)
Fall, 1945 - No. 2, 1945
Margood Publishing Co. (Timely)

	Good	Fine	Mint
1,2-Super Rabbit	2.00	5.00	10.00

ANNETTE (See 4-Color Comics No. 905)

ANNETTE'S LIFE STORY (See 4-Color No. 1100)

ANNIE OAKLEY
Spring, 1948 - No. 4, 11/48; No. 5, 6/55 - No. 11, 6/56
Marvel/Atlas Comics(MPI No. 1-4/CDS No. 5 on)

	Good	Fine	Mint
1 (1st Series)(1948)	7.00	20.00	40.00
2-Kurtzman-a	6.00	18.00	36.00
3,4	4.00	12.00	24.00
5 (2nd Series)(1955)	2.50	7.00	14.00
6-8: 8-Woodbridge-a	1.50	4.50	9.00
9-Williamson-a, 4 pgs.	3.00	8.00	16.00
10,11	1.20	3.50	7.00

ANNIE OAKLEY AND TAGG
1953 - 1965
Dell Publishing Co./Gold Key

	Good	Fine	Mint
4-Color 438	2.00	5.00	10.00
4-Color 481,575	1.50	4.00	8.00
4(7-9/55)-10	1.20	3.50	7.00
11-18(1-3/59): 13-Manning-a	1.00	3.00	6.00
1(7/65-Gold Key)-Photo-c	.40	1.20	2.40

ANOTHER WORLD (See Strange Stories From . . .)

ANTHRO (See Showcase)
July-Aug, 1968 - No. 6, July-Aug, 1969
National Periodical Publications

	Good	Fine	Mint
1-Howie Post-a in all	.40	1.20	2.40
2-6: 6-Wood inks		.50	1.00

ANTONY AND CLEOPATRA (See Ideal, a Classical Comic)

A-1 COMICS (A-1 appears on covers No. 1-17 only)(See individual title listings. 1st two issues not numbered.)
1944 - No. 139, Sept-Oct, 1955
Life's Romances Publ.-No. 1/Compix/Magazine Ent.

	Good	Fine	Mint
nn-Kerry Drake, Johnny Devildog, Rocky, Streamer Kelly	7.00	20.00	40.00
1-Dotty Dripple(1 pg.), Mr. Ex, Bush Berry, Rocky, Lew Loyal (20 pgs.)	1.20	3.50	7.00
2-8,10-Texas Slim & Dirty Dalton, The Corsair, Teddy Rich, Dotty Dripple, Inca Dinca, Tommy Tinker, Little Mexico & Tugboat Tim, The Masquerader & others	1.20	3.50	7.00
9-Texas Slim (all)	1.20	3.50	7.00
11,12-Teena	1.50	4.00	8.00
13-Guns of Fact & Fiction (1948). Used in **SOTI**, pg. 19; narcotics, junkie mentioned; Ingels & J. Craig-a	8.00	23.00	46.00
14-Tim Holt Western Adventures No. 1 (1948)	15.00	45.00	90.00
15-Teena	1.50	4.00	8.00
16-Vacation Comics	.85	2.50	5.00
17-Tim Holt No. 2. Last issue to carry A-1 on cover	10.00	27.00	54.00
18-Jimmy Durante	6.00	18.00	36.00
19-Tim Holt No. 3	6.00	18.00	36.00
20-Jimmy Durante	5.00	14.00	28.00
21-Joan of Arc(1949)-Whitney-a	6.00	18.00	36.00
22-Dick Powell(1949)	4.00	11.00	22.00
23-Cowboys 'N' Indians No. 6	.85	2.50	5.00
24-Trail Colt No. 1-Frazetta, r-in Manhunt No. 13; Ingels-c; L. B. Cole-a	17.00	50.00	100.00
25-Fibber McGee & Molly(1949)	1.50	4.50	9.00
26-Trail Colt No. 2-Ingels-c	10.00	30.00	60.00
27-Ghost Rider No. 1(1950)-Origin Ghost Rider	20.00	55.00	110.00
28-Christmas-(Koko & Kola No. 6)(5/47)	.85	2.50	5.00
29-Ghost Rider No. 2-Frazetta-c (1950)	20.00	55.00	110.00
30-Jet No. 1-Powell-a	8.00	24.00	48.00
31-Ghost Rider No. 3-Frazetta-c & origin (1951)	20.00	55.00	110.00
32-Jet Powers No. 2	6.00	18.00	36.00
33-Muggsy Mouse No. 1(1951)	.70	2.00	4.00
34-Ghost Rider No. 4-Frazetta-c (1951)	20.00	55.00	110.00
35-Jet Powers No. 3-Williamson/Evans-a	15.00	45.00	90.00
36-Muggsy Mouse No. 2	.70	2.00	4.00
37-Ghost Rider No. 5-Frazetta-c (1951)	20.00	55.00	110.00
38-Jet Powers No. 4-Williamson & Wood-a	15.00	45.00	90.00
39-Muggsy Mouse No. 3	.70	2.00	4.00
40-Dogface Dooley No. 1('51)	.85	2.50	5.00
41-Cowboys 'N' Indians No. 7	.85	2.50	5.00
42-Best of the West No. 1	10.00	30.00	60.00
43-Dogface Dooley No. 2	.85	2.50	5.00
44-Ghost Rider No. 6	6.00	18.00	36.00
45-American Air Forces No. 5	1.50	4.50	9.00
46-Best of the West No. 2	4.00	12.00	24.00
47-Thun'da, King of the Congo No. 1-Frazetta-c/a('52)	150.00	400.00	800.00
48-Cowboys 'N' Indians No. 8	.85	2.50	5.00
49-Dogface Dooley No. 3	.85	2.50	5.00
50-Danger Is Their Business No. 11 (1952)	2.50	7.00	14.00
51-Ghost Rider No. 7 ('52)	6.00	18.00	36.00
52-Best of the West No. 3	4.00	12.00	24.00
53-Dogface Dooley No. 4	.85	2.50	5.00
54-American Air Forces No. 6(8/52)	1.50	4.50	9.00
55-U.S. Marines No. 5-Powell-a	2.00	6.00	12.00
56-Thun'da No. 2	12.00	32.00	64.00
57-Ghost Rider No. 8	5.00	14.00	28.00
58-American Air Forces No. 7	1.50	4.50	9.00
59-Best of the West No. 4	4.00	12.00	24.00
60-The U.S. Marines No. 6	2.00	6.00	12.00
61-Space Ace No. 5(1953)-Guardineer-a	7.00	20.00	40.00
62-Starr Flagg, Undercover Girl No. 5	10.00	30.00	60.00
63-Manhunt No. 13-Frazetta reprinted from A-1 No. 24	12.00	35.00	70.00
64-Dogface Dooley No. 5	.85	2.50	5.00
65-American Air Forces No. 8	1.50	4.50	9.00
66-Best of the West No. 5	4.00	12.00	24.00
67-American Air Forces No. 9	1.50	4.50	9.00
68-U.S. Marines No. 7	2.00	6.00	12.00
69-Ghost Rider No. 9(10/52)	5.00	14.00	28.00
70-Best of the West No. 6	2.50	7.00	14.00

A-1 COMICS (continued)

	Good	Fine	Mint
71-Ghost Rider No. 10(12/52)	5.00	14.00	28.00
72-U.S. Marines No. 8	2.00	6.00	12.00
73-Thun'da No. 3	9.00	25.00	50.00
74-American Air Forces No. 10	1.50	4.50	9.00
75-Ghost Rider No. 11(3/52)	4.00	12.00	24.00
76-Best of the West No. 7	2.50	7.00	14.00
77-Manhunt No. 14 (classic cover)	7.00	20.00	40.00
78-Thun'da No. 4	9.00	25.00	50.00
79-American Air Forces No. 11	1.50	4.50	9.00
80-Ghost Rider No. 12(6/52)	4.00	12.00	24.00
81-Best of the West No. 8	2.50	7.00	14.00
82-Cave Girl No. 11(1953)-Powell-a; origin	14.00	40.00	80.00
83-Thun'da No. 5	7.00	20.00	40.00
84-Ghost Rider No. 13(8/53)	4.00	12.00	24.00
85-Best of the West No. 9	2.50	7.00	14.00
86-Thun'da No. 6	7.00	20.00	40.00
87-Best of the West No. 10	2.50	7.00	14.00
88-Bobby Benson's B-Bar-B Riders No. 20	2.00	6.00	12.00
89-Home Run No. 3-Powell-a	2.00	5.00	10.00
90-Red Hawk No. 11(1953)-Powell-a	2.00	5.00	10.00
91-American Air Forces No. 12	1.50	4.50	9.00
92-Dream Book of Romance No. 5-photo-c; Guardineer-a	2.00	5.00	10.00
93-Great Western No. 8('54)-Origin The Ghost Rider	5.00	14.00	28.00
94-White Indian No. 11-Frazetta-a(r)	17.00	50.00	100.00
95-Muggsy Mouse No. 4	.70	2.00	4.00
96-Cave Girl No. 12, with Thun'da; Powell-a	10.00	28.00	56.00
97-Best of the West No. 11	2.50	7.00	14.00
98-Undercover Girl No. 6	9.00	25.00	50.00
99-Muggsy Mouse No. 5	.70	2.00	4.00
100-Badmen of the West No. 1-Meskin-a(?)	5.00	15.00	30.00
101-White Indian No. 12-Frazetta-a(r)	17.00	50.00	100.00
102-Dream Book of Romance No. 6	1.50	4.50	9.00
103-Best of the West No. 12	2.50	7.00	14.00
104-White Indian No. 13-Frazetta-a(r) ('54)	17.00	50.00	100.00
105-Great Western No. 9-Ghost Rider app.; Powell-a, 6 pgs.; Bolle-c	2.00	6.00	12.00
106-Dream Book of Love No. 1-Powell, Bolle-a	2.50	7.00	14.00
107-Hot Dog No. 1	.70	2.00	4.00
108-Red Fox No. 15 (1954)	5.00	15.00	30.00
109-Dream Book of Romance No. 7 (7-8/54)	1.50	4.50	9.00
110-Dream Book of Romance No. 8	1.50	4.50	9.00
111-I'm a Cop No. 1 ('54); drug mention story	3.50	10.00	20.00
112-Ghost Rider No. 14 ('54)	4.00	12.00	24.00
113-Great Western No. 10	2.00	6.00	12.00
114-Dream Book of Love No. 2-Guardineer, Bolle-a	2.00	5.00	10.00
115-Hot Dog No. 3	.70	2.00	4.00
116-Cave Girl No. 13	10.00	28.00	56.00
117-White Indian No. 14	5.00	15.00	30.00
118-Undercover Girl No. 7	9.00	25.00	50.00
119-Straight Arrow's Fury No. 1	3.00	8.00	16.00
120-Badmen of the West No. 2	3.00	9.00	18.00
121-Mysteries of Scotland Yard No. 1; r-from Manhunt	3.50	10.00	20.00
122-Black Phantom No. 1(11/54)	8.00	24.00	48.00
123-Dream Book of Love No. 3(10-11/54)	1.50	4.50	9.00
124-Dream Book of Romance No. 8(10-11/54)	1.50	4.50	9.00
125-Cave Girl No. 14	10.00	28.00	56.00
126-I'm a Cop No. 2-Powell-a	1.50	4.50	9.00
127-Great Western No. 11('54)	2.00	6.00	12.00
128-I'm a Cop No. 3-Powell-a	1.50	4.50	9.00
129-The Avenger No. 1('55)	8.00	23.00	46.00
130-Strongman No. 1	5.00	15.00	30.00
131-The Avenger No. 2('55)	4.00	12.00	24.00
132-Strongman No. 2	4.00	12.00	24.00
133-The Avenger No. 3	4.00	12.00	24.00
134-Strongman No. 3	4.00	12.00	24.00
135-White Indian No. 15	5.00	15.00	30.00
136-Hot Dog No. 4	.70	2.00	4.00
137-Africa No. 1	7.00	20.00	40.00
138-The Avenger No. 4	4.00	12.00	24.00
139-Strongman No. 4-Powell-a	4.00	12.00	24.00

NOTE: ***Bolle** a-110. Photo-c-110.*

APACHE
1951
Fiction House Magazines

	Good	Fine	Mint
1-Baker-c	3.50	10.00	20.00
I.W. Reprint No. 1	.70	2.00	4.00

APACHE HUNTER
1954 (18 pgs. in color) (promo copy) (saddle stitched)
Creative Pictorials

	Good	Fine	Mint
Severin; Heath stories	15.00	45.00	90.00

APACHE KID (Formerly Reno Browne; Western Gunfighters No. 20 on)(Also see Two-Gun Western)
No. 53, 12/50 - No. 10, 1/52; No. 11, 12/54 - No. 19, 4/56
Marvel/Atlas Comics(MPC No. 53-10/CPS No. 11 on)

	Good	Fine	Mint
53(No.1)	2.50	7.50	15.00
2-5	1.50	4.00	8.00
6-10 (1951-52)	1.20	3.50	7.00
11-19 (1954-56)	.85	2.50	5.00

Note: ***Heath** c-11. **Maneely** c-15.*

APACHE MASSACRE (See Chief Victorio's. . .)

APACHE TRAIL
Sept, 1957 - No. 4, June, 1958
Steinway/America's Best

	Good	Fine	Mint
1	1.50	4.00	8.00
2-4: 2-Tuska-a	.70	2.00	4.00

APPROVED COMICS
March, 1954 - No. 12, Aug, 1954 (All painted-c)(no c-price)
St. John Publishing Co.

	Good	Fine	Mint
1-The Hawk No. 5-r	2.00	6.00	12.00
2-Invisible Boy-r(3/54)-Origin; Saunders-c	3.00	8.00	16.00
3-Wild Boy of the Congo No. 11-r(4/54); bondage-c	2.00	6.00	12.00
4-Kid Cowboy-r	2.00	6.00	12.00
5-Fly Boy-r	2.00	6.00	12.00
6-Daring Adv.-r(5/54); Krigstein-a(2); Baker-c	3.00	8.00	16.00
7-The Hawk No. 6-r	2.00	6.00	12.00
8-Crime on the Run; Powell-a	1.50	4.50	9.00
9-Western Bandit Trails No. 3-r, with new-c; Baker c/a	3.00	9.00	18.00
11-Fightin' Marines-r; Kanteen Kate app; Baker-c/a	3.00	9.00	18.00
12-Northwest Mounties No. 4-r(8/54); new Baker-c; drug mention	3.00	9.00	18.00

AQUAMAN (See Showcase, Brave & the Bold, Super DC Giant, Adventure, DC Super-Stars No. 7, Detective, DC Comics Presents No. 5, DC Special Series No. 1, DC Special No. 28, and World's Finest)

AQUAMAN
Jan-Feb, 1962 - No. 56, Mar-Apr, 1971; No. 57, Aug-Sept, 1977 - No. 63, Aug-Sept, 1978
National Periodical Publications/DC Comics

	Good	Fine	Mint
1-Intro. Quisp	7.00	20.00	40.00
2,3	3.50	10.00	20.00
4-10	1.50	4.50	9.00
11-20: 11-Intro. Mera. 18-Aquaman weds Mera	.70	2.00	4.00

A-1 #111, © ME

Approved Comics #6, © STJ

Aquaman #4, © DC

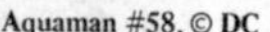
Aquaman #58, © DC

Arak #1, © DC

Archie Comics #85, © AP

AQUAMAN (continued)

	Good	Fine	Mint
21-30: 23-Birth of Aquababy. 29-Intro. Ocean Master, Aquaman's step-brother	.50	1.40	2.80
31,32,34-40	.35	1.00	2.00
33-Intro. Aqua-Girl	.40	1.20	2.40
41-47,49	.30	.90	1.80
48-Origin reprinted	.35	1.00	2.00
50-52-Adams Deadman	2.00	5.00	10.00
53-56('71): 56-Intro Crusader		.50	1.00
57('77),59,60-63		.30	.60
58-Origin retold		.40	.80

NOTE: ***Aparo*** *a-40-59; c-57-60, 63.* ***Newton*** *a-60-63.*

AQUANAUTS (See 4-Color No. 1197)

ARAK/SON OF THUNDER
Sept, 1981 - Present
DC Comics

	Good	Fine	Mint
1-4		.30	.60

ARCHIE AND ME
Oct, 1964 - Present
Archie Publications

	Good	Fine	Mint
1	3.50	10.00	20.00
2-5	1.50	4.00	8.00
6-10	.85	2.50	5.00
11-30	.45	1.40	2.80
31-42		.50	1.00
43-63-(All Giants)		.40	.80
64-124-(Regular size)		.30	.60

ARCHIE AND MR. WEATHERBEE
1980 (59¢)
Spire Christian Comics (Fleming H. Revell Co.)

	Good	Fine	Mint
nn		.40	.80

ARCHIE...ARCHIE ANDREWS, WHERE ARE YOU?
Feb, 1977 - Present (Digest size, 160 pages)
Archie Publications

	Good	Fine	Mint
1	.30	.80	1.60
2,3,5,7-9-Adams-a; 8-Reprints origin The Fly by S&K. 9-Superhero reprint	.35	1.00	2.00
4,6		.50	1.00
10-20		.50	1.00

ARCHIE AS PUREHEART THE POWERFUL (...As Capt. Pureheart No. 4-6)
Sept, 1966 - No. 6, Nov, 1967
Archie Publications (Radio Comics)

	Good	Fine	Mint
1	1.50	4.00	8.00
2-6	.70	2.00	4.00

NOTE: *Evilheart cameos in all. Title: ...As Capt. Pureheart the Powerful-No. 4,6; ...As Capt. Pureheart-No. 5.*

ARCHIE AT RIVERDALE HIGH
Aug, 1972 - Present
Archie Publications

	Good	Fine	Mint
1	.85	2.50	5.00
2-10	.30	.80	1.60
11-30		.40	.80
31-78		.30	.60

ARCHIE COMICS (Archie No. 177 on)(See Everything's..., Jackpot, Oxydol-Dreft, and Pep)(First Teen-age comic)
Winter, 1942-43 - Present
MLJ Magazines/Archie Publications No. 20 on

	Good	Fine	Mint
1-Veronica app.	150.00	400.00	800.00
2	55.00	150.00	250.00
3	35.00	100.00	180.00
4,5	20.00	60.00	100.00
6-10	17.00	50.00	90.00
11-20	10.00	30.00	50.00
21-30	7.00	20.00	36.00
31-40	3.50	10.00	20.00
41-50	2.50	7.00	14.00
51-70: 69-Katy Keene story	2.00	5.00	10.00
71-100	1.20	3.50	7.00
101-130	.70	2.00	4.00
131-200	.40	1.20	2.40
201-240		.40	.80
241-282		.30	.60
283-Cover/story plugs "International Children's Appeal" which was a fraudulent charity, according to TV's 20/20 news program broadcast July 20, 1979.		.50	1.00
284-299,301-310		.25	.50
300-Anniversary issue		.30	.60
Annual 1('50)-116 pgs. (Rare)	25.00	75.00	150.00
Annual 2('51)	10.00	30.00	60.00
Annual 3-5(1952-54)	6.00	18.00	36.00
Annual 6-10(1955-59)	3.00	9.00	18.00
Annual 11-15(1960-65)	1.50	4.50	9.00
Annual 16-26(1966-75)	.70	2.00	4.00
Annual 27	.25	.70	1.40
Annual Digest 27('75)-36(4/80): 29-196 pgs., rest are 160 pgs.	.35	1.00	2.00
...All-Star Specials(Winter '75)-$1.25; 6 remaindered Archie comics rebound in each; titles: "The World of Giant Comics," "Giant Grab Bag of Comics," "Triple Giant Comics," and "Giant Spec. Comics"	.50	1.50	3.00
Mini-Comics (1970-Fairmont Potato Chips Giveaway-Miniature)(8 issues-nn's., 8 pgs. each)	1.00	3.00	6.00
Official Boy Scout Outfitter(1946)-9½x6½", 16 pgs., B. R. Baker Co.	5.50	16.00	32.00

ARCHIE COMICS DIGEST
Aug, 1973 - Present (Small size, 160 pages)
Archie Publications

	Good	Fine	Mint
1	.85	2.50	5.00
2-10	.35	1.00	2.00
11-31		.40	.80
32-The Fly reprint by S&K		.45	.90
33-45: 36-Katy Keene story		.30	.60

NOTE: ***Adams*** *a-1,2,4,5,19-21,24,25,27,29,31,33.*

ARCHIE GETS A JOB
1977
Spire Christian Comics (Fleming H. Revell Co.)

	Good	Fine	Mint
		.40	.80

ARCHIE GIANT SERIES MAGAZINE
1954 - Present (No No. 36-135, no No. 252-451)
Archie Publications

	Good	Fine	Mint
1-Archie's Christmas Stocking	11.00	32.00	64.00
2,3-Archie's Christmas Stocking	5.00	15.00	30.00
4-6-Archie's Christmas Stocking	4.00	12.00	24.00
7-Katy Keene Holiday Fun(9/60)	4.00	12.00	24.00
8-Betty & Veronica Summer Fun ('60)			
9-The World of Jughead (12/60)			
10-Archie's Christmas Stocking (1/61)			
11-Betty & Veronica Spectacular (6/61)			
12-Katy Keene Holiday Fun (9/61)			
13-Betty & Veronica Summer Fun (10/61)			
14-The World of Jughead (12/61) each....	2.50	7.50	15.00
15-Archie's Christmas Stocking (1/62)			
16-Betty & Veronica Spectacular (6/62)			
17-Archie's Jokes (9/62)			
18-Betty & Veronica Summer Fun (10/62)			
19-The World of Jughead (12/62)			
20-Archie's Christmas Stocking (1/63) each....	2.00	6.00	12.00
21-Betty & Veronica Spectacular (6/63)			
22-Archie's Jokes (9/63)			
23-Betty & Veronica Summer Fun (10/63)			

ARCHIE GIANT SERIES MAG. (continued)
24-The World of Jughead (12/63)
25-Archie's Christmas Stocking (1/64)
26-Betty & Veronica Spectacular (6/64)
27-Archie's Jokes (8/64)
28-Betty & Veronica Summer Fun (9/64)
29-Around the World with Archie (10/64)
30-The World of Jughead (12/64)
31-Archie's Christmas Stocking (1/65)
32-Betty & Veronica Spectacular (6/65)
33-Archie's Jokes
34-Betty & Veronica Summer Fun (9/65)
35-Around the World with Archie (10/65) — **Good** **Fine** **Mint**
each.... 2.00 5.00 10.00
136-The World of Jughead (12/65)
137-Archie's Christmas Stocking (1/66)
138-Betty & Veronica Spectacular (6/66)
139-Archie's Jokes (6/66)
140-Betty & Veronica Summer Fun (8/66)
141-Around the World with Archie (9/66)
each.... 1.00 3.00 6.00
142-Archie's Super-Hero Special - Origin Capt. Pureheart, Capt. Hero, and Evilheart 1.50 4.00 8.00
143-The World of Jughead (12/66)
144-Archie's Christmas Stocking (1/67)
145-Betty & Veronica Spectacular (6/67)
146-Archie's Jokes (6/67)
147-Betty & Veronica Summer Fun (8/67)
148-World of Archie (9/67)
149-World of Jughead (10/67)
150-Archie's Christmas Stocking (1/68)
151-World of Archie (2/68)
152-World of Jughead (2/68)
153-Betty & Veronica Spectacular (6/68)
154-Archie Jokes (6/68)
155-Betty & Veronica Summer Fun (8/68)
156-World of Archie (10/68)
157-World of Jughead (12/68)
158-Archie's Christmas Stocking (1/69)
159-Betty & Veronica Christmas Spect. (1/69)
160-World of Archie (2/69)
each.... .80 2.40 4.80
161-World of Jughead (2/69)
162-Betty & Veronica Spectacular (6/69)
163-Archie's Jokes (8/69)
164-Betty & Veronica Summer Fun (9/69)
165-World of Archie (9/69)
166-World of Jughead (9/69)
167-Archie's Christmas Stocking (1/70)
168-Betty & Veronica Christmas Spect. (1/70)
169-Archie's Christmas Love-In (1/70)
170-Jughead's Eat-Out Comic Book Mag. (12/69)
171-World of Archie (2/70)
172-World of Jughead (2/70)
173-Betty & Veronica Spectacular (6/70)
174-Archie's Jokes (8/70)
175-Betty & Veronica Summer Fun (9/70)
176-Li'l Jinx Giant Laugh-Out (8/70)
177-World of Archie (9/70)
178-World of Jughead (9/70)
179-Archie's Christmas Stocking (1/71)
180-Betty & Veronica Christmas Spect. (1/71)
181-Archie's Christmas Love-In (1/71)
182-World of Archie (2/71)
183-World of Jughead (2/71)
184-Betty & Veronica Spectacular (6/71)
185-Li'l Jinx Giant Laugh-Out (6/71)
186-Archie's Jokes (8/71)
187-Betty & Veronica Summer Fun (9/71)
188-World of Archie (9/71)
189-World of Jughead (9/71)
190-Archie's Christmas Stocking (12/71)
191-Betty & Veronica Christmas Spect. (2/72)
192-Archie's Christmas Love-In (1/72)
193-World of Archie (3/72)
194-World of Jughead (4/72)
195-Li'l Jinx Christmas Bag (1/72)
196-Sabrina's Christmas Magic (1/72)
197-Betty & Veronica Spectacular (6/72)
198-Archie's Jokes (8/72)
199-Betty & Veronica Summer Fun
200-World of Archie (10/72)
each.... .40 1.20 2.40
201-Betty & Veronica Spectacular (10/72)
202-World of Jughead (11/72)
203-Archie's Christmas Stocking (12/72)
204-Betty & Veronica Christmas Spect. (2/73)
205-Archie's Christmas Love-In (1/73)
206-Li'l Jinx Christmas Bag (12/72)
207-Sabrina's Christmas Magic (12/72)
208-World of Archie (3/73)
209-World of Jughead (4/73)
210-Betty & Veronica Spectacular (6/73)
211-Archie's Jokes (8/73)
212-Betty & Veronica Summer Fun (9/73)
213-World of Archie (10/73)
214-Betty & Veronica Spectacular
215-World of Jughead
216-Archie's Christmas Stocking (12/73)
217-Betty & Veronica Christmas Spect. (2/74)
218-Archie's Christmas Love-In (1/74)
219-Li'l Jinx Christmas Bag (12/73)
220-Sabrina's Christmas Magic (12/73)
221-Betty & Veronica Spectacular (Advertised as World of Archie) (6/74)
222-Archie's Jokes (Advertised as World of Jughead)(8/74)
223-Li'l Jinx (8/74)
224-Betty & Veronica Summer Fun (9/74)
225-World of Archie (9/74)
226-Betty & Veronica Spectacular (10/74)
227-World of Jughead (10/74)
228-Archie's Christmas Stocking (12/74)
229-Betty & Veronica Christmas Spect. (12/74)
230-Archie's Christmas Love-In (11/74)
231-Sabrina's Christmas Magic (1/75)
232-World of Archie (3/75)
233-World of Jughead (4/75)
234-Betty & Veronica Spectacular (6/75)
235-Archie's Jokes (8/75)
236-Betty & Veronica Summer Fun (9/75)
237-World of Archie (9/75)
238-Betty & Veronica Spectacular (10/75)
239-World of Jughead (10/75)
240-Archie's Christmas Stocking (12/75)
241-Betty & Veronica Christmas Spectacular (12/75)
242-Archie's Christmas Love-In (1/76)
243-Sabrina's Christmas Magic (1/76)
244-World of Archie (3/76)
245-World of Jughead (4/76)
246-Betty & Veronica Spectacular (6/76)
247-Archie's Jokes (8/76)
248-Betty & Veronica Summer Fun (9/76)
249-World of Archie (9/76)
250-Betty & Veronica Spectacular (10/76)
251-World of Jughead (10/76) — **Good** **Fine** **Mint**
each.... .40 .80
452-Archie's Christmas Stocking (12/76)
453-Betty & Veronica Christmas Spect. (12/76)
454-Archie's Christmas Love-In (1/77)
455-Sabrina's Christmas Magic (1/77)
456-World of Archie (3/77)
457-World of Jughead (4/77)
458-Betty & Veronica Spectacular (6/77)
459-Archie's Jokes (8/77)-Shows 8/76 in error
460-Betty & Veronica Summer Fun (9/77)
461-World of Archie (9/77)
462-Betty & Veronica Spectacular (10/77)
463-World of Jughead (10/77)
464-Archie's Christmas Stocking (12/77)
465-Betty & Veronica Christmas Spectacular (12/77)
466-Archie's Christmas Love-In (1/78)
467-Sabrina's Christmas Magic (1/78)
468-World of Archie (2/78)
469-World of Jughead (2/78)
470-Betty & Veronica Spectacular (6/78)
471-Archie's Jokes (8/78)
472-Betty & Veronica Summer Fun (9/78)
473-World of Archie (9/78)
474-Betty & Veronica Spectacular (10/78)
475-World of Jughead (10/78)
476-Archie's Christmas Stocking (12/78)
477-Betty & Veronica Christmas Spectacular (12/78)
478-Archie's Christmas Love-In (1/79)
479-Sabrina Christmas Magic (1/79)
480-The World of Archie (3/79)
481-World of Jughead (4/79)
482-Betty & Veronica Spectacular (6/79)
483-Archie's Jokes (8/79)
484-Betty & Veronica Summer Fun (9/79)
485-The World of Archie (9/79)
486-Betty & Veronica Spectacular (10/79)
487-The World of Jughead (10/79)
488-Archie's Christmas Stocking (1/80)
489-Betty & Veronica Christmas Spect. (1/80)
490-Archie's Christmas Love-in (1/80)
491-Sabrina's Christmas Magic (1/80)
492-The World of Archie (2/80)
493-The World of Jughead (2/80)
494-Betty & Veronica Spectacular (6/80)
495-Archie's Jokes (8/80)
496-Betty & Veronica Summer Fun (9/80)
497-The World of Archie (9/80)
498-Betty & Veronica Spectacular (10/80)
499-The World of Jughead (10/80)
500-Archie's Christmas Stocking (12/80)
501-Betty & Veronica Christmas Spect. (12/80)
502-Archie's Christmas Love-in (1/81)
503-Sabrina Christmas Magic (1/81)
504-The World of Archie (3/81)

Archie's Girls, Betty & Veronica #49, © AP

Archie's Joke Book Mag. #24, © AP

Archie's Pal Jughead #2, © AP

ARCHIE GIANT SERIES MAG. (continued)
505-The World of Jughead (4/81)
506-Betty & Veronica Spectacular (6/81)
507-Archie's Jokes (8/81)
508-Betty & Veronica Summer Fun (9/81)
509-The World of Archie (9/81)
510-Betty & Vernonica Spectacular (9/81)

	Good	Fine	Mint
511-The World of Jughead (10/81) each....		.30	.60

ARCHIE'S CAR
1979 (49¢)
Spire Christian Comics (Fleming H. Revell Co.)

	Good	Fine	Mint
nn		.40	.80

ARCHIE'S CHRISTMAS LOVE-IN (See Archie Giant Series Mag. No. 169,181,192,205,218,230,242,454,466,478,490,502)

ARCHIE'S CHRISTMAS STOCKING (See Archie Giant Series Mag. No. 10,15,20,25,31,137,144,150,158,167,179,190,203,216,228,240, 452,464,476,488,500)

ARCHIE'S CLEAN SLATE
1973 (35-49 cents)
Spire Christian Comics (Fleming H. Revell Co.)

	Good	Fine	Mint
1		.50	1.00

ARCHIE'S FAMILY ALBUM
1978 (36 pages) (39 cents)
Spire Christian Comics (Fleming H. Revell Co.)

	Good	Fine	Mint
		.40	.80

ARCHIE'S FESTIVAL
1980 (49 cents)
Spire Christian Comics (Fleming H. Revell Co.)

	Good	Fine	Mint
		.30	.60

ARCHIE'S GIRLS, BETTY AND VERONICA
1950 - Present
Archie Publications

	Good	Fine	Mint
1	30.00	80.00	150.00
2	14.00	40.00	80.00
3-5	10.00	30.00	60.00
6-10	5.50	16.00	32.00
11-20: 14-Katy Keene app.	4.00	12.00	24.00
21-30	3.00	8.00	16.00
31-60	2.00	6.00	12.00
61-74,76-100	1.00	3.00	6.00
75-Betty & Veronica sell soul to devil	2.00	5.00	10.00
101-140: 118-Origin Superteen. 119-Last Superteen story	.50	1.50	3.00
141-180	.30	.80	1.60
181-220		.50	1.00
221-299,301-311		.30	.60
300-Anniversary issue		.40	.80
Annual 1 (1953)	10.00	30.00	60.00
Annual 2-5 (1958)	5.50	16.00	32.00
Annual 6-8 (1960)	3.50	10.00	20.00

ARCHIE SHOE-STORE GIVEAWAY
1944-45 (12-15 pgs. of games, puzzles, stories like Superman-Tim books, No nos. - came out monthly)
Archie Publications

	Good	Fine	Mint
	7.00	20.00	40.00

ARCHIE'S JOKEBOOK COMICS DIGEST ANNUAL (See Jokebook . .)

ARCHIE'S JOKE BOOK MAGAZINE (See Joke Book . . .)
1953 - No. 3, Summer, 1954; No. 15, 1954 - Present
Archie Publications

	Good	Fine	Mint
1953-One Shot(No.1)	15.00	50.00	90.00
2,3 (nn.4-14)	7.00	20.00	40.00
15-30: 16,17-Katy Keene app. (No. 15 formerly Archie's Rival Reggie)	3.50	10.00	20.00
31-40,42,43	2.00	5.00	10.00
41-1st professional comic work by Neal Adams ('59), 1 pg.; see Nutra Child	5.50	16.00	32.00
44-47-Adams-a in all, 1-2 pgs.	3.00	8.00	16.00
48-Four pgs. Adams-a	3.00	8.00	16.00
49-60	1.00	3.00	6.00
61-100	.50	1.50	3.00
101-140	.35	1.00	2.00
141-200		.50	1.00
201-282		.30	.60
Drug Store Giveaway (No. 39 with new cover)	1.20	3.50	7.00

ARCHIE'S JOKES (See Archie Giant Series Mag. No. 17,22,27,33, 139,146,154,163,174,186,198,211,222,235,247,459,471,483,495)

ARCHIE'S LOVE SCENE
1973 (35-49 cents)
Spire Christian Comics (Fleming H. Revell Co.)

	Good	Fine	Mint
1		.50	1.00

ARCHIE'S MADHOUSE (Madhouse Ma-ad No. 67 on)
Sept, 1959 - No. 66, Feb, 1969
Archie Publications

	Good	Fine	Mint
1-Archie begins	7.00	20.00	40.00
2	4.00	12.00	24.00
3-5	3.50	10.00	20.00
6-10	3.00	8.00	16.00
11-16 (Last w/regular characters)	2.00	6.00	12.00
17-21,23-40 (New format)	.70	2.00	4.00
22-1st app. Sabrina, the Teen-age Witch (9/62)	2.00	5.00	10.00
41,42,44-66		.50	1.00
43-Mighty Crusaders cameo		.60	1.20
Annual 1 (1962-63)	1.50	4.50	9.00
Annual 2-6('64-69)(Becomes Madhouse Ma-ad Annual No. 7 on)	.50	1.50	3.00

NOTE: *Cover title to 61-65 is "Madhouse" and to 66 is "Madhouse Ma-ad Jokes."*

ARCHIE'S MECHANICS
Sept, 1954 - 1955
Archie Publications

	Good	Fine	Mint
1-(15 cents; 52 pgs.)	17.00	50.00	100.00
2,3-(10 cents)	14.00	40.00	80.00

ARCHIE'S ONE WAY
1972 (35 cents, 39 cents, 49 cents) (36 pages)
Spire Christian Comics (Fleming H. Revell Co.)

	Good	Fine	Mint
nn		.50	1.00

ARCHIE'S PAL, JUGHEAD (Jughead No. 127 on)
1949 - No. 126, Nov, 1965
Archie Publications

	Good	Fine	Mint
1	40.00	100.00	200.00
2	14.00	40.00	80.00
3-5: 5-Intro. Moose & Midge	10.00	30.00	60.00
6-10	7.00	20.00	40.00
11-20	4.00	12.00	24.00
21-40	3.00	8.00	16.00
41-60	2.00	6.00	12.00
61-80	1.75	5.00	10.00
81-100	1.00	3.00	6.00
101-126	.80	2.40	4.80
Annual 1 (1953)	8.00	24.00	48.00
Annual 2-5 (1954-56)	4.00	12.00	24.00
Annual 6-8 (1957-60)	3.00	8.00	16.00

ARCHIE'S PALS 'N' GALS
1952-53 - No. 6, 1957-58; No. 7, 1958 - Present
Archie Publications

	Good	Fine	Mint
1-(116 pages)	12.00	36.00	72.00
2(Annual)(1957)	7.00	20.00	40.00

ARCHIE'S PALS 'N' GALS (continued)

	Good	Fine	Mint
3-7(Annual, '57-58)	4.00	12.00	24.00
8(1958)-10	3.00	8.00	16.00
11-20	2.00	5.00	10.00
21-40	1.00	3.00	6.00
41-60	.50	1.50	3.00
61-90		.50	1.00
91-146		.30	.60

ARCHIE'S PARABLES
1973, 1975 (36 pages) (39-49 cents)
Spire Christian Comics (Fleming H. Revell Co.)

	Good	Fine	Mint
By Al Hartley		.50	1.00

ARCHIE'S RIVAL REGGIE (See Reggie)

ARCHIE'S RIVAL REGGIE (Archie's Joke Book Mag. & Reggie No. 15 on)
1950 - No. 14, Aug, 1954
Archie Publications

	Good	Fine	Mint
1	20.00	60.00	120.00
2	10.00	28.00	56.00
3-5	5.50	16.00	32.00
6-14: Katy Keene app. No. 10-14	3.50	10.00	20.00

ARCHIE'S SOMETHING ELSE
1975 (36 pages) (39-49 cents)
Spire Christian Comics (Fleming H. Revell Co.)

	Good	Fine	Mint
nn		.50	1.00

ARCHIE'S SONSHINE
1973, 1974 (36 pages) (39-49 cents)
Spire Christian Comics (Fleming H. Revell Co.)

	Good	Fine	Mint
nn		.50	1.00

ARCHIE'S SUPER HERO SPECIAL (See Archie Giant Series Magazine No. 142)

ARCHIE'S SUPER-HERO SPECIAL DIGEST (. . Comics Digest Mag. 2)
Jan, 1979 - No. 2, Aug, 1979 (160 pages, .95 cents)
Archie Publications(Red Circle)

	Good	Fine	Mint
1-Simon & Kirby r-/Double Life of Pvt. Strong No. 1,2		.50	1.00
2-Contains contents to the never published Black Hood No. 1; origin Black Hood; Adams, Wood, Morrow, S&K(r)-a; Adams-c		.50	1.00

ARCHIE'S TV LAUGH-OUT
Dec, 1969 - Present
Archie Publications

	Good	Fine	Mint
1	1.50	4.00	8.00
2-5	.70	2.00	4.00
6-10	.35	1.00	2.00
11-20		.50	1.00
21-75		.30	.60

ARCHIE'S WORLD
1973, 1976 (39-49 cents)
Spire Christian Comics (Fleming H. Revell Co.)

	Good	Fine	Mint
		.50	1.00

ARISTOCATS (See Movie Comics & Walt Disney Showcase No. 16)

ARISTOKITTENS, THE (. . . Meet Jiminy Cricket No. 1)(Disney)
Oct, 1971 - No. 9, Oct, 1975 (No. 6: 52 pages)
Gold Key

	Good	Fine	Mint
1		.40	.80
2-9		.25	.50

ARIZONA KID, THE
March, 1951 - No. 6, Jan, 1952
Marvel/Atlas Comics(CSI)

	Good	Fine	Mint
1	3.00	9.00	18.00
2-4	2.00	6.00	12.00

	Good	Fine	Mint
5,6	1.75	5.00	10.00

ARK, THE (See The Crusaders)

ARMY AND NAVY (Supersnipe No. 6 on)
May, 1941 - No. 5, Sept, 1942
Street & Smith Publications

	Good	Fine	Mint
1-Cap Fury & Nick Carter	9.00	25.00	50.00
2-Cap Fury & Nick Carter	5.00	14.00	28.00
3,4	4.00	12.00	24.00
5-Supersnipe app.; see Shadow V2No.3 for 1st app.	12.00	35.00	70.00

ARMY AT WAR (Also see Our Army at War, Cancelled Comic Cavalcade)
Oct-Nov, 1978
DC Comics

	Good	Fine	Mint
1		.30	.60

ARMY ATTACK
July, 1964 - No. 47, Feb, 1967
Charlton Comics

	Good	Fine	Mint
V1No.1	.30	.80	1.60
2-5		.40	.80
V2No.38(7/65)-47 (formerly U.S. Air Force No. 1-37)		.30	.60

NOTE: ***Glanzman** a-1-3. **Montes/Bache** a-44.*

ARMY WAR HEROES
Dec, 1963 - No. 38, June, 1970
Charlton Comics

	Good	Fine	Mint
1	.50	1.50	3.00
2-20		.50	1.00
21-38: 23-Origin & 1st app. Iron Corporal series by Glanzman. 24-Intro. Archer & Corp. Jack series		.40	.80

NOTE: ***Montes/Bache** a-1,16,17,21,23-25,27-30.*

AROUND THE BLOCK WITH DUNC & LOO (See Dunc and Loo)

AROUND THE WORLD IN 80 DAYS (See 4-Color Comics No. 784 and A Golden Picture Classic)

AROUND THE WORLD UNDER THE SEA (See Movie Classics)

AROUND THE WORLD WITH ARCHIE (See Archie Giant Series Mag. No. 29,35,141)

AROUND THE WORLD WITH HUCKLEBERRY & HIS FRIENDS (See Dell Giant No. 44)

ARRGH! (Satire)
Dec, 1974 - No. 5, Sept, 1975
Marvel Comics Group

	Good	Fine	Mint
1-Everett-a(r)	.30	.80	1.60
2-5		.40	.80

NOTE: ***Alcala** a-2; c-3. **Everett** a-2r. **Maneely** a-4r.*

ARROW, THE
Oct, 1940 - No. 3, Oct, 1941
Centaur Publications

	Good	Fine	Mint
1-The Arrow begins(r/Funny Pages)	30.00	85.00	170.00
2	20.00	55.00	120.00
3-Origin Dash Darwell, the Human Meteor; origin The Rainbow; bondage-c	20.00	55.00	120.00

NOTE: ***Gustavson** a-1,2; c-3.*

ARROWHEAD
April, 1954 - No. 4, Nov, 1954
Atlas Comics (CPS)

	Good	Fine	Mint
1-Sinnott-a in all	2.00	6.00	12.00
2-4	1.50	4.00	8.00

ASTONISHING (Marvel Boy No. 1,2)
No. 3, April, 1951 - No. 63, Aug, 1957

Archie's Pals 'N' Gals #5, © AP

Army At War #1, © DC

Arrgh! #1, © MCG

Astonishing #60, © MCG

Astonishing Tales #31, © MCG

The Atom #3, © DC

ASTONISHING (continued)
Marvel/Atlas Comics(20CC)

	Good	Fine	Mint
3-Marvel Boy cont'd.	10.00	30.00	60.00
4-6-Last Marvel Boy; 4-Stan Lee app.	8.00	24.00	48.00
7-10	2.00	6.00	12.00
11,12,15,17,18,20	2.00	5.00	10.00
13,14,16,19-Krigstein-a	2.50	7.00	14.00
21-24	1.50	4.00	8.00
25-Crandall-a	2.00	6.00	12.00
26-29	1.50	4.00	8.00
30-Tentacled eyeball story; last pre-code ish	2.00	6.00	12.00
31-43,46,49-52,56,58,59	.85	2.50	5.00
44-Crandall swipe/Weird Fantasy 22	2.00	6.00	12.00
45,47-Krigstein-a	2.00	6.00	12.00
48-Matt Fox-a	1.50	4.00	8.00
53-Crandall-a	1.50	4.00	8.00
54-Torres-a	1.50	4.00	8.00
55-Crandall, Torres-a	2.00	6.00	12.00
57-Williamson/Krenkel-a, 4 pgs.	3.50	10.00	20.00
60-Williamson/Mayo-a, 4 pgs.	3.50	10.00	20.00
61,63	1.00	3.00	6.00
62-Torres, Powell-a	1.50	4.00	8.00

NOTE: ***Berg** a-53, 56. **Cameron** a-30, 50. **Gene Colan** a-29. **Ditko** a-50, 53. **Drucker** a-41. **Everett** a-3-6, 12, 37, 47, 48, 58, 61; c-4, 5, 15, 16, 18, 29, 47, 51, 53, 55, 57, 59-62. **Fuge** a-11. **Heath** c/a-8. **Kirby** a-56. **Maneely** c-33. **Moldoff** a-33. **Morrow** a-52, 61. **Orlando** a-47, 58, 61. **Powell** a-44, 48. **Ravielli** a-28. **J. Romita** a-7, 43, 57. **Roussos** a-55. **Sekowsky** a-13. **Moldoff** a-33. **Woodbridge** a-62, 63. Canadian reprints exist.*

ASTONISHING TALES (See Ka-Zar)
Aug, 1970 - No. 36, July, 1976
Marvel Comics Group

	Good	Fine	Mint
1-Ka-Zar by Kirby(p) & Dr. Doom by Wood begin	.50	1.50	3.00
2-Kirby, Wood-a	.35	1.00	2.00
3-6: Smith-a; Wood-a-No. 3,4; Everett inks-No. 6	.50	1.50	3.00
7-9: 8-Last Dr. Doom. (52 pgs.)	.30	.80	1.60
10-Smith/Sal Buscema-a	.50	1.50	3.00
11-Origin Ka-Zar	.30	.80	1.60
12-Man Thing by Adams	.50	1.50	3.00
13-Man Thing app.	.25	.70	1.40
14-18,20: 20-Last Ka-Zar		.60	1.20
19-Starlin (p), 4pgs.	.25	.70	1.40
21-24: 21-It! the Living Colossus begins, ends No. 24		.40	.80
25-Deathlok the Demolisher begins	.35	1.00	2.00
26-30: 29-Guardians of the Galaxy app.		.50	1.00
31-Wrightson-c(i)		.50	1.00
32-36		.30	.60

NOTE: ***John Buscema** a-9. **Ditko** a-21r. **McWilliams** a-30i. **Sutton & Trimpe** a-8.*

ASTRO BOY (TV) (Also see March of Comics No. 285)
August, 1965
Gold Key

	Good	Fine	Mint
1(10151-508)	2.00	5.00	10.00

ASTRO COMICS
1969 - 1979 (Giveaway)
American Airlines (Harvey)

	Good	Fine	Mint
nn-Has Harvey's Casper, Spooky, Hot Stuff, Stumbo the Giant, Little Audrey, Little Lotta, & Richie Rich reprints	.70	2.00	4.00

ATLANTIS, THE LOST CONTINENT (See 4-Color No. 1188)

ATLAS (See First Issue Special)

ATOM, THE (See Action, All-American, Brave & the Bold, D.C. Special Series No. 1, Detective, Showcase, & World's Finest)

ATOM, THE (. . . & the Hawkman No. 39 on)
June-July, 1962 - No. 38, Aug-Sept, 1968
National Periodical Publications

	Good	Fine	Mint
1	7.00	20.00	40.00
2	3.50	10.00	20.00
3-1st Time Pool story; 1st app. Chronos (origin)	3.00	8.00	16.00
4,5: 4-Snapper Carr x-over	2.00	5.00	10.00
6-10: 7-Hawkman x-over. 8-Justice League; Dr. Light app.	1.50	4.00	8.00
11-20: 19-Zatanna x-over	.80	2.40	4.80
21-30: 29-Golden Age Atom x-over	.50	1.50	3.00
31-38: 31-Hawkman x-over. 36-G.A. Atom x-over. 37-Intro. Major Mynah; Hawkman cameo	.35	1.00	2.00

NOTE: ***Anderson** a-1-11i, 13, 39p; c-inks-1-25, 31-35, 37. **Gil Kane** a-1-37; c-1-37. **Kubert** a-40i, 41i, 43, 44; c-39-45. Pool stories also in 6, 9, 12, 17, 21, 27, 35.*

ATOM AGE (See Classics Special)

ATOM-AGE COMBAT
June, 1952 - No. 5, April, 1953
St. John Publishing Co.

	Good	Fine	Mint
1	7.00	20.00	40.00
2-Atomic bomb-c	5.00	15.00	30.00
3,5: 3-Mayo-a, 6 pgs.	3.50	10.00	20.00
4 (Scarce)	4.00	12.00	24.00
1(2/58-St. John)	3.00	8.00	16.00

ATOM-AGE COMBAT
Nov, 1958 - No. 3, March, 1959
Fago Magazines

	Good	Fine	Mint
1	4.00	12.00	24.00
2,3	3.00	8.00	16.00

ATOMAN
Feb, 1946 - No. 2, April, 1946
Spark Publications

	Good	Fine	Mint
1-Origin Atoman; Robinson/Meskin-a; Kidcrusaders, Wild Bill Hickok, Marvin the Great app.	11.00	32.00	70.00
2: Robinson/Meskin-a	5.50	16.00	34.00

ATOM AND THE HAWKMAN, THE (Formerly The Atom)
No. 39, Oct-Nov, 1968 - No. 45, Oct-Nov, 1969
National Periodical Publications

	Good	Fine	Mint
39,42-45: 43-1st app. Gentlemen Ghost, origin-44	.30	.90	1.80
40,41-Hawkman by Kubert; c-39-45	.35	1.00	2.00

NOTE: ***Anderson** a-39,43; with Kubert-40,41,44*

ATOM ANT (TV)
January, 1966 (Hanna-Barbera)
Gold Key

	Good	Fine	Mint
1(10170-601)	.70	2.00	4.00

ATOMIC ATTACK (Part of Attack series?)
1952 - No. 8, Oct, 1953
Youthful Magazines

	Good	Fine	Mint
1 (Exist?)	5.50	16.00	32.00
2-4,6-8	3.00	8.00	16.00
5-Atomic bomb cover	5.50	16.00	32.00

ATOMIC BOMB
1942
Jay Burtis Publications

	Good	Fine	Mint
1-Airmale & Stampy	4.00	12.00	24.00

ATOMIC BUNNY
1958 - No. 19, Dec, 1959
Charlton Comics

	Good	Fine	Mint
12-19	1.00	3.00	6.00

ATOMIC COMICS
1946 (Reprints)
Daniels Publications (Canadian)

	Good	Fine	Mint
1-Rocketman, Yankee Boy, Master Key; bondage-c	4.00	12.00	24.00
2-4	3.00	8.00	16.00

ATOMIC COMICS
Jan, 1946 - No. 4, July-Aug, 1946
Green Publishing Co.

1-Radio Squad by Siegel & Shuster; Barry O'Neal app.; Fu Manchu cover	8.00	24.00	48.00
2-Inspector Dayton; Kid Kane by Matt Baker; Lucky Wings, Congo King, Prop Powers (only app.) begin	8.00	24.00	48.00
3,4: 3-Zero Ghost Detective app.; Baker-a(2) each; 4-Kamen-c	5.00	14.00	28.00

ATOMIC MOUSE (See Blue Bird & Giant Comics)
March, 1953 - No. 54, June, 1963
Capitol Stories/Charlton Comics

1-Origin	3.00	9.00	18.00
2-10	2.00	5.00	10.00
11-14,16-25,27-54	1.00	3.00	6.00
15-Hoppy The Marvel Bunny reprt.	1.00	3.00	6.00
26-(68 pages)	2.00	5.00	10.00

ATOMIC RABBIT
August, 1955 - No. 11, March, 1958
Charlton Comics

1-Origin; Al Fago-a	3.00	9.00	18.00
2-10-Fago-a in most	1.75	5.00	10.00
11-(68 pages)	2.00	6.00	12.00

ATOMIC SPY CASES
Mar-Apr, 1950
Avon Periodicals

1	8.00	24.00	48.00

ATOMIC THUNDERBOLT, THE
Feb, 1946 - No. 2, April, 1946
Regor Company

1,2: 1-Intro. Atomic Thunderbolt & Mr. Murdo	5.00	14.00	28.00

ATOMIC WAR!
Nov, 1952 - No. 4, April, 1953
Ace Periodicals (Junior Books)

1-Atomic bomb cover	22.00	65.00	140.00
2,3: 3-Atomic bomb cover	14.00	42.00	90.00
4-Used in **POP**, pg. 96 & illo.	17.00	50.00	100.00

ATOM THE CAT
Aug, 1955 - No. 17, Jun, 1959
Charlton Comics

1	1.20	3.50	7.00
2-10,13-17	.85	2.50	5.00
11-(64 pages), 12(100 pages)	1.00	3.00	6.00

ATTACK
May, 1952 - No. 7, 1953
Youthful Mag./Trojan

1-Extreme violence issue	3.00	9.00	18.00
2,3,5-7	1.50	4.00	8.00
4-Krenkel-a, 7 pgs.	2.50	7.00	14.00

ATTACK
No. 54, 1958 - No. 50, Nov, 1959
Charlton Comics

54(100 pages)	.70	2.00	4.00
55-60	.25	.75	1.50

ATTACK! (Attack at Sea V4No.5)(Also see Special War Series No. 2)
1962 - No. 4, Oct, 1967; 9/71 - No. 15, 3/75; 8/79 - Present
Charlton Comics

	Good	Fine	Mint
nn(No. 1)-('62) Special Edition	.35	1.00	2.00
2('63), 3(Fall, '64)		.50	1.00
V4No.2(10/65), 3(10/66), 4(10/67)		.30	.60
1(9/71)		.50	1.00
2-15(3/75): 4-American Eagle app.		.40	.80
16-23('80), 24-32('81)		.30	.60

ATTACK!
1975 (39 cents, 49 cents) (36 pages)
Spire Christian Comics (Fleming H. Revell Co.)

nn		.50	1.00

ATTACK AT SEA (Formerly Attack!, 1967)
October, 1968
Charlton Comics

V4No.5		.30	.60

ATTACK ON PLANET MARS
1951
Avon Periodicals

nn-Infantino, Fawcette, Kubert & Wood-a; adaptation of Tarrano the Conqueror by Ray Cummings	40.00	120.00	240.00

AUDREY & MELVIN (Formerly Little. . .)
No. 62, September, 1974
Harvey Publications

62		.30	.60

AUGIE DOGGIE (TV) (See Whitman Comic Books)
October, 1963 (Hanna-Barbera)
Gold Key

1	.70	2.00	4.00

AURORA COMIC SCENES INSTRUCTION BOOKLET
1974 (Slick paper, 8 pgs.)(6¼x9¾'')(in full color)
(Included with superhero model kits)
Aurora Plastics Co.

181-140-Tarzan; Adams-a	.70	2.00	4.00
182-140-Spider-Man; 183-140-Tonto(Gil Kane art); 184-140-Hulk; 185-140-Superman; 186-140-Superboy; 187-140-Batman; 188-140-The Lone Ranger(1974-by Gil Kane); 192-140-Captain America (1975); 193-140-Robin each. . . .	.25	.70	1.40

AUTHENTIC POLICE CASES
Feb, 1948 - No. 38, Mar, 1955
St. John Publishing Co.

1-Hale the Magician by Tuska begins; bondage-c	5.50	16.00	32.00
2-Lady Satan, Johnny Rebel app.	3.50	10.00	20.00
3-Veiled Avenger app.; blood drainage story plus 2 Lucky Coyne stories; used in **SOTI**, illo. from Red Seal No. 16; bondage-c	15.00	45.00	90.00
4,5: 5-Late 1930s Jack Cole-a(r); transvestism story. 4-Masked Black Jack app.	3.50	10.00	20.00
6-Matt Baker-c; used in **SOTI**, illo-''An invitation to learning'', r-in Fugitives From Justice No. 3; Jack Cole-a; also used by the N.Y. Legis. Comm.	17.00	50.00	100.00
7,8,10-14: 7-Jack Cole-a; Matt Baker art begins No. 8; Vic Flint in No. 10-14	4.50	13.00	26.00
9-Drug mention story (r-in No. 34); no Vic Flint	6.00	18.00	36.00
15-Drug c/story; Vic Flint app.; Baker-c	2.50	15.00	30.00
16,18,20,21,23,24	2.50	7.00	14.00
17,19,22-Baker-c. 19-Heroin mention	3.00	8.00	16.00
25-28 (All 100 pages): 27-Junkie mention	5.50	16.00	32.00
29,30,33	1.75	5.00	10.00

Atomic War! #2, © ACE

Authentic Police Cases #12, © STJ

Authentic Police Cases #27, © STJ

Authentic Police Cases #35, © STJ

The Avengers #16, © MCG

The Avengers #57, © MCG

AUTHENTIC POLICE CASES (continued) — Good / Fine / Mint

31,32,37-Baker-c 2.00 6.00 12.00
34-Drug mention story r/No. 9; drug-c by Baker 3.50 10.00 20.00
35-Baker c/a(2) 3.00 8.00 16.00
36-Vic Flint strip-r; Baker-c 2.00 6.00 12.00
38-Baker c/a 3.00 8.00 16.00

NOTE: ***Matt Baker*** *c-7-16, 22, 36-38; a-13, 16.*

AVENGER, THE (See A-1 Comics)
1955 - No. 4, Aug-Sept, 1955
Magazine Enterprises

1(A-1 129)-Origin 8.00 23.00 46.00
2(A-1 131), 3(A-1 133), 4(A-1 138) 4.00 12.00 24.00
IW Reprint No. 9('64)-Reprints No. 1 (new cover) 1.20 3.50 7.00

NOTE: ***Powell*** *a-2-4; c-1-4.*

AVENGERS, THE
Sept, 1963 - Present
Marvel Comics Group

1-Origin The Avengers (Thor, Iron Man, Hulk, Ant-Man, Wasp) 55.00 160.00 340.00
2 20.00 60.00 120.00
3 14.00 40.00 80.00
4-Revival of Captain America who joins the Avengers 20.00 60.00 120.00
4-Reprint from the Golden Record Comic set .50 1.50 3.00
With Record.... .70 2.00 4.00
5-Hulk leaves 7.00 20.00 40.00
6-10: 6-Intro The Masters of Evil. 8-Intro Kang. 9-Intro Wonder Man who dies in same story 5.50 16.00 32.00
11-15: 15-Death of Zemo 3.50 10.00 20.00
16-19: 16-New Avengers line-up (Hawkeye, Quicksilver, Scarlet Witch join; Thor, Iron Man, Giant-Man & Wasp leave.) 19-Intro. Swordsman; origin Hawkeye 2.50 7.00 14.00
20-22: Wood inks 1.50 4.50 9.00
23-30: 28-Giant-Man becomes Goliath .85 2.50 5.00
31-40 .70 2.00 4.00
41-50: 48-Intro/Origin new Black Knight .50 1.50 3.00
51,52,54-56: 52-Black Panther joins; Intro The Grim Reaper. 54-Intro new Masters of Evil. .50 1.50 3.00
53-X-Men app. .70 2.00 4.00
57-Intro. The Vision 2.50 7.50 15.00
58-Origin The Vision 2.50 7.50 15.00
59-65,68-70: 59-Intro. Yellowjacket. 60-Wasp & Yellowjacket wed. 63-Goliath becomes Yellowjacket; Hawkeye becomes the new Goliath .80 2.40 4.80
66,67: Smith-a 1.50 4.00 8.00
71-1st Invaders; Black Knight joins .75 2.20 4.40
72-80: 80-Intro. Red Wolf .70 2.00 4.00
81,82,84-91: 87-Origin The Black Panther .70 2.00 4.00
83-Intro. The Liberators (Wasp, Valkyrie, Scarlet Witch, Medusa & the Black Widow) .75 2.20 4.40
92-Adams-c .85 2.50 5.00
93-(52 pgs.)-Adams c/a 5.00 15.00 30.00
94-96-Adams c/a 2.50 7.50 15.00
97-G.A. Capt. America, Sub-Mariner, Human Torch, Patriot, Vision, Blazing Skull, Fin, Angel, & New Capt. Marvel x-over; 1.00 3.00 6.00
98-Goliath becomes Hawkeye; Smith c/a w/Buscema 2.00 5.00 10.00
99-Smith c/a 2.00 5.00 10.00
100-Smith c/a; featuring everyone who was an Avenger 3.50 10.00 20.00
101-106,108,109 .70 2.00 4.00
107-Starlin-a(p) .75 2.20 4.40
110-X-Men app. .75 2.20 4.40
111,113-119: 116-18-Defenders/Silver Surfer app. .50 1.50 3.00
112-1st app. Mantis .60 1.80 3.60
120-Starlin-c(p) .60 1.80 3.60

Good / Fine / Mint

121-130: 123-Origin Mantis .50 1.40 2.80
131-140: 134,135-True origin The Vision .40 1.20 2.40
141-149: 144-Origin & 1st app. Hellcat .35 1.10 2.20
150-Kirby-a(r); new line-up begins: Capt. America, Scarlet Witch, Iron Man, Wasp, Yellowjacket, Vision & The Beast .40 1.20 2.40
151-160: 151-Wonderman returns with new costume .40 1.10 2.20
161-166-Byrne-a .50 1.40 2.80
167-170: 151-Wonderman returns with new costume .35 1.00 2.00
171-180 .25 .75 1.50
181-191-Byrne-a. 181-New line-up; Capt. America, Scarlet Witch, Iron Man, Wasp, Vision, The Beast & The Falcon. 187-Origin Quicksilver & Scarlet Witch .40 1.10 2.20
192-199: 196-1st Taskmaster .50 1.00
200-Double size .25 .75 1.50
201-215: 211-New line-up: Capt. America, Iron Man, Tigra, Thor, Wasp & Yellowjacket. 213-Yellowjacket leaves .40 .80
Annual 7(11/77)-Starlin c/a; Warlock dies. .75 2.20 4.40
Annual 8(10/78) .35 1.00 2.00
Annual 9(10/79)-Newton art .25 .75 1.50
Annual 10(10/81)-Golden c/a .50 1.00
Special 1(9/67) 2.00 6.00 12.00
Special 2(9/68) 1.00 3.00 6.00
Special 3(9/69) 1.00 3.00 6.00
Special 4(1/71), 5(1/72) .75 2.20 4.40
Special 6(11/76) .50 1.50 3.00
Giant Size 1(8/74) .70 2.00 4.00
Giant Size 2(11/74)(death of the Swordsman), 3(2/75) .40 1.20 2.40
Giant Size 4(6/75), 5(12/75) .35 1.00 2.00

NOTE: ***Austin*** *c-inks-No. 157, 168, 170-77, 181, 183-88, 198-201, Annual 8.* ***John Buscema*** *a-41-44p, 46p, 47p, 49-62p, 65, 68-77, 79-85, 87-91, 97, 98, 105p, 121p, 124p, 125p, 152, 153; c-41-66, 68-91, 97, 98, 178.* ***Byrne*** *a-161-166p, 181-191p; c-186-190p, 202p.* ***Cockrum*** *a-Gnt Size 2; c-169, 175, 177, 202.* ***Infantino*** *a-178p, 197, 203; c-203.* ***Kane*** *c-37p.* ***Kane/Everett*** *c-97.* ***Kirby*** *a-1-8, 16; c-1-30, 148, 151-158; layouts-14, 15.* ***Marcos*** *a-inks-163-65, 167, 168, 170, 171, 173-77, Annual 8; c-163i.* ***Miller*** *c-193p.* ***Mooney*** *a-179p, 180p.* ***Nebres*** *a-178i.* ***Newton*** *a-204p,* ***Perez*** *a-(p)-144, 167, 168, 170, 171, 191-196, 198-202, Annual 8; c-163, 164, 167, 168, 170-74, 181, 183-85, 191-on(most), Annual 8.* ***Starlin*** *c-121.* ***Tuska*** *a-140p, 163p, 178p.*

AVENGERS, THE (TV)
Nov, 1968 (''John Steed & Emma Peel'' cover title)
Gold Key

1 2.00 5.00 10.00

NOTE: *''The Avengers'' is official title on inside.*

AVIATION ADVENTURES & MODEL BUILDING
Dec, 1946 - No. 17, Feb, 1947 (True Aviation Adv. . . . No. 15)
Parents' Magazine Institute

16,17-Half comics and half pictures 2.00 5.00 10.00

AVIATION CADETS
1943
Street & Smith Publications

2.00 6.00 12.00

AWFUL OSCAR (Formerly Oscar)
No. 12, Aug, 1949 - No. 13, Oct, 1949
Marvel Comics Group

12,13 1.50 4.00 8.00

BABE (. . . , Darling of the Hills, later issues)(Also see Big Shot, Sparky Watts)
June-July, 1948 - No. 11, Apr-May, 1950
Prize/Headline/Feature

BABE (continued)

	Good	Fine	Mint
1-Boody Rogers-a	4.50	13.00	26.00
2-11-All by Boody Rogers	3.00	9.00	18.00

BABE AMAZON OF OZARKS
No. 5, 1948
Standard Comics

5	2.50	7.50	15.00

BABE RUTH SPORTS COMICS
April, 1949 - No. 11, Feb, 1951
Harvey Publications

1-Powell-a	3.50	10.00	20.00
2-11: Powell-a in most	2.00	6.00	12.00

BABES IN TOYLAND (See 4-Color No. 1282 and Golden Pix Story Book ST-3)

BABY HUEY AND PAPA (See Paramount Animated . . .)
May, 1962 - No. 33, Jan, 1968
Harvey Publications

1	7.00	20.00	40.00
2	3.50	10.00	20.00
3-5	2.00	6.00	12.00
6-10	1.50	4.00	8.00
11-20	.70	2.00	4.00
21-33	.35	1.00	2.00

BABY HUEY IN DUCKLAND
Nov, 1962 - No. 15, Nov, 1966 (25 cent Giant)
Harvey Publications

1	4.00	12.00	24.00
2-5	2.00	5.00	10.00
6-15	.85	2.50	5.00

BABY HUEY, THE BABY GIANT (Also see Casper, Harvey Hits No. 22, Comics Hits No. 60, & Paramount Animated Comics)
9/56 - No. 97, 10/71; No. 98, 10/72; No. 99, 10/80 - No. 101
Harvey Publications

1	15.00	45.00	100.00
2	10.00	30.00	60.00
3-Baby Huey gets high on uppers & downers	5.50	16.00	32.00
4,5	4.00	12.00	24.00
6-10	2.00	6.00	12.00
11-20	1.50	4.00	8.00
21-40	1.00	3.00	6.00
41-60	.70	2.00	4.00
61-84,86-98	.35	1.00	2.00
85-Giant issue	.50	1.50	3.00
99-101		.50	1.00

BABY SNOOTS (Also see March of Comics No. 359,371,396,401, 474)
Aug, 1970 - No. 22, Nov, 1975
Gold Key

1	.35	1.00	2.00
2-22: 22-Titled Snoots, the Forgetful Elefink		.50	1.00

BACHELOR FATHER (TV)
1962
Dell Publishing Co.

4-Color 1332 (No. 1)	1.00	3.00	6.00
2-Written by Stanley	1.50	4.00	8.00

BACHELOR'S DIARY
1949
Avon Periodicals

1(Scarce)-King Features panel cartoons & text-r; pin-up, girl wrestling photos	11.00	32.00	70.00

BADGE OF JUSTICE
No. 22, 1/55 - No. 23, 3/55; 4/55 - No. 4, 10/55
Charlton Comics

	Good	Fine	Mint
22(1/55), 23(3/55), 1	.85	2.50	5.00
2-4	.70	2.00	4.00

BADMEN OF THE WEST
1951 (Giant - 132 pages)
Avon Periodicals

1-Contains rebound copies of Jesse James, King of the Bad Men of Deadwood, Badmen of Tombstone; other combinations possible Issues with Kubert-a. . . .	8.00	24.00	48.00

BADMEN OF THE WEST! (See A-1 Comics)
1953 - No. 3, 1954
Magazine Enterprises

1(A-1 100)-Meskin-a?	5.00	15.00	30.00
2(A-1 120), 3	3.00	9.00	18.00

BADMEN OF TOMBSTONE
1950
Avon Periodicals

nn	4.00	12.00	24.00

BAFFLING MYSTERIES (Formerly Indian Braves No. 1-4; Heroes of the Wild Frontier No. 26-28)
No. 5, Nov, 1951 - No. 26(10/55),29,30, 1955
Periodical House (Ace Magazines)

5	3.00	9.00	18.00
6,7,9,10: 10-E.C. Crypt Keeper swipe on-c	2.00	6.00	12.00
8-Harrison/Wood-a?	3.50	10.00	20.00
11-20: 20-Bondage-c	2.00	6.00	12.00
21-25 (26,29,30-Exist?)	1.50	4.50	9.00

NOTE: ***Cameron*** *a-16,17,20,22.* ***Colan*** *a-5, 11, 25r/5.* ***Sekowsky*** *a-5, 22.*

BALBO (See Mighty Midget Comics)

BALOO & LITTLE BRITCHES
April, 1968 (Walt Disney)
Gold Key

1-From the Jungle Book	.70	2.00	4.00

BALTIMORE COLTS
1950 (Giveaway)
American Visuals Corp.

Eisner-c	10.00	30.00	60.00

BAMBI (See 4-Color No. 12,30,186, Movie Comics, Movie Classics, and Walt Disney Showcase No. 31)

BAMBI (Disney)
1941, 1942
K. K. Publications (Giveaway)

1941-Horlick's Malted Milk & various toy stores - text & pictures; most copies mailed out with store stickers on cover	14.00	40.00	80.00
1942-Same as 4-Color 12, but no price (Same as '41 issue?) (Scarce)	20.00	60.00	120.00

BAMM BAMM & PEBBLES FLINTSTONE
Oct, 1964 (Hanna-Barbera)
Gold Key

1	.70	2.00	4.00

BANANA OIL
1924 (52 pages)(Black & White)
MS Publ. Co.

Milt Gross-a; not reprints	6.00	17.00	34.00

BANANA SPLITS, THE (TV) (See March of Comics No. 364)
Feb, 1969 - No. 8, Oct, 1971 (Hanna-Barbera)
Gold Key

Baffling Mysteries #12, © ACE

Baffling Mysteries #24, © ACE

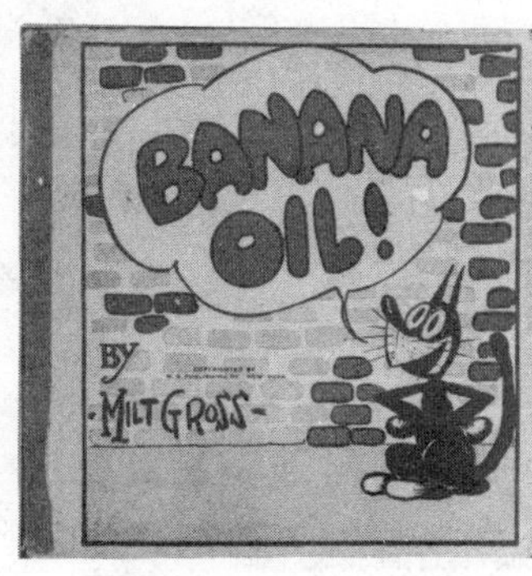

Banana Oil nn, © Milt Gross

Banner Comics #4, © ACE

The Barbarians #1, © Atlas

Barney Google & Sparkplug #2, © News Synd.

BANANA SPLITS (continued)

	Good	Fine	Mint
1	.70	2.00	4.00
2-8	.35	1.00	2.00

BAND WAGON (See Hanna-Barbera . . .)

BANG-UP COMICS
Dec, 1941 - No. 3, June, 1942
Progressive Publications

	Good	Fine	Mint
1-Cosmo Mann & Lady Fairplay begin; Buzz Balmer by Rick Yager in all	20.00	50.00	100.00
2,3	10.00	30.00	60.00

BANNER COMICS (Captain Courageous No. 6)
No. 3, May, 1941 - No. 5, Jan, 1942
Ace Magazines

	Good	Fine	Mint
3-Captain Courageous & Lone Warrior & Sidekick Dicky begin	25.00	65.00	130.00
4,5	20.00	50.00	100.00

BARBARIANS, THE
June, 1975
Atlas Comics/Seaboard Periodicals

	Good	Fine	Mint
1-Origin, only app. Andrax; Iron Jaw app.	.25	.75	1.50

BARBIE & KEN
May-July, 1962 - No. 5, Nov-Jan, 1963-64
Dell Publishing Co.

	Good	Fine	Mint
01-053-207(No. 1)	1.00	3.00	6.00
2-5	.70	2.00	4.00

BARKER, THE
Autumn, 1946 - No. 15, Dec, 1949
Quality Comics Group/Comic Magazine

	Good	Fine	Mint
1	2.50	7.00	14.00
2	1.50	4.00	8.00
3-10	1.20	3.50	7.00
11-14	.70	2.00	4.00
15-Jack Cole-a(p)	1.50	4.00	8.00

NOTE: ***Jack Cole*** *art in some issues.*

BARNEY AND BETTY RUBBLE (Flintstones' Neighbors)
Jan, 1973 - No. 23, Dec, 1976 (Hanna-Barbera)
Charlton Comics

	Good	Fine	Mint
1	.70	2.00	4.00
2-23	.35	1.00	2.00

BARNEY BAXTER
1938 - 1956
David McKay/Dell Publishing Co.

	Good	Fine	Mint
Feature Book 15(McKay-1938)	9.00	25.00	55.00
4-Color 20(1942)	8.00	22.00	44.00
4,5	5.00	14.00	28.00
1,2(1956-Argo)	1.50	5.00	10.00

BARNEY BEAR HOME PLATE
1979 (49 cents)
Spire Christian Comics (Fleming H. Revell Co.)

	Good	Fine	Mint
		.30	.60

BARNEY BEAR OUT OF THE WOODS
1980 (49 cents)
Spire Christian Comics (Fleming H. Revell Co.)

	Good	Fine	Mint
nn		.40	.80

BARNEY BEAR SUNDAY SCHOOL PICNIC
1981 (69 cents)
Spire Christian Comics (Fleming H. Revell Co.)

	Good	Fine	Mint
nn		.40	.80

BARNEY BEAR THE SWAMP GANG!
1980 (59 cents)
Spire Christian Comics (Fleming H. Revell Co.)

	Good	Fine	Mint
nn		.40	.80

BARNEY BEAR WAKES UP
1977 (39 cents)
Spire Christian Comics (Fleming H. Revell Co.)

	Good	Fine	Mint
nn		.40	.80

BARNEY GOOGLE AND SPARKPLUG (See Comic Monthly & Giant Comic Album)
1923 - 1928 (Daily strip reprints; B&W) (52 pages)
Cupples & Leon Co.

	Good	Fine	Mint
1-By Billy DeBeck	9.00	27.00	54.00
2-6	7.00	20.00	40.00

NOTE: *Started in 1918 as newspaper strip; Spark Plug began 1922, 1923.*

BARNEY GOOGLE & SNUFFY SMITH
1942 - April, 1964
Dell Publishing Co./Gold Key

	Good	Fine	Mint
4-Color 19('42)	10.00	30.00	60.00
4-Color 40('43)	5.00	15.00	30.00
Large Feature Comic 11(1943)	8.00	25.00	50.00
1(1950-Dell)-Exist?	2.50	7.50	15.00
2,3-Exist?	2.00	5.00	10.00
1(10113-404)-Gold Key, 4/64	1.20	3.50	7.00

BARNEY GOOGLE & SNUFFY SMITH
May, 1951 - No. 4, Feb, 1952 (Reprints)
Toby Press

	Good	Fine	Mint
1	3.00	9.00	18.00
2,3	2.00	6.00	12.00
4-Kurtzman-a "Pot Shot Pete," 5 pgs.; reprints/John Wayne No. 5	3.00	8.00	16.00

BARNEY GOOGLE AND SNUFFY SMITH
March, 1970 - No. 6, Jan, 1971
Charlton Comics

	Good	Fine	Mint
1	1.00	3.00	6.00
2-6	.70	2.00	4.00

BARNYARD
1944 - 1950; 1957
Nedor/Polo Mag./Standard(Animated Cartoons)

	Good	Fine	Mint
1	3.50	10.00	20.00
2-12,16	1.00	3.00	6.00
13-15,17,20,21,23,26,27,29-All contain Frazetta text illos	2.50	7.50	15.00
18,19,22,24,25-All contain Frazetta-a & text illos	7.00	20.00	40.00
28,30,31	.70	2.00	4.00
10(1957)	.35	1.00	2.00

BARRY M. GOLDWATER
March, 1965 (Complete life story)
Dell Publishing Co.

	Good	Fine	Mint
12-055-503	3.00	6.00	12.00

BASEBALL COMICS
Spring, 1949
Will Eisner Productions

	Good	Fine	Mint
1-Will Eisner c/a	15.00	45.00	100.00

BASEBALL HEROES
1952 (One Shot)
Fawcett Publications

	Good	Fine	Mint
nn (Scarce)	9.00	26.00	60.00

BASEBALL THRILLS
1951 - No. 10, Summer, 1952
Ziff-Davis Publ. Co.

	Good	Fine	Mint
1	5.00	15.00	30.00

BASEBALL THRILLS (continued)

	Good	Fine	Mint
2-Powell-a(2)	3.50	10.00	20.00
3-Kinstler c/a	3.50	10.00	20.00
4-10	3.00	8.00	16.00

BASIC HISTORY OF AMERICA ILLUSTRATED
1976 (B&W)
Pendulum Press

		Mint
07-1999	America Becomes a World Power 1890-1920	
07-2251	The Industrial Era 1865-1915	
07-226x	Before the Civil War 1830-1860	
07-2278	Americans Move Westward 1800-1850	
07-2286	The Civil War 1850-1876 - Redondo-a	
07-2294	The Fight for Freedom 1750-1783	
07-2308	The New World 1500-1750	
07-2316	Problems of the New Nation 1800-1830	
07-2324	Roaring Twenties and the Great Depression 1920-1940	
07-2332	The United States Emerges 1783-1800	
07-2340	America Today 1945-1976	
07-2359	World War II 1940-1945	
	Softcover	1.50
	Hardcover	4.50

BASIL (. . . the Royal Cat)
Jan, 1953 - No. 4, Sept, 1953
St. John Publishing Co.

	Good	Fine	Mint
1	1.00	3.00	6.00
2-4	.50	1.50	3.00

BAT LASH (See DC Special Series No. 16, Showcase No. 76)
Oct-Nov, 1968 - No. 7, Oct-Nov, 1969
National Periodical Publications

	Good	Fine	Mint
1	.50	1.50	3.00
2-7	.35	1.00	2.00

BATMAN (See Aurora, The Best of DC No. 2, The Brave & the Bold. Detective, 80-Page Giants, Giant Comics to Color, Limited Coll. Ed., 100-Page Super Spec., 3-D Batman, & World's Finest)

BATMAN
Spring, 1940 - Present
National Periodical Publ./Detective Comics/DC Comics

	Good	Fine	Mint
1-Origin The Batman retold by Bob Kane; see Detective No. 33 for 1st origin; 1st app. Joker & Catwoman; has Batman story without Robin originally planned for Detective No. 38; reprinted in Famous First Editions	700.00	2100.00	5000.00
(Prices vary widely on this book)			
2	200.00	550.00	1200.00
3-1st Catwoman in costume	115.00	340.00	700.00
4	100.00	280.00	575.00
5	70.00	200.00	425.00
6-10: 8-Infinity-c	45.00	130.00	275.00
11-15: 13-Jerry Siegel, creator of Superman appears in a Batman story	35.00	100.00	225.00
16-Intro. Alfred	40.00	120.00	250.00
17-20	20.00	60.00	120.00
21-26,28-30: 24-Last app. of Tweedledum & Tweedledee. 25-Only Joker-Penguin team-up	17.00	50.00	100.00
27-Christmas-c	20.00	60.00	120.00
31,32,34-40: 32-Origin Robin retold	12.00	36.00	72.00
33-Christmas-c	14.00	40.00	80.00
41-46	10.00	30.00	60.00
47-Origin The Batman retold	30.00	80.00	170.00
48-1001 Secrets of Bat Cave	11.00	32.00	64.00
49,50: 49-1st Vicki Vale. 50-Two-Face app.	10.00	30.00	60.00
51-60: 57-Centerfold is a 1950 calendar	7.00	20.00	45.00
61-Origin Batman Plane II	8.00	22.00	44.00
62-Origin Catwoman	10.00	28.00	56.00
63-70: 68-Two-Face app.	6.00	18.00	36.00
71-73,75-77,79,80	6.00	18.00	36.00
74-Used in **POP**, pg. 90	7.00	20.00	40.00
78-(9/53)-Ron Kar, The Man Hunter from Mars story-the 1st lawman of mars to come to earth (Green skinned)	7.00	20.00	40.00
81-89: 81-Two-Face app; 86-Intro Batmarine (Batman's submarine). 89-Last Pre-Code ish.	5.00	15.00	30.00
90-99	4.00	12.00	24.00
100	14.00	40.00	90.00
101-110	3.50	10.00	20.00
111-120	3.00	8.00	16.00
121-130: 127-Superman app.	2.00	6.00	12.00
131-140: 131-Intro. 2nd Batman & Robin series. 134-Origin & 1st app. Dummy. 139-Intro. old Bat-Girl	2.00	5.00	10.00
141-150	1.50	4.00	8.00
151-170: 164-New look & Mystery Analysts series begins	1.00	3.00	6.00
171-Riddler app. (5/65), 1st since 12/48	1.00	3.00	6.00
172-180: 176-Giant G-17	.70	2.00	4.00
(80-Pg. Giant G-17)	1.00	3.00	6.00
181-190: 181-Batman & Robin poster insert; Intro Poison Ivy. 182-Giant G-24. 185-Giant G-27. 187-Giant G-30	.40	1.20	2.40
(80-Pg. Giant G-24,27,30)	.50	1.50	3.00
191-200: 193-Giant G-37. 197-New Bat-Girl app. 198-Giant G-43, r-origin. 200-Retells origin of Batman & Robin	.35	1.00	2.00
(80-Pg. Giant G-37,43)	.40	1.20	2.40
201-210: 203-Giant G-49. 208-Giant G-55; new Gil Kane-a	.30	.90	1.80
(80-Pg. Giant G-49,55)	.35	1.00	2.00
211-218: 213-Giant G-61; origin Alfred; new origin of Robin. 216-Alfred given a new last name-''Pennyworth.''(see Det. 96). 218-Giant G-67		.60	1.20
(80-Pg. Giant G-61,67)	.30	.90	1.80
219-Adams-a	1.00	3.00	6.00
220		.60	1.20
221,223-231: 223-Giant G-73. 228-Giant G-79		.50	1.00
(80-Pg. Giant G-73,79)	.30	.80	1.60
222-Beatles take-off	.70	2.00	4.00
232-Adams-a; Intro Ras Al Ghul	1.00	3.00	6.00
233,235,236,238-242: 233-Giant G-85. 238-DC-8 100 Pg. Super Spec.; unpubbed G.A. Atom, Sargon, Plastic Man stories; Doom Patrol origin-r; Adams-c. 241-r-Batman No. 5		.50	1.00
(80-Pg. Giant G-85)	.30	.80	1.60
(100-Pg. DC-8)	.45	1.30	2.60
234,237: Adams-a. 234-52pg. ish begin, end No. 242	1.00	3.00	6.00
243-245-Adams-a	.70	2.00	4.00
246-250		.50	1.00
251-Adams-a; Joker app.	.70	2.00	4.00
252,253: 253-Shadow app.		.50	1.00
254-100pg. editions begin	.30	.80	1.60
255-Adams-a	.70	2.00	4.00
256-261-Last 100pg. issue	.30	.80	1.60
262-68pgs.		.50	1.00
263-280: 266-Catwoman returns to old costume		.40	.80
281-299		.30	.60
300(52pgs.)-302		.50	1.00
303-305(44 pgs.)		.40	.80
306-342: 311-Batgirl reteams with Batman		.30	.60
Annual 1(8-10/61)-Swan cover	5.50	16.00	32.00
Annual 2	3.00	8.00	16.00
Annual 3(Summer, '62)	2.00	6.00	12.00
Annual 4-7(7/64)	1.50	4.00	8.00
Pizza Hut giveaway(12/77)-exact reprints of No. 122 & 123		.40	.80
Prell Shampoo giveaway('66)-16 pgs. ''The Joker's Practical Jokes'' (6-7/8''x3-3/8'')	.50	1.50	3.00

NOTE: ***Adams** c-200, 203, 210, 217, 219, 220-22, 224-27, 229, 230, 232, 234, 236-41, 243-46, 251, 255.* ***Anderson** a-254i; c-218,*

Batman #2, © DC

Batman #100, © DC

Batman #251, © DC

Battle #12, © MCG

Battle Action #3, © MCG

Battle Classics #1, © DC

BATMAN (continued)
223, 228. ***Aparo*** *c-284, 286, 291-95, 297-99, 301-309, 324-326, 329, 331-338, 340, 341.* ***Buckler*** *a-239-242, 265p, 297.* ***Burnley*** *a-10, 12-18, 20, 25, 27; c-28.* ***J. Cole*** *a-238r.* ***Giordano*** *c-249, 263, 265-67, 271, 300, 315, 316.* ***Golden*** *a-295, 303p.* ***Grell*** *a-287-89; c-287-89.* ***Infantino*** *a-234, 235, 255r, 261r; c-164-75, 177-81, 183, 184, 188-92, 194-99.* ***Kaluta*** *c-242, 248, 253.* ***Bob Kane*** *a-1, 2; c-1-5, 7.* ***G. Kane*** *a-(R)-254, 255, 259, 261.* ***Kubert*** *a-238r; c-310, 319, 327, 328.* ***Lopez*** *c-272, 311, 313, 314, 318.* ***Mooney*** *a-255r.* ***Newton*** *a-305, 306, 328p, 331-333p, 337p, 338p.* ***Robinson/Roussos*** *a-12-17, 20, 22, 24, 25, 27, 28, 31, 33, 37.* ***Robinson*** *a-12, 14, 18, 22-32, 34, 36, 37, 255r, 261r; c-6, 8-10, 12-15, 18, 21, 24, 26, 27, 30, 37, 39.* ***Simonson*** *a-300p, 312p, 321; c-312.* ***Staton*** *a-334.* ***Wrightson*** *a-265i; c-320r.*

BATMAN (Kellogg's Poptarts comics)
1966 (set of 6) (16 pages)
National Periodical Publications

	Good	Fine	Mint
"The Man in the Iron Mask," "The Penguin's Fowl Play," "The Joker's Happy Victims," "The Catwoman's Catnapping Caper," "The Mad Hatter's Hat Crimes," "The Case of the Batman II" each....	.70	2.00	4.00

NOTE: ***Infantino*** *art on Catwoman and Joker issues.*

BATMAN FAMILY, THE
Sept-Oct, 1975 - No. 20, Oct-Nov, 1978 (No.1-4: 68 pages)
(Combined with Detective Comics with No. 481)
National Periodical Publications/DC Comics

	Good	Fine	Mint
1-Origin Batgirl-Robin team-up (The Dynamite Duo); reprints plus one new story begins; Adams-a(r).	.50	1.50	3.00
2-5		.60	1.20
6-10,14-16		.40	.80
11-13: Rogers-a. 11-New stories begin; Man-Bat begins	.30	.80	1.60
17-($1.00 size)-Starlin-a		.60	1.20
18-20: Huntress by Staton in all		.60	1.20

NOTE: ***Aparo*** *a-17; c-11-14, 16.* ***Chaykin*** *a-14p.* ***Michael Golden*** *a-15-20.* ***Grell*** *a-1; c-1.* ***Infantino*** *a-2r,4r, 9r.* ***Gil Kane*** *a-2r.* ***Kaluta*** *c-17, 19.* ***Newton*** *a-13.* ***Robinson*** *a-1r ,9r.* ***Russell*** *a-18i, 19i.* ***Starlin*** *c-18, 20.*

BATMAN MINIATURE (See Batman Kellogg's)

BATMAN RECORD COMIC
1966 (One Shot)
National Periodical Publications

	Good	Fine	Mint
1	.50	1.50	3.00

BATMAN SPECTACULAR (See DC Special Series No. 15)

BAT MASTERSON (TV)
Aug-Oct, 1959; Dec-Jan, 1959-60 - No. 9, Nov-Jan, 1961-62
Dell Publishing Co.

	Good	Fine	Mint
4-Color 1013 (8-10/59)	1.00	3.00	6.00
2-9	.70	2.00	4.00

BATS (See Tales Calculated to Drive You . . .)

BATTLE
March, 1951 - No. 70, June, 1960
Marvel/Atlas Comics(FPI No. 1-62/Male No. 63 on)

	Good	Fine	Mint
1	3.00	9.00	18.00
2-10: 4-1st Buck Pvt. O'Toole	1.50	4.00	8.00
11-20	.85	2.50	5.00
21,23-Krigstein-a	2.00	5.00	10.00
22,24-35,38-40	.50	1.50	3.00
36-Everett, Anderson-a	.70	2.00	4.00
37-Kubert-a	1.50	4.00	8.00
41-Kubert/Moskowitz-a	1.50	4.00	8.00
42-48	.50	1.50	3.00
49-Davis-a	2.00	5.00	10.00
50-54,56-58	.40	1.20	2.40
55-Williamson-a, 5 pgs.	2.50	7.00	14.00
59-Torres-a	1.20	3.50	7.00
60-62: Combat Kelly app.-No. 60,62; Combat Casey app.-No. 61	.35	1.00	2.00
63-65: 63-Ditko-a. 64,65-Kirby-a	1.20	3.50	7.00
66-Kirby, Davis-a	1.50	4.00	8.00
67-Williamson/Crandall-a, 4 pgs; Kirby, Davis-a	2.50	7.00	14.00
68-Kirby/Williamson-a, 4 pgs; Kirby/Ditko-a	2.50	7.00	14.00
69-Kirby-a	1.00	3.00	6.00
70-Kirby/Ditko-a	1.00	3.00	6.00

NOTE: ***Anderson*** *a-36.* ***Berg*** *a-8, 14, 60, 62.* ***Everett*** *a-36, 50, 70; c-56, 57.* ***Heath*** *c/a-6.* ***Kirby*** *c-64-69.* ***Maneely*** *c/a-4.* ***Orlando*** *a-47.* ***Powell*** *a-53, 55.* ***Robinson*** *a-9, 39.* ***Severin*** *a-28, 32, 34; c-36.* ***Woodbridge*** *a-52, 55.*

BATTLE ACTION
Feb, 1952 - No. 12, 5/53; No. 13, 10/54 - No. 31, 9/57
Atlas Comics (NPI)

	Good	Fine	Mint
1	3.00	8.00	16.00
2-4,6,7,9,10: 6-Robinson c/a	1.00	3.00	6.00
5-Used in **POP**, pg. 93,94	1.50	4.00	8.00
8-Krigstein-a	2.00	5.00	10.00
11-26,28,29,31	.70	2.00	4.00
27,30-Torres-a	1.50	4.00	8.00

NOTE: *Battle Brady app. 5,6,10-12.* ***Woodbridge*** *a-28,30.*

BATTLE ATTACK
Oct, 1952 - No. 8, Dec, 1955
Stanmor Publications

	Good	Fine	Mint
1	2.00	5.00	10.00
2-8	1.00	3.00	6.00

BATTLE BRADY (Men in Action No. 1-9)
No. 10, Jan, 1953 - No. 14, June, 1953
Atlas Comics (IPC)

	Good	Fine	Mint
10	1.50	4.00	8.00
11-Used in **POP**, pg. 95 plus B&W & color illos.	2.00	5.00	10.00
12-14	1.00	3.00	6.00

BATTLE CLASSICS (See Cancelled Comic Cavalcade)
Sept-Oct, 1978 (44 pages)
DC Comics

	Good	Fine	Mint
1-Kubert-r, new Kubert-c		.40	.80

BATTLE CRY
1952 - No. 20, Sept, 1955
Stanmor Publications

	Good	Fine	Mint
1	2.00	6.00	12.00
2,3,5-10: 8-Pvt. Ike begins, ends No. 12,17	1.00	3.00	6.00
4-Classic E.C. swipe	1.50	4.00	8.00
11-Opium-c	2.00	5.00	10.00
12-20	.70	2.00	4.00

NOTE: ***Hollingsworth*** *a-9.*

BATTLEFIELD (War Adventures on the . . .)
April, 1952 - No. 11, May, 1953
Atlas Comics (ACI)

	Good	Fine	Mint
1	2.00	6.00	12.00
2-5	1.00	3.00	6.00
6-11	.70	2.00	4.00

BATTLEFIELD ACTION (Formerly Foreign Intrigues)
No. 16, Nov, 1957 - No. 62, Feb-Mar, 1966; No. 63, 7/80-Present
Charlton Comics

	Good	Fine	Mint
16	.30	.80	1.60
17,18,20-30		.40	.80
19-Check-a	.50	1.50	3.00
31-62(1966)		.30	.60

BATTLEFIELD ACTION (continued)

	Good	Fine	Mint
63-72(1981)		.30	.60

NOTE: ***Montes/Bache*** *a-43,55,62.*

BATTLE FIRE
April, 1955 -No. 7, 1955
Aragon Magazine/Stanmor Publications

	Good	Fine	Mint
1	1.20	3.50	7.00
2-7	.70	2.00	4.00

BATTLEFRONT
June, 1952 - No. 48, Aug, 1957
Atlas Comics (FPI)

	Good	Fine	Mint
1-Heath-c	3.00	9.00	18.00
2,5	1.50	4.50	9.00
3,4-Robinson book-length story in each	1.50	4.50	9.00
6-10: Combat Kelly in all	1.20	3.50	7.00
11-30: Battle Brady in No. 14,16	.70	2.00	4.00
31-39	.50	1.50	3.00
40,42-Williamson-a	2.50	7.00	14.00
41,44-47	.40	1.20	2.40
43-Check-a	.70	2.00	4.00
48-Crandall-a	1.20	3.50	7.00

NOTE: ***Drucker*** *a-28.* ***Everett*** *a-44.* ***Morrow*** *a-41.* ***Orlando*** *a-47.* ***Powell*** *a-21, 25, 47.* ***Robinson*** *a-1, 2, 4, 5; c-4.* ***Severin*** *c-40.* ***Woodbridge*** *a-45, 46.*

BATTLEFRONT
No. 5, June, 1952
Standard Comics

	Good	Fine	Mint
5-Toth-a	3.00	8.00	16.00

BATTLE GROUND
Sept, 1954 - No. 20, Sept, 1957
Atlas Comics (OMC)

	Good	Fine	Mint
1	2.00	6.00	12.00
2-Jack Katz-a	1.50	4.00	8.00
3-8,10	.70	2.00	4.00
9-Krigstein-a	2.00	5.00	10.00
11,13,18-Williamson-a in each (4 pgs. No. 11)	2.50	7.00	14.00
12,15-17,19,20	.50	1.50	3.00
14-Kirby-a	.85	2.50	5.00

NOTE: ***Colan*** *a-11.* ***Drucker*** *a-7, 12, 13.* ***Orlando*** *a-17.* ***Pakula*** *a-11.* ***Severin*** *a-19.* ***Tuska*** *a-11.*

BATTLE HEROES
Sept, 1966 - No. 2, Nov, 1966 (25 cents)
Stanley Publications

	Good	Fine	Mint
1,2	.30	.80	1.60

BATTLE OF THE BULGE (See Movie Classics)

BATTLE OF THE PLANETS
June, 1979 - Present (Based on syndicated cartoon by Sandy Frank)
Gold Key/Whitman No. 6 on

	Good	Fine	Mint
1		.40	.80
2-11		.30	.60

BATTLE REPORT
Aug, 1952 - No. 6, June, 1953
Ajax/Farrell Publications

	Good	Fine	Mint
1	1.50	4.00	8.00
2-6	.85	2.50	5.00

BATTLE SQUADRON
April, 1955 - No. 5, Dec, 1955
Stanmor Publications

	Good	Fine	Mint
1	1.20	3.50	7.00
2-5	.70	2.00	4.00

BATTLESTAR GALACTICA (Also see Marvel Super Spec. No. 8)
March, 1979 - No. 23, January, 1981
Marvel Comics Group

	Good	Fine	Mint
1	.25	.70	1.40
2,3: 1-3-Partial-r		.50	1.00
4-10		.40	.80
11-23		.30	.60

Note: ***Austin*** *c-9i.* ***Simonson*** *a(p)-4,5,11-20,22,23.*

BATTLE STORIES
1952 - No. 11, 1953
Fawcett Publications

	Good	Fine	Mint
1-Evans-a	3.00	9.00	18.00
2-11	1.50	4.00	8.00

BATTLE STORIES
1963 - 1964
Super Comics

	Good	Fine	Mint
Reprints No. 10-12,15-18; Jet Powers in No. 15 by Powell	.35	1.00	2.00

BEACH BLANKET BINGO (See Movie Classics)

BEAGLE BOYS, THE (Walt Disney)
Nov, 1964 - No. 47, Feb, 1979
Gold Key

	Good	Fine	Mint
1	.85	2.50	5.00
2-5	.50	1.50	3.00
6-10	.30	.80	1.60
11-20: 11,14-Reprints		.50	1.00
21-47		.30	.60

BEAGLE BOYS VS. UNCLE SCROOGE
March, 1979 - No. 12, Feb, 1980
Gold Key

	Good	Fine	Mint
1		.50	1.00
2-12: 9-Reprints		.30	.60

BEANBAGS
Winter, 1951 - No. 2, Spring, 1952
Ziff-Davis Publ. Co. (Approved Comics)

	Good	Fine	Mint
1,2	2.00	5.00	10.00

BEANIE THE MEANIE
1958 - No. 3, May, 1959
Fago Publications

	Good	Fine	Mint
1-3	.70	2.00	4.00

BEANY AND CECIL (TV) (Bob Clampett's. . .)
Jan, 1952 - 1955; July-Sept, 1962 - No. 5, July-Sept, 1963
Dell Publishing Co.

	Good	Fine	Mint
4-Color 368	3.00	9.00	18.00
4-Color 414,448,477,530,570,635	2.00	6.00	12.00
01-057-209	2.00	6.00	12.00
2-5	1.50	4.00	8.00

BEAR COUNTRY (Disney) (See 4-Color No. 758)

BEATLES, THE (See Strange Tales No. 130, My Little Margie No. 54, Jimmy Olsen No. 79, Summer Love)

BEATLES, LIFE STORY, THE
Sept-Nov, 1964 (35 cents)
Dell Publishing Co.

	Good	Fine	Mint
1-Stories with color photo pin-ups	11.00	32.00	70.00

BEATLES YELLOW SUBMARINE (See Movie Comics under *Yellow. . .*)

BEAVER VALLEY (See 4-Color No. 625)

BEDKNOBS & BROOMSTICKS (See Walt Disney Showcase No. 6)

BEE 29, THE BOMBARDIER

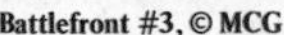
Battlefront #3, © MCG

Battlestar Galactica #1, © MCG

Battle Stories #4, © FAW

Beep Beep, The Road Runner #14, © DELL

Best Comics #1, © BP

Best Love #33, © MCG

BEE 29, THE BOMBARDIER (continued)
February, 1945
Neal Publications

	Good	Fine	Mint
1-(Funny animal)	2.00	5.00	10.00

BEEP BEEP, THE ROAD RUNNER (TV)(Also see Daffy)
July, 1958 - No. 14, Aug-Oct, 1962; Oct, 1966 - Present
Dell Publishing Co./Gold Key No. 1-88/Whitman No. 89 on

	Good	Fine	Mint
4-Color 918,1008,1046	.70	2.00	4.00
4(2-4/60)-14(Dell)	.35	1.00	2.00
1	.70	2.00	4.00
2-5	.35	1.00	2.00
6-18		.60	1.20
19-with pull-out poster		.60	1.20
20-40		.50	1.00
41-60		.40	.80
61-90		.30	.60
Florida Power & Light, PG&E Kite Giveaway ('67, '71), 8pgs.	.30	.80	1.60

(See March of Comics No. 351,353,375,387,397)
NOTE: *5,8-10,35,59-65,68 are reprints.*

BEETLE BAILEY (Also see Comics Reading Library)
No. 469, 5/53 - No. 38, 5-7/62; No. 39, 11/62 - No. 53, 5/66; No. 54, 8/66 - No. 66, 1968; No. 67, 2/69 - No. 119, 11/76; No. 120, April, 1978 - No. 132, April, 1980
Dell Publishing Co./Gold Key No. 39-53/King No. 54-66/Charlton No. 67-119/Gold Key No. 120-131/Whitman No. 132 on

	Good	Fine	Mint
4-Color 469,521,552,622	.70	2.00	4.00
5-10	.35	1.00	2.00
11-50	.25	.70	1.40
51-132		.30	.60
Bold Detergent Giveaway(1969)-same as regular ish (No. 67) minus price		.40	.80
Cerebral Palsy Assn. Giveaway V2No.71(1969)-V2No.73(1/70)		.40	.80
Giant Comic Album(1972, 59 cents, 11x14'') Color cover, B&W interior, modern promotions (reprints)		.40	.80
Red Cross giveaway, 16pp, 5x7'', 1969, paper cover		.40	.80

BEHIND PRISON BARS
1952
Realistic Comics (Avon)

	Good	Fine	Mint
1-Kinstler-c	7.50	22.00	44.00

BEHOLD THE HANDMAID
1954 (Religious) (25 cents with a 20 cent sticker price)
George Pflaum

	Good	Fine	Mint
	5.00	15.00	30.00

NOTE: *Several copies surfaced in 1979 with prices varying widely.*

BELIEVE IT OR NOT (See Ripley's . . .)

BEN AND ME (See 4-Color No. 539)

BEN BOWIE & HIS MOUNTAIN MEN
1952 - No. 17, Nov-Jan, 1958-59
Dell Publishing Co.

	Good	Fine	Mint
4-Color 443	1.00	3.00	6.00
4-Color 513,557,599,626,657	.85	2.50	5.00
7(5-7/56)-10	.70	2.00	4.00
11-Intro. & origin Yellow Hair	.50	1.50	3.00
12-17	.35	1.00	2.00

BEN CASEY (TV)
June-July, 1962 - No. 10, June-Aug, 1965
Dell Publishing Co.

	Good	Fine	Mint
12-063-207	.85	2.50	5.00
2(10/62)-10	.50	1.50	3.00

BEN CASEY FILM STORY
November, 1962
Gold Key

	Good	Fine	Mint
30009-211-All photos	2.00	6.00	12.00

BENEATH THE PLANET OF THE APES (See Movie Comics)

BEN FRANKLIN KITE FUN BOOK
1975, 1977 (16 pages; 5-1/8''x6-5/8'')
Southern Calif. Edison Co./PG&E('77)

	Good	Fine	Mint
	.30	.80	1.60

BEN HUR (See 4-Color No. 1052)

BEN ISRAEL
1974 (39 cents)
Logos International

	Good	Fine	Mint
		.50	1.00

BEOWULF
April-May, 1975 - No. 6, Feb-Mar, 1976
National Periodical Publications

	Good	Fine	Mint
1	.30	.80	1.60
2-6		.50	1.00

BERRYS, THE
May, 1956
Argo Publ.

	Good	Fine	Mint
1-Reprints daily & Sunday strips & daily Animal Antics by Ed Nofziger	1.20	3.50	7.00

BEST COMICS
Nov, 1939 - 1940 (small size, reads sideways)
Better Publications

	Good	Fine	Mint
1-Red Mask begins	10.00	30.00	60.00
2-4	6.00	18.00	36.00

BEST FROM BOY'S LIFE, THE
Oct, 1957 - No. 5, Oct, 1958 (35 cents)
Gilberton Company

	Good	Fine	Mint
1-Space Conquerors & Kam of the Ancient Ones app.; also No. 3	1.00	3.00	6.00
2-5	.70	2.00	4.00

BEST LOVE (Formerly Sub-Mariner No. 32)
No. 33, Aug, 1949 - No. 36, April, 1950
Marvel Comics (MPI)

	Good	Fine	Mint
33,34	1.50	4.00	8.00
35,36-Everett-a	2.00	6.00	12.00

NOTE: *Photo-c-No. 35.*

BEST OF BUGS BUNNY, THE
Oct, 1966 - No. 2, Oct, 1968
Gold Key

	Good	Fine	Mint
1,2	.70	2.00	4.00

BEST OF DC, THE (Blue Ribbon Digest) (See Limited Coll. Ed. C-52)
Sept-Oct, 1979 - Present (100 pages; all reprints)
DC Comics

	Good	Fine	Mint
1-Superman reprints; Orlando-c		.60	1.20
2-Batman reprints; Adams-a(r)		.60	1.20
3-Super Friends, 4-Rudolph		.50	1.00
5-The Years Best Comics Stories		.50	1.00
6-Daily Planet, 7-Superboy		.50	1.00
8-Superman		.50	1.00
9-Batman; Aparo-c		.50	1.00
10-Super Villians; Penguin origin		.50	1.00
11-Year's Best in Comic Stores		.50	1.00
12-Superman-r		.50	1.00
13-D.C. Comics Presents; Superman-r		.50	1.00
14-Batman's Villians; Rogers-a		.50	1.00
15-Superboy-r		.50	1.00
16-Superman-r; anniversary ish		.50	1.00
17-Supergirl		.50	1.00
18-The New Teen Titans		.50	1.00

BEST OF DC (continued)

	Good	Fine	Mint
19-Superman-r		.50	1.00
20-J.S.A.-r w/origin		.50	1.00

NOTE: ***Anderson** a-1.* ***Aparo** a-14r; c-9, 14.* ***Infantino** a-18.* ***Newton** a-5.* ***Perez** c-18.* ***Staton** a-5.*

BEST OF DENNIS THE MENACE, THE
Summer, 1959 - No. 5, Spring, 1961 (100 pages)
Hallden/Fawcett Publications

	Good	Fine	Mint
1	1.20	3.50	7.00
2-5	.85	2.50	5.00

BEST OF DONALD DUCK, THE
Nov, 1965 (36 pages)
Gold Key

	Good	Fine	Mint
1-Reprints 4-Color 223 by Barks	5.00	15.00	30.00

BEST OF DONALD DUCK & UNCLE SCROOGE, THE
Nov, 1964 - No. 2, Sept, 1967 (25 cents)
Gold Key

	Good	Fine	Mint
1(30022-411)('64)-Reprints 4-Color 189 & 408 by Carl Barks No. 189-c redrawn by Barks	8.00	24.00	36.00
2(30022-709)('67)-Reprints 4-Color 256 & "Seven Cities of Cibola" & U.S. 8 by Barks	6.00	18.00	30.00

BEST OF MARMADUKE, THE
1960 (a dog)
Charlton Comics

	Good	Fine	Mint
1-Brad Anderson's strip reprints	.50	1.50	3.00

BEST OF THE WEST (See A-1 Comics)
1951 - No. 12, April-June, 1954
Magazine Enterprises

	Good	Fine	Mint
1(A-1 42)-Ghost Rider, Durango Kid, Straight Arrow, Bobby Benson begin	10.00	30.00	60.00
2(A-1 46), 3(A-1 52), 4(A-1 59), 5(A-1 66)	4.00	12.00	24.00
6(A-1 70), 7(A-1 76), 8(A-1 81), 9(A-1 85), 10(A-1 87), 11(A-1 97), 12(A-1 103)	2.50	7.00	14.00

NOTE: ***Borth** a-12.* ***Powell** a-1,12.*

BEST OF UNCLE SCROOGE & DONALD DUCK, THE
November, 1966 (25 cents)
Gold Key

	Good	Fine	Mint
1(30030-611)-Reprints part 4-Color 159 & 456 & Uncle Scrooge 6,7 by Carl Barks	5.00	15.00	30.00

BEST OF WALT DISNEY COMICS, THE
1974 (In color; $1.50; 52 pages) (Walt Disney)
8½x11" cardboard covers; 32,000 printed of each
Western Publishing Co.

	Good	Fine	Mint
96170-Reprints 1st two stories less 1 pg. each from 4-Color 62	1.00	3.00	6.00
96171-Reprints Mickey Mouse and the Bat Bandit of Inferno Gulch from 1934 (strips) by Gottfredson	1.00	3.00	6.00
96172-Reprints Uncle Scrooge 386 & two other stories	1.00	3.00	6.00
96173-Reprints "Ghost of the Grotto" (from 4-Color 159) & "Christmas on Bear Mtn." (from 4-Color 178)	1.00	3.00	6.00

BEST ROMANCE
No. 5, Feb-Mar, 1952 - No. 7, Aug, 1952
Standard Comics (Visual Editions)

	Good	Fine	Mint
5-Toth-a	2.50	7.00	14.00
6,7-Photo-c	1.00	3.00	6.00

BEST SELLER COMICS (See Tailspin Tommy)

BEST WESTERN (Formerly Terry Toons?) (Western Outlaws & Sheriffs No. 60 on)
No. 58, June, 1949 - No. 59, Aug, 1949
Marvel Comics (IPC)

	Good	Fine	Mint
58,59-Black Rider	2.50	7.00	14.00

BETTY AND HER STEADY (Going Steady with Betty No. 1)
No. 2, Mar-Apr, 1950
Avon Periodicals

	Good	Fine	Mint
2	3.50	10.00	20.00

BETTY AND ME
Aug, 1965 - Present (Giants No. 36 on)
Archie Publications

	Good	Fine	Mint
1	3.50	10.00	20.00
2-5: 3-Origin Superteen; in new costume No. 4-7; dons new helmet No. 5, ends No. 8	1.50	4.00	8.00
6-10	.70	2.00	4.00
11-35	.35	1.00	2.00
36-55 (52 pages)		.40	.80
56-116		.30	.60

BETTY AND VERONICA (See Archie's Girls . . .)

BETTY & VERONICA ANNUAL DIGEST
November, 1980 - Present
Archie Publications

	Good	Fine	Mint
1, 2(11/81)		.40	.80

BETTY & VERONICA CHRISTMAS SPECTACULAR (See Archie Giant Series Mag. No. 159,168,180,191,204,217,229,241,453,465,477, 489,501)

BETTY & VERONICA SPECTACULAR (See Archie Giant Series Mag. No.11,16,21,26,32,138,145,153,162,173,184,197,201,210,214, 221,226,234,238,246,250,458,462,470,482,486,494,498,506, 510)

BETTY & VERONICA SUMMER FUN (See Archie Giant Series Mag. No. 8,13,18,23,28,34,140,147,155,164,175,187,199,212,224,236, 248,460,484,496,508)

BEVERLY HILLBILLIES (TV)
Apr-June, 1963 - No. 21, Oct, 1971
Dell Publishing Co.

	Good	Fine	Mint
1	1.50	4.00	8.00
2-10	.70	2.00	4.00
11-21	.50	1.50	3.00

NOTE: *No. 11-14,17,18 are photo covers.*

BEWARE (Formerly Fantastic; Chilling Tales No. 13 on)
No. 10, June, 1952 - No. 12, Oct, 1952
Youthful Magazines

	Good	Fine	Mint
10-Pit & the Pendulum adaptation; Wildey, Harrison-a	4.00	12.00	24.00
11-Harrison-a; Ambrose Bierce adapt.	3.50	10.00	20.00
12-Used in **SOTI**, pg. 388; Harrison-a	5.00	14.00	28.00

BEWARE
Jan, 1953 - No. 15, May, 1955
Trojan Magazines/Merit Publ.

	Good	Fine	Mint
13(No. 1)-Harrison-a	4.00	12.00	24.00
14(No. 2)	3.50	10.00	20.00
15,16(No. 3,4)-Harrison-a	3.00	8.00	16.00
5,9,12	3.00	8.00	16.00
6-Ill. in **SOTI**-"His tongue. . . it's been ripped out"	8.00	24.00	48.00
7,8-Check-a	3.50	10.00	20.00
10-Frazetta/Check-c; Disbrow, Check-a	17.00	50.00	100.00
11-Disbrow-a	3.50	10.00	20.00
13,15-Harrison-a	3.50	10.00	20.00
14-Krenkel/Harrison-c	3.50	10.00	20.00

NOTE: ***Hollingsworth** a-16(4),9; c-16(4),8,9.*

BEWARE! (Tomb of Darkness No. 9 on)
March, 1973 - No. 8, May, 1974
Marvel Comics Group

The Best Of U.S. & D.D. #1, © WDP

Beverly Hillbillies #16, © DELL

Beware #10, © YM

Beware Terror Tales #3, © FAW

The Beyond #18, © ACE

Big Shot Comics #32, © CCG

BEWARE! (continued)

	Good	Fine	Mint
1		.50	1.00
2-6,8		.30	.60
7-Torres r-/Mystical Tales No. 7		.30	.60

BEWARE TERROR TALES
May, 1952 - 1953
Fawcett Publications

	Good	Fine	Mint
1-E.C. art swipe/Haunt of Fear No. 5	3.50	10.00	20.00
2-8: 8-Tothish-a	2.00	6.00	12.00
9-11-(Exist?)	1.75	5.00	10.00

NOTE: ***Bernard Bailey*** a-1; c-1,2,4,5. ***Powell*** *a-1,2,8.* ***Sekowsky*** *a-2*

BEWARE THE CREEPER (See Adventure, Brave & the Bold, First Issue Special, Showcase, and World's Finest)
May-June, 1968 - No. 6, March-April, 1969
National Periodical Publications

	Good	Fine	Mint
1-Ditko-a	.60	1.80	3.60
2-6-Ditko-a	.40	1.20	2.40

BEWITCHED (TV)
April-June, 1965 - No. 14, Oct, 1969
Dell Publishing Co.

	Good	Fine	Mint
1	.85	2.50	5.00
2-14: Photo-c No. 3-10	.50	1.50	3.00

BEYOND, THE
Nov, 1950 - No. 33, 1955
Ace Magazines

	Good	Fine	Mint
1-Bakerish-a(p)	5.00	14.00	28.00
2-Bakerish-a(p)	3.50	10.00	20.00
3-5,7-9	2.50	7.00	14.00
6-Bakerish-a	3.50	10.00	20.00
10-Harrison/Wood?-a	3.50	10.00	20.00
11-17,19,20	1.75	5.00	10.00
18-Used in **POP**, pgs. 81,82	2.00	6.00	12.00
21-33	1.50	4.00	8.00

NOTE: ***Cameron*** *a-20-26,30; c-20.* ***Colan*** *a-13.* ***Sekowsky*** *a-3, 5, 7, 11, 19p, 20p. No. 1 was to appear as Challenge of the Unknown No. 7.*

BEYOND THE GRAVE
July, 1975 - No. 6, June, 1976
Charlton Comics

	Good	Fine	Mint
1-Ditko-a	.30	.80	1.60
2,4-6-Ditko-a		.60	1.20
3-No Ditko-a		.30	.60

NOTE: ***Ditko*** *c-2,3,6.*

BIBLE TALES FOR YOUNG FOLK
Aug, 1953 - No. 5, Mar, 1954
Atlas Comics (OMC)

	Good	Fine	Mint
1	3.50	10.00	20.00
2-Everett, Krigstein-a	3.50	10.00	20.00
3-5	2.50	7.00	14.00

BIG ALL-AMERICAN COMIC BOOK, THE
1944 (One Shot) (132 pages)
All-American/National Periodical Publ.

	Good	Fine	Mint
1-Wonder Woman, Green Lantern, Flash, The Atom, Wildcat, Scribbly, The Whip, Ghost Patrol, Hawkman by Kubert (1st on Hawkman), Hop Harrigan, Johnny Thunder, Little Boy Blue, Mr. Terrific, Mutt & Jeff app.; Sargon on cover only	85.00	250.00	500.00

BIG BOOK OF FUN COMICS
Spring, 1936 (52 pages)
National Periodical Publications

	Good	Fine	Mint
1 (Rare) - Large size; reprints New Fun No. 1-5 (1st DC Annual)	60.00	180.00	400.00

BIG BOOK ROMANCES
February, 1950(no date given) (148 pages)
Fawcett Publications

	Good	Fine	Mint
1-Contains remaindered Fawcett romance comics - several combinations possible	5.00	14.00	28.00

BIG BOY (See Adventures of the . . .)

BIG CHIEF WAHOO
1942
Eastern Color Printing/George Dougherty

	Good	Fine	Mint
1-Newspaper reprints	6.00	18.00	36.00
2-Steve Roper app.	3.50	10.00	20.00
3-5	2.50	7.00	14.00
6-10	2.00	5.00	10.00
11-23	1.50	4.00	8.00

NOTE: *Kerry Drake in some issues.*

BIG CIRCUS, THE (See 4-Color No. 1036)

BIG COUNTRY, THE (See 4-Color No. 946)

BIG DADDY ROTH
Oct-Nov, 1964 - No. 4, Apr-May, 1965 (Magazine; 35 cents)
Millar Publications

	Good	Fine	Mint
1-Toth-a	3.00	8.00	16.00
2-4-Toth-a	2.00	6.00	12.00

BIG HERO ADVENTURES (See Jigsaw)

BIG JIM'S P.A.C.K.
No date (16 pages)
Mattel, Inc. (Marvel Comics)

	Good	Fine	Mint
Giveaway with Big Jim doll		.15	.30

BIG JOHN AND SPARKIE (Formerly Sparkie, Radio Pixie)
1952
Ziff-Davis Publ. Co.

	Good	Fine	Mint
4	3.00	8.00	16.00

BIG LAND, THE (See 4-Color No. 812)

BIG RED (See Movie Comics)

BIG SHOT COMICS
May, 1940 - No. 104, Aug, 1949
Columbia Comics Group

	Good	Fine	Mint
1-Intro. Skyman; The Face (Tony Trent), The Cloak (Spy Master), Marvelo, Monarch of Magicians, Joe Palooka begin	30.00	90.00	180.00
2-Origin Skyman	14.00	40.00	80.00
3-The Cloak called Spy Chief	10.00	30.00	60.00
4,5	7.00	20.00	40.00
6-10	5.00	15.00	30.00
11-13	4.00	12.00	24.00
14-Origin Sparky Watts	5.00	14.00	28.00
15-Origin The Cloak	5.00	15.00	30.00
16-20	4.00	12.00	24.00
21-30: 29-Intro. Capt. Yank; Bo (a dog) newspaper strip reprints by Frank Beck begins, ends No. 104	3.00	8.00	16.00
31-40: 32-Vic Jordan newspaper strip reprints begin, ends No. 50	2.50	7.00	14.00
41-50: 42-No Skyman. 50-Origin The Face retold	2.00	6.00	12.00
51-60	1.50	4.00	8.00
61-70: 63 on-Tony Trent, the Face	1.00	3.00	6.00
71-80: 73-The Face cameo. 74,80: The Face app. in Tony Trent. 78-Last Charlie Chan strip reprints	1.00	3.00	6.00
81-90: 85-Tony Trent marries Babs Walsh	.95	2.80	5.60
91-104	.85	2.50	5.00

(Skyman in Outer Space No. 69-94)

NOTE: ***Mart Bailey*** *art on ''The Face''-No. 1-104. Sparky Watts by* ***Boody Rogers****-No. 14-42,77-104, (by others No. 43-76). Others than Tony Trent wear ''The Face'' mask in No. 46-63,93. Skyman by* ***Ogden Whitney****-No. 1,2,4,12-37,49,70-101. Skyman covers-No. 1,*

BIG SHOT COMICS (continued)
6,10,11,14,16,20,27,89,95,100.

BIG TEX
June, 1953
Toby Press

	Good	Fine	Mint
1-Contains (3) John Wayne stories-r with name changed to Big Tex	2.00	5.00	10.00

BIG-3
Fall, 1940 - No. 7, Jan, 1942
Fox Features Syndicate

1-Blue Beetle, The Flame, & Samson begin	30.00	90.00	180.00
2	15.00	45.00	90.00
3-5	11.00	32.00	70.00
6-Last Samson	9.00	26.00	60.00
7-V-Man app.	9.00	26.00	60.00

BIG TOP COMICS, THE
1951 (no month)
Toby Press

1,2	1.00	3.00	6.00

BIG TOWN (Radio/TV)
Jan, 1951 - No. 50, Mar-Apr, 1958
National Periodical Publications

1	6.00	18.00	36.00
2	3.00	8.00	16.00
3-10	2.00	5.00	10.00
11-20	1.00	3.00	6.00
21-30	.80	2.40	4.80
31-50	.70	2.00	4.00

BIG VALLEY, THE (TV)
June, 1966 - No. 6, Oct, 1969
Dell Publishing Co.

1: Photo-c No. 1-5	.85	2.50	5.00
2-6: 6 reprints No. 1	.50	1.50	3.00

BILL BARNES COMICS (Air Ace V2No.1 on)
Oct, 1940(No. month given) - No. 12, Oct, 1943
Street & Smith Publications

1	12.00	35.00	70.00
2-Barnes as The Phantom Flyer app.	9.00	25.00	50.00
3-5	5.00	15.00	30.00
6-12	3.50	10.00	20.00

BILL BATTLE, THE ONE MAN ARMY
Oct, 1952 - 1953
Fawcett Publications

1-Photo-c	1.50	4.00	8.00
2-6: 5,6(Exist?)	.85	2.50	5.00

BILL BOYD WESTERN
Feb, 1950 - No. 23, June, 1952
Fawcett Publications

1	7.00	20.00	40.00
2-10	4.00	12.00	24.00
11-23	3.00	8.00	16.00

BILL BUMLIN (See Treasury of Comics No. 3)

BILL ELLIOTT (See Wild Bill Elliott)

BILL STERN'S SPORTS BOOK
Spring-Summer, 1951 - V2No.2, Winter, 1952
Ziff-Davis Publ. Co.(Approved Comics)

V1No.10(1951)	2.00	6.00	12.00
2(Sum'52-reg. size)	1.50	4.00	8.00
V2No.2(1952,96 pgs.)-Krigstein, Kinstler-a	3.50	10.00	20.00

BILLY AND BUGGY BEAR
1958; 1964
I.W. Enterprises/Super

	Good	Fine	Mint
I.W. Reprint No. 1(Early Timely funny animal), No. 7(1958)	.35	1.00	2.00
Super Reprint No. 10(1964)	.35	1.00	2.00

BILLY BUCKSKIN WESTERN (Two-Gun Western No. 4)
Nov, 1955 - No. 3, March, 1956
Atlas Comics (IMC No. 1/MgPC No. 2,3)

1-Mort Drucker-a	2.50	7.00	14.00
2-Mort Drucker-a	1.20	3.50	7.00
3-Williamson, Drucker-a	3.00	9.00	18.00

BILLY BUNNY (Black Cobra No. 6 on)
Feb-Mar, 1954 - No. 5, Oct-Nov, 1954
Excellent Publications

1	.85	2.50	5.00
2-5	.50	1.50	3.00

BILLY BUNNY'S CHRISTMAS FROLICS
1952 (100 pages)
Farrell Publications

1	2.00	6.00	12.00

BILLY MAKE BELIEVE (See Single Series No. 14)

BILLY THE KID (Formerly Masked Raider)
No. 9, 1957 - No. 121, Dec, 1976; No. 122, Sept, 1977 - No. 123, Oct, 1977; No. 124, Feb, 1978 - Present
Charlton Publ. Co.

9-12,14,17-19: 11-(68 pages, origin, 1st app. The Ghost Train)	1.20	3.50	7.00
13-Torres-a	1.50	4.00	8.00
15-Origin	1.50	4.00	8.00
16-Two pgs. Williamson	2.00	6.00	12.00
20-22-Severin-a(3)	2.00	6.00	12.00
23-40	.35	1.00	2.00
41-60		.50	1.00
61-80: 66-Bounty Hunter series begins. Not in No. 79,82,84-86		.40	.80
81-123: 87-Last Bounty Hunter. 111-Origin & 1st app. The Ghost Train; Sutton-a. 117-Gunsmith & Co., The Cheyenne Kid app.		.30	.60
124(2/78)-129		.30	.60
130-136		.30	.60
Modern Comics 109 (1977 reprint)		.15	.30

Note: ***Severin** a-121-129,134.*

BILLY THE KID ADVENTURE MAGAZINE
Oct, 1950 - No. 30, 1955
Toby Press

1-Williamson/Frazetta, 2 pgs.	7.00	20.00	45.00
2,4,5,7,8,10	1.50	4.50	9.00
3-Williamson/Frazetta "The Claws of Death," 4 pgs. plus Williamson-a	11.00	32.00	70.00
6-Frazetta story assist on 'Nightmare'	3.00	9.00	18.00
9-Kurtzman Pot-Shot Pete	3.50	10.00	20.00
11,12,15-20	1.20	3.50	7.00
13-Kurtzman r-/John Wayne 12 (Genius)	2.00	5.00	10.00
14-Williamson/Frazetta; r-of No. 1, 2 pgs.	3.50	10.00	20.00
21,23-30	.85	2.50	5.00
22-One pg. Williamson/Frazetta r-/No. 1	1.50	4.00	8.00

BILLY THE KID AND OSCAR
Winter, 1945 - No. 3, Summer, 1946 (funny animal)
Fawcett Publications

1	1.50	4.00	8.00
2,3	.85	2.50	5.00

BILLY WEST (Bill West No. 9,10)

Bill Barnes Comics #1, © S&S

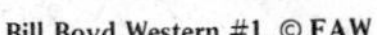
Bill Boyd Western #1, © FAW

Billy The Kid #13, © TOBY

Black & White #2, © News Synd.

Black Cat Comics #5, © HARV

Black Cat Mystic #60, © HARV

BILLY WEST (continued)
1949 - No. 9, Feb, 1951; No. 10, Feb, 1952
Standard Comics (Visual Editions)

	Good	Fine	Mint
1	2.00	5.00	10.00
2-10: 7,8-Schomburg-c	1.20	3.50	7.00

NOTE: ***Celardo*** *a-1-6,9; c-2,3.* ***Moreira*** *a-3.* ***Roussos*** *a-2.*

BING CROSBY (See Feature Films)

BINGO (. . . Comics) (H. C. Blackerby)
1945 (Reprints National material)
Howard Publ.

	Good	Fine	Mint
1-L. B. Cole opium-c	7.00	20.00	40.00

BINGO, THE MONKEY DOODLE BOY
Aug, 1951; Oct, 1953
St. John Publishing Co.

	Good	Fine	Mint
1(8/51)-by Eric Peters	1.50	4.00	8.00
1(10/53)	1.00	3.00	6.00

BINKY (Formerly Leave It to. . .)
No. 72, 4-5/70 - No. 81, 10-11/71; No. 82, Summer/77
National Periodical Publ./DC Comics

	Good	Fine	Mint
72-81		.50	1.00
82('77)-(One Shot)		.30	.60

BINKY'S BUDDIES
Jan-Feb, 1969 - No. 12, Nov-Dec, 1970
National Periodical Publications

	Good	Fine	Mint
1	.35	1.00	2.00
2-12		.50	1.00

BIONIC WOMAN, THE (TV)
October, 1977 - No. 5, June, 1978
Charlton Publications

	Good	Fine	Mint
1-5		.50	1.00

BLACK AND WHITE (Large Feature Comics No. 25 on)
1939 - 1941 (All strip reprints)
Dell Publishing Co.

	Good	Fine	Mint
1-Dick Tracy Meets the Blank	70.00	200.00	400.00
2-Terry & the Pirates	35.00	100.00	200.00
3-Heigh-Ho Silver! The Lone Ranger (text & ill.)(76 pgs.)	30.00	90.00	200.00
4-Dick Tracy Gets His Man	40.00	120.00	240.00
5-Tarzan by Harold Foster (origin); reprints 1st dailies from '29	90.00	250.00	500.00
6-Terry & the Pirates & The Dragon Lady; reprints dailies from 1936	35.00	90.00	180.00
7-(Scarce)-52 pgs.; The Lone Ranger-Hi-Yo Silver the Lone Ranger to the Rescue	50.00	140.00	280.00
8-Dick Tracy Racket Buster	30.00	100.00	200.00
9-King of the Royal Mounted	14.00	40.00	80.00
10-(Scarce)-Gangbusters (No. appears on inside front cover)	30.00	60.00	120.00
11-Dick Tracy Foils the Mad Doc Hump	35.00	100.00	200.00
12-Smilin' Jack	14.00	40.00	80.00
13-Dick Tracy & Scotty	35.00	100.00	200.00
14-Smilin' Jack	14.00	40.00	80.00
15-Dick Tracy & the Kidnapped Princess	35.00	100.00	200.00
16-Donald Duck-1st app. Daisy Duck on back cover (6/41-Disney)	200.00	600.00	1200.00
(Prices vary widely on this book)			
17-Gangbusters (1941)	14.00	40.00	80.00
18-Phantasmo	14.00	40.00	80.00
19-Dumbo Comic Paint Book (Disney); partial reprint 4-Color 17	70.00	185.00	400.00
20-Donald Duck Comic Paint Book (Rarer than No. 16) (Disney)	300.00	800.00	1600.00
(Prices vary widely on this book)			
21-Private Buck	5.00	15.00	30.00
22-Nuts & Jolts	5.00	15.00	30.00
23-The Nebbs	5.00	15.00	30.00
24-Popeye (Thimble Theatre) ½ by Segar	30.00	80.00	160.00

NOTE: *The Black & White Feature Books are oversized 8½x11-3/8'' comics with color covers and black and white interiors. The first nine (9) issues all have rough, heavy stock covers and, except for No. 7, all have 76 pages, including covers. No. 7 and No. 10-24 all have 52 pages. Beginning with No. 10 the covers are slick and thin and, because of their size, are difficult to handle without damaging. For this reason, they are seldom found in fine to mint condition. The paper stock, unlike Wow No. 1 and Capt. Marvel No. 1, is itself not unstable . . . just thin.*

BLACKBEARD'S GHOST (See Movie Comics)

BLACK BEAUTY (See 4-Color No. 440)

BLACK CAT COMICS (. . West. No. 16-19; . . Mystery No. 30 on)
June-July, 1946 - No. 29, June, 1951
Harvey Publications (Home Comics)

	Good	Fine	Mint
1-Kubert-a	24.00	70.00	140.00
2-Kubert-a	14.00	40.00	80.00
3	10.00	28.00	56.00
4-The Red Demons begin (The Demon No. 4 & 5)	10.00	28.00	56.00
5,6-The Scarlet Arrow app.; S&K-a in both; Powell-a No. 6	11.00	32.00	64.00
7-Vagabond Prince by S&K plus 1 more story	11.00	32.00	64.00
8-S&K-a	10.00	28.00	56.00
9-Origin Stuntman (r-/Stuntman No. 1); Kerry Drake begins, ends No. 12	14.00	40.00	80.00
10-20: 10,13-Kerry Drake app. 14,15,17-Mary Worth app. plus Invisible Scarlett O'Neil-No. 15,20,24	6.00	18.00	36.00
21-26,28	5.00	15.00	30.00
27-Used in **SOTI**, pg. 193; X-Mas-c	7.00	20.00	40.00
29-Black Cat bondage-c; Black Cat stories	5.00	14.00	28.00

BLACK CAT MYSTERY (Formerly Black Cat; . . . Western Mystery No. 54; . . . Western No. 55,56; . . . Mystery No. 57; . . . Mystic No. 58-62; Black Cat No. 63-65)
No. 30, Aug, 1951 - No. 65, April, 1963
Harvey Publications

	Good	Fine	Mint
30-Black Cat on cover only	4.00	12.00	24.00
31,32,34,35,37,38,40	3.50	10.00	20.00
33-Used in **POP**, pg. 89; electrocution-c	4.00	12.00	24.00
36,39-Used in **SOTI**: No. 36-Pgs. 270,271; No. 39-Pgs. 386, 387,388	11.00	32.00	64.00
41-43	3.00	9.00	18.00
44,46-49,51-Nostrand-a in all	3.50	10.00	20.00
45-Classic ''Colorama'' by Powell; Nostrand-a	5.00	15.00	30.00
50-Check-a; Lee Elias?-c showing a mans face burning away	5.00	15.00	30.00
52,53	3.00	9.00	18.00
54-Two Black Cat stories	3.50	10.00	20.00
55,56-Black Cat app.	3.00	8.00	16.00
57(7/56)-Simon?-c	3.00	8.00	16.00
58-60-Kirby-a(4)	3.50	10.00	20.00
61-Nostrand-a & classic ''Colorama'' reprinted from 45	3.00	8.00	16.00
62(3/58)-E.C. story swipe	2.50	7.00	14.00
63-65(10/62-4/63)-All Giants (25 cents)-Black Cat app.	3.50	10.00	20.00

NOTE: ***Meskin*** *a-51.* ***Palais*** a-30, 31(2), 32(2), 34, 38, 40. ***Powell*** *a-32-35, 36(2), 40, 41, 43-52, 57. Bondage-c-No. 32, 34, 43.*

BLACK COBRA (Formerly Billy Bunny)
No. 1, 10-11/54; No. 6(No. 2), 12-1/54-55; No. 3, 2-3/55
Ajax/Farrell Publications

	Good	Fine	Mint
1	4.00	12.00	24.00
6(No. 2)-Formerly Billy Bunny	3.00	9.00	18.00
3	3.00	9.00	18.00

BLACK DIAMOND WESTERN (Desperado No. 1-8)
No. 9, Mar, 1949 - No. 60, Feb, 1956
Lev Gleason Publications

	Good	Fine	Mint
9-Origin	3.50	10.00	20.00
10-15	2.00	5.00	10.00
16-28-Wolverton's Bing Bang Buster	3.00	8.00	16.00
29,30,32-60	.70	2.00	4.00
31-One pg. Frazetta	1.50	4.00	8.00

BLACK FURY (Wild West No. 58) (See Blue Bird)
May, 1955 - No. 57, Mar-Apr, 1966 (Horse stories)
Charlton Comics Group

	Good	Fine	Mint
1	1.20	3.50	7.00
2-15	.35	1.00	2.00
16-18-Ditko-a	1.20	3.50	7.00
19-57		.50	1.00

BLACK GOLD
1945? (8 pgs. in color)
Esso Service Station (Giveaway)

	Good	Fine	Mint
Reprints from True Comics	3.00	9.00	18.00

BLACK GOLIATH
Feb, 1976 - No. 5, Nov, 1976
Marvel Comics Group

	Good	Fine	Mint
1		.50	1.00
2-5		.40	.80

BLACKHAWK (Formerly Uncle Sam No. 1-8)
No. 9, Winter, 1944 - No. 243, Oct-Nov, 1968; No. 244, Jan-Feb, 1976 - No. 250, Jan-Feb, 1977
Comic Magazines(Quality)No. 9-107; National Periodical Publ. No. 108(1/57) on

	Good	Fine	Mint
9 (1944)	50.00	140.00	280.00
10 (1946)	24.00	70.00	140.00
11-15: 14-Ward-a; Fear app.	17.00	50.00	100.00
16-20	11.00	32.00	64.00
21-30	9.00	25.00	50.00
31-40	6.00	18.00	36.00
41-49,51-60	4.00	12.00	24.00
50-1st Killer Shark; origin in text	5.00	15.00	30.00
61-Used in **POP**, pg. 91	5.00	15.00	30.00
62-Used in **POP**, pg. 92 & color illo	5.00	15.00	30.00
63-65,67-70,72-80: 70-Return of Killer Shark. 75-Intro. Blackie the Hawk	3.50	10.00	20.00
66-B&W and color illos in **POP**	5.50	16.00	32.00
71-Origin retold	4.00	12.00	24.00
81-92,94-107	3.00	8.00	16.00
93-Origin in text	3.50	10.00	20.00
108-Re-intro. Blackie, the Hawk, their mascot; not in No. 115	4.00	12.00	30.00
109-117	2.00	5.00	10.00
118-Frazetta r-/Jimmy Wakely 4, 3 pgs.	5.00	14.00	28.00
119-130	1.20	3.50	7.00
131-142,144-160: 133-Intro. Lady Blackhawk	.70	2.00	4.00
143-Kurtzman r-/Jimmy Wakely 4	1.00	3.00	6.00
161-163,165-190	.40	1.10	2.20
164-Origin retold	.70	2.00	4.00
191-197,199-202,204-210: Combat Diary series begins. 197-New look for Blackhawks	.30	.80	1.60
198-Origin retold	.35	1.00	2.00
203-Origin Chop Chop	.35	1.00	2.00
211-243(1968): 228-Batman, Green Lantern, Superman, The Flash cameos. 230-Blackhawks become superheroes. 242-Return to old costumes	.30	.80	1.60
244,245('76)-Kubert-c; Evans-a each		.50	1.00
246-250: 250-Chuck dies; Evans-a(p)		.50	1.00

NOTE: ***Crandall** a-10, 11, 16, 18-20, 22-26, 30-33, 39-44, 46-50, 52-58, 60, 63, 64, 66, 67; c-18-20, 22-on(most). **Kubert** c-245. **Ward** a-16-27(Chop Chop, 8pgs. ea.); pencilled stories-No. 17-63(approx.).*

BLACKHAWK INDIAN TOMAHAWK WAR, THE
1951
Avon Periodicals

	Good	Fine	Mint
nn-Kinstler-c; Kit West story	3.50	10.00	20.00

BLACK HOLE
March, 1980 - Present (54 pgs.; $1.50; 11-1/16x8-7/16")
Whitman Publ. Co.

	Good	Fine	Mint
1,2,3-Reprints; photo-c		.75	1.50
4,5		.50	1.00

BLACK HOOD COMICS (Formerly Hangman No. 2-8; Laugh Comics No. 20 on)
No. 9, Winter, 1944 - No. 19, Summer, 1946
MLJ Magazines

	Good	Fine	Mint
9-The Hangman & The Boy Buddies cont'd	12.00	35.00	70.00
10-The Hangman & Dusty, the Boy Detective app.	7.00	20.00	40.00
11-Dusty app.; no Hangman	5.00	15.00	30.00
12-18: 17-Bondage-c	5.00	15.00	30.00
19-I.D. exposed	6.00	18.00	36.00

(Also see Archie's Super-Hero Special Digest No. 2)

BLACK JACK (Rocky Lane's . . ., formerly Jim Bowie)
No. 20, Nov, 1957 - No. 30, Nov, 1959
Charlton Comics

	Good	Fine	Mint
20,21	.60	1.80	3.60
22-(68 pages)	.85	2.50	5.00
23-Williamson-a	2.50	7.00	14.00
24,26,28-Ditko-a	1.20	3.50	7.00
25,27,29,30	.60	1.80	3.60

BLACK KNIGHT, THE
1952 - 1953
Toby Press

	Good	Fine	Mint
1 (1952)	4.00	12.00	24.00
1 (5/53-Toby)-Bondage-c	3.00	9.00	18.00
Super Reprint No. 11 (1963)	.85	2.50	5.00

BLACK KNIGHT, THE
May, 1955 - No. 5, April, 1956
Atlas Comics (MgPC)

	Good	Fine	Mint
1	14.00	40.00	80.00
2-5	10.00	30.00	60.00

BLACK LIGHTNING (See Cancelled Comic Cavalcade, DC Comics Presents No. 16, and World's Finest)
April, 1977 - No. 11, Sept-Oct, 1978
National Periodical Publications/DC Comics

	Good	Fine	Mint
1		.45	.90
2-11: 4,5-Superman, J. Olsen x-over; Intro Cyclotronic Man-No. 4		.30	.60

NOTE: ***Buckler** c-2, 3, 6-11.*

BLACK MAGIC (. . . Magazine) (Becomes Cool Cat)
10-11/50 - V7No.3, 7-8/60; V7No.4, 9-10/60 - V8No.5, 11-12/61
V1No.1-5, 52pgs.; V1No.6, V2No.1-12, 48pgs.
Crestwood Publ. To V4No.5/Headline to V7No.2/Crestwood(Prize)

	Good	Fine	Mint
V1No.1-S&K story, 10 pgs.; 2 Meskin stories	9.00	25.00	50.00
2-S&K c/a, 17 pgs.	5.00	14.00	28.00
3(2-3/51)-S&K-a	4.00	12.00	24.00
4-S&K c/a, 9 pgs.	4.00	12.00	24.00
5-S&K-a	3.50	10.00	20.00
6-S&K c/a, 5 pgs.	3.50	10.00	20.00
V2No.1(10-11/51),4,5,7(6/52, No. 13 on cover)-S&K-a	3.00	8.00	16.00
2,3,6,10,11-S&K-c only	2.00	5.00	10.00

Blackhawk #50, © DC

Blackhawk #203, © DC

Black Lightning #1, © DC

Black Magic V4#3, © PRIZE

Black Terror #22, © BP

Blast-Off #1, © HARV

BLACK MAGIC (continued)

	Good	Fine	Mint
8,9,12-S&K-a	2.50	7.00	14.00
V3No.1-6(5/53)-S&K c/a in all(No. 19-24)	2.00	6.00	12.00
V4No.1(6-7/53),2,6(5-6/54)-S&K c/a in all(No.25,26,30)	2.00	6.00	12.00
V4No.3-5-Ditko-a(No.27-29)	3.50	10.00	20.00
V5No.1-3(11-12/54)(no No.4-6)-S&K c/a(No.31-33)	2.00	6.00	12.00
V6No.1(9-10/57)-No.6(7-8/58)	1.00	3.00	6.00
V7No.1(9-10/58), 2(11-12/58), 3(7-8/60)	.70	2.00	4.00
4(9-10/60), 5(11-12/60)-Torres-a in all	1.20	3.50	7.00
6(1-2/61)	.55	1.60	3.20
V8No.1(3-4/61)	.55	1.60	3.20
2(5-6/61)-E.C. story swipe, Ditko-a	1.00	3.00	6.00
3(7-8/61)-E.C. swipe/W.F. 22	1.00	3.00	6.00
4,5	.55	1.60	3.20

NOTE: *__Ditko__ a-V2No.2. __Meskin__ a-1(2), 2, 4, 5(2), 6, V2No.1, 2(2), 11(2)6. __Nostrand__ a-V4No.4. __Orlando__ a-V6No.1. __Tuska__ a-most early ish. __Wildey__ a-V6No.1.*

BLACK MAGIC
Oct-Nov, 1973 - No. 9, Apr-May, 1975
National Periodical Publications

	Good	Fine	Mint
1-S&K reprints		.40	.80
2-9-S&K reprints		.25	.50

BLACKMAIL TERROR (See Harvey Comics Library)

BLACKMAN
No Date (1981)
Leader Comics Group

	Good	Fine	Mint
V1No.1		.30	.60

BLACKOUTS (See Broadway Hollywood . . .)

BLACK PANTHER, THE (Also see Jungle Action)
January, 1977 - No. 15, May, 1979
Marvel Comics Group

	Good	Fine	Mint
1-Kirby c/a		.60	1.20
2-Kirby c/a		.40	.80
3-15: Kirby-c/a-3-11		.40	.80

NOTE: *__J. Buscema__ c-15. __Layton__ c-13i.*

BLACK PHANTOM (See Wisco)
Nov, 1954 - No. 2, 1955
Magazine Enterprises

	Good	Fine	Mint
1 (A-1 122)	8.00	24.00	48.00
2 (Rare)	12.00	35.00	70.00

BLACK RIDER (Formerly Western Winners; Western Tales of Black Rider No. 28-31; Gunsmoke Western No. 32 on)
No. 8, 3/50 - No. 18, 1/52; No. 19, 11/53 - No. 27, 3/55
Marvel/Atlas Comics(CDS No. 8-17/CPS No. 19 on)

	Good	Fine	Mint
8 (No. 1)	7.00	20.00	40.00
9	4.00	12.00	24.00
10-Origin Black Rider	5.00	14.00	28.00
11-20: 15-Jack Keller-a	3.00	8.00	16.00
21-27: 21,23-Two-Gun Kid story. 24-Arrowhead story. 26,27-Kid Colt Outlaw story	2.00	6.00	12.00

BLACK RIDER RIDES AGAIN!
September, 1957
Atlas Comics (CPS)

	Good	Fine	Mint
1-Kirby-a(3); Powell-a; Severin-c	3.00	9.00	18.00

BLACKSTONE (See Wisco Giveaways & Super Magician Comics)

BLACKSTONE, MASTER MAGICIAN COMICS
Mar-Apr, 1946 - No. 3, July-Aug, 1946
Vital Publications/Street & Smith Publ.

	Good	Fine	Mint
1	4.00	12.00	24.00
2,3	3.50	10.00	20.00

BLACKSTONE, THE MAGICIAN
No. 2, May, 1948 - No. 4, Sept, 1948 (no No.1)
Marvel Comics (CnPC)

	Good	Fine	Mint
2-4-The Blonde Phantom in all (. . . Detective on cover only-No. 3,4); 3-Bondage-c	10.00	30.00	60.00

BLACKSTONE, THE MAGICIAN DETECTIVE FIGHTS CRIME
Fall, 1947
E. C. Comics

	Good	Fine	Mint
1-1st app. Happy Houlihans	17.00	50.00	100.00

BLACK SWAN COMICS
1945
MLJ Magazines

	Good	Fine	Mint
1-The Black Hood reprints from Black Hood No. 14	5.00	15.00	30.00

BLACK TARANTULA (See Feature Presentations No. 5)

BLACK TERROR (See Exciting & America's Best)
1942 - No. 27, June, 1949
Better Publications/Standard

	Good	Fine	Mint
1-Black Terror, Crime Crusader begin	30.00	80.00	180.00
2	14.00	40.00	90.00
3	10.00	30.00	70.00
4,5	8.00	24.00	55.00
6-10: 7-The Ghost app.	6.00	18.00	36.00
11-19	5.00	15.00	30.00
20-The Scarab app.	5.00	15.00	30.00
21-Miss Masque app.	6.00	18.00	36.00
22-Part Frazetta-a on one Black Terror story	7.00	20.00	40.00
23	5.00	15.00	30.00
24-¼ pg. Frazetta-a	5.00	15.00	30.00
25-27	5.00	15.00	30.00

NOTE: *Most issues have __Schomburg (Xela)__ covers. Bondage covers-17,24. __Meskin__ a-27. __Moreira__ a-27. __Robinson/Meskin__ a-23, 24(3), 25, 26. __Roussos/Mayo__ a-24. __Tuska__ a-27.*

BLAKE HARPER (See City Surgeon . . .)

BLAST (Satire Magazine)
Feb, 1971 - No. 2, May, 1971
G & D Publications

	Good	Fine	Mint
1-Wrightson & Kaluta-a	1.50	4.00	8.00
2-Kaluta-a	1.00	3.00	6.00

BLAST-OFF (Three Rocketeers)
October, 1965
Harvey Publications (Fun Day Funnies)

	Good	Fine	Mint
1-Kirby/Williamson-a(2); Williamson/Crandall-a(2); Williamson/Torres/Krenkel-a	3.00	8.00	16.00

BLAZE CARSON (Rex Hart No. 6 on) (See Wisco)
Sept, 1948 - No. 5, June, 1949
Marvel Comics (USA)

	Good	Fine	Mint
1	3.50	10.00	20.00
2,4,5	2.00	6.00	12.00
3-Used by N.Y. State Legis. Comm.(Injury to eye splash)	3.00	9.00	18.00

BLAZE THE WONDER COLLIE (My Love No. 1)
No. 2, Oct, 1949 - No. 3, Feb, 1950
Marvel Comics

	Good	Fine	Mint
2(No.1), 3-photo-c (Scarce)	5.00	15.00	30.00

BLAZING BATTLE TALES
July, 1975
Seaboard Periodicals (Atlas)

	Good	Fine	Mint
1-Intro. Sgt. Hawk & the Sky Demon; McWilliams-a; Thorne-c		.30	.60

BLAZING COMBAT (Magazine) (35 cents)
Oct, 1965 - No. 4, July, 1966 (Black & White)

BLAZING COMBAT (continued)
Warren Publishing Co.

	Good	Fine	Mint
1-Frazetta-c	7.00	20.00	40.00
2-4-All Frazetta-c; 4-Frazetta ½ pg.	2.50	7.50	15.00
. . . Anthology (reprints from No. 1-4)	.30	.80	1.60

NOTE: *Above has art by* ***Crandall, Evans, Morrow, Orlando, Severin, Torres, Toth, Williamson,*** *and* ***Wood.***

BLAZING COMICS
June, 1944 - No. 6(V2No.3), 1955?
Enwil Associates/Rural Home

1-The Green Turtle, Red Hawk, Black Buccaneer begin; origin Jun-Gal	5.00	15.00	30.00
2-4	3.50	10.00	20.00

5(1955?)-Black Buccaneer-c, 6(V2No.3-inside, 1955)-Indian/Jap-c
Note: No. 5 & 6 contain remaindered comics rebound and the contents can vary. Cloak & Daggar, Will Rogers, Superman 64, Star Spangled 130, Kaanga known. Value would be half of contents.

BLAZING SIXGUNS
December, 1952
Avon Periodicals

1-Kinstler c/a; Larsen/Alascia-a(2)	7.50	15.00	30.00

BLAZING SIXGUNS
1964
I.W./Super Comics

I.W. Reprint No. 1,8,9: 8-Kinstler-c; 9-Ditko-a	.40	1.20	2.40
Super Reprint No. 10,11,15,16(Buffalo Bill, Swift Deer),17(1964)	.35	1.00	2.00
12-Reprints Bullseye No. 3; S&K-a	2.00	6.00	12.00
18-Powell's Straight Arrow	.85	2.50	5.00

BLAZING SIX-GUNS
Feb, 1971 - No. 2, April, 1971 (52 pages)
Skywald Comics

1-The Red Mask, Sundance Kid begin, Avon's Geronimo reprint by Kinstler		.50	1.00
2-Wild Bill Hickok, Jesse James, Kit Carson reprints		.40	.80

BLAZING WEST (Hooded Horseman No. 23 on)
Fall, 1948 - No. 22, Mar-Apr, 1952
American Comics Group(B&I Publ./Michel Publ.)

1-Origin & 1st app. Injun Jones, Tenderfoot & Buffalo Belle; Texas Tim & Ranger begins, ends No. 13	3.00	8.00	16.00
2,3,5	1.50	4.00	8.00
4-Origin & 1st app. Little Lobo; Starr-a	1.50	4.00	8.00
6-10	1.20	3.50	7.00
11-13	1.00	3.00	6.00
14-Origin & 1st app. The Hooded Horseman; Whitney-c	1.20	3.50	7.00
15-22	.85	2.50	5.00

BLAZING WESTERN
Jan, 1954 - No. 5, Sept, 1954
Timor Publications

1-Text story by Bruce Hamilton	1.20	3.50	7.00
2-4	.85	2.50	5.00
5-Disbrow-a	1.00	3.00	6.00

BLESSED PIUS X
No date (32 pages; ½ text, ½ comics) (Paper cover)
Catechetical Guild (Giveaway)

	3.00	8.00	16.00

BLITZKRIEG!
Jan-Feb, 1976 - No. 5, Sept-Oct, 1976
National Periodical Publications

	Good	Fine	Mint
1-Kubert-c on all		.40	.80
2-5		.30	.60

BLONDE PHANTOM (Formerly All-Select No. 1-11; Lovers No. 23 on) (Also see Blackstone and Marvel Mystery)
No. 12, Winter, 1946-47 - No. 22, March, 1949
Marvel Comics (MPC)

12-Miss America begins, ends No. 14	20.00	60.00	130.00
13-Sub-Mariner begins	14.00	40.00	90.00
14,15; 14-Bondage-c. 15-Kurtzman's 'Hey Look'	12.00	35.00	75.00
16-Captain America with Bucky app.; Kurtzman's "Hey Look"	12.00	35.00	75.00
17-22	10.00	30.00	65.00

BLONDIE (See Dagwood, Daisy & Her Pups, Eat Right to Work. . . , & Comics Reading Libraries)
1942 - 1946
David McKay Publications

Feature Book 12 (Rare)	30.00	80.00	160.00
Feature Book 27-29,31,34(1940)	5.00	14.00	28.00
Feature Book 36,38,40,42,43,45,47	3.50	10.00	20.00

BLONDIE & DAGWOOD FAMILY
Oct, 1963 - No. 4, Dec, 1965 (68 pages)
Harvey Publications (King Features Synd.)

1	1.00	3.00	6.00
2-4	.70	2.00	4.00

BLONDIE COMICS (. . . Monthly No. 16-141)
Spring, 1947 - No. 163, Nov, 1965; No. 164, Aug, 1966 - No. 175, Dec, 1967; No. 177, Feb, 1969 - No. 222, Nov, 1976
David McKay No. 1-15/Harvey No. 16-163/King No. 164-175/ Charlton No. 177 on

1	5.00	15.00	30.00
2-5	3.00	8.00	16.00
6-10	2.00	5.00	10.00
11-20(No. 16, 3/50)	1.20	3.50	7.00
21-30	.55	1.60	3.20
31-50	.40	1.20	2.40
51-80	.30	.80	1.60
81-100		.60	1.20
101-130		.50	1.00
131-139		.40	.80
140-(80 pages)	.30	.80	1.60
141-166(No. 148,155,157-159,161-163 are 68 pgs.)		.60	1.20
167-One pg. Williamson ad		.40	.80
168-175,177-222(No No. 176)		.30	.60
Blondie, Dagwood & Daisy 1(100 pgs., 1953)	3.00	9.00	18.00
1950 Giveaway	1.20	3.50	7.00
1962,1964 Giveaway	.40	1.20	2.40
N. Y. State Dept. of Mental Hygiene Giveaway-('50,'56,'61) Regular size (Diff. issues) 16 pages; no No.	1.00	3.00	6.00

BLOOD IS THE HARVEST
1950 (32 pages) (paper cover)
Catechetical Guild

(Scarce)-Anti-communism(13 known copies)	135.00	400.00	800.00
Black & white version (5 known copies), saddle stitched	50.00	150.00	300.00

Untrimmed version (only one known copy); estimated value-$1800
NOTE: *In 1979 nine copies of the color version surfaced from the old Guild's files plus the five black & white copies.*

BLUE BEETLE, THE (Also see Mystery Men & Weekly Comic Mag.)
Winter, 1939-40 - No. 60, Aug, 1950
Fox Publ. No. 1-11, 31-60; Holyoke No. 12-30

1-Reprints from Mystery Men 1-5; Blue Beetle origin; Yarko the

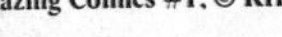
Blazing Comics #1, © RH

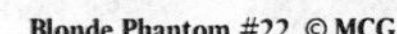
Blonde Phantom #22, © MCG

Blondie Comics #9, © KING

Blue Beetle #5, © FOX

Blue Bolt #5, © NOVP

Blue Bolt Weird #117, © STAR

BLUE BEETLE (continued) Good Fine Mint

Great reprints from Wonderworld 2-5 all by Eisner; Master Magician app.; (Blue Beetle in 4 different costumes) 50.00 150.00 300.00
2 25.00 75.00 150.00
3-Simon-c 17.00 50.00 100.00
4-Marijuana drug mention story 14.00 40.00 80.00
5 11.00 32.00 65.00
6-Dynamite Thor begins; origin Blue Beetle 9.00 25.00 50.00
7,8-Dynamo app. in both. 8-Last Thor 9.00 25.00 50.00
9,10-The Blackbird & The Gorilla app. in both 7.00 20.00 40.00
11-The Gladiator app. 7.00 20.00 40.00
12-The Black Fury app. 7.00 20.00 40.00
13-V-Man begins, ends No. 18; Kubert-a 7.00 20.00 40.00
14,15-Costumed aide, Sparky called Spunky No. 15-19 7.00 20.00 40.00
16-19: 19-Kubert-a 5.00 15.00 32.00
20-Origin/1st app. Tiger Squadron; Arabian Nights begin 6.00 18.00 36.00
21-26: 24-Intro. & only app. The Halo 4.50 14.00 28.00
27-Tamra, Jungle Prince app. 4.00 12.00 24.00
28-30 3.00 10.00 20.00
31-40: "The Threat from Saturn" serial in No. 34-37 3.00 9.00 18.00
41-45 2.50 7.00 14.00
46-The Puppeteer app; bondage-c. 2.50 7.00 14.00
47-Kamen/Baker c/a begin; The Puppeteer app. 12.00 36.00 72.00
48-50 11.00 32.00 64.00
51,53 9.00 25.00 50.00
52-Kamen bondage-c 12.00 35.00 70.00
54-Used in **SOTI**. Illo-"Children call these 'headlights' comics;" Heroin drug mention story 35.00 110.00 240.00
55,57-Last Kamen issue 10.00 30.00 60.00
56-Used in **SOTI**, pg. 145 17.00 50.00 100.00
58-60-No Kamen-a 3.00 8.00 16.00

NOTE: ***Kamen** a-47-51, 53, 55-57; c-47, 49-52. **Powell** a-4(2).*

BLUE BEETLE (Formerly The Thing; becomes Mr. Muscles No. 22 on) (See Space Adventures)
No. 18, Feb, 1955 - No. 21, Aug, 1955
Charlton Comics

18,19-(Pre-1942-r) 2.00 5.00 10.00
20-Joan Mason by Kamen 3.00 9.00 18.00
21-New material 2.00 5.00 10.00

BLUE BEETLE (Unusual Tales No. 1-49; becomes Ghostly Tales No. 55 on)
V2No.1, 6/64 - V2No.5, 3-4/65; V3No.50, 7/65 - V3No.54, 2-3/66; No. 1, 6/67 - No. 5, 10/68?
Charlton Comics

V2No.1-Origin Dan Garrett-Blue Beetle 1.50 4.00 8.00
2-5, V3No.50-54 1.00 3.00 6.00
1(1967)-Question series begins by Ditko 1.50 4.00 8.00
2-Origin Ted Kord-Blue Beetle; Dan Garrett x-over .85 2.50 5.00
3-5 (No. 1-5-Ditko-a) .70 2.00 4.00
1,3(Modern Comics-1977)-Reprints .15 .30

NOTE: *No. 6 only appeared in the fanzine 'The Charlton Portfolio.'*

BLUE BIRD COMICS
Late 1940's - 1964 (Giveaway)
Various Shoe Stores/Charlton Comics

nn(1947-50)(36 pgs.)-Several issues; Human Torch, Sub-Mariner app. in some 3.50 10.00 20.00
1959-Wild Bill Hickok No. 1 .70 2.00 4.00
1959-(6 titles; all No. 2) Black Fury No. 1,4,5, Freddy No. 4, Li'l Genius, Timmy the Timid Ghost No. 4, Masked Raider No. 4, Wild Bill Hickok (Charlton) .70 2.00 4.00
1960-(6 titles)(All No. 4) Black Fury No. 8,9, Masked Raider, Freddy No. 8,9, Timmy the Timid Ghost No. 9, Li'l Genius No. 9 (Charlton) .30 .80 1.60
1961,1962-(All No. 10's) Atomic Mouse No. 12,13,16, Black Fury No. 12, Freddy, Li'l Genius, Masked Raider, Six Gun Heroes, Timmy the Ghost, Wild Bill Hickok, Wyatt Earp No. 3,12,13,16-18 (Charlton) .50 1.00
1963-Texas Rangers No. 17 (Charlton) .40 .80
1964-Mysteries of Unexplored Worlds No. 18, War Heroes No. 18 (Charlton) .30 .60
1965-War Heroes No. 18 .25 .50

NOTE: *More than one issue of each character could have been published each year. Numbering is sporatic.*

BLUE BIRD CHILDREN'S MAGAZINE, THE
1957 (16 pages; soft cover; regular size)
Graphic Information Service

V1No.2-6: Pat, Pete & Blue Bird app. .40 1.20 2.40

BLUE BOLT
June, 1940 - No. 101 (V10No.2), Sept-Oct, 1949
Funnies, Inc. No. 1/Novelty Press/Premium Group of Comics

V1No.1-Origin Blue Bolt by Joe Simon, Sub-Zero, White Rider & Super Horse, Dick Cole, Wonder Boy & Sgt. Spook 55.00 160.00 320.00
2-S&K-a (1st S&K teamup) 40.00 120.00 240.00
3-Wolverton, 1 pg.; S&K c/a 30.00 90.00 180.00
4,5-S&K-a in each; 5-Everett-a begins on Sub-Zero 24.00 70.00 140.00
6,8-10-S&K-a 20.00 60.00 120.00
7-S&K c/a 24.00 70.00 140.00
11,12 8.00 24.00 48.00
V2No.1-Origin Dick Cole & The Twister 3.50 10.00 20.00
2-Origin The Twister retold in text 3.50 10.00 20.00
3-5: 5-Intro. Freezum 3.00 8.00 16.00
6-Origin Sgt. Spook retold 2.00 6.00 12.00
7-12: 7-Lois Blake becomes Blue Bolt's costume aide; last Twister 1.75 5.00 10.00
V3No.1-3 1.75 5.00 10.00
4-12: 4-Blue Bolt abandons costume 1.50 4.00 8.00
V4No.1-12: 8-Last Sub-Zero 1.00 3.00 6.00
V5No.1-8 .70 2.00 4.00
V6No.1-3,5-10, V7No.1-12 .70 2.00 4.00
V6No.4-Racist cover .85 2.50 5.00
V8No.1-6,8-12, V9No.1-5,7,8: V8No.9-Last Blue Bolt .55 1.60 3.20
V8No.7,V9No.6,9-L. B. Cole-c 1.50 4.00 8.00
V10No.1,2: 1-Last Dick Cole .55 1.60 3.20

NOTE: ***Everett** c-V1No.4, 11, V2No.1. **Gustavson** a-V1No.1-12, V2No.1-7. **Rico** a-V7No.4.*

BLUE BOLT (Becomes Ghostly Weird Stories No. 120 on; continuation of Novelty Blue Bolt)
No. 102, Nov-Dec, 1949 - No. 119, May-June, 1953
Star Publications

102-104-The Chameleon app.; last Target-No. 104 5.50 16.00 32.00
105-Origin Blue Bolt (from No. 1) retold by Simon; Chameleon & Target app.; opium den story 15.00 45.00 90.00
106-Blue Bolt by S&K begins; Spacehawk reprints from Target by Wolverton begins, ends No. 110; Sub-Zero begins; ends No. 108 14.00 40.00 80.00
107-110: 108-Last S&K Blue Bolt reprint. 109-Wolverton-c(r)/Spacehawk story. 110-Target app. 14.00 40.00 80.00
111-Red Rocket & The Mask-r; last Blue Bolt; 1pg. L. B. Cole-a 15.00 45.00 90.00
112-Last Torpedo Man app. 14.00 40.00 80.00
113-Wolverton's Spacehawk r-/Target V3No.7 14.00 40.00 80.00
114,116: 116-Jungle Jo-r 14.00 40.00 80.00
115-Sgt. Spook app. 15.00 45.00 90.00
117-Jo-Jo & Blue Bolt-r 14.00 40.00 80.00
118-"White Spirit" by Wood 15.00 45.00 90.00

BLUE BOLT (continued) Good Fine Mint
119-Disbrow/Cole-c; Jungle Jo-r 14.00 40.00 80.00
Accepted Reprint No. 103(1957?, no date) 2.00 6.00 12.00

NOTE: *L. B. Cole c-102 on. Disbrow a-112(2), 113(3), 114(2), 115(2), 116-118. Hollingsworth a-117. Palais a-112r.*

BLUE CIRCLE COMICS
June, 1944 - No. 6, April, 1945
Enwil Associates/Rural Home

1-The Blue Circle begins; origin Steel Fist 3.00 8.00 16.00
2-5: Last steel Fist 2.00 5.00 10.00
6-Colossal Features-r 2.00 6.00 12.00

BLUE PHANTOM, THE
June-Aug, 1962
Dell Publishing Co.

1(01-066-208)-by Fred Fredericks .85 2.50 5.00

BLUE RIBBON COMICS (. . . Mystery Comics No. 9-18)
Nov, 1939 - No. 22, March, 1942
MLJ Magazines

1-Dan Hastings, Ricky the Amazing Boy, Rang-A-Tang the Wonder Dog begin; Little Nemo app. (not by W. McCay); Jack Cole-a
50.00 150.00 300.00
2-Bob Phantom, Silver Fox (both in No. 3), Rang-A-Tang Club & Cpl. Collins begin; Jack Cole-a 17.00 50.00 100.00
3 12.00 35.00 75.00
4-Doc Strong, The Green Falcon, & Hercules begin; origin & 1st app. The Fox & Ty-Gor, Son of the Tiger 11.00 32.00 65.00
5-8: 8-Last Hercules 8.00 24.00 48.00
9-(Scarce)-Origin & 1st app. Mr. Justice 50.00 150.00 320.00
10-12: 12-Last Doc Strong 22.00 65.00 130.00
13-Inferno, the Flame Breather begins, ends No. 19
22.00 65.00 130.00
14,15,17,18: 15-Last Green Falcon 20.00 55.00 110.00
16-Origin & 1st app. Captain Flag 45.00 125.00 250.00
19-22: 20-Last Ty-Gor. 22-Origin Mr. Justice retold
15.00 45.00 90.00

BLUE RIBBON COMICS (Teen-Age Diary Secrets No. 6)
Feb, 1949 - No. 6, Aug, 1949 (See Heckle & Jeckle)
Blue Ribbon (St. John)

1,3-Heckle & Jeckle 2.00 5.00 10.00
2(4/49)-Diary Secrets; Baker-c 4.00 12.00 24.00
4(6/49)-Teen-Age Diary Secrets; Baker c/a(2)
5.00 14.00 28.00
5(8/49)-Teen-Age Diary Secrets; photo-c; Baker-a(2)
5.00 14.00 28.00
6-Dinky Duck(8/49) .85 2.50 5.00

BLUE STREAK (See Holyoke One-Shot No. 8)

BLYTHE (See 4-Color No. 1072)

B-MAN (See Double-Dare Adventures)

BO (Also see Big Shot No. 32)
June, 1955 - No. 3, Oct, 1955
Charlton Comics Group

1-3-(a dog) Newspaper reprints by Frank Beck
1.20 3.50 7.00

BOATNIKS, THE (See Walt Disney Showcase No. 1)

BOB & BETTY & SANTA'S WISHING WELL
1941 (12 pages) (Christmas giveaway)
Sears Roebuck & Co.

6.00 18.00 36.00

BOBBY BENSON'S B-BAR-B RIDERS (See Model Fun)
May-June, 1950 - No. 20, 1953
Magazine Enterprises

1-Powell-a 5.50 16.00 32.00

Good Fine Mint
2 3.00 9.00 18.00
3-5: 4-Lemonade Kid-c 2.50 7.00 14.00
6-8,10 2.00 6.00 12.00
9,11,13-Frazetta-c; Ghost Rider in No. 13-15. 13-Drug story
11.00 32.00 66.00
12,15-20(A-1 88) 2.00 6.00 12.00
14-Bondage-c 3.50 8.00 16.00
. . . in the Tunnel of Gold-(5¼x8''; 84 pgs.) Radio giveaway by Hecker-H.O. Company(H.O. Oats); contains only 12 color pages of comics, rest in novel form 3.50 8.00 16.00
. . . And The Lost Herd-22pgs. comics, otherwise same as above
2.50 7.00 14.00

NOTE: *Powell a-1-14; c-1-8,10,12,16.*

BOBBY COMICS
May, 1946
Universal Phoenix Features

1-by S. M. Iger 1.50 4.00 8.00

BOBBY SHELBY COMICS
1949
Shelby Cycle Co./Harvey Publications

1.50 4.00 8.00

BOBBY SHERMAN (TV)
Feb, 1972 - No. 7, Oct, 1972
Charlton Comics

1-7-Based on TV show ''Getting Together'' .85 2.50 5.00

BOBBY THATCHER & TREASURE CAVE
1932 (86 pages; B&W; hardcover; 7x9'')
Altemus Co.

Reprints; Storm-a 4.00 12.00 24.00

BOB COLT WESTERN
Nov, 1950 - No. 10, May, 1952
Fawcett Publications

1 7.00 20.00 40.00
2-10 4.00 12.00 24.00

BOB HOPE (See Adventures of . . .)

BOBMAN & TEDDY (See The Great Society)
1966
Parallax Publications

Bob & Ted Kennedy - political satire 1.20 3.50 7.00

BOB SCULLY, TWO-FISTED HICK DETECTIVE
No date (1930's) (36 pages; 9½x12''; B&W; paper cover)
Humor Publ. Co.

By Howard Dell; not reprints 3.50 10.00 20.00

BOB SON OF BATTLE (See 4-Color No. 729)

BOB STEELE WESTERN
Dec, 1950 - No. 10, June, 1952
Fawcett Publications

1 7.00 20.00 40.00
2-5 4.00 12.00 24.00
6-10 3.00 8.00 16.00

BOB SWIFT (Boy Sportsman)
May, 1951 - No. 5, Jan, 1952
Fawcett Publications

1 1.20 3.50 7.00
2-5: Saunders painted-c No. 1-5 .70 2.00 4.00

BOLD STORIES (Also see Candid Tales, It Rhymes With Lust)
Mar, 1950 - July, 1950 (Digest size; 144 pgs.; full color)
Kirby Publishing Co.

March issue (Very Rare) - Contains ''The Ogre of Paris'' by Wood

Blue Ribbon Comics #2, © MLJ

Bobby Benson's B-Bar-B Riders #9, © ME

Bob Steele Western #1, © FAW

Bomber Comics #2, © EP

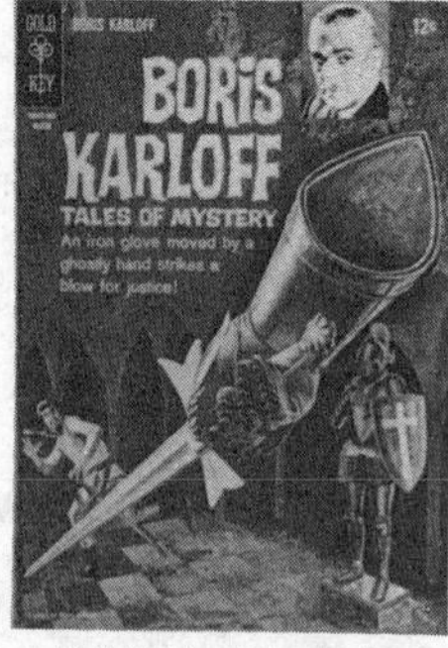

Boris Karloff Tales of Mystery #9, © GK

Boy Comics #21, © LEV

BOLD STORIES (continued) — Good / Fine / Mint
30.00 80.00 160.00
May issue (Very Rare) - Contains "The Cobra's Kiss" by Graham Ingels (21 pgs.) 20.00 60.00 120.00
July issue (Very Rare) - Contains "The Ogre of Paris" by Wood
24.00 70.00 140.00

BOMBARDIER (See Bee 29, the Bombardier)

BOMBA, THE JUNGLE BOY
Sept-Oct, 1967 - No. 7, Sept-Oct, 1968
National Periodical Publications

1-Infantino/Anderson-c .25 .70 1.40
2-7 .40 .80

BOMBER COMICS
March, 1944 - No. 4, Winter, 1944-45
Melverne Herald/Elliot Publ./Farrell/Sunrise Times

1-Origin Wonder Boy; Kismet, Man of Fate begins
4.00 12.00 24.00
2-4 3.00 8.00 16.00

BONANZA (TV)
June-Aug, 1960 - No. 37, Aug, 1970
Dell/Gold Key

4-Color 1110,1221,1283, also No. 01070-207, 01070-210
1.50 4.50 9.00
1(12/62-Gold Key) 1.00 3.00 6.00
2-10 .70 2.00 4.00
11-37 .35 1.00 2.00
NOTE: *Photo covers-No. 11,13-28.*

BONGO (See Story Hour Series)

BONGO & LUMPJAW (See 4-Color No. 706,886, and Walt Disney Showcase No. 3)

BON VOYAGE (See Movie Classics)

BOOK OF ALL COMICS
1945 (196 pages)
William H. Wise

Green Mask, Puppeteer 7.00 20.00 40.00

BOOK OF COMICS, THE
No date (1944) (132 pages) (25 cents)
William H. Wise

nn-Captain V app. 7.00 20.00 40.00

BOOK OF LOVE
1950 (132 pages)
Fox Features Syndicate

nn-See Fox Giants. Contents can vary and determines price.

BOOTS AND HER BUDDIES
No. 5, 1948 - No. 9, 1949; Dec, 1955 - No. 3, 1956
Standard Comics/Visual/Argo

5,6,8 2.00 6.00 12.00
7-Spanking panels(3) 5.50 16.00 32.00
9-(Scarce)-Frazetta-a, 2 pgs. 9.00 26.00 60.00
1-3(Argo-1955-56)-Reprints 1.20 3.50 7.00

BOOTS & SADDLES (See 4-Color No. 919,1029,1116)

BORDER PATROL
May-June, 1951 - No. 3, Sept-Oct, 1951
P. L. Publishing Co.

1 2.00 5.00 10.00
2,3 1.00 3.00 6.00

BORIS KARLOFF TALES OF MYSTERY (. . . Thriller No. 1,2)
No. 3, April, 1963 - No. 97, Feb, 1980
Gold Key

3-8,10-(Two No. 5's, 10/63,11/63) .50 1.50 3.00
9-Wood-a 1.00 3.00 6.00

Good / Fine / Mint
11-Williamson-a, Orlando-a, 8 pgs. 1.00 3.00 6.00
12-Torres, McWilliams-a; Orlando-a(2) .70 2.00 4.00
13,14,16-20 .25 .70 1.40
15-Crandall-a .50 1.50 3.00
21-Jones-a .50 1.50 3.00
22-50: 23-Reprint .50 1.00
51-73 .30 .60
74-Origin & 1st app. Taurus .30 .60
75-79,87-97: 78,81-86,88,90,92,95,97-Reprints .30 .60
80-86-(52 pages) .30 .60
Story Digest 1(7/70-Gold Key)-All text .45 .90
(See Mystery Comics Digest No. 2,5,8,11,14,17,20,23,26)
NOTE: ***Bolle*** *a-51-54, 56, 58, 59.* ***McWilliams*** *a-12, 14, 18, 19.* ***Orlando*** *a-11-15, 21.*

BORIS KARLOFF THRILLER (TV) (Becomes Boris Karloff Tales of Mystery No. 3)
Oct, 1962 - No. 2, Jan, 1963 (80 pages)
Gold Key

1-Photo-c 1.00 3.00 6.00
2 .50 1.50 3.00

BORN AGAIN
1978 (39 cents)
Spire Christian Comics (Fleming H. Revell Co.)

Watergate, Nixon, etc. .60 1.20

BOUNCER, THE (Formerly Green Mask?)
1944 - No. 14, Jan, 1945
Fox Features Syndicate

nn(1944)-Same as No. 14 3.00 8.00 16.00
11(No.1)(9/44)-Origin 3.00 8.00 16.00
12-14 2.50 7.00 14.00

BOUNTY GUNS (See 4-Color No. 739)

BOY AND THE PIRATES, THE (See 4-Color No. 1117)

BOY COMICS (Captain Battle No. 1&2; Boy Illustories No. 43-108)
(Stories by Charles Biro)
No. 3, April, 1942 - No. 119, March, 1956
Lev Gleason Publications

3(No.1)-Origin Crimebuster, Bombshell & Young Robin Hood; Yankee Longago, Case 1001-1008, Swoop Storm, & Boy Movies begin; intro. Iron Jaw 50.00 140.00 280.00
4 24.00 70.00 140.00
5 20.00 60.00 120.00
6-Origin Iron Jaw; origin & death of Iron Jaw's son; Little Dynamite begins, ends No. 39 40.00 120.00 250.00
7,9: 7-Flag-c 15.00 45.00 100.00
8-Death of Iron Jaw 20.00 55.00 120.00
10-Return of Iron Jaw; classic Biro-c 24.00 70.00 150.00
11-14 10.00 30.00 60.00
15-Death of Iron Jaw 14.00 40.00 80.00
16,18-20 7.00 20.00 40.00
17-Flag-c 8.00 24.00 48.00
21-28: 28-Yankee Longago ends 5.00 14.00 28.00
29-68 pages 5.00 15.00 30.00
30-Origin Crimebuster retold 6.00 18.00 36.00
31-40: 32(68pgs.)-Swoop Storm, Young Robin Hood ends. 34-Suicide c/story 2.50 7.00 14.00
41-50 2.00 5.00 10.00
51-59: 57-Dilly Duncan begins, ends No. 71 1.20 3.50 7.00
60-Iron Jaw returns 1.50 4.00 8.00
61-Origin Crimebuster & Iron Jaw retold 2.00 5.00 10.00
62-Death of Iron Jaw explained 1.50 4.00 8.00
63-72: 71-Drug story 1.00 3.00 6.00
73-Frazetta 1-pg. ad 1.20 3.50 7.00
74-80: 80-1st app. Rocky X of the Rocketeers; becomes "Rocky X" No. 101; Iron Jaw, Sniffer & the Deadly Dozen begins, ends No. 118 .85 2.50 5.00
81-88 .85 2.50 5.00

BOY COMICS (continued)

	Good	Fine	Mint
89-92-The Claw serial app. in all	1.20	3.50	7.00
93-Claw cameo; Check-a(Rocky X)	2.00	5.00	10.00
94-97,99,100	.85	2.50	5.00
98-Rocky X by Sid Check	2.00	5.00	10.00
101-107,109,111,119: 111-Crimebuster becomes Chuck Chandler. 119-Last Crimebuster	.85	2.50	5.00
108,110,112-118-Kubert-a	1.50	4.00	8.00

(See Giant Boy Book of Comics)

NOTE: *Boy Movies in 3-5,40,41. Iron Jaw app.-3, 4, 6, 8, 10, 11, 13-15; returns-60-62, 68, 69, 72-79, 81-118.* ***Fuje*** *a-55, 18 pages. pages.*

BOY COMMANDOS (See Detective Comics)
Winter, 1942-43 - No. 36, Nov-Dec, 1949
National Periodical Publications

	Good	Fine	Mint
1-Origin Liberty Belle; The Sandman & The Newsboy Legion x-over in Boy Commandos; S&K-a, 48 pgs.	70.00	200.00	420.00
2-Last Liberty Belle; S&K-a, 46 pgs.	40.00	110.00	225.00
3-S&K-a, 45 pgs.	24.00	70.00	150.00
4,5	12.00	35.00	75.00
6-10: 6-S&K-a	9.00	26.00	56.00
11-Infinity-c	7.00	20.00	40.00
12-14,16-20	5.00	14.00	28.00
15-S&K-a	7.00	20.00	40.00
21,22,24-28,30	2.50	7.00	14.00
23-S&K-a(2)	5.00	14.00	28.00
29,31-S&K-a	4.00	12.00	24.00
32-35: 34-Intro. Wolf, their mascot	2.50	7.00	14.00
36	3.50	10.00	20.00

NOTE: *Most issues signed by* ***Simon & Kirby*** *are not by them.* ***S&K*** *c-1-9.*

BOY COMMANDOS
Sept-Oct, 1973 - No. 2, Nov-Dec, 1973
National Periodical Publications

	Good	Fine	Mint
1,2-S&K reprints		.45	.90

BOY DETECTIVE
May-June, 1951 - No. 4, May, 1952
Avon Periodicals

	Good	Fine	Mint
1	5.00	15.00	30.00
2,3: 3-Kinstler-c	3.50	10.00	20.00
4-Wood-a	7.00	20.00	40.00

BOY EXPLORERS COMICS
May-June, 1946 - No. 2, Sept-Oct, 1946
Harvey Publications

	Good	Fine	Mint
1-Kirby-a, 12 pgs; S&K-c	30.00	80.00	200.00
2-(Rare)-Small size (5½x8½''; B&W; 32 pgs.) Distributed to mail subscribers only; S&K-a			

During 1979 it has been reported that several copies have emerged and are now being offered at reduced prices. $500.00

(Also see All New No. 15, Flash Gordon No. 5, and Stuntman No. 3)

BOY ILLUSTORIES (See Boy Comics)

BOY LOVES GIRL (Boy Meets Girl No. 1-24)
No. 25, July, 1952 - No. 57, June, 1956
Lev Gleason Publications

	Good	Fine	Mint
25(No.1)	1.50	4.00	8.00
26,27,29-42	1.00	3.00	6.00
28-Drug propaganda story	2.50	7.00	14.00
43-Toth-a	2.50	7.00	14.00
44-57: 57-Ann Brewster-a	.70	2.00	4.00

BOY MEETS GIRL (Boy Loves Girl No. 25 on)
Feb, 1950 - No. 24, June, 1952
Lev Gleason Publications

	Good	Fine	Mint
1-Guardineer-a	1.50	4.00	8.00
2-10: 7-Fuje-c	1.00	3.00	6.00
11-23: 11-Painted-c	.85	2.50	5.00
24-Briefer-a	.85	2.50	5.00

BOYS' AND GIRLS' MARCH OF COMICS (See March of Comics)

BOYS' RANCH (Also see Witches' Western Tales)
Oct, 1950 - No. 6, Aug, 1951 (No.1-3, 52 pgs.; No. 4-6, 36 pgs.)
Harvey Publications

	Good	Fine	Mint
1-S&K-a(3)	22.00	65.00	130.00
2-S&K-a(3)	17.00	50.00	100.00
3-S&K-a(2); Meskin-a	12.00	35.00	70.00
4-S&K-c/a, 5pgs.	8.00	23.00	45.00
5,6-S&K splashes & centerspread only; Meskin-a	5.50	16.00	32.00
Shoe Store Giveaway No. 5,6 (Identical to regular issues except S&K centerfold replaced with ad)	5.00	14.00	28.00

NOTE: ***Simon & Kirby*** *c-1-6.*

BOZO THE CLOWN (TV)
July, 1950 - No. 4, Oct-Dec, 1963
Dell Publishing Co.

	Good	Fine	Mint
4-Color 285	1.50	4.00	8.00
2(7-9/51)-7(10-12/52)	.70	2.00	4.00
4-Color 464,508,551,594	.70	2.00	4.00
1-4(1963)	.50	1.00	2.00

BRADY BUNCH, THE (TV)
Feb, 1970 - No. 2, May, 1970
Dell Publishing Co.

	Good	Fine	Mint
1,2	.70	2.00	4.00
Kite Fun Book (PG&E, 1976)	.35	1.00	2.00

BRAIN, THE
Sept, 1956 - 1958
Sussex Publ. Co./Magazine Enterprises

	Good	Fine	Mint
1	.85	2.50	5.00
2,3	.50	1.50	3.00
4-7	.35	1.00	2.00
I.W. Reprints No. 1,3,4,8,9,10('63),14	.30	.80	1.60
I.W. Reprint No. 2-Reprints Sussex No. 2 with new cover added	.30	.80	1.60
Super Reprint No. 17,18(no date)	.30	.80	1.60

BRAIN BOY
April-June, 1962 - No. 6, Sept-Nov, 1963
Dell Publishing Co.

	Good	Fine	Mint
4-Color 1330-Gil Kane-a; origin	1.50	4.00	8.00
2(7-9/62),4-6: 4-origin retold	.70	2.00	4.00
3-Drug mention story	.70	2.00	4.00

BRAND ECHH (See Not Brand Echh)

BRAND OF EMPIRE (See 4-Color No. 771)

BRAVADOS, THE (See Wild Western Action)
August, 1971 (52 pages) (One-Shot)
Skywald Publ. Corp.

	Good	Fine	Mint
1-Red Mask, The Durango Kid, Billy Nevada reprints		.40	.80

BRAVE AND THE BOLD, THE (See Super DC Giant)
Aug-Sept, 1955 - Present
National Periodical Publications/DC Comics

	Good	Fine	Mint
1-Kubert Viking Prince, Silent Knight, Golden Gladiator begin	60.00	180.00	375.00
2	32.00	85.00	175.00
3,4	20.00	60.00	120.00
5-Robin Hood begins	15.00	45.00	90.00
6-10: 6-Kubert Robin Hood; G. Gladiator last app.; Silent Knight; no V. Prince	12.00	36.00	75.00
11-22: 22-Last Silent Knight	9.00	26.00	55.00
23-Kubert Viking Prince origin	11.00	32.00	70.00

Boy Commandos #9, © DC

Boy Loves Girl #27, © LEV

Brave & The Bold #22, © DC

Brave & The Bold #42, © DC

Brave & The Bold #67, © DC

Brave & The Bold #100, © DC

BRAVE AND THE BOLD (continued)	Good	Fine	Mint
24-Last Kubert Viking Prince	11.00	32.00	70.00
25-27-Suicide Squad	2.50	7.00	14.00
28-Justice League intro.; origin Snapper Carr	45.00	130.00	275.00
29,30-Justice League	17.00	50.00	100.00
31-33-Cave Carson	2.50	7.00	14.00
34-Origin Hawkman & Byth by Kubert	9.00	25.00	50.00
35,36-Kubert Hawkman; origin Shadow Thief No. 36	4.00	12.00	24.00
37-39-Suicide Squad	2.00	5.00	10.00
40,41-Cave Carson Inside Earth; No. 40 has Kubert art	2.00	6.00	12.00
42,44-Kubert Hawkman	2.50	7.50	14.00
43-Origin Hawkman by Kubert	3.50	10.00	20.00
45-49-Infantino Strange Sports Stories	.70	2.00	4.00
50-Green Arrow & J'onn J'onzz	.75	2.20	4.40
51-Aquaman & Hawkman	.75	2.20	4.40
52-Kubert Sgt. Rock, Haunted Tank, Johnny Cloud, & Mlle. Marie	1.20	3.50	7.00
53-Toth Atom & Flash	1.20	3.50	7.00
54-Kid Flash, Robin & Aqualad; 1st app./origin Teen Titans	2.00	5.00	10.00
55-Metal Men & The Atom	.50	1.40	2.80
56-Flash & Jonn' Jonzz'	.50	1.40	2.80
57-Intro & Origin Metamorpho	.50	1.40	2.80
58-Metamorpho by Fradon	.50	1.40	2.80
59-Batman & Green Lantern	.50	1.40	2.80
60-Teen Titans	.50	1.40	2.80
61,62-Starman & Black Canary by Anderson	.85	2.50	5.00
63-Supergirl & Wonder Woman	.50	1.40	2.80
64-Batman & Eclipso	.50	1.40	2.80
65-Flash & Doom Patrol	.50	1.40	2.80
66-Metamorpho & Metal Men	.50	1.40	2.80
67-Infantino Batman & The Flash	.50	1.50	3.00
68-Batman & Metamorpho	.50	1.40	2.80
69-Batman & Green Lantern	.50	1.40	2.80
70-Batman & Hawkman; Craig-a(p)	.50	1.40	2.80
71-Batman & Green Arrow	.50	1.40	2.80
72-Infantino Flash & Spectre	.50	1.50	3.00
73-Aquaman-Atom	.40	1.20	2.40
74-Batman-Metal Men	.40	1.20	2.40
75-Batman-The Spectre	.40	1.20	2.40
76-Batman-Plastic Man	.40	1.20	2.40
77-Batman-Atom	.40	1.20	2.40
78-Batman-Wonder Woman-Batgirl	.40	1.20	2.40
79-Batman-Deadman by Adams	2.00	5.00	10.00
80-Batman-Creeper; Adams-a	1.50	4.00	8.00
81-Batman-Flash; Adams-a	1.50	4.00	8.00
82-Batman-Aquaman; Adams-a; origin Ocean Master retold	1.50	4.00	8.00
83-Batman-Teen Titans; Adams-a	1.50	4.00	8.00
84-Batman-Sgt. Rock; Adams-a	1.50	4.00	8.00
85-Batman-Green Arrow; new costume for Green Arrow by Adams	1.50	4.00	8.00
86-Batman-Deadman; Adams-a	1.50	4.00	8.00
87-Batman-Wonder Woman	.40	1.20	2.40
88-Batman-Wildcat	.40	1.20	2.40
89-Batman-Phantom Stranger	.40	1.20	2.40
90-Batman-Adam Strange	.40	1.20	2.40
91-Batman-Black Canary	.40	1.20	2.40
92-Batman-Intro. the Bat Squad	.35	1.10	2.20
93-Batman-House of Mystery; Adams-a	1.50	4.00	8.00
94-Batman-Teen Titans	.50	1.50	3.00
95-Batman-Plastic Man	.35	1.10	2.20
96-Batman-Sgt. Rock	.35	1.10	2.20
97-Batman-Wildcat; 52 pgs. begin, end No. 102; 1st Deadman reprint/Strange Adv. No. 205	.40	1.20	2.40
98-Batman-Phantom Stranger	.35	1.10	2.20
99-Batman-Flash; Adams-c; Kubert Viking Prince	.35	1.10	2.20
100-Batman-Gr. Lantern-Gr. Arrow-Black Canary-Robin; Adams-a	1.00	3.00	6.00
101-Batman-Metamorpho; Kubert Viking Prince	.30	.90	1.80
102-Batman-Teen Titans; Adams-a(p)	.50	1.50	3.00
103-Batman-Metal Men	.25	.75	1.50
104-Batman-Aparo Deadman	.25	.75	1.50
105-Batman-Wonder Woman	.25	.75	1.50
106-Batman-Green Arrow	.25	.75	1.50
107-Batman-Black Canary	.25	.75	1.50
108-Batman-Sgt. Rock	.25	.75	1.50
109-Batman-Demon	.25	.75	1.50
110-Batman-Wildcat	.25	.75	1.50
111-Batman-The Joker		.60	1.20
112-Batman-Mr. Miracle; 100-pg. issues begin, end No. 117		.60	1.20
113-Batman-Metal Men; Kubert-a; Hawkman origin reprint from No. 34; origin Multi-Man/Challengers of the Unknown No. 14		.60	1.20
114-Batman-Aquaman		.60	1.20
115-Batman-Atom; Kubert origin Viking Prince/No. 23		.60	1.20
116-Batman-Spectre		.60	1.20
117-Batman-Sgt. Rock; last 100-pg. issue		.45	.90
118-Batman-Wildcat-Joker		.45	.90
119-Batman-ManBat		.45	.90
120-Batman-Kamandi-(68 pgs.)		.45	.90
121-Batman-Metal Men		.45	.90
122-Batman-Swamp Thing		.45	.90
123-Batman-Plastic Man-Metamorpho		.45	.90
124-Batman-Sgt. Rock		.45	.90
125-Batman-Flash		.45	.90
126-Batman-Aquaman		.45	.90
127-Batman-Wildcat		.45	.90
128-Mr. Miracle		.45	.90
129-Batman-Green Arrow-The Atom, Part 1 (also Two-Face & The Joker)		.45	.90
130-Batman-Green Arrow-The Atom, Part 2 (also Two-Face & The Joker)		.45	.90
131-Batman-Wonder Woman		.45	.90
132-Batman-Kung-Fu Fighter		.45	.90
133-Batman-Deadman		.45	.90
134-Batman-Green Lantern		.45	.90
135-Batman-Metal Men		.40	.80
136-Batman-Metal Men-Green Arrow		.40	.80
137-Batman-The Demon		.40	.80
138-Batman-Mr. Miracle		.40	.80
139-Batman-Hawkman		.40	.80
140-Batman-Wonder Woman		.40	.80
141-Batman-Black Canary (vs. The Joker)	.30	.60	1.20
142-Batman-Aquaman	.30	.60	1.20
143-Batman-Creeper; Human Target origin story (44 pgs.)		.60	1.20
144-Batman-Green Arrow; Human Target story (44 pgs.)		.40	.80
145-Batman-Phantom Stranger		.40	.80
146-G.A. Batman-Unknown Soldier		.40	.80
147-Batman-Supergirl		.40	.80
148-Batman-Plastic Man; Staton-a		.40	.80
149-Batman-Teen Titans		.60	1.20
150-Batman-Superman; Gil Kane-a		.40	.80
151-Batman-Flash		.30	.60
152-Batman-Atom		.30	.60
153-Batman-The Red Tornado		.30	.60
154-Batman-Metamorpho		.30	.60
155-Batman-Green Lantern		.30	.60
156-Batman-Dr. Fate		.30	.60
157-Batman vs. Kamandi		.30	.60
158-Batman-Wonder Woman		.30	.60
159-Batman-Ra's Al Ghul		.30	.60
160-Batman-Supergirl		.30	.60
161-Batman-Adam Strange		.30	.60

BRAVE AND THE BOLD (continued)

	Good	Fine	Mint
162-Batman-Sgt. Rock		.30	.60
163-Batman-Black Lightning		.30	.60
164-Batman-Hawkman		.30	.60
165-Batman-Man-Bat		.30	.60
166-Batman-Black Canary		.30	.60
167-Batman-Black Knight; origin Nemesis		.30	.60
168-Batman-Green Arrow		.30	.60
169-Batman-Zatanna		.30	.60
170-Batman-Nemesis		.30	.60
171-Batman-Scalphunter		.30	.60
172-Batman-Firestorm		.30	.60
173-Batman-Nemesis		.30	.60
174-Batman-Green Lantern-Nemesis		.30	.60
175-Batman-Lois Lane		.30	.60
176-Batman-Swamp Thing		.30	.60
177-Batman-Elongated Man		.30	.60
178-Batman-Creeper		.30	.60
179-Batman-Legion		.30	.60
180-Batman-Spectre-Nemesis		.30	.60
181-Batman-The Hawk-Nemesis		.30	.60
182-Batman-Robin		.30	.60
183-Batman-The Riddler-Nemesis		.30	.60
184-Batman-Huntress		.30	.60
185-Batman-Hawkman		.30	.60

NOTE: ***Adams** a-79-86, 93, 100r, 102; c-75, 76, 79-86, 88-90, 93, 95, 99, 100r. **Anderson** a-115r. **Aparo** a-98, 100-02, 104-36, 138-45, 147-52, 154-163, 168-178, 180-182, 184; inks-126, 148; c-105-09, 111-157, 168-178, 180-184. **Buckler** c-137. **Giordano** a-143, 144. **Infantino** a-67, 97r, 98r, 172-p, 183; c-45-49, 67, 69, 70, 72, 98r; w/**Anderson**-96. **Kaluta** c-176. **Kane** a-115r. **Kubert &/or Heath** a-1-24; reprints-101, 113, 115, 117. **Kubert** c-22-24, 34-36, 40, 42-44, 52. **Mooney** a-114r. **Newton** a-153, 156p, 165p. **Roussos** a-114r. **Staton** a-148.*

BRAVE AND THE BOLD SPECIAL, THE (See DC Special Series No. 8)

BRAVE EAGLE (See 4-Color No. 705,770,816,879,929)

BRAVE ONE, THE (See 4-Color No. 773)

BREEZE LAWSON, SKY SHERIFF (See Sky Sheriff)

BRENDA LEE STORY, THE
September, 1962
Dell Publishing Co.

	Good	Fine	Mint
01-078-209	3.00	9.00	18.00

BRENDA STARR (Also see All Great)
No. 13, 9/47; No. 14, 3/48; V2No.3, 6/48 - V2No.12, 12/49
Four Star Comic Corp./Superior Comics Ltd.

	Good	Fine	Mint
V1No.13-By Dale Messick; classic bondage-c	9.00	25.00	50.00
14-Kamen? bondage-c	10.00	28.00	60.00
V2No.3-Kamen?-c; Baker-a	8.00	24.00	50.00
4-Used in **SOTI**, pg. 21; Kamen? bondage-c	14.00	42.00	70.00
5-10-Kamen?-c	5.50	16.00	34.00
11,12 (Scarce)-Kamen?-c	8.00	24.00	50.00

NOTE: *Newspaper reprints plus original material through No. 6. All original No. 7 on.*

BRENDA STARR (. . . Reporter)
No. 13, June, 1955 - No. 15, Oct, 1955
Charlton Comics

	Good	Fine	Mint
13-15-Newspaper reprints	3.50	10.00	20.00

BRENDA STARR REPORTER
October, 1963
Dell Publishing Co.

	Good	Fine	Mint
1	2.50	7.00	14.00

BRER RABBIT (See 4-Color No. 129,208,693, Walt Disney Showcase No. 28, and Wheaties)

BRER RABBIT IN "A KITE TAIL"
1956 (14 pages) (Walt Disney) (Premium)
Pacific Gas & Electric Co.

	Good	Fine	Mint
(Rare)	14.00	40.00	80.00

BRER RABBIT IN "ICE CREAM FOR THE PARTY"
1955 (14 pages) (Walt Disney) (Premium)
American Dairy Association

	Good	Fine	Mint
(Rare)	7.00	20.00	40.00

BRICK BRADFORD
1948 - 1949 (Ritt & Grey reprints)
King Features Syndicate/Standard

	Good	Fine	Mint
5	5.00	15.00	30.00
6-8: 7-Schomburg-c	4.75	14.00	28.00

BRIDE'S DIARY
No. 4, May, 1955 - No. 10, Aug, 1956
Ajax/Farrell Publ.

	Good	Fine	Mint
4-9	1.20	3.50	7.00
10-Disbrow-a	2.00	5.00	10.00

BRIDES IN LOVE (Summer Love No. 46 on)
Aug, 1956 - No. 45, Jan, 1965
Charlton Comics

	Good	Fine	Mint
1	1.20	3.50	7.00
2-10	.70	2.00	4.00
11-45	.30	.90	1.80

BRIDES ROMANCES
1953 - No. 23, Dec, 1956
Quality Comics Group

	Good	Fine	Mint
1	3.00	9.00	18.00
2-10	1.50	4.00	8.00
11-17,19-22	.85	2.50	5.00
18-Baker-a	1.50	4.00	8.00
23-Baker c/a	2.00	6.00	12.00

BRIDE'S SECRETS
Mar-Apr, 1954 - No. 19, Mar, 1958
Ajax/Farrell(Excellent Publ.)/Four-Star Comic

	Good	Fine	Mint
1	3.00	9.00	18.00
2-5	1.50	4.00	8.00
6-19: 12-Disbrow-a	1.00	3.00	6.00

BRIDE-TO-BE ROMANCES (See True. . .)

BRIGAND, THE (See Fawcett Movie Comics No. 18)

BRINGING UP FATHER (See Large Feature Comic No. 9 and 4-Color Comics No. 37)

BRINGING UP FATHER
1917 (16½x5½"; cardboard cover; 100 pages; B&W)
Star Co. (King Features)

	Good	Fine	Mint
(Rare) Daily strip reprints by George McManus (no price on cover)	17.00	50.00	100.00

BRINGING UP FATHER
1919 - 1934 (by George McManus)
(10x10"; stiff cardboard covers; B&W; daily strip reprints; 52 pgs.)
Cupples & Leon Co.

	Good	Fine	Mint
1	10.00	30.00	60.00
2-10	5.00	14.00	28.00
11-26 (Scarcer)	7.00	20.00	40.00
The Big Book 1(1926)-Thick book (hardcover)	14.00	40.00	80.00
The Big Book 2(1929)	10.00	30.00	60.00

NOTE: *The Big Books contain 3 regular issues rebound and probably with dust jackets.*

Brenda Starr V2#11, © SUPR

Brides Romances #8, © QUA

Bringing Up Father Series 1, © KING

Broncho Bill #12, © UFS

Brother Power The Geek #1, © DC

Buccaneers #20, © QUA

BRINGING UP FATHER, THE TROUBLE OF
1921 (9x15'') (Sunday reprints in color)
Embee Publ. Co.

	Good	Fine	Mint
(Rare)	17.00	50.00	100.00

BROADWAY HOLLYWOOD BLACKOUTS
Mar-Apr, 1954 - No. 3, July-Aug, 1954
Stanhall (Trojan)

1-3 2.00 5.00 10.00

BROADWAY ROMANCES
January, 1950 - No. 9, 1951
Quality Comics Group

1-Ward c/a, 9pgs.; Gustavson-a 10.00 30.00 60.00
2-Ward-a, 9pgs. 7.00 20.00 40.00
3-9 3.00 9.00 18.00

BROKEN ARROW (See 4-Color No. 855,947)

BROKEN CROSS, THE (See The Crusaders)

BRONCHO BILL
1939 - 1940; 1949 - 1950
United Features Syndicate/Standard/Visual

Single Series 2 ('39) 10.00 30.00 60.00
Single Series 19 ('40)(No.2 on cvr) 8.00 24.00 48.00
1(1949-Standard) 6.00 12.00 24.00
2 3.50 7.00 14.00
3-10 2.00 4.00 8.00
11-16 1.75 3.50 7.00
NOTE: *Schomburg c-7,9-13,16.*

BROTHER POWER, THE GEEK
Sept-Oct, 1968 - No. 2, Nov-Dec, 1968
National Periodical Publications

1-Origin; Simon-a .50 1.00
2-Simon-a .30 .60

BROTHERS, HANG IN THERE, THE
1979 (49 cents)
Spire Christian Comics (Fleming H. Revell Co.)

.40 .80

BROTHERS OF THE SPEAR (Also see Tarzan)
June, 1972 - No. 17, Feb, 1976
Gold Key

1 .70 2.00 4.00
2-10 .30 .80 1.60
11-17 .40 .80

BROWNIES (See 4-Color No. 192,244,293,337,365,398,436,482, 522,605)

BRUCE GENTRY
Jan, 1948 - No. 2, Nov, 1948; No. 3, Jan, 1949 - No. 8, July, 1949
Better/Standard/Four Star Publ./Superior No. 3

1-Ray Bailey strip reprints begin, end No. 3; E. C. emblem appears as a monogram on stationery in story; negligee panels
12.00 35.00 70.00
2,3-Feldstein?-a (No.2: 5 pgs.) 9.00 25.00 50.00
4-8 5.50 16.00 32.00
NOTE: *Kamenish a-4,6,7; c-1-4,6-8.*

BRUTE, THE
Feb, 1975 - No. 3, July, 1975
Seaboard Publ. (Atlas)

1-Origin & 1st app. .50 1.00
2 .30 .60
3-Brunner?/Weiss-a(p) .40 .80

BUCCANEER
No date (1963)
I. W. Enterprises

	Good	Fine	Mint

I.W. Reprint No. 1(reprints Quality No. 20), No. 8(reprints No. 23)
1.00 3.00 6.00
Super Reprint No. 12('64, reprints No. 21)-Crandall art
1.00 3.00 6.00

BUCCANEERS (Formerly Kid Eternity)
No. 19, Jan, 1950 - No. 27, May, 1951 (No.24-27: 52 pages)
Quality Comics Group

19-Captain Daring, Black Roger, Eric Falcon & Spanish Man begin; Crandall-a 8.00 24.00 48.00
20,23-Crandall-a 8.00 24.00 48.00
21-Crandall c/a 10.00 30.00 60.00
22-Bondage-c 4.00 12.00 24.00
24,26: 24-Adam Peril, U.S.N. begins; last Spanish Man
4.00 12.00 24.00
25-Origin & 1st app. Corsair Queen 4.00 12.00 24.00
27-Crandall c/a 9.00 25.00 50.00

BUCCANEERS, THE (See 4-Color No. 800)

BUCK DUCK
June, 1953 - No. 4, Dec, 1953
Atlas Comics (ANC)

1-4 (funny animal) 1.00 3.00 6.00

BUCK JONES
No. 2, Apr-June, 1951 - No. 8, Oct-Dec, 1952
Dell Publishing Co.

4-Color 299(No.1)(1950) 3.00 9.00 18.00
2(4-6/51) 2.00 6.00 12.00
3-8 1.50 4.50 9.00
4-Color 460,500,546,589 1.50 4.50 9.00
4-Color 652,733,850 1.00 3.00 6.00

BUCK ROGERS (In the 25th Century)
1933 (36 pages in color) (6x8'')
Kelloggs Corn Flakes Giveaway

(Rare) by Phil Nolan & Dick Calkins; 1st Buck Rogers radio premium
20.00 60.00 120.00

BUCK ROGERS (Also see Famous Funnies, Pure Oil Comics, Salerno Carnival of Comics, 24 Pages of Comics, & Vicks Comics)
Winter, 1940-41 - No. 6, Sept, 1943
Famous Funnies

1-Sunday strip reprints by Rick Yager; begins with strip No. 190
60.00 160.00 320.00
2 35.00 105.00 220.00
3,4 30.00 85.00 180.00
5-Story continues with Famous Funnies No. 80; ½ Buck Rogers, ½ Sky Roads 22.00 65.00 130.00
6-Reprints of 1939 dailies; contain B.R. story "Crater of Doom" (2 pgs.) by Calkins not reprinted from Famous Funnies
22.00 65.00 130.00

BUCK ROGERS
No. 100, Jan, 1951 - No. 9, May-June, 1951
Toby Press

100(7), 101(8), 9-All Anderson-a? 6.00 18.00 36.00

BUCK ROGERS
October, 1964; No. 2, July, 1979 - Present (no No. 10)
Gold Key/Whitman No. 7 on

1(10128-410) 2.00 5.00 10.00
2(7/79)-Movie adaptation .50 1.00
3-9,11: 3,4-Movie adaptation; 5-new stories .30 .60
Giant Movie Edition 11296(64pp, Whitman, $1.50), reprints GK No. 2-4 minus cover .35 1.00 2.00
NOTE: *Bolle, McWilliams a-2-4,11.*

BUCKSKIN (See 4-Color No. 1011,1107 (Movie))

BUDDIES IN THE U.S. ARMY

BUDDIES IN THE U.S. ARMY (continued)
Nov, 1952 - No. 2, 1953
Avon Periodicals

	Good	Fine	Mint
1	4.50	13.00	26.00
2-Mort Lawrence c/a	4.00	11.00	22.00

BUDDY TUCKER & HIS FRIENDS
1906 (11x17") (In color)
Cupples & Leon Co.

	Good	Fine	Mint
1905 Sunday strip reprints by R. F. Outcault	10.00	30.00	60.00

BUFFALO BEE (See 4-Color No. 957,1002,1061)

BUFFALO BILL (Formerly Super Western Comics)
No. 5, April, 1951 - No. 9, Dec, 1951
Youthful Magazines

	Good	Fine	Mint
5-9	1.00	3.00	6.00

BUFFALO BILL CODY (See Cody of the Pony Express)

BUFFALO BILL, JR. (TV)
Jan, 1956 - No. 13, Aug-Oct, 1959; 1965
Dell Publishing Co./Gold Key

	Good	Fine	Mint
4-Color 673,742,766,798,828,856(11/57)	1.00	3.00	6.00
7(2-4/58)-13	.70	2.00	4.00
1(6/65-Gold Key)	.50	1.50	3.00

BUFFALO BILL'S PICTURE STORIES
1909 (Soft cardboard cover)
Street & Smith Publications

	Good	Fine	Mint
	7.00	20.00	40.00

BUFFALO BILL'S PICTURE STORIES
June-July, 1949 - No. 2, Aug-Sept, 1949
Street & Smith Publications

	Good	Fine	Mint
1,2-Wildey, Powell-a in each	2.00	5.00	10.00

BUGALOOS (TV)
Sept, 1971 - No. 4, Feb, 1972
Charlton Comics

	Good	Fine	Mint
1-4	.35	1.00	1.50

NOTE: *No. 3(1/72) went on sale late in 1972 (after No. 4) with the 1/73 issues.*

BUGHOUSE
Mar-Apr, 1954 - No. 4, Sept-Oct, 1954
Ajax/Farrell (Excellent Publ.)

	Good	Fine	Mint
V1No.1	3.50	10.00	15.00
2-4	2.50	7.00	10.50

BUGHOUSE FABLES
1921 (48 pgs.) (4x4½") (10 cents)
Embee Distributing Co. (King Features)

	Good	Fine	Mint
1-Barney Google	4.00	12.00	24.00

BUG MOVIES
1931 (52 pages) (B&W)
Dell Publishing Co.

	Good	Fine	Mint
Not reprints; Stookie Allen-a	4.00	12.00	24.00

BUGS BUNNY
1942 - Present
Dell Publishing Co./Gold Key No. 86-218/Whitman No. 219 on

	Good	Fine	Mint
Large Feature Comic 8(1942)-(Rarely found in fine-mint condition)	55.00	160.00	320.00
4-Color 33 ('43)	24.00	70.00	140.00
4-Color 51	15.00	45.00	90.00
4-Color 88	7.00	20.00	40.00
4-Color 123('46),142,164	4.00	12.00	24.00
4-Color 187,200,217,233	3.00	9.00	18.00
4-Color 250-Used in **SOTI**, pg. 309	3.00	9.00	18.00
4-Color 266,274,281,289,298('50)	2.00	6.00	12.00
4-Color 307,317(No.1),327(No.2),338,347,355,366,376,393	1.50	4.00	8.00
4-Color 407,420,432	1.20	3.50	7.00
28(12-1/52-53)-30	.60	1.80	3.60
31-50	.40	1.20	2.40
51-85(6-7/62)	.30	.80	1.60
86(10/62)-88-Bugs Bunny's Showtime-(80 pgs.)(25 cents)	.50	1.50	3.00
89-120		.50	1.00
121-140		.40	.80
141-170		.30	.60
171-230		.25	.50

NOTE: *Reprints- 100,102,104,123,143,144,147,167,173,175-77, 179-85,187,190*

	Good	Fine	Mint
Christmas Funnies 1('50)	4.00	12.00	24.00
Christmas Funnies 2-5('51-54) (Becomes Christmas Party No. 6)	2.00	6.00	12.00
Christmas Funnies 7-9(12/56-12/58)	1.75	5.00	10.00
Christmas Party 6('55)(Formerly Christmas Funnies No. 5)(Giant)	1.75	5.00	10.00
. . . Comic-Go-Round 11196-(224 pgs.)($1.95)(Golden Press, 1979)	.40	1.20	2.40
County Fair 1('57)(Giant)	1.75	5.00	10.00
Florida Power & Light Giveaway('60,'68)	.35	1.00	2.00
Halloween Parade 1('53)(Giant)	3.50	10.00	20.00
Halloween Parade 2('54)(Trick 'N' Treat Halloween Fun No. 3 on)	1.75	5.00	10.00
Trick 'N' Treat Halloween Fun 3('55), 4(10/56)(Formerly Halloween Fun)	1.75	5.00	10.00
Vacation Funnies 1('51)-112 pgs.	4.00	12.00	24.00
Vacation Funnies 2-9('52-'59)-100 pgs.	1.75	5.00	10.00
Winter Fun 1(12/67-Gold Key)	.35	1.00	2.00

BUGS BUNNY (See The Best of. . .; Comic Album No. 2,6,10,14; Dell Giant No. 28,32,46; Golden Comics Digest No. 1,3,5,6,8,10,14, 15,17,21,26,30,34,39,42,47; March of Comics No. 44,59,75,83,97, 115,132,149,160,179,188,201,220,231,245,259,273,287,301,315, 329,343,363,367,380,392,403; Puffed Wheat, Super Book No. 14,26; and Whitman Comic Books)

BUGS BUNNY (Puffed Rice Giveaway)
1949 (32 pages each, 3-1/8x6-7/8")
Quaker Cereals

A1-Traps the Counterfeiters, A2-Aboard Mystery Submarine, A3-Rocket to the Moon, A4-Lion Tamer, A5-Rescues the Beautiful Princess, B1-Buried Treasure, B2-Outwits the Smugglers, B3-Joins the Marines, B4-Meets the Dwarf Ghost, B5-Finds Aladdin's Lamp, C1-Lost in the Frozen North, C2-Secret Agent, C3-Captured by Cannibals, C4-Fights the Man from Mars, C5-And the Haunted Cave

	Good	Fine	Mint
each. . . .	2.00	5.00	10.00

BUGS BUNNY (3-D)
1953 (Pocket size) (15 titles)
Cheerios Giveaway

	Good	Fine	Mint
each. . . .	3.00	8.00	16.00

BUGS BUNNY & PORKY PIG
Sept, 1965 (100 pages; paper cover; giant)
Gold Key

	Good	Fine	Mint
1(30025-509)	1.20	3.50	7.00

BUGS BUNNY'S ALBUM (See 4-Color No. 498,585,647,724)

BUGS BUNNY LIFE STORY ALBUM (See 4-Color No. 838)

BUGS BUNNY MERRY CHRISTMAS (See 4-Color No. 1064)

BULLETMAN (See Master Comics, Fawcett Miniatures and Mighty Midget Comics)
1941 - No. 16, Fall, 1946 (nn 13)

Buddies In The U.S. Army #1, © AVON

Buffalo Bill Jr. #1, © GK

Bugs Bunny #29, © L. Schlesinger

BULLETMAN (continued)
Fawcett Publications

	Good	Fine	Mint
1	60.00	180.00	375.00
2	40.00	120.00	250.00
3	30.00	85.00	175.00
4,5	24.00	70.00	150.00
6-10	20.00	60.00	125.00
11,12,14-16 (nn 13)	17.00	50.00	100.00
...Well Known Comics (Scarce) (1942)-Paper cover, glued binding (Bestmaid/Samuel Lowe giveaway)	15.00	45.00	90.00

NOTE: *No. 2,3,5 have **Mac Raboy** covers.*

BULLS-EYE (Cody of The Pony Express No. 8 on)
July-Aug, 1954 - No. 7, Jul-Aug, 1955
Mainline(Prize) No. 1-5/Charlton No. 6,7

	Good	Fine	Mint
1-S&K-c, 2 pages	14.00	40.00	80.00
2-S&K c/a	14.00	40.00	80.00
3-5-S&K c/a(2)	8.00	23.00	46.00
6-S&K c/a	7.00	20.00	40.00
7-S&K c/a(3)	8.00	23.00	45.00
Great Scott Shoe Store giveaway-Reprints No. 2 with new cover	5.00	15.00	30.00

BULLS-EYE COMICS
No. 11, 1944
Harry 'A' Chesler

	Good	Fine	Mint
11-Origin K-9, Green Knight's sidekick, Lance; The Green Knight, Lady Satan, Yankee Doodle Jones app.	5.00	15.00	30.00

BULLWHIP GRIFFIN (See Movie Comics)

BULLWINKLE (TV) (See March of Comics No. 233, and Rocky & Bullwinkle)
3-5/62 - No. 11, 4/74; No. 12, 6/76 - No. 19, 3/78; No. 20, 4/79 - No. 25, 2/80
Dell/Gold Key

	Good	Fine	Mint
4-Color 1270 (3-5/62)	.70	2.00	4.00
01-090-209 (Dell, 7-9/62)	.70	2.00	4.00
1,2 (2/63-Gold Key)	.70	2.00	4.00
3(4/72)-11(4/74-Gold Key)	.30	.80	1.60
12(6/76)-reprints		.40	.80
13(9/76), 14-new stories		.50	1.00
15-25		.30	.60
Mother Moose Nursery Pomes 01-530-207 (5-7/62-Dell)	1.25	2.50	5.00

NOTE: *Reprints-6,7,20-24*

BULLWINKLE (TV)
July, 1970 - No. 7, July, 1971
Charlton Comics

	Good	Fine	Mint
1	.70	2.00	4.00
2-7	.35	1.00	2.00

BUNNY
Dec, 1966 - No. 20, Dec, 1971; No. 21, Nov, 1976
Harvey Publications

	Good	Fine	Mint
1	1.00	3.00	6.00
2-8,10-12,14,17-21	.50	1.50	3.00
9,13,15,16-All Giants	1.00	3.00	6.00

BURKE'S LAW (TV)
Jan-Mar, 1964 - No. 3, Mar-May, 1965
Dell Publishing Co.

	Good	Fine	Mint
1	.85	2.50	5.00
2,3	.70	2.00	4.00

BURNING ROMANCES
1949 (132 pages)
Fox Feature Publications (Hero Books)

1-See Fox Giants. Contents can vary and determines price.

BUSTER BEAR
Dec, 1953 - No. 10, June, 1955
Quality Comics Group (Arnold Publ.)

	Good	Fine	Mint
1	.85	2.50	5.00
2-10	.70	2.00	4.00
I.W. Reprint No. 9,10 (Super on inside)	.30	.80	1.60

BUSTER BROWN
1903 - 1906 (11x17'' strip reprints in color)
Frederick A. Stokes Co.

	Good	Fine	Mint
...& His Resolutions (1903) by R. F. Outcault	25.00	75.00	150.00
...Abroad (1904)-86 pgs.; hardback; 8x10¼''; B&W; by R. F. Outcault(76pgs.)	20.00	60.00	120.00
...His Dog Tige & Their Troubles (1904)	20.00	60.00	120.00
...Pranks (1905)	20.00	60.00	120.00
...Antics (1906)-11x17'', 30 pages color strip reprints	20.00	60.00	120.00
...Mary Jane & Tige (1906)	20.00	60.00	120.00
...His Dog Tige & Their Jolly Times (1906)	20.00	60.00	120.00
...My Resolutions (1906)-68 pgs.; B&W; hardcover; Sunday panel reprints	20.00	60.00	120.00
...Latest Frolics (1907), 21pp	20.00	60.00	120.00
Collection of Buster Brown Comics (1908)	20.00	60.00	120.00
Buster Brown Up to Date (1909)	20.00	60.00	120.00

NOTE: *Rarely found in fine or mint condition.*

BUSTER BROWN
1908 - 1917 (11x17'' strip reprints in color)
Cupples & Leon Co./N. Y. Herald Co.
(By R. F. Outcault)

	Good	Fine	Mint
...Amusing Capers (1908)	15.00	45.00	90.00
...And His Pets (1909)	15.00	45.00	90.00
...On His Travels (1910)	15.00	45.00	90.00
...Happy Days (1911)	15.00	45.00	90.00
...In Foreign Lands (1912)	15.00	45.00	80.00
...And the Cat (1917)	12.00	35.00	70.00

NOTE: *Rarely found in fine or mint condition.*

BUSTER BROWN COMICS
1945 - 1959 (No. 5: paper cover)
Brown Shoe Co.

	Good	Fine	Mint
1	4.00	12.00	24.00
2-10	1.50	4.00	8.00
11-20	.85	2.50	5.00
21-24,26-28	.60	1.80	3.60
25,31,33-37,40-42-Crandall-a in all	3.00	9.00	18.00
29,30,32-''Interplanetary Police Vs. the Space Siren'' by Crandall	3.00	9.00	18.00
38,39,43	.60	1.80	3.60
...Goes to Mars ('58-Western Printing)	.85	2.50	5.00
...In ''Buster Makes the Team!'' (1959-Custom Comics)	.70	2.00	4.00
...Of the Safety Patrol ('60-Custom Comics)	.70	2.00	4.00
...Out of This World ('59-Custom Comics)	.70	2.00	4.00
...Safety Coloring Book (1958)-Slick paper, 16 pages	.70	2.00	4.00

BUSTER BUNNY
Nov, 1949 - No. 16, Oct, 1953
Standard Comics(Animated Cartoons)/Pines

	Good	Fine	Mint
1-Frazetta 1 pg. text illos. in both	2.00	5.00	10.00
2-16	.70	2.00	4.00

BUSTER CRABBE
Nov, 1951 - No. 12, 1953
Famous Funnies

	Good	Fine	Mint
1-Frazetta drug pusher back-c	10.00	30.00	60.00
2-Williamson/Evans-c	14.00	40.00	80.00
3-Williamson/Evans c/a	15.00	45.00	90.00

Bulletman #4, © FAW

Buster Brown #7, © Buster Brown

Buster Bunny #14, © STD

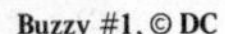
Buzzy #1, © DC

Calling All Kids #18, © PMI

Campus Romances #3, © AVON

BUSTER CRABBE (continued)

	Good	Fine	Mint
4-Frazetta c/a, 1pg.; bondage-c	20.00	55.00	110.00
5-Frazetta-c; Williamson/Krenkel/Orlando-a, 11pgs. (per Mr. Williamson) (Scarce)	150.00	400.00	750.00
6,8,10-12	2.50	7.00	14.00
7,9-One pg. of Frazetta in each	3.00	9.00	18.00

BUSTER CRABBE (The Amazing Adventures of. .)
Dec, 1953 - No. 4, June, 1954
Lev Gleason Publications

	Good	Fine	Mint
1	3.50	10.00	20.00
2,3-Toth-a	5.00	14.00	28.00
4-Flash Gordon-c	3.50	10.00	20.00

BUTCH CASSIDY
June, 1971 - No. 3, Oct, 1971 (52 pages)
Skywald Comics

	Good	Fine	Mint
1-Red Mask reprint, retitled Maverick; Bolle-a		.40	.80
2-Whip Wilson reprint		.30	.60
3-Dead Canyon Days reprint/Crack Western No. 63; Sundance Kid app.; Crandall-a		.30	.60

BUTCH CASSIDY (. . . & the Wild Bunch)
1951
Avon Periodicals

	Good	Fine	Mint
1-Kinstler c/a	7.00	20.00	40.00

NOTE: ***Reinman** story; Issue No. on inside spine.*

BUTCH CASSIDY (See Fun-In No. 11)

BUZ SAWYER
June, 1948 - 1949
Standard Comics

	Good	Fine	Mint
1-Roy Crane-a	4.00	12.00	24.00
2-5	3.50	8.00	16.00

BUZ SAWYER'S PAL, ROSCOE SWEENEY (See Sweeney)

BUZZY
Winter, 1944-45 - No. 75, 1-2/57; No. 76, 10/57; No. 77, 10/58
National Periodical Publications/Detective Comics

	Good	Fine	Mint
1	5.50	16.00	32.00
2-5	3.50	8.00	16.00
6-10	2.00	5.00	10.00
11-40: 33-Scribbly by Mayer	1.00	3.00	6.00
41-77	.50	1.50	3.00

BUZZY THE CROW (See Harvey Hits No. 18)

CADET GRAY OF WEST POINT
1958 (Giant)
Dell Publishing Co.

	Good	Fine	Mint
1-Williamson-a, 10 pgs.	3.00	9.00	18.00

CAIN'S HUNDRED (TV)
May-June, 1962 - No. 2, Sept-Nov, 1962
Dell Publishing Co.

	Good	Fine	Mint
nn(01-094-207)-Heroin drug story	.85	2.50	5.00
2	.50	1.50	3.00

CALL FROM CHRIST
1952 (36 pages)
Catechetical Educational Society (Giveaway)

	Good	Fine	Mint
	3.00	8.00	16.00

CALLING ALL BOYS (Tex Granger No. 18 on)
Jan, 1946 - No. 17, May, 1948
Parents' Magazine Institute

	Good	Fine	Mint
1	2.00	5.00	10.00
2-17	1.00	3.00	6.00

CALLING ALL GIRLS
Sept, 1941 - No. 72, April, 1948 (Part magazine, part comic)
Parents' Magazine Institute

	Good	Fine	Mint
1,2	2.00	5.00	10.00
3-10	1.00	3.00	6.00
11-20	.60	1.80	3.60
21-43(10-11/45)-Last issue with comics	.35	1.00	2.00
44-51(7/46)-Last comic book size issue		.40	.80
52-72		.30	.60

NOTE: ***Jack Sparling** art in many issues.*

CALLING ALL KIDS
Dec-Jan, 1945-46 - No. 26, Aug, 1949
Parents' Magazine/Quality Comics

	Good	Fine	Mint
1	1.50	4.00	8.00
2	.85	2.50	5.00
3-10	.35	1.00	2.00
11-26	.30	.80	1.60

CALVIN (See Li'l Kids)

CALVIN & THE COLONEL (TV)
1962 - No. 2, July-Sept, 1962
Dell Publishing Co.

	Good	Fine	Mint
4-Color 1354	1.00	3.00	6.00
2	.70	2.00	4.00

CAMERA COMICS
July, 1944 - No. 9, 1946
U.S. Camera Publishing Corp.

	Good	Fine	Mint
nn (7/44 & 9/44 issues)	2.00	5.00	10.00
1(10/44)-The Grey Comet	2.00	5.00	10.00
2-9: All ½ photos	1.50	4.00	8.00

CAMP COMICS
Feb, 1942 - No. 3, April, 1942
Dell Publishing Co.

	Good	Fine	Mint
1-''Seaman Sy Wheeler'' by Kelly, 7 pgs.; Bugs Bunny app.	30.00	90.00	180.00
2-Kelly-a, 12 pgs.; Bugs Bunny app.	20.00	60.00	120.00
3-(Scarce)-Kelly-a	30.00	90.00	180.00

CAMP RUNAMUCK (TV)
April, 1966
Dell Publishing Co.

	Good	Fine	Mint
1	.85	2.50	5.00

CAMPUS LOVES
Dec, 1949 - No. 5, Aug, 1950
Quality Comics Group (Comic Magazines)

	Good	Fine	Mint
1-Ward c/a, 9 pgs.	10.00	30.00	60.00
2-Ward c/a	8.00	24.00	48.00
3-5: 5-Spanking panels (2)	4.00	12.00	24.00

NOTE: ***Gustavson** a-1-5. Photo-c-3-5.*

CAMPUS ROMANCE (. . . Romances on cover)
Sept-Oct, 1949 - No. 3, Feb-Mar, 1950
Avon Periodicals

	Good	Fine	Mint
1-Walter Johnson-a; c-/Avon paperback 348	7.00	20.00	40.00
2-Grandenetti-a; c-/Avon paperback 151	7.00	20.00	40.00
3-c-/Avon paperback 201	7.00	20.00	40.00

CANADA DRY PREMIUMS (See Swamp Fox, The)

CANCELLED COMIC CAVALCADE
Summer, 1978 - No. 2, Fall, 1978 (8½x11''; B&W)
(Xeroxed pages on one side only w/blue cover and taped spine)
DC Comics, Inc.

1-(412 pages) Contains xeroxed copies of art for: Black Lightning No. 12, cover to No. 13; Claw No. 13,14; The Deserted No. 1; Doorway to Nightmare No. 6; Firestorm No. 6; The Green Team No. 2,3.
2-(532 pages) Contains xeroxed copies of art for: Kamandi No. 60

CANCELLED COMIC CAVALCADE (cont'd.)
(including Omac), No. 61; Prez No. 5; Shade No. 9 (including The Odd Man); Showcase No. 105 (Deadman), 106 (The Creeper); The Vixen No. 1; and covers to Army at War No. 2, Battle Classics No. 3, Demand Classics No. 1 & 2, Dynamic Classics No. 3, Mr. Miracle No. 26, Ragman No. 6, Weird Mystery No. 25 & 26, & Western Classics No. 1 & 2. (Rare)
(One set sold in 1980 for $500.00)
NOTE: *In June, 1978, DC cancelled several of their titles. For copyright purposes, the unpublished original art for these titles was xeroxed, bound in the above books, published and distributed. Only 35 copies were made.*

CANDID TALES (Also see Bold Stories & It Rhymes With Lust)
April, 1950, June, 1950 (Digest size) (144 pages) (Full color)
Kirby Publishing Co.

	Good	Fine	Mint
(Scarce) Contains Woodish Female Pirate story, 15 pgs., and 14 pgs. in June issue	30.00	80.00	160.00

NOTE: *Another version exists with Dr. Kilmore by Wood; no female pirate story.*

CANDY
Fall, 1944 - No. 3, Spring, 1945
William H. Wise & Co.

	Good	Fine	Mint
1-Two Scoop Scuttle stories by Basil Wolverton	9.00	25.00	50.00
2,3-Scoop Scuttle by Basil Wolverton (2-4 pgs.)	7.00	20.00	40.00

CANDY
Fall, 1947 - No. 64, July, 1956
Quality Comics Group

	Good	Fine	Mint
1	3.50	10.00	20.00
2-10	2.00	5.00	10.00
11-63	1.20	3.50	7.00
64-Ward-c(p)?	1.50	4.00	8.00
Super Reprint No. 2,10,12,16,17,18('63-'64)	.50	1.50	3.00

NOTE: ***Jack Cole** 1-2pg. art in many issues.*

CANNONBALL COMICS
Feb, 1945 - No. 2, Mar, 1945
Rural Home Publishing Co.

	Good	Fine	Mint
1-The Crash Kid, Thunderbrand, The Captive Prince & Crime Crusader begin	12.00	35.00	70.00
2	7.00	20.00	40.00

CANTEEN KATE (Also see All Picture All True Love Story & Fightin' Marines)
June, 1952 - No. 3, Nov, 1952
St. John Publishing Co.

	Good	Fine	Mint
1-Matt Baker c/a	25.00	75.00	150.00
2-Matt Baker c/a	20.00	60.00	120.00
3-Used in **POP**, pg. 75; Baker c/a (Rare)	30.00	80.00	160.00

CAP'N CRUNCH COMICS (See Quaker Oats)
1963; 1965 (16 pgs.; miniature giveaways; 2½x5½'')
Quaker Oats Co.

	Good	Fine	Mint
(4 titles)-''The Picture Pirates,'' ''The Fountain of Youth,'' ''I'm Dreaming of a Wide Isthmus,'' ''Bewitched, Betwitched, & Betweaked''('65)		.60	1.20

CAPTAIN ACTION
Oct-Nov, 1968 - No. 5, June-July, 1969
National Periodical Publications

	Good	Fine	Mint
1-Origin; Wood-a; Superman cameo	.35	1.00	2.00
2,3,5-Kane/Wood-a	.30	.80	1.60
4-Gil Kane-a		.50	1.00
. . . & Action Boy('67)-Ideal Toy Co. giveaway		.40	.80

CAPTAIN AERO COMICS (Samson No. 1-6)
V1No.7(No.1), Dec, 1941 - V2No.4(No.10), Jan, 1943; V3No.9(No. 11), Sept, 1943 - V4No.3(No.17), Oct, 1944; No. 21, Dec, 1944 - No. 26, Aug, 1946 (no No. 18-20)
Holyoke Publishing Co.

	Good	Fine	Mint
V1No.7(No.1)-Flag-Man & Solar, Master of Magic, Captain Aero, Cap Stone, Adventurer begin	24.00	70.00	140.00
8(No.2)-Pals of Freedom app.	12.00	35.00	70.00
9(No.3)-Alias X begins; Pals of Freedom app.	12.00	35.00	70.00
10(No.4)-Origin The Gargoyle; Kubert-a	12.00	35.00	70.00
11,12(No.5,6)-Kubert-a; Miss Victory app. in No. 6	10.00	30.00	60.00
V2No.1(No.7)	7.00	20.00	40.00
2(No.8)-Origin The Red Cross	7.00	20.00	40.00
3(No.9)-Miss Victory app.	4.50	13.00	26.00
4(No.10)	4.00	11.00	22.00
V3No.9 - V3No.13(No.11-15): 11,15-Miss Victory app.	2.00	6.00	12.00
V4No.2, V4No.3(No.16,17)	2.00	6.00	12.00
21	2.00	5.00	10.00
22-24,26-L. B. Cole-c	5.00	15.00	30.00
25-L. B. Cole S/F-c	7.00	20.00	40.00

NOTE: ***Hollingsworth** a-23. **Infantino** a-23.*

CAPTAIN AMERICA (See All-Select, All Winners, Aurora, Giant Comics to Color, The Invaders, Marvel Super Heroes, Marvel Super-Action, Marvel Team-Up, Marvel Treasury Special, & USA Comics)

CAPTAIN AMERICA (Tales of Suspense No. 1-99; . . . and the Falcon No. 134-223)
No. 100, April, 1968 - Present
Marvel Comics Group

	Good	Fine	Mint
100-Flashback on Cap's revival with Avengers & Sub-Mariner	2.00	6.00	12.00
101-108	1.00	3.00	6.00
109-Origin Capt. America	1.20	3.50	7.00
110,111,113-Steranko c/a. 110-Rick becomes Cap's partner. 111-Death of Steve Rogers. 113-Cap's funeral	1.50	4.00	8.00
112,114-116,118-120	.40	1.20	2.40
117-1st app. The Falcon	.50	1.50	3.00
121-130	.40	1.20	2.40
131-139: 133-The Falcon becomes Cap's partner; origin Modok. 137,138-Spider-Man x-over	.35	1.00	2.00
140-Origin Grey Gargoyle retold	.40	1.20	2.40
141-143,145-150: 143-(52 pgs.)	.30	.80	1.60
144-Drug propaganda story; Nixon & Agnew app.	.30	.80	1.60
151-154,156-159,161-163,165-171,177-179		.60	1.20
155-Origin r-/Young Men No. 24	.30	.80	1.60
160-1st app. Solarr	.30	.80	1.60
164-1st app. Nightshade	.30	.80	1.60
172-175-X-Men x-over	.60	1.80	3.60
176-End of Captain America	.30	.80	1.60
180-Intro & origin of Nomad	.30	.80	1.60
181-Intro & origin of new Capt. America	.30	.80	1.60
182,184,185,187-192		.60	1.20
183-Death of New Cap; Nomad becomes Cap		.60	1.20
186-True origin The Falcon	.30	.80	1.60
193-199,201-230		.40	.80
200	.40	1.10	2.20
231-236,238-242,244-251,254,256-260,262-265: 245-No Code. 250-Reagan & Carter app.		.30	.60
237-Death of Sharon Carter		.30	.60
243-Origin Adonis		.30	.60
252,253-Byrne-a	.30	.80	1.60
255-Origin redrawn by Byrne	.35	1.00	2.00
261-Nomad app.		.30	.60

Cannonball Comics #2, © RH

Captain Aero Comics #4, © HOKE

Captain America #109, © MCG

Captain America Comics #15, © MCG

Captain America Comics #37, © MCG

Captain Battle #3, © LEV

CAPTAIN AMERICA (continued) — Good / Fine / Mint

Giant Size 1(12/75) .40 1.10 2.20
Special 1(1/71) .55 1.60 3.20
Special 2(1/72) .50 1.50 3.00
Annual 3(4/76), 4(8/77)-Kirby c/a .30 .80 1.60

NOTE: ***Austin*** *c-225.* ***Buckler*** *a-243p.* ***Buscema*** *a-115p, 217; c-136p, 217.* ***Byrne*** *part c-223, 238, 239, 247-54; a-247-255p.* ***Everett*** *a-136i, 137i; c-126i.* ***Infantino*** *a-245.* ***Gil Kane*** *a-145p; c-172-174, 176, 180, 215, 216, 220, 221.* ***Kirby*** *a-100-109, 112, 193-214, 216, Giant Size 1, Special 1,2, Annual 3,4; c-100-109, 112, 126p, 193-214.* ***Miller*** *c-255p.* ***Morrow*** *a-144.* ***Perez*** *c-243p.* ***Starlin/Sinnott*** *c-162.* ***Tuska*** *a-215p.* ***Wood*** *a-127i*

CAPTAIN AMERICA COMICS
Mar, 1941 - No. 75, Jan, 1950; No. 76, 5/54 - No. 78, 9/54
(No. 74 & 75 titled Capt. America's Weird Tales)
Timely No. 1-75/Atlas No. 76-78 (CCC/MJMC/CMPS)

1-Origin & 1st app. Captain America & Bucky by S&K; Hurricane, Tuk the Caveboy begin by S&K; Red Skull app.
800.00 2200.00 4500.00
(Prices vary widely on this book)
2-S&K Hurricane; Tuk by Avison (Kirby splash)
300.00 850.00 1700.00
3-Red Skull app; Stan Lee's 1st text. 200.00 550.00 1150.00
4 125.00 370.00 750.00
5 120.00 325.00 650.00
6-Origin Father Time; Tuk the Caveboy ends
100.00 280.00 550.00
7-Red Skull app; bondage-c 100.00 280.00 550.00
8-10-Last S&K issue, (S&K centerfold No. 6-10)
90.00 250.00 500.00
11-Last Hurricane, Headline Hunter; Al Avison Captain America begins, ends No. 20 55.00 160.00 320.00
12-The Imp begins, ends No. 16; Last Father Time
55.00 160.00 320.00
13-Origin The Secret Stamp; classic-c 60.00 175.00 350.00
14,15: 15-Bondage-c 45.00 130.00 260.00
16-Red Skull app; bondage-c. 50.00 135.00 270.00
17-The Fighting Fool only app. 45.00 130.00 260.00
18,19-Human Torch begins No. 19; not in No. 20
35.00 100.00 200.00
20-Sub-Mariner app. 32.00 95.00 190.00
21-25 27.00 80.00 160.00
26-30: 27-Last Secret Stamp 24.00 70.00 140.00
31-36,38-40 22.00 65.00 130.00
37-Red Skull app. 25.00 75.00 150.00
41-50 20.00 60.00 120.00
51-58,60 19.00 55.00 110.00
59-Origin retold 25.00 75.00 150.00
61-Red Skull app. 20.00 60.00 120.00
62-65,67: 63-Intro Asbestos Lady 19.00 55.00 110.00
66-Origin Golden Girl; Kurtzman's "Hey Look"
30.00 90.00 180.00
68-70-Sub-Mariner in all 19.00 55.00 110.00
71-73: 71-Bucky app. 15.00 45.00 90.00
74-(Rare)(1949)-Titled "C.A.'s Weird Tales;" Red Skull app.
45.00 140.00 280.00
75(2/50)-Titled "C.A.'s Weird Tales;" no C.A. app.; horror cover/stories 24.00 70.00 140.00
76-78(1954) 14.00 40.00 80.00
128-Pg. Issue (B&W-1942) 60.00 180.00 320.00
Shoestore Giveaway No. 77 8.00 24.00 48.00

NOTE: ***Crandall*** *a-2i, 3i.* ***Schomburg*** *c-41, 42.* ***S&K*** *c-1, 2, 5-7, 9, 10. A Canadian 132 page issue exists in black & white.*

CAPTAIN AND THE KIDS, THE (See Famous Comics Cartoon Books)

CAPTAIN AND THE KIDS, THE (See Comics on Parade)
1938 - 4-Color No. 881, Feb, 1958
United Features Syndicate

Single Series 1('38) 14.00 40.00 80.00
Single Series 1(Reprint)(12/39-"Reprint" on cover)

Good / Fine / Mint
10.00 30.00 60.00
Okay 1(7/46) 4.00 12.00 24.00
50th Anniversary issue('48)-Contains a 2 page history of the strip, including an account of the famous Supreme Court decision allowing both Pulitzer & Hearst to run the same strip under different names.
1.50 4.00 8.00
Special Summer issue, Fall issue (1948) 1.20 3.50 7.00
4-Color 881 .85 2.50 5.00

CAPTAIN ATOM
1950 - 1951 (5x7¼") (5 cents)
Nationwide Publishers

1-7 1.20 3.50 7.00

CAPTAIN ATOM (Strange Suspense Stories No. 1-77)
No. 78, Dec, 1965 - No. 89, Dec, 1967 (Also see Space Advs.)
Charlton Comics

78-Origin retold 2.50 4.00 8.00
79-81 1.20 3.50 7.00
82-Intro. Nightshade 1.20 3.50 7.00
83-86,88,89: 83-Ted Kord Blue Beetle begins, ends No. 86.
1.00 3.00 6.00
87-Nightshade begins 1.00 3.00 6.00
83-85(Modern Comics-1977)-reprints .15 .30

NOTE: ***Ditko*** *c/a 78-87. No. 90 only published in fanzine 'The Charlton Bullseye' No. 1,2.*

CAPTAIN BATTLE (Boy No. 3 on) (See Silver Streak)
Summer, 1941 - No. 2, Fall, 1941
Comic House/Fun

1-Origin Blackout; Captain Battle begins 20.00 60.00 120.00
2 14.00 40.00 80.00

CAPTAIN BATTLE (2nd Series)
1943 - No. 5, Summer, 1943 (No.3: 52pgs., no date)(No.5: 68pgs.)
Magazine Press

3-Origin Silver Streak retold; Simon-a(r) 8.00 24.00 48.00
4 7.00 20.00 40.00
5-Origin Blackout retold 7.00 20.00 40.00

CAPTAIN BATTLE, JR.
Fall, 1943 - No. 2, Winter, 1943-44
Comic House

1-The Claw vs. The Ghost 17.00 50.00 100.00
2-Wolverton's Scoop Scuttle; Don Rico-a; The Green Claw story
17.00 50.00 100.00

CAPTAIN BRITAIN (Also see Marvel Team-Up No. 65,66)
Oct. 13, 1976 - No. 39, 1977 (Weekly)
Marvel Comics International

1-Origin; with Capt. Britain's face mask inside
.85 2.50 5.00
2-Origin, conclusion; Britain's Boomerang inside
.70 2.00 4.00
3-Vs. Bank Robbers .40 1.20 2.40
4-7-Vs. Hurricane .40 1.20 2.40
8-Vs. Bank Robbers .40 1.20 2.40
9-13-Vs. Dr. Synne .35 1.00 2.00
14,15-Vs. Mastermind .35 1.00 2.00
16-20-With Capt. America; 17 misprinted & color section reprinted in No. 18 .35 1.00 2.00
21-23,25,26-With Capt. America .35 1.00 2.00
24-With C.B.'s Jet Plane inside .70 2.00 4.00
27-Origin retold .35 1.00 2.00
28-32-Vs. Lord Hawk .30 .80 1.60
33-35-More on origin .35 1.00 2.00
36-Star Sceptre .30 .80 1.60
37-39-Vs. Highwayman & Munipulator .30 .80 1.60
Annual(1978,Hardback,64pgs.)-Reprints No. 1-7 with pin-ups of Marvel characters 1.50 4.00 8.00

CAPTAIN BRITAIN (continued)
NOTE: *No. 1,2, & 24 are rarer in mint due to inserts. Distributed in Great Britain only. Story from No. 39 continues in Super Spider-Man (British weekly) No. 231-247. Following cancellation of his series, new Captain Britain stories appeared in "Super Spider-Man" (British weekly) No. 231-247. Captain Britain stories which appear in Super-Spider-Man No. 248-253 are reprints of Marvel Team-Up No. 65&66.*

CAPTAIN CANUCK — Good / Fine / Mint
7/75 - No. 4, 7/77; No. 4, 7-8/79 - No. 14, 3-4/81
Comely Comix (Canada) (Distr. in U. S. No. 9 on)

1-1st app. Bluefox — .30 .80 1.60
2-1st app. Dr. Walker, Redcoat & Kebec — .50 1.00
3(5-7/76)-1st app. Heather — .50 1.00
4(1st printing-2/77)-10x14½"; ($5.00); B&W; 300 copies serially numbered and signed with one certificate of authenticity. — 4.50 13.00 26.00
4(2nd printing-7/77)-11x17", B&W; only 15 copies printed; signed by creator Richard Comely, serially numbered and two certificates of authenticity inserted; orange cardboard covers (Very Rare) — 10.00 30.00 60.00
4(7-8/79)-1st app. Tom Evans & Mr. Gold; origin The Catman — .25 .50
5-Origin Capt. Canuck's powers; 1st app. Earth Patrol & Chaos Corps — .25 .50
6-14: 8-Jonn 'The Final Chapter'. 9-1st World Beyond. 11-1st 'Chariots of Fire' story. — .25 .50
Summer Special 1(7-9/80, 95 cents, 64pgs.) — .50 1.00
NOTE: *30,000 copies of No. 2 were destroyed in Winnipeg.*

CAPTAIN CARVEL AND HIS CARVEL CRUSADERS
(See Carvel Comics)

CAPTAIN COURAGEOUS (Banner No. 3-5)
March, 1942
Ace Magazines

6-Origin & 1st app. The Sword; Lone Warrior, Capt. Courageous app. — 15.00 45.00 90.00

CAPT'N CRUNCH COMICS (See Cap'n. . .)

CAPTAIN DAVY JONES (See 4-Color No. 598)

CAPTAIN EASY
1939 - No. 17, Sept, 1949; April, 1956
Dell Publ./Standard(Visual Editions)/Argo

Hawley(1939)-Contains reprints from The Funnies & 1938 Sunday strips by Roy Crane — 12.00 35.00 70.00
4-Color 24 (1943) — 10.00 30.00 60.00
4-Color 111 — 4.00 12.00 24.00
10(Standard-10/47) — 2.50 7.00 14.00
11-17: All contain 1930's & '40's strip-r — 2.00 5.00 10.00
Argo 1(4/56)-(r) — 1.50 4.00 8.00

CAPTAIN EASY & WASH TUBBS (See Famous Comics Cartoon Books)

CAPTAIN FEARLESS COMICS (Also see Holyoke One-Shot No. 6)
August, 1941 - No. 2, Sept, 1941
Holyoke Publishing Co.

1-Origin Mr. Miracle, Alias X, Captain Fearless, Citizen Smith, Son of the Unknown Soldier; Miss Victory begins — 12.00 35.00 70.00
2 — 7.00 20.00 40.00

CAPTAIN FLASH
Nov, 1954 - No. 4, July, 1955
Sterling Comics

1-Origin by Mike Sekowsky(not Toth); Tomboy begins — 5.00 14.00 28.00
2-4 — 3.50 10.00 20.00

CAPTAIN FLEET
Fall, 1952
Ziff-Davis Publishing Co.

Good / Fine / Mint
1 — 3.00 9.00 18.00

CAPTAIN FLIGHT COMICS
Mar, 1944 - No. 11, Feb-Mar, 1947
Four Star Publications

nn — 3.50 10.00 20.00
2 — 2.00 6.00 12.00
3-5: 4-Rock Raymond begins, ends No. 7. 5-Red Rocket begins; the Grenade app. — 1.75 5.00 10.00
6,7 — 2.50 7.00 14.00
8-Yankee Girl, Black Cobra begin; intro. Cobra Kid — 5.00 14.00 28.00
9-Torpedoman app.; last Yankee Girl; Kinstler-a — 5.00 14.00 28.00
10-Deep Sea Dawson, Zoom of the Jungle, Rock Raymond, Red Rocket, & Black Cobra app; L. B. Cole bondage-c — 5.00 14.00 28.00
11-Torpedoman, Blue Flame app.; last Black Cobra, Red Rocket; L. B. Cole-c — 5.00 14.00 28.00
NOTE: ***L. B. Cole** c-7-11.*

CAPTAIN FORTUNE PRESENTS
1955 - 1959 (16 pages; 3¼x6-7/8") (Giveaway)
Vital Publications

"Davy Crockett in Episodes of the Creek War," "Davy Crockett at the Alamo," "In Sherwood Forest Tells Strange Tales of Robin Hood" ('57), "Meets Bolivar the Liberator"('59), "Tells How Buffalo Bill Fights the Dog Soldiers"('57), "Young Davy Crockett" — .85 2.50 5.00

CAPTAIN GALLANT (. . . of the Foreign Legion) (TV)
1955 - 1956
Charlton Comics

1-Buster Crabbe — 2.50 7.00 14.00
2-4 — 1.50 4.00 8.00
Heinz Foods Premium(1955; regular size)-U.S. Pictorial; contains Buster Crabbe photos; Don Heck-a — 1.20 3.50 7.00
Non-Heinz version (same as above except pictures of show replaces ads) — 1.20 3.50 7.00

CAPTAIN HERO (See Jughead as. . .)

CAPTAIN HERO COMICS DIGEST MAGAZINE
Sept, 1981 - Present
Archie Publications

1-Reprints of Jughead as Super-Guy — .30 .60

CAPTAIN HOBBY COMICS
Feb, 1948 (Canadian)
Export Publication Ent. Ltd. (Dist. in U.S. by Kable News Co.)

1 — 1.20 3.50 7.00

CAPTAIN HOOK & PETER PAN (See 4-Color No. 446 and Peter Pan)

CAPTAIN JET (Fantastic Fears No. 7 on)
May, 1952 - No. 5, Jan, 1953
Comic Media/Four Star Publ./Farrell

1 — 2.50 7.00 14.00
2-5,6(?) — 2.00 5.00 10.00

CAPTAIN KANGAROO (See 4-Color No. 721,780,872)

CAPTAIN KIDD (Formerly Dagar)
1949
Fox Features Syndicate

24,25 — 2.50 7.00 14.00

CAPTAIN MARVEL (See All Hero, All-New Coll. Ed., America's Greatest, Fawcett Min., Gift, Limited Coll. Ed., Marvel Family, Master No. 21, Mighty Midget Comics, Shazam, Whiz, Wisco, and X-Mas)

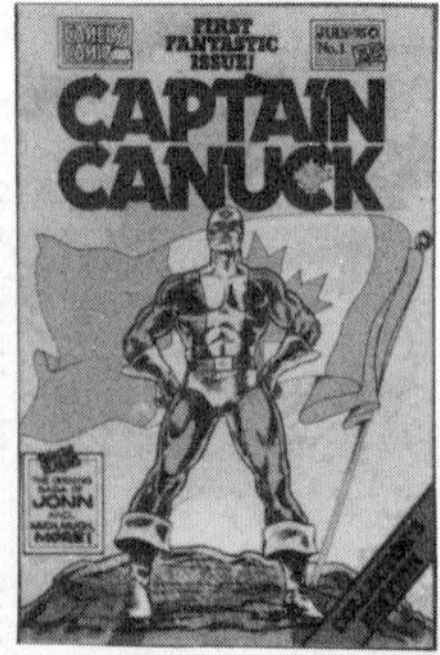

Captain Canuck #1, © Comely Comix

Captain Easy #1, © NEA Services, Inc.

Captain Flight #2, © STAR

Captain Marvel #25, © MCG

Captain Marvel Advs. #14, © FAW

Captain Marvel Jr. #4, © FAW

CAPTAIN MARVEL (. . . Presents the Terrible 5 No. 5)
April, 1966 - No. 4, Nov, 1966 (25 cents)
M. F. Enterprises

	Good	Fine	Mint
nn-(No.1 on page 5)-Origin	.35	1.00	2.00
2,4		.60	1.20
3-(No.3 on page 4)-Fights the Bat		.60	1.20

CAPTAIN MARVEL (See Marvel Spotlight & Marvel Super-Heroes 12)
May, 1968 - No. 19, Dec, 1969; No. 20, June, 1970 - No. 21, Aug, 1970; No. 22, Sept, 1972 - No. 62, May, 1979
Marvel Comics Group

	Good	Fine	Mint
1	2.00	5.00	10.00
2-5	.60	1.80	3.60
6-10	.40	1.20	2.40
11-Smith/Trimpe-c; Death of Una	.60	1.80	3.60
12-20: 17-New costume	.30	.80	1.60
21-24	.30	.80	1.60
25-Starlin c/a	1.20	3.50	7.00
26-Starlin c/a	.85	2.50	5.00
27-34-Starlin c/a. 29-C.M. gains added powers.	.60	1.80	3.60
35,37-40: 39-Origin Watcher		.60	1.20
36-Starlin-a, 3pgs.	.30	.80	1.60
41,43-Wrightson part inks; cover No. 43(inks)		.60	1.20
42,44-48,50		.50	1.00
49-Starlin in part		.60	1.20
51-62: 53-Inhumans app.		.40	.80
Giant-Size 1 (12/75)	.40	1.20	2.40

NOTE: ***Alcala*** *a-35.* ***Gil Kane*** *a-17-22; c-17-25.* ***McWilliams*** *a-40*

CAPTAIN MARVEL ADVENTURES
1941 - No. 150, Nov, 1953
Fawcett Publications

	Good	Fine	Mint
nn(No.1)-Captain Marvel & Sivana by Jack Kirby. The cover was printed on unstable paper stock and is rarely found in Fine or Mint condition	600.00	1900.00	4200.00
(Prices vary widely on this book)			
2-Art by George Tuska	150.00	400.00	800.00
3	70.00	190.00	380.00
4-Three Lt. Marvels app.	50.00	130.00	260.00
5	40.00	110.00	220.00
6-10	30.00	90.00	180.00
11-15: 13-Two-pg. Capt. Marvel pin-up. 15-Comic cards on back cover begin, end No. 26	20.00	60.00	120.00
16,17	17.00	50.00	100.00
18-Origin & 1st app. Mary Marvel & Marvel Family; painted-c (12/11/42)	24.00	70.00	140.00
19-Mary Marvel x-over; Christmas-c	14.00	42.00	85.00
20,21-With miniature comic still attached to cover; miniature's cover same as Whiz No. 22 (other variations possible)(See Fawcett Miniatures & Mighty Midget) with comic attached	19.00	55.00	110.00
20,21-Without miniature	12.00	36.00	72.00
22-Mr. Mind serial begins	25.00	75.00	150.00
23-25	12.00	36.00	72.00
26-30: 26-U.S.A.-Flag-c	10.00	30.00	60.00
31-35: 35-Origin Radar	9.50	28.00	56.00
36-40: 37-Mary Marvel x-over	8.00	24.00	48.00
41-46: 42-Christmas-c. 43-Captain Marvel 1st meets Uncle Marvel; Mary Batson cameo. 46-Mr. Mind serial ends	7.00	20.00	40.00
47-50	5.50	16.00	32.00
51-53,55-60: 52-Origin & 1st app. Sivana Jr.; Capt. Marvel Jr. x-over	4.00	12.00	24.00
54-Special oversize 68-pg. issue	5.00	14.00	28.00
61-The Cult of the Curse serial begins	6.00	18.00	36.00
62-66-Serial ends; Mary Marvel x-over in No. 65	3.50	10.00	20.00
67-77,79: 69-Billy Batson's Christmas; Uncle Marvel, Mary Marvel, Capt. Marvel Jr. x-over. 71-Three Lt. Marvels app. No. 79-Origin Mr. Tawny	3.50	10.00	20.00
78-Origin Mr. Atom	4.00	12.00	24.00
80-Origin Capt. Marvel retold	5.50	16.00	32.00
81-84,86-90: 81,90-Mr. Atom app. 82-Infinity-c. 86-Mr. Tawny app.	4.00	12.00	24.00
85-Freedom Train issue	4.75	14.00	28.00
91-99: 96-Mr. Tawny app.	3.00	8.00	16.00
100-Origin retold	5.00	15.00	30.00
101-120	2.75	8.00	16.00
121-Origin retold	3.00	9.00	18.00
122-141,143-149	2.50	7.00	14.00
142-Used in **POP**, pgs. 92,96	3.00	9.00	18.00
150-(Low distribution)	7.00	20.00	40.00
Bond Bread Giveaways-(24 pgs.; pocket size-7¼x3½''; paper cover): ". . . & the Stolen City," "The Boy Who Never Heard of C.M."-(1950)(reprint). . . .each. . . .	12.00	35.00	70.00

CAPTAIN MARVEL ADVENTURES (Also see Whiz)
1945 (6x8'') (Full color, paper cover)
Fawcett Publications (Wheaties Giveaway)

	Good	Fine	Mint
"Captain Marvel & the Threads of Life" plus 2 other stories (32pgs.)	10.00	30.00	70.00

NOTE: *All copies were taped at each corner to a box of Wheaties and are never found in Fine or Mint condition.*

CAPTAIN MARVEL AND THE GOOD HUMOR MAN
1950
Fawcett Publications

	Good	Fine	Mint
nn	9.00	26.00	60.00

CAPTAIN MARVEL AND HIS LTS. OF SAFETY
1950 - 1951 (3 issues - no No.'s)
Fawcett Publications

	Good	Fine	Mint
"Danger Flies a Kite," "Danger Smashes the Lights," "Danger Takes to Climbing" (Scarce)	5.00	15.00	34.00

CAPTAIN MARVEL COMIC STORY PAINT BOOK (See Comic Story Paint Book)

CAPTAIN MARVEL, JR. (See Fawcett Miniatures, Marvel Family, Master Comics, Mighty Midget Comics, and Shazam)

CAPTAIN MARVEL, JR.
Nov, 1942 - No. 119, June, 1953 (nn 34)
Fawcett Publications

	Good	Fine	Mint
1-Origin Capt. Marvel Jr. retold (Whiz No. 25); Capt. Nazi app.	70.00	200.00	400.00
2-Vs. Capt. Nazi; origin Capt. Nippon	40.00	110.00	225.00
3,4	30.00	85.00	170.00
5-Vs. Capt. Nazi	22.00	65.00	130.00
6-10: 8-Vs. Capt. Nazi. 9-Flag-c	17.00	50.00	100.00
11,12,15-Capt. Nazi app.	12.00	35.00	70.00
13,14,16-20: 16-Capt. Marvel & Sivana x-over	8.00	24.00	50.00
21-30	5.50	16.00	32.00
31-33,36-40: 37-Infinity-c	3.00	9.00	20.00
35-No. 34 on inside; the cover shows origin of Sivana Jr. which is not on inside. Evidently the cover to No. 35 was printed out of sequence and bound with contents to No. 34	3.50	10.00	20.00
41-50	2.50	7.50	15.00
51-70	2.50	7.50	15.00
71-103,105-114,116-119	2.00	6.00	12.00
104-Used in **POP**, pg. 89	2.50	7.50	15.00
115-Injury to eye-c; Eyeball story	2.50	7.50	15.00

NOTE: ***Mac Raboy*** *c-1-10,12,13,16,19,31 among others.*

CAPTAIN MARVEL JR. WELL KNOWN COMICS
1944 (12 pages; 8½x10½'') (Printed in blue)
(paper cover; glued binding)
Bestmaid/Samuel Lowe (Giveaway)

	Good	Fine	Mint
	15.00	45.00	90.00

NOTE: *Several copies surfaced during 1980.*

CAPTAIN MARVEL PRESENTS THE TERRIBLE FIVE
Aug, 1966; V2No.5, Sept, 1967 (no No.2-4) (25 cents)
M. F. Enterprises

CAPT. MARVEL PRESENTS... (continued)

	Good	Fine	Mint
1	.35	1.00	1.50
V2No.5-(Formerly Capt. Marvel)	.30	.80	1.20

CAPTAIN MARVEL'S FUN BOOK
1944 (½'' thick) (cardboard covers)
Samuel Lowe Co.

Puzzles, games, magic, etc.; infinity-c	5.00	15.00	30.00

CAPTAIN MARVEL SPECIAL EDITION (See Special Edition)

CAPTAIN MARVEL STORY BOOK
Summer, 1946 - 1948
Fawcett Publications

1	15.00	45.00	90.00
2-4	10.00	30.00	60.00

CAPTAIN MARVEL THRILL BOOK (Large-Size)
1941 (Black & White; color cover)
Fawcett Publications

1-Reprints from Whiz No. 8,10, & Special Edition No. 1 (Rare)	150.00	450.00	900.00

NOTE: *Rarely found in Fine or Mint condition.*

CAPTAIN MARVEL WELL KNOWN COMICS
1944 (12 pages; 8½x10½'') (Printed in red)
(paper cover; glued binding)
Bestmaid/Samuel Lowe Co. (Giveaway)

(Scarce)	25.00	70.00	120.00

CAPTAIN MIDNIGHT (Sweethearts No. 68 on)
Sept, 1942 - No. 67, Fall, 1948
Fawcett Publications

1-Origin Captain Midnight; Captain Marvel cameo on cover	40.00	120.00	240.00
2	20.00	60.00	120.00
3-5	14.00	40.00	80.00
6-10: 10-Flag-c	9.00	25.00	50.00
11-20	5.00	15.00	30.00
21-30	3.50	10.00	20.00
31-40	2.50	7.50	15.00
41-67	2.00	6.00	12.00

(See Super Book No. 3)

CAPTAIN NICE (TV)
Nov, 1967 (One Shot)
Gold Key

1(10211-711)-Photo-c	.70	2.00	4.00

CAPTAIN PUREHEART (See Archie as...)

CAPTAIN ROCKET
November, 1951
P. L. Publ. (Canada)

1	9.00	25.00	50.00

CAPTAIN SAVAGE (... & His Leatherneck Raiders)
Jan, 1968 - No. 19, Mar, 1970 (See Sgt. Fury No. 10)
Marvel Comics Group

1-Sgt. Fury & Howlers cameo	.30	.80	1.60
2-Origin Hydra		.40	.80
3-10		.30	.60
11-19: Severin art No. 8,9,16-19. 11-Sgt. Fury & Howlers x-over		.30	.60

CAPTAIN SCIENCE (Fantastic No. 8 on)
Nov, 1950 - No. 7, Dec, 1951
Youthful Magazines

1-Wood-a; origin	30.00	90.00	180.00
2,3,6,7; 6,7-Bondage-c	10.00	30.00	60.00
4,5-Wood & Orlando-c/a(2) each	30.00	85.00	170.00

CAPTAIN SILVER'S LOG OF SEA HOUND (See Sea Hound)

CAPTAIN SINDBAD (Movie Adaptation) (See Movie Comics)

CAPTAIN STEVE SAVAGE
1950 - No. 13, May-June, 1956
Avon Periodicals

	Good	Fine	Mint
nn(1st series)-Wood art, 22 pgs. (titled-''...Over Korea'')	12.00	35.00	70.00
1(4/51)-Reprints nn ish (Canadian)	6.00	18.00	36.00
2-Kamen-a	3.50	10.00	20.00
3-11	2.00	5.00	10.00
12-Wood-a, 6pp	3.50	10.00	20.00
13-Check, Lawrence-a	3.00	8.00	16.00

NOTE: ***Kinstler** c-2-5, 7-9, 11. **Ravielli** a-9.*

1(1954-2nd series)	2.50	7.00	14.00
2-Wood-a, 6pp	4.00	12.00	24.00
3-5,7('55)	1.50	4.00	8.00
6-Reprints nn ish; Wood-a	4.00	12.00	24.00
8-13	1.00	3.00	6.00

CAPTAIN STONE (See Holyoke One-Shot No. 10)

CAPTAIN STORM
May-June, 1964 - No. 18, Mar-Apr, 1967
National Periodical Publications

1-Origin	.50	1.50	3.00
2-18: 12-Kubert-c	.35	1.00	2.00

CAPTAIN 3-D
December, 1953
Harvey Publications

1-Kirby/Ditko-a	3.00	8.00	16.00

NOTE: *Many copies surfaced in 1979, causing a set-back in price.*

CAPTAIN TOOTSIE & THE SECRET LEGION (Advs. of..)
Oct, 1950 - No. 2, 1950
Toby Press

1-Not Beck-a	5.00	14.00	30.00
2-Not Beck-a	3.00	9.00	20.00

CAPTAIN VENTURE & THE LAND BENEATH THE SEA
Oct, 1968 - No. 2, Oct, 1969
Gold Key (See Space Family Robinson)

1,2	1.00	3.00	6.00

CAPTAIN VICTORY AND THE GALACTIC RANGERS
Nov, 1981 - Present ($1.00) (36 pgs.)
Pacific Comics (Sold only through comic shops)

1-Kirby c/a		.50	1.00
2-Kirby c/a		.50	1.00

CAPTAIN VIDEO (TV)
Feb, 1951 - No. 6, Dec, 1951
Fawcett Publications

1-George Evans-a(2)	12.00	35.00	75.00
2-Used in **SOTI**, pg. 382	9.00	27.00	60.00
3-6-All Evans-a	7.50	22.00	50.00

NOTE: *Minor **Williamson** assist on most issues.*

CAPTAIN WIZARD (Also see Meteor)
1946
Rural Home

1-Capt. Wizard dons new costume; Impossible Man, Race Wilkins app.	3.00	8.00	18.00

CARDINAL MINDSZENTY (The Truth Behind the Trial of...)
1949 (24 pages; paper cover, in color)
Catechetical Guild Education Society

nn-Anti-communism	12.00	35.00	70.00

Captain Midnight #8, © FAW

Captain Steve Savage #4, © AVON

Captain Wizard #1, © RH

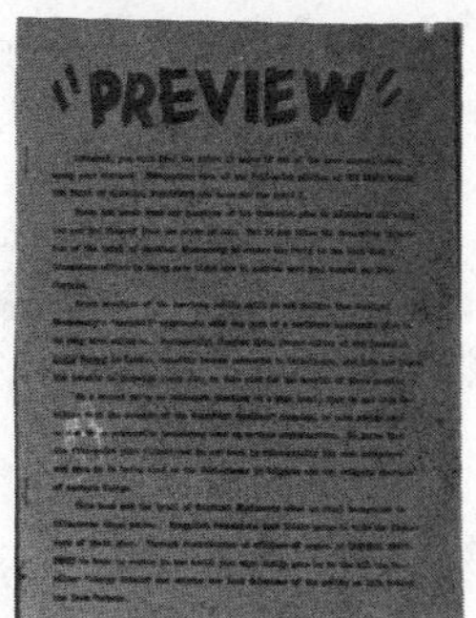

Cardinal Mindszenty-Preview Copy, © CG

Caroline Kennedy nn, © CC

Casey-Crime Photographer #4, © MCG

CARDINAL MINDSZENTY (continued) — Good / Fine / Mint

Press Proof-(Very Rare)-(Full color, 7½x11¾", untrimmed)
Only two known copies — 200.00

Preview Copy (B&W, stapled), 18 pgs.; contains first 13 pgs. of Cardinal Mindszenty and was sent out as an advance promotion.
Only one known copy — $200.00 - $400.00

NOTE: *Regular edition also printed in French.*

CAREER GIRL ROMANCES (Formerly Three Nurses)
Jan, 1965 - No. 77, 1972
Charlton Comics

	Good	Fine	Mint
V4No.24-77		.40	.80

CAR 54, WHERE ARE YOU? (TV)
Mar-May, 1962 - No. 7, Sept-Nov, 1963; 1964 - 1965
Dell Publishing Co.

	Good	Fine	Mint
4-Color 1257(3-5/62)	.70	2.00	4.00
2(7-9/62)-7	.50	1.50	3.00
2,3(10-12/64), 4(1-3/65)-Reprints No. 2,3,&4 of 1st series	.35	1.00	2.00

CARNATION MALTED MILK GIVEAWAYS (See Wisco)

CARNIVAL COMICS
1945
Harry 'A' Chesler/Pershing Square Publ. Co.

	Good	Fine	Mint
1	1.50	4.00	10.00

CARNIVAL OF COMICS
1954 (Giveaway)
Fleet-Air Shoes

	Good	Fine	Mint
nn-Contains a comic bound with new cover; several combinations possible; Charlton's Eh! known	1.00	3.00	6.00

CAROLINE KENNEDY
1961 (One Shot)
Charlton Comics

	Good	Fine	Mint
	3.50	10.00	20.00

CAROUSEL COMICS
V1No.8, April, 1948
F. E. Howard, Toronto

	Good	Fine	Mint
V1No.8	.85	2.50	5.00

CARTOON KIDS
1957
Atlas Comics (CPS)

	Good	Fine	Mint
1	.85	2.50	5.00

CARTOONS (Magazine) (Also see Drag Cartoons)
1960 - Present (52 pages) (Automobile humor)
Petersen Publ. Co.

	Good	Fine	Mint
1,2(Digest size, 1960)	.85	2.50	5.00
1(Regular size)	.85	2.50	5.00
2-20	.35	1.00	2.00
21-25		.45	.90
26-Toth-a	.85	2.50	5.00
27-101		.40	.80

CARVEL COMICS (Amazing Advs. of Capt. Carvel)
1975 (25 cents; No.3-5: 35 cents) (No.4,5: 3¼x5")
Carvel Corp. (Ice Cream)

	Good	Fine	Mint
1-3		.15	.30
4,5(1976)-Baseball theme	.85	2.50	5.00

CASE OF THE SHOPLIFTER'S SHOE (See Feature Book No. 50
McKay, (Perry Mason)

CASE OF THE WASTED WATER, THE
1972? (Giveaway)
Rheem Water Heating

	Good	Fine	Mint
Neal Adams-a	2.00	6.00	12.00

CASE OF THE WINKING BUDDHA, THE
1950 (132 pgs.; 25 cents; B&W; 5½x7-5½8")
St. John Publ. Co.

	Good	Fine	Mint
Charles Raab-a; reprinted in Authentic Police Cases No. 25	5.00	15.00	30.00

CASEY-CRIME PHOTOGRAPHER (Two-Gun Western No. 5 on)
Aug, 1949 - No. 4, Feb, 1950
Marvel Comics (BFP)

	Good	Fine	Mint
1: Photo-c	3.00	9.00	18.00
2-4: Photo-c	2.00	6.00	12.00

CASEY JONES (See 4-Color No. 915)

CASPER AND NIGHTMARE (See Harvey Hits No. 37,45,52,56,62,65, 68,75)

CASPER AND NIGHTMARE (Nightmare & Casper No. 1-5) (25 cents)
No. 6, 11/64 - No. 44, 10/73; No. 45, 6/74 - No. 46, 10/74?
Harvey Publications

	Good	Fine	Mint
6	2.00	6.00	12.00
7-10	1.00	3.00	6.00
11-20	.50	1.50	3.00
21-46	.35	1.00	2.00

CASPER AND SPOOKY (See Harvey Hits No. 20)
Oct, 1972 - No. 7, Oct, 1973
Harvey Publications

	Good	Fine	Mint
1	.70	2.00	4.00
2-7	.30	.90	1.80

CASPER AND THE GHOSTLY TRIO
Nov, 1972 - No. 7, Nov, 1973
Harvey Publications

	Good	Fine	Mint
1	.70	2.00	4.00
2-7	.30	.90	1.80

CASPER AND WENDY
Sept, 1972 - No. 8, Nov, 1973
Harvey Publications

	Good	Fine	Mint
1	.70	2.00	4.00
2-8	.30	.90	1.80

CASPER CAT
1958; 1963
I. W. Enterprises/Super

	Good	Fine	Mint
1,7-Reprint, Super No. 14('63)	.35	1.00	2.00

CASPER DIGEST STORIES
February, 1980 - Present (95 cents; 132 pgs.; digest size)
Harvey Publications

	Good	Fine	Mint
1		.60	1.20
2-4		.50	1.00

CASPER DIGEST WINNERS
April, 1980 - No. 3, June, 1980 (95 cents; 132 pgs.; digest size)
Harvey Publications

	Good	Fine	Mint
1		.60	1.20
2,3		.50	1.00

CASPER HALLOWEEN TRICK OR TREAT
January, 1976
Harvey Publications

	Good	Fine	Mint
1	.30	.80	1.60

CASPER IN SPACE (Formerly Casper Spaceship)
No. 6, June, 1973 - No. 8, Oct, 1973
Harvey Publications

	Good	Fine	Mint
6-8	.30	.80	1.60

CASPER'S GHOSTLAND
Winter, 1958-59 - No. 97, 8/77; No. 98, 12/79 (25 cents)
Harvey Publications

CASPER'S GHOSTLAND (continued)	Good	Fine	Mint
1	5.50	16.00	32.00
2	3.50	10.00	20.00
3-10	3.00	8.00	16.00
11-20	2.00	5.00	10.00
21-40	1.00	3.00	6.00
41-60	.70	2.00	4.00
61-80	.35	1.00	2.00
81-97	.30	.80	1.60
98		.30	.60

CASPER SPACESHIP (Casper in Space No. 6 on)
Aug, 1972 - No. 5, April, 1973
Harvey Publications

1	.70	2.00	4.00
2-5	.30	.80	1.60

CASPER STRANGE GHOST STORIES
October, 1974 - No. 15, March, 1977
Harvey Publications

1	.55	1.60	3.20
2-14: 13-(40 cents)	.30	.80	1.60

CASPER'S T.V. SHOWTIME
October, 1979 - Present
Harvey Comics

1		.60	1.20
2-5		.40	.80

CASPER, THE FRIENDLY GHOST (See Famous TV Funday Funnies, The Friendly Ghost . . ., Comics Hits No. 61, Nightmare & . . ., Richie Rich, & Tastee-Freez)

CASPER, THE FRIENDLY GHOST
Sept, 1949 - No. 5, May, 1951
St. John Publishing Co.

1(1949)-Origin & 1st app. Baby Huey	25.00	70.00	140.00
2-5	14.00	40.00	80.00

CASPER, THE FRIENDLY GHOST (Paramount Picture Star . . .)
No. 7, Dec, 1952 - No 70, July, 1958
Harvey Publications (Family Comics)

7-Baby Huey app.	11.00	32.00	64.00
8-10	7.00	20.00	40.00
11-19	5.50	16.00	32.00
20-Wendy the Witch begins (1st app, 5/54)	6.00	18.00	36.00
21-30: 24-Infinity-c	5.00	14.00	28.00
31-40	4.00	12.00	24.00
41-50	3.50	10.00	20.00
51-70	3.00	8.00	16.00
American Dental Association (Giveaways):			
. . .'s Dental Health Activity Book-1977	.30	.80	1.60
. . . Presents Space Age Dentistry-1972	.40	1.20	2.40
. . ., His Den, & Their Dentist Fight the Tooth Demons-1974	.40	1.20	2.40

NOTE: *No. 6 is Comics Hits no. 61(10/52).*

CASTILIAN (See Movie Classics)

CAT, T.H.E. (TV) (See T.H.E. Cat)

CAT, THE (See Movie Classics)

CAT, THE
Nov, 1972 - No. 4, June, 1973
Marvel Comics Group

1-Origin The Cat; Wally Wood inks	.70	2.00	4.00
2-Mooney/Marie Severin-a	.50	1.50	3.00
3-Everett inks	.50	1.50	3.00
4-Starlin/Weiss-a	.50	1.50	3.00

CATHOLIC COMICS (See Heroes All Catholic . . .)
June, 1946 - V3No.10, July, 1949
Catholic Publications

	Good	Fine	Mint
1	4.00	12.00	24.00
2-12	2.00	6.00	12.00
V2No.1-10	1.20	3.50	7.00
V3No.1-10	.85	2.50	5.00

CATHOLIC PICTORIAL
1947
Catholic Guild

1-Toth-a(2) (Rare)	14.00	40.00	80.00

CATMAN COMICS (Crash No. 1-5)
5/41 - No. 17, 1/43; No. 18, 7/43 - No. 22, 12/43; No. 23, 3/44 - No. 26, 11/44; No. 27, 4/45 - No. 30, 12/45; No. 31, 6/46 - No. 32, 8/46
Holyoke Publishing Co.

1(V1No.6)-Origin The Deacon & Sidekick Mickey, Dr. Diamond & Rag-Man; The Black Widow app.; The Catman by Chas. Quinlan & Blaze Baylor begin	25.00	70.00	145.00
2(V1No.7)	14.00	42.00	85.00
3(V1No.8), 4(V1No.9): 3-The Pied Piper begins	10.00	30.00	60.00
5(V2No.10)-Origin Kitten; The Hood begins, 6,7(V2No.11,12)	7.00	20.00	40.00
8(V2No.13,3/42)-Origin Little Leaders; Volton by Kubert begins (his 1st comic book work)	12.00	35.00	70.00
9(V2No.14)	6.00	18.00	36.00
10(V2No.15)-Origin Blackout; Phantom Falcon begins	6.00	18.00	36.00
11(V3No.1), 12(V3No.2, 7/42))-15(V3No.13), 16-18(V3No.8, 7/43), 19(V2No.6), 20(V2No.7)	5.00	15.00	30.00
21(V2No.8), 22(V2No.9), 23(V3No.13, 5/44)-Kirbyish-a	4.00	12.00	24.00
24(V2No.12, 7/44)	4.00	12.00	24.00
25-The Reckoner begins	3.50	10.00	20.00
26(V3No.2)-Origin The Golden Archer; Leatherface app.; L. B. Cole-c	11.00	32.00	70.00
27-Origin Kitten retold; L. B. Cole Flag-c	11.00	32.00	70.00
28-Catman learns Kitten's I.D.; Dr. Macabre, Deacon app.; L. B. Cole-c/a	15.00	45.00	90.00
29-32-L. B. Cole-c; bondage-No. 30	11.00	32.00	70.00

CAUGHT
Aug, 1956 - No. 5, April, 1957
Atlas Comics (VPI)

1	1.50	4.00	8.00
2,4	.85	2.50	5.00
3-Torres-a	2.00	5.00	10.00
5-Crandall, Krigstein-a	2.50	7.00	14.00

CAVALIER COMICS
1945; 1952 (Early DC reprints)
A. W. Nugent Publ. Co.

2(1945)-Speed Saunders, Fang Gow	2.50	7.50	15.00
2(1952)	1.50	4.50	9.00

CAVE GIRL
1953 - 1954
Magazine Enterprises

11(A-1 82)-Origin	14.00	40.00	80.00
12(A-1 96), 13(A-1 116), 14(A-1 125)-Thunda by Powell	10.00	28.00	56.00

NOTE: ***Powell** c/a in all.*

CAVE KIDS
Feb, 1963 - No. 16, Mar, 1967 (Hanna-Barbera)
Gold Key

1	.85	2.50	5.00
2-5	.50	1.50	3.00
6-16	.35	1.00	2.00

Casper, The Friendly Ghost #20, © HARV

Catman Comics #2, © HOKE

Catman Comics #30, © HOKE

Challengers Of The Unknown #74, © DC

Chamber Of Chills #18, © HARV

Champ Comics #15, © HARV

CENTURION OF ANCIENT ROME, THE
1958 (no month listed) (36 pages) (B&W)
Zondervan Publishing House

	Good	Fine	Mint
(Rare) All by Jay Disbrow Estimated Value....			200.00

CENTURY OF COMICS
1933 (100 pages) (Probably the 3rd comic book)
Eastern Color Printing Co.

Bought by Wheatena, Milk-O-Malt, John Wanamaker, Kinney Shoe Stores, & others to be used as premiums and radio giveaways. No. publisher listed.

nn-Mutt & Jeff, Joe Palooka, etc. reprints	100.00	300.00	600.00

CHALLENGE OF THE UNKNOWN (Formerly Real Life Secrets?)
No. 6, Sept, 1950 - No. 7, 1950 (See Web Of Mystery No. 19)
Ace Magazines

6-'Village of the Vampire' used in N.Y. Joint Legislative Comm. Publ; Sekowsky-a	4.00	12.00	24.00
7	3.00	8.00	16.00

CHALLENGER, THE
1945 - No. 4, Oct-Dec, 1946
Interfaith Publications

nn; No date; 32 pgs.; Origin the Challenger Club; Anti-Fascist with funny animal filler	5.00	15.00	32.00
2-4-Kubert-a	7.00	20.00	45.00

CHALLENGERS OF THE UNKNOWN (See Showcase, Super DC Giant, and Super Team Family)
4-5/58 - No.77, 12-1/70-71; No.78, 2/73 - No.80, 6-7/73; No.81, 6-7/77 - No.87, 6-7/78
National Periodical Publications/DC Comics

1-Kirby/Stein-a(2)	40.00	110.00	220.00
2-Kirby/Stein-a(2)	17.00	50.00	100.00
3-Kirby/Stein-a(2)	14.00	40.00	80.00
4-8-Kirby/Wood-a plus c-No. 8	10.00	30.00	60.00
9,10	6.00	12.00	24.00
11-20: 14-Origin Multi-Man. 18-Intro. Cosmo, the Challs Spacepet	2.00	5.00	10.00
21-40: 31-Retells origin of the Challengers	1.00	3.00	6.00
41-60: 48-Doom Patrol app. 49-Intro. Challenger Corps. 51-Sea Devils app. 55-Death of Red Ryan. 60-Red Ryan returns	.70	2.00	4.00
61-63,66-73: 69-Intro. Corinna	.30	.80	1.60
64,65-Kirby origin-r, parts 1 & 2	.35	1.00	2.00
74-Deadman by Adams; Wrightson-a	1.20	3.50	7.00
75-80		.40	.80
81-83(1977)		.30	.60
84-87-Swamp Thing, Deadman app. in all		.40	.80

NOTE: ***Adams** c-67, 68, 70, 72, 74i, 81i. **Buckler** c-84. **Kirby** a-75-80r; c-75, 77, 78. **Kubert** c-64, 66, 69, 76, 79. **Nasser** a-81, 82; c-81, 82. **Wood** r-76.*

CHALLENGE TO THE WORLD
1951 (36 pages) (10 cents)
Catechetical Guild

nn	5.00	14.00	28.00

CHAMBER OF CHILLS (...of Clues No. 27 on)
No. 21, June, 1951 - No. 26, Dec, 1954
Harvey Publications/Witches Tales

21-Excessive violence, torture	5.00	15.00	30.00
22,23-Excessive violence, torture	3.50	10.00	20.00
24-Bondage-c, excessive violence	3.50	10.00	20.00
5(2/52)-Decapitation, acid in face scene	3.50	10.00	20.00
6,8-10	3.00	8.00	16.00
7-Used in **SOTI**, pg. 389	3.50	10.00	20.00
11,12,14	2.50	7.00	14.00
13,15-23-Nostrand-a in all; c-No. 20	5.00	14.00	28.00
24-26	1.50	4.00	8.00

NOTE: *This title is filled with bondage, torture, sadism, perversion, gore, cannabalism, eyes ripped out, acid in face, etc. **Palais** a-21(1)-24(4). **Powell** a-21, 23-25('51), 5-8, 11, 13, 18-21. Bondage-c-21('51), 7. 25 r-No. 5; 26 r-No. 9.*

CHAMBER OF CHILLS
Nov, 1972 - No. 25, Nov, 1976
Marvel Comics Group

	Good	Fine	Mint
1		.60	1.20
2,3: 2-Brak The Barbarian story		.50	1.00
4-Brunner, Chaykin-a		.50	1.00
5-7-Last new story		.40	.80
8-10,12-20,22-25		.30	.60
11-Everett-a r-/Menace No. 3		.30	.60
21-8pg. Everett Venus r-/Venus No. 18		.30	.60

NOTE: ***Adkins** a-1i, 2i. **Brunner** a-2-4. **Ditko** r-14, 16, 19, 23, 24. **Everett** a-3i. **Russell** a-2. **Robert E. Howard** horror story adaptation-2,3.*

CHAMBER OF CLUES (Formerly Chamber of Chills)
Feb, 1955 - No. 28, April, 1955
Harvey Publications

27-Kerry Drake r-/No. 19-heroin story; Powell-a	5.00	15.00	30.00
28-Kerry Drake	3.00	8.00	16.00

CHAMBER OF DARKNESS (Monsters on the Prowl No. 9)
Oct, 1969 - No. 8, Dec, 1970
Marvel Comics Group

1-Buscema-a	.30	.80	1.60
2-Adams script	.30	.80	1.60
3-Smith, Gil Kane-a	.40	1.20	2.40
4-A Conanesque tryout by Smith; reprinted in Conan No. 16	3.00	8.00	16.00
5,6,8	.30	.80	1.60
7-Wrightson c/a (his 1st work at Marvel); Wrightson draws himself in 1st & last panels	.60	1.80	3.60
1(1/72-25 cent Special)	.25	.70	1.40

NOTE: ***Adkins/Everett** a-8. **Craig** a-5. **Ditko** a-6-8r. **Kirby** a-4, 5, 7. **Kirby/Everett** c-5. **Severin/Everett** c-6. **Wrightson** c-7, 8.*

CHAMP COMICS (Champion No. 1-10)
No. 11, Oct, 1940 - No. 29, March, 1944
Champ Publ./Greenwald/Harvey Publications

11-Human Meteor cont'd.	14.00	40.00	80.00
12-18: 14,15-Crandall-c	10.00	30.00	60.00
19-The Wasp app.; Kirby-c	10.00	30.00	60.00
20-The Green Ghost app.	10.00	30.00	60.00
21-29: 22-The White Mask app.	7.00	20.00	40.00

CHAMPION (See Gene Autry's...)

CHAMPION COMICS (Champ No. 11 on)
No. 2, Dec, 1939 - No. 10, Aug, 1940 (no No.1)
Worth Publ. Co./Harvey Publications

2-The Champ, The Blazing Scarab, Neptina, Liberty Lads, Jungleman, Bill Handy, Swingtime Sweetie begin	15.00	45.00	90.00
3-7: 7-The Human Meteor begins?	10.00	30.00	60.00
8-10-Kirby-c; bondage No. 10	13.00	37.00	75.00

CHAMPIONS, THE
October, 1975 - No. 17, Jan, 1978
Marvel Comics Group

1-The Angel, Black Widow, Ghost Rider, Hercules, Ice Man (The Champions) begin; Kane/Adkins-c; Venus x-over	.75	2.20	4.40
2-5: 2,3-Venus x-over	.30	.80	1.60
6-10: 6-Kirby-c		.60	1.20
11-15,17-Byrne-a	.40	1.10	2.20
16		.30	.60

CHAMPION SPORTS

CHAMPION SPORTS (continued)
Oct-Nov, 1973 - No. 3, Feb-Mar, 1974
National Periodical Publications

	Good	Fine	Mint
1-3		.30	.60

CHAOS (See The Crusaders)

CHARLIE CHAN (See The New Advs. of. . .)

CHARLIE CHAN (The Adventures of) (Zaza The Mystic No. 10 on)
6-7/48 - No.5, 2-3/49; No.6, 6/55 - No.9, 3/56
Crestwood(Prize) No.1-5; Charlton No.6(6/55) on

	Good	Fine	Mint
1-S&K-c, 2 pages; Infantino-a	8.00	24.00	48.00
2-5-All S&K-c	5.00	14.00	28.00
6(6/55-Charlton)-S&K-c	3.00	8.00	16.00
7-9	2.50	7.00	14.00

CHARLIE CHAN
Oct-Dec, 1965 - No. 4, July-Sept, 1966
Dell Publishing Co.

	Good	Fine	Mint
1-Springer-a	1.20	3.50	7.00
2-4	.70	2.00	4.00

CHARLIE CHAPLIN
1917 (9x16''; large size; softcover; B&W)
Essanay/M. A. Donohue & Co.

	Good	Fine	Mint
Series 1, No. 315-Comic Capers. No. 316-In the Movies	25.00	70.00	140.00
Series 1, No. 317-Up in the Air. No. 318-In the Army	25.00	70.00	140.00
. . . Funny Stunts-(12½x16-3/8'') in color	12.00	35.00	70.00

NOTE: *No. 315-318: partially by* ***Segar*** *- pre-Thimble Theatre.*

CHARLIE McCARTHY (See Edgar Bergan Presents. . .)
1947 - 1954
Dell Publishing Co.

	Good	Fine	Mint
4-Color 171,196, 1	2.00	6.00	12.00
2-9	1.50	4.00	8.00
4-Color 445,478,527,571	1.00	3.00	6.00

CHARLTON CLASSICS
April, 1980 - Present
Charlton Comics

	Good	Fine	Mint
1		.30	.60
2-5		.25	.50

CHARLTON CLASSICS LIBRARY (1776)
V10No.1, March, 1973 (One Shot)
Charlton Comics

	Good	Fine	Mint
1776 (title) - Adaptation of the film musical ''1776''	.35	1.00	2.00

CHARLTON PREMIERE (Formerly Marine War Heroes)
V1No.19, July, 1967; V2No.1, Sept, 1967 - No. 4, May, 1968
Charlton Comics

	Good	Fine	Mint
V1No.19-Marine War Heroes		.40	.80
V2No.1-Trio; intro. Shape, Tyro Team, & Spookman		.40	.80
V2No.2-Children of Doom		.40	.80
3-Sinistro Boy Fiend; Blue Beetle Peacemaker x-over		.40	.80
4-Unlikely Tales; Ditko, Aparo-a		.40	.80

CHARLTON SPORT LIBRARY - PROFESSIONAL FOOTBALL
Winter, 1969-70 (Jan. on cover) (68 pages)
Charlton Comics

	Good	Fine	Mint
1	.50	1.50	3.00

CHASING THE BLUES
1912 (52 pages) (7½x10''; B&W; hardcover)
Doubleday Page

	Good	Fine	Mint
by Rube Goldberg	10.00	30.00	60.00

CHECKMATE (TV)
Oct, 1962 - No. 2, Dec, 1962
Gold Key

	Good	Fine	Mint
1,2	.85	2.50	5.00

CHEERIOS PREMIUMS (Disney)
1947 (32 pages) (Pocket size; 16 titles)
Walt Disney Productions

	Good	Fine	Mint
Set ''W''-Donald Duck & the Pirates	3.50	10.00	20.00
Pluto Joins the F.B.I.	2.00	6.00	12.00
Bucky Bug & the Cannibal King	2.00	6.00	12.00
Mickey Mouse & the Haunted House	3.00	8.00	16.00
Set ''X''-Donald Duck, Counter Spy	3.00	8.00	16.00
Goofy Lost in the Desert	2.00	6.00	12.00
Br'er Rabbit Outwits Br'er Fox	2.00	6.00	12.00
Mickey Mouse at the Rodeo	3.00	8.00	16.00
Set ''Y''-Donald Duck's Atom Bomb by Carl Barks	85.00	210.00	420.00
Br'er Rabbit's Secret	2.00	6.00	12.00
Dumbo & the Circus Mystery	3.00	8.00	16.00
Mickey Mouse Meets the Wizard	3.00	8.00	16.00
Set ''Z''-Donald Duck Pilots a Jet Plane (not by Barks)	3.00	8.00	16.00
Pluto Turns Sleuth Hound	2.00	6.00	12.00
The Seven Dwarfs & the Enchanted Mtn.	3.00	8.00	16.00
Mickey Mouse's Secret Room	3.00	8.00	16.00

CHEERIOS 3-D GIVEAWAYS (Disney)
1954 (Pocket size) (24 titles)
Walt Disney Productions
(Glasses were cut-outs on boxes)

	Good	Fine	Mint
Glasses only. . . .	3.00	8.00	16.00

(Set 1)
1-Donald Duck & Uncle Scrooge, the Firefighters
2-Mickey Mouse & Goofy, Pirate Plunder
3-Donald Duck's Nephews, the Fabulous Inventors
4-Mickey Mouse, Secret of the Ming Vase
5-Donald Duck with Huey, Dewey, & Louie; . . . the Seafarers (title on 2nd page)
6-Mickey Mouse, Moaning Mountain
7-Donald Duck, Apache Gold
8-Mickey Mouse, Flight to Nowhere

	Good	Fine	Mint
(per book). . . .	3.50	10.00	20.00

(Set 2)
1-Donald Duck, Treasure of Timbuktu
2-Mickey Mouse & Pluto, Operation China
3-Donald Duck in the Magic Cows
4-Mickey Mouse & Goofy, Kid Kokonut
5-Donald Duck, Mystery Ship
6-Mickey Mouse, Phantom Sheriff
7-Donald Duck, Circus Adventures
8-Mickey Mouse, Arctic Explorers

	Good	Fine	Mint
(per book). . . .	3.50	10.00	20.00

(Set 3)
1-Donald Duck & Witch Hazel
2-Mickey Mouse in Darkest Africa
3-Donald Duck & Uncle Scrooge, Timber Trouble
4-Mickey Mouse, Rajah's Rescue
5-Donald Duck in Robot Reporter
6-Mickey Mouse, Slumbering Sleuth
7-Donald Duck in the Foreign Legion
8-Mickey Mouse, Airwalking Wonder

	Good	Fine	Mint
(per book). . . .	3.50	10.00	20.00

CHESTY AND COPTIE
1946 (4 pages) (Giveaway) (Disney)
Los Angeles Community Chest

Charlie Chan #1, © PRIZE

Charlie McCarthy #7, © DELL

Charlton Premiere #2, © CC

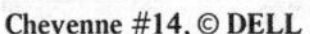
Cheyenne #14, © DELL

Chilling Tales #15, © YM

Choice Comics #2, © GP

CHESTY AND COPTIE (continued) — Good / Fine / Mint
(Very Rare) by Floyd Gottfredson 8.00 24.00 48.00

CHEYENNE (TV)
Oct, 1956 - No. 25, Dec-Jan, 1961-62
Dell Publishing Co.

4-Color 734,772,803 1.50 4.00 8.00
4(8-10/57) - 12 1.00 3.00 6.00
13-25 .85 2.50 5.00

CHEYENNE AUTUMN (See Movie Classics)

CHEYENNE KID (Wild Frontier No. 1-7)
No. 8, 1957 - No. 99, Nov, 1973
Charlton Comics

8,9,13,15-17,19,20 .40 1.20 2.40
10-Williamson/Torres-a(3); Ditko-c 4.00 12.00 24.00
11,12-Williamson/Torres-a(2) each; 11-(68 pgs.)
4.00 12.00 24.00
14,18-Williamson-a, 5 pgs.? 3.00 8.00 16.00
21,25-Severin c/a(3) each 1.50 4.00 8.00
22-24,27-29 .35 1.00 2.00
26,30-Severin-a .70 2.00 4.00
31-59 .50 1.00
60-99: 66-Wander begins, ends No. 87. Apache Red begins No. 88, origin No. 89 .30 .60

CHICAGO MAIL ORDER (See C-M-O Comics)

CHICAGO SUNDAY TRIBUNE COMIC BOOK MAGAZINE
1940 - 1943 (Similar to Spirit Sections)
(7¾x10¾''; full color; 16-24 pages each)
Chicago Tribune

1940 issues 5.00 15.00 30.00
1941, 1942 issues 4.00 12.00 24.00
1943 issues 3.50 10.00 20.00

NOTE: *Published weekly. Texas Slim, Kit Carson, Spooky, Josie, Nuts & Jolts, Lew Loyal, Brenda Starr, Daniel Boone, Captain Storm, Rocky, Smokey Stover, Tiny Tim, Little Joe, Fu Manchu appear among others. Early issues had photo stories with pictures from the movies; later issues had comic art.*

CHIEF, THE (Indian Chief No. 3 on)
1950, 1951
Dell Publishing Co.

4-Color 290, 2 1.50 4.00 8.00

CHIEF CRAZY HORSE
1950
Avon Periodicals

nn: Fawcette-c 7.00 20.00 40.00

CHIEF VICTORIO'S APACHE MASSACRE
1951
Avon Periodicals

nn-Williamson/Frazetta-a, 7 pgs.; Larsen-a; Kinstler-c
25.00 75.00 160.00

CHILDREN'S BIG BOOK
1945 (68 pages; stiff covers) (25 cents)
Dorene Publ. Co.

Comics & fairy tales; David Icove-a 3.00 8.00 16.00

CHILI (Millie's Rival)
May, 1969 - No. 26, Dec, 1973
Marvel Comics Group

1 .50 1.50 3.00
2-5 .30 .80 1.60
6-15 .40 .80
16-26 .25 .50
Special 1(12/71) .25 .50

CHILLING ADVENTURES IN SORCERY (. . . as Told by Sabrina No. 1, 2) (Red Circle Sorcery No. 6 on)
9/72 - No. 2, 10/72; No. 3, 10/73 - No. 5, 2/74
Archie Publications (Red Circle Prod.)

	Good	Fine	Mint
1,2-Sabrina cameo in both	.50	1.50	3.00
3-Morrow c/a, all	.35	1.00	2.00
4,5-Morrow c/a, 5,6 pgs.	.35	1.00	2.00

CHILLING TALES (Formerly Beware)
No. 13, Dec, 1952 - No. 17, Oct, 1953
Youthful Magazines

13(No.1)-Harrison-a; Matt Fox c/a 5.00 14.00 28.00
14-Harrison-a 3.50 10.00 20.00
15,17-Matt Fox-c. 15-Harrison-a. 17-Sir Walter Scott & Poe adapt.
3.50 10.00 20.00
16-Poe adaptation-'Metzengerstein'; bondage-c
3.50 10.00 20.00

CHILLING TALES OF HORROR (Magazine)
V1No.1, 6/69 - V1No.7, 12/70; V2No.2, 2/71 - V2No.5, 10/71
(52 pages; black & white) (50 cents)
Stanley Publications

V1No.1 .50 1.50 3.00
2-7: 7-Cameron-a .35 1.00 2.00
V2No.2-Spirit of Frankenstein r-/Adv. into Unknown No. 16;
V2No.3,5 .35 1.00 2.00
V2No.4-r-9 pg. Feldstein-a from Adv. into Unknown No. 3
.50 1.50 3.00

NOTE: *Two issues of V2No.2 exist, Feb, 1971 and April, 1971.*

CHILLY WILLY (See 4-Color No. 740,852,967,1017,1074,1122, 1177,1212,1281)

CHINA BOY (See Wisco)

CHIP 'N' DALE (Walt Disney)
Nov, 1953 - No. 30, June-Aug, 1962; Sept, 1967 - Present
Dell Publishing Co./Gold Key/Whitman No. 65 on

4-Color 517,581,636 .70 2.00 4.00
4(12/55-2/56)-10 .35 1.00 2.00
11-30 .60 1.20
1(Gold Key reprints, 1967) .60 1.20
2-10 .40 .80
11-20 .30 .60
21-70: 46,66-Reprints .25 .50

NOTE: *All Gold Key issues have reprints except No. 32-35,38-41, 45-47. No. 23-28,30-42,45-47,49 have new covers.*

CHITTY CHITTY BANG BANG (See Movie Comics)

CHOICE COMICS
Dec, 1941 - No. 3, Feb, 1942
Great Publications

1-Origin Secret Circle; Atlas the Mighty app.; Zomba, Jungle Fight, Kangaroo Man, & Fire Eater begin 12.00 36.00 80.00
2 9.00 26.00 60.00
3-Features movie 'The Lost City'' classic cover; continues in Great Comics No. 3 20.00 55.00 120.00

CHOO CHOO CHARLIE
Dec, 1969
Gold Key

1-John Stanley-a 1.50 4.00 8.00

CHOPPERTOONS (Magazine)
Summer, 1971 - No. 2, Fall, 1971 (52 pages)
TRM Publications

1,2 (Motorcycle humor) .50 1.50 3.00

CHRISTIAN HEROES OF TODAY
1964 (36 pages)
David C. Cook

.70 2.00 4.00

CHRISTMAS (See A-1 No. 28)

CHRISTMAS ADVENTURE, A
1969
Gilberton (Stacey's & other Dept. Stores Giveaway)

	Good	Fine	Mint
Some Alex Blum-a - r-/Picture Parade No. 4 with new-c (1953)	1.20	3.50	7.00

CHRISTMAS ADVENTURE, THE
1963 (16 pages)
S. Rose (H. L. Green Giveaway)

	Good	Fine	Mint
	.85	2.50	5.00

CHRISTMAS ALBUM (See March of Comics No. 312)

CHRISTMAS & ARCHIE ($1.00)
Jan, 1975 (68 pages) (10¼x13¼'')
Archie Comics

	Good	Fine	Mint
1	1.20	3.50	7.00

CHRISTMAS AT THE ROTUNDA (Titled Ford Rotunda Christmas Book 1957 on) (Regular size)
Given away every Christmas at one location
1954 - 1961
Ford Motor Co. (Western Printing)

	Good	Fine	Mint
1954-56 issues (nn's)	2.00	5.00	10.00
1957-61 issues (nn's)	.85	2.50	5.00

CHRISTMAS BELLS (See March of Comics No. 297)

CHRISTMAS CARNIVAL
1952 (100 pages) (One Shot)
Ziff-Davis Publ. Co./St. John Publ. Co. No. 2

	Good	Fine	Mint
nn	3.50	10.00	20.00
2-Reprints Ziff-Davis issue plus-c	3.00	8.00	16.00

CHRISTMAS CAROL, A (See March of Comics No. 33)

CHRISTMAS CAROL, A
No date (1942-43) (32 pgs.; 8¼x10¾''; paper cover)
Sears Roebuck & Co. (Giveaway)

	Good	Fine	Mint
nn-Comics & coloring book	5.00	15.00	30.00

CHRISTMAS CAROL, A
1940s ? (20 pgs.)
Sears Roebuck & Co. (Christmas giveaway)

	Good	Fine	Mint
Comic book & animated coloring book	3.50	10.00	20.00

CHRISTMAS CAROLS
1959 ? (16 pgs.)
Hot Shoppes Giveaway

	Good	Fine	Mint
	1.20	3.50	7.00

CHRISTMAS COLORING FUN
1964 (20 pgs.; slick cover; B&W inside)
H. Burnside

	Good	Fine	Mint
	.40	1.20	2.40

CHRISTMAS DREAM, A
1950 (16 pages) (Kinney Shoe Store Giveaway)
Promotional Publishing Co.

	Good	Fine	Mint
nn	1.50	4.00	8.00

CHRISTMAS DREAM, A
1952? (16 pgs.; paper cover)
J. J. Newberry Co. (Giveaway)

	Good	Fine	Mint
	1.50	4.00	8.00

CHRISTMAS DREAM, A
1952 (16 pgs.; paper cover)
Promotional Publ. Co. (Giveaway)

	Good	Fine	Mint
	1.50	4.00	8.00

CHRISTMAS EVE, A (See March of Comics No. 212)

CHRISTMAS FUN AROUND THE WORLD
No date (early 50's) (16 pages; paper cover)
No publisher

	Good	Fine	Mint
	2.00	6.00	12.00

CHRISTMAS IN DISNEYLAND
Dec, 1957 (25 cents) (Disney)
Dell Publishing Co.

	Good	Fine	Mint
1-Barks-a, 18 pgs.	7.00	20.00	40.00

CHRISTMAS JOURNEY THROUGH SPACE
1960
Promotional Publishing Co.

	Good	Fine	Mint
Reprints 1954 issue Jolly Christmas Book with new slick cover	1.20	3.50	7.00

CHRISTMAS ON THE MOON
1958 (20 pgs.; slick cover)
W. T. Grant Co. (Giveaway)

	Good	Fine	Mint
	2.00	5.00	10.00

CHRISTMAS PARADE (Walt Disney's)
Nov, 1949 - No. 9, Dec, 1958 (25 cents; No.9: 35 cents)
Dell Publishing Co.

	Good	Fine	Mint
1-Barks-a, 25 pgs; r-in G.K. Christmas Parade No. 5	25.00	75.00	160.00
2-Barks-a, 25 pgs; r-in G.K. Christmas Parade No. 6	14.00	42.00	90.00
3-7	3.00	9.00	18.00
8(12/56)-Barks-a, 8pgs.	7.00	20.00	40.00
9(12/58)-Barks-a, 20 pgs.	9.00	25.00	50.00

CHRISTMAS PARADE (See March of Comics No. 284, Dell Giant No. 26, and Walt Disney's. .)

CHRISTMAS PARADE (Walt Disney's)
1962 (no month) - No. 9, 1/72 (No.1,5: 80pgs.; No.2-4,7-9: 36pgs.)
Gold Key

	Good	Fine	Mint
1 (30018-301)	2.50	7.00	14.00
2-Reprints 4-Color 367 by Barks	3.50	10.00	20.00
3-Reprints 4-Color 178 by Barks	3.50	10.00	20.00
4-Reprints 4-Color 203 by Barks	3.50	10.00	20.00
5-Reprints Christmas Parade 1(Dell) by Barks	3.50	10.00	20.00
6-Reprints Christmas Parade 2(Dell) by Barks(64pp)	3.00	9.00	16.00
7,9: 7-Pull-out poster	1.50	4.00	8.00
8-Reprints 4-Color 367 by Barks; pull-out poster	3.50	10.00	20.00

CHRISTMAS PARTY (See March of Comics No. 256)

CHRISTMAS PLAY BOOK
1946 (16 pgs.; paper cover)
Gould-Stoner Co. (Giveaway)

	Good	Fine	Mint
	3.00	8.00	16.00

CHRISTMAS ROUNDUP
1960
Promotional Publishing Co.

	Good	Fine	Mint
Marv Levy c/a	1.00	3.00	6.00

CHRISTMAS STORY (See March of Comics No. 326)

CHRISTMAS STORY BOOK (See Woolworth's Christmas Book)

CHRISTMAS STORY CUT-OUT BOOK, THE
1951 (36 pages) (15 cents)
Catechetical Guild

	Good	Fine	Mint
393-½ text, ½ comics	3.00	8.00	16.00

Christmas On The Moon, 1958

Christmas Parade #4 (GK), © WDP

Christmas Play Book, 1946

Cinderella Love #25, © ZD

Circus Comics #2, © Farm Women's

The Cisco Kid #16, © DELL

CHRISTMAS TREASURY, A (See March of Comics No. 227)
1954 (100 pages)
Dell Publishing Co.

	Good	Fine	Mint
1	3.50	10.00	20.00

CHRISTMAS USA (Through 300 Years) (Also see Uncle Sam's . . .)
1956
Promotional Publ. Co. (Giveaway)

Marv Levy c/a	1.00	3.00	6.00

CHRISTMAS WITH ARCHIE
1973, 1974 (52 pages) (49 cents)
Spire Christian Comics (Fleming H. Revell Co.)

nn	.30	.80	1.60

CHRISTMAS WITH MOTHER GOOSE (See 4-Color No. 90,126,172, 201,253)

CHRISTMAS WITH SANTA (See March of Comics No. 92)

CHRISTMAS WITH SNOW WHITE AND THE SEVEN DWARFS
1953 (16 pages, paper cover)
Kobackers Giftstore of Buffalo, N.Y.

	3.00	8.00	16.00

CHRISTOPHERS, THE
1951 (36 pages)
Catechetical Guild (Giveaway)

	50.00	150.00	300.00

CHUCKLE, THE GIGGLY BOOK OF COMIC ANIMALS
1945 (132 pages) (One Shot)
R. B. Leffingwell Co.

1-Funny animal	2.00	6.00	12.00

CHUCK WAGON (See Sheriff Bob Dixon's . . .)

CICERO'S CAT
July-Aug, 1959 - No. 2, Sept-Oct, 1959
Dell Publishing Co.

1,2	1.50	4.00	8.00

CIMARRON STRIP (TV)
January, 1968
Dell Publishing Co.

1	.85	2.50	5.00

CINDERELLA (See 4-Color No. 272,786, & Movie Comics)

CINDERELLA IN "FAIREST OF THE FAIR"
1955 (14 pages) (Walt Disney)
American Dairy Association (Premium)

nn	4.50	13.00	26.00

CINDERELLA LOVE
10-11/49 - No.11, 4-5/51; No.12, 9/51; No.12, 2/54 - No.15, 8/54; No.25, 12/54 - No.29, 10/55 (2 No.12's) (no No. 16-24)
Ziff-Davis/St. John Publ. Co. No. 12 on

1 (1st Series)	2.00	6.00	12.00
2-8,12(9/51)	1.20	3.50	7.00
9-Kinstler-a	2.00	6.00	12.00
10-Whitney painted-c	1.75	5.00	10.00
11-Crandall-a; Saunders painted-c	3.00	8.00	16.00
12(St. John-10/53)-No.14	1.00	3.00	6.00
15-Matt Baker-c	2.50	7.00	14.00
25(2nd Series)(Formerly Romantic Marriage)	1.00	3.00	6.00
26-Baker-c	3.00	8.00	16.00
27,28	.70	2.00	4.00
29-Matt Baker-c	2.50	7.00	14.00

CINDY (. . . Smith No. 40; Crime Can't Win No. 41) (Formerly Krazy Komics)
No. 27, Fall, 1947 - No. 40, July, 1950
Timely Comics

	Good	Fine	Mint
27-Kurtzman-a, 3 pgs.	3.50	10.00	20.00
28-31-Kurtzman-a	2.00	6.00	12.00
32-40	1.00	3.00	6.00

NOTE: ***Kurtzman's*** *"Hey Look"-No. 27,29-31; "Giggles 'N' Grins"-No. 28.*

CINEMA COMICS HERALD
1941 - 1942 (4-pg. movie "trailers") (paper cover)

"Mr. Bug Goes to Town"-(1941)	2.50	7.50	15.00
"Bedtime Story"	2.50	7.50	15.00
"Thunder Birds"-(1942)	2.50	7.50	15.00
"They All Kissed the Bride"	2.50	7.50	15.00

CIRCUS (. . . the Comic Riot)
June, 1938 - No. 3, Aug, 1938
Globe Syndicate

1-(Scarce)-Spacehawk (2 pgs.), & Disk Eyes by Wolverton (2 pgs.), Pewee Throttle by Cole (1st comic book work), Beau Gus, Ken Craig & The Lords of Crillon, Jack Hinton by Eisner, Van Bragger by Kane; Everett-a	60.00	180.00	360.00
2,3-(Scarce)-Eisner, Cole, Wolverton, Bob Kane-a in each	30.00	90.00	180.00

CIRCUS BOY (See 4-Color No. 759,785,813)

CIRCUS COMICS
1945 - No. 2, June, 1945; Winter, 1948-49
Farm Women's Publishing Co./D. S. Publ.

1	1.00	3.00	6.00
2	.70	2.00	4.00
1(1948)-D.S. Publ.; 2 pgs. Frazetta	7.00	20.00	40.00

CIRCUS OF FUN COMICS
1945 - 1947 (a book of games & puzzles)
A. W. Nugent Publishing Co.

1-3	1.50	4.00	8.00

CIRCUS WORLD (See Movie Classics)

CISCO KID
Winter, 1944 - No. 3, 1945
Bernard Bailey/Swappers Quarterly

1-Giunta-a	7.00	20.00	40.00
2,3	5.00	14.00	28.00

CISCO KID, THE (TV)
July, 1950 - No. 41, Oct-Dec, 1958
Dell Publishing Co.

4-Color 292(No.1)-7/50	3.00	8.00	16.00
2(1/51)-5	2.00	5.00	10.00
6-20	1.20	3.50	7.00
21-41	.70	2.00	4.00

CITIZEN SMITH (See Holyoke One-Shot No. 9)

CITY OF THE LIVING DEAD (See Fantastic Tales No. 1)
1952
Avon Periodicals

nn-Hollingsworth c/a	10.00	30.00	60.00

CITY SURGEON (Blake Harper . . .)
August, 1963
Gold Key

1(10075-308)	.70	2.00	4.00

CIVIL WAR MUSKET, THE (Kadets of America Handbook)
1960 (36 pages) (Half-size; 25 cents)
Custom Comics, Inc.

nn	.85	2.50	5.00

CLAIRE VOYANT (Also see Keen Teens)
1946 - 1947 (Sparling strip reprints)

CLAIRE VOYANT (continued)
Leader Publ./Standard/Pentagon Publ.

	Good	Fine	Mint
nn	25.00	60.00	120.00
2-Kamen-c	18.00	45.00	90.00
3-Kamen bridal-c; contents mentioned in ***Love and Death***, a book by Gershom Legman('49) referenced by Dr. Wertham	30.00	75.00	150.00
4-Kamen bondage-c	18.00	45.00	90.00

CLANCY THE COP
1930 - 1931 (52 pages; B&W) (not reprints)
Dell Publishing Co.

1,2-Vep-a	4.00	12.00	24.00

EXPLAINING THE CLASSICS SERIES
by Jim Sands

The **Classics Comics** and **Classics Illustrated** series is one of the most complex and difficult to understand. This all new approach to listing will be a certain improvement to collectors and dealers alike. No longer will there be any uncertainty about exactly which issue of **Rip Van Winkle** you wish to locate. Under the old system you had to sift through up to nine sections. Now you can be certain that the comic can be found immediately with no error of getting a Line Drawn Cover mixed up with a Painted Cover. Each issue is now clearly listed under only one section. That is, all issues of No. 12 **Rip Van Winkle** can be found under one heading. This radical and simple process is possible for only one reason:

All issues have been listed in accordance with the highest reorder number (hereafter referred to as HRN). The HRN is critical in knowing exactly what issue is being discussed.

The HRN is simply the highest number found on that reorder list which every Classic carried, usually on the back cover. Over a 30 year period the Classics series saw many changes in covers, page size, interior art, and exterior logos. One thing that remained constant is the reorder list which gave the reader a unique opportunity to purchase Classics missed or wanted. In the case of reprints, this reorder list is often the only reliable means of determining age.

One very unique aspect to the Classics series is the multiplicity of issues, with the same title, over a 30 year period from 1941-1971. The aspect to collecting and selling can be rather difficult if one does not know how to distinguish between reprints and first editions (originals).

Originals or First Editions always have an ad for the next issue. Reprints, over the entire 30 year period, never contained this "Coming Next" ad. The only exception to this rule is No. 55 and No. 57 which had reprints which carried "Coming Next" ad but the HRN can easily indicate these two issues' real age and placement in the series of reprints. This all new guide to explaining the Classics will make it very easy to see at one glance **every issue** of whatever title is being researched.

For many it is difficult to determine whether an issue is a Line Drawn or Painted Cover. This innovative new guide will take away all guesswork as every issue will be listed in terms of the oldest issues first and the newer issues last. Again, it is important to stress the number of the last title on that reorder list which is also known as the HRN or Highest Reorder Number.

CLASSIC COMICS (See America in Action, Stories by Famous Authors, Story of the Commandos, & The World Around Us)

CLASSIC COMICS (. . .'s Illustrated No. 35 on)
10/41 - No. 34, 2/47; No. 35, 3/47 - No. 169, Winter/71
(Painted Covers No. 81 on)
Gilberton Publications

Abbreviations:
A—Art C or c—Cover CC—Classic Comics CI—Classics Ill. Ed—Edition LDC—Line Drawn Cover PC—Painted Cover r—Reprint

1. The Three Musketeers

Ed	HRN	Date	Details	A	C	Good	Fine	Mint
1	—	11/41	Original	1	1	75.00	225.00	450.00
2	10	5/43	10¢ price removed CC-r	1	1	6.00	18.00	36.00
3	15	11/43	Long Isl. Ind. Ed.; CC-r	1	1	5.00	14.00	28.00
4	18/20	6/44	Sunrise Times Ed.; CC-r	1	1	5.00	14.00	28.00
5	21	7/44	Richmond Courier Ed.; CC-r	1	1	4.00	12.00	24.00
6	28	6/46	CC-r	1	1	3.00	8.00	16.00
7	36	4/47	LDC-r	1	1	1.00	3.00	6.00
8	60	6/49	LDC-r	1	1	.70	2.00	4.00
9	64	10/49	LDC-r	1	1	.70	2.00	4.00
10	78	12/50	C-price 15¢; LDC-r	1	1	.70	2.00	4.00
11	93	3/52	LDC-r	1	1	.70	2.00	4.00
12	114	11/53	Last LDC-r	1	1	.70	2.00	4.00
13	134	9/56	New-c; old-a; 64 pg. PC-r	1	2	.80	2.40	4.80
14	143	3/58	Old-a; PC-r; 64 pg.	1	2	.80	2.40	4.80
15	150	5/59	New-a; PC-r; Evans/Crandall-a	2	2	.50	1.50	3.00
16	149	3/61	PC-r	2	2	.50	1.50	3.00
17	167	'62/63	PC-r	2	2	.50	1.50	3.00
18	167	4/64	PC-r	2	2	.50	1.50	3.00
19	167	1/65	PC-r	2	2	.50	1.50	3.00
20	167	3/66	PC-r	2	2	.50	1.50	3.00
21	166	11/67	PC-r	2	2	.50	1.50	3.00
22	166	Spr/69	New 25¢ price; stiff-c; PC-r	2	2	.40	1.20	2.40
23	169	Spr/71	PC-r; stiff-c	2	2	.40	1.20	2.40

2. Ivanhoe

Ed	HRN	Date	Details	A	C	Good	Fine	Mint
1	—	1941	Original	1	1	35.00	100.00	200.00
2	10	5/43	'Presents' removd. from cover; CC-r	1	1	5.00	14.00	28.00
3	15	11/43	Long Isl. Ind. ed.; CC-r	1	1	4.00	12.00	24.00
4	20	6/44	Sunrise Times ed.; CC-r	1	1	4.00	12.00	24.00
5	21	7/44	Richmond Courier ed.; CC-r	1	1	3.50	10.00	20.00
6	28	6/46	Last 'Comics'-r	1	1	3.00	9.00	18.00
7	36	4/47	1st LDC-r	1	1	.80	2.40	4.80
8	60	6/49	LDC-r	1	1	.70	2.00	4.00
9	64	10/49	LDC-r	1	1	.70	2.00	4.00
10	78	12/50	C-price 15¢; LDC-r	1	1	.70	2.00	4.00
11	89	11/51	LDC-r	1	1	.70	2.00	4.00
12	106	4/53	LDC-r	1	1	.70	2.00	4.00
13	121	7/54	Last LDC-r	1	1	.70	2.00	4.00
14	136	1/57	New-c&a; PC-r	2	2	1.00	3.00	6.00
15	142	1/58	PC-r	2	2	.50	1.50	3.00
16	153	11/59	PC-r	2	2	.50	1.50	3.00
17	149	3/61	PC-r	2	2	.50	1.50	3.00
18	167	'62/63	PC-r	2	2	.50	1.50	3.00
19	167	5/64	PC-r	2	2	.50	1.50	3.00
20	167	1/65	PC-r	2	2	.50	1.50	3.00
21	167	3/66	PC-r	2	2	.50	1.50	3.00
22	166	9/67	PC-r	2	2	.50	1.50	3.00
23	166	R/1968	Twin Circle ed.; PC-r	2	2	.50	1.50	3.00
24	166	R/1968	PC-r	2	2	.50	1.50	3.00
25	169	Win/69	Stiff-c	2	2	.40	1.20	2.40
26	169	Win/71	PC-r	2	2	.40	1.20	2.40

3. The Count of Monte Cristo

Ed	HRN	Date	Details	A	C	Good	Fine	Mint
1	—	3/42	Original	1	1	30.00	80.00	160.00
2	10	5/43	CC-r	1	1	5.00	14.00	28.00
3	15	11/43	Long Isl. Ind. ed.; CC-r	1	1	4.00	12.00	24.00

Claire Voyant #1, © STD

Classic Comics #2(HRN-18), © GIL

Classic Comics #3(HRN-20), © GIL

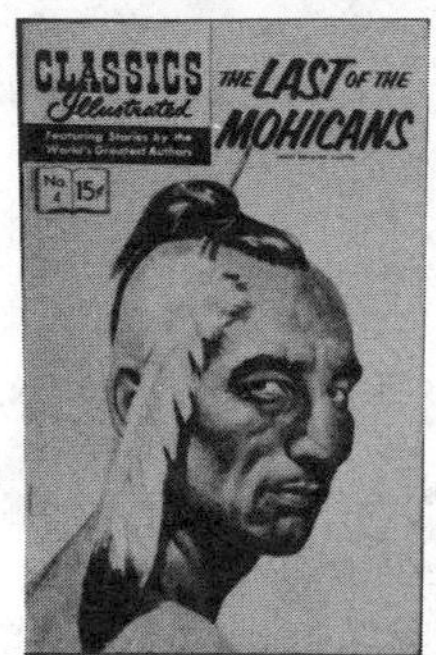

Classic Comics #4(HRN-167), © GIL

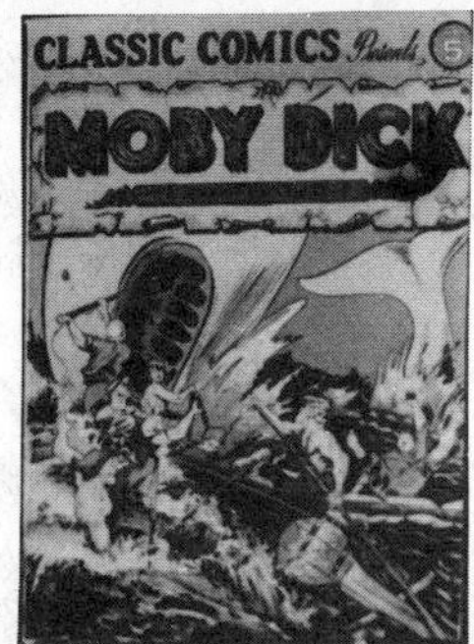

Classic Comics #5(HRN-36), © GIL

Classic Comics #6(HRN-20), © GIL

CLASSIC COMICS (continued)

Ed	HRN	Date	Details	A	C	Good	Fine	Mint
4	18/20	6/44	Sunrise Times ed.; CC-r	1	1	4.00	12.00	24.00
5	20	6/44	Sunrise Times ed.; CC-r	1	1	3.50	10.00	20.00
6	21	7/44	Richmond Courier ed.; CC-r	1	1	3.00	9.00	18.00
7	28	6/46	CC-r	1	1	3.00	9.00	18.00
8	36	4/47	1st LDC-r	1	1	1.00	3.00	6.00
9	60	6/49	LDC-r	1	1	.70	2.00	4.00
10	62	8/49	LDC-r	1	1	.70	2.00	4.00
11	71	5/50	LDC-r	1	1	.70	2.00	4.00
12	87	9/51	Price 15¢; LDC-r	1	1	.70	2.00	4.00
13	113	11/53	LDC-r	1	1	.70	2.00	4.00
14	135	11/56	New-c&a; PC-r	2	2	.50	1.50	3.00
15	143	3/58	PC-r	2	2	.50	1.50	3.00
16	153	11/59	PC-r	2	2	.50	1.50	3.00
17	161	3/61	PC-r	2	2	.50	1.50	3.00
18	167	'62/63	PC-r	2	2	.50	1.50	3.00
19	167	7/64	PC-r	2	2	.50	1.50	3.00
20	167	7/65	PC-r	2	2	.50	1.50	3.00
21	167	7/66	PC-r	2	2	.50	1.50	3.00
22	166	R/1968	Price 25¢; PC-r	2	2	.40	1.20	2.40
23	169	Win/69	Stiff-c; PC-r	2	2	.40	1.20	2.40

4. The Last of the Mohicans

Ed	HRN	Date	Details	A	C	Good	Fine	Mint
1	—	8/42	Original	1	1	20.00	60.00	120.00
2	12	6/43	Price balloon deleted; CC-r	1	1	5.00	14.00	28.00
3	15	11/43	Long Isl. Ind. ed.; CC-r	1	1	4.00	12.00	24.00
4	20	6/44	Long Isl. Ind. ed.; CC-r	1	1	4.00	12.00	24.00
5	21	7/44	Queens Home News ed.; CC-r	1	1	3.00	9.00	18.00
6	28	6/46	Last CC-r	1	1	3.00	9.00	18.00
7	36	4/47	1st LDC-r	1	1	1.00	3.00	6.00
8	60	6/49	LDC-r	1	1	.70	2.00	4.00
9	64	10/49	LDC-r	1	1	.70	2.00	4.00
10	78	12/50	New price 15¢; LDC-r	1	1	.85	2.50	4.00
11	89	11/51	LDC-r	1	1	.85	2.50	4.00
12	117	3/54	Last LDC-r	1	1	.85	2.50	4.00
13	135	11/56	New-c; PC-r	1	2	.50	1.50	3.00
14	141	11/57	PC-r	1	2	.50	1.50	3.00
15	150	5/59	New-a; PC-r; Severin, L.B. Cole-a	2	2	.50	1.50	3.00
16	161	3/61	PC-r	2	2	.50	1.50	3.00
17	167	'62/63	PC-r	2	2	.50	1.50	3.00
18	167	6/64	PC-r	2	2	.50	1.50	3.00
19	167	8/65	PC-r	2	2	.50	1.50	3.00
20	167	8/66	PC-r	2	2	.50	1.50	3.00
21	166	R/1967	Twin Circle ed.; PC-r	2	2	.50	1.50	3.00
22	166	R/1967	New price 25¢; PC-r	2	2	.40	1.20	2.40
23	169	Spr/69	Stiff-c; PC-r	2	2	.40	1.20	2.40

5. Moby Dick

Ed	HRN	Date	Details	A	C	Good	Fine	Mint
1	—	9/42	Original	1	1	20.00	60.00	120.00
2	10	5/43	C-price removed; CC-r; Conray Products ed.	1	1	5.00	14.00	28.00
3	15	11/43	Long Isl. Ind. ed.; CC-r	1	1	4.00	12.00	24.00
4	18/20	6/44	Sunrise Times ed.; CC-r	1	1	3.00	9.00	18.00
5	20	7/44	Sunrise Times ed.; CC-r	1	1	3.00	9.00	18.00
6	21	7/44	Sunrise Times ed.; CC-r	1	1	3.00	9.00	18.00
7	28	6/46	CC-r	1	1	3.00	9.00	18.00
8	36	4/47	1st LDC-r	1	1	1.00	3.00	6.00
9	60	6/49	LDC-r	1	1	.70	2.00	4.00
10	62	8/49	LDC-r	1	1	.70	2.00	4.00
11	71	5/50	LDC-r	1	1	.70	2.00	4.00
12	87	9/51	New price 15¢; LDC-r	1	1	.70	2.00	4.00
13	118	4/54	LDC-r	1	1	.70	2.00	4.00
14	131	3/56	New c&a; PC-r	2	2	.50	1.50	3.00
15	138	5/57	PC-r	2	2	.50	1.50	3.00
16	148	1/59	PC-r	2	2	.50	1.50	3.00
17	158	9/60	PC-r	2	2	.50	1.50	3.00
18	167	'62/63	PC-r	2	2	.50	1.50	3.00
19	167	6/64	PC-r	2	2	.50	1.50	3.00
20	167	7/65	PC-r	2	2	.50	1.50	3.00
21	167	3/66	PC-r	2	2	.50	1.50	3.00
22	166	9/67	PC-r	2	2	.50	1.50	3.00
23	166	Win/69	New-c&price 25¢; PC-r	2	3	.40	1.20	2.40
24	169	Win/71	PC-r	2	3	.40	1.20	2.40

6. A Tale of Two Cities

Ed	HRN	Date	Details	A	C	Good	Fine	Mint
1	—	11/42	Original	1	1	15.00	45.00	90.00
2	14	9/43	C-price deleted; CC-r	1	1	5.00	14.00	28.00
3	18	3/44	Long Isl. Ind. ed.; CC-r	1	1	4.00	12.00	24.00
4	20	6/44	Sunrise Times ed.; CC-r	1	1	4.00	12.00	24.00
5	28	6/46	Last CC-r	1	1	3.00	9.00	18.00
6	51	9/48	1st LDC-r	1	1	1.00	3.00	6.00
7	64	10/49	LDC-r	1	1	.70	2.00	4.00
8	78	12/50	C-price now 15¢; LDC-r	1	1	.70	2.00	4.00
9	89	11/51	LDC-r	1	1	.70	2.00	4.00
10	117	3/54	LDC-r	1	1	.70	2.00	4.00
11	132	5/56	New-c&a; PC-r; Joe Orlando-a	2	2	.50	1.50	3.00
12	140	9/57	PC-r	2	2	.50	1.50	3.00
13	147	11/57	PC-r	2	2	.50	1.50	3.00
14	152	9/59	PC-r	2	2	.50	1.50	3.00
15	153	11/59	PC-r	2	2	.50	1.50	3.00
16	149	3/61	PC-r	2	2	.50	1.50	3.00
17	167	'62/63	PC-r	2	2	.50	1.50	3.00
18	167	6/64	PC-r	2	2	.50	1.50	3.00
19	167	8/65	PC-r	2	2	.50	1.50	3.00
20	166	5/67	PC-r	2	2	.50	1.50	3.00
21	166	Fall/68	PC-r	2	2	.50	1.50	3.00
22	166	Fall/68	New-c&price 25¢; PC-r	2	3	.40	1.20	2.40
23	169	Sum-70	Stiff-c; PC-r	2	3	.40	1.20	2.40

7. Robin Hood

Ed	HRN	Date	Details	A	C	Good	Fine	Mint
1	—	12/42	Original	1	1	16.00	48.00	96.00
2	12	6/43	P.D.C. on cvr. deleted; CC-r	1	1	5.00	14.00	28.00
3	18	3/44	Long Isl. Ind. ed.; CC-r	1	1	4.00	12.00	24.00
4	20	6/44	Nassau Bulletin ed.; CC-r	1	1	3.50	10.00	20.00
5	22	10/44	Queens Cty. Times ed.; CC-r	1	1	3.50	10.00	20.00
6	—	—	Saks 34th Ave. X-Mas Giveaway			14.00	40.00	80.00
7	28	6/46	CC-r	1		3.50	10.00	20.00
8	—	—	Robin Hood & His Merry Men, The Ill. Story of (Flour Giveaway)			12.00	36.00	72.00

CLASSIC COMICS (continued)

Ed	HRN	Date	Details	A	C	Good	Fine	Mint
9	51	9/48	LDC-r	1	1	1.00	3.00	6.00
10	60	6/49	LDC-r	1	1	.80	2.40	4.80
11	64	10/49	LDC-r	1	1	.80	2.40	4.80
12	78	12/50	LDC-r	1	1	.80	2.40	4.80
13	97	7/52	LDC-r	1	1	.80	2.40	4.80
14	106	3/53	LDC-r	1	1	.80	2.40	4.80
15	121	7/54	LDC-r	1	1	.80	2.40	4.80
16	129	11/55	New-c; PC-r	1	2	.70	2.00	4.00
17	136	1/57	New-a; PC-r	2	2	.50	1.50	3.00
18	143	3/58	PC-r	2	2	.50	1.50	3.00
19	153	11/59	PC-r	2	2	.50	1.50	3.00
20	164	10/61	PC-r	2	2	.50	1.50	3.00
21	167	'62/63	PC-r	2	2	.50	1.50	3.00
22	167	6/64	PC-r	2	2	.50	1.50	3.00
23	167	5/65	PC-r	2	2	.50	1.50	3.00
24	167	7/66	PC-r	2	2	.50	1.50	3.00
25	166	12/67	PC-r	2	2	.50	1.50	3.00
26	169	Sum-69	Stiff-c; PC-r	2	2	.40	1.20	2.40

8. Arabian Nights

Ed	HRN	Date	Details	A	C	Good	Fine	Mint
1	—	2/43	Original	1	1	40.00	110.00	220.00
2	14	9/43	CC-r	1	1	14.00	40.00	80.00
3	17	1/44	Long Isl. ed.; CC-r	1	1	9.00	26.00	52.00
4	20	6/44	Nassau Bulletin ed.; 'Three Men Named Smith;' 64 pgs.; CC-r	1	1	9.00	26.00	52.00
5	28	6/46	CC-r	1	1	6.00	18.00	36.00
6	51	9/48	LDC-r	1	1	4.50	14.00	28.00
7	64	10/49	LDC-r	1	1	4.50	14.00	28.00
8	78	12/50	LDC-r	1	1	4.00	12.00	24.00
9	164	10/61	New-c&a; PC-r	2	2	2.75	8.00	16.00

9. Les Miserables

Ed	HRN	Date	Details	A	C	Good	Fine	Mint
1	—	3/43	Original	1	1	14.00	40.00	80.00
2	14	9/43	CC-r	1	1	5.00	16.00	32.00
3	18	3/44	Nassau Bulletin ed.; CC-r	1	1	4.00	12.00	24.00
4	20	6/44	Richmond Courier ed.; CC-r	1	1	3.50	10.00	20.00
5	28	6/46	CC-r	1	1	3.00	8.00	16.00
6	51	9/48	LDC-r	1	1	1.50	4.00	8.00
7	71	5/50	LDC-r	1	1	1.00	3.00	6.00
8	87	9/51	New price 15¢; LDC-r	1	1	.85	2.50	5.00
9	161	3/61	New-c&a; PC-r	2	2	.70	2.00	4.00
10	167	9/63	PC-r	2	2	.50	1.50	3.00
11	167	12/65	PC-r	2	2	.50	1.50	3.00
12	166	R/1968	New-c&price 25¢; PC-r	2	3	.40	1.20	2.40

10. Robinson Crusoe (Used in **SOTI**, pg. 142)

Ed	HRN	Date	Details	A	C	Good	Fine	Mint
1	—	4/43	Original	1	1	17.00	50.00	100.00
2	14	9/43	CC-r	1	1	5.00	14.00	28.00
3	18	3/44	Nassau Bulletin ed.; pg.64 has Bill of Rights; CC-r	1	1	4.00	12.00	24.00
4	20	6/44	Queens Home News ed.; CC-r	1	1	3.50	10.00	20.00
5	28	6/46	CC-r	1	1	3.00	8.00	16.00
6	51	9/48	LDC-r	1	1	1.00	3.00	6.00
7	64	10/49	LDC-r	1	1	1.00	3.00	6.00
8	78	12/50	New price 15¢; LDC-r	1	1	.70	2.00	4.00
9	97	7/52	LDC-r	1	1	.70	2.00	4.00
10	114	12/53	LDC-r	1	1	.70	2.00	4.00
11	130	1/56	New-c; PC-r	1	2	.60	1.80	3.60
12	140	9/57	New-a; PC-r	2	2	.50	1.50	3.00
13	153	11/59	PC-r	2	2	.50	1.50	3.00
14	164	10/61	PC-r	2	2	.50	1.50	3.00
15	167	'62/63	PC-r	2	2	.50	1.50	3.00
16	167	7/64	PC-r	2	2	.50	1.50	3.00
17	167	5/65	PC-r	2	2	.50	1.50	3.00
18	167	6/66	PC-r	2	2	.50	1.50	3.00
19	166	Fall/68	New price 25¢; PC-r	2	2	.40	1.20	2.40
20	166	R/68	Twin Circle ed.; PC-r	2	2	.40	1.20	2.40
21	169	Sm/70	Stiff-c; PC-r	2	2	.40	1.20	2.40

11. Don Quixote

Ed	HRN	Date	Details	A	C	Good	Fine	Mint
1	—	5/43	Original	1	1	16.00	46.00	92.00
2	18	3/44	Nassau Bulletin ed.; CC-r	1	1	4.00	12.00	24.00
3	21	7/44	Queens Home News ed.; CC-r	1	1	3.00	10.00	20.00
4	28	6/46	CC-r	1	1	3.00	8.00	16.00
5	110	8/53	New-PC; PC-r	1	2	1.00	3.00	6.00
6	156	5/60	Pgs. reduced 64 to 48; PC-r	1	2	.50	1.50	3.00
7	165	1962	PC-r	1	2	.50	1.50	3.00
8	167	1/64	PC-r	1	2	.50	1.50	3.00
9	167	11/65	PC-r	1	2	.50	1.50	3.00
10	166	R/1968	New-c&price 25¢; PC-r	1	3	.50	1.50	3.00

12. Rip Van Winkle and the Headless Horseman

Ed	HRN	Date	Details	A	C	Good	Fine	Mint
1	—	6/43	Original	1	1	17.00	50.00	100.00
2	15	11/43	Long Isl. Ind. ed.; CC-r	1	1	5.00	14.00	28.00
3	20	6/44	Long Isl. Ind. ed.;	1	1	4.00	12.00	24.00
4	22	10/44	Queens Cty. Times ed.; CC-r	1	1	4.00	12.00	24.00
5	28	6/46	CC-r	1	1	3.50	10.00	20.00
6	60	6/49	1st LDC-r	1	1	1.00	3.00	6.00
7	62	8/49	LDC-r	1	1	.85	2.50	5.00
8	71	5/50	LDC-r	1	1	.85	2.50	5.00
	89	11/51	Coward Shoe Give-away	1	1	3.00	8.00	16.00
9	89	11/51	New price 15¢; LDC-r	1	1	.70	2.00	4.00
10	118	4/54	LDC-r	1	1	.70	2.00	4.00
11	132	5/56	New-c; PC-r	1	2	.70	2.00	4.00
12	150	5/59	New-a; PC-r	2	2	.50	1.50	3.00
13	158	9/60	PC-r	2	2	.50	1.50	3.00
14	167	'62/63	PC-r	2	2	.50	1.50	3.00
15	167	12/63	PC-r	2	2	.50	1.50	3.00
16	167	4/65	PC-r	2	2	.50	1.50	3.00
17	167	4/66	PC-r	2	2	.50	1.50	3.00
18	166	R/1968	New-c&price 25¢; PC-r	2	3	.30	.80	1.60
19	169	Sm/70	PC-r	2	3	.30	.80	.160

13. Dr. Jekyll and Mr. Hyde (Used in **SOTI**, pg. 143)

Ed	HRN	Date	Details	A	C	Good	Fine	Mint
1	—	8/43	Original	1	1	17.00	50.00	100.00
2	15	11/43	Long Isl. Ind. ed.; CC-r	1	1	5.00	14.00	28.00
3	20	6/44	Long Isl. Ind. ed.; CC-r	1	1	4.00	12.00	24.00
4	28	6/46	No c-price; CC-r	1	1	3.00	8.00	16.00
5	60	6/49	New-c; Pgs. reduced from 56 to 48; H.C. Kiefer-c; LDC-r	1	2	.70	2.00	4.00

Classic Comics #8(HRN-20), © GIL

Classic Comics #10(HRN-14), © GIL

Classic Comics #12(HRN-20), © GIL

Classic Comics #14(HRN-21), © GIL

Classic Comics #16(Orig.), © GIL

Classic Comics #18(Orig.), © GIL

CLASSIC COMICS (continued)

Ed	HRN	Date	Details	A	C	Good	Fine	Mint
6	62	8/49	LDC-r	1	2	.70	2.00	4.00
7	71	5/50	LDC-r	1	2	.70	2.00	4.00
8	87	9/51	Date returns (erroneous); LDC-r	1	2	.70	2.00	4.00
9	112	10/53	New-c&a; PC-r	2	3	.50	1.50	3.00
10	153	11/59	PC-r	2	3	.50	1.50	3.00
11	161	3/61	PC-r	2	3	.50	1.50	3.00
12	167	'62/63	PC-r	2	3	.50	1.50	3.00
13	167	8/64	PC-r	2	3	.50	1.50	3.00
14	167	11/65	PC-r	2	3	.50	1.50	3.00
15	166	R/1968	New price 25¢; PC-r	2	3	.40	1.20	2.40
16	166	R/1968	Twin Circle ed.; PC-r	2	3	.40	1.20	2.40
17	169	Wn/69	PC-r	2	3	.30	.80	1.60

14. Westward Ho!

Ed	HRN	Date	Details	A	C	Good	Fine	Mint
1	—	9/43	Original	1	1	40.00	120.00	240.00
2	15	11/43	Long Isl. Ind. ed.; CC-r	1	1	14.00	40.00	80.00
3	21	7/44	Pg.56 new; CC-r	1	1	10.00	30.00	60.00
4	28	6/46	No c-price; Pg.56 new; CC-r	1	1	7.00	20.00	40.00
5	53	11/48	Pgs. reduced from 56 to 48; LDC-r	1	1	5.00	15.00	30.00

15. Uncle Tom's Cabin (Used in **SOTI**, pgs. 102, 103)

Ed	HRN	Date	Details	A	C	Good	Fine	Mint
1	—	11/43	Original	1	1	16.00	46.00	92.00
2	15	11/43	Price circle blank; Long Isl. Ind. ed; CC-r	1	1	7.00	20.00	40.00
3	21	7/44	Nassau Bulletin ed.; CC-r	1	1	6.00	18.00	36.00
4	28	6/46	No c-price; CC-r	1	1	3.00	9.00	18.00
5	53	11/48	1st pgs. reduced 56 to 48; LDC-r	1	1	2.00	5.00	10.00
6	71	5/50	LDC-r	1	1	1.20	3.50	7.00
7	89	11/51	New price 15¢; LDC-r	1	1	1.00	3.00	6.00
8	117	3/54	New-c/a/lettering changes; PC-r	2	2	.70	2.00	4.00
9	128	9/55	'Picture Progress' promo; PC-r	2	2	.50	1.50	3.00
10	137	3/57	PC-r	2	2	.50	1.50	3.00
11	146	9/58	PC-r	2	2	.50	1.50	3.00
12	154	1/60	PC-r	2	2	.50	1.50	3.00
13	161	3/61	PC-r	2	2	.50	1.50	3.00
14	167	'62/63	PC-r	2	2	.50	1.50	3.00
15	167	6/64	PC-r	2	2	.50	1.50	3.00
16	167	5/65	PC-r	2	2	.50	1.50	3.00
17	166	5/67	PC-r	2	2	.50	1.50	3.00
18	166	Wn/69	New-c; PC-r	2	3	.35	1.00	2.00
19	169	Sm/70	PC-r	2	3	.30	.80	1.60

16. Gullivers Travels

Ed	HRN	Date	Details	A	C	Good	Fine	Mint
1	—	12/43	Original	1	1	12.00	36.00	72.00
2	18/20	6/44	Price deleted; Queens Home News ed; CC-r	1	1	4.00	12.00	24.00
3	22	10/44	Queens Cty. Times ed.; CC-r	1	1	4.00	12.00	24.00
4	28	6/46	CC-r	1	1	3.00	9.00	18.00
5	60	6/49	Pgs. reduced to 48; LDC-r	1	1	1.00	3.00	6.00
6	62	8/49	LDC-r	1	1	.70	2.00	4.00
7	64	10/49	LDC-r	1	1	.70	2.00	4.00
8	78	12/50	New c-price 15¢; LDC-r	1	1	.60	1.80	3.60
9	89	11/51	LDC-r	1	1	.60	1.80	3.60
10	155	3/60	New-c; PC-r	1	2	.50	1.50	3.00
11	165	1962	PC-r	1	2	.50	1.50	3.00
12	167	5/64	PC-r	1	2	.50	1.50	3.00
13	167	11/65	PC-r	1	2	.50	1.50	3.00
14	166	R/1968	New price 25¢; PC-r	1	2	.45	1.40	2.80
15	166	R/1968	Twin Circle ed.; PC-r	1	2	.45	1.40	2.80
16	169	Wn/69	PC-r	1	2	.40	1.20	2.40

17. The Deerslayer

Ed	HRN	Date	Details	A	C	Good	Fine	Mint
1	—	1/44	Original	1	1	10.00	30.00	60.00
2	18	3/44	Price removd; CC-r	1	1	3.50	10.00	20.00
3	22	10/44	Queens Cty. Times ed.; CC-r	1	1	3.00	8.00	16.00
4	28	6/46	CC-r	1	1	2.00	6.00	12.00
5	60	6/49	Pgs.reduced to 48; LDC-r	1	1	.85	2.50	5.00
6	64	10/49	LDC-r	1	1	.85	2.50	5.00
7	85	7/51	C-price 15¢; LDC-r	1	1	.70	2.00	4.00
8	118	4/54	LDC-r	1	1	.70	2.00	4.00
9	132	5/56	LDC-r	1	1	.60	1.80	3.60
10	167	11/66	Last LDC-r	1	1	.60	1.80	3.60
11	166	R/1968	New-c&price 25¢; PC-r	1	2	.50	1.50	3.00
12	169	Spr/71	Stiff-c; letters from parents & educators; PC-r	1	2	.40	1.20	2.40

18. The Hunchback of Notre Dame

Ed	HRN	Date	Details	A	C	Good	Fine	Mint
1	—	3/44	Orig.; Gilberton ed.	1	1	14.00	40.00	80.00
2	—	3/44	Orig.; Island Pub. Co. ed.	1	1	12.00	36.00	72.00
3	18/20	6/44	Queens Home News ed.; CC-r	1	1	3.50	10.00	20.00
4	22	10/44	Queens Cty. Times ed.; CC-r	1	1	3.00	8.00	16.00
5	28	6/46	CC-r	1	1	2.00	6.00	12.00
6	60	6/49	New-c; 8pgs. deleted; Kiefer-c; LDC-r	1	2	.85	2.50	5.00
7	62	8/49	LDC-r	1	2	.85	2.50	5.00
8	78	12/50	C-price 15¢; LDC-r	1	2	.70	2.00	4.00
9	89	11/51	LDC-r	1	2	.70	2.00	4.00
10	118	4/54	LDC-r	1	2	.70	2.00	4.00
11	140	9/57	New-c; PC-r	1	3	1.00	3.00	6.00
12	146	9/58	PC-r	1	3	1.00	3.00	6.00
13	158	9/60	New-c&a; PC-r; Evans/Crandall-a	2	4	.30	.80	1.60
14	165	1962	PC-r	2	4	.30	.80	1.60
15	167	9/63	PC-r	2	4	.30	.80	1.60
16	167	10/64	PC-r	2	4	.30	.80	1.60
17	167	4/66	PC-r	2	4	.30	.80	1.60
18	166	R/1968	New price 25¢; PC-r	2	4	.25	.70	1.40
19	169	Sm/70	Stiff-c; PC-r	2	4	.25	.70	1.40

19. Huckleberry Finn

Ed	HRN	Date	Details	A	C	Good	Fine	Mint
1	—	4/44	Orig.; Gilberton ed.	1	1	9.00	26.00	52.00
2	—	4/44	Orig.; Island Pub. Co. ed.	1	1	5.00	15.00	30.00
3	18	3/44	Nassau Bulletin ed.; CC-r	1	1	3.50	10.00	20.00
4	22	10/44	Queens Cty. Times ed.; CC-r	1	1	3.00	8.00	16.00
5	28	6/46	CC-r	1	1	2.50	7.00	14.00

CLASSIC COMICS (continued)

Ed	HRN	Date	Details	A	C	Good	Fine	Mint
6	60	6/49	Pgs. reduced to 48; LDC-r	1	1	.85	2.50	5.00
7	62	8/49	LDC-r	1	1	.85	2.50	5.00
8	78	12/50	LDC-r	1	1	.70	2.00	4.00
9	89	11/51	LDC-r	1	1	.70	2.00	4.00
10	117	3/54	LDC-r	1	1	.70	2.00	4.00
11	131	3/56	New-c&a; PC-r	2	2	.50	1.50	3.00
12	140	9/57	PC-r	2	2	.50	1.50	3.00
13	150	5/59	PC-r	2	2	.50	1.50	3.00
14	158	9/60	PC-r	2	2	.50	1.50	3.00
15	165	1962	PC-r	2	2	.50	1.50	3.00
16	167	'62/63	PC-r	2	2	.50	1.50	3.00
17	167	6/64	PC-r	2	2	.50	1.50	3.00
18	167	6/65	PC-r	2	2	.50	1.50	3.00
19	167	10/65	PC-r	2	2	.50	1.50	3.00
20	166	9/67	PC-r	2	2	.50	1.50	3.00
21	166	Win/69	New price 25¢; PC-r	2	2	.40	1.20	2.40
22	169	Sm/70	PC-r	2	2	.40	1.20	2.40

20. The Corsican Brothers

Ed	HRN	Date	Details	A	C	Good	Fine	Mint
1	—	6/44	Orig.; Gilberton ed.	1	1	11.00	32.00	64.00
2	—	6/44	Orig.; Courier ed.	1	1	10.00	28.00	56.00
3	—	6/44	Orig.; Long Island Ind. ed.; CC-r	1	1	10.00	28.00	56.00
4	22	10/44	Queens Cty. Times ed.; CC-r	1	1	5.00	14.00	28.00
5	28	6/46	CC-r	1	1	4.00	12.00	24.00
6	60	6/49	Cl logo; no price; 48 pgs.; LDC-r	1	1	3.00	8.00	16.00
7	62	8/49	LDC-r	1	1	3.00	8.00	16.00
8	78	12/50	C-price 15¢; LDC-r	1	1	2.00	6.00	12.00
9	97	7/52	LDC-r	1	1	2.00	6.00	12.00

21. 3 Famous Mysteries (''The Sign of the 4,'' ''The Murders in the Rue Morgue,'' ''The Flayed Hand'')

Ed	HRN	Date	Details	A	C	Good	Fine	Mint
1	—	7/44	Orig.; Gilberton ed.	1	1	17.00	50.00	100.00
2	—	7/44	Original; Island Pub. Co. ed.	1	1	17.00	50.00	100.00
3	—	7/44	Original; Richmond Courier Ed.	1	1	17.00	50.00	100.00
4	22	10/44	Nassau Bulletin ed.; CC-r	1	1	6.00	18.00	36.00
5	30	9/46	CC-r	1	1	6.00	16.00	32.00
6	55	1/49	1st pgs. reduced 56 to 48; LDC-r	1	1	3.50	10.00	20.00
7	62	8/49	LDC-r	1	1	3.00	8.00	16.00
8	70	4/50	LDC-r	1	1	3.00	8.00	16.00
9	85	7/51	Price 15¢; LDC-r	1	1	3.00	8.00	16.00
10	114	12/53	New-c; PC-r	1	2	3.00	8.00	16.00

22. The Pathfinder

Ed	HRN	Date	Details	A	C	Good	Fine	Mint
1	—	10/44	Orig.; Gilberton ed.	1	1	8.00	24.00	48.00
2	—	10/44	Original; Island Pub. Co. ed.	1	1	7.00	20.00	40.00
3	—	10/44	Original; Queens County Times ed.	1	1	7.00	20.00	40.00
4	30	9/46	C-price removed; CC-r	1	1	5.00	14.00	28.00
5	60	6/49	Pgs. reduced to 48; LDC-r	1	1	.85	2.50	5.00
6	62	8/49	LDC-r	1	1	.80	2.30	4.60
7	70	4/50	LDC-r	1	1	.80	2.30	4.60
8	85	7/51	15¢ c-price; LDC-r	1	1	.55	1.60	3.20
9	118	4/54	LDC-r	1	1	.55	1.60	3.20
10	132	5/56	LDC-r	1	1	.55	1.60	3.20
11	146	9/58	LDC-r	1	1	.55	1.60	3.20
12	167	11/63	New-c; PC-r	1	2	.50	1.50	3.00
13	167	12/65	PC-r	1	2	.50	1.50	3.00
14	166	8/67	PC-r	1	2	.50	1.50	3.00

23. Oliver Twist

Ed	HRN	Date	Details	A	C	Good	Fine	Mint
1	—	7/45	Original	1	1	7.00	20.00	40.00
2	30	9/46	Price circle blank; CC-r	1	1	2.50	7.00	14.00
3	60	6/49	Pgs. reduced to 48; LDC-r	1	1	.85	2.50	5.00
4	62	8/49	LDC-r	1	1	.85	2.50	5.00
5	71	5/50	LDC-r	1	1	.70	2.00	4.00
6	85	7/51	15¢ c-price; LDC-r	1	1	.55	1.60	3.20
7	94	4/52	LDC-r	1	1	.55	1.60	3.20
8	118	4/54	LDC-r	1	1	.55	1.60	3.20
9	136	1/57	New-PC, old-a; PC-r	1	2	1.00	3.00	6.00
10	150	5/59	Old-a; PC-r	1	2	1.00	3.00	6.00
11	164	1961	Old-a; PC-r	1	2	1.00	3.00	6.00
12	164	1961	New-a; PC-r; Evans/Crandall-a	2	2	.50	1.50	3.00
13	167	'62/63	PC-r	2	2	.50	1.50	3.00
14	167	8/64	PC-r	2	2	.50	1.50	3.00
15	167	12/65	PC-r	2	2	.50	1.50	3.00
16	166	R/1968	New price 25¢; PC-r	2	2	.40	1.20	2.40
17	169	Win/69	Stiff-c; PC-r	2	2	.40	1.20	2.40

24. A Connecticut Yankee in King Arthur's Court

Ed	HRN	Date	Details	A	C	Good	Fine	Mint
1	—	9/45	Original	1	1	7.00	20.00	40.00
2	30	9/46	Price circle blank; CC-r	1	1	3.00	8.00	16.00
3	60	6/49	8 pgs. deleted; LDC-r	1	1	.85	2.50	5.00
4	62	8/49	LDC-r	1	1	.85	2.50	5.00
5	71	5/50	LDC-r	1	1	.70	2.00	4.00
6	87	9/51	15¢ c-price; LDC-r	1	1	.70	2.00	4.00
7	121	7/54	LDC-r	1	1	.70	2.00	4.00
8	140	9/57	New-c&a; PC-r	2	2	.50	1.50	3.00
9	153	11/59	PC-r	2	2	.50	1.50	3.00
10	164	1961	PC-r	2	2	.50	1.50	3.00
11	167	'62/63	PC-r	2	2	.50	1.50	3.00
12	167	7/64	PC-r	2	2	.50	1.50	3.00
13	167	6/66	PC-r	2	2	.50	1.50	3.00
14	166	R/1968	New price 25¢; PC-r	2	2	.40	1.20	2.40
15	169	Spr/71	PC-r	2	2	.40	1.20	2.40

25. Two Years Before the Mast

Ed	HRN	Date	Details	A	C	Good	Fine	Mint
1	—	10/45	Original; Webb/Heames-a&c	1	1	9.00	27.00	54.00
2	30	9/46	Price circle blank; CC-r	1	1	2.50	7.00	14.00
3	60	6/49	8 pgs. deleted; LDC-r	1	1	.85	2.50	5.00
4	62	8/49	LDC-r	1	1	.85	2.50	5.00
5	71	5/50	LDC-r	1	1	.70	2.00	4.00
6	85	7/51	15¢c-price; LDC-r	1	1	.70	2.00	4.00
7	114	12/53	LDC-r	1	1	.70	2.00	4.00
8	156	5/60	3 pgs. replaced by fillers; new-c; PC-r	1	2	.60	1.80	3.60
9	167	12/63	PC-r	1	2	.50	1.50	3.00
10	167	12/65	PC-r	1	2	.50	1.50	3.00
11	166	9/67	PC-r	1	2	.50	1.50	3.00
12	169	Win/69	New price 25¢; stiff-c; PC-r	1	2	.40	1.20	2.40

26. Frankenstein

Classic Comics #20(Orig.), © GIL

Classic Comics #22(HRN-85), © GIL

Classic Comics #24(Orig.), © GIL

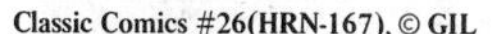
Classic Comics #26(HRN-167), © GIL

Classic Comics #30(HRN-167), © GIL

Classic Comics #34(HRN-167), © GIL

CLASSIC COMICS (continued)

Ed	HRN	Date	Details	A	C	Good	Fine	Mint
1	—	12/45	Original; Webb/Brewster a&c	1	1	17.00	50.00	100.00
2	30	9/46	Price circle blank; CC-r	1	1	7.00	20.00	40.00
3	60	6/49	LDC-r	1	1	2.00	5.00	10.00
4	62	8/49	LDC-r	1	1	2.00	5.00	10.00
5	71	5/50	LDC-r	1	1	2.00	5.00	10.00
6	82	4/51	15¢ c-price; LDC-r	1	1	1.50	4.00	8.00
7	117	3/54	LDC-r	1	1	1.50	4.00	8.00
8	146	9/58	New-c; PC-r	1	2	.50	1.50	3.00
9	153	11/59	PC-r	1	2	.50	1.50	3.00
10	160	1/61	PC-r	1	2	.50	1.50	3.00
11	165	1962	PC-r	1	2	.50	1.50	3.00
12	167	'62/63	PC-r	1	2	.50	1.50	3.00
13	167	6/64	PC-r	1	2	.50	1.50	3.00
14	167	6/65	PC-r	1	2	.50	1.50	3.00
15	167	10/65	PC-r	1	2	.50	1.50	3.00
16	166	9/67	PC-r	1	2	.50	1.50	3.00
17	169	Fall/69	New price 25¢; PC-r	1	2	.40	1.20	2.40
18	169	Spr/71	PC-r	1	2	.40	1.20	2.40

27. The Adventures of Marco Polo

Ed	HRN	Date	Details	A	C	Good	Fine	Mint
1	—	4/46	Original	1	1	8.00	24.00	48.00
2	30	9/46	Last 'Comics' reprint; CC-r	1	1	3.00	8.00	16.00
3	70	4/50	8 pgs. deleted; no c-price; LDC-r	1	1	.70	2.00	4.00
4	87	9/51	15¢c-price; LDC-r	1	1	.70	2.00	4.00
5	117	3/54	LDC-r	1	1	.70	2.00	4.00
6	154	1/60	New-c; PC-r	1	2	.50	1.50	3.00
7	165	1962	PC-r	1	2	.50	1.50	3.00
8	167	4/64	PC-r	1	2	.50	1.50	3.00
9	167	6/66	PC-r	1	2	.50	1.50	3.00
10	169	Spr/69	New price 25¢; stiff-c; PC-r	1	2	.40	1.20	2.40

28. Michael Strogoff

Ed	HRN	Date	Details	A	C	Good	Fine	Mint
1	—	6/46	Original	1	1	8.00	24.00	48.00
2	51	9/48	8 pgs. cut; LDC-r	1	1	3.50	10.00	20.00
3	115	1/54	New-c; PC-r	1	2	.50	1.50	3.00
4	155	3/60	PC-r	1	2	.50	1.50	3.00
5	167	11/63	PC-r	1	2	.50	1.50	3.00
6	167	7/66	PC-r	1	2	.50	1.50	3.00
7	169	Sm/69	PC-r	1	3	.70	2.00	4.00

29. The Prince and the Pauper

Ed	HRN	Date	Details	A	C	Good	Fine	Mint
1	—	7/46	Orig.; "Horror"-c	1	1	14.00	40.00	80.00
2	60	6/49	8 pgs. cut; new-c; LDC-r	1	2	1.00	3.00	6.00
3	62	8/49	LDC-r	1	2	.85	2.50	5.00
4	71	5/50	LDC-r	1	2	.85	2.50	5.00
5	93	3/52	LDC-r	1	2	.70	2.00	4.00
6	114	12/53	LDC-r	1	2	.70	2.00	4.00
7	128	9/55	New-c; PC-r; H.C. Kiefer-c	1	3	.50	1.50	3.00
8	138	5/57	PC-r	1	3	.50	1.50	3.00
9	150	5/59	PC-r	1	3	.50	1.50	3.00
10	164	1961	PC-r	1	3	.50	1.50	3.00
11	167	'62/63	PC-r	1	3	.50	1.50	3.00
12	167	7/64	PC-r	1	3	.50	1.50	3.00
13	167	11/65	PC-r	1	3	.50	1.50	3.00
14	166	R/1968	New price 25¢; PC-r	1	3	.40	1.20	2.40
15	169	Sm/70	PC-r	1	3	.40	1.20	2.40

30. The Moonstone

Ed	HRN	Date	Details	A	C	Good	Fine	Mint
1	—	9/46	Original	1	1	7.00	20.00	40.00
2	60	6/49	LDC-r	1	1	2.00	5.00	10.00
3	70	4/50	LDC-r	1	1	1.20	3.50	7.00
4	155	3/60	New L.B. Cole-c; PC-r	1	2	3.00	8.00	16.00
5	165	1962	PC-r; L.B. Cole-c	1	2	1.50	4.00	8.00
6	167	1/64	PC-r; L.B. Cole-c	1	2	1.00	3.00	6.00
7	167	9/65	PC-r; L.B. Cole-c	1	2	.70	2.00	4.00
8	166	R/1968	New price 25¢; PC-r	1	2	.50	1.50	3.00

31. The Black Arrow

Ed	HRN	Date	Details	A	C	Good	Fine	Mint
1	—	10/46	Original	1	1	7.00	20.00	40.00
2	51	9/48	CI logo; LDC-r	1	1	1.00	3.00	6.00
3	64	10/49	LDC-r	1	1	1.00	3.00	6.00
4	87	9/51	15¢ c-price; LDC-r	1	1	.70	2.00	4.00
5	108	6/53	LDC-r	1	1	.70	2.00	4.00
6	125	3/55	LDC-r	1	1	.70	2.00	4.00
7	131	3/56	New-c; PC-r	1	2	.70	2.00	4.00
8	140	9/57	PC-r	1	2	.50	1.50	3.00
9	148	1/59	PC-r	1	2	.50	1.50	3.00
10	161	3/61	PC-r	1	2	.50	1.50	3.00
11	167	'62/63	PC-r	1	2	.50	1.50	3.00
12	167	7/64	PC-r	1	2	.50	1.50	3.00
13	167	11/65	PC-r	1	2	.50	1.50	3.00
14	166	R/1968	25¢ new price; PC-r	1	2	.40	1.20	2.40

32. Lorna Doone

Ed	HRN	Date	Details	A	C	Good	Fine	Mint
1	—	12/46	Original; Matt Baker c&a	1	1	8.00	24.00	48.00
2	53/64	10/49	8 pgs. deleted; LDC-r	1	1	3.50	10.00	20.00
3	85	7/51	15¢ price, LDC-r; Baker c&a	1	1	3.00	8.00	16.00
4	118	4/54	LDC-r	1	1	1.50	4.00	8.00
5	138	5/57	New-c; old-c becomes new title pg.; PC-r	1	2	1.00	3.00	6.00
6	150	5/59	PC-r	1	2	.70	2.00	4.00
7	167	'62/63	PC-r	1	2	.70	2.00	4.00
8	167	1/64	PC-r	1	2	.70	2.00	4.00
9	167	11/65	PC-r	1	2	.70	2.00	4.00
10	166	R/1968	New-c; PC-r	1	3	.50	1.50	3.00

33. The Adventures of Sherlock Holmes

Ed	HRN	Date	Details	A	C	Good	Fine	Mint
1	—	1/47	Original; Kiefer-c	1	1	25.00	75.00	150.00
2	53	11/48	'A Study in Scarlet' (17 pgs.) deleted; LDC-r	1	1	7.00	20.00	40.00
3	71	5/50	LDC-r	1	1	6.00	18.00	36.00
4	89	11/51	15¢ price; LDC-r	1	1	6.00	18.00	36.00

34. Mysterious Island

Ed	HRN	Date	Details	A	C	Good	Fine	Mint
1	—	2/47	Original; Last 'Classic Comic.'	1	1	8.00	24.00	48.00
2	60	6/49	8 pgs. deleted; LDC-r	1	1	1.00	3.00	6.00
3	62	8/49	LDC-r	1	1	.85	2.50	5.00
4	71	5/50	LDC-r	1	1	.85	2.50	5.00
5	78	12/50	15¢ price circle; LDC-r	1	1	.70	2.00	4.00
6	92	2/52	LDC-r	1	1	.70	2.00	4.00
7	117	3/54	LDC-r	1	1	.70	2.00	4.00
8	140	9/57	New-c; PC-r	1	2	.50	1.50	3.00
9	156	5/60	PC-r	1	2	.50	1.50	3.00
10	167	10/63	PC-r	1	2	.50	1.50	3.00

CLASSIC COMICS (continued)

Ed	HRN	Date	Details	A	C	Good	Fine	Mint
11	167	5/64	PC-r	1	2	.50	1.50	3.00
12	167	6/66	PC-r	1	2	.50	1.50	3.00
13	166	R/1968	New price 25¢; PC-r	1	2	.40	1.20	2.40

35. Last Days of Pompeii

Ed	HRN	Date	Details	A	C	Good	Fine	Mint
1	—	3/47	Original; 1st 'Classics Illus.;'' LDC c-H.C. Kiefer	1	1	8.00	24.00	48.00
2	161	3/61	New c&a; 15¢; PC-r; Jack Kirby-a	2	2	1.50	4.00	8.00
3	167	1/64	PC-r	2	2	.85	2.50	5.00
4	167	7/66	PC-r	2	2	.85	2.50	5.00
5	169	Spr/70	New price 25¢; stiff-c; PC-r	2	2	.85	2.50	5.00

36. Typee

Ed	HRN	Date	Details	A	C	Good	Fine	Mint
1	—	4/47	Original	1	1	4.50	13.00	26.00
2	64	10/49	No c-price; 8 pg. ed.; LDC-r	1	1	2.00	6.00	12.00
3	155	3/60	New-c; PC-r	1	2	1.20	3.50	7.00
4	167	9/63	PC-r	1	2	1.20	3.50	7.00
5	167	7/65	PC-r	1	2	1.20	3.50	7.00
6	169	Sm/69	New price 25¢; stiff-c; PC-r	1	2	.50	1.50	3.00

37. The Pioneers

Ed	HRN	Date	Details	A	C	Good	Fine	Mint
1	—	5/47	Original	1	1	4.00	12.00	24.00
2	62	8/49	8 pgs. cut; LDC-r	1	1	2.00	6.00	12.00
3	70	4/50	LDC-r	1	1	.70	2.00	4.00
4	92	2/52	15¢ c-price; LDC-r	1	1	.50	1.50	3.00
5	118	4/54	LDC-r	1	1	.50	1.50	3.00
6	131	3/56	LDC-r	1	1	.50	1.50	3.00
7	132	5/56	LDC-r	1	1	.50	1.50	3.00
8	153	11/59	LDC-r	1	1	.50	1.50	3.00
9	167	5/64	LDC-r	1	1	.50	1.50	3.00
10	167	6/66	LDC-r	1	1	.50	1.50	3.00
11	166	R/1968	New-c&price 25¢; PC-r	1	2	.70	2.00	4.00

38. Adventures of Cellini

Ed	HRN	Date	Details	A	C	Good	Fine	Mint
1	—	6/47	Original	1	1	7.50	22.00	44.00
2	164	1961	New-c&a; PC-r	2	2	.85	2.50	5.00
3	167	12/63	PC-r	2	2	.85	2.50	5.00
4	167	7/66	PC-r	2	2	.85	2.50	5.00
5	169	Spr/70	Stiff-c; new price 25¢; PC-r	2	2	.70	2.00	4.00

39. Jane Eyre

Ed	HRN	Date	Details	A	C	Good	Fine	Mint
1	—	7/47	Original	1	1	7.00	20.00	40.00
2	60	6/49	No c-price; 8 pgs. cut; LDC-r	1	1	2.00	6.00	12.00
3	71	5/50	LDC-r	1	1	2.00	6.00	12.00
4	92	2/52	15¢ c-price; LDC-r	1	1	.85	2.50	5.00
5	118	4/54	LDC-r	1	1	.85	2.50	5.00
6	142	1/58	New-c; old-a; PC-r	1	2	1.50	4.00	8.00
7	154	1/60	Old-a; PC-r	1	2	1.50	4.00	8.00
8	165	1962	New-a; PC-r	2	2	1.00	3.00	6.00
9	167	12/63	PC-r	2	2	1.00	3.00	6.00
10	167	4/65	PC-r	2	2	1.00	3.00	6.00
11	167	8/66	PC-r	2	2	1.00	3.00	6.00
12	166	R/1968	New-c; PC-r	2	3	.50	1.50	3.00

40. Mysteries (''The Pit and the Pendulum,'' ''The Advs. of Hans Pfall,'' ''The Fall of the House of Usher'')

Ed	HRN	Date	Details	A	C	Good	Fine	Mint
1	—	8/47	Original; Kiefer-a/c	1	1	14.00	40.00	80.00
2	62	8/49	LDC-r	1	1	5.00	14.00	28.00
3	75	9/50	LDC-r	1	1	4.00	12.00	24.00
4	92	2/52	15¢ c-price; LDC-r	1	1	3.50	10.00	20.00

41. Twenty Years After

Ed	HRN	Date	Details	A	C	Good	Fine	Mint
1	—	9/47	Original; 'horror'-c	1	1	12.00	36.00	72.00
2	62	8/49	New-c; no c-price 8 pgs. cut; LDC-r; Kiefer-c	1	2	1.00	3.00	6.00
3	78	12/50	C-price 15¢; LDC-r	1	2	.85	2.50	5.00
4	156	5/60	New-c; PC-r	1	3	.70	2.00	4.00
5	167	12/63	PC-r	1	3	.50	1.50	3.00
6	167	11/66	PC-r	1	3	.50	1.50	3.00
7	169	Spr/70	New price 25¢; stiff-c; PC-r	1	3	.40	1.20	2.40

42. Swiss Family Robinson

Ed	HRN	Date	Details	A	C	Good	Fine	Mint
1	42	10/47	Orig.; Kiefer a&c	1	1	4.50	13.00	26.00
2	62	8/49	No c-price; 8 pgs. cut; LDC-r	1	1	1.50	4.00	7.00
3	75	9/50	LDC-r	1	1	1.00	3.00	6.00
4	93	3/52	LDC-r	1	1	1.00	3.00	6.00
5	117	3/54	LDC-r	1	1	1.00	3.00	6.00
6	131	3/56	New-c; old-a; PC-r	1	2	2.00	5.00	10.00
7	137	3/57	Old-a; PC-r	1	2	2.00	5.00	10.00
8	141	11/57	Old-a; PC-r	1	2	2.00	5.00	10.00
9	152	9/59	New-a; PC-r	2	2	.85	2.50	5.00
10	158	9/60	PC-r	2	2	.85	2.50	5.00
11	165	1962	PC-r	2	2	.85	2.50	5.00
12	165	12/63	PC-r	2	2	.85	2.50	5.00
13	167	12/63	PC-r	2	2	.80	2.20	4.40
14	167	4/65	PC-r	2	2	.50	1.50	3.00
15	166	11/67	PC-r	2	2	.50	1.50	3.00
16	169	Spr/69	PC-r	2	2	.50	1.50	3.00
17	169	Spr/70	New price 25¢; stiff-c; PC-r	2	2	.40	1.20	2.40
18	169	Sm/70	Stiff-c; PC-r	2	2	.40	1.20	2.40

43. Great Expectations (Used in **SOTI**, pg. 311)

Ed	HRN	Date	Details	A	C	Good	Fine	Mint
1	—	11/47	Original; Kiefer-a/c (Scarce)	1	1	30.00	80.00	160.00
2	62	8/49	No c-price; 8 pgs. cut; LDC-r	1	1	15.00	45.00	90.00

44. Mysteries of Paris (Used in **SOTI**, pg. 323)

Ed	HRN	Date	Details	A	C	Good	Fine	Mint
1	44	12/47	Original; 56 pgs.; Kiefer-a/c	1	1	14.00	40.00	80.00
2	62	8/47	No c-price; 8 pgs. cut; LDC-r; not all have 'gift box' ad	1	1	5.00	14.00	28.00
3	78	12/50	C-price 15¢; LDC-r	1	1	4.00	12.00	24.00

45. Tom Brown's School Days

Ed	HRN	Date	Details	A	C	Good	Fine	Mint
1	44	1/48	Original; 1st 48pg. issue	1	1	4.00	12.00	24.00
2	64	10/49	No c-price; LDC-r	1	1	2.50	7.00	14.00
3	161	3/61	New-c&a; PC-r	2	2	.85	2.50	5.00
4	167	2/64	PC-r	2	2	.85	2.50	5.00
5	167	8/66	PC-r	2	2	.70	2.00	4.00
6	166	R/1968	New price 25¢; PC-r	2	2	.50	1.50	3.00

46. Kidnapped

Classics Ill. #36(Orig.), © GIL

Classics Ill. #42(HRN-42), © GIL

Classics Ill. #43(Orig.), © GIL

Classics Ill. #49(HRN-47), © GIL

Classics Ill. #50(HRN-51), © GIL

Classics Ill. #52(HRN-53), © GIL

CLASSICS ILLUSTRATED (continued)

Ed	HRN	Date	Details	A	C	Good	Fine	Mint
1	47	4/48	Original; Webb-a	1	1	4.00	12.00	24.00
2	62	8/49	Price circle blank; LDC-r	1	1	1.20	3.50	7.00
3	78	12/50	15¢ price; LDC-r	1	1	.85	2.50	5.00
4	87	9/51	LDC-r	1	1	.85	2.50	5.00
5	118	4/54	LDC-r	1	1	.75	2.20	4.40
6	131	3/56	New-c; PC-r	1	2	.70	2.00	4.00
7	140	9/57	PC-r	1	2	.70	2.00	4.00
8	150	5/59	PC-r	1	2	.70	2.00	4.00
9	156	5/60	PC-r	1	2	.70	2.00	4.00
10	164	1961	Reduced pg.width; PC-r	1	2	.50	1.50	3.00
11	167	'62/63	PC-r	1	2	.50	1.50	3.00
12	167	3/64	PC-r	1	2	.50	1.50	3.00
13	167	6/65	PC-r	1	2	.50	1.50	3.00
14	167	12/65	PC-r	1	2	.50	1.50	3.00
15	167	9/67	PC-r	1	2	.50	1.50	3.00
16	166	Win/69	New price 25¢; PC-r	1	2	.40	1.20	2.40
17	169	Sm/70	PC-r	1	2	.40	1.20	2.40

47. Twenty Thousand Leagues Under the Sea

Ed	HRN	Date	Details	A	C	Good	Fine	Mint
1	47	5/48	Orig.; Kiefer-a&c	1	1	4.00	12.00	24.00
2	64	10/49	No c-price; LDC-r	1	1	1.20	3.50	7.00
3	78	12/50	15¢ price; LDC-r	1	1	.85	2.50	5.00
4	94	4/52	LDC-r	1	1	.85	2.50	5.00
5	118	4/54	LDC-r	1	1	.85	2.50	5.00
6	128	9/55	New-c; PC-r	1	2	.80	2.40	4.80
7	133	7/56	PC-r	1	2	.80	2.40	4.80
8	140	9/57	PC-r	1	2	.80	2.40	4.80
9	148	1/59	PC-r	1	2	.80	2.40	4.80
10	156	5/60	PC-r	1	2	.80	2.40	4.80
11	165	'62/63	PC-r	1	2	.80	2.40	4.80
12	167	3/64	PC-r	1	2	.80	2.40	4.80
13	167	8/65	PC-r	1	2	.70	2.00	4.00
14	167	10/66	PC-r	1	2	.70	2.00	4.00
15	166	R/1968	New price 25¢; new-c; PC-r	1	3	.50	1.50	3.00
16	169	Spr/70	Stiff-c; PC-r	1	3	.40	1.20	2.40

48. David Copperfield

Ed	HRN	Date	Details	A	C	Good	Fine	Mint
1	47	6/48	Original; Kiefer a/c	1	1	4.00	12.00	24.00
2	64	10/49	Price circle replaced by motif of boy reading; LDC-r	1	1	1.20	3.50	7.00
3	87	9/51	15¢ c-price; LDC-r	1	1	.85	2.50	5.00
4	121	7/54	New-c; PC-r	1	2	.85	2.50	5.00
5	130	1/56	PC-r	1	2	.85	2.50	5.00
6	140	9/57	PC-r	1	2	.85	2.50	5.00
7	148	1/59	PC-r	1	2	.85	2.50	5.00
8	156	5/60	PC-r	1	2	.85	2.50	5.00
9	167	'62/63	PC-r	1	2	.70	2.00	4.00
10	167	4/64	PC-r	1	2	.70	2.00	4.00
11	167	6/65	PC-r	1	2	.70	2.00	4.00
12	166	5/67	PC-r	1	2	.70	2.00	4.00
13	166	R/1967	Twin Circle ed.; no c-price; PC-r	1	2	.85	2.50	5.00
14	166	Spr/69	New price 25¢; PC-r	1	2	.40	1.20	2.40
15	169	Win/69	Stiff-c; PC-r	1	2	.40	1.20	2.40

49. Alice in Wonderland

Ed	HRN	Date	Details	A	C	Good	Fine	Mint
1	47	7/48	Original; 1st Blum a & c	1	1	7.00	20.00	40.00
2	64	10/49	No c-price; LDC-r	1	1	1.50	4.00	8.00
3	85	7/51	15¢ c-price; LDC-r	1	1	1.20	3.50	7.00
4	155	3/60	New PC, similar to orig.; PC-r	1	2	1.00	3.00	6.00
5	165	1962	PC-r	1	2	.85	2.50	5.00
6	167	3/64	PC-r	1	2	.85	2.50	5.00
7	167	6/66	PC-r	1	2	.85	2.50	5.00
8	166	Fall/68	New-c; soft-c; 25¢ price; PC-r	1	3	1.20	3.50	7.00
9	166	Fall/68	Stiff-c; PC-r	1	3	1.00	3.00	6.00

50. Adventures of Tom Sawyer (Used in **SOTI**, pg. 37)

Ed	HRN	Date	Details	A	C	Good	Fine	Mint
1	51	8/48	Original; Aldo Rubano a&c	1	1	5.00	15.00	30.00
2	51	9/48	Original	1	1	3.50	10.00	20.00
3	64	10/49	No c-price; LDC-r	1	1	2.00	5.00	10.00
4	78	12/50	15¢ price; LDC-r	1	1	.75	2.20	4.40
5	94	4/52	LDC-r	1	1	.75	2.20	4.40
6	114	12/53	LDC-r	1	1	.75	2.20	4.40
7	117	3/54	LDC-r	1	1	.75	2.20	4.40
8	132	5/56	LDC-r	1	1	.75	2.20	4.40
9	140	9/57	New-c; PC-r	1	2	.70	2.00	4.00
10	150	5/59	PC-r	1	2	.70	2.00	4.00
11	164	1961	New-a; PC-r	2	2	.50	1.50	3.00
12	167	'62/63	PC-r	2	2	.50	1.50	3.00
13	167	1/65	PC-r	2	2	.50	1.50	3.00
14	167	5/66	PC-r	2	2	.50	1.50	3.00
15	166	12/67	PC-r	2	2	.50	1.50	3.00
16	169	Fall/69	New price 25¢; PC-r	2	2	.40	1.20	2.40
17	169	Win/71	PC-r	2	2	.40	1.20	2.40

51. The Spy

Ed	HRN	Date	Details	A	C	Good	Fine	Mint
1	51	9/48	Original; maroon-c	1	1	3.00	8.00	16.00
2	51	9/48	Original; violet-c	1	1	3.00	8.00	16.00
3	89	11/51	New price 15¢; LDC-r	1	1	.75	2.20	4.40
4	121	7/54	LDC-r	1	1	.75	2.20	4.40
5	139	7/57	New-c; PC-r	1	2	.75	2.20	4.40
6	156	5/60	PC-r	1	2	.50	1.50	3.00
7	167	11/63	PC-r	1	2	.50	1.50	3.00
8	167	7/66	PC-r	1	2	.50	1.50	3.00
9	166	Win/69	New price 25¢; stiff-c; PC-r	1	2	.40	1.20	2.40

52. The House of the Seven Gables

Ed	HRN	Date	Details	A	C	Good	Fine	Mint
1	53	10/48	Orig.; Griffiths a&c	1	1	3.00	8.00	16.00
2	89	11/51	New price 15¢; LDC-r	1	1	.70	2.00	4.00
3	121	7/54	LDC-r	1	1	.70	2.00	4.00
4	142	1/58	New-c&a; PC-r	2	2	.50	1.50	3.00
5	156	5/60	PC-r	2	2	.50	1.50	3.00
6	165	1962	PC-r	2	2	.50	1.50	3.00
7	167	5/64	PC-r	2	2	.50	1.50	3.00
8	167	3/66	PC-r	2	2	.50	1.50	3.00
9	166	R/1968	New price 25¢; PC-r	2	2	.40	1.20	2.40
10	169	Spr/70	Stiff-c; PC-r	2	2	.40	1.20	2.40

53. A Christmas Carol

Ed	HRN	Date	Details	A	C	Good	Fine	Mint
1	53	11/48	Original & only ed; Kiefer-a,c	1	1	5.50	16.00	32.00

54. Man in the Iron Mask

Ed	HRN	Date	Details	A	C	Good	Fine	Mint
1	55	12/48	Original; Froehlich-a, Kiefer-c	1	1	3.00	8.00	16.00
2	93	3/52	New price 15¢; LDC-r	1	1	.70	2.00	4.00

CLASSICS ILLUSTRATED (continued)

Ed	HRN	Date	Details	A	C	Good	Fine	Mint
3	111	9/53	LDC-r	1	1	.70	2.00	4.00
4	142	1/58	New-c&a; PC-r	2	2	.50	1.50	3.00
5	154	1/60	PC-r	2	2	.50	1.50	3.00
6	165	1962	PC-r	2	2	.50	1.50	3.00
7	167	5/64	PC-r	2	2	.50	1.50	3.00
8	167	4/66	PC-r	2	2	.50	1.50	3.00
9	166	Win/69	New price 25¢; stiff-c; PC-r	2	2	.50	1.50	3.00

55. Silas Marner (Used in **SOTI**, pgs. 311, 312)

Ed	HRN	Date	Details	A	C	Good	Fine	Mint
1	55	1/49	Original	1	1	4.00	12.00	24.00
2	75	9/50	Price circle blank; 'Coming Next' ad; LDC-r	1	1	.70	2.00	4.00
3	97	7/52	LDC-r	1	1	.70	2.00	4.00
4	121	7/54	New-c; PC-r	1	2	.50	1.50	3.00
5	130	1/56	PC-r	1	2	.50	1.50	3.00
6	140	9/57	PC-r	1	2	.50	1.50	3.00
7	154	1/60	PC-r	1	2	.50	1.50	3.00
8	165	1962	PC-r	1	2	.50	1.50	3.00
9	167	5/64	PC-r	1	2	.50	1.50	3.00
10	167	6/65	PC-r	1	2	.50	1.50	3.00
11	166	5/67	PC-r	1	2	.50	1.50	3.00
12	166	Win/69	New price 25¢; PC-r	1	2	.40	1.20	2.40

56. The Toilers of the Sea

Ed	HRN	Date	Details	A	C	Good	Fine	Mint
1	55	2/49	Original; A.M. Froehlich a,c	1	1	5.50	16.00	32.00
2	165	1962	New-c&a; PC-r; Angelo Torres-a	2	2	1.50	4.00	8.00
3	167	3/64	PC-r	2	2	1.50	4.00	8.00
4	167	10/66	PC-r	2	2	1.50	4.00	8.00

57. The Song of Hiawatha

Ed	HRN	Date	Details	A	C	Good	Fine	Mint
1	55	3/49	Original; Alex Blum a&c	1	1	3.00	8.00	16.00
2	75	9/50	No c-price; 'Coming Next'ad; LDC-r	1	1	.70	2.00	4.00
3	94	4/52	15¢ c-price; LDC-r	1	1	.60	1.80	3.60
4	118	4/54	LDC-r	1	1	.60	1.80	3.60
5	134	9/56	New-c; PC-r	1	2	.50	1.50	3.00
6	139	7/57	PC-r	1	2	.50	1.50	3.00
7	154	1/60	PC-r	1	2	.50	1.50	3.00
8	167	'62/63	Has orig.date; PC-r	1	2	.50	1.50	3.00
9	167	9/64	PC-r	1	2	.50	1.50	3.00
10	167	10/65	PC-r	1	2	.50	1.50	3.00
11	166	R/1968	New price 25¢; PC-r	1	2	.40	1.20	2.40

58. The Prairie

Ed	HRN	Date	Details	A	C	Good	Fine	Mint
1	60	4/49	Original	1	1	3.00	8.00	16.00
2	62	8/49	LDC-r	1	1	1.50	4.00	8.00
3	78	12/50	15¢ price in double circle; LDC-r	1	1	1.50	4.00	8.00
4	114	12/53	LDC-r	1	1	.75	2.20	4.40
5	131	3/56	LDC-r	1	1	.70	2.00	4.00
6	132	5/56	LDC-r	1	1	.70	2.00	4.00
7	146	9/58	New-c; PC-r	1	2	.50	1.50	3.00
8	155	3/60	PC-r	1	2	.50	1.50	3.00
9	167	5/64	PC-r	1	2	.50	1.50	3.00
10	167	4/66	PC-r	1	2	.50	1.50	3.00
11	169	Sm/69	New price 25¢; stiff-c; PC-r	1	2	.45	1.40	2.80

59. Wuthering Heights

Ed	HRN	Date	Details	A	C	Good	Fine	Mint
1	60	5/49	Original; Kiefer a/c	1	1	5.00	14.00	28.00
2	62	8/49	LDC-r	1	1	2.00	5.00	10.00
3	85	7/51	15¢ price; LDC-r	1	1	2.00	5.00	10.00
4	156	5/60	New-c; PC-r	1	2	1.20	3.50	7.00
5	167	10/66	PC-r	1	2	.50	1.50	3.00
6	167	10/66	PC-r	1	2	.50	1.50	3.00
7	169	Sm/69	New price 25¢; stiff-c; PC-r	1	2	.40	1.20	2.40

60. Black Beauty

Ed	HRN	Date	Details	A	C	Good	Fine	Mint
1	62	6/49	Original; Froehlich a & c	1	1	2.50	7.00	14.00
2	62	8/49	LDC-r	1	1	2.00	5.00	10.00
3	85	7/51	New price 15¢ LDC-r	1	1	2.00	5.00	10.00
4	158	9/60	New-c&a; PC-r	2	2	1.20	3.50	7.00
5	167	2/64	PC-r	2	2	1.20	3.50	7.00
6	167	3/66	PC-r	2	2	.85	2.50	5.00
7	167	3/66	'Open book'blank; came with record; PC-r	2	2	.85	2.50	5.00
8	166	R/1968	New-c&price, 25¢; PC-r	2	3	.50	1.50	3.00

61. The Woman in White

Ed	HRN	Date	Details	A	C	Good	Fine	Mint
1	62	7/49	Original; Blum-a,c	1	1	3.00	9.00	18.00
2	156	5/60	New-c; PC-r	1	2	1.20	3.50	7.00
3	167	1/64	PC-r	1	2	1.20	3.50	7.00
4	166	R/1968	New price 25¢; stiff-c; PC-r	1	2	.85	2.50	5.00

62. Western Stories (''The Luck of Roaring Camp'' and ''The Outcasts of Poker Flat'')

Ed	HRN	Date	Details	A	C	Good	Fine	Mint
1	62	8/49	Original; Kiefer-a,c	1	1	4.00	12.00	24.00
2	89	11/51	New price 15¢; LDC-r	1	1	.85	2.50	5.00
3	121	7/54	LDC-r	1	1	.70	2.00	4.00
4	137	3/57	New-c; PC-r	1	2	.70	2.00	4.00
5	152	9/59	PC-r	1	2	.70	2.00	4.00
6	167	10/63	PC-r	1	2	.70	2.00	4.00
7	167	6/64	PC-r	1	2	.50	1.50	3.00
8	167	11/66	PC-r	1	2	.50	1.50	3.00
9	166	R/1968	New-c&price 25¢; PC-r	1	3	1.20	3.50	7.00

63. The Man Without a Country

Ed	HRN	Date	Details	A	C	Good	Fine	Mint
1	62	9/49	Original; Kiefer-a,c	1	1	3.00	8.00	16.00
2	78	12/50	C-price 15¢ in double circle; LDC-r	1	1	1.75	5.00	10.00
3	156	5/60	New-c, old-a; PC-r	1	2	2.00	6.00	12.00
4	165	1962	New-a & text pgs.; PC-r; A. Torres-a	2	2	.75	2.20	4.40
5	167	3/64	PC-r	2	2	.70	2.00	4.00
6	167	8/66	PC-r	2	2	.70	2.00	4.00
7	169	Sm/69	New price 25¢; stiff-c; PC-r	2	2	.50	1.50	3.00

64. Treasure Island

Ed	HRN	Date	Details	A	C	Good	Fine	Mint
1	62	10/49	Original; Blum-a,c	1	1	3.00	9.00	18.00
2	82	4/51	New price 15¢; LDC-r	1	1	.75	2.20	4.40
3	117	3/54	LDC-r	1	1	.70	2.00	4.00
4	131	3/56	New-c; PC-r	1	2	.60	1.80	3.60
5	138	5/57	PC-r	1	2	.50	1.50	3.00

Classics Ill. #56(HRN-55), © GIL

Classics Ill. #58(HRN-60), © GIL

Classics Ill. #64(HRN-62), © GIL

Classics Ill. #66(HRN-67), © GIL

Classics Ill. #71(HRN-71), © GIL

Classics Ill. #74(HRN-75), © GIL

CLASSICS ILLUSTRATED (continued)

Ed	HRN	Date	Details	A	C	Good	Fine	Mint
6	146	9/58	PC-r	1	2	.50	1.50	3.00
7	158	9/60	PC-r	1	2	.50	1.50	3.00
8	165	1962	PC-r	1	2	.50	1.50	3.00
9	167	'62/63	PC-r	1	2	.50	1.50	3.00
10	167	6/64	PC-r	1	2	.50	1.50	3.00
11	167	12/65	PC-r	1	2	.50	1.50	3.00
12	166	10/67	PC-r	1	2	.50	1.50	3.00
13	169	Spr/69	New price 25¢; stiff-c; PC-r	1	2	.40	1.20	2.40

65. Benjamin Franklin

Ed	HRN	Date	Details	A	C	Good	Fine	Mint
1	64	11/49	Original	1	1	3.00	8.00	16.00
2	—	———	Ben Franklin Store Giveaway; diff-c; same interior-a	1		3.50	10.00	20.00
3	131	3/56	New-c; PC-r	1	2	.70	2.00	4.00
4	154	1/60	PC-r	1	2	.50	1.50	3.00
5	167	2/64	PC-r	1	2	.50	1.50	3.00
6	167	4/66	PC-r	1	2	.50	1.50	3.00
7	169	Fall/69	New price 25¢; stiff-c; PC-r	1	2	.40	1.20	2.40

66. The Cloister and the Hearth

Ed	HRN	Date	Details	A	C	Good	Fine	Mint
1	67	12/49	Original & only ed; Kiefer-a & c	1	1	6.00	18.00	36.00

67. The Scottish Chiefs

Ed	HRN	Date	Details	A	C	Good	Fine	Mint
1	67	1/50	Original; Blum-a&c	1	1	2.50	7.00	14.00
2	85	7/51	New price 15¢; LDC-r	1	1	.70	2.00	4.00
3	118	4/54	LDC-r	1	1	.70	2.00	4.00
4	136	1/57	New-c; PC-r	1	2	.60	1.80	3.60
5	154	1/60	PC-r	1	2	.50	1.50	3.00
6	167	11/63	PC-r	1	2	.50	1.50	3.00
7	167	8/65	PC-r	1	2	.50	1.50	3.00

68. Julius Caesar (Used in **SOTI**, pgs. 36, 37)

Ed	HRN	Date	Details	A	C	Good	Fine	Mint
1	70	2/50	Original; Kiefer-a,c	1	1	4.00	12.00	24.00
2	85	7/51	New price 15¢; LDC-r	1	1	.75	2.20	4.40
3	108	6/53	LDC-r	1	1	.70	2.00	4.00
4	156	5/60	New-c; PC-r	1	2	.75	2.20	4.40
5	165	1962	New-a; PC-r	2	2	.50	1.50	3.00
6	167	2/64	PC-r	2	2	.50	1.50	3.00
7	167	10/65	Tarzan books inside cover; PC-r	2	2	.50	1.50	3.00
8	166	R/1967	PC-r	2	2	.50	1.50	3.00
9	166	R/168	Twin Circle ed.; PC-r	2	2	.70	2.00	4.00
10	169	Win/69	PC-r	2	2	.40	1.20	2.40

69. Around the World in 80 Days

Ed	HRN	Date	Details	A	C	Good	Fine	Mint
1	70	3/50	Original; Kiefer-a/c	1	1	3.50	10.00	20.00
2	87	9/51	New price 15¢; LDC-r	1	1	.85	2.50	5.00
3	125	3/55	LDC-r	1	1	.80	2.30	4.60
4	136	1/57	New-c; PC-r	1	2	.70	2.00	4.00
5	146	9/58	PC-r	1	2	.70	2.00	4.00
6	152	9/59	PC-r	1	2	.70	2.00	4.00
7	164	1961	PC-r	1	2	.70	2.00	4.00
8	167	'62/63	PC-r	1	2	.70	2.00	4.00
9	167	7/64	PC-r	1	2	.70	2.00	4.00
10	167	11/65	PC-r	1	2	.70	2.00	4.00
11	166	7/67	PC-r	1	2	.50	1.50	3.00
12	169	Spr/69	New price 25¢; stiff-c; PC-r	1	2	.40	1.20	2.40

70. The Pilot

Ed	HRN	Date	Details	A	C	Good	Fine	Mint
1	71	4/50	Original; Blum-a,c	1	1	1.50	4.00	8.00
2	92	2/52	New price 15¢; LDC-r	1	1	.85	2.50	5.00
3	125	3/55	LDC-r	1	1	.75	2.20	4.40
4	156	5/60	New-c; PC-r	1	2	.70	2.00	4.00
5	167	2/64	PC-r	1	2	.70	2.00	4.00
6	167	5/66	PC-r	1	2	.70	2.00	4.00

71. The Man Who Laughs

Ed	HRN	Date	Details	A	C	Good	Fine	Mint
1	71	5/50	Original; Blum-a,c	1	1	3.50	10.00	20.00
2	165	1962	New-c&a; PC-r	2	2	2.50	7.00	14.00
3	167	4/64	PC-r	2	2	2.50	7.00	14.00

72. The Oregon Trail

Ed	HRN	Date	Details	A	C	Good	Fine	Mint
1	73	6/50	Original; Kiefer-a,c	1	1	1.50	4.00	8.00
2	89	11/51	New price 15¢; LDC-r	1	1	.75	2.20	4.40
3	121	7/54	LDC-r	1	1	.70	2.00	4.00
4	131	3/56	New-c; PC-r	1	2	.75	2.20	4.40
5	140	9/57	PC-r	1	2	.75	2.20	4.40
6	150	5/59	PC-r	1	2	.70	2.00	4.00
7	164	1961	PC-r	1	2	.70	2.00	4.00
8	167	'62/63	PC-r	1	2	.70	2.00	4.00
9	167	8/64	PC-r	1	2	.70	2.00	4.00
10	167	10/65	PC-r	1	2	.70	2.00	4.00
11	166	R/1968	New price 25¢; PC-r	1	2	.50	1.50	3.00

73. The Black Tulip

Ed	HRN	Date	Details	A	C	Good	Fine	Mint
1	75	7/50	1st & only ed.; Alex Blum-a & c	1	1	5.50	16.00	32.00

74. Mr. Midshipman Easy

Ed	HRN	Date	Details	A	C	Good	Fine	Mint
1	75	8/50	1st & only edition	1	1	5.50	16.00	32.00

75. The Lady of the Lake

Ed	HRN	Date	Details	A	C	Good	Fine	Mint
1	75	9/50	Original; Kiefer-a/c	1	1	2.50	7.00	14.00
2	85	7/51	New price 15¢; LDC-r	1	1	.70	2.00	4.00
3	118	4/54	LDC-r	1	1	.70	2.00	4.00
4	139	7/57	New-c; PC-r	1	2	.50	1.50	3.00
5	154	1/60	PC-r	1	2	.50	1.50	3.00
6	165	1962	PC-r	1	2	.50	1.50	3.00
7	167	4/64	PC-r	1	2	.50	1.50	3.00
8	167	5/66	PC-r	1	2	.50	1.50	3.00
9	169	Spr/69	New price 25¢; stiff-c; PC-r	1	2	.40	1.20	2.40

76. The Prisoner of Zenda

Ed	HRN	Date	Details	A	C	Good	Fine	Mint
1	75	10/50	Original; Kiefer-a,c	1	1	2.00	5.00	10.00
2	85	7/51	New price 15¢; LDC-r	1	1	1.20	3.50	7.00
3	111	9/53	LDC-r	1	1	.85	2.50	5.00
4	128	9/55	New-c; PC-r	1	2	.50	1.50	3.00
5	152	9/59	PC-r	1	2	.50	1.50	3.00
6	165	1962	PC-r	1	2	.50	1.50	3.00
7	167	4/64	PC-r	1	2	.50	1.50	3.00
8	167	9/66	PC-r	1	2	.50	1.50	3.00
9	169	Fall/69	New price 25¢; stiff-c; PC-r	1	2	.50	1.50	3.00

77. The Iliad

Ed	HRN	Date	Details	A	C	Good	Fine	Mint
1	78	11/50	Original; Blum-a,c	1	1	1.50	4.00	8.00

CLASSICS ILLUSTRATED (continued)

Ed	HRN	Date	Details	A	C	Good	Fine	Mint
2	87	9/51	New price 15¢; LDC-r	1	1	.85	2.50	5.00
3	121	7/54	LDC-r	1	1	.75	2.20	4.40
4	139	7/57	New-c; PC-r	1	2	.70	2.00	4.00
5	150	5/59	PC-r	1	2	.50	1.50	3.00
6	165	1962	PC-r	1	2	.50	1.50	3.00
7	167	10/63	PC-r	1	2	.50	1.50	3.00
8	167	7/64	PC-r	1	2	.50	1.50	3.00
9	167	5/66	PC-r	1	2	.50	1.50	3.00
10	166	R/1968	New price 25¢; PC-r	1	2	.40	1.20	2.40

78. Joan of Arc

Ed	HRN	Date	Details	A	C	Good	Fine	Mint
1	78	12/50	Original; Kiefer-a,c	1	1	1.50	4.00	8.00
2	87	9/51	New price 15¢; LDC-r	1	1	.70	2.00	4.00
3	113	11/53	LDC-r	1	1	.70	2.00	4.00
4	128	9/55	New-c; PC-r	1	2	.60	1.80	3.60
5	140	9/57	PC-r	1	2	.50	1.50	3.00
6	150	5/59	PC-r	1	2	.50	1.50	3.00
7	159	11/60	PC-r	1	2	.50	1.50	3.00
8	167	'62/63	PC-r	1	2	.50	1.50	3.00
9	167	12/63	PC-r	1	2	.50	1.50	3.00
10	167	6/65	PC-r	1	2	.50	1.50	3.00
11	166	6/67	PC-r	1	2	.50	1.50	3.00
12	169	Win/69	New-c&price, 25¢; PC-r	1	3	.45	1.40	2.80

79. Cyrano de Bergerac

Ed	HRN	Date	Details	A	C	Good	Fine	Mint
1	78	1/51	Orig.; movie promo inside front-c; Blum-a & c	1	1	1.50	4.00	8.00
2	85	7/51	New price 15¢; LDC-r	1	1	.80	2.30	4.60
3	118	4/54	LDC-r	1	1	.80	2.30	4.60
4	133	7/56	New-c; PC-r	1	2	.70	2.00	4.00
5	156	5/60	PC-r	1	2	.70	2.00	4.00

80. White Fang (Last line drawn cover)

Ed	HRN	Date	Details	A	C	Good	Fine	Mint
1	79	2/51	Original; last issue w/LDC; Blum-a, c	1	1	2.00	6.00	12.00
2	87	9/51	LDC-r	1	1	.70	2.00	4.00
3	125	3/55	LDC-r	1	1	.70	2.00	4.00
4	132	5/56	New-c; PC-r	1	2	.60	1.80	3.60
5	140	9/57	PC-r	1	2	.50	1.50	3.00
6	153	11/59	PC-r	1	2	.50	1.50	3.00
7	167	'62/63	PC-r	1	2	.50	1.50	3.00
8	167	9/64	PC-r	1	2	.50	1.50	3.00
9	167	7/65	PC-r	1	2	.50	1.50	3.00
10	166	6/67	PC-r	1	2	.50	1.50	3.00
11	169	Fall/69	New price 25¢; PC-r	1	2	.40	1.20	2.40

81. The Odyssey (1st painted cover)

Ed	HRN	Date	Details	A	C	Good	Fine	Mint
1	82	3/51	Original	1	1	1.50	4.00	8.00
2	167	8/64	PC-r	1	1	.70	2.00	4.00
3	167	10/66	PC-r	1	1	.70	2.00	4.00
4	169	Spr/69	New, stiff-c; PC-r	1	2	.40	1.20	2.40

82. The Master of Ballantrae

Ed	HRN	Date	Details	A	C	Good	Fine	Mint
1	82	4/51	Original; Blum-c	1	1	1.50	4.00	8.00
2	167	8/64	PC-r	1	1	.85	2.50	5.00
3	166	Fall/68	New, stiff-c; PC-r	1	2	.40	1.20	2.40

83. The Jungle Book

Ed	HRN	Date	Details	A	C	Good	Fine	Mint
1	85	5/51	Original; Blum-a&c	1	1	1.50	4.00	8.00
2	110	8/53	PC-r	1	1	.50	1.50	3.00
3	125	3/55	PC-r	1	1	.40	1.20	2.40
4	134	5/56	PC-r	1	1	.40	1.20	2.40
5	142	1/58	PC-r	1	1	.40	1.20	2.40
6	150	5/59	PC-r	1	1	.40	1.20	2.40
7	159	11/60	PC-r	1	1	.40	1.20	2.40
8	167	'62/63	PC-r	1	1	.40	1.20	2.40
9	167	3/65	PC-r	1	1	.40	1.20	2.40
10	167	11/65	PC-r	1	1	.40	1.20	2.40
11	167	5/66	PC-r	1	1	.40	1.20	2.40
12	166	R/1968	New c&a; stiff-c; PC-r	2	2	.30	.90	1.80

84. The Gold Bug and Other Stories ("The Gold Bug," "The Tell-Tale Heart," "The Cask of Amontillado")

Ed	HRN	Date	Details	A	C	Good	Fine	Mint
1	85	6/51	Original	1	1	3.00	8.00	16.00
2	167	7/64	PC-r	1	1	1.50	4.00	8.00

85. The Sea Wolf

Ed	HRN	Date	Details	A	C	Good	Fine	Mint
1	85	8/51	Original; Blum-a&c	1	1	1.50	4.00	8.00
2	121	7/54	PC-r	1	1	.70	2.00	4.00
3	132	5/56	PC-r	1	1	.70	2.00	4.00
4	141	11/57	PC-r	1	1	.70	2.00	4.00
5	161	3/61	PC-r	1	1	.70	2.00	4.00
6	167	2/64	PC-r	1	1	.70	2.00	4.00
7	167	11/65	PC-r	1	1	.70	2.00	4.00
8	169	Fall/69	New price 25¢; stiff-c; PC-r	1	1	.40	1.20	2.40

86. Under Two Flags

Ed	HRN	Date	Details	A	C	Good	Fine	Mint
1	87	8/51	Original; first DelBourgo-a	1	1	1.50	4.00	8.00
2	117	3/54	PC-r	1	1	.40	1.50	3.00
3	139	7/57	PC-r	1	1	.50	1.50	3.00
4	158	9/60	PC-r	1	1	.50	1.50	3.00
5	167	2/64	PC-r	1	1	.50	1.50	3.00
6	167	8/66	PC-r	1	1	.50	1.50	3.00
7	169	Sm/69	New price 25¢; stiff-c; PC-r	1	1	.40	1.20	2.40

87. A Midsummer Nights Dream

Ed	HRN	Date	Details	A	C	Good	Fine	Mint
1	87	9/51	Original	1	1	2.00	5.00	10.00
2	161	3/61	PC-r	1	1	.70	2.00	4.00
3	167	4/64	PC-r	1	1	.70	2.00	4.00
4	167	5/66	PC-r	1	1	.70	2.00	4.00
5	169	Sm/69	New price 25¢; stiff-c; PC-r	1	1	.50	1.50	3.00

88. Men of Iron

Ed	HRN	Date	Details	A	C	Good	Fine	Mint
1	89	10/51	Original	1	1	1.00	3.00	6.00
2	154	1/60	PC-r	1	1	.50	1.50	3.00
3	167	1/64	PC-r	1	1	.50	1.50	3.00
4	166	4/1968	New price 25¢; stiff-c; PC-r	1	1	.45	1.40	2.80

89. Crime and Punishment (Cover illo. in **POP**)

Ed	HRN	Date	Details	A	C	Good	Fine	Mint
1	89	11/51	Original	1	1	2.00	6.00	12.00
2	152	9/59	PC-r	1	1	.70	2.00	4.00
3	167	4/64	PC-r	1	1	.70	2.00	4.00
4	167	5/66	PC-r	1	1	.70	2.00	4.00
5	169	Fall/69	New price 25¢ stiff-c; PC-r	1	1	.50	1.50	3.00

Classics Ill. #78(HRN-128), © GIL

Classics Ill. #84(HRN-167), © GIL

Classics Ill. #87(HRN-87), © GIL

Classics Ill. #94(HRN-94), © GIL

Classics Ill. #98(HRN-98), © GIL

Classics Ill. #101(HRN-101), © GIL

CLASSICS ILLUSTRATED (continued)

90. Green Mansions

Ed	HRN	Date	Details	A C	Good	Fine	Mint
1	89	12/51	Original; Blum-a&c	1 1	1.75	5.00	10.00
2	148	1/59	New-c; PC-r	1 2	.30	.80	1.60
3	165	1962	PC-r	1 2	.30	.80	1.60
4	167	4/64	PC-r	1 2	.30	.80	1.60
5	167	9/66	PC-r	1 2	.30	.80	1.60
6	169	Sm/69	New price 25¢; stiff-c; PC-r	1 2		.50	1.00

91. The Call of the Wild

Ed	HRN	Date	Details	A C	Good	Fine	Mint
1	92	1/52	Original	1 1	1.20	3.50	7.00
2	112	10/53	PC-r	1 1	.50	1.50	3.00
3	125	3/55	'Picture Progress' on back-c; PC-r	1 1	.50	1.50	3.00
4	134	9/56	PC-r	1 1	.50	1.50	3.00
5	143	3/58	PC-r	1 1	.50	1.50	3.00
6	165	1962	PC-r	1 1	.40	1.20	2.40
7	167	1962	PC-r	1 1	.40	1.20	2.40
8	167	4/65	PC-r	1 1	.40	1.20	2.40
9	167	3/66	PC-r	1 1	.40	1.20	2.40
10	167	3/66	Record ed.; PC-r	1 1	.40	1.20	2.40
11	166	11/67	PC-r	1 1	.40	1.20	2.40
12	169	Spr/70	New price 25¢; stiff-c; PC-r	1 1	.30	.80	1.60

92. The Courtship of Miles Standish

Ed	HRN	Date	Details	A C	Good	Fine	Mint
1	92	2/52	Original; Blum-a&c	1 1	1.50	4.00	8.00
2	165	1962	PC-r	1 1	.50	1.50	3.00
3	167	3/64	PC-r	1 1	.50	1.50	3.00
4	166	5/67	PC-r	1 1	.50	1.50	3.00
5	169	Win/69	New price 25¢ stiff-c; PC-r	1 1	.40	1.20	2.40

93. Pudd'nhead Wilson

Ed	HRN	Date	Details	A C	Good	Fine	Mint
1	94	3/52	Orig.; Kiefer-a&c;	1 1	1.20	3.50	7.00
2	165	1962	New-c; PC-r	1 2	.50	1.50	3.00
3	167	3/64	PC-r	1 2	.40	1.20	2.40
4	166	R/1968	New price 25¢; soft-c; PC-r	1 2	.30	.80	1.60

94. David Balfour

Ed	HRN	Date	Details	A C	Good	Fine	Mint
1	94	4/52	Original	1 1	1.00	3.00	6.00
2	167	5/64	PC-r	1 1	.50	1.50	3.00
3	166	R/1968	New price 25¢; PC-r	1 1	.40	1.20	2.40

95. All Quiet on the Western Front

Ed	HRN	Date	Details	A C	Good	Fine	Mint
1	96	5/52	Orig.; DelBourgo-a	1 1	3.00	8.00	16.00
2	99	5/52	Original; checklist to 99	1 1	3.00	8.00	16.00
3	167	10/64	PC-r	1 1	.70	2.00	4.00
4	167	11/66	PC-r	1 1	.60	1.80	3.60

96. Daniel Boone

Ed	HRN	Date	Details	A C	Good	Fine	Mint
1	97	6/52	Original; Blum-a	1 1	2.00	5.00	10.00
2	117	3/54	PC-r	1 1	.50	1.50	3.00
3	128	9/55	PC-r	1 1	.50	1.50	3.00
4	132	5/56	PC-r	1 1	.50	1.50	3.00
5	134	———	'Story of Jesus' on back-c; PC-r	1 1	.50	1.50	3.00
6	158	9/60	PC-r	1 1	.50	1.50	3.00
7	167	1/64	PC-r	1 1	.50	1.50	3.00
8	167	5/65	PC-r	1 1	.50	1.50	3.00
9	167	11/66	PC-r	1 1	.50	1.50	3.00
10	166	Win/69	New-c; price 25¢; PC-r	1 2	.40	1.20	2.40

97. King Solomon's Mines

Ed	HRN	Date	Details	A C	Good	Fine	Mint
1	96	7/52	Orig.; Kiefer a&c	1 1	2.00	5.00	10.00
2	118	4/54	PC-r	1 1	.70	2.00	4.00
3	131	3/56	PC-r	1 1	.50	1.50	3.00
4	141	9/51	PC-r	1 1	.50	1.50	3.00
5	158	9/60	PC-r	1 1	.50	1.50	3.00
6	167	2/64	PC-r	1 1	.50	1.50	3.00
7	167	9/65	PC-r	1 1	.50	1.50	3.00
8	169	Sm/69	New price 25¢; stiff-c; PC-r	1 1	.50	1.50	3.00

98. The Red Badge of Courage

Ed	HRN	Date	Details	A C	Good	Fine	Mint
1	98	8/52	Original	1 1	1.50	4.00	8.00
2	118	4/54	PC-r	1 1	.50	1.50	3.00
3	132	5/56	PC-r	1 1	.50	1.50	3.00
4	142	1/58	PC-r	1 1	.50	1.50	3.00
5	152	9/59	PC-r	1 1	.50	1.50	3.00
6	161	3/61	PC-r	1 1	.50	1.50	3.00
7	167	'62/63	Has orig.date; PC-r	1 1	.50	1.50	3.00
8	167	9/64	PC-r	1 1	.50	1.50	3.00
9	167	10/65	PC-r	1 1	.50	1.50	3.00
10	166	R/1968	New-c&price 25¢; PC-r	1 2	.85	2.50	5.00
11	166	Fall/68	PC-r	1 2	.85	2.50	5.00

99. Hamlet (Used in **POP**, pg. 102)

Ed	HRN	Date	Details	A C	Good	Fine	Mint
1	98	9/52	Original; Blum-a&c	1 1	1.50	5.00	10.00
2	121	7/54	PC-r	1 1	.50	1.50	3.00
3	141	11/57	PC-r	1 1	.50	1.50	3.00
4	158	9/60	PC-r	1 1	.50	1.50	3.00
5	167	'62/63	Has orig.date; PC-r	1 1	.50	1.50	3.00
6	167	7/65	PC-r	1 1	.50	1.50	3.00
7	166	4/67	PC-r	1 1	.50	1.50	3.00
8	169	Spr/69	New-c&price 25¢; PC-r	1 2	.40	1.20	2.40

100. Mutiny on the Bounty

Ed	HRN	Date	Details	A C	Good	Fine	Mint
1	100	10/52	Original	1 1	1.20	3.50	7.00
2	117	3/54	PC-r	1 1	.50	1.50	3.00
3	132	5/56	PC-r	1 1	.50	1.50	3.00
4	142	1/58	PC-r	1 1	.50	1.50	3.00
5	155	3/60	PC-r	1 1	.50	1.50	3.00
6	167	'62/63	Has orig.date; PC-r	1 1	.50	1.50	3.00
7	167	5/64	PC-r	1 1	.50	1.50	3.00
8	167	3/66	PC-r	1 1	.50	1.50	3.00
9	167	3/66	No # or price; came w/LP record; PC-r	1 1	1.20	3.50	7.00
10	169	Spr/70	PC-r	1 1	.40	1.20	2.40

101. William Tell

Ed	HRN	Date	Details	A C	Good	Fine	Mint
1	101	11/52	Original	1 1	1.20	3.50	7.00
2	118	4/54	PC-r	1 1	.50	1.50	3.00
3	141	11/57	PC-r	1 1	.40	1.20	2.40
4	158	9/60	PC-r	1 1	.40	1.20	2.40
5	167	'62/63	Has orig.date; PC-r	1 1	.40	1.20	2.40
6	167	11/64	PC-r	1 1	.40	1.20	2.40
7	166	4/67	PC-r	1 1	.40	1.20	2.40
8	169	Win/69	New price 25¢; stiff-c; PC-r	1 1	.35	1.00	2.00

102. The White Company

Ed	HRN	Date	Details	A C	Good	Fine	Mint
1	101	12/52	Original	1 1	1.20	3.50	7.00

CLASSICS ILLUSTRATED (continued)

Ed	HRN	Date	Details	A	C	Good	Fine	Mint
2	165	1962	PC-r	1	1	.70	2.00	4.00
3	167	4/64	PC-r	1	1	.50	1.50	3.00

103. Men Against the Sea

Ed	HRN	Date	Details	A	C	Good	Fine	Mint
1	104	1/53	Original (if has 'Coward Shoe' ad, add 150%)	1	1	1.20	3.50	7.00
2	114	12/53	PC-r	1	1	.70	2.00	4.00
3	131	3/56	New-c; PC-r	1	2	.50	1.50	3.00
4	149	3/59	PC-r	1	2	.50	1.50	3.00
5	158	9/60	PC-r	1	2	.50	1.50	3.00
6	167	3/64	PC-r	1	2	.50	1.50	3.00

104. Bring 'Em Back Alive

Ed	HRN	Date	Details	A	C	Good	Fine	Mint
1	105	2/53	Original (if has 'Coward Shoe' ad, add 150%); Kiefer a&c	1	1	1.20	3.50	7.00
2	118	4/54	PC-r	1	1	.50	1.40	2.80
3	133	7/56	PC-r	1	1	.50	1.40	2.80
4	150	5/59	PC-r	1	1	.50	1.40	2.80
5	158	9/60	PC-r	1	1	.50	1.40	2.80
6	167	10/63	PC-r	1	1	.50	1.40	2.80
7	167	9/65	PC-r	1	1	.40	1.20	2.40
8	169	Win/69	New price 25¢; stiff-c; PC-r	1	1	.40	1.20	2.40

105. From the Earth to the Moon

Ed	HRN	Date	Details	A	C	Good	Fine	Mint
1	106	3/53	Original	1	1	1.20	3.50	7.00
2	118	4/54	PC-r	1	1	.50	1.40	2.80
3	132	3/56	PC-r	1	1	.50	1.40	2.80
4	141	11/57	PC-r	1	1	.50	1.40	2.80
5	146	9/58	PC-r	1	1	.50	1.40	2.80
6	156	5/60	PC-r	1	1	.50	1.40	2.80
7	167	'62/63	Has orig.date; PC-r	1	1	.50	1.40	2.80
8	167	5/64	PC-r	1	1	.50	1.40	2.80
9	167	5/65	PC-r	1	1	.50	1.40	2.80
10	166	10/67	PC-r	1	1	.50	1.40	2.80
11	169	Sm/69	New price 25¢; stiff-c; PC-r	1	1	.40	1.20	2.40
12	169	Spr/71	PC-r	1	1	.40	1.20	2.40

106. Buffalo Bill

Ed	HRN	Date	Details	A	C	Good	Fine	Mint
1	107	4/53	Orig.; DelBourgo-a	1	1	1.20	3.50	7.00
2	118	4/54	PC-r	1	1	.50	1.40	2.80
3	132	3/56	PC-r	1	1	.50	1.40	2.80
4	142	1/58	PC-r	1	1	.50	1.40	2.80
5	161	3/61	PC-r	1	1	.50	1.40	2.80
6	167	3/64	PC-r	1	1	.50	1.40	2.80
7	166	7/67	PC-r	1	1	.50	1.40	2.80
8	169	Fall/69	PC-r	1	1	.40	1.20	2.40

107. King of the Khyber Rifles

Ed	HRN	Date	Details	A	C	Good	Fine	Mint
1	108	5/53	Original	1	1	1.00	3.00	6.00
2	118	4/54	PC-r	1	1	.50	1.40	2.80
3	146	9/58	PC-r	1	1	.50	1.40	2.80
4	158	9/60	PC-r	1	1	.50	1.40	2.80
5	167	'62/63	Has orig.date; PC-r	1	1	.50	1.40	2.80
6	167	'62/63	PC-r	1	1	.40	1.20	2.40
7	167	10/66	PC-r	1	1	.40	1.20	2.40

108. Knights of the Round Table

Ed	HRN	Date	Details	A	C	Good	Fine	Mint
1	108	6/53	Original; Blum-a	1	1	2.00	5.00	10.00
2	117	3/54	PC-r	1	1	.50	1.40	2.80
3	153	11/59	PC-r	1	1	.50	1.40	2.80
4	165	1962	PC-r	1	1	.50	1.40	2.80
5	167	4/64	PC-r	1	1	.50	1.40	2.80
6	166	4/67	PC-r	1	1	.50	1.40	2.80
7	169	Sm/69	New price 25¢; stiff-c; PC-r	1	1	.40	1.20	2.40

109. Pitcairn's Island

Ed	HRN	Date	Details	A	C	Good	Fine	Mint
1	110	7/53	Original	1	1	2.50	7.00	14.00
2	165	1962	PC-r	1	1	.50	1.50	3.00
3	167	3/64	PC-r	1	1	.50	1.50	3.00
4	166	6/67	PC-r	1	1	.50	1.50	3.00

110. A Study in Scarlet

Ed	HRN	Date	Details	A	C	Good	Fine	Mint
1	111	8/53	Original	1	1	3.00	8.00	16.00
2	165	1962	PC-r	1	1	1.20	3.50	7.00

111. The Talisman

Ed	HRN	Date	Details	A	C	Good	Fine	Mint
1	112	9/53	Original; last H.C. Kiefer-a	1	1	3.50	10.00	20.00
2	165	1962	PC-r	1	1	.50	1.50	3.00
3	167	5/64	PC-r	1	1	.50	1.50	3.00
4	166	R/1968	New price 25¢; PC-r	1	1	.50	1.40	2.80

112. Adventures of Kit Carson

Ed	HRN	Date	Details	A	C	Good	Fine	Mint
1	113	10/53	Original	1	1	2.00	6.00	12.00
2	129	11/55	PC-r	1	1	.50	1.40	2.80
3	141	11/57	PC-r	1	1	.50	1.40	2.80
4	152	9/59	PC-r	1	1	.50	1.40	2.80
5	161	3/61	PC-r	1	1	.50	1.40	2.80
6	167	'62/63	PC-r	1	1	.50	1.40	2.80
7	167	2/65	PC-r	1	1	.50	1.40	2.80
8	167	5/66	PC-r	1	1	.50	1.40	2.80
9	166	Win/69	New-c&price 25¢; PC-r	1	2	.50	1.50	3.00

113. The Forty-Five Guardsmen

Ed	HRN	Date	Details	A	C	Good	Fine	Mint
1	114	11/53	Original	1	1	2.00	6.00	12.00
2	166	7/67	PC-r	1	1	.70	2.00	4.00

114. The Red Rover

Ed	HRN	Date	Details	A	C	Good	Fine	Mint
1	115	12/53	Original	1	1	2.00	6.00	12.00
2	166	7/67	PC-r	1	1	.70	2.00	4.00

115. How I Found Livingstone

Ed	HRN	Date	Details	A	C	Good	Fine	Mint
1	116	1/54	Original	1	1	1.50	4.00	8.00
2	167	1/67	PC-r	1	1	.70	2.00	4.00

116. The Bottle Imp

Ed	HRN	Date	Details	A	C	Good	Fine	Mint
1	117	2/54	Original	1	1	2.00	5.00	10.00
2	167	1/67	PC-r	1	1	.70	2.00	4.0

117. Captains Courageous

Ed	HRN	Date	Details	A	C	Good	Fine	Mint
1	118	3/54	Original	1	1	1.50	4.00	8.0
2	167	2/67	PC-r	1	1	.70	2.00	4.0
3	169	Fall/69	New price 25¢; stiff-c; PC-r	1	1	.50	1.50	3.0

118. Rob Roy

Ed	HRN	Date	Details	A	C	Good	Fine	Mint
1	119	4/54	Original	1	1	2.00	6.00	12.0

Classics Ill. #105(HRN-167), © GIL

Classics Ill. #109(HRN-110), © GIL

Classics Ill. #115(HRN-116), © GIL

Classics Ill. #124(HRN-167), © GIL

Classics Ill. #130(HRN-167), © GIL

Classics Ill. #133(HRN-167), © GIL

LASSICS ILLUSTRATED (continued)

Ed	HRN	Date	Details	A	C	Good	Fine	Mint
2	167	2/67	PC-r	1	1	.70	2.00	4.00

19. Soldiers of Fortune

Ed	HRN	Date	Details	A	C	Good	Fine	Mint
1	120	5/54	Original	1	1	1.50	4.00	8.00
2	166	3/67	PC-r	1	1	.70	2.00	4.00
3	169	Spr/70	New price 25¢; stiff-c; PC-r	1	1	.50	1.50	3.00

20. The Hurricane

Ed	HRN	Date	Details	A	C	Good	Fine	Mint
1	121	1954	Original	1	1	1.50	4.00	8.00
2	166	3/67	PC-r	1	1	.70	2.00	4.00

21. Wild Bill Hickok

Ed	HRN	Date	Details	A	C	Good	Fine	Mint
1	122	7/54	Original	1	1	2.00	5.00	10.00
2	132	5/56	PC-r	1	1	.50	1.50	3.00
3	141	11/57	PC-r	1	1	.50	1.50	3.00
4	154	1/60	PC-r	1	1	.50	1.50	3.00
5	167	'62/63	PC-r	1	1	.50	1.50	3.00
6	167	8/64	PC-r	1	1	.50	1.50	3.00
7	166	4/67	PC-r	1	1	.40	1.20	2.40
8	169	Win/69	PC-r	1	1	.40	1.20	2.40

22. The Mutineers

Ed	HRN	Date	Details	A	C	Good	Fine	Mint
1	123	9/54	Original	1	1	1.00	3.00	6.00
2	136	1/57	PC-r	1	1	.50	1.50	3.00
3	146	9/58	PC-r	1	1	.50	1.50	3.00
4	158	9/60	PC-r	1	1	.50	1.50	3.00
5	167	11/63	PC-r	1	1	.50	1.50	3.00
6	167	3/65	PC-r	1	1	.50	1.50	3.00
7	166	8/67	PC-r	1	1	.40	1.20	2.40

23. Fang and Claw

Ed	HRN	Date	Details	A	C	Good	Fine	Mint
1	124	11/54	Original	1	1	2.00	6.00	12.00
2	133	7/56	PC-r	1	1	.50	1.40	2.80
3	143	3/58	PC-r	1	1	.50	1.40	2.80
4	154	1/60	PC-r	1	1	.50	1.40	2.80
5	167	'62/63	Has orig.date; PC-r	1	1	.50	1.40	2.80
6	167	9/65	PC-r	1	1	.50	1.40	2.80

24. The War of the Worlds

Ed	HRN	Date	Details	A	C	Good	Fine	Mint
1	125	1/55	Original	1	1	1.50	4.00	8.00
2	131	3/56	PC-r	1	1	.50	1.40	2.80
3	141	11/57	PC-r	1	1	.50	1.40	2.80
4	148	1/59	PC-r	1	1	.50	1.40	2.80
5	156	5/60	PC-r	1	1	.50	1.40	2.80
6	165	1962	PC-r	1	1	.50	1.40	2.80
7	167	'62/63	PC-r	1	1	.50	1.40	2.80
8	167	11/64	PC-r	1	1	.50	1.40	2.80
9	167	11/65	PC-r	1	1	.50	1.40	2.80
10	166	R/1968	New price 25¢; PC-r	1	1	.40	1.20	2.40
11	169	Sm/70	PC-r	1	1	.40	1.20	2.40

25. The Ox Bow Incident

Ed	HRN	Date	Details	A	C	Good	Fine	Mint
1	—	3/55	Original	1	1	.85	2.50	5.00
2	143	3/58	PC-r	1	1	.50	1.40	2.80
3	152	9/59	PC-r	1	1	.50	1.40	2.80
4	149	3/61	PC-r	1	1	.50	1.40	2.80
5	167	'62/63	PC-r	1	1	.50	1.40	2.80
6	167	11/64	PC-r	1	1	.50	1.40	2.80
7	166	4/67	PC-r	1	1	.50	1.40	2.80
8	169	Win/69	New price 25¢; stiff-c; PC-r	1	1	.40	1.20	2.40

26. The Downfall

Ed	HRN	Date	Details	A	C	Good	Fine	Mint
1	—	5/55	Orig.; 'Picture Progress' replaces reorder list	1	1	1.20	3.50	7.00
2	167	8/64	PC-r	1	1	.50	1.50	3.00
3		R/1968	New price 25¢; PC-r	1	1	.50	1.40	2.80

127. The King of the Mountains

Ed	HRN	Date	Details	A	C	Good	Fine	Mint
1	128	7/55	Original	1	1	.85	2.50	5.00
2	167	6/64	PC-r	1	1	.70	2.00	4.00
3	166	F/1968	New price 25¢; PC-r	1	1	.50	1.50	3.00

128. Macbeth (Used in **POP**, pg. 102)

Ed	HRN	Date	Details	A	C	Good	Fine	Mint
1	128	9/55	Orig.; last Blum-a	1	1	1.50	4.00	8.00
2	143	3/58	PC-r	1	1	.50	1.50	3.00
3	158	9/60	PC-r	1	1	.50	1.50	3.00
4	167	'62/63	PC-r	1	1	.50	1.50	3.00
5	167	6/64	PC-r	1	1	.50	1.50	3.00
6	166	4/67	PC-r	1	1	.50	1.50	3.00
7	166	R/1968	Twin Circle ed.; PC-r	1	1	.40	1.20	2.40
8	169	Spr/70	New price 25¢; stiff-c; PC-r	1	1	.40	1.20	2.40

129. Davy Crockett

Ed	HRN	Date	Details	A	C	Good	Fine	Mint
1	129	11/55	Original	1	1	1.50	4.00	8.00
2	167	9/66	PC-r	1	1	.85	2.50	5.00

130. Caesar's Conquests

Ed	HRN	Date	Details	A	C	Good	Fine	Mint
1	130	1/56	Original; Orlando-a	1	1	1.20	3.50	7.00
2	142	1/58	PC-r	1	1	.50	1.40	2.80
3	152	9/59	PC-r	1	1	.50	1.40	2.80
4	149	3/61	PC-r	1	1	.50	1.40	2.80
5	167	'62/63	PC-r	1	1	.50	1.40	2.80
6	167	10/64	PC-r	1	1	.50	1.40	2.80
7	167	4/66	PC-r	1	1	.50	1.40	2.80

131. The Covered Wagon

Ed	HRN	Date	Details	A	C	Good	Fine	Mint
1	131	3/56	Original	1	1	1.50	4.00	8.00
2	143	3/58	PC-r	1	1	.50	1.40	2.80
3	152	9/59	PC-r	1	1	.50	1.40	2.80
4	158	9/60	PC-r	1	1	.50	1.40	2.80
5	167	'62/63	PC-r	1	1	.50	1.40	2.80
6	167	11/64	PC-r	1	1	.50	1.40	2.80
7	167	4/66	PC-r	1	1	.50	1.40	2.80
8	169	Win/69	New price 25¢; stiff-c; PC-r	1	1	.40	1.20	2.40

132. The Dark Frigate

Ed	HRN	Date	Details	A	C	Good	Fine	Mint
1	132	5/56	Original	1	1	1.50	4.00	8.00
2	150	5/59	PC-r	1	1	.50	1.40	2.80
3	167	1/64	PC-r	1	1	.50	1.40	2.80
4	166	5/67	PC-r	1	1	.50	1.40	2.80

133. The Time Machine

Ed	HRN	Date	Details	A	C	Good	Fine	Mint
1	132	7/56	Original	1	1	1.50	4.00	8.00
2	142	1/58	PC-r	1	1	.50	1.40	2.80
3	152	9/59	PC-r	1	1	.50	1.40	2.80
4	158	9/60	PC-r	1	1	.50	1.40	2.80
5	167	'62/63	PC-r	1	1	.50	1.40	2.80
6	167	6/64	PC-r	1	1	.50	1.40	2.80
7	167	3/66	PC-r	1	1	.50	1.40	2.80
8	167	3/66	No # or price; record ed.; PC-r	1	1	2.00	5.00	10.00

CLASSICS ILLUSTRATED (continued)

Ed	HRN	Date	Details	A	C	Good	Fine	Mint
9	166	12/67	PC-r	1	1	.40	1.20	2.40
10	169	Win/71	New price 25¢; stiff-c; PC-r	1	1	.40	1.20	2.40

134. Romeo and Juliet

Ed	HRN	Date	Details	A	C	Good	Fine	Mint
1	134	9/56	Original; Evans-a	1	1	.85	2.50	5.00
2	161	3/61	PC-r	1	1	.70	2.00	4.00
3	167	5/65	PC-r	1	1	.70	2.00	4.00
4	166	6/67	PC-r	1	1	.70	2.00	4.00
5	166	Win/69	New c&price 25¢; stiff-c; PC-r	1	2	.40	1.20	2.40

135. Waterloo

Ed	HRN	Date	Details	A	C	Good	Fine	Mint
1	135	11/56	Orig.; G. Ingels-a	1	1	.85	2.50	5.00
2	153	11/59	PC-r	1	1	.50	1.40	2.80
3	167	'62/63	PC-r	1	1	.50	1.40	2.80
4	167	9/64	PC-r	1	1	.50	1.40	2.80
5	166	R/1968	New price 25¢; PC-r	1	1	.40	1.20	2.40

136. Lord Jim

Ed	HRN	Date	Details	A	C	Good	Fine	Mint
1	136	1/57	Original; Evans-a	1	1	.85	2.50	5.00
2	165	'62/63	PC-r	1	1	.50	1.40	2.80
3	167	3/64	PC-r	1	1	.50	1.40	2.80
4	167	9/66	PC-r	1	1	.50	1.40	2.80
5	169	Sm/69	New price 25¢; stiff-c; PC-r	1	1	.40	1.20	2.40

137. The Little Savage

Ed	HRN	Date	Details	A	C	Good	Fine	Mint
1	136	3/57	Original; Evans-a	1	1	1.50	4.00	8.00
2	148	1/59	PC-r	1	1	.50	1.40	2.80
3	156	5/60	PC-r	1	1	.50	1.40	2.80
4	167	'62/63	PC-r	1	1	.50	1.40	2.80
5	167	10/64	PC-r	1	1	.50	1.40	2.80
6	166	8/67	PC-r	1	1	.50	1.40	2.80
7	169	Spr/70	New price 25¢; stiff-c; PC-r	1	1	.40	1.20	2.40

138. A Journey to the Center of the Earth

Ed	HRN	Date	Details	A	C	Good	Fine	Mint
1	136	5/57	Original	1	1	1.50	4.00	8.00
2	146	9/58	PC-r	1	1	.40	1.20	2.40
3	156	5/60	PC-r	1	1	.40	1.20	2.40
4	158	9/60	PC-r	1	1	.40	1.20	2.40
5	167	'62/63	PC-r	1	1	.40	1.20	2.40
6	167	6/64	PC-r	1	1	.40	1.20	2.40
7	167	4/66	PC-r	1	1	.40	1.20	2.40
8	166	R/1968	New price 25¢; PC-r	1	1	.35	1.00	2.00

139. In the Reign of Terror

Ed	HRN	Date	Details	A	C	Good	Fine	Mint
1	139	7/57	Original; Evans-a	1	1	1.00	3.00	6.00
2	154	1/60	PC-r	1	1	.40	1.20	2.40
3	167	'62/63	Has orig.date; PC-r	1	1	.40	1.20	2.40
4	167	7/64	PC-r	1	1	.40	1.20	2.40
5	166	R/1968	New price 25¢; PC-r	1	1	.35	1.00	2.00

140. On Jungle Trails

Ed	HRN	Date	Details	A	C	Good	Fine	Mint
1	140	9/57	Original	1	1	1.00	3.00	6.00
2	150	5/59	PC-r	1	1	.40	1.20	2.40
3	160	1/61	PC-r	1	1	.40	1.20	2.40
4	167	9/63	PC-r	1	1	.40	1.20	2.40
5	167	9/65	PC-r	1	1	.40	1.20	2.40

141. Castle Dangerous

Ed	HRN	Date	Details	A	C	Good	Fine	Mint
1	141	11/57	Original	1	1	1.50	4.00	8.00
2	152	9/59	PC-r	1	1	.70	2.00	4.00
3	167	'62/63	PC-r	1	1	.50	1.50	3.00
4	166	7/67	PC-r	1	1	.50	1.50	3.00

142. Abraham Lincoln

Ed	HRN	Date	Details	A	C	Good	Fine	Mint
1	142	1/58	Original	1	1	1.50	4.00	8.00
2	154	1/60	PC-r	1	1	.70	2.00	4.00
3	158	9/60	PC-r	1	1	.70	2.00	4.00
4	167	10/63	PC-r	1	1	.70	2.00	4.00
5	167	7/65	PC-r	1	1	.70	2.00	4.00
6	166	11/67	PC-r	1	1	.70	2.00	4.00
7	169	Fall/69	New price 25¢; stiff-c; PC-r	1	1	.50	1.50	3.00

143. Kim

Ed	HRN	Date	Details	A	C	Good	Fine	Mint
1	143	3/58	Original; Orlando-a	1	1	.70	2.00	4.00
2	165	'62/63	PC-r	1	1	.40	1.20	2.40
3	167	11/63	PC-r	1	1	.40	1.20	2.40
4	167	8/65	PC-r	1	1	.40	1.20	2.40
5	169	Win/69	New price 25¢; stiff-c; PC-r	1	1	.35	1.00	2.00

144. The First Men in the Moon

Ed	HRN	Date	Details	A	C	Good	Fine	Mint
1	143	5/58	Original; Williamson/Woodbridge-a	1	1	2.00	6.00	12.00
2	153	11/59	PC-r	1	1	.50	1.40	2.80
3	161	3/61	PC-r	1	1	.50	1.40	2.80
4	167	'62/63	PC-r	1	1	.50	1.40	2.80
5	167	12/65	PC-r	1	1	.50	1.40	2.80
6	166	Fall/68	New-c&price 25¢; PC-r	1	2	.30	.80	1.60
7	169	Win/69	Stiff-c; PC-r	1	2	.30	.80	1.60

145. The Crisis

Ed	HRN	Date	Details	A	C	Good	Fine	Mint
1	143	7/58	Original; Evans-a	1	1	.70	2.00	4.00
2	156	5/60	PC-r	1	1	.40	1.20	2.40
3	167	10/63	PC-r	1	1	.40	1.20	2.40
4	167	3/65	PC-r	1	1	.40	1.20	2.40
5	166	R/1968	New price 25¢; PC-r	1	1	.35	1.00	2.00

146. With Fire and Sword

Ed	HRN	Date	Details	A	C	Good	Fine	Mint
1	143	9/58	Original; Woodbridge-a	1	1	1.00	3.00	6.00
2	156	5/60	PC-r	1	1	.70	2.00	4.00
3	167	11/63	PC-r	1	1	.70	2.00	4.00
4	167	3/65	PC-r	1	1	.70	2.00	4.00

147. Ben-Hur

Ed	HRN	Date	Details	A	C	Good	Fine	Mint
1	147	11/58	Original; Orlando-a	1	1	1.50	4.00	8.00
2	153	11/59	PC-r	1	1	.50	1.40	2.80
3	158	9/60	PC-r	1	1	.50	1.40	2.80
4	167	'62/63	Orig.date; but PC-r	1	1	.50	1.40	2.80
5	167	———	PC-r	1	1	.50	1.40	2.80
6	167	2/65	PC-r	1	1	.50	1.40	2.80
7	167	9/66	PC-r	1	1	.50	1.40	2.80
8	166	Fall/68	New-c&price 25¢; PC-r; has both hard & stiff-c	1	2	.30	.80	1.60

148. The Buccaneer

Classics Ill. #138(HRN-136), © GIL

Classics Ill. #140(HRN-160), © GIL

Classics Ill. #148(HRN-148), © GIL

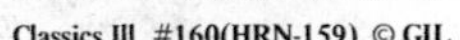
Classics Ill. #160(HRN-159), © GIL

Classics Ill. #161(HRN-167), © GIL

Classics Ill. #162(HRN-167), © GIL

CLASSICS ILLUSTRATED (continued)

Ed	HRN	Date	Details	A	C	Good	Fine	Mint
1	148	1/59	Original; Evans/ Jenny-a	1	1	1.50	4.00	8.00
2	568	——	Juniors list only PC-r	1	1	.50	1.40	2.80
3	167	'62/63	PC-r	1	1	.50	1.40	2.80
4	167	9/65	PC-r	1	1	.50	1.40	2.80
5	169	Sm/69	New price 25¢; PC-r	1	1	.40	1.20	2.40

149. Off on a Comet

Ed	HRN	Date	Details	A	C	Good	Fine	Mint
1	149	3/59	Orig.; G.McCann-a	1	1	1.20	3.50	7.00
2	155	3/60	PC-r	1	1	.50	1.50	3.00
3	149	3/61	PC-r	1	1	.50	1.50	3.00
4	167	12/63	PC-r	1	1	.50	1.50	3.00
5	167	2/65	PC-r	1	1	.50	1.50	3.00
6	167	10/66	PC-r	1	1	.50	1.50	3.00
7	166	Fall/68	New-c&price 25¢; PC-r	1	2	.50	1.40	2.80

150. The Virginian

Ed	HRN	Date	Details	A	C	Good	Fine	Mint
1	150	5/59	Original	1	1	1.50	4.00	8.00
2	164	1961	PC-r	1	1	.70	2.00	4.00
3	167	'62/63	PC-r	1	1	.70	2.00	4.00
4	167	12/65	PC-r	1	1	.70	2.00	4.00

151. Won By the Sword

Ed	HRN	Date	Details	A	C	Good	Fine	Mint
1	150	7/59	Original	1	1	1.00	3.00	6.00
2	164	1961	PC-r	1	1	.70	2.00	4.00
3	167	10/63	PC-r	1	1	.50	1.50	3.00
4	167	1963	PC-r	1	1	.50	1.50	3.00
5	166	7/67	PC-r	1	1	.50	1.50	3.00

152. Wild Animals I Have Known

Ed	HRN	Date	Details	A	C	Good	Fine	Mint
1	152	9/59	Orig.; L.B. Cole-a	1	1	1.50	4.00	8.00
2	149	3/61	PC-r	1	1	.85	2.50	5.00
3	167	9/63	PC-r	1	1	.70	2.00	4.00
4	167	8/65	PC-r	1	1	.70	2.00	4.00
5	169	Fall/69	New price 25¢; stiff-c; PC-r	1	1	.50	1.50	3.00

153. The Invisible Man

Ed	HRN	Date	Details	A	C	Good	Fine	Mint
1	153	11/59	Original	1	1	1.00	3.00	6.00
2	149	3/61	PC-r	1	1	.50	1.40	2.80
3	167	'62/63	PC-r	1	1	.50	1.40	2.80
4	167	2/65	PC-r	1	1	.50	1.40	2.80
5	167	9/66	PC-r	1	1	.50	1.40	2.80
6	166	Win/69	New price 25¢; PC-r	1	1	.40	1.20	2.40
7	169	Spr/71	Stiff-c; letters spelling 'Invisible Man' are 'solid' not 'invisible;' PC-r	1	1	.35	1.00	2.00

154. The Conspiracy of Pontiac

Ed	HRN	Date	Details	A	C	Good	Fine	Mint
1	154	1/60	Original	1	1	1.00	3.00	6.00
2	167	11/63	PC-r	1	1	.75	2.20	4.40
3	167	7/64	PC-r	1	1	.70	2.00	4.00
4	166	12/67	PC-r	1	1	.70	2.00	4.00

155. The Lion of the North

Ed	HRN	Date	Details	A	C	Good	Fine	Mint
1	154	3/60	Original	1	1	1.00	3.00	6.00
2	167	1/64	PC-r	1	1	.70	2.00	4.00
3	166	R/1967	New price 25¢; PC-r	1	1	.50	1.50	3.00

156. The Conquest of Mexico

Ed	HRN	Date	Details	A	C	Good	Fine	Mint
1	156	5/60	Orig.; Bruno Premiani-a&c	1	1	1.50	4.00	8.00
2	167	1/64	PC-r	1	1	.50	1.50	3.00
3	166	8/67	PC-r	1	1	.50	1.50	3.00
4	169	Spr/70	New price 25¢; stiff-c; PC-r	1	1	.45	1.40	2.80

157. Lives of the Hunted

Ed	HRN	Date	Details	A	C	Good	Fine	Mint
1	156	7/60	Original	1	1	1.00	3.00	6.00
2	167	2/64	PC-r	1	1	.70	2.00	4.00
3	166	10/67	PC-r	1	1	.50	1.50	3.00

158. The Conspirators

Ed	HRN	Date	Details	A	C	Good	Fine	Mint
1	156	9/60	Original	1	1	1.00	3.00	6.00
2	167	7/64	PC-r	1	1	.70	2.00	4.00
3	166	10/67	PC-r	1	1	.70	2.00	4.00

159. The Octopus

Ed	HRN	Date	Details	A	C	Good	Fine	Mint
1	159	11/60	Orig.; Gray Morrow & Geo. Evans-a	1	1	1.00	3.00	6.00
2	167	2/64	PC-r	1	1	.50	1.50	3.00
3	166	R/1967	New price 25; PC-r	1	1	.40	1.20	2.40

160. The Food of the Gods

Ed	HRN	Date	Details	A	C	Good	Fine	Mint
1	159	1/61	Original	1	1	1.50	4.00	8.00
2	160	1/61	Original; same, except for HRN	1	1	.50	1.50	3.00
3	167	1/64	PC-r	1	1	.50	1.40	2.80
4	166	6/67	PC-r	1	1	.50	1.40	2.80

161. Cleopatra

Ed	HRN	Date	Details	A	C	Good	Fine	Mint
1	161	3/61	Original	1	1	2.00	6.00	12.00
2	167	1/64	PC-r	1	1	1.20	3.50	7.00
3	166	8/67	PC-r	1	1	1.20	3.50	7.00

162. Robur the Conqueror

Ed	HRN	Date	Details	A	C	Good	Fine	Mint
1	162	5/61	Original	1	1	1.50	4.00	8.00
2	167	7/64	PC-r	1	1	.50	1.50	3.00
3	166	8/67	PC-r	1	1	.50	1.50	3.00

163. Master of the World

Ed	HRN	Date	Details	A	C	Good	Fine	Mint
1	163	7/61	Original; Gray Morrow-a	1	1	1.00	3.00	6.00
2	167	1/65	PC-r	1	1	.50	1.40	2.80
3	166	R/1968	New price 25¢; PC-r	1	1	.40	1.20	2.40

164. The Cossack Chief

Ed	HRN	Date	Details	A	C	Good	Fine	Mint
1	164	(1961)	Original; undated	1	1	1.00	3.00	6.00
2	167	4/65	PC-r	1	1	.50	1.50	3.00
3	166	Fall/68	New price 25¢ PC-r	1	1	.45	1.40	2.80

165. The Queen's Necklace

Ed	HRN	Date	Details	A	C	Good	Fine	Mint
1	164	1/62	Original; Morrow-a	1	1	1.50	4.00	8.00
2	167	4/65	PC-r	1	1	.50	1.50	3.00
3	166	Fall/68	New price 25¢; PC-r	1	1	.50	1.40	2.80

166. Tigers and Traitors

CLASSICS ILLUSTRATED (continued)

Ed	HRN	Date	Details	A C	Good	Fine	Mint
1	165	5/62	Original	1 1	2.00	5.00	10.00
2	167	2/64	PC-r	1 1	.70	2.00	4.00
3	166	6/67	PC-r	1 1	.50	1.50	3.00

167. Faust

Ed	HRN	Date	Details	A C	Good	Fine	Mint
1	165	8/62	Original	1 1	3.50	10.00	20.00
2	167	2/64	PC-r	1 1	1.50	4.00	8.00
3	166	6/67	PC-r	1 1	1.50	4.00	8.00

168. In Freedom's Cause

Ed	HRN	Date	Details	A C	Good	Fine	Mint
1	169	Win/69	Original; Evans/ Crandall-a	1 1	1.50	4.00	8.00

169. Negro Americans—The Early Years

Ed	HRN	Date	Details	A C	Good	Fine	Mint
1	166	Spr/69	Orig. & last issue	1 1	4.00	12.00	24.00
2	169	Spr/69		1 1	2.00	6.00	12.00

CLASSIC COMICS LIBRARY GIFT BOX (Later boxes titled Classics Illustrated . . .)

These Gift Boxes first appeared in November 1943. They were (at least according to the advertising) designed with the boys in the service in mind. The buyer was told that "the boys relax with Classic Comics." The boxes held five Classics. They began to sell for 50 cents and ceased publication at a price of 79 cents. The earlier series is worth more and are more colorful.

Classic Comics boxes:
- Box A,B,C,D — 25.00 75.00 150.00
- 1952 Christmas Box: held No. 64,76,83 & 98 (reprints) — 17.00 50.00 100.00

NOTE: *These boxes were priced at 50 cents. Box A held reprints of No. 1-5; Box B-No. 6-10; Box C-No. 11-15; & Box D-No. 16-20.*

Classics Illustrated boxes:
- Boxes with 59 cent price — 17.00 50.00 100.00
- Boxes with 69 cent price — 14.00 40.00 80.00
- Boxes with 79 cent price — 14.00 40.00 80.00

NOTE: *Condition of box should be graded, also.*

CLASSICS ILLUSTRATED LIBRARY GIFT BOX (See Classics Comics . . .)

CLASSICS ILLUSTRATED EDUCATIONAL SERIES
1951; 1953 (16 pages)
Gilberton Corp.

1-Shelter Through the Ages (Ruberoid Co.)(1951; 15 cents) Kiefer-a — 10.00 30.00 60.00
nn-The Westinghouse Story-The Dreams of a Man (Westinghouse Co.-1953) H. C. Kiefer-a — 10.00 30.00 60.00

CLASSICS ILLUSTRATED GIANTS
February, 1950 (One-Shots - "OS")
Gilberton Publications

These Giant Editions were on sale for two years, beginning in 1950. They were 50 cents on the newsstand and 60 cents by mail. They are actually four classics in one volume. All the stories are reprints of the Classics Illustrated Series.

"An Illustrated Library of Great Adventure Stories" - reprints of No. 6,7,8,10 — 20.00 60.00 150.00
"An Illustrated Library of Exciting Mystery Stories" - reprints of No. 30,21,40,13 — 30.00 80.00 175.00
"An Illustrated Library of Great Indian Stories" - reprints of No. 4,17, 22,37 — 20.00 60.00 150.00

CLASSICS ILLUSTRATED "GOLDEN RECORDS GREAT LITERATURE SERIES" ($2.49 retail for comic and record)
Mar, 1966 (All issues) (Record with comic sets)
Gilberton (Comics)/A. A. Records (Records) — Good Fine Mint

SLP-189: Black Beauty, SLP-190: Mutiny on the Bounty, SLP-191: The Time Machine, SLP-192: The Call of the Wild
Comic & Record . . . . each . . . . — 12.00

NOTE: *Comics are all dated March, 1966 and the last reorder number on the back is 167.*

CLASSICS ILLUSTRATED JUNIOR
Oct, 1953 - Spring, 1971
Famous Authors Ltd. (Gilberton Publications)

Original editions have ad for the next issue. Reprints are worth 50 per cent less than originals. Prices listed are for originals.

	Good	Fine	Mint
501-Snow White & the Seven Dwarfs; Alex Blum-a	7.00	20.00	40.00
502-The Ugly Duckling	3.50	10.00	20.00
503-Cinderella	1.50	4.00	8.00
504-The Pied Piper	1.50	4.00	8.00
505-The Sleeping Beauty	1.50	4.00	8.00
506-The Three Little Pigs	1.50	4.00	8.00
507-Jack & the Beanstalk	2.00	5.00	10.00
508-Goldilocks & the Three Bears	1.50	4.00	8.00
509-Beauty and the Beast	2.00	5.00	10.00
510-Little Red Riding Hood	2.00	5.00	10.00
511-Puss-N-Boots	1.20	3.50	7.00
512-Rumpel Stiltskin	2.00	5.00	10.00
513-Pinocchio	3.50	10.00	20.00
514-The Steadfast Tin Soldier	2.50	7.00	14.00
515-Johnny Appleseed	2.00	5.00	10.00
516-Aladdin and His Lamp	3.50	10.00	20.00
517-The Emperor's New Clothes	2.00	5.00	10.00
518-The Golden Goose	1.20	3.50	7.00
519-Paul Bunyan	1.20	3.50	7.00
520-Thumbelina	2.00	5.00	10.00
521-King of the Golden River	2.00	5.00	10.00
522-The Nightingale	2.00	5.00	10.00
523-The Gallant Tailor	1.20	3.50	7.00
524-The Wild Swans	1.20	3.50	7.00
525-The Little Mermaid	1.20	3.50	7.00
526-The Frog Prince	2.00	5.00	10.00
527-The Golden-Haired Giant	1.20	3.50	7.00
528-The Penny Prince	1.20	3.50	7.00
529-The Magic Servants	1.20	3.50	7.00
530-The Golden Bird	1.20	3.50	7.00
531-Rapunzel	2.00	5.00	10.00
532-The Dancing Princesses	1.20	3.50	7.00
533-The Magic Fountain	1.20	3.50	7.00
534-The Golden Touch	1.20	3.50	7.00
535-The Wizard of Oz	3.50	10.00	20.00
535-Twin Circle edition	4.00	12.00	24.00
536-The Chimney Sweep	1.20	3.50	7.00
537-The Three Fairies	1.20	3.50	7.00
538-Silly Hans	1.20	3.50	7.00
539-The Enchanted Fish	1.50	4.00	8.00
540-The Tinder-Box	3.50	10.00	20.00
541-Snow White & Rose Red	2.00	5.00	10.00
542-The Donkey's Tale	2.50	7.00	14.00
543-The House in the Woods	1.20	3.50	7.00
544-The Golden Fleece	3.50	10.00	20.00
545-The Glass Mountain	2.00	5.00	10.00
546-The Elves & the Shoemaker	2.00	5.00	10.00
547-The Wishing Table	1.20	3.50	7.00
548-The Magic Pitcher	1.20	3.50	7.00
549-Simple Kate	1.20	3.50	7.00
550-The Singing Donkey	1.20	3.50	7.00
551-The Queen Bee	1.20	3.50	7.00
552-The Three Little Dwarfs	3.00	8.00	16.00
553-King Thrushbeard	1.20	3.50	7.00
554-The Enchanted Deer	1.20	3.50	7.00

Classics Ill. #166(HRN-167), © GIL

Classics Ill. Jr. #518-Orig., © GIL

Classics Ill. Jr. #522-Orig., © GIL

Classics Ill. Special #129A, © GIL

Claw #6, © DC

Clown Comics #2, © HARV

CLASSICS ILLUSTRATED JUNIOR (cont'd.)

	Good	Fine	Mint
555-The Three Golden Apples	1.50	4.00	8.00
556-The Elf Mound	.85	2.50	5.00
557-Silly Willy	.85	2.50	5.00
558-The Magic Dish	.85	2.50	5.00
559-The Japanese Lantern; 1 pg. Ingels-a	2.00	5.00	10.00
560-The Doll Princess	.85	2.50	5.00
561-Hans Humdrum	.85	2.50	5.00
562-The Enchanted Pony	1.20	3.50	7.00
563-The Wishing Well	1.20	3.50	7.00
564-The Salt Mountain	.85	2.50	5.00
565-The Silly Princess	1.00	3.00	6.00
566-Clumsy Hans	.85	2.50	5.00
567-The Bearskin Soldier	.85	2.50	5.00
568-The Happy Hedgehog	1.20	3.50	7.00
569-The Three Giants	1.20	3.50	7.00
570-The Pearl Princess	.85	2.50	5.00
571-How Fire Came to the Indians	1.20	3.50	7.00
572-The Drummer Boy	.85	2.50	5.00
573-The Crystal Ball	.85	2.50	5.00
574-Brightboots	.85	2.50	5.00
575-The Fearless Prince	1.20	3.50	7.00
576-The Princess Who Saw Everything	1.50	4.00	8.00
577-The Runaway Dumpling	2.00	6.00	12.00

NOTE: *Last reprint - Spring, 1971.*

CLASSICS ILLUSTRATED SPECIAL ISSUE
Dec, 1955 - July, 1962 (100 pages) (35 cents)
Gilberton Co. (Came out semi-annually)

	Good	Fine	Mint
129A-The Story of Jesus (titled ...Special Edition) "Jesus on Mountain" cover	2.00	6.00	12.00
"Three Camels" cover(12/58)	3.50	10.00	20.00
132A-The Story of America (6/56)	1.50	4.00	8.00
135A-The Ten Commandments(12/56)	3.00	9.00	18.00
138A-Adventures in Science(6/57)	2.50	7.00	14.00
141A-The Rough Rider (Teddy Roosevelt)(12/57)	1.50	4.00	8.00
144A-Blazing the Trails West(6/58)- 73 pages of Crandall/Evans plus Severin-a	1.50	4.00	8.00
147A-Crossing the Rockies(12/58)-Crandall/Evans-a	2.00	6.00	12.00
150A-Royal Canadian Police(6/59)-Ingels, Sid Check-a	2.00	6.00	12.00
153A-Men, Guns & Cattle(12/59)-Evans-a, 26 pgs.	1.75	5.00	10.00
156A-The Atomic Age(6/60)-Crandall/Evans, Torres-a	1.75	5.00	10.00
159A-Rockets, Jets and Missiles(12/60)-Evans, Morrow-a	2.00	6.00	12.00
162A-War Between the States(6/61)-Kirby & Crandall/Evans-a	1.75	5.00	10.00
165A-To the Stars(12/61)-Torres, Crandall/Evans, Kirby-a	2.00	6.00	12.00
166A-World War II('62)-Torres, Crandall/Evans, Kirby-a	1.75	5.00	10.00
167A-Prehistoric World(7/62)-Torres & Crandall/Evans-a	2.50	7.00	14.00
nn Special Issue-The United Nations (50 cents); (Scarce)-Not Williamson-a	3.50	10.00	20.00

NOTE: *158A appeared as DC's Showcase No. 43, "Dr. No" and was only published in Great Britain as 158A with different cover.*

CLASSICS LIBRARY (see King Classics)

CLAW THE UNCONQUERED (See Cancelled Comic Cavalcade)
5-6/75 - No. 9, 9-10/76; No. 10, 4-5/78 - No. 12, 8-9/78
National Periodical Publications/DC Comics

	Good	Fine	Mint
1	.30	.80	1.60
2,3		.50	1.00
4-12: 9-Origin		.30	.60

NOTE: ***Kubert** c-10-12.*

CLAY CODY, GUNSLINGER
Fall, 1957
Pines Comics

	Good	Fine	Mint
1	.85	2.50	5.00

CLEAN FUN, STARRING "SHOOGAFOOTS JONES"
1944 (24 pgs.; B&W; oversized covers) (10 cents)
Specialty Book Co.

	Good	Fine	Mint
Humorous situations involving Negroes in the Deep South			
White cover issue....	2.75	8.00	16.00
Dark grey cover issue....	3.00	9.00	18.00

CLEMENTINA THE FLYING PIG (See Dell Jr. Treasury)

CLEOPATRA (See Ideal, a Classical Comic No. 1)

CLIFF MERRITT SETS THE RECORD STRAIGHT
Giveaway (2 different issues)
Brotherhood of Railroad Trainsmen

	Good	Fine	Mint
...and the Very Candid Candidate by Al Williamson	.40	1.20	2.40
...Sets the Record Straight by Al Williamson (2 diff.-c: one by Williamson, the other by McWilliams)	.40	1.20	2.40

CLIFFORD BRIDE'S IMMORTAL NAPOLEON AND UNCLE ELBY
1932 (12x17"; softcover cartoon book)
The Castle Press

	Good	Fine	Mint
Intro. by Don Herod	5.00	14.00	28.00

CLIMAX!
July, 1955
Gilmor

	Good	Fine	Mint
1,2 (Mystery)	1.50	4.00	8.00

CLINT & MAC (See 4-Color No. 889)

CLOAK AND DAGGER
Fall, 1952
Ziff-Davis Publishing Co.

	Good	Fine	Mint
1-Saunders painted-c	7.00	20.00	40.00

CLOSE SHAVES OF PAULINE PERIL, THE
June, 1970 - No. 4, March, 1971
Gold Key

	Good	Fine	Mint
1-4	.70	2.00	4.00

CLOWN COMIC BOOK
1945
Clown Comics

	Good	Fine	Mint
nn	1.50	4.00	8.00

CLOWN COMICS
May-June, 1946 - No. 3, Sept-Oct, 1946
Home Comics/Harvey Publications

	Good	Fine	Mint
1-3	1.50	4.00	8.00

CLUBHOUSE PRESENTS
June, 1956
Sussex Publ. Co./Magazine Enterprises

	Good	Fine	Mint
1	1.00	3.00	6.00

CLUBHOUSE RASCALS
June, 1956 - No. 2, Oct, 1956
Sussex Publ. Co. (Magazine Enterprises)

	Good	Fine	Mint
1,2: 2-The Brain app.	1.00	3.00	6.00

CLUB "16"
June, 1948 - No. 4, Dec, 1948
Famous Funnies

	Good	Fine	Mint
1	1.50	4.00	8.00
2-4	1.00	3.00	6.00

CLUE COMICS (Real Clue Crime V2No.4 on)
Jan, 1943 - No. 15(V2No.3), May, 1947

CLUE COMICS (continued)
Hillman Periodicals

	Good	Fine	Mint
1-Origin The Boy King, Nightmare, Micro-Face, Twilight, & Zippo	20.00	60.00	125.00
2	12.00	35.00	70.00
3	9.00	25.00	50.00
4	7.00	20.00	40.00
5	5.00	15.00	30.00
6-9	4.50	13.00	26.00
10-Origin The Gun Master	4.50	13.00	26.00
11	3.00	9.00	18.00
12-Origin Rackman	4.50	13.00	26.00
V2No.1-Nightro new origin; Iron Lady app.; Simon & Kirby-a	5.00	15.00	30.00
V2No.2-S&K-a(2), Infantino-a	5.00	15.00	30.00
V2No.3-S&K-a(3)	5.50	16.00	32.00

CLUTCHING HAND, THE
July-Aug, 1954
American Comics Group

	Good	Fine	Mint
1	3.00	8.00	16.00

CLYDE BEATTY
October, 1953 (84 pages)
Commodore Productions

	Good	Fine	Mint
1	4.50	13.00	26.00
. . . African Jungle Book('53)-Richfield Oil Co. giveaway	3.00	9.00	18.00

CLYDE CRASHCUP (TV)
Aug-Oct, 1963 - No. 5, Sept-Nov, 1964
Dell Publishing Co.

	Good	Fine	Mint
1-5: Written by John Stanley	.85	2.50	5.00

C-M-O COMICS
1942
Chicago Mail Order Co.

	Good	Fine	Mint
1-Invisible Terror, Super Ann, & Plymo the Rubber Man app. (All Centaur costume heroes)	3.50	10.00	20.00
2-Invisible Terror, Super Ann app.	3.00	9.00	18.00

COCOMALT BIG BOOK OF COMICS
1938 (Regular size; full color)
Harry 'A' Chesler

	Good	Fine	Mint
1-(Scarce)-Biro-c; Little Nemo, Dan Hastings; Guardineer-a	17.00	50.00	100.00

CODE NAME: ASSASSIN (See First Issue Special)

CODY OF THE PONY EXPRESS (See Colossal Feature Magazine)
Sept, 1950 - No. 3, Jan, 1951
Fox Features Syndicate

	Good	Fine	Mint
1-3 (actually No. 3-5)	2.50	7.00	14.00

CODY OF THE PONY EXPRESS (Buffalo Bill. . .) (Outlaws of the West No. 11 on; Formerly Bullseye) (See Colossal Features Magazine)
No. 8, Oct, 1955; No. 9, Jan, 1956; No. 10, June, 1956
Charlton Comics

	Good	Fine	Mint
8-Bullseye on splash pg; not S&K-a	1.00	3.00	6.00
9,10	.70	2.00	4.00

CO-ED ROMANCES
November, 1951
P. L. Publishing Co.

	Good	Fine	Mint
1	1.50	4.00	8.00

COLLECTORS ITEM CLASSICS (See Marvel Collectors Item Classics)

COLOSSAL FEATURES MAGAZINE (Formerly I Loved) (See Cody of the Pony Express)
No. 33, May, 1950 - No. 34, July, 1950; No. 3, Sept, 1950
Fox Features Syndicate

	Good	Fine	Mint
33,34-Cody of the Pony Express begins (based on serial)	2.50	7.00	14.00
3-Authentic criminal cases	3.00	9.00	18.00

COLOSSAL SHOW, THE (TV)
October, 1969
Gold Key

	Good	Fine	Mint
1	.85	2.50	5.00

COLOSSUS COMICS (Also see Green Giant & Motion Pic. Fun. Wkly)
March, 1940
Sun Publications (Funnies, Inc.?)

	Good	Fine	Mint
1-(Scarce)-Tulpa of Tsang (hero); Colossus app.	50.00	150.00	300.00

NOTE: *Cover by artist that drew Colossus in Green Giant Comics.*

COLT 45 (TV)
1958 - Nov-Jan, 1960; No. 4, Feb-Apr, 1960 - No. 9, May-July, 1961
Dell Publishing Co.

	Good	Fine	Mint
4-Color 924,1004,1058; No. 4,5,7-9	1.50	4.00	8.00
6-Toth-a	2.00	6.00	12.00

COLUMBIA, THE GEM OF THE COMICS
1943
William H. Wise Co.

	Good	Fine	Mint
1-Joe Palooka, Charlie Chan, Capt. Yank, Sparky Watts, Dixie Dugan begin	5.00	14.00	28.00
2-4	3.50	10.00	20.00

COMANCHE (See 4-Color No. 1350)

COMANCHEROS, THE (See 4-Color No. 1300)

COMBAT
June, 1952 - No. 11, April, 1953
Atlas Comics (ANC)

	Good	Fine	Mint
1	2.00	6.00	12.00
2,3,5-9,11	1.00	3.00	6.00
4-Krigstein-a	2.00	6.00	12.00
10-B&W and color illos. in **POP**	2.00	6.00	12.00

NOTE: *Combat Casey in 7,8,10,11.*

COMBAT
Oct-Nov, 1961 - No. 40, Oct, 1973 (no No.9)
Dell Publishing Co.

	Good	Fine	Mint
1	1.00	3.00	6.00
2-7: 4-JFK c/story	.55	1.60	3.20
8(4-6/63), 8(7-9/63)	.35	1.00	2.00
10-27: 23-Roosevelt & Churchill app		.50	1.00
28-40(reprints No. 1-14): 30-J. F. Kennedy c/story		.30	.60

NOTE: ***Glanzman** c/a-1-27.*

COMBAT CASEY (Formerly War Combat)
No. 6, Jan, 1953 - No. 34, July, 1957
Atlas Comics (SAI)

	Good	Fine	Mint
6	2.00	5.00	10.00
7,9	1.00	3.00	6.00
8-Used in **POP**, pg. 94	2.00	5.00	10.00
10,13-16,18,19-Violent art by R. Q. Sale; Battle Brady x-over No.10	1.50	4.00	8.00
11,12,20-34	.70	2.00	4.00
17-Opium mention story; R. Q. Sale-a	2.00	5.00	10.00

NOTE: ***Everett** a-6. **Heath** c-10, 30. **Powell** a-29(4), 30(2), 34. **Severin** c-26.*

COMBAT KELLY
Nov, 1951 - No. 44, Aug, 1957
Atlas Comics (SPI)

	Good	Fine	Mint
1-Heath-a	3.50	10.00	20.00
2-10	1.50	4.00	8.00

Clue Comics #1, © HILL

Colt .45 #5, © DELL

Combat #3, © DELL

Comic Album #18, © DELL

Comic Cavalcade #4, © DC

Comic Cavalcade #42, © DC

COMBAT KELLY (continued) — Good / Fine / Mint

11-Used in **POP**, pages 94,95 plus color illo. 2.00 6.00 12.00
12-Color illo. in **POP** 3.00 8.00 16.00
13-16 .70 2.00 4.00
17-Violent art by R. Q. Sale; Combat Casey app.
2.00 5.00 10.00
18-20,22-44: 18-Battle Brady app. 38-Green Berets story(8/56)
.85 2.50 5.00
21-Transvestite-c 1.00 3.00 6.00

NOTE: ***Berg*** *a-12-14, 17, 19-23, 25, 26, 28, 31-36, 42,43.* ***Colan*** *a-42.* ***Severin*** *c-42.* ***Whitney*** *a-5.*

COMBAT KELLY (and the Deadly Dozen)
June, 1972 - No. 9, Oct, 1973
Marvel Comics Group

1-Intro. Combat Kelly .60 1.20
2,3: 3-Origin Combat Kelly .40 .80
4-Sgt. Fury x-over .30 .60
5-9: 9-Deadly Dozen dies .30 .60

COMBINED OPERATIONS (See The Story of the Commandos)

COMEDY CARNIVAL
no date (1950's) (100 pages)
St. John Publishing Co.

nn-Contains rebound St. John comics 5.00 15.00 30.00

COMEDY COMICS (1st Series) (Daring Mystery No. 1-8)
(Margie No. 35 on)
No. 9, April, 1942 - No. 34, Fall, 1946
Timely Comics

9-(Scarce)-The Fin by Everett, Capt. Dash, Citizen V, & The Silver Scorpion app.; Wolverton-a; 1st app. Comedy Kid; satire on Hitler & Stalin 50.00 140.00 280.00
10-(Scarce)-Origin The Fourth Musketeer, Victory Boys; Monstro, the Mighty app. 30.00 90.00 180.00
11-Vagabond app. 10.00 30.00 60.00
12,13,15-32 2.00 6.00 12.00
14-Origin & 1st app. Super Rabbit 10.00 30.00 60.00
33-Kurtzman-a, 5 pgs. 3.50 10.00 20.00
34-Wolverton-a, 5 pgs. 5.00 14.00 28.00

COMEDY COMICS (2nd Series)
May, 1948 - No. 10, 1949
Marvel Comics (ACI)

1,3,4-Hedy, Tessie, Millie begin; Kurtzman's "Hey Look"
5.00 15.00 30.00
2 1.50 4.00 8.00
5-10 .85 2.50 5.00

COMIC ALBUM
Mar-May, 1958 - No. 18, June-Aug, 1962
Dell Publishing Co.

1-Donald Duck 2.00 5.00 10.00
2-Bugs Bunny .70 2.00 4.00
3-Donald Duck 1.50 4.00 8.00
4-Tom & Jerry .50 1.50 3.00
5-Woody Woodpecker .50 1.50 3.00
6-Bugs Bunny .50 1.50 3.00
7-Popeye .70 2.00 4.00
8-Tom & Jerry .50 1.50 3.00
9-Woody Woodpecker .50 1.50 3.00
10-Bugs Bunny .50 1.50 3.00
11-Popeye (9-11/60) .70 2.00 4.00
12-Tom & Jerry .50 1.50 3.00
13-Woody Woodpecker .50 1.50 3.00
14-Bugs Bunny .50 1.50 3.00
15-Popeye .70 2.00 4.00
16-Flintstones .50 1.50 3.00
17-Space Mouse .50 1.50 3.00
18-Three Stooges .85 2.50 5.00

COMIC BOOK (Also see Comics From Weatherbird)
1954 (Giveaway)
American Juniors Shoe

Contains a comic rebound with new cover. Several combinations possible. Contents determines price.

COMIC BOOKS (Series 1)
1950 (16 pgs.; 5¼x8½''; full color; bound at top; paper cover)
Metropolitan Printing Co. (Giveaway) — Good / Fine / Mint

1-Boots and Saddles; intro. The Masked Marshal
2.50 7.00 14.00
1-The Green Jet; Green Lama by Raboy 15.00 45.00 90.00
1-My Pal Dizzy (Teen-age) 1.50 4.00 8.00
1-New World; origin Atomaster (costumed hero)
3.50 10.00 20.00
1-Talullah (Teen-age) 1.50 4.00 8.00

COMIC CAPERS
1944 - No. 6, Summer, 1946
Red Circle Mag./Marvel Comics

1-Super Rabbit begins 2.00 6.00 12.00
2-6 1.50 4.00 8.00

COMIC CAVALCADE
Winter, 1942-43 - No. 63, June-July, 1954
(Contents change with No. 30, Dec-Jan, 1948 on)
All-American/National Periodical Publications

1-The Flash, Green Lantern, Wonder Woman, Wildcat, The Black Pirate by Moldoff (also No. 2), Ghost Patrol, and Red White & Blue begin; Scribbly app., Minute Movies 70.00 200.00 425.00
2-Mutt & Jeff begin; last Ghost Patrol & Black Pirate; Minute Movies
40.00 115.00 230.00
3-Hop Harrigan & Sargon, the Sorcerer begin; The King app.
30.00 80.00 175.00
4-The Gay Ghost, The King, Scribbly, & Red Tornado app.
24.00 70.00 150.00
5-Christmas-c 20.00 60.00 125.00
6-10: 7-Red Tornado & Black Pirate app.; last Scribbly. 9-Christmas-c 17.00 50.00 100.00
11,12,14-20: 12-Last Red White & Blue. 15-Johnny Peril begins, ends No. 29 14.00 40.00 80.00
13-Solomon Grundy app. 30.00 80.00 160.00
21-23 14.00 40.00 80.00
24-Solomon Grundy x-over in Green Lantern 15.00 45.00 90.00
25-29: 25-Black Canary app. 26-28-Johnny Peril app. 28-Last Mutt & Jeff. 29-Last Flash, Wonder Woman, Green Lantern & Johnny Peril 10.00 30.00 60.00
30-The Fox & the Crow begin 8.00 22.00 45.00
31-35: 31-Post-a 4.00 12.00 24.00
36-49 3.00 9.00 18.00
50-62(Scarce) 5.00 14.00 28.00
63(Rare) 8.00 24.00 48.00
Giveaway (1945, 16 pages, paper-c, in color)-Movie "Tomorrow The World" (Nazi theme) 14.00 40.00 80.00

NOTE: ***Toth*** *a-26-28(Green Lantern); c-23, 27. Atom app.-22, 23.*

COMIC COMICS
April, 1946 - No. 10, 1947
Fawcett Publications

1-Captain Kidd 2.50 7.00 14.00
2-10-Wolverton-a, 4 pgs. each 4.00 12.00 24.00

COMIC CUTS (Also see The Funnies)
5/19/34 - 7/28/34 (5 cents; 24 pages) (Tabloid size in full color)
(Not reprints; published weekly; created for newsstand sale)
H. L. Baker Co., Inc.

V1No.1 - V1No.7(6/30/34), V1No.8(7/14/34), V1No.9(7/28/34)-Idle Jack strips 5.50 16.00 32.00

COMIC LAND
March, 1946
Fact and Fiction

1-Sandusky & the Senator, Sam Stuper, Marvin the Great, Sir Pass-

COMIC LAND (continued) Good Fine Mint
er, Phineas Gruff app.; Irv Tirman & Perry Williams art
2.00 5.00 10.00

COMIC MONTHLY
Jan, 1922 - No. 7, July, 1922 (28 pgs.)(8½x9'')(10 cents)
(1st monthly newsstand comic publication) (Reprints 1921 B&W dailies)
Embee Dist. Co.

	Good	Fine	Mint
1-Polly & Her Pals	30.00	80.00	160.00
2-Mike & Ike	5.50	16.00	32.00
3-S'Matter, Pop?	5.50	16.00	32.00
4-Barney Google	10.00	30.00	60.00
5-Tillie the Toiler	8.00	24.00	48.00
6-Indoor Sports	4.00	12.00	24.00
7-Little Jimmy	4.00	12.00	24.00

COMIC PAGES (Formerly Funny Picture Stories)
V3No.4, July, 1939 - V3No.6, Dec, 1939
Centaur Publications

	Good	Fine	Mint
V3No.4-6	5.00	14.00	30.00

COMIC PAINTING AND CRAYONING BOOK
1917 (32 pages)(10x13½'')(No price on cover)
Saalfield Publ. Co.

	Good	Fine	Mint
Tidy Teddy by F. M. Follett, Clarence the Cop, Mr. & Mrs. Butt-In. Regular comic stories to read or color	5.00	15.00	30.00

COMICS (See All Good)

COMICS, THE
March, 1937 - No. 11, 1938 (Newspaper strip reprints)
Dell Publishing Co.

	Good	Fine	Mint
1-Wash Tubbs, Tom Mix, Tom Beatty, & Arizona Kid begin	14.00	40.00	80.00
2	8.00	24.00	48.00
3-11: 3-Alley Oop	7.00	20.00	40.00

COMICS CALENDAR, THE (The 1946. . .)
1946 (116 pgs.; 25 cents)(Stapled at top)
True Comics Press (ordered through the mail)

	Good	Fine	Mint
(Rare) Has a ''strip'' story for every day of the year in color	10.00	30.00	60.00

COMICS DIGEST (Pocket size)
Winter, 1942-43 (100 pages) (Black & White)
Parents' Magazine Institute

	Good	Fine	Mint
1-Reprints from True Comics (non-fiction World War II stories)	3.00	8.00	16.00

COMIC SELECTIONS (Shoe store giveaway)
1944-46 (Reprints from Calling All Girls, True Comics, True Aviation, & Real Heroes)
Parents' Magazine Press

	Good	Fine	Mint
1	1.00	3.00	6.00
2-5	.85	2.50	5.00

COMICS FOR KIDS
1945
London Publishing Co./Timely

	Good	Fine	Mint
1,2	1.50	4.00	8.00

COMICS FROM WEATHER BIRD (Also see Comic Book, Free Comics to You, Weather Bird & Edward's Shoes)
1954 - 1957 (Giveaway)
Weather Bird Shoes

Contains a comic bound with new cover. Many combinations possible. Contents would determine price. Some issues do not contain complete comics, but only parts of comics. Value equals 40 to 60 percent of contents.

COMICS HITS
Oct, 1951 - No. 61, Oct, 1952
Harvey Publications

	Good	Fine	Mint
51-The Phantom	7.00	20.00	40.00
52-Steve Canyon	6.00	18.00	36.00
53-Mandrake the Magician	7.00	20.00	40.00
54-Tim Tyler's Tales of Jungle Terror	6.00	18.00	36.00
55-Mary Worth	3.00	9.00	18.00
56-The Phantom; bondage-c	6.00	18.00	36.00
57-Rip Kirby -''Kidnap Racket''; entire book by Alex Raymond	10.00	30.00	60.00
58-Girls in White	3.00	9.00	18.00
59-Tales of the Invisible Scarlet O'Neil	7.00	20.00	40.00
60-Paramount Animated Comics No.1(2nd app. Baby Huey)	15.00	45.00	90.00
61-Casper the Friendly Ghost; 1st Harvey Casper	14.00	42.00	85.00

COMICS MAGAZINE, THE (Funny Pages No. 6 on)
Apr, 1936 - No. 5, Sept, 1936 (Paper covers)
Quality Comics Group

	Good	Fine	Mint
1: Federal Agent by Siegel & Shuster; 1pg. Kelly-a; Dr. Mystic begins	20.00	60.00	120.00
2: Siegel & Shuster-a; 1pg. Kelly-a	12.00	35.00	70.00
3-5	10.00	30.00	60.00

COMICS MAN, THE
1937 (One Shot)
Centaur/Comics Corp.?

	Good	Fine	Mint
1	10.00	30.00	60.00

COMICS NOVEL (Anarcho, Dictator of Death)
1947
Fawcett Publications

	Good	Fine	Mint
1-All Radar	10.00	30.00	60.00

COMICS ON PARADE (No. 30 on, continuation of Single Series)
April, 1938 - No. 104, Feb, 1955
United Features Syndicate

	Good	Fine	Mint
1-Tarzan by Foster; Captain & the Kids, Little Mary Mixup, Abbie & Slats, Ella Cinders, Broncho Bill, Li'l Abner begin	50.00	140.00	280.00
2	25.00	70.00	140.00
3	17.00	50.00	100.00
4,5	10.00	30.00	60.00
6-10	8.00	24.00	48.00
11-20	7.00	20.00	40.00
21-29: 22-Son of Tarzan begins. 29-Last Tarzan issue	6.00	18.00	36.00
30-Li'l Abner	4.00	12.00	24.00
31-The Captain & the Kids	3.00	8.00	16.00
32-Nancy & Fritzi Ritz	1.75	5.00	10.00
33-Li'l Abner	4.00	12.00	24.00
34-The Captain & the Kids	2.50	7.00	14.00
35-Nancy & Fritzi Ritz	1.75	5.00	10.00
36-Li'l Abner	4.00	12.00	24.00
37-The Captain & the Kids	2.00	6.00	12.00
38-Nancy & Fritzi Ritz; infinity-c	1.75	5.00	10.00
39-Li'l Abner	4.00	12.00	24.00
40-The Captain & the Kids	2.00	6.00	12.00
41-Nancy & Fritzi Ritz	1.50	4.00	8.00
42-Li'l Abner	3.50	10.00	20.00
43-The Captain & the Kids	2.00	6.00	12.00
44-Nancy & Fritzi Ritz	1.50	4.00	8.00
45-Li'l Abner	3.50	10.00	20.00
46-The Captain & the Kids	2.00	6.00	12.00
47-Nancy & Fritzi Ritz	1.50	4.00	8.00
48-Li'l Abner	3.50	10.00	20.00
49-The Captain & the Kids	2.00	6.00	12.00
50-Nancy & Fritzi Ritz	1.50	4.00	8.00

Comics Hits #57, © HARV

The Comics Magazine #2, © QUA

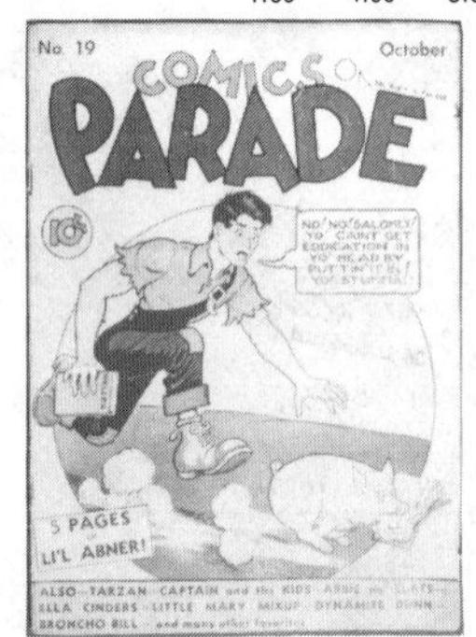

Comics On Parade #19, © UFS

Comics On Parade #59, © UFS

Comic Story Paint Book #1055, © S. Lowe

Complete Comics #2, © MCG

COMICS ON PARADE (continued)

	Good	Fine	Mint
51-Li'l Abner	2.50	7.00	14.00
52-The Captain & the Kids	1.50	4.00	8.00
53-Nancy & Fritzi Ritz	1.50	4.00	8.00
54-Li'l Abner	2.50	7.00	14.00
55-Nancy & Fritzi Ritz	1.50	4.00	8.00
56-The Captain & the Kids (r-/Sparkler)	1.50	4.00	8.00
57-Nancy & Fritzi Ritz	1.50	4.00	8.00
58-Li'l Abner	2.50	7.00	14.00
59-The Captain & the Kids	1.50	4.00	8.00
60-70-Nancy & Fritzi Ritz	1.50	4.00	8.00
71-76-Nancy only	1.00	3.00	6.00
77-104-Nancy & Sluggo	1.00	3.00	6.00
Special Issue, 7/46; Summer, 1948 - The Capt. & the Kids app.	1.00	3.00	6.00
Bound Volume (Very Rare) includes No. 1-12; bound by publisher in pictorial comic boards & distributed at the 1939 World's Fair and through mail order from ads in comic books (Also see Tip Top)	100.00	280.00	560.00

NOTE: *Li'l Abner reprinted from Tip Top.*

COMICS READING LIBRARIES (Educational Series)
1973, 1977, 1979 (36 pages in color) (Giveaways)
King Features (Charlton Publ.)

	Good	Fine	Mint
R-01-Tiger, Quincy		.15	.30
R-02-Beetle Bailey, Blondie & Popeye		.15	.30
R-03-Blondie, Beetle Baily		.30	.60
R-04-Tim Tyler's Luck, Felix the Cat		.30	.60
R-05-Quincy, Henry		.15	.30
R-06-The Phantom, Mandrake	.35	1.00	2.00
1977 reprint(R-04)	.20	.60	1.20
R-07-Popeye, Little King	.25	.70	1.40
R-08-Prince Valiant(Foster), Flash Gordon	4.00	12.00	24.00
1977 reprint	1.50	4.00	8.00
R-09-Hagar the Horrible, Boner's Ark		.15	.30
R-10-Redeye, Tiger		.15	.30
R-11-Blondie, Hi & Lois		.25	.50
R-12-Popeye-Swee'pea, Brutus		.30	.60
R-13-Beetle Bailey, Little King		.15	.30
R-14-Quincy-Hamlet		.15	.30
R-15-The Phantom, The Genius	.35	1.00	2.00
R-16-Flash Gordon, Mandrake	4.00	12.00	24.00
1977 reprint	1.50	4.00	8.00
Other 1977 editions....		.15	.30
1979 editions(68pgs.)		.20	.40

NOTE: *Above giveaways available with purchase of $45.00 in merchandise. Used as a reading skills aid for small children.*

COMICS REVUE
June, 1947 - No. 5, Jan, 1948
St. John Publ. Co. (United Features Synd.)

	Good	Fine	Mint
1-Ella Cinders & Blackie	2.00	5.00	10.00
2-Hap Hopper (7/47)	2.00	5.00	10.00
3-Iron Vic (8/47)	1.20	3.50	7.00
4-Ella Cinders (9/47)	1.20	3.50	7.00
5-Gordo No. 1 (1/48)	1.20	3.50	7.00

COMIC STORY PAINT BOOK
1943 (68 pages) (Large size)
Samuel Lowe Co.

	Good	Fine	Mint
1055-Captain Marvel & a Captain Marvel Jr. story to read & color; 3 panels in color per page (reprints)	20.00	60.00	125.00

COMIX BOOK (B&W Magazine - $1.00)
1974 - No. 5, 1976
Marvel Comics Group/Krupp Comics Works No. 4

	Good	Fine	Mint
1-Underground comic artists; 2 pg. Wolverton-a	.50	1.50	3.00
2	.40	1.20	2.40
3-Low distribution (3/75)	.50	1.50	3.00
4(2/76), 4(5/76), 5	.40	1.20	2.40

NOTE: *Print run No. 1-3: 200-250M; No. 4&5: 10M each.*

COMIX INTERNATIONAL
July, 1974 - No. 5, Spring, 1977 (Full color)
Warren Magazines

	Good	Fine	Mint
1-Low distribution; all Corben remainders from Warren	3.50	10.00	20.00
2-Wood, Wrightson-r	1.20	3.50	7.00
3-5	.70	2.00	4.00

NOTE: *No. 4 had two printings with extra* **Corben** *story in one.*

COMMANDER BATTLE AND THE ATOMIC SUB
July-Aug, 1954 - No. 7, July-Aug, 1955
American Comics Group (Titan Publ. Co.)

	Good	Fine	Mint
1 (3-D effect)	6.00	18.00	36.00
2-7: 3-H-Bomb-c. 7-Landau-a	3.00	8.00	16.00

COMMANDMENTS OF GOD
1954, 1958
Catechetical Guild

	Good	Fine	Mint
300-Same contents in both editions; different-c	3.00	8.00	16.00

COMMANDO ADVENTURES
June, 1957 - No. 2, Aug, 1957
Atlas Comics (MMC)

	Good	Fine	Mint
1,2-Severin-c; 2-Drucker-a	1.20	3.50	7.00

COMMANDO YANK (See Mighty Midget Comics)

COMPLETE BOOK OF COMICS AND FUNNIES
1944 (196 pages) (One Shot)
Better Publications

	Good	Fine	Mint
1-Origin Brad Spencer, Wonderman; The Magnet, The Silver Knight by Kinstler, & Zudo the Jungle Boy app.	7.00	20.00	40.00

COMPLETE BOOK OF TRUE CRIME COMICS
No date (Mid 1940's) (132 pages) (25 cents)
William H. Wise & Co.

	Good	Fine	Mint
nn-Contains Crime Does Not Pay rebound (includes No. 22)	25.00	75.00	150.00

COMPLETE COMICS (Formerly Amazing No. 1)
Winter, 1944-45
Marvel Comics

	Good	Fine	Mint
2-The Destroyer, The Whizzer, The Young Allies & Sergeant Dix	25.00	75.00	150.00

COMPLETE LOVE MAGAZINE (Formerly a pulp with same title)
V26No.2, May-June, 1951 - V32No.4(No.191), Sept, 1956
Ace Periodicals (Periodical House)

	Good	Fine	Mint
V26No.2-Painted-c	1.20	3.50	7.00
V26No.3-6(2/52), V27No.1-6	.85	2.50	5.00
V28No.1-6, V29No.1-6	.85	2.50	5.00
V30No.1(No.176, 4/54) - V30No.6(No.181, 1/55)	.85	2.50	5.00
V31No.1(No.182, 3/55) - V31No.6(No.187, 1/56)	.50	1.50	3.00
V32No.1(No.188, 3/56) - V32No.4(No.191, 9/56)	.50	1.50	3.00

NOTE: *Photo-c-179.*

COMPLETE MYSTERY (True Complete Mystery No. 5 on)
Aug, 1948 - No. 4, Feb, 1949 (Full length stories)
Marvel Comics (PrPI)

	Good	Fine	Mint
1-Seven Dead Men	5.00	15.00	30.00
2-Jigsaw of Doom!	4.00	12.00	24.00
3-Fear in the Night; Burgos-a	4.00	12.00	24.00
4-A Squealer Dies Fast	4.00	12.00	24.00

COMPLETE ROMANCE
1949
Avon Periodicals

	Good	Fine	Mint
1-(Scarce)-Reprinted as Women to Love	17.00	50.00	100.00

COMPLIMENTARY COMICS
No date (1950's)
Sales Promotion Publ. (Giveaway)

	Good	Fine	Mint
1-Strongman by Powell, 3 stories	3.50	10.00	20.00

CONAN (See Chamber of Darkness No. 4, King Conan, Savage Sword of Conan, and Savage Tales)

CONAN, THE BARBARIAN
Oct, 1970 - Present
Marvel Comics Group

	Good	Fine	Mint
1-Origin Conan by Barry Smith; Kull app.	12.00	32.00	65.00
2	5.00	14.00	30.00
3-(low distribution in some areas)	7.00	20.00	46.00
4,5	4.00	12.00	24.00
6-10: 10-52 pgs.; Black Knight-r; Kull by Severin app.	3.00	8.00	16.00
11-13: 12-Wrightson c-inks	2.00	6.00	12.00
14,15-Elric app.	3.00	8.00	16.00
16-20: 16-Conan reprint from Savage Tales No. 1	1.50	4.50	9.00
21,22,24: 22-has r-from No. 1. 24-Last Smith issue; Red Sonja's 2nd app.	1.40	4.00	8.00
23-1st app. Red Sonja	2.00	5.00	10.00
25-Buscema-a begins	1.00	3.00	6.00
26-30	.50	1.50	3.00
31-36,38-40	.40	1.20	2.40
37-Adams c/a	.80	2.40	4.80
41-43,46,49	.30	.90	1.80
44,45-Adams inks, c-45; Red Sonja app. No. 43,44,48	.40	1.10	2.20
47-Wood-a(r)	.30	.90	1.80
48-Origin retold	.30	.90	1.80
50	.40	1.20	2.40
51-56,60	.30	.80	1.60
57-Ploog-a	.30	.80	1.60
58-1st Belit app.	.40	1.20	2.40
59-Origin Belit		.50	1.00
61-70: 64 r-/Savage Tales No. 5; Starlin-a on Conan		.50	1.00
71-80: 78-r-/Savage Sword of Conan No. 1		.50	1.00
81-99: 87-R-/Savage Sword of Conan No. 3		.50	1.00
100-Death of Belit	.40	1.20	2.40
101-114,117-129		.40	.80
115-double size	.30	.80	1.60
116-Adams c/a		.40	.80

NOTE: ***Austin*** *a-125, 126; c-125i, 126i.* ***Buckler*** *a-40; c-40.* ***Buscema*** *a-25-36, 38, 39, 41-56, 58-63, 65-68, 70-78, 83-91, 93-126; c-26, 36, 44, 46, 52, 56, 58, 59, 64, 72, 78, 79, 83-91, 93-102, 105-26.* ***Chaykin*** *a-79-83.* ***Kane*** *a-12, 127, 128, Giant Size 1-4; c-12p, 17(w/****Brunner****), 18, 23, 25, 27-32, 34, 35, 38, 39, 41-43, 45-51, 53-55, 57, 60-63, 65-71, 127, 128, Giant Size 1, 3, 4.* ***Gil Kane*** *a/c-129.* ***Smith*** *a-1-16, 19-21, 23, 24; layouts only-21; c-1-11, 13-16, 19-22, 24.* ***Sutton*** *inks-Giant Size 1-3. Issues No. 3-5, 7-9, 11, 16-18, 21, 23, 25, 27-30, 35, 37, 38, 42, 45, 52, 57, 58, 65, 69-71, 73, 79-83, 99, 100, 104, 114, Annual 2 have original Robert E. Howard stories adapted. Issues No. 32-34 adapted from Norvell Page's novel* ***Flame Winds.***

	Good	Fine	Mint
Giant Size 1(9/74)-Smith r-/No. 3; start adaptation of Howard's "Hour of the Dragon"	.70	2.00	4.00
Giant Size 2(12/74)-Smith r-/No. 5; Sutton-a; Buscema-c	.70	2.00	4.00
Giant Size 3(1975-Smith r-/No. 6; Sutton-a), Giant Size 4(6/75; Smith r-/No. 7), Giant Size 5('75; Smith r-/No. 14,15; Kirby-c)	.30	.90	1.80
King Size 1(9/73-35 cents)-Smith r-/No. 2,4; Smith-c	1.00	3.00	6.00
Annual 2(6/76)-50 cents; new stories	.40	1.20	2.40
Annual 3(2/78)-reprints	.30	.80	1.60
Annual 4(10/78), 5(12/79)-Buscema-a/part-c	.25	.70	1.40
Annual 6(10/81)-Kane c/a	.25	.70	1.40

CONDORMAN
Oct, 1981 - No. 3
Whitman Publ.

	Good	Fine	Mint
1-3-Movie adaptation		.30	.60

CONFESSIONS ILLUSTRATED (Magazine)
Jan-Feb, 1956 - No. 2, Spring, 1956
E. C. Comics

	Good	Fine	Mint
1-Craig, Kamen, Wood, Orlando-a	5.00	15.00	30.00
2-Craig, Crandall, Kamen, Orlando-a	7.00	20.00	40.00

CONFESSION OF LOVE
No. 2, July, 1950 (25 cents; 132 pgs. in color)(7¼x5¼'')
Artful Publ.

	Good	Fine	Mint
2-Art & text; Bakerish-a	7.00	20.00	40.00

CONFESSIONS OF LOVE (Confessions of Romance No. 7)
No. 11, July, 1952 - No. 6, Aug, 1953
Star Publications

	Good	Fine	Mint
11	2.50	7.00	14.00
12,13-Disbrow-a	3.00	9.00	18.00
14, 6	2.00	6.00	12.00
4-Disbrow-a	3.00	8.00	16.00
5-Wood/?-a	4.00	12.00	24.00

NOTE: *All have* ***L. B. Cole*** *covers.*

CONFESSIONS OF ROMANCE (Formerly Confessions of Love)
No. 7, Nov, 1953 - No. 11, Nov, 1954
Star Publications

	Good	Fine	Mint
7,8	3.00	8.00	14.00
9-Wood-a	6.00	18.00	36.00
10,11-Disbrow-a	3.00	9.00	18.00

NOTE: ***L. B. Cole*** *covers on all.*

CONFESSIONS OF THE LOVELORN (Formerly Lovelorn)
No. 52, Aug, 1954 - No. 114, June, 1960
American Comics Group (Regis Publ./Best Synd. Features)

	Good	Fine	Mint
52-54 (3-D effect)	3.50	10.00	20.00
55,57-90	1.20	3.50	7.00
56-Communist propaganda sty, 10pgs.	1.50	4.50	9.00
91-Williamson-a	3.50	10.00	20.00
92-114	.85	2.50	5.00

NOTE: ***Whitney*** *a-most issues. 106,107-painted-c.*

CONFIDENTIAL DIARY (Formerly High School Confidential Diary; Three Nurses No. 18 on)
No. 13, July, 1962 - No. 17, March, 1963
Charlton Comics

	Good	Fine	Mint
13-17	.35	1.00	2.00

CONGO BILL (See Action Comics)
Aug-Sept, 1954 - No. 7, Aug-Sept, 1955
National Periodical Publications

	Good	Fine	Mint
1-(Scarce)	9.00	26.00	60.00
2-7 (Scarce)	8.00	22.00	50.00

CONNECTICUT YANKEE, A (See King Classics)

CONQUEROR, THE (See 4-Color No. 690)

CONQUEROR COMICS
Winter, 1945
Albrecht Publishing Co.

	Good	Fine	Mint
nn	2.00	6.00	12.00

CONQUEST
1953 (6 cents)
Store Comics

	Good	Fine	Mint
1-Richard the Lion Hearted, Beowulf, Swamp Fox	1.50	4.00	8.00

Conan The Barbarian #2, © MCG

Confessions Of Love #6, © STAR

Confessions Of Romance #8, © STAR

Contact Comics #1, © Aviation Press

Coo Coo Comics #13, © STD

The Cougar #1, © ATLAS

CONQUEST
Spring, 1955
Famous Funnies

	Good	Fine	Mint
1-Crandall-a, 1 pg.; contains contents of 1953 issue	2.00	5.00	10.00

CONTACT COMICS
July, 1944 - No. 12, May, 1946
Aviation Press

	Good	Fine	Mint
nn-Black Venus, Flamingo, Golden Eagle, Tommy Tomahawk begin	5.50	16.00	32.00
2-5: 3-Last Flamingo. 3,4-Black Venus by L. B. Cole. 5-The Phantom Flyer app.	7.00	20.00	40.00
6,11-Kurtzman's Black Venus; 11-Last Golden Eagle, last Tommy Tomahawk; Palais-a, 4 pgs; Feldstein-a	8.00	24.00	48.00
7-10,12: 12-Sky Rangers, Air Kids, Ace Diamond app.	5.50	16.00	32.00

NOTE: ***L. B. Cole*** *a-9; c-1-12.* ***Giunta*** *a-3.* ***Infantino*** *a-4.* ***Palais*** *a-11,12.*

CONTEMPORARY MOTIVATORS
1977 - 1978 (5-3/8x8'')(31 pgs., B&W, $1.45)
Pendelum Press

14-3002 The Caine Mutiny; 14-3010 Banner in the Sky; 14-3029 God Is My Co-Pilot; 14-3037 Guadalcanal Diary; 14-3045 Hiroshima; 14-3053 Hot Rod; 14-3061 Just Dial a Number; 14-307x Star Wars; 14-3088 The Diary of Anne Frank; 14-3096 Lost Horizon — 1.50

NOTE: *Also see Now Age III. Above may have been dist. the same.*

COO COO COMICS (. . . the Bird Brain No. 57 on)
Oct, 1942 - 1952
Nedor Comics/Standard (Animated Cartoons)

	Good	Fine	Mint
1-Super Mouse origin	3.50	10.00	20.00
2-10	1.20	3.50	7.00
11-33	.85	2.50	5.00
34-40,43-46,48-50-Text illos by Frazetta in all	2.00	6.00	12.00
41-Frazetta-a(2)	6.00	18.00	36.00
42,47-Frazetta-a & text illos.	5.00	14.00	28.00
51-62	.70	2.00	4.00

"COOKIE"
April, 1946 - No. 55, Aug-Sept, 1955
Michel Publ./American Comics Group(Regis Publ.)

	Good	Fine	Mint
1	2.00	6.00	12.00
2-10	.85	2.50	5.00
11-20	.50	1.50	3.00
21-34,36-55	.35	1.00	2.00
35-Starlett O'Hara story	.40	1.20	2.40

COOL CAT (Formerly Black Magic)
V8No.6, Mar-Apr, 1962 - V9No.2, July-Aug, 1962
Prize Publications

	Good	Fine	Mint
V8No.6, No No.(V9No.1), V9No.2	.70	2.00	4.00

COPPER CANYON (See Fawcett Movie Comics)

CORKY & WHITE SHADOW (See 4-Color No. 707)

CORLISS ARCHER (See Meet. . .)

CORPORAL RUSTY DUGAN (See Rusty Dugan)

CORPSES OF DR. SACOTTI, THE (See Ideal a Classical Comic)

CORSAIR, THE (See A-1 Comics No. 5,7,10)

COSMO CAT
July-Aug, 1946 - 1949; 1959
Fox Publications/Green Publ. Co./Norlen Mag.

	Good	Fine	Mint
1	2.00	6.00	12.00
2-10	1.50	4.00	8.00
2-4(1957-Green Publ. Co.)	.70	2.00	4.00
2-4(1959-Norlen Mag.)	.50	1.50	3.00
I.W. Reprint No. 1	.35	1.00	2.00

COSMO THE MERRY MARTIAN
Sept, 1958 - No. 6, Oct, 1959
Archie Publications (Radio Comics)

	Good	Fine	Mint
1-Bob White-a in all	3.50	10.00	20.00
2-6	2.50	7.00	14.00

COTTON WOODS (See 4-Color No. 837)

COUGAR, THE
April, 1975 - No. 2, June, 1975
Seaboard Periodicals (Atlas)

	Good	Fine	Mint
1-Adkins-a		.45	.90
2-Origin		.30	.60

COUNTDOWN (See Movie Classics)

COUNT OF MONTE CRISTO, THE (See 4-Color No. 794)

COURAGE COMICS
1945
J. Edward Slavin

	Good	Fine	Mint
1,2,77	1.00	3.00	6.00

COURTSHIP OF EDDIE'S FATHER (TV)
Jan, 1970 - No. 2, May, 1970
Dell Publishing Co.

	Good	Fine	Mint
1,2	.70	2.00	4.00

COVERED WAGONS, HO (See 4-Color No. 814)

COWBOY ACTION (Western Thrillers No. 1-4; Quick Trigger Western No. 12 on)
No. 5, March, 1955 - No. 11, March, 1956
Atlas Comics (ACI)

	Good	Fine	Mint
5-10	1.20	3.50	7.00
11-Williamson-a, 4 pgs., Baker-a	3.00	9.00	18.00

COWBOY COMICS (. . Stories No. 14, formerly Star Rangers)
No. 13, July, 1938 - No. 14, Sept?, 1938
Centaur Publishing Co.

	Good	Fine	Mint
13-(Rare)-Gustavson-a	12.00	35.00	80.00
14	8.00	22.00	48.00

COWBOY IN AFRICA (TV)
March, 1968
Gold Key

	Good	Fine	Mint
1(10219-803)	1.00	3.00	6.00

COWBOY LOVE (Becomes Range Busters?)
July, 1949 - V2No.8, 1955
Fawcett Publications/Charlton Comics

	Good	Fine	Mint
V1No.1-(52 pgs.)	3.00	8.00	16.00
V1No.2,3	1.50	4.00	8.00
V1No.4,6-27, V1No.28,29(4/55), 30	.85	2.50	5.00
5-Photo-c; Hopalong Cassidy photo back cover	1.20	3.50	7.00
V2No.7-Williamson/Evans-a	3.50	10.00	20.00
V2No.8	.85	2.50	5.00

NOTE: ***Powell*** *a-10. Photo c-6.*

COWBOY ROMANCES (Young Men No. 4 on)
Oct, 1949 - No. 3, Mar, 1950
Marvel Comics (IPC)

	Good	Fine	Mint
1-Photo-c	4.00	12.00	24.00
2,3	3.00	8.00	16.00

COWBOYS 'N' INJUNS COMICS
1946 - 1952
Compix/Magazine Enterprises

	Good	Fine	Mint
1	.85	2.50	5.00

COWBOYS 'N' INJUNS COMICS (continued) — Good / Fine / Mint

2-5 .60 1.80 3.60
6(A-1 23), 7(A-1 41), 8(A-1 48) .85 2.50 5.00
I.W. Reprint No. 1,7 (reprinted in Canada by Superior, No. 7)
.35 1.00 2.00

COWBOY WESTERN COMICS (Formerly Jack In The Box; Becomes Space Western No. 40-45 & Wild Bill Hickok & Jingles No. 68 on; title: . . . Heroes No. 47; Cowboy Western No. 48 on)
No. 17, 1948 - No. 67, Jan, 1958 (nn 40-45)
Charlton(Capitol Stories)

17,20 1.50 4.00 8.00
18-Orlando c/a, 4pgs. 2.00 5.00 10.00
19-Orlando c/a 2.00 5.00 10.00
21-25,28-30 1.20 3.50 7.00
26,27-Photo-c 2.00 5.00 10.00
31-39,46-50 (nn 40-45) .85 2.50 5.00
51-66 .70 2.00 4.00
67-Williamson/Torres-a, 5 pgs. 4.00 12.00 24.00
NOTE: Many issues trimmed 1'' shorter.

COWGIRL ROMANCES (Formerly Jeanie)
No. 28, Jan, 1950
Marvel Comics (CCC)

28(No.1)-Photo-c 4.00 12.00 24.00

COWGIRL ROMANCES
1950 - No. 12, Winter, 1952-53
Fiction House Magazines

1-Kamen-a 6.00 18.00 36.00
2-5 3.00 9.00 18.00
6-9,11,12 2.50 7.00 14.00
10-Frazetta/Williamson-a; Kamen/Baker-a 10.00 30.00 60.00

COW PUNCHER (. . . Comics)
Jan, 1947 - 1949
Avon Periodicals

1-Clint Cortland, Texas Ranger, Kit West, Pioneer Queen begin; Kubert-a; Alabam stories begin 10.00 30.00 60.00
2-Kubert, Kamen/Feldstein-a; Kamen bondage-c
9.00 25.00 50.00
3-5,7: 3-Kiefer story 7.00 20.00 40.00
6-Opium drug mention story; bondage, headlight-c
8.00 24.00 48.00

COWPUNCHER
1953 (nn) (Reprints Avon's No. 2)
Realistic Publications

Kubert-a 3.50 10.00 20.00

COWSILLS, THE (See Harvey Pop Comics)

CRACKAJACK FUNNIES (Giveaway)
1937 (32 pgs.; full size; soft cover; full color)(Before No. 1?)
Malto-Meal

Features Dan Dunn, G-Man, Speed Bolton, Freckles, Buck Jones, Clyde Beatty, The Nebbs, Major Hoople, Wash Tubbs
20.00 60.00 120.00

CRACKAJACK FUNNIES
June, 1938 - No. 43, Jan, 1942
Dell Publishing Co.

1-Dan Dunn, Freckles, Myra North, Wash Tubbs, Apple Mary, The Nebbs, Don Winslow, Tom Mix, Buck Jones begin
35.00 100.00 200.00
2 17.00 50.00 100.00
3 12.00 35.00 70.00
4,5 9.00 26.00 52.00
6-10: 9-Red Ryder begins 7.00 20.00 40.00
11-14 6.00 17.00 34.00
15-Tarzan text feature begins; not in No. 26,35

Good / Fine / Mint
7.00 20.00 40.00
16-24 5.00 15.00 30.00
25-The Owl begins; in new costume No. 26 by Frank Thomas
12.00 35.00 70.00
26-30 9.00 26.00 52.00
31-Owl covers begin 7.00 20.00 40.00
32-Origin Owl Girl 9.00 26.00 52.00
33-39: 36-Last Tarzan ish. 39-Andy Panda begins
6.00 17.00 35.00
40-43: 42-Last Owl cover 5.00 15.00 30.00
NOTE: ***McWilliams*** *art in most issues.*

CRACK COMICS (. . . Western No. 63 on)
May, 1940 - No. 62, Sept, 1949
Quality Comics Group

1-Origin The Black Condor by Lou Fine, Madame Fatal, Red Torpedo & The Space Legion; The Clock, Alias the Spider, Wizard Wells, & Ned Bryant begin; Powell-a 120.00 320.00 650.00
2 50.00 150.00 300.00
3 45.00 130.00 260.00
4 40.00 110.00 225.00
5-10: 10-Tor, the Magic Master begins 30.00 90.00 180.00
11-18-Last Fine Black Condor 25.00 75.00 150.00
19,20 12.00 36.00 75.00
21-26 11.00 32.00 65.00
27-Origin Captain Triumph by Alfred Andriola (Kerry Drake artist)
20.00 60.00 120.00
28-30 10.00 28.00 55.00
31-39 5.00 15.00 30.00
40-47 3.50 11.00 22.00
48-57,60-Capt. Triumph by Crandall 4.00 12.00 24.00
58,59,61,62 3.00 9.00 18.00
NOTE: *Black Condor by* ***Fine****: No. 1,2,4-6,8,10-18; by* ***Sultan****: No. 3,7,22; by* ***Fugitani****: No. 9, 19.* ***Guardineer*** *a-17.* ***Gustavson*** *a-17.* ***McWilliams*** *art-No. 15-21, 23-27.*

CRACKED (Magazine) (See Biggest Greatest . . .) (Satire)
Feb-Mar, 1958 - Present
Major Magazines

1-One pg. Williamson 4.00 12.00 24.00
2-1st Shut-Ups & Bonus Cut-Outs 2.00 6.00 12.00
3-6 1.00 3.00 6.00
7-Reprints 1st 6 covers on cover .70 2.00 4.00
8-12,14-17,19,20: 10-Last ish edited by Sol Brodsky
.70 2.00 4.00
13-(nn, 3/60) .50 1.50 3.00
18-(nn, 2/61) .35 1.00 2.00
21-27(11/62) .30 .80 1.60
27(No.28, 2/63; misnumbered) .30 .80 1.60
29(5/63), 30 .30 .80 1.60
31-60 .60 1.20
61-98,100 .40 .80
99-Alfred E. Neuman featured on cover .40 .80
101-145 .30 .60
Biggest . . . (Winter, 1977) .60 1.20
Biggest, Greatest . . . nn('65) .60 1.20
Biggest, Greatest . . . 2('66)-No.12('76) .40 .80
Extra Special . . . 1('76), 2('76) .40 .80
Giant . . . nn('65) .30 .80 1.60
Giant . . . 2('66)-12('76), nn(9/77),
King Sized . . . 1('67) .40 .80
King Sized . . . 2('68)-11('77) .30 .60
Super . . . 1('68) .40 .80
Super . . . 2('69)-10('77): 2-Spoof on Beatles movie by Severin
.30 .60

NOTE: ***Burgos*** *a-1-10.* ***Davis*** *a-5, 11-18, 24, 80; c-12-14, 16.* ***Elder*** *a-5, 6, 10-13; c-10.* ***Everett*** *a-1-10, 23-25, 61; c-1.* ***Heath*** *a-1-3, 6, 13, 14, 17, 110; c-6.* ***Jaffee*** *a-5, 6.* ***Morrow*** *a-8-10.* ***Reinman (Paul)*** *a-1-4.* ***Severin*** *a-in most all issues No. 1 on.* ***Shores*** *a-3-7.*

Cowboy Western #28, © CC

Crackajack Funnies #8, © DELL

Crack Comics #46, © QUA

Crack Western #68, © QUA

Creatures On The Loose #22, © MCG

Creepy #1, © WP

CRACKED (continued)
***Stone** a-16, 17. **Torres** a-7-10. **Ward** a-143, 144, 156. **Williamson** a-1 (1 pg.). **Wolverton** a-10 (2 pgs.),Giant nn('65).*

CRACKED COLLECTORS' EDITION (Formerly . . . Special)
No. 4, 1973 - Present
Major Magazines

	Good	Fine	Mint
4	.30	.80	1.60
5-27		.40	.80

CRACKED SHUT-UPS (Cracked Special No. 3)
Feb, 1972 - No. 2, 1972
Major Magazines

	Good	Fine	Mint
1,2	.30	.80	1.60

CRACKED SPECIAL (Formerly Cracked Shut-Ups; . . . Collectors' Edition No. 4 on)
No. 3, 1973
Major Magazines

	Good	Fine	Mint
3	.30	.80	1.60

CRACK WESTERN (Formerly Crack; Jonesy No. 85 on)
No. 63, Nov, 1949 - No. 84, May, 1953
Quality Comics Group

	Good	Fine	Mint
63-Origin & 1st app. Two-Gun Lil (ends No. 84), Arizona Ames, Frontier Marshal, & Dead Canyon Days	3.50	10.00	20.00
64,65,67,69-Crandall-a; 65-Two-Gun Lil story. 67-Arizona Ames becomes A. Raines. 69-Last Dead Canyon Days.	3.00	9.00	18.00
66,68,72-81: 75,78,81-Crandall-c	2.00	5.00	10.00
70-Origin & 1st app. The Whip; Crandall-a	3.00	9.00	18.00
71,83-Crandall c/a	3.50	10.00	20.00
82,84-Crandall-a	3.00	9.00	18.00

CRASH COMICS (Catman No. 6 on)
May, 1940 - No. 5, Nov, 1940
Tem Publishing Co.

	Good	Fine	Mint
1-The Blue Streak, Strongman (origin), The Perfect Human begin; Simon & Kirby-a	30.00	90.00	180.00
2-Simon & Kirby-a	20.00	60.00	120.00
3-Simon & Kirby-a	14.00	40.00	80.00
4-Origin & 1st app. The Catman; S&K-a	20.00	60.00	120.00
5-S&K-a	14.00	40.00	80.00

NOTE: *Solar Legion by **Kirby** No. 1-5 (5 pgs. each).*

CRAZY
Dec, 1953 - No. 7, July, 1954
Atlas Comics (CSI)

	Good	Fine	Mint
1-Everett c/a	3.00	9.00	18.00
2-7	2.00	6.00	12.00

NOTE: ***Berg** a-2. **Drucker** a-6. **Everett** a-1,4. **Maneely** a-6.*

CRAZY (People Who Buy This Magazine Is . . .) (Formerly This Magazine Is . . .)
V3No.3, Nov, 1957 - V4No.8, Feb, 1959 (Magazine) (Satire)
Charlton Publications

	Good	Fine	Mint
V3No.3 - V4No.7	.50	1.50	3.00
V4No.8-Davis-a, 8 pgs.	1.00	3.00	6.00

CRAZY (Satire)
Feb, 1973 - No. 3, June, 1973
Marvel Comics Group

	Good	Fine	Mint
1-Not Brand Echh-r begin		.40	.80
2,3: 3-Kirby-a(r)		.30	.60

CRAZY (Magazine) (Satire)
Oct, 1973 - Present (40 cents) (Black & White)
Marvel Comics Group

	Good	Fine	Mint
1-Wolverton(1 pg.), Ploog, Bode-a; 3 pg. photo story of Adams & Giordano	.30	.90	1.80
2-Adams-a; Kurtzman's "Hey Look" reprint, 2 pgs.; Buscema-a		.60	1.20
3,5,6,8: 3-Drucker-a		.40	.80
4,7-Ploog-a		.40	.80
9-16-Eisner-a		.40	.80
17-82: 76-Best of . . Super Special		.30	.60
Super Special 1(Summer,'75, 100pgs)-Ploog, Adams-r	.30	.80	1.60

NOTE: ***Buscema** a-82. **Cardy** c-7,8. **Freas** c-1,2,4,6; a-7. **Rogers** a-82.*

CRAZY, MAN, CRAZY (Magazine) (Satire)
June, 1956
Humor Magazines

	Good	Fine	Mint
V2No.2-Wolverton-a, 3pgs.	3.00	9.00	18.00

CREATURE, THE (See Movie Classics)

CREATURES ON THE LOOSE (Tower of Shadows No. 1-9)
No. 10, March, 1971 - No. 37, Sept, 1975
Marvel Comics Group

	Good	Fine	Mint
10-First King Kull story; Wrightson-a	2.00	6.00	12.00
11-15: 13-Crandall-a	.30	.80	1.60
16-Origin Warrior of Mars	.40	1.10	2.20
17-20		.50	1.00
21,22: Steranko-c; Thongor begins No. 22, ends No. 29		.50	1.00
23-29		.50	1.00
30-Manwolf begins		.40	.80
31-37		.40	.80

NOTE: ***Ditko** r-15, 17, 18, 20, 22, 24, 27, 28. **Everett** a-16r. **Gil Kane** c-25, 29. **Morrow** a-20, 21. **Perez** a-33-37.*

CREEPER, THE (See Beware. . . & First Issue Special)

CREEPY (Magazine)
1964 - Present
Warren Publishing Co.

	Good	Fine	Mint
1-Frazetta-a	1.00	3.00	6.00
2	.85	2.50	5.00
3-13	.70	2.00	4.00
14-Adams 1st Warren work	.85	2.50	5.00
15-25	.50	1.50	3.00
26-40: 37-1st story on Atlantis series	.40	1.20	2.40
41-60	.35	1.10	2.20
61-80	.30	.90	1.80
81-112,114-118,120-124	.30	.80	1.60
113-All Wrightson-r	.30	.80	1.60
119-All Nino-r	.30	.80	1.60
Year Book 1968, 1969	.85	2.50	5.00
Year Book 1970-Adams, Ditko-a(r)	.70	2.00	4.00
Annual 1971-Ditko-a(r)	.50	1.50	3.00
Annual 1972,1973	.40	1.20	2.40
Annual 1974-All Crandall-r	.40	1.20	2.40

(NOTE: Annuals are included in regular numbering.)

NOTE: *Above books contain many good artists works: **Adams, Brunner, Corben, Craig (Taycee), Crandall, Ditko, Evans, Frazetta, Heath, Jeff Jones, Krenkel, McWilliams, Morrow, Nino, Orlando, Ploog, Severin, Torres, Toth, Williamson, Wood,** & **Wrightson;** covers by **Crandall, Davis, Frazetta, Morrow, SanJulian, Todd/Bode;** Otto Binder's "Adam Link" stories in No. 2,4,6,8,9,12,13,15 with **Orlando** art.*

CREEPY THINGS
July, 1975 - No. 6, June, 1976
Charlton Comics

	Good	Fine	Mint
1		.50	1.00
2-6		.40	.80
3-1977 reprint-Modern Comics		.25	.50

NOTE: ***Ditko** a-3,5. **Sutton** c-3,4.*

CRIME AND JUSTICE (Rookie Cop No. 27 on)
March, 1951 - No. 26, Sept, 1955
Capitol Stories/Charlton Comics

Crime & Justice #2, © CC

Crime & Justice #18, © CC

Crime & Punishment #61, © LEV

CRIME AND JUSTICE (continued)	Good	Fine	Mint
1-Spanking panel	3.50	10.00	20.00
2-8,10,13: 6-Negligee panels	1.20	3.50	7.00
9-Classic story ''Comics Vs. Crime''	2.50	7.00	14.00
11-Narcotics plus drug mention story; bondage-c	3.00	8.00	16.00
12-Bondage-c; heroin drug mention	3.00	8.00	16.00
14-Color illos in **POP**; gory story of man who beheads women	4.00	12.00	24.00
15-17,19,20,22-26	1.00	3.00	6.00
18-Ditko-a	4.00	12.00	24.00
21-Opium mention story	3.00	9.00	18.00

NOTE: ***Shuster** a-19-21; c-19.*

CRIME AND PUNISHMENT
April, 1948 - No. 74, Aug, 1955
Lev Gleason Publications

	Good	Fine	Mint
1	5.00	14.00	28.00
2,4,5	2.50	7.00	14.00
3-Used in **SOTI**, pg. 112; injury-to-eye panel	4.00	12.00	24.00
6-10	1.50	4.50	9.00
11-20	1.20	3.50	7.00
21-26,29: 24-Sgt. Spook app.	.85	2.50	5.00
27,28-Drug story	3.00	8.00	16.00
30-Tuska-a	1.00	3.00	6.00
31-38,40-44	.70	2.00	4.00
39-Drug mention story ''The 5 Dopes''	3.00	9.00	18.00
45-''Hophead Killer'' drug story	3.00	8.00	16.00
46-One page Frazetta	1.50	4.50	9.00
47-57,60-65,70-74	.70	2.00	4.00
58-Used in **POP**, pg. 79	2.00	6.00	12.00
59-Used in **SOTI**, illo-''What comic-book America stands for''	7.00	20.00	40.00
66-Toth c/a(4); 3-D effect ish	8.00	24.00	48.00
67-''Monkey on His Back''-heroin story; 3-D effect ish.	6.00	16.00	32.00
68-3-D effect ish.	1.50	4.00	8.00
69-''The Hot Rod Gang''-dope crazy kids	5.00	14.00	28.00

NOTE: ***Everett** a-31. **Fuje** a-13, 17, 18, 27. **Guardineer** a-2, 3, 10, 17, 18, 27, 28, 40-44. **Kinstler** c-69. **McWilliams** a-41, 48, 49. **Tuska** a-28.*

CRIME CAN'T WIN (Formerly Cindy Smith)
No. 41, 9/50 - No. 43, 2/51; No. 4, 4/51 - No. 12, 9/53
Marvel/Atlas Comics (CCC)

	Good	Fine	Mint
41,42	1.20	3.50	7.00
43-Tuska-a; horror story	2.00	5.00	10.00
4(4/51), 5-9,11,12	1.20	3.50	7.00
10-Possible use in **SOTI**, pg. 161	2.00	6.00	12.00

NOTE: ***Robinson** a-9-11.*

CRIME CASES (Formerly Willie Comics)
No. 24, 8/50 - No. 27, 3/51; No. 5, 5/51 - No. 12, 7/52
Marvel/Atlas Comics(CnPC No.24-8/MJMC No.9-12)

	Good	Fine	Mint
24-26	1.20	3.50	7.00
27-Everett-a	1.50	4.00	8.00
5-12: 11-Robinson-a	.85	2.50	5.00

CRIME CLINIC, THE
1951 - No. 11, Sept-Oct, 1951
Ziff-Davis Publishing Co.

	Good	Fine	Mint
1-Painted-c	4.00	12.00	24.00
2,4-11-Painted-c	3.00	8.00	16.00
3-Used in **SOTI**, pg. 18	4.00	12.00	24.00

NOTE: *Painted covers by **Saunders.***

CRIME DETECTIVE COMICS
Mar-Apr, 1948 - V3No.8, 1952
Hillman Periodicals

	Good	Fine	Mint
V1No.1	3.00	8.00	16.00
2-4,7,10-12	1.20	3.50	7.00
5-Krigstein-a	2.50	7.00	14.00
6-McWilliams-a	1.20	3.50	7.00
8-Kirbyish-a	2.00	6.00	12.00
9-Used in **SOTI**, pg. 16 & ''Caricature of the author in a position comic book publishers wish he were in permanently'' illo.	14.00	40.00	80.00
V2No.1,4,7-Krigstein-a	2.00	5.00	10.00
2,3,5,6,8-10	.85	2.50	5.00
V3No.1,3-8	.70	2.00	4.00
2-Kinstler-a	.85	2.50	5.00

NOTE: ***Powell** a-11.*

CRIME DETECTOR
Jan, 1954 - No. 5, Sept, 1954
Timor Publications

	Good	Fine	Mint
1	3.00	8.00	16.00
2-4: 3-2pg. drug text	1.50	4.00	8.00
5-Disbrow-a (classic)	3.50	10.00	20.00

CRIME DOES NOT PAY (Silver Streak No. 1-21)
No. 22, June, 1942 - No. 147, July, 1955 (1st crime comic)
Comic House/Lev Gleason/Golfing

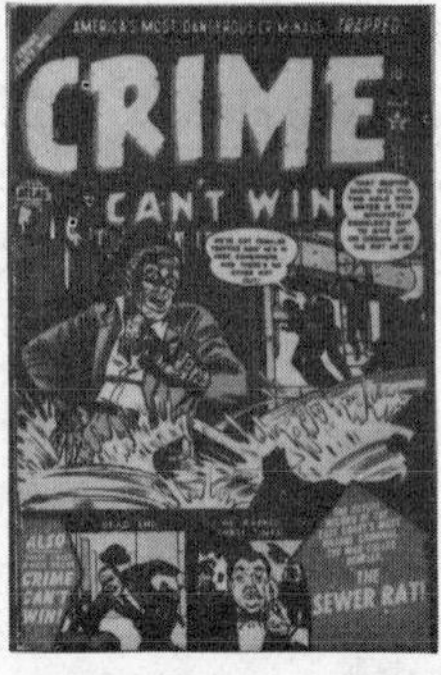

Crime Can't Win #12, © MCG

Crime Cases #8, © MCG

Crime Detective V3#1, © HILL

Crime Does Not Pay #34, © LEV

Crime Does Not Pay #91, © LEV

Crimefighters #7, © MCG

CRIME DOES NOT PAY (continued)

	Good	Fine	Mint
22-Origin The War Eagle & only app.; Chip Gardner begins; No. 22 rebound in True Crime, Complete Book of (Scarce)	40.00	120.00	240.00
23 (Scarce)	24.00	70.00	140.00
24-Intro. & 1st app. Mr. Crime (Scarce); cocaine story	20.00	60.00	120.00
25,27-30	10.00	30.00	60.00
26-Three drug mentions	12.00	32.00	64.00
31-40	5.50	16.00	32.00
41,43-46,48-50	3.50	10.00	20.00
42-Electrocution-c	5.00	14.00	28.00
47-Electric chair-c	5.00	14.00	28.00
51-62,64-70	2.00	6.00	12.00
63-Contains Biro-Gleason's self code of 12 listed restrictions	2.00	6.00	12.00
71-100: 87-Chip Gardner begins, ends No. 99,102. 98-Bondage-c	1.00	3.00	6.00
101-104,107	.70	2.00	4.00
105-Used in **POP**, pg. 84	2.00	6.00	12.00
106,114-Frazetta, 1 pg.	1.50	4.50	9.00
108-110,112,113,115-120,122-130	.85	2.50	5.00
111-Used in **POP**, pgs. 80,81	2.00	6.00	12.00
121-Drug mention story	1.20	3.50	7.00
131-140,144-147	.70	2.00	4.00
141-143-Kubert-a, one each	2.00	5.00	10.00
1(Golfing-1945)	.70	2.00	4.00
The Best of . . .(1944)-128 pgs.; Series contains 4 rebound issues	14.00	40.00	80.00
1945 issue	10.00	30.00	60.00
1946-48 issues	8.00	24.00	48.00
1949-50 issues	7.00	20.00	40.00
1951-53 issues	6.00	16.00	32.00

NOTE: ***Kubert*** *c-143.* ***McWilliams*** *a-91, 93, 95, 102. Whodunnit by* ***Guardineer****-40-104, 108-110; Chip Gardner by* ***Bob Fujitani. (Fuje)****-88-103; c-103.* ***Landau****-a-118.* ***McWilliams*** *a-103.* ***Powell*** *a-146.* ***Tuska*** *a-61, 63, 64.*

CRIME EXPOSED
Dec, 1950 - No. 14, June, 1952
Marvel/Atlas Comics(PrPI/PPI)

	Good	Fine	Mint
1	2.00	5.00	10.00
2,3,5-9,11,14: 11-Robinson-a	1.00	3.00	6.00
4-Tuska-a	1.20	3.50	7.00
10-Used in **POP**, pg. 81	2.00	5.00	10.00
12-Krigstein & Robinson-a	2.00	5.00	10.00
13-Used in **POP**, pg. 81; Krigstein-a	2.50	7.00	14.00

CRIMEFIGHTERS
April, 1948 - No. 10, Nov, 1949
Marvel Comics (CmPS/CCC No.4-10)

	Good	Fine	Mint
1	3.00	9.00	18.00
2	1.20	3.50	7.00
3-Morphine addict story	2.50	7.00	14.00
4-10: 9,10-Photo-c	.85	2.50	5.00

CRIME FIGHTERS (. . . Always Win)
No. 11, Sept, 1954 - No. 13, Jan, 1955
Atlas Comics (CnPC)

	Good	Fine	Mint
11,12	1.20	3.50	7.00
13-Pakula, Reinman, Severin-a	1.50	4.00	8.00

CRIME FIGHTING DETECTIVE (Shock Detective Cases No. 20 on; formerly Criminals on the Run?)
No. 11, Apr-May, 1950 - No. 19, June, 1952
Star Publishing Co.

	Good	Fine	Mint
11-L. B. Cole c/a, 2pgs.	2.50	7.00	14.00
12,13,15-19: 17-Young King Cole & Dr. Doom app.; L. B. Cole-c on all	2.00	6.00	12.00
14-L. B. Cole-c/a, r-/Law-Crime No. 2	3.00	9.00	18.00

CRIME FILES
No. 5, Sept, 1952 - No. 6, Nov, 1952
Standard Comics

	Good	Fine	Mint
5-Alex Toth-a; used in **SOTI**, pg. 4 (text)	4.50	13.00	26.00
6-Sekowsky-a	2.00	6.00	12.00

CRIME ILLUSTRATED (Magazine)
Nov-Dec, 1955 - No. 2, Spring, 1956
E. C. Comics

	Good	Fine	Mint
1-Ingels & Crandall-a	7.00	20.00	40.00
2-Ingels & Crandall-a	6.00	16.00	32.00

NOTE: ***Craig*** *a-2.* ***Crandall*** *a-1, 2; c-2.* ***Evans*** *a-1.* ***Davis*** *a-2.* ***Ingels*** *a-1, 2.* ***Krigstein/Crandall*** *a-1.* ***Orlando*** *a-1, 2; c-1.*

CRIME INCORPORATED (Formerly Crimes Incorporated)
No. 2, Aug, 1950; No. 3, Aug, 1951
Fox Features Syndicate

	Good	Fine	Mint
2	3.00	9.00	18.00
3(1951)	2.50	7.00	14.00

CRIME MACHINE (Magazine)
Feb, 1971 - No. 2, May, 1971 (B&W)
Skywald Publications

	Good	Fine	Mint
1-Kubert-a(2)(r)(Avon)	.85	2.50	5.00

Crime Fighting Detective #12, © STAR

Crime Fighting Detective #19, © STAR

Crime Illustrated #2, © WMG

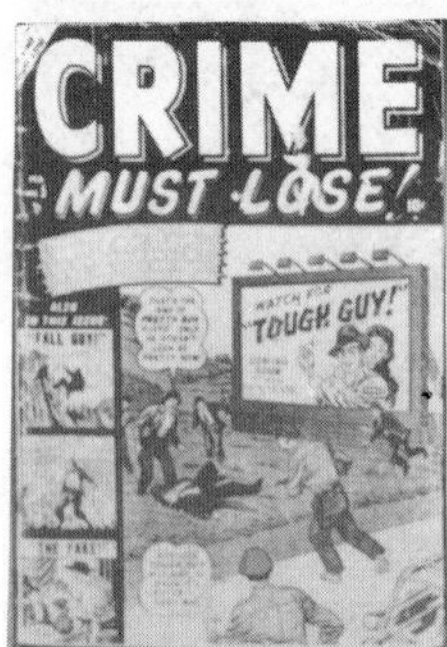

Crime Must Lose #5, © MCG

Crime Must Pay The Penalty #16, © ACE

Crime Mysteries #5, © TM

CRIME MACHINE (continued)

	Good	Fine	Mint
2-Torres, Wildey-a; Violent c/a	.60	1.80	3.60

CRIME MUST LOSE! (Formerly Sports Action?)
No. 4, Oct, 1950 - No. 12, April, 1952
Sports Action (Atlas Comics)

	Good	Fine	Mint
4-10,12: Ann Brewster-a	1.50	4.00	8.00
11-Used in **POP**, pg. 89	2.00	5.00	10.00

CRIME MUST PAY THE PENALTY (Formerly Four Favorites; Penalty No. 47,48)
No. 33, Feb, 1948 - No. 48, Jan, 1956
Ace Magazines (Current Books)

	Good	Fine	Mint
33(2/48)-Drug story; becomes Four Teeners No. 34?	4.00	12.00	24.00
34(Exist?)	1.50	4.00	8.00
2(6/48)-Extreme violence; J. Cole-a?	2.50	7.00	14.00
3,6,7,9,10	1.20	3.50	7.00
4,5-J. Cole-a? 4-Transvestism story	2.00	5.00	10.00
8-Transvestism story	2.00	5.00	10.00
11,12,14-17,20	.85	2.50	5.00
13-Heroin drug story	1.50	4.00	8.00
18-2pg. text on cocaine	1.20	3.50	7.00
19-Narcotics drug story	1.50	4.00	8.00
21-32,35-40,42-48	.70	2.00	4.00
33(7/53)-''Dell Fabry-Junk King''-drug story	2.50	7.00	14.00
34-Drug story	2.50	7.00	14.00
41-Drug story-''Dealers in White Death''	2.50	7.00	14.00

NOTE: ***Cameron*** *a-30,32,34,39,40.*

CRIME MUST STOP
October, 1952
Hillman Periodicals

	Good	Fine	Mint
V1No.1(Scarce)-Similar to Monster Crime; Mort Lawrence-a	14.00	40.00	80.00

CRIME MYSTERIES (Secret Mysteries No. 16 on)
May, 1952 - No. 15, Sept, 1954
Ribage Publishing Corp. (Trojan Magazines)

	Good	Fine	Mint
1-Transvestism story	8.00	24.00	48.00
2-Marijuana story (7/52)	10.00	28.00	56.00
3-One pg. Frazetta	6.00	18.00	36.00
4-Cover shows girl in bondage having her blood drained; 1 pg. Frazetta	10.00	28.00	56.00
5,7,9	4.50	13.00	26.00
6,8,10-Heroin drug mention stories	5.00	15.00	30.00
11-14	3.50	10.00	20.00
15-Acid in face-c	5.50	16.00	32.00

NOTE: ***Hollingsworth*** *a-10-12, 15; c-12, 15.* ***Woodbridge*** *a-13. Bondage-c-1, 8, 12.*

CRIME ON THE RUN (See Approved Comics)
1949
St. John Publishing Co.

	Good	Fine	Mint
8	1.50	4.00	8.00

CRIME ON THE WATERFRONT (Formerly Famous Gangsters)
No. 4, May, 1952 (Painted cover)
Realistic Publications

	Good	Fine	Mint
4-Drug mention story/cover	7.00	20.00	40.00

CRIME PATROL (International No. 1-5; International Crime Patrol No. 6, becomes Crypt of Terror No. 17 on)
No. 7, Summer, 1948 - No. 16, Feb-Mar, 1950
E. C. Comics

	Good	Fine	Mint
7-14: 12-Ingels-a	17.00	50.00	100.00
15-Intro. of Crypt Keeper & Crypt of Terror; used by N.Y. Legis. Comm.-last pg. Feldstein-a	60.00	145.00	290.00
16-2nd Crypt Keeper app.	40.00	110.00	220.00

NOTE: ***Craig*** *c/a in most.*

CRIME PHOTOGRAPHER (See Casey. . .)

CRIME REPORTER
Aug, 1948 - No. 3, Dec, 1948 (Shows Oct.)
St. John Publ. Co.

	Good	Fine	Mint
1-Drug club story	10.00	28.00	56.00
2-Used in **SOTI**: illo-''Children told me what the man was going to do with the red-hot poker;'' r-/Dynamic No. 17 with editing; morphine story; Baker-c; Tuska-a	25.00	75.00	150.00
3-Morphine story; Baker-c; Tuska-a	8.00	24.00	48.00

CRIMES BY WOMEN
June, 1948 - No. 15, 1949; 1954
Fox Features Syndicate

	Good	Fine	Mint
1	14.00	40.00	80.00
2	8.00	24.00	48.00
3-Used in **SOTI**, pg. 234	10.00	28.00	56.00
4,5,7,9,11-15:11-Opium text story	7.00	20.00	40.00
6-Classic girl fight-c	8.00	24.00	48.00
8-Used in **POP**	8.00	24.00	48.00
10-Used in **SOTI**, pg. 72	8.00	24.00	48.00
54(M.S. Publ.-'54)-Reprint; (formerly My Love Secret)	5.00	15.00	30.00

CRIMES INCORPORATED (Formerly My Past)
No. 12, June, 1950 (Crime Incorporated No. 2 on)

Crime Patrol #8, © WMG

Crime Reporter #1, © STJ

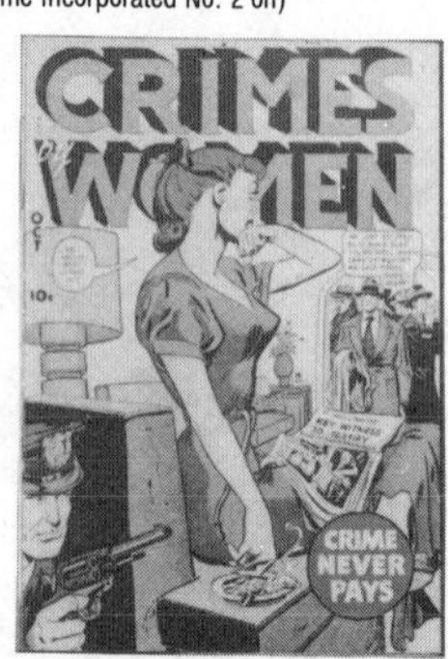

Crimes By Women #9, © FOX

Crime SuspenStories #10, © WMG

Criminals On The Run #10, © NOVP

Crown Comics #13, © McCombs

CRIMES INCORPORATED (continued)
Fox Features Syndicate

	Good	Fine	Mint
12	2.50	7.00	14.00

CRIMES INCORPORATED
1950 (132 pages)
Fox Features Syndicate

nn-See Fox Giants. Contents can vary and determines price.

CRIME SMASHER
Summer, 1948 (One Shot)
Fawcett Publications

	Good	Fine	Mint
1 (Spy Smasher)	8.00	16.00	32.00

CRIME SMASHERS (Secret Mysteries No. 16 on)
Oct, 1950 - No. 15, Sept, 1954
Ribage Publishing Corp.(Trojan Magazines)

	Good	Fine	Mint
1-Used in **SOTI**, pg. 19,20, & illo-''A girl raped and murdered;'' Sally the Sleuth begins; drug mention story	15.00	45.00	90.00
2-Kubert-c	8.00	24.00	48.00
3-Cocaine drug story	9.00	25.00	50.00
4	6.00	18.00	36.00
5-Wood-a	10.00	28.00	56.00
6,8-Drug stories (morphine-No. 8)	6.00	18.00	36.00
7-Bondage-c; heroin story	6.00	18.00	36.00
9-Bondage-c	5.00	15.00	30.00
10,11-Drug mention stories	6.00	18.00	36.00
12-Injury to eye panel; 1pg. Frazetta	6.00	18.00	36.00
13-Used in **POP**, pgs. 79,80; 1pg. Frazetta	6.00	18.00	36.00
14,15: 14-Hollingsworth-a	4.00	12.00	24.00

CRIME SUSPENSTORIES (Formerly Vault of Horror No. 12-14)
No. 15, Oct-Nov, 1950 - No. 27, Feb-Mar, 1955
E. C. Comics

15-Identical to No. 1 in content; No. 1 printed on outside front cover. No. 15 (formerly ''The Vault of Horror'') printed and blackened out on inside front cover with Vol. 1, No. 1 printed over it. Evidently, several of No. 15 were printed before a decision was made not to drop the Vault of Horror and Haunt of Fear series. The print run was stopped on No. 15 and continued on No. 1. All of No. 15 were changed as described above.

	Good	Fine	Mint
	65.00	170.00	340.00
1	50.00	150.00	300.00
2	30.00	85.00	175.00
3-5	20.00	60.00	125.00
6-10	14.00	40.00	85.00
11,12,14,15	11.00	32.00	65.00
13,16-Williamson-a	14.00	40.00	85.00
17-Williamson/Frazetta-a, 6 pgs.	17.00	50.00	110.00
18	9.00	25.00	50.00
19-Used in **SOTI**, pg. 235	10.00	30.00	60.00
20-Cover used in **SOTI**, illo-''Cover of a children's comic book''	14.00	40.00	80.00
21,24-27	7.00	20.00	40.00
22,23-Used in Senate investigation on juvenile delinquency	10.00	30.00	60.00

NOTE: ***Craig** a-1-21; c-1-18,20-22. **Crandall** a-18-26. **Davis** a-4, 5, 7, 9-12, 20. **Elder** a-17, 18. **Evans** a-15, 19, 21, 23, 25, 27; c-23, 24. **Feldstein** c-19. **Ingels** a-1-12, 14, 15, 27. **Kamen** a-2, 4-18, 20-27; c-25-27. **Krigstein** a-22, 24, 25, 27. **Kurtzman** a-1, 3. **Orlando** a-16, 22, 24, 26. **Wood** a-1, 3. Issues No. 11-15 have E. C. ''quickie'' stories. No. 25 contains the famous ''Are You a Red Dupe?'' editorial.*

CRIMINALS ON THE RUN (Formerly Young King Cole)
(Crime Fighting Detective No. 11 on?)
Aug-Sept, 1948 - No. 10, Dec-Jan, 1949-50
Premium Group (Novelty Press)

	Good	Fine	Mint
V4No.1-Young King Cole begins	4.00	12.00	24.00
2-6: 6-Dr. Doom app.;	3.50	10.00	20.00
7-Classic ''Fish in the Face'' cover by L. B. Cole	6.00	18.00	36.00
V5No.1,2	3.50	10.00	20.00
10-L. B. Cole-c	3.50	10.00	20.00

NOTE: *Most issues have **L. B. Cole** covers.* ***McWilliams*** a-V4No.6,7, V5No.2; c-V4No.5

CROSLEY'S HOUSE OF FUN
1950 (32 pgs.; full color; paper cover)
Crosley Div. AVCO Mfg. Corp. (Giveaway)

	Good	Fine	Mint
Strips revolve around Crosley appliances	2.00	5.00	10.00

CROSS AND THE SWITCHBLADE, THE
1972 (35-49 cents)
Spire Christian Comics/Fleming H. Revell Co.

	Good	Fine	Mint
1		.50	1.00

CROSSFIRE
1973 (39,49 cents)
Spire Christian Comics (Fleming H. Revell Co.)

	Good	Fine	Mint
nn		.50	1.00

CROSSING THE ROCKIES (See Classics Special)

CROWN COMICS
Winter, 1944-45 - No. 19, July, 1949
Golfing/McCombs Publ.

	Good	Fine	Mint
1-''The Oblong Box'' story	6.00	18.00	36.00
2	3.00	9.00	18.00
3-Baker-a	6.00	18.00	36.00
4-6-Baker c/a; Voodah app. No. 4,5	6.00	18.00	36.00
7-Feldstein, Baker, Kamen-a	5.00	15.00	30.00
8-Baker-a; Voodah app.	5.00	15.00	30.00
9,11,14-19: Voodah in No. 10-19	3.00	9.00	18.00
10-Drug mention story	3.50	10.00	20.00
12-Feldstein?, Starr-a	4.00	12.00	24.00
13-Leonard Starr-a	3.00	9.00	18.00

NOTE: ***Bolle** a-13,18,19. **Powell** a-19.*

CRUSADER FROM MARS (See Tops in Adventure)
Jan-Mar, 1952 - No. 2, Fall, 1952
Ziff-Davis Publ. Co.

	Good	Fine	Mint
1	15.00	45.00	90.00
2-Bondage-c	12.00	35.00	70.00

CRUSADER RABBIT (See 4-Color No. 735,805)

CRUSADERS, THE
1974 - 1979 (36 pages) (39,59 cents) (Religious)
Chick Publications

	Good	Fine	Mint
Vol. 1-Operation Bucharest('74). Vol. 2-The Broken Cross('74). Vol. 3-Scarface('74). Vol. 4-Exorcists('75). Vol. 5-Chaos('75). each....		.40	.80
Vol. 6-Primal Man('76)-(Disputes evolution theory). Vol. 7-The Ark-(Claims proof of existence, destroyed by Bolsheviks). Vol. 8-The Gift-(Life story of Christ). Vol. 9-Angel of Light-(Story of the Devil). Vol. 10-Spellbound-(Tells how rock music is Satanical & produced by witches). 11-Sabotage. 12-Alberto.(No. 6-12 low in distribution; Loaded in religious propaganda.)		.40	.80

CRYIN' LION, THE
Fall, 1944 - No. 3, Spring, 1945
William H. Wise Co.

	Good	Fine	Mint
1-3	1.00	3.00	6.00

CRYPT OF SHADOWS
Jan, 1973 - No. 21, Nov, 1975
Marvel Comics Group

	Good	Fine	Mint
1-Wolverton-a r-/Advs. Into Terror No. 7	.25	.70	1.40
2-10		.40	.80
11-21		.30	.60

NOTE: ***Briefer** a-2. **Ditko** a-13r, 18-20r. **Everett** a-6, 14r. **Moldoff** a-8. **Powell** a-12r, 14r.*

CRYPT OF TERROR (Tales From the Crypt No. 20 on; formerly Crime Patrol)
No. 17, Apr-May, 1950 - No. 19, Aug-Sept, 1950
E. C. Comics

	Good	Fine	Mint
17	70.00	200.00	400.00
18,19	50.00	135.00	275.00

NOTE: *Craig c/a-17-19.* ***Feldstein*** *a-17-19.* ***Ingels*** *a-19.* ***Kurtzman*** *a-18.* ***Wood*** *a-18. Canadian reprints known; see Table of Contents.*

CUPID
Jan, 1950 - No. 2, Mar, 1950
Marvel Comics (U.S.A.)

	Good	Fine	Mint
1,2	2.00	6.00	12.00

CURIO
1930's(?) (Tabloid size, 16-20 pages)
Harry 'A' Chesler

	Good	Fine	Mint
	4.50	13.00	26.00

CURLY KAYOE COMICS
1946 - 1948; 1948 - 1950
United Features Syndicate/Dell Publ. Co.

	Good	Fine	Mint
1 (1946)	2.50	7.50	15.00
2-8	1.20	3.50	7.00
United Presents. . . (Fall, 1948)	1.50	4.00	8.00
4-Color 871 (Dell)	1.20	3.50	7.00

CUSTER'S LAST FIGHT
1950
Avon Periodicals

	Good	Fine	Mint
nn-Partial reprint of Cowpuncher No. 1	5.50	16.00	32.00

CUTIE PIE
May, 1955 - No. 5, Aug, 1956
Junior Reader's Guild/Lev Gleason

	Good	Fine	Mint
1	1.25	2.50	5.00
2-5	.90	1.80	3.60

CYCLONE COMICS
June, 1940 - No. 5, Nov, 1940
Bilbara Publishing Co.

	Good	Fine	Mint
1-Origin Tornado Tom; Volton begins, Mister Q app.	15.00	45.00	90.00
2	8.00	24.00	48.00
3-5	6.00	18.00	36.00

CYNTHIA DOYLE, NURSE IN LOVE (Formerly and becomes Sweetheart Diary No. 74 on)
No. 66, Oct, 1962 - No. 73, Dec, 1963
Charlton Publications

	Good	Fine	Mint
66-73	.30	.80	1.60

DAFFY (. . . Duck No. 18 on)
1953 - No. 30, 7-9/62; No. 31, 10-12/62 - Present (no No. 132,133)
Dell Publishing Co./Gold Key No. 31-127/Whitman No. 128 on

	Good	Fine	Mint
4-Color 457,536,615('55)Elmer Fudd x-overs begin	.60	1.80	3.60
4-11(1956-57)	.50	1.50	3.00
12-19(1958-59)	.30	.90	1.80
20-40(1960-64)		.60	1.20
41-60(1964-68)		.50	1.00
61-90(1969-73)Road Runner in most		.30	.60
91-131,134-136(1974-81)		.25	.50
Mini-Comic 1 (1976; 3¼x6½'')		.25	.50

NOTE: *Reprint issues-No.41-46,48,50,53-55,58,59,67,69,73,81,96,103-08,110.*
(See March of Comics No. 277,288,313,331,347,357,375,387,397,402,413)

DAFFYDILS
1911 (52 pgs.; 6x8''; B&W; hardcover)
Cupples & Leon Co.

	Good	Fine	Mint
by Tad	5.00	15.00	30.00

DAFFY TUNES COMICS
June, 1947 - No. 2, Aug, 1947
Four Star Publications

	Good	Fine	Mint
nn	.85	2.50	5.00
2-Al Fago c/a	1.20	3.50	7.00

DAGAR, DESERT HAWK (Capt. Kidd No. 24; formerly All Great)
No. 14, Feb, 1948 - No. 23, Apr, 1949 (No No.17,18)
Fox Features Syndicate

	Good	Fine	Mint
14-Tangi & Safari Cary begin; Edmond Good bondage-c/a	14.00	40.00	80.00
15,16-E. Good-a; 15-Bondage-c	10.00	30.00	60.00
19,20,22	8.00	24.00	48.00
21-'Bombs & Bums Away' panel in 'Flood of Death' story used in **SOTI**	10.00	30.00	60.00
23-Bondage-c	10.00	30.00	60.00

NOTE: *Tangi by* ***Kamen****-14-16,19; c-21.*

DAGAR THE INVINCIBLE (Tales of Sword & Sorcery. . .)
Oct, 1972 - No. 18, Dec, 1976 (See Dan Curtis)
Gold Key

	Good	Fine	Mint
1-Origin; intro. Villains Olstellon & Scorpio	.85	2.50	5.00
2-5: 3-Intro. Graylin, Dagar's woman; Jarn x-over	.40	1.20	2.40
6-1st Dark Gods story	.30	.80	1.60
7-10: 9-Intro. Torgus. 10-1st Three Witches story	.30	.80	1.60
11-18: 13-Durak & Torgus x-over; story continues in Dr. Spektor No. 15. 14-Dagar's origin retold. 18-Origin retold		.50	1.00

NOTE: *Durak app.-7,12,13. Tragg app.-5,11.*

DAGWOOD (Chic Young's) (Also see Blondie)
Sept, 1950 - No. 140, Nov, 1965
Harvey Publications

	Good	Fine	Mint
1	5.00	14.00	28.00
2-10	2.50	7.00	14.00
11-30	1.20	3.50	7.00
31-70	.70	2.00	4.00
71-100	.50	1.50	3.00
101-128,130,135		.50	1.00
129,131-134,136-140-All are 68-pg. issues	.30	.80	1.60

NOTE: *Popeye and other one page strips appeared in early issues.*

DAGWOOD SPLITS THE ATOM (Also see Topix V8No.4)
1949 (Science comic with King Features characters) (Giveaway)
King Features Syndicate

	Good	Fine	Mint
nn-½ comic, ½ text; Popeye, Olive Oyl, Henry, Mandrake, Little King, Katzenjammer Kids app.	3.00	8.00	16.00

DAISY AND DONALD (See Walt Disney Showcase No. 8)
May, 1973 - Present (no No. 48)
Gold Key/Whitman No. 42 on

	Good	Fine	Mint
1-Barks r-/WDC&S No. 308	.30	.80	1.60
2,3,5		.50	1.00
4-Barks r-/WDC&S No. 224		.50	1.00
6-10		.40	.80
11-47,49-: 32-r-/WDC&S 308		.30	.60

DAISY & HER PUPS (Blondie's Dogs)
No. 21, 7/51 - No. 27, 7/52; No. 8, 9/52 - No. 25, 7/55
Harvey Publications

	Good	Fine	Mint
21-27: 26,27 have No. 6 & 7 on cover but No. 26 & 27 on inside	1.00	3.00	6.00
8-25	.85	2.50	5.00

Cyclone Comics #4, © Bilbara Publ.

Dagar Desert Hawk #19, © FOX

Dagwood #4, © KING

Dale Evans Comics #18, © DC

Danger #16, © SUPER

Danger Is Our Business #1, © TOBY

DAISY COMICS
Dec, 1936 (Small size: 5¼x7½'')
Eastern Color Printing Co.

	Good	Fine	Mint
Joe Palooka, Buck Rogers (2 pgs. from Famous Funnies No. 18), Napoleon Flying to Fame, Butty & Fally	12.00	35.00	70.00

DAISY DUCK & UNCLE SCROOGE PICNIC TIME (See Dell Giant No.33)

DAISY DUCK & UNCLE SCROOGE SHOW BOAT (See Dell Giant No.55)

DAISY DUCK'S DIARY (See 4-Color No. 600,659,743,858,948,1055, 1150,1247)

DAISY HANDBOOK
1946 - 1948 (132 pgs.)(10 cents)(Pocket-size)
Daisy Manufacturing Co.

1-Buck Rogers, Red Ryder	9.00	25.00	50.00
2-Captain Marvel & Ibis the Invincible, Red Ryder, Boy Commandos, & Robotman; 2 pgs. Wolverton-a; contains 8pg. color catalog.	9.00	25.00	50.00

DAISY LOW OF THE GIRL SCOUTS
1954, 1965 (16 pgs.; paper cover)
Girl Scouts of America

1954-Story of Juliette Gordon Low	2.00	5.00	10.00
1965	.50	1.50	3.00

DAISY MAE (See Oxydol-Dreft)

DAISY'S RED RYDER GUN BOOK
1955 (132 pages)(25 cents)(Pocket-size)
Daisy Manufacturing Co.

Boy Commandos, Red Ryder, 1 pg. Wolverton-a	7.00	20.00	40.00

DAKOTA LIL (See Fawcett Movie Comics)

DAKTARI (Ivan Tors) (TV)
July, 1967 - No. 4, 1969
Dell Publishing Co.

1	.70	2.00	4.00
2-4	.35	1.00	2.00

DALE EVANS (See Queen of the West . . .)

DALE EVANS COMICS
Sept-Oct, 1948 - No. 24, July-Aug, 1952
National Periodical Publications

1-Sierra Smith begins by Alex Toth	9.00	25.00	50.00
2-11-Alex Toth-a	5.00	15.00	30.00
12-24	2.50	7.00	14.00

DALTON BOYS, THE
1951
Avon Periodicals

1-(No. on spine)-Kinstler-c	6.00	18.00	36.00

DAN CURTIS GIVEAWAYS
1974 (24 pages) (3x6'') (in color, all reprints)
Western Publishing Co.

1-Dark Shadows, 2-Star Trek, 3-The Twilight Zone, 4-Ripley's Believe It or Not! True Ghost Stories, 5-Turok, Son of Stone, 6-Star Trek, 7-The Occult Files of Dr. Spektor, 8-Dagar the Invincible, 9-Grimm's Ghost Stories Set . . .	.50	1.50	3.00

DANDEE
1947
Four Star Publications

	1.50	4.00	8.00

DAN DUNN (See Nickel Books, Super Book(No No.), & Detective Dan)

DANDY COMICS (Also see Happy Jack Howard)
Spring, 1947 - No. 7, Spring, 1948
E. C. Comics

	Good	Fine	Mint
1-Vince Fago-a	10.00	30.00	60.00
2-7-Vince Fago-a	8.00	24.00	48.00

DANGER
January, 1953 - No. 11, 1954
Comic Media/Allen Hardy Assoc.

1-Heck-a	2.50	7.00	14.00
2,3,5-7,9-11	1.50	4.00	8.00
4-Marijuana cover/story	4.00	12.00	24.00
8-Bondage/torture/headlights panels	1.50	4.00	8.00

DANGER (Jim Bowie No. 15 on)
No. 12, June, 1954 - No. 14, Nov, 1954
Charlton Comics

12(No.1)-Nyoka begins	2.00	6.00	12.00
13,14	1.50	4.00	8.00

DANGER
1964
Super Comics

Super Reprint No. 10-12 (Black Dwarf; No. 11-reprints from Johnny Danger), No. 15,16 (Yankee Girl & Johnny Rebel), No. 17 (Capt. Courage & Enchanted Dagger), No. 18(no date) (Gun-Master, Annie Oakley, The Chameleon; L.B. Cole-a)	.70	2.00	4.00

DANGER AND ADVENTURE (Formerly This Magazine is Haunted; Robin Hood and His Merry Men No. 28 on)
No. 22, 1956 - No. 27, Feb, 1957
Charlton Comics

22-Ibis the Invincible app.	1.00	3.00	6.00
23-Lance O'Casey app.	.85	2.50	5.00
24-27: 24-Mike Danger & Johnny Adventure begin	.60	1.80	3.60

DANGER IS OUR BUSINESS!
Dec, 1953 - No. 10, June, 1955
Toby Press

1-Williamson/Frazetta-a, 6 pgs. (Science Fiction)	20.00	60.00	120.00
2-10	2.50	7.00	14.00
I.W. Reprint No. 9('64)-Williamson/Frazetta-a r-/No. 1; Kinstler-c	6.00	18.00	36.00

DANGER IS THEIR BUSINESS (See A-1 Comics No. 50)

DANGER MAN (See 4-Color No. 1231)

DANGER TRAIL
July-Aug, 1950 - No. 5, Mar-Apr, 1951
National Periodical Publications

1-King Farrady begins, ends No. 4; Toth-a	15.00	45.00	90.00
2-5-Toth-a in all; Johnny Peril app. No. 5	10.00	30.00	60.00

DANIEL BOONE (See The Exploits of. . ., 4-Color No. 1163, The Legends of. . ., Frontier Scout. . ., Fighting. . ., & March of Comics No. 306)

DAN'L BOONE
Sept, 1955 - No. 8, Sept, 1957
Magazine Enterprises/Sussex Publ. Co. No. 2 on

1	1.50	4.00	8.00
2-8	.85	2.50	5.00

DANIEL BOONE (TV) (See March of Comics No. 306)
Jan, 1965 - No. 15, Apr, 1969
Gold Key

1('64)(TV)	.70	2.00	4.00
2-15	.40	1.20	2.40

DANNY BLAZE (Nature Boy No. 3 on)
Aug, 1955 - No. 2, Oct, 1955
Charlton Comics

1,2	2.00	5.00	10.00

DANNY DINGLE (See Single Series No. 17)

DANNY KAYE'S BAND FUN BOOK
1959
H & A Selmer (Giveaway)

	Good	Fine	Mint
	1.50	4.00	8.00

DANNY THOMAS SHOW, THE (See 4-Color No. 1180,1249)

DARBY O'GILL & THE LITTLE PEOPLE (See 4-Color No. 1024 & Movie Comics)

DAREDEVIL (. . . & the Black Widow No. 92-107)
April, 1964 - Present
Marvel Comics Group

	Good	Fine	Mint
1-Origin Daredevil	24.00	70.00	150.00
2-Fantastic Four cameo	12.00	35.00	80.00
3-Origin, 1st app. The Owl	7.50	22.00	50.00
4,5: 5-dons new costume	5.00	14.00	28.00
6,7,9,10: 7-dons new costume	3.50	10.00	20.00
8-Origin & 1st app. Stilt-Man	3.50	10.00	20.00
11-17,19,20: 13-Facts about Ka-Zar's origin; Kirby-a; Romita's 1st work at Marvel	1.50	4.50	9.00
18-Origin & 1st app. Gladiator	1.50	4.50	9.00
21-30: 30-Titor x-over	.75	2.20	4.40
31-40	.50	1.50	3.00
41-49: 42-Death Mike Murdock. 43-vs. Capt. America	.40	1.20	2.40
50-52-Smith-a	.80	2.30	4.60
53-Origin retold	.50	1.50	3.00
54-56,58-60	.40	1.10	2.20
57-Reveals i.d. to Karen Page	.40	1.10	2.20
61-81: 81-Oversize issue; Black Widow begins	.30	.80	1.60
82-90: 83-Smith layouts. 86-Karen Page leaves		.60	1.20
91-98,101-106,108-113,115-120		.50	1.00
99-Avengers x-over		.60	1.20
100-Origin retold	.50	1.50	3.00
107-Starlin-c	.30	.80	1.60
114-1st app. Deathstalker	.30	.80	1.60
121-140: 124-1st app. Copperhead; Black Widow leaves. 126-1st New Torpedo. 131-1st app. & origin Bullseye		.50	1.00
141,143-149		.50	1.00
142-Nova cameo		.50	1.00
150-1st app. Paladin		.50	1.00
151-Reveals i.d. to Heather Glenn		.50	1.00
152-157		.40	.80
158-Frank Miller art begins; origin & death of Deathstalker	4.00	12.00	24.00
159	2.00	6.00	12.00
160,161	1.50	4.50	9.00
162	.35	1.00	2.00
163-167,169,170: 164-Origin retold	1.00	3.00	6.00
168-Intro/origin Elektra	2.50	7.50	15.00
171-176: 174-176-Elektra app.	.60	1.80	3.60
177-182: 181-Death of Elektra	.30	.90	1.80
183,184-Angel dust story	.25	.75	1.50
Giant Size 1 ('75)	.30	.90	1.80
Special 1(9/67)-new art	.50	1.50	3.00
Special 2(2/71)(Wood-r), 3(1/72)-r	.30	.90	1.80
Annual 4(10/76)	.30	.90	1.80

NOTE: ***John Buscema*** *a-136, 137; c-136i, 142.* ***Byrne*** *a-138.* ***Craig*** *a-50i, 52i.* ***Ditko*** *c/a-162.* ***Everett*** *a/c-1; inks-21, 67, 81, 83.* ***Infantino*** *a-150-152.* ***Gil Kane*** *a-146.* ***Kirby*** *c-2-4, 5p, 13p, 136p.* ***Miller*** *script-168-177; a-158-161p, 163-177p; c-158-161, 163-177.* ***Orlando*** *a-2-4.* ***Powell*** *a-9p, 11p.* ***Wood*** *a-5-10, 11i; c-5i, 6-11, 164i.*

DAREDEVIL COMICS (See Silver Streak)
July, 1941 - No. 134, Sept, 1956 (Charles Biro stories)
Lev Gleason Publications (Funnies, Inc. No. 1)
(No. 1 titled "Daredevil Battles Hitler")

	Good	Fine	Mint
1-The Silver Streak, Lance Hale, Dickey Dean, Pirate Prince & Cloud Curtis team up with Daredevil and battle Hitler; Daredevil battles the Claw; Origin of Hitler feature story	175.00	450.00	850.00
2-London, Pat Patriot, Nightro, Real American No. 1, Dickie Dean, Pirate Prince, & Times Square begin; intro. & only app. The Pioneer, Champion of America	90.00	250.00	500.00
3-Origin of 13	50.00	140.00	280.00
4	40.00	120.00	240.00
5-Intro. Sniffer & Jinx; Ghost vs. Claw begins by Bob Wood, ends No. 20	35.00	100.00	200.00
6-10: 8-Nightro ends	30.00	80.00	150.00
11-London, Pat Patriot end; bondage/torture-c	20.00	60.00	120.00
12-Origin of The Claw; Scoop Scuttle by Wolverton begins (2-4 pgs.), ends No. 22, not in No. 21	30.00	80.00	165.00
13-Intro. of Little Wise Guys	30.00	80.00	165.00
14	15.00	45.00	90.00
15-Death of Meatball	22.00	65.00	145.00
16,17	15.00	40.00	80.00
18-New origin of Daredevil-Not same as Silver Streak No. 6	35.00	90.00	180.00
19,20	12.00	34.00	64.00
21-Reprints cover of Silver Streak No. 6(on inside) plus intro. of The Claw from Silver Streak No. 1	20.00	55.00	110.00
22-30	6.00	16.00	32.00
31-Death of The Claw	10.00	28.00	56.00
32-37: 34-Two Daredevil stories begin, end No. 68	4.50	13.00	26.00
38-Origin Daredevil retold from No. 18	8.00	24.00	48.00
39,40	4.50	13.00	26.00
41-50: 42-Intro. Kilroy in Daredevil	3.00	8.00	16.00
51-58,60-69-Last Daredevil ish.	1.50	4.50	9.00
59-Two page dope text story	2.00	5.00	10.00
70-Little Wise Guys take over book; McWilliams-a; Hot Rock Flanagan begins, ends No. 80	1.00	3.00	6.00
71-79,81: 79-Daredevil returns	1.00	3.00	6.00
80-Daredevil x-over	1.00	3.00	6.00
82,90-One page Frazetta ad in both (No. 82 is an anti-drug ad)	1.50	4.00	8.00
83-89,91-134	.85	2.50	5.00

NOTE: ***Wolverton's*** *Scoop Scuttle-12-20, 22.* ***Bolle*** *a-125.* ***McWilliams*** *a-73, 75, 79, 80.*

DARING ADVENTURES (Also see Approved Comics)
No. 7, July?, 1954 - 1956
St. John Publishing Co.

	Good	Fine	Mint
7-10	1.50	4.00	8.00
11-18	1.00	3.00	6.00
3-D 1(11/53)-Reprints lead story/Son of Sinbad No. 1 by Kubert	10.00	30.00	60.00

DARING ADVENTURES
1963 - 1964
I.W. Enterprises/Super Comics

	Good	Fine	Mint
I.W. Reprint No. 9-Disbrow-a(3)	2.00	6.00	12.00
Super Reprint No. 10,11('63)-Dynamic Man; 11-Marijuana story; Yankee boy app.	1.00	3.00	6.00
Super Reprint No. 12('64)-Phantom Lady from Fox(reprints No. 14, 15)	6.00	18.00	36.00
Super Reprint No. 15('64)-Hooded Menace	5.00	15.00	30.00
Super Reprint No. 16('64)-Mr. E, Dynamic Man/Dynamic No. 11	1.00	3.00	6.00
Super Reprint No. 17('64)-Green Lama by Raboy from Green Lama No. 3	2.00	6.00	12.00
Super Reprint No. 18-Origin Atlas	1.00	3.00	6.00

DARING COMICS (Formerly Daring Mystery) (Jeanie No. 13 on)
No. 9, Fall, 1944 - No. 12, Fall, 1945
Timely Comics

	Good	Fine	Mint
9-Human Torch & Sub-Mariner begin	20.00	55.00	120.00

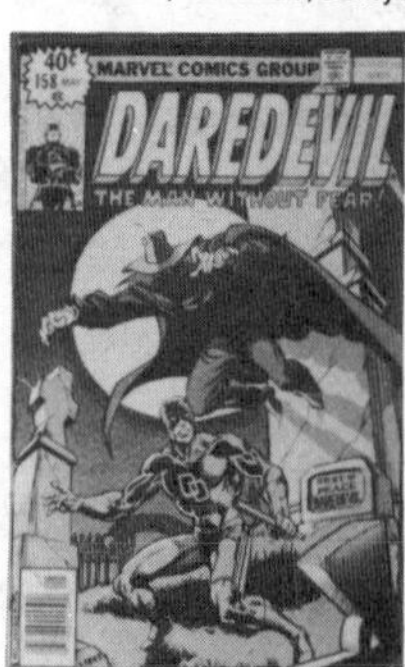

Daredevil #158, © MCG

Daredevil Comics #16, © LEV

Daredevil Comics #27, © LEV

Daring Comics #12, © MCG

Daring Love #1, © Gillmore

Dark Mysteries #14, © Master

DARING COMICS (continued)

	Good	Fine	Mint
10-The Angel only app.	15.00	45.00	100.00
11,12-The Destroyer app.	15.00	45.00	100.00

DARING CONFESSIONS (Formerly Youthful Hearts)
No. 4, 1952 - No. 7, May, 1953
Youthful Magazines

	Good	Fine	Mint
4-Doug Wildey-a	2.00	6.00	12.00
5-7: 6-Wildey-a	2.00	6.00	12.00

DARING LOVE (Radiant Love No. 2 on)
Sept-Oct, 1953
Gillmore Magazines

	Good	Fine	Mint
1	2.50	7.00	14.00

DARING LOVE (Formerly Youthful Romances)
No. 15, Dec, 1952 - No. 17, Apr, 1953
Ribage/Pix

	Good	Fine	Mint
15-17	2.00	5.00	10.00

DARING LOVE STORIES
1950 (25 cents) (132 pages)
Fox Features Syndicate

nn-See Fox Giants. Contents can vary and determines price.

DARING MYSTERY COMICS (Comedy No. 9 on; title changed to Daring with No. 9)
Jan, 1940 - No. 8, Jan, 1942
Timely Comics

	Good	Fine	Mint
1-Origin The Fiery Mask by Joe Simon; Monako, Prince of Magic, John Steele, Soldier of Fortune, Doc Doyle begin; Flash Foster & Barney Mullen, Sea Rover only app; bondage-c	250.00	700.00	1600.00
2-(Rare)-Origin The Phantom Bullet & only app.; The Laughing Mask & Mr. E only app.; Trojak the Tiger Man begins, ends No. 6; Zephyr Jones & K-4 & His Sky Devils app., also No. 4	150.00	425.00	900.00
3-The Phantom Reporter, Dale of FBI, Breeze Barton, Captain Strong & Marvex the Super-Robot only app.; The Purple Mask begins	100.00	275.00	650.00
4-Last Purple Mask; Whirlwind Carter begins; Dan Gorman, G-Man app.	80.00	225.00	475.00
5-The Falcon begins; The Fiery Mask, Little Hercules app. by Sagendorf in the Segar style: bondage-c	70.00	200.00	420.00
6-Origin & only app. Marvel Boy by S&K; Flying Flame, Dynaman, & Stuporman only app.; The Fiery Mask by S&K; S&K-c	90.00	250.00	525.00
7-Origin The Blue Diamond, Captain Daring by S&K, The Challenger, The Fin by Everett, The Silver Scorpion & The Thunderer by Burgos; Mr. Millions app.	100.00	270.00	550.00
8-Origin Citizen V; Last Fin, Silver Scorpion, Capt. Daring by Borth, Blue Diamond & The Thunderer; S&K-c; Rudy the Robot only app.	70.00	200.00	400.00

NOTE: ***Schomburg*** *c-1.* ***Simon*** *a-2,3,5.*

DARK MANSION OF FORBIDDEN LOVE, THE (Becomes Forbidden Tales of Dark Mansion No. 5 on)
Sept-Oct, 1971 - No. 4, Mar-Apr, 1972
National Periodical Publications

	Good	Fine	Mint
1	.30	.80	1.60
2-Adams-c	.35	1.00	2.00
3-Jeff Jones-c	.35	1.00	2.00
4		.50	1.00

DARK MYSTERIES
June-July, 1951 - No. 30, 1955
''Master''-''Merit'' Publications

	Good	Fine	Mint
1-Wood c/a, 8 pgs.	14.00	40.00	80.00
2-Wood c/a w/Harrison, 8 pgs.	10.00	30.00	60.00
3-9: 7-Harrison-a	3.00	8.00	16.00
10-Cannibalism story; bondage-c	3.00	9.00	18.00
11-13,15-18	2.00	6.00	12.00
14-Several E.C. Craig swipes	3.00	8.00	16.00
19-Injury to eye panel; bondage-c	3.50	10.00	20.00
20-Female bondage, blood drainage story	2.50	7.00	14.00
21,22-Last pre-code ish, mis-dated 3/54 instead of 3/55	2.00	5.00	10.00
23-25	1.25	3.75	7.50
26-30(Exist?)			

NOTE: ***Cameron*** *a-1, 2.* ***Hollingsworth*** *a-7-17, 20, 21, 23.*

DARK SHADOWS
October, 1957 - 1958
Steinway Comic Publications (Ajax)

	Good	Fine	Mint
1	2.00	6.00	12.00
2,3	1.00	3.00	6.00

DARK SHADOWS (TV) (See Dan Curtis)
May, 1969 - No. 35, Feb, 1976
Gold Key

	Good	Fine	Mint
1(30039-903)-with pull-out poster	1.00	3.00	6.00
2-5: 3-with pull-out poster; photo-c No. 1-5	.50	1.50	3.00
6-10	.35	1.00	2.00
11-20		.50	1.00
21-35		.50	1.00
Story Digest 1 (6/70)	.25	.70	1.40

DARLING LOVE
Oct-Nov, 1949 - No. 11, 1952 (no month)
Close Up/Archie Publ. (A Darling Magazine)

	Good	Fine	Mint
1	3.00	8.00	16.00
2-8,10,11: 5-photo-c	2.00	5.00	10.00
9-Krigstein-a	3.00	8.00	16.00

DARLING ROMANCE
Sept-Oct, 1949 - No. 7, 1951
Close Up (MLJ Publications)

	Good	Fine	Mint
1	3.00	8.00	16.00
2-7	2.00	5.00	10.00

DASTARDLY & MUTTLEY IN THEIR FLYING MACHINES (See Fun-In No. 1-4,6)

DASTARDLY & MUTTLEY KITE FUN BOOK (Giveaway)
1969 (16 pages) (5x7'') (Hanna-Barbera's)
Florida Power & Light Co./Sou. Calif. Edison/Pacific Gas & Electric

	Good	Fine	Mint
	.50	1.50	3.00

DATE WITH DANGER
No. 5, Dec, 1952 - No. 6, Feb, 1953
Standard Comics

	Good	Fine	Mint
5,6	1.50	4.00	8.00

DATE WITH DEBBI
1-2/69 - No. 17, 9-10/71; No. 18, 10-11/72
National Periodical Publications

	Good	Fine	Mint
1	.85	2.50	5.00
2-18	.50	1.50	3.00

DATE WITH JUDY, A (Radio/TV)
Oct-Nov, 1947 - No. 79, Oct-Nov, 1960
National Periodical Publications

	Good	Fine	Mint
1	6.00	18.00	36.00
2	3.00	9.00	18.00
3-10	2.00	6.00	12.00
11-20	1.00	3.00	6.00
21-40	.70	2.00	4.00
41-79: 79-Drucker c/a	.50	1.50	3.00

DATE WITH MILLIE, A (Life With Millie No. 8 on)
Oct, 1956 - No. 7, Aug, 1957; Oct, 1959 - No. 7, Oct, 1960
Atlas/Marvel Comics (MPC)

	Good	Fine	Mint
1(10/56)-(1st Series)	3.00	8.00	16.00

DATE WITH MILLIE (continued) — Good / Fine / Mint
2-7 — 1.50 / 4.00 / 8.00
1(10/59)-(2nd Series) — 2.00 / 5.00 / 10.00
2-7 — 1.00 / 3.00 / 6.00

DATE WITH PATSY, A
September, 1957
Atlas Comics

1 — 2.00 / 6.00 / 12.00

DAVID AND GOLIATH (See 4-Color No. 1205)

DAVID CASSIDY
Feb, 1972 - No. 14, Sept, 1973
Charlton Comics

1 — 1.00 / 3.00 / 6.00
2-14 — .70 / 2.00 / 4.00

DAVID LADD'S LIFE STORY (See Movie Classics)

DAVY CROCKETT (See Fightin. . ., Frontier Fighters, It's Game Time, & Western Tales)

DAVY CROCKETT
1951
Avon Periodicals

nn-Ingels?, Reinman-a; Fawcette-c — 5.50 / 16.00 / 32.00

DAVY CROCKETT (TV)
May, 1955 - No. 2, Nov, 1963 (Walt Disney)
Dell Publishing Co./Gold Key

4-Color 631,639 — 1.00 / 3.00 / 6.00
4-Color 664,671(Marsh-a) — 1.50 / 4.00 / 8.00
. . King of the Wild Frontier Annual 1('55-25 cents; Marsh-a; 100 pages) — 4.50 / 13.00 / 26.00
1(9/63-Gold Key) — .60 / 1.80 / 3.60
2 — .35 / 1.00 / 2.00
. . Christmas Book (no date, 16pgs, paper-c) Sears giveaway — 1.25 / 3.75 / 7.50
. . In the Raid at Piney Creek (1955, 16pgs, 5x7¼'')American Motors giveaway — 2.50 / 7.50 / 15.00
. . Safety Trails (1955, 16pgs, 3¼x7'') Cities Service giveaway — 2.00 / 6.00 / 12.00

DAVY CROCKETT FRONTIER FIGHTER (Kid Montana No. 9 on)
Aug, 1955 - No. 8, 1957
Charlton Comics

1 — 1.00 / 3.00 / 6.00
2-8 — .60 / 1.80 / 3.60
Hunting With. . .('55, 16 pgs.)-Ben Franklin Store giveaway (Publ.-S. Rose) — .70 / 2.00 / 4.00

DAYS OF THE MOB (See **In** the Days of the Mob)

DAZEY'S DIARY
June-Aug, 1962
Dell Publishing Co.

01-174-208 — .70 / 2.00 / 4.00

DAZZLER, THE (Also see X-Men No. 130)
March, 1981 - Present
Marvel Comics Group

1-X-Men app; Alcala art — .50 / 1.00
2-X-Men app. — .30 / .60
3-10 — .30 / .60

NOTE: *No. 1 distributed only through comic shops.*

DC COMICS PRESENTS
July-Aug, 1978 - Present
DC Comics

1-Superman/Flash — .50 / 1.50 / 3.00
2-Superman/Flash(Legion x-over), 3-Superman/Adam Strange, 4-Superman/Metal Men, 5-Superman/Aquaman each. . . . — .30 / .90 / 1.80
6-Superman/Green Lantern, 7-Superman/Red Tornado, 8-Superman/Swamp Thing, 9-Superman/Wonder Woman, 10-Superman/Sgt. Rock each. . . . — .25 / .75 / 1.50
11-Superman/Hawkman, 12-Superman/Mr. Miracle, 13-Superman/Legion of Super Heroes, 14-Superman/Superboy, 15-Superman/Atom, 16-Superman/Black Lightning, 17-Superman/Firestorm, 18-Superman/Zatanna, 19-Superman/Batgirl, 20-Superman/Green Arrow each. . . . — .60 / 1.20
21-Superman/Elongated Man, 22-Superman/Capt. Comet, 23-Superman/Dr. Fate, 24-Superman/Deadman, 25-Superman/Phantom Stranger each. . . . — .50 / 1.00
26-Superman/Green Lantern; intro Cyborg, Starfire, Raven, New Teen Titans; Starlin-c/a — 2.50 / 7.50 / 15.00
27,28-Superman/Supergirl, 29-Superman/Spectre, 30-Superman/Black Canary each. . . . — .40 / .80
31-Superman/Robin, 32-Superman/Wonder Woman, 33-Superman/Capt. Marvel, 34-Superman/Marvel Family, 35-Superman/Man-Bat, 36-Superman/Starman, 37-Superman/Hawkgirl; Rip Hunter origin, 38-Superman/Flash, 39-Superman/Plastic Man, 40-Superman/Metamorpho each. . . . — .30 / .60

NOTE: ***Anderson** a-5, 8. **Buckler** a-12. **Gil Kane** a-28, 35. **Lopez** a-1-4, 17; c-1-4, 8, 17, 31p. **Perez** a-26p, 38; c-38. **Starlin** a-26-29, 36, 37; c-26-29, 36, 37. **Staton** a(p)-9-11, 15, 16, 19, 20p, 21p, 23, 39; c-15.*

DC 100 PAGE SUPER SPECTACULAR (50 cents)
1971 - No. 13, 6/72; No. 14, 2/73 - No. 22, 11/73 (No No.1-3)
National Periodical Publications

4-Weird Mystery Tales-Johnny Peril & Phantom Stranger; cover & splashes by Wrightson; origin Jungle Boy of Jupiter — .40 / 1.20 / 2.40
5-Love stories; Wood Inks, 7pgs. — .50 / 1.50 / 3.00
6-''World's Greatest Super-Heroes''-JLA, JSA, Spectre, Johnny Quick, Vigilante, Wildcat & Hawkman; Adams wrap-around-c — .70 / 2.00 / 4.00
7-(See Superman No. 245),8-(See Batman No. 238)
9-(See Our Army at War No. 242),10-(See Adventure No. 416)
11-(See Flash No. 214),12-(See Superboy No. 185)
13-(See Superman No. 252)
14-Batman-(reprints Detective No. 31,32); Dollman, Wonder Woman, The Atom, Wildcat, & Blackhawk-r — .35 / 1.00 / 2.00
15-Superboy, Boy Commandos, Sandman, & Aquaman-r; S&K-a; Hawk & Dove-r — .30 / .80 / 1.60
16-Sgt. Rock & Capt. Storm-r — .35 / 1.00 / 2.00
17-JLA-Sandman & All-Star No. 37-r — .30 / .80 / 1.60
18-Superman, Hourman, Captain Triumph, The G.A. Atom-r — .30 / .80 / 1.60
19-Tarzan newspaper-r by Russ Manning — .35 / 1.00 / 2.00
20-Batman origin Two-Face; Dr. Mid-Nite, Wildcat, Starman, Black Canary, Blackhawk, The Spectre-r — .30 / .80 / 1.60
21-Superboy-r — .30 / .80 / 1.60
22-The Flash-r — .30 / .80 / 1.60

NOTE: ***Anderson** a-11, 14, 22. **Crandall** a-14. **Drucker** a-4r. **Infantino** a-17, 20, 22. **Kubert** a-6, 7, 16, 17; c-16,19. **Meskin** a-4, 22. **Toth** a-14, 17, 20.*

DC SPECIAL (Also see Super DC. . .)
10-12/68 - No. 15, 11-12/71; No. 16, Spr/75 - No. 29, 8-9/77
National Periodical Publications

1-All Infantino ish; Flash, Batman, Adam Strange-r — .50 / 1.50 / 3.00
2-Teen Favorites — .30 / .80 / 1.60
3-All heroine ish. Unpubbed G.A. Black Canary & Wonder Woman story — .35 / 1.00 / 2.00
4-Mystery Tales — .25 / .70 / 1.40
5-All Kubert ish. Viking Prince, Sgt. Rock-r — .40 / 1.20 / 2.40
6-Wild Frontier — .30 / .80 / 1.60

DC Comics Presents #26, © DC

DC 100pg. Super Spec. #14, © DC

DC Special #1, © DC

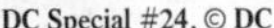
DC Special #24, © DC

DC Special Series #2, © DC

DC Super Stars #1, © DC

DC SPECIAL (continued) — Good / Fine / Mint

7-Strange Sports Stories .25 .70 1.40
8-Wanted .30 .80 1.60
9-Strange Sports Stories .30 .80 1.60
10-Stop! In the Name of the Law; r-/Showcase No. 1,5 .30 .80 1.60
11-The Monsters Are Here; Adams/Wrightson-c; Kirby-a(2) .30 .80 1.60
12-Viking Prince; Kubert-c; r-/Brave & the Bold No. 1,5,9,16; new Kubert splashes .40 1.20 2.40
13-Strange Sports Stories .30 .80 1.60
14-Wanted .30 .80 1.60
15-G.A. Plastic Man origin r-Police No. 1; origin Woozy by Cole .70 2.00 4.00
16-Super Heroes Battle Super Gorillas .30 .80 1.60
17-Green Lantern .30 .80 1.60
18-Earth Shaking Stories-Flash, Green Lantern, Captain Marvel .30 .80 1.60
19-War Against the Giants .30 .80 1.60
20-Green Lantern .35 1.00 2.00
21-War Against the Monsters .25 .70 1.40
22-25-The 3 Musketeers(new) & Robin Hood (reprints) .25 .70 1.40
26-Enemy Ace r-/Kubert .25 .70 1.40
27-Captain Comet, Tommy Tomorrow; Adams-i .25 .70 1.40
28-Earth Shattering Disaster Stories; Legion of Super-Heroes story .30 .80 1.60
29-Secret Origin of the Justice Society .25 .70 1.40

NOTE: ***Adams*** *c-3, 4, 6, 11, 29.* ***Anderson*** *c-7i, 8, 9, 13, 14.* ***Infantino*** *a-13; c-7p.* ***Buckler*** *a-27p; c-27.* ***Grell*** *c-20.* ***G. Kane*** *a-20r.* ***Kubert*** *a-22.* ***Staton*** *a-29p.* ***Toth*** *a-13.*

DC SPECIAL BLUE-RIBBON DIGEST
Mar-Apr, 1980 - Present
DC Comics

1-Legion-r/Adventure 247, 2-Flash-r, 3-JSA-r, 4-Green Lantern-r, 5-Zatanna, Justice League,The Demon, Deadman, & Wondergirl origin-r, 6-Ghosts-r, 7-Sgt. Rock-r, 8-Legion-r, 9-Secret Origins of Super Heroes-r, 10-Warlord-r, 11-J.L.A.-r, 12-Haunted Tank-r, 13-Strange Sports Stories-r, 14-U.F.O. Invaders-r, 15-Secret Origins of Super Villains-r, 16-Green Lantern-r each.... .50 1.00

NOTE: ***Adams*** *a-16(6)r; c-16.* ***Heath*** *a-14.* ***Infantino*** *a(r)-2, 14.* ***Kubert*** *a-3; c-7, 12, 14.* ***Orlando*** *c-1.* ***Wood*** *a-3.* ***Wrightson*** *a-16r.*

DC SPECIAL SERIES
Sept, 1977 - No. 16, Fall, 1978; No. 17, Aug, 1979 - Present
National Periodical Publications/DC Comics

1-Five-Star Super-Hero Spectacular; Atom, Flash, Green Lantern, Aquaman, Batman, Kobra app.; Adams-c; Staton, Nasser-a .30 .80 1.60
2(No.1)-Original Swamp Thing Saga, The(9-10/77)-reprints Swamp Thing No. 1&2 by Wrightson; Wrightson wrap-around-c .30 .80 1.60
3(No.2)-Sgt. Rock Special(10/77)-Kubert-c .25 .70 1.40
4(No.1)-Unexpected Annual, The(10/77) .25 .70 1.40
5(nn)-Superman Spectacular(11/77, 68 pgs.) .25 .70 1.40
6-Secret Society of Super-Villains Special(11/77) .25 .70 1.40
7(nn)-Ghosts Special(12/77) .25 .70 1.40
8(nn)-Brave & the Bold Special with Batman/Deadman/Sgt. Rock/Sherlock Holmes; Aparo-c .25 .70 1.40
9(nn)-Wonder Woman Spectacular(3/78)-Heath, Ditko-a .40 .80
10(nn)-Secret Origins of Super-Heroes(4/78)-Staton, Newton, Nasser-a .40 .80
11-The Flash Spectacular(5/78)-Anderson, Wood-a .40 .80
12-Secrets of Haunted House Special(6/78)-Starlin-c .40 .80
13(nn)-Sgt. Rock Spectacular(Summer/78)-Kubert-c .40 .80
14(nn)-Original Swamp Thing Saga(Summer/78)-Wrightson wrap-around-c .40 .80
15-Batman Spectacular(Summer/78)-Golden, Newton, Nasser-a Rogers c/a .40 .80
16-Jonah Hex Spectacular(Fall/78)-Bat Lash, Scalphunter stories Heath-a .40 .80
17-The Original Swamp Thing Saga(9/79)-(68 pgs.; $1.00 size); Batman app.; Wrightson c/a; r-/Swamp Thing No. 5-7 .50 1.00
18-Sgt. Rock's Prize Battle Tales(10-11/79)-(100 pg.; digest size); reprints; Kubert-c .50 1.00
19-Secret Origins of Super Heroes(10-11/79)-(100 pg.; digest size); reprints; new origin of Wonder Woman; Kubert-r .50 1.00
20-Swamp Thing(2/80)-Wrightson c/a(r) .50 1.00
21-Superstar Holiday Special-New art .50 1.00
22-G. I. Combat(9/80) .50 1.00
23-The Flash and His Friends(2-3/81)-Infantino-a(r) .50 1.00
24-World's Finest Comics Digest(2-3/81)-Kirby-a .50 1.00
25-Superman II The Adventure Continues (Sum '81) .50 1.00
26-Superman and His Incredible Fortress of Solitude (Sum '81) .50 1.00
27-Batman vs. The Incredible Hulk(12/81) .50 1.00

NOTE: *Number shown in parentheses is the cover number; the actual number is on inside.*

DC SUPER-STARS
March, 1976 - No. 18, Winter, 1978 (No.3-18: 52 pgs.)
National Periodical Publications/DC Comics

1-Teen Titans (68 pgs.) .35 1.00 2.00
2-Adam Strange, Hawkman (68 pgs.) .50 1.00
3-Superman, Legion of Super-Heroes .50 1.00
4-Adam Strange .50 1.00
5-The Flash .50 1.00
6-Adam Strange, Capt. Comet, Tommy Tomorrow, Space Cabby .50 1.00
7-Aquaman .50 1.00
8-Adam Strange, Star Rovers, Space Ranger .50 1.00
9-Superman, Nighthawk .50 1.00
10-Strange Sports; Super-Heroes vs. Super-Villains .50 1.00
11-Magic; Morrow-c; Zatanna, Flash-r .50 1.00
12-Superboy .50 1.00
13-Aragones c/a .50 1.00
14-Secret Origins of Super-Villains; new origin of Two-Face .50 1.00
15-War Heroes-Kubert-c .50 1.00
16-Star Hunters(1st app.)-Newton c/a .60 1.20
17-Secret Origins of Super-Heroes(1st app. & origin of The Huntress) Legion app. .50 1.00
18-Deadman & The Phantom Stranger .50 1.00

NOTE: ***Anderson*** *a-2, 4, 6, 12(i).* ***Aparo*** *c-7, 14, 18.* ***Buckler*** *a-14p; c-10.* ***Davis*** *a-14.* ***Grell*** *a-17.* ***Infantino*** *a-2, 4-6, 8, 11.* ***G. Kane*** *a-1r, 10r.* ***Nasser*** *a-11.* ***Staton*** *a-17; c-17. No. 10, 12-18 contain all new material; the rest are reprints.*

D-DAY (Also see Special War Series)
Summer, 1963 - No. 6, Nov, 1968
Charlton Comics

1(1963)-Montes/Bache-c .30 .80 1.60
2(Fall,'64)-Wood-a(3) .85 2.50 5.00
3-6('68)-Montes/Bache-a No. 5 .50 1.00

DEAD END CRIME STORIES
April, 1949 (52 pages)
Kirby Publishing Co.

nn-(Scarce)-Powell, Roussos-a 10.00 30.00 60.00

DEAD EYE CRIME STORIES
1950
Hillman Periodicals

	Good	Fine	Mint
1-(Scarce)-Roussos-a	7.00	20.00	40.00

DEAD-EYE WESTERN COMICS
Nov-Dec, 1948 - V3No.1, 1953
Hillman Periodicals

V1No.1(1948-52 pgs.)-Krigstein-a	3.00	8.00	16.00
nn(3-4/49, 52 pgs.)	1.50	4.00	8.00
V1No.2-12	.85	2.50	5.00
V2No.1,2,5-8,10-12	.60	1.80	3.60
3,4-Krigstein-a	2.00	5.00	10.00
9-One pg. Frazetta ad	1.20	3.50	7.00
V3No.1	.50	1.50	3.00

NOTE: ***Briefer** a-V1No.8. Kinstleresque stories by **McCann**-12, V2No.1,2, V3No.1.*

DEADLIEST HEROES OF KUNG FU
Summer, 1975 (Magazine)
Marvel Comics Group

1	.35	1.00	2.00

DEADLY HANDS OF KUNG FU, THE
April, 1974 - No. 33, Feb, 1977 (75 cents) (B&W - Magazine)
Marvel Comics Group

1(V1No.4 listed in error)-Origin Sons of the Tiger; Shang-Chi, Master of Kung Fu begins; Bruce Lee photo pin-up	.70	2.00	4.00
2,3,5	.40	1.20	2.40
4-Bruce Lee painted-c by Adams; 8 pg. biog of B. Lee	.50	1.50	3.00
6-14	.35	1.10	2.20
15-(Annual 1, Summer '75)	.40	1.20	2.40
16-27,29-33	.30	.90	1.80
28-Origin Jack of Hearts; Bruce Lee life story	.35	1.10	2.20
Special Album Edition 1(Summer, '74)-Adams-i	.40	1.20	2.40

NOTE: ***Adams** c-1, 2-4, 11, 12, 14, 17. **Rogers** a-32, 33. **Starlin** a-1, 2, 4p, 15r. **Staton** a-31, 32. Sons of the Tiger in 1, 3, 4, 6-9.*

DEAD OF NIGHT
Dec, 1973 - No. 11, Aug, 1975
Marvel Comics Group

1-Reprints		.40	.80
2-10: 9-Kirby-r		.30	.60
11-Intro. & 1st app. The Scarecrow; Kane/Wrightson-c		.60	1.20

NOTE: ***Ditko** a-7r, 10r.*

DEAD WHO WALK, THE
1952 - No. 3, 1952
Realistic Comics

nn-3	12.00	36.00	72.00

DEADWOOD GULCH
1931 (52 pages) (B&W)
Dell Publishing Co.

By Gordon Rogers	5.00	14.00	28.00

DEAN MARTIN & JERRY LEWIS (See Adventures of . . .)

DEAR BEATRICE FAIRFAX
Nov, 1949 - No. 9, Sept, 1951 (Vern Greene art)
Best/Standard Comics(King Features)

1	2.00	5.00	10.00
2-9	1.50	4.00	8.00

NOTE: ***Schomburg** air brush-c-1-9.*

DEAR HEART (Formerly Lonely Heart)

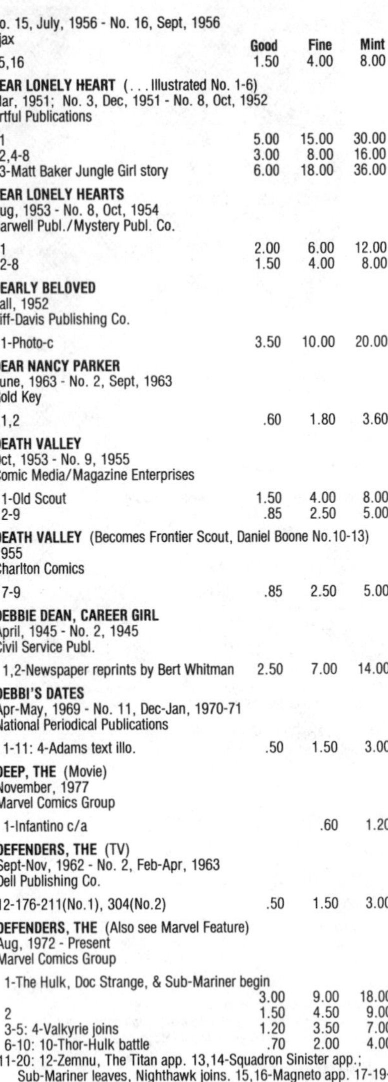

No. 15, July, 1956 - No. 16, Sept, 1956
Ajax

	Good	Fine	Mint
15,16	1.50	4.00	8.00

DEAR LONELY HEART (. . . Illustrated No. 1-6)
Mar, 1951; No. 3, Dec, 1951 - No. 8, Oct, 1952
Artful Publications

1	5.00	15.00	30.00
2,4-8	3.00	8.00	16.00
3-Matt Baker Jungle Girl story	6.00	18.00	36.00

DEAR LONELY HEARTS
Aug, 1953 - No. 8, Oct, 1954
Harwell Publ./Mystery Publ. Co.

1	2.00	6.00	12.00
2-8	1.50	4.00	8.00

DEARLY BELOVED
Fall, 1952
Ziff-Davis Publishing Co.

1-Photo-c	3.50	10.00	20.00

DEAR NANCY PARKER
June, 1963 - No. 2, Sept, 1963
Gold Key

1,2	.60	1.80	3.60

DEATH VALLEY
Oct, 1953 - No. 9, 1955
Comic Media/Magazine Enterprises

1-Old Scout	1.50	4.00	8.00
2-9	.85	2.50	5.00

DEATH VALLEY (Becomes Frontier Scout, Daniel Boone No.10-13)
1955
Charlton Comics

7-9	.85	2.50	5.00

DEBBIE DEAN, CAREER GIRL
April, 1945 - No. 2, 1945
Civil Service Publ.

1,2-Newspaper reprints by Bert Whitman	2.50	7.00	14.00

DEBBI'S DATES
Apr-May, 1969 - No. 11, Dec-Jan, 1970-71
National Periodical Publications

1-11: 4-Adams text illo.	.50	1.50	3.00

DEEP, THE (Movie)
November, 1977
Marvel Comics Group

1-Infantino c/a		.60	1.20

DEFENDERS, THE (TV)
Sept-Nov, 1962 - No. 2, Feb-Apr, 1963
Dell Publishing Co.

12-176-211(No.1), 304(No.2)	.50	1.50	3.00

DEFENDERS, THE (Also see Marvel Feature)
Aug, 1972 - Present
Marvel Comics Group

1-The Hulk, Doc Strange, & Sub-Mariner begin	3.00	9.00	18.00
2	1.50	4.50	9.00
3-5: 4-Valkyrie joins	1.20	3.50	7.00
6-10: 10-Thor-Hulk battle	.70	2.00	4.00
11-20: 12-Zemnu, The Titan app. 13,14-Squadron Sinister app.; Sub-Mariner leaves, Nighthawk joins. 15,16-Magneto app. 17-19-Wrecking Crew app.	.50	1.50	3.00

21-26,28-30: 26-29-Guardians of the Galaxy app.

The Dead Who Walk nn, © REAL

Dear Lonely Heart #4, © Artful

The Defenders #2, © MCG

The Defenders #47, © MCG

The Demon #2, © DC

Demon-Hunter #1, © ATLAS

DEFENDERS (continued)	Good	Fine	Mint
	.35	1.00	2.00
27-1st app. Starhawk	.40	1.20	2.40
31,32-Origin Nighthawk	.30	.80	1.60
33-40: 35-Intro. New Red Guardian	.30	.80	1.60
41-46: 44-Hellcat joins. 45-Dr. Strange leaves		.60	1.20
47-51-Moon Night x-over; 47-Wonderman app.		.60	1.20
52,55-60		.50	1.00
53,54-Golden-a(p)		.50	1.00
61,65-70		.50	1.00
62-64-Nova & others cameo		.60	1.20
71-99: 99-Silver Surfer app.		.40	.80
100-Double size		.50	1.00
101-103		.30	.60

NOTE: ***J. Buscema*** *c-66.* ***Golden*** *a-54p; c-94, 96.* ***Infantino*** *a-55, 56; c-56.* ***Kirby*** *c-42-45.* ***Nasser*** *c-88.* ***Rogers*** *c-98, 99. Silver Surfer in No. 2, 3, 6, 8-11.*

	Good	Fine	Mint
Annual 1(11/76)	.45	1.30	2.60
Giant Size 1(7/74)-Silver Surfer app.; Starlin-a; Everett & Ditko-r	.70	2.00	4.00
Giant Size 2(10/74)-G. Kane-a	.30	.80	1.60
Giant Size 3(1/75)-Starlin-a	.30	.80	1.60
Giant Size 4(4/75), 5(7/75)-Guardians app.	.30	.80	1.60

NOTE: ***Ditko*** *a-Giant Size 1-4r.*

DELECTA OF THE PLANETS (See Fawcett Miniatures & Don Fortune)

DELLA VISION
April, 1955 - No. 3, Aug, 1955
Atlas Comics

	Good	Fine	Mint
1	3.00	8.00	16.00
2,3	2.00	5.00	10.00

DELL GIANT COMICS
No. 21, Sept, 1959 - No. 55, Sept, 1961 (Most 80 pages, 25 cents)
Dell Publishing Co.

	Good	Fine	Mint
21-Tom & Jerry Picnic Time	.70	2.00	4.00
22-Huey, Dewey & Louie Back to School(10/59)	1.50	4.00	8.00
23-Little Lulu & Tubby Halloween Fun	4.00	12.00	24.00
24-Woody Woodpecker Family Fun (11/59)	.70	2.00	4.00
25-Tarzan's Jungle World(11/59)-Marsh-a	2.50	7.00	14.00
26-Christmas Parade-Barks-a(16pgs.,Disney)	7.00	20.00	40.00
27-Man in Space r-/4-Color 716,866, & 954 (100 pages, 35 cents) (Disney)	1.50	4.00	8.00
28-Bugs Bunny's Winter Fun (2/60)	.70	2.00	4.00
29-Little Lulu & Tubby in Hawaii (4/60)	3.50	10.00	20.00
30-Disneyland USA(6/60)-Reprinted in Vacation in Disneyland	1.20	3.50	7.00
31-Huckleberry Hound Summer Fun (7/60)	.60	1.80	3.60
32-Bugs Bunny Beach Party	.70	2.00	4.00
33-Daisy Duck & Uncle Scrooge Picnic Time (9/60)	2.00	5.00	10.00
34-Nancy & Sluggo Summer Camp (8/60)	.85	2.50	5.00
35-Huey, Dewey & Louie Back to School (10/60)	1.20	3.50	7.00
36-Little Lulu & Witch Hazel Halloween Fun(10/60)-(two different back covers)	3.00	9.00	18.00
37-Tarzan, King of the Jungle(11/60)-Marsh-a	2.00	5.00	10.00
38-Uncle Donald & His Nephews Family Fun (11/60)	1.20	3.50	7.00
39-Walt Disney's Merry Christmas(12/60)-Not by Barks	1.50	4.00	8.00
40-Woody Woodpecker Christmas Parade(12/60)	.60	1.80	3.60
41-Yogi Bear's Winter Sports (12/60)	.60	1.80	3.60
42-Little Lulu & Tubby in Australia (1961)	2.50	7.00	14.00
43-Mighty Mouse in Outer Space (5/61)	1.50	4.00	8.00
44-Around the World with Huckleberry & His Friends (7/61)	.60	1.80	3.60
45-Nancy & Sluggo Summer Camp (8/61)	1.20	3.50	7.00
46-Bugs Bunny Beach Party	1.00	3.00	6.00
47-Mickey & Donald in Vacationland (8/61)	1.50	4.00	8.00
48-The Flintstones (Bedrock Bedlam)(7/61)	.60	1.80	3.60
49-Huey, Dewey & Louie Back to School (9/61)	1.20	3.50	7.00
50-Little Lulu & Witch Hazel Trick 'N' Treat (10/61)	3.00	9.00	18.00
51-Tarzan, King of the Jungle by Jesse Marsh (11/61)	1.50	4.00	8.00
52-Uncle Donald & His Nephews Dude Ranch (11/61)	1.50	4.00	8.00
53-Donald Duck Merry Christmas(12/61)-Not by Barks	1.50	4.00	8.00
54-Woody Woodpecker Christmas Party(12/61)-issued after No. 55	.60	1.80	3.60
55-Daisy Duck & Uncle Scrooge Showboat (9/61)	1.50	4.00	8.00

DELL JUNIOR TREASURY (15 cents)
June, 1955 - No. 10, Oct, 1957
Dell Publishing Co.

	Good	Fine	Mint
1-Alice in Wonderland-Reprints 4-Color 331 (52 pgs.)	3.00	8.00	16.00
2-Aladdin & the Wonderful Lamp	2.50	7.00	14.00
3-Gulliver's Travels(1/56)	2.00	6.00	12.00
4-Advs. of Mr. Frog & Miss Mouse	2.50	7.00	14.00
5-The Wizard of Oz(7/56)	2.50	7.00	14.00
6-Heidi (10/56)	2.00	6.00	12.00
7-Santa & the Angel	2.00	6.00	12.00
8-Raggedy Ann & the Camel with the Wrinkled Knees	2.00	6.00	12.00
9-Clementina the Flying Pig	2.00	6.00	12.00
10-Advs. of Tom Sawyer	2.50	7.00	14.00

DEMON, THE (See Detective No. 482-485)
Aug-Sept, 1972 - No. 16, Jan, 1974
National Periodical Publications

	Good	Fine	Mint
1-Origin; Kirby-a in all	.30	.90	1.80
2-5		.50	1.00
6-16		.30	.60

DEMON-HUNTER
September, 1975
Seaboard Periodicals (Atlas)

	Good	Fine	Mint
1-Origin; drug mention		.40	.80

DENNIS THE MENACE (See The Best of. . . & The Very Best of. . .)
8/53 - No. 14, 1/56; No. 15, 3/56 - No. 31, 11/58; No. 32 -Present
Standard Comics/Pines No.15-31/Hallden(Fawcett) No. 32 on

	Good	Fine	Mint
1	12.00	36.00	75.00
2	5.50	16.00	35.00
3-10	3.50	10.00	20.00
11-20	2.00	6.00	12.00
21-40	1.00	3.00	6.00
41-60	.70	2.00	4.00
61-90	.50	1.50	3.00
91-160	.30	.80	1.60
. . . & Dirt('59,'68)-Soil Conservation giveaway	.25	.70	1.40
. . . Away We Go('70)-Caladayl giveaway	.25	.70	1.40
. . . Takes a Poke at Poison('61)-Food & Drug Assn. giveaway (revised 1/66, 11/70, 1972)	.25	.70	1.40

DENNIS THE MENACE (Giants) (No. 1 titled Giant Vacation Special; becomes Bonus Magazine No. 76 on)
(No. 1-8,18,23,25,30,38: 100 pgs.; rest to No. 41: 84 pgs.; No. 42-75: 68 pgs.)
Summer, 1955 - No. 75, 1970
Standard/Pines/Hallden(Fawcett)

	Good	Fine	Mint
nn-Giant Vacation Special(Summer '55-Standard)	3.00	8.00	16.00

DENNIS THE MENACE (continued)
nn-Christmas issue (Winter '55)
2-Giant Vacation Special (Summer '56-Pines)
3-Giant Christmas issue (Winter '56-Pines)
4-Giant Vacation Special (Summer '57-Pines)
5-Giant Christmas issue (Winter '57-Pines)
6-In Hawaii (Giant Vacation Special)(Summer '58-Pines)-Reprinted Summer '60 plus 3 more times
6-Giant Christmas issue (Winter '58)
7-In Hollywood (Winter '59-Hallden)
8-In Mexico (Winter '60, 100 pgs.-Hallden/Fawcett)
9-Goes to Camp (Summer '61, 84 pgs., 2nd printing-Summer '62)-1st CCA approved ish.
10-X-Mas issue (Winter '61)

	Good	Fine	Mint
each....	1.20	3.50	7.00

11-Giant Christmas issue (Winter '62)
12-Triple Feature (Winter '62)
13-Best of Dennis the Menace (Spring '63)-Reprints
14-And His Dog Ruff (Summer '63)
15-In Washington, D.C. (Summer '63)
16-Goes to Camp (Summer '63)-Reprints No. 9
17-& His Pal Joey (Winter '63)
18-In Hawaii (Reprints No. 6)
19-Giant Christmas issue (Winter '63)
20-Spring Special (Spring '64)
each.... .85 2.50 5.00
21-The Best of... (Spring '64)-Reprints
22-T.V. Special (Spring '64)
23-In Hollywood (Summer '64, 100 pgs.)-Reprints No. 7
24-Goes to Camp (Summer '64)-Reprints No. 9
25-In Mexico (Reprints No. 8)
26-In Washington, D.C. (Summer '64)-Reprints No. 15
27-Giant Christmas issue (Winter '64)
28-Triple Feature (Spring '65)
29-Best of... (Spring '65)-Reprints
30-In Hawaii (Summer '65)-Reprints No. 6
31-All Year 'Round (Summer '65)
32-And His Pal Joey! (Summer '65)-Reprints No. 17
33-In California (Summer '65)
34-And His Dog Ruff (Summer '65)-Reprints all No. 14
35-Christmas Special (Winter '65)
36-Spring Special (Spring '66)
37-Television Special (Spring '66)
38-In Mexico (Summer '66)-Reprints No. 8
39-Goes to Camp (Summer '66)-Reprints No. 9
40-In Washington, D.C. (Summer '66)-Reprints No. 15
each.... .60 1.80 3.60
41-From A to Z (Summer '66)
42-In Hollywood (Summer '66)-Reprints No. 7
43-Christmas Special (Winter '66)
44-Around the Clock (Spring '67)
45-And His Pal Joey! (Spring '67)
46-Triple Feature (Summer '67)-Reprints No. 28
47-In California (Summer '67)-Reprints most No. 33
48-Way Out Stories (Summer '67)
49-All Year 'Round (Fall '67)-Reprints No. 31
50-At the Circus (Summer '67)
51-Christmas Special (Winter '67)
52-Sports Special (Spring '68)-last CCA approved ish.
53-Spring Special (Spring '68)-Reprints most No. 36
54-And His Dog Ruff (Summer '68)-Reprints most No. 14
55-Tall Stories (Spring '68)
56-Television Special (Spring '68)-Reprints TV show scripts
57-Pet Parade (Summer '68)
58-The Best of... (Summer '68)-Reprints
59-Day By Day (Summer '68)
60-In Hollywood (Fall '68)-Reprints most No. 7
61-Christmas Favorites (Winter '68)
62-Fun Book (Winter '68)-Reprints most D.T.M. Fun Book No. 1
63-& His Wish I Was Book (Winter '69)
64-In Mexico (Spring '69)-Reprints most No. 8
65-Around the Clock (Spring '69)-Reprints No. 44
66-Gags 'n' Games (Summer '69)
67-Goes to Camp (Summer '69)-Reprints most No. 16
68-In Hawaii (Summer '69)-Part reprint No. 6
69-The Best of... (Aug, '69)-Reprints
70-Tangled Tales (Aug, '69)
71-Highlights (Sept, '69)-Reprints
72-In Washington, D.C. (Aug, '69)-Reprints most No. 15
73-Way-Out Stories (Sept, '69)-Reprints No. 48
74-Mr. Wilson & His Gang at Christmas (Dec, '69)-Reprints
75-Merry Christmas to You (Dec, '69)
each.... .30 .80 1.60

DENNIS THE MENACE
Nov, 1981 - Present
Marvel Comics Group

1,2 .30 .60

DENNIS THE MENACE AND HIS DOG RUFF
Summer, 1961
Hallden/Fawcett

1 2.00 6.00 12.00

DENNIS THE MENACE AND HIS FRIENDS
1969; No. 5, Jan, 1970 - Present
Fawcett Publications

	Good	Fine	Mint
Dennis T.M. & Joey No. 2 (7/69)	1.50	4.00	8.00
Dennis T.M. & Ruff No. 2 (9/69)	1.00	3.00	6.00
Dennis T.M. & Mr. Wilson No. 1 (10/69)	1.00	3.00	6.00
Dennis & Margaret No. 1 (Winter '69)	.50	1.50	3.00
5-10: No. 5-Dennis T.M. & Margaret. No. 6-& Joey. No. 7-& Ruff. No. 8-& Mr. Wilson	.25	.70	1.40
11-20	.25	.70	1.40
21-37		.60	1.20
38(begin digest size, 148 pgs., 4/78, 95 cents) - 42		.60	1.20

NOTE: *Titles rotate every four issues, beginning with No. 5.*

DENNIS THE MENACE AND HIS PAL JOEY
Summer, 1961 (10 cents) (See Dennis the Menace Giants No. 45)
Fawcett Publications

1 2.00 6.00 12.00

DENNIS THE MENACE AND THE BIBLE KIDS
1977 (36 pages)
Word Books

1-Jesus. 2-Joseph. 3-David. 4-The Bible Girls. 5-Moses. 6-More About Jesus.
each.... .25 .50

DENNIS THE MENACE BONUS MAGAZINE
No. 76, 1970 - Present (No. 76-124: 68 pgs.; No. 125-163: 52 pgs.; No. 164 on: 36 pgs.)
Fawcett Publications

76-In the Carribean (1/70)
77-Sports Special (2/70)-Reprints No. 52
78-Spring Special (3/70)-Reprints most No. 20
79-Tall Stories (4/70)-Reprints No. 55
80-Day By Day (5/70)-Reprints No. 59
81-Summer Funner (6/70)
82-In California (6/70)-Reprints most No. 33
83-Mama Goose (7/70)
84-At the Circus (7/70)-Reprint
85-The Fall Ball (8/70)
86-Mr. Wilson & His Gang at Christmas (10/70)-Reprints
87-Christmas Special (10/70)
88-In London (1/71)
89-Spring Fling (2/71)
90-Highlights (3/71)-Reprints
each.... .25 .70 1.40
91-Fun Book (4/71)-Reprints most D.T.M. Fun Book No. 1
92-In Hollywood (5/71)-Reprints most No. 7
93-Visits Paris (6/71)
94-Jackpot (6/71)-Reprint
95-That's Our Boy (7/71)-Reprints
96-(Some numbered No. 95)-Summer Games (7/71)
97-Comicapers (8/71)
98-Mr. Wilson & His Gang at Christmas (10/71)
99-Christmas Special (10/71)
100-Up in the Air (1/72)
101-Rise and Shine (2/72)
102-Wish-I-Was Book (3/72)-Reprints No. 63
103-Short Stuff Special (4/72)
104-In Mexico (5/72)-Reprints most No. 8
105-Birthday Special (6/72)-Reprints part D.T.M. No. 1
106-Fast & Funny (6/72)
107-Around the Clock (7/72)-Reprints No. 44
108-Goes to Camp (7/72)-Reprints most No. 9
109-Gags and Games (7/72)-Reprints No. 66 with new cover
110-Mr. Wilson & His Gang at Christmas (10/72)
each.... .50 1.00
111-Christmas Special (10/72)
112-Go-Go Special (1/73)
113-Tangled Tales (2/73)-Reprints No. 70
114-In Hawaii (3/73)-Reprints No. 68 with new cover
115-Ting-A-Ling Special (4/73)
116-In Washington, D.C. (5/73)-Reprints most No. 15
117-Encore (6/73)-Reprints No. 69 with new cover
118-Here's How (6/73)
119-The Summer Number (7/73)
120-Strikes Back (7/73)
121-Way-Out Stories (8/73)-Reprints No. 48
122-& Mr. Wilson & His Gang at Christmas (10/73)
123-Christmas Special (10/73)
124-Happy Holidays! (1/74)
125-In London (2/74)-Reprints most No. 88
126-Sports Special (3/74)-Reprints most No. 52
127-Visits Paris (4/74)-Partially reprints No. 93
128-Visits the Queen (Queen Mary) (5/74)
129-At the Circus (6/74)-Part reprint No. 50
130-In Hollywood (6/74)-Reprints half No. 7
131-What in the World?! (7/74)
132-Follow the Leader (7/74)-Reprints
133-That's the Spirit! (8/74)
134-Christmas Special (10/74)
135-& Mr. Wilson & His Gang at Christmas (10/74)-Reprints
136-"Crazy Daze" (1/75)
137-"Up and at 'Em" (2/75)

The Destructor #2, © ATLAS

Detective Comics #14, © DC

Detective Comics #27, © DC

DENNIS T.M. BONUS MAG. (continued)

	Good	Fine	Mint
138-Fun Book (3/75)-Reprints half D.T.M. Fun Book No. 1			
139-Jackpot (4/75)-Reprints most No. 94			
140-Big Deal (5/75) each....		.40	.80
141-Gags & Games (6/75)-Reprints most No. 109			
142-Just Kidding (6/75)-Intro. Hot Dog (Dennis' cat)			
143-Ireland (7/75)			
144-In Washington, D.C. (7/75)(Bicentennial)-Reprints most No. 116			
145-Yankee Doodle Dennis 1776-1976 (8/75)			
146-Christmas Special (10/75)			
147-& Mr. Wilson & His Gang at Christmas (10/75)			
148-In Florida (1/76)			
149-The Cookie Kid! (2/76)-Reprints			
150-The Daffy Dozen (3/76)			
151-Yearbook (4/76)			
152-The Best of... (5/76)-Reprints			
153-Yankee Doodle Dennis 1776-1976 (6/76)-Reprints No. 145			
154-Yours Truly Dennis (6/76)-Reprints part No. 101,106			
155-Making Movies! (Summer Special, 7/76)			
156-Pretty Tricky! (7/76)-Reprints			
157-Dare-Devil Dennis (8/76)-Reprints			
158-Christmas Special (10/76)			
159-& Mr. Wilson & His Gang at Christmas (10/76)			
160-Yearbook (1/77)			
161-Off and Running! (2/77)-Reprints half D.T.M. Fun Book No. 1			
162-At Marriott's Great America (3/77)			
163-Cherry Blossom Festival (4/77)			
164-''Just Kid-ding'' (5/77)-Reprints			
165-The Best of Dennis (6/77)-Reprints			
166-Vacation Sensation (6/77)-Reprints			
167-At the National Air & Space Museum of the Smithsonian Institute, Washington, D.C. (6/77)			
168-Tough and Tricky (7/77)-Reprints each....		.30	.60
169-He's All Yours (7/77)-Reprints			
170-A Special Christmas (10/77)			
171-Mr. Wilson & His Gang at Christmas (10/77)			
172-All Year Long (1/78)			
173-Best of... (2/78)-Reprints			
174-In Hawaii (Maui) (3/78)-New			
175-In the Soup (4/78)-Reprints			
176-Cookie Capers (5/78)-Reprints			
177-Fair Enough (6/78)			
178-The Short Sport (6/78)-Reprints			
179-Triple Trouble (7/78)-Reprints			
180-Going and Coming (7/78)-Reprints			
181-Dennis In San Diego California (8/78)			
182-Mr. Wilson & His Gang at Christmas (10/78)			
183-Christmas Special (10/78)			
184-Visits the United Nations (1/79)			
185-Best of... (2/79)-Reprints			
186-Returns to San Diego (3/79)			
187-The One and Only (4/79)-Reprints			
188-Dennis Carries On (5/79)			
189-Fore (6/79)			
190-Dennis in Hawaii (6/79) each....		.30	.60

DENNIS THE MENACE FUN BOOK
1960 (100 pages)
Standard Comics

	Good	Fine	Mint
1	2.00	6.00	12.00

DENNIS THE MENACE POCKET FULL OF FUN!
Spring, 1969 - Present (196 pages) (Digest size)
Fawcett Publications (Hallden)

	Good	Fine	Mint
1-Reprints in all issues	.35	1.00	2.00
2-10		.50	1.00
11-28		.30	.60
29-41: 35,40-Sunday strip reprints		.40	.80

NOTE: *No. 1-28 are 196 pgs.; No. 29-36: 164 pgs.; No. 37: 148 pgs.; No. 38 on: 132 pgs. No. 8,11,15,21,25,29 all contain strip reprints.*

DENNIS THE MENACE TELEVISION SPECIAL
Summer, 1961 - No. 2, Spring, 1962 (Giant)
Fawcett Publications (Hallden Div.)

	Good	Fine	Mint
1	1.50	4.00	8.00
2	1.00	3.00	6.00

DENNIS THE MENACE TRIPLE FEATURE
Winter, 1961 (Giant)
Fawcett Publications

	Good	Fine	Mint
1	1.50	4.00	8.00

DEPUTY, THE (See 4-Color No. 1077,1130,1225)

DEPUTY DAWG (TV) (Also see New Terrytoons)
Oct-Dec, 1961 - No. 1, Aug, 1965
Dell Publishing Co./Gold Key

	Good	Fine	Mint
4-Color 1238,1299	1.00	3.00	6.00
1(10164-508)	.70	2.00	4.00

DEPUTY DAWG PRESENTS DINKY DUCK AND HASHIMOTO SAN
August, 1965
Gold Key

	Good	Fine	Mint
1(10159-508)	.85	2.50	5.00

DESIGN FOR SURVIVAL (Gen. Thomas S. Power's...)
1968 (36 pages in color) (25 cents)
American Security Council Press

	Good	Fine	Mint
nn-Propaganda against the Threat of Communism-Aircraft cover	3.00	8.00	16.00
Twin Circle edition-cover shows panels from inside	2.00	5.00	10.00

DESPERADO (Black Diamond Western No. 9 on)
June, 1948 - No. 8, Feb, 1949
Lev Gleason Publications

	Good	Fine	Mint
1-Biro-a	3.00	8.00	16.00
2-8: 7-Guardineer-a	1.50	4.00	8.00

DESTINATION MOON (See Fawcett Movie Comics & Strange Adventures No. 1)

DESTRUCTOR, THE
February, 1975 - No. 4, Aug, 1975
Atlas/Seaboard

	Good	Fine	Mint
1-Origin; Ditko/Wood-a	.30	.80	1.60
2-4: 2,3-Ditko/Wood-a; 4-Ditko-a(p)		.50	1.00

DETECTIVE COMICS
March, 1937 - Present
National Periodical Publications/DC Comics

	Good	Fine	Mint
1-(Scarce)-Slam Bradley & Spy by Siegel & Shuster, Speed Saunders by Guardineer, Flat Foot Flannigan by Gustavson, Cosmo, the Phantom of Disguise, Buck Marshall, Bruce Nelson begin; Fu Manchu-c	300.00	800.00	1800.00
2 (Rare)	130.00	380.00	800.00
3 (Rare)	100.00	280.00	575.00
4,5	50.00	130.00	275.00
6,7,9,10	35.00	100.00	215.00
8-Fu Manchu-c	50.00	150.00	300.00
11-17,19	25.00	75.00	150.00
18-Fu Manchu-c	40.00	120.00	240.00
20-The Crimson Avenger begins (intro. & 1st app.)	40.00	120.00	240.00
21,23-25	17.00	50.00	100.00
22-Crimson Avenger-c	24.00	70.00	140.00
26	18.00	54.00	108.00
27-1st app. The Batman & Commissioner Gordon by Bob Kane; No. 27 reprinted in Famous First Edition	1200.00	3600.00	7500.00
(Prices vary widely on this book)			
28	400.00	1000.00	2000.00

Detective Comics #41, © DC

Detective Comics #68, © DC

Detective Comics #100, © DC

DETECTIVE COMICS (continued)	Good	Fine	Mint
29-Batman-c; Doctor Death app; Larry Steele begins	190.00	550.00	1100.00
30,32: 30-Dr. Death app.	100.00	280.00	560.00
31-Batman-c; 1st Julie Madison	170.00	450.00	925.00
33-Origin The Batman; Batman-c	275.00	750.00	1600.00
34-Steve Malone begins	75.00	200.00	450.00
35-37: Batman-c. 35-Hypo-c. 36-Origin Hugo Strange. 37-Cliff Crosby begins	75.00	200.00	450.00
38-Origin/1st app. Robin the Boy Wonder	230.00	650.00	1400.00
39	70.00	185.00	390.00
40-Origin & 1st app. Clay Face	50.00	145.00	310.00
41-Robin's 1st solo	45.00	135.00	280.00
42-45: 44-Crimson Avenger dons new costume	30.00	80.00	160.00
46-50: 48-1st time car called Batmobile; Gotham City 1st mention. 49-Last Clay Face	24.00	70.00	150.00
51-57,59: 59-Last Steve Malone; 2nd Penguin; Wing becomes Crimson Avenger's aide	20.00	60.00	120.00
58-1st Penguin app.; last Speed Saunders	30.00	85.00	180.00
60-Intro. Air Wave	22.00	65.00	130.00
61-63: 63-Last Cliff Crosby; 1st app. Mr. Baffle	19.00	55.00	110.00
64-Origin & 1st app. Boy Commandos by Simon & Kirby	65.00	180.00	400.00
65-Boy Commandos-c	35.00	85.00	170.00
66-Origin & 1st app. Two-Face	35.00	85.00	170.00
67,69,70	15.00	45.00	90.00
68-Two-Face app.	19.00	55.00	110.00
71-75: 74-1st Tweedledum & Tweedledee; S&K-a	14.00	40.00	80.00
76-Newsboy Legion & The Sandman x-over in Boy Commandos; S&K-a	19.00	55.00	110.00
77-79: All S&K-a	14.00	40.00	80.00
80-Two-Face app.; S&K-a	15.00	45.00	90.00
81,82,84-90: 81-1st Cavalier app. 85-Last Spy. 89-Last Crimson Avenger	12.00	35.00	70.00
83-1st ''Skinny'' Alfred; last S&K Boy Commandos? Note: most issues No. 84 on signed S&K are not by them	14.00	40.00	80.00
91-99: 96-Alfred's last name 'Beagle' revealed, later changed to 'Pennyworth'-Batman 214	11.00	32.00	64.00
100	20.00	60.00	120.00
101-120: 114-1st small logo(7/46)	10.00	30.00	60.00
121-130	9.00	25.00	50.00
131-137,139: 137-Last Air Wave	8.00	23.00	46.00
138-Origin Robotman (See Star Spangled No. 7, 1st app.)	15.00	45.00	90.00

	Good	Fine	Mint
140-1st app. The Riddler	24.00	70.00	140.00
141,143-150: 150-Last Boy Commandos	8.00	23.00	46.00
142-2nd Riddler app.	11.00	32.00	64.00
151-Origin & 1st app. Pow Wow Smith	9.00	25.00	50.00
152,154,155,157-160: 152-Last Slam Bradley	8.00	23.00	46.00
153-1st Roy Raymond app.	9.00	25.00	50.00
156(2/50)-The new classic Batmobile	9.00	25.00	50.00
161-167,169-180	7.00	20.00	40.00
168-Origin the Joker	24.00	70.00	140.00
181-189,191-199,201-204,206-212: 187-Two-Face app. 202-Last Robotman & Pow Wow Smith	5.50	16.00	32.00
190-Origin Batman retold	6.00	18.00	36.00
200	8.00	23.00	46.00
205-Origin Batcave	7.00	20.00	40.00
213-Origin Mirror Man	6.00	18.00	36.00
214-224: 218-Last pre-code ish.	5.00	14.00	28.00
225-Intro. & 1st app. Martian Manhunter-John Jones, later changed to J'onn J'onzz (1st National Silver Age hero); also see Batman 78	60.00	180.00	360.00
226	12.00	35.00	70.00
227-229	8.00	24.00	48.00
230-1st app. Mad Hatter	10.00	30.00	60.00
231-Origin Martian Manhunter retold	5.00	14.00	28.00
232,234-240	4.00	12.00	24.00
233-Origin & 1st app. Batwoman	7.00	20.00	40.00
241-260: 246-Intro. Diane Meade, J. Jones' girl. 257-Intro. & 1st app. Whirly Bats	3.50	10.00	20.00
261-264,266,268-270: 261-1st app. Dr. Double. 262-Origin Jackal	2.50	7.00	14.00
265-Batman's origin retold	3.50	10.00	20.00
267-Origin & 1st app. Bat-Mite	3.50	10.00	20.00
271-280	2.00	5.00	10.00
281-297,299,300: 292-Last Roy Raymond. 293-Aquaman begins, ends No. 300	1.50	4.00	8.00
298-1st modern Clayface	2.00	5.00	10.00
301-327,329,330: 311-Intro. Zook in J'onn J'onzz; 1st app. Catman. 322-Batgirl's only app. in Detective. 326-Last J'onn J'onzz; intro. Idol-Head of Diabolu. 327-Elongated Man begins; new batman costume	.85	2.50	5.00
328-Death of Alfred	1.00	3.00	6.00
331-368,370: 345-Intro The Black Buster. 351-Elongated Man new costume. 355-Zatanna x-over in Elongated Man. 356-Alfred brought back in Batman. 359-Intro/origin new Batgirl	.70	2.00	4.00
369-Adams-a	2.00	5.00	10.00
371-390: 383-Elongated Man series ends. 387-r/1st Batman story			

Detective Comics #151, © DC

Detective Comics #168, © DC

Detective Comics #323, © DC

Detective Comics #437, © DC

Detective Comics #500, © DC

Devil Kids #12, © HARV

DETECTIVE COMICS (continued) Good Fine Mint
from No. 27 .50 1.50 3.00
391-394,396,398,399,401,403,405,406,409,411-420: 414-52 pgs. begin, end No. 424. 418-Creeper x-over
.40 1.20 2.40
395,397,400,402,404,407,408,410-Adams-a. 400-Origin & 1st app. Man-Bat 1.50 4.00 8.00
421-436: 424-Last Batgirl. 425-1st Jason Bard. 426-Elongated Man begins, ends No. 436. 428,434-Hawkman begins, ends No. 467 .30 .90 1.80
437-Manhunter begins by Simonson, ends No. 443
.30 .90 1.80
438-439(100 pgs.): 439-Origin Manhunter .30 .80 1.60
440(100 pgs.)-G.A. Manhunter, Hawkman, Dollman, Gr. Lantern; Toth-a .30 .80 1.60
441(100 pgs.)-G.A. Plastic Man .30 .80 1.60
442(100 pgs.)-G.A. Newsboy Legion, Bl. Canary, Elongated Man, Dr. Fate new 12 pgs. Toth-a .30 .90 1.80
443(100 pgs.)-Origin The Creeper-r .30 .80 1.60
444,445(100 pgs.): 444-Elongated Man begins
.30 .80 1.60
446-456,458-460: 446-Hawkman begins, ends No. 455. 448-The Creeper app. 458,459-Man-Bat app. 460-Tim Trench begins
.60 1.20
457-Origin retold & updated .60 1.20
461-465,469,470,480: 469-Intro Dr. Phosperous .40 .80
466-468,471-476,478,479-Rogers-a with Adams-i-No. 466
.50 1.50 3.00
477-Adams-a(r); Rogers-a, 3pgs. .40 1.20 2.40
481-(Combined with Batman Family, 12/78-1/79)(Begin $1.00 issues)-Man-Bat app.; Robin, Batgirl begin; Starlin/Russell, Rogers-a; Starlin wrap-around c/a .35 1.00 2.00
482-Starlin/Russell, Golden-a; Demon begins, ends No. 485
.30 .80 1.60
483-40th Anniversary ish.; origin retold; Newton Batman begins; The Human Target begins, ends No. 484,486 .60 1.20
484,486,488-489,491-495: 491(492 on inside). 492-Intro General Sear .60 1.20
485-Death of Kathy Kane, the Batwoman; Man-Bat app.
.60 1.20
487-The Odd Man by Ditko begins; Roy Raymond returns
.60 1.20
490-Black Lightning begins .60 1.20
496-499,501-510 .30 .60
500-($1.50)-Batman/Deadman team-up .30 .80 1.60
Special Edition(1944)-Giveaway-(68 pgs.) Regular comic format
24.00 70.00 140.00

NOTE: ***Adams** c-369, 370, 372, 385, 389, 391, 392, 394-422, 439. **Anderson** a-359, 360, 377, 390, 440, 442, 480; c-329, 333, 347, 351, 352, 359, 361-365, 369, 371, 431, 433. **Aparo** a-437, 438, 444-46, 500; c-437, 440-46, 448, 468, 480, 484(back), 493-7, 499, 501-03, 508, 509. **Baily** a-443r. **Buckler** a-446, 479; c-482. **Chaykin** a-441, 483. **Ditko** a-443r, 483-85, 487. **Giordano** a-457, 484, 486, 487p; c-450, 457, 483(back), 485, 486. **Grell** a-445, 455; c-455. **Infantino** a-327-357, 361-63, 366, 367, 369, 439r, 442, 445r, 500; c-327-331, 333-347, 351-68, 371. **Kaluta** c-423, 424, 426-28, 431, 434, 438, 484, 486. **Bob Kane** a-Most early ish. No. 27 on, 297r, 438r, 439r, 443r. **Gil Kane** a-368, 370-74, 384, 385, 388-407, 438r, 439r. **Kubert** a-438r, 439r, 500; c-348-50. **Lopez** a-455; c-483, 487, 500p. **Meskin** a-420r. **Mooney** a-444r. **Moreira** a-153, 419r, 444r, 445r. **Newton** a-480, 481, 483-99, 501-09. **Robinson** a-part: 66, 68, 71-73; all: 74-76, 79, 80; c-62, 64, 66, 68-74, 76, 79, 82, 86, 88. **Rogers** c-471-79. **Roussos** Airwave-76-105(most). **Schaffenberger** a-456, 457, 483-86. **Simon/Kirby** a-440, 442. **Simonson** a(p)-437-43, 450, 469, 470, 500. **Starlin** c-503, 504. **Starr** a-444r. **Toth** a-414r, 416r, 418r, 424, 440-42, 443r, 444r. **Tuska** a-486, 490. **Wrightson** c-425*

DETECTIVE DAN, SECRET OP. 48
1933 (36 pgs.; 9½x12") (B&W; Softcover)
Humor Publ. Co.

By Norman Marsh; forerunner of Dan Dunn 5.00 14.00 28.00

DETECTIVE EYE
Nov, 1940 - No. 2, Dec, 1940
Centaur Publications
Good Fine Mint
1-Air Man & The Eye Sees begins; The Masked Marvel app.
30.00 80.00 160.00
2-Opium smuggling story 20.00 60.00 135.00

DETECTIVE PICTURE STORIES (Keen Det. Funnies No. 8 on?)
Dec, 1936 - No. 7, 1937
Quality Comics Group

1 20.00 60.00 120.00
2 12.00 35.00 70.00
3-The Clock begins 12.00 35.00 70.00
4-Eisner, Siegel & Shuster-a 12.00 35.00 70.00
5-7: 5-Kane-a 10.00 30.00 60.00

DETECTIVES, THE (See 4-Color No. 1168,1219,1240)

DEVIL DINOSAUR
April, 1978 - No. 9, Dec, 1978
Marvel Comics Group

1 .50 1.00
2-9 .40 .80

NOTE: *All **Kirby** c/a. **Kirby/Byrne** c-9.*

DEVIL-DOG DUGAN (Tales of the Marines No. 4 on)
July, 1956 - No. 3, Nov, 1956
Atlas Comics (OPI)

1-Severin-c 2.00 6.00 12.00
2-Iron Mike McGraw x-over; Severin-c 1.50 4.00 8.00
3 1.50 4.00 8.00

DEVIL DOGS
1942
Street & Smith Publishers

1-Boy Rangers 4.00 12.00 24.00

DEVILINA
Feb, 1975 - No. 2, May, 1975 (Magazine) (B&W)
Atlas/Seaboard

1,2 .70 2.00 4.00

DEVIL KIDS STARRING HOT STUFF
July, 1962 - Present
Harvey Publications (Illustrated Humor)

1 7.00 20.00 45.00
2 3.50 10.00 21.00
3-10 2.50 7.00 14.00
11-20 1.50 4.00 8.00
21-30 1.00 3.00 6.00
31-50 .70 2.00 4.00
51-70 .40 1.20 2.40
71-90 .30 .80 1.60
91-102 .30 .60

DEXTER COMICS
Summer, 1948 - No. 5, July, 1949
Dearfield Publ.

1 1.50 4.00 8.00
2-5 .85 2.50 5.00

DEXTER THE DEMON (Formerly Melvin the Monster)
No. 6, July, 1957 - No. 7, Sept, 1957
Atlas Comics (HPC)

6,7 .50 1.50 3.00

DIARY CONFESSIONS (Formerly Ideal Romance)
May, 1955 - 1956
Stanmor/Key Publ.

9-14 1.00 3.00 6.00

DIARY LOVES (G. I. Sweethearts No. 32 on)
Nov, 1949 - No. 31, April, 1953

DIARY LOVES (continued)
Quality Comics Group

	Good	Fine	Mint
1-Crandall, Colan-a	6.00	18.00	36.00
2-Ward c/a, 9 pgs.	8.00	22.00	44.00
3,5-7,10	2.00	5.00	10.00
4-Crandall-a	4.00	12.00	24.00
8,9-Ward-a 6,8 pgs. plus Gustavson-No. 8	5.00	14.00	28.00
11,13,14,17-20	1.50	4.00	8.00
12,15,16-Ward-a 9,7,8 pgs.	4.00	12.00	24.00
21-Ward-a, 7 pgs.	3.50	10.00	20.00
22-31: 31-Whitney-a	.85	2.50	5.00

NOTE: *Most early issues have photo covers.*

DIARY OF HORROR
December, 1952
Avon Periodicals

1-Hollingsworth c/a	7.00	20.00	40.00

DIARY SECRETS (Formerly Teen-Age Diary Secrets)
No. 10, June, 1950 - No. 30, Sept, 1955
St. John Publishing Co.

10	5.00	14.00	28.00
11-Spanking panel	5.50	16.00	32.00
12-16,18,19	4.00	12.00	24.00
17,20-Kubert-a	5.00	14.00	28.00
21-30	2.50	7.00	14.00
Annual (nn)(25 cents)	7.00	20.00	40.00

NOTE: ***Baker** c/a most issues.*

DICK COLE (Sport Thrills No. 11 on)
Dec-Jan, 1948-49 - No. 10, June-July, 1950
Curtis Publ./Star Publications

1-Sgt. Spook; L. B. Cole-c; McWilliams-a; Curt Swan's 1st work	3.00	9.00	18.00
2	2.50	7.00	14.00
3-10	2.50	7.00	14.00
Accepted Reprint No. 7(V1No.6 on cover)(1950's)-Reprints No. 9	1.20	3.50	7.00

NOTE: *All have **L. B. Cole** covers. Dick Cole in 1,2 only*

DICKIE DARE
1941
Eastern Color Printing Co.

1-Caniff-a, Everett-c	6.00	18.00	36.00
2,3	4.00	12.00	24.00
4-Half Scorchy Smith by Noel Sickles who was very influential in Milton Caniff's development	5.00	14.00	28.00

DICK POWELL (See A-1 Comics No. 22)

DICK QUICK, ACE REPORTER (Formerly Picture News)
Jan-Feb, 1947
Lafayette St. Corp.

10-Krigstein, Milt Gross-a	3.00	9.00	18.00

DICK'S ADVENTURES IN DREAMLAND (See 4-Color No. 245)

DICK TRACY (See Merry Christmas, Popular Comics, Super Comics, Tastee-Freez, Limited Coll. Ed.,Harvey Comics Library, & Super Book No. 1,7,13,25)

DICK TRACY
1939 - No. 24, Dec, 1949
Dell Publishing Co.

	Good	Fine	Mint
Black & White 1(1939)	70.00	200.00	400.00
Black & White 4	40.00	120.00	240.00
Black & White 8,11,13,15	35.00	100.00	200.00
4-Color 1(1939)('35 reprint)	75.00	200.00	400.00
4-Color 6(1940)('37 reprint)-(Scarce)	40.00	120.00	240.00
4-Color 8(1940)('38-'39 reprint)	30.00	80.00	160.00
Large Feature Comics 3(1941)	30.00	80.00	160.00
4-Color 21('41)('38 reprint)	24.00	70.00	140.00
4-Color 34('43)('39-'40 reprint)	17.00	50.00	100.00
4-Color 56('44)('40 reprint)	12.00	35.00	70.00
4-Color 96('46)('40 reprint)	9.00	25.00	50.00
4-Color 133('47)('40-'41 reprint)	7.00	20.00	40.00
4-Color 163('47)('41 reprint)	6.00	16.00	32.00
4-Color 215('48)-Titled "Sparkle Plenty," Tracy reprints	5.00	14.00	28.00
Buster Brown Shoes giveaway-36 pgs. in color (1938 reprints)	17.00	50.00	100.00
Gillmore Giveaway-(See Super Book)			
...Hatful of Fun(no date, 1950-52)-32 pgs.; 8½x10''-Dick Tracy hat promotion; D. Tracy games, magic tricks. Miller Bros. premium	5.00	14.00	28.00
Motorola Giveaway('53)-Reprints Harvey Comics Library No. 2	5.00	14.00	28.00
Popped Wheat Giveaway('47)-'40 reprint; 16 pgs. in color; Sig Feuchtwanger publ.; Gould-a	.85	2.50	5.00
...Presents the Family Fun Book-Tip Top Bread Giveaway, no date, number (1940); 16 pgs. in color; Spy Smasher, Ibis, Lance O'Casey app. Fawcett Publ.	20.00	60.00	120.00
Same as above but without app. of heroes & Dick Tracy on cover only	7.00	20.00	40.00
Service Station giveaway(1958)-16 pgs. in color, regular size; Harvey Info. Press(slick cover)	2.00	5.00	10.00
1(1/48)('34 reprints)	20.00	55.00	110.00
2,3	10.00	30.00	60.00
4-10	9.00	25.00	50.00
11-18	6.00	18.00	36.00
19-24-Not by Gould	3.50	10.00	20.00

DICK TRACY (Cont'd. from Dell series)
No. 25, Mar, 1950 - No. 145, April, 1961
Harvey Publications

25	10.00	28.00	56.00
26-29	8.00	24.00	48.00
30-1st app. Gravel Gertie	10.00	28.00	56.00
31,32,34,35,37-40	7.00	20.00	40.00
33-"Measles the Teen-Age Dope Pusher"	8.00	24.00	48.00
36-1st app. B. O. Plenty	10.00	28.00	56.00
41-50	5.00	15.00	30.00
51-56,58-80: 51-2pgs Powell-a	4.75	14.00	28.00
57-1st app. Sam Catchem	7.00	20.00	40.00
81-140	3.50	10.00	20.00
141-145 (25 cents)	4.00	12.00	24.00

NOTE: *No. 110-120,141-145 are all reprints from earlier issues.*

DICK TRACY
May, 1937 - Jan, 1938
David McKay Publications

Feature Book nn - 100 pgs., part reprinted as 4-Color No. 1 (appeared before Black & Whites, 1st Dick Tracy comic book) (Very Rare-three known copies) Estimated Value....	300.00	800.00	1600.00
Feature Book 4 - Reprints nn issue but with new cover added	70.00	180.00	360.00
Feature Book 6,9	60.00	140.00	280.00

DICK TRACY & DICK TRACY JR. CAUGHT THE RACKETEERS, HOW
1933 (88 pages) (7x8½'') (Hardcover)
Cupples & Leon Co.

2-(numbered on pg. 84)-Continuation of Stooge Viller book (daily strip reprints from 8/3/33 thru 11/8/33) (Rarer than No. 1)	35.00	100.00	200.00
with dust jacket....	50.00	140.00	280.00

DICK TRACY & DICK TRACY JR. AND HOW THEY CAPTURED "STOOGE" VILLER (See Treasure Box of Famous Comics)
1933 (7x8½'') (Hard cover; One Shot; 100 pgs.)
Reprints 1932 & 1933 Dick Tracy daily strips

Diary Of Horror #1, © AVON

Diary Secrets #17, © STJ

Dick Tracy #33, © N.Y. News Synd.

Ding Dong #1, © ME

Dixie Dugan #1, © McNaught Synd.

Doc Savage #5, © S&S

DICK TRACY & D. TRACY JR.... (cont'd.)
Cupples & Leon Co.

Good / Fine / Mint
nn(No.1)-1st app. of ''Stooge'' Viller 24.00 70.00 140.00
with dust jacket.... 35.00 100.00 200.00

DICK TRACY, EXPLOITS OF
1946 (Strip reprints) (Hardcover) ($1.00)
Rosdon Books, Inc.

1-Reprints the complete case of ''The Brow'' from early 1940's 17.00 50.00 100.00
with dust jacket.... 25.00 75.00 150.00

DICK TRACY SHEDS LIGHT ON THE MOLE
1949 (16 pgs.) (Ray-O-Vac Flashlights giveaway)
Western Printing Co.

Not by Gould 4.00 12.00 24.00

DICK TURPIN (See Legend of Young...)

DICK WINGATE OF THE U.S. NAVY
1951; 1953
Toby Press/Superior Publ.

nn-U.S. Navy giveaway .85 2.50 5.00
1(1953) 1.50 4.00 8.00

DIE, MONSTER, DIE (See Movie Classics)

DIG 'EM
1973 (16 pgs.) (2-3/8x6'')
Kellogg's Sugar Smacks Giveaway

4 different .50 1.00

DILLY (The Little Wise Guys)
May, 1953 - No. 3, Sept, 1953
Lev Gleason Publications

1-3: 2,3-Biro-c 1.20 3.50 7.00

DIME COMICS
1945; 1951
Newsbook Publ. Corp.

1-Silver Streak app.; L. B. Cole c/a 30.00 80.00 160.00
1(1951), 5 1.50 4.00 8.00

DINGBATS (See First Issue Special)

DING DONG
1946
Compix/Magazine Enterprises

1 .85 2.50 5.00
2-5 .70 2.00 4.00

DINKY DUCK (Paul Terry's...) (See Blue Ribbon Comics)
11/51 - No. 16, 9/55; No. 16, Fall/'56; No. 17, 5/57 - No. 19, Summer/'58
St. John Publishing Co./Pines No. 16 on

1 1.00 3.00 6.00
2-10 .70 2.00 4.00
11-16(9/55) .40 1.20 2.40
16(Fall,'56) - 19 .30 .80 1.60

DINKY DUCK & HASHIMOTO SAN (See Deputy Dawg Presents...)

DINO (The Flintstones)
Aug, 1973 - No. 20, Jan, 1977
Charlton Publications

1 .50 1.50 3.00
2-20 .50 1.00

DINOSAURUS (See 4-Color No. 1120)

DIPPY DUCK
October, 1957
Atlas Comics (OPI)

1-Maneely-a 1.00 3.00 6.00

DIRTY DOZEN (See Movie Classics)

DISNEYLAND BIRTHDAY PARTY
1958 (25 cents)
Dell Publishing Co.

Good / Fine / Mint
1-Carl Barks-a, 16 pgs. 7.00 20.00 40.00

DISNEYLAND, USA (See Dell Giant No. 30)

DIVER DAN
Feb-Apr, 1962 - No. 2, June-Aug, 1962
Dell Publishing Co.

4-Color 1254, 2 1.00 3.00 6.00

DIXIE DUGAN
July, 1942 - 1949
McNaught Syndicate/Columbia/Publication Ent.

1-Joe Palooka x-over in Dixie Dugan by Ham Fisher, 3.50 10.00 20.00
2,3 2.50 7.00 14.00
4,5(1945-46) 1.50 4.00 8.00
6-13(1948-49) 1.00 3.00 6.00

DIXIE DUGAN
Nov, 1951 - 1954
Prize Publications (Headline)

V3No.1-4 1.20 3.50 7.00
V4No.1-4(No.5-8) .85 2.50 5.00

DIZZY DAMES
Sept-Oct, 1952 - No. 6, July-Aug, 1953
American Comics Group (B&M Distr. Co.)

1 1.20 3.50 7.00
2-6 .85 2.50 5.00

DIZZY DON
1942 - No. 20, 1947 (B&W)
F. E. Howard Publications (Canada)

1 1.20 3.50 7.00
2-20 .85 2.50 5.00

DIZZY DUCK
No. 32, Nov, 1950 - No. 39, 1952
Standard Comics

32-39 .50 1.50 3.00

DOBERMAN (See Sgt. Bilko's Private...)

DOBIE GILLIS (See The Many Loves of...)

DOC CARTER VD COMICS
1949 (16 pages in color) (Paper cover)
Health Publications Institute, Raleigh, N. C. (Giveaway)

14.00 40.00 80.00

DOC SAVAGE (...Comics)
May, 1940 - No. 20, Oct, 1943
Street & Smith Publications

1-Doc Savage, Cap Fury, Danny Garrett, Mark Mallory, The Whisperer, Captain Death, Billy the Kid, Sheriff Pete & Treasure Island begin; Norgil, the Magician app. 60.00 160.00 325.00
2-Origin & 1st app. Ajax, the Sun Man; Danny Garrett, The Whisperer end 25.00 75.00 150.00
3 20.00 60.00 120.00
4-Treasure Island ends 15.00 45.00 90.00
5-Origin & 1st app. Astron, the Crocodile Queen, not in No. 9 & 11; Norgil the Magician app. 12.00 35.00 70.00
6-9: 6-Cap Fury ends; origin & only app. Red Falcon in Astron story. 8-Mark Mallory ends. 9-Supersnipe app. 10.00 30.00 60.00
10-Origin & only app. The Thunderbolt 10.00 30.00 60.00
11,12 8.00 22.00 44.00
V2No.1-8(No.13-20): 16-The Pulp Hero, The Avenger app. 17-Sun Man ends; Nick Carter begins 8.00 22.00 44.00

DOC SAVAGE
November, 1966
Gold Key

	Good	Fine	Mint
1-Adaptation of the Thousand-Headed Man; James Bama-c	2.00	5.00	10.00

DOC SAVAGE
Oct, 1972 - No. 8, Jan, 1974
Marvel Comics Group

	Good	Fine	Mint
1	.40	1.20	2.40
2,3-Steranko-c	.30	.80	1.60
4-8		.50	1.00
Giant-Size 1(1975)-Reprints No. 1 & 2	.30	.80	1.60

DOC SAVAGE (Magazine)
Aug, 1975 - No. 8, 1976 (Black & White)
Marvel Comics Group

	Good	Fine	Mint
1-Cover from movie poster	.50	1.50	3.00
2(10/75),3-8	.35	1.00	2.00

NOTE: ***John Buscema** a-1-3.*

DR. ANTHONY KING, HOLLYWOOD LOVE DOCTOR
Jan, 1952 - No. 3, May, 1953; No. 4, May, 1954
Minoan Publishing Corp.

	Good	Fine	Mint
1	2.00	6.00	12.00
2-4	1.50	4.00	8.00

DR. ANTHONY LOVE CLINIC (See Mr. Anthony's. . .)

DR. BOBBS (See 4-Color No. 212)

DR. FATE (See More Fun, First Issue Special, Showcase, & Justice League)

DR. FU MANCHU (See The Mask of. . .)
1964
I.W. Enterprises

	Good	Fine	Mint
1-Reprints Avon's ''Mask of Dr. Fu Manchu;'' Wood-a	7.00	20.00	40.00

DOCTOR GRAVES (See The Many Ghosts of. . .)

DR. JEKYLL AND MR. HYDE (See A Star Presentation)

DR. KILDARE (TV)
1962 - No. 9, April-June, 1965
Dell Publishing Co.

	Good	Fine	Mint
4-Color 1337('62)	1.00	3.00	6.00
2-9	.70	2.00	4.00

DR. MASTERS (See The Adventures of Young. . .)

DOCTOR SOLAR, MAN OF THE ATOM
10/62 - No. 27, 4/69; No. 28, 4/81 - Present
Gold Key/Whitman No. 28 on

	Good	Fine	Mint
1-Origin Dr. Solar (1st Gold Key comic-No. 10000-210)	2.00	5.00	10.00
2-Prof. Harbinger begins	.85	2.50	5.00
3-5: 5-Intro. Man of the Atom in costume	.55	1.60	3.20
6-10	.40	1.20	2.40
11-14,16-27	.35	1.00	2.00
15-Origin retold	.40	1.20	2.40
28		.30	.60

NOTE: ***Frank Bolle** a-6-19. **Bob Fugitani** a-in early issues. **Al McWilliams** a-20-23.*

DOCTOR SPEKTOR (See The Occult Files of. . .)

DOCTOR STRANGE (Strange Tales No. 1-168)
No. 169, June, 1968 - No. 183, Nov, 1969; June, 1974 - Present
Marvel Comics Group (Also see Marvel Premiere)

	Good	Fine	Mint
169(No.1)	.85	2.50	5.00
170-183: 177-New costume for Dr. Strange	.40	1.20	2.40
1(6/74)-Brunner c/a	1.00	3.00	6.00
2-Brunner c/a	.40	1.20	2.40
3-Ditko-a(r), Brunner c/a 2 pgs.	.40	1.20	2.40
4,5-Brunner c/a end	.40	1.20	2.40
6-Brunner-c	.30	.80	1.60
7-20		.60	1.20
21-Origin/Str. Tales 169		.60	1.20
22-Brunner-c		.60	1.20
23-26-Starlin-a(p)-No.24,25; c-25,26		.60	1.20
27,30-32,34-40		.40	.80
28,29,33-Brunner-c		.50	1.00
41-47,49,50		.40	.60
48-Rogers-a		.50	1.00

NOTE: ***Alcala** a-19. **Austin** a(i)-47-50. **Brunner** c-30. **Ditko** a-179r, 3r. **Golden** a-46p; c-42-44, 46. **Rogers** a/c(p)-47-50. **Russell** a-34.*

	Good	Fine	Mint
Annual 1(1976)-Russell-a	.35	1.00	2.00
Giant Size(11/75)	.40	1.20	2.40

DR. TOM BRENT, YOUNG INTERN
Feb, 1963 - No. 5, Oct, 1963
Charlton Publications

	Good	Fine	Mint
1	.30	.80	1.60
2-5		.50	1.00

DR. VOLTZ (See Mighty Midget Comics)

DR. WHO & THE DALEKS (See Movie Classics)

DO-DO
1951 (5x7¼'' Miniature) (5 cents)
Nation Wide Publishers

	Good	Fine	Mint
1-7	.40	1.20	2.40

DODO & THE FROG, THE (Formerly Funny Stuff)
9-10/54 - No. 88, 1-2/56; No. 89, 8-9/56; No. 90, 10-11/56; No. 91, 9/57; No. 92, 11/57
National Periodical Publications

	Good	Fine	Mint
80-91: Doodles Duck by Sheldon Mayer in many issues	.70	2.00	4.00
92-(Scarce)	1.50	4.00	8.00

DOGFACE DOOLEY
1951 - 1953
Magazine Enterprises

	Good	Fine	Mint
1(A-1 40)	.85	2.50	5.00
2(A-1 43), 3(A-1 49), 4(A-1 53), 5(A-1 64)	.85	2.50	5.00
I.W. Reprint No. 1('64), Super Reprint No. 17	.60	1.80	3.60

DOG OF FLANDERS, A (See 4-Color No. 1088)

DOGPATCH (See Al Capp's. . . & Mammy Yokum)

DOINGS OF THE DOO DADS, THE
1922 (34 pgs.; 7¾x7¾''; B&W) (50 cents)
(Red & White cover; square binding)
Detroit News (Universal Feat. & Specialty Co.)

	Good	Fine	Mint
Reprints 1921 newspaper strip ''Text & Pictures'' given away as prize in the Detroit News Doo Dads contest; by Arch Dale	5.00	14.00	28.00

DOLLFACE & HER GANG (See 4-Color No. 309)

DOLL MAN
Fall, 1941 - No. 7, Fall, '43; No. 8, Spring, '46 - No. 47, Oct, 1953
Quality Comics Group

	Good	Fine	Mint
1-Dollman (by Cassone) & Just 'N' Wright begin	55.00	160.00	320.00
2-The Dragon begins; Crandall-a(5)	35.00	95.00	190.00
3	20.00	60.00	120.00
4	15.00	45.00	90.00
5-Crandall-a	13.00	37.00	75.00

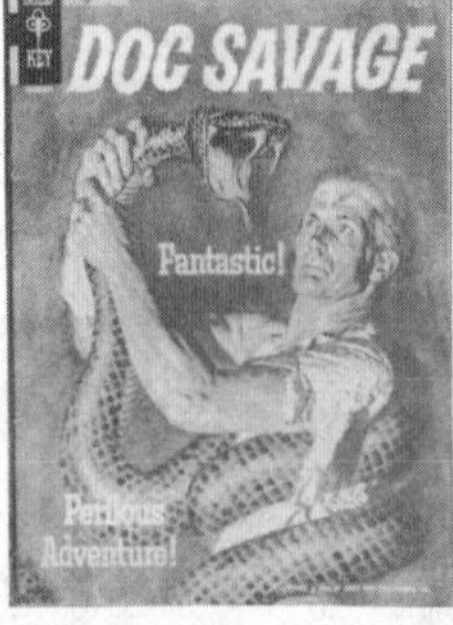

Doc Savage #1, © GK

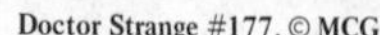
Doctor Strange #177, © MCG

Dogface Dooley #3, © ME

Doll Man #10, © QUA

Donald & Mickey In Disneyland #1, © WDP

Donald Duck 4C-238, © WDP

DOLL MAN (continued) — Good / Fine / Mint

6,7(1943) 9.00 25.00 50.00
8(1946)-1st app. Torchy by Bill Ward 12.00 35.00 70.00
9 8.00 24.00 48.00
10-20 7.00 20.00 40.00
21-30 5.50 16.00 32.00
31-36,38,40: Jeb Rivers app. No. 32-34 4.00 12.00 24.00
37-Origin Dollgirl; Dollgirl bondage-c 5.50 16.00 32.00
39-''Narcotics. . . the Death Drug''-cover/story
5.00 14.00 28.00
41-47 3.00 9.00 18.00
I.W. Reprint No. 1('63)-Crandall-a 1.00 3.00 6.00
Super Reprint No. 11('64),15(reprints No.23),17,18: Torchy app.-No.15,17 1.50 4.00 8.00

NOTE: ***Ward*** *Torchy in 8,9,11,12,14-24,27; by* ***Fox****-No. 30, 35-47.* ***Crandall*** *a-2,5,10,13 & Super No. 11,17,18.*

DOLLY DILL
1945
Marvel Comics/Newsstand Publ.

1 3.00 9.00 18.00

DOLLY DIMPLES & BOBBY BOONCE'
1933
Cupples & Leon Co.

4.00 12.00 24.00

DONALD AND MICKEY IN DISNEYLAND
1958 (25 cents)
Dell Publishing Co.

1 (Giant) 2.00 5.00 10.00

DONALD AND MICKEY MERRY CHRISTMAS (Formerly Famous Gang)
1943 - 1949 (20 pgs.)(Giveaway) Put out each Christmas; 1943 issue titled ''Firestone Presents Comics'' (Disney)
K. K. Publ./Firestone Tire & Rubber Co.

1943-Donald Duck reprint from WDC&S No. 32 by Carl Barks
70.00 190.00 380.00
1944-Donald Duck reprint from WDC&S No. 35 by Barks
65.00 180.00 360.00
1945-''Donald Duck's Best Christmas,'' 8 pgs. Carl Barks; intro. & 1st app. Grandma Duck in comic books
90.00 240.00 480.00
1946-Donald Duck in ''Santa's Stormy Visit,'' 8 pgs. Carl Barks
60.00 170.00 340.00
1947-Donald Duck in ''Three Good Little Ducks,'' 8 pgs. Carl Barks
55.00 150.00 300.00
1948-Donald Duck in ''Toyland,'' 8 pgs. Carl Barks
55.00 150.00 300.00
1949-Donald Duck in ''New Toys,'' 8 pgs. Carl Barks
60.00 170.00 340.00

DONALD AND THE WHEEL (See 4-Color No. 1190)

DONALD DUCK (See Cheerios, Uncle Scrooge, Walt Disney Comics & Stories, Whitman Comic Books)

DONALD DUCK (Also see The Wise Little Hen)
1935, 1936 (Linen-like text & color pictures; 1st Donald Duck book ever) (9½x13'')
Whitman Publishing Co./Grosset & Dunlap/K.K.

978(1935)-16 pgs.; story book 40.00 120.00 240.00
nn(1936)-36 pgs.; reprints '35 edition with expanded ill. & text
30.00 90.00 180.00
with dust jacket. . . . 40.00 120.00 240.00

DONALD DUCK (Walt Disney's) (10 cents)
1938 (B&W) (8½x11½'') (Cardboard covers)
Whitman/K.K. Publications
(Has Donald Duck with bubble pipe on front cover)

nn-The first Donald Duck comic book; 1936 & 1937 Sunday strip reprints(in black and white); same format as Black & Whites
(Prices vary widely on this book) 100.00 300.00 600.00

Good / Fine / Mint

DONALD DUCK (See 4-Color listings for titles)
1940 - No. 84, 7-8/62; No. 85, 12/62 - Present
Dell Publishing Co./Gold Key No. 85-216/Whitman No. 217 on

4-Color 4(1940)-Daily 1939 strip reprints by Al Taliaferro
300.00 700.00 1400.00
Black & White 16(1/41?)-1940 Sunday strips-r in B&W
200.00 600.00 1200.00
Black & White 20('41) 300.00 800.00 1600.00
4-Color 9('42)-''Finds Pirate Gold;''-68 pgs. by Carl Barks & Jack Hannah (pgs. 1,2,5,12-40 are by Barks)
400.00 1150.00 2200.00
4-Color 29(9/43)-''Mummy's Ring'' by Carl Barks; reprinted in Uncle Scrooge & Donald Duck No. 1('65) & W.D. Comics Digest No. 44('73) 325.00 800.00 1600.00
(Prices vary widely on all above books)
4-Color 62(1/45)-''Frozen Gold;'' 52 pgs. by Carl Barks, reprinted in The Best of W.D. Comics 150.00 400.00 800.00
4-Color 108(1946)-''Terror of the River;'' 52 pgs. by Carl Barks
100.00 240.00 480.00
4-Color 147(5/47)-in ''Volcano Valley'' by Carl Barks
70.00 160.00 320.00
4-Color 159(8/47)-in ''The Ghost of the Grotto;'' 52 pgs. by Carl Barks-reprinted in Best of Uncle Scrooge & Donald Duck No. 1 ('66) & The Best of W.D. Comics; two Barks stories
60.00 140.00 280.00
4-Color 178(12/47)-1st Uncle Scrooge by Carl Barks; reprinted in Gold Key Christmas Parade No. 3 & The Best of W.D. Comics
60.00 140.00 280.00
4-Color 189(6/48)-by Carl Barks; reprinted in Best of Donald Duck & Uncle Scrooge No. 1('64) 60.00 140.00 280.00
4-Color 199(10/48)-by Carl Barks; mentioned in **Love and Death**
60.00 140.00 280.00
4-Color 203(12/48)-by Barks; reprinted as Gold Key Christmas Parade No. 4 40.00 90.00 180.00
4-Color 223(4/49)-by Barks; reprinted as Best of Donald Duck No. 1('65) 50.00 125.00 250.00
4-Color 238(8/49), 256(12/49)-by Barks; No. 256-reprinted in Best of Donald Duck & Uncle Scrooge No. 2('67) & W.D. Comics Digest No. 44('73) 30.00 70.00 140.00
4-Color 263(2/50)-Two Barks stories 30.00 70.00 140.00
4-Color 275(5/50), 282(7/50), 291(9/50), 300(11/50)-All by Carl Barks; No. 275,282 reprinted in W.D. Comics Digest No. 44('73)
25.00 60.00 120.00
4-Color 308(1/51), 318(3/51)-by Barks; No. 318-reprinted in W.D. Comics Digest No. 34 18.00 45.00 90.00
4-Color 328(5/51)-by Carl Barks (drug issue)
20.00 55.00 110.00
4-Color 339(7-8/51), 379-not by Barks 3.50 10.00 20.00
4-Color 348(9-10/51), 356,394-Barks-c only 4.50 13.00 26.00
4-Color 367(1-2/52)-by Barks; reprinted as Gold Key Christmas Parade No. 2 & again as No. 8 18.00 45.00 90.00
4-Color 408(7-8/52), 422(9-10/52)-All by Carl Barks. No. 408-reprinted in Best of Donald Duck & Uncle Scrooge No. 1('64)
15.00 40.00 80.00
26(11-12/52)-In ''Trick or Treat''(Barks-a, 36pgs.) 1st story r-/Walt Disney Digest No. 16 15.00 40.00 80.00
27-30-Barks-c only 3.50 10.00 20.00
31-40 2.00 5.00 10.00
41-44,47-50 1.20 3.50 7.00
45-Barks-a, 6 pgs. & 9 pgs. (2 variations exist)
5.00 15.00 30.00
46-''Secret of Hondorica'' by Barks, 24 pgs.; reprinted in Donald Duck No. 98 & 154 7.00 20.00 40.00
51-Barks, ½ pg. 1.50 4.00 8.00
52-''Lost Peg-Leg Mine'' by Barks, 10 pgs. 5.00 15.00 30.00
53,55-59 1.00 3.00 6.00
54-''Forbidden Valley'' by Barks, 26 pgs. 7.00 20.00 40.00
60-''D.D. & the Titanic Ants'' by Barks, 20 pgs. plus 6 more pgs.
6.00 18.00 36.00
61-67,69,70 .70 2.00 4.00
68-Barks-a, 5 pgs. 3.00 9.00 18.00
71-Barks-r, ½ pg. 1.20 3.50 7.00

DONALD DUCK (continued)

	Good	Fine	Mint
72-78,80,82-97,100: 96-Donald Duck Album	.70	2.00	4.00
79,81-Barks-a, 1pg.	1.20	3.50	7.00
98-Reprints No. 46 (Barks)	2.00	5.00	10.00
99-Xmas Album	.85	2.50	5.00
101-133: 112-1st Moby Duck	.30	.80	1.60
134-Barks-r plus a WDC&S-r	.85	2.50	5.00
135-Barks-r, 19 pgs.	.50	1.50	3.00
136-153		.50	1.00
154-Barks-r(No.46)	.50	1.50	3.00
155,156,158		.50	1.00
157-Barks-r(No.45)	.30	.80	1.60
159-Reprints/WDC&S No. 192		.50	1.00
160-Barks-r(No.26)	.30	.80	1.60
161-163,165-170		.50	1.00
164-Barks-r(No.79)	.30	.80	1.60
171,177-Reprints		.40	.80
172,173,175,176		.30	.60
174-Reprints 4-Color 394		.40	.80
178-187,189-191		.30	.60
188-Five pg. Barks-r		.40	.80
192-Barks-r(40 pgs.) from Donald Duck No. 60 & WDC&S No. 226,234(52 pgs.)		.40	.80
193-200,202-207,209-211,213-218: 217 has 216 on-c		.30	.60
201-Barks-r/Christ. Parade 26, 16pgs.		.30	.60
208,212-Barks-r		.40	.80
219-Barks-r(2)		.30	.60
220-228,230-233		.30	.60
229-Barks-r/F.C. 282		.30	.60
Mini-Comic No. 1(1976)-(3¼x6½''); Reprints/Donald Duck No. 150		.25	.50

NOTE: ***Carl Barks** wrote all issues he illustrated, but No. 117, 126, 138 contain his script only. Issues 4-Color No.189, 199, 203, 223, 238, 256, 263, 275, 282, 308, 348, 356, 367, 394, 408, 422, 26-30, 35, 44, 46, 52, 55, 57, 60, 65, 70- 73, 77-80, 83, 101, 103, 105, 106, 111, 126 all have **Barks** covers. No. 96 titled ''Comic Album,'' No. 99-''Christmas Album.'' Reprint issues-No.147, 166, 168, 180, 181, 183-86, 189-213, 215-221.*

DONALD DUCK
1944 (16 pg. Christmas giveaway)(paper cover)(2 versions)
K. K. Publications

	Good	Fine	Mint
Kelly cover reprint	50.00	125.00	250.00

DONALD DUCK ALBUM (See Duck Album & Comic Album No. 1,3)
May-July, 1959 - Oct, 1963
Dell Publishing Co./Gold Key

	Good	Fine	Mint
4-Color 995,1182, 01204-207 (1962-Dell)	1.00	3.00	6.00
4-Color 1099,1140,1239-Barks-c	1.20	3.50	7.00
1(8/63-Gold Key)	.70	2.00	4.00
2(10/63)	.35	1.00	2.00

DONALD DUCK AND THE BOYS (Also see Story Hour Series)
1948 (Hardcover book; 5¼x5½'') 100pgs., ½art, ½text
Whitman Publishing Co.

	Good	Fine	Mint
845-Partial r-/WDC&S No. 74 by Barks	15.00	45.00	90.00

(Prices vary widely on this book)

DONALD DUCK AND THE RED FEATHER
1948 (4 pages) (8½x11'') (Black & White)
Red Feather Giveaway

	Good	Fine	Mint
	3.50	10.00	20.00

DONALD DUCK BEACH PARTY
1954 - 1959; Sept, 1965 (25 cents)
Dell Publishing Co./Gold Key('65)

	Good	Fine	Mint
1	3.00	8.00	16.00
2-6	2.00	6.00	12.00
1(G.K. No. 10158-509)-Reprints Barks story from WDC&S No. 45	2.50	7.00	14.00

DONALD DUCK BOOK (See Story Hour Series)

DONALD DUCK COMIC PAINT BOOK (See Black & White No. 20)

DONALD DUCK FUN BOOK (Annual)
1953 - 1954 (100 pages) (25 cents)
Dell Publishing Co.

	Good	Fine	Mint
1('53), 2('54)	2.50	7.00	14.00

DONALD DUCK IN DISNEYLAND
1955 (Giant)
Dell Publishing Co.

	Good	Fine	Mint
1	2.00	6.00	12.00

DONALD DUCK IN ''THE LITTERBUG''
1963 (15 pages) (Disney giveaway)
Keep America Beautiful

	Good	Fine	Mint
	2.00	5.00	10.00

DONALD DUCK MARCH OF COMICS
1947 - 1951 (Giveaway) (Disney)
K. K. Publications

	Good	Fine	Mint
nn(No.4)-''Maharajah Donald;'' 30 pgs. by Carl Barks-(1947)	500.00	1200.00	2400.00
20-''Darkest Africa'' by Carl Barks-(1948); 22 pgs.	325.00	800.00	1600.00
41-''Race to South Seas'' by Carl Barks-(1949); 22 pgs.	240.00	600.00	1200.00
56-(1950)-Not Barks	20.00	60.00	120.00
69-(1951)-Not Barks	15.00	45.00	90.00
263	3.50	10.00	20.00

DONALD DUCK MERRY XMAS (See Dell Giant No. 53)

DONALD DUCK PICNIC PARTY (See Picnic Party)

DONALD DUCK ''PLOTTING PICNICKERS''
1962 (14 pages) (Disney)
Fritos Giveaway

	Good	Fine	Mint
	2.00	5.00	10.00

DONALD DUCK'S SURPRISE PARTY
1948 (16 pgs.) (Giveaway for Icy Frost Twins Ice Cream Bars)
Walt Disney Productions

	Good	Fine	Mint
(Rare)Kelly c/a	120.00	350.00	600.00

DONALD DUCK TELLS ABOUT KITES
1954 (Giveaway) (8 pgs. - no cover) (Disney)
Southern California Edison Co./Pacific Gas & Electric Co./Florida Power & Light Co.

	Good	Fine	Mint
Fla. Power & S.C.E. issue-Barks pencils-8 pgs.; inks-7 pgs. (Rare)	600.00	1300.00	2500.00
P.G.&E. issue-7th page redrawn changing middle 3 panels to show P.G.&E. in story line; (All Barks; last page Barks pencils only) (Scarce)	500.00	1200.00	2200.00

(Prices vary widely on above books)

NOTE: *These books appeared one month apart in the fall and were distributed on the West and East Coasts.*

DONALD DUCK, THIS IS YOUR LIFE (See 4-Color No. 1109)

DONALD DUCK XMAS ALBUM (See regular Donald Duck No. 99)

DONALD IN MATHMAGIC LAND (See 4-Color No. 1051, 1198)

DONDI (See 4-Color No. 1176,1276)

DON FORTUNE MAGAZINE
Aug, 1946 - No. 6, Feb, 1947
Don Fortune Publishing Co.

	Good	Fine	Mint
1-Delecta of the Planets by C. C. Beck in all	3.50	10.00	20.00
2-6	2.50	7.00	14.00

Donald Duck 4C-308, © WDP

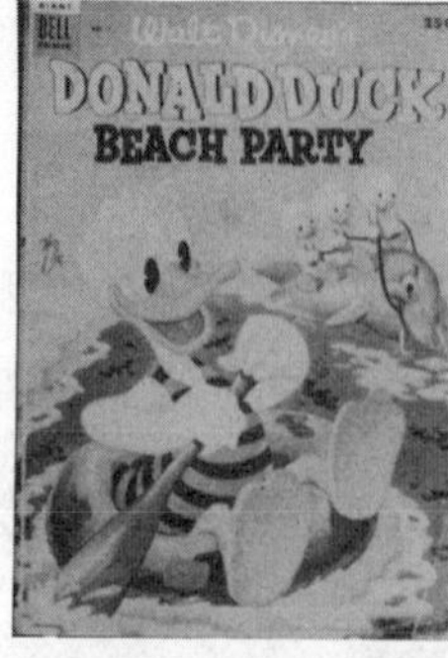

Donald Duck Beach Party #1, © WDP

Don Fortune #2, © Don Fortune

Don Winslow #44, © FAW

Doom Patrol #100, © DC

Doomsday +1 #1, © CC

DON NEWCOMBE
1950 (Baseball)
Fawcett Publications

	Good	Fine	Mint
nn	6.00	16.00	32.00

DON'T GIVE UP THE SHIP (See 4-Color No. 1049)

DON WINSLOW OF THE NAVY (See 4-Color No. 2,22, & Super Book No. 5,6)

DON WINSLOW OF THE NAVY (See TV Teens)
Feb, 1943 - No. 73, Sept, 1955 (Fightin' Navy No. 74)
Fawcett Publications/Charlton No. 70 on

1-Captain Marvel on cover	17.00	50.00	100.00
2	8.00	24.00	48.00
3	5.00	15.00	30.00
4,5	3.50	10.00	20.00
6-10	3.00	9.00	18.00
11-20	2.50	7.00	14.00
21-40	1.50	4.00	8.00
41-64(12/48)	1.20	3.50	7.00
65(1/51)-73: 70(3/55),71,&72 reprints No. 26,58,&59	.85	2.50	5.00

DOOM PATROL (My Greatest Adv. No. 1-85; see Showcase No. 94-96)
3/64 - No. 121, 9-10/68; 2/73 - No. 124, 6-7/73
National Periodical Publications

86	.80	2.30	4.60
87-99: 88-Origin The Chief. 91-Intro. Mento. 99-Intro. Beast Boy who later became the Changeling in the New Teen Titans	.35	1.10	2.20
100-Origin Beast Boy; Robot-Maniac series begins	.35	1.10	2.20
101-110: 105-Robot-Maniac series ends. 106-Negative Man begins (origin).	.30	.90	1.80
111-120	.25	.70	1.40
121-Death of Doom Patrol; Orlando-c		.60	1.20
122-124(reprints)		.40	.80

DOOMSDAY + 1
7/75 - No. 6, 5/76; No. 7, 6/68 - No. 12, 5/79
Charlton Comics

1	1.00	3.00	6.00
2	.50	1.50	3.00
3-6: 4-Intro Lor	.70	2.00	4.00
V3No.7-12 (reprints No. 1-6)	.30	.80	1.60
5 (Modern Comics reprint, 1977)		.20	.40

NOTE: ***Byrne** c/a-1-12; Painted covers-2-7. **Ditko** a-5, 11r.*

DOORWAY TO NIGHTMARE (See Cancelled Comic Cavalcade)
Jan-Feb, 1978 - No. 5, Sept-Oct, 1978
DC Comics

1		.60	1.20
2-5: 4-Craig-a		.40	.80

NOTE: ***Kaluta** covers on all. Merged into The Unexpected with No. 190.*

DOPEY DUCK COMICS (Wacky Duck No. 3) (See Super Funnies)
Fall, 1945 - No. 2, April, 1946
Timely Comics (NPP)

1,2	5.00	14.00	28.00

DOROTHY LAMOUR - JUNGLE PRINCESS (Formerly Jungle Lil)
No. 2, June, 1950 - No. 3, Aug, 1950
Fox Features Syndicate

2,3-Wood-a(3) each, photo-c	5.00	14.00	28.00

DOT AND DASH AND THE LUCKY JINGLE PIGGIE
1942 (12 pages)
Sears Roebuck Christmas giveaway

Contains a war stamp album and a punch out Jingle Piggie bank	3.50	10.00	20.00

DOT DOTLAND (Formerly Little Dot. . .)
No. 62, Sept, 1974 - No. 63, November, 1974
Harvey Publications

	Good	Fine	Mint
62,63		.60	1.20

DOTTY (. . .& Her Boy Friends) (Formerly Four Teeners; Glamorous Romances No. 41 on)
No. 35, July, 1948 - No. 40, May, 1949
Ace Magazines (A. A. Wyn)

35-40: 37-Transvestite story	1.20	3.50	7.00

DOTTY DRIPPLE (Horace & Dotty Dripple No. 25 on)
1944 - No. 24, June, 1952
Magazine Ent.(Life's Romances)/Harvey No. 3 on

1 (no date, 1946?)	1.20	3.50	7.00
nn (no date) (10 cents)	1.20	3.50	7.00
A-1 No.1 (no date) (M.E.-1944)	1.20	3.50	7.00
2-24	.60	1.80	3.60

DOTTY DRIPPLE
Aug, 1955 - 1958
Dell Publishing Co.

4-Color 646,691,718,746,801,903	1.00	3.00	6.00
7-11(Exist?)	.70	2.00	4.00

DOUBLE ACTION COMICS
No. 2, Jan, 1940 (Regular size; 68 pgs.; B&W, color cover)
National Periodical Publications

2-Contains original stories(?); no costume heroes; same cover as Adventure No. 37. (Six known copies)
Estimated value. . . . 4500.00

NOTE: *The cover to this book was probably reprinted as Adventure No. 37. No. 1 exists as an ash can copy with B&W cover; contains a coverless comic on inside with 1st & last page missing.*

DOUBLE COMICS
1940 - 1944 (132 pages)
Elliot Publications

1940 issues	30.00	90.00	180.00
1941 issues	20.00	60.00	120.00
1942 issues	14.00	40.00	80.00
1943,44 issues	10.00	30.00	60.00

NOTE: Double Comics consisted of an almost endless combination of pairs of remaindered, unsold issues of comics representing most publishers and usually mixed publishers in the same book; e.g., a Captain America with a Silver Streak, or a Feature with a Detective, etc., could appear inside the same cover. The actual contents would have to determine its price. Prices listed are for average contents. Any containing rare origin or first issues are worth much more. Covers also vary in same year. Value would be approximately 50 percent of contents.

DOUBLE-DARE ADVENTURES
Dec, 1966 - No. 2, March, 1967 (35-25 cents)
Harvey Publications

1-Origin Bee-Man, Glowing Gladiator, & Magic-Master; Kirby-a	.70	2.00	4.00
2-Williamson/Crandall-a; r-/Alarming Adv. No. 3('63)	1.00	3.00	6.00

DOUBLE LIFE OF PRIVATE STRONG, THE
June, 1959 - No. 2, Aug, 1959
Archie Publications/Radio Comics

1-Origin The Shield by Simon & Kirby	10.00	30.00	60.00
2-S&K Shield	7.00	20.00	40.00

DOUBLE TALK (Also see Two-Faces)
No date (1962?) (32 pgs.; full color; slick cover)
Christian Anti-Communism Crusade (Giveaway)
Feature Publications

	15.00	45.00	90.00

DOUBLE TROUBLE

DOUBLE TROUBLE (continued)
Nov, 1957 - No. 2, Jan, 1958?
St. John Publishing Co.

	Good	Fine	Mint
1,2	.85	2.50	5.00

DOUBLE TROUBLE WITH GOOBER
1952 - 1953
Dell Publishing Co.

	Good	Fine	Mint
4-Color 417,471,516,556, 1	.70	2.00	4.00

DOUBLE UP
1941 (200 pages) (Pocket size)
Elliott Publications

	Good	Fine	Mint
1-Contains rebound copies of digest sized issues of Pocket Comics, Speed Comics, & Spitfire Comics	20.00	60.00	120.00

DOVER BOYS (See Adventures of the. . .)

DOVER THE BIRD
Spring, 1955
Famous Funnies Publishing Co.

	Good	Fine	Mint
1	.85	2.50	5.00

DOWN WITH CRIME
Nov, 1952 - No. 7, Nov, 1953
Fawcett Publications

	Good	Fine	Mint
1	4.00	12.00	24.00
2,4,7	2.50	7.00	14.00
3-Used in **POP**, pg. 106; heroin drug cover/story	6.00	18.00	36.00
5-Bondage-c	3.50	10.00	20.00
6-Used in **POP**, pg. 80	3.00	9.00	18.00

DO YOU BELIEVE IN NIGHTMARES?
Nov, 1957 - No. 2, Jan, 1958
St. John Publishing Co.

	Good	Fine	Mint
1-Ditko c/a(most)	5.00	14.00	28.00
2-Ayers-a	2.50	7.00	14.00

DRACULA (See Tomb of. . . & Movie Classics under Universal Presents as well as Dracula)

DRACULA (See Movie Classics for No. 1)
11/66 - No. 4, 3/67; No. 6, 7/72 - No. 8, 7/73 (No No.5)
Dell Publishing Co.

	Good	Fine	Mint
2-Origin Dracula (11/66)		.60	1.20
3,4-Intro. Fleeta No. 4('67)		.50	1.00
6-('72)-reprints No. 2		.40	.80
7,8: 7 reprints No.3, 8 - No.4		.30	.60

DRACULA (Magazine)
1979 (120 pages) (full color)
Warren Publishing Co.

	Good	Fine	Mint
Book 1-Maroto art; Spanish material translated into English	1.20	3.50	7.00

DRACULA LIVES! (Magazine)
1973(no month) - No. 14, Sept, 1975 (B&W) (75 cents)
Marvel Comics Group (No. 14 exist?)

	Good	Fine	Mint
1-Buckler-a; Boris-c	.50	1.50	3.00
2-Origin; Adams c/a; Starlin-a	.50	1.50	3.00
3-Adams-a(i)	.50	1.50	3.00
4-Ploog-a	.40	1.20	2.40
5(V2No.1)-14: 7-Evans-a. 9-Alcala-a	.35	1.00	2.00
Annual 1('75)-Adams-a(r)	.35	1.00	2.00

DRAG CARTOONS (Magazine)
No. 1, 6-7/63; No. 2, 12/63 - 1970's (Later issues-no numbers)
Millar Publ./Professional Serv./Lopez Publ.

	Good	Fine	Mint
1-Manning, Warren Tufts-a	1.50	4.00	8.00
2-Manning-a	1.00	3.00	6.00
3-5,7,9-11,13-24	.35	1.00	2.00
6,8-Toth-a	.60	1.80	3.60
12-Griffin, Toth-a	2.00	5.00	10.00
25-49: Wonder Wart-Hog by Gilbert Shelton in all; The Adventures of Bull O' Fuzz & other strips	.70	2.00	4.00
50-60		.50	1.00

DRAG 'N' WHEELS (Formerly Top Eliminator)
No. 30, Sept, 1968 - No. 59, May, 1973
Charlton Comics

	Good	Fine	Mint
30-59-Scot Jackson feat.		.40	.80

DRAGONSLAYER
October, 1981 - Present
Marvel Comics Group

	Good	Fine	Mint
1-Paramount Disney movie adaptation		.30	.60

DRAGOON WELLS MASSACRE (See 4-Color No. 815)

DRAGSTRIP HOTRODDERS (World of Wheels No. 17 on)
Nov-Dec, 1963 - No. 16, May-June, 1967
Charlton Comics

	Good	Fine	Mint
1		.50	1.00
2-16		.40	.80

DRAMA OF AMERICA, THE
1973 (224 pages) ($1.95)
Action Text

	Good	Fine	Mint
1-''Students' Supplement to History''	.50	1.50	3.00

DREAM BOOK OF LOVE (See A-1 Comics No. 106,114,123)

DREAM BOOK OF ROMANCE (See A-1 No. 92,102,109,110,124)

DREAM OF LOVE
1958 (Reprints)
I. W. Enterprises

	Good	Fine	Mint
1,2,8,9: 8-Kinstler-c	.50	1.50	3.00

DREAMS OF THE RAREBIT FIEND
1904?

By Winsor McCay (Very Rare) (Two copies known to exist)
Estimated value. . . . $200.00—$600.00

DRIFT MARLO
May-July, 1962 - No. 2, Oct-Dec, 1962
Dell Publishing Co.

	Good	Fine	Mint
01-232-207, 2(12-232-212)	.85	2.50	5.00

DRISCOLL'S BOOK OF PIRATES
1934 (124 pgs.) (B&W; hardcover; 7x9'')
David McKay Publ. (Not reprints)

	Good	Fine	Mint
By Montford Amory	5.00	14.00	28.00

DRUM BEAT (See 4-Color No. 610)

DUCK ALBUM (See Donald Duck Album)
Oct, 1951 - Sept, 1957
Dell Publishing Co.

	Good	Fine	Mint
4-Color 353,450: Barks-c	2.00	5.00	10.00
4-Color 492,531,560,586	1.20	3.50	7.00
4-Color 611,649,686	1.20	3.50	7.00
4-Color 726,782,840	.85	2.50	5.00

DUDLEY
Nov-Dec, 1949 - No. 3, Mar-Apr, 1950
Feature/Prize Publications

	Good	Fine	Mint
1-By Boody Rogers	1.20	3.50	7.00
2,3	.85	2.50	5.00

DUDLEY DO-RIGHT (TV)

Down With Crime #1, © FAW

Do You Believe In Nightmares #1, © STJ

Dracula #2, © DELL

PRIDE
Congratulations, Bob,
ON YOUR 12th EDITION
C·C·BECK
JERRY De FUCCIO
and THE CAPTAIN

LAZINESS · INJUSTICE
C.C.BEC
1981

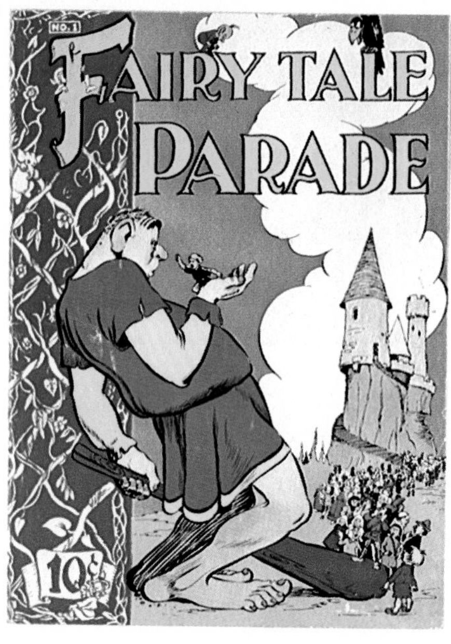

Fairy Tale Parade No. 1, 1942. Walt Kelly cover art. © Oscar Lebeck

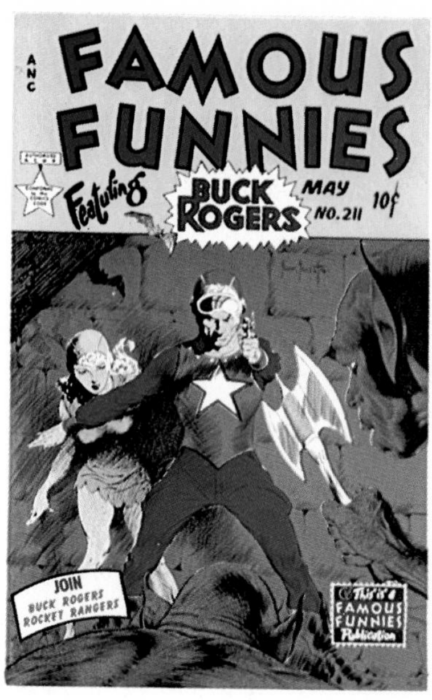

Famous Funnies No. 211, 1954. Cover by Frank Frazetta. © John S. Dille Co.

Famous Stars No. 5, 1951. Elizabeth Taylor photo cover. © Z-D

Fantastic Comics No. 1, 1939. Cover by Lou Fine. © Fox

Fawcett Movie Comic No. 15, 1952. © Faw

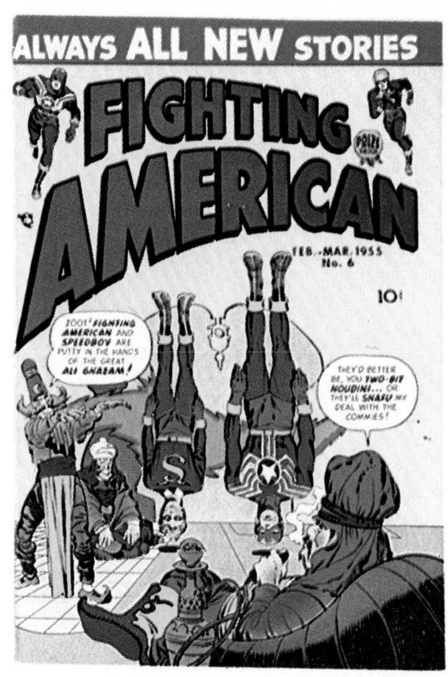

Fighting American No. 6, 1955. Cover and art by Simon & Kirby. © Prize

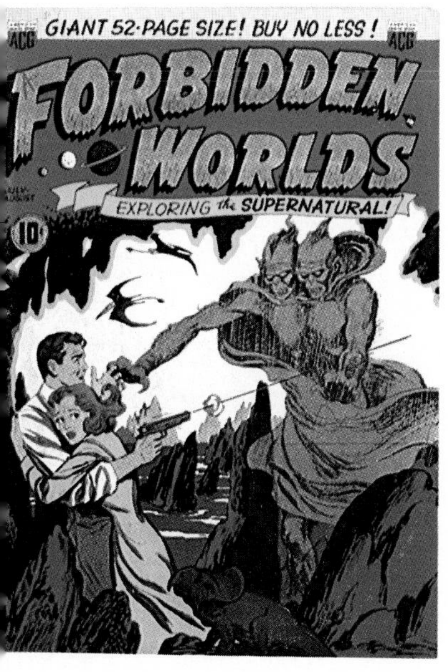

Forbidden Worlds No. 1, 1951. © ACG

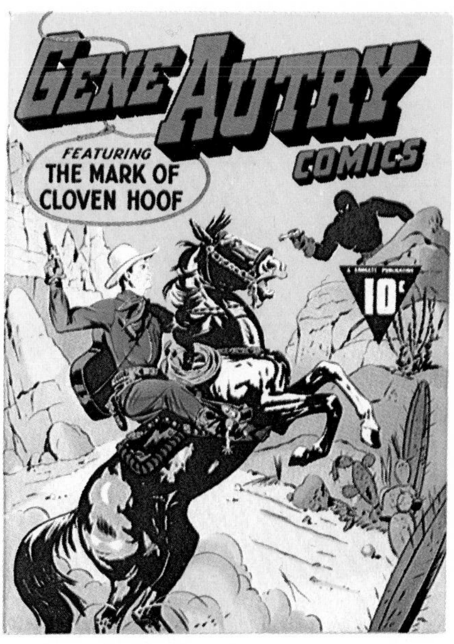

Gene Autry No. 1, 1941. © Gene Autry

Hit Comics No. 5, 1940. Cover by Lou Fine. © Qua

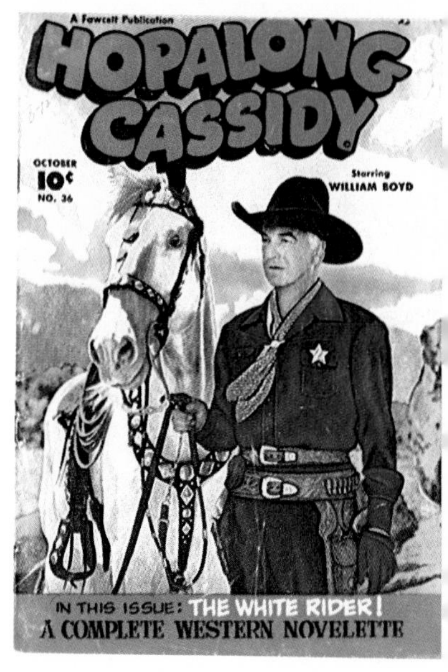

Hopalong Cassidy No. 36, 1949. © Faw

Joan of Arc A-1 No. 21, 1949. © ME

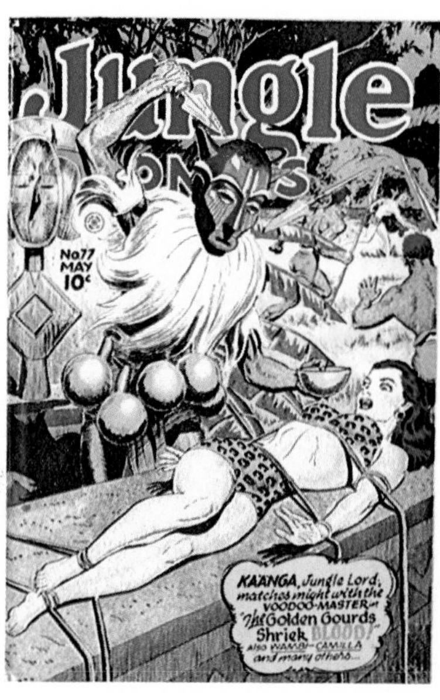

Jungle Comics No. 77, 1946. © FH

King Comics No. 59, 1941. © King

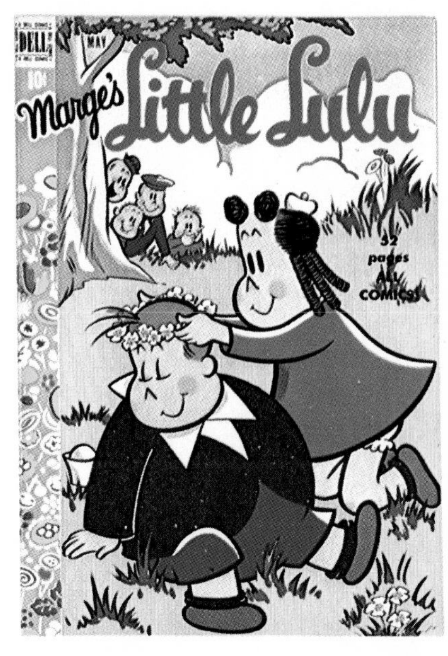

Little Lulu No. 23, 1950. © Marjorie Buell

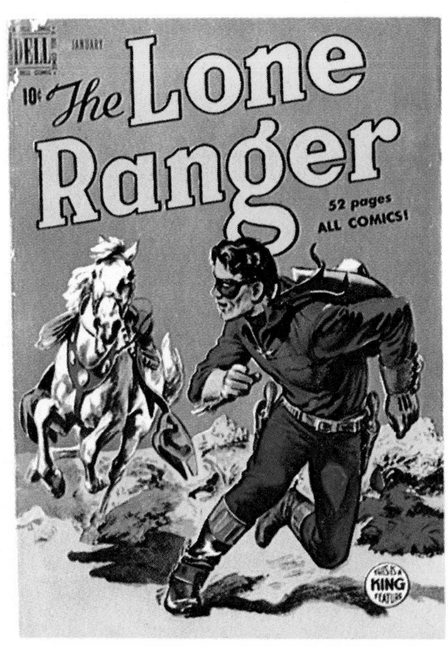

The Lone Ranger No. 19, 1950. © The Lone Ranger, Inc.

The Marvel Family No. 77, 1952. © Faw

GREETINGS FROM THE...
MARVEL® COMICS GROUP
©1981 MCG
CARVEL COMICS?! WHO'RE THEY TRYIN' TO FOOL?!
HOW MUCH FOR COSMO THE MERRY MARTIAN #3?
IS THAT IN FINE OR MINT CONDITION?
I'LL TRADE YA!
SHEESH, I DIDN'T KNOW JACK KIRBY GUEST-STARRED IN MILLIE THE MODEL #107.
HAS ANYONE SEEN MY COPY OF A MEDAL FOR BOWSER?
I THINK I KNOW WHERE A DOZEN COPIES OF BIG CHIEF WAHOO HAVE BEEN STASHED AWAY!
I'LL TRADE MY WHOLE SET OF McKEEVER AND THE COLONEL'S FOR BINGO, THE MONKEY DOODLE BOY #1...
I DIDN'T KNOW STARLIN DID THE COVER FOR ADVENTURES ON THE PLANET OF THE APES #6...
WHO LEFT A COPY OF NEGRO ROMANCE BACK AT AVENGERS MANSION?
KRAVEN THE HUNTER'S WILLING TO TRADE ANIMAL CRACKERS #s 4-20 --IF ANYONE'S INTERESTED...
HEY! NIGHT NURSE #1 IS UP TO A WHOLE DOLLAR!
ONLY 69 COMICS BEGIN WITH "CAPTAIN" IN THE TITLE? I THOUGHT THERE WERE MORE...
GRIT
THE COMIC BOOK PRICE GUIDE

Durango Kid #11, © ME

Dynamic Comics #8, © CHES

Dynamo #4, © TC

DUDLEY DO-RIGHT (continued)
Aug, 1970 - No. 7, Aug, 1971 (Jay Ward)
Charlton Comics

	Good	Fine	Mint
1	.70	2.00	4.00
2-7	.35	1.00	2.00

DUKE OF THE K-9 PATROL
April, 1963
Gold Key

1 (10052-304)	1.00	3.00	6.00

DUMBO (See 4-Color No. 17,234,668, Movie Comics, & Walt Disney Showcase No. 12)

DUMBO (Walt Disney's. . .)
1941 (K.K. Publ. Giveaway)
Weatherbird Shoes/Ernest Kern Co.(Detroit)

16 pgs., 9x10'' (Rare)	20.00	60.00	120.00
52 pgs., 5½x8½'', slick cover in color; B&W interior; half text, half reprints/4-Color No. 17	12.00	35.00	70.00

DUMBO COMIC PAINT BOOK (See Black & White No. 19)

DUMBO WEEKLY
1942 (Premium supplied by Diamond D-X Gas Stations)
Walt Disney Productions

1	10.00	30.00	60.00
2-16	5.00	15.00	30.00

NOTE: *A cover and binder came separate at gas stations.*

DUNC AND LOO (No. 1 titled ''Around the Block with Dunc and Loo'')
1961 - No. 8, Oct-Dec, 1963
Dell Publishing Co.

1	2.00	5.00	10.00
2-8	1.00	3.00	6.00

NOTE: *Written by* ***John Stanley; Bill Williams*** *art.*

DURANGO KID (Also see White Indian)
Oct-Nov, 1949 - No. 41, 1955
Magazine Enterprises

1-White Indian by Frazetta begins (origin); Frazetta-a continues through No. 16	25.00	75.00	150.00
2-5	14.00	40.00	80.00
6-16-Last Frazetta ish.	10.00	28.00	56.00
17-Origin Durango Kid	5.00	15.00	30.00
18-30	2.50	7.00	14.00
31-41	1.50	4.00	8.00

NOTE: *No. 6,8,14,15 contain* ***Frazetta*** *art not reprinted in White Indian.* ***Frazettaish*** *a-35 (not by him).* ***Guardineer*** *c-35; a-35.*

DWIGHT D. EISENHOWER
December, 1969
Dell Publishing Co.

01-237-912 - Life story	2.00	6.00	12.00

DYNABRITE COMICS
1978 - 1979 (69 cents; 48 pgs.)(10x7-1/8''; cardboard covers)
(Blank inside covers)
Whitman Publishing Co.

11350 - Disney's Mickey & the Beanstalk (4-C 157)
11350-1 - Mickey Mouse Album (4-C 1057,1151,1246)
11351 - Mickey Mouse & His Sky Adventure (4-C 214,343)
11352 - Donald Duck (4-C 408, Donald Duck 45,52)-Barks
11352-1 - Donald Duck (4-C 318, 10 pg. Barks/WDC&S 125,128)-Barks-c(r)
11353 - Daisy Ducks Diary (4-C 1055,1150) - Barks-a
11354 - Goofy: A Gaggle of Giggles
11354-1 - Super Goof Meets Super Thief
11355 - Uncle Scrooge (Barks-a/U.S. 12,33)
11355-1 - Uncle Scrooge (Barks-a/U.S. 13,16) - Barks-c(r)
11356 - Bugs Bunny(?)
11357 - Star Trek (r-Star Trek 33 & ?)
11358 - Star Trek (r-Star Trek 34,36)
11359 - Bugs Bunny-r
11360 - Winnie the Pooh Fun and Fantasy (Disney-r)
11361 - Gyro Gearloose & the Disney Ducks (4-C 1047,1184) Barks-c(r)

	Good	Fine	Mint
each....		.40	.80

DYNAMIC ADVENTURES
No. 8,9, 1964
I. W. Enterprises

8	1.20	3.50	7.00
9-Reprints Avon's ''Escape From Devil's Island''	1.50	4.00	8.00
nn(no date)-Reprints Risks Unlimited with Rip Carson, Senorita Rio	1.20	3.50	7.00

DYNAMIC CLASSICS (See Cancelled Comic Cavalcade)
Sept-Oct, 1978
DC Comics

1-Adams Batman, Simonson Manhunter-r		.30	.60

DYNAMIC COMICS (No No.4-7)
Oct, 1941 - No. 3, Feb, 1942; No. 8, 1944 - No. 25, May, 1948
Harry 'A' Chesler

1-Origin Major Victory by Charles Sultan (reprinted in Major Victory No. 1), Dynamic Man & Hale the Magician; The Black Cobra only app.	24.00	70.00	150.00
2-Origin Dynamic Boy & Lady Satan; intro. The Green Knight & sidekick Lance Cooper	14.00	40.00	80.00
3	10.00	30.00	60.00
8-Dan Hastings, The Echo, The Master Key, Yankee Boy begin; Yankee Doodle Jones app; hypo story.	10.00	30.00	60.00
9-Mr. E begins; Mac Raboy-c	12.00	34.00	68.00
10-Drug story	8.00	24.00	48.00
11-14	5.50	16.00	32.00
15-Morphine drug dealing story; The Sky Chief app.	7.00	20.00	40.00
16-Marijuana story; bondage-c	8.00	24.00	48.00
17(1/46)-Illustrated in **SOTI**, ''The children told me what the man was going to do with the hot poker,'' but Wertham saw this in Crime Reporter No. 2 (this is a morphine drug story)	10.00	30.00	60.00
18,19,21,22,24,25	5.00	14.00	28.00
20-Drug story; bare-breasted woman-c	5.50	16.00	32.00
23-Yankee Girl app.	5.50	16.00	32.00
I.W. Reprint No. 1-Yankee Girl('64), No. 8	.70	2.00	4.00

NOTE: ***Kinstler*** *c-IW No. 1.* ***Tuska*** *art in many issues, No. 3, 9, 11, 12, 16, 19.*

DYNAMITE (Johnny Dynamite No. 10 on)
May, 1953 - No. 9, Sept, 1954
Comic Media/Allen Hardy Publ.

1-Morphine drug mention story; Pete Morisi-a	3.50	10.00	20.00
2	2.00	6.00	12.00
3-Marijuana, heroin drug story; Johnny Dynamite begins by Pete Morisi-a	3.00	8.00	16.00
4-Injury-to-eye, prostitution; Morisi-a	2.00	6.00	12.00
5-9-Morisi-a in all	1.50	4.50	9.00

DYNAMO
Aug, 1966 - No. 4, June, 1967 (25 cents)
Tower Comics

1-Crandall, Ditko-a; Weed series begins; NoMan & Lightning cameos; Wood c/a	.85	2.50	5.00
2-4: Wood c/a in all; Ditko-a No. 4	.60	1.80	3.60

DYNOMUTT (TV)
Nov, 1977 - No. 8, Jan, 1979
Marvel Comics Group

1-8		.50	1.00

EAGLE, THE (1st Series)

EAGLE (continued)
July, 1941 - No. 4, Jan, 1942
Fox Features Syndicate

	Good	Fine	Mint
1-The Eagle begins; Rex Dexter of Mars app.	25.00	75.00	150.00
2-The Spider Queen begins (origin)	13.00	38.00	75.00
3-Joe Spook begins (origin)	11.00	32.00	65.00
4	11.00	32.00	65.00

EAGLE (2nd Series)
Feb-Mar, 1945 - No. 2, Apr-May, 1945
Rural Home Publ.

	Good	Fine	Mint
1-Aviation stories	4.00	12.00	24.00
2-Lucky Aces	4.00	12.00	24.00

NOTE: ***L. B. Cole** c/a.*

EARTH MAN ON VENUS (An . . .) (Also see Strange Planets)
1951
Avon Periodicals

	Good	Fine	Mint
nn-Wood-a, 26 pgs.	100.00	250.00	500.00

EASTER BONNET SHOP (See March of Comics No. 29)

EASTER WITH MOTHER GOOSE (See 4-Color No. 103,140,185,220)

EAT RIGHT TO WORK AND WIN
1942 (16 pages) (Giveaway)
Swift & Company

Blondie, Henry, Flash Gordon by Alex Raymond, Toots & Casper, Thimble Threatre (Popeye), Tillie the Toiler, The Phantom, The Little King, & Bringing Up Father - original strips just for this book - (in daily strip form which shows what foods we should eat and why)

	Good	Fine	Mint
	17.00	50.00	100.00

E. C. CLASSIC REPRINTS
May, 1973 - No. 12, 1976 (E. C. Comics reprinted in full color minus ads)
East Coast Comix Co.

	Good	Fine	Mint
1-The Crypt of Terror No. 1 (Tales From the Crypt No. 46)	1.00	3.00	6.00
2-Weird Science No. 15('52)	.70	2.00	4.00
3-Shock SuspenStories No. 12	.35	1.00	2.00
4-Haunt of Fear No. 12	.35	1.00	2.00
5-Weird Fantasy No. 13('52)	.35	1.00	2.00
6-Crime SuspenStories No. 25	.35	1.00	2.00
7-Vault of Horror No. 26	.35	1.00	2.00
8-Shock SuspenStories No. 6	.35	1.00	2.00
9-Two-Fisted Tales No. 34	.35	1.00	2.00
10-Haunt of Fear No. 23	.35	1.00	2.00
11-Weird Science No. 12(No.1)	.35	1.00	2.00
12-Shock SuspenStories No. 2	.35	1.00	2.00

E. C. 3-D CLASSICS (See Three Dimensional . . .)

EDDIE STANKY (Baseball Hero)
1951 (New York Giants)
Fawcett Publications

	Good	Fine	Mint
nn	7.00	20.00	40.00

EDGAR BERGEN PRESENTS CHARLIE McCARTHY
1938 (36 pgs.; 15x10½''; in color)
Whitman Publishing Co. (Charlie McCarthy Co.)

	Good	Fine	Mint
764 (Scarce)	24.00	70.00	160.00

EDWARD'S SHOES GIVEAWAY
1954 (Has clown on cover)
Edward's Shoe Store

Contains comic with new cover. Many combinations possible. Contents determines price, 50-60 percent of original. (Similar to Comics From Weatherbird & Free Comics to You)

ED WHEELAN'S JOKE BOOK STARRING FAT & SLAT (See Fat & Slat)

EERIE (Strange Worlds No. 18 on)
No. 1, Jan, 1947; No. 1, May-June, 1951 - No. 17, Aug-Sept, 1954
Avon Periodicals

	Good	Fine	Mint
1(1947)-1st horror comic; Kubert, Fugitani-a; bondage-c	17.00	50.00	100.00
1(1951)-Reprints story/'47 No. 1	10.00	28.00	56.00
2-Wood c/a; bondage-c	12.00	34.00	68.00
3-Wood-c, Kubert, Wood/Orlando-a	12.00	34.00	68.00
4,5-Wood-c	10.00	30.00	60.00
6,13,14	4.00	12.00	24.00
7-Wood/Orlando-c; Kubert-a	7.00	20.00	40.00
8-Kinstler-a; bondage-c	5.00	14.00	28.00
9-Kubert-a; Check-c	5.50	16.00	32.00
10,11-Kinstler-a	5.00	14.00	28.00
12-25-pg. Dracula story from novel	6.00	18.00	36.00
15-Reprints No. 1('51)minus-c(bondage)	3.00	8.00	16.00
16-Wood-a r-/No. 2	4.00	12.00	24.00
17-Wood/Orlando & Kubert-a; reprints No. 3 minus inside & outside Wood-c	5.00	15.00	30.00

NOTE: ***Hollingsworth** a-9-11; c-10,11.*

EERIE
1964
I. W. Enterprises

	Good	Fine	Mint
I.W. Reprint No. 1(1964)-Wood-c(r)	1.20	3.50	7.00
I.W. Reprint No. 2,6,8: 8-Dr. Drew by Grandenetti from Ghost No. 9	.85	2.50	5.00
I.W. Reprint No. 9-From Eerie No. 2(Avon); Wood-c	1.50	4.00	8.00

EERIE (Magazine)
No. 1, Sept, 1965; No. 2, Mar, 1966 - Present
Warren Publishing Co.

1-24 pgs., black & white, small size (5¼x7¼''), low distribution; cover from inside back cover of Creepy No. 2; stories reprinted from Creepy No. 7, 8. At least three different versions exist.

First Printing - B&W, 5¼'' wide x 7¼'' high, evenly trimmed. On page 18, panel 5, in the upper left-hand corner, the large rear view of a bald headed man blends into solid black and is unrecognizable. Overall printing quality is poor.

	Good	Fine	Mint
	25.00	75.00	150.00

Second Printing - B&W, 5¼x7¼'', with uneven, untrimmed edges (if one of these were trimmed evenly, the size would be less than as indicated). The figure of the bald headed man on page 18, panel 5 is cleared and discernible. The staples have a ¼'' blue stripe.

	Good	Fine	Mint
	8.00	24.00	48.00

Other unauthorized reproductions for comparison's sake would be practically worthless. One known version was probably shot off a first printing copy with some loss of detail; the finer lines tend to disappear in this version which can be determined by looking at the lower right-hand corner of page one, first story. The roof of the house is shaded with straight lines. These lines are sharp and distinct on original, but broken on this version.

	Good	Fine	Mint
	2.00	5.00	10.00

NOTE: ***The Comic Book Price Guide** recommends that, before buying, you consult an expert.*

	Good	Fine	Mint
2-Frazetta-c	1.50	4.00	8.00
3-Frazetta-c, 1 pg.	.85	2.50	5.00
4-10: 4-Frazetta ½ page	.70	2.00	4.00
11-16,18,19	.60	1.80	3.60
17-Low distribution	1.00	3.00	6.00
20-25	.50	1.50	3.00
26-42: 39-1st Dax by Maroto. 42-Williamson-a(r)	.40	1.20	2.40
43-46	.35	1.10	2.20
47-54,56-78: 78-The Mummy reprints	.35	1.10	2.20
55-Color Spirit story by Eisner	.40	1.20	2.40
79,80-Origin Darklon the Mystic by Starlin	.35	1.00	2.00
81-124	.30	.80	1.60
125-Neal Adams r-Special	.30	.80	1.60
Year Book 1970-Reprints	1.00	3.00	6.00

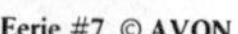
Eerie #7, © AVON

Eerie #1, © I.W.

Eerie #1, © WP

Eerie Tales #10, © SUPER

Eh! #7, © CC

80 Page Giant #6, © DC

EERIE (continued)

	Good	Fine	Mint
Year Book 1971-Reprints	.85	2.50	5.00
Year Book 1972,1973-Reprints	.60	1.80	3.60
Year Book 1974,1975-Reprints	.40	1.20	2.40

NOTE: *The above books contain art by many good artists:* ***Adams, Brunner, Corben, Craig (Taycee), Crandall, Ditko, Eisner, Evans, Jeff Jones, Kinstler, Krenkel, McWilliams, Morrow, Orlando, Ploog, Severin, Starlin, Torres, Toth, Williamson, Wood,*** *and* ***Wrightson;*** *covers by* ***Bode', Corben, Davis, Frazetta, Morrow, and Orlando.***

EERIE ADVENTURES
Winter, 1951
Ziff-Davis Publ. Co.

1-Powell-a(2), Kinstler-a; used in **SOTI**; bondage-c
3.00 9.00 18.00

NOTE: Title dropped due to similarity to Avon's Eerie & legal action.

EERIE TALES (Magazine)
1959 (Black & White)
Hastings Associates

1-Williamson, Torres, Powell(2), & Morrow(2)-a
4.00 12.00 24.00

EERIE TALES
1964
Super Comics

Super Reprint No. 10,11,12,18: Purple Claw in No. 11,12; No. 12 r-Avon Eerie No. 1('51) .70 2.00 4.00
15-Wolverton-art-Spacehawk reprint/Blue Bolt Weird Tales No. 113
2.00 6.00 12.00

EGBERT
Spring, 1946 - No. 20, 1950
Arnold Publications/Quality Comics Group

1	2.00	6.00	12.00
2-10	1.00	3.00	6.00
11-20	.70	2.00	4.00

EH! (. . . Dig This Crazy Comic) (From Here to Insanity No. 8 on)
Dec, 1953 - No. 7, Nov-Dec, 1954 (Satire)
Charlton Comics

1	4.00	12.00	24.00
2-7: 5-Classic sexual inuendo-c	3.00	9.00	18.00

80 PAGE GIANT (. . . Magazine No. 1-15) (25 cents)
8/64 - No. 15, 10/65; No. 16, 11/65 - No. 89, 7/71
National Periodical Publications (No.57-89: 68 pages)

1-Superman	4.00	12.00	24.00
2-Jimmy Olsen	1.50	4.00	8.00
3-Lois Lane	1.00	3.00	6.00
4-Flash-G.A. reprint; Infantino-a	1.00	3.00	6.00
5-Batman	1.00	3.00	6.00
6-Superman	1.00	3.00	6.00
7-Sgt. Rock's Prize Battle Tales; Kubert c/a	1.00	3.00	6.00
8-More Secret Origins-origins of JLA, Aquaman, Robin, Atom, & Superman; Infantino-a	3.00	8.00	16.00
9-Flash(reprints Flash No. 123)-Infantino-a	1.00	3.00	6.00
10-Superboy	1.00	3.00	6.00
11-Superman	.55	1.60	3.20
12-Batman	.55	1.60	3.20
13-Jimmy Olsen	.55	1.60	3.20
14-Lois Lane	.55	1.60	3.20
15-Superman and Batman	.55	1.60	3.20

Continued as part of regular series under each title in which that particular book came out, a Giant being published instead of the regular size. Issues No. 16 to No. 89 are listed for your information. See individual titles for prices.

16-JLA No. 39 (11/65)
17-Batman No. 176
18-Superman No. 183
19-Our Army at War No. 164
20-Action No. 334
21-Flash No. 160
22-Superboy No. 129
23-Superman No. 187
24-Batman No. 182
25-Jimmy Olsen No. 95
26-Lois Lane No. 68
27-Batman No. 185
28-World's Finest No. 161
29-JLA No. 48
30-Batman No. 187
31-Superman No. 193
32-Our Army at War No. 177
33-Action No. 347
34-Flash No. 169
35-Superboy No. 138
36-Superman No. 197
37-Batman No. 193
38-Jimmy Olsen No. 104
39-Lois Lane No. 77
40-World's Finest No. 170
41-JLA No. 58
42-Superman No. 202
43-Batman No. 198
44-Our Army at War No. 190
45-Action No. 360
46-Flash No. 178
47-Superboy No. 147
48-Superman No. 207
49-Batman No. 203
50-Jimmy Olsen No. 113
51-Lois Lane No. 86
52-World's Finest No. 179
53-JLA No. 67
54-Superman No. 212
55-Batman No. 208
56-Our Army at War No. 203
57-Action No. 373
58-Flash No. 187
59-Superboy No. 156
60-Superman No. 217
61-Batman No. 213
62-Jimmy Olsen No. 122
63-Lois Lane No. 95
64-World's Finest No. 188
65-JLA No. 76
66-Superman No. 222
67-Batman No. 218
68-Our Army at War No. 216
69-Adventure No. 390
70-Flash No. 196
71-Superboy No. 165
72-Superman No. 227
73-Batman No. 223
74-Jimmy Olsen No. 131
75-Lois Lane No. 104
76-World's Finest No. 197
77-JLA No. 85
78-Superman No. 232
79-Batman No. 228
80-Our Army at War No. 229
81-Adventure No. 403
82-Flash No. 205
83-Superboy No. 174
84-Superman No. 239
85-Batman No. 233
86-Jimmy Olsen No. 140
87-Lois Lane No. 113
88-World's Finest No. 206
89-JLA No. 93

87TH PRECINCT (TV)
Apr-June, 1962 - No. 2, July-Sept, 1962
Dell Publishing Co.

	Good	Fine	Mint
4-Color 1309; Krigstein-a	3.00	9.00	18.00
2-Drug story	2.75	8.00	16.00

EL BOMBO COMICS
1946
Standard Comics/Frances M. McQueeny

nn(1946)	3.00	6.00	12.00
1(no date)	3.00	6.00	12.00

EL CID (See 4-Color No. 1259)

EL DORADO (See Movie Classics)

ELLA CINDERS (See Famous Comics Cartoon Book)

ELLA CINDERS
1938 - 1940
United Features Syndicate

Single Series 3(1938) 10.00 28.00 56.00
Single Series 21(No.2 on cover, No.21 on inside), 28('40)
7.00 20.00 40.00

ELLA CINDERS (See Comics Revue No. 1,4)
March, 1948 - No. 5, 1949
United Features Syndicate

1	3.00	8.00	16.00
2-5	2.00	5.00	10.00

ELLERY QUEEN
May, 1949 - No. 4, Nov, 1949
Superior Comics Ltd.

1-Kamen c/a	10.00	28.00	56.00
2	6.00	18.00	36.00
3-Drug use stories(2)	7.00	20.00	40.00
4-Kamen-a	6.00	18.00	36.00

NOTE: ***Kamen*** *c-1-4.*

ELLERY QUEEN
1-3/52 - No. 2, Summer/52 (Saunders painted covers)
Ziff-Davis Publishing Co.

	Good	Fine	Mint
1-Saunders-c	10.00	28.00	56.00
2-Saunders bondage, torture-c	10.00	28.00	56.00

ELLERY QUEEN (See 4-Color No. 1165,1243,1289)

ELMER FUDD (Also see Daffy)
May, 1953 - No. 1293, Mar-May, 1962
Dell Publishing Co.

4-Color 470,558,628,689('56)	.85	2.50	5.00
4-Color 725,783,841,888,938,977,1032,1081,1131,1171,1222, 1293('61)	.60	1.80	3.60

(See Super Book No. 10,22, & No No.)

ELMO
January, 1948
St. John Publishing Co.

1-Daily newspaper strip reprints	2.00	5.00	10.00

ELSIE THE COW
Oct-Nov, 1949 - No. 3, July-Aug, 1950
D. S. Publishing Co.

1-(36 pages)	10.00	28.00	56.00
2,3	6.00	18.00	36.00
Borden Milk Giveaway-(16 pgs., nn) (3 issues, 1957)	3.00	8.00	16.00
Elsie's Fun Book(1950; Borden Milk)	4.00	12.00	24.00
Everyday Birthday Fun With. . .(1957; 20 pgs.)(100th Anniversary); Kubert-a	3.00	8.00	16.00

ELVIS PRESLEY (See I Love You 60 & Young Lovers 18)

E-MAN
Oct, 1973 - No. 10, Sept, 1975
Charlton Comics

1-Origin E-Man; Staton c/a in all	.85	2.50	5.00
2-Ditko-a	.50	1.50	3.00
3,4: 3-Howard-a. 4-Ditko-a	.50	1.50	3.00
5-Miss Liberty Belle app. by Ditko	.40	1.10	2.20
6-Byrne's 1st work	.60	1.80	3.60
7,9,10-Byrne-a in all	.60	1.80	3.60
8-Full-length story; Nova begins as E-Man's partner	.70	2.00	4.00
1-5,9,10(Modern Comics reprints, '77)		.15	.30

NOTE: *Killjoy app.-No. 1,2,4. Liberty Belle app.-No. 5. Rog 2000 app.-No. 6, 7, 9, 10. Travis app.-No. 3.*

EMERGENCY (Magazine)
June, 1976 - No. 4, Jan, 1977 (B&W)
Charlton Comics

1-Adams c/a	.50	1.50	3.00
2-Adams-c	.30	.80	1.60
3-Adams c/a	.35	1.00	2.00
4	.30	.80	1.60

EMERGENCY (TV)
June, 1976 - No. 4, Dec, 1976
Charlton Comics

1-Staton-c, Byrne-a	.50	1.50	3.00
2-4: 2-Staton-c		.50	1.00

EMERGENCY DOCTOR
Summer, 1963 (One Shot)
Charlton Comics

1	.30	.80	1.60

EMIL & THE DETECTIVES (See Movie Comics)

EMMA PEEL & JOHN STEED (See The Avengers)

ENCHANTMENT VISUALETTES (Magazine)
Dec, 1949 - No. 5, April, 1950
World Editions

	Good	Fine	Mint
1-Contains two romance comic strips each; painted-c	8.00	24.00	48.00
2-5	6.00	18.00	36.00

ENCHANTING LOVE
Oct, 1949 - No. 6, July, 1950
Kirby Publishing Co.

1	3.00	8.00	16.00
2-4,6: 2-Powell-a	2.00	5.00	10.00
5-Ingels-a, 9 pgs.; photo-c	7.00	20.00	40.00

ENEMY ACE (See Star-Spangled War Stories)

ENSIGN O'TOOLE (TV)
Aug-Oct, 1963 - No. 2, 1964
Dell Publishing Co.

1,2	.85	2.50	5.00

ENSIGN PULVER (See Movie Classics)

EPIC ILLUSTRATED (Magazine)
May, 1981 - Present (B&W/Color)
Marvel Comics Group

1-8		.50	1.00

NOTE: ***Adams** a-7; c-6. **Buscema** a-1. **Chaykin** a-2; c-8. **Conrad** a-1,4, 5, 7, 8. **Corbin** c-2. **Davis** a-4. **Frazetta** c-1. **Golden** a-3. **Gulacy** c-3. **Kaluta** c-4. **Smith** c/a-7. **Starlin** a-1-8.*

ERNIE COMICS (Formerly Monkeyshines?; All Love Romances No. 26 on)
Sept, 1948 - No. 25, Mar, 1949
Current Books/Ace Periodicals

nn(9/48,11/48)	1.50	4.00	8.00
24,25	.85	2.50	5.00

ESCAPADE IN FLORENCE (See Movie Comics)

ESCAPE FROM DEVIL'S ISLAND
1952
Avon Periodicals

1-Kinstler-c; r/as Dynamic Adv. No. 9	12.00	35.00	70.00

ESCAPE FROM FEAR
1962 (8 pages)
Planned Parenthood of America (Giveaway)

On birth control	14.00	40.00	80.00

ESCAPE TO WITCH MOUNTAIN (See Walt Disney Showcase No. 29)

ESPIONAGE (TV)
May-July, 1964 - No. 2, Aug-Oct, 1964
Dell Publishing Co.

1,2	.85	2.50	5.00

ETERNAL BIBLE, THE
1946 (Large size) (16 pages in color)
Authentic Publications

1	4.00	12.00	24.00

ETERNALS, THE
July, 1976 - No. 19, Jan, 1978
Marvel Comics Group

1-Origin		.60	1.20
2-19: 2-1st app. Ajak & The Celestials. 14-16-Hulk app.		.40	.80
Annual 1(10/77)		.40	.80

NOTE: ***Kirby** c/a in all. Price changed from 25 cents to 30 cents during run of No. 1.*

Elsie The Cow nn, © Borden Milk

E-Man #6, © CC

The Eternals #15, © MCG

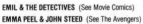

Exciting Comics #7, © BP

Exciting Comics #40, © BP

Exposed #6, © DS

ETTA KETT
No. 11, Dec, 1948 - No. 14, Sept, 1949
King Features Syndicate/Standard

	Good	Fine	Mint
11-14	2.00	5.00	10.00

EVA THE IMP
1957
Red Top Comic/Decker

	Good	Fine	Mint
1,2	.85	2.50	5.00

EVEL KNIEVEL
1974 (16 pages) (Giveaway)
Marvel Comics Group (Ideal Toy Corp.)

	Good	Fine	Mint
nn-Sekowsky-a		.50	1.00

EVERYBODY'S COMICS
1944 - 1947
Fox Features Syndicate

	Good	Fine	Mint
1(1944)-The Green Mask, The Puppeteer; 194 pgs.	5.00	15.00	30.00
1(1946)-Contents vary-Green Lama, The Puppeteer app.	4.00	12.00	24.00
1(1946)-Same as the 1945 Ribtickler	1.50	4.00	8.00
1947 (132 pages)	5.00	15.00	30.00

EVERYTHING HAPPENS TO HARVEY
Sept-Oct, 1953 - No. 7, Sept-Oct, 1954
National Periodical Publications

	Good	Fine	Mint
1	4.50	13.00	26.00
2-7	3.00	9.00	18.00

EVERYTHING'S ARCHIE
May, 1969 - Present
Archie Publications

	Good	Fine	Mint
1 (Giant)	1.50	4.00	8.00
2-10 (Giants)	.50	1.50	3.00
11-20		.50	1.00
21-89		.30	.60

EVERYTHING'S DUCKY (See 4-Color No. 1251)

EXCITING COMICS
April, 1940 - No. 69, Sept, 1949
Nedor/Better Publications/Standard Comics

	Good	Fine	Mint
1-Origin The Mask, Jim Hatfield, Sgt. Bill King, Dan Williams begin	35.00	100.00	200.00
2-The Sphinx begins; The Masked Rider app.	15.00	45.00	90.00
3	13.00	37.00	75.00
4	9.00	27.00	54.00
5	7.00	20.00	40.00
6-8	5.00	15.00	30.00
9-Origin/1st app. of The Black Terror & sidekick Tim; bondage-c	40.00	110.00	220.00
10-13: 12-Drug mention story	15.00	45.00	90.00
14-Last Sphinx, Dan Williams	9.00	27.00	54.00
15-Origin The Liberator	11.00	32.00	65.00
16-20: 20-The Mask ends	7.00	21.00	42.00
21,23-30: 28-Crime Crusader begins, ends No. 58	7.00	21.00	42.00
22-Origin The Eaglet; The American Eagle begins	7.00	21.00	42.00
31-38: 35-Liberator ends, not in 31-33	5.50	16.00	32.00
39-Origin Kara, Jungle Princess	8.00	23.00	46.00
40-50: 42-The Scarab begins. 49-Last Kara, Jungle Princess. 50-Last American Eagle	7.00	20.00	40.00
51-Miss Masque begins	10.00	30.00	60.00
52-54: Miss Masque ends	7.00	20.00	40.00
55-Judy of the Jungle begins(origin), ends No. 69; 1 pg. Ingels-a	10.00	30.00	60.00
56-58: All airbrush-c	7.00	20.00	40.00
59-Frazetta art in Caniff style; signed Frank Frazeta (one t), 9 pgs; bondage-c	14.00	40.00	80.00
60-65: 60-Rick Howard, the Mystery Rider begins	7.00	20.00	40.00
66-Cocaine drug story	8.00	24.00	48.00
67-69	5.00	14.00	28.00

NOTE: ***Schomburg (Xela)*** *c-42, 56-66. No. 66-last airbrush cover. Black Terror by* ***R. Moreira****-No. 65. Bondage covers are common.*

EXCITING ROMANCES
1949 - 1953
Fawcett Publications

	Good	Fine	Mint
1	2.00	6.00	12.00
2-12	1.00	3.00	6.00

NOTE: ***Powell*** *a-8-10.*

EXCITING ROMANCE STORIES
1949 (132 pages)
Fox Features Syndicate

nn-See Fox Giants. Contents can vary and determines price.

EXCITING WAR
No. 5, Sept, 1952 - No. 8, May, 1953; No. 9, Nov, 1953
Standard Comics (Better Publ.)

	Good	Fine	Mint
5-7,9	1.00	3.00	6.00
8-Toth-a	2.00	6.00	12.00

EXORCISTS (See The Crusaders)

EXOTIC ROMANCES (Formerly True War Romances)
No. 22, Oct, 1955 - No. 31, Nov, 1956
Quality Comics Group (Comic Magazines)

	Good	Fine	Mint
22-26,29	1.50	4.00	8.00
27,31-Baker c/a	3.50	10.00	20.00
28,30-Baker-a	3.00	8.00	16.00

EXPLOITS OF DANIEL BOONE
Nov, 1955 - No. 8, Dec, 1956
Quality Comics Group

	Good	Fine	Mint
1	3.00	8.00	16.00
2-8	1.50	4.00	8.00

EXPLOITS OF DICK TRACY (See Dick Tracy)

EXPLORER JOE
Winter, 1951 - No. 2, Oct-Nov, 1952
Ziff-Davis Publ. Co.

	Good	Fine	Mint
1-Saunders painted-c	2.50	7.00	14.00
2-Krigstein-a	3.50	10.00	20.00

EXPOSED (. . . True Crime Cases)
Mar-Apr, 1948 - No. 9, July-Aug, 1949
D. S. Publishing Co.

	Good	Fine	Mint
1	3.50	10.00	20.00
2-Giggling killer story with excessive blood; two eye injury panels	3.50	10.00	20.00
3,8,9	2.00	5.00	10.00
4-Orlando-a	3.00	8.00	16.00
5-Breeze Lawson, Sky Sheriff by E. Good	2.00	5.00	10.00
6-Ingels-a; used in **SOTI**, illo.-''How to prepare an alibi.''	10.00	28.00	56.00
7-Illo. in **SOTI**, ''Diagram for housebreakers''; used by N.Y. Legis. Comm.	9.00	25.00	50.00

EXTRA (Magazine)
1948
Magazine Enterprises

	Good	Fine	Mint
1-Funny Man by Siegel & Shuster, Space Ace, Undercover Girl	8.00	23.00	46.00

EXTRA!
Mar-Apr, 1955 - No. 5, Nov-Dec, 1955

EXTRA! (continued)
E. C. Comics

	Good	Fine	Mint
1	7.00	20.00	40.00
2-5	5.00	14.00	28.00

NOTE: ***Craig, Crandall, Severin** art in all.*

FACE, THE (Tony Trent, the Face No. 3 on)
1941
Columbia Comics Group

1-The Face	14.00	40.00	80.00
2	9.00	25.00	50.00

FAIRY TALE PARADE (See Famous Fairy Tales)
June-July, 1942 - 1946 (All by Walt Kelly)
Dell Publishing Co.

1-All by Kelly	90.00	250.00	525.00
2(1943)	50.00	140.00	290.00
3-5	35.00	90.00	180.00
6-9	25.00	70.00	140.00
4-Color 50('44)	20.00	60.00	120.00
4-Color 69('45)	15.00	45.00	90.00
4-Color 87('45)	14.00	40.00	80.00
4-Color 104,114('46)	12.00	34.00	68.00
4-Color 121('46)-Not Kelly	7.00	20.00	40.00

NOTE: *No. 1-9, 4-Color No. 50,69 have **Kelly** c/a; 4-Color No. 87, 104, 114-**Kelly** art only. No. 9 has a redrawn version of The Reluctant Dragon.*

FAIRY TALES
No. 10, 1951 - No. 11, June-July, 1951
Ziff-Davis Publ. Co. (Approved Comics)

10,11	3.00	8.00	16.00

FAITHFUL
November, 1949 - No. 2, Jan, 1950?
Marvel Comics/Lovers' Magazine

1,2	2.00	5.00	10.00

FALLING IN LOVE
Sept-Oct, 1955 - No. 143, Oct-Nov, 1973
Arleigh Publ. Co./National Periodical Publications

1	4.00	12.00	24.00
2-10	2.00	6.00	12.00
11-20	1.00	3.00	6.00
21-40	.70	2.00	4.00
41-100	.35	1.00	2.00
101-143 (143-exist?)		.50	1.00

FALL OF THE ROMAN EMPIRE (See Movie Comics)

FAMILY AFFAIR (TV)
Feb, 1970 - No. 4, Oct, 1970 (25 cents)
Gold Key

1-Pull-out poster	1.00	3.00	6.00
2-4	.70	2.00	4.00

FAMILY FUNNIES
No. 9, Aug-Sept, 1946
Parents' Magazine Institute

9	1.20	3.50	7.00

FAMILY FUNNIES
Sept, 1950 - No. 10, June, 1951
Harvey Publications

1-Mandrake	3.00	8.00	16.00
2-10: 4-Flash Gordon	2.50	7.00	14.00
1(black & white)	1.20	3.50	7.00

FAMOUS AUTHORS ILL. (See Stories by. . .)

FAMOUS COMICS
No date; Mid 1930's (24 pages) (paper cover)
Zain-Eppy/United Features Syndicate

	Good	Fine	Mint
Reprinted from 1934 newspaper strips in color; Joe Palooka, Hair-breadth Harry, Napoleon, The Nebbs, etc.	15.00	45.00	90.00

FAMOUS COMICS
1934 (100 pgs., daily newspaper reprints)
(3½x8½''; paper cover) (came in a box)
King Features Syndicate (Whitman Publ. Co.)

684(No.1)-Little Jimmy, Katzenjammer Kids, & Barney Google	15.00	45.00	90.00
684(No.2)-Polly, Little Jimmy, Katzenjammer Kids	10.00	30.00	60.00
684(No.3)-Little Annie Rooney, Polly, Katzenjammer Kids	10.00	30.00	60.00
. . . . Box price. . . .	4.00	12.00	24.00

FAMOUS COMICS CARTOON BOOKS
1934 (72 pgs.; 8x7¼''; daily strip reprints)
Whitman Publishing Co. (B&W; hardbacks)

1200-The Captain & the Kids; Dirks reprints credited to Bernard Dibble	8.00	24.00	48.00
1202-Captain Easy & Wash Tubbs by Roy Crane	12.00	36.00	72.00
1203-Ella Cinders	8.00	24.00	48.00
1204-Freckles & His Friends	7.00	20.00	40.00

NOTE: *Called Famous Funnies Cartoon Books inside.*

FAMOUS CRIMES
June, 1948 - No. 19, Sept, 1950
Fox Features Syndicate

1-Blue Beetle app. & crime story reprint/Phantom Lady No. 16	6.00	18.00	36.00
2,4-6	3.50	10.00	20.00
3-Injury-to-eye story used in **SOTI**, pg. 112; has two electrocution stories	6.00	18.00	36.00
7-''Tarzan, the Wyoming Killer'' used in **SOTI**, pg. 44; drug trial/possession story	6.00	18.00	36.00
8-10,12,14-19	3.50	8.00	16.00
11,13-Drug story in ea.(heroin; opium)	4.00	12.00	24.00
51(no date)-Morphine drug story	3.50	10.00	20.00
52	2.00	5.00	10.00

FAMOUS FAIRY TALES
1943 (32 pgs.); 1944 (16 pgs.) (Soft covers)
K. K. Publ. Co. (Giveaway)

1942-Reprints from Fairy Tale Parade No. 2,3; Kelly inside art	50.00	140.00	240.00
1944-Kelly inside art	30.00	80.00	160.00

FAMOUS FEATURE STORIES
1938 (68 pgs., 7½x11'')
Dell Publishing Co.

1-Tarzan, Terry & the Pirates, King of the Royal Mtd., Buck Jones, Dick Tracy, Smilin' Jack, Dan Dunn, Don Winslow, G-Man, Tail-spin Tommy, Mutt & Jeff, & Little Orphan Annie reprints - all illustrated text	24.00	70.00	140.00

FAMOUS FIRST EDITION (See Limited Collectors Edition)
($1.00; 10x13½''-Giant Size)(72pgs.; No.6-8, 68 pgs.)
1974 - No. 8, Aug-Sept, 1975; C-61, Sept, 1978 - Present
National Periodical Publications/DC Comics

C-26-Action No. 1	1.00	3.00	6.00
C-28-Detective No. 27	.80	2.30	4.60
C-30-Sensation No. 1(1974)	.70	2.00	4.00
F-4-Whiz No. 2(No.1)(10-11/74)-Cover not identical to original	.70	2.00	4.00
F-5-Batman No. 1(F-6 on inside)	.50	1.50	3.00
F-6-Wonder Woman No. 1	.50	1.50	3.00
F-7-All-Star Comics No. 3	.50	1.50	3.00

Extra! #2, © WMG

Famous Comics #684, © KING

Famous Crimes #12, © FOX

F.F. A Carnival Of Comics, © EAS

Famous Funnies #23, © EAS

Famous Funnies #134, © EAS

FAMOUS FIRST EDITION (continued) Good Fine Mint

F-8-Flash No. 1(8-9/75) .50 1.50 3.00

C-61-Superman No. 1(9/78) .50 1.50 3.00

Hardbound editions w/dust jackets ($5.00) (Lyle Stuart, Inc.)
C-26,C-28,C-30,F-4,F-6 known 1.50 4.00 8.00

Warning: The above books are **exact** reprints of the originals that they represent except for the Giant-Size format. None of the originals are Giant-Size. The first five issues and C-61 were printed with two covers. Reprint information can be found on the outside cover, but not on the inside cover which was reprinted exactly like the original (inside and out).

FAMOUS FUNNIES
1933 - No. 218, July, 1955
Eastern Color/Dell Publ./Eastern Color

A Carnival of Comics (probably the second comic book), 36 pgs., no date given, no publisher, no number; contains strip reprints of The Bungle Family, Dixie Dugan, Hairbreadth Harry, Joe Palooka, Keeping Up With the Jones, Mutt & Jeff, Reg'lar Fellers, S'Matter Pop, Strange As It Seems, and others. This book was sold by M. C. Gaines to Wheatena, Milk-O-Malt, John Wanamaker, Kinney Shoe Stores, & others to be given away as premiums and radio giveaways (1933).
130.00 340.00 600.00

Series 1-(No date-early 1934)(68 pgs.) No publisher given; sold in chain stores for 10 cents. 35,000 print run (produced by Eastern Color for Dell Publ. Co.). Contains Sunday strip reprints of Mutt & Jeff, Reg'lar Fellers, Nipper, Hairbreadth Harry, Strange As It Seems, Joe Palooka, Dixie Dugan, The Nebbs, Keeping Up With the Jones, and others. Inside front and back covers and pages 1-16 of Famous Funnies Series 1, Nos. 49-64 reprinted from **Famous Funnies, A Carnival of Comics**, and most of pages 17-48 reprinted from **Funnies on Parade.** This was the first comic book sold. 120.00 320.00 560.00

No. 1 (7/34-on stands 5/34) - Eastern Color Printing Co. First monthly newsstand comic book. Contains Sunday strip reprints of Toonerville Folks, Mutt & Jeff, Hairbreadth Harry, S'Matter Pop, Nipper, Dixie Dugan, The Bungle Family, Connie, Ben Webster, Tailspin Tommy, The Nebbs, Joe Palooka, & others. 90.00 240.00 480.00

2 30.00 80.00 160.00

3-Buck Rogers Sunday strip reprints by Rick Yager begins, ends No. 218; not in No. 191-208; the number of the 1st strip reprinted is pg. 190, Series No. 1 50.00 130.00 260.00

4 20.00 55.00 110.00

5 14.00 40.00 80.00

6-10 12.00 35.00 70.00

11,12,18-Four pgs. of Buck Rogers in each issue, completes stories in Buck Rogers No. 1 which lacks these pages; No. 18-Two pgs. of Buck Rogers reprinted in Daisy Comics No. 1
13.00 38.00 76.00

13-17,19,20: 14-Has two Buck Rogers panels missing
10.00 28.00 56.00

21,23-30: 27-War on Crime begins 6.00 18.00 36.00

22-Four pgs. of Buck Rogers needed to complete stories in Buck Rogers No. 1 9.00 25.00 50.00

31-34,36,37,39,40 5.00 15.00 30.00

35-Two pgs. Buck Rogers omitted in Buck Rogers No. 2
9.00 25.00 50.00

38-Full color portrait of Buck Rogers 6.00 18.00 36.00

41-60 5.00 14.00 28.00

61-64,66,67,69,70 4.00 12.00 24.00

65,68-Two pgs. Kirby-a-"Lightnin & the Lone Rider"
5.00 14.00 28.00

71,73,77-80: 80-Buck Rogers story continues from B. R. No. 5
3.00 9.00 18.00

72-Speed Spaulding begins by Marvin Bradley (artist), ends No. 88. This series was written by Edwin Balmer & Philip Wylie and later appeared as film & book "When Worlds Collide."
4.00 12.00 24.00

74-76-Two pgs. Kirby-a in all 3.50 10.00 20.00

81-Origin Invisible Scarlet O'Neil; strip begins No. 82, ends No. 167
3.00 9.00 18.00

82-Buck Rogers-c 4.00 12.00 24.00

83-87,90: 87 has last Buck Rogers full page reprint
3.00 9.00 18.00

Good Fine Mint

88-Buck Rogers in "Moon's End" by Calkins, 2 pgs.(not reprints). Beginning with No. 88, all Buck Rogers pages have rearranged panels 4.00 12.00 24.00

89-Origin Fearless Flint, the Flint Man 4.00 12.00 24.00

91-93,95,96,98-110: 105-Series 2 begins (Strip Page No. 1)
3.00 8.00 16.00

94-Buck Rogers in "Solar Holocaust" by Calkins, 3 pgs.(not reprints)
3.50 10.00 20.00

97-War Bond promotion, Buck Rogers by Calkins, 2 pgs.(not reprints)
3.50 10.00 20.00

111-130 2.00 6.00 12.00

131-150: 137-Strip page No. 110½ omitted 1.75 5.00 10.00

151-169 1.50 4.00 8.00

170-Two text illos. by Williamson, his 1st comic book work
3.50 10.00 20.00

171-180: 171-Strip pgs. 227,229,230, Series 2 omitted. 172-Strip Pg. 232 omitted 1.50 4.00 8.00

181-190: Buck Rogers ends with start of strip pg. 302, Series 2
1.00 3.00 6.00

191-197,199,201,203,206-208: No Buck Rogers
.85 2.50 5.00

198,200,202,205-One pg. Frazetta ads; no Buck Rogers
1.20 3.50 7.00

204-Used in **POP**, pgs. 79,99 2.00 5.00 10.00

209-Buck Rogers begins with strip pg. 480, Series 2; Frazetta-c
20.00 60.00 120.00

210-216: Frazetta-c. 211-Buck Rogers ads by Anderson begins, ends No. 217. No. 215-Contains Buck Rogers strip pg. 515-518, Series 2 followed by pgs. 179-181, Series 3
20.00 60.00 120.00

217,218-Buck Rogers ends with pg. 199, Series 3
1.00 3.00 6.00

NOTE: ***Rick Yager*** *did the Buck Rogers Sunday strips reprinted in Famous Funnies. The Sundays were formerly done by Russ Keaton and Lt. Dick Calkins did the dailies, but would sometimes assist Yager on a panel or two from time to time. Strip No. 169 is Yager's first full Buck Rogers page. Yager did the strip until 1958 when* ***Murphy Anderson*** *took over.* ***Tuska*** *art from 4/26/59 - 1965. Virtually every panel was rewritten for Famous Funnies. Not identical to the original Sunday page. The Buck Rogers reprints run continuously through Famous Funnies issue No. 190 (Strip No. 302) with no break in story line. The story line has no continuity after No. 190. The Buck Rogers newspaper strips came out in four series: Series 1, 3/30/30 - 9/21/41 (No. 1 - 600); Series 2, 9/28/41 -10/21/51 (No. 1 - 525)(Strip No. 110½ (½ pg.) published in only a few newspapers); Series 3, 10/28/51 - 2/9/58 (No. 100-428)(No No. 1-99); Series 4, 2/16/58 - 6/13/65 (No numbers, dates only).*

FAMOUS FUNNIES
1964
Super Comics

Reprint No. 15-18 .40 1.20 2.40

FAMOUS GANG BOOK OF COMICS (Donald & Mickey Merry Christmas 1943 on)
1942 (32 pgs.; paper cover) (Christmas giveaway)
Firestone Tire & Rubber Co.

(Rare)-Porky Pig, Bugs Bunny; r-/Looney Tunes
100.00 270.00 500.00

FAMOUS GANGSTERS (Crime on the Waterfront No. 4)
April, 1951 - No. 3, Feb, 1952
Avon Periodicals/Realistic

1-Narcotics mentioned; Capone, Dillinger; c-/Avon paperback No. 329 7.00 20.00 40.00

2-Wood-c, 1 pg.; r-/Saint No. 7 & retitled "Mike Strong"
8.00 24.00 48.00

3-Lucky Luciano & Murder, Inc; drug story; c-/Avon paperback 66
8.00 24.00 48.00

FAMOUS INDIAN TRIBES
July-Sept, 1962; July, 1972

FAMOUS INDIAN TRIBES (continued)
Dell Publishing Co.

	Good	Fine	Mint
12-264-209 (The Sioux)	.50	1.50	3.00
2(7/72)-Reprints above		.50	1.00

FAMOUS STARS
Nov-Dec, 1950 - No. 6, Spring, 1952
Ziff-Davis Publ. Co.

	Good	Fine	Mint
1-Shelley Winters, Susan Peters, Ava Gardner, Shirley Temple Photo-c	7.00	20.00	40.00
2-Betty Hutton, Bing Crosby, Colleen Townsend, Gloria Swanson; Everett-a(2)	5.00	14.00	28.00
3-Farley Granger, Judy Garland's ordeal, Alan Ladd	5.50	16.00	32.00
4-Al Jolson, Bob Mitchum, Ella Raines, Richard Conte, Vic Damone; Crandall-a, 6pgs.	5.00	14.00	28.00
5-Liz Taylor, Betty Grable, Esther Williams, George Brent; Krigstein-a	5.50	16.00	32.00
6-Gene Kelly, Hedy Lamar, June Allyson, William Boyd, Janet Leigh, Gary Cooper	4.00	12.00	24.00

NOTE: ***Whitney** a-1,3.*

FAMOUS STORIES (. . . Book No. 2)
1942
Dell Publishing Co.

	Good	Fine	Mint
1-Treasure Island	6.00	18.00	36.00
2-Tom Sawyer	6.00	18.00	36.00

FAMOUS TV FUNDAY FUNNIES
1961
Harvey Publications

	Good	Fine	Mint
1-Casper the Ghost	3.00	8.00	16.00

FAMOUS WESTERN BADMEN (Formerly Redskin)
No. 13, Dec, 1952 - No. 15, 1953
Youthful Magazines

	Good	Fine	Mint
13-15	1.50	4.50	9.00

FANTASTIC (Formerly Capt. Science; Beware No. 10 on)
No. 8, Feb, 1952 - No. 9, April, 1952
Youthful Magazines

	Good	Fine	Mint
8-Capt. Science by Harrison	5.00	14.00	28.00
9-Harrison-a	3.00	9.00	18.00

FANTASTIC (Fantastic Fears No. 1-9)
No. 10, Nov-Dec, 1954 - No. 11, Jan-Feb, 1955
Ajax/Farrell Publ.

	Good	Fine	Mint
10,11	2.00	6.00	12.00

FANTASTIC ADVENTURES
1963 - 1964 (Reprints)
Super Comics

	Good	Fine	Mint
9-12,15,16,18: 11-Reprints Disbrow/Blue Bolt No. 118. 16-Briefer-a. 18-Reprints/Superior Stories No. 1	1.00	3.00	6.00
17-South Sea Girl by Baker	1.50	4.00	8.00

FANTASTIC COMICS
Dec, 1939 - No. 23, Nov, 1941
Fox Features Syndicate

	Good	Fine	Mint
1-Origin Samson; Stardust, The Super Wizard, Space Smith, Sub Saunders, Capt. Kidd begin	50.00	140.00	280.00
2	24.00	70.00	140.00
3-5	20.00	60.00	120.00
6-9: 6,7-Simon-c	17.00	50.00	100.00
10-Intro. David	14.00	40.00	80.00
11-17: 16-Stardust ends	8.00	24.00	48.00
18-Intro. Black Fury & sidekick Chuck; ends No. 23	10.00	30.00	60.00
19,20	8.00	24.00	48.00
21-The Banshee begins(origin); ends No. 23	10.00	30.00	60.00
22	8.00	24.00	48.00
23-Origin The Gladiator	10.00	30.00	60.00

NOTE: ***Lou Fine** c-1-5.*

FANTASTIC FEARS (Formerly Captain Jet) (Fantastic No. 10 on)
No. 7, May, 1953 - No. 9, Sept-Oct, 1954
Ajax/Farrell Publ.

	Good	Fine	Mint
7(5/53)	3.50	10.00	20.00
8(7/53)	2.50	7.00	14.00
3,4	2.00	5.00	10.00
5-1st Ditko story written by Bruce Hamilton reprinted in Weird V2No.8	8.00	24.00	48.00
6-Decapitation of girl's head with paper cutter (classic)	4.00	12.00	24.00
7(5-6/54), 9(9-10/54)	2.00	5.00	10.00
8(7-8/54)-Contains story intended for Jo-Jo; name changed to Kaza; decapitation story	3.00	8.00	16.00

FANTASTIC FOUR
Nov, 1961 - Present
Marvel Comics Group

	Good	Fine	Mint
1-Origin & 1st app. The Fantastic Four (Reed Richards: Mr. Fantastic, Johnny Storm: The Human Torch, Sue Storm: The Invisible Girl, & Ben Grimm: The Thing); origin The Mole Man	175.00	550.00	1200.00
1-Reprint from the Golden Record Comic Set	.80	2.40	4.80
with record....	1.00	3.00	6.00
2-Vs. The Skrulls	80.00	220.00	440.00
3-Fantastic Four don costumes & establish Headquarters	55.00	160.00	320.00
4-1st Silver Age Sub-Mariner app.	45.00	130.00	260.00
5-Origin & 1st app. Doctor Doom	30.00	80.00	190.00
6-10: 6-Sub-Mariner, Dr. Doom team up. 7-1st app. Kurrgo. 8-1st app. Puppet-Master & Alicia Masters	17.00	50.00	110.00
11-Origin The Impossible Man	14.00	40.00	90.00
12-Fantastic Four Vs. The Hulk	14.00	40.00	90.00
13-15: 13-Intro. The Watcher; 1st app. The Red Ghost	10.00	30.00	68.00
16-20: 18-Origin The Super Skrull. 19-Intro. Rama-Tut. 20-Origin The Molecule Man	7.00	20.00	44.00
21-30: 21-Intro. The Hate Monger. 25,26-The Thing Vs. the Hulk 30-Intro. Diablo	4.50	13.00	26.00
31-40: 31-Avengers x-over. 33-1st app. Attoma. 35-Intro/1st app. Dragon Man. 36-Intro/1st app. Madam Medusa & the Frightful Four (Sandman, Wizard, Paste Pot Pete). 39-Wood inks on Daredevil	2.50	7.00	14.00
41-47: 41-43-Frightful Four app. 44-Intro. Gorgan. 45-Intro. The Inhumans	2.00	5.00	10.00
48-Intro. & 1st app. The Silver Surfer	5.00	15.00	30.00
49,50-Silver Surfer x-over	2.50	7.00	14.00
51-60: 52-Intro. The Black Panther; origin-No. 53. Silver Surfer x-over in No. 55-60,61(cameo). 54,60-Inhumans cameo	1.50	4.00	8.00
61-65,68-70	1.00	3.00	6.00
66,67-1st app. & origin Him (Warlock)	1.50	4.00	8.00
71,73,78-80	.70	2.00	4.00
72,74-77: Silver Surfer app.	1.50	4.00	8.00
81-90: 81-Crystal joins & dons costume. 84-87-Dr. Doom app.	.70	2.00	4.00
91-99,101,102: 94-Intro. Agatha Harkness. Last Kirby issue No. 102,108	.60	1.80	3.60
100	2.00	5.00	10.00
103-111	.40	1.20	2.40
112-Hulk Vs. Thing	.70	2.00	4.00
113-120: 116-(52 pgs.)	.35	1.00	2.00
121-123-Silver Surfer x-over. 123-Nixon on c/story	.60	1.80	3.60
124-127,129-140: 126-Origin F.F. retold. 129-Intro. Thundra.			

Famous Stars #5, © ZD

Fantastic Four #48, © MCG

Fantastic Four #100, © MCG

Fantastic Four #200, © MCG

Fan. Voyages Of Sindbad #1, © GK

Fantasy Masterpieces V2#1, © MCG

FANTASTIC FOUR (continued) — Good / Fine / Mint

130-Sue leaves F.F. 132-Medusa joins. 133-Thundra Vs. Thing — .35 / 1.00 / 2.00
128-Four pg. glossy insert of F.F. Friends & Fiends — .50 / 1.50 / 3.00
141-149,151-154,158-160: 142-Kirbyish art by Buckler begins. 151-Origin Thundra. 159-Medusa leaves, Sue rejoins — .30 / .80 / 1.60
150-Crystal & Quicksilver's wedding — .35 / 1.00 / 2.00
155-157: Silver Surfer in all — .35 / 1.00 / 2.00
161-180: 164-The Crusader (old Marvel Boy) revived; origin No. 165. 176-Re-intro Impossible Man; Marvel artists app. — .50 / 1.00
181-190: 190-191-F.F. breaks up — .40 / .80
191-196 — .30 / .60
197-199-Son of Dr. Doom app. — .30 / .60
200-Giant size-FF re-united — .50 / 1.50 / 3.00
201-207,209-216,218-219 — .30 / .60
208-Nova app. — .30 / .60
217-Dazzler app. by Byrne — .40 / 1.20 / 2.40
220-Brief origin & explains powers of F.F.; Vindicator app. — .30 / .60
221-231 — .30 / .60
232-Byrne-a — .60 / 1.20
233-235,347-up: Byrne-a — .25 / .70 / 1.40
236-20th Anniversary issue(11/81, 64pgs., $1.00) — .60 / 1.20
Giant-Size 2(8/74) - 4: Formerly G-S Super-Stars — .50 / 1.50 / 3.00
Giant-Size 5(5/75), 6(8/75) — .30 / .80 / 1.60
Special 1('63)-Origin F.F.; Ditko-a — 7.00 / 20.00 / 40.00
Special 2('64)-Dr. Doom origin & x-over — 4.00 / 12.00 / 24.00
Special 3('65)-Reed & Sue wed — 2.00 / 6.00 / 12.00
Special 4(11/66)-G.A. Torch x-over & origin retold — 1.00 / 3.00 / 6.00
Special 5(11/67)-Intro. Pscho-Man; no reprints; Silver Surfer app. — .70 / 2.00 / 4.00
Special 6(11/68)-Intro. Annihilus; no reprints; birth of Franklin Richards — .50 / 1.50 / 3.00
Special 7(11/69), 8(12/70), 9(12/71), 10('73) — .35 / 1.00 / 2.00
Annual 11(6/76), 12(2/78) — .25 / .70 / 1.40
Annual 13(10/78), 14(1/80) — .60 / 1.20
Annual 15(10/80) — .50 / 1.00
Annual 16(10/81)-1st app. Dragon Lord — .40 / .80

NOTE: ***Austin** c-232-235i. **Buckler** a-142-144, 147-153, 155, 156, 158, 159, 161-163, 168, 169; c-140, 142, 144, 147-149, 151, 156, 159, 162, 165, 169, 216. **John Buscema** a-107, 108(w/**Kirby** & **Romita**),109-132, 134-141, 160, (172-175 pencils), 202, Annual 11, 13, Giant-Size 1-4; c-107-122, 124-129, 133-139, 202, Special 10. **Byrne** a-209-218p, 220, 221, 232-37p. c-216, 221, 232-236, 237. **Ditko** a-13i, Gnt Size 2r, Annual 16. **Kirby** a-1-102, 108, 189r, 236p, Special 1-10, Giant-Size 5, 6r; c-1-101, 164, 167, 171-177, 180, 181, 190, 200, Annual 11, Giant-Size 5, Special 1-7, 9. **Marcos** a-Annual 14i. **Perez** a-164-167, 170-172, 176-178, 184-188, 191, Annual 14p, 15p; c-187, 188, 191, 192, 194-197. **Simonson** c-212. **Steranko** c-130-132.*

FANTASTIC GIANTS (Konga No. 1-23)
September, 1966 (25 cents)
Charlton Comics

V2No.24-Origin Konga & Gorgo reprinted; two new Ditko stories — 2.00 / 6.00 / 12.00

FANTASTIC TALES
1958 (no date) (Reprint)
I. W. Enterprises

1-Reprints Avon's "City of the Living Dead" — 1.50 / 4.00 / 8.00

FANTASTIC VOYAGE (See Movie Comics)
Aug, 1969 - No. 2, Dec, 1969
Gold Key

1,2 (TV) — 1.00 / 3.00 / 6.00

FANTASTIC VOYAGES OF SINDBAD, THE
Oct, 1965 - No. 2, June, 1967
Gold Key — Good / Fine / Mint

1,2 — 1.50 / 4.00 / 8.00

FANTASTIC WORLDS
No. 5, Sept, 1952 - No. 7, Jan, 1953
Standard Comics

5-Toth, Anderson-a — 5.00 / 14.00 / 28.00
6-Toth story — 4.00 / 12.00 / 24.00
7 — 3.00 / 8.00 / 16.00

FANTASY MASTERPIECES (Marvel Super Heroes No. 12 on)
Feb, 1966 - No. 11, Oct, 1967; Dec, 1979 - No. 14, Jan, 1981
Marvel Comics Group

1-Photo of Stan Lee — .50 / 1.50 / 3.00
2 — .40 / 1.20 / 2.40
3-G.A. Captain America reprints begin; 1st 25 cent ish. — .40 / 1.20 / 2.40
4-6-Capt. America reprints — .40 / 1.20 / 2.40
7-Begin G.A. Sub-Mariner, Torch reprint — .35 / 1.10 / 2.20
8-Torch battles the Sub-Mariner r-/Marvel Mystery No. 9 — .35 / 1.10 / 2.20
9-Origin Human Torch r-/Marvel Comics No.1 — .35 / 1.10 / 2.20
10-All Winners reprint — .35 / 1.10 / 2.20
11-Reprint of origin Toro & Black Knight — .35 / 1.10 / 2.20
V2No.1(12/79)-48 pgs.; 75 cents; reprints origin Silver Surfer from Silver Surfer No. 1 with editing; J. Buscema-a — .50 / 1.50 / 3.00
2-4-Silver Surfer reprints — .40 / 1.20 / 2.40
5-14-Silver Surfer reprints — .50 / 1.00

NOTE: ***Buscema** c-V2No.7-9(in part). **Ditko** a-1-3r, 7r, 9r. **Starlin** a-9-13r.*

FANTOMAN (Formerly Amazing Adv. Funnies)
No. 2, Aug, 1940 - No. 4, Dec, 1940
Centaur Publications

2-The Fantom of the Fair-r; The Arrow app.; Burgos, Everett, J. Cole, Gustavson-a — 20.00 / 60.00 / 130.00
3,4: Gustavson-a(r) — 14.00 / 40.00 / 90.00

FARGO KID (Formerly Justice Traps the Guilty)
V11No.3(No.1), June-July, 1958 - V11No.5, Oct-Nov, 1958
Prize Publications

V11No.3(No.1)-Origin Fargo Kid, Severin-c; Williamson-a(2) — 4.00 / 12.00 / 24.00
V11No.4,5-Severin c/a — 2.50 / 7.00 / 14.00

FARMER'S DAUGHTER, THE
2-3/54 - No. 3, 6-7/54; 8-9/54 - No. 4, 2-3/55
Stanhall Publ./Trojan Magazines

1-Lingerie, nudity panel — 3.50 / 10.00 / 20.00
2,3('54)(Stanhall) — 2.00 / 6.00 / 12.00
1(Trojan) — 2.00 / 6.00 / 12.00
2-4 — 1.50 / 4.00 / 8.00

FASTEST GUN ALIVE, THE (See 4-Color No. 741)

FAST FICTION (. . . Action) (Stories by Famous Authors Illustrated No. 6 on)
March, 1950 - No. 5, July, 1950
Seaboard Publ./Famous Authors Ill.

1-Scarlet Pimpernel; Jim Lavery-a — 7.00 / 20.00 / 40.00
2-Captain Blood; H. C. Kiefer-a — 6.00 / 18.00 / 36.00
3-She, by Rider Haggard; Vincent Napoli-a — 10.00 / 30.00 / 60.00
4-The 39 Steps; Lavery-a — 4.00 / 12.00 / 24.00
5-Beau Geste; Kiefer-a — 4.00 / 12.00 / 24.00

FAST WILLIE JACKSON
October, 1976 - No. 7, 1977
Fitzgerald Periodicals, Inc.

1 — .50 / 1.00
2-7 — .40 / .80

FAT ALBERT (. . . & the Cosby Kids) (TV)
March, 1974 - No. 29, Feb, 1979
Gold Key

	Good	Fine	Mint
1		.50	1.00
2-29		.30	.60

FAT AND SLAT (Ed Wheelan) (Gunfighter No. 5 on)
Summer, 1947 - No. 4, Spring, 1948
E. C. Comics

	Good	Fine	Mint
1	10.00	28.00	56.00
2-4	8.00	22.00	44.00

FAT AND SLAT JOKE BOOK
Summer, 1944 (One Shot, 52 pages)
All-American Comics (William H. Wise)

	Good	Fine	Mint
by Ed Wheelan	7.00	20.00	40.00

FATE (See Hand of Fate, & Thrill-O-Rama)

FATHER OF CHARITY
No date (32 pgs.; paper cover)
Catechetical Guild Giveaway

	Good	Fine	Mint
	2.00	6.00	12.00

FATMAN, THE HUMAN FLYING SAUCER
April, 1967 - No. 3, Aug-Sept, 1967
Lightning Comics

	Good	Fine	Mint
1-Origin Fatman & Tinman by C. C. Beck	2.00	5.00	10.00
2-Beck-a	2.00	5.00	10.00
3-(Scarce)-Beck-a	3.00	8.00	16.00

FAUNTLEROY COMICS (Superduck Presents . . .)
1950
Close-Up/Archie Publications

	Good	Fine	Mint
1	1.50	4.00	8.00
2,3	.70	2.00	4.00

FAWCETT MINIATURES (See Mighty Midget)
1946 (12-24 pgs.; 3¾x5'') (Wheaties giveaways)
Fawcett Publications

	Good	Fine	Mint
Captain Marvel-''And the Horn of Plenty;'' Bulletman story	2.00	6.00	12.00
Captain Marvel-''& the Raiders From Space;'' Golden Arrow story	2.00	6.00	12.00
Captain Marvel Jr.-''The Case of the Poison Press!'' Bulletman story	2.00	6.00	12.00
Delecta of the Planets-C. C. Beck art; B&W inside; 12 pgs.; 3 different issues	5.00	15.00	30.00

FAWCETT MOTION PICTURE COMICS (See Motion Picture Comics)

FAWCETT MOVIE COMICS
1949 - No. 20, Dec, 1952
Fawcett Publications

	Good	Fine	Mint
nn-''Dakota Lil''-George Montgomery & Rod Cameron('49)	8.00	24.00	48.00
nn-''Copper Canyon''-Ray Milland & Hedy Lamarr('50)	7.00	20.00	40.00
nn-''Destination Moon''-(1950)	30.00	80.00	160.00
nn-''Montana''-Errol Flynn & Alexis Smith('50)	7.00	20.00	40.00
nn-''Pioneer Marshal''-Monte Hale(1950)	7.00	20.00	40.00
nn-''Powder River Rustlers''-Rocky Lane(1950)	7.00	20.00	40.00
nn-''Singing Guns''-Vaughn Monroe & Ella Raines(1950)	7.00	20.00	40.00
7-''Gunmen of Abilene''-Rocky Lane; Bob Powell-a(1950)	7.00	20.00	40.00
8-''King of the Bullwhip''-Lash LaRue; Bob Powell-a(1950)	8.00	24.00	48.00
9-''The Old Frontier''-Monte Hale; Bob Powell-a(2/51)	7.00	20.00	40.00
10-''The Missourians''-Monte Hale(4/51)	7.00	20.00	40.00
11-''The Thundering Trail''-Lash LaRue(6/51)	8.00	24.00	48.00
12-''Rustlers on Horseback''-Rocky Lane(8/51)	7.00	20.00	40.00
13-''Warpath''-Edmond O'Brien & Forrest Tucker(10/51)	7.00	20.00	40.00
14-''Last Outpost''-Ronald Reagan(12/51)	12.00	35.00	80.00
15-(Scarce)-''The Man From Planet X''-Robert Clark; Shaffenberger-a (2/52)	75.00	200.00	420.00
16-''10 Tall Men''-Burt Lancaster	5.50	16.00	32.00
17-''Rose of Cimarron''-Jack Buetel & Mala Powers	5.50	16.00	32.00
18-''The Brigand''-Anthony Dexter; Shaffenberger-a	5.50	16.00	32.00
19-''Carbine Williams''-James Stewart; Costanza-a	6.00	18.00	36.00
20-''Ivanhoe''-Liz Taylor	7.00	20.00	40.00

FAWCETT'S FUNNY ANIMALS (No. 1-26, 86 on titled ''Funny Animals'')
Dec, 1942 - No. 91, Feb, 1956
Fawcett Publications/Charlton Comics No. 83? on

	Good	Fine	Mint
1-Capt. Marvel on cover	10.00	30.00	60.00
2-10: 8-Flag-c	3.50	10.00	20.00
11-20	2.00	6.00	12.00
21-40	2.00	5.00	10.00
41-88,90,91	1.50	4.00	8.00
89-Merry Mailman ish	2.00	5.00	10.00

NOTE: *Marvel Bunny in all issues to at least No. 57.*

F.B.I., THE
April-June, 1965
Dell Publishing Co.

	Good	Fine	Mint
1-Sinnott-a	.70	2.00	4.00

F.B.I. STORY, THE (See 4-Color No. 1069)

FEAR (Adventure into . . .)
Nov, 1970 - No. 31, Dec, 1975 (No.1-6 - Giant Size)
Marvel Comics Group

	Good	Fine	Mint
1-Reprints Fantasy & Sci-Fi stories	.30	.80	1.60
2-6		.40	.80
7-9: 9-Everett-a		.40	.80
10-Man-Thing begins; Morrow c/a(p)	1.00	3.00	6.00
11-Adams-c	.40	1.20	2.40
12-Starlin-a	.40	1.20	2.40
13-18		.60	1.20
19-Intro. Howard the Duck by Val Mayerick	2.00	6.00	12.00
20-Morbius, the Living Vampire begins, ends No. 31; Gulacy-a(p)		.50	1.00
21-31: 30-Evans-a		.40	.80

NOTE: ***Brunner*** *c-15-17.* ***Chaykin*** *a-10.* ***Ditko*** *a-6-8r.* ***Kirby*** *a-8r, 9r.* ***Russell*** *a-23p, 24p.* ***Severin*** *c-8.*

FEAR IN THE NIGHT (See Complete Mystery No. 3)

FEARLESS FAGAN (See 4-Color No. 441)

FEATURE BOOK (Dell) (See Black & White and Large Feature Book)

FEATURE BOOK (All newspaper reprints)
May, 1937 - No. 57, 1947
David McKay Publications

	Good	Fine	Mint
nn-Popeye & the Jeep; thought to be reprinted as Feature Book No. 3 (Very Rare) Estimated value . . .	200.00	600.00	1200.00
nn-Dick Tracy-Reprinted as Feature Book No. 4 (100 pgs.) & in part as 4-Color No. 1 (Very Rare, only three known copies) Estimated Value	300.00	800.00	1600.00

NOTE: *Above books were advertised together with different covers from Feature Books No. 3 & 4.*

Fatman #3, © Lightning Comics

Fawcett Movie Comics #14, © FAW

Fear #19, © MCG

Feature Book #9, © N.Y. News Synd.

Feature Comics #36, © QUA

Feature Funnies #3, © QUA

FEATURE BOOK (continued)	Good	Fine	Mint
1-King of the Royal Mtd.	25.00	75.00	150.00
2-Popeye(6/37) by Segar	40.00	120.00	240.00
3-Popeye(7/37) by Segar	35.00	100.00	200.00
4-Dick Tracy(8/37)-Same as nn issue listed but a new cover added	70.00	180.00	360.00
5-Popeye(9/37) by Segar	25.00	70.00	140.00
6-Dick Tracy(10/37)	60.00	140.00	280.00
7-Little Orphan Annie (Very Rare)	70.00	180.00	360.00
8-Secret Agent X-9-Not by Raymond	14.00	40.00	80.00
9-Dick Tracy(1/38)	60.00	140.00	280.00
10-Popeye(2/38)	25.00	70.00	140.00
11-Little Annie Rooney	10.00	30.00	60.00
12-Blondie(4/38) (Rare)	30.00	80.00	160.00
13-Inspector Wade	6.00	18.00	36.00
14-Popeye(6/38) by Segar (Scarce)	40.00	120.00	240.00
15-Barney Baxter(7/38)	9.00	25.00	55.00
16-Red Eagle	6.00	18.00	36.00
17-Gangbusters	12.00	35.00	70.00
18,19-Mandrake	14.00	40.00	80.00
20-Phantom	25.00	75.00	150.00
21-Lone Ranger	25.00	75.00	150.00
22-Phantom	25.00	75.00	150.00
23-Mandrake	20.00	60.00	120.00
24-Lone Ranger(1941)	25.00	75.00	150.00
25-Flash Gordon-Reprints not by Raymond	45.00	125.00	250.00
26-Prince Valiant(1941)-Harold Foster-a; newspaper strips reprinted, pgs. 1-28,30-63	100.00	260.00	420.00
27-29,31,34-Blondie	5.00	14.00	28.00
30,32,37,41,44-Katzenjammer Kids	3.50	10.00	20.00
33-(Title unknown)			
35-Katzenjammer Kids; has photo & biog of Harold H. Knerr(1883-1949) who took over strip from Rudolph Dirks in 1914	4.00	12.00	24.00
36,38,40,42,43,45,47-Blondie	3.50	10.00	20.00
39-Phantom	14.00	40.00	80.00
46-Mandrake In the Fire World-(58 pgs.)	10.00	30.00	60.00
48-Maltese Falcon('46)	10.00	30.00	60.00
49,50-Perry Mason	5.00	14.00	28.00
51,54-Rip Kirby by Raymond; origin-No. 51	10.00	30.00	60.00
52,55-Mandrake	9.00	25.00	50.00
53,56,57-Phantom	10.00	30.00	60.00

NOTE: *All Feature Books through No. 25 are over-sized 8½x11-3/8" comics with color covers and black and white interiors. The covers are rough, heavy stock. The page counts, including covers, are as follows: nn, No.3,4-100 pgs.; No.1,2-52 pgs.; No.5-25 are all 76 pgs.*

FEATURE COMICS (Formerly Feature Funnies)
No. 21, June, 1939 - No. 144, May, 1950
Quality Comics Group

	Good	Fine	Mint
21-26: 23-Charlie Chan begins	6.00	18.00	36.00
26-(nn, nd)-c-in one color, 10 cents	3.50	10.00	20.00
27-Origin & 1st app. of Dollman by Eisner	90.00	250.00	500.00
28-1st Fine Dollman	40.00	110.00	225.00
29,30	25.00	75.00	150.00
31-Last Clock & Charlie Chan issue	20.00	55.00	110.00
32-37: 32-Rusty Ryan & Samar begin. 37-Last Fine Dollman	15.00	45.00	90.00
38-41: 38-Origin the Ace of Space. 39-Origin The Destroying Demon, ends No. 40. 40-Bruce Blackburn in costume	10.00	30.00	60.00
42-USA, the Spirit of Old Glory begins	6.00	18.00	36.00
43,45-50: 46-Intro. Boyville Brigadiers in Rusty Ryan. 48 USA ends	6.00	18.00	36.00
44-Dollman by Crandall begins, ends No. 63; Crandall-a(2)	8.00	24.00	48.00
51-55	5.50	16.00	32.00
56-Marijuana story in "Swing Session"	6.00	18.00	36.00
57-Spider Widow begins	5.50	16.00	32.00
58-60: 60-Raven begins, ends No. 71	5.50	16.00	32.00
61-68	4.00	12.00	24.00
69,70-Phantom Lady x-over in Spider Widow	5.50	16.00	32.00
71-80: 71-Dollman app. 72-Spider Widow ends	3.00	8.00	16.00
81-100	2.50	7.00	14.00
101-144: 140-Intro. Stuntman Stetson	2.00	5.00	10.00

NOTE: ***Celardo** a-37-43. **Crandall** a-44-60, 62, 63(most). **Gustavson** a-(Rusty Ryan)-32-47. **Powell** a-34, 64-73.*

FEATURE FILMS
Mar-Apr, 1950 - No. 4, Sept-Oct, 1950
National Periodical Publications

	Good	Fine	Mint
1-"Captain China" with John Payne & Gail Russell	10.00	30.00	60.00
2-"Riding High" with Bing Crosby	8.00	24.00	48.00
3-"The Eagle & the Hawk" with John Payne, Rhonda Fleming & D. O'Keefe	8.00	24.00	48.00
4-"Fancy Pants"-Bob Hope & Lucille Ball	8.00	24.00	48.00

FEATURE FUNNIES (Feature Comics No. 21 on)
Oct, 1937 - No. 20, May, 1939
Quality Comics Group

	Good	Fine	Mint
1-Joe Palooka, Mickey Finn, The Bungles, Jane Arden, Dixie Dugan, Big Top, Ned Bryant, Strange As It Seems, & Off the Record strip reprints begin	35.00	100.00	180.00
2-The Clock begins(11/37)-Masked hero	20.00	60.00	120.00
3-Hawks of Seas begins by Eisner, ends No. 12	10.00	30.00	60.00
4,5	8.00	24.00	48.00
6-12: 11-Archie O'Toole by Bud Thomas begins, ends No. 22	5.50	16.00	32.00
13-Espionage, Starring Black X begins by Eisner, ends No. 22	7.00	20.00	40.00
14-20	6.00	18.00	36.00

FEATURE PRESENTATION, A (Feature Presentation Mag. No. 6)
(Formerly Women in Love) (Also see Startling Terror Tales No. 11)
No. 5, April, 1950
Fox Features Syndicate

	Good	Fine	Mint
5-Black Tarantula	10.00	30.00	60.00

FEATURE PRESENTATIONS MAGAZINE (Formerly A Feature Presentation No. 5; becomes Feature Stories Mag. No. 3 on)
No. 6, July, 1950
Fox Features Syndicate

	Good	Fine	Mint
6-Moby Dick; Wood-c	8.00	22.00	44.00

FEATURE STORIES MAGAZINE (Formerly Feat. Present. Mag. No. 6)
No. 3, Aug, 1950 - No. 4, Oct, 1950
Fox Features Syndicate

	Good	Fine	Mint
3-Jungle Lil, Zegra stories	6.00	18.00	36.00
4	5.00	14.00	28.00

FEDERAL MEN COMICS
1945 - No. 5, 1946 (DC reprints from 1930's)
Gerard Publ. Co.

	Good	Fine	Mint
1,3-5	4.00	12.00	24.00
2-Siegel & Shuster-a; cover redrawn from Detective No. 9	4.00	12.00	24.00

FELIX THE CAT
1927 - 1931 (24 pgs.; 8x10¼")(1926,'27 color strip reprints)
McLoughlin Bros.

	Good	Fine	Mint
260-(Rare)-by Otto Messmer	30.00	85.00	190.00

FELIX THE CAT (See Inky & Dinky and March of Comics)
1943 - No. 12, July-Sept, 1965
Dell Publ. No.1-19/Toby No.20-61/Harvey No.62-118/Dell

	Good	Fine	Mint
4-Color 15	20.00	60.00	120.00
4-Color 46('44)	15.00	45.00	90.00
4-Color 77('45)	12.00	35.00	70.00
4-Color 119('46)	9.00	25.00	50.00

FELIX THE CAT (continued)

	Good	Fine	Mint
4-Color 135('46)	7.00	20.00	40.00
4-Color 162('47)	5.00	15.00	30.00
1(2-3/48)(Dell)	8.00	24.00	48.00
2	4.00	12.00	24.00
3-5	3.50	10.00	20.00
6-19(2-3/51-Dell)	2.00	6.00	12.00
20-30(Toby): 28-2/52 has No. 29 on cover, No. 28 on inside	2.00	5.00	10.00
31-61(6/55-Toby)-Last Messmer ish.	1.50	4.00	8.00
62(8/55)-100 (Harvey)	.70	2.00	4.00
101-118(11/61)	.55	1.60	3.20
12-269-211(9-11/62)(Dell)	1.00	3.00	6.00
2-12(7-9/65)(Dell)	.55	1.60	3.20
. . . & His Friends 1(12/53-Toby)	2.00	6.00	12.00
. . . & His Friends 2-4	1.50	4.00	8.00
3-D Comic Book 1(1953-One Shot)	10.00	30.00	60.00
Summer Annual 2('52)-Early 1930's Sunday strip reprints	14.00	40.00	80.00
Summer Annual nn('53, 100 pgs., Toby)	8.00	24.00	48.00
Winter Annual 2('54)	5.50	16.00	32.00

(See March of Comics No. 24,36,51)

NOTE: *4-Color No. 15,46,77 are all daily or Sunday newspaper reprints from the 1930's drawn by Otto Messmer, who created Felix in 1915 for the Sullivan animation studio. He drew Felix from the beginning under contract to Pat Sullivan. In 1946 he went to work for Dell and wrote and drew most of the stories through the Toby Press issues. He did not work for Harvey or the 1960's Dells. No. 107 reprints No. 71 interior; No. 110 reprints No. 56 interior.*

FERDINAND THE BULL
1938 (10 cents)(Large size; some color, rest B&W)
Dell Publishing Co.

	Good	Fine	Mint
nn	5.00	15.00	30.00

FIBBER McGEE & MOLLY (See A-1 Comics No. 25)

FICTION ILLUSTRATED (Digest size)
Jan, 1976 - Present (4¾x6¾'') ($1.00)
Pyramid Publ. (Byron Preiss Visual Publ.)

	Good	Fine	Mint
Vol. 1-Schlomo Raven, Detective begins, Vol 2-Starfawn, Vol. 3-Chandler	.30	.90	1.80

55 DAYS AT PEKING (See Movie Comics)

FIGHT AGAINST CRIME (Fight Against the Guilty No. 22)
May, 1951 - No. 21, Sept, 1954
Story Comics

	Good	Fine	Mint
1	3.00	9.00	18.00
2,3	2.00	5.00	10.00
4-Drug story-''Hopped Up Killers''	4.00	12.00	24.00
5-Frazetta, 1 pg.	1.50	4.00	8.00
6-Used in **POP**, pgs. 83,84	2.50	7.00	14.00
7-Heroin drug story	3.00	8.00	16.00
8-Last crime format issue	1.50	4.00	8.00

NOTE: *No. 9-21 contain violent, gruesome stories with blood, dismemberment, decapitation, E.C. style plot twists and several E.C. swipes.*

	Good	Fine	Mint
9-11,13	3.50	10.00	20.00
12-Morphine drug story-''The Big Dope''	5.00	14.00	28.00
14-Tothish art by Ross Andru	3.50	10.00	20.00
15-B&W & color illos in **POP**	4.00	12.00	24.00
16-E.C. story swipe/Haunt of Fear No. 19; Tothish-a by Ross Andru; bondage-c	4.00	12.00	24.00
17-Wildey E.C. swipe/Shock SuspenStories No. 9	4.00	12.00	24.00
18,19	3.50	10.00	20.00
20-Decapitation cover; contains hanging, ax murder, blood & violence	8.00	24.00	48.00
21-E.C. swipe; bondage-c	4.00	12.00	24.00

NOTE: ***Cameron** a-5. **Hollingsworth** a-3, 9, 10, 13. **Wildey** a-15, 16.*

FIGHT AGAINST THE GUILTY (Formerly Fight Against Crime)
No. 22, Dec, 1954 - No. 23, Mar, 1955
Story Comics

	Good	Fine	Mint
22-Tothish-a by Ross Andru; E.C. story swipe	2.00	6.00	12.00
23-Hollingsworth-a	1.50	4.50	9.00

FIGHT COMICS
Jan, 1940 - No. 86, Summer, 1953
Fiction House Magazines

	Good	Fine	Mint
1-Origin Spy Fighter, Starring Saber; Fine/Eisner-c	40.00	110.00	225.00
2	20.00	55.00	110.00
3-Rip Regan, the Power Man begins	15.00	45.00	90.00
4,5: 4-Fine-c	12.00	35.00	70.00
6-10	8.00	24.00	48.00
11-14: Rip Regan ends	7.00	20.00	40.00
15-1st Super American	12.00	35.00	70.00
16-Captain Fight begins; Spy Fighter ends	12.00	35.00	70.00
17,18: Super American ends	10.00	28.00	56.00
19-Captain Fight ends; origin & 1st app. Senorita Rio; Rip Carson, Chute Trooper begins	10.00	28.00	56.00
20	7.00	20.00	40.00
21-30	5.50	16.00	32.00
31,33-35	4.00	12.00	24.00
32-Tiger Girl begins	5.50	16.00	32.00
36-47,49,50: 44-1st Capt. Fight	5.00	14.00	28.00
48-Used in **Love and Death** by Legman	5.50	16.00	32.00
51-Origin Tiger Girl	7.00	20.00	40.00
52-60: 54-Lingerie panels	3.50	10.00	20.00
61-Origin Tiger Girl retold	4.00	12.00	24.00
62-65-Last Baker issue	3.50	10.00	20.00
66-77	3.00	8.00	16.00
78-Used in **POP**, pg. 99	3.50	10.00	20.00
79-The Space Rangers app.	3.00	8.00	16.00
80-85	2.00	6.00	12.00
86-Two Tigerman stories by Evans; Moreira-a	3.00	8.00	16.00

NOTE: *Bondage cover-No. 40. Tiger Girl by **Baker**-No. 36-60,62-65; Kayo Kirby by **Baker**-No. 52-64, 67. **Eisner** covers-No. 1-3, 5. **Kamen** a-54?, 57?. **Tuska** a-5, 8.*

FIGHT FOR FREEDOM
1949, 1951 (16 pgs.) (Giveaway)
National Association of Mfgrs./General Comics

	Good	Fine	Mint
Dan Barry-a; used in **POP**, pg. 102	5.00	15.00	30.00

FIGHT FOR LOVE
1952 (no month)
United Features Syndicate

	Good	Fine	Mint
nn-(Scarce)-Abbie & Slats newspaper-r	3.00	9.00	18.00

FIGHTING AIR FORCE (See U. S. Fighting Air Force)

FIGHTIN' AIR FORCE (War and Attack No. 54 on)
No. 3, Feb, 1956 - No. 53, Feb, 1966
Charlton Comics

	Good	Fine	Mint
V1No.3-10,11(68 pgs., 3/58)	.70	2.00	4.00
12-(100 pgs.)	.70	2.00	4.00
13-50: 50-American Eagle begins		.40	.80
51-53		.30	.60

FIGHTING AMERICAN
Apr-May, 1954 - No. 7, Apr-May, 1955
Headline Publications/Prize

	Good	Fine	Mint
1-Origin Fighting American & Speedboy; S&K c/a(3)	30.00	90.00	200.00
2-S&K-a(3)	20.00	55.00	120.00
3,4-S&K-a(3)	15.00	45.00	100.00
5-S&K-a(2), Kirby/?-a	15.00	45.00	100.00
6-Four pg. reprint of origin, plus 2 pgs. by S&K	14.00	42.00	90.00
7-Kirby-a	12.00	35.00	80.00

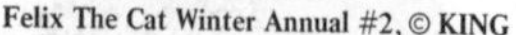
Felix The Cat Winter Annual #2, © KING

Fight Comics #32, © FH

Fight Comics #53, © FH

Fighting American #1, © HARV

Fightin' Marines #84, © CC

Fighting Yank #2, © BP

FIGHTING AMERICAN (continued)
NOTE: ***Simon & Kirby*** *covers on all.*

FIGHTING AMERICAN
October, 1966 (25 cents)
Harvey Publications

	Good	Fine	Mint
1-Origin Fighting American & Speedboy by S&K-r; S&K-a(3); 1 pg. Adams ad	2.00	5.00	10.00

FIGHTIN' ARMY (Formerly Soldier and Marine Comics)
No. 16, 1/56 - No. 127, 12/76; No. 128, 9/77 - Present
Charlton Comics

	Good	Fine	Mint
16-19,21-30	.30	.80	1.60
20-Ditko-a	.35	1.10	2.20
31-60		.40	.80
61-80: 75-The Lonely War of Willy Schultz begins, ends No. 92		.30	.60
81-155: 89,90,92-Ditko-a; Devil Brigade in No. 79,82,83		.30	.60
108(Modern Comics-1977)-Reprint		.15	.30

NOTE: ***Montes/Bache*** *a-48,49,51,69,75,76.*

FIGHTING DANIEL BOONE
1953
Avon Periodicals

	Good	Fine	Mint
nn-Kinstler c/a, 22 pgs.	5.00	15.00	30.00
I.W. Reprint No. 1-Kinstler c/a; Lawrence/Alascia-a	1.00	3.00	6.00

FIGHTING DAVY CROCKETT (Formerly Kit Carson)
No. 9, Oct-Nov, 1955
Avon Periodicals

	Good	Fine	Mint
9-Kinstler-c	2.50	7.00	14.00

FIGHTIN' 5, THE (Formerly Space War)
July, 1964 - No. 41, Jan, 1967; No. 42, Oct, 1981 - Present
Charlton Comics

	Good	Fine	Mint
V2No.28-Origin Fightin' Five	.25	.70	1.40
29-39,41		.40	.80
40-Peacemaker begins	.30	.80	1.60
42-44: Reprints		.30	.60

FIGHTING FRONTS!
Aug, 1952 - No. 5, Jan, 1953
Harvey Publications

	Good	Fine	Mint
1	1.75	5.00	10.00
2-Extreme violence; Powell-a	2.00	6.00	12.00
3-5: 3-Powell-a	1.20	3.50	7.00

FIGHTING INDIAN STORIES (See Midget Comics)

FIGHTING INDIANS OF THE WILD WEST!
Mar, 1952 - No. 2, Nov, 1952
Avon Periodicals

	Good	Fine	Mint
1-Kinstler, Larsen-a	5.50	16.00	32.00
2-Kinstler-a	3.50	10.00	20.00
100 Pg. Annual(1952, 25 cents)-Contains three comics rebound	7.00	20.00	40.00

FIGHTING LEATHERNECKS
Feb, 1952 - No. 6, Dec, 1952
Toby Press

	Good	Fine	Mint
1-''Duke's Diary''-full pg. pin-ups by Sparling	3.00	8.00	16.00
2-''Duke's Diary''	2.50	7.00	14.00
3-5-''Gil's Gals''-full pg. pin-ups	2.50	7.00	14.00
6-(Same as No. 3-5?)	1.50	4.00	8.00

FIGHTING MAN, THE
May, 1952 - No. 8, July, 1953
Ajax/Farrell Publications(Excellent Publ.)

	Good	Fine	Mint
1	2.00	5.00	10.00
2-8	.85	2.50	5.00
Annual 1 (132 pgs.)	5.00	15.00	30.00

FIGHTING MAN MANUAL, THE
1952
Ajax/Farrell Publications

	Good	Fine	Mint
1 (Same is Fighting Man Annual?)	5.00	14.00	28.00

FIGHTIN' MARINES (Also see Approved Comics)
No. 15, 8/51 - No. 132, 11/76; No. 133, 10/77 - Present
St. John(Approved Comics)/Charlton Comics

	Good	Fine	Mint
15(No.1)-Matt Baker c/a ''Leatherneck Jack''	5.00	14.00	28.00
2-1st Canteen Kate by Baker	6.00	18.00	36.00
3-9-Canteen Kate by Matt Baker; Baker c-No. 2,3,5-9	5.00	14.00	28.00
10,15-Baker-c	1.50	4.00	8.00
11-R-/No. 3 inside; Canteen Kate by Baker(r); Baker-c	3.50	10.00	20.00
12,13,16,18-20-Not Baker-c	.70	2.00	4.00
14,17-Canteen Kate by Baker	3.50	10.00	20.00
21-24	.40	1.20	2.40
25-(68 pgs.)	.70	2.00	4.00
26-(100 pgs.)(8/58)	1.50	4.00	8.00
27-50		.60	1.20
51-100: 78-Shotgun Harker & the Chicken series begin		.40	.80
101-121		.30	.60
122-Pilot issue for ''War'' title (Fightin' Marines Presents War)		.30	.60
123-160		.30	.60
120(Modern Comics reprint, 1977)		.20	.40

NOTE: *No. 14 & 16 (CC) reprints St. John issue; No. 16 reprints St. John insignia on cover.* ***Montes/Bache*** *a-48,53,55,64,65,72-74, 77-83.*

FIGHTING MARSHAL OF THE WILD WEST (See The Hawk)

FIGHTIN' NAVY (Formerly Don Winslow)
No. 74, May, 1956 - No. 125, Apr-May, 1966
Charlton Comics

	Good	Fine	Mint
74	.30	.80	1.60
75-81		.40	.80
82-Sam Glanzman-a	.30	.90	1.80
83-125		.30	.60

NOTE: ***Montes/Bache*** *a-109.*

FIGHTING PRINCE OF DONEGAL, THE (See Movie Comics)

FIGHTIN' TEXAN (Formerly The Texan)
No. 16, Oct, 1952 - No. 17, Dec, 1952
St. John Publishing Co.

	Good	Fine	Mint
16,17-Tuska-a each. 17-Cameron-a	1.50	4.00	8.00

FIGHTING UNDERSEA COMMANDOS
1952 - No. 5, April, 1953
Avon Periodicals

	Good	Fine	Mint
1	3.00	8.00	16.00
2-5: 4-Kinstler-c	2.50	7.00	14.00

FIGHTING WAR STORIES
Aug, 1952 - 1953
Men's Publications

	Good	Fine	Mint
1	1.00	3.00	6.00
2-5	.70	2.00	4.00

FIGHTING YANK (See Startling & America's Best)
Sept, 1942 - No. 29, Aug, 1949
Nedor/Better Publ./Standard

	Good	Fine	Mint
1-The Fighting Yank begins; Mystico, the Wonder Man app; bondage-c	30.00	80.00	160.00
2	14.00	40.00	80.00
3	10.00	30.00	60.00

FIGHTING YANK (continued)

	Good	Fine	Mint
4	8.00	24.00	48.00
5,6,8-10	7.00	20.00	40.00
7-The Grim Reaper app.	7.00	20.00	40.00
11-The Oracle app.	5.00	15.00	30.00
12-17: 12-Hirohito bondage-c	5.00	15.00	30.00
18-The American Eagle app.	4.00	12.00	24.00
19,20	4.00	12.00	24.00
21-24: 21-Kara, Jungle Princess app. 22,24-Miss Masque app.	6.00	18.00	36.00
25-Robinson/Meskin-a; strangulation, lingerie panel; The Cavalier app.	6.00	18.00	36.00
26-29: 26-28-Robinson/Meskin-a. 28-One pg. Williamson-a	6.00	18.00	36.00

NOTE: *Many issues have* ***Schomburg (Xela)*** *covers.*

FIGHT THE ENEMY
Aug, 1966 - No. 3, Mar, 1967 (25 cents)
Tower Comics

	Good	Fine	Mint
1-Lucky 7 & Mike Manly begin; Grandenetti-a	.40	1.20	2.40
2-Boris Vallejo story	1.00	3.00	6.00
3-Wood-a ½pg; McWilliams-a	.30	.80	1.60

FILM FUNNIES
Nov, 1949 - No. 2, Feb, 1950
Marvel Comics (CPC)

	Good	Fine	Mint
1	3.00	9.00	18.00
2	2.50	7.00	14.00

FILM STARS ROMANCES
Jan-Feb, 1950 - No. 3, May-June, 1950
Star Publications

	Good	Fine	Mint
1-Rudy Valentino story; L. B. Cole-c	8.00	24.00	48.00
2-Liz Taylor/Robert Taylor photo-c	8.00	24.00	48.00
3-Photo-c	7.00	20.00	40.00

FIRE AND BLAST
1952 (16 pgs.; paper cover) (Giveaway)
National Fire Protection Assoc.

	Good	Fine	Mint
Mart Baily A-Bomb cover; about fire prevention	8.00	24.00	48.00

FIRE BALL XL5 (See Steve Zodiac)

FIRE CHIEF AND THE SAFE OL' FIREFLY, THE
1952 (16 pgs.)
National Board of Fire Underwriters (produced by American Visuals Corp.) (Eisner)

	Good	Fine	Mint
(Rare) Eisner c/a; safety brochure given away at schools	6.00	18.00	36.00

FIREHAIR COMICS (Pioneer West Romances No. 3-6)
Winter/48-49 - No. 2, Spr/49; No. 7, Spr/51 - No. 11, Spr/52
Fiction House Magazines

	Good	Fine	Mint
1	5.00	15.00	30.00
2,7-11	3.50	10.00	20.00
I.W. Reprint 8-Kinstler-c; reprints Rangers No. 57; Dr. Drew story by Grandenetti (no date)	.85	2.50	5.00

FIRESTONE (See Donald & Mickey)

FIRESTORM (See Cancelled Comic Cavalcade & DC Comics Presents)
March, 1978 - No. 5, Oct-Nov, 1978
DC Comics

	Good	Fine	Mint
1-Origin & 1st app.		.40	.80
2-5: 2-Origin Multiplex. 3-Origin Killer Frost. 4-1st app. Hyena		.30	.60

FIRST AMERICANS, THE (See 4-Color No. 843)

FIRST CHRISTMAS, THE (3-D)
1953 (25 cents) (Oversized - 8¼x10¼'')
Fiction House Magazines (Real Adv. Publ. Co.)

	Good	Fine	Mint
nn-Kelly Freas-c	10.00	30.00	60.00

FIRST ISSUE SPECIAL
April, 1975 - No. 13, April, 1976
National Periodical Publications

	Good	Fine	Mint
1-Intro. Atlas by Kirby	.25	.70	1.40
2-Green Team (See Cancelled Comic Cavalcade)		.40	.80
3-Metamorpho		.40	.80
4-Lady Cop		.40	.80
5-Manhunter by Kirby		.50	1.00
6-Dingbats by Kirby		.50	1.00
7-The Creeper by Fleisher/Ditko	.30	.80	1.60
8-The Warlord (origin)	2.00	5.00	10.00
9-Dr. Fate; Kubert-c; Simonson-a	.25	.70	1.40
10-The Outsiders		.40	.80
11-Code Name: Assassin; Redondo-a		.40	.80
12-New Starman-Kubert-c		.60	1.20
13-Return of the New Gods		.40	.80

FIRST KISS (For Lovers Only No. 39 on)
Dec, 1957 - No. 36, Feb, 1964
Charlton Comics

	Good	Fine	Mint
V1No.1	.50	1.50	3.00
V1No.2-10	.30	.90	1.80
11-36 (37,38-exist?)		.50	1.00

FIRST LOVE ILLUSTRATED
2/49 - No. 86, 3/58; No. 87, 9/58 - No. 88, 11/58; No. 89, 11/62, No. 90, 2/63
Harvey Publications(Home Comics)(True Love)

	Good	Fine	Mint
1-Powell-a(2)	3.00	9.00	18.00
2,4-10	1.75	5.00	10.00
3-''Was I Too Fat To Be Loved'' story	2.00	6.00	12.00
11-29	1.00	3.00	6.00
30-Lingerie panel	1.00	3.00	6.00
31-34,36,37,39-90	.85	2.50	5.00
35-Used in **SOTI**, illo-''The title of this comic book is First Love;''	7.00	20.00	40.00
38-Nostrand-a	2.00	5.00	10.00

NOTE: ***Disbrow*** *a-13.* ***Powell*** *a-1, 3-5, 7, 10, 11, 13-17, 19, 21-24, 26-29, 33, 35-41, 43, 45, 46, 50, 54, 57, 58, 61-63, 65, 71-73, 76, 82,84,88.*

FIRST MEN IN THE MOON (See Movie Comics)

FIRST ROMANCE MAGAZINE
8/49 - No. 6, 6/50; No. 7, 6/51 - No. 50, 2/58; No. 51, 9/58 - No. 52, 11/58
Home Comics(Harvey Publ.)/True Love

	Good	Fine	Mint
1	3.50	10.00	20.00
2-5	2.00	5.00	10.00
6-10	1.50	4.00	8.00
11-20	1.00	3.00	6.00
21-27,29-52	.70	2.00	4.00
28-Nostrand-a(Powell swipe)	2.00	5.00	10.00

NOTE: ***Powell*** *a-1-5,8-10,14,18,20-22,24,25,28,36,46,48,51.*

FIRST TRIP TO THE MOON (See Space Advs. No. 20)

5-STAR SUPER-HERO SPEC. (See DC Special Series No. 1)

FLAME, THE
Summer, 1940 - No. 8, Jan, 1942
Fox Features Syndicate

	Good	Fine	Mint
1-Flame stories from WonderWorld No. 6-9; origin The Flame; Lou Fine-a, 36 pgs.	60.00	160.00	320.00
2-Fine-a(2)	30.00	80.00	160.00
3-8	14.00	40.00	80.00

FLAME, THE (Formerly Lone Eagle)

Fighting Yank #15, © BP

Fight The Enemy #2, © TC

First Romance Magazine #37, © HARV

The Flash #137, © DC

Flash Comics #7, © DC

Flash Comics #97, © DC

FLAME (continued)
No. 5, Dec-Jan, 1954-55 - No. 4, June-July, 1955
Ajax/Farrell Publications (Excellent Publ.)

	Good	Fine	Mint
5(No.1)	5.00	14.00	28.00
2-4	3.00	8.00	16.00

FLAMING LOVE
Dec, 1949 - No. 6, Oct, 1950 (Photo covers No. 2-6)
Quality Comics Group (Comic Magazines)

	Good	Fine	Mint
1-Ward-c, 9 pgs.	10.00	30.00	60.00
2,5,6	3.00	12.00	24.00
3-Ward-a, 9 pgs.; Crandall-a	9.00	25.00	50.00
4-Gustavson-a	4.00	12.00	24.00

FLAMING WESTERN ROMANCES
Nov-Dec, 1949 - No. 3, Mar-Apr, 1950
Star Publications

	Good	Fine	Mint
1-L. B. Cole-c	8.00	24.00	48.00
2-L. B. Cole-c	5.50	16.00	32.00
3-Robert Taylor, Arlene Dahl photo-c with biographies inside; L. B. Cole-c; spanking panel	8.00	24.00	48.00

FLASH, THE (Formerly Flash Comics)(See Adventure, The Brave & the Bold, DC Comics Presents, DC Special Series, DC Super-Stars, Green Lantern, Showcase, Super Team Family, & World's Finest)
No. 105, Feb-Mar, 1959 - Present
National Periodical Publications/DC Comics

	Good	Fine	Mint
105-Origin Flash(retold), & Mirror Master	60.00	160.00	320.00
106-Origin Grodd & Pied Piper	25.00	70.00	140.00
107-110: 110-Intro. & origin Kid Flash & The Weather Wizard	10.00	30.00	60.00
111,115	5.50	16.00	32.00
112-Intro & Origin Elongated Man	6.00	18.00	36.00
113-Origin Trickster	5.50	16.00	32.00
114-Intro & origin Captain Cold	5.50	16.00	32.00
116-120: 117-Origin Capt. Boomerang. 119-Elongated Man marries Sue Dearborn	4.00	12.00	24.00
121	3.00	8.00	16.00
122-Origin & 1st app. The Top	3.00	8.00	16.00
123-Re-intro. Golden Age Flash; origins of both Flashes; 1st mention of an Earth II where DC Golden Age heroes live	4.00	12.00	24.00
124-128,130: 128-Origin Abra Kadabra	1.75	5.00	10.00
129-G.A. Flash x-over	2.00	6.00	12.00
131-136,138-140: 136-1st Dexter Miles. 139-Origin Prof. Zoom. 140-Origin & 1st app. Heat Wave	1.00	3.00	6.00
137-G.A. Flash x-over; J.S.A. cameo (1st since 2-3/51); 1st app. Vandal Savage	1.20	3.50	7.00
141-150	.80	2.30	4.60
151-160: 151-G.A. Flash x-over. 160-25 cent ish G-21: G.A.-r of Flash & Johnny Quick	.50	1.50	3.00
(84 pg. Giant G-21)	.70	2.00	4.00
161-170: 162-Giant size. 165-Silver Age Flash weds Iris West. 167-New facts about Flash's origin. 169-25 cent ish G-34. 170-Dr. Mid-Nite, Dr. Fate, G.A. Flash x-over	.35	1.00	2.00
(84 pg. Giant G-34)	.40	1.20	2.40
171-180: 171-JLA, Green Lantern, Atom flashbacks. 173-G.A. Flash x-over. 174-Barry Allen reveals I.D. to wife. 175-2nd Superman/Flash race; JLA cameo. 178-25 cent ish G-46	.30	.80	1.60
(84 pg. Giant G-46)	.35	1.00	2.00
181-190: 186-Re-intro. Sargon. 187-25 cent ish G-58		.60	1.20
(84 pg. Giant G-58)	.30	.80	1.60
191-200: 196-25 cent ish G-70		.60	1.20
(84 pg. Giant G-70)	.30	.80	1.60
201-210: 201-New G.A. Flash story. 205-25 cent ish G-82. 208-52 pg. begin, end No. 213,215,216. 214-Origin Metal Men-r		.50	1.00
(64 pg. Giant G-82)	.30	.80	1.60
211-216,220: 211-G.A. Flash origin (No.104). 213-All-r. 214-50 cent DC-11, origin Metal Men. 215-G.A. Flash x-over, r-in No. 216		.40	.80
(Giant DC-11)	.30	.90	1.80
217-219: Adams-a in all. 217-Green Lantern/Green Arrow series begins. 219-Last Green Arrow	.85	2.50	5.00
221,222,224,225,227,228,230,231		.40	.80
223-Adams-a(i)	.60	1.80	3.60
226-Adams-a	.60	1.80	3.60
229,232-(100 pgs. each)	.30	.80	1.60
233-250: 243-Death of the Top. 246-Last Green Lantern		.40	.80
251-270: 265-67-(44 pgs.). 265,266-Kid Flash app.		.30	.60
271-274,284-288,290-293		.30	.60
275,276-Iris West Allen dies	.30	.80	1.60
277,278-Drug ish.(angel dust).		.40	.80
279-283-Drug mention		.30	.60
289-Perez 1st DC art		.40	.80
294-296-Starlin-a		.30	.60
297-299,301-305: 303-The Top returns		.30	.60
300-52 page ish	.30	.80	1.60
Annual 1(10-12/63)-Origin Elongated Man & Kid Flash-r	2.00	6.00	12.00
Wheaties Giveaway (1946, 32 pgs., 6½x8¼")-Johnny Thunder, Ghost Patrol, The Flash & Kubert Hawkman app. NOTE: *All known copies were taped to Wheaties boxes and never found in fine or mint condition.*	15.00	55.00	120.00

NOTE: ***Adams*** *c-194, 195, 202-204, 206-208, 211, 213, 215, 246.* ***Anderson*** *inks-110, 111, 114, 115, 117-119, 148-150, 168, 176, 194, 200-204, 206-208, 210; c-165, 176, 196, 205, 210, 212, 232.* ***Buckler*** *a-271, 272; c-247-50, 252, 255, 258, 259, 262, 265-67, 269-71.* ***Giordano*** *c-275-79.* ***Grell*** *a-238, 240, 242.* ***Infantino*** *a-105-174, 178, 187, 194, 196, 200, 201, 203, 209, 210, 212-215, 229, 232r, 296-304, Annual 1; c-105-164, 166-176, 200, 201, 296-303.* ***G. Kane*** *a-232r.* ***Kubert*** *a-108p; c-189-191.* ***Lopez*** *c-272.* ***Meskin*** *a-229r, 232r.* ***Perez*** *a-290-293p; c-293.* ***Staton*** *c-263, 264. Green Lantern x-over-131, 143, 168, 171, 191.*

FLASH COMICS (The Flash No. 105 on) (Also see All-Flash)
Jan, 1940 - No. 104, Feb, 1949
National Periodical Publications/All-American

	Good	Fine	Mint
1-Origin The Flash by Harry Lampert, Hawkman by Garner Fox, The Whip & Johnny Thunder; Cliff Cornwall by Moldoff, Minute Movies begin; Moldoff (Shelly) cover; 1st app. Shiera Sanders who later becomes Hawkgirl, No. 24; reprinted in Famous First Edition	250.00	750.00	1600.00
2-Rod Rian begins, ends No. 11	100.00	280.00	600.00
3-The King begins, ends No. 41	70.00	190.00	400.00
4-Moldoff (Shelly) Hawkman begins	60.00	160.00	340.00
5	50.00	145.00	310.00
6,7	40.00	120.00	250.00
8-10: 8-Male bondage-c	35.00	95.00	200.00
11-20: 12-Les Watts begins; "Sparks" No. 16 on. 17-Last Cliff Cornwall	25.00	70.00	145.00
21-23	17.00	50.00	100.00
24-Shiera becomes Hawkgirl	25.00	70.00	140.00
25-30: 28-Last Les Sparks. 29-Ghost Patrol begins(origin), ends No. 104	16.00	48.00	100.00
31-40: 35-Origin Shade	14.00	40.00	80.00
41-50	12.00	36.00	72.00
51-61: 59-Last Minute Movies. 61-Last Moldoff Hawkman	8.00	24.00	48.00
62-Hawkman by Kubert begins	14.00	40.00	80.00
63-70: 66-68-Hop Harrigan in all	10.00	30.00	60.00
71-80: 80-Atom begins, ends No. 104	10.00	30.00	60.00
81-85	10.00	30.00	60.00
86-Intro. The Black Canary in Johnny Thunder	30.00	80.00	160.00
87-90: 88-Origin Ghost	14.00	40.00	80.00
91,93-99: 98-Atom dons new costume	17.00	50.00	100.00
92-1st solo Black Canary	30.00	80.00	160.00
100(Scarce)	35.00	100.00	200.00

FLASH COMICS (continued)

	Good	Fine	Mint
101-103(Scarce)	30.00	80.00	160.00
104-Origin The Flash retold (Rare)	120.00	300.00	580.00

NOTE: ***Infantino*** *a-90, 93-95, 99-104.* ***Kinstler*** *a-87, 89(Hawkman).* ***Krigstein*** *a-94.* ***Kubert*** *a-62-76, 83, 85, 86, 88-104; c-63, 65, 67, 70, 71, 73, 75, 83, 85, 86, 88, 89, 91, 94, 96, 98, 100, 104.*

FLASH GORDON (See Eat Right to Work . . ., Feature Book No. 25 (McKay), King Classics, King Comics, March of Comics No. 118,133, 142, and Street Comix)

FLASH GORDON
No. 10, 1943 - No. 512, Nov, 1953
Dell Publishing Co.

	Good	Fine	Mint
4-Color 10(1943)-by Alex Raymond; reprints/''The Ice Kingdom''	60.00	150.00	280.00
4-Color 84(1945)-by Alex Raymond; reprints/''The Fiery Desert''	35.00	90.00	180.00
4-Color 173,190	8.00	24.00	48.00
4-Color 204,247	6.00	18.00	36.00
4-Color 424	4.00	12.00	24.00
2(5-7/53-Dell)-Evans-a	3.00	8.00	16.00
4-Color 512	3.00	8.00	16.00
Macy's Giveaway(1943)-(Rare)-20 pgs.; not by Raymond	60.00	160.00	320.00

FLASH GORDON
Oct, 1950 - April, 1951
Harvey Publications

	Good	Fine	Mint
1-Alex Raymond-a; bondage-c	20.00	60.00	120.00
2-4-Alex Raymond	14.00	40.00	80.00

5-(Rare)-Small size-5½x8½''; B&W; 32 pgs.; Distributed to some mail subscribers only Estimated value. . . . $400.00—$600.00

(Also see All-New No. 15, Boy Explorers No. 2, and Stuntman No. 3)

FLASH GORDON
1952? (Paper cover; 16 pgs. in color; regular size)
Harvey Comics (Gordon Bread giveaway)

	Good	Fine	Mint
1938, 1941? Reprints by Raymond each. . . .	10.00	30.00	60.00

FLASH GORDON
June, 1965
Gold Key

	Good	Fine	Mint
1 (1947 reprint)	1.20	3.50	7.00

FLASH GORDON (Also see Comics Reading Libraries)
9/66 - No. 18, 1/70; No. 19, 10-11/78 - Present
King, No.1-11(12/67)/Charlton, No.12(2/69)-18/Gold Key, No.19-27/Whitman No. 28 on

	Good	Fine	Mint
1-Army giveaway(1968)(''Complimentary'' on cover)(Same as regular No. 1 minus Mandrake story & back cover)	1.50	4.00	8.00
1-Williamson c/a(2); Mandrake app.	1.50	4.00	8.00
2-Bolle, Gil Kane-a	1.20	3.50	7.00
3-Williamson-c, Estrada-a	1.50	4.00	8.00
4-Secret Agent X-9 begins, Williamson-c/a	1.50	4.00	8.00
5-Williamson c/a	1.50	4.00	8.00
6,8-Crandall-a. 6-Crandall-c. 8-Aparo-a	1.20	3.50	7.00
7-Raboy-a	1.00	3.00	6.00
9,10-Raymond-r, Buckler-a	1.20	3.50	7.00
11-Crandall-a	.85	2.50	5.00
12-Crandall c/a	1.00	3.00	6.00
13-Jeff Jones-a	.85	2.50	5.00
14-17: 17-Brick Bradford app.	.40	1.20	2.40
18-Kaluta-a	.70	2.00	4.00
19(10-11/78, G.K.), 20-30		.30	.60
31-33: Movie adapt; Williamson-a		.30	.60

FLASH GORDON GIANT COMIC ALBUM
1972 (11x14''; cardboard covers; 48 pgs.; B&W; 59 cents)
Modern Promotions, N. Y.

	Good	Fine	Mint
Reprints 1968, 1969 dailies by Dan Barry	.25	.70	1.40

FLASH SPECTACULAR, THE (See DC Special Series No. 11)

FLAT TOP
Nov, 1953 - No. 6, July, 1954
Mazie Comics/Harvey Publ.(Magazine Publ.)

	Good	Fine	Mint
1	.85	2.50	5.00
2-6	.50	1.50	3.00

FLINTSTONES, THE (TV)(See Dell Giant No.48 for No. 1)
No. 2, Nov-Dec, 1961 - No. 60, Sept, 1970 (Hanna-Barbera)
Dell Publ. Co./Gold Key No. 7 (10/62) on

	Good	Fine	Mint
2	.50	1.50	3.00
3-10	.30	.90	1.80
11-30: 11-1st app. Pebbles(6/63)		.50	1.00
31-60(9/70): 34-1st app. The Great Gazoo. 39-Reprints		.30	.60
At N. Y. World's Fair('64)-J.W. Books(25 cents), re-issued in 1965 (1965 on-c)	.70	2.00	4.00
Bigger & Boulder 1(30013-211)G.K. Giant(25 cents); 84 pgs.	.85	2.50	5.00
Bigger & Boulder 2-(25 cents)(1966)-reprints B&B No. 1	.50	1.50	3.00
Pebbles & Bamm Bamm(100 pgs.)-30028-511 (paper cover-25 cents)	.50	1.50	3.00

(See Comic Album No. 16, Bamm-Bamm & Pebbles Flintstone, Dell Giant 48, March of Comics No. 229,243,271,289,299,317,327, 341, Pebbles Flintstone, and Whitman Comic Books.)

FLINTSTONES, THE (. . . & Pebbles)
Nov, 1970 - No. 50, Feb, 1977
Charlton Comics

	Good	Fine	Mint
1	.70	2.00	4.00
2-7,9-50	.35	1.00	2.00
8-''Flintstones Summer Vacation,'' 52 pgs. (Summer, 1971)	.40	1.20	2.40

(Also see Barney & Betty Rubble, Dino, The Great Gazoo, and Pebbles & Bamm-Bamm)

FLINTSTONES, THE (TV)
October, 1977 - No. 9, Feb, 1979
Marvel Comics Group

	Good	Fine	Mint
1		.50	1.00
2-9		.30	.60

FLINTSTONES CHRISTMAS PARTY, THE (See The Funtastic World of Hanna-Barbera No. 1)

FLIP
April, 1954 - No. 2, June, 1954 (Satire)
Harvey Publications

	Good	Fine	Mint
1,2-Nostrand-a in each	4.00	12.00	24.00

FLIPPER (TV)
April, 1966 - No. 3, Nov, 1967
Gold Key

	Good	Fine	Mint
1-3	.70	2.00	4.00

FLIPPITY & FLOP
12-1/51-52 - No. 46, 8-10/59; No. 47, 9-11/60
National Periodical Publ. (Signal Publ. Co.)

	Good	Fine	Mint
1	4.00	12.00	24.00
2-5	2.00	5.00	10.00
6-10	1.50	4.00	8.00
11-47	.85	2.50	5.00

FLY, THE (See The Adventures of. .)

FLY BOY (Also see Approved Comics)
Spring, 1952 - No. 4, 1954

Flash Comics #102, © DC

Flash Gordon #3, © KING

The Flintstones #3, © Hanna-Barbera

Flyman #36, © AP

Forbidden Love #2, © QUA

Forbidden Worlds #11, © ACG

FLY BOY (continued)
Ziff-Davis Publ. Co. (Approved)

	Good	Fine	Mint
1-Saunders painted-c	2.00	5.00	10.00
2-4-Saunders painted-c	1.50	4.00	8.00

FLYING ACES
July, 1955 - 1956
Key Publications

	Good	Fine	Mint
1	1.00	3.00	6.00
2-5	.70	2.00	4.00

FLYING A'S RANGE RIDER (TV) (See 4-Color No. 404 for No. 1)
No. 2, June-Aug, 1953 - No. 24, Dec-Feb, 1959
Dell Publishing Co.

	Good	Fine	Mint
2	1.20	3.50	7.00
3-10	.85	2.50	5.00
11-16,18-24	.70	2.00	4.00
17-Toth-a	2.00	5.00	10.00

FLYING CADET (WW II Plane Photos)
Jan, 1943 - 1947 (½ photos, ½ comics)
Flying Cadet Publishing Co.

	Good	Fine	Mint
V1No.1-9	1.20	3.50	7.00
V2No.1-8(No.10-17)	.85	2.50	5.00

FLYIN' JENNY
1946 - 1947 (1945 strip reprints)
Pentagon Publ. Co.

	Good	Fine	Mint
nn	3.00	8.00	16.00
2-Baker-c	3.50	10.00	20.00

FLYING MODELS
May, 1954 (16 pgs.) (5 cents)
H-K Publ. (not Harvey Kurtzman)

	Good	Fine	Mint
V61No.3 (Rare)	2.50	7.00	14.00

FLYING NUN (TV)
Feb, 1968 - No. 4, Nov, 1968
Dell Publishing Co.

	Good	Fine	Mint
1-4	.50	1.50	3.00

FLYING NURSES (See Sue & Sally Smith. . .)

FLYING SAUCERS
1950 - 1953
Avon Periodicals/Realistic

	Good	Fine	Mint
1(1950)-Wood-a, 21 pgs.	35.00	85.00	170.00
nn(1952)-Cover altered plus 2 pgs. of Wood-a not in original	30.00	80.00	160.00
nn(1953)-Reprints above	17.00	50.00	90.00

FLYING SAUCERS (Comics)
April, 1967 - No. 4, Nov, 1967; No. 5, Oct, 1969
Dell Publishing Co.

	Good	Fine	Mint
1	.70	2.00	4.00
2-5	.50	1.40	2.80

FLYMAN (Formerly Adv. of The Fly; Mighty Comics. . . No. 40 on)
No. 32, July, 1965 - No. 39, Sept, 1966
Mighty Comics Group (Radio Comics) (Archie)

	Good	Fine	Mint
32,33-Comet, Shield, Black Hood x-over; re-intro. Wizard, Hangman-No. 33	.50	1.50	3.00
34-Shield begins	.50	1.50	3.00
35-Origin Black Hood	.50	1.50	3.00
36-Hangman x-over in Shield; re-intro. & origin of Web	.50	1.50	3.00
37-Hangman, Wizard x-over in Flyman; last Shield issue	.50	1.50	3.00
38-Web story	.50	1.50	3.00
39-Steel Sterling story	.50	1.50	3.00

FOLLOW THE SUN (TV)
May-July, 1962 - No. 2, Sept-Nov, 1962
Dell Publishing Co.

	Good	Fine	Mint
01-280-207(No.1), 208(No.2)	.70	2.00	4.00

FOODINI (See The Great. . . , Pinhead &. . . , & Jingle Dingle)
March, 1950 - No. 5, 1950
Continental Publications (Holyoke)

	Good	Fine	Mint
1	1.50	4.50	9.00
2-5	1.00	3.00	6.00

FOOEY (Magazine) (Satire)
Feb, 1961 - No. 4, May, 1961
Scoff Publishing Co.

	Good	Fine	Mint
1	1.50	4.00	8.00
2-4	.85	2.50	5.00

FOOTBALL THRILLS
Fall-Winter, 1951-52 - No. 2, 1952
Ziff-Davis Publ. Co.

	Good	Fine	Mint
1-Powell a(2); Saunders painted-c	3.00	8.00	16.00
2-Saunders painted-c	2.00	6.00	12.00

FOR A NIGHT OF LOVE
1951
Avon Periodicals

	Good	Fine	Mint
nn-Two stories adapted from the works of Emile Zola; Astarita, Ravielli-a; Kinstler-c	10.00	30.00	60.00

FORBIDDEN LOVE
Mar, 1950 - No. 4, Sept, 1950
Quality Comics Group

	Good	Fine	Mint
1-(Scarce)Classic photo-c; Crandall-a	80.00	200.00	340.00
2,3(Scarce)-Photo-c	20.00	60.00	120.00
4-(Scarce)Ward/Cuidera-a; photo-c	25.00	70.00	140.00

FORBIDDEN LOVE (See Dark Mansion of. . .)

FORBIDDEN TALES OF DARK MANSION (Dark Mansion of Forbidden Love No. 1-4)
No. 5, May-June, 1972 - No. 15, Feb-Mar, 1974
National Periodical Publications

	Good	Fine	Mint
5-15: 13-Kane/Howard-a		.40	.80

NOTE: ***Alcala*** *a-9-11, 13.* ***Chaykin*** *a-7-15.* ***Kaluta*** *c-7-13.* ***G. Kane*** *a-13.* ***Kirby*** *a-6.* ***Nino*** *a-8, 12, 15.* ***Redondo*** *a-14.*

FORBIDDEN WORLDS (. . . Presents Herbie No. 114,116)
7-8/51 - No. 34, 10-11/54; No. 35, 8/55 - No. 145, 8/67
(No.1-5: 52 pgs.; No.6-8: 44 pgs.)
American Comics Group

	Good	Fine	Mint
1-Williamson/Frazetta-a, 10pgs.	30.00	85.00	170.00
2	9.00	25.00	50.00
3-Williamson/Wood-a, 7pgs.	12.00	35.00	70.00
4	5.00	15.00	30.00
5-Williamson/Krenkel-a, 8pgs.	12.00	35.00	70.00
6-Harrison/Williamson-a, 8pgs.	10.00	30.00	60.00
7,8,10	3.00	8.00	16.00
9-A-Bomb explosion story	3.00	9.00	18.00
11-20	2.00	6.00	12.00
21-33	1.50	4.00	8.00
34(10-11/54)(Becomes Young Heroes No. 35 on)-Last pre-code ish; A-Bomb explosion story	2.00	5.00	10.00
35(8/55)-62	1.00	3.00	6.00
63,69,76,78-Williamson-a in all	3.00	9.00	18.00
64,66-68,70-72,74,75,77,79-90	.85	2.50	5.00
65-''There's a New Moon Tonight'' listed in No. 114 as holding 1st record fan mail response	1.00	3.00	6.00
73-Intro., 1st app. Herbie by Whitney	12.00	36.00	72.00
91-93,95,97-100	.70	2.00	4.00
94-Herbie app.	4.00	12.00	24.00
96-Williamson-a	2.50	7.00	14.00
101-109,111-113,115,117-120	.50	1.50	3.00
110,114,116-Herbie app. 114 contains list of editor's top 20 ACG stories	2.00	6.00	12.00

FORBIDDEN WORLDS (continued) — Good / Fine / Mint

121-124: 124-Magic Agent app. .40 1.20 2.40

125-Magic Agent app.; intro. & origin Magicman series, ends No. 141 .50 1.50 3.00

126-130 .40 1.10 2.20

131,132,134-141: 136-Nemesis x-over in Magicman. 140-Mark Midnight app. by Ditko .30 .90 1.80

133-Origin & 1st app. Dragonia in Magicman (1-2/66); returns No. 138 .30 .90 1.80

142-145 .25 .70 1.40

NOTE: ***Buscema*** *a-75, 79, 81, 82.* ***Disbrow*** *a-10.* ***Ditko*** *a-137, 138, 140.* ***Landau*** *a-24, 28, 31-34, 48, 86r, 96, 143-45.* ***Moldoff*** *a-31.*

FORD ROTUNDA CHRISTMAS BOOK (See Christmas at the Rotunda)

FOREIGN INTRIGUES (Formerly Johnny Dynamite; Battlefield Action No. 16 on)
1956
Charlton Comics

13-15-Johnny Dynamite continues 1.50 4.00 8.00
2-15 1.20 3.50 7.00

FOREVER, DARLING (See 4-Color No. 681)

FOREVER PEOPLE
Feb-Mar, 1971 - No. 11, Oct-Nov, 1972
National Periodical Publications

1-Superman x-over; Kirby-a begins .80 2.30 4.60
2 .40 1.20 2.40
3-5: 4-G.A. reprints begin .35 1.10 2.20
6-8,11 .30 .80 1.60
9,10-Deadman x-over .35 1.00 2.00

NOTE: ***Kirby*** *c/a-1-11; No. 4-9 contain Sandman reprints from Adventure No. 85, 84, 75, 80, 77, 74 in that order.*

FOR GIRLS ONLY
Nov, 1953 (Digest size, 100 pgs.)
Bernard Bailey Enterprises

1-½ comic book, ½ magazine 3.00 8.00 16.00

FORGOTTEN STORY BEHIND NORTH BEACH, THE
No date (8 pgs.; paper cover)
Catechetical Guild

3.00 9.00 18.00

FOR LOVERS ONLY (Formerly First Kiss)
No. 39, 1969 - No. 98, Nov, 1976
Charlton Comics

39-98 .25 .50

40 BIG PAGES OF MICKEY MOUSE
1936 (44 pgs.; 10¼x12½''; cardboard cover)
Whitman Publishing Co.

945-Reprints Mickey Mouse Magazine No. 1, but with a different cover. Ads were eliminated and some illustrated stories had expanded text. The book is ¾'' shorter than Mickey Mouse Mag. No. 1, but the reprints are the same size. (Rare) 35.00 100.00 200.00

48 FAMOUS AMERICANS
1947 (Giveaway) (Half-size in color)
J. C. Penney Co. (Cpr. Edwin H. Stroh)

Simon & Kirby-a 7.00 20.00 40.00

FOR YOUR EYES ONLY
October, 1981 - Present
Marvel Comics Group

1-James Bond movie adaptation .30 .60
2-Concluding half of movie adaptation .30 .60

NOTE: ***Chaykin*** *c/a(p)-1, 2.*

FOUR COLOR
1939 - No. 1354, 1962
Dell Publishing Co.

NOTE: *Four Color only appears on issues No. 19-25, 1-99. Dell Publishing Co. filed these as Series I, No. 1-25, and Series II, No. 1-1354. Later issues were printed with and without ads on back cover. Issues without ads are worth more.*

SERIES I: — Good / Fine / Mint

1(nn)-Dick Tracy 75.00 200.00 400.00
2(nn)-Don Winslow (Rare) 35.00 100.00 200.00
3(nn)-Myra North 8.00 24.00 48.00
4-Donald Duck by Al Taliaferro('40)(Disney) 300.00 700.00 1400.00
(Prices vary widely on this book)
5-Smilin' Jack 17.00 50.00 100.00
6-Dick Tracy (Scarce) 40.00 120.00 240.00
7-Gangbusters 8.00 24.00 48.00
8-Dick Tracy 30.00 80.00 160.00
9-Terry & the Pirates-Reprints No. 5 & The Pirate from Super No. 9-29 30.00 80.00 160.00
10-Smilin' Jack 17.00 50.00 100.00
11-Smitty 10.00 28.00 56.00
12-Little Orphan Annie 17.00 50.00 100.00
13-Reluctant Dragon('41)-Contains 2 pages of photos from film; 2 pg. foreword to Fantasia by Leopold Stokowski; Donald Duck, Goofy, Baby Weems & Mickey Mouse (as the Sorcerer's Apprentice) app. 40.00 120.00 240.00
14-Moon Mullins 8.00 24.00 48.00
15-Tillie the Toiler 8.00 24.00 48.00
16-Mickey Mouse (Disney) by Gottfredson 300.00 800.00 1600.00
(Prices vary widely on this book)
17-Dumbo(1941)-Mickey Mouse, Donald Duck, & Pluto app. (Disney) 60.00 160.00 300.00
18-Jiggs & Maggie(1936-'38 reprints) 10.00 30.00 60.00
19-Barney Google-(1st issue with Four Color on the cover) 10.00 30.00 60.00
20-Tiny Tim 10.00 30.00 60.00
21-Dick Tracy 24.00 70.00 140.00
22-Don Winslow 7.00 20.00 40.00
23-Gangbusters 7.00 20.00 40.00
24-Captain Easy 10.00 30.00 60.00
25-Popeye 30.00 80.00 160.00

SERIES II:

1-Little Joe 12.00 34.00 68.00
2-Harold Teen 8.00 24.00 48.00
3-Alley Oop 17.00 50.00 100.00
4-Smilin' Jack 17.00 50.00 100.00
5-Raggedy Ann & Andy 15.00 45.00 90.00
6-Smitty 7.00 20.00 40.00
7-Smokey Stover 10.00 30.00 60.00
8-Tillie the Toiler 5.50 16.00 32.00
9-Donald Duck ''Finds Pirate Gold'' by Carl Barks & Jack Hannah (Disney) (1942) 400.00 1150.00 2200.00
(Prices vary widely on this book)
10-Flash Gordon by Alex Raymond-Reprints from ''The Ice Kingdom'' 60.00 150.00 280.00
11-Wash Tubbs 12.00 34.00 64.00
12-Bambi (Disney) 20.00 60.00 120.00
13-Mr. District Attorney 7.00 20.00 40.00
14-Smilin' Jack 14.00 40.00 80.00
15-Felix the Cat 20.00 60.00 120.00
16-Porky Pig(1942)-''Secret of the Haunted House'' 30.00 80.00 160.00
17-Popeye 20.00 60.00 120.00
18-Little Orphan Annie's Jr. Commandos; Flag-c 14.00 40.00 80.00
19-Thumper Meets the 7 Dwarfs (Disney)-Reprinted in Silly Symphonies 20.00 60.00 120.00
20-Barney Baxter 8.00 22.00 44.00
21-Oswald the Rabbit 14.00 40.00 80.00

Forever People #10, © DC

Four Color #7, © N.Y. News Synd.

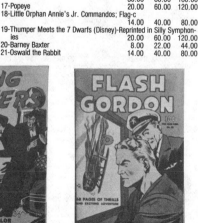

Four Color #10, © KING

Four Color #30, © WDP

OSWALD
THE RABBIT
10¢
DELL
BY
WALTER LANTZ

Four Color #39, © Walter Lantz

Four Color #61, © DELL

FOUR COLOR (continued)	**Good**	**Fine**	**Mint**
22-Tillie the Toiler	5.00	14.00	28.00
23-Raggedy Ann	13.00	38.00	76.00
24-Gangbusters	7.00	20.00	40.00
25-Andy Panda	15.00	45.00	90.00
26-Popeye	17.00	50.00	100.00
27-Mickey Mouse & the 7 Colored Terror (Disney)	50.00	120.00	240.00
28-Wash Tubbs	8.00	24.00	48.00
29-Donald Duck-''Mummy's Ring'' by Carl Barks (Disney) (9/43)	325.00	800.00	1600.00
(Prices vary widely on this book)			
30-Bambi's Children(1943)-Disney	20.00	60.00	120.00
31-Moon Mullins	6.00	18.00	36.00
32-Smitty	4.00	12.00	24.00
33-Bugs Bunny-Public Nuisance No. 1	24.00	70.00	140.00
34-Dick Tracy	17.00	50.00	100.00
35-Smokey Stover	5.50	16.00	32.00
36-Smilin' Jack	7.00	20.00	40.00
37-Bringing Up Father	5.50	16.00	32.00
38-Roy Rogers	25.00	70.00	140.00
39-Oswald the Rabbit('44)	10.00	30.00	60.00
40-Barney Google	5.00	15.00	30.00
41-Mother Goose & Nursery Rhyme Comics-All by Kelly	12.00	35.00	70.00
42-Tiny Tim (1934 reprints)	5.50	16.00	32.00
43-Popeye (1938-'42 reprints)	10.00	30.00	60.00
44-Terry & the Pirates	15.00	45.00	90.00
45-Raggedy Ann	10.00	28.00	56.00
46-Felix the Cat & the Haunted Castle	15.00	45.00	90.00
47-Gene Autry	14.00	40.00	80.00
48-Porky Pig of the Mounties by Carl Barks (7/44)	90.00	220.00	440.00
49-Snow White & the 7 Dwarfs	17.00	50.00	100.00
50-Fairy Tale Parade-Walt Kelly art (1944)	20.00	60.00	120.00
51-Bugs Bunny	15.00	45.00	90.00
52-Little Orphan Annie	8.00	24.00	48.00
53-Wash Tubbs	5.00	14.00	28.00
54-Andy Panda	10.00	28.00	56.00
55-Tillie the Toiler	3.50	10.00	20.00
56-Dick Tracy	12.00	35.00	70.00
57-Gene Autry	12.00	35.00	70.00
58-Smilin' Jack	7.00	20.00	40.00
59-Mother Goose & Nursery Rhyme Comics-Kelly c/a	8.00	24.00	48.00
60-Tiny Folks Funnies	5.50	16.00	32.00
61-Santa Claus Funnies(11/44)-Kelly art	15.00	45.00	90.00
62-Donald Duck-''Frozen Gold'' by Carl Barks (Disney) (1/45)	150.00	400.00	800.00
63-Roy Rogers	15.00	45.00	90.00
64-Smokey Stover	3.50	10.00	20.00
65-Smitty	3.50	10.00	20.00
66-Gene Autry	12.00	35.00	70.00
67-Oswald the Rabbit	7.00	20.00	40.00
68-Mother Goose by Walt Kelly	12.00	35.00	70.00
69-Fairy Tale Parade by Walt Kelly	15.00	45.00	90.00
70-Popeye and Wimpy	8.00	24.00	48.00
71-Three Caballeros by Walt Kelly(1945)-(Disney)	70.00	160.00	300.00
72-Raggedy Ann & Andy	8.00	24.00	48.00
73-The Gumps	3.00	8.00	16.00
74-Little Lulu	80.00	180.00	340.00
75-Gene Autry	10.00	30.00	60.00
76-Little Orphan Annie	7.00	20.00	40.00
77-Felix the Cat	12.00	35.00	70.00
78-Porky Pig & the Bandit Twins	7.00	20.00	40.00
79-Mickey Mouse in The Riddle of the Red Hat by Carl Barks(8/45) (Disney)	70.00	170.00	340.00
80-Smilin' Jack	5.00	15.00	30.00
81-Moon Mullins	3.50	10.00	20.00
82-Lone Ranger	12.00	35.00	70.00
83-Gene Autry	10.00	30.00	60.00
84-Flash Gordon by Alex Raymond-Reprints from ''The Fiery Desert''	35.00	90.00	180.00
85-Andy Panda & the Mad Dog Mystery	5.50	16.00	32.00
86-Roy Rogers	11.00	32.00	64.00
87-Fairy Tale Parade by Walt Kelly; Dan Noonan cover	14.00	40.00	80.00
88-Bugs Bunny	7.00	20.00	40.00
89-Tillie the Toiler	3.00	9.00	18.00
90-Xmas with Mother Goose by Walt Kelly (11/45)	12.00	35.00	70.00
91-Santa Claus Funnies by Walt Kelly (11/45)	12.00	35.00	70.00
92-Pinocchio(1945); Donald Duck by Kelly, 16 pgs. (Disney)	17.00	50.00	100.00
93-Gene Autry	8.00	24.00	48.00
94-Winnie Winkle (1945)	4.00	12.00	24.00
95-Roy Rogers	11.00	32.00	64.00
96-Dick Tracy	9.00	25.00	50.00
97-Little Lulu (1946)	40.00	90.00	160.00
98-Lone Ranger	10.00	30.00	60.00
99-Smitty	3.00	8.00	16.00
100-Gene Autry	8.00	24.00	48.00
101-Terry & the Pirates	10.00	28.00	56.00

Four Color #81, © N.Y. News Synd.

Four Color #96, © N.Y. News Synd.

Four Color #99, © N.Y. News Synd.

Four Color #103, © DELL

Four Color #128, © DELL

Four Color #143, © Walter Lantz

FOUR COLOR (continued)

NOTE: *No. 101 is last issue to carry ''Four Color'' logo on cover; all issues beginning with No. 100 are marked ''. . . O. S.'' (One Shot) which can be found in the bottom left-hand panel on the first page; the numbers following ''O. S.'' relate to the year/month issued.*

	Good	Fine	Mint
102-Oswald the Rabbit-Walt Kelly art, 1 pg.	7.00	20.00	40.00
103-Easter with Mother Goose by Walt Kelly	12.00	34.00	68.00
104-Fairy Tale Parade by Walt Kelly	12.00	34.00	68.00
105-Albert the Alligator & Pogo Possum by Kelly (4/46)	40.00	120.00	240.00
106-Tillie the Toiler	2.50	7.00	14.00
107-Little Orphan Annie	5.00	15.00	30.00
108-Donald Duck-''Terror of the River'' by Carl Barks (Disney) (1946)	100.00	240.00	480.00
109-Roy Rogers	8.00	24.00	48.00
110-Little Lulu	20.00	55.00	110.00
111-Captain Easy	4.00	12.00	24.00
112-Porky Pig's Adv. in Gopher Gulch	5.00	14.00	28.00
113-Popeye	3.50	10.00	20.00
114-Fairy Tale Parade by Walt Kelly	12.00	34.00	68.00
115-Little Lulu	20.00	55.00	110.00
116-Mickey Mouse & ''The House of Many Mysteries'' (Disney)	10.00	28.00	56.00
117-Roy Rogers	5.50	16.00	32.00
118-The Lone Ranger	10.00	30.00	60.00
119-Felix the Cat	9.00	25.00	50.00
120-Little Lulu	18.00	45.00	90.00
121-Fairy Tale Parade-(not Kelly)	7.00	20.00	40.00
122-Henry (10/46)	1.50	4.00	8.00
123-Bugs Bunny's Dangerous Venture	4.00	12.00	24.00
124-Roy Rogers	5.50	16.00	32.00
125-The Lone Ranger	7.00	20.00	40.00
126-Christmas with Mother Goose by Walt Kelly (1946)	10.00	28.00	56.00
127-Popeye	3.50	10.00	20.00
128-Santa Claus Funnies-''Santa & the Angel'' by Gollub; ''A Mouse in the House'' by Kelly	10.00	28.00	56.00
129-Uncle Remus & Tales of Brer Rabbit(1946)(Disney)	8.00	24.00	48.00
130-Andy Panda	3.00	8.00	16.00
131-Little Lulu	18.00	45.00	90.00
132-Tillie the Toiler('47)	2.50	7.00	14.00
133-Dick Tracy	7.00	20.00	40.00
134-Tarzan & the Devil Ogre	25.00	70.00	140.00
135-Felix the Cat	7.00	20.00	40.00
136-The Lone Ranger	7.00	20.00	40.00
137-Roy Rogers	5.50	16.00	32.00
138-Smitty	2.00	6.00	12.00

	Good	Fine	Mint
139-Little Lulu (1947)	14.00	40.00	80.00
140-Easter with Mother Goose by Walt Kelly	10.00	28.00	56.00
141-Mickey Mouse & the Submarine Pirates (Disney)	10.00	28.00	56.00
142-Bugs Bunny & the Haunted Mtn.	4.00	12.00	24.00
143-Oswald the Rabbit	3.00	8.00	16.00
144-Roy Rogers (1947)	5.50	16.00	32.00
145-Popeye	3.50	10.00	20.00
146-Little Lulu	14.00	40.00	80.00
147-Donald Duck in ''Volcano Valley'' by Carl Barks (Disney)(5/47)	70.00	160.00	320.00
148-Albert the Alligator & Pogo Possum by Walt Kelly	35.00	100.00	200.00
149-Smilin' Jack	4.00	12.00	24.00
150-Tillie the Toiler (6/47)	2.00	6.00	12.00
151-The Lone Ranger	5.50	16.00	32.00
152-Little Orphan Annie	4.00	12.00	24.00
153-Roy Rogers	4.00	12.00	24.00
154-Andy Panda	3.00	8.00	16.00
155-Henry (7/47)	1.50	4.00	8.00
156-Porky Pig & the Phantom	3.50	10.00	20.00
157-Mickey Mouse & ''The Beanstalk'' (Disney)	8.00	22.00	44.00
158-Little Lulu	14.00	40.00	80.00
159-Donald Duck in ''The Ghost of the Grotto'' by Carl Barks (Disney) (8/47)	60.00	140.00	280.00
160-Roy Rogers	4.00	12.00	24.00
161-Tarzan & the Fires of Tohr	20.00	60.00	120.00
162-Felix the Cat (9/47)	5.00	15.00	30.00
163-Dick Tracy	6.00	16.00	32.00
164-Bugs Bunny ''Finds the Frozen Kingdom''	4.00	12.00	24.00
165-Little Lulu	18.00	45.00	90.00
166-Roy Rogers	4.00	12.00	24.00
167-The Lone Ranger	5.50	16.00	32.00
168-Popeye (10/47)	3.50	10.00	20.00
169-Woody Woodpecker-''Manhunter in the North''; drug use story	3.00	9.00	18.00
170-Mickey Mouse on ''Spook's Island'' (11/47)(Disney)-reprinted in M. M. No. 103	8.00	22.00	44.00
171-Charlie McCarthy	2.00	6.00	12.00
172-Christmas with Mother Goose by Walt Kelly (11/47)	10.00	28.00	56.00
173-Flash Gordon	8.00	24.00	48.00
174-Winnie Winkle	2.50	7.00	14.00
175-Santa Claus Funnies by Walt Kelly ('47)	10.00	28.00	56.00
176-Tillie the Toiler (12/47)	2.00	6.00	12.00

Four Color #157, © WDP

Four Color #166, © Roy Rogers

Four Color #171, © DELL

Four Color #186, © WDP

Four Color #191, © L. Schlesinger

Four Color #195, © KING

FOUR COLOR (continued)	Good	Fine	Mint
177-Roy Rogers	4.00	12.00	24.00
178-Donald Duck in "Christmas on Bear Mtn." by Carl Barks; 1st app. Uncle Scrooge (Disney)(12/47)	60.00	140.00	280.00
179-Uncle Wiggily-Walt Kelly cover	5.00	14.00	28.00
180-Ozark Ike	4.00	12.00	24.00
181-Mickey Mouse in "Jungle Magic" (Disney)	8.00	22.00	44.00
182-Porky Pig (2/48)	3.50	10.00	20.00
183-Oswald the Rabbit	3.00	8.00	16.00
184-Tillie the Toiler	2.00	6.00	12.00
185-Easter with Mother Goose by Walt Kelly (1948)	10.00	28.00	56.00
186-Bambi (Disney)-Reprinted as Bambi No. 3('56)	5.00	14.00	28.00
187-Bugs Bunny-"The Dreadful Dragon"	3.00	9.00	18.00
188-Woody Woodpecker (5/48)	2.50	7.50	15.00
189-Donald Duck in "The Old Castle's Secret" by Carl Barks (Disney) (6/48)	60.00	140.00	280.00
190-Flash Gordon ('48)	8.00	24.00	48.00
191-Porky Pig "To the Rescue"	3.50	10.00	20.00
192-The Brownies by Walt Kelly (7/48)	8.00	24.00	48.00
193-Tom & Jerry (1948)	4.00	12.00	24.00
194-Mickey Mouse in "The World Under the Sea" (Disney)-Reprinted in M.M. No. 101	8.00	22.00	44.00
195-Tillie the Toiler	2.00	5.00	10.00
196-Charlie McCarthy	2.00	6.00	12.00
197-Spirit of the Border (Zane Grey) (1948)	3.00	8.00	16.00
198-Andy Panda	3.00	8.00	16.00
199-Donald Duck in "Sheriff of Bullet Valley" by Carl Barks; Barks draws himself on wanted poster, last page; used in ***Love & Death*** (Disney) (10/48)	60.00	140.00	280.00
200-Bugs Bunny-Super Sleuth (10/48)	3.00	9.00	18.00
201-Christmas with Mother Goose by Walt Kelly	7.00	20.00	40.00
202-Woody Woodpecker	1.50	4.00	8.00
203-Donald Duck in "The Golden Christmas Tree" by Carl Barks (Disney) (12/48)	40.00	90.00	180.00
204-Flash Gordon (1948)	6.00	18.00	36.00
205-Santa Claus Funnies by Walt Kelly	8.00	24.00	48.00
206-Little Orphan Annie	3.50	10.00	20.00
207-King of the Royal Mounted	5.50	16.00	32.00
208-Brer Rabbit Does It Again (Disney) (1/49)	5.00	14.00	28.00
209-Harold Teen	1.00	3.00	6.00
210-Tippie & Cap Stubbs	1.00	3.00	6.00
211-Little Beaver	2.00	5.00	10.00
212-Dr. Bobbs	1.00	3.00	6.00

	Good	Fine	Mint
213-Tillie the Toiler	2.00	5.00	10.00
214-Mickey Mouse & "His Sky Adventure"(2/49)(Disney)-Reprinted in M.M. No. 105	5.00	15.00	30.00
215-Sparkle Plenty (Dick Tracy reprints by Gould)	5.00	14.00	28.00
216-Andy Panda	1.50	4.50	9.00
217-Bugs Bunny in "Court Jester"	3.00	9.00	18.00
218-The Three Little Pigs (Disney)(3/49)	4.00	12.00	24.00
219-Swee'pea	4.00	12.00	24.00
220-Easter with Mother Goose by Walt Kelly	8.00	23.00	46.00
221-Uncle Wiggily-Walt Kelly cover in part	3.50	10.00	20.00
222-West of the Pecos (Zane Grey)	3.00	8.00	16.00
223-Donald Duck "Lost in the Andes" by Carl Barks (Disney-4/49) (Square egg story)	50.00	125.00	250.00
224-Little Iodine (4/49)	3.00	8.00	16.00
225-Oswald the Rabbit	2.00	5.00	10.00
226-Porky Pig & Spoofy, the Spook	2.50	7.00	14.00
227-Seven Dwarfs (Disney)	5.00	14.00	28.00
228-Mark of Zorro ('49)	6.00	18.00	36.00
229-Smokey Stover	1.50	4.00	8.00
230-Sunset Pass (Zane Grey)	3.00	8.00	16.00
231-Mickey Mouse & "The Rajah's Treasure" (Disney)	5.00	15.00	30.00
232-Woody Woodpecker (6/49)	1.50	4.00	8.00
233-Bugs Bunny-"Sleepwalking Sleuth"	3.00	9.00	18.00
234-Dumbo in "Sky Voyage" (Disney)	3.50	10.00	20.00
235-Tiny Tim	2.00	6.00	12.00
236-Heritage of the Desert (Zane Grey)('49)	3.00	8.00	16.00
237-Tillie the Toiler	2.00	5.00	10.00
238-Donald Duck in "Voodoo Hoodoo" by Carl Barks (Disney) (8/49)	30.00	70.00	140.00
239-Adventure Bound (8/49)	1.50	4.00	8.00
240-Andy Panda	1.50	4.50	9.00
241-Porky Pig	2.50	7.00	14.00
242-Tippie & Cap Stubbs	1.00	3.00	6.00
243-Thumper Follows His Nose (Disney)	3.50	10.00	20.00
244-The Brownies by Walt Kelly	8.00	24.00	48.00
245-Dick's Adventures in Dreamland (9/49)	2.00	5.00	10.00
246-Thunder Mountain (Zane Grey)	2.00	6.00	12.00
247-Flash Gordon	6.00	18.00	36.00
248-Mickey Mouse & "The Black Sorcerer" (Disney)	5.00	15.00	30.00
249-Woody Woodpecker-"The Globetrotter" (10/49)	1.50	4.00	8.00
250-Bugs Bunny-Used in **SOTI**, pg. 309	3.00	9.00	18.00
251-Hubert at Camp Moonbeam	1.50	4.00	8.00
252-Pinocchio(Disney)-not Kelly; origin	5.00	14.00	28.00

Four Color #201, © DELL

Four Color #224, © DELL

Four Color #232, © Walter Lantz

Four Color #261, © WDP

Four Color #271, © L. Schlesinger

Four Color #282, © WDP

FOUR COLOR (continued)	Good	Fine	Mint
253-Christmas with Mother Goose by Walt Kelly	7.00	20.00	40.00
254-Santa Claus Funnies by Walt Kelly; Pogo & Albert story by Kelly (11/49)	8.00	24.00	48.00
255-The Ranger (Zane Grey) (1949)	2.00	6.00	12.00
256-Donald Duck in "Luck of the North" by Carl Barks (Disney) (12/49)-Shows No. 257 on inside	30.00	70.00	140.00
257-Little Iodine	3.00	8.00	16.00
258-Andy Panda & "The Balloon Race"	1.50	4.50	9.00
259-Santa & the Angel (Gollub art-condensed from No. 128) & Santa at the Zoo (12/49)-two books in one	2.50	7.00	14.00
260-Porky Pig-"Hero of the Wild West" (12/49)	2.50	7.00	14.00
261-Mickey Mouse & "The Missing Key" (Disney)	5.00	15.00	30.00
262-Raggedy Ann & Andy	2.50	7.00	14.00
263-Donald Duck in "Land of the Totem Poles" by Carl Barks (Disney)(2/50)-has two Barks stories	30.00	70.00	140.00
264-Woody Woodpecker in "The Magic Lantern"	1.50	4.00	8.00
265-King of the Royal Mounted	4.00	12.00	24.00
266-Bugs Bunny-"Isle of Hercules"(2/50)-Reprinted in Best of B.B. No. 1	2.00	6.00	12.00
267-Little Beaver	1.20	3.50	7.00
268-Mickey Mouse's "Surprise Visitor" (1950) (Disney)	5.00	15.00	30.00
269-Johnny Mack Brown	3.50	10.00	20.00
270-Drift Fence (Zane Grey) (3/50)	2.00	6.00	12.00
271-Porky Pig-"Phantom of the Plains"	2.50	7.00	14.00
272-Cinderella (Disney)(4/50)	3.50	10.00	20.00
273-Oswald the Rabbit	2.00	5.00	10.00
274-Bugs Bunny-"Hair Brained Reporter"	2.00	6.00	12.00
275-Donald Duck in "Ancient Persia" by Carl Barks (Disney) (5/50)	25.00	60.00	120.00
276-Uncle Wiggily	2.00	6.00	12.00
277-Porky Pig-"Desert Adventure" (5/50)	2.50	7.00	14.00
278-Bill Elliott	3.00	8.00	16.00
279-Mickey Mouse & Pluto Battle the Giant Ants (Disney)-Reprinted in M.M. No. 102	4.00	12.00	24.00
280-Andy Panda	1.50	4.50	9.00
281-Bugs Bunny-"In the Great Circus Mystery"	2.00	6.00	12.00
282-Donald Duck and "The Pixilated Parrot" by Carl Barks (Disney)	25.00	60.00	120.00
283-King of the Royal Mounted (7/50)	4.00	12.00	24.00
284-Porky Pig-"Kingdom of Nowhere"	2.50	7.00	14.00
285-Bozo the Clown & His Minikin Circus (TV)	1.50	4.00	8.00
286-Mickey Mouse-"& the Uninvited Guest" (Disney)	4.00	12.00	24.00
287-Gene Autry's Champion	1.50	4.50	9.00
288-Woody Woodpecker-"Klondike Gold"	1.50	4.00	8.00
289-Bugs Bunny in Indian Trouble	2.00	6.00	12.00
290-The Chief	1.50	4.00	8.00
291-Donald Duck in "The Magic Hourglass" by Carl Barks (Disney) (9/50)	25.00	60.00	120.00
292-The Cisco Kid	3.00	8.00	16.00
293-The Brownies-Kelly cover/art	8.00	24.00	48.00
294-Little Beaver	1.20	3.50	7.00
295-Porky Pig in "President Porky" (9/50)	2.50	7.00	14.00
296-Mickey Mouse in "Private Eye for Hire" (Disney)	4.00	12.00	24.00
297-Andy Panda (10/50)	1.50	4.50	9.00
298-Bugs Bunny "Sheik for a Day"	2.00	6.00	12.00
299-Buck Jones	3.00	9.00	18.00
300-Donald Duck in "Big-Top Bedlam" by Carl Barks (Disney) (11/50)	25.00	60.00	120.00
301-The Mysterious Rider (Zane Grey)	2.00	6.00	12.00
302-Santa Claus Funnies (11/50)	1.50	4.50	9.00
303-Porky Pig in "The Land of the Monstrous Flies"	1.50	4.00	8.00
304-Mickey Mouse in "Tom-Tom Island" (Disney) (12/50)	3.50	10.00	20.00
305-Woody Woodpecker	1.20	3.50	7.00
306-Raggedy Ann	2.00	6.00	12.00
307-Bugs Bunny-"Lumber Jack Rabbit"	1.50	4.00	8.00
308-Donald Duck in "Dangerous Disguise" by Carl Barks (Disney) (1/51)	18.00	45.00	90.00
309-Dollface & Her Gang ('51)	1.20	3.50	7.00
310-King of the Royal Mounted (1/51)	3.00	8.00	16.00
311-Porky Pig in "Midget Horses of Hidden Valley"	1.50	4.00	8.00
312-Tonto (No.1)	3.50	10.00	20.00
313-Mickey Mouse(No.1) in "The Mystery of the Double-Cross Ranch" (Disney)	3.50	10.00	20.00
314-Ambush (Zane Grey)	2.00	6.00	12.00
315-Oswald the Rabbit	1.00	3.00	6.00
316-Rex Allen (No.1)	3.00	8.00	16.00
317-Bugs Bunny in "Hare Today Gone Tomorrow" (No.1)	1.50	4.00	8.00
318-Donald Duck in "No Such Varmint" by Carl Barks (No. 1) (Disney)	18.00	45.00	90.00
319-Gene Autry's Champion	1.50	4.00	8.00
320-Uncle Wiggily	1.50	4.50	9.00

Four Color #294, © KING

Four Color #307, © L. Schlesinger

Four Color #315, © Walter Lantz

Four Color #322, © L. Schlesinger

Four Color #345, © Walter Lantz

Four Color #355, © L. Schlesinger

FOUR COLOR (continued)	Good	Fine	Mint
321-The Little Scouts	.85	2.50	5.00
322-Porky Pig (No.1)	1.50	4.00	8.00
323-Suzie Q. Smith (3/51)	1.00	3.00	6.00
324-I Met a Handsome Cowboy (3/51)	3.00	8.00	16.00
325-Mickey Mouse (No.2) in "The Haunted Castle" (Disney)(4/51)	3.50	10.00	20.00
326-Andy Panda	1.00	3.00	6.00
327-Bugs Bunny	1.50	4.00	8.00
328-Donald Duck in "Old California"(No.2) by Carl Barks-Peyote drug use issue (Disney) (5/51)	20.00	55.00	110.00
329-Trigger (5/51)-Photo-c	2.50	7.00	14.00
330-Porky Pig (No.2)	1.50	4.00	8.00
331-Alice in Wonderland (Disney) (1951)	3.50	10.00	20.00
332-Little Beaver	1.20	3.50	7.00
333-Wilderness Trek (Zane Grey) (5/51)	2.00	6.00	12.00
334-Mickey Mouse & "Yukon Gold" (Disney) (6/51)	3.50	10.00	20.00
335-Francis the Mule	.80	2.40	4.80
336-Woody Woodpecker	1.20	3.50	7.00
337-The Brownies-not by Walt Kelly	2.00	5.00	10.00
338-Bugs Bunny	1.50	4.00	8.00
339-Donald Duck and "The Magic Fountain"-not by Carl Barks (Disney) (7-8/51)	3.50	10.00	20.00
340-King of the Royal Mounted (7/51)	3.00	8.00	16.00
341-Unbirthday Party with Alice in Wonderland (Disney) (7/51)	3.50	10.00	20.00
342-Porky Pig	.85	2.50	5.00
343-Mickey Mouse in "The Ruby Eye of Homar-Guy-Am" (Disney)-Reprinted in M.M. No. 104	3.00	8.00	16.00
344-Sgt. Preston (TV)	2.00	5.00	10.00
345-Andy Panda in Scotland Yard (8-10/51)	1.00	3.00	6.00
346-Hideout (Zane Grey)	2.00	6.00	12.00
347-Bugs Bunny-"The Frigid Hare" (8-9/51)	1.50	4.00	8.00
348-Donald Duck "The Crocodile Collector"-Barks cover only (Disney) (9-10/51)	4.50	13.00	26.00
349-Uncle Wiggily	1.50	4.50	9.00
350-Woody Woodpecker	1.20	3.50	7.00
351-Porky Pig-"Grand Canyon Giant" (9-10/51)	.85	2.50	5.00
352-Mickey Mouse-"The Mystery of Painted Valley" (Disney)	3.00	8.00	16.00
353-Duck Album-Barks cover (Disney)	2.00	5.00	10.00
354-Raggedy Ann & Andy	2.00	6.00	12.00
355-Bugs Bunny Hot-Rod Hare	1.50	4.00	8.00
356-Donald Duck in "Rags to Riches"-Barks cover only (Disney)	4.50	13.00	26.00

	Good	Fine	Mint
357-Comeback (Zane Grey)	1.50	4.00	8.00
358-Andy Panda (11-1/52)	1.00	3.00	6.00
359-Frosty the Snowman	1.00	3.00	6.00
360-Porky Pig-"In Tree of Fortune" (11-12/51)	.85	2.50	5.00
361-Santa Claus Funnies	1.50	4.50	9.00
362-Mickey Mouse & "The Smuggled Diamonds" (Disney)	3.00	8.00	16.00
363-King of the Royal Mounted	2.50	7.00	14.00
364-Woody Woodpecker	.85	2.50	5.00
365-The Brownies-not by Kelly	2.00	5.00	10.00
366-Bugs Bunny-"Uncle Buckskin Comes to Town" (12-1/52)	1.50	4.00	8.00
367-Donald Duck in "A Christmas for Shacktown" by Carl Barks (Disney) (1-2/52)	18.00	45.00	90.00
368-Beany & Cecil (1/52)	3.00	9.00	18.00
369-The Lone Ranger's Famous Horse Hi-Yo Silver; Silver's origin	2.00	5.00	10.00
370-Porky Pig "Trouble in the Big Trees"	.85	2.50	5.00
371-Mickey Mouse-"The Inca Idol Case" ('52) (Disney)	3.00	8.00	16.00
372-Riders of the Purple Sage (Zane Grey)	2.00	4.00	8.00
373-Sgt. Preston (TV)	2.00	5.00	10.00
374-Woody Woodpecker	.85	2.50	5.00
375-John Carter of Mars (E. R. Burroughs)-Jesse Marsh art; origin	7.00	20.00	40.00
376-Bugs Bunny	1.50	4.00	8.00
377-Suzie Q. Smith	1.00	3.00	6.00
378-Tom Corbett, Space Cadet (TV)-McWilliams art	2.50	7.00	14.00
379-Donald Duck in "Southern Hospitality"-not by Barks (Disney)	3.50	10.00	20.00
380-Raggedy Ann & Andy	2.00	6.00	12.00
381-Tubby (No.1)	8.00	24.00	48.00
382-Snow White & 7 Dwarfs (Disney)-origin; partial reprint of 4-Color No. 49 (Movie)	4.00	12.00	24.00
383-Andy Panda	.70	2.00	4.00
384-King of the Royal Mounted (3/52)	2.50	7.00	14.00
385-Porky Pig-"The Isle of Missing Ships" (3-4/52)	.85	2.50	5.00
386-Uncle Scrooge No. 1 by Carl Barks (Disney) in "Only a Poor Old Man" (3/52)	100.00	240.00	400.00
387-Mickey Mouse in "High Tibet" (Disney) (4-5/52)	3.00	8.00	16.00
388-Oswald the Rabbit	1.00	3.00	6.00
389-Andy Hardy	1.00	3.00	6.00
390-Woody Woodpecker	.85	2.50	5.00

Four Color #361, © DELL

Four Color #374, © Walter Lantz

Four Color #387, © WDP

Four Color #394, © WDP

Four Color #403, © WDP

Four Color #413, © WDP

FOUR COLOR (continued)	Good	Fine	Mint
391-Uncle Wiggily	1.20	3.50	7.00
392-Hi-Yo Silver	2.00	5.00	10.00
393-Bugs Bunny	1.50	4.00	8.00
394-Donald Duck in ''Malayalaya''-Barks cover only (Disney)	4.50	13.00	26.00
395-Forlorn River (Zane Grey) (1952)-First Nevada (5/52)	1.50	4.00	8.00
396-Tales of the Texas Rangers (TV)	2.00	6.00	12.00
397-Sgt. Preston (TV)(5/52)	2.00	5.00	10.00
398-The Brownies-not by Kelly	2.00	5.00	10.00
399-Porky Pig in ''The Lost Gold Mine''	.85	2.50	5.00
400-Tom Corbett-Space Cadet (TV)-McWilliams art	2.50	7.00	14.00
401-Mickey Mouse & Goofy's Mechanical Wizard (Disney) (6-7/52)	2.00	6.00	12.00
402-Mary Jane & Sniffles	2.00	5.00	10.00
403-Li'l Bad Wolf (Disney) (6/52)	1.50	4.00	8.00
404-The Range Rider (TV)	1.50	4.00	8.00
405-Woody Woodpecker	.85	2.50	5.00
406-Tweety & Sylvester	.70	2.00	4.00
407-Bugs Bunny ''Foreign-Legion Hare''	1.20	3.50	7.00
408-Donald Duck and ''The Golden Helmet'' by Carl Barks (Disney) (7-8/52)	15.00	40.00	80.00
409-Andy Panda (7-9/52)	.70	2.00	4.00
410-Porky Pig in ''The Water Wizard''	.85	2.50	5.00
411-Mickey Mouse & ''The Old Sea Dog'' (Disney) (8-9/52)	2.00	6.00	12.00
412-Nevada (Zane Grey)	1.50	4.00	8.00
413-Robin Hood (Disney-Movie) (8/52)	2.00	5.00	10.00
414-Beany & Cecil (TV)('52)	2.00	6.00	12.00
415-Rootie Kazootie (TV)	1.20	3.50	7.00
416-Woody Woodpecker	.85	2.50	5.00
417-Double Trouble with Goober	.70	2.00	4.00
418-Rusty Riley-A Boy, a Horse, and a Dog-Frank Godwin art (strip reprints) (8/52)	1.00	3.00	6.00
419-Sgt. Preston (TV)	2.00	5.00	10.00
420-Bugs Bunny-''Mysterious Buckaroo'' (8-9/52)	1.20	3.50	7.00
421-Tom Corbett-Space Cadet (TV)-McWilliams art	2.50	7.00	14.00
422-Donald Duck and ''The Gilded Man'' by Carl Barks (Disney) (9-10/52) (No.423 on inside)	15.00	40.00	80.00
423-Rhubarb, Owner of the Brooklyn Ball Club (The Millionaire Cat)	.70	2.00	4.00
424-Flash Gordon-Test Flight in Space (9/52)	4.00	12.00	24.00
425-Zorro, the Return of	3.50	10.00	20.00

	Good	Fine	Mint
426-Porky Pig in ''The Scalawag Leprechaun''	.85	2.50	5.00
427-Mickey Mouse & ''The Wonderful Whizzix'' (Disney) (10-11/52)-reprinted in M.M. No. 100	2.00	6.00	12.00
428-Uncle Wiggily	1.00	3.00	6.00
429-Pluto in ''Why Dogs Leave Home'' (Disney)(10/52)	1.20	3.50	7.00
430-Tubby	4.00	12.00	24.00
431-Woody Woodpecker (10/52)	.85	2.50	5.00
432-Bugs Bunny & ''The Rabbit Olympics''	1.20	3.50	7.00
433-Wildfire (Zane Grey)	1.50	4.00	8.00
434-Rin Tin Tin-''In Dark Danger'' (11/52)	1.20	3.50	7.00
435-Frosty the Snowman	1.00	3.00	6.00
436-The Brownies-not by Kelly (11/52)	1.50	4.00	8.00
437-John Carter of Mars (E. R. Burroughs)-art by Marsh	5.50	16.00	32.00
438-Annie Oakley (TV)	2.00	5.00	10.00
439-Little Hiawatha (Disney) (12/52)	1.50	4.00	8.00
440-Black Beauty (12/52)	1.50	4.00	8.00
441-Fearless Fagan	.85	2.50	5.00
442-Peter Pan (Disney) (Movie)	3.50	10.00	20.00
443-Ben Bowie	1.00	3.00	6.00
444-Tubby	4.00	12.00	24.00
445-Charlie McCarthy	1.00	3.00	6.00
446-Captain Hook & Peter Pan (Disney) (Movie) (1/53)	3.50	10.00	20.00
447-Andy Hardy	.70	2.00	4.00
448-Beany & Cecil (TV)	2.00	6.00	12.00
449-Tappan's Burro (Zane Grey) (2-4/53)	1.50	4.00	8.00
450-Duck Album-Barks cover (Disney)	2.00	5.00	10.00
451-Rusty Riley-Frank Godwin art (strip reprints) (2/53)	1.00	3.00	6.00
452-Raggedy Ann & Andy ('53)	2.00	6.00	12.00
453-Suzie Q. Smith (2/53)	.85	2.50	5.00
454-Krazy Kat-not by Herriman (2/53)	1.50	4.00	8.00
455-Johnny Mack Brown (3/53)	1.50	4.00	8.00
456-Uncle Scrooge in ''Back to the Klondike'' (No.2) by Barks (3/53)	50.00	120.00	200.00
457-Daffy Duck	.60	1.80	3.60
458-Oswald the Rabbit	.70	2.00	4.00
459-Rootie Kazootie (TV)	1.20	3.50	7.00
460-Buck Jones (4/53)	1.50	4.50	9.00
461-Tubby	4.00	12.00	24.00
462-Little Scouts	.50	1.50	3.00
463-Petunia Pig (4/53)	.85	2.50	5.00
464-Bozo (4/53)	.70	2.00	4.00
465-Francis the Mule	.50	1.50	3.00

Four Color #433, © DELL

Four Color #455, © DELL

Four Color #463, © L. Schlesinger

Four Color #473, © WDP

Four Color #485, © DELL

Four Color #501, © DELL

FOUR COLOR (continued)	Good	Fine	Mint
466-Rhubarb, the Millionaire Cat	.55	1.60	3.20
467-Desert Gold (Zane Grey) (5-7/53)	1.50	4.00	8.00
468-Goofy (Disney)	1.20	3.50	7.00
469-Beetle Bailey (5/53)	.70	2.00	4.00
470-Elmer Fudd	.85	2.50	5.00
471-Double Trouble With Goober	.70	2.00	4.00
472-Wild Bill Elliott (6/53)	1.50	4.50	9.00
473-Li'l Bad Wolf (Disney)	1.00	3.00	6.00
474-Mary Jane & Sniffles	1.50	4.00	8.00
475-The Two Mouseketeers	.50	1.50	3.00
476-Rin Tin Tin	1.20	3.50	7.00
477-Beany & Cecil (TV)	2.00	6.00	12.00
478-Charlie McCarthy	1.00	3.00	6.00
479-Dale Evans	2.00	6.00	12.00
480-Andy Hardy	.70	2.00	4.00
481-Annie Oakley (TV)	1.50	4.00	8.00
482-Brownies-not by Kelly	1.00	3.00	6.00
483-Little Beaver ('53)	1.00	3.00	6.00
484-River Feud (Zane Grey) (8-10/53)	1.50	4.00	8.00
485-The Little People-Walt Scott	1.00	3.00	6.00
486-Rusty Riley-Frank Godwin strip reprints	1.00	3.00	6.00
487-Mowgli, the Jungle Book (Rudyard Kipling's)	1.50	4.00	8.00
488-John Carter of Mars (Burroughs)-Marsh art	5.00	14.00	28.00
489-Tweety & Sylvester	.70	2.00	4.00
490-Jungle Jim	1.50	4.00	8.00
491-Silvertip (Max Brand)-Kinstler art (8/53)	2.00	5.00	10.00
492-Duck Album (Disney)	1.20	3.50	7.00
493-Johnny Mack Brown	1.50	4.00	8.00
494-The Little King	.85	2.50	5.00
495-Uncle Scrooge (No.3)(Disney)-by Carl Barks (9/53)	35.00	90.00	160.00
496-The Green Hornet	3.50	10.00	20.00
497-Zorro (Sword of . . .)	3.50	10.00	20.00
498-Bugs Bunny's Album (9/53)	.85	2.50	5.00
499-Spike & Tyke (9/53)	.70	2.00	4.00
500-Buck Jones	1.50	4.50	9.00
501-Francis the Mule	.50	1.50	3.00
502-Rootie Kazootie (TV)	1.20	3.50	7.00
503-Uncle Wiggily (10/53)	1.00	3.00	6.00
504-Krazy Kat-not by Herriman	1.50	4.00	8.00
505-The Sword & the Rose (Disney) (10/53) (TV)	1.50	4.00	8.00
506-The Little Scouts	.50	1.50	3.00
507-Oswald the Rabbit	.70	2.00	4.00
508-Bozo (10/53)	.70	2.00	4.00

	Good	Fine	Mint
509-Pluto (Disney) (10/53)	1.20	3.50	7.00
510-Son of Black Beauty	1.00	3.00	6.00
511-Outlaw Trail (Zane Grey)-Kinstler-a	2.00	5.00	10.00
512-Flash Gordon (11/53)	3.00	8.00	16.00
513-Ben Bowie's Mountain Men (11/53)	.85	2.50	5.00
514-Frosty the Snowman	.85	2.50	5.00
515-Andy Hardy	.70	2.00	4.00
516-Double Trouble With Goober	.70	2.00	4.00
517-Chip 'N' Dale (Disney)	.70	2.00	4.00
518-Rivets (11/53)	.70	2.00	4.00
519-Steve Canyon-not by Milton Caniff	2.00	6.00	12.00
520-Wild Bill Elliott	1.50	4.50	9.00
521-Beetle Bailey (12/53)	.70	2.00	4.00
522-The Brownies	1.00	3.00	6.00
523-Rin Tin Tin	1.20	3.50	7.00
524-Tweety & Sylvester	.70	2.00	4.00
525-Santa Claus Funnies	.70	2.00	4.00
526-Napoleon	.70	2.00	4.00
527-Charlie McCarthy	1.00	3.00	6.00
528-Dale Evans	2.00	5.00	10.00
529-Little Beaver	1.00	3.00	6.00
530-Beany & Cecil (1/54)	2.00	6.00	12.00
531-Duck Album (Disney)	1.20	3.50	7.00
532-The Rustlers (Zane Grey) (2-4/54)	1.50	4.00	8.00
533-Raggedy Ann & Andy	2.00	6.00	12.00
534-Western Marshal (Ernest Haycox's)-Kinstler-a	2.00	6.00	12.00
535-I Love Lucy (TV) (2/54)	1.50	4.00	8.00
536-Daffy (3/54)	.60	1.80	3.60
537-Stormy, the Thoroughbred . . . (Disney-Movie) on top ⅔ of each page; Pluto story on bottom ⅓ of each page (2/54)	2.00	5.00	10.00
538-Zorro (Mask of . . .)-Kinstler-a	4.00	12.00	24.00
539-Ben & Me (Disney)	.85	2.50	5.00
540-Knights of the Round Table (3/54) (Movie)	2.00	6.00	12.00
541-Johnny Mack Brown	1.50	4.00	8.00
542-Super Circus Featuring Mary Hartline (TV) (3/54)	1.00	3.00	6.00
543-Uncle Wiggily (3/54)	1.00	3.00	6.00
544-Rob Roy (Disney-Movie)-Manning-a	2.00	5.00	10.00
545-Pinocchio-Partial reprint of 4-Color 92 (Disney-Movie)	2.00	6.00	12.00
546-Buck Jones	1.50	4.50	9.00
547-Francis the Mule	.50	1.50	3.00
548-Krazy Kat-not by Herriman (4/54)	1.20	3.50	7.00
549-Oswald the Rabbit	.70	2.00	4.00

Four Color #536, © DELL

Four Color #540, © DELL

Four Color #549, © Walter Lantz

FOUR COLOR (continued)	Good	Fine	Mint
550-The Little Scouts	.50	1.50	3.00
551-Bozo (4/54)	.70	2.00	4.00
552-Beetle Bailey	.70	2.00	4.00
553-Suzie Q. Smith	.85	2.50	5.00
554-Rusty Riley (Frank Godwin strip reprints)	1.00	3.00	6.00
555-Range War (Zane Grey)	1.50	4.00	8.00
556-Double Trouble With Goober (5/54)	.70	2.00	4.00
557-Ben Bowie & His Mountain Men	.85	2.50	5.00
558-Elmer Fudd (5/54)	.85	2.50	5.00
559-I Love Lucy (TV)	1.50	4.00	8.00
560-Duck Album (Disney)	1.20	3.50	7.00
561-Mr. Magoo (5/54)	1.20	3.50	7.00
562-Goofy (Disney)	1.20	3.50	7.00
563-Rhubarb, the Millionaire Cat (6/54)	.50	1.50	3.00
564-Li'l Bad Wolf (Disney)	1.00	3.00	6.00
565-Jungle Jim	1.50	4.00	8.00
566-Son of Black Beauty	1.00	3.00	6.00
567-Prince Valiant-by Bob Fuje (Movie)	4.00	12.00	24.00
568-Gypsy Colt (Movie)	1.50	4.00	8.00
569-Priscilla's Pop	.55	1.60	3.20
570-Beany & Cecil (TV)	2.00	6.00	12.00
571-Charlie McCarthy	1.00	3.00	6.00
572-Silvertip (Max Brand)(7/54)	1.20	3.50	7.00
573-The Little People by Walt Scott	.70	2.00	4.00
574-Zorro (Hand of . . .)	3.50	10.00	20.00
575-Annie Oakley (TV)	1.50	4.00	8.00
576-Angel (8/54)	.55	1.60	3.20
577-Spike & Tyke	.70	2.00	4.00
578-Steve Canyon (8/54)	2.00	6.00	12.00
579-Francis the Talking Mule	.50	1.50	3.00
580-Six Gun Ranch (Luke Short-8/54)	1.00	3.00	6.00
581-Chip 'N' Dale (Disney)	.70	2.00	4.00
582-Mowgli-Jungle Book	1.00	3.00	6.00
583-The Lost Wagon Train (Zane Grey)	1.50	4.00	8.00
584-Johnny Mack Brown	1.50	4.00	8.00
585-Bugs Bunny's Album	.85	2.50	5.00
586-Duck Album (Disney)	1.20	3.50	7.00
587-The Little Scouts	.50	1.50	3.00
588-King Richard & the Crusaders (Movie) (10/54) Matt Baker-a	2.00	6.00	12.00
589-Buck Jones	1.50	4.50	9.00
590-Hansel & Gretel	1.50	4.00	8.00
591-Western Marshal (Ernest Haycox's)-Kinstler-a	2.00	6.00	12.00
592-Super Circus (TV)	1.00	3.00	6.00
593-Oswald the Rabbit	.70	2.00	4.00
594-Bozo (10/54)	.70	2.00	4.00
595-Pluto (Disney)	.70	2.00	4.00
596-Turok, Son of Stone (No.1)	8.00	24.00	48.00
597-The Little King	.70	2.00	4.00
598-Captain Davy Jones	.85	2.50	5.00
599-Ben Bowie & His Mountain Men (11/54)	.85	2.50	5.00
600-Daisy Duck's Diary (Disney) (11/54)	1.00	3.00	6.00
601-Frosty the Snowman	.85	2.50	5.00
602-Mr. Magoo & Gerald McBoing-Boing	1.20	3.50	7.00
603-The Two Mouseketeers	.50	1.50	3.00
604-Shadow on the Trail (Zane Grey)	1.50	4.00	8.00
605-The Brownies-not by Kelly (12/54)	1.00	3.00	6.00
606-Sir Lancelot (not TV)-J. Buscema-a	2.00	6.00	12.00
607-Santa Claus Funnies	.70	2.00	4.00
608-Silvertip-Valley of Vanishing Men (Max Brand)-Kinstler-a	2.00	5.00	10.00
609-The Littlest Outlaw (Disney-Movie) (1/55)	2.00	5.00	10.00
610-Drum Beat (Movie); Alan Ladd photo-c	1.00	3.00	6.00
611-Duck Album (Disney)	1.20	3.50	7.00
612-Little Beaver (1/55)	.70	2.00	4.00
613-Western Marshal (Ernest Haycox's) (2/55)-Kinstler-a	2.00	6.00	12.00
614-20,000 Leagues Under the Sea (Disney) (Movie) (2/55)	2.00	6.00	12.00
615-Daffy	.60	1.80	3.60
616-To the Last Man (Zane Grey)	1.50	4.00	8.00
617-Zorro (Quest of . . .)	3.50	10.00	20.00
618-Johnny Mack Brown	1.50	4.00	8.00
619-Krazy Kat-not by Herriman	1.20	3.50	7.00
620-Mowgli-Jungle Book	1.00	3.00	6.00
621-Francis the Talking Mule (4/55)	.50	1.50	3.00
622-Beetle Bailey	.70	2.00	4.00
623-Oswald the Rabbit	.50	1.50	3.00
624-Treasure Island (Disney-Movie) (4/55)	1.50	4.00	8.00
625-Beaver Valley (Disney-Movie)	.85	2.50	5.00
626-Ben Bowie & His Mountain Men	.85	2.50	5.00
627-Goofy (Disney) (5/55)	1.20	3.50	7.00
628-Elmer Fudd	.85	2.50	5.00
629-Lady & the Tramp with Jock (Disney) (5/55)	1.50	4.00	8.00
630-Priscilla's Pop	.55	1.60	3.20
631-Davy Crockett (Disney)(5/55)(. . . Indian Fighter)(TV)	1.00	3.00	6.00
632-Fighting Caravans (Zane Grey)	1.50	4.00	8.00
633-The Little People by Walt Scott	.70	2.00	4.00
634-Lady & the Tramp Album (Disney) (6/55)	1.20	3.50	7.00
635-Beany & Cecil (TV)	2.00	6.00	12.00
636-Chip 'N' Dale (Disney)	.70	2.00	4.00
637-Silvertip (Max Brand)-Kinstler-a	2.00	5.00	10.00
638-Spike & Tyke (8/55)	.70	2.00	4.00
639-Davy Crockett (Disney) (7/55) (. . . at the Alamo) (TV)	1.00	3.00	6.00
640-Western Marshal (Ernest Haycox's)-Kinstler-a	2.00	6.00	12.00
641-Steve Canyon ('55)-by Caniff	2.00	6.00	12.00
642-The Two Mouseketeers	.50	1.50	3.00
643-Wild Bill Elliott	1.50	4.50	9.00
644-Sir Walter Raleigh (5/55)-Based on movie "The Virgin Queen"	2.00	5.00	10.00
645-Johnny Mack Brown	1.50	4.00	8.00
646-Dotty Dripple & Taffy	1.00	3.00	6.00
647-Bugs Bunny Album (9/55)	.70	2.00	4.00
648-Texas Rangers (Jace Pearson's)	1.50	4.00	8.00
649-Duck Album (Disney)	1.20	3.50	7.00
650-Prince Valiant - by Bob Fuje	3.00	8.00	16.00
651-King Colt (Luke Short)(9/55)-Kinstler-a	1.20	3.50	7.00
652-Buck Jones	1.00	3.00	6.00
653-Smokey the Bear (10/55)	.70	2.00	4.00
654-Pluto (Disney)	.70	2.00	4.00
655-Francis the Talking Mule (10/55)	.50	1.50	3.00
656-Turok, Son of Stone (No.2) (10/55)	6.00	16.00	32.00
657-Ben Bowie & His Mountain Men	.85	2.50	5.00
658-Goofy (Disney)	1.20	3.50	7.00
659-Daisy Duck's Diary	1.00	3.00	6.00
660-Little Beaver	.70	2.00	4.00
661-Frosty the Snowman	.85	2.50	5.00
662-Zoo Parade (TV)-Marlin Perkins (11/55)	.55	1.60	3.20
663-Winky Dink (TV)	.50	1.50	3.00
664-Davy Crockett in the Great Keelboat Race (TV) (Disney)(11/55)	1.50	4.00	8.00
665-The African Lion (Disney-Movie) (11/55)	1.00	3.00	6.00
666-Santa Claus Funnies	.70	2.00	4.00
667-Silvertip & the Stolen Stallion (Max Brand) (12/55)-Kinstler-a	1.20	3.50	7.00
668-Dumbo (Disney) (12/55)	1.50	4.00	8.00
668-Dumbo (Disney) (1/58) different cover, same contents	1.50	4.00	8.00
669-Robin Hood (Disney-Movie) (12/55)-reprint of No. 413	1.50	4.00	8.00
670-M.G.M's Mouse Musketeers (1/56)-Formerly the Two Mouseketeers	.50	1.50	3.00
671-Davy Crockett & the River Pirates (TV) (Disney) (12/55)-Jesse Marsh art	1.50	4.00	8.00

Four Color #628, © L. Schlesinger

Four Color #640, © DELL

Four Color #660, © KING

Four Color #685, © DELL

Four Color #734, © DELL

Four Color #778, © DELL

FOUR COLOR (continued)	Good	Fine	Mint
672-Quentin Durward (1/56) (Movie)	2.00	5.00	10.00
673-Buffalo Bill, Jr. (TV)	1.00	3.00	6.00
674-The Little Rascals	.70	2.00	4.00
675-Steve Donovan, Western Marshal (TV)-Kinstler-a	1.50	4.50	9.00
676-Will-Yum!	.55	1.60	3.20
677-Little King	.70	2.00	4.00
678-The Last Hunt (Movie)	1.50	4.00	8.00
679-Gunsmoke (TV)	1.00	3.00	6.00
680-Out Our Way with the Worry Wart (2/56)	.70	2.00	4.00
681-Forever, Darling (Movie) with Lucille Ball & Desi Arnaz (2/56)	1.00	3.00	6.00
682-When Knighthood Was in Flower (Disney-Movie)-Reprint of No. 505	2.00	5.00	10.00
683-Hi & Lois (3/56)	.55	1.60	3.20
684-Helen of Troy (Movie)-Buscema-a	3.00	8.00	16.00
685-Johnny Mack Brown	1.50	4.00	8.00
686-Duck Album (Disney)	1.20	3.60	7.00
687-The Indian Fighter (Movie)	1.50	4.00	8.00
688-Alexander the Great (Movie) (5/56) Buscema-a; photo-c	2.00	5.00	10.00
689-Elmer Fudd (3/56)	.85	2.50	5.00
690-The Conqueror (Movie) - John Wayne	2.00	6.00	12.00
691-Dotty Dripple & Taffy	1.00	3.00	6.00
692-The Little People-Walt Scott	.70	2.00	4.00
693-Song of the South (Disney)(1956)-Partial reprint of No. 129	1.50	4.00	8.00
694-Super Circus (TV)	1.00	3.00	6.00
695-Little Beaver	.70	2.00	4.00
696-Krazy Kat-not by Herriman (4/56)	1.20	3.50	7.00
697-Oswald the Rabbit	.50	1.50	3.00
698-Francis the Talking Mule	.50	1.50	3.00
699-Prince Valiant-by Bob Fuje	3.00	8.00	16.00
700-Water Birds & the Olympic Elk (Disney-Movie)(4/56)	1.50	4.00	8.00
701-Jiminy Crickett (Disney) (5/56)	1.00	3.00	6.00
702-The Goofy Success Story (Disney)	.85	2.50	5.00
703-Scamp (Disney)	.55	1.60	3.20
704-Priscilla's Pop (5/56)	.55	1.60	3.20
705-Brave Eagle	.85	2.50	5.00
706-Bongo & Lumpjaw (Disney)(6/56)	.85	2.50	5.00
707-Corky & White Shadow (Disney)(5/56)-Mickey Mouse Club (TV)	.85	2.50	5.00
708-Smokey the Bear	.70	2.00	4.00
709-The Searchers (Movie) - John Wayne	2.00	6.00	12.00
710-Francis the Mule	.50	1.50	3.00
711-M.G.M's Mouse Musketeers	.50	1.50	3.00
712-The Great Locomotive Chase (Disney-Movie) (9/56)	2.00	5.00	10.00
713-The Animal World (Movie) (8/56)	1.50	4.00	8.00
714-Spin & Marty (TV)(Disney)-Mickey Mouse Club (6/56)	.85	2.50	5.00
715-Timmy (8/56)	.50	1.50	3.00
716-Man in Space (Disney-Movie)	1.50	4.00	8.00
717-Moby Dick (Movie)	2.00	6.00	12.00
718-Dotty Dripple & Taffy	1.00	3.00	6.00
719-Prince Valiant - by Bob Fuje	3.00	8.00	16.00
720-Gunsmoke (TV)	.85	2.50	5.00
721-Capt. Kangaroo (TV)	.85	2.50	5.00
722-Johnny Mack Brown	1.50	4.00	8.00
723-Santiago (Movie)-Kinstler-a(9/56); Alan Ladd photo-c	2.00	6.00	12.00
724-Bugs Bunny's Album	.70	2.00	4.00
725-Elmer Fudd (9/56)	.60	1.80	3.60
726-Duck Album	.85	2.50	5.00
727-The Nature of Things (TV) (Disney)-Jesse Marsh-a	1.50	4.00	8.00
728-M.G.M's Mouse Musketeers	.50	1.50	3.00
729-Bob, Son of Battle	.85	2.50	5.00
730-Smokey Stover	1.00	3.00	6.00
731-Silvertip-the Fighting Four (Max Brand)-Kinstler-a	2.00	5.00	10.00
732-Zorro, the Challenge of (10/56)	3.50	10.00	20.00
733-Buck Jones	1.00	3.00	6.00
734-Cheyenne (TV) (10/56)	1.50	4.00	8.00
735-Crusader Rabbit	.70	2.00	4.00
736-Pluto (Disney)	.60	1.80	3.60
737-Steve Canyon	2.00	6.00	12.00
738-Westward Ho, the Wagons (Disney-Movie)	1.50	4.00	8.00
739-Bounty Guns (Luke Short)-Drucker-a	1.00	3.00	6.00
740-Chilly Willy (Walter Lantz)	.50	1.50	3.00
741-The Fastest Gun Alive (Movie) (9/56)	2.00	5.00	10.00
742-Buffalo Bill, Jr. (TV)	1.00	3.00	6.00
743-Daisy Duck's Diary (Disney) (11/56)	1.00	3.00	6.00
744-Little Beaver	.70	2.00	4.00
745-Francis the Famous Talking Mule	.50	1.50	3.00
746-Dotty Dripple & Taffy	1.00	3.00	6.00
747-Goofy (Disney)	.85	2.50	5.00
748-Frosty the Snowman (11/56)	.70	2.00	4.00
749-Secrets of Life (Disney-Movie)	1.50	4.00	8.00
750-The Great Cat Family (Disney-Movie)	1.50	4.00	8.00
751-Our Miss Brooks (TV)	1.00	3.00	6.00
752-Mandrake the Magician	2.00	6.00	12.00
753-Walt Scott's Little People (11/56)	.70	2.00	4.00
754-Smokey the Bear	.70	2.00	4.00
755-The Littlest Snowman (12/56)	.70	2.00	4.00
756-Santa Claus Funnies	.70	2.00	4.00
757-The True Story of Jesse James (Movie)	1.50	4.00	8.00
758-Bear Country (Disney-Movie)	1.00	3.00	6.00
759-Circus Boy (TV)	.70	2.00	4.00
760-The Hardy Boys (TV) (Disney)-Mickey Mouse Club	1.00	3.00	6.00
761-Howdy Doody (TV) (1/57)	1.20	3.50	7.00
762-The Sharkfighters (Movie)(1/57)(Scarce)	3.00	8.00	16.00
763-Grandma Duck's Farm Friends (Disney)	1.00	3.00	6.00
764-M.G.M's Mouse Musketeers	.50	1.50	3.00
765-Will-Yum!	.55	1.60	3.20
766-Buffalo Bill, Jr. (TV)	1.00	3.00	6.00
767-Spin & Marty (TV)(Disney)-Mickey Mouse Club (2/57)	.85	2.50	5.00
768-Steve Donovan, Western Marshal (TV)-Kinstler-a	1.50	4.50	9.00
769-Gunsmoke (TV)	.85	2.50	5.00
770-Brave Eagle	.85	2.50	5.00
771-Brand of Empire (Luke Short)(3/57)-Drucker-a	1.00	3.00	6.00
772-Cheyenne (TV)	1.50	4.00	8.00
773-The Brave One (Movie)	1.00	3.00	6.00
774-Hi & Lois (3/57)	.55	1.60	3.20
775-Sir Lancelot (TV)-Buscema-a	2.00	6.00	12.00
776-Johnny Mack Brown	1.50	4.00	8.00
777-Scamp (Disney)	.55	1.60	3.20
778-The Little Rascals	.70	2.00	4.00
779-Lee Hunter, Indian Fighter (3/57)	.70	2.00	4.00
780-Capt. Kangaroo (TV)	.85	2.50	5.00
781-Fury (TV) (3/57)	1.00	3.00	6.00
782-Duck Album (Disney)	.85	2.50	5.00
783-Elmer Fudd	.60	1.80	3.60
784-Around the World in 80 Days (Movie) (2/57)	2.00	6.00	12.00
785-Circus Boy (TV) (4/57)	.70	2.00	4.00
786-Cinderella (Disney) (3/57)-Partial reprint of No. 272	1.50	4.00	8.00
787-Little Hiawatha (Disney) (4/57)	1.00	3.00	6.00
788-Prince Valiant - by Bob Fuje	3.00	8.00	16.00
789-Silvertip-Valley Thieves (Max Brand) (4/57)-Kinstler-a	1.20	3.50	7.00
790-The Wings of Eagles (Movie) (John Wayne)-Toth-a	3.50	10.00	20.00
791-The 77th Bengal Lancers (TV)	1.50	4.00	8.00
792-Oswald the Rabbit	.50	1.50	3.00

FOUR COLOR (continued)	Good	Fine	Mint
793-Morty Meekle	.70	2.00	4.00
794-The Count of Monte Cristo (5/57) (Movie)-Buscema-a	3.50	10.00	20.00
795-Jiminy Cricket (Disney)	1.00	3.00	6.00
796-Ludwig Bemelman's Madeleine & Genevieve	1.20	3.50	7.00
797-Gunsmoke (TV)	.85	2.50	5.00
798-Buffalo Bill, Jr. (TV)	1.00	3.00	6.00
799-Priscilla's Pop	.55	1.60	3.20
800-The Buccaneers (TV)	1.50	4.00	8.00
801-Dotty Dripple & Taffy	1.00	3.00	6.00
802-Goofy (Disney) (5/57)	.85	2.50	5.00
803-Cheyenne (TV)	1.50	4.00	8.00
804-Steve Canyon (1957)	2.00	6.00	12.00
805-Crusader Rabbit	.70	2.00	4.00
806-Scamp (Disney) (6/57)	.55	1.60	3.20
807-Savage Range (Luke Short)-Drucker-a	1.00	3.00	6.00
808-Spin & Marty (TV)(Disney)-Mickey Mouse Club	.85	2.50	5.00
809-The Little People-Walt Scott	.70	2.00	4.00
810-Francis the Mule	.50	1.50	3.00
811-Howdy Doody (TV) (7/57)	1.20	3.50	7.00
812-The Big Land (Movie); Alan Ladd photo-c	1.50	4.00	8.00
813-Circus Boy (TV)	.70	2.00	4.00
814-Covered Wagons, Ho! (Disney)-Donald Duck (6/57)	1.50	4.00	8.00
815-Dragoon Wells Massacre (Movie)	1.50	4.00	8.00
816-Brave Eagle	.85	2.50	5.00
817-Little Beaver	.70	2.00	4.00
818-Smokey the Bear (6/57)	.70	2.00	4.00
819-Mickey Mouse in Magicland (Disney) (7/57)	1.50	4.00	8.00
820-The Oklahoman (Movie)	1.50	4.00	8.00
821-Wringle Wrangle (Disney)-Based on movie "Westward Ho, the Wagons"-Marsh-a	2.00	5.00	10.00
822-Paul Revere's Ride with Johnny Tremain (TV)(Disney)-Toth-a	3.00	8.00	16.00
823-Timmy	.50	1.50	3.00
824-The Pride & the Passion (Movie) (8/57)	1.50	4.00	8.00
825-The Little Rascals	.55	1.60	3.20
826-Spin & Marty & Annette (TV)(Disney)-Mickey Mouse Club	.85	2.50	5.00
827-Smokey Stover (8/57)	1.00	3.00	6.00
828-Buffalo Bill, Jr. (TV)	1.00	3.00	6.00
829-Tales of the Pony Express (TV) (8/57)	1.00	3.00	6.00
830-The Hardy Boys (TV)(Disney)-Mickey Mouse Club (8/57)	1.00	3.00	6.00
831-No Sleep 'Til Dawn (Movie) (9/57)	1.50	4.00	8.00
832-Lolly & Pepper	.70	2.00	4.00
833-Scamp (Disney) (9/57)	.55	1.60	3.20
834-Johnny Mack Brown	1.50	4.00	8.00
835-Silvertip-The Fake Rider (Max Brand)	1.20	3.50	7.00
836-Man in Flight (Disney) (9/57)	1.00	3.00	6.00
837-All-American Athlete Cotton Woods	.70	2.00	4.00
838-Bugs Bunny's Life Story Album (9/57)	.70	2.00	4.00
839-The Vigilantes (Movie)	2.00	5.00	10.00
840-Duck Album (Disney)	.85	2.50	5.00
841-Elmer Fudd	.60	1.80	3.60
842-The Nature of Things (Disney-Movie)('57)-Jesse Marsh-a (TV series)	1.50	4.00	8.00
843-The First Americans (Disney)-Jesse Marsh-a	1.50	4.00	8.00
844-Gunsmoke (TV)	.85	2.50	5.00
845-The Land Unknown (Movie)-Alex Toth-a	4.00	12.00	24.00
846-Gun Glory (Movie)-by Alex Toth	3.50	10.00	20.00
847-Perri (squirrels) (Disney-Movie)-Two different covers published	1.00	3.00	6.00
848-Marauder's Moon	1.50	4.00	8.00
849-Prince Valiant-by Bob Fuje	3.00	8.00	16.00

	Good	Fine	Mint
850-Buck Jones	1.00	3.00	6.00
851-The Story of Mankind (Movie) (1/58)	1.50	4.00	8.00
852-Chilly Willy (2/58)	.50	1.50	3.00
853-Pluto (Disney) (10/57)	.60	1.80	3.60
854-The Hunchback of Notre Dame (Movie)	3.00	8.00	16.00
855-Broken Arrow (TV)	1.00	3.00	6.00
856-Buffalo Bill, Jr. (TV)	1.00	3.00	6.00
857-The Goofy Adventure Story (Disney) (11/57)	.85	2.50	5.00
858-Daisy Duck's Diary (Disney) (11/57)	1.00	3.00	6.00
859-Topper & Neil (11/57)	.55	1.60	3.20
860-Wyatt Earp (TV)-Manning-a	2.00	5.00	10.00
861-Frosty the Snowman	.70	2.00	4.00
862-The Truth About Mother Goose (Disney-Movie) (11/57)	2.00	5.00	10.00
863-Francis the Mule	.50	1.50	3.00
864-The Littlest Snowman	.70	2.00	4.00
865-Andy Burnett (TV) (Disney) (12/57)	1.00	3.00	6.00
866-Mars & Beyond (Disney-Movie)	1.50	4.00	8.00
867-Santa Claus Funnies	.70	2.00	4.00
868-Walt Scott's Little People (12/57)	.70	2.00	4.00
869-Old Yeller (Disney-Movie) (1/58)	2.00	5.00	10.00
870-Little Beaver (1/58)	.70	2.00	4.00
871-Curly Kayoe	1.20	3.50	7.00
872-Capt. Kangaroo (TV)	.85	2.50	5.00
873-Grandma Duck's Farm Friends (Disney)	1.00	3.00	6.00
874-Old Ironsides (Disney-Movie with J. Tremain) (1/58)	1.50	4.00	8.00
875-Trumpets West (Luke Short) (2/58)	1.00	3.00	6.00
876-Tales of Wells Fargo (TV) (2/58)	1.00	3.00	6.00
877-Frontier Doctor with Rex Allen (TV)-Alex Toth-a	3.00	8.00	16.00
878-Peanuts-Schulz-c only (2/58)	2.00	6.00	12.00
879-Brave Eagle (2/58)	.85	2.50	5.00
880-Steve Donovan, Western Marshal-Drucker-a	1.00	3.00	6.00
881-The Capt. & the Kids	.85	2.50	5.00
882-Zorro (Disney)-1st Disney issue by Alex Toth (TV) (2/58)	3.00	8.00	16.00
883-The Little Rascals	.55	1.60	3.20
884-Hawkeye & the Last of the Mohicans (TV)	.85	2.50	5.00
885-Fury (TV) (3/58)	1.00	3.00	6.00
886-Bongo & Lumpjaw (Disney)	.85	2.50	5.00
887-The Hardy Boys (Disney)(TV)-Mickey Mouse Club (1/58)	1.00	3.00	6.00
888-Elmer Fudd (3/58)	.60	1.80	3.60
889-Clint & Mac (Disney)(TV)-Alex Toth-a (3/58)	3.00	8.00	16.00
890-Hugh O'Brian Famous Marshal Wyatt Earp (TV)-by Russ Manning	2.00	5.00	10.00
891-Light in the Forest (Disney-Movie) (3/58)	1.50	4.00	8.00
892-Maverick (TV) (4/58)	1.20	3.50	7.00
893-Jim Bowie (TV)	.85	2.50	5.00
894-Oswald the Rabbit	.50	1.50	3.00
895-Wagon Train (TV) (3/58)	1.00	3.00	6.00
896-Tinker Bell (Disney)	2.00	6.00	12.00
897-Jiminy Cricket (Disney)	1.00	3.00	6.00
898-Silvertip's Trap (Max Brand)-Kinstler-a (5/58)	2.00	5.00	10.00
899-Goofy (Disney)	.85	2.50	5.00
900-Prince Valiant-by Bob Fuje	3.00	8.00	16.00
901-Little Hiawatha (Disney)	1.00	3.00	6.00
902-Will-Yum!	.55	1.60	3.20
903-Dotty Dripple & Taffy	1.00	3.00	6.00
904-Lee Hunter, Indian Fighter	.70	2.00	4.00
905-Annette (Disney)(TV)-Mickey Mouse Club	3.50	10.00	20.00
906-Francis the Mule	.50	1.50	3.00
907-Sugarfoot (TV)-Toth-a	3.00	8.00	16.00

Four Color #807, © DELL

Four Color #843, © WDP

Four Color #890, © DELL

Four Color #916, © KING

Four Color #987, © WDP

Four Color #1024, © WDP

FOUR COLOR (continued)	Good	Fine	Mint
908-The Little People-Walt Scott (5/58)	.70	2.00	4.00
909-Smitty & Herby	.70	2.00	4.00
910-The Vikings (Movie)-Buscema-a	2.00	5.00	10.00
911-The Gray Ghost of the Confederacy (TV)(Movie)	2.00	5.00	10.00
912-Leave It to Beaver (TV)	1.00	3.00	6.00
913-The Left-Handed Gun (Movie) (7/58); Paul Newman photo-c	2.00	5.00	10.00
914-No Time For Sergeants (Movie)	1.20	3.50	7.00
915-Casey Jones (TV)	.70	2.00	4.00
916-Red Ryder	1.50	4.00	8.00
917-The Life of Riley (TV)	.85	2.50	5.00
918-Beep Beep, the Roadrunner (7/58)-Two different back covers published	.70	2.00	4.00
919-Boots & Saddles (TV)	.70	2.00	4.00
920-Zorro (Disney)(TV)-Alex Toth-a (6/58)	3.00	8.00	16.00
921-Hugh O'Brian Famous Marshal Wyatt Earp (TV)-Manning-a	2.00	5.00	10.00
922-Johnny Mack Brown by Russ Manning	2.00	6.00	12.00
923-Timmy	.50	1.50	3.00
924-Colt 45 (TV) (8/58)	1.50	4.00	8.00
925-Last of the Fast Guns (Movie) (8/58)	1.50	4.00	8.00
926-Peter Pan (Disney)-Reprint of No. 442	1.50	4.00	8.00
927-Top Gun (Luke Short)Buscema-a	1.00	3.00	6.00
928-Sea Hunt (TV)	1.50	4.00	8.00
929-Brave Eagle	.85	2.50	5.00
930-Maverick (TV) (7/58)	1.20	3.50	7.00
931-Have Gun, Will Travel (TV)	1.00	3.00	6.00
932-Smokey the Bear-origin	.70	2.00	4.00
933-Zorro (Disney)-by Alex Toth (9/58)	3.00	8.00	16.00
934-The Restless Gun (TV)	1.00	3.00	6.00
935-King of the Royal Mounted	2.00	5.00	10.00
936-The Little Rascals	.55	1.60	3.20
937-Ruff and Reddy (TV)(Hanna-Barbera) (9/58)	.85	2.50	5.00
938-Elmer Fudd (9/58)	.60	1.80	3.60
939-Steve Canyon - not by Caniff	2.00	5.00	10.00
940-Lolly & Pepper	.70	2.00	4.00
941-Pluto (Disney) (10/58)	.60	1.80	3.60
942-Pony Express (TV)	1.00	3.00	6.00
943-White Wilderness (Disney-Movie) (10/58)	1.50	4.00	8.00
944-The 7th Voyage of Sindbad (Movie) (9/58)-Buscema-a	5.00	14.00	28.00
945-Maverick (TV)	1.20	3.50	7.00
946-The Big Country (Movie)	1.50	4.00	8.00
947-Broken Arrow (TV)	1.00	3.00	6.00
948-Daisy Duck's Diary (Disney) (11/58)	1.00	3.00	6.00
949-High Adventures (Lowell Thomas')(TV)	.85	2.50	5.00
950-Frosty the Snowman	.70	2.00	4.00
951-The Lennon Sisters Life Story - 36 pgs.; Toth-a	3.50	10.00	20.00
952-Goofy (Disney) (11/58)	.85	2.50	5.00
953-Francis the Mule	.50	1.50	3.00
954-Man in Space (Disney-Movie)	1.50	4.00	8.00
955-Hi & Lois (11/58)	.55	1.60	3.20
956-Ricky Nelson (TV)	2.50	7.00	14.00
957-Buffalo Bee (TV)	.70	2.00	4.00
958-Santa Claus Funnies	.60	1.80	3.60
959-Walt Scott's Christmas Stories-(Little People)(1951-56 strip re-prints)	.70	2.00	4.00
960-Zorro (Disney)(TV)(12/58)-Toth art	3.00	8.00	16.00
961-Jace Pearson's Tales of the Texas Rangers (TV)-Toth-a	2.00	6.00	12.00
962-Maverick (TV) (1/59)	1.20	3.50	7.00
963-Johnny Mack Brown	1.50	4.00	8.00
964-The Hardy Boys (TV)(Disney)-Mickey Mouse Club (1/59)	1.00	3.00	6.00
965-Grandma Duck's Farm Friends (Disney) (1/59)	1.00	3.00	6.00
966-Tonka-Starring Sal Mineo (Disney-Movie)	1.50	4.00	8.00

	Good	Fine	Mint
967-Chilly Willy (2/59)	.50	1.50	3.00
967-Johnny Mack Brown	1.50	4.00	8.00
968-Tales of Wells Fargo (TV)	1.00	3.00	6.00
969-Peanuts (2/59)	2.00	6.00	12.00
970-Lawman (TV)	1.00	3.00	6.00
971-Wagon Train (TV)	1.00	3.00	6.00
972-Tom Thumb (Movie)-George Pal	2.00	6.00	12.00
973-Sleeping Beauty & the Prince (Disney) (5/59)	2.00	5.00	10.00
974-The Little Rascals (3/59)	.55	1.60	3.20
975-Fury (TV)	1.00	3.00	6.00
976-Zorro (Disney)(TV)-Toth-a	3.00	8.00	16.00
977-Elmer Fudd	.60	1.80	3.60
978-Lolly & Pepper	.70	2.00	4.00
979-Oswald the Rabbit	.50	1.50	3.00
980-Maverick (TV) (4-6/59)	1.20	3.50	7.00
981-Ruff & Reddy (TV)(Hanna-Barbera)	.85	2.50	5.00
982-Tinker Bell (TV-Disney)	2.00	6.00	12.00
983-Have Gun, Will Travel (TV) (4-6/59)	1.00	3.00	6.00
984-Sleeping Beauty's Fairy Godmothers (Disney)	1.50	4.00	8.00
985-Shaggy Dog (Disney-Movie) (5/59)	1.50	4.00	8.00
986-Restless Gun (TV)	1.00	3.00	6.00
987-Goofy (Disney) (7/59)	.85	2.50	5.00
988-Little Hiawatha (Disney)	1.00	3.00	6.00
989-Jiminy Cricket (Disney) (5-7/59)	1.00	3.00	6.00
990-Huckleberry Hound (TV) (Hanna-Barbera)	.50	1.50	3.00
991-Francis the Mule	.50	1.50	3.00
992-Sugarfoot (TV)-Toth-a	3.00	8.00	16.00
993-Jim Bowie (TV)	.85	2.50	5.00
994-Sea Hunt (TV)	1.50	4.00	8.00
995-Donald Duck Album (Disney) (5-7/59)	1.00	3.00	6.00
996-Nevada (Zane Grey)	1.50	4.00	8.00
997-Walt Disney Presents-Tales of Texas John Slaughter (TV-Disney)	.85	2.50	5.00
998-Ricky Nelson (TV)	2.50	7.00	14.00
999-Leave It To Beaver (TV)	1.00	3.00	6.00
1000-The Gray Ghost of the Confederacy (Movie) (6-8/59)	1.50	4.00	8.00
1001-Lowell Thomas' High Adventure (TV) (8-10/59)	.85	2.50	5.00
1002-Buffalo Bee (TV)	.70	2.00	4.00
1003-Zorro (TV) (Disney)	2.00	5.00	10.00
1004-Colt 45 (TV) (6-8/59)	1.50	4.00	8.00
1005-Maverick (TV)	1.20	3.50	7.00
1006-Hercules (Movie)-Buscema-a	3.50	10.00	20.00
1007-John Paul Jones (Movie) (7-9/59)	1.20	3.50	7.00
1008-Beep Beep, the Road Runner (7-9/59)	.70	2.00	4.00
1009-The Rifleman (TV)	2.00	5.00	10.00
1010-Grandma Duck's Farm Friends (Disney)-by Carl Barks	4.00	12.00	24.00
1011-Buckskin (TV)	.85	2.50	5.00
1012-Last Train from Gun Hill (Movie) (7/59)	1.50	4.00	8.00
1013-Bat Masterson (TV) (8/59)	1.00	3.00	6.00
1014-The Lennon Sisters - Toth-a	3.50	8.00	16.00
1015-Peanuts-cover by Schulz	2.00	6.00	12.00
1016-Smokey the Bear	.50	1.50	3.00
1017-Chilly Willy	.50	1.50	3.00
1018-Rio Bravo (Movie)(6/59)-John Wayne; Toth-a	4.00	12.00	24.00
1019-Wagon Train (TV)	1.00	3.00	6.00
1020-Jungle Jim-McWilliams-a	1.00	3.00	6.00
1021-Jace Pearson's Tales of the Texas Rangers (TV)	1.00	3.00	6.00
1022-Timmy	.50	1.50	3.00
1023-Tales of Wells Fargo (TV) (8-10/59)	1.00	3.00	6.00
1024-Darby O'Gill & the Little People (Disney-Movie)-Toth-a	3.00	8.00	16.00
1025-Vacation in Disneyland (8-10/59)-Carl Barks-a	6.00	16.00	32.00
1026-Spin & Marty (TV)(Disney)-Mickey Mouse Club (9-11/59)			

FOUR COLOR (continued)	Good	Fine	Mint
	.70	2.00	4.00
1027-The Texan (TV)	.85	2.50	5.00
1028-Rawhide (TV); photo-c	1.00	3.00	6.00
1029-Boots & Saddles (TV)	.70	2.00	4.00
1030-Spanky & Alfalfa, the Little Rascals	.55	1.60	3.20
1031-Fury (TV)	1.00	3.00	6.00
1032-Elmer Fudd	.60	1.80	3.60
1033-Steve Canyon - not by Caniff	2.00	5.00	10.00
1034-Nancy & Sluggo Summer Camp (9-11/59)	.70	2.00	4.00
1035-Lawman (TV)	1.00	3.00	6.00
1036-The Big Circus (Movie)	1.00	3.00	6.00
1037-Zorro (Disney)(TV)-Tufts-a; Annette Funicello photo-c	2.00	5.00	10.00
1038-Ruff & Reddy (TV)(Hanna-Barbera)(1959)	.85	2.50	5.00
1039-Pluto (Disney) (11-1/60)	.60	1.80	3.60
1040-Quick Draw McGraw (TV)(Hanna-Barbera)(12-2/60)	.50	1.50	3.00
1041-Sea Hunt (TV)-Toth-a	2.00	6.00	12.00
1042-The Three Chipmunks (Alvin, Simon & Theodore) (10-12/59)	.40	1.20	2.40
1043-The Three Stooges	1.50	4.50	9.00
1044-Have Gun, Will Travel (TV) (10-12/59)	1.00	3.00	6.00
1045-The Restless Gun (TV)	1.00	3.00	6.00
1046-Beep Beep, the Road Runner (11-1/60)	.70	2.00	4.00
1047-Gyro Gearloose (Disney)-Barks c/a	4.00	12.00	24.00
1048-The Horse Soldiers (Movie) (John Wayne)Sekowsky-a	3.50	10.00	20.00
1049-Don't Give Up the Ship (Movie) (8/59)	1.00	3.00	6.00
1050-Huckleberry Hound (TV)(Hanna-Barbera)(10-12/59)	.50	1.50	3.00
1051-Donald in Mathmagic Land (Disney-Movie)	1.50	4.00	8.00
1052-Ben Hur (Movie) (11/59)-by Russ Manning	3.50	8.00	16.00
1053-Goofy (Disney) (11-1/60)	.85	2.50	5.00
1054-Huckleberry Hound Winter Fun (TV)(Hanna-Barbera)(12/59)	.50	1.50	3.00
1055-Daisy Duck's Diary (Disney)-by Carl Barks (11-1/60)	4.00	12.00	24.00
1056-Yellowstone Kelly (Movie) (11-1/60)	1.50	4.00	8.00
1057-Mickey Mouse Album (Disney)	1.00	3.00	6.00
1058-Colt 45 (TV) (11-1/60)	1.50	4.00	8.00
1059-Sugarfoot (TV)	.85	2.50	5.00
1060-Journey to the Center of the Earth (Movie)	3.50	8.00	16.00
1061-Buffalo Bee (TV)	.70	2.00	4.00
1062-Walt Scott's Christmas Stories-Little People (strip reprints)	.70	2.00	4.00
1063-Santa Claus Funnies	.60	1.80	3.60
1064-Bugs Bunny's Merry Christmas (12/59)	.70	2.00	4.00
1065-Frosty the Snowman	.70	2.00	4.00
1066-77 Sunset Strip (TV)-Toth-a (1-3/60)	2.00	5.00	10.00
1067-Yogi Bear (TV)(Hanna-Barbera)	.50	1.50	3.00
1068-Francis the Talking Mule (11-1/59-60)	.50	1.50	3.00
1069-The FBI Story (Movie)-Toth-a	3.50	8.00	16.00
1070-Solomon & Sheba (Movie) Sekowsky-a; photo-c	2.00	5.00	10.00
1071-The Real McCoys (TV)	1.00	3.00	6.00
1072-Blythe (Marge's)	1.00	3.00	6.00
1073-Grandma Duck's Farm Friends-Barks c/a (Disney)	4.00	12.00	24.00
1074-Chilly Willy	.50	1.50	3.00
1075-Tales of Wells Fargo (TV) (2-4/60)	1.00	3.00	6.00
1076-The Rebel (TV)-Sekowsky-a	1.50	4.00	8.00
1077-The Deputy (TV)-Buscema-a; Henry Fonda photo-c	2.00	5.00	10.00
1078-The Three Stooges	1.50	4.50	9.00
1079-The Little Rascals (Spanky & Alfalfa)	.55	1.60	3.20

	Good	Fine	Mint
1080-Fury (TV)	1.00	3.00	6.00
1081-Elmer Fudd	.60	1.80	3.60
1082-Spin & Marty (Disney)	.70	2.00	4.00
1083-Men into Space (TV)-Anderson-a	1.50	4.00	8.00
1084-Speedy Gonzales	.70	2.00	4.00
1085-The Time Machine (Movie) (3/60)-Alex Toth-a	3.50	10.00	20.00
1086-Lolly & Pepper	.70	2.00	4.00
1087-Peter Gunn (TV)	1.00	3.00	6.00
1088-A Dog of Flanders (Movie) (4/60)	1.00	3.00	6.00
1089-Restless Gun (TV)	1.00	3.00	6.00
1090-Francis the Mule	.50	1.50	3.00
1091-Jacky's Diary (4-6/60)	1.50	4.00	8.00
1092-Toby Tyler (Disney-Movie) (3/60)	1.50	4.00	8.00
1093-MacKenzie's Raiders (Movie) (6-8/60)	1.50	4.00	8.00
1094-Goofy (Disney)	.85	2.50	5.00
1095-Gyro Gearloose (Disney)-Barks-c/a (4-6/60)	4.00	12.00	24.00
1096-The Texan (TV)	.85	2.50	5.00
1097-Rawhide (TV)-Manning-a; photo-c	1.00	3.00	6.00
1098-Sugarfoot (TV)	.85	2.50	5.00
1099-Donald Duck Album (Disney) (5-7/60) - Barks-c	1.20	3.50	7.00
1100-Annette's Life Story (Disney-Movie)	3.50	10.00	20.00
1101-Kidnapped (Disney-Movie) (5/60)	1.50	4.00	8.00
1102-Wanted: Dead or Alive (TV) (5-7/60); Steve McQueen photo-c	1.50	4.00	8.00
1103-Leave It To Beaver (TV)	1.00	3.00	6.00
1104-Yogi Bear Goes to College (TV)(Hanna-Barbera)(6-8/60)	.50	1.50	3.00
1105-Oh, Susanna (TV)-Toth art	3.50	8.00	16.00
1106-77 Sunset Strip (TV)(6-8/60)-Toth-a	2.00	5.00	10.00
1107-Buckskin (Movie)	1.50	4.00	8.00
1108-The Troubleshooters (TV)	.85	2.50	5.00
1109-This Is Your Life, Donald Duck (Disney) (8-10/60)-Gyro flash-back written by Carl Barks	1.50	4.00	8.00
1110-Bonanza (TV) (6-8/60)	1.50	4.50	9.00
1111-Shotgun Slade (TV)	1.50	4.00	8.00
1112-Pixie & Dixie & Mr. Jinks (TV)(Hanna-Barbera)(7-9/60)	.70	2.00	4.00
1113-Tales of Wells Fargo (TV)	1.00	3.00	6.00
1114-Huckleberry Finn (Movie) (7/60)	1.00	3.00	6.00
1115-Ricky Nelson (TV)-Manning-a	3.00	8.00	16.00
1116-Boots & Saddles (TV)	.70	2.00	4.00
1117-The Boy & the Pirates (Movie)	1.50	4.00	8.00
1118-The Sword & the Dragon (Movie) (6/60)	1.50	4.00	8.00
1119-Smokey the Bear	.50	1.50	3.00
1120-Dinosaurus (Movie)	1.50	4.00	8.00
1121-Hercules Unchained (Movie)(8/60)-Crandall/Evans-a	2.00	6.00	12.00
1122-Chilly Willy	.50	1.50	3.00
1123-Tombstone Territory (TV)	1.00	3.00	6.00
1124-Whirlybirds (TV)	.85	2.50	5.00
1125-Laramie (TV)	1.00	3.00	6.00
1126-Hotel DeParee-Sundance (TV) (8-10/60)	.85	2.50	5.00
1127-The Three Stooges	1.50	4.50	9.00
1128-Rocky & His Friends (Jay Ward) (8-10/60)	1.00	3.00	6.00
1129-Pollyanna (Disney-Movie) (8/60)	2.00	6.00	12.00
1130-The Deputy (TV)-Buscema-a	2.00	5.00	10.00
1131-Elmer Fudd (9-11/60)	.60	1.80	3.60
1132-Space Mouse (8-10/60)	.50	1.50	3.00
1133-Fury (TV)	1.00	3.00	6.00
1134-Real McCoys (TV)-Toth-a	2.50	7.00	14.00
1135-M.G.M's Mouse Musketeers	.50	1.50	3.00
1136-Jungle Cat (Disney-Movie) (9-11/60)	1.50	4.00	8.00
1137-The Little Rascals	.85	1.60	3.20
1138-The Rebel (TV)	1.50	4.00	8.00
1139-Spartacus (Movie) (11/60)-Buscema-a	3.00	8.00	16.00

Four Color #1058, © DELL

Four Color #1081, © L. Schlesinger

Four Color #1104, © Hanna-Barbera

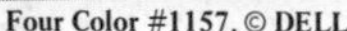
Four Color #1157, © DELL

Four Color #1186, © DELL

Four Color #1240, © DELL

FOUR COLOR (continued)	Good	Fine	Mint
1140-Donald Duck Album (Disney) (10-12/60) - Barks-c	1.20	3.50	7.00
1141-Huckleberry Hound for President (TV)(Hanna-Barbera)(10/60)	.50	1.50	3.00
1142-Johnny Ringo (TV)	.85	2.50	5.00
1143-Pluto (Disney)	.60	1.80	3.60
1144-The Story of Ruth (Movie)	1.50	4.00	8.00
1145-The Lost World (Movie)-Gil Kane-a	2.00	5.00	10.00
1146-The Restless Gun (TV)	1.00	3.00	6.00
1147-Sugarfoot (TV)	.85	2.50	5.00
1148-I Aim at the Stars-the Wernher Von Braun Story (Movie) (11-1/61)	1.00	3.00	6.00
1149-Goofy (Disney) (11-1/61)	.85	2.50	5.00
1150-Daisy Duck's Diary (Disney) (12-1/61) by Carl Barks	4.00	12.00	24.00
1151-Mickey Mouse Album (Disney) (11-1/61)	1.00	3.00	6.00
1152-Rocky & His Friends (Jay Ward) (TV) (12-2/61)	1.00	3.00	6.00
1153-Frosty the Snowman	.55	1.60	3.20
1154-Santa Claus Funnies	.60	1.80	3.60
1155-North to Alaska (Movie) - J. Wayne	3.00	8.00	16.00
1156-Swiss Family Robinson (Disney-Movie) (12/60)	2.00	5.00	10.00
1157-Master of the World (Movie) (7/61)	2.00	5.00	10.00
1158-Three Worlds of Gulliver (2 issues with different covers) (Movie)	2.00	5.00	10.00
1159-77 Sunset Strip (TV)-Toth-a	2.00	5.00	10.00
1160-Rawhide (TV); photo-c	1.00	3.00	6.00
1161-Grandma Duck's Farm Friends (Disney) by Carl Barks (2-4/61)	4.00	12.00	24.00
1162-Yogi Bear Joins the Marines (TV)(Hanna-Barbera)(5-7/61)	.50	1.50	3.00
1163-Daniel Boone (3-5/61); Marsh-a	1.00	3.00	6.00
1164-Wanted: Dead or Alive (TV); Steve McQueen photo-c	1.50	4.00	8.00
1165-Ellery Queen	2.00	6.00	12.00
1166-Rocky & His Friends (Jay Ward) (TV) (3-5/61)	1.00	3.00	6.00
1167-Tales of Wells Fargo (TV)	1.00	3.00	6.00
1168-The Detectives (TV)	1.00	3.00	6.00
1169-New Adventures of Sherlock Holmes	4.00	12.00	24.00
1170-The Three Stooges	1.50	4.50	9.00
1171-Elmer Fudd	.60	1.80	3.60
1172-Fury (TV)	1.00	3.00	6.00
1173-The Twilight Zone by Reed Crandall (TV) (5/61)	3.00	8.00	16.00
1174-The Little Rascals	.55	1.60	3.20
1175-M.G.M's Mouse Musketeers (3-5/61)	.50	1.50	3.00
1176-Dondi (Movie)-Origin	1.00	3.00	6.00
1177-Chilly Willy (4-6/61)	.50	1.50	3.00
1178-Ten Who Dared (Disney-Movie) (12/60)	1.50	4.00	8.00
1179-The Swamp Fox (TV)(Disney)(3-5/61)	1.50	4.00	8.00
1180-The Danny Thomas Show (TV)	2.00	6.00	12.00
1181-Texas John Slaughter (TV)(Disney)(4-6/61)	1.00	3.00	6.00
1182-Donald Duck Album (Disney) (5-7/61)	1.00	3.00	6.00
1183-101 Dalmatians (Disney-Movie) (3/61)	1.50	4.00	8.00
1184-Gyro Gearloose; Barks c/a (Disney) (5-7/61) Two variations exist	4.00	12.00	24.00
1185-Sweetie Pie	1.00	3.00	6.00
1186-Yak Yak (No.1) by Jack Davis (2 versions - one minus 3-pg. Davis-a)	2.00	5.00	10.00
1187-The Three Stooges (6/61)	1.50	4.50	9.00
1188-Atlantis the Lost Continent (Movie) (5/61)	2.00	6.00	12.00
1189-Greyfriars Bobby (Disney-Movie) (11/61)	1.50	4.00	8.00
1190-Donald & the Wheel (Disney-Movie) (11/61); Barks-c	2.00	5.00	10.00
1191-Leave It To Beaver (TV)	1.00	3.00	6.00
1192-Ricky Nelson (TV)-Manning-a	3.00	8.00	16.00
1193-The Real McCoys (TV)	1.00	3.00	6.00
1194-Pepe (Movie) (4/61)	.85	2.50	5.00
1195-National Velvet (TV)	.85	2.50	5.00
1196-Pixie & Dixie & Mr. Jinks (TV)(Hanna-Barbera)(7-9/61)	.70	2.00	4.00
1197-The Aquanauts (TV)	1.00	3.00	6.00
1198-Donald in Mathmagic Land - reprint of No. 1051 (Disney-Movie)	1.00	3.00	6.00
1199-The Absent-Minded Professor (Disney-Movie) (4/61)	1.50	4.00	8.00
1200-Hennessey (TV) (8-10/61)-Gil Kane-a	1.00	3.00	6.00
1201-Goofy (Disney) (8-10/61)	.85	2.50	5.00
1202-Rawhide (TV); photo-c	1.00	3.00	6.00
1203-Pinocchio (Disney) (3/62)	1.50	4.00	8.00
1204-Scamp (Disney)	.40	1.20	2.40
1205-David & Goliath (Movie) (7/61)	1.50	4.00	8.00
1206-Lolly & Pepper (9-11/61)	.70	2.00	4.00
1207-The Rebel (TV)-Sekowsky-a	2.00	5.00	10.00
1208-Rocky & His Friends (Jay Ward) (TV)	1.00	3.00	6.00
1209-Sugarfoot (TV)	.85	2.50	5.00
1210-The Parent Trap (Disney-Movie)(8/61)(Haley Mills)	2.50	7.00	14.00
1211-77 Sunset Strip (TV)-Manning-a	2.00	4.00	8.00
1212-Chilly Willy (7-9/61)	.50	1.50	3.00
1213-Mysterious Island (Movie)	2.00	5.00	10.00
1214-Smokey the Bear	.50	1.50	3.00
1215-Tales of Wells Fargo (TV) (10-12/61)	1.00	3.00	6.00
1216-Whirlybirds (TV)	.85	2.50	5.00
1218-Fury (TV)	1.00	3.00	6.00
1219-The Detectives (TV)	1.00	3.00	6.00
1220-Gunslinger (TV)	1.00	3.00	6.00
1221-Bonanza (TV) (9-11/61)	1.50	4.50	9.00
1222-Elmer Fudd (9-11/61)	.60	1.80	3.60
1223-Laramie (TV)-Gil Kane-a	1.00	3.00	6.00
1224-The Little Rascals	.55	1.60	3.20
1225-The Deputy (TV)	1.00	3.00	6.00
1226-Nikki, Wild Dog of the North (Disney-Movie) (9/61)	1.00	3.00	6.00
1227-Morgan the Pirate (Movie)	2.00	6.00	12.00
1229-Thief of Baghdad (Movie)-Evans-a	4.00	12.00	24.00
1230-Voyage to the Bottom of the Sea (Movie)	2.00	5.00	10.00
1231-Danger Man (TV); Patrick McGoohan photo-c	1.00	3.00	6.00
1232-On the Double (Movie)	1.00	3.00	6.00
1233-Tammy Tell Me True (Movie) (1961)	2.00	5.00	10.00
1234-The Phantom Planet (Movie) (1961)	2.00	5.00	10.00
1235-Mister Magoo (12-2/62)	.85	2.50	5.00
1235-Mister Magoo (3-5/65) 2nd printing - reprints of '61 issue	.50	1.50	3.00
1236-King of Kings (Movie)	1.50	4.00	8.00
1237-The Untouchables (TV)-not by Toth	1.00	3.00	6.00
1238-Deputy Dawg (TV)	1.00	3.00	6.00
1239-Donald Duck Album (Disney) (10-12/61)-Barks-c	1.20	3.50	7.00
1240-The Detectives (TV)	1.00	3.00	6.00
1241-Sweetie Pie	1.00	3.00	6.00
1242-King Leonardo (TV) (11-1/62)	.85	2.50	5.00
1243-Ellery Queen	2.00	6.00	12.00
1244-Space Mouse (11-1/62)	.50	1.50	3.00
1245-New Adventures of Sherlock Holmes	4.00	12.00	24.00
1246-Mickey Mouse Album (Disney) (11-1/62)	1.00	3.00	6.00
1247-Daisy Duck's Diary (Disney) (12-2/62)	1.00	3.00	6.00
1248-Pluto (Disney)	.60	1.80	3.60
1249-The Danny Thomas Show (TV)-Manning-a	2.50	7.00	14.00
1250-The Four Horsemen of the Apocalypse (Movie)	2.00	5.00	10.00
1251-Everything's Ducky (Movie) (1961)	1.50	4.00	8.00
1252-Andy Griffith (TV)	1.00	3.00	6.00

FOUR COLOR (continued)	Good	Fine	Mint
1253-Space Man (1-3/62)	1.00	3.00	6.00
1254-Diver Dan (TV) (2-4/62)	1.00	3.00	6.00
1255-The Wonders of Aladdin (Movie) (1961)	1.50	4.00	8.00
1256-Kona, Monarch of Monster Isle (2-4/62)	1.50	4.00	8.00
1257-Car 54, Where Are You? (TV) (3-5/62)	.70	2.00	4.00
1258-The Frogmen-Evans-a	2.00	6.00	12.00
1259-El Cid (Movie) (1961)	2.00	5.00	10.00
1260-The Horsemasters (TV, Movie - Disney) (12-2/62)	2.00	5.00	10.00
1261-Rawhide (TV); photo-c	1.00	3.00	6.00
1262-The Rebel (TV)	1.50	4.00	8.00
1263-77 Sunset Strip (TV) (12-2/62)-Manning-a	1.50	4.00	8.00
1264-Pixie & Dixie & Mr. Jinks (TV)(Hanna-Barbera)	.70	2.00	4.00
1265-The Real McCoys (TV)	1.00	3.00	6.00
1266-Spike & Tyke (12-2/62)	.35	1.00	2.00
1267-Gyro Gearloose; Barks c/a, 4 pgs. (Disney) (12-2/62)	3.00	9.00	18.00
1268-Oswald the Rabbit	.50	1.50	3.00
1269-Rawhide (TV); photo-c	1.00	3.00	6.00
1270-Bullwinkle & Rocky (Jay Ward)(TV)(3-5/62)	.70	2.00	4.00
1271-Yogi Bear Birthday Party (TV)(Hanna-Barbera)(11/61)	.50	1.50	3.00
1272-Frosty the Snowman	.55	1.60	3.20
1273-Hans Brinker (Disney-Movie) (1962)	1.50	4.00	8.00
1274-Santa Claus Funnies	.60	1.80	3.60
1275-Rocky & His Friends (Jay Ward) (TV) (12-2/62)	1.00	3.00	6.00
1276-Dondi	.85	2.50	5.00
1278-King Leonardo (TV)	.85	2.50	5.00
1279-Grandma Duck's Farm Friends (Disney) (2-4/62)	1.00	3.00	6.00
1280-Hennessey (TV)	1.00	3.00	6.00
1281-Chilly Willy (4-6/62)	.50	1.50	3.00
1282-Babes in Toyland (Disney-Movie) (1/62); Annette Funicello photo-c	2.00	5.00	10.00
1283-Bonanza (TV) (2-4/62)	1.50	4.50	9.00
1284-Laramie (TV)-Heath-a	1.00	3.00	6.00
1285-Leave It To Beaver (TV)	1.00	3.00	6.00
1286-The Untouchables (TV)	1.00	3.00	6.00
1287-Man From Wells Fargo (TV)	1.00	3.00	6.00
1288-The Twilight Zone (TV) (4/62)-Crandall/Evans c/a	3.00	8.00	16.00
1289-Ellery Queen	2.00	6.00	12.00
1290-M.G.M's Mouse Musketeers	.50	1.50	3.00
1291-77 Sunset Strip (TV)-Manning-a	1.50	4.00	8.00
1293-Elmer Fudd (3-5/62)	.60	1.80	3.60
1294-Ripcord (TV)	.85	2.50	5.00
1295-Mister Ed (TV) (3-5/62)	1.00	3.00	6.00
1296-Fury (TV) (3-5/62)	1.00	3.00	6.00
1297-Spanky, Alfalfa & the Little Rascals	.55	1.60	3.20
1298-The Hathaways (TV)	.85	2.50	5.00
1299-Deputy Dawg (TV)	1.00	3.00	6.00
1300-The Comancheros (Movie) (1961)-John Wayne	2.50	7.00	14.00
1301-Adventures in Paradise (TV) (2-4/62)	.70	2.00	4.00
1302-Johnny Jason, Teen Reporter (2-4/62)	.60	1.80	3.60
1303-Lad: A Dog (Movie)	1.00	3.00	6.00
1304-Nellie the Nurse (3-5/62)-John Stanley-a	3.00	8.00	16.00
1305-Mister Magoo (3-5/62)	.70	2.00	4.00
1306-Target: the Corrupters (TV) (3-5/62)	1.00	3.00	6.00
1307-Margie (TV) (3-5/62)	.85	2.00	4.00
1308-Tales of the Wizard of Oz (TV) (3-5/62)	2.50	7.00	14.00
1309-87th Precinct (TV) (4-6/62)-Krigstein-a	3.00	9.00	18.00
1310-Huck & Yogi Winter Sports (TV)(Hanna-Barbera)(3/62)	.70	2.00	4.00
1311-Rocky & His Friends (Jay Ward) (TV)	1.00	3.00	6.00
1312-National Velvet (TV)	.85	2.50	5.00
1313-Moon Pilot (Disney-Movie) (3/62)	1.50	4.00	8.00
1324-The Underwater City (Movie)-Evans-a	2.50	7.00	14.00
1328-The Underwater City (Movie)-Evans-a (1961)	2.50	7.00	14.00
1330-Brain Boy-Gil Kane-a	1.50	4.00	8.00
1332-Bachelor Father (TV)	1.00	3.00	6.00
1333-Short Ribs	.85	2.50	5.00
1335-Aggie Mack	.70	2.00	4.00
1336-On Stage - not by Leonard Starr	.70	2.00	4.00
1337-Dr. Kildare (TV)	1.00	3.00	6.00
1341-Andy Griffith (TV)	1.00	3.00	6.00
1348-Yak Yak (No.2)-by Jack Davis	2.50	5.00	10.00
1349-Yogi Bear Visits the U.N. (TV)(Hanna-Barbera)(1/62)	.50	1.50	3.00
1350-Comanche (Disney-Movie)(1962)-Reprints 4-Color 966 (title change from "Tonka" to "Comanche")(4-6/62)	.85	2.50	5.00
1354-Calvin & the Colonel (TV)	1.00	3.00	6.00

NOTE: *Missing numbers probably do not exist.*

FOUR FAVORITES (Crime Must Pay the Penalty No. 33 on)
Sept, 1941 - No. 32, Dec, 1947
Ace Magazines

	Good	Fine	Mint
1-Vulcan, Lash Lightning, Magno the Magnetic Man & The Raven begin; Flag-c	20.00	60.00	120.00
2-The Black Ace only app.	10.00	30.00	60.00
3-Last Vulcan	9.00	25.00	50.00
4,5: 4-The Raven & Vulcan end; Unknown Soldier begins, ends No. 28. 5-Captain Courageous begins, ends No. 28	7.00	20.00	40.00
6-8	5.00	15.00	30.00
9,11-Kurtzman-a; 11-L.B. Cole-a	8.00	24.00	48.00
10-Classic Kurtzman c/a	10.00	28.00	56.00
12-L.B. Cole-a	5.00	15.00	30.00
13-20	4.00	12.00	24.00
21	3.00	8.00	16.00
22-Captain Courageous drops costume	3.00	8.00	16.00
23-26: 23-Unknown Soldier drops costume. 26-Last Magno	3.00	8.00	16.00
27-32	2.00	5.00	10.00

FOUR HORSEMEN OF THE APOCALYPSE, THE (See 4-Color No. 1250)

FOUR MOST (. . . Boys No. 38-41)
Winter, 1941-42 - V8No.5(No. 36), 9-10/49; No. 37, 11-12/49 - No. 41, 6-7/50
Novelty Publications/Star Publications V8No.1 on

	Good	Fine	Mint
V1No.1-The Target, The Cadet & Dick Cole begin w/origins retold, Wonder Boy begins	20.00	60.00	120.00
2,3: 3-Flag-c	10.00	28.00	56.00
4-1pg. Dr. Seuss(signed)	8.00	22.00	44.00
V2No.1-4, V3No.1-4	1.50	4.00	8.00
V4No.1-4	1.00	3.00	6.00
V5No.1-The Target & Targeteers app.	.85	2.50	5.00
2-5	.85	2.50	5.00
V6No.1-White Rider & Super Horse begins	.85	2.50	5.00
2-4,6	.85	2.50	5.00
5-L. B. Cole-c	3.00	9.00	18.00
V7No.1,3-5, V8No.1	.85	2.50	5.00
2,6-L. B. Cole-c. 6-Last Dick Cole	3.00	8.00	16.00
V8No.2-5-L. B. Cole c/a	3.50	10.00	20.00
37-41	3.50	10.00	20.00

FOUR STAR BATTLES TALES
Feb-Mar, 1973 - No. 5, Nov-Dec, 1973
National Periodical Publications

	Good	Fine	Mint
1-All reprints		.40	.80

Four Color #1281, © DELL

Four Favorites #3, © ACE

Four Most V8#2, © STAR

Foxhole #1, © PRIZE

Foxy Fagan #7, © Dearfield

Frankenstein Comics #5, © PRIZE

FOUR STAR BATTLES TALES (continued)

	Good	Fine	Mint
2-4		.30	.60
5-Krigstein-a(r)		.30	.60

NOTE: ***Drucker** a-1,3-5r. **Kubert** a-4r; c-2.*

FOUR STAR SPECTACULAR
Mar-Apr, 1976 - No. 6, Jan-Feb, 1977
National Periodical Publications

	Good	Fine	Mint
1-Superboy, Wonder Woman reprints begin		.50	1.00
2-6: 2-Infinity cover		.40	.80

NOTE: *All contain DC Superhero reprints. No. 1 has 68 pages; No. 2-6, 52 pages. No. 1,4-Hawkman app.; No. 2-Flash app.; No. 3-Green Lantern app; No. 4-Wonder Woman, Superboy app; No. 6-Blackhawk G.A. reprint.*

FOUR TEENERS (Formerly Crime Must Pay The Penalty?; Dotty No. 35 on)
April, 1948 (Teen-age comic)
A. A. Wyn

	Good	Fine	Mint
34	1.20	3.50	7.00

FOX AND THE CROW (Stanley & His Monster No. 109 on) (See Real Screen Comics)
Dec-Jan, 1951-52 - No. 108, Feb-Mar, 1968
National Periodical Publications

	Good	Fine	Mint
1	30.00	80.00	160.00
2(Scarce)	14.00	40.00	80.00
3-5	8.00	24.00	48.00
6-10	5.50	16.00	32.00
11-20	3.50	10.00	20.00
21-40	2.00	6.00	12.00
41-60	1.50	4.00	8.00
61-94,96-108	.85	2.50	5.00
95-Stanley & His Monster begins(origin)	.85	2.50	5.00

NOTE: *Many covers by **Mort Drucker.***

THE FOX AND THE HOUND
August, 1981 - Present
Whitman Publishing Co.

	Good	Fine	Mint
1-Based on new animated movie		.30	.60
2		.30	.60

FOX GIANTS

Each of these usually contain four remaindered Fox books minus covers. Since these missing covers often had the first page of the first story, most Giants therefore are incomplete. The value should be approximately 50 percent of the listed price of each individual title included in the Giant.

FOXHOLE
Sept-Oct, 1954 - No. 7, Sept-Oct?, 1955
Simon & Kirby Publ.(Prize)/Charlton Comics No. 5 on

	Good	Fine	Mint
1-Kirby-c	3.00	8.00	16.00
2-Kirby c/a(2)	3.50	10.00	20.00
3,5-Kirby-c only	1.50	4.00	8.00
4(3-4/54),7	.85	2.50	5.00
6-Kirby c/a(2)	3.00	8.00	16.00
Super Reprints No. 10-12,15-18	.30	.80	1.60

NOTE: ***Kirby** a(r)-Super No. 11,12,18. **Powell** a(r)-Super No. 15,16.*

FOXY FAGAN
Dec, 1946 - No. 7, Summer, 1948
Dearfield Publishing Co.

	Good	Fine	Mint
1-Foxy Fagan & Little Buck begin	2.00	6.00	12.00
2-7	1.50	4.00	8.00

FOXY GRANDPA
1901 - 1916 (Hardcover; strip reprints)
N. Y. Herald/Frederick A. Stokes Co./M. A. Donahue & Co./Bunny Publ.

	Good	Fine	Mint
1901-9x15'' in color-N. Y. Herald	20.00	60.00	130.00
1902-''Latest Larks of . . .,'' 32 pgs. in color, 9½x15½''	20.00	60.00	130.00
1903-''Latest Advs.,'' 9x15'', 24 pgs. in color, Hammersly Co.	20.00	60.00	130.00
1903-'' . . .'s New Advs.,'' 10x15, 32 pgs. in color, Stokes	20.00	60.00	130.00
1904-''Up to Date,'' 10x15'', 28 pgs. in color, Stokes	20.00	60.00	130.00
1905-''The Latest Advs. of,'' 9x15'', 24 pgs., in color, M.A. Donohue Co; re-issue of 1902 ish	10.00	30.00	60.00
1905-''Merry Pranks of,'' 9½x15½'', 24 pgs. in color, Donahue	12.00	35.00	70.00
1905-''Latest Larks of,'' 9½x15½'', 32 pgs. in color, Donahue	12.00	35.00	70.00
1906-''Frolics,'' 10x15'', 30 pgs. in color, Stokes	12.00	35.00	70.00
1907	7.00	20.00	40.00
1908?-''Triumphs,'' 10x15''	7.00	20.00	40.00
1908?-''& Little Brother,'' 10x15''	7.00	20.00	40.00
1908?-''& Flip Flaps,'' 10x15''	7.00	20.00	40.00
1911-''Latest Tricks,'' R-1910,1911 Sundays in color-Stokes Co.	10.00	30.00	60.00
1914-9½x15½'', 24 pgs., 6 color cartoons/page, Bunny Publ.	7.00	20.00	40.00
1916-''Merry Book,'' 10x15'', 30 pgs. in color, Stokes	7.00	20.00	40.00

FOXY GRANDPA SPARKLETS SERIES
1908 (6½x7¾''; 24 pgs. in color)
M. A. Donahue & Co.

	Good	Fine	Mint
'' . . . Rides the Goat,'' '' . . . & His Boys,'' '' . . . Playing Ball,'' '' . . . Fun on the Farm,'' '' . . . Fancy Shooting,'' '' . . . Show the Boys Up Sports,'' '' . . . Plays Santa Claus'' each. . . .	14.00	40.00	80.00
900- . . . Playing Ball; Bunny illos; 8 pgs., linen like pgs., no date	5.50	16.00	32.00

FRACTURED FAIRY TALES
October, 1962
Gold Key

	Good	Fine	Mint
1 (10022-210)	1.00	3.00	6.00

FRANCIS, BROTHER OF THE UNIVERSE
1980 (75 cents) (52 pgs.) (One Shot)
Marvel Comics Group

	Good	Fine	Mint
Buscema/Marie Severin-a; story of Francis Bernadone celebrating his 800th birthday in 1982		.40	.80

FRANCIS THE FAMOUS TALKING MULE (All based on movie) (See 4-Color No. 335,465,501,547,579,621,655,698,710,745,810,863, 906,953,991,1068,1090)

FRANK BUCK (Formerly My True Love)
No. 70, May, 1950 - No. 3, Sept, 1950
Fox Features Syndicate

	Good	Fine	Mint
70, 3-Wood a(p)?	5.50	16.00	32.00
71,72	3.50	10.00	20.00

FRANKENSTEIN (See Movie Classics)
Aug-Oct, 1964; No. 2, Sept, 1966 - No. 4, Mar, 1967
Dell Publishing Co.

	Good	Fine	Mint
1(12-283-410)(1964)	.70	2.00	4.00
2-Intro. & origin super-hero character (9/66)	.35	1.00	2.00
3,4		.50	1.00

FRANKENSTEIN COMICS
Sum, 1945 - V5No.5(No.33), Oct-Nov, 1954
Prize Publications (Crestwood/Feature)

	Good	Fine	Mint
1-Frankenstein begins by Dick Briefer (origin)	10.00	30.00	60.00
2	7.00	20.00	40.00
3-10: 7-S&K a(r)/Headline Comics. 8(7-8/47)-Superman satire	5.00	15.00	30.00

11-17(1-2/49)-11-Boris Karloff parody c/story. 17-Last humor issue

FRANKENSTEIN COMICS (continued)

	Good	Fine	Mint
	3.50	10.00	20.00
18(3/52)-New origin, horror series begins	4.00	12.00	24.00
19,20(V3No.4, 8-9/52)	3.00	9.00	18.00
21(V3No.5), 22(V3No.6)	3.00	9.00	18.00
23(V4No.1)-No.28(V4No.6)	2.75	8.00	16.00
29(V5No.1)-No.33(V5No.5)	2.75	8.00	16.00

NOTE: ***Meskin** a-21, 29.*

FRANKENSTEIN (The Monster of . . .)
Jan, 1973 - No. 18, Sept, 1975
Marvel Comics Group

	Good	Fine	Mint
1-Ploog-a begins	.30	.80	1.60
2-6-Last Ploog-a		.40	.80
7-17		.40	.80
18-Wrightson-c		.40	.80
Power Record giveaway-(12¼x12¼''; 16 pgs.); Adams, Ploog-a	.30	.80	1.60

NOTE: ***Ditko** a-12r.*

FRANKENSTEIN, JR. (. . . & the Impossibles) (TV)
January, 1967 (Hanna-Barbera)
Gold Key

	Good	Fine	Mint
1	.70	2.00	4.00

FRANKIE (. . . & Lana) (Formerly Movie Tunes; Frankie Fuddle No. 16 on)
No. 4, Spring, 1947 - No. 15, June, 1949
Marvel Comics (MgPC)

	Good	Fine	Mint
4-8	.85	2.50	5.00
9-Transvestite story	1.00	3.00	6.00
10-15	.70	2.00	4.00

FRANKIE DOODLE (See Single Series No. 7 and Sparkler No. 2)

FRANKIE FUDDLE (Formerly Frankie & Lana) (Li'l Willie No. 20 on)
1949 - No. 17, Nov, 1949 (No. 18,19 exist?)
Marvel Comics

	Good	Fine	Mint
16,17	.70	2.00	4.00

FRANK LUTHER'S SILLY PILLY COMICS (See Jingle Dingle . . .)
1950 (10 cents)
Children's Comics

	Good	Fine	Mint
1-Characters from radio, records, & TV	2.00	5.00	10.00

FRANK MERRIWELL AT YALE (Speed Demons No. 5 on?)
June, 1955 - No. 4, Dec, 1955
Charlton Comics

	Good	Fine	Mint
1	.70	2.00	4.00
2-4	.50	1.50	3.00

FRANTIC (Magazine) (See Zany & Ratfink)
Oct, 1958 - V2No.2, April, 1959 (Satire)
Pierce Publishing Co.

	Good	Fine	Mint
V1No.1,2	.85	2.50	5.00
V2No.1,2	.50	1.50	3.00

FRECKLES AND HIS FRIENDS (See Famous Comics Cartoon Book & Honeybee Birdwhistle . . .)

FRECKLES AND HIS FRIENDS
No. 5, 11/47 - No. 12, 8/49; 11/55 - No. 4, 6/56
Standard Comics/Argo

	Good	Fine	Mint
5-12-Reprints; 11-Lingerie panels	2.00	5.00	10.00

NOTE: *Some copies of No. 8 & 9 contain a printing oddity. The negatives were elongated in the engraving process, probably to conform to page dimensions on the filler pages. Those pages only look normal when viewed at a 45 degree angle.*

	Good	Fine	Mint
1(Argo,'55)-Reprints	1.20	3.50	7.00
2-4	.85	2.50	5.00

FREDDY (See Blue Bird)
March, 1958 - No. 47, Feb, 1965
Charlton Comics

	Good	Fine	Mint
V2No.12-47	.30	.80	1.60
Schiff's Shoes Presents . . . No. 1(1959)-Giveaway		.60	1.20

FREDDY
May-July, 1963 - No. 3, Oct-Dec, 1964
Dell Publishing Co.

	Good	Fine	Mint
1-3	.30	.80	1.60

FREE COMICS TO YOU FROM . . . (name of shoe store) (Has clown on cover & another with a rabbit) (Like comics from Weather Bird & Edward's Shoes)
Circa 1956
Shoe Store Giveaway

Contains a comic bound with new cover - several combinations possible; contents determines price.

FREEDOM AGENT (Also see John Steele)
April, 1963
Gold Key

	Good	Fine	Mint
1 (10054-304)	.50	1.50	3.00

FREEDOM FIGHTERS (See Justice League No. 107,108)
Mar-Apr, 1976 - No. 15, July-Aug, 1978
National Periodical Publications/DC Comics

	Good	Fine	Mint
1-Uncle Sam, The Ray, Black Condor, Doll Man, Human Bomb, & Phantom Lady begin	.25	.70	1.40
2,3		.40	.80
4-10: 4,5-Wonder Woman app. 8,9-The Crusaders app. 10-Origin Doll Man reprint		.40	.80
11-15: 11-Origin The Ray reprint. 12-Origin Firebrand. 13-Origin Black Condor retold. 14,15-Batgirl & Batwoman app. 15-Origin Phantom Lady		.30	.60

NOTE: ***Buckler** c-14.*

FREEDOM TRAIN
1948 (Giveaway)
Street & Smith Publ.

	Good	Fine	Mint
Powell-c	2.00	5.00	10.00

FRENZY (Magazine) (Satire)
April, 1958 - No. 6, March, 1959
Picture Magazine

	Good	Fine	Mint
1	.85	2.50	5.00
2-6	.50	1.50	3.00

FRIDAY FOSTER
October, 1972
Dell Publishing Co.

	Good	Fine	Mint
1	.50	1.50	3.00

FRIENDLY GHOST, CASPER, THE (See Casper . . .)
Aug, 1958 - Present
Harvey Publications

	Good	Fine	Mint
1-Infinity-c	11.00	32.00	64.00
2	7.00	20.00	40.00
3-10	4.00	12.00	24.00
11-20	3.50	8.00	16.00
21-50	1.20	3.50	7.00
51-100	.55	1.60	3.20
101-150		.50	1.00
151-218: 173,179,185-Cub Scout Specials		.30	.60
American Dental Assoc. giveaway-Small size (1967, 16 pgs.)	.40	1.20	2.40

FRIGHT
June, 1975 (August on inside)

Frankenstein #6, © MCG

Freckles & His Friends #8, © NEA Service

Freedom Fighters #7, © DC

Fright #1, © ATLAS

Frisky Animals #54, © STAR

Frogman Comics #7, © HILL

FRIGHT (continued)
Atlas/Seaboard Periodicals — Good Fine Mint

1-Origin The Son of Dracula; Frank Thorne c/a — .40 .80

FRISKY ANIMALS (Formerly Frisky Fables)
No. 44, Jan, 1951 - No. 58, 1954
Star Publications

44,46-51,53-58-Super Cat 4.00 12.00 24.00
45-Classic L. B. Cole-c 7.00 20.00 40.00
52-L. B. Cole c/a, 3pgs. 4.50 13.00 26.00
NOTE: *All have* ***L. B. Cole****-c. No. 47-No Super Cat.* ***Disbrow*** *a-49,52.*

FRISKY ANIMALS ON PARADE (Formerly Parade; becomes Super-spook)
Sept, 1957 - No. 3, Dec/Jan, 1957-1958
Ajax-Farrell Publ. (Four Star Comic Corp.)

1-3: L. B. Cole-c 2.50 7.00 14.00

FRISKY FABLES (Frisky Animals No. 44 on)
Spring, 1945 - No. 44, Oct-Nov, 1949
Premium Group/Novelty/Star Publ.

V1No.1 3.00 8.00 16.00
2,3(1945) 1.50 4.00 8.00
4-7(1946) .85 2.50 5.00
V2No.1-9,11,12(1947) .70 2.00 4.00
10-Christmas-c .75 2.25 4.50
V3No.1-12(1948) .50 1.50 3.00
V4No.1-7 .50 1.50 3.00
36-45(V4No.8-12, V5No.1-4 (10-11/49))-L. B. Cole-c 5.00 14.00 20.00

FRITZI RITZ (See Single Series No. 5,1(reprint), United Comics and Comics on Parade)

FRITZI RITZ
Fall/48 - No. 55, 9-11/57; No. 56, 12-2/57-58 - No. 59, 9-11/58
United Features Synd./St. John/Dell No. 56 on

nn(1948)-Special fall ish. 2.00 6.00 12.00
2-5 1.00 3.00 6.00
6-10: 7-Lingerie panel .70 2.00 4.00
11-19,21-28,30-59 .50 1.50 3.00
20-Strange As It Seems; Russell Patterson Cheescake-a; negligee panel 1.00 3.00 6.00
29-Five pg. Abbie & Slats; 1 pg. Mamie by Russell Patterson .50 1.50 3.00

NOTE: *Abbie & Slats in No. 7, 8, 11, 18, 20, 27, 29. Li'l Abner in No. 35.*

FROGMAN COMICS
Jan-Feb, 1952 - No. 11, May, 1953
Hillman Periodicals

1 2.00 5.00 10.00
2-4,6-11: 4-Meskin-a 1.00 3.00 6.00
5-Krigstein, Torres-a 2.50 7.00 14.00

FROGMEN, THE
No. 1258, Feb-Apr, 1962 - No. 12, Feb-Mar, 1965
Dell Publishing Co.

4-Color 1258-Evans-a 2.00 6.00 12.00
2,3-Evans-a; part Frazetta inks in No. 2,3 3.00 8.00 16.00
4,6-12 .70 2.00 4.00
5-Toth-a 2.00 5.00 10.00

FROM BEYOND THE UNKNOWN
10-11/69 - No.25, 11-12/73 (No.7-11: 64 pgs.; No.12-17: 52 pgs.)
National Periodical Publications

1 .60 1.20
2-5 .40 .80
6-10: 7-Intro. Col. Glenn Merrit; Anderson art No. 7,8 .40 .80
11-25: Star Rovers reprints begin No. 18,19. Space Museum in No.
23-25 — Good Fine Mint — .30 .60

NOTE: ***Adams*** *c-3, 6, 8, 9.* ***Anderson*** *c-2, 4, 5, 10, 11i, 15- 17, 22; reprints-3, 4, 6-8, 10, 11, 13-16, 24, 25.* ***Infantino*** *reprints-1-5, 7-19, 23-25; c-11p.* ***Kaluta*** *c-18,19.* ***Kubert*** *c-1,7, 12-14.* ***Toth*** *a-2r.* ***Wood*** *a-13i.*

FROM HERE TO INSANITY (Satire) (Eh No. 1-7)
(See Frantic & Frenzy)
No. 8, Feb, 1955 - V3No.1, 1956
Charlton Comics

8,9 2.00 5.00 10.00
10-Ditko-c/a, 3 pgs. 3.50 10.00 20.00
11,12-All Kirby except 4 pgs. 5.00 14.00 28.00
V3No.1(1956)-Ward-c/a(2)(signed McCartney); 5 pgs. Wolverton; 3 pgs. Ditko; magazine format 10.00 28.00 56.00

FRONTIER DAYS
1956 (Giveaway)
Robin Hood Shoe Store (Brown Shoe)

1 .70 2.00 4.00

FRONTIER DOCTOR (See 4-Color No. 877)

FRONTIER FIGHTERS
Sept-Oct, 1955 - No. 8, Nov-Dec, 1956
National Periodical Publications

1-Davy Crockett, Buffalo Bill by Kubert, Kit Carson begin 6.00 18.00 36.00
2-8 3.50 10.00 20.00
NOTE: *Buffalo Bill by* ***Kubert*** *in all.*

FRONTIER ROMANCES
Nov-Dec, 1949 - No. 2, Jan-Feb, 1950
Avon Periodicals/I. W.

1-Used in **SOTI**, pg. 180(General reference) & illo. ''Erotic spanking in a western comic book;'' 25.00 70.00 140.00
2 (Scarce) 10.00 30.00 60.00
1-I.W.(reprints Avon's No. 1) 3.00 8.00 16.00
I.W. Reprint No. 9 1.50 4.00 8.00

FRONTIER SCOUT; DAN'L BOONE (Formerly Death Valley; The Masked Raider No. 14 on)
No. 10, Jan, 1956 - No. 13, 1956; No. 14, March, 1965
Charlton Comics

10-13(1956) .60 1.80 3.60
V2No.14(3/65) .25 .70 1.40

FRONTIER TRAIL (The Rider No. 1-5)
No. 6, May, 1958
Ajax/Farrell Publ.

6 .70 2.00 4.00

FRONTIER WESTERN
Feb, 1956 - No. 10, Aug, 1957
Atlas Comics (PrPI)

1 2.50 7.00 14.00
2,3,6-Williamson-a, 4 pgs. each 3.00 9.00 18.00
4,7,9,10 1.20 3.50 7.00
5-Crandall, Baker, Wildey, Davis-a 2.50 7.00 14.00
8-Crandall, Morrow, & Wildey-a 1.50 4.00 8.00
NOTE: ***Drucker*** *a-3,4.* ***Heath*** *c-5.* ***Severin*** *c-6. Ringo Kid in No. 4.*

FRONTLINE COMBAT
July-Aug, 1951 - No. 15, Jan, 1954
E. C. Comics

1 40.00 100.00 200.00
2 25.00 70.00 140.00
3 20.00 50.00 100.00
4-Used in **SOTI**, pg. 257; contains ''Airburst'' by Kurtzman which is his personal all-time favorite story 15.00 40.00 80.00
5 12.00 35.00 70.00

FRONTLINE COMBAT (continued) — Good / Fine / Mint

6-10 9.00 25.00 50.00
11-15 7.00 20.00 40.00

NOTE: *Davis a-in all; c-11,12. Evans a-10-15. Heath a-1. Kubert a-14. Kurtzman a-1-5; c-1-9. Severin a-5-7, 9, 13, 15. Severin/Elder a-2-11; c-10. Toth a-8, 12. Wood a-1-4, 6-10, 12-15; c-13-15. Special issues: No. 7 (Iwo Jima), No. 9 (Civil War), No. 12 (Air Force). (Canadian reprints known; see Table of Contents.)*

FRONT PAGE COMIC BOOK
1945
Harvey Publications

1-Kubert-a; intro. & 1st app. Man in Black by Powell; Fuje-c 7.00 20.00 40.00

FROSTY THE SNOWMAN
1951 - 1961
Dell Publishing Co.

4-Color 359,435 1.00 3.00 6.00
4-Color 514,601,661 .85 2.50 5.00
4-Color 748,861,950,1065 .70 2.00 4.00
4-Color 1153,1272 .55 1.60 3.20

FRUITMAN SPECIAL
Dec, 1969 (68 pages)
Harvey Publications

1-Funny super hero .50 1.50 3.00

F-TROOP (TV)
Aug, 1966 - No. 7, Aug, 1967 (All have photo-c)
Dell Publishing Co.

1 .70 2.00 4.00
2-7 .35 1.00 2.00

FUGITIVES FROM JUSTICE
Feb, 1952 - No. 5, Oct, 1952
St. John Publishing Co.

1 3.00 8.00 16.00
2-Matt Baker-a; Vic Flint strip reprints begin, end No. 5 3.50 10.00 20.00
3-Reprints panel from Authentic Police Cases that was used in **SOTI** with changes; Tuska-a 6.00 18.00 36.00
4 2.00 6.00 12.00
5-Bondage-c 3.00 8.00 16.00

FULL COLOR COMICS
1946
Fox Features Syndicate

nn 2.50 7.00 14.00

FULL OF FUN
Aug, 1957 - No. 2, Nov, 1957; 1964
Red Top (Decker Publ.)(Farrell)/I. W. Enterprises

1(1957)-Dave Berg-a .50 1.50 3.00
2-Reprints Bingo, the Monkey Doodle Boy .50 1.50 3.00
8-I.W. Reprint('64) .30 .80 1.60

FUN AT CHRISTMAS (See March of Comics No. 138)

FUN CLUB COMICS (See Interstate Theatres . . .)

FUN COMICS (Mighty Bear No. 13 on)
Jan, 1953 - No. 12, Oct, 1953
Star Publications

9(Giant)-L. B. Cole-c 3.00 9.00 18.00
10-12-L. B. Cole-c 2.50 7.00 14.00

FUNDAY FUNNIES (See Famous TV . . ., and Harvey Hits No. 35,40)

FUN-IN (Hanna-Barbera)
Feb, 1970 - No. 10, Jan, 1972; No. 11, 4/74 - No. 15, 12/74
Gold Key

Good / Fine / Mint

1-4,6-Dastardly & Muttley in Their Flying Machines; Perils of Penelope Pitstop in No. 1-4; It's the Wolf in all; Cattanooga Cats in No. 2-4 .25 .50
5,7-Motormouse & Autocat, Dastardly & Muttley in both; It's the Wolf in No. 7 .20 .40
8,10-The Harlem Globetrotters, Dastardly & Muttley in No. 10 .20 .40
9-Where's Huddles?, Dastardly & Muttley, Motormouse & Autocat app. .20 .40
11-Butch Cassidy .20 .40
12,15-Speed Buggy; No. 15: 52 pgs. .20 .40
13-The Hair Bear Bunch .20 .40
14-Inch High Private Eye .20 .40

NOTE: *52 pg. issues had 16 pgs. of advertising added.*

FUNKY PHANTOM, THE (TV)
Dec, 1971 - No. 13, Mar, 1975 (Hanna-Barbera)
Gold Key

1 .35 1.00 2.00
2-13 .50 1.00

FUNLAND
No date (25 cents)
Ziff-Davis (Approved Comics)

Contains games, puzzles, etc. 1.20 3.50 7.00

FUNLAND COMICS
1945
Croyden Publishers

1 1.20 3.50 7.00

FUNNIES, THE (Also see Comic Cuts)
1929 - No. 36, 10/18/30 (10 cents; 5 cents No.22 on) (16 pgs.)
Full tabloid size in color; not reprints; published every Saturday
Dell Publishing Co.

1-My Big Brudder, Johnathan, Jazzbo & Jim, Foxy Grandpa, Sniffy, Jimmy Jams & other strips begin; first four-color comic newsstand publication; also contains magic, puzzles & stories 30.00 70.00 140.00
2-21 (1930, 30 cents) 10.00 24.00 48.00
22(nn-7/12/30-5 cents) 6.00 16.00 32.00
23(nn-7/19/30-5 cents), 24(nn-7/26/30-5 cents), 25(nn-8/2/30), 26(nn-8/9/30), 27(nn-8/16/30), 28(nn-8/23/30), 29(nn-8/30/30), 30(nn-9/6/30), 31(nn-9/13/30), 32(nn-9/20/30), 33(nn-9/27/30), 34(nn-10/4/30), 35(nn-10/11/30), 36(nn, no date-10/18/30) each. . . . 6.00 16.00 32.00

FUNNIES, THE (New Funnies No. 65 on)
Oct, 1936 - No. 64, May, 1942
Dell Publishing Co.

1-Tailspin Tommy, Mutt & Jeff, Alley Oop, Capt. Easy, Don Dixon begin 30.00 80.00 160.00
2: Scribbly by Mayer 14.00 40.00 80.00
3 10.00 30.00 60.00
4 7.00 20.00 40.00
5 6.00 18.00 36.00
6-10 5.50 16.00 32.00
11-29 5.00 14.00 28.00
30-John Carter of Mars (origin) begins by Edgar Rice Burroughs 30.00 80.00 150.00
31-44: 33-John Coleman Burroughs art begins on John Carter 14.00 40.00 70.00
45-Origin Phantasmo, the Master of the World & intro. his sidekick Whizzer McGee 10.00 30.00 48.00
46-50: 46-The Black Knight begins, ends No. 62 7.00 20.00 36.00
51-56-Last ERB John Carter of Mars 7.00 20.00 36.00
57-Intro. & origin Captain Midnight 17.00 50.00 80.00
58-60 7.00 20.00 36.00

Frontline Combat #10, © WMG

Funland Comics #1, © Croyden

The Funnies #57, © DELL

Funnyman #3, © ME

Funny Pages #38, © QUA

Funny Stuff #56, © DC

FUNNIES (continued)

	Good	Fine	Mint
61-Andy Panda begins by Walter Lantz	8.00	24.00	40.00
62,63-Last Captain Midnight cover	7.00	20.00	36.00
64-Format change; Oswald the Rabbit, Felix the Cat, Li'l Eight Ball app.; origin & 1st app. Woody Woodpecker in Andy Panda; last Capt. Midnight & Phantasmo	20.00	60.00	120.00

NOTE: ***McWilliams** art in many issues on "Rex King of the Deep."*

FUNNIES ANNUAL, THE
1959 ($1.00)(B&W; tabloid-size, approx. 7x10")
Avon Periodicals

1-(Rare)-Features the best newspaper comic strips of the year: Archie, Snuffy Smith, Beetle Baily, Henry, Blondie, Steve Canyon, Buz Sawyer, The Little King, Hi & Lois, Popeye, & others. Also has a chronological history of the comics from 2000 B.C. to 1959.	17.00	50.00	90.00

FUNNIES ON PARADE (Premium)
1933 (Probably the 1st comic book) (36 pgs.; slick cover)
No date or publisher listed
Eastern Color Printing Co.

nn-Contains Sunday page reprints of Mutt & Jeff, Joe Palooka, Hairbreadth Harry, Reg'lar Fellers, Skippy, & others (10,000 print run). This book was printed for Proctor & Gamble to be given away & came out before Famous Funnies or Century of Comics.	150.00	350.00	620.00

FUNNY ANIMALS (See Fawcett's Funny Animals)

FUNNYBONE
1944 (132 pages)
La Salle Publishing Co.

	1.50	4.00	8.00

FUNNY BOOK (. . . Magazine) (Hocus Pocus No. 9)
Dec, 1942 - No. 9, Aug-Sept, 1946
Parents' Magazine Press

1-Funny animal	2.00	5.00	10.00
2-9	1.20	3.50	7.00

FUNNY COMICS (7 cents)
1955 (36 pgs.; 5x7"; in color)
Modern Store Publ.

1-Funny animal	.40	1.20	2.40

FUNNY COMIC TUNES (See Funny Tunes)

FUNNY FABLES
Aug, 1957 - V2No. 2, Nov, 1957
Decker Publications (Red Top Comics)

V1No.1	.30	.90	1.80
V2No.1,2		.50	1.00

FUNNY FILMS
Sept-Oct, 1949 - No. 29, May-June, 1954
American Comics Group(Michel Publ./Titan Publ.)

1	2.00	5.00	10.00
2-10	1.00	3.00	6.00
11-29	.80	2.30	4.60

FUNNY FOLKS (Hollywood . . . on cover only No. 17-27; becomes Hollywood Funny Folks No. 28? on)
April-May, 1946 - No. 27, 1950
National Periodical Publications

1-1st app. Nutsy Squirrel	5.50	16.00	32.00
2-5	3.00	8.00	16.00
6-10	2.00	5.00	10.00
11-27	1.00	3.00	6.00

NOTE: ***Sheldon Mayer** a-in some issues.*

FUNNY FROLICS
Summer, 1945 - No. 5, Dec, 1946
Timely/Marvel Comics (SPI)

	Good	Fine	Mint
1-4	1.50	4.00	8.00
5-Kurtzman-a	3.00	8.00	16.00

FUNNY FUNNIES
April, 1943 (68 pages)
Nedor Publishers

1	2.00	5.00	10.00

FUNNYMAN
Dec, 1947; No. 1, Jan, 1948 - No. 7, Aug, 1948
Magazine Enterprises

nn(12/47)-Prepublication B&W undistributed copy by Siegel & Shuster-(5¾x8"), 16 pgs.; Sold in San Francisco in 1976 for $300.00			
1-By Siegel & Shuster	6.00	18.00	36.00
2-5-By Siegel & Shuster	5.00	14.00	28.00
6,7-(No. 7 exist?)	2.00	6.00	12.00

FUNNY MOVIES (See 3-D Funny Movies)

FUNNY PAGES (Formerly The Comics Magazine)
No. 6, Nov, 1936 - No. 42, Oct, 1940
Quality Comics Group

V1No.6-The Clock begins (2 pgs.), ends No. 11	10.00	28.00	60.00
7-11	6.00	18.00	40.00
V2No.1-9(No. 12-20)	5.50	16.00	36.00
10(No. 21)-(Scarce)-1st app. of The Arrow by Gustavson	20.00	60.00	135.00
11,12(No. 22,23)	10.00	30.00	75.00
V3No.1-10(No. 24-33)	10.00	30.00	75.00
V4No.1(No. 34, 1/40)-(Rare)-The Owl & The Phantom Rider app.; origin Mantoka, Maker of Magic by Jack Cole; the Arrow app. on cover; Tarpe Mills-a	20.00	65.00	145.00
35-42-Last Arrow	10.00	30.00	75.00

NOTE: ***Jack Cole** a-V2No.3, 8, 10, 11, V3No.6, 7, 9, 10, V4No.1, 37. **Eisner** a-V1No.7, 8, 10. **Everett** a-V2No.11 (text illos). **Sid Greene** a-39. **Gustavson** a-V2No.5, 11, V3No.6, 9. **McWilliams** a-V3No.6. **Tarpe Mills** a-V3No.8-V4No.1; c-V3No.9. **Bob Wood** a-V2No.11(3), V3No.6, 9.*

FUNNY PICTURE STORIES
Nov, 1936 - V3No.6, 1939
Centaur Publications

V1No.1-The Clock begins	20.00	60.00	120.00
2	10.00	28.00	60.00
3,5-9	6.00	18.00	40.00
4-Eisner-a	8.00	22.00	48.00
V2No.1-Jack Strand begins	5.00	14.00	30.00
2-11	4.00	12.00	26.00
V3No.1-6	4.00	12.00	26.00

FUNNY STUFF (Becomes The Dodo & the Frog No. 80)
Summer, 1944 - No. 79, July-Aug, 1954
All-American/National Periodical Publications No. 7 on

1-The Three Mouseketeers & The "Terrific Whatzit" begin-Sheldon Mayer-a	12.00	35.00	70.00
2-Sheldon Mayer-a	7.00	20.00	40.00
3-5	4.00	12.00	24.00
6-10	3.00	8.00	16.00
11-20	2.00	6.00	12.00
21,23-30: 24-Infinity-c	1.50	4.00	8.00
22-Superman cameo	4.00	12.00	24.00
31-79-Dodo & the Frog. 75-Bo Bunny by Mayer	1.00	3.00	6.00
Wheaties Giveaway(1946, 6½x8¼") (Scarce)	4.00	12.00	24.00

NOTE: **Mayer** *a-1, 2, 55, 68, 75.*

FUNNY 3-D
December, 1953
Harvey Publications

FUNNY 3-D (continued)

	Good	Fine	Mint
1	8.00	24.00	48.00

FUNNY TUNES (Animated Funny Comic Tunes No. 16-22; Funny Comic Tunes No. 23, on covers only; formerly Human Torch; Oscar No. 24 on)
No. 16, Summer, 1944 - No. 23, Fall, 1946
U.S.A. Comics Magazine Corp. (Timely)

	Good	Fine	Mint
16-22	1.50	4.00	8.00
23-Kurtzman-a	3.00	8.00	16.00

FUNNY TUNES
Aug-Sept, 1953 - No. 3, Dec-Jan, 1953-54
Avon Periodicals

	Good	Fine	Mint
1-Space Mouse	1.50	4.00	8.00
2,3-Space Mouse-No.3	1.20	3.50	7.00

FUNNY WORLD
1947 - 1948
Marbak Press

	Good	Fine	Mint
1-3-Newspaper strip reprints	1.50	4.00	8.00

FUNTASTIC WORLD OF HANNA-BARBERA, THE
Dec, 1977 - No. 3, 1978 ($1.25) (Oversized)
Marvel Comics Group

	Good	Fine	Mint
1-The Flintstones Christmas Party(12/77); 2-Yogi Bear's Easter Parade(3/78); 3-Laff-a-lympics(6/78) each....	.30	.80	1.60

FUN TIME
1953 - No. 4, Winter, 1953-54
Ace Periodicals

	Good	Fine	Mint
1,2	.85	2.50	5.00
3,4 (100 pgs. each)	2.00	6.00	12.00

FUN WITH SANTA CLAUS (See March of Comics No. 11,108,325)

FURY (Straight Arrow's Horse...) (See A-1 No. 119)

FURY (TV)
Aug, 1957 - 1962
Dell Publishing Co./Gold Key

	Good	Fine	Mint
4-Color 781,885,975	1.00	3.00	6.00
4-Color 1031,1080,1133,1172,1218,1296, 01292-208(No.1-'62)	1.00	3.00	6.00
10020-211(11/62-G.K.)	1.00	3.00	6.00

(See March of Comics No. 200)

FUTURE COMICS
June, 1940 - No. 4, Sept, 1940
David McKay Publications

	Good	Fine	Mint
1-(Scarce)-Origin The Phantom; The Lone Ranger, & Saturn Against the Earth begin	100.00	300.00	600.00
2	20.00	60.00	120.00
3,4	15.00	45.00	90.00

FUTURE WORLD COMICS
Summer, 1946 - No. 2, Fall, 1946
George W. Dougherty

	Good	Fine	Mint
1,2	4.00	12.00	24.00

FUTURE WORLD COMIX (Warren Presents... on cover)
September, 1978
Warren Publications

	Good	Fine	Mint
1		.50	1.00

G-8 (See G-Eight)

GABBY (Formerly Ken Shannon)
No. 11, July, 1953; No. 2, Sept, 1953 - No. 9, Sept, 1954
Quality Comics Group

	Good	Fine	Mint
11(No.1)(7/53)	1.20	3.50	7.00
2-9	.85	2.50	5.00

GABBY GOB (See Harvey Hits No. 85,90,94,97,100,103,106,109)

GABBY HAYES WESTERN
Nov, 1948 - No. 50, Jan, 1953; Dec, 1954 - No. 59, Jan, 1957
Fawcett/Toby Press/Charlton Comics No. 51 on

	Good	Fine	Mint
1	8.00	24.00	48.00
2-10	3.50	10.00	20.00
11-20	2.50	7.00	14.00
21-50	2.00	5.00	10.00
51-59(Charlton '54-57)	1.50	4.00	8.00
1(Toby)(12/53)	3.50	10.00	20.00
Quaker Oats Giveaway No. 1-5(1951)	2.50	7.00	14.00

GAGS
July, 1937; July, 1942 (13¾x10¾'')
United Features Synd./Triangle Publ. No. 9

	Good	Fine	Mint
1(7/37)-52 pgs.; 20 pgs. Grin & Bear It, Fellow Citizen	3.00	8.00	16.00
V1No.9 (36 pgs.; 15 cents)	2.00	5.00	10.00

GAG STRIPS
Aug, 1942 (13¾x10¾''; 36 pgs.; 15 cents)
Triangle Publications

	Good	Fine	Mint
V1No.1-Comic strips by 24 different cartoonists	2.00	5.00	10.00

GALACTIC WARS COMIX (Warren Presents... on cover)
December, 1978
Warren Publications

	Good	Fine	Mint
1		.50	1.00

GALLANT MEN, THE (TV)
October, 1963
Gold Key

	Good	Fine	Mint
1(10085-310)-Manning-a	.85	2.50	5.00

GALLEGHER, BOY REPORTER (TV)
May, 1965 (Disney)
Gold Key

	Good	Fine	Mint
1(10149-505)	.85	2.50	5.00

GANDY GOOSE
Mar, 1953 - No. 5, Nov, 1953; No. 5, Fall, 1956 - No. 6, Summ/58
St. John Publ. Co./Pines No. 5,6

	Good	Fine	Mint
1	.85	2.50	5.00
2-5(1953)(St. John)	.70	2.00	4.00
5,6(1956-58)(Pines)	.35	1.00	2.00

GANG BUSTERS
1938 - 1943
David McKay/Dell Publishing Co.

	Good	Fine	Mint
Feature Book 17(McKay)('38)	12.00	35.00	70.00
Black & White 10('39)-(Scarce)	20.00	60.00	120.00
Black & White 17('41)	14.00	40.00	80.00
4-Color 7(1940)	8.00	24.00	48.00
4-Color 23,24('42-43)	7.00	20.00	40.00

GANG BUSTERS (Radio/TV)
Dec-Jan, 1947-48 - No. 67, Dec-Jan, 1958-59
National Periodical Publications

	Good	Fine	Mint
1	10.00	30.00	60.00
2	5.00	14.00	28.00
3-10: 8-Barry, Infantino-a	3.50	10.00	20.00
11-13,15,16,18-30	2.00	5.00	10.00
14,17-Frazetta-a, 8 pgs. each	10.00	30.00	60.00
31-50	1.20	3.50	7.00
51-67: 51-Drucker-a	.85	2.50	5.00

Future Comics #1, © DMP

Gabby Hayes Western #2, © FAW

Gang Busters #20, © DC

Gangsters & Gun Molls #4, © AVON

Gay Comics #27, © MCG

Gene Autry Comics #18, © DELL

GANGSTERS AND GUN MOLLS
Sept, 1951 - No. 4, June, 1952
Avon Periodical/Realistic Comics

	Good	Fine	Mint
1-Wood-a, 1 pg; c-/Avon paperback 292	10.00	30.00	60.00
2-Check-a, 8 pgs.; Kamen-a	8.00	24.00	48.00
3-Marijuana mention story; used in **POP**, pg. 84-85; Kinstler-c	2.00	24.00	48.00
4	7.00	20.00	40.00

GANGSTERS CAN'T WIN
Feb-Mar, 1948 - 1951
D. S. Publishing Co.

1	5.00	14.00	28.00
2	2.50	7.50	15.00
3-Two bra & panties panels	3.50	10.00	20.00
4-Narcotics mentioned; acid in face story	3.50	10.00	20.00
5,6-Ingels-a	4.00	12.00	24.00
7-McWilliams-a	2.00	6.00	12.00
8-10	2.00	6.00	12.00

GANG WORLD
No. 5, Nov, 1952 - No. 6, Jan, 1953
Standard Comics

5-Bondage-c	3.50	10.00	20.00
6-Opium story	2.50	7.00	14.00

GARRISON'S GORILLAS (TV)
Jan, 1968 - No. 5, Oct, 1969
Dell Publishing Co.

1	.70	2.00	4.00
2-5: 5-Reprints No. 1	.35	1.00	2.00

GASOLINE ALLEY
1929 (B&W daily strip reprints)(7x8¾''; hardcover)
Reilly & Lee Publishers

By King (96 pgs.)	7.00	20.00	40.00

GASOLINE ALLEY
Oct, 1950 - No. 2, 1950 (Newspaper reprints)
Star Publications

1-Contains 1 pg. intro. history of the strip (The Life of Skeezix); reprints 15 scenes of highlights from 1921-1935, plus an adventure from 1935 and 1936 strips; a 2-pg. filler is included on the life of the creator Frank King, with photo of the cartoonist.	6.00	18.00	36.00
2-(1936-37 reprints)-L. B. Cole-c	7.00	20.00	40.00

(See Super Book No. 21)

GASP!
March, 1967 - No. 4, Aug, 1967
American Comics Group

1-L.S.D. drug mention	.85	2.50	5.00
2-4	.50	1.50	3.00

GAY COMICS (Honeymoon No. 41)
1944 (no month) - No. 40, Oct, 1949 (No. 2-17 exist?)
Timely Comics/USA Comic Mag. Co. No. 18-24

1-Wolverton's Powerhouse Pepper; Tessie the Typist begins	10.00	28.00	56.00
18-29-Wolverton-a in all; Kurtzman in No. 24, 29	5.00	15.00	30.00
30,31,33,36,37-Kurtzman's ''Hey Look''	1.50	4.00	8.00
32,35,38-40	1.00	3.00	6.00
34-Three Kurtzman's ''Hey Look''	2.50	7.00	14.00

GAY COMICS (Also see Tickle, Smile, & Whee Comics)
1955 (52 pgs.; 5x7¼''; 7 cents)
Modern Store Publ.

1	.50	1.50	3.00

GAY PURR-EE (See Movie Comics)

GEEK, THE (See Brother Power. . .)

G-8 AND HIS BATTLE ACES
October, 1966
Gold Key

	Good	Fine	Mint
1 (10184-610)	1.50	4.00	8.00

GEM COMICS
April, 1942; 1945
Spotlight Publishers

1(1942)-Bondage-c	3.50	10.00	20.00
1(1945)-Little Mohee, Steve Strong app.	3.50	10.00	20.00

GENE AUTRY (See March of Comics No. 25,28,39,54,78,90,104, 120,135,150)

GENE AUTRY COMICS (Dell takes over with No. 11)
1941 - 1944 (68 pgs.)
Fawcett Publications

1 (Rare)	60.00	170.00	350.00
2	25.00	70.00	140.00
3-5	20.00	55.00	110.00
6-10	14.00	45.00	90.00

GENE AUTRY COMICS (. . . & Champion No. 102 on)
June, 1946 - No. 121, Jan, 1959
Dell Publishing Co.

11,12(1943-44)-Continuation of Fawcett series	14.00	40.00	80.00
4-Color 47(1944)	14.00	40.00	80.00
4-Color 57('44),66('45)	12.00	35.00	70.00
4-Color 75,83('45)	10.00	30.00	60.00
4-Color 93,100('45-46)	8.00	24.00	48.00
1(5-6/46)	14.00	40.00	80.00
2(7-8/46)	7.00	20.00	40.00
3-5	5.00	14.00	28.00
6-10	4.00	12.00	24.00
11-30: 20-Panhandle pete begins	3.00	8.00	16.00
31-60	2.00	5.00	10.00
61-80	1.50	4.00	8.00
81-121: 87-Blank inside-c	1.00	3.00	6.00
Pillsbury Premium('47)-36 pgs., 6½x7½''; games, comics, puzzles	5.50	16.00	32.00
Quaker Oats Giveaway(1950)-2½x6¾''; 5 different versions each. . . .	3.00	8.00	16.00
3-D Giveaway(1953)-Pocket-size; 5 different	3.00	8.00	16.00

NOTE: ***Manning*** *a-118.* ***Jesse Marsh*** *art: 4-Color No. 66, 75, 93, 100, No. 1-25, 27-37, 39, 40.*

GENE AUTRY TIM (Formerly Superman-Tim) (Becomes Tim in Space)
1950 (Half-size) (Black & White Giveaway)
Tim Stores

Several issues (All Scarce)	5.00	14.00	21.00

GENE AUTRY'S CHAMPION
1950; No. 3, Aug-Oct, 1951 - No. 19, Aug, 1955
Dell Publishing Co.

4-Color 287('50)	1.50	4.50	9.00
4-Color 319('51), 3	1.50	4.00	8.00
4-19	1.00	3.00	6.00

GENERAL DOUGLAS MACARTHUR
1951
Fox Features Syndicate

nn	5.00	14.00	28.00

GENTLE BEN (TV)
Feb, 1968 - No. 5, Oct, 1969
Dell Publishing Co.

1	.70	2.00	4.00
2-5: 5-Reprints No. 1	.35	1.00	2.00

GEORGE OF THE JUNGLE (TV)
Feb, 1969 - No. 2, Oct, 1969 (Jay Ward)
Gold Key

GEORGE OF THE JUNGLE (continued)

	Good	Fine	Mint
1,2	.50	1.50	3.00

GEORGE PAL'S PUPPETOONS
Dec, 1945 - No. 18, 1947; No. 19, 1950
Fawcett Publications

1-Captain Marvel on cover	8.00	24.00	48.00
2-10	4.00	12.00	24.00
11-19	3.00	8.00	16.00

GEORGIE (. . . & Judy No. 26-35?)
Spring, 1945 - No. 39, Oct, 1952
Timely Comics/GPI No. 1-34

1-Dave Berg-a	3.50	10.00	20.00
2-8	2.00	5.00	10.00
9,10-Kurtzman's "Hey Look"	3.00	8.00	16.00
11,12	.85	2.50	5.00
13-Kurtzman's "Hey Look," 3 pgs.	2.50	7.00	14.00
14-Wolverton art, 1 pg. & Kurtzman's "Hey Look"	3.00	8.00	16.00
15,16,18-24,26-39	.60	1.70	3.40
17-Kurtzman's "Hey Look," 1 pg.	1.50	4.00	8.00
25-Painted cover by classic pin-up artist Peter Driben	2.00	5.00	10.00

GERALD McBOING-BOING AND THE NEARSIGHTED MR. MAGOO
(Mr. Magoo No. 6)
Aug-Oct, 1952 - No. 5, Aug-Oct, 1953
Dell Publishing Co.

1	2.00	5.00	10.00
2-5	1.20	3.50	7.00

GERONIMO
1950 - No. 4, Feb, 1952
Avon Periodicals

1-Indian Fighter; Maneely-a; Texas Rangers r-/Cowpuncher No. 1	5.50	16.00	32.00
2-On the Warpath; Kit West app.; Kinstler c/a	4.00	12.00	24.00
3-And His Apache Murderers; Kinstler c/a(2); Kit West, drug story r-Cowpuncher No. 6	4.00	12.00	24.00
4-Savage Raids of; Kinstler c/a(3)	3.50	10.00	20.00

GERONIMO JONES
Sept, 1971 - No. 9, Jan, 1973
Charlton Comics

1		.30	.60
2-9		.20	.40

GET LOST
Feb-Mar, 1954 - No. 3, June-July, 1954 (Satire)
Mikeross Publications

1	3.50	10.00	20.00
2-Has 4 pg. E. C. parady featuring the "Sewer Keeper"	3.00	8.00	16.00
3	2.00	6.00	12.00

GET SMART (TV)
June, 1966 - No. 8, Sept, 1967 (No. 1-7 have photo-c)
Dell Publishing Co.

1-Photo-c	1.00	3.00	6.00
2-Ditko-a	1.50	4.00	8.00
3-8	.70	2.00	4.00

GHOST
Winter, 1950-51 - No. 11, Summer, 1954
Fiction House Magazines

1	6.00	18.00	36.00
2-9: 3,6,7-Bondage-c	4.00	12.00	24.00
10,11-Dr. Drew by Grandenetti in each, reprinted from Rangers; Evans-a-No. 11	5.00	14.00	28.00

GHOST BREAKERS (Also see (CC) Sherlock Holmes & Racket Squad in Action)
Sept, 1948 - No. 2, Nov, 1948 (52 pages)
Street & Smith Publications

	Good	Fine	Mint
1-Powell-a; Dr. Neff (magician) app.	6.00	18.00	36.00
2-Powell-c/a; Maneely-a	5.00	15.00	30.00

GHOST CASTLE (See Tales of. . .)

GHOSTLY HAUNTS (Formerly Ghost Manor)
No. 20, 9/71 - No. 53, 12/76; No. 54, 9/77 - No. 55, 10/77; No. 56, 1/78 - No. 58, 4/78
Charlton Comics

20,21		.40	.80
22-41,43-58: 27-Dr. Graves x-over. 39-Origin & 1st app. Destiny Fox		.40	.80
42-Newton c/a		.30	.60
40(Modern Comics reprint, 1977)		.15	.30

NOTE: ***Ditko*** *a-22-28, 30-34, 36-41, 43-48, 50, 52, 54, 56r; c-22-27, 30, 33-38, 47, 54, 56.* ***Glanzman*** *a-20.* ***Howard*** *a-27, 42.* ***Sutton*** *c-39.*

GHOSTLY TALES (Blue Beetle No. 50-54)
No. 55, 4-5/66 - No. 124, 12/76; No. 125, 9/77 - Present
Charlton Comics

55-Intro. & origin Dr. Graves		.60	1.20
56-70-Dr. Graves ends		.40	.80
71-106,108-113,115-146		.30	.60
107-Sutton, Wood-a		.40	.80
114-Newton-a		.30	.60

NOTE: ***Aparo*** *c-71.* ***Ditko*** *a-55, 57, 58, 60, 61, 67, 69-73, 75-90, 92-97, 99-116, 118, 120-122, 125r, 126r, 131-33r, 136-41r, 144r; c-67, 69, 73, 77, 78, 83, 84, 86-90, 92-97, 99, 102, 102, 107, 109, 111, 118, 120-22, 125, 131-33.* ***Howard*** *a-95, 98, 99, 117; c-98, 107, 120, 121.* ***Newton*** *c-115.* ***Sutton*** *a-112, 113.*

GHOSTLY WEIRD STORIES (Formerly Blue Bolt Weird)
No. 120, Sept, 1953 - No. 124, Sept, 1954
Star Publications

120,121-Jo-Jo reprints	7.00	20.00	40.00
122-The Mask, Rulah reprint	6.00	18.00	36.00
123-Jo-Jo; Disbrow-a(2)	6.00	18.00	36.00
124-Torpedo Man	6.00	18.00	36.00

NOTE: ***Disbrow*** *a-120-124.* ***L. B. Cole*** *covers-all issues.*

GHOST MANOR (Ghostly Haunts No. 20 on)
July, 1968 - No. 19, July, 1971
Charlton Comics

1		.40	.80
2-12,17		.30	.60
13-16,18,19-Ditko-a; c-15,18,19		.60	1.20

GHOST MANOR (2nd Series)
Oct, 1971 - No. 32, Dec, 1976; No. 33, Sept, 1977 - Present
Charlton Comics

1		.40	.80
2-7,9,10		.30	.60
8-Wood-a		.40	.80
11-17,19		.30	.60
18,22-Newton c/a		.40	.80
20-Newton-a		.30	.60
21-E-Man, Blue Beetle, Capt. Atom cameos		.40	.80
23-39,41-56,58-60: 28-Nudity panels		.30	.60
40-Torture & drug use		.30	.60
57-Wood, Ditko, Howard-a		.30	.60
19(Modern Comics reprint, 1977)		.20	.40

NOTE: ***Ditko*** *a-18, 20-22, 24-26, 28, 29, 31, 37r, 38r, 40r, 42-44r, 46r, 51r, 52r, 57; c-2-7, 9, 11, 14-16, 28, 31, 37, 38, 42, 43, 46, 51, 52.* ***Howard*** *a-4, 20, 21, 57.*

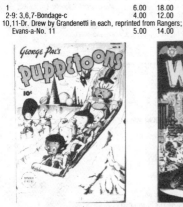

George Pal's Puppetoons #8, © FAW

Ghostly Weird Stories #121, © STAR

Ghost Manor #22, © CC

Ghost Rider #13, © ME

Ghost Rider #35, © MCG

Ghosts #88, © DC

GHOST RIDER (See A-1 Comics & Great Western)
1950 - 1954
Magazine Enterprises

	Good	Fine	Mint
1(A-1 27)-Origin Ghost Rider	20.00	55.00	110.00
2(A-1 29), 3(A-1 31), 4(A-1 34), 5(A-1 37)-All Frazetta-c only	20.00	55.00	110.00
6(A-1 44), 7(A-1 51)	6.00	18.00	36.00
8(A-1 57), 10(A-1 71)	5.00	14.00	28.00
9(A-1 69)-L.S.D. story	5.00	14.00	28.00
11(A-1 75), 12(A-1 80, bondage-c), 13(A-1 84), 14(A-1 112)	4.00	12.00	24.00

NOTE: ***Dick Ayers** art in all.*

GHOST RIDER (See Night Rider)
Feb, 1967 - No. 7, Nov, 1967
Marvel Comics Group

	Good	Fine	Mint
1-Origin Ghost Rider; Kid Colt reprint	.40	1.10	2.20
2-7		.60	1.20

GHOST RIDER (See Marvel Spotlight)
Sept, 1973 - Present (Super-hero)
Marvel Comics Group

	Good	Fine	Mint
1	1.20	3.50	7.00
2-5	.55	1.70	3.40
6-9	.50	1.50	3.00
10-Ploog-a	.50	1.50	3.00
11-20	.40	1.10	2.20
21-34,36-49: 36-Drug mention	.30	.80	1.60
35-Starlin-c/a	.30	.90	1.80
50-Double size; Night Rider app.		.60	1.20
51-63		.40	.80

NOTE: ***Byrne** a-20. **Infantino** a-43, 44, 51. **Kirby** c-21-23. **Mooney** a-6,8. **Newton** a-23.*

GHOSTS (Ghost No. 1)
Sept-Oct, 1971 - Present (No. 1-5: 52 pgs.)
National Periodical Publications/DC Comics

	Good	Fine	Mint
1	.40	1.10	2.20
2-Wood-a	.40	1.10	2.20
3-10		.50	1.00
11-30		.40	.80
31-70: 40-68 pgs.		.30	.60
71-87,89-96: 74-Orlando-a		.30	.60
88-Golden-a		.30	.60
97-99-The Spectre app.		.40	.80
100-Infinity-c		.30	.60
101-107		.30	.60

NOTE: ***Alcala** a-9, 15, 17-19, 21, 23-25, 28, 33, 34. **Aparo** a-1; c-97, 98. **Ditko** a-77. **Golden** a-88. **Kaluta** c-7, 93, 101. **Kubert** c-105, 107. **Nasser** a-97. **Newton** a-92p, 94. **Nino** a-35, 37, 57. **Orlando** c-80. **Redondo** a-8, 13, 45.*

GHOSTS SPECIAL (See DC Special Series No. 7)

GHOST STORIES (See Amazing Ghost Stories)

GHOST STORIES
Sept-Nov, 1962; No. 2, Apr-June, 1963 - No. 37, Oct, 1973
Dell Publishing Co.

	Good	Fine	Mint
12-295-211-Written by John Stanley	1.50	4.00	8.00
2-10: Two No. 6's exist with diff. c/a(12-295-406,12-295-503)	.25	.70	1.40
11-37		.40	.80

NOTE: *No. 21-34,36,37 all reprint earlier issues.*

GHOUL TALES (Magazine)
Nov, 1970 - No. 5, July, 1971 (52 pages) (B&W)
Stanley Publications

	Good	Fine	Mint
1-Aragon pre-code reprints; Mr. Mystery as host; bondage-c	.40	1.20	2.40
2-(1/71)Reprint/Climax No. 1		.60	1.20
3-(3/71)		.60	1.20
4-(5/71)Reprints story "The Way to a Man's Heart" used in **SOTI**	.85	2.50	5.00
5-ACG reprints		.60	1.20

NOTE: *No. 1-4 contain pre-code Aragon reprints.*

GIANT BOY BOOK OF COMICS (See Boy)
1945 (Hardcover) (240 pages)
Newsbook Publications (Gleason)

	Good	Fine	Mint
1-Crimebuster & Young Robin Hood	17.00	50.00	100.00

GIANT COMIC ALBUM
1972 (52 pgs.; 11x14''; B&W; 59 cents)
King Features Syndicate

	Good	Fine	Mint
Newspaper reprints: Little Iodine, Katzenjammer Kids, Henry, Mandrake the Magician ('59 Falk), Popeye, Beetle Bailey, Barney Google, Blondie, Flash Gordon ('68-69 Dan Barry), & Snuffy Smith	1.00	3.00	6.00

GIANT COMICS
Summer, 1957 - No. 3, Winter, 1957 (100 pgs.) (25 cents)
Charlton Comics

	Good	Fine	Mint
1-Atomic Mouse, Hoppy app.	1.00	3.00	6.00
2,3-Atomic Mouse, Rabbit, Christmas Book	1.00	3.00	6.00

GIANT COMICS (See Wham-O Giant Comics)

GIANT COMICS EDITION (See Terry-Toons)
1947 - No. 17, 1950 (All 100-164 pgs.) (25 cents)
St. John Publishing Co.

	Good	Fine	Mint
1-Mighty Mouse	8.00	24.00	48.00
2	4.00	12.00	24.00
3-Terry-Toons Album; 100 pgs.	5.50	16.00	32.00
4-Crime comics; contains Red Seal No. 16, used & illo. in **SOTI**	12.00	36.00	72.00
5-Police Case Book(4/49)-Contents varies; contains remaindered St. John books - some volumes contain 5 copies rather than 4, with 160 pages; Matt Baker-c	10.00	30.00	60.00
5A-Terry-Toons Album, 132 pgs.	5.50	16.00	32.00
6-Western Picture Stories; Baker-c/a(3); The Sky Chief, Blue Monk, Ventrilo app.; Tuska-a	8.00	24.00	48.00
7-Contains a teen-age romance plus 3 Mopsy comics	7.00	20.00	40.00
8-The Advs. of Mighty Mouse (10/49)	7.00	20.00	40.00
9-Romance and confession stories; Kubert-a(4); Baker-a; photo-c	10.00	30.00	60.00
9-Same as above but with Baker-c	17.00	50.00	100.00
10-Terry-Toons	5.50	16.00	32.00
11-Western Picture Stories-Baker c/a(4); The Sky Chief, Desperado, & Blue Monk app.; another version with Son of Sinbad by Kubert	8.00	24.00	48.00
12-Diary Secrets; Baker prostitute-c; 4 St. John romance comics; Baker-a	40.00	100.00	200.00
13-Romances; Baker, Kubert-a	10.00	30.00	60.00
14-Mighty Mouse Album	5.50	16.00	32.00
15-Romances (4 love comics)	10.00	30.00	60.00
16-Little Audrey, Abbott & Costello, Casper	5.50	16.00	32.00
17-Mighty Mouse Album (nn, no date, but did follow No. 16); 100 pgs. on cover but has 148 pgs.	5.50	16.00	32.00

NOTE: *The above books contain remaindered comics and contents could vary with each issue. No. 11,12 have part photo mag. insides.*

GIANT COMICS EDITIONS
1940's (132 pages)
United Features Syndicate

	Good	Fine	Mint
1-Abbie & Slats, Abbott & Costello, Jim Hardy, Ella Cinders, Iron Vic	5.50	16.00	32.00
2-Jim Hardy & Gordo	5.00	14.00	28.00

NOTE: *Above books contain rebound copies; contents can vary.*

GIANT COMICS TO COLOR
1975 - 1976 (16x11'') (69 cents)

GIANT COMICS TO COLOR (continued)
Whitman Publishing Co.

	Good	Fine	Mint
1714-Wonder Woman "The Menace of the Mole Men" (1975)			
1715-Shazam! "Double Trouble" (1975)			
1716-Superman "Luthor's Lost Land" (1975)			
1717-Batman "Comedy of Tears" (1975)			
1642-Spider-Man "Weather Forecast: Danger" (1976)			
1663-Captain America "The Challenge of Super Sport" (1976)			
1664-Superman "Braniac's Biggest Plot" (1976)			
1671-Batman "Four Birds of a Feather" (1976)			
each....		.60	1.20

GIANT GRAB BAG OF COMICS (See Archie All-Star Specials under Archie Comics)

GIANTS (See Thrilling True Stories of...)

GIANT-SIZE (Avengers, Captain America, Captain Marvel, Conan, Daredevil, Defenders, Fantastic Four, Hulk, Invaders, Iron Man, Kid Colt, Man-Thing, Master of Kung Fu, Power Man, Spider-Man, Super-Villain Team-Up, Thor, Werewolf, and X-Men are listed under their own titles.)

GIANT-SIZE CHILLERS (Giant-Size Dracula No. 2)
June, 1974; Feb, 1975 - No. 3, Aug, 1975 (35 cents)
Marvel Comics Group

	Good	Fine	Mint
1-(6/74)-Tomb of Dracula (52 pgs.); Origin & 1st app. Lilith, Dracula's daughter	.30	.80	1.60
1-(2/75)(50 cents)(68 pgs.)-Alcala-a		.60	1.20
2-(5/75)		.50	1.00
3-(8/75)-Wrightson c/a; Smith-a(r)	.30	.80	1.60

NOTE: ***Everett*** *reprint-No. 2/Advs. Into Weird Worlds No. 10.*

GIANT SIZE CREATURES (Giant-Size Werewolf No. 2)
July, 1974 (52 pgs.) (35 cents)
Marvel Comics Group

	Good	Fine	Mint
1-Werewolf, Tigra app.; Crandall-a(r)		.50	1.00

GIANT-SIZE DRACULA (Formerly Giant-Size Chillers)
No. 2, Sept, 1974 - No. 5, June, 1975 (50 cents)
Marvel Comics Group

	Good	Fine	Mint
2	.30	.80	1.60
3-Fox-a/Uncanny Tales No. 6		.60	1.20
4-Ditko-a(2)(r)		.50	1.00
5-1st Byrne-a at Marvel	2.00	5.00	10.00

GIANT-SIZE SUPER HEROES
June, 1974 (35 cents)
Marvel Comics Group

	Good	Fine	Mint
1-Spider-Man vs. Man-Wolf; Ditko-a(r)	.35	1.00	2.00

GIANT-SIZE SUPER-STARS (Giant-Size Fantastic Four No. 2)
May, 1974 (35 cents)
Marvel Comics Group

	Good	Fine	Mint
1-Fantastic Four, Thing, Hulk by Buckler; Kirbyish-a	.40	1.20	2.40

GIANT SPECTACULAR COMICS (See Archie All-Star Special under Archie Comics)

GIANT SUMMER FUN BOOK (See Terry-Toons...)

GIANTS (Baseball) (See New York...)

G. I. COMBAT
Oct, 1952 - No. 43, Dec, 1956
Quality Comics Group

	Good	Fine	Mint
1-Crandall-c	6.00	18.00	36.00
2,7-9	3.00	9.00	18.00
3-5,10-Crandall c/a	4.00	12.00	24.00
6-Crandall-a	3.50	10.00	20.00
11-20	2.00	5.00	10.00
21-33,35-43: 32-Nuclear attack-c	1.50	4.50	9.00
34-Crandall-a	3.00	9.00	18.00

G. I. COMBAT
No. 44, Jan, 1957 - Present
National Periodical Publications/DC Comics

	Good	Fine	Mint
44	10.00	30.00	60.00
45	5.50	16.00	32.00
46-50	3.00	8.00	16.00
51-60	2.00	5.00	10.00
61-66,68-80	1.20	3.50	7.00
67-1st Tank Killer	3.50	10.00	20.00
81,82,84-86,88-100	.60	1.80	3.60
83-1st Big Al, Little Al, & Charlie Cigar	2.00	5.00	10.00
87-1st Haunted Tank	3.00	9.00	18.00
101-113,115-120	.40	1.20	2.40
114-Origin Haunted Tank	1.00	3.00	6.00
121-137,139,140		.60	1.20
138-Intro. The Losers (Capt. Storm, Gunner/Sarge, Johnny Cloud) in Haunted Tank	.35	1.00	2.00
141-150,152,154		.50	1.00
151,153-Medal of Honor series by Maurer		.50	1.00
155-203,207,208		.40	.80
204-206,209-236 ($1.00 size)		.60	1.20

NOTE: ***Adams*** *c-168, 201, 202.* ***Drucker*** *a-48, 61, 63, 66, 71, 72, 76, 134, 140, 141, 144, 147, 148, 153.* ***Evans*** *a-135, 138, 158, 164, 166, 202, 204, 205, 215.* ***Kubert/Heath*** *stories in many issues.* ***Morrow*** *a-159-161(2 pgs.).* ***Redondo*** *a-189.* ***Wildey*** *a-153. Johnny Cloud app.-No. 112, 115, 120. Mlle. Marie app.-No. 123, 132, 200. Sgt. Rock app.-No. 111-113, 115, 120, 125, 141, 146, 147, 149, 200. USS Stevens by* ***Glanzman****-No. 145, 150-153, 157.*

G. I. COMICS (Also see Jeep & Overseas Comics)
1945 (distributed to U. S. armed forces)
Giveaways

	Good	Fine	Mint
33-49-Contains Prince Valiant by Foster, Blondie, Smilin' Jack, Mickey Finn, Terry & the Pirates, Donald Duck, Alley Oop, Moon Mullins, & Capt. Easy strip reprints	2.00	6.00	12.00

GIDGET (TV)
April, 1966 - No. 2, Dec, 1966
Dell Publishing Co.

	Good	Fine	Mint
1,2	.70	2.00	4.00

GIFT (See The Crusaders)

GIFT COMICS (50 cents)
1941 - No. 4, 1949 (No.1-3: 324 pgs.; No. 4: 152 pgs.)
Fawcett Publications

	Good	Fine	Mint
1-Captain Marvel, Bulletman, Golden Arrow, Ibis the Invincible, Mr. Scarlet, & Spy Smasher app.	70.00	210.00	420.00
2	55.00	165.00	340.00
3	40.00	110.00	240.00
4-The Marvel Family, Captain Marvel, etc.; each issue can vary in contents	19.00	55.00	120.00

GIFTS FROM SANTA (See March of Comics No. 137)

GIGGLE COMICS (Spencer Spook No. 100) (Also see Ha Ha)
Oct, 1943 - No. 99, Feb, 1955
Creston No.1-63/American Comics Group No. 64 on

	Good	Fine	Mint
1	3.00	8.00	16.00
2-5	1.50	4.00	8.00
6-20: 9-1st Superkatt	.85	2.50	5.00
21-40	.70	2.00	4.00
41-54,56-59,61-99	.40	1.20	2.40
55,60-Milt Gross-a	.80	2.30	4.60

G-I IN BATTLE (G-I No. 1 only)
Aug, 1952 - No. 9, July, 1953; Mar, 1957 - No. 6, May, 1958
Ajax-Farrell Publ./Four Star

	Good	Fine	Mint
1	2.00	5.00	10.00

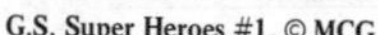

G.S. Super Heroes #1, © MCG

G.I. Combat #1, © DC

Giggle Comics #51, © ACG

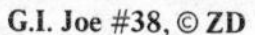

G.I. Joe #38, © ZD

Girls' Love Stories #44, © DC

G.I. War Brides #7, © SUPR

G-I IN BATTLE (continued)

	Good	Fine	Mint
2-9	.85	2.50	5.00
Annual(1953)-100 pgs.	4.00	12.00	24.00
1(1957-Ajax)	1.00	3.00	6.00
2-6	.60	1.80	3.60

G. I. JANE
May, 1953 - No. 13, Aug-Sept, 1955
Trojan Magazines

	Good	Fine	Mint
1	2.00	5.00	10.00
2-13	1.20	3.50	7.00

G. I. JOE (Also see Advs. of . . . & Showcase No. 53,54)
1950 - No. 51, June, 1957
Ziff-Davis Publ. Co.

	Good	Fine	Mint
10(No.1)	2.00	5.00	10.00
11-13('51)	1.20	3.50	7.00
14-Pin-ups	1.50	4.00	8.00
V2No.6(12/51)-17,19,20	1.20	3.50	7.00
18-(100 pg. Giant-'52)	3.00	9.00	18.00
21-28,30-34,36,37,39-47,49-51	.70	2.00	4.00
29,35,38-Bondage-c	.85	2.50	5.00
48-Atom bomb story	.85	2.50	5.00

NOTE: ***Norman Saunders*** *painted c-6-11, 13, 14, 30.* ***Powell*** *a-7, 8, 11.*

G. I. JOE (America's Movable Fighting Man)
1967 (32 pages) (5-1/8''x8-3/8'')
Custom Comics

	Good	Fine	Mint
Schaffenberger-a		.40	.80

G. I. JUNIORS (See Harvey Hits No. 86,91,95,98,101,104,107,110, 112,114,116,118,120,122)

GIL THORP
May-July, 1963
Dell Publishing Co.

	Good	Fine	Mint
1-Caniffish-a	1.00	3.00	6.00

GINGER (Li'l Jinx No. 11 on?)
1951 - No. 10, Summer, 1954
Archie Publications

	Good	Fine	Mint
1	3.00	9.00	18.00
2-10: 8-Katy Keene story	2.00	5.00	10.00

GIRL COMICS (Girl Confessions No. 13 on)
Nov, 1949 - No. 12, Jan, 1952
Marvel/Atlas Comics(CnPC)

	Good	Fine	Mint
1	4.00	12.00	24.00
2-Kubert-a	3.00	8.00	16.00
3-Everett-a	2.00	6.00	12.00
4-11	1.50	4.00	8.00
12-Krigstein-a	3.00	8.00	16.00

GIRL CONFESSIONS (Formerly Girl Comics)
No. 13, Mar, 1952 - No. 35, Aug, 1954
Atlas Comics (CnPC/ZPC)

	Good	Fine	Mint
13,16-18-Everett-a	2.00	5.00	10.00
14,15,19,20	1.20	3.50	7.00
21-35	1.00	3.00	6.00

GIRL FROM U.N.C.L.E., THE (TV)
Oct, 1966 - No. 5, Oct, 1967
Gold Key

	Good	Fine	Mint
1-McWilliams-a	.70	2.00	4.00
2-5-Leonard Swift-Courier No. 5	.35	1.00	2.00

GIRLS' FUN & FASHION MAGAZINE (Formerly Polly Pigtails)
V5No.44, Jan, 1950 - V5No.47, July, 1950
Parents' Magazine Institute

	Good	Fine	Mint
V5No.44-47	.50	1.50	3.00

GIRLS IN LOVE (Formerly G. I. Sweethearts No. 45)
May, 1950 - No. 57, Dec, 1956
Fawcett No. 1/Quality Comics Group No. 46 on

	Good	Fine	Mint
1	2.50	7.00	14.00
2-10	1.20	3.50	7.00
11-56: 54-'Commie' story	.85	2.50	5.00
57-Matt Baker c/a	3.00	8.00	16.00

GIRLS IN WHITE (See Comics Hits No. 58)

GIRLS' LIFE
Jan, 1954 - No. 6, 1954
Atlas Comics (BFP)

	Good	Fine	Mint
1-Patsy Walker	1.50	4.00	8.00
2-6	.85	2.50	5.00

GIRLS' LOVE STORIES
Aug-Sept, 1949 - No. 180, Nov-Dec, 1973
National Periodical Publ.(Signal Publ. No.28-65/Arleigh No.83-117)

	Good	Fine	Mint
1-Toth, Kinstler-a, 8 pgs. each	7.00	20.00	40.00
2	4.00	12.00	24.00
3-10	2.00	6.00	12.00
11-20	1.50	4.00	8.00
21-30	1.00	3.00	6.00
31-50	.75	2.20	4.40
51-100	.50	1.50	3.00
101-146: 113-117-April O'Day app.	.25	.70	1.40
147-151-''Confessions'' serial		.40	.80
152-180		.30	.60

GIRLS' ROMANCES
Feb-Mar, 1950 - No. 160, Oct, 1971
National Per. Publ.(Signal Publ. No.32-79/Arleigh No.84)

	Good	Fine	Mint
1	7.00	20.00	40.00
2,3: 2-Photo-c	3.50	10.00	20.00
4-10	2.00	6.00	12.00
11-20	1.50	4.00	8.00
21-30	1.00	3.00	6.00
31-50	.75	2.20	4.40
51-100	.50	1.50	3.00
101-133,135-160	.25	.70	1.40
134-Adams-c	.30	.80	1.60

G. I. SWEETHEARTS (Formerly Diary Loves; Girls In Love No. 46 on)
No. 32, June, 1953 - No. 45, May, 1955
Quality Comics Group

	Good	Fine	Mint
32-45	1.20	3.50	7.00

G. I. TALES (Sgt. Barney Barker No. 1-3)
No. 4, Feb, 1957 - No. 6, July, 1957
Atlas Comics (MCI)

	Good	Fine	Mint
4-Severin-a(4)	1.50	4.00	8.00
5	.85	2.50	5.00
6-Orlando, Powell, & Woodbridge-a	1.20	3.50	7.00

G. I. WAR BRIDES
April, 1954 - No. 8, June, 1955
Superior Publishers Ltd.

	Good	Fine	Mint
1	1.50	4.00	8.00
2,3,5-8	.85	2.50	5.00
4-Kamenesque-a; lingerie panels	.85	2.50	5.00

G. I. WAR TALES
Mar-Apr, 1973 - No. 4, Oct-Nov, 1973
National Periodical Publications

	Good	Fine	Mint
1-Reprints		.15	.30
2-Adams-a(r)		.40	.80
3-Reprints		.10	.20
4-Krigstein-a(r)		.30	.60

NOTE: ***Drucker*** *a-3r,4r.* ***Kubert*** *a-2,3.*

GJDRKZLXCBWQ COMICS
Oct, 1973 (36 pgs.; 50 cents; small size; black & white)

GJDRKZLXCBWQ COMICS (continued)
Glenn Bray

	Good	Fine	Mint
Wolverton-a	.25	.70	1.40

GLAMOROUS ROMANCES (Formerly Dotty)
No. 41, Sept, 1949 - No. 90, Oct, 1956
Ace Magazines (A. A. Wyn)

	Good	Fine	Mint
41-72,74-90: 53-Painted-c	.85	2.50	5.00
73-L.B. Cole-a	1.50	4.00	8.00

GNOME MOBILE, THE (See Movie Comics)

GOD IS
1973, 1975 (35-49 Cents)
Spire Christian Comics (Fleming H. Revell Co.)

	Good	Fine	Mint
By Al Hartley		.50	1.00

GOD'S HEROES IN AMERICA
1956 (nn) (68 pgs.) (25 cents; 35 cents)
Catechetical Guild Educational Society

	Good	Fine	Mint
307	2.00	6.00	12.00

NOTE: *Warehouse find in 1979.*

GOD'S SMUGGLER (Religious)
1972 (35-49 cents)
Spire Christian Comics/Fleming H. Revell Co.

	Good	Fine	Mint
1-Two variations exist		.50	1.00

GODZILLA
August, 1977 - No. 24, July, 1979
Marvel Comics Group

	Good	Fine	Mint
1		.60	1.20
2		.40	.80
3-Champions x-over		.40	.80
4,5-Sutton-a		.40	.80
6-24		.40	.80

GO-GO
June, 1966 - No. 9, Oct, 1967
Charlton Comics

	Good	Fine	Mint
1-Miss Bikini Luv begins; Rolling Stones, Beatles, Elvis, Sonny & Cher, Sinatra, Bob Dylan parody; Herman's Hermits pin-ups	.85	2.50	5.00
2-Ringo Starr, David McCallum, Beatles photo cover; Beatles story and photos	.50	1.50	3.00
3-Blooperman begins, ends No. 6	.50	1.50	3.00
4	.50	1.50	3.00
5-Super Hero & TV satire by J. Aparo & Grass Green begin	.85	2.50	5.00
6-9	.50	1.50	3.00

GO-GO AND ANIMAL (See Tippy's Friends . . .)

GOING STEADY (Formerly Teen-Age Temptations)
No. 10, 1954 - No. 13, June, 1955; No. 14, Oct, 1955; V3No.3, Jan-Feb, 1960; V3No.4, Sept-Oct, 1960 - No. 6, Jan-Feb, 1961
St. John Publishing Co./Prize (Headline)

	Good	Fine	Mint
10(1954)-Matt Baker c/a	4.00	12.00	24.00
11(2/55), 12(4/55)-Baker-c	2.00	6.00	12.00
13(6/55)-Baker c/a	3.50	10.00	20.00
14(10/55)-Matt Baker-c/a, 25 pgs.	4.00	12.00	24.00
V3No.3-6(1960-61)		.30	.60

GOING STEADY WITH BETTY (Betty & Her Steady No. 2)
Nov-Dec, 1949
Avon Periodicals

	Good	Fine	Mint
1	5.00	14.00	28.00

GOLDEN ARROW (See Fawcett Miniatures & Mighty Midget Comics)

GOLDEN ARROW (. . . Western No. 6)
1942 - No. 6, Spring, 1947
Fawcett Publications

	Good	Fine	Mint
1-Golden Arrow begins	7.00	20.00	40.00
2	4.00	12.00	24.00
3-5	2.50	7.00	14.00
6-Krigstein-a	3.00	9.00	18.00

GOLDEN ARROW WELL KNOWN COMICS
1944 (12 pgs.; 8½x10½''; paper cover; glued binding)
Bestmaid/Samuel Lowe (Giveaway)

	Good	Fine	Mint
	10.00	30.00	50.00

GOLDEN COMICS DIGEST
May, 1969 - No. 48, Jan, 1976
Gold Key

NOTE: *Whitman editions exist of many titles and are generally valued less.*

	Good	Fine	Mint
1-Tom & Jerry, Woody Woodpecker, Bugs Bunny	1.50	3.00	6.00
2-Hanna-Barbera TV Fun Favorites		.60	1.20
3-Tom & Jerry, Woody Woodpecker	.30	.80	1.60
4-Tarzan; Manning & Marsh-a	1.00	3.00	6.00
5,8-Tom & Jerry, Woody Woodpecker, Bugs Bunny	.30	.80	1.60
6-Bugs Bunny	.30	.80	1.60
7-Hanna-Barbera TV Fun Favorites		.60	1.20
9-Tarzan	1.00	3.00	6.00
10-Bugs Bunny		.60	1.20
11-Hanna-Barbera TV Fun Favorites		.40	.80
12-Tom & Jerry, Bugs Bunny, Woody Woodpecker Journey to the Sun		.40	.80
13-Tom & Jerry		.40	.80
14-Bugs Bunny Fun Packed Funnies		.40	.80
15-Tom & Jerry, Woody Woodpecker, Bugs Bunny		.40	.80
16-Woody Woodpecker Cartoon Special		.40	.80
17-Bugs Bunny		.40	.80
18-Tom & Jerry; Barney Bear-r by Barks	.80	1.60	2.40
19-Little Lulu	1.50	4.00	8.00
20-Woody Woodpecker Falltime Funtime		.40	.80
21-Bugs Bunny Showtime		.40	.80
22-Tom & Jerry Winter Wingding		.40	.80
23-Little Lulu & Tubby Fun Fling	1.50	4.00	8.00
24-Woody Woodpecker Fun Festival		.40	.80
25,28-Tom & Jerry		.40	.80
26-Bugs Bunny Halloween Hulla-Boo-Loo; Dr. Spektor article, also No. 25		.40	.80
27-Little Lulu & Tubby in Hawaii	1.20	3.50	7.00
29-Little Lulu & Tubby	1.20	3.50	7.00
30-Bugs Bunny Vacation Funnies		.40	.80
31-Turok, Son of Stone; reprints 4-Color No. 596,656	.70	2.00	4.00
32-Woody Woodpecker Summer Fun		.40	.80
33-Little Lulu & Tubby Halloween Fun; Dr. Spektor app.	1.50	4.00	8.00
34-Bugs Bunny Winter Funnies		.40	.80
35-Tom & Jerry Snowtime Funtime		.40	.80
36-Little Lulu & Her Friends	1.50	4.00	8.00
37-Woody Woodpecker County Fair		.40	.80
38-The Pink Panther		.50	1.00
39-Bugs Bunny Summer Fun		.30	.60
40-Little Lulu & Tubby Trick or Treat; all by Stanley	1.50	4.00	8.00
41-Tom & Jerry Winter Carnival		.30	.60
42-Bugs Bunny		.30	.60
43-Little Lulu in Paris	1.50	4.00	8.00
44-Woody Woodpecker Family Fun Festival		.30	.60
45-The Pink Panther		.50	1.00
46-Little Lulu & Tubby	1.20	3.50	7.00
47-Bugs Bunny		.30	.60
48-The Lone Ranger		.50	1.00

Godzilla #4, © MCG

Going Steady With Betty #1, © AVON

Golden Arrow #3, © FAW

Golden West Rodeo Treasury #1, © DELL

Gold Key Champion #1, © GK

Goofy Comics #29, © STD

GOLDEN COMICS DIGEST (continued)
NOTE: *No. 1-30, 164 pages; No. 31 on, 132 pages.*

GOLDEN LAD
July, 1945 - No. 5, June, 1946
Spark Publications

	Good	Fine	Mint
1-Origin Golden Lad & Swift Arrow	14.00	40.00	80.00
2-Mort Meskin-a	6.00	24.00	48.00
3-Mort Meskin-a	7.00	20.00	40.00
4	7.00	20.00	40.00
5-Origin Golden Girl; Shaman & Flame app.	6.00	24.00	48.00

NOTE: *All **Robinson, Meskin,** and **Roussos** art.*

GOLDEN LEGACY
1966 - 1972 (Black History) (25 cents)
Fitzgerald Publishing Co.

	Good	Fine	Mint
1-Toussaint L'Ouverture (1966)			
2-Harriet Tubman (1967)			
3-Crispus Attucks & the Minutemen (1967)			
4-Benjamin Banneker (1968)			
5-Matthew Henson (1969)			
6-Alexander Dumas & Family (1969)			
7-Frederick Douglass, Part 1 (1969)			
8-Frederick Douglass, Part 2 (1970)			
9-Robert Smalls (1970)			
10-J. Cinque & the Amistad Mutiny (1970)			
11-The Life of Alexander Pushkin (1971)			
12-Black Cowboys (1972)			
13-The Life of Martin Luther King, Jr. (1972)			
14-Men of Action: White, Marshall J. Wilkins (1972)			
15-Ancient African Kingdoms (1972)			
each....		.50	1.00
1-10,12,13,15(1976)-Reprints		.15	.30

GOLDEN LOVE STORIES (Formerly Golden West Love)
No. 4, April, 1950
Kirby Publishing Co.

	Good	Fine	Mint
4-Powell-a; cover features picture of Glenn Ford and Janet Leigh	3.50	10.00	20.00

GOLDEN PICTURE CLASSIC, A
1957 (Text stories w/illustrations in color; 100 pgs. each)
(Softcover 50 cents; hardcover $1.00)
Western Printing Co. (Simon & Shuster)

CL-401: Treasure Island; CL-402: Tom Sawyer; CL-403: Black Beauty; CL-404: Little Women; CL-405: Heidi; CL-406: Ben Hur; CL-407: Around the World in 80 Days; CL-408: Sherlock Holmes; CL-409: The Three Musketeers; CL-410: The Merry Advs. of Robin Hood; CL-411: Hans Brinker; CL-412: The Count of Monte Cristo

	Good	Fine	Mint
Softcover editions....	.50	1.50	3.00
Hardcover editions....	1.00	3.00	6.00

NOTE: *Hardcover editions were numbered CL-101 thru CL-112.*

GOLDEN PICTURE STORY BOOK
Dec, 1961 (52 pgs.; 50 cents; large size) (Disney)
Racine Press (Western)

	Good	Fine	Mint
ST-1-Huckleberry Hound	.70	2.00	4.00
ST-2-Yogi Bear	.70	2.00	4.00
ST-3-Babes in Toyland (Walt Disney's...)	2.00	5.00	10.00
ST-4-(...of Disney Ducks)-Walt Disney's Wonderful World of Ducks (Donald Duck, Uncle Scrooge, Donald's Nephews, Grandma Duck, Ludwig Von Drake, & Gyro Gearloose stories)	3.50	10.00	20.00

GOLDEN WEST LOVE (Golden Love Stories No. 4)
Sept-Oct, 1949 - No. 3, Feb, 1950
Kirby Publishing Co.

	Good	Fine	Mint
1-Powell-a No. 1-3	3.50	10.00	20.00
2,3: 3-Photo-c	2.50	7.00	14.00

GOLDEN WEST RODEO TREASURY
1957 (25 cents) (Giant)
Dell Publishing Co.

	Good	Fine	Mint
1	3.00	8.00	16.00

GOLDILOCKS (See March of Comics No. 1)

GOLDILOCKS & THE THREE BEARS
1943 (Giveaway)
K. K. Publications

	Good	Fine	Mint
	7.00	20.00	40.00

GOLD KEY CHAMPION
Mar, 1978 - No. 2, May-June, 1978 (52 pages) (50 cents)
Gold Key

	Good	Fine	Mint
1-Space Family Robinson reprints		.40	.80
2-Mighty Samson reprints		.40	.80

GOLD KEY SPOTLIGHT
May, 1976 - No. 11, Feb, 1978
Gold Key

	Good	Fine	Mint
1-Tom, Dick & Harriet		.30	.60
2-Wacky Advs. of Cracky		.30	.60
3-Wacky Witch		.30	.60
4-Tom, Dick & Harriet		.30	.60
5-Wacky Advs. of Cracky		.30	.60
6-Dagar the Invincible; Santos-a; origin Demonomicon		.40	.80
7-Wacky Witch & Greta Ghost		.30	.60
8-The Occult Files of Dr. Spektor, Simbar, Lu-sai; Santos-a		.40	.80
9-Tragg		.40	.80
10-O. G. Whiz		.30	.60
11-Tom, Dick & Harriet		.30	.60

GOLD MEDAL COMICS
1945 (132 pages)
Cambridge House

	Good	Fine	Mint
nn-Captain Truth by Fugitani	3.50	10.00	20.00
2-5	2.50	7.00	14.00

GOMER PYLE (TV)
July, 1966 - No. 3, Jan, 1967
Gold Key

	Good	Fine	Mint
1-3	.70	2.00	4.00

GOODBYE, MR. CHIPS (See Movie Comics)

GOOFY
May, 1953 - Sept-Nov, 1962
Dell Publishing Co.

	Good	Fine	Mint
4-Color 468,562,627,658	1.20	3.50	7.00
4-Color 747,802,899,952,987,1053,1094,1149,1201	.85	2.50	5.00
12-308-211(Dell, 9-11/62)	.30	.80	1.60

GOOFY ADVENTURE STORY (See 4-Color No. 857)

GOOFY COMICS
June, 1943 - 1953
Nedor Publ. Co. No. 1-14/Standard No. 18-48(Animated Cartoons)

	Good	Fine	Mint
1	3.00	8.00	16.00
2	1.50	4.00	8.00
3-19	.85	2.50	5.00
20-35-Frazetta text illos in all	2.50	7.00	14.00
36-48	.70	2.00	4.00

GOOFY SUCCESS STORY (See 4-Color No. 702)

GOOSE (Humor magazine)
Sept, 1976 - No. 3, 1976 (52 pgs.) (75 cents)
Cousins Publ. (Fawcett)

	Good	Fine	Mint
1-3		.50	1.00

GORDO (See Comics Revue No. 5)

GORGO (Based on movie) (See Return of...)
May, 1961 - No. 23, Sept, 1965

GORGO (continued)
Charlton Comics

	Good	Fine	Mint
1-Ditko-a, 22 pgs.	7.00	20.00	40.00
2,3-Ditko c/a	3.50	10.00	20.00
4-10: 4-Ditko-c	2.00	6.00	12.00
11,13-16-Ditko-a	2.00	5.00	10.00
12,17-23: 12-Reptisaurus x-over; Montes/Bache-a-No. 17-23	.85	2.50	5.00
Gorgo's Revenge('62)-Becomes Return of Gorgo	2.00	5.00	10.00

GOSPEL BLIMP, THE
1973 (36 pgs.) (35, 39 cents)
Spire Christian Comics (Fleming H. Revell Co.)

nn .50 1.00

GOTHIC ROMANCES
January, 1975 (B&W Magazine) (75 cents)
Atlas/Seaboard Publ.

1-Adams-a .30 .90 1.80

GOVERNOR & J. J., THE (TV)
Feb, 1970 - No. 3, Aug, 1970
Gold Key

1 .50 1.50 3.00
2,3 .30 .80 1.60

GRANDMA DUCK'S FARM FRIENDS (See 4-Color No. 763,873,965, 1010,1073,1161,1279)

GRAND PRIX (Formerly Hot Rod Racers)
1967 - No. 44, May, 1972
Charlton Comics

16-44: Features Rick Roberts .25 .50

GRAY GHOST, THE (See 4-Color No. 911,1000)

GREAT ACTION COMICS
1958 (Reprints)
I. W. Enterprises

1-Captain Truth 1.00 3.00 6.00
8,9-Phantom Lady No. 15 & (?) 5.50 16.00 32.00

GREAT AMERICAN COMICS PRESENTS - THE SECRET VOICE
1945 (10 cents)
Peter George 4-Star Publ./American Features Syndicate

1-All anti-Nazi 5.00 14.00 28.00

GREAT CAT FAMILY, THE (See 4-Color No. 750)

GREAT COMICS
Nov, 1941 - No. 3, Jan, 1942
Great Publications

1-Origin The Great Zarro; Madame Strange begins
15.00 45.00 90.00
2 10.00 30.00 60.00
3-Futuro Takes Hitler to Hell; movie story cont'd./Choice No. 3
20.00 60.00 120.00

GREAT COMICS
1945
Novack Publishing Co./Jubilee Comics

1-The Defenders, Capt. Power app.; L. B. Cole-c
4.00 12.00 24.00
1-Same cover; Boogey Man, Satanas, & The Sorcerer & His Apprentice 3.00 8.00 16.00

GREAT DOGPATCH MYSTERY (See Mammy Yokum & the. . .)

GREAT EXPLOITS
October, 1957
Decker Publ./Red Top

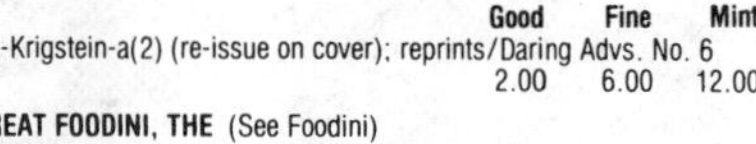
Good Fine Mint
1-Krigstein-a(2) (re-issue on cover); reprints/Daring Advs. No. 6
2.00 6.00 12.00

GREAT FOODINI, THE (See Foodini)

GREAT GAZOO, THE (The Flintstones)
Aug, 1973 - No. 20, Jan, 1977 (Hanna-Barbera)
Charlton Comics

1 .30 .60
2-20 .20 .40

GREAT GRAPE APE, THE
Sept, 1976 - No. 2, Nov, 1976 (Hanna-Barbera)
Charlton Comics

1,2 .25 .50

GREAT LOCOMOTIVE CHASE, THE (See 4-Color No. 712)

GREAT LOVER ROMANCES
March, 1951 - No. 22, May, 1955
Toby Press

1-Jon Juan reprint/J.J. No. 1 by Schomburg; Dr. Anthony King app.
3.50 10.00 20.00
2-5,7,9-22: 2-Jon Juan, Dr. Anthony King app.
.85 2.50 5.00
6-Kurtzman-a 2.50 7.00 14.00
8-Five full pgs. of ''Pin-Up Pete'' by Sparling
3.00 8.00 16.00

GREAT PEOPLE OF GENESIS, THE
No date (64 pgs.) (Religious giveaway)
David C. Cook Publ. Co.

Reprint/Sunday Pix Weekly 1.50 4.00 8.00

GREAT RACE, THE (See Movie Classics)

GREAT SACRAMENT, THE
1953 (36 pages)
Catechetical Guild giveaway

2.00 6.00 12.00

GREAT SCOTT SHOE STORE (See Bulls-Eye)

GREAT SOCIETY, THE (Political Satire)
1966 ($1.00) (Also see Bobman & Teddy)
Parallax

Along Ranger; Captain Marvelous; Colonel America; Phantasm; Super LBJ; Wonderbird 1.00 3.00 6.00

GREAT WEST (Magazine)
1969 (52 pages) (Black & White)
M. F. Enterprises

V1No.1 .40 .80

GREAT WESTERN
Jan-Mar, 1954 - No. 11, Oct-Dec, 1954
Magazine Enterprises

8(A-1 93)-Origin The Ghost Rider 5.00 14.00 28.00
9(A-1 105), 10(A-1 113), 11(A-1 127)-Ghost Rider in No. 9,11; Durango Kid in all 2.00 6.00 12.00
I.W. Reprint No. 1,2 9: Straight Arrow app. in No. 1,2
.70 2.00 4.00
I.W. Reprint No. 8-Origin Ghost Rider(Tim Holt No.11); Tim Holt app.; Bolle-a 1.20 3.50 7.00

GREEN ARROW (See Adventure, Action, Brave & the Bold, Flash, Green Lantern, Leading, More Fun, and World's Finest)

GREEN BERET, THE (See Tales of. . .)

GREEN GIANT COMICS (Also see Colossus Comics)
1940 (no price on cover)
Pelican Publications (Funnies, Inc.?)

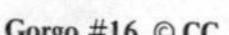
Gorgo #16, © CC

Great Lover Romances #3, © TOBY

Great Western #11, © ME

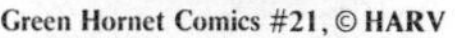
Green Hornet Comics #21, © HARV

WINTER ISSUE No. 10
GREEN LANTERN
10¢
THE MAN WHO WANTED THE WORLD!

Green Lantern #10, © DC

Green Lantern #5, © DC

GREEN GIANT COMICS (continued)

	Good	Fine	Mint
1-Dr. Nerod, Green Giant, Black Arrow, Mundoo & Master Mystic app; origin Colossus (Rare, currently only 5 copies known)	300.00	700.00	1200.00

NOTE: *The idea for this book came about by a stroll through a grocery store. Printed by Moreau Publ. of Orange, N.J. as an experiment to see if they could profitably use the idle time of their 40-page Hoe color press. The experiment failed due to the difficulty of obtaining good quality color registration and Mr. Moreau believes the book never reached the stands. The book has no price or date which lends credence to this. Contains five pages reprinted from Motion Picture Funnies Weekly.*

GREEN HORNET (TV)
Feb, 1967 - No. 3, Aug, 1967
Gold Key

	Good	Fine	Mint
1	2.00	6.00	12.00
2,3	1.50	4.50	9.00

GREEN HORNET (See 4-Color No. 496)

GREEN HORNET COMICS (. . . Fights Crime No. 37)
Dec, 1940 - No. 47, Sept, 1949
Helnit Publ.(Holyoke) No. 1/Harvey Publ.

	Good	Fine	Mint
1-Green Hornet begins	50.00	150.00	320.00
2	25.00	70.00	140.00
3	17.00	50.00	100.00
4,5	12.00	36.00	72.00
6	10.00	30.00	60.00
7-Origin The Zebra; Robin Hood & Spirit of 76 begin	14.00	40.00	80.00
8-10	10.00	30.00	60.00
11,12-Mr. Q in both	8.00	24.00	48.00
13-20: 14,18-Bondage-c	7.00	20.00	40.00
21-30: 24-Sci-Fi-c	6.00	18.00	36.00
31-The Man in Black Called Fate begins	7.00	20.00	40.00
32-36: 36-Bondage-c; spanking panel	6.00	18.00	36.00
37-Shock Gibson app. by Powell; S&K Kid Adonis reprinted from Stuntman No. 3	8.00	24.00	48.00
38-Shock Gibson, Kid Adonis app.	7.00	20.00	40.00
39-Stuntman story by S&K	12.00	35.00	70.00
40,41	5.50	16.00	32.00
42-45,47-Kerry Drake in all	5.50	16.00	32.00
46-"Case of the Marijuana Racket" cover/story; Kerry Drake app.	6.00	18.00	36.00

NOTE: ***Fuje*** *a-23, 24, 26.* ***Kubert*** *a-20, 30.* ***Powell*** *a-7-10, 12, 14, 16-19, 21, 30, 31(2), 32(3), 33, 34(3), 35, 36, 37(2), 38.* ***Robinson*** *a-27.* ***Schomburg*** *c-15, 17-23. Kirbyish c-7, 9.*

GREEN JET COMICS, THE (See Comic Books, Series 1)

GREEN LAMA (Also see Comic Books, Series 1)
Dec, 1944 - No. 8, March, 1946
Spark Publications

	Good	Fine	Mint
1-Intro. The Green Lama, Lt. Hercules & The Boy Champions; Mac Raboy-a No. 1-8	20.00	60.00	120.00
2-Lt. Hercules borrows the Human Torch's powers for one panel	14.00	40.00	80.00
3,6-8: 7-Christmas-c	10.00	30.00	60.00
4-Dick Tracy take-off in Lt. Hercules story by H. L. Gold (sci-fiction writer)	10.00	30.00	60.00
5-Lt. Hercules story; Little Orphan Annie, Smilin' Jack & Snuffy Smith take-off	10.00	30.00	60.00

NOTE: ***Robinson*** *a-3-5.*

GREEN LANTERN (1st Series) (See All-American)
Fall, 1941 - No. 38, May-June, 1949
National Periodical Publications/All-American

	Good	Fine	Mint
1-Origin retold	160.00	440.00	900.00
2-1st book-length story	90.00	240.00	480.00
3	60.00	160.00	320.00
4	45.00	120.00	240.00
5	40.00	100.00	200.00
6,7	30.00	80.00	160.00
8-Hop Harrigan begins	30.00	80.00	160.00
9	25.00	70.00	140.00
10-Origin Vandal Savage	25.00	70.00	140.00
11-17,19,20: 12-Origin Gambler	20.00	60.00	120.00
18-Christmas-c	22.00	65.00	130.00
21-29: 27-Origin Sky Pirate	17.00	50.00	100.00
30-Origin/1st app. Streak the Wonder Dog by Toth	17.00	50.00	100.00
31-35	14.00	40.00	80.00
36-38: 37-Sargon the Sorcerer app.	17.00	50.00	100.00

NOTE: *Book-length stories No. 2-8.* ***Toth*** *a-28, 30, 31, 34-38; c-30, 34, 36-38.*

GREEN LANTERN (2nd Series) (See Adventure, DC Special, DC Special Series, Flash, and Showcase)
7-8/60 - No. 89, 4-5/72; No. 90, 8-9/76 - Present
National Periodical Publications/DC Comics

	Good	Fine	Mint
1-Origin retold; Gil Kane-a begins	30.00	90.00	200.00
2-1st Pieface	14.00	40.00	80.00
3	10.00	30.00	60.00
4,5: 5-Origin & 1st app. Hector Hammond; 1st 5700 A.D. story	8.00	24.00	48.00
6-10: 6-Intro Tomar-re the alien G.L. 7-Origin Sinestro. 9-1st Jordan Brothers	4.00	12.00	24.00
11-20: 13-Flash x-over. 14-Origin Sonar. 16-Origin Star Sapphire 20-Flash x-over	2.50	7.00	14.00
21-30: 21-Origin Dr. Polaris. 23-1st Tattooed Man. 24-Origin Shark. 29-JLA cameo; 1st Blackhand	2.00	5.00	10.00
31-40: 40-G.A. Green Lantern x-over; origin The Guardians	1.00	3.00	6.00
41-50: 42-Zatanna x-over. 43-Flash x-over. No. 45-G.A. Green Lantern x-over	.70	2.00	4.00
51-75: 52,61-G.A. Green Lantern x-over. 67-G.A. Green Lantern origin retold. 69-Wood inks	.50	1.50	3.00
76-Begin Green Lantern/Green Arrow series by Neal Adams	10.00	28.00	56.00
77	5.00	14.00	28.00
78-80	4.00	12.00	24.00
81,82: 82-One pg. Wrightson inks	3.00	8.00	16.00
83-G.L. reveals i.d. to Carol Ferris	3.00	8.00	16.00
84-Adams/Wrightson-a	3.00	8.00	16.00
85,86(52 pgs.)-Drug propaganda books	4.00	12.00	24.00
87,89(52 pgs.): 89-G.A. Green Lantern stories	2.50	7.00	14.00
88(52 pgs.,'72)-One page Adams-a	.70	2.00	4.00
90('76)-99		.50	1.00
100-(Giant)-1st app. new Air Wave	.40	1.10	2.20
101-107,113,114		.40	.80
108-110(44 pgs.)-G.A. Gr. Lant. stories		.40	.80
111-Orgin retold		.40	.80
112-G.A. Gr. Lant. origin retold		.40	.80
115-Origin Crumbler		.40	.80
116-118,120-128,130: 117-Kari Limbo begins. 122-JLA x-over; 123-Last Green Arrow		.30	.60
119-Drug propaganda story		.50	1.00
129,133-Starlin-c		.40	.80
131,132,134-149: 132-Adam Strange begins new series		.30	.60
150-Anniversary ish., 48 pgs.		.40	.80

NOTE: ***Adams*** *a-76-87, 89; c-63, 76-89.* ***Anderson*** *inks-1, 4, 9, 10, 16, 21, 71, 73, 74, 87, 88, 137; c-inks-2, 9, 10, 12, 14-16, 19-44, 52-56, 59, 61, 66, 69.* ***Giordano*** *c-120, 121.* ***Grell*** *a-90, 93, 94, 97-100, 106, 108-110; c-90, 93, 94, 97-102, 104-106, 108-112.* ***Infantino*** *a-53, 88, 137p, 145p-147p; c-53.* ***Gil Kane*** *a-1-61, 68-75, 85, 87, 88; c-1-52, 54-61, 67-75, 123-126.* ***Lopez*** *c-113.* ***Perez*** *c-132, 141-144.* ***Staton*** *a-117-119, 123-147, 150; c-107, 117-119, 135(i), 136-144, 145p, 146, 147.* ***Toth*** *a-86r.*

GREEN MASK, THE (The Bouncer No. 11 on?)
Summer, 1940 - No. 9, 2/42; No. 10, 8/44 - No. 11, 11/44;

GREEN MASK (continued)
V2No.1, Spr, 1945 - No. 6, 10-11/46; 1955
Fox Features Syndicate

	Good	Fine	Mint
V1No.1-Origin The Green Mask & Domino; reprints/Mystery Men No. 1-3,5-7	35.00	100.00	200.00
2	15.00	45.00	90.00
3-Powell-a; Marijuana story	10.00	30.00	60.00
4-Navy Jones begins, ends No. 6	8.00	24.00	48.00
5	8.00	24.00	48.00
6-The Nightbird begins, ends No. 9	7.00	20.00	40.00
7-9	5.50	16.00	32.00
10,11: 10-Origin One Round Hogan & Rocket Kelly	5.50	16.00	32.00
V2No.1-6	4.00	12.00	24.00
1(1955-2nd Series)	3.00	8.00	16.00

GREEN PLANET, THE
1962 (One Shot)
Charlton Comics

	Good	Fine	Mint
nn	1.00	3.00	6.00

GREEN TEAM (See First Issue Special)

GREETINGS FROM SANTA (See March of Comics No. 48)

GREYFRIARS BOBBY (See 4-Color No. 1189)

GRIM GHOST, THE
Jan, 1975 - No. 3, July, 1975
Atlas/Seaboard Publ.

	Good	Fine	Mint
1-Origin		.40	.80
2,3-Heath-c		.30	.60

GRIMM'S GHOST STORIES (See Dan Curtis)
Jan, 1972 - Present
Gold Key

	Good	Fine	Mint
1		.60	1.20
2-4,6,7,9,10		.40	.80
5,8-Williamson-a	.30	.90	1.80
11-16,18-20		.30	.60
17-Crandall-a		.60	1.20
21-35: 25-Bolle-a; No. 32,34-reprints		.30	.60
36-56: 43,44-(52 pgs.)		.25	.50
Mini-Comic No. 1 (3¼x6½'', 1976)		.30	.60

NOTE: *Reprints-No. 39,43,44,53.*

GRIN (The American Funny Book) (Magazine)
Nov, 1972 - No. 3, April, 1973 (52 pgs.) (Satire)
APAG House Pubs

	Good	Fine	Mint
1		.60	1.20
2,3		.40	.80

GRIN & BEAR IT (See Large Feature Comic No. 28)

GRIT GRADY (See Holyoke One-Shot No. 1)

GROOVY (Cartoon Comics - not CCA approved)
March, 1968 - No. 3, July, 1968
Marvel Comics Group

	Good	Fine	Mint
1-3	.50	1.50	3.00

GUADALCANAL DIARY (Also see American Library)
1945 (One Shot)
David McKay Publishing Co.

	Good	Fine	Mint
nn-B&W text & pictures	4.00	12.00	24.00

GUERRILLA WAR (Formerly Jungle War Stories)
No. 12, July-Sept, 1965 - No. 14, Mar, 1966
Dell Publishing Co.

	Good	Fine	Mint
12-14	.30	.60	1.20

GUILTY (See Justice Traps the Guilty)

GULF FUNNY WEEKLY (Gulf Comic Weekly No. 1-4)
1933 - No. 422, 5/23/41 (in full color; 4 pgs.; tabloid size to 2/3/39; 2/10/39 on, regular comic book size)(early issues undated)
Gulf Oil Company (Giveaway)

	Good	Fine	Mint
1	5.50	16.00	32.00
2-30	3.50	10.00	20.00
31-100	2.00	6.00	12.00
101-196	2.00	5.00	10.00
197-Wings Winfair begins(1/29/37); by Fred Meagher beginning in 1938	12.00	35.00	70.00
198-300 (Last tabloid size)	5.00	15.00	30.00
301-350 (Regular size)	3.00	8.00	16.00
351-422	2.00	5.00	10.00

GULLIVER'S TRAVELS (See Dell Jr. Treasury No. 3)
Sept-Nov, 1965 - No. 3, May, 1966
Dell Publishing Co.

	Good	Fine	Mint
1-3	.85	2.50	5.00

GUMPS, THE
1918 - No. 8, 1931 (10x10'')(52 pgs.; black & white)
Landfield-Kupfer/Cupples & Leon No. 2

	Good	Fine	Mint
Book No.2(1918)-(Rare); 5¼x13⅓''; paper cover; 36 pgs. daily strip reprints by Sidney Smith	10.00	30.00	60.00
nn(1924)-by Sidney Smith	7.00	20.00	40.00
2,3	5.50	16.00	32.00
4-7	4.00	12.00	24.00
8-(10x14''); 36 pgs.; B&W; National Arts Co.	4.00	12.00	24.00

GUMPS, THE (. . . in Radioland)
1937 (95 pgs.) (Mostly text)
Pebco Tooth Paste Premium

	Good	Fine	Mint
	5.00	15.00	30.00

GUMPS, THE (Also see Merry Christmas . . .)
Mar-Apr, 1947 - No. 5, Nov-Dec, 1947
Dell Publ. Co./Bridgeport Herald Corp.

	Good	Fine	Mint
4-Color 73 (Dell)	3.00	8.00	16.00
1 (1947)	3.00	8.00	16.00
2-5	2.00	6.00	12.00

GUNFIGHTER (Fat & Slat No. 1-4) (Becomes Haunt of Fear No.15 on)
No. 5, Summer, 1948 - No. 14, Mar-Apr, 1950
E. C. Comics

	Good	Fine	Mint
5,6-Moon Girl in each	25.00	70.00	140.00
7-14	17.00	50.00	100.00

NOTE: ***Craig** & **H. C. Kiefer** art in most issues. **Feldstein/Craig** a-10. **Feldstein** a-7-11. **Ingels** a-5-14; c-7-12. **Wood** a-13, 14.*

GUNFIGHTERS, THE
1963 - 1964
Super Comics (Reprints)

	Good	Fine	Mint
10,11(Billy the Kid), 12(Swift Arrow), 15(Straight Arrow), 16,18-All reprints	.50	1.50	3.00

GUNFIGHTERS, THE (Formerly Kid Montana)
No. 51, 10/66 - No. 52, 10/67; No. 53, 6/79 - Present
Charlton Comics

	Good	Fine	Mint
51,52	.30	.80	1.60
53,54-Williamson a(r)/Wild Bill Hickok		.40	.80
55,57-70		.30	.60
56-Williamson/Severin-c/a; r-Sheriff of Tombstone		.40	.80

GUN GLORY (See 4-Color No. 846)

GUNHAWK, THE (Whip Wilson No. 10,11)
No. 12, Nov, 1950 - No. 18, Dec, 1951
Marvel Comics/Atlas (MCI)

	Good	Fine	Mint
12-18	2.00	5.00	10.00

GUNHAWKS, THE (The Gunhawk No. 7)

Green Mask #3, © FOX

Green Planet nn, © CC

The Gumps nn, 1924, © News Synd.

Guns Against Gangsters #3, © NOVP

Gunsmoke #7, © P.L. Publ.

Hand Of Fate #25(12/54), © ACE

GUNHAWKS (continued)
October, 1972 - No. 7, October, 1973
Marvel Comics Group

	Good	Fine	Mint
1-Reno Jones, Kid Cassidy		.60	1.20
2-5		.40	.80
6-Kid Cassidy dies, 7-Reno Jones solo		.40	.80

GUNMASTER (Judo Master No. 89 on; formerly Six-Gun Heroes)
Sept, 1964; Mar-Apr, 1966 - No. 89, Oct, 1967 (two No.89's)
Charlton Comics

	Good	Fine	Mint
V1No.1	.35	1.00	2.00
2-4,V5No.84-86: 4-Blank inside-c		.60	1.20
V5No.87-89		.50	1.00

NOTE: *Vol. 5 was originally cancelled with No. 88 (3-4/66). No. 89 on, became Judo Master, then later in 1967, Charlton issued No. 89 as a Gunmaster one-shot.*

GUNS AGAINST GANGSTERS
Sept-Oct, 1948 - V2No.2, 1949
Curtis Publications/Novelty Press

	Good	Fine	Mint
1-Toni Gayle begins by Schomburg	6.00	18.00	36.00
2-5	5.00	15.00	30.00
6-Toni Gayle cover	5.00	15.00	30.00
V2No.1,2	5.00	15.00	30.00

NOTE: ***L. B. Cole** c-1-6; a-1,2,3(2),4-6.*

GUNSLINGER (See 4-Color No. 1220)

GUNSLINGER (Formerly Tex Dawson. . .)
No. 2, April, 1973 - No. 3, June, 1973
Marvel Comics Group

	Good	Fine	Mint
2,3		.40	.80

GUNSMOKE
Apr-May, 1949 - No. 16, Jan, 1952
P. L. Publishing Co./Western Comics

	Good	Fine	Mint
1-Gunsmoke, Masked Marvel begin, both by Ingels, plus Ingels bondage-c	8.00	24.00	48.00
2-Ingels c/a(2)	6.00	18.00	36.00
3,4-Ingels-a each	4.00	12.00	24.00
5,6	3.00	8.00	16.00
7-16	2.00	5.00	10.00

NOTE: ***Ingels** c-1-6; bondage-1,3.*

GUNSMOKE (TV)
1955 - No. 27, June-July, 1961; Feb, 1969 - No. 6, Feb, 1970
Dell Publishing Co./Gold Key

	Good	Fine	Mint
4-Color 679	1.00	3.00	6.00
4-Color 720,769,797,844	.85	2.50	5.00
6(11/57), 7	.85	2.50	5.00
8,9,11,12-Williamson-a in all, 4 pgs. each	2.00	6.00	12.00
10-Williamson/Crandall-a, 4 pgs.	2.00	6.00	12.00
13-27	.40	1.20	2.40
Gunsmoke Film Story (11/62-G.K. Giant) No. 30008-211	1.00	3.00	6.00
1 (G.K.)	.40	1.20	2.40
2-6('69-70)		.60	1.20

GUNSMOKE TRAIL
June, 1957 - No. 4, 1957
Ajax-Farrell Publ./Four Star Comic Corp.

	Good	Fine	Mint
1	1.50	4.00	8.00
2-4	.85	2.50	5.00

GUNSMOKE WESTERN (Formerly Western Tales of Black Rider)
Dec, 1955 - No. 77, July, 1963
Atlas Comics No. 32-35(CPS/NPI); Marvel No. 36 on

	Good	Fine	Mint
32	2.00	6.00	12.00
33,35,36-Williamson-a in each: 5,6 & 4 pgs. plus Drucker No. 33	3.00	9.00	18.00
34-Baker-a, 3pgs.	1.50	4.00	8.00
37-Davis-a(2); Williamson text illo	2.00	5.00	10.00
38,39	.85	2.50	5.00
40-Williamson/Mayo-a, 4 pgs.	3.00	9.00	18.00
41,42,45-49,51-55,57-59: 49,52-Kid From Texas story. 57-1st Two Gun Kid by Severin. 60-Sam Hawk app. in Kid Colt	.85	2.50	5.00
43,44-Torres-a	1.50	4.00	8.00
50,60,61-Crandall-a	1.50	4.00	8.00
56-Matt Baker-a	1.50	4.00	8.00
62-77: 72-Origin Kid Colt	.85	2.50	5.00

NOTE: ***Colan** a-37. **Davis** a-37, 52, 54, 55; c-50, 54. **Ditko** a-56, 66. **Kirby** a-47, 50, 51, 59, 62(3), 63, 65-67, 69, 71, 73, 77; c-56(w/**Ditko**), 57, 58, 61(w/**Ayers**), 62, 63, 66, 68, 69, 71-77. **Severin** c-43. **Wildey** a-10, 37, 42, 57. Kid Colt in all. Two-Gun Kid in No. 57, 59, 60-63, 66. Wyatt Earp in No. 45, 48, 49, 52, 54, 55, 58.*

GUNS OF FACT & FICTION (See A-1 Comics No. 13)

GUN THAT WON THE WEST, THE
1956 (24 pgs.; regular size) (Giveaway)
Winchester-Western Division & Olin Mathieson Chemical Corp.

	Good	Fine	Mint
nn-Painted-c	1.20	3.50	7.00

GYPSY COLT (See 4-Color No. 568)

GYRO GEARLOOSE (See Walt Disney Showcase No. 18)
Nov, 1959 - May-July, 1962 (Disney)
Dell Publishing Co.

	Good	Fine	Mint
4-Color 1047,1095,1184-All by Carl Barks	4.00	12.00	24.00
4-Color 1267-Barks c/a, 4 pgs.	3.00	9.00	18.00
No. 01329-207, 5-7/62-Barks-c only	2.00	6.00	12.00

HAGAR THE HORRIBLE (See Comics Reading Libraries)

HA HA COMICS (Teepee Tim No. 100 on) (Also see Giggle)
Oct, 1943 - No. 99, Jan, 1955
Scope Mag.(Creston Publ.) No. 1-80/American Comics Group

	Good	Fine	Mint
1	3.00	9.00	18.00
2-5	1.50	4.00	8.00
6-20	.85	2.50	5.00
21-40	.70	2.00	4.00
41-99: 95-3-D effect-c	.50	1.40	2.80

HAIR BEAR BUNCH, THE (TV) (See Fun-In No. 13)
Feb, 1972 - No. 9, Feb, 1974 (Hanna-Barbera)
Gold Key

	Good	Fine	Mint
1-9		.50	1.00

HALLELUJAH TRAIL, THE (See Movie Classics)

HAND OF FATE (Formerly Men Against Crime)
No. 8, Dec, 1951 - No. 26, March, 1955
Ace Magazines

	Good	Fine	Mint
8: Surrealistic text story	3.50	10.00	20.00
9,10	2.50	7.50	15.00
11-18,20,22,23	2.00	6.00	12.00
19-Bondage, hypo needle scenes	2.00	6.00	12.00
21-Necronomicon story; drug belladonna used	2.50	7.50	15.00
24-Electric Chair-c	2.50	7.50	15.00
25(11/54), 25(12/54), 26-All Nostrand-a	2.50	7.50	15.00

NOTE: ***Cameron** art-No. 19-25. **Sekowsky** a-8, 13.*

HANDS OF THE DRAGON
June, 1975
Seaboard Periodicals (Atlas)

	Good	Fine	Mint
1-Origin; Mooney inks		.50	1.00

HANGMAN COMICS (Special No. 1; Black Hood No. 9 on)
No. 2, Spring, 1942 - No. 8, Fall, 1943
MLJ Magazines

	Good	Fine	Mint
2-The Hangman, Boy Buddies begin	30.00	90.00	180.00
3-8	17.00	50.00	100.00

HANK

HANK (continued)
1946
Pentagon Publications

	Good	Fine	Mint
nn-Coulton Waugh's newspaper reprint	1.00	3.00	6.00

HANNA-BARBERA (See Golden Comics Digest No. 2,7,11)

HANNA-BARBERA BAND WAGON
Oct, 1962 - No. 3, April, 1963
Gold Key

1,2-Giants, 84 pgs.	.70	2.00	4.00
3-Regular size	.50	1.50	3.00

HANNA-BARBERA HI-ADVENTURE HEROES (See Hi-Adventure . . .)

HANNA-BARBERA PARADE
Sept, 1971 - No. 10, Dec, 1972
Charlton Comics

1-6,8-10	.50	1.50	3.00
7-"Summer Picnic"-52 pgs.	.70	2.00	4.00

NOTE: *No. 4 (1/72) went on sale late in 1972 with the January 1973 issues.*

HANNA-BARBERA SPOTLIGHT (See Spotlight)

HANNA-BARBERA SUPER TV HEROES
April, 1968 - No. 7, Oct, 1969 (Hanna-Barbera)
Gold Key

1-The Birdman, The Herculoids, Moby Dick, Samson & Goliath, and The Mighty Mightor begin	1.50	4.00	8.00
2-The Galaxy Trio only app.; Shazzan begins; no Samson & Goliath	1.00	3.00	6.00
3-7: 3-The Space Ghost app.; also No. 3,6,7, no Herculoids; no Samson & Goliath in No. 4-7	.85	2.50	5.00

HANNA-BARBERA (TV STARS) (See TV Stars)

HANS AND FRITZ
1929 (16 pgs.; 10x13½''; B&W Sunday strip reprints)
The Saalfield Publishing Co.

193-(Very Rare)-By R. Dirks; contains B&W Sunday strip reprints of Katzenjammer Kids & Hawkshaw the Detective from 1916	17.00	50.00	100.00

HANS BRINKER (See 4-Color No. 1273)

HANS CHRISTIAN ANDERSEN
1953 (100 pgs. - Special Issue)
Ziff-Davis Publ. Co.

nn-Danny Kaye (movie)	5.00	14.00	28.00

HANSEL & GRETEL (See 4-Color No. 590)

HANSI, THE GIRL WHO LOVED THE SWASTIKA
1973, 1976 (39-49 cents)
Spire Christian Comics (Fleming H. Revell Co.)

		.50	1.00

HAP HAZARD COMICS (Real Love No. 25 on)
1944 - No. 24, Feb, 1949
Ace Magazines (Readers' Research)

1	2.00	5.00	10.00
2-10	1.20	3.50	7.00
11-13,15-24	.85	2.50	5.00
14-Feldstein-c (4/47)	3.00	8.00	16.00

HAP HOPPER (See Comics Revue No. 2)

HAPPIEST MILLIONAIRE, THE (See Movie Comics)

HAPPINESS AND HEALING FOR YOU (Also see Oral Roberts' True Stories)
1955 (36 pgs.; slick cover) (Oral Roberts Giveaway)
Commercial Comics

	Good	Fine	Mint
	3.50	10.00	20.00

NOTE: *The success of this book prompted Oral Roberts to go into the publishing business himself to produce his own material.*

HAPPI TIM (See March of Comics No. 182)

HAPPY COMICS (Happy Rabbit No. 41 on)
1943 - No. 40, Dec, 1950
Nedor Publ./Standard Comics (Animated Cartoons)

1	3.00	9.00	18.00
2	1.50	4.50	9.00
3-10	.85	2.50	5.00
11-19	.70	2.00	4.00
20-31,34-37-Frazetta text illos in all; 2 in No. 34, 3 in No. 30	2.00	5.00	10.00
32-Frazetta-a, 7 pgs. plus text illos; Roussos-a	6.00	18.00	36.00
33-Two Frazetta stories, 6 pgs. each (Scarce)	12.00	35.00	70.00
38-40	.50	1.50	3.00

HAPPY DAYS
March, 1979 - No. 6, Feb, 1980
Gold Key

1		.50	1.00
2-6		.30	.60
. . . With the Fonz Kite Fun Book(6¾x5¼'','78)-PG&E	.30	.80	1.60

HAPPY HOLIDAY (See March of Comics No. 181)

HAPPY HOOLIGAN (See Alphonse . . .)
1903 (18 pgs.) (Sunday strip reprints in color)
Hearst's New York American-Journal

Book 1-by Fred Opper	17.00	50.00	100.00
50 Pg. Edition(1903)-10x15'' in color	24.00	62.00	125.00

HAPPY HOOLIGAN (Handy . . .)
1908 (32 pgs. in color) (10x15''; cardboard covers)
Frederick A. Stokes Co.

	14.00	40.00	80.00

HAPPY HOOLIGAN (Story of . . .)
1932 (16 pgs.; 9½x12''; softcover)
McLoughlin Bros.

281-Three-color text, pictures on heavy paper	5.00	15.00	30.00

HAPPY HOULIHANS (Saddle Justice No. 3 on)
Fall, 1947 - No. 2, Winter, 1947-48
E. C. Comics

1-Origin Moon Girl	17.00	50.00	100.00
2	8.00	24.00	48.00

HAPPY JACK
August, 1957 - No. 2, Nov, 1957
Red Top (Decker)

V1No.,1,2	.85	2.50	5.00

HAPPY JACK HOWARD
1957
Red Top (Farrell)/Decker

nn-Reprints Handy Andy story from E. C. Dandy Comics No. 5, renamed "Happy Jack"	1.50	4.00	8.00

HAPPY RABBIT (Formerly Happy Comics)
No. 41, 1950 - No. 48, April, 1952
Standard Comics (Animated Cartoons)

41-48	.85	2.50	5.00

HAPPY TIME XMAS BOOK

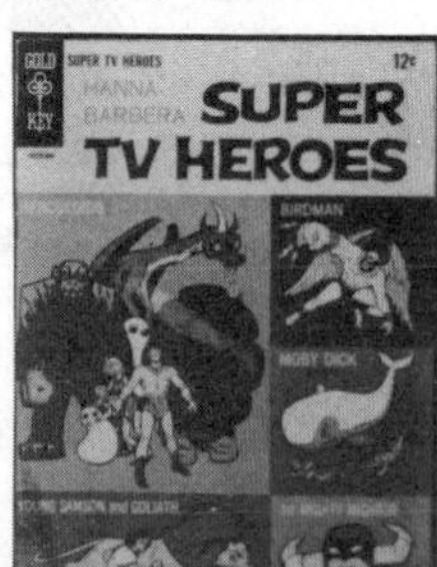

Hanna-Barbera Super TV Heroes #1, © Hanna-Barbera

Hans Christian Andersen nn, © ZD

Happy Houlihans #1, © WMG

Harvey Comics Library #1, © HARV

Harvey Hits #9, © HARV

Harvey Hits #50, © HARV

HAPPY TIME XMAS BOOK (continued)
1952 (Christmas Giveaway)
F. W. Woolworth Co.

	Good	Fine	Mint
	3.00	8.00	16.00

HARDY BOYS, THE (See 4-Color No. 760,830,887,964-Disney)

HARDY BOYS, THE (TV)
April, 1970 - No. 4, Jan, 1971
Gold Key

	Good	Fine	Mint
1	.70	2.00	4.00
2-4	.35	1.00	2.00

HARLEM GLOBETROTTERS (TV) (See Fun-In No. 8,10)
April, 1972 - No. 12, Jan, 1975 (Hanna-Barbera)
Gold Key

	Good	Fine	Mint
1-12		.50	1.00

NOTE: *No. 4, 8, and 12 contain 16 extra pages of advertising.*

HAROLD TEEN (See 4-Color No. 2, 209, & Treasure Box of Famous Comics)

HAROLD TEEN (Adv. of. . .)
1929-31 (36-52 pgs.) (Paper covers)
Cupples & Leon Co.

	Good	Fine	Mint
B&W daily strip reprints by Carl Ed	6.00	18.00	36.00

HARVEY
Oct, 1970; No. 2, 12/70; No. 3, 6/72 - No. 6, 12/72
Marvel Comics Group

	Good	Fine	Mint
1-6		.40	.80

HARVEY COLLECTORS COMICS (Richie Rich Collectors Comics No. 10 on, cover title only)
9/75 - No. 15, 1/78; No. 16, 10/79 - Present (52 pgs.)
Harvey Publications

	Good	Fine	Mint
1-Reprints Richie Rich No. 1,2	.70	2.00	4.00
2-10	.40	1.20	2.40
11-19: 16-Sad Sack-r		.50	1.00

NOTE: *All reprints: Casper-No. 2,7, Richie Rich-No. 1,3,5,6,8-15, Wendy-No. 4. No. 6 titled 'Richie Rich. . . on inside.*

HARVEY COMICS HITS (See Comics Hits)

HARVEY COMICS LIBRARY
April, 1952 - No. 2, 1952
Harvey Publications

	Good	Fine	Mint
1-Teen-Age Dope Slaves as exposed by Rex Morgan, M.D.; drug propaganda story; used in **SOTI**, pg. 27 *(Prices vary widely on this book)*	70.00	200.00	400.00
2-Sparkle Plenty (Dick Tracy in "Blackmail Terror")	12.00	35.00	70.00

HARVEY HITS
Sept, 1957 - No. 122, Nov, 1967
Harvey Publications

	Good	Fine	Mint
1-The Phantom	10.00	28.00	56.00
2-Rags Rabbit(10/57)	1.50	4.00	8.00
3-Richie Rich(11/57)-r/Little Dot; 1st book devoted to Richie Rich; see Little Dot for 1st app.	60.00	160.00	320.00
4-Little Dot's Uncles	8.00	24.00	48.00
5-Stevie Mazie's Boy Friend	1.50	4.00	8.00
6-The Phantom; Kirby-c	5.00	14.00	28.00
7-Wendy the Witch	8.00	24.00	48.00
8-Sad Sack	3.00	8.00	16.00
9-Richie Rich's Golden Deeds-r (2nd book devoted to Richie Rich)	25.00	75.00	150.00
10-Little Lotta	6.00	18.00	36.00
11-Little Audrey Summer Fun (7/58)	4.50	13.00	26.00
12-The Phantom; Kirby-c	4.00	12.00	24.00
13-Little Dot's Uncles (9/58); Richie Rich 1 pg.	5.50	16.00	32.00
14-Herman & Katnip (10/58)	1.50	4.00	8.00
15-The Phantom (1958)	3.00	9.00	18.00
16-Wendy the Witch (1/59)	4.00	12.00	24.00
17-Sad Sack's Army Life (2/59)	1.50	4.00	8.00
18-Buzzy & the Crow	1.50	4.00	8.00
19-Little Audrey	3.00	8.00	16.00
20-Casper & Spooky	4.00	12.00	24.00
21-Wendy the Witch	3.00	9.00	18.00
22-Sad Sack's Army Life	1.00	3.00	6.00
23-Wendy the Witch	3.00	9.00	18.00
24-Little Dot's Uncles (9/59); Richie Rich 1 pg.	4.00	12.00	24.00
25-Herman & Katnip (10/59)	1.00	3.00	6.00
26-The Phantom (11/59)	3.00	9.00	18.00
27-Wendy the Good Little Witch	3.00	9.00	18.00
28-Sad Sack's Army Life	.50	1.50	3.00
29-Harvey-Toon (1960); Casper, Buzzy	2.00	6.00	12.00
30-Wendy the Witch (3/60)	3.00	8.00	16.00
31-Herman & Katnip (4/60)	.70	2.00	4.00
32-Sad Sack's Army Life	.50	1.50	3.00
33-Wendy the Witch (6/60)	3.00	8.00	16.00
34-Harvey-Toon (7/60)	1.00	3.00	6.00
35-Funday Funnies (8/60)	.70	2.00	4.00
36-The Phantom (1960)	2.00	6.00	12.00
37-Casper & Nightmare	2.00	6.00	12.00
38-Harvey-Toon	1.50	4.00	8.00
39-Sad Sack's Army Life (12/60)	.50	1.50	3.00
40-Funday Funnies	.50	1.50	3.00
41-Herman & Katnip	.50	1.50	3.00
42-Harvey-Toon (3/61)	.80	2.30	4.60
43-Sad Sack's Army Life (4/61)	.35	1.00	2.00
44-The Phantom	2.00	6.00	12.00
45-Casper & Nightmare	2.00	5.00	10.00
46-Harvey-Toon	.80	2.30	4.60
47-Sad Sack's Army Life (8/61)	.40	1.20	2.40
48-The Phantom (1961)	2.00	6.00	12.00
49-Stumbo the Giant (1st app.)	5.00	14.00	28.00
50-Harvey-Toon (11/61)	.80	2.30	4.60
51-Sad Sack's Army Life (12/61)	.40	1.20	2.40
52-Casper & Nightmare	2.00	5.00	10.00
53-Harvey-Toons (2/62)	.70	2.00	4.00
54-Stumbo the Giant	3.00	8.00	16.00
55-Sad Sack's Army Life (4/62)	.40	1.20	2.40
56-Casper & Nightmare	2.00	5.00	10.00
57-Stumbo the Giant	3.00	8.00	16.00
58-Sad Sack's Army Life	.40	1.20	2.40
59-Casper & Nightmare (7/62)	2.00	5.00	10.00
60-Stumbo the Giant (9/62)	3.00	8.00	16.00
61-Sad Sack's Army Life	.40	1.20	2.40
62-Casper & Nightmare	1.50	4.00	8.00
63-Stumbo the Giant	3.00	8.00	16.00
64-Sad Sack's Army Life (1/63)	.40	1.20	2.40
65-Casper & Nightmare	1.50	4.00	8.00
66-Stumbo The Giant	3.00	8.00	16.00
67-Sad Sack's Army Life (4/63)	.40	1.20	2.40
68-Casper & Nightmare	1.50	4.00	8.00
69-Stumbo the Giant (6/63)	3.00	8.00	16.00
70-Sad Sack's Army Life (7/63)	.40	1.20	2.40
71-Nightmare (8/63)	.40	1.20	2.40
72-Stumbo the Giant	3.00	8.00	16.00
73-Little Sad Sack (10/63)	.40	1.20	2.40
74-Sad Sack's Muttsy. . . (11/63)	.40	1.20	2.40
75-Casper & Nightmare	1.00	3.00	6.00
76-Little Sad Sack	.40	1.20	2.40
77-Sad Sack's Muttsy. . .	.40	1.20	2.40
78-Stumbo the Giant	3.00	8.00	16.00
79-Little Sad Sack (4/64)	.40	1.20	2.40
80-Sad Sack's Muttsy. . . (5/64)	.40	1.20	2.40
81-Little Sad Sack	.40	1.20	2.40
82-Sad Sack's Muttsy. . .	.40	1.20	2.40
83-Little Sad Sack (8/64)	.40	1.20	2.40
84-Sad Sack's Muttsy. . .	.40	1.20	2.40
85-Gabby Gob (10/64)	.40	1.20	2.40
86-G. I. Juniors	.40	1.20	2.40

HARVEY HITS (continued)

	Good	Fine	Mint
87-Sad Sack's Muttsy . . .	.40	1.20	2.40
88-Stumbo the Giant (1/65)	3.00	8.00	16.00
89-Sad Sack's Muttsy . . .	.40	1.20	2.40
90-Gabby Gob	.35	1.00	2.00
91-G. I. Juniors	.35	1.00	2.00
92-Sad Sack's Muttsy . . . (5/65)	.35	1.00	2.00
93-Sadie Sack (6/65)	.35	1.00	2.00
94-Gabby Gob	.35	1.00	2.00
95-G. I. Juniors	.35	1.00	2.00
96-Sad Sack's Muttsy . . . (9/65)	.35	1.00	2.00
97-Gabby Gob	.35	1.00	2.00
98-G. I. Juniors	.35	1.00	2.00
99-Sad Sack's Muttsy . . . (12/65)	.35	1.00	2.00
100-Gabby Gob	.35	1.00	2.00
101-G. I. Juniors (2/66)	.35	1.00	2.00
102-Sad Sack's Muttsy . . . (3/66)	.35	1.00	2.00
103-Gabby Gob	.35	1.00	2.00
104-G. I. Juniors	.35	1.00	2.00
105-Sad Sack's Muttsy . . .	.35	1.00	2.00
106-Gabby Gob (7/66)	.35	1.00	2.00
107-G. I. Juniors (8/66)	.35	1.00	2.00
108-Sad Sack's Muttsy . . .	.35	1.00	2.00
109-Gabby Gob?	.35	1.00	2.00
110-G. I. Juniors(11/66)	.35	1.00	2.00
111-Sad Sack's Muttsy . . . (12/66)	.35	1.00	2.00
112-G. I. Juniors	.35	1.00	2.00
113-Sad Sack's Muttsy . . .	.35	1.00	2.00
114-G. I. Juniors	.35	1.00	2.00
115-Sad Sack's Muttsy . . .	.35	1.00	2.00
116-G. I. Juniors	.35	1.00	2.00
117-Sad Sack's Muttsy . . .	.35	1.00	2.00
118-G. I. Juniors	.35	1.00	2.00
119-Sad Sack's Muttsy . . . (8/67)	.35	1.00	2.00
120-G. I. Juniors	.35	1.00	2.00
121-Sad Sack's Muttsy . . . (10/67)	.35	1.00	2.00
122-G. I. Juniors	.35	1.00	2.00

HARVEY POP COMICS (Teen Humor)
Oct, 1968 - No. 2, Nov, 1969
Harvey Publications

	Good	Fine	Mint
1,2-The Cowsills	.85	2.50	5.00

HARVEY 3-D HITS (See Sad Sack)

HARVEY-TOON (. . . S) (See Harvey Hits No. 29,34,38,42,46,50,53)

HATARI (See Movie Classics)

HATHAWAYS, THE (See 4-Color No. 1298)

HAUNTED (See This Magazine Is Haunted)

HAUNTED (. . . Library No. 21 on)
Sept, 1971 - No. 30, Nov, 1976; No. 31, Sept, 1977 - Present
Charlton Comics

	Good	Fine	Mint
1		.60	1.20
2-5		.50	1.00
6-16,18-20,22-59		.40	.80
17,21-Newton-a		.40	.80

NOTE: ***Ditko** a-1-8, 11-16, 18, 23, 24, 28, 30, 34r, 36r, 39-42r, 47r, 49-51r. c-1-7, 11, 13, 14, 16, 30, 41, 47, 49-51. **Howard** a-18. **Newton** c-21, 22. **Staton** a-18, 30; c-18. No. 51 reprints No. 1; No. 49 reprints Tales/Myst. Traveler No. 4.*

HAUNTED LOVE
April, 1973 - No. 11, Sept, 1975
Charlton Comics

	Good	Fine	Mint
1-Tom Sutton-a, 16 pgs.		.50	1.00
2,3,6-11		.30	.60
4,5-Ditko-a		.40	.80
Modern Comics No. 1(1978)		.20	.40

NOTE: ***Howard** a-8. **Newton** c-8,9.*

HAUNTED THRILLS
June, 1952 - No. 21, Nov, 1954
Ajax/Farrell Publications

	Good	Fine	Mint
1	4.00	12.00	24.00
2	4.00	12.00	24.00
3-5: 3-Drug use story	2.50	7.00	14.00
6-11	2.00	5.00	10.00
12-Kiefer-a	2.50	7.00	12.00
13,16,17,19-21	1.50	4.00	8.00
14-Jesus Christ apps. in story	1.50	4.00	8.00
15-Jo-Jo-r	3.00	8.00	16.00
18-Lingerie panels	1.00	3.00	6.00

NOTE: *Kamenish art in most issues.*

HAUNT OF FEAR (Formerly Gunfighter)
No. 15, May-June, 1950 - No. 28, Nov-Dec, 1954
E. C. Comics

	Good	Fine	Mint
15(1950)	90.00	250.00	500.00
16	50.00	135.00	270.00
17-Origin of Crypt of Terror, Vault of Horror, & Haunt of Fear; used in **SOTI**, pg. 43; last pg. Ingels-a used by N.Y. Legis. Comm.	50.00	120.00	240.00
4	40.00	100.00	200.00
5	30.00	75.00	150.00
6-10	20.00	60.00	120.00
11-13,15-18	15.00	40.00	80.00
14-Origin Old Witch by Ingels	20.00	60.00	120.00
19-Used in **SOTI**, ill.-"A comic book baseball game" & Senate investigation on juvenile delinq.	20.00	60.00	120.00
20-Feldstein r-/Vault of Horror No. 12	12.00	35.00	70.00
21,22,24-28	8.00	24.00	48.00
23-Used in **SOTI**, pg. 241	10.00	28.00	56.00

(Canadian reprints known; see Table of Contents.)

NOTE: ***Craig** a-15-17, 5, 7, 10, 12, 13; c-15-17, 5-7. **Crandall** a-20, 21, 26, 27. **Davis** a-4-26, 28. **Evans** a-15-19, 22-25, 27. **Feldstein** a-15-17, 20; c-4, 8-10. **Ingels** a-16, 17, 4-28; c-11-28. **Kamen** a-16, 4, 6, 7, 9-11, 13-19, 21-28. **Krigstein** a-28. **Kurtzman** a-15/1, 17/3. **Orlando** a-9, 12. **Wood** a-15, 16, 4-6.*

HAUNT OF HORROR, THE (Magazine)
6/73 - No. 2, 8/73; 5/74 - No. 5, 1/75 (75 cents) (B&W)
Cadence Comics Publ. (Marvel)

	Good	Fine	Mint
1,2(6/73-8/73,B&W) digest size	.50	1.50	3.00
1-Alcala-a	.40	1.20	2.40
2-Origin & 1st app. Gabriel the Devil Hunter; Satana begins	.30	.80	1.60
3	.30	.80	1.60
4-Adams-a	.40	1.20	2.40
5-Evans-a(2)	.30	.80	1.60

HAVE GUN, WILL TRAVEL (TV)
1958 - No. 14, July-Sept, 1962
Dell Publishing Co.

	Good	Fine	Mint
4-Color 931,983,1044	1.00	3.00	6.00
4-14	.85	2.50	5.00

HAWAIIAN EYE (TV)
July, 1963
Gold Key

	Good	Fine	Mint
1 (10073-307)	.85	2.50	5.00

HAWAIIAN ILLUSTRATED LEGENDS SERIES
1975 (B&W)(Cover printed w/blue, yellow, and green)
Hogarth Press

	Good	Fine	Mint
1-Kalelealuaka, the Mysterious Warrior		.60	1.20
2,3		.40	.80

HAWK, THE (Also see Approved Comics)

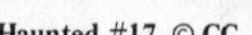
Haunted #17, © CC

Haunted Thrills #4, © AJAX

Haunt Of Fear #19, © WMG

The Hawk & The Dove #5, © DC

Hawkman #4, © DC

Heart Throbs #3, © QUA

HAWK (continued)
Winter, 1951 - No. 12, May, 1955
Ziff-Davis/St. John Publ. Co. No. 3 on

	Good	Fine	Mint
1-Anderson-a	4.00	12.00	24.00
2-Kubert, Infantino-a	3.00	8.00	16.00
3-8,10-11: 8-Reprints No. 3 with diff.-c. 10-Reprints one story/ No. 2. 11-Buckskin Belle app.	2.00	6.00	12.00
9-Baker c/a; Kubert-a(r)/No. 2	2.50	7.00	14.00
12-Baker c/a	2.50	7.00	14.00
3-D 1(11/53)-Baker-c	8.00	24.00	48.00

NOTE: ***Baker** c-8,9,11. **Tuska** a-9.*

HAWK & THE DOVE, THE (See Showcase)
Aug-Sept, 1968 - No. 6, June-July, 1969
National Periodical Publications

	Good	Fine	Mint
1-Ditko c/a	.40	1.20	2.40
2-Ditko c/a	.35	1.00	2.00
3-6: 5-Teen Titans cameo	.30	.80	1.60

NOTE: ***Gil Kane** c/a-3-6.*

HAWKEYE & THE LAST OF THE MOHICANS (See 4-Color No. 884)

HAWKMAN (See Atom & Hawkman, The Brave & the Bold, DC Comics Presents, Detective, Mystery in Space, Showcase, & World's Finest)
Apr-May, 1964 - No. 27, Aug-Sept, 1968
National Periodical Publications

	Good	Fine	Mint
1	5.50	16.00	32.00
2	3.00	8.00	16.00
3-5: 4-Zatanna x-over(origin-1st app.)	1.50	4.00	8.00
6-10: 9-Atom cameo; Hawkman & Atom learn each other's I.D.; 2nd app. Shadow Thief	1.00	3.00	6.00
11-15	.70	2.00	4.00
16-27: Adam Strange x-over No. 18, cameo No. 19. 25-G.A. Hawkman reprint	.40	1.20	2.40

NOTE: ***Anderson** a-1-21; c-1-21. **Kubert** c-27.*

HAWKSHAW THE DETECTIVE (See Okay)
1917 (24 pgs.; B&W; 10½x13½'') (Sunday strip reprints)
The Saalfield Publishing Co.

	Good	Fine	Mint
By Gus Mager	5.50	16.00	24.00

HAWTHORN-MELODY FARMS DAIRY COMICS
No date (1950's) (Giveaway)
Everybody's Publishing Co.

	Good	Fine	Mint
Cheerie Chick, Tuffy Turtle, Robin Koo Koo, Donald & Longhorn Legends	1.00	3.00	4.50

HEADLINE COMICS (. . . Crime No. 32-39)
Feb, 1943 - No. 22, Nov-Dec, 1946; 1947 - No. 77, Oct, 1956
Prize Publications

	Good	Fine	Mint
1-Yank & Doodle x-over in Junior Rangers	8.00	24.00	48.00
2	4.00	12.00	24.00
3-Used in **POP**, pg. 84	5.00	14.00	28.00
4-10: 10-Hitler story	3.00	8.00	16.00
11,12,17,18	2.00	5.00	10.00
13-15-Blue Streak in all	2.00	6.00	12.00
16-Origin Atomic Man	3.00	8.00	16.00
19-S&K-a	7.00	20.00	40.00
20,21: 21-Atomic Man ends	2.00	5.00	10.00
22	1.50	4.00	8.00
23-(All S&K-a)	8.00	24.00	48.00
24-(All S&K-a); dope-crazy killer story	8.00	24.00	48.00
25-35-S&K c/a	4.00	12.00	24.00
36-S&K-a; opium drug mention story	3.00	8.00	16.00
37-One pg. S&K, Severin-a	2.00	6.00	12.00
38,40-Meskin-a	1.50	4.00	8.00
39,41-43,45-48,50,51,53-55: 51-Kirby-c	.70	2.00	4.00
44-S&K-c; Severin/Elder, Meskin-a	3.00	8.00	16.00
49-Meskin-a	1.00	3.00	6.00
52-One pg. drug ad	2.00	6.00	12.00
56,57-S&K-a	2.00	6.00	12.00
58-69,71-77	.70	2.00	4.00
70-Drug mention story	2.00	6.00	12.00

HEAP, THE
Sept, 1971 (52 pages)
Skywald Publications

	Good	Fine	Mint
1-Kinstler-a, r-/Strange Worlds No. 8	.50	1.50	3.00

HEART AND SOUL
April-May, 1954 - No. 2, June-July, 1954
Mikeross Publications

	Good	Fine	Mint
1,2	2.00	5.00	10.00

HEART THROBS (Love Stories No. 147 on)
Aug, 1949 - No. 146, Oct, 1972
Quality/National No. 47(4-5/57) on (Arleigh No. 48-101)

	Good	Fine	Mint
1-Classic Ward-c, Gustavson-a, 9pgs.	15.00	45.00	90.00
2-Ward c/a, 9 pgs; Gustavson-a	10.00	28.00	56.00
3-Gustavson-a	3.50	10.00	20.00
4,6,8-Ward-a, 8-9 pgs.	5.00	15.00	30.00
5,7,9	2.00	5.00	10.00
10,15-Ward-a	4.00	12.00	24.00
11-14,16-20	1.20	3.50	7.00
21-Ward-c	3.00	9.00	18.00
22,23-Ward-a(p)	2.50	7.00	14.00
24-39	.85	2.50	5.00
40-Ward-a; r-7 pgs./No.21	2.00	5.00	10.00
41-50	.70	2.00	4.00
51-70	.40	1.20	2.40
71-100,102-119,121-146: 102-123-(Serial)-Three Girls, Their Lives, Their Loves		.50	1.00
101-The Beatles app. on cover	.50	1.50	3.00
120-Adams-c	.35	1.00	2.00

NOTE: ***Gustavson** a-8.*

HEAVY METAL (Magazine)
April, 1977 - Present ($1.50)
HM Communications

	Good	Fine	Mint
1	1.00	3.00	6.00
2-5	.70	2.00	4.00
6-10	.50	1.50	3.00
11-20	.40	1.20	2.40
21-30	.30	.90	1.80
31-44		.50	1.00

NOTE: ***Bode'** a-1-4. **Chaykin** a-50-54. **Nino** a-11,14-17. **Rogers** a-26. **Steranko** a-50-54. **Wrightson** a-39.*

HECKLE AND JECKLE (See Blue Ribbon Comics)
10/51 - No. 24, 10/55; No. 25, Fall/56 - No. 34, 6/59
St. John Publ. Co. No. 1-24/Pines No. 25 on

	Good	Fine	Mint
1	5.50	16.00	32.00
2-5	3.00	8.00	16.00
6-10	2.00	6.00	12.00
11-20	1.50	4.00	8.00
21-34	.70	2.00	4.00

HECKLE AND JECKLE (TV) (See New Terrytoons)
Nov, 1962 - No. 4, Aug, 1963
Gold Key

	Good	Fine	Mint
1-4	.70	2.00	4.00

(See March of Comics No. 379,472)

HECKLE AND JECKLE (TV)(Also see New Terrytoons)
May, 1966 - No. 2, Oct, 1966; No. 3, Aug, 1967
Dell Publishing Co.

	Good	Fine	Mint
1-3	.55	1.60	3.20

HECTOR COMICS
1953 - 1954
Key Publications

	Good	Fine	Mint
1-3	.85	2.50	5.00

HECTOR HEATHCOTE (TV)
March, 1964
Gold Key

	Good	Fine	Mint
1 (10111-403)	.70	2.00	4.00

HEDY DEVINE COMICS (Formerly USA No. 17) (Hedy of Hollywood No. 36 on)
No. 22, Aug, 1947 - No. 50, Sept, 1952 (No. 18-21 exist?)
Marvel Comics (RCM)

22	1.50	4.00	8.00
23-Wolverton-a, 1 pg; Kurtzman's "Hey Look," 2 pgs., 24,25,27-30-"Hey Look" by Kurtzman, 1-3 pgs.	4.00	12.00	24.00
26-"Giggles & Grins" by Kurtzman	2.50	7.00	14.00
31-34,36-50	1.00	3.00	6.00
35-Four pgs. "Rusty" by Kurtzman	3.00	8.00	16.00

HEDY-MILLIE-TESSIE COMEDY (See Comedy)

HEDY WOLFE
August, 1957
Atlas Publishing Co. (Emgee)

1	2.00	5.00	10.00

HEE HAW (TV)
July, 1970 - No. 7, Aug, 1971
Charlton Press

1-7	.50	1.50	3.00

HEIDI (See Dell Jr. Treasury No. 6)

HELEN OF TROY (See 4-Color No. 684)

HELLO I'M JOHNNY CASH
1976 (39-49 cents)
Spire Christian Comics (Fleming H. Revell Co.)

nn		.40	.80

HELLO PAL COMICS (Short Story Comics)
Jan, 1943 - No. 3, May, 1943
Harvey Publications

1-Rocketman & Rocketgirl begin; Yankee Doodle Jones app.; Mickey Rooney cover	9.00	25.00	50.00
2-Charlie McCarthy cover	6.00	18.00	36.00
3-Bob Hope cover	6.00	18.00	36.00

HELL-RIDER (Magazine)
Aug, 1971 - No. 2, Oct, 1971 (B&W)
Skywald Publications

1-Origin & 1st app.; Butterfly & Wildbunch begins; heroin drug story	.80	2.40	3.60
2-Drug mention story	.70	2.00	3.00

NOTE: *No. 3 advertised in Psycho No. 5 but did not come out.* ***Buckler*** *a-1,2.* ***Morrow*** *c-3.*

HELP! (Magazine)
Aug, 1960 - No. 12, Sept, 1961; V2No.1(No.13), Feb, 1962 - V2No.8(No.20), Feb, 1964; No. 21, Oct, 1964 - No. 26, Sept, 1965
Edited by Harvey Kurtzman
General Promotions/Warren Publishing Co.

V1No.1	7.00	20.00	40.00
2	3.50	10.00	20.00
3,4	2.00	6.00	12.00
5,9-Little Nemo-r by Winsor McCay (3 pgs. & 2 pgs.)	2.00	5.00	10.00
6-8,10,12	1.50	4.00	8.00
11-Krazy Kat by George Herriman (2 pgs.)	2.00	5.00	10.00
V2No.1(No.13, 2/62)-Spirit-r by Eisner (7 pgs.)	3.50	10.00	20.00
2-8(No.14-20): 2-The Humor of Charles Dana Gibson (6 pgs.). 5-Miss Lace by Caniff (5 pgs.). 6-Skippy by P. Crosby (6 pgs.). 8-Mutt & Jeff by Ham Fisher (4 pgs.)	1.00	3.00	6.00
21-(75 cent Annual-10/64)	1.00	3.00	6.00
22(1/65)-Robert Crumb-Fritz the Cat (2 pgs.) in Public Gallery (early underground comix development)	2.00	6.00	12.00
23,26	.85	2.50	5.00
24-Fritz the Cat, 2 pgs.	2.00	6.00	12.00
25-Sketchbook-Life in Bulgaria	2.00	5.00	10.00

NOTE: ***Robert Crumb*** *a-22,24,25.* ***Gilbert Sheldon's*** *Wonder Warthog-V2No.4(16),V2No.6(18),V2No.8(20),22-26. Covers feature photos of: No. 1-Sid Caesar, No. 2-Ernie Kovacs, No. 3-Jerry Lewis, No. 4-Mort Sahl, No. 5-Dave Garroway, No. 6-Jonathan Winters, No. 7-Tom Poston, No. 8-Hugh Downs, No. 9-Phil Ford/Mime Hines, No. 10-Jackie Gleason.*

HE-MAN
Fall, 1952
Ziff-Davis Publ. Co. (Approved Comics)

1-Kinstler-c	3.50	10.00	20.00

HE-MAN
May, 1954 - No. 2, July, 1954
Toby Press

1	3.00	8.00	16.00
2	2.00	6.00	12.00

HENNESSEY (See 4-Color No. 1200,1280)

HENRY
1935 (52 pages) (Daily B&W strip reprints)
David McKay Publications

1-by Carl Anderson	5.00	14.00	28.00

HENRY
1946 - No. 65, Apr-June, 1961
Dell Publishing Co.

4-Color 122,155	1.50	4.00	8.00
1	1.50	4.00	8.00
2	.50	1.50	3.00
3-10	.30	.80	1.60
11-20	.25	.70	1.40
21-Infinity-c	.35	1.00	2.00
22-65		.60	1.20

HENRY (See March of Comics No. 43,58,84,101,112,129,147,162, 178,189 and Giant Comic Album)

HENRY ALDRICH COMICS
Aug-Sept, 1950 - No. 22, 1954
Dell Publishing Co.

1-Series written by John Stanley; Bill Williams-a	2.00	5.00	10.00
2-5	1.20	3.50	7.00
6-22	.70	2.00	4.00

HENRY BREWSTER
Feb, 1966 - V2No.7, Sept, 1967 (All Giants)
Country Wide (M.F. Ent.)

1-6(12/66)-Powell-a in most		.40	.80
V2No.7		.30	.60

HERBIE (See Forbidden Worlds)
April-May, 1964 - No. 23, Feb, 1967
American Comics Group

1	7.00	20.00	40.00
2-4	3.50	10.00	20.00
5-Beatles, Dean Martin, F. Sinatra app.	4.00	12.00	24.00
6,7,9,10	2.00	6.00	12.00
8-Origin The Fat Fury	3.00	9.00	18.00
11-22: 14-Nemesis & MagicMan app.	1.50	4.00	8.00

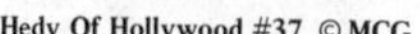
Hedy Of Hollywood #37, © MCG

Henry #11, © DELL

Herbie #11, © ACG

Hercules Unbound #3, © DC

Heroes All V1#2, © CG

Heroic Comics #37, © EAS

HERBIE (continued)

	Good	Fine	Mint
23-Reprints 1st story/F.W. No.73	1.50	4.00	8.00

NOTE: *All have* ***Whitney*** *c/a.*

HERBIE GOES TO MONTE CARLO, HERBIE RIDES AGAIN See Walt Disney Showcase No. 24,41)

HERCULES
Oct, 1967 - No. 13, Sept, 1970; Dec, 1968
Charlton Comics

	Good	Fine	Mint
1-Thane of Bagarth series begins	.40	1.10	2.20
2-13	.30	.80	1.60
8-(Low distribution)(12/68)-35 cents; magazine format; B&W; reprints	2.50	7.00	14.00
Modern Comics reprint No. 10('77)		.15	.30

HERCULES (See The Mighty . . .)

HERCULES UNBOUND
Oct-Nov, 1975 - No. 12, Aug-Sept, 1977
National Periodical Publications

	Good	Fine	Mint
1-Wood inks begin		.50	1.00
2-5		.40	.80
6-12: 10-Atomic Knights x-over		.30	.60

NOTE: ***Layton*** *inks-No. 9, 10.* ***Simonson*** *a-11, 12; c-7i, 8i, 10-12.* ***Wood*** *inks-1-8; c-7i, 8i.*

HERCULES UNCHAINED (See 4-Color No. 1006,1121)

HERE COMES SANTA (See March of Comics No. 30,213,340)

HERE IS SANTA CLAUS
1930s (16 pgs., 8 in color) (stiff paper covers)
Goldsmith Publishing Co. (Kann's in Washington, D.C.)

	Good	Fine	Mint
nn	3.00	9.00	18.00

HERE'S HOW AMERICA'S CARTOONISTS HELP TO SELL U.S. SAVINGS BONDS
1950? (16 pgs.; paper cover)
Harvey Comics giveaway

	Good	Fine	Mint
Contains: Joe Palooka, Donald Duck, Archie, Kerry Drake, Red Ryder, Blondie & Steve Canyon	10.00	28.00	56.00

HERE'S HOWIE
Jan-Feb, 1952 - No. 20, Mar-Apr, 1955
National Periodical Publications

	Good	Fine	Mint
1	4.00	12.00	24.00
2-5	2.50	7.00	14.00
6-10	2.00	5.00	10.00
11-20 (19,20-exist?)	1.00	3.00	6.00

HERMAN & KATNIP (See Harvey Hits No. 14,25,31,41)

HEROES ALL CATHOLIC ACTION ILLUSTRATED
1943 - V6No.5, March 10, 1948 (paper covers)
Heroes All Co.

	Good	Fine	Mint
V1No.1,2-(16 pgs., 8x11")	3.50	10.00	20.00
V2No.1(1/44)-3(3/44)-(16 pgs., 8x11")	2.50	7.00	14.00
V3No.1(1/45)-10(10/45)-(16 pgs., 8x11")	2.00	5.00	10.00
V4No.1-35 (12/20/46)-(16 pgs.)	1.20	3.50	7.00
V5No.1(1/10/47)-8(2/28/47)-(16 pgs.)	.85	2.50	5.00
V5No.9(3/7/47)-20(11/25/47)-(32 pgs.)	.85	2.50	5.00
V6No.1(1/10/48)-5(3/10/48)-(32 pgs.)	.85	2.50	5.00

HEROES, INC. PRESENTS CANNON
1969 - No. 2, 1976 (Sold at Army PX's)
Wally Wood/CPL/Gang Publ. No. 2

	Good	Fine	Mint
nn-Wood/Ditko-a	3.00	8.00	16.00
2-Wood-c; Ditko & Wood-a; 8½x10½"; B&W; $2.00	.50	1.50	3.00

NOTE: *First issue not distributed by publisher; it is rumored that 9,000 copies were stored in a warehouse and stolen.*

HEROES OF THE WILD FRONTIER (Formerly Baffling Mysteries)
No. 26, Mar, 1955 - No. 2, April, 1956
Ace Periodicals

	Good	Fine	Mint
26(No.1),27,28	.85	2.50	5.00
2	.70	2.00	4.00

HERO FOR HIRE (Power Man No. 17 on)
June, 1972 - No. 16, Dec, 1973
Marvel Comics Group

	Good	Fine	Mint
1-Origin Luke Cage retold; marijuana mention	.80	2.40	4.80
2-10	.30	.90	1.80
11-16: 14-Origin retold. 15-Everett Subby-r('53). 16-Origin Stilletto; death of Rackham	.30	.80	1.60

HEROIC ADVENTURES (See Adventures)

HEROIC COMICS (Reg'lar Fellas No. 1-15; New Heroic No. 41 on)
Aug, 1940 - No. 97, June, 1955
Eastern Color Printing Co./Famous Funnies(Funnies, Inc. No. 1)

	Good	Fine	Mint
1-Hydroman(origin) by Bill Everett, The Purple Zombie(origin) & Mann of India by Tarpe Mills begins	25.00	70.00	140.00
2	14.00	40.00	80.00
3,4	10.00	30.00	60.00
5,6	8.00	24.00	48.00
7-Origin Man O'Metal, 1 pg.	8.00	24.00	48.00
8-10: 10-Lingerie panels	5.00	14.00	28.00
11,13: 13-Crandall/Fine-a	4.00	12.00	24.00
12-Music Master(origin) begins by Everett, ends No. 31; last Purple Zombie & Mann of India	5.50	16.00	32.00
14-Hydroman x-over in Rainbow Boy; also in No. 15; origin Rainbow Boy	5.50	16.00	32.00
15-Intro. Downbeat	5.00	14.00	28.00
16-20: 17-Rainbow Boy x-over in Hydroman. 19-Rainbow Boy x-over in Hydroman & vice versa	3.50	10.00	20.00
21-30: No. 25-Rainbow Boy x-over in Hydroman. 28-Last Man O'Metal. 29-Last Hydroman	2.00	5.00	10.00
31,34	1.00	3.00	6.00
32,33,35-38-Toth-a	2.00	6.00	12.00
39-Ingels-a	2.00	6.00	12.00
40-42-Toth, Ingels-a	2.00	5.00	10.00
43-47,49,50-Toth-a	1.50	4.00	8.00
48,52-55,57,59	.70	2.00	4.00
51-Williamson-a; Kiefer-c	3.00	9.00	18.00
56,58-Toth-c	1.00	3.00	6.00
60,61,64-Everett-a	.70	2.00	4.00
62,63-Everett-c	.60	1.80	3.60
65-Williamson/Frazetta-a; Evans-a, 2 pgs.	4.00	12.00	24.00
66,75,94-Frazetta (2 pgs.) in each	1.50	4.00	8.00
67,73-Frazetta-a(2), 4 pgs. each	2.50	7.00	14.00
68,74,76-80,84,85,88-93,95-97	.40	1.20	2.40
69,72-Frazetta-a(2) (6 & 8 pgs. each)	4.00	12.00	24.00
70,71,86,87-Frazetta, 3-4 pgs. each; 1 pg. drug mention by Frazetta in No. 70	2.50	7.00	14.00
81,82-One pg. Frazetta art	.85	2.50	5.00
83-Frazetta-a, ½ pg.	.85	2.50	5.00

NOTE: ***Everett*** *a-(Hydroman-No. 1-9), 44, 60; c-1-9, 62, 63.* ***Sid Greene*** *a-46.* ***Kiefer*** *a-46; c-46, 80.* ***Tarpe Mills*** *a-3(2), 10.*

HEY THERE, IT'S YOGI BEAR (See Movie Comics)

HI-ADVENTURE HEROES (Hanna-Barbera)
May, 1969 - No. 2, Aug, 1969
Gold Key

	Good	Fine	Mint
1-Three Musketeers, Gulliver, Arabian Knights stories	.50	1.50	3.00
2-Three Musketeers, Micro-Venture, Arabian Knights	.30	.80	1.60

HI AND LOIS (See 4-Color No. 683,774,955)

HI AND LOIS
Nov, 1969 - No. 11, July, 1971
Charlton Comics

	Good	Fine	Mint
1		.40	.80
2-11		.20	.40

HICKORY
Oct, 1949 - No. 6, Aug, 1950
Quality Comics Group

	Good	Fine	Mint
1-Sahl c/a; Feldstein?-a	3.00	8.00	16.00
2,4-6	2.00	6.00	12.00
3-Wardish-c by Sahl	3.00	8.00	16.00

HIDDEN CREW, THE (See The United States A. F.)

HIDE-OUT (See 4-Color No. 346)

HIDING PLACE, THE
1973 (35-49 cents)
Spire Christian Comics/Fleming H. Revell Co.

nn		.40	.80

HIGH ADVENTURE
October, 1957
Red Top(Decker) Comics (Farrell)

1-Krigstein-r from Explorer Joe (re-issue on cover)	1.50	4.00	8.00

HIGH ADVENTURE (See 4-Color No. 949,1001)

HIGH CHAPPARAL (TV)
August, 1968
Gold Key

1 (10226-808)	.85	2.50	5.00

HIGH SCHOOL CONFIDENTIAL DIARY (Confidential Diary No. 13 on)
June, 1960 - No. 11, March, 1962
Charlton Comics

1	.70	2.00	4.00
2-11	.35	1.00	2.00

HI-HO COMICS
1946
Four Star Publications

1-L. B. Cole-c	3.50	10.00	20.00
2,3: 2-L. B. Cole-c	2.50	7.00	14.00

HI-JINX
July-Aug, 1947 - 1949
B&I Publ. Co.(American Comics Group)/Creston/LaSalle

1-3	2.00	5.00	10.00
4-7-Milt Gross	2.50	7.00	14.00
132 Pg. issue, nn, no date (LaSalle)	3.00	9.00	18.00

HI-LITE COMICS
Fall, 1945
E. R. Ross Publishing Co.

1-Miss Shady	3.50	10.00	20.00

HILLBILLY COMICS
Aug, 1955 - No. 4, July, 1956 (Satire)
Charlton Comics

1	.85	2.50	5.00
2-4	.70	2.00	4.00

HIP-IT-TY HOP (See March of Comics No. 15)

HI-SCHOOL ROMANCE DATE BOOK
Nov, 1962 - No. 3, Mar, 1963 (25 cent Giant)
Harvey Publications

1-Powell, Baker-a	2.50	7.00	14.00
2,3	1.00	3.00	6.00

HI-SCHOOL ROMANCE (. . . Romances No. 41 on)
Oct, 1949 - No. 5, June, 1950; No. 6, Dec, 1950 - No. 73, Mar, 1958; No. 74, Sept, 1958 - No. 75, Nov, 1958
Harvey Publications/True Love(Home Comics)

	Good	Fine	Mint
1	3.00	9.00	18.00
2-9,11-20	1.50	4.00	8.00
10-Rape story	2.00	5.00	10.00
21-31	.85	2.50	5.00
32-''Unholy passion'' story	1.50	4.00	8.00
33-75	.50	1.50	3.00

NOTE: ***Powell** a-1-3,5,8,12-14,16,18.21-23,25-27,30-34,36, 37,39,45-48,50,57,58,60,65,67,69.*

HIS NAME IS SAVAGE (Magazine format)
No. 1, June, 1968 (One Shot)
Adventure House Press

1-Gil Kane-a	2.00	5.00	10.00

HI-SPOT COMICS (Red Ryder No. 1 & No. 3 on)
No. 2, Nov, 1940
Hawley Publications

2-David Innes of Pellucidar; art by J. C. Burroughs; written by Edgar R. Burroughs	40.00	120.00	240.00

HIT COMICS
July, 1940 - No. 65, July, 1950
Quality Comics Group

1-Origin Neon, the Unknown & Hercules; intro. The Red Bee; Blaze Barton, the Strange Twins, X-5 Super Agent, Casey Jones, Jack & Jill (ends No.7), & Bob & Swab begin	130.00	320.00	640.00
2-The Old Witch begins, ends No. 14	60.00	160.00	340.00
3-Casey Jones ends; transvestite story-'Jack & Jill'	45.00	130.00	280.00
4-Super Agent (ends No. 17), & Betty Bates (ends No. 65) begin; X-5 ends	40.00	110.00	235.00
5-Classic cover	50.00	140.00	300.00
6-10: 10-Old Witch by Crandall, 4 pgs.-1st work in comics	35.00	100.00	180.00
11-17: 13-Bob & Swab, Blaze Barton ends. 17-Last Neon; Crandall Hercules in all	28.00	80.00	160.00
18-Origin Stormy Foster, the Great Defender; The Ghost of Flanders begins; Crandall-c	35.00	100.00	180.00
19,20	28.00	80.00	160.00
21-24: 21-Last Hercules. 24-Last Red Bee & Strange Twins	25.00	70.00	140.00
25-Origin Kid Eternity by Moldoff	30.00	90.00	180.00
26-Blackhawk x-over in Kid Eternity	20.00	60.00	120.00
27-29	12.00	36.00	72.00
30,31-''Bill the Magnificent'' by Kurtzman, 11 pgs. in each	10.00	30.00	60.00
32-40: 32-Plastic Man x-over. 34-Last Stormy Foster	5.00	15.00	30.00
41-50	4.00	12.00	24.00
51-60-Last Kid Eternity	3.50	10.00	20.00
61,63-Crandall c/a; Jeb Rivers begins No. 61	4.00	12.00	24.00
62	3.00	8.00	16.00
64,65-Crandall-a	3.50	10.00	20.00

NOTE: ***Crandall** a-11-17(Hercules), 23, 24(Stormy Foster); c-18-20, 23, 24. **Fine** c-1-14, 16, 17(most). **Ward** c-33.*

HI-YO SILVER (See Lone Ranger's Famous Horse. . ., March of Comics No. 215, and The Lone Ranger)

HOCUS POCUS (Formerly Funny Book)
No. 9, Aug-Sept, 1946
Parents' Magazine Press

9	.80	2.40	4.80

HOGAN'S HEROES (TV) (No. 1-7 have photo-c)
June, 1966 - No. 9, Oct, 1969
Dell Publishing Co.

1	.85	2.50	5.00
2,4-9: No. 9-Reprints No. 1	.35	1.00	2.00

Hickory #2, © QUA

Hi-Ho Comics #2, © Four Star

Hit Comics #26, © QUA

Holiday Comics #5, © STAR

Hollywood Diary #3, © QUA

Holyoke One-Shot #3, © HOKE

HOGAN'S HEROES (continued)

	Good	Fine	Mint
3-Ditko-a(p)	.70	2.00	4.00

HOLIDAY COMICS
1942 (196 pages) (25 cents)
Fawcett Publications

	Good	Fine	Mint
1-Reprints three Fawcett comics; Capt. Marvel, Nyoka (No.1), & Whiz	45.00	140.00	280.00

HOLIDAY COMICS
January, 1951 - No. 8, Aug, 1952?
Star Publications

	Good	Fine	Mint
1,3-8-Funny animal contents (Frisky Fables); L. B. Cole-c	5.50	16.00	32.00
2-Classic L. B. Cole-c	7.00	20.00	40.00

HOLI-DAY SURPRISE (Formerly Summer Fun)
1967 (25 cents)
Charlton Comics

	Good	Fine	Mint
V2No.55-Giant		.40	.80

HOLLYWOOD COMICS
1944
New Age Publications

	Good	Fine	Mint
1	3.50	10.00	20.00

HOLLYWOOD CONFESSIONS
Oct, 1949 - No. 2, Dec, 1949
St. John Publishing Co.

	Good	Fine	Mint
1-Kubert c/a(3)	9.00	25.00	50.00
2-Kubert c/a(2) (Scarce)	17.00	50.00	80.00

HOLLYWOOD DIARY
Dec, 1949 - No. 5, July-Aug, 1950
Quality Comics Group

	Good	Fine	Mint
1	5.50	16.00	32.00
2-5: 2,3-Photo-c	3.50	10.00	20.00

HOLLYWOOD FILM STORIES
April, 1950 - No. 4, Sept, 1950?
Feature Publications/Prize

	Good	Fine	Mint
1	5.00	14.00	28.00
2,4	3.50	10.00	20.00
3-A movie magazine; no comics	3.50	10.00	20.00

HOLLYWOOD FUNNY FOLKS (Formerly Funny Folks; Nutsy Squirrel No. 61 on)
No. 28, 1950 - No. 60, July-Aug, 1954
National Periodical Publications

	Good	Fine	Mint
28-40	1.00	3.00	6.00
41-60	.70	2.00	4.00

NOTE: ***Sheldon Mayer** a-28, 49.*

HOLLYWOOD LOVE DOCTOR (See Doctor Anthony King. . .)

HOLLYWOOD PICTORIAL (. . . Romances on cover)
No. 3, January, 1950
St. John Publishing Co.

	Good	Fine	Mint
3-Matt Baker-a	5.50	16.00	32.00

(Becomes a movie magazine - Hollywood Pictorial West. with No. 4.)

HOLLYWOOD ROMANCES
V2No. 46, Nov, 1966; V2No. 47, Oct, 1967 - No. 59, June, 1971
Charlton Comics

	Good	Fine	Mint
V2No. 46-Rolling Stones c/story	.30	.80	1.60
V2No. 47-59: 56-''Born to Heart Break'' begins		.30	.60

HOLLYWOOD SECRETS
Nov, 1949 - No. 6, Sept, 1950
Quality Comics Group

	Good	Fine	Mint
1-Ward-c/a, 9pgs.	14.00	40.00	80.00
2-Crandall-a, Ward c/a, 9 pgs.	8.00	24.00	48.00
3-6: All photo-c	3.50	10.00	20.00

	Good	Fine	Mint
. . . of Romance, I.W. Reprint No. 9	.85	2.50	5.00

HOLYOKE ONE-SHOT
1944 - 1945 (All reprints)
Holyoke Publishing Co. (Tem Publ.)

	Good	Fine	Mint
1-Grit Grady (on cover only), Miss Victory, Alias X (origin)-All reprints from Captain Fearless	3.00	8.00	16.00
2-Rusty Dugan (Corporal); Capt. Fearless (origin), Mr. Miracle (origin), app.	3.00	8.00	16.00
3-Miss Victory-Crash No. 4 reprints; Cat Man (origin), Solar Legion by Kirby app.; Miss Victory on cover only (1945)	8.00	24.00	48.00
4-Mr. Miracle-The Blue Streak app.	3.00	8.00	16.00
5-U.S. Border Patrol Comics (Sgt. Dick Carter of the . . .), Miss Victory (story matches cover No. 3), Citizen Smith, & Mr. Miracle app.	3.50	10.00	20.00
6-Capt. Fearless, Alias X, Capt. Stone (splash used as cover-No.10); Diamond Jim & Rusty Dugan (splash from cover-No.2)	3.00	8.00	16.00
7-Z-2, Strong Man, Blue Streak (story matches cover-No.8)-Reprints from Crash No. 2	4.00	12.00	24.00
8-Blue Streak, Strong Man (story matches cover-No.7)-Crash reprints	3.00	8.00	16.00
9-Citizen Smith, The Blue Streak, Solar Legion by Kirby & Strongman, the Perfect Human app.; reprints from Crash No. 4 & 5; Citizen Smith on cover only-from story in No. 5(1944-before No.3)	5.00	14.00	28.00
10-Captain Stone (Crash reprints); Solar Legion by S&K	5.00	14.00	28.00

HOMER COBB (See Adventures of. . .)

HOMER HOOPER
July, 1953 - No. 3, Sept, 1953
Atlas Comics

	Good	Fine	Mint
1-3	.85	2.50	5.00

HOMER, THE HAPPY GHOST (See Adventures of. . .)
3/55 - No. 22, 11/58; V2No.1, 11/69 - V2No.5, 7/70
Atlas(ACI/PPI/WPI)/Marvel Comics

	Good	Fine	Mint
V1No.1	1.50	4.00	8.00
2-22	.85	2.50	5.00
V2No.1 - V2No.5 (1969-70)	.50	1.50	3.00

HOME RUN (See A-1 Comics No. 89)

HONEYBEE BIRDWHISTLE AND HER PET PEPI (Introducing)
1969 (24 pgs.; B&W; slick cover)
Newspaper Enterprise Association (Giveaway)

	Good	Fine	Mint
nn-Contains Freckles newspaper strips with a short biography of Henry Fornhals (artist) & Fred Fox (writer) of the strip.	3.00	8.00	16.00

HONEYMOON (Formerly Gay Comics)
No. 41, January, 1950
A Lover's Magazine(USA) (Marvel)

	Good	Fine	Mint
41	.85	2.50	5.00

HONEYMOON ROMANCE
April, 1950 - No. 2, July, 1950 (25 cents) (digest size)
Artful Publications(Canadian)

	Good	Fine	Mint
1,2-(Rare)	14.00	40.00	80.00

HONEY WEST (TV)
September, 1966
Gold Key

	Good	Fine	Mint
1 (10186-609)	1.00	3.00	6.00

HONG KONG PHOOEY (Hanna-Barbera)
June, 1975 - No. 9, Nov, 1976
Charlton Comics

	Good	Fine	Mint
1-9		.40	.80

HOODED HORSEMAN, THE (Formerly Blazing West)
No.23, 5-6/52 - No.27, 1-2/53; No.18, 12-1/54-55 - No.27, 6-7/56
American Comics Group (Michel Publ.)

	Good	Fine	Mint
23(5-6/52)-Hooded Horseman, Injun Jones continues	3.00	9.00	18.00
24-27(1-2/53)	2.00	5.00	10.00
18(11-12/54)(Formerly Out of the Night)	2.00	5.00	10.00
19-3-D effect-c	2.00	5.00	10.00
20-Origin Johnny Injun	2.00	5.00	10.00
21-25,27(6-7/56)	1.50	4.00	8.00
26-Origin & 1st app. Cowboy Sahib; 11 pgs. Starr-a; bondage-c	2.00	5.00	10.00

NOTE: ***Whitney** c/a-20-22.*

HOODED MENACE, THE (Also see Daring Advs.)
1951 (One Shot)
Realistic/Avon Periodicals

	Good	Fine	Mint
nn-Based on a band of hooded outlaws in the Pacific Northwest, 1900-1906; reprinted in Daring Advs. No. 15	40.00	110.00	225.00

HOODS UP
1953 (16 pgs.; 15 cents)
Fram Corp. (Dist. to service station owners)

	Good	Fine	Mint
1-(Very Rare; only 2 known)-Eisner-c/a	14.00	40.00	80.00
2-6-(Very Rare; only 1 known of each)-Eisner-c/a	10.00	30.00	60.00

NOTE: *Convertible Connie gives tips for service stations, selling Fram oil filters.*

HOOT GIBSON WESTERN (Formerly My Love Story)
No. 5, May, 1950 - No. 3, Sept, 1950
Fox Features Syndicate

	Good	Fine	Mint
5,6(No. 1,2)	3.50	10.00	20.00
3-Wood-a	7.00	20.00	40.00
Western Roundup('50)(25 cents; 132 pgs.)	7.00	20.00	40.00

HOPALONG CASSIDY (Also see Master Comics)
1943 - No. 85, Jan, 1954
Fawcett Publications

	Good	Fine	Mint
1	25.00	70.00	140.00
2	10.00	30.00	60.00
3-5	7.00	20.00	40.00
6-14	5.50	16.00	32.00
15-30	3.50	10.00	20.00
31-50	2.50	7.00	14.00
51-85	2.00	5.00	10.00
Grape Nuts Flakes giveaway(1950,9x6'')	3.00	8.00	16.00
. . . & the Mad Barber(1951 Bond Bread giveaway)-7x5''; used in **SOTI**, pgs. 308,309	10.00	30.00	60.00
. . . & The Stampede(1950,5x5'')52 pgs.; Color; Samuel Lowe Co. No. 511-5, ½ art/½ text	3.00	8.00	16.00
. . . & The Stolen Treasure(1950,5x5'')52 pgs.; Color; Samuel Lowe Co. No. 511-5, ½ art/½ text	3.00	8.00	16.00
. . . in the Strange Legacy	5.00	14.00	28.00
. . . Gives a Helping Hand(1951)-52 pgs.; B&W; Samuel Lowe Co. No. 517-5	3.00	8.00	16.00
. . . Meets the Brend Brothers Bandits	3.50	10.00	20.00
White Tower Giveaway (1946, 16pgs., paper-c)	3.50	10.00	20.00

HOPALONG CASSIDY
No. 86, Feb, 1954 - No. 135, May-June, 1959
National Periodical Publications

	Good	Fine	Mint
86	3.00	8.00	16.00
87-100	1.50	4.00	8.00
101-135	1.00	3.00	6.00

NOTE: ***Gil Kane** art-1956 up.*

HOPE SHIP
June-Aug, 1963
Dell Publishing Co.

	Good	Fine	Mint
1	.50	1.50	3.00

HOPPY THE MARVEL BUNNY (See Fawcett Funny Animal)
Dec, 1945 - 1947
Fawcett Publications

	Good	Fine	Mint
1	5.00	14.00	28.00
2-15	2.00	6.00	12.00
. . . Well Known Comics (1944,8½x10½'',paper-c) Bestmaid/Samuel Lowe	7.00	20.00	40.00

HORACE & DOTTY DRIPPLE (Dotty Dripple No. 1-24)
No. 25, Aug, 1952 - No. 43, Oct, 1955
Harvey Publications

	Good	Fine	Mint
25-43	.70	2.00	4.00

HORIZONTAL LIEUTENANT, THE (See Movie Classics)

HORRIFIC (Terrific No. 14 on)
Sept, 1952 - No. 13, Sept, 1954
Artful/Comic Media/Harwell/Mystery

	Good	Fine	Mint
1	4.00	12.00	24.00
2	2.50	7.00	14.00
3-Bullet in head-c	3.50	10.00	20.00
4-7,9,10	1.75	5.00	10.00
8-Origin & 1st app. The Teller(E.C. parody)	2.00	6.00	12.00
11-Swipe/Witches Tales No. 6,27	1.50	4.00	8.00
12,13	1.50	4.00	8.00

NOTE: ***Don Heck** a-8; c-3-13. **Hollingsworth** a-4. **Morisi** a-8. **Palais** a-8, 11.*

HORROR FROM THE TOMB (Mysterious Stories No. 2)
Sept, 1954
Premier Magazine Co.

	Good	Fine	Mint
1-Woodbridge/Torres-a	5.00	14.00	28.00

HORRORS, THE
No. 11, Jan, 1953 - No. 15, Apr, 1954
Star Publications

	Good	Fine	Mint
11-Horrors of War; Disbrow-a(2)	6.00	18.00	36.00
12-Horrors of War; color illo in **POP**	7.00	20.00	40.00
13-Horrors of Mystery; crime stories	6.00	18.00	36.00
14,15-Horrors of the Underworld	6.00	18.00	36.00

NOTE: *All have **L. B. Cole** covers. **Hollingsworth** a-13. **Palais** a-13r.*

HORROR TALES (Magazine)
V1No.7, 6/69 - V6No.6, 12/74; V7No.2, 5/76 - Present
(V1-V6, 52 pgs.; V7, V8No.2, 112 pgs.; V8No.4 on, 68 pgs.)
(No V5No.3, V7No.1, V8No.1,3)
Eerie Publications

	Good	Fine	Mint
V1No.7-9		.60	1.20
V2No.1-6('70), V3No.1-6('71)		.40	.80
V4No.1-3,5-7('72)		.40	.80
V4No.4-LSD story reprint/Weird V3No.5	.70	2.00	4.00
V5No.1,2,4,5(6/73),5(10/73)		.40	.80
V6No.1-6('74),V7No.2,4('76)		.40	.80
V7No.3('76)-Giant issue		.50	1.00
V8No.2,4,5('77)		.40	.80

NOTE: *Bondage-c-V6No.1,3.*

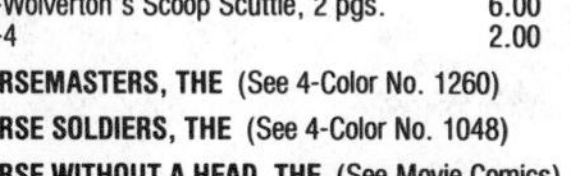

HORSE FEATHERS COMICS
November, 1945
Lev Gleason Publications

	Good	Fine	Mint
1-Wolverton's Scoop Scuttle, 2 pgs.	6.00	18.00	36.00
2-4	2.00	5.00	10.00

HORSEMASTERS, THE (See 4-Color No. 1260)

HORSE SOLDIERS, THE (See 4-Color No. 1048)

HORSE WITHOUT A HEAD, THE (See Movie Comics)

Hopalong Cassidy #3, © FAW

Horrific #10, © Artful

The Horrors #11, © STAR

Hot Rod & Speedway Comics #5, © HILL

Hot Rods & Racing Cars #4, © CC

House Of Mystery #143, © DC

HOT DOG
June-July, 1954 - No. 4, Dec-Jan, 1954-55
Magazine Enterprises

	Good	Fine	Mint
1(A-1 107),2,3(A-1 115),4(A-1 136)	.70	2.00	4.00

HOTEL DEPAREE - SUNDANCE (See 4-Color No. 1126)

HOT ROD AND SPEEDWAY COMICS
Feb-Mar, 1952 - No. 5, Apr-May, 1953
Hillman Periodicals

	Good	Fine	Mint
1	1.50	4.00	8.00
2-Krigstein-a	2.50	7.00	14.00
3-5	.70	2.00	4.00

HOT ROD CARTOONS (Magazine)
Nov, 1964 - No. 60, Sept, 1974 (35 cents)
Petersen Publ. Co.

	Good	Fine	Mint
1	1.00	3.00	6.00
2-5,8,9	.40	1.20	2.40
6,7,10-12,15-Toth-a	1.00	3.00	6.00
13,14,16-20		.60	1.20
21-46,48-59		.50	1.00
47-Toth-a, 2 pgs.	.85	2.50	5.00
60-Robert Williams-a	.85	2.50	5.00

HOT ROD COMICS
Nov, 1951 - V2No.7, Feb, 1953
Fawcett Publications

	Good	Fine	Mint
V1No.1-Powell-a in all	2.50	7.00	14.00
2-6, V2No.7	1.50	4.00	8.00

"HOT ROD" KING
Fall, 1952
Ziff-Davis Publ. Co.

	Good	Fine	Mint
1-Giacoia-a	3.00	9.00	18.00

HOT ROD RACERS (Grand Prix No. 16 on)
Dec, 1964 - No. 15, 1967
Charlton Comics

	Good	Fine	Mint
1		.30	.60
2-15		.20	.40

HOT RODS AND RACING CARS
Nov, 1951 - No. 120, June, 1973
Charlton Comics (Motor Mag. No. 1)

	Good	Fine	Mint
1	1.50	4.00	8.00
2-10	.70	2.00	4.00
11-20	.35	1.00	2.00
21-50		.50	1.00
51-120		.30	.60

HOT SHOT CHARLIE
1947 (Lee Elias)
Hillman Periodicals

	Good	Fine	Mint
1	1.20	3.50	7.00

HOT STUFF CREEPY CAVES
Nov, 1974 - No. 7, Nov, 1975
Harvey Publications

	Good	Fine	Mint
1	.55	1.60	3.20
2-5	.30	.80	1.60
6,7		.40	.80

HOT STUFF SIZZLERS
July, 1960 - No. 59, March, 1974
Harvey Publications

	Good	Fine	Mint
1	4.00	12.00	24.00
2-5	1.50	4.00	8.00
6-10	1.00	3.00	6.00
11-20	.70	2.00	4.00
21-59	.35	1.00	2.00

HOT STUFF, THE LITTLE DEVIL
Oct, 1957 - Present
Harvey Publications (Illustrated Humor)

	Good	Fine	Mint
1	10.00	30.00	60.00
2-5	5.00	14.00	28.00
6-10	3.50	8.00	16.00
11-20	1.20	3.50	7.00
21-40	.70	2.00	4.00
41-60	.55	1.60	3.20
61-100	.30	.80	1.60
101-163		.40	.80
Shoestore Giveaway('63)	.35	1.00	2.00

HOT WHEELS (TV)
Mar-Apr, 1970 - No. 6, Jan-Feb, 1971
National Periodical Publications

	Good	Fine	Mint
1	.70	2.00	4.00
2,4,5	.40	1.20	2.40
3-Adams-c	1.00	3.00	6.00
6-Adams c/a	1.50	4.00	8.00

NOTE: ***Toth*** *a-1-5; c-1,4,5.*

HOUSE OF MYSTERY (See Limited Collectors' Edition & Super DC Giant)

HOUSE OF MYSTERY
Dec-Jan, 1951-52 - Present
National Periodical Publications/DC Comics

	Good	Fine	Mint
1	14.00	40.00	90.00
2,3	7.00	20.00	45.00
4,5	5.50	16.00	35.00
6-15	4.00	12.00	25.00
16-35(2/55)-Last pre-code ish; No. 30-Woodish-a	2.50	7.00	14.00
36-49,51-60	1.20	3.50	7.00
50-Text story of Orson Welles' War of the Worlds broadcast	1.50	4.00	8.00
61,65,66,72-Kirby-a	1.50	4.00	8.00
62-64,67-71,73-75	.70	2.00	4.00
76,82,84,85-Kirby-a	1.00	3.00	6.00
77-81,83,86-100	.50	1.50	3.00
101-108,110-119	.35	1.00	2.00
109,120-Toth-a; Kubert No. 109	.70	2.00	4.00
121-142		.60	1.20
143-J'onn J'onzz, Manhunter begins, ends No. 173 (6/64); story continues/Detective No. 326	.40	1.20	2.40
144-148,150		.60	1.20
149-Toth-a	.40	1.10	2.20
151-155,157,159		.40	.80
156-Origin Robby Reed in Dial H for Hero (begins; ends No. 173)	.30	.80	1.60
158-Origin & last app. Diabolu Idol-Head in J'onn J'onzz		.50	1.00
160-Intro. Marco Xavier (Martian Manhunter) & Vulture Crime Organization in J'onn J'onzz (7/66), ends No. 173; Plastic Man x-over		.50	1.00
161-168,170		.50	1.00
169-Origin & 1st app. Gem Girl in Dial H for Hero		.40	.80
171-177: 174-Mystery format begins		.40	.80
178-Adams-a	.85	2.50	5.00
179-Adams/Orlando, Wrightson-a (1st pro work)	1.50	4.00	8.00
180,181,183: Wrightson-a. 180,183-Wood-a	.60	1.80	3.60
182-Toth-a(r)		.60	1.20
184-Kane/Wood, Toth-a	.50	1.50	3.00
185-Williamson/Kaluta-a; 3 pgs. Wood-a	.80	2.40	4.80
186-Adams, Wrightson-a	.80	2.40	4.80
187,190-Toth-a(r)		.60	1.20
188-Wrightson-a	.80	2.40	4.80
189-Wood-a, Toth-a(r)	.40	1.20	2.40
191,195-Wrightson-a; 195-Redondo-a	.80	2.40	4.80
192,193,198,200		.40	.80
194-Toth-a(r); Kirby, Redondo-a	.40	1.20	2.40

HOUSE OF MYSTERY (continued)	Good	Fine	Mint
196-Toth-a(r)		.60	1.20
197-Redondo-a	.30	.80	1.60
199-Wood, Kirby-a	.55	1.60	3.20
201,205,206,208-210		.30	.60
202,203,211-Redondo-a in all		.40	.80
204-Wrightson-a, 9 pgs.	.60	1.80	3.60
207-Wrightson, Starlin, Redondo-a	.50	1.50	3.00
212,213,215,216,218,220,222,223,225		.30	.60
214,217,219-Redondo-a		.40	.80
221-Wrightson/Kaluta-a	.50	1.50	3.00
224-Adams inks & Wrightson-a; begin 100 pg. issues; Phantom Stranger reprint	.70	2.00	4.00
226-Wrightson, Redondo-a; Phantom Stranger reprint	.30	.90	1.80
227-Redondo-a		.40	.80
228-Adams inks; Wrightson-r	.60	1.80	3.60
229-Wrightson-a(r); Redondo, Toth-a; last 100 pg. issue	.30	.90	1.80
230-234,237-240,242,243: 230-68 pgs.		.30	.60
235-Redondo-a		.40	.80
236-Adams inks, Ditko-a		.60	1.20
241-Redondo-a		.40	.80
244-Spectre app.		.40	.80
245-250		.30	.60
251-($1.00 size)-Wood-a	.30	.80	1.60
252-253,255,256,258		.60	1.20
254,274,277-Rogers-a	.30	.80	1.60
257,259-Golden-a; last $1.00 size	.30	.80	1.60
260-273,275,276,278-281,283-299		.60	1.20
282-Starlin-a		.60	1.20

NOTE: ***Adams*** *c-175-192, 196, 197, 199, 251-254.* ***Alcala*** *a-209, 211-215, 217, 219, 220, 222, 224-228.* ***Aparo*** *a-201, 209; c-269.* ***Chaykin*** *a-277.* ***Craig*** *a-263, 275, 295.* ***Ditko*** *a-236, 247, 254, 258, 276, 277; c-277.* ***Drucker*** *a-37.* ***Howard*** *a-182, 187, 254.* ***Infantino*** *a-110, 111, 294, 296; c-296p.* ***Kaluta*** *a-109, 195, 200, 202, 250; c-200-202, 210, 212, 233, 260, 261, 263, 265, 267, 268, 273, 276, 284, 287, 288, 293-295.* ***Bob Kane*** *a-84.* ***Kirby*** *a-194r, 199r; c-65, 76, 78, 79, 85.* ***Kubert*** *c-286, 289-294, 297-299.* ***Meskin*** *a-144.* ***Moreira*** *a-20-50, 79, 201r; c-50.* ***Morrow*** *a-192, 196, 255.* ***Nasser*** *a-276.* ***Newton*** *a-259, 272.* ***Nino*** *a-204, 212, 213, 220, 224, 225, 245, 250, 252, 253, 255, 256, 283.* ***Orlando*** *a-175(2 pgs.); c-262, 264, 270-272, 274, 275, 278, 296i.* ***Reese*** *a-195, 200, 205i.* ***Redondo*** *a-287.* ***Roussos*** *a-65, 84.* ***Starlin*** *a-207(2 pgs.); c-281.* ***Leonard Starr*** *a-9.* ***Sutton*** *a-271.* ***Tuska*** *a-293, 294.* ***Wrightson*** *c-193-195, 204, 207, 209, 211, 213, 214, 217, 221, 226r, 231, 236, 255, 256.*

HOUSE OF SECRETS
11-12/56 - No. 80, 9-10/66; No. 81, 8-9/69 - No. 140, 2-3/76; No. 141, 8-9/76 - No. 154, 10-11/78
National Periodical Publications/DC Comics

	Good	Fine	Mint
1-Drucker-a	13.00	38.00	85.00
2-Moreira-a	6.00	18.00	40.00
3-Kirby c/a	6.00	18.00	40.00
4,8-Kirby-a	4.00	12.00	24.00
5-7,9-11	3.50	10.00	20.00
12-Kirby c/a	4.00	12.00	24.00
13-20	2.00	6.00	12.00
21,22,24-47,49,50	1.50	4.00	8.00
23-Origin Mark Merlin	2.00	5.00	10.00
48-Toth-a	2.00	5.00	10.00
51-60,62: 58-Origin Mark Merlin retold	.70	2.00	4.00
61-First Eclipso	.80	2.40	4.80
63-67-Toth-a	1.20	3.50	7.00
68-80: 73-Mark Merlin ends, Prince Ra-Man begins. 80-Eclipso, Prince Ra-Man end		.60	1.20
81,84,86,88,89: 81-Mystery format begins		.40	.80
82-Adams-c(i)	.80	2.40	4.80
83-Toth-a	.70	2.00	4.00
85-Adams-a(i)	.80	2.40	4.80
87-Wrightson & Kaluta-a	.80	2.40	4.80
90-Buckler-a (1st comic art)/Adams-a	.80	2.40	4.80
91-Wood-a	.70	2.00	4.00
92-Intro. Swamp Thing; Wrightson-a (6-7/71); J. Jones part inks	4.00	12.00	24.00
93,96,98-Toth-a(r). 96-Wood-a	.40	1.20	2.40
94-Wrightson inks; Toth-a(r)	.80	2.40	4.80
95,99,102,104-Redondo-a		.50	1.00
97,100,101,103,105-112,114,115		.40	.80
113,116-Redondo-a		.50	1.00
117,119-122,124-130		.40	.80
118-Evans-a		.50	1.00
123-Toth-a, 12 pgs.		.50	1.00
131-133,136-138		.30	.60
134-Redondo-a		.40	.80
135,139-Wrightson-c. 139-Redondo-a		.40	.80
140-Origin The Patchworkman; Redondo-a	.30	.80	1.60
141-150,152-154: 150-Phantom Stranger, Dr. 13 app.		.30	.60
151-Golden, Suydam-a		.40	.80

NOTE: ***Adams*** *c-81, 82, 84-88, 90, 91.* ***Alcala*** *a-100, 105, 107, 109, 115, 117, 119, 120, 122, 125.* ***Anderson*** *a-91.* ***Aparo*** *a-93, 97, 105; c-153.* ***Colan*** *a-63.* ***Dezuniga*** *a-93, 94, 111, 120.* ***Ditko*** *a-139, 148.* ***Finley*** *a-7.* ***Infantino*** *a-43, 53.* ***Kaluta*** *a-87, 98, 99; c-98, 99, 101, 102, 151, 154.* ***Bob Kane*** *a-18, 21.* ***Kirby*** *c-11.* ***Kubert*** *a-29, 30, 39(with* ***Meskin****).* ***Meskin*** *a-22.* ***Morrow*** *a-86, 89, 90; c-89, 147, 148.* ***Nino*** *a-101, 103, 106, 109, 115, 117, 126, 128, 131, 147, 153.* ***Suydam*** *a-119, 131, 151.* ***Starlin*** *c-150.* ***Wrightson*** *c-92-94, 96, 100, 103, 106, 107, 135, 139.*

HOUSE OF TERROR (3-D)
October, 1953
St. John Publishing Co.

	Good	Fine	Mint
1-Kubert, Baker-a	6.00	18.00	36.00

HOUSE OF YANG, THE (See Yang)
July, 1975 - No. 6, June, 1976
Charlton Comics

	Good	Fine	Mint
1-Opium propaganda story		.40	.80
2-6		.30	.60
Modern Comics No. 1(1978)		.30	.60

HOWARD THE DUCK (See Fear, Man-Thing, & Marvel Treasury Ed.)
Jan, 1976 - No, 31, May, 1979
Marvel Comics Group

	Good	Fine	Mint
1-Brunner c/a; Spider-Man x-over (low distribution)	2.00	5.00	10.00
2-Brunner c/a, Starlin-a (low distr.)	.85	2.50	5.00
3-Buscema-a	.40	1.20	2.40
4,5	.30	.90	1.80
6-9: 8-Dr. Strange app.	.30	.80	1.60
10-15: 10-Spider-Man x-over; Dr. Strange app. 12-1st app. Kiss		.60	1.20
16-Album issue; all text; 3pg. comics	.30	.80	1.60
17-20		.50	1.00
21-31: 22-Man-Thing app.		.40	.80
Annual 1(9/77)		.60	1.20

NOTE: ***Colan*** *a-4-15, 17-20, 24-28.* ***Infantino*** *a-1, 20.* ***Leialoha*** *a-4-13i.* ***Mayerik*** *a-23, 24; c-23.*

HOWARD THE DUCK MAGAZINE
October, 1979 - No. 9, March, 1981
Marvel Comics Group

	Good	Fine	Mint
1	.30	.80	1.60
2,3,5-9		.45	.90
4-Beatles, John Lennon, Elvis, Kiss & Devo cameos; Hitler app.		.60	1.20

NOTE: ***Buscema*** *a-4.* ***Davis*** *c-3.* ***Golden*** *a-1, 5p, 6p(51pgs.).* ***Rogers*** *a-7, 8.* ***Simonson*** *a-7.*

House Of Mystery #251, © DC

House Of Secrets #87, © DC

Howard The Duck #4, © MCG

Howdy Doody #4, © DELL

The Human Fly #9, © MCG

The Human Torch #3, © MCG

HOW BOYS AND GIRLS CAN HELP WIN THE WAR
1942 (One Shot) (10 cents)
The Parents' Magazine Institute

	Good	Fine	Mint
1	5.00	14.00	28.00

HOWDY DOODY (TV)
1949 - No. 38, July-Sept, 1956
Dell Publishing Co.

	Good	Fine	Mint
1	4.50	13.00	26.00
2-5	2.00	6.00	12.00
6-Used in **SOTI**, pg. 309	3.00	9.00	18.00
7-10	1.20	3.50	7.00
11-38	1.20	2.50	5.00
4-Color 761,811	1.20	3.50	7.00

HOW IT BEGAN (See Single Series No. 15)

HOW SANTA GOT HIS RED SUIT (See March of Comics No. 2)

HOW STALIN HOPES WE WILL DESTROY AMERICA
1951 (16 pgs.) (Giveaway)
Joe Lowe Co. (Pictorial News)

	Good	Fine	Mint
	50.00	150.00	300.00

(Prices vary widely on this book)

HOW TO DRAW FOR THE COMICS
No date (1942?) (32 pgs.; B&W & color) (10 Cents)
Street and Smith

	Good	Fine	Mint
nn-Art by Winsor McCay, George Marcoux(Supersnipe artist), Vernon Greene(The Shadow artist), Jack Binder(with biog), Thorton Fisher, Jon Small, & Jack Farr	8.00	24.00	48.00

HOW THE WEST WAS WON (See Movie Comics)

H. R. PUFNSTUF (TV)
Oct, 1970 - No. 8, July, 1972
Gold Key

	Good	Fine	Mint
1-8		.50	1.00

(See March of Comics No. 360)

HUBERT (See 4-Color No. 251)

HUCK & YOGI JAMBOREE (TV)
March, 1961 (116 pgs.; $1.00) (B&W original material)
(6¼x9''; cardboard cover; high quality paper)
Dell Publishing Co.

	Good	Fine	Mint
		1.00	2.00

HUCK & YOGI WINTER SPORTS (See 4-Color No. 1310)

HUCK FINN (See New Advs. of. . .)

HUCKLEBERRY FINN (See 4-Color No. 1114)

HUCKLEBERRY HOUND (See Dell Giant No. 31,44, March of Comics No. 199,214,235, Whitman Comic Books & Golden Picture Story Book)

HUCKLEBERRY HOUND (TV)
May-July, 1959 - No. 43, Oct, 1970 (Hanna-Barbera)
Dell/Gold Key No. 18 (10/62) on

	Good	Fine	Mint
4-Color 990,1050	.50	1.50	3.00
3(1-2/60)-17	.30	.80	1.60
18-20: All titled Huckleberry Hound Chuckleberry Tales; No. 18,19-84 pgs.		.40	.80
21-43: 37-reprints		.30	.60
4-Color 1054,1141	.50	1.50	3.00
. . . Kite Fun Book(1961)-16 pgs.; small size	.70	2.00	4.00

HUCKLEBERRY HOUND (TV)
Nov, 1970 - No. 8, Jan, 1972 (Hanna-Barbera)
Charlton Comics

	Good	Fine	Mint
1-8		.50	1.00

HUCKLEBERRY HOUND
Sept, 1978 - Present
Marvel Comics Group

	Good	Fine	Mint
1		.30	.60
2		.25	.50

HUCKLEBERRY HOUND CHUCKLEBERRY TALES (See No. 18-20 in regular series)

HUEY, DEWEY, & LOUIE BACK TO SCHOOL
1958 (25 cents) (See Dell Giant No. 22,35,49)
Dell Publishing Co.

	Good	Fine	Mint
1-Giant	2.00	6.00	12.00

HUEY, DEWEY, AND LOUIE JUNIOR WOODCHUCKS
Aug, 1966 - Present (Disney)
Gold Key No. 1-61/Whitman No. 62 on

	Good	Fine	Mint
1-Written by Carl Barks	2.00	6.00	12.00
2,3(12/68)-Written by Carl Barks	1.50	4.00	8.00
4,5(4/70)-Barks-r	1.00	3.00	6.00
6-17,19-Written by Barks	.85	2.50	5.00
18,20,21,27-30	.40	1.20	2.40
22-26-Barks-r	.55	1.60	3.20
31-57,60-66: 41-Reprints		.50	1.00
58,59-Barks-r		.60	1.20

NOTE: ***Barks** story reprints-No. 24,35,42,45,51.*

HUGH O'BRIAN FAMOUS MARSHAL WYATT EARP (Also see 4-Color 860)
1958; No. 4, Sept-Nov, 1958 - No. 13, Dec-Jan, 1960-61
Dell Publishing Co.

	Good	Fine	Mint
4-Color 890,921-All Manning-a	2.00	5.00	10.00
4-12-Manning-a	1.50	4.00	8.00
13-Toth-a?	1.00	3.00	6.00

HULK, THE (See The Incredible Hulk)

HULK, THE (Formerly The Rampaging Hulk)
No. 11, 10/78 - No. 27, June, 1981 (Magazine)($1.50)(in color)
Marvel Comics Group

	Good	Fine	Mint
11-Moon Knight app.	.50	1.50	3.00
12-27	.30	.80	1.60

NOTE: ***Alcala** a-15, 18-20, 22, 24-27. **Buscema** a-23; c-26. **Chaykin** a-21-25. **Simonson** a-27; c-23.*

HUMAN FLY
1963 - 1964 (Reprints)
I.W. Enterprises/Super

	Good	Fine	Mint
I.W. Reprint No. 1-Reprints Blue Beetle No. 44('46)	.70	2.00	4.00
Super Reprint No. 10-Reprints Blue Beetle No. 46('47)	.70	2.00	4.00

HUMAN FLY, THE
Sept, 1977 - No. 19, Mar, 1979
Marvel Comics Group

	Good	Fine	Mint
1-Origin; Spider-Man x-over		.60	1.20
2-Infantino-a(p); Ghost Rider x-over		.40	.80
3-19: 9-Daredevil x-over; Byrne/Austin-c		.40	.80

HUMAN TORCH, THE (Red Raven No. 1) (See Marvel Mystery)
No. 2, Fall, 1940 - No. 15, Spring, 1944 (becomes Funny Tunes);
No. 16, Fall, 1944 - No. 35, Mar, 1949 (becomes Love Tales);
No. 36, April, 1954 - No. 38, Aug, 1954
Timely Comics No.1-35(SnPC No.16-35)/Atlas No. 36-38

	Good	Fine	Mint
2(No.1)-Intro & Origin Toro; The Falcon, The Fiery Mask, Mantor the Magician, & Microman only app.; Human Torch by Burgos, Sub-Mariner by Everett begin (origin of each in text)	300.00	900.00	2000.00

(Prices vary widely on this book)

	Good	Fine	Mint
3(No.2)-Bondage-c; 40pg. H.T. story	130.00	390.00	800.00
4(No.3)-The Patriot app.; last Everett Sub-Mariner; Sid Greene-a	100.00	280.00	575.00
5(No.4)-The Patriot app. (Summer, 1941)	65.00	190.00	400.00

HUMAN TORCH (continued)	Good	Fine	Mint
5-Human Torch battles Sub-Mariner (Fall,'41)	120.00	320.00	750.00
6,7,9	40.00	120.00	260.00
8-Human Torch battles Sub-Mariner; Wolverton-a, 1 pg.	70.00	200.00	420.00
10-Human Torch battles Sub-Mariner; Wolverton-a, 1 pg.	55.00	160.00	340.00
11-15: 12-Bondage-c	35.00	100.00	210.00
16-20: 19-Bondage-c	25.00	70.00	150.00
21-30	20.00	55.00	120.00
31-Namora x-over in Sub-Mariner (also No. 30); last Toro	15.00	45.00	100.00
32-Sungirl, Namora app.	15.00	45.00	100.00
33-Capt. America x-over in Sub-Mariner	15.00	45.00	100.00
34-Sungirl solo	15.00	45.00	100.00
35-Captain America & Sungirl app. (1949)	15.00	45.00	100.00
36-38(1954)-Sub-Mariner in all issues except No. 34 & 35	12.00	36.00	72.00

NOTE: ***Burgos*** *c-36.* ***Powell*** *a-36.* ***Schomburg*** *c-12, 14, 15, 19. Since there is a six month delay between No. 15 & 16, it is believed that Funny Tunes No. 16 continued after Human Torch No. 15.*

HUMAN TORCH, THE
Sept, 1974 - No. 8, Nov, 1975
Marvel Comics Group

	Good	Fine	Mint
1-Kirby-a(r)	.30	.80	1.60
2-8		.40	.80

NOTE: *Golden age Torch-r No. 1-8.* ***Kirby*** *a-2-5,8r.*

HUMBUG (Satire by Harvey Kurtzman)
Aug, 1957 - No. 11, Oct, 1958
Humbug Publications

	Good	Fine	Mint
1	4.00	12.00	24.00
2-9	2.00	5.00	10.00
10,11-Magazine format	2.00	5.00	10.00
Bound Volume(No.1-6)-Sold by publisher	14.00	40.00	80.00
Bound Volume(No.1-9)	17.00	50.00	100.00

NOTE: ***Davis*** *a-1-11.* ***Elder*** *a-2-4, 6-9, 11.* ***Heath*** *a-2, 4-8, 10.* ***Jaffee*** *a-2, 4-9.* ***Kurtzman*** *a-11.* ***Wood*** *a-1.*

HUMDINGER
May-June, 1946 - 1947
Novelty Press/Premium Group

	Good	Fine	Mint
1-Jerkwater Line, Mickey Starlight by Don Rico, Dink begin	2.00	5.00	10.00
2-6,V2No.1,2	.85	2.50	5.00

HUMOR (See All Humor Comics)

HUMPHREY COMICS
October, 1948 - No. 40, 1954
Harvey Publications

	Good	Fine	Mint
1-Joe Palooka's pal (reprints); Powell-a	3.50	10.00	20.00
2,3	2.00	5.00	10.00
4-Boy Heroes app.	3.50	10.00	20.00
5-10: 7-Little Dot app.	1.50	4.00	8.00
11-20	1.00	3.00	6.00
21-40	.70	2.00	4.00

HUNCHBACK OF NOTRE DAME, THE (See 4-Color No. 854)

HUNK
August, 1961 - 1963
Charlton Comics

	Good	Fine	Mint
1-11		.40	.80

HUNTED (Formerly My Love Memoirs)
No. 13, July, 1950 - No. 2, Sept, 1950
Fox Features Syndicate

	Good	Fine	Mint
13(No.1)-Used in **SOTI**, pg. 42 & illo.-''Treating police contemptuously'' (lower left); Hollingsworth bondage-c	8.00	24.00	48.00
2	3.50	10.00	20.00

HURRICANE COMICS
1945
Cambridge House

	Good	Fine	Mint
1-(Humor)	1.50	4.00	8.00

HYPER MYSTERY COMICS
May, 1940 - No. 2, June, 1940
Hyper Publications

	Good	Fine	Mint
1-Hyper, the Phenomenal begins	15.00	45.00	100.00
2	12.00	35.00	75.00

I AIM AT THE STARS (See 4-Color No. 1148)

IBIS, THE INVINCIBLE (See Fawcett Min., Mighty Midget & Whiz)
1942 - No. 6, Spring, 1948
Fawcett Publications

	Good	Fine	Mint
1-Origin Ibis; Raboy-c	35.00	100.00	220.00
2-Bondage-c	25.00	70.00	140.00
3-Wolverton-a No. 3-6 (4 pgs. each)	17.00	50.00	100.00
4-6: 5-Bondage-c	14.00	40.00	80.00

IDAHO
June-Aug, 1963 - No. 8, July-Sept, 1965
Dell Publishing Co.

	Good	Fine	Mint
1	.70	2.00	4.00
2-8	.40	1.20	2.40

IDEAL (. . . a Classical Comic) (2nd Series) (Love Romances No. 6?)
July, 1948 - No. 5, March, 1949
Timely Comics

	Good	Fine	Mint
1-Antony & Cleopatra	8.00	24.00	48.00
2-The Corpses of Dr. Sacotti	5.50	16.00	32.00
3-Joan of Arc; used in **SOTI**, pg. 308-'Boer War'	5.50	16.00	32.00
4-Richard the Lion-hearted; titled ''. . . the World's Greatest Comics;'' The Witness app.	7.00	20.00	40.00
5-Ideal Love & Romance	4.00	12.00	24.00

(Feature-length stories in all)

IDEAL COMICS (1st Series) (Willie No. 5 on)
Fall, 1944 - No. 4, Spring, 1946
Timely Comics (MgPC)

	Good	Fine	Mint
1	3.00	8.00	16.00
2-4-Super Rabbit	2.00	5.00	10.00

IDEAL LOVE & ROMANCE (See Ideal, A Classical Comic)

IDEAL ROMANCE (Formerly Tender Romance)
April, 1954 - No. 7, Dec, 1954 (Diary Confessions No. 9 on)
Key Publications

	Good	Fine	Mint
3	1.50	4.50	9.00
4-7	1.00	3.00	6.00

IDEAL ROMANCES
1950
Stanmor

	Good	Fine	Mint
6	1.50	4.00	8.00

I DREAM OF JEANNIE (TV)
1966 - No. 2, Dec, 1966
Dell Publishing Co.

	Good	Fine	Mint
1,2: 1-Photo-c	.85	2.50	5.00

IF THE DEVIL WOULD TALK
1950; 1958 (32 pgs.; paper cover; in full color)
Roman Catholic Catechetical Guild/Impact Publ.

nn-(Scarce)-About secularism (20-30 copies known to exist); very

The Human Torch #37, © MCG

Humbug #2, © Humbug Publ.

Ibis The Invincible #5, © FAW

Impact #2, © WMG

The Incredible Hulk #177, © MCG

Incredible Science Fiction #32, © WMG

IF THE DEVIL WOULD TALK (continued)

	Good	Fine	Mint
low distribution	100.00	300.00	600.00
1958 Edition-(Rare)-(Impact Publ.); art & script changed to meet church criticism of earlier edition; only 4 known copies exist	100.00	300.00	600.00
Black & White version of nn edition; small size; only 4 known copies exist	50.00	150.00	300.00

NOTE: *The original edition of this book was printed and killed by the Guild's board of directors. It is believed that a very limited number of copies were distributed. The 1958 version was a complete bomb with very limited, if any, circulation. In 1979, 11 original, 4 1958 reprints, and 4 B&W's surfaced from the Guild's old files in St. Paul, Minnesota.*

ILLUSTRATED GAGS (See Single Series No. 16)

ILLUSTRATED LIBRARY OF. . . , AN (See Classics Illustrated Giants)

ILLUSTRATED STORIES OF THE OPERAS
1943 (16 pgs.; B&W) (25 cents) (cover-B&W & red)
Baily (Bernard) Publ. Co.

	Good	Fine	Mint
nn-(Rare)-Faust (part reprinted in Cisco Kid No. 1)	10.00	30.00	60.00
nn-(Rare)-Aida	10.00	30.00	60.00
nn-(Rare)-Carmen; Baily-a	10.00	30.00	60.00
nn-(Rare)-Rigoleito	10.00	30.00	60.00

ILLUSTRATED STORY OF ROBIN HOOD & HIS MERRY MEN, THE (See Robin Hood)

ILLUSTRATED TARZAN BOOK, THE (See Tarzan Book)

I LOVED (Formerly Rulah; Colossal Feature Mag. No. 33 on)
No. 28, July, 1949 - No. 32, Mar, 1950
Fox Features Syndicate

	Good	Fine	Mint
28-32	2.00	6.00	12.00

I LOVE LUCY COMICS (TV)
Summer, 1953; Aug-Oct, 1954 - No. 35, Apr-June, 1962
Dell Publishing Co.

	Good	Fine	Mint
3-D (Summer, 1953)	10.00	30.00	60.00
4-Color 535,559	1.50	4.00	8.00
3-10	1.00	3.00	6.00
11-35	.70	2.00	4.00

I LOVE YOU
June, 1950 - No. 6, 1951
Fawcett Publications

	Good	Fine	Mint
1	3.50	10.00	20.00
2-6	2.00	5.00	10.00

I LOVE YOU (Formerly In Love)
No. 7, 9/55 - No. 121, 12/76; No. 122, 3/79 - No. 130, 5/80
Charlton Comics

	Good	Fine	Mint
7-Kirby-c, Powell-a	3.00	9.00	18.00
8-20	.70	2.00	4.00
21-25,27-50	.35	1.00	2.00
26-Torres-a	.85	2.50	5.00
51-130: 113-Jonnie Love app.		.40	.80
60(1/66)-Elvis Presley drawn c/story	1.00	3.00	6.00

I'M A COP
1954
Magazine Enterprises

	Good	Fine	Mint
1(A-1 111)-Drug mention stories	3.50	10.00	20.00
2(A-1 126), 3(A-1 128), 4	1.50	4.50	9.00

NOTE: ***Powell** c/a-1,2.*

I'M DICKENS - HE'S FENSTER (TV)
May-July, 1963 - No. 2, Aug-Oct, 1963
Dell Publishing Co.

	Good	Fine	Mint
1,2	1.00	2.00	4.00

I MET A HANDSOME COWBOY (See 4-Color No. 324)

IMPACT
Mar-Apr, 1955 - No. 5, Nov-Dec, 1955
E. C. Comics

	Good	Fine	Mint
1	7.00	20.00	40.00
2-5: 4-Crandall-a	5.00	14.00	28.00

NOTE: ***Crandall** a-1-4. **Davis** a-2-4; c-1-5. **Evans** a-1, 4, 5. **Ingels** a-in all. **Kamen** a-3. **Krigstein** a-1, 5. **Orlando** a-2, 5.*

INCREDIBLE HULK, THE (See Aurora and Rampaging Hulk)
May, 1962 - No. 6, Mar, 1963; No. 102, Apr, 1968 - Present
Marvel Comics Group

	Good	Fine	Mint
1-Origin	100.00	300.00	625.00
2	40.00	120.00	250.00
3-Origin retold	20.00	60.00	130.00
4,5	14.00	40.00	85.00
6-Intro. Teen Brigade	14.00	40.00	85.00
102-(Formerly Tales to Astonish)-Origin retold	2.00	6.00	12.00
103-110: 105-1st Missing Link	1.00	3.00	6.00
111-115	.75	2.20	4.40
116-125	.65	1.90	3.80
126,127,129-140: 126-1st Barbara Norriss (Valkyrie). 131-1st Jim Wilson, Hulk's new sidekick. 136-1st Xeron, The Star-Slayer. 140-1st Jarella, Hulk's love	.50	1.50	3.00
128-Avengers app.	.75	2.20	4.40
141-1st app. Doc Samson	.65	1.90	3.80
142-160: 145-52 pgs. 149-1st The Inheritor. 152-Nixon & Agnew app. 155-1st app. Shaper	.40	1.20	2.40
161,163-175,179: 163-1st app. The Gremlin. 164-1st app. Capt. Omen & Colonel John D. Armbruster. 166-1st Zzzax. 168-1st The Harpy. 169-1st Bi-Beast. 172-X-Men cameo; origin Juger-nalt retold	.30	.90	1.80
162-1st The Wendigo; Beast app.; the Mimic dies	.60	1.80	3.60
176-178-Warlock app.	.80	2.40	4.80
180-1st app. Wolverine(cameo)	1.00	3.00	6.00
181-Wolverine app.	4.00	8.00	16.00
182-Wolverine cameo; 1st Crackajack Jackson	1.00	3.00	6.00
183-199: 185-Death of Col. Armbruster.	.30	.80	1.60
200-Silver Surfer app.	.50	1.50	3.00
201-221,223-237,239,240: 212-1st The Constrictor		.60	1.20
222-Starlin-a		.60	1.20
238-Jimmy Carter, Jerry Brown app.		.60	1.20
241-249,252,253-266		.40	.80
250-Giant size; Silver Surfer app.		.60	1.20
251-Golden-c		.40	.80
Giant-Size 1 ('75)	.40	1.10	2.20
Special 1 (10/68)-New material; Steranko-c	1.20	3.50	7.00
Special 2 (10/69)-Origin retold	.70	2.00	4.00
Special 3(1/71)	.50	1.50	3.00
Annual 4 (1/72),5(10/76)	.30	.90	1.80
Annual 6 (11/77)	.30	.80	1.60
Annual 7(8/78)-Byrne-a; Iceman & Angel app.	.40	1.20	2.40
8(11/79), 9(9/80)	.30	.80	1.60

NOTE: ***Alcala** a-222i, Annual 8. **Buscema** c-202. **Ditko** a-2, 6, 249, Annual 2r, 3r, 9p(r); c-2, 6, 235, 249. **Kirby** a-1-5; c-1-5, Annual 5. **Starlin** c-217. **Staton** a-207-209. **Wrightson** c-197.*

INCREDIBLE MR. LIMPET, THE (See Movie Classics)

INCREDIBLE SCIENCE FICTION (Formerly Weird Science-Fantasy)
July-Aug, 1955 - No. 33, Jan-Feb, 1956
E. C. Comics

	Good	Fine	Mint
30,33: 33-Story-r/W.F. No. 18	17.00	50.00	100.00
31,32-Williamson/Krenkel-a each. 31-Wood-a(2)	25.00	70.00	120.00

NOTE: ***Davis** a-30, 32, 33; c-30-32. **Krigstein** a-in all. **Orlando** a-30, 32, 33(''Judgement Day'' reprint). **Wood** a-30, 31, 33; c-33.*

INDIAN BRAVES (Baffling Mysteries No. 5 on)
March, 1951 - No. 4, Sept, 1951
Ace Magazines

INDIAN BRAVES (continued) | Good | Fine | Mint

1 | 1.50 | 4.00 | 8.00
2-4 | .85 | 2.50 | 5.00
I.W. Reprint No. 1 (no date) | .50 | 1.50 | 3.00

INDIAN CHIEF (White Eagle . . .) (Formerly The Chief)
No. 3, July-Sept, 1951 - No. 33, Jan-Mar, 1959
Dell Publishing Co.

3-11: 6-White Eagle app. | .85 | 2.50 | 5.00
12-1st White Eagle(10-12/53)-Not same as earlier character | 1.00 | 3.00 | 6.00
13-29 | .50 | 1.50 | 3.00
30-33-Buscema-a | .85 | 2.50 | 5.00

INDIAN CHIEF (See March of Comics No. 94,110,127,140,159, 170,187)

INDIAN FIGHTER, THE (See 4-Color No. 687)

INDIAN FIGHTER
May, 1950 - No. 11, Jan, 1952
Youthful Magazines

1 | 1.50 | 4.00 | 8.00
2-11: 2-4-Wildey-a; c-No.2(bondage) | .85 | 2.50 | 5.00

INDIAN LEGENDS OF THE NIAGARA (See American Graphics)

INDIANS
Spring, 1950 - No. 17, 1953
Fiction House Magazines (Wings Publ. Co.)

1-Manzar, White Indian, Long Bow & Orphan of the Storm begin | 3.50 | 10.00 | 20.00
2-Starlight begins | 2.50 | 7.00 | 14.00
3-5 | 2.00 | 5.00 | 10.00
6-17 | 1.20 | 3.50 | 7.00

INDIANS OF THE WILD WEST
Circa 1958? (no date)
I. W. Enterprises

9-Reprints | .50 | 1.50 | 3.00

INDIANS ON THE WARPATH
No date (132 pages)
St. John Publishing Co.

nn-Matt Baker-c; contains St. John comics rebound. Many combinations possible | 5.00 | 15.00 | 30.00

INDIAN TRIBES (See Famous Indian Tribes)

INDIAN WARRIORS (Formerly White Rider . . .)
No. 7, June, 1951 - No. 11, 1952
Star Publications

7-11: 11-White Rider & Superhorse app.; L. B. Cole-c | 2.50 | 7.00 | 14.00
3-D 1(12/53)-L. B. Cole-c | 8.00 | 24.00 | 48.00
Accepted Reprint(nn)(inside cover shows White Rider & Superhorse No. 11)-Reprints cover/No. 7; origin White Rider & . . . ; | 1.20 | 3.50 | 7.00
Accepted Reprint No. 8-L. B. Cole-c | 1.20 | 3.50 | 7.00

INDOORS-OUTDOORS (See Wisco)

INDOOR SPORTS
No date (64 pgs.; 6x9''; B&W reprints; hardcover)
National Specials Co.

By Tad | 3.50 | 10.00 | 20.00

INFERIOR FIVE, THE (. . . 5 No. 11,12) (See Showcase)
3-4/67 - No. 10, 9-10/68; No. 11, 8-9/72 - No. 12, 10-11/72
National Periodical Publications

1 | .70 | 2.00 | 4.00
2-Plastic Man app. | .35 | 1.00 | 2.00
3-9 | | .50 | 1.00
10-Superman x-over | .30 | .80 | 1.60
11,12-Orlando c/a; both reprints Showcase No. 62,63 | | .40 | .80

INFORMER, THE
April, 1954 - No. 5, Dec, 1954
Feature Television Productions

1-Sekowsky-a begins | 1.50 | 4.00 | 8.00
2-Drug mention story | 2.50 | 7.00 | 14.00
3-5 | 1.00 | 3.00 | 6.00

IN HIS STEPS
1973, 1977 (39, 49 cents)
Spire Christian Comics (Fleming H. Revell Co.)

nn | | .50 | 1.00

INHUMANS, THE (See Amazing Advs.)
Oct, 1975 - No. 12, Aug, 1977
Marvel Comics Group

1 | .50 | 1.50 | 3.00
2-5 | .25 | .70 | 1.40
6-12: 9-Reprints | | .40 | .80

NOTE: ***Gil Kane** a-5-7; c-7.*

INKY & DINKY (Felix's Nephews)
Sept, 1957 - No. 7, Oct, 1958
Harvey Publications

1-Cover shows Inky's left eye with 2 pupils | 3.00 | 8.00 | 16.00
2-7 | 1.50 | 4.00 | 8.00

NOTE: *Contains no **Messmer** art.*

IN LOVE (I Love You No. 7 on)
Sept, 1954 - No. 6, July, 1955
Prime Publ./Mainline(Prize)/Charlton No. 5 on

1-Simon & Kirby-a | 5.50 | 16.00 | 32.00
2-S&K-a | 3.00 | 8.00 | 16.00
3,4-S&K-a | 2.50 | 7.00 | 14.00
5-S&K-c only | 1.50 | 4.00 | 8.00
6-No S&K-a | .85 | 2.50 | 5.00

IN LOVE WITH JESUS
1952 (36 pages) (Giveaway)
Catechetical Educational Society

| 3.50 | 10.00 | 20.00

IN SEARCH OF THE CASTAWAYS (See Movie Comics)

INSIDE CRIME (Formerly My Intimate Affair)
1950; No. 3, July, 1950 - No. 2, Sept, 1950
Fox Features Syndicate (Hero Books)

nn(no publ. listed; I.W. reprint?) | 3.50 | 8.00 | 16.00
3-Wood-a, 10 pgs.; L. B. Cole-c | 7.00 | 20.00 | 40.00
2(9/50)-Used in **SOTI**, pg. 182-3; Lingerie panel; r-/Spook No. 24 | 5.50 | 16.00 | 32.00

INSPECTOR, THE (Also see The Pink Panther)
July, 1974 - No. 19, Feb, 1978
Gold Key

1 | .30 | .80 | 1.60
2-5 | | .50 | 1.00
6-19: 11-Reprints | | .30 | .60

INSPECTOR WADE (See Feature Book No. 13, McKay)

INTERNATIONAL COMICS (. . . Crime Patrol No. 6)
Spring, 1947 - No. 5, Nov-Dec, 1947
E. C. Comics

1 | 17.00 | 50.00 | 100.00
2-5 | 14.00 | 40.00 | 80.00

INTERNATIONAL CRIME PATROL (Formerly International Comics

Indian Fighter #6, © YM

Inferior Five #2, © DC

The Inhumans #4, © MCG

Intimate Confessions #7, © REAL

Intimate Secrets Of Romance #1, © STAR

The Invaders #20, © MCG

INTERNATIONAL CRIME PATROL (cont'd.)
No. 1-5; becomes Crime Patrol No. 7 on)
Spring, 1948
E. C. Comics

	Good	Fine	Mint
6-Moon Girl app.	20.00	60.00	120.00

INTERSTATE THEATRES' FUN CLUB COMICS
Mid 1940's (10 cents on cover) (B&W cover) (Premium)
Interstate Theatres

Cover features MLJ characters looking at a copy of Top-Notch Comics, but contains an early Detective Comic on inside; many combinations possible	5.50	16.00	24.00

IN THE DAYS OF THE MOB (Magazine)
Fall, 1971 (Black & White)
Hampshire Dist. Ltd. (National)

1-Kirby-a; has John Dillinger wanted poster inside	.80	2.40	3.60

IN THE PRESENCE OF MINE ENEMIES
1973 (35-49 cents)
Spire Christian Comics/Fleming H. Revell Co.

		.50	1.00

INTIMATE (Teen-Age Love No. 4 on?)
December, 1957 - No. 3, May, 1958
Charlton Comics

1-3	1.20	3.50	5.25

INTIMATE CONFESSIONS
1950 (132 pages)
Fox Features Syndicate

nn-See Fox Giants. Contents could vary and determines price.

INTIMATE CONFESSIONS
July-Aug, 1951 - No. 8, Mar, 1953
Realistic Comics

1-Kinstler-c/a; c/Avon paperback 222	80.00	230.00	400.00
2	10.00	30.00	56.00
3-c/Avon paperback 250; Kinstler-c/a	14.00	40.00	72.00
4-c/Avon paperback 304; Kinstler-c	10.00	30.00	56.00
5,7: 7-Spanking panel	10.00	30.00	56.00
6-c/Avon paperback 120	10.00	30.00	56.00
8-c/Avon paperback 375; Kinstler-a	10.00	30.00	56.00

INTIMATE CONFESSIONS
1964
I. W. Enterprises/Super Comics

I.W. Reprint No. 9	.70	2.00	4.00
Super Reprint No. 12,18	.70	2.00	4.00

INTIMATE LOVE
1950 - No. 28, Aug, 1954
Standard Comics

5	1.50	4.00	8.00
6-8-Severin/Elder-a	2.00	6.00	12.00
9,10	.85	2.50	5.00
11-18,20,23,25,27,28	.70	2.00	4.00
19,21,22,24,26-Toth-a	3.50	8.00	16.00

NOTE: ***Celardo** a-8, 10. **Colletta** a-23. **Moreira** a-13(2). Photo-c-7, 14, 18, 20, 24.*

INTIMATE ROMANCES
1950 - 1954
Standard Comics

1	2.00	5.00	10.00
2-19	1.20	3.50	7.00

INTIMATE SECRETS OF ROMANCE
Sept, 1953 - No. 2, April, 1954
Star Publications

	Good	Fine	Mint
1,2-L. B. Cole-c	4.00	12.00	24.00

INTRIGUE
January, 1955
Quality Comics Group

1-Horror; Jack Cole reprt/Web of Evil	5.00	15.00	30.00

INVADERS, THE (TV)
Oct, 1967 - No. 4, Oct, 1968 (All have photo-c)
Gold Key

1	.85	2.50	5.00
2-4	.50	1.50	3.00

INVADERS, THE (Also see Avengers No. 71)
August, 1975 - No. 41, Sept, 1979
Marvel Comics Group

1-Captain America, Sub-Mariner & Human Torch begin	1.00	3.00	6.00
2-1st app. Mailbag & Brain-Drain	.50	1.50	3.00
3-5: 3-Intro U-Man	.30	.90	1.80
6-10: 6-Liberty Legion app; intro/1st app. Union Jack. 7-Intro Baron Blood; Human Torch origin retold. 9-Origin Baron Blood	.30	.80	1.60
11-Origin Spitfire; intro The Blue Bullet	.30	.80	1.60
12-19: 14-1st app. The Crusaders. 16-Re-intro The Destroyer. 17-Intro Warrior Woman. 18-Re-intro The Destroyer w/new origin. 19-New Union Jack app.		.50	1.00
20-Reprints Sub-Mariner story/Motion Picture Funnies Weekly with brief write-up about MPFW	.50	1.50	3.00
21-Reprint/Marvel Mystery No. 10		.50	1.00
22-30: 22-New origin Toro. 24-Reprint/Marvel Mystery No. 17. 28-Intro new Human Top & Golden Girl. 29-Intro Teutonic Knight		.50	1.00
31-40(5/79): 34-Mighty Destroyer joins		.50	1.00
41-Giant size		.40	.80
Giant Size . . . 1(6/75)-50 cents; origin; GA Sub-Mariner r-/Sub-Mariner 1; intro Master-Man	.70	2.00	4.00
Annual 1(9/77)-Schomburg, Rico stories; Schomburg-c; Avengers app; re-intro The Shark & The Hyena.	.30	.80	1.60

NOTE: ***Buckler** a-5. **Everett** a-21r(1940), Annual 1. **Gil Kane** c-13, 17, 18, 20-27. **Kirby** c-3-9, 10(part), 11, 12, 14-16, 32, 33. **Mooney** a-5, 16, 22.*

INVISIBLE BOY (See Approved Comics)

INVISIBLE MAN, THE (See Superior Stories No. 1)

INVISIBLE SCARLET O'NEIL (Also see Comics Hits No. 59)
Dec, 1950 - No. 3, April, 1951
Famous Funnies (Harvey)

1	8.00	24.00	48.00
2,3	5.50	16.00	32.00

IRON FIST (Also see Marvel Premiere)
Nov, 1975 - No. 15, Sept, 1977
Marvel Comics Group

1-McWilliams-a; Iron Man app.	1.50	4.00	8.00
2	.80	2.30	4.60
3-5	.65	1.90	3.80
6-10: 8-Origin retold	.50	1.50	3.00
11,13,14	.40	1.20	2.40
12-Captain America app.	.40	1.20	2.40
15-New X-Men app.	2.00	6.00	12.00

NOTE: ***Adkins** c/a-8i. **Byrne** a-1-15; c-8p.*

IRON HORSE (TV)
March, 1967 - No. 2, June, 1967
Dell Publishing Co.

1,2	.50	1.50	3.00

IRON JAW (Also see The Barbarians)
Jan, 1975 - No. 4, July, 1975

IRON JAW (continued)
Atlas/Seaboard Publ.

	Good	Fine	Mint
1-Adams-c	.30	.80	1.60
2-Adams-c		.60	1.20
3,4-Origin		.40	.80

IRON MAN
May, 1968 - Present
Marvel Comics Group

	Good	Fine	Mint
1-Origin	5.50	16.00	32.00
2	2.50	7.00	14.00
3-5	1.50	4.00	8.00
6-10	1.00	3.00	6.00
11-15	.70	2.00	4.00
16-20	.60	1.80	3.60
21-40: 22-Death of Janice Cord. 27-Intro Fire Brand. 33-Intro Spymaster	.50	1.50	3.00
41,42,44-46,48-50: 46-The Guardsman dies. 50-1st Princess Python	.40	1.20	2.40
43(52 pgs.)-Intro The Guardsman	.50	1.40	2.80
47-Origin retold; Smith-a	1.00	3.00	6.00
51,52	.30	.80	2.00
53-Starlin-p(part)	.50	1.50	3.00
54-Everett Sub-Mariner in part	.40	1.20	2.40
55,56-Starlin-a; 55-Starlin-c	.85	2.50	4.00
57-67,69,70: 65-Origin Dr. Spectrum	.40	1.20	2.40
68-Starlin-c; origin retold	.40	1.20	2.40
71,73-80: 76 reprints No. 9	.30	.80	1.60
72-Adams draws Mike Fredrick's head, pg. 14, panel 1	.30	.90	1.80
81-85,88-90	.30	.90	1.80
86-1st app. Blizzard	.35	1.00	2.00
87-Origin Blizzard	.35	1.00	2.00
91-99	.30	.80	1.60
100-Starlin-c	.40	1.20	2.40
101-117: 101-Intro DreadKnight. 110-Origin Jack of Hearts retold	.30	.80	1.60
118-Byrne-a	.50	1.50	3.00
119,120,123-128-Tony Stark recovers from alcohol problem		.60	1.20
121,122,129-149,151-153: 122-Origin		.40	.80
150-Double size		.40	.80
Giant Size 1('75)-Ditko-a(r)	.35	1.00	2.00
Special 1(8/70)-Everett-c	.70	2.00	4.00
Special 2(11/71)	.35	1.00	2.00
Annual 3(6/76)-Manthing app.	.30	.80	1.60
King Size 4(8/77)-Newton-a(i); Champions app.	.30	.80	1.60

NOTE: ***Alcala*** *a-112i.* ***Austin*** *c-151i.* ***Byrne*** *a-109p, 118p.* ***Cockrum*** *c-122.* ***Craig*** *a-1i, 2-4, 5-14i, 15, 16-19i, 24p, 25p, 26-28i; c-2-4.* ***Infantino*** *a-108p, 109p, 122p, 129.* ***Kirby*** *c-80p, 90, 92-95.* ***Layton*** *a-117-128i, 130, 131i-135i, 137, 138p, 139, 140, 141i-153i; c-118, 119i, 120, 121, 122i, 123, 124i, 125, 126i, 127, 128, 130, 131-148, 149p-153p.* ***Tuska*** *a-38-69p, 97.*

IRON MAN AND SUBMARINER
April, 1968 (One Shot)
Marvel Comics Group

	Good	Fine	Mint
1-Craig inks-Iron Man	1.50	4.00	8.00

IRON VIC (See Comics Revue No. 3)
1940; Aug, 1947 - No. 3, 1947
United Features Syndicate/St. John Publ. Co.

	Good	Fine	Mint
Single Series 22	7.00	20.00	40.00
2,3(St. John)	1.50	4.00	8.00

ISIS (TV) (Also see Shazam)
Oct-Nov, 1976 - No. 8, Dec-Jan, 1977-78
National Periodical Publications/DC Comics

	Good	Fine	Mint
1-Wood inks		.50	1.00
2-4: 2-Nasser-a		.40	.80
5-Begin new look for Isis		.30	.60
6-8: 7-Origin		.30	.60

ISLAND AT THE TOP OF THE WORLD (See Walt Disney Showcase 27)

ISLAND OF DR. MOREAU, THE (Movie)
October, 1977
Marvel Comics Group

	Good	Fine	Mint
1		.50	1.00

I SPY (TV)
Aug, 1966 - No. 6, Sept, 1968
Gold Key

	Good	Fine	Mint
1	1.00	3.00	6.00
2-6: 3,4-McWilliams-a	.70	2.00	4.00

IS THIS TOMORROW?
1947 (One Shot) (3 editions) (52 pages)
Catechetical Guild

	Good	Fine	Mint
1-Theme of communists taking over the USA; (no price on cover) Used in **POP**, pg. 102	17.00	50.00	80.00
1-(10 cents on cover)	35.00	90.00	150.00
1-Has blank circle with no price on cover	35.00	90.00	150.00
Black & White advance copy titled "Confidential"-(52 pgs.)-Contains script and art edited out of the color edition, including one page of extreme violence showing mob nailing a Cardinal to a door; (only two known copies)	75.00	200.00	340.00

NOTE: *The original color version first sold for 10 cents. Since sales were good, it was later printed as a giveaway. Approximately four million in total were printed. The two black and white copies listed plus two other versions as well as a full color untrimmed version surfaced in 1979 from the Guild's old files in St. Paul, Minnesota.*

IT! (See Supernatural Thrillers No.1 & Astonishing Tales No.21-24)

IT HAPPENS IN THE BEST FAMILIES
1920 (52 pages) (B&W Sundays)
Powers Photo Engraving Co.

	Good	Fine	Mint
By Briggs	4.00	12.00	24.00
Special Railroad Edition(30 Cents)-R-/strips from 1914-1920	3.50	10.00	20.00

IT REALLY HAPPENED
1944 - No. 11, Oct, 1947
William H. Wise No. 1,2/Standard (Visual Editions)

	Good	Fine	Mint
1	3.00	9.00	18.00
2-7,9,10	2.00	5.00	10.00
8-Story of Roy Rogers	3.00	9.00	18.00
11-Ward?, Baker-a	3.00	9.00	18.00

NOTE: ***Guardineer*** *a-7(2), 8(2), 11.* ***Schomburg*** *c-4, 6, 9, 11.*

IT RHYMES WITH LUST (Also see Bold Stories, Candid Tales)
1950 (Digest size) (128 pages)
St. John Publishing Co.

	Good	Fine	Mint
(Rare)-Matt Baker & Ray Osrin-a	25.00	70.00	140.00

IT'S ABOUT TIME (TV)
January, 1967
Gold Key

	Good	Fine	Mint
1 (10195-701)-Photo-c	1.00	3.00	6.00

IT'S A DUCK'S LIFE
Feb, 1950 - No. 11, Feb, 1952
Marvel Comics/Atlas(MMC)

	Good	Fine	Mint
1-Buck Duck, Super Rabbit begin	2.00	6.00	12.00
2-11	1.00	3.00	6.00

IT'S FUN TO STAY ALIVE (Giveaway)
1948 (16 pgs.) (heavy stock paper)
National Automobile Dealers Association

Ironjaw #2, © ATLAS

Iron Man #47, © MCG

It's About Time #1, © GK

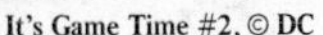
It's Game Time #2, © DC

Jack & Jill Visit Toyland--nn

Jackpot Comics #5, © MLJ

IT'S FUN TO STAY ALIVE (continued) — Good / Fine / Mint
Featuring: Bugs Bunny, The Berrys, Dixie Dugan, Elmer, Tim Tyler, Bruce Gentry, Abbie & Slats, Joe Jinks, The Toodles, & Cokey; all art copyright 1946-48 drawn especially for this book.
8.00 24.00 48.00

IT'S GAME TIME
Sept-Oct, 1955 - No. 4, Mar-Apr, 1956
National Periodical Publications

1-(Scarce)-Davy Crockett app. in puzzle 14.00 40.00 80.00
2-4(Scarce): 2-Dodo & The Frog 10.00 30.00 60.00

IT'S LOVE, LOVE, LOVE
November, 1957 - No. 2, Jan, 1958 (10 cents)
St. John Publishing Co.

1,2 2.00 5.00 10.00

IVANHOE (See Fawcett Movie Comics No. 20)

IVANHOE
July-Sept, 1963
Dell Publishing Co.

1 (12-373-309) 1.00 3.00 6.00

IWO JIMA (See A Spectacular Feature)

JACE PEARSON (See Tales of the Texas Rangers)

JACK & JILL VISIT TOYTOWN WITH ELMER THE ELF
1949 (16 pgs.) (paper cover)
Butler Brothers (Toytown Stores Giveaway)
2.00 5.00 10.00

JACK ARMSTRONG
11/47 - No. 9, 9/48; No. 10, 3/49 - No. 13, Sept, 1949
Parents' Magazine Institute

1 3.50 10.00 20.00
2-5 2.50 7.00 14.00
6-13 2.00 5.00 10.00
12-Premium version(distr. in Chicago only); Free printed on upper right-c; no price(Rare) 5.50 16.00 32.00

JACKIE GLEASON
1948; Sept, 1955 - No. 5, Dec, 1955
St. John Publishing Co.

1(1948) 7.00 20.00 40.00
2(1948) 4.00 12.00 24.00
1(1955) 3.00 8.00 16.00
2-5 2.00 5.00 10.00

JACKIE GLEASON & THE HONEYMOONERS (TV)
June-July, 1956 - No. 12, Apr-May, 1958
National Periodical Publications

1 5.50 16.00 32.00
2-12 4.00 12.00 24.00

JACKIE JOKERS (Also see Richie Rich &. . .)
March, 1973 - No. 4, Sept, 1973
Harvey Publications

1-4; 2-President Nixon app. .20 .40

JACKIE ROBINSON (Famous Plays of. . .)
1949; May, 1950 - No. 6, 1952 (Baseball hero)
Fawcett Publications

nn 10.00 30.00 60.00
1 (Exist?) 8.00 24.00 48.00
2-6 7.00 20.00 40.00

JACK IN THE BOX (Formerly Yellowjacket No. 1-10)
(Cowboy Western Comics No. 17 on)
Feb, 1946; No. 11, 1946 - No. 16, 1947
Frank Comunale/Charlton Comics No. 12 on

1-Stitches, Marty Mouse & Nutsy McKrow 2.00 5.00 10.00
11-Yellowjacket 2.50 7.00 14.00

Good / Fine / Mint
12,14-16 1.20 3.50 7.00
13-Wolverton-a 7.00 20.00 40.00

JACKPOT COMICS (Jolly Jingles No. 10 on)
Spring, 1941 - No. 9, Spring, 1943
MLJ Magazines

1-The Black Hood, Mr. Justice, Steel Sterling & Sgt. Boyle begin; Biro-c 50.00 130.00 260.00
2 22.00 65.00 130.00
3,5 20.00 55.00 110.00
4-Archie begins (on sale 12/41)-(Also see Pep Comics No. 22); Montana-c 60.00 160.00 325.00
6-9: 6,7-Bondage-c 17.00 50.00 100.00

JACK Q FROST (See Unearthly Spectaculars)

JACK THE GIANT KILLER (See Movie Classics)

JACK THE GIANT KILLER (New Advs. of. . .)
Aug-Sept, 1953
Bimfort & Co.

V1No.1-H. C. Kiefer-a 5.50 16.00 32.00

JACKY'S DIARY (See 4-Color No. 1091)

JAGUAR, THE (See The Advs. of. . .)

JAMBOREE
Feb, 1946(no mo. given) - No. 3, April, 1946
Round Publishing Co.

1-3 .85 2.50 5.00

JANE ARDEN (See Pageant of Comics)
March, 1948 - No. 2, June, 1948
St. John (United Features Syndicate)

1-Newspaper reprints 5.00 15.00 30.00
2 3.50 10.00 20.00

JANN OF THE JUNGLE (Jungle Tales No. 1-7)
No. 8, Nov, 1955 - No. 17, June, 1957
Atlas Comics (CSI)

8(No.1) 4.50 13.00 26.00
9,11-15 3.50 10.00 20.00
10-Williamson/Colleta-c 4.50 13.00 26.00
16,17-Williamson/Mayo-a(3), 5 pgs. each 7.00 20.00 40.00

JASON & THE ARGONAUTS (See Movie Classics)

JAWS 2 (See Marvel Super Special, A)

JEANIE COMICS (Cowgirl Romances No. 28) (Formerly Daring)
No. 13, April, 1947 - No. 27, Oct, 1949
Marvel Comics/Atlas(CPC)

13 3.00 9.00 18.00
14,15 2.00 5.00 10.00
16-Used in **Love and Death** by Legman; Kurtzman's "Hey Look" 5.00 14.00 28.00
17-19,22-Kurtzman's "Hey Look," 1-3 pgs. each 2.50 7.00 14.00
20,21,23-27 1.20 3.50 7.00

JEEP COMICS (Also see G.I. and Overseas Comics)
Winter, 1944 - No. 3, Mar-Apr, 1948
R. B. Leffingwell & Co.

1-3-Capt. Power in No. 1,2; Criss Cross & Jeep & Peep (costumed) in all 3.00 8.00 16.00
1-29(Giveaway)-Strip reprints in all; Tarzan, Flash Gordon, Blondie, The Nebbs, Little Iodine, Red Ryder, Don Winslow, The Phantom, Johnny Hazard, Katzenjammer Kids; distributed to U.S. Armed Forces in mid 1940's 3.50 10.00 20.00

NOTE: ***L. B. Cole*** *c-3.*

JEFF JORDAN, U.S. AGENT
Dec, 1947 - Jan, 1948
D. S. Publishing Co.

JEFF JORDAN, U.S. AGENT (continued) Good Fine Mint
1 2.50 7.00 14.00

JERRY DRUMMER (Formerly Soldier & Marine V2No.9)
1957
Charlton Comics

V2No.10,11, V3No.12 .70 2.00 4.00

JERRY LEWIS (See Adventures of. . .)

JESSE JAMES (See 4-Color No. 757 & The Legend of. . .)

JESSE JAMES (Also see Badmen of the West)
Aug, 1950 - No. 29, Aug-Sept, 1956
Avon Periodicals

1-Kubert Alabam r-/Cowpuncher No. 1 8.00 24.00 48.00
2-Kubert-a(3) 6.00 18.00 36.00
3-Kubert Alabam r-/Cowpuncher No. 2 5.00 15.00 30.00
4-No Kubert 2.50 7.00 14.00
5,6-Kubert Jesse James-a(3); one pg. Wood-a, No. 5
5.50 16.00 32.00
7-Kubert Jesse James-a(2) 5.00 14.00 28.00
8-Kinstler-a(3) 3.50 10.00 20.00
9,10-No Kubert 2.50 7.00 14.00
11-14 2.00 5.00 10.00
15-Kinstler r-/No. 3 2.00 5.00 10.00
16-Kinstler r-/No. 3 & Sheriff Bob Dixon's Chuck Wagon No. 1
with name changed to Sheriff Tom Wilson 2.00 6.00 12.00
17-Jesse James r-/No. 4; Kinstler-c idea from Kubert splash in No. 6
1.50 4.00 8.00
18-Kubert Jesse James r-/No. 5 1.50 4.00 8.00
19-Kubert Jesse James-r 1.50 4.00 8.00
20-Williamson/Frazetta-a; r-Chief Vic. Apache Massacre; Kubert
Jesse James r-/No. 6 7.00 20.00 40.00
21-Two Jesse James r-/No. 4, Kinstler r-/No. 4
1.50 4.00 8.00
22,23-No Kubert 1.20 3.50 7.00
24-New McCarty strip by Kinstler plus Kinstler r-/No. 9
1.20 3.50 7.00
25-New McCarty Jesse James strip by Kinstler; Kinstler J. James r-/
No. 7,9 1.20 3.50 7.00
26,27-New McCarty J. James strip plus a Kinstler/McCann Jesse
James-r 1.20 3.50 7.00
28-Reprints most of Red Mountain, Featuring Quantrells Raiders
1.20 3.50 7.00
29 1.20 3.50 7.00
Annual(nn; 1952; 25 cents)-". . . Brings Six-Gun Justice to the
West"(100 pgs.)-3 earlier issues rebound; Kubert, Kinstler-a
10.00 30.00 60.00

NOTE: *Mostly reprints No. 10 on.* ***Kinstler*** *a-3, 4, 7-9, 15r, 16(2), 21-27; c-3, 4, 9, 17, 18, 20-27.*

JESSE JAMES
July, 1953
Realistic Publications

nn-Reprints Avon's No. 1, same cover, colors different
3.00 9.00 18.00

JEST (Kayo No. 12) (Formerly Snap)
1944
Harry 'A' Chesler

10-Johnny Rebel & Yankee Boy app. in text 2.50 7.00 14.00
11-Little Nemo in Adventure Land 3.00 8.00 16.00

JESTER
1945
Harry 'A' Chesler

10 2.00 6.00 12.00

JESUS
1979 (49 cents)
Good Fine Mint
Spire Christian Comics (Fleming H. Revell Co.)

.30 .60

JET (Jet Powers No. 1-4) (Space Ace No. 5)
1950 - 1951
Magazine Enterprises

1(A-1 30)-Powell-a begins 8.00 24.00 48.00
2(A-1 32) 6.00 18.00 36.00
3(A-1 35)-Williamson/Evans-a 15.00 45.00 90.00
4(A-1 38)-Williamson/Wood-a; "The rain of sleep" drug story
15.00 45.00 90.00

JET ACES
1952 - 1953
Fiction House Magazines

1 3.00 8.00 16.00
2-4 2.00 5.00 10.00

JET DREAM (. . .& Her Stuntgirl Counterspies)
June, 1968
Gold Key

1 .70 2.00 4.00

JET FIGHTERS
No. 5, Nov, 1952 - No. 7, Mar, 1953
Standard Magazines

5,7-Toth-a 3.00 9.00 18.00
6-Celardo-a 1.50 4.00 8.00

JETMAN
1950's
Superior Publ. Ltd.

1 (Exist?) 3.50 10.00 20.00

JET POWER (Jet Powers No. 1) (See Jet)
1963
I. W. Enterprises

1,2-Powell art; reprints Jet No. 1 & 2 1.00 3.00 6.00

JET POWERS (See Jet)

JET PUP (See 3-D Features)

JETSONS, THE (TV)
Jan, 1963 - No. 36, Oct, 1970 (Hanna-Barbera)
Gold Key

1 .85 2.50 5.00
2-10 .50 1.50 3.00
11-36 .35 1.00 2.00
(See March of Comics No. 276,330,348)

JETSONS, THE (TV) (Hanna-Barbera)
Nov, 1970 - No. 20, Dec, 1973
Charlton Comics

1 .50 1.50 3.00
2-20 .35 1.00 2.00

JETTA OF THE 21ST CENTURY
No. 5, 1952 - 1953 (Teen-age Archie type)
Standard Comics

5-7 2.00 6.00 12.00

JIGGS & MAGGIE (See 4-Color No. 18)

JIGGS & MAGGIE
No. 11, 1949 - No. 21, 2/53; No. 22, 4/53 - No. 27, 2-3/54
Standard Comics/Harvey Publications No. 22 on

11 2.00 6.00 12.00
12-15,17-20 1.50 4.00 8.00
16-Wood text illos. 2.50 7.00 14.00

Jeff Jordan #1, © DS

Jesse James #25, © AVON

Jet Power #1, © I.W.

Jigsaw #1, © HARV

Jingle Jangle #34, © EAS

Joe Louis #2, © FAW

JIGGS & MAGGIE (continued)

	Good	Fine	Mint
21-25,27	1.50	4.00	8.00
26-Four pgs. partially in 3-D	5.50	16.00	32.00

NOTE: *Sunday page reprints by* ***McManus*** *loosely blended into story continuity. Advertised on covers as "All New."*

JIGSAW (Big Hero Adventures)
Sept, 1966 - No. 2, Dec, 1966
Harvey Publications (Funday Funnies)

1-Origin; Crandall-a	.70	2.00	4.00
2-Man From S.R.A.M.	.35	1.00	2.00

JIGSAW OF DOOM (See Complete Mystery No. 2)

JIM BOWIE (Formerly Danger; Black Jack No. 20 on)
No. 15, 1955? - No. 19, April, 1957
Charlton Comics

15-19	.50	1.50	3.00

JIM BOWIE (See 4-Color No. 893,993, & Western Tales)

JIM DANDY
May, 1956 - No. 3, Sept, 1956 (Charles Biro)
Dandy Magazine (Lev Gleason)

1	.85	2.50	5.00
2,3	.70	2.00	4.00

JIM HARDY (Also see Treasury of Comics & Sparkler)
1939 - 1940; 1947; Jan, 1948
United Features Syndicate/Spotlight Publ./St. John

Single Series 6	9.00	25.00	50.00
Single Series 27('40)	7.00	20.00	40.00
1('47)-Spotlight Publ.	2.00	6.00	12.00
2	1.50	4.00	8.00
1(1/48-St. John)-Feat. Windy & Paddles	1.50	4.00	8.00

JIM HARDY
1944; 1948 (132 pages) (25 cents - Giant)
(Tip Top, Sparkler reprints)
Spotlight/United Features Syndicate

(1944)-Origin Mirror Man; Triple Terror app.	5.50	16.00	30.00
(1948)	3.50	10.00	20.00

JIMINY CRICKET (See 4-Color No. 701,795,897,989 & Walt Disney Showcase No. 37)

JIMMY (James Swinnerton)
1905 (10x15") (40 pages in color)
N. Y. American & Journal

	10.00	30.00	60.00

JIMMY DURANTE (See A-1 Comics No. 18,20)

JIMMY OLSEN (See Superman's Pal . . .)

JIMMY WAKELY
Sept-Oct, 1949 - No. 18, July-Aug, 1952
National Periodical Publications

1-Alex Toth-a; Kit Colby Girl Sheriff begins	10.00	30.00	60.00
2-Toth-a	8.00	24.00	48.00
3,4,6,7-Frazetta art in all, 3 pgs. each; Kurtzman in No. 4; Toth in all	10.00	30.00	60.00
5,8-15,18-Toth-a; 12,14-Kubert-a, 3 & 2 pgs.	7.00	20.00	40.00
16,17	4.00	12.00	24.00

JIM RAY'S AVIATION SKETCH BOOK
Mar-Apr, 1946 - No. 2, May-June, 1946
Vital Publishers

1,2-Picture stories about planes and pilots	3.50	10.00	20.00

JIM SOLAR (See Wisco/Klarer)

JINGLE BELLS (See March of Comics No. 65)

JINGLE BELLS CHRISTMAS BOOK
1971 (20 pgs.; B&W inside; slick cover)
Montgomery Ward (Giveaway)

	Good	Fine	Mint
		.40	.80

JINGLE DINGLE CHRISTMAS STOCKING COMICS
V2No.1, 1951 (no date listed) (100 pgs.; giant-size)(25 cents)
Stanhall Publications (Publ.-annually)

V2No.1-Foodini & Pinhead, Silly Pilly plus games & puzzles	2.50	7.00	14.00

JINGLE JANGLE COMICS (Also see Puzzle Fun)
Feb, 1942 - No. 42, Dec, 1949
Eastern Color Printing Co.

1-Pie-Face Prince of Old Pretzleburg, & Jingle Jangle Tales by George Carlson, Hortense, & Benny Bear begin	17.00	50.00	100.00
2,3-No Pie-Face Prince	8.00	24.00	48.00
4-Pie-Face Prince cover	8.00	24.00	48.00
5	7.00	20.00	40.00
6-10: 8-No Pie-Face Prince	5.50	16.00	32.00
11-15	3.50	10.00	20.00
16-30: 17,18-No Pie-Face Prince	3.00	8.00	16.00
31-42	2.00	6.00	12.00

NOTE: ***George Carlson*** *a-(2) in all except No. 2, 3, 8, 17, 18; c-1-6.* ***Carlson*** *1 pg. puzzles in 9, 10, 12-15, 18, 20.* ***Carlson*** *illustrated a series of Uncle Wiggily books in 1930's.*

JING PALS
1946
Victory Magazine Corporation

1-4	1.50	4.00	8.00

JINKS, PIXIE, AND DIXIE (See Whitman Comic. . .)
1965 (Giveaway) (Hanna-Barbera)
Florida Power & Light

		.50	1.00

JOAN OF ARC (See A-1 Comics No. 21 & Ideal a Classical Comic)

JOAN OF ARC
No date (28 pages)
Catechetical Guild (Topix) (Giveaway)

	7.00	20.00	40.00

NOTE: *Unpublished version exists which came from the Guild's files.*

JOE COLLEGE
1949 - No. 2, Winter, 1950
Hillman Periodicals

1,2-Powell-a; 1-Briefer-a	1.50	4.00	8.00

JOE JINKS (See Single Series No. 12)

JOE LOUIS
Sept, 1950 - No. 2, Nov, 1950
Fawcett Publications

1	8.00	24.00	48.00
2	6.00	18.00	36.00

JOE PALOOKA
1933 (B&W daily strip reprints) (52 pages)
Cupples & Leon Co.

1-(Scarce)-by Fisher	17.00	50.00	100.00

JOE PALOOKA (1st Series)
1942 - 1944
Columbia Comic Corp.

1	14.00	40.00	80.00
2	7.00	20.00	40.00
3,4	5.50	16.00	32.00

JOE PALOOKA (2nd Series) (Battle Adv. No. 68-73; . . . Advs. No. 74-115)
Nov, 1945 - No. 118, Mar, 1961

JOE PALOOKA (continued)
Harvey Publications

	Good	Fine	Mint
1	10.00	30.00	60.00
2	5.00	14.00	28.00
3,4,6	4.00	12.00	24.00
5-Boy Explorers by S&K (7-8/46)	7.00	20.00	40.00
7-1st Powell Flyin' Fool, ends No. 25	3.50	10.00	20.00
8-Opium drug story; lingerie panel	3.50	10.00	20.00
9,10	3.00	8.00	16.00
11-14,16-20	3.00	8.00	16.00
15-Origin Humphrey; Super heroine Atoma app. by Powell	4.00	12.00	24.00
21-30: 30-Nude female painting	2.00	5.00	10.00
31-61: 31-Drug story. 44-Joe Palooka marries Ann Howe. 50-Bondage -c	1.50	4.00	8.00
62-S&K Boy Explorers-r	2.00	6.00	12.00
63-80: 66,67-'commie' torture story	1.20	3.50	7.00
81-115	.85	2.50	5.00
116-S&K Boy Explorers (reprt,giant,1960)	2.50	7.00	14.00
117,118-Giants	2.00	6.00	12.00
Joe Palooka Fights His Way Back (1945 Giveaway, 24 pgs.) Family Comics	12.00	36.00	72.00
. . . Visits the Lost City(1945)(One Shot)(nn)(50 cents)-164 page continuous story strip reprint. Has biography & photo of Ham Fisher; possibly the single longest comic book story published (159 pgs.?)	22.00	65.00	140.00

NOTE: ***Powell** a-8, 19, 26-45, 47-53 at least. Black Cat text stories No. 8, 13, 19.*

JOE YANK
March, 1952 - 1954
Standard Comics (Visual Editions)

	Good	Fine	Mint
5,7	1.20	3.50	7.00
6-Toth plus Severin/Elder-a	3.00	8.00	16.00
8-Toth-c	2.50	7.00	14.00
9-16	.85	2.50	5.00

JOHN CARTER OF MARS (See 4-Color No. 375,437,488)

JOHN CARTER OF MARS
April, 1964 - No. 3, Oct, 1964
Gold Key

	Good	Fine	Mint
1(10104-404)-Reprints 4-Color 375; Jesse Marsh-a	2.50	7.00	12.00
2(407), 3(410)-Reprints 4-Color 437 & 488; Marsh-a	2.00	5.00	10.00

JOHN CARTER OF MARS
1970 (72 pgs.; paper cover; 10½x16½''; B&W)
House of Greystroke

	Good	Fine	Mint
1941-42 Sunday strip reprints; John Coleman Burroughs-a	2.50	7.00	14.00

JOHN CARTER, WARLORD OF MARS
June, 1977 - No. 28, Oct, 1979
Marvel Comics Group

	Good	Fine	Mint
1-Origin by Gil Kane	.40	1.10	2.20
2-5	.30	.80	1.60
6-10-Last Kane issue		.50	1.00
11-Origin Dejah Thoris		.60	1.20
12-17,19,20		.50	1.00
18-Bryne/Nebres-c	.30	.80	1.60
21-28		.40	.80
Annual 1(10/77), 2(9/78), 3(10/79)	.30	.90	1.80

NOTE: ***Austin** c-24i. **Cockrum** a-11. **Infantino** a-12-14. **Gil Kane** a-1-10p. **Perez** c-24p. **Simonson** a-15.*

JOHN F. KENNEDY, CHAMPION OF FREEDOM
1964 (no month) (25 cents)
Worden & Childs

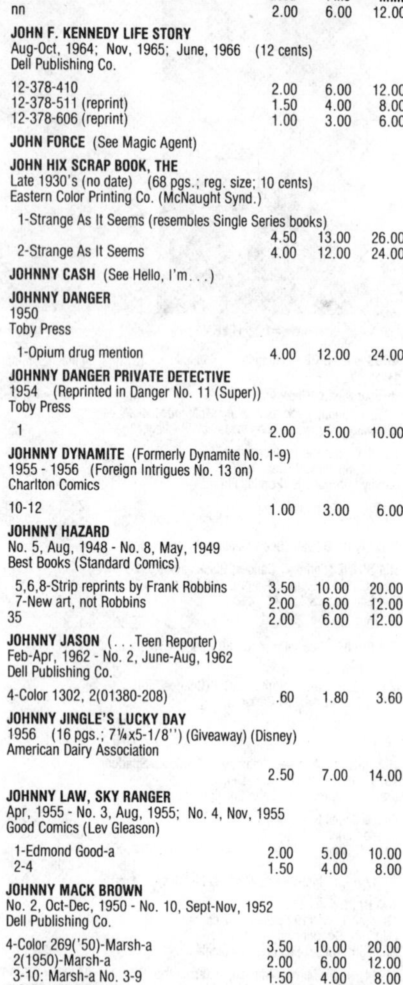

	Good	Fine	Mint
nn	2.00	6.00	12.00

JOHN F. KENNEDY LIFE STORY
Aug-Oct, 1964; Nov, 1965; June, 1966 (12 cents)
Dell Publishing Co.

	Good	Fine	Mint
12-378-410	2.00	6.00	12.00
12-378-511 (reprint)	1.50	4.00	8.00
12-378-606 (reprint)	1.00	3.00	6.00

JOHN FORCE (See Magic Agent)

JOHN HIX SCRAP BOOK, THE
Late 1930's (no date) (68 pgs.; reg. size; 10 cents)
Eastern Color Printing Co. (McNaught Synd.)

	Good	Fine	Mint
1-Strange As It Seems (resembles Single Series books)	4.50	13.00	26.00
2-Strange As It Seems	4.00	12.00	24.00

JOHNNY CASH (See Hello, I'm. . .)

JOHNNY DANGER
1950
Toby Press

	Good	Fine	Mint
1-Opium drug mention	4.00	12.00	24.00

JOHNNY DANGER PRIVATE DETECTIVE
1954 (Reprinted in Danger No. 11 (Super))
Toby Press

	Good	Fine	Mint
1	2.00	5.00	10.00

JOHNNY DYNAMITE (Formerly Dynamite No. 1-9)
1955 - 1956 (Foreign Intrigues No. 13 on)
Charlton Comics

	Good	Fine	Mint
10-12	1.00	3.00	6.00

JOHNNY HAZARD
No. 5, Aug, 1948 - No. 8, May, 1949
Best Books (Standard Comics)

	Good	Fine	Mint
5,6,8-Strip reprints by Frank Robbins	3.50	10.00	20.00
7-New art, not Robbins	2.00	6.00	12.00
35	2.00	6.00	12.00

JOHNNY JASON (. . . Teen Reporter)
Feb-Apr, 1962 - No. 2, June-Aug, 1962
Dell Publishing Co.

	Good	Fine	Mint
4-Color 1302, 2(01380-208)	.60	1.80	3.60

JOHNNY JINGLE'S LUCKY DAY
1956 (16 pgs.; 7¼x5-1/8'') (Giveaway) (Disney)
American Dairy Association

	Good	Fine	Mint
	2.50	7.00	14.00

JOHNNY LAW, SKY RANGER
Apr, 1955 - No. 3, Aug, 1955; No. 4, Nov, 1955
Good Comics (Lev Gleason)

	Good	Fine	Mint
1-Edmond Good-a	2.00	5.00	10.00
2-4	1.50	4.00	8.00

JOHNNY MACK BROWN
No. 2, Oct-Dec, 1950 - No. 10, Sept-Nov, 1952
Dell Publishing Co.

	Good	Fine	Mint
4-Color 269('50)-Marsh-a	3.50	10.00	20.00
2(1950)-Marsh-a	2.00	6.00	12.00
3-10: Marsh-a No. 3-9	1.50	4.00	8.00
4-Color 455,493	1.50	4.00	8.00
4-Color 541,584,618,645,685,722,776,834,963,967	1.50	4.00	8.00
4-Color 922-Manning-a	2.00	6.00	12.00

JOHNNY RINGO (See 4-Color No. 1142)

JOHNNY STARBOARD (See Wisco)

Joe Palooka #3, © HARV

John Carter, Warlord--#18, © MCG

Johnny Mack Brown #10, © DELL

John Wayne #25, © TOBY

Jo-Jo Comics #21, © FOX

Jonah Hex #16, © DC

JOHNNY THUNDER
Feb-Mar, 1973 - No. 3, July-Aug, 1973
National Periodical Publications

	Good	Fine	Mint
1-Johnny Thunder & Nighthawk reprints begin		.50	1.00
2,3: 2-Trigger Twins app.		.40	.80

NOTE: ***Drucker*** *a-2, 3.* ***Infantino*** *a-2.* ***Toth*** *a-1, 3. Also see All-American & All-Star Western.*

JOHN PAUL JONES
Sept, 1959 - 1959
Dell Publishing Co.

	Good	Fine	Mint
4-Color 1007, 1(Exist?)	1.20	3.50	7.00

JOHN STEED & EMMA PEEL (See The Avengers)

JOHN STEELE SECRET AGENT
December, 1964 (Freedom Agent)
Gold Key

	Good	Fine	Mint
1	.85	2.50	5.00

JOHN WAYNE ADVENTURE COMICS (See Oxydol-Dreft)
Winter, 1949 - No. 31, May, 1955
Toby Press

	Good	Fine	Mint
1	11.00	32.00	64.00
2-Williamson/Frazetta-a(2) (one reprint/Billy the Kid No. 1), 6 & 2 pgs.	15.00	45.00	90.00
3,4-Williamson/Frazetta-a(2), 16 pgs. total each	15.00	45.00	90.00
5-Kurtzman-a-(Alfred "L" Newman in Potshot Pete)	7.00	20.00	40.00
6,7-Williamson/Frazetta-a in both; Kurtzman-a in No. 6	12.00	35.00	70.00
8-Williamson/Frazetta-a(2), 12 & 9 pgs.	14.00	40.00	80.00
9-11,13-15	4.00	12.00	24.00
12-Kurtzman-a	5.00	15.00	30.00
16-Williamson/Frazetta r-from Billy the Kid No. 1	8.00	22.00	44.00
17,19-24,26-28,30	4.00	12.00	24.00
18-Williamson/Frazetta-a r-/John Wayne No. 4 & 8	10.00	28.00	56.00
25-Williamson/Frazetta-a r-/Billy the Kid No. 3	10.00	28.00	56.00
29-Williamson/Frazetta-a r-/No. 4	10.00	28.00	56.00
31-Williamson/Frazetta-a r-/No. 2	10.00	28.00	56.00

NOTE: *Williamsonish art in later issues by* ***Gerald McCann.***

JO-JO COMICS (. . . Congo King No. 7-29; My Desire No. 30 on)
(Also see Fantastic Fear and Jungle Jo)
1945 - No. 29, July, 1949 (two No.7's; no No. 13)
Fox Features Syndicate

	Good	Fine	Mint
nn(1945)-Funny animal	1.20	3.50	7.00
2(Sum,'46)-6: Funny animal; 2-Ten pg. Electro story	1.00	3.00	6.00
7(7/47)-Jo-Jo, Congo King begins	12.00	35.00	70.00
7(No.8) (9/47)	10.00	30.00	60.00
8-10(No.9-11): 8-Tanee begins	9.00	25.00	50.00
11,12(No.12,13),14,16	7.00	20.00	40.00
15-Cited by Dr. Wertham in 5/47 Saturday Review of Literature	9.00	25.00	50.00
17-Kamen bondage-c	9.00	25.00	50.00
18-20	7.00	20.00	40.00
21-29	6.00	17.00	34.00

NOTE: *Many bondage-c/a by* ***Baker/Kamen/Feldstein/Good.*** *No. 7's have Princesses Gwenna, Geesa, Yolda, & Safra before settling down on Tanee.*

JO-JOY (Adventures of . . .)
1945 - 1953 (Christmas gift comic)
W. T. Grant Dept. Stores

	Good	Fine	Mint
1945-53 issues	.70	2.00	4.00

JOKEBOOK COMICS DIGEST ANNUAL
Oct, 1977 - Present (192 pgs.-Digest Size)
Archie Publications

	Good	Fine	Mint
1(10/77)-Reprints; Adams-a		.60	1.20
2(4/78)-8(6/81)		.60	1.20

JOKER, THE (See Batman, Brave & the Bold, and Detective)
May, 1975 - No. 9, Sept-Oct, 1976
National Periodical Publications

	Good	Fine	Mint
1-Two-Face app.		.50	1.00
2-4: 3-The Creeper app. 4-Green Arrow, Black Canary app.		.40	.80
V2No.5-9: 5-The Royal Flush Gang. 6-Sherlock Holmes. 7-Luthor app. 8-The Scarecrow. 9-Catwoman app.		.40	.80

JOKER COMICS (Adventures Into Terror No. 43 on)
April, 1942 - No. 42, March, 1950
Timely/Marvel Comics No. 36 on

	Good	Fine	Mint
1-(Rare)-1st app. Powerhouse Pepper by Wolverton; Stuporman app. from Daring	50.00	150.00	320.00
2-Wolverton-a continued	25.00	75.00	150.00
3-5-Wolverton-a	15.00	45.00	90.00
6-10-Wolverton-a	10.00	28.00	56.00
11-20-Wolverton-a	8.00	22.00	44.00
21,22,24-27,29,30-Wolverton cont'd. & Kurtzman's "Hey Look" in No. 23-27	6.00	18.00	36.00
23-1st "Hey Look" by Kurtzman; Wolverton-a	8.00	22.00	44.00
28,32,34,37-42	1.20	3.50	7.00
31-Last Powerhouse Pepper; not in No. 28	5.00	15.00	30.00
33,35,36-Kurtzman's "Hey Look"	2.50	7.00	14.00

JOLLY CHRISTMAS, A (See March of Comics No. 269)

JOLLY CHRISTMAS BOOK (See Christmas Journey Through Space)
1951; 1954; 1955 (36 pgs.; 24 pgs.)
Promotional Publ. Co.

	Good	Fine	Mint
1951-(Woolworth giveaway)-slightly oversized; no slick cover; Marv Levy c/a	2.00	5.00	10.00
1954-(Hot Shoppes giveaway)-regular size-reprints 1951 issue; slick cover added; 24 pgs.; no ads	2.00	5.00	10.00
1955-(J. M. McDonald Co. giveaway)-regular size	1.50	4.00	8.00

JOLLY COMICS
1947
Four Star Publishing Co.

	Good	Fine	Mint
1	2.00	5.00	10.00

JOLLY JINGLES (Formerly Jackpot)
No. 10, Sum, 1943 - 1945
MLJ Magazines

	Good	Fine	Mint
10-Super Duck begins (origin & 1st app.)	5.00	15.00	30.00
11-25	1.50	4.00	8.00

JONAH HEX (See All-Star Western and Weird Western Tales)
Mar-Apr, 1977 - Present
National Periodical Publications/DC Comics

	Good	Fine	Mint
1	1.00	3.00	6.00
2-6,8,10: 10-Morrow-c	.45	1.40	2.80
7-Explains Hex's face disfigurement	.50	1.50	3.00
9-Wrightson-c	.50	1.50	3.00
11,13-20		.50	1.00
12-Starlin-c		.50	1.00
21-30: 23-Intro Mei Ling		.40	.80
31-55: 31,32-Origin retold. 40-Scalphunter begins. 42-1st app. Jeremiah Hart. 45-Jonah Hex marries Mei Ling		.40	.80

NOTE: ***Cruz*** *a-26, 28, 29.* ***Kubert*** *c-45, 46.* ***Lopez*** *a-32.* ***Spiegle*** *a-34(Tothish).*

JONAH HEX AND OTHER WESTERN TALES (Blue Ribbon Digest)

JONAH HEX & OTHER. . . (continued)
Sept-Oct, 1979 - No. 3, Jan-Feb, 1980 (100 pgs.)
DC Comics

	Good	Fine	Mint
1-Origin Scalphunter-r; painted-c		.50	1.00
2-Reprints from Weird Western Tales; Adams, Toth, Aragones, Gil Kane, Dezuniga-a		.50	1.00
3		.50	1.00

JONAH HEX SPECTACULAR (See DC Special Series No. 16)

JONESY (Formerly Crack Western)
No. 85, Aug, 1953; No. 2, Oct, 1953 - No. 8, 1954
Comic Favorite/Quality Comics Group

85(No.1)	.85	2.50	5.00
2-8	.50	1.50	3.00

JON JUAN (Also see Great Lover Romances)
Spring, 1950
Toby Press

1-All Schomburg-a (signed Al Reid on-c); written by Siegel; used in **SOTI**, pg. 38	8.00	24.00	48.00

JONNY QUEST (TV)
December, 1964 (Hanna-Barbera)
Gold Key

1 (10139-412)	1.00	3.00	6.00

JOSEPH & HIS BRETHREN (See The Living Bible)

JOSIE (She's. . . No. 1-16) (. . . & the Pussycats No. 45 on)
Feb, 1963 - Present
Archie Publications/Radio Comics

1	3.00	8.00	16.00
2-10	1.50	4.00	8.00
11-20	1.00	3.00	6.00
21,23-30	.70	2.00	4.00
22-Mighty Man & Mighty (Josie Girl) app.	.40	1.20	2.40
31-54	.30	.80	1.60
55-74(52pg. ish.)		.40	.80
75-102		.30	.60

JOURNAL OF CRIME
1949 (132 pages)
Fox Features Syndicate

nn-See Fox Giants. Contents can vary and determines price.

JOURNEY INTO FEAR
May, 1951 - No. 21, Sept, 1954
Superior-Dynamic Publications

1-Baker-a(2)	8.00	24.00	48.00
2-4	4.00	12.00	24.00
5-10	3.50	10.00	20.00
11-Mad artist kills prostitutes	3.50	10.00	20.00
12-14,16-21	3.00	8.00	16.00
15-Used in **SOTI**, pg. 389	5.00	14.00	28.00

NOTE: *Feldsteinish, Kamenish, 'headlight'-a most issues.* ***Robinson*** *a-10.*

JOURNEY INTO MYSTERY (1st Series) (Thor No. 126 on)
6/52 - No. 48, 8/57; No. 49, 11/58 - No. 125, 2/66
Atlas(CPS No.1-48/AMI No.49-82/Marvel No.83 on)

1	35.00	100.00	210.00
2	17.00	50.00	110.00
3,4	12.00	36.00	75.00
5-11: Last pre-code issue	8.00	24.00	48.00
12-20,22: 22-Davisesque-a	5.50	16.00	32.00
21-Kubert-a; Tothish-a by Andru	6.00	18.00	36.00
23-32,35-38,40: 24-Torres?-a	3.00	8.00	16.00
33-Williamson-a	6.00	18.00	36.00
34-Williamson, Krigstein-a	6.00	18.00	36.00
39-Wood-a	5.50	16.00	32.00
41-Crandall-a; Frazettaesque-a by Morrow	3.50	10.00	20.00
42-Torres-a	3.00	8.00	16.00
43,44-Williamson/Mayo-a in both	3.50	10.00	20.00
45,47-49,52,53: 49-Check-a	2.00	6.00	12.00
46-Torres & Krigstein-a	3.50	10.00	20.00
50-Davis-a	2.00	6.00	12.00
51-Kirby/Wood-a	2.00	6.00	12.00
54-Williamson-a	2.00	6.00	12.00
55-61,63-73: 66-Return of Xemu	2.00	5.00	10.00
62-1st app. Xemu (Titan) called ''The Hulk''	3.50	10.00	20.00
74-82-Contents change to fantasy with No. 74	1.20	3.50	7.00
83-Reprint from the Golden Record Comic Set	.70	2.00	4.00
with the record. . . .	1.50	4.00	8.00
83-Origin & 1st app. The Mighty Thor by Kirby (8/62)	90.00	240.00	480.00
84	25.00	70.00	140.00
85-1st app. Loki & Heimdall	15.00	45.00	90.00
86-1st app. Odin	10.00	30.00	60.00
87,88	8.00	24.00	48.00
89-Origin Thor reprint/No. 83	8.00	24.00	48.00
90-No Kirby-a; Aunt Mary proto-type	6.00	18.00	36.00
91,92,94-96-Sinnott-a	4.75	14.00	28.00
93,97-Kirby-a; Tales of Asgard series begins No. 97(Origin which concludes No. 99)	5.00	15.00	30.00
98-100-Kirby/Heck-a. 99-1st app. Surtur & Mr. Hyde	4.50	13.00	26.00
101,103,104,110	2.00	6.00	12.00
102-Intro Sif	3.00	9.00	18.00
105-109-Ten extra pages Kirby-a. 107-1st app. Grey Gargoyle	3.00	9.00	18.00
111,113,114,116-124: 119-Intro Hegun, Fandrall, Volstagg	1.20	3.50	7.00
112-Thor Vs. Hulk(1st battle); origin Loki begins; ends No. 113	2.00	6.00	12.00
115-Detailed origin Loki	2.00	6.00	12.00
125-Thor reveals i.d. to Jane Foster	1.50	4.00	8.00
Annual 1('65)-1st app. Hercules; Kirby c/a	2.50	7.00	14.00

NOTE: ***Bailey*** *a-43.* ***Briefer*** *a-5, 12.* ***Check*** *a-17.* ***Colan*** *a-23, 81.* ***Ditko*** *a-50-96; c-71.* ***Ditko/Kirby*** *a-38, 50-83.* ***Everett*** *a-20, 40; c-4-6, 9, 37, 39, 40, 41, 44, 45.* ***Russ Heath*** *c-51.* ***Kirby*** *a-83-89, 93, 97, 98-100(w/Heck), 101-125; c-50-82(w/****Ditko****), 83, 84, 86, 87, 89, 90, 92, 94, 97-125.* ***Leiber/Fox*** *a-93, 98, 99.* ***Morrow*** *a-41, 42.* ***Orlando*** *a-30, 45, 57.* ***Mac Pakula****(Tothish) a-9.* ***Robinson*** *a-9.* ***Wildey*** *a-16.*

JOURNEY INTO MYSTERY (2nd Series)
Oct, 1972 - No. 19, Oct, 1975
Marvel Comics Group

1-Robert Howard adaptation; Kane, Starlin/Ploog, Reese-a	.25	.70	1.40
2-Robert Bloch adaptation		.50	1.00
3,5-Bloch adaptation; 5-Last new story		.40	.80
4-H. P. Lovecraft adaptation		.40	.80
6-19: 16-Orlando-a(r)		.30	.60

NOTE: ***Ditko*** *a(r)-7, 10, 12, 14, 15, 19; c-10.* ***Everett*** *a-9r.* ***G. Kane*** *c-3p.* ***Kirby*** *a-7r, 13r, 18r, 19r; c-7.* ***Orlando*** *a-16r.* ***Starlin*** *a-3p.* ***Wildey*** *a-9r, 14r.*

JOURNEY INTO UNKNOWN WORLDS (Formerly Teen)
No. 36, 9/50 - No. 38, 2/51; No. 4, 4/51 - No. 59, 8/57
Atlas Comics (WFP)

36(No.1)-Science fiction	13.00	38.00	76.00
37(No.2)-Science fiction; Everett c/a	10.00	28.00	56.00
38(No.3)-Science fiction	7.00	20.00	40.00
4-6,8-10-All horror stories	3.50	10.00	20.00
7-Wolverton-a-''Planet of Terror,'' 6 pgs; electric chair c-inset/story	17.00	50.00	100.00
11,12-Krigstein-a	5.00	14.00	28.00

Journey Into Fear #3, © SUPR

Journey Into Mystery #41, © MCG

Journey Into Unk. Worlds #37(#2), © MCG

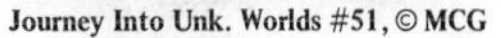
Journey Into Unk. Worlds #51, © MCG

Judy Canova #23, © FOX

Juke Box Comics #1, © EAS

JOURNEY INTO UNK. WORLDS (continued)

	Good	Fine	Mint
13,16,17,20	2.00	6.00	12.00
14-Wolverton-a-''One of Our Graveyards Is Missing,'' 4 pgs; Tuska-a	17.00	50.00	100.00
15-Wolverton-a-''They Crawl By Night,'' 5 pgs.	17.00	50.00	100.00
18,19-Matt Fox-a	3.00	9.00	18.00
21-26,28-33,36,37,39,40,42	1.50	4.00	8.00
27-Sid Check-a	2.00	6.00	12.00
34-Kubert, Torres-a	3.00	9.00	18.00
35-Torres-a	1.75	5.00	10.00
38-Severin-a	1.75	5.00	10.00
41-Matt Fox, Frazettaish-a	2.00	6.00	12.00
43-Krigstein, Baker-a	3.00	8.00	16.00
44-Davis-a	3.00	8.00	16.00
45,55,59-Williamson-a in all with Mayo No. 55,59 plus Crandall-a, No. 55	4.50	13.00	26.00
46,47,49,52,56-58	1.20	3.50	7.00
48,53-Crandall-a; Check-a, No. 48	4.00	11.00	22.00
50-Davis, Crandall-a	3.00	9.00	18.00
51-Wood-a	3.00	9.00	18.00
54-Torres-a	2.50	7.00	14.00

NOTE: ***Berg** a-38(No.3). **Lou Cameron** a-33. **Colan** a-37(No.2), 6. **Ditko** a-31, 51; c-31. **Everett** a-11, 14, 41, 47, 55; c-13, 14, 17, 22, 28, 47, 48p, 50, 53-55, 59. **Heath** a-36(No.1), 4, 6-8, 36i. **Maneely** c-25. **Morrow** a-48. **Orlando** a-44, 57. **Powell** a-53, 54. **Rico** a-21. **Sekowsky** a-4, 5. **Severin** a-51; c-48i. **Wildey** a-25, 44.*

JOURNEY OF DISCOVERY WITH MARK STEEL (See Mark Steel)

JOURNEY TO THE CENTER OF THE EARTH (See 4-Color No. 1060)

JUDE, THE FORGOTTEN SAINT
1954 (16 pgs.; 8x11''; full color; paper cover)
Catechetical Guild Education Society

	Good	Fine	Mint
nn	1.50	4.00	8.00

JUDGE COLT
Oct, 1969 - No. 4, Sept, 1970
Gold Key

	Good	Fine	Mint
1	.50	1.50	3.00
2-4	.30	.80	1.60

JUDGE PARKER
Feb, 1956
Argo

	Good	Fine	Mint
1	1.50	4.00	8.00
2	1.00	3.00	6.00

JUDO JOE
Aug, 1953 - No. 3, Dec, 1953
Jay-Jay Corp.

	Good	Fine	Mint
1-Drug ring story	3.00	8.00	16.00
2,3: 3-Hypo needle story	1.20	3.50	7.00

JUDOMASTER (Gun Master No. 84-89) (See Special War Series)
No. 89, May-June, 1966 - No. 98, Dec, 1967 (two No. 89's)
Charlton Comics

	Good	Fine	Mint
89-98: 91-Sarge Steel begins. 93-Intro. Tiger	.50	1.50	3.00
93-98(Modern Comics reprint, 1977)		.15	.30

JUDY CANOVA (Formerly My Experience)
May, 1950 - No. 3, Sept, 1950
Fox Features Syndicate

	Good	Fine	Mint
23(No.1)-Wood-c (signed); Wood-a(p)	5.00	14.00	28.00
24-Wood-a(p)	5.00	14.00	28.00
3-Wood-c; Wood/Orlando-a	7.00	20.00	40.00

JUDY GARLAND (See Famous Stars)

JUDY JOINS THE WAVES
1951 (For U.S. Navy)
Toby Press

	Good	Fine	Mint
nn	1.50	4.00	8.00

JUGHEAD (Formerly Archie's Pal. . .)
No. 127, Dec, 1965 - Present
Archie Publications

	Good	Fine	Mint
127-130	.50	1.50	3.00
131,133,135-160	.30	.90	1.80
132-Shield-c; The Fly & Black Hood app.	.50	1.40	2.80
134-Shield-c & app.	.50	1.40	2.80
161-240		.50	1.00
241-318		.30	.60

JUGHEAD AS CAPTAIN HERO
Oct, 1966 - No. 7, Nov, 1967
Archie Publications

	Good	Fine	Mint
1	1.50	4.00	8.00
2-7	.85	2.50	5.00

JUGHEAD JONES COMICS DIGEST
June, 1977 - Present (160 pages)
Archie Publications

	Good	Fine	Mint
1-Adams-a; Capt. Hero-r	.55	1.60	3.20
2(9/77)-Adams-a	.35	1.00	2.00
3-5,8-12,14,15		.50	1.00
6-Origin Jaguar-r		.50	1.00
7-Adams-a		.50	1.00
13-Reprints 1957 Jughead's Folly		.50	1.00

JUGHEAD'S EAT-OUT COMIC BOOK MAGAZINE (See Archie Giant Series Mag. No. 170)

JUGHEAD'S FANTASY
Aug, 1960 - No. 3, Dec, 1960
Archie Publications

	Good	Fine	Mint
1	5.50	16.00	32.00
2,3	3.50	10.00	20.00

JUGHEAD'S FOLLY
1957
Archie Publications (Close-Up)

	Good	Fine	Mint
1-Jughead a la Elvis	7.00	20.00	40.00

JUGHEAD'S JOKES
Aug, 1967 - Present
(No. 1-8, 38 on: reg. size; No. 9-23: 68 pgs.; No. 24-37: 52 pgs.)
Archie Publications

	Good	Fine	Mint
1	2.00	6.00	12.00
2	1.00	3.00	6.00
3-10	.70	2.00	4.00
11-30	.30	.90	1.80
31-50		.40	.80
51-70		.30	.60

JUGHEAD'S SOUL FOOD
1979 (49 cents)
Spire Christian Comics (Fleming H. Revell Co.)

	Good	Fine	Mint
		.30	.60

JUGHEAD WITH ARCHIE DIGEST (. . . Plus Betty & Veronica & Reggie Too No. 1,2)
March, 1974 - Present (Digest Size; 160 pgs.)
Archie Publications

	Good	Fine	Mint
1	.70	2.00	4.00
2-10	.35	1.00	2.00
11-20: Capt. Hero r-in No. 14-16; Pureheart the Powerful No. 18,21,22; Capt. Pureheart No. 17,19		.50	1.00
21-47		.30	.60

JUKE BOX COMICS
March, 1948 - No. 6, 1949
Famous Funnies

	Good	Fine	Mint
1-Toth c/a; Hollingsworth-a	12.00	35.00	70.00
2-6: 2-Transvestism story	5.50	16.00	32.00

JUMBO COMICS

Jumbo Comics #1, © FH

Jumbo Comics #46, © FH

Jumbo Comics #87, © FH

JUMBO COMICS (continued)
Sept, 1938 - No. 167, Apr, 1953 (No.1-3: 68 pgs.; No.4-8: 52 pgs.)
(No. 1-8 oversized-10½x14½''; black & white)
Fiction House Magazines (Real Adv. Publ. Co.)

	Good	Fine	Mint
1-(Rare)-Sheena Queen of the Jungle by Meskin, The Hawk by Eisner, The Hunchback by Dick Briefer(ends No.8) begin; 1st comic art by Jack Kirby (Count of Monte Cristo & Wilton of the West); Mickey Mouse appears (1 panel) with brief biography of Walt Disney	125.00	375.00	750.00
2-(Scarce)-Diary of Dr. Hayward by Kirby (also No.3) plus 2 other stories; contains strip from Universal Film featuring Edgar Bergen and Charlie McCarthy	60.00	180.00	380.00
3-Last Kirby issue	40.00	115.00	250.00
4-(Scarce)-Origin The Hawk by Eisner; Wilton of the West by Fine (ends No.14)(1st comic work); Count of Monte Cristo by Fine (ends No.15); The Diary of Dr. Hayward by Fine (cont'd. No. 8,9)	50.00	140.00	300.00
5	30.00	90.00	200.00
6-8-Last B&W issue. No. 8 was a N. Y. World's Fair Special Edition	28.00	80.00	170.00
9-Stuart Taylor begins by Fine; Fine-c; 1st color issue(8-9/39)-8¼x10¼''(oversized in width only)	25.00	75.00	150.00
10-14: 10-Regular size 68 pg. issues begin	20.00	60.00	120.00
15-Lightning begins	15.00	45.00	90.00
16-20	12.00	35.00	70.00
21-30: 22-1st Tom, Dick & Harry; origin The Hawk retold	10.00	30.00	60.00
31-40: 35 shows V2No.11 (correct number does not appear)	10.00	30.00	60.00
41-50	8.00	24.00	48.00
51-60: 52-Last Tom, Dick & Harry	7.00	20.00	40.00
61-70: 68-Sky Girl begins, ends No. 130; not in No. 79	5.50	16.00	32.00
71-80	5.00	14.00	28.00
81-93,95-100: 89-ZX5 becomes a private eye	5.00	14.00	28.00
94-Used in **Love and Death** by Legman	6.00	18.00	36.00
101-110: 103-Lingerie panel	3.50	10.00	20.00
111-140	3.00	8.00	16.00
141-149-Two Sheena stories. 141-Long Bow, Indian Boy begins, ends No. 160	3.50	10.00	20.00
150-154,156-158	3.00	8.00	16.00
155-Used in **POP**, pg. 98	3.50	10.00	20.00
159-163: Space Scouts serial in all; 163-Suicide Smith app.	3.00	8.00	16.00
164-The Star Pirate begins, ends No. 165	3.00	8.00	16.00
165-167: 165,167-Space Rangers app.	3.00	8.00	16.00

NOTE: *Bondage covers, negligee panels, torture, etc. are common in this series. Hawks of the Seas, Inspector Dayton, Spies in Action, Sports Shorts, & Uncle Otto by* ***Eisner****, No. 1-7. Hawk by* ***Eisner****-No. 10-15;* ***Eisner*** *c-1, 3-6, 12, 13, 15. 1pg. Patsy pin-ups in 92-97, 99-101. Sheena by* ***Meskin****-No. 1, 4; by* ***Powell****-No. 2, 3, 5-28. Sky Girl by* ***Matt Baker****-No. 69-78, 80-124.* ***Bailey*** *a-3-8.* ***Briefer*** *a-1-8, 10.* ***Fine*** *c-8-11.* ***Kamen*** *a-101, 105, 123, 132; c-105.* ***Bob Kane*** *a-1-8.*

JUMPING JACKS PRESENTS THE WHIZ KIDS
1978 (In 3-D) with glasses (4 pages)
Jumping Jacks Stores giveaway

	Good	Fine	Mint
nn		.40	.80

JUNGLE ACTION
Oct, 1954 - No. 6, Aug, 1955
Atlas Comics (IPC)

	Good	Fine	Mint
1-Leopard Girl begins; Maneely c/a	5.50	16.00	32.00
2-(3-D effect cover)	5.50	16.00	32.00
3-6: 5-Maneely-c	4.00	12.00	24.00

JUNGLE ACTION
Oct, 1972 - No. 24, Nov, 1976
Marvel Comics Group

	Good	Fine	Mint
1-Lorna, Jann-r		.50	1.00
2,4		.40	.80
3-Tharn-r; Starlin-c(p)		.40	.80
5-Black Panther begins		.40	.80
6-10-All new stories		.40	.80
11-18: All new stories. 18-Kirby-c		.40	.80
19-22-KKK x-over		.40	.80
23,24: 23-R-/No. 22. 24-1st Wind Eagle		.40	.80

NOTE: ***Buckler*** *a-22.* ***Buscema*** *c-22.* ***Gil Kane*** *c-13-17, 19, 24.* ***Kirby*** *c-18.*

JUNGLE ADVENTURES
1963 - 1964 (Reprints)
Super Comics

	Good	Fine	Mint
10,12(Rulah), 15(Kaanga/Jungle No. 152)	1.50	4.00	8.00
17(Jo-Jo)	1.50	4.00	8.00
18-Reprints/White Princess of the Jungle No. 1; no Kinstler-a; origin of both White Princess & Cap'n Courage	2.00	5.00	10.00

JUNGLE ADVENTURES
March, 1971 - No. 3, June, 1971
Skywald Comics

	Good	Fine	Mint
1-Zangar origin; reprints of Jo-Jo, Blue Gorilla(origin)/White Princess No. 3, Kinstler-a/White Princess No. 2	.50	1.50	3.00
2-Zangar, Sheena/Sheena No. 17 & Jumbo No. 162, Jo-Jo, origin Slave Girl Princess-r	.50	1.50	3.00

Jumbo Comics #158, © FH

Jungle Action #1, © MCG

Jungle Adventures #1, © SKY

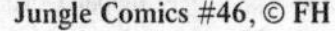
Jungle Comics #46, © FH

Jungle Tales Of Tarzan #2, © CC

Junior Comics #13, © FOX

JUNGLE ADVENTURES (continued) — Good / Fine / Mint
3-Zangar, Jo-Jo, White Princess-r .50 1.50 3.00

JUNGLE BOOK, THE (See Movie Comics)

JUNGLE CAT (See 4-Color No. 1136)

JUNGLE COMICS
Jan, 1940 - No. 163, Summer, 1954
Fiction House Magazines

1-Origin The White Panther, Kaanga, Lord of the Jungle, Tabu, Wizard of the Jungle; Wambi, the Jungle Boy & Camilla begin 60.00 175.00 350.00
2-Fantomah, Mystery Woman of the Jungle begins 35.00 100.00 200.00
3,4 30.00 80.00 160.00
5 20.00 60.00 120.00
6-10 14.00 40.00 80.00
11-20 10.00 30.00 60.00
21-30: 25 shows V2No.1 (correct number does not appear). No. 27-New origin Fantomah, Daughter of the Pharoahs; Camilla dons new costume 8.00 24.00 48.00
31-40 7.00 20.00 40.00
41,43-50 5.50 16.00 32.00
42-Kaanga by Crandall, 12 pgs. 7.00 20.00 40.00
51-60 5.00 14.00 28.00
61-70 4.00 12.00 24.00
71-80: 79-New origin Tabu; part nudity panel 3.50 10.00 20.00
81-97,99-106,108-110 3.00 8.00 16.00
98-Used in **SOTI**, pg. 185 & illo-''In ordinary comic books, there are pictures within pictures for children who know how to look''; used by N.Y. Legis. Comm. 10.00 28.00 56.00
107-Baker-a; nudity panel 3.50 10.00 20.00
111-142,144,146-150: 135-Desert Panther begins in Terry Thunder (origin), not in No. 137; ends (dies) No. 138 3.00 8.00 16.00
143,145-Used in **POP**, pg. 99 3.50 10.00 20.00
151-157,159-163: 152-Tiger Girl begins 3.00 8.00 16.00
158-Sheena app. 4.00 12.00 24.00
I.W. Reprint No. 1,9: 9-r-/No. 151 1.00 3.00 6.00

NOTE: *Bondage covers, negligee panels, torture, etc. are common to this series. Camilla by* ***Fran Hopper****-No. 73, 78, 80-90; by* ***Baker****-No. 103, 106, 107, 111, 112. Kaanga by* ***John Celardo****-No. 80-110; by* ***Maurice Whitman****-No. 124-163. Tabu by* ***Whitman****-No. 93-110.* ***Celardo*** *a-78; c-98, 99, 106, 109, 112.* ***Eisner*** *c-2, 5.* ***Fine*** *c-1.* ***Larsen*** *a-65, 66, 72, 74, 75, 79, 83, 84, 87-90. Bondage covers are common.*

JUNGLE GIRL (See Lorna, . . .)

JUNGLE GIRL (Nyoka, Jungle Girl No. 2 on)
Fall, 1942 (No month listed)
Fawcett Publications

1-Bondage-c 20.00 60.00 120.00

JUNGLE JIM
Jan, 1949 - No. 20, Apr, 1951
Standard Comics (Best Books)

11-20 1.50 4.00 8.00

JUNGLE JIM
1953 - No. 1020, Aug-Oct, 1959
Dell Publishing Co.

4-Color 490,565(1953-54) 1.50 4.00 8.00
3(10-12/54)-5 .85 2.50 5.00
6-20(4-6/59) .70 2.00 4.00
4-Color 1020(No.21) 1.00 3.00 6.00

JUNGLE JIM
December, 1967
King Features Syndicate

5-Reprints Dell No. 5; Wood-c .50 1.50 3.00

JUNGLE JIM (Continued from Dell)
No. 22, Feb, 1969 - No. 28, Feb, 1970 (no No. 21)
Charlton Comics — Good / Fine / Mint

22-Dan Flagg begins, ends No. 23; Wood & Ditko-a .85 2.50 5.00
23-28: 23-Wood-c. 24-Jungle People begin. 27-Wood, Ditko-a. 28-Ditko-a .50 1.50 3.00

JUNGLE JO
Mar, 1950 - No. 6, Mar, 1951
Fox Features Syndicate (Hero Books)

nn-Jo-Jo blanked out, leaving Congo King; came out after Jo-Jo No. 29 (intended as Jo-Jo No. 30?) 7.00 20.00 40.00
1-Tangi begins; part Wood-a 8.00 22.00 44.00
2-6 5.00 15.00 30.00

JUNGLE LIL (Dorothy Lamour, Jungle Princess No. 2 on) (Also see Feature Stories Magazine)
April, 1950
Fox Features Syndicate/Hero Books

1 8.00 22.00 44.00

JUNGLE TALES (Jann of the Jungle No. 8 on)
Sept, 1954 - No. 7, Sept, 1955
Atlas Comics (CSI)

1-Jann of the Jungle 5.50 16.00 32.00
2-7 4.00 12.00 24.00

JUNGLE TALES OF TARZAN
Dec, 1964 - No. 5, 1965
Charlton Comics

1 1.50 4.00 8.00
2-4 1.00 3.00 6.00
5-(Exist?)-Cardboard covers in color; Glanzman-a; this series was unauthorized and killed after No. 5 was printed - all but a few issues of No. 5 were destroyed?
Estimated value. . . . $300.00—$500.00

NOTE: ***Glanzman*** *did not get his art back; was told had to be destroyed with other Tarzan art.*

JUNGLE TERROR (See Comics Hits No. 54)

JUNGLE THRILLS (Terrors of the Jungle No. 17)
No. 16, February, 1952
Fox Features Syndicate/Star Publications

16-Phantom Lady & Rulah story-reprint/All Top No. 15; used in **POP**, pg. 98; L. B. Cole-c 12.00 35.00 70.00
3-D 1(12/53)-Jungle Lil & Jungle Jo appear; L. B. Cole-c 14.00 40.00 80.00

JUNGLE TWINS, THE (Tono & Kono)
April, 1972 - No. 17, Nov, 1975
Gold Key

1 .60 1.20
2-5 .40 .80
6-17: 12-16pgs. ads extra .30 .60

JUNGLE WAR STORIES (Guerrilla War No. 12 on)
July-Sept, 1962 - No. 11, Apr-June, 1965
Dell Publishing Co.

01-384-209 .30 .80 1.60
2-11 .60 1.20

JUNIE PROM
Winter, 1947-48 - No. 7, Aug, 1949
Dearfield Publishing Co.

1 2.00 6.00 12.00
2-7 1.50 4.00 8.00

JUNIOR COMICS
No. 9, Sept, 1947 - No. 16, July, 1948
Fox Features Syndicate

9-16-Feldstein c/a 20.00 60.00 120.00

JUNIOR FUNNIES (Formerly Tiny Tot Funnies No. 9)
No. 10, Aug, 1951 - No. 13, Feb, 1952
Harvey Publications (King Features Synd.)

	Good	Fine	Mint
10-13: Partial reprints-Blondie, Popeye, Felix, Katzenjammer Kids	1.20	3.50	7.00

JUNIOR HOP COMICS (Junior Hopp)
1952 - No. 3, July, 1952
Atlas Comics/SPM Publ.

	Good	Fine	Mint
1-3: 3-Dave Berg-a	1.00	3.00	6.00

JUNIOR MEDICS OF AMERICA, THE
1957 (15 cents)
E. R. Squire & Sons

	Good	Fine	Mint
1359	1.00	3.00	6.00

JUNIOR MISS
Winter, 1944 - No. 39, Aug, 1950 (No. 2-23 exist?)
Timely/Marvel Comics (CnPC)

	Good	Fine	Mint
1-Frank Sinatra life story	4.00	12.00	24.00
24-38	.70	2.00	4.00
39-Kurtzman-a	1.50	4.00	8.00

JUNIOR PARTNERS (Formerly Oral Roberts' True Stories)
No. 120, Aug, 1959 - V3No.12, Dec, 1961
Oral Roberts Evangelistic Assn.

	Good	Fine	Mint
120(No.1)	1.50	4.00	8.00
2(9/59)	.85	2.50	5.00
3-12(7/60)	.35	1.00	2.00
V2No.1(8/60)-5(12/60)		.50	1.00
V3No.1(1/61)-12		.40	.80

JUNIOR TREASURY (See Dell Junior . . .)

JUNIOR WOODCHUCKS (See Huey, Dewey & Louie . . .)

JUSTICE COMICS (Tales of Justice No. 58 on; formerly Wacky Duck)
No. 7, Fall/47 - No. 9, 6/48; No. 4, 8/48 - No. 53, 5/55
Atlas(NPP No. 7-19/CnPC No. 20-23/MgMC No. 24-37/Male No. 38-62)

	Good	Fine	Mint
7-9('47-48)	1.75	5.00	10.00
4-Dope dealing story	2.00	6.00	12.00
5-7,9,10	1.00	3.00	6.00
8-Anti Wertham editorial	1.50	4.00	8.00
11-30	.70	2.00	4.00
31-40,42,43,45-47,49-53	.50	1.50	3.00
41-Electrocution cover	1.50	4.00	8.00
44-Drug story	2.00	6.00	12.00
48-Pakula & Tuska-a	1.00	3.00	6.00

NOTE: ***Everett** a-53. **Louis Ravielli** a-39. **Robinson** a-22, 25, 41. **Wildey** a-52.*

JUSTICE, INC. (The Avenger)
May-June, 1975 - No. 4, Nov-Dec, 1975
National Periodical Publications

	Good	Fine	Mint
1-McWilliams-a; origin		.60	1.20
2-4		.40	.80

NOTE: ***Kirby** c-2, 3; a-2-4. **Kubert** c-1, 4.*

JUSTICE LEAGUE OF AMERICA (See Brave & the Bold)
Oct-Nov, 1960 - Present
National Periodical Publications/DC Comics

	Good	Fine	Mint
1-Origin Despero	35.00	100.00	200.00
2-1st app. Kanjar Ro	20.00	60.00	120.00
3-Origin Kanja Ro	14.00	40.00	80.00
4,5: 4-Green Arrow joins JLA. 5-Origin Dr. Destiny	9.00	25.00	50.00
6-8,10: 6-Origin Prof. Amos Fortune. 10-Origin Felix Faust	5.50	16.00	32.00
9-Origin J.L.A.	7.00	20.00	40.00
11-13,15: 12-Origin & 1st app. Dr. Light. 13-Speedy app.	3.00	8.00	16.00
14-Atom joins JLA	3.00	8.00	16.00
16-20: 17-Adam Strange flashback	2.00	6.00	12.00
21,22: 21-Re-intro. of JSA. 22-JSA x-over	1.75	5.00	10.00
23-28: 28-Robin app.	1.50	4.00	8.00
29,30-JSA x-over	1.50	4.00	8.00
31-Hawkman joins JLA, Hawkgirl cameo	1.00	3.00	6.00
32-Intro & Origin Brain Storm	1.00	3.00	6.00
33-36,40	.85	2.50	5.00
37,38-JSA x-over	1.00	3.00	6.00
39-25 cent Giant G-16	1.20	3.50	7.00
41-Intro & Origin The Key	.75	2.20	4.40
42-45: 42-Metamorpho app.	.60	1.80	3.60
46,47-JSA x-over	.75	2.20	4.40
48-25 cent Giant G-29	.75	2.20	4.40
49,50: 50-Robin app.	.60	1.80	3.60
51-54,57,59,60	.60	1.80	3.60
55-Intro. Earth 2 Robin; JSA x-over	.60	1.80	3.60
56-JSA x-over	.60	1.80	3.60
58-25 cent Giant G-41	.60	1.80	3.60
61-63,66,68-70: 69-Wonder Woman quits. 70-Creeper x-over	.35	1.00	2.00
64,65-JSA x-over; intro. & origin Red Tornado No. 64	.40	1.20	2.40
67-25 cent Giant G-53	.45	1.30	2.60
71,72,75,77-80: 71-Manhunter leaves JLA. 78-Re-intro. Vigilante 79-Vigilante x-over	.30	.90	1.80
73,74-JSA x-over; 74-Black Canary leaves JSA & joins JLA	.35	1.00	2.00
76-25 cent Giant G-65	.40	1.20	2.40
81,84,86-90	.30	.80	1.60
82-JSA x-over	.30	.90	1.80
83-JSA x-over; death of Spectre (revived later)	.30	.90	1.80
85-25 cent Giant G-77	.35	1.00	2.00
91-JSA x-over; Hourman-r; 52 pgs. begin, end No. 99	.30	.80	1.60
92-JSA x-over; Flash-r	.30	.80	1.60
93-25 cent Giant G-89	.30	.90	1.80
94-Origin Sandman (Adv. No. 40) & Starman (Adv. No. 61); Deadman x-over; Adams-a	1.50	4.00	8.00
95-Origin Dr. Fate & Dr. Midnight reprint (More Fun No. 67, All-American No. 25)	.40	1.20	2.40
96-Origin Hourman reprint (Adventure No. 48)	.40	1.20	2.40
97-Origin JLA retold	.35	1.00	2.00
98,99: 98-G.A. Sargon, Starman-r. 99-G.A. Sandman, Atom-r	.30	.90	1.80
100	.40	1.10	2.20
101,102-JSA, 7 Soldiers & others x-over; 102-Red Tornado dies	.30	.90	1.80
103-106: 103-Phantom Stranger joins. 105-Elongated Man joins. 106-New Red Tornado joins		.60	1.20
107,108-JSA & G.A. Uncle Sam, Black Condor, The Ray, Dollman, Phantom Lady, & The Human Bomb x-over	.30	.80	1.60
109-Hawkman resigns		.60	1.20
110-116: All 100 pg. issues; JSA Tale No. 110 & Toth-r. No. 113,115-JSA/JLA team up		.60	1.20
117-120: 117-Hawkman rejoins		.50	1.00
121-Adam Strange marries Alanna		.40	.80
122,125-130: 128-Wonder Woman rejoins. 129-Death of Red Tornado		.40	.80
123,124-JSA x-over		.40	.80
131,132		.40	.80
133,134-Part 2 & 3 of Despero		.40	.80
135,136: JSA & G.A. Bulletman, Bulletgirl, Spy Smasher, Mr. Scarlet, Pinky & Ibis x-over in all		.40	.80
137-Same as above plus Superman battles G.A. Capt. Marvel		.45	.90
138,139-Adams-c; 139-begin 52 pg. issues, end No. 157		.45	.90

Justice Comics #33, © MCG

Justice League #5, © DC

Justice League #94, © DC

Justice Traps The Guilty #12, © PRIZE

Kamandi #4, © DC

Karate Kid #2, © DC

JUSTICE LEAGUE OF AMERICA (continued)

	Good	Fine	Mint
140-150: 144-Origin retold; origin J'onn J'onnz. 145-Red Tornado resurrected. 147,148-JSA & Legion x-over		.40	.80
151-170: 153-Origin & 1st app. Ultraa. 157-Atom marries Jean Loring. 158-160-(44 pgs.). 159,160-JSA x-over; Miss Liberty app. 161-Zatanna joins & new costume. 166-168-Defeat of Secret Society of Super-Villains		.30	.60
171-176,181,182,184,186-190: 171-Mr. Terrific murdered. 171,172, 175-JSA x-over. 181-Gr. Arrow leaves		.30	.60
177-180,183-Starlin-c. 179-Firestorm joins JLA		.30	.60
185-Starlin/Smith-c		.30	.60
191,192,194-199: 195-JSA x-over		.30	.60
193-1st All-Star Squadron		.60	1.20
200-Anniversary ish. (80pgs., $1.50)	.30	.90	1.80

NOTE: ***Adams** c-63, 66, 67, 70, 74, 79, 81, 82, 86-89, 91, 92, 94, 96-98, 138, 139. **Anderson** c-1-4, 10, 12-14, 16, 17, 19, 24, 69, 75-77, 80, 83-85, 90i, 95. **Aparo** a-200. **Buckler** c-140, 142, 151, 156, 158, 159, 161, 163, 164, 193p. **Giordano** c-118, 119, 127, 166, 172. **Grell** c-122. **Infantino** a-110r, 200; c-56-58, 90p. **Kaluta** c-154. **Gil Kane** a-200. **Krigstein** a-96(r-Sensation No. 84.) **Kubert** c-72, 73, 200. **Lopez** c-165. **Orlando** c-151i. **Perez** a-192-196; c-192-195, 196p, 197p. **Starlin** c-179, 180, 183, 185. **Staton** c-157. **Tuska** a-153.*

THE JUSTICE MACHINE
June, 1981 ($2.00)
Capital City

	Good	Fine	Mint
1-Byrne-c(p)		1.00	2.00

JUSTICE TRAPS THE GUILTY (Fargo Kid V11No.3 on)
Oct-Nov, 1947 - V11No.2(No.92), Apr-May, 1958
Prize/Headline Publications

	Good	Fine	Mint
V2No.1-S&K c/a	6.00	18.00	36.00
2-5-S&K c/a	3.50	10.00	20.00
6-S&K c/a; Feldstein-a	4.00	12.00	24.00
7,9-S&K c/a	2.00	6.00	12.00
8,10-S&K c/a; Krigstein-a	3.00	8.00	16.00
11,19-S&K-c	1.20	3.50	7.00
12,14-17,20-No S&K	1.00	3.00	6.00
13-Used in **SOTI**, pg. 110-111	3.00	8.00	16.00
18-S&K-c, Elder-a	1.20	3.50	7.00
21-S&K c/a	1.20	3.50	7.00
22,23,27-S&K-c	1.00	3.00	6.00
24-26,28-50	.70	2.00	4.00
51-57,59-70	.60	1.80	3.60
58-Illo. in **SOTI**, "Treating police contemptuously"(top left); text on heroin	6.00	18.00	36.00
71-75,77-92	.50	1.50	3.00
76-Orlando-a	.60	1.80	3.60

NOTE: ***Bailey** a-12. **Kirby** a-19p. **Meskin** a-19i, 27. **Robinson** a-19p. **Severin** a-11p.*

JUST KIDS
1932 (16 pages; 9½x12''; paper cover)
McLoughlin Bros.

	Good	Fine	Mint
283-Three-color text, pictures on heavy paper	4.00	12.00	24.00

JUST MARRIED
January, 1958 - No. 114, Dec, 1976
Charlton Comics

	Good	Fine	Mint
1	.85	2.50	5.00
2-20	.30	.90	1.80
21-50		.30	.60
51-114		.20	.40

KA'A'NGA COMICS (. . . Jungle King)
Spring, 1949 - No. 20, Summer, 1954
Fiction House Magazines (Glen-Kel Publ. Co.)

	Good	Fine	Mint
1-Ka'a'nga, Lord of the Jungle begins	10.00	30.00	60.00
2-4	6.00	18.00	36.00
5-Camilla app.	3.50	10.00	20.00
6-9: 7-Tuska-a. 9-Tabu, Wizard of the Jungle app.	3.00	8.00	16.00
10-Used in **POP**, pg. 99	3.50	10.00	20.00
11-15	2.00	6.00	12.00
16-Sheena app.	2.50	7.00	14.00
17-20	2.00	5.00	10.00
I.W. Reprint No. 1 (r-/No. 18) Kinstler-c	.70	2.00	4.00
I.W. Reprint No. 8 (reprints No. 10)	.70	2.00	4.00

KAMANDI, THE LAST BOY ON EARTH (Also see Cancelled Comic Cavalcade and Brave & the Bold No. 120)
Oct-Nov, 1972 - No. 59, Oct-Nov, 1978
National Periodical Publications/DC Comics

	Good	Fine	Mint
1-Origin	.40	1.20	2.40
2-5: 4-Intro. Prince Tuftan of the Tigers	.30	.90	1.80
6-10	.30	.80	1.60
11-20: 15-Watergate tapes used as weapon		.60	1.20
21-31: 29-Superman, Legend x-over. 31-Intro Pyra		.50	1.00
32-Giant; origin from No. 1		.60	1.20
33-40-Last Kirby issue		.40	.80
41,42,47-58: 49-1st pre-disaster years story. 58-Karate Kid x-over		.20	.40
43-46-Tales of the Great Disaster feat.		.20	.40
59-Starlin c/a		.40	.80

NOTE: ***Alcala** a-47-52. **Kirby** a-1-40; c-1-33. **Kubert** c-34-41. **Nasser** a-45, 46. **Starlin** c-57.*

KARATE KID (See Action, Adventure, Legion of Super-Heroes, & Superboy)
Mar-Apr, 1976 - No. 15, July-Aug, 1978
National Periodical Publications/DC Comics

	Good	Fine	Mint
1-Meets Iris Jacobs; Estrada/Staton-a		.50	1.00
2-15: 2- Intro villain Major Disaster. 15-Continued into Kamandi No. 58		.40	.80

NOTE: ***Buckler** c-14. **Staton** a-1-9i. Legion x-over-No. 1, 2, 4, 6, 10, 12, 13. Princess Projectra x-over-No. 8, 9*

KASCO KOMICS
1945; 1949 (regular size; paper cover)
Kasko Grainfeed (Giveaway)

	Good	Fine	Mint
1(1945)-Similar to Katy Keene; Bill Woggan-a; 28 pgs.; 6-7/8''x9-7/8''	10.00	28.00	56.00
2(1949)	8.00	24.00	48.00

KATHY
September, 1949 - 1953
Standard Comics

	Good	Fine	Mint
1	1.50	4.00	8.00
2-5	.85	2.50	5.00
6-16	.60	1.80	3.60

KATHY
Oct, 1959 - No. 27, Feb, 1964
Atlas Comics/Marvel (ZPC)

	Good	Fine	Mint
1	.85	2.50	5.00
2-27	.50	1.50	3.00

KAT KARSON
No date (Reprint)
I. W. Enterprises

	Good	Fine	Mint
1-Funny animals	.50	1.50	3.00

KATY AND KEN VISIT SANTA WITH MISTER WISH
1948 (16 pgs.; paper cover)
S. S. Kresge Co. (Giveaway)

	Good	Fine	Mint
	2.50	7.00	14.00

KATY KEENE (Also see Kasco Komics, Laugh, Pep, Suzie, & Wilbur)
1949 - No. 4, 1951; No. 5, 3/52 - No. 62, Oct, 1961
Archie Publ./Close-Up/Radio Comics

KATY KEENE (continued)

	Good	Fine	Mint
1-Bill Woggan-a begins	25.00	70.00	140.00
2	14.00	40.00	80.00
3-5	10.00	30.00	60.00
6-10	8.00	24.00	48.00
11-20	5.50	16.00	32.00
21-40	4.00	12.00	24.00
41-62	3.00	8.00	16.00
Annual 1('54)-Negligee panels	12.00	32.00	64.00
Annual 2-6('55-59)	5.50	16.00	32.00
3-D 1(1953-Large size)	12.00	32.00	64.00
Charm 1(9/58)	5.00	14.00	28.00
Glamour 1(1957)	5.00	14.00	28.00
Spectacular 1('56)	5.50	16.00	32.00

KATY KEENE FASHION BOOK MAGAZINE
1955 - No. 13, Sum, '56 - No. 23, Wint, '58-59
Radio Comics/Archie Publications

	Good	Fine	Mint
1	10.00	30.00	60.00
2	6.00	18.00	36.00
3-10(nn's)	5.00	14.00	28.00
11-17	4.00	12.00	24.00
18-Photo of Bill Woggon	4.00	12.00	24.00
19-23	3.00	8.00	16.00

KATY KEENE HOLIDAY FUN (See Archie Giant Series Mag. No. 7,12)

KATY KEENE PINUP PARADE
1955 - No. 15, Spring, 1961 (25 cents)
Radio Comics/Archie Publications

	Good	Fine	Mint
1	10.00	30.00	60.00
2-10,12-14: 8-Mad parody	4.00	12.00	24.00
11-Story of how comics get CCA approved, narrated by Katy	5.00	14.00	28.00
15(Rare)-Picture of artist & family	5.50	16.00	32.00

KATZENJAMMER KIDS, THE
1903 (50 pgs.; 10x15¼''; in color)
New York American & Journal
(by Rudolph Dirks, strip 1st appeared in 1898)

	Good	Fine	Mint
1903 (Rare)	20.00	60.00	120.00
1905-Tricks of. . .(10x15)	15.00	45.00	90.00
1906-Stokes-10x16'', 32 pgs. in color	15.00	45.00	90.00
1910-The Komical. . .(10x15)	15.00	45.00	90.00
1921-Embee Dist. Co., 10x16'', 20 pgs. in color	12.00	35.00	70.00

KATZENJAMMER KIDS, THE (See Giant Comic Album)
1945-1946; Summer, 1947 - No. 27, Feb-Mar, 1954
David McKay Publ./Standard No.12-21(Spring/'50 - 53)/Harvey No. 22, 4/53 on

	Good	Fine	Mint
Feature Book 30,32,37('45),41,44('46)	3.50	10.00	20.00
Feature Book 35	4.00	12.00	24.00
1(1947)	3.50	10.00	20.00
2-11	2.00	6.00	12.00
12-14(Standard)	1.50	4.00	8.00
15-21(Standard)	1.00	3.00	6.00
22-25,27(Harvey)	1.00	3.00	6.00
26-½ in 3-D	5.50	16.00	32.00

KAYO (Formerly Jest?)
March, 1945
Harry 'A' Chesler

	Good	Fine	Mint
12-Green Knight, Capt. Glory, Little Nemo (not by McCay)	2.00	6.00	12.00

KA-ZAR
Aug, 1970 - No. 3, Mar, 1971 (Giant-Size)
Marvel Comics Group

	Good	Fine	Mint
1-Reprints earlier Ka-Zar stories; Avengers x-over in Hercules; hidden profanity-c	.40	1.10	2.20
2,3-Ka-Zar origin No. 2; Angel in both	.25	.70	1.40

KA-ZAR
Jan, 1974 - No. 20, Feb, 1977 (Regular Size)
Marvel Comics Group

	Good	Fine	Mint
1	.30	.90	1.80
2-10: 4-Brunner-c		.60	1.20
11-20		.50	1.00

NOTE: ***Alcala*** *a-6i, 8i.* ***J. Buscema*** *a-8p.* ***Heath*** *a-12.* ***Gil Kane*** *c-11, 15, 20.* ***Kirby*** *c-12.*

KA-ZAR
April, 1981 - Present (Regular size)
Marvel Comics Group

	Good	Fine	Mint
1		.60	1.20
2-9		.40	.80

NOTE: ***Anderson***-*a(p)-1-9; c-1-9. (No. 10 on will be sold only in comic shops with no ads.)*

KEEN DETECTIVE FUNNIES (Formerly Det. Picture Stories?)
No. 8, July, 1938 - No. 24, Sept, 1940
Centaur Publications

	Good	Fine	Mint
V1No.1	20.00	60.00	120.00
8-The Clock continues	14.00	40.00	80.00
9-11: 9-Tex Martin by Eisner	10.00	30.00	60.00
V2No.1,2-The Eye Sees by Frank Thomas begins; ends No. 23(Not in V2No.3). 2-Jack Cole-a	10.00	28.00	56.00
3-TNT Todd begins	10.00	28.00	56.00
4,5-The Clock app.	10.00	28.00	56.00
6,9-11: 6-Eisner a(r)	10.00	28.00	56.00
7-The Masked Marvel by Ben Thompson begins	17.00	50.00	100.00
8(No. 19)-Nudist ranch panel w/ four girls	10.00	28.00	56.00
12-Origin The Eye Sees	12.00	35.00	70.00
V3No.1-6	11.00	32.00	65.00
22-24	11.00	32.00	65.00

NOTE: ***Burgos*** *a-V2No.2.* ***Ken Ernst*** *a-V2No.9.*

KEEN KOMICS
V2No.1, May, 1939 - V2No.3, Nov, 1939
Centaur Publications

	Good	Fine	Mint
V2No.1	8.50	25.00	50.00
V2No.2,3	7.00	20.00	40.00

NOTE: ***Burgos*** *a-V2No.2,3.* ***Gustavson*** *a-V2No.2.*

KEEN TEENS
1945
Life's Romances Publ./Leader/Magazine Enterprises

	Good	Fine	Mint
nn-14 pgs. Claire Voyant (cont'd. in other nn issue); movie photos; Dotty Dripple, Gertie O'Grady & Sissy	5.50	16.00	32.00
nn-16 pgs. Claire Voyant & 16 pgs. movie photos	5.50	16.00	32.00
3-5: 5-Perry Como-c (M.E.)	2.00	5.00	10.00

KEEPING UP WITH THE JONESES
1920 - No. 2, 1921 (48 pgs.; 9½x9½''; B&W daily strip reprints)
Cupples & Leon Co.

	Good	Fine	Mint
1,2-By Pop Momand	4.00	12.00	24.00

KELLYS, THE (Formerly Rusty; Spy Cases No. 26 on)
No. 23, Jan, 1950 - No. 25, June, 1950
Marvel Comics (HPC)

	Good	Fine	Mint
23-25	1.00	3.00	6.00

KEN MAYNARD WESTERN
Sept, 1950 - No. 8, Feb, 1952
Fawcett Publications

	Good	Fine	Mint
1-with photos	8.00	24.00	48.00

Katy Keene #6, © AP

Katzenjammer Kids #5, © KING

Kazar #1(1974), © MCG

Kent Blake #13, © MCG

Kerry Drake #15, © HARV

Key Ring #1, © DELL

KEN MAYNARD WESTERN (continued)

	Good	Fine	Mint
2	5.50	16.00	32.00
3-8	4.00	12.00	24.00

KEN SHANNON (Gabby No. 11)
Oct, 1951 - No. 15, 1953 (a private eye)
Quality Comics Group

	Good	Fine	Mint
1-Crandall-a; drug mention story	7.00	20.00	40.00
2-Crandall c/a(2); text on narcotics	6.00	18.00	36.00
3-5-Crandall-a	4.00	12.00	24.00
6,7	3.00	8.00	16.00
8-Opium den drug use story	4.00	12.00	24.00
9,10-Crandall-c	3.50	10.00	20.00
11-15	2.00	5.00	10.00

NOTE: ***Jack Cole*** *a-1-9. No. 11-15 published after title change to Gabby.*

KEN STUART
1948
Publication

	Good	Fine	Mint
1-Frank Borth-a	1.50	4.00	8.00

KENT BLAKE OF THE SECRET SERVICE (War)
May, 1951 - No. 14, July, 1953
Marvel/Atlas Comics(20CC)

	Good	Fine	Mint
1-Injury to eye, bondage, torture	2.50	7.00	14.00
2-Two drug mention stories	2.00	6.00	12.00
3-14	1.00	3.00	6.00

KERRY DRAKE (Also see Green Hornet)
Jan, 1956 - No. 2, March, 1956
Argo

	Good	Fine	Mint
1,2-Newspaper-r	2.00	5.00	10.00

KERRY DRAKE DETECTIVE CASES (. . . Racket Buster No. 32,33)
(Also see Chamber of Clues)
1944; No. 6, Jan, 1948 - No. 33, Aug, 1952
Life's Romances/Magazine Ent. No.1-5/Harvey No.6 on

	Good	Fine	Mint
nn(1944)(A-1 Comics)	7.00	20.00	40.00
2-5(1944)	5.00	14.00	28.00
6,8(1948); 8-Bondage-c	3.50	10.00	20.00
7-Kubert-a; biog of Andriola	4.00	12.00	24.00
9,10-Two-part marijuana story; Kerry smokes marijuana-No. 10	7.00	20.00	40.00
11-15	3.00	9.00	18.00
16-18,21-33	2.50	7.00	14.00
19,20-Two-part drug mention story	4.50	13.00	26.00
. . . in the Case of the Sleeping City-(1951-Publishers Synd.)-16 pg. giveaway for armed forces; paper cover	2.50	7.00	14.00

NOTE: ***Berg*** *a-5.* ***Powell*** *a-11-13, 23.*

KEWPIES
1949
Will Eisner Publications

	Good	Fine	Mint
1-Feiffer-a; used in **SOTI** in a non-seductive context, pg. 35	10.00	30.00	60.00

KEY COMICS
Jan, 1944 - No. 5, Aug, 1946
Consolidated Magazines

	Good	Fine	Mint
1-The Key, Will-O-The-Wisp begin	3.00	8.00	16.00
2-5	2.00	5.00	10.00

KEY COMICS
1951 - 1956 (32 pages) (Giveaway)
Key Clothing Co./Peterson Clothing

Contains a comic from different publishers bound with new cover. Cover changed each year. Many combinations possible. Distributed in Nebraska, Iowa, & Kansas. Contents would determine price, 40-60 percent of original.

KEY RING COMICS
1941 (16 pgs.; two colors) (sold 5 for 10 cents)
Dell Publishing Co.

	Good	Fine	Mint
1-Sky Hawk	2.00	6.00	12.00
1-Viking Carter	2.00	6.00	12.00
1-Features Sleepy Samson	2.00	6.00	12.00
1-Origin Greg Gilday r-/War Comics No. 2	2.50	7.00	14.00
1-Radior(Super hero)	2.50	7.00	14.00

NOTE: *Each book has two holes in spine to put in binder.*

KID CARROTS
September, 1953
St. John Publishing Co.

	Good	Fine	Mint
1	1.00	3.00	6.00

KID COLT OUTLAW (. . . Hero of the West No. 1-?) (Also see Wisco)
Aug, 1948 - No. 139, Mar, 1968; No. 140, Nov, 1969 - Present
No. 1-102, Marvel/Atlas(LMC); No. 103 on, Marvel

	Good	Fine	Mint
1	14.00	40.00	80.00
2	7.00	20.00	40.00
3-5	4.00	12.00	24.00
6-10	3.00	8.00	16.00
11-Origin	3.50	10.00	20.00
12-30	1.75	5.00	10.00
31-47,49,50	1.50	4.00	8.00
48-Kubert-a	1.75	5.00	10.00
51-53,55,56	1.00	3.00	6.00
54-Williamson/Maneely-c	2.00	6.00	12.00
57-60,66: 4-pg. Williamson-a in all. 59-Reprint Rawhide Kid No. 79	3.00	9.00	18.00
61-63,67-78,80-85	.70	2.00	4.00
64,65-Crandall-a	1.00	3.00	6.00
79-Origin retold	1.00	3.00	6.00
86-Kirby-a(r)	.70	2.00	4.00
87-Davis-a(r)	1.00	3.00	6.00
88,89-Williamson-a in both (4 pgs.). 89-Redrawn Matt Slade No. 2	2.00	6.00	12.00
90-92,94,95,97-118,120	.40	1.20	2.40
93,96,119-Kirby-a	.50	1.40	2.80
121-140: 121-Rawhide Kid x-over. 125-Two-Gun Kid x-over. 130-132 -68pg. issues with one new story each; 130-Origin. 132-Last Jack Keller ish. 140-Reprints begin		.60	1.20
141-146,148-160: 141-New Two-Gun Kid story. 156-Giant; reprints		.50	1.00
147-Williamson-a(r)		.60	1.20
161-169,171		.30	.60
170,172-Williamson-a(r); origin retold No. 170		.40	.80
173-200		.30	.60
201-227		.30	.60
. . . Album (no date; 1950's; Atlas Comics)-132 pgs.; random binding, cardboard cover, B&W stories; contents can vary	4.00	12.00	24.00
Giant Size 1(1/75), 2(4/75), 3(7/75)		.60	1.20

NOTE: ***Crandall*** *a-140r, 167r.* ***Everett*** *a-137i.* ***Kirby*** *a-176(part); c-87, 92-95, 97, 99-112, 114-117, 121-123, 197r.* ***Morrow*** *a-173r.* ***Severin*** *c-58.* ***Whitney*** *a-141r.* ***Wildey*** *a-82.* ***Woodbridge*** *a-64, 81. Black Rider in No. 33, 35-37, 41, 44, 74, 86. Iron Mask in No. 110, 114, 121, 127. Sam Hawk in No. 84, 101, 111, 121, 146, 174, 181, 188.*

KID COWBOY (Also see Approved Comics No. 4)
1950 - 1954 (painted covers)
Ziff-Davis Publ./St. John (Approved Comics)

	Good	Fine	Mint
1-Lucy Belle begins	2.00	6.00	12.00
2-14: 11-Bondage-c	1.50	4.00	8.00

NOTE: ***Berg*** *a-5.* ***Maneely*** *c-2.*

KIDDIE KAPERS
Oct, 1957; 1963 - 1964
Decker Publ. (Red Top-Farrell)

	Good	Fine	Mint
1(no date, 1945-46?)	.50	1.50	3.00
1(10/57)(Decker)-Little Bit reprints from Kiddie Karnival	.50	1.50	3.00

KIDDIE KAPERS (continued)

	Good	Fine	Mint
Super Reprint No. 10('63), 14('63), 15,17('64), 18('64)	.35	1.00	2.00

KIDDIE KARNIVAL
1952 (100 pgs.) (One Shot)
Ziff-Davis Publ. Co. (Approved Comics)

nn-Rebound Little Bit No. 1,2	3.00	8.00	16.00

KID ETERNITY (Becomes Buccaneers) (See Hit)
Spring, 1946 - No. 18, Nov, 1949
Quality Comics Group

1	30.00	80.00	160.00
2	11.00	32.00	64.00
3-Mac Raboy-a	12.00	36.00	72.00
4-10	5.50	16.00	32.00
11-18	4.00	12.00	24.00

KID FROM DODGE CITY, THE
July, 1957 - No. 2, Sept, 1957
Atlas Comics (MMC)

1	1.00	3.00	6.00
2-Everett-c	.70	2.00	4.00

KID FROM TEXAS, THE (A Texas Ranger)
June, 1957 - No. 2, Aug, 1957
Atlas Comics (CSI)

1-Powell-a	1.50	4.00	8.00
2	.85	2.50	5.00

KID KOKO
1958
I. W. Enterprises

Reprint No. 1,2-(reprints M.E.'s Koko & Kola No. 4, 1947)	.50	1.50	3.00

KID KOMICS (. . . Movie Komics No. 11)
Feb, 1943 - No. 10, Spring, 1946
Timely Comics

1-Origin Captain Wonder & sidekick Tim Mullrooney; intro. Subbie, the Sea-Going Lad, Pinto Pete, & Trixy Trouble; Knuckles & Whitewash Jones only app.; Wolverton art, 7 pgs.	75.00	225.00	450.00
2-The Young Allies, Red Hawk, & Tommy Tyme begin; last Captain Wonder & Subbie	45.00	130.00	260.00
3-The Vision & Daredevils app.	30.00	90.00	180.00
4-The Destroyer begins; Sub-Mariner app.; Red Hawk & Tommy Tyme end	25.00	70.00	140.00
5,6	17.00	50.00	100.00
7-10: The Whizzer app. 7; Destroyer not in No. 7,8; 10-Last Destroyer, Young Allies & Whizzer	12.00	35.00	70.00

KID MONTANA (Formerly Davy Crockett Frontier Fighter; The Gunfighters No. 51 on)
V2No.9, Nov, 1957 - No. 50, Mar, 1965
Charlton Comics

V2No.9,10	.30	.80	1.60
11-20		.50	1.00
21-50		.40	.80

NOTE: *Title change to Montana Kid on cover only on No. 44; remained Kid Montana on inside.*

KID MOVIE KOMICS (Formerly Kid Komics; Rusty No. 12 on)
No. 11, Summer, 1946
Timely Comics

11-Silly Seal & Ziggy Pig; 2 pgs. Kurtzman ''Hey Look'' plus 6 pg. story	5.50	16.00	32.00

KIDNAPPED (See 4-Color No. 1101 & Movie Comics)

KIDNAP RACKET (See Comics Hits No. 57)

KID SLADE GUNFIGHTER (Formerly Matt Slade. . .)
No. 5, Jan, 1957 - No. 8, July, 1957
Atlas Comics (SPI)

	Good	Fine	Mint
5-Severin-a	1.20	3.50	7.00
6,8	.85	2.50	5.00
7-Williamson/Mayo-a, 4 pgs.	3.00	8.00	16.00

KID ZOO COMICS
July, 1948
Street & Smith Publications

1	.85	2.50	5.00

KILLERS, THE
1947 - 1948 (No month)
Magazine Enterprises

1-Mr. Zin, the Hatchet Killer; mentioned in **SOTI**, pgs. 179,180; Used by N. Y. Legis. Comm. L. B. Cole-c	50.00	150.00	300.00
2-(Scarce)-Hashish smoking story; ''Dying, Dying, Dead'' drug story; Whitney, Ingels-a; Whitney hanging-c	50.00	150.00	300.00

KILROYS, THE
June-July, 1947 - No. 54, June-July, 1955
B&I Publ. Co. No. 1-19/American Comics Group

1	3.00	8.00	16.00
2-5	1.50	4.00	8.00
6-10: 8-Milt Gross's Moronica	.85	2.50	5.00
11-30	.70	2.00	4.00
31-47,50-54	.35	1.00	2.00
48,49-(3-D effect)	2.00	6.00	12.00

KING CLASSICS
1977 (85 cents each) (36 pages, cardboard covers)
King Features (Printed in Spain for U.S. distr.)

1-Connecticut Yankee, 2-Last of the Mohicans, 3-Moby Dick, 4-Robin Hood, 5-Swiss Family Robinson, 6-Robinson Crusoe, 7-Treasure Island, 8-20,000 Leagues, 9-Christmas Carol, 10-Huck Finn, 11-Around the World in 80 Days, 12-Davy Crockett, 13-Don Quixote, 14-Gold Bug, 15-Ivanhoe, 16-Three Musketeers, 17-Baron Munchausen, 18-Alice in Wonderland, 19-Black Arrow, 20-Five Weeks in a Balloon, 21-Great Expectations, 22-Gulliver's Travels, 23-Prince & Pauper, 24-Lawrence of Arabia each. 50 1.00

NOTE: *The first eight issues were not numbered. Issues No. 25-32 were advertised but not published.*

KING COLT (See 4-Color No. 651)

KING COMICS (Strip reprints)
Apr, 1936 - No. 159, Feb, 1952 (Winter on cover)
David McKay Publications/Standard No. 159

1-Flash Gordon by Alex Raymond; Brick Bradford, Mandrake the Magician & Popeye begin	100.00	300.00	600.00
2	50.00	150.00	300.00
3	35.00	100.00	200.00
4	20.00	70.00	140.00
5	17.00	55.00	110.00
6-10	14.00	40.00	80.00
11-20	10.00	30.00	60.00
21-30	8.00	24.00	48.00
31-49: 33-Last Segar Popeye	7.00	20.00	40.00
50-The Lone Ranger begins	7.00	20.00	40.00
51-60: 52-Barney Baxter begins?	5.50	16.00	32.00
61-The Phantom begins	5.00	14.00	28.00
62-100	4.00	12.00	24.00
101-115-Last Raymond issue	3.50	10.00	20.00
116-145	2.50	7.00	14.00
146,147-Prince Valiant in both	2.00	6.00	12.00
148-155-Flash Gordon ends	2.00	6.00	12.00
156-159	1.75	5.00	10.00

KING CONAN

Kid Komics #3, © MCG

The Kilroys #37, © ACG

King Comics #147, © DMP

King Conan #1, © MCG

King Of The Royal Mtd. #14, © DELL

Kobra #4, © DC

KING CONAN (continued)
March, 1980 - Present
Marvel Comics Group

	Good	Fine	Mint
1	.40	1.10	2.20
2-8: 4-Death of Thoth Amon		.60	1.20

NOTE: ***Buscema*** *a-1p-8p; c-1-5, 7, 8.* ***Simonson*** *c-6.*

KING KONG (See Movie Comics)

KING LEONARDO & HIS SHORT SUBJECTS (TV)
1962 - No. 4, Sept, 1963
Dell Publishing Co./Gold Key

	Good	Fine	Mint
4-Color 1242,1278	.85	2.50	5.00
01390-207(5-7/62)(Dell)	.85	2.50	5.00
1-4(10/62-63)	.70	2.00	4.00

KING LOUIE & MOWGLI
May, 1968 (Disney)
Gold Key

	Good	Fine	Mint
1 (10223-805)	.70	2.00	4.00

KING OF BAD MEN OF DEADWOOD
1950
Avon Periodicals

	Good	Fine	Mint
nn-Kinstler-c; Kamen/Feldstein-a r-/Cowpuncher 2	7.00	20.00	40.00

KING OF DIAMONDS (TV)
July-Sept, 1962
Dell Publishing Co.

	Good	Fine	Mint
01-391-209-Photo-c	1.00	3.00	6.00

KING OF KINGS (See 4-Color No. 1236)

KING OF THE ROYAL MOUNTED (See Black & White No. 9, Feature Book No. 1 (McKay), Nickel Books, & Super Book No. 2,6)

KING OF THE ROYAL MOUNTED (Zane Grey's)
No. 8, June-Aug, 1952 - No. 28, Mar-May, 1958
Dell Publishing Co.

	Good	Fine	Mint
4-Color 207('48)	5.50	16.00	32.00
4-Color 265,283	4.00	12.00	24.00
4-Color 310,340	3.00	8.00	16.00
4-Color 363,384	2.50	7.00	14.00
8-28('58)	2.00	5.00	10.00
4-Color 935('58)	2.00	5.00	10.00

NOTE: *4-Color No. 207,265,283,310,340,363,384 are all newspaper reprints with* ***Jim Gary*** *art. No. 8 on are all Dell originals.*

KING RICHARD & THE CRUSADERS (See 4-Color No. 588)

KING SOLOMON'S MINES
1951 (Movie)
Avon Periodicals

	Good	Fine	Mint
nn(No.1 on 1st page)	17.00	50.00	100.00

KISS (See Marvel Comics Super Special & Howard the Duck No. 12)

KIT CARSON (See Frontier Fighters)

KIT CARSON (Formerly All True Detective Cases No. 4; Fighting Davy Crockett No. 9)
6/51 - No. 3, 12/51; No. 5, 11-12/54 - No. 8, 9/55
Avon Periodicals

	Good	Fine	Mint
nn(No.1)	3.50	10.00	20.00
2(8/51), 3(12/51)	2.50	7.00	14.00
5-6,8(1954)	2.00	6.00	12.00
7-Kinstler-a(2)	2.50	7.00	14.00
I.W. Reprint No. 10('63)	.85	2.50	5.00

NOTE: ***Kinstler*** *c-1,3,5,6-8.*

KIT CARSON & THE BLACKFEET WARRIORS
1953
Realistic

	Good	Fine	Mint
nn-Reprint; Kinstler-c	3.00	9.00	18.00

KIT KARTER
May-July, 1962
Dell Publishing Co.

	Good	Fine	Mint
1	.85	2.50	5.00

KITTY
October, 1948
St. John Publishing Co.

	Good	Fine	Mint
1-Lily Renee-a	1.20	3.50	7.00

KLARER GIVEAWAYS (See Wisco)

KNIGHTS OF THE ROUND TABLE (See 4-Color No. 540)

KNIGHTS OF THE ROUND TABLE
No. 10, April, 1957
Pines Comics

	Good	Fine	Mint
10	.70	2.00	4.00

KNIGHTS OF THE ROUND TABLE
Nov-Jan, 1964
Dell Publishing Co.

	Good	Fine	Mint
1 (12-397-401)	1.00	3.00	6.00

KNOCK KNOCK
1936 (32 pages) (B&W)
Gerona Publications

	Good	Fine	Mint
1-Bob Dunn-a	4.00	12.00	24.00

KNOCKOUT ADVENTURES
1954
Fiction House Magazines

	Good	Fine	Mint
1-Reprints/Fight Comics No. 53	2.00	5.00	10.00

KNOW YOUR MASS
1958 (100 Pg. Giant) (35 cents) (square binding)
Catechetical Guild

	Good	Fine	Mint
303-In color	3.50	10.00	20.00

KOBRA (See DC Special Series No. 1)
Feb-Mar, 1976 - No. 7, Mar-Apr, 1977
National Periodical Publications

	Good	Fine	Mint
1-Art plotted by Kirby		.50	1.00
2-7: 2-Adams-a, 1pg. ad		.30	.60

NOTE: ***Kubert*** *c-4.* ***Nasser*** *a-6, 7.*

KOKEY KOALA
May, 1952
Toby Press

	Good	Fine	Mint
1	1.50	4.00	8.00

KOKO & KOLA
Fall, 1946 - No. 5, May, 1947; No. 6, 1950
Compix/Magazine Enterprises

	Good	Fine	Mint
1-5,6(A-1 28)	.85	2.50	5.00

KO KOMICS
October, 1945
Gerona Publications

	Good	Fine	Mint
1-The Duke of Darkness & The Menace (hero)	3.50	10.00	20.00

KOMIC KARTOONS
Fall, 1945 - No. 2, Winter, 1945
Timely Comics

	Good	Fine	Mint
1,2	3.50	10.00	20.00

KOMIK PAGES
April, 1945
Harry 'A' Chesler, Jr. (Our Army, Inc.)

KOMIK PAGES (continued)

	Good	Fine	Mint
10(No.1 on inside)-Land O' Nod by Rick Yager (2 pgs.), Animal Crackers, Foxy GrandPa, Tom, Dick & Mary, Cheerio Minstrels, Red Starr plus other 1-2 pg. strips; Cole-a; all-r	3.50	10.00	20.00

KONA (. . . Monarch of Monster Isle)
Feb-Apr, 1962 - No. 21, Jan-Mar, 1967
Dell Publishing Co.

4-Color 1256	1.50	4.00	8.00
2-10: 4-Anak begins	.70	2.00	4.00
11-21	.40	1.20	2.40

KONGA (Fantastic Giants No. 24) (See Return of. . .)
1960; No. 2, Aug, 1961 - No. 23, Nov, 1965
Charlton Comics

1(1960)-Based on movie	9.00	18.00	36.00
2-5	3.50	10.00	20.00
6-15	2.00	5.00	10.00
16-23	.85	2.50	5.00

NOTE: ***Ditko*** *a-1, 3-15; c-4, 6-9.* ***Glanzman*** *a-12.* ***Montes & Bache*** *a-16-23.*

KONGA'S REVENGE (Formerly Return of. . .)
No. 2, Summer, 1963 - No. 3, Fall, 1954; Dec, 1968
Charlton Comics

2,3: 2-Ditko c/a	2.00	5.00	10.00
1('68)-Reprints Konga's Revenge No. 3	.85	2.50	5.00

KONG THE UNTAMED
June-July, 1975 - No. 5, Feb-Mar, 1976
National Periodical Publications

1	.30	.80	1.60
2-5		.50	1.00

NOTE: ***Alcala*** *a-1-3.* ***Wrightson*** *c-1,2.*

KOOKIE
Feb-Apr, 1962 - No. 2, May-July, 1962
Dell Publishing Co.

1,2-Written by John Stanley; Bill Williams-a	1.50	4.00	8.00

K. O. PUNCH, THE (Also see Lucky Fights It Through)
1948 (Educational giveaway)
E. C. Comics

Feldstein-splash; Kamen-a	150.00	300.00	600.00

KORAK, SON OF TARZAN (Edgar Rice Burroughs)
Jan, 1964 - No. 45, Jan, 1972
Gold Key

1-Russ Manning-a	2.00	6.00	12.00
2-11-Russ Manning-a	1.00	3.00	6.00
12-21: 14-Jon of the Kalahari ends. 15-Mabu, Jungle Boy begins; Manning-a No. 21	.50	1.50	3.00
22-30	.40	1.20	2.40
31-45	.30	.90	1.80

KORAK, SON OF TARZAN (Tarzan Family No. 60 on)
No. 46, May-June, 1972 - No. 56, Feb-Mar, 1974; No. 57, May-June, 1975 - No. 59, Sept-Oct, 1975 (Edgar Rice Burroughs)
National Periodical Publications

46-(52 pgs.)-Carson of Venus begins (origin); Pellucidar feature	.40	1.20	2.40
47,48,50	.30	.80	1.60
49-Origin Korak retold	.30	.80	1.60
51-56-Carson of Venus ends		.60	1.20
57-59		.50	1.00

NOTE: ***Anderson*** *a-52-56.* ***Kaluta*** *a-46-56. All have covers by* ***Joe Kubert.*** ***Manning*** *strip reprints-No. 57-59.*

KORG: 70,000 B. C.
May, 1975 - No. 9, Nov, 1976 (Hanna-Barbera)
Charlton Comics

	Good	Fine	Mint
1		.50	1.00
2-9		.40	.80

KORNER KID COMICS
1947
Four Star Publications

1	1.20	3.50	7.00

KOSHER COMICS
1966 ($1.00)
Parallax

"Supermax" & "Tishman of the Apes"	1.50	4.50	9.00

KRAZY KAT
1946 (Hardcover)
Holt

Reprints daily & Sunday strips by Herriman	25.00	75.00	150.00
with dust jacket (Rare). . . .	35.00	100.00	200.00

KRAZY KAT (. . .& Ignatz the Mouse early issues)
May-June, 1951 - Jan, 1964 (None by Herriman)
Dell Publishing Co./Gold Key

1(1951)	3.00	8.00	16.00
2-5	2.00	5.00	10.00
4-Color 454,504	1.50	4.00	8.00
4-Color 548,619,696	1.20	3.50	7.00
1(10098-401)(1/64-Gold Key)	1.00	3.00	6.00

KRAZY KAT (See March of Comics No. 72,87)

KRAZY KOMICS (1st Series) (Cindy No. 27 on)
July, 1942 - No. 26, 1946
Timely Comics (USA No. 1-21/JPC No. 22-26)

1	9.00	25.00	50.00
2-Wolverton-a, 5pgs.	5.00	14.00	28.00
3-10	3.00	8.00	16.00
11,13,14	1.50	4.50	9.00
12-Timely's entire art staff drew themselves into a Creeper story	3.00	8.00	16.00
15-Has "Super Soldier" by Pfc. Stan Lee	1.50	4.50	9.00
16-24,26	1.20	3.50	7.00
25-Kurtzman-a, 6 pgs.	3.00	8.00	16.00

KRAZY KOMICS (2nd Series) (Also see Ziggy Pig)
Aug, 1948 - No. 6, 1949
Timely/Marvel Comics

1-Wolverton (10 pgs.) & Kurtzman (8 pgs.)-a	12.00	35.00	70.00
2-Wolverton-a, 10 pgs.	6.00	18.00	36.00
3-6	1.20	3.50	7.00

KRAZY KROW
Summer, 1945 - No. 7, 1946
Marvel Comics (ZPC)

1	1.50	4.00	8.00
2-7	.70	2.00	4.00
I.W. Reprint No. 1('57), 2('58), 7	.30	.80	1.60

KRAZYLIFE
1945 (no month)
Fox Features Syndicate

1-Funny animal	1.50	4.00	8.00

KRIM-KO COMICS
1936 - 1939 (4 pg. giveaway) (weekly)
Krim-ko Chocolate Drink

Lola, Secret Agent; 184 issues - all original stories each. . . .	1.50	4.00	8.00

Kona #11, © DELL

Konga #13, © CC

Korak #2, © GK

Krypton Chronicles #1, © DC

Lady Luck #89, © QUA

Land Of The Lost #2, © WMG

KROFFT SUPERSHOW
April, 1978 - No. 6, Jan, 1979
Gold Key

	Good	Fine	Mint
1		.30	.60
2-6		.15	.30

KRYPTON CHRONICLES
Sept, 1981 - Present
DC Comics

1		.50	1.00
2,3		.40	.80

KULL & THE BARBARIANS (Magazine)
May, 1975 - No. 3, Sept, 1975 (B&W) ($1.00)
Marvel Comics Group

1-Andru/Wood-r/Kull No. 1; 2 pgs. Adams; Gil Kane, Severin-a	.60	1.80	3.60
2-Red Sonja by Chaykin begins; Adams-i; Gil Kane-a	.50	1.50	3.00
3-Origin Red Sonja by Chaykin; Adams-a; Solomon Kane app.	.50	1.50	3.00

KULL THE CONQUEROR (. . . the Destroyer No. 11 on)
June, 1971 - No. 2, Aug, 1971; No. 3, July, 1972 - No. 15, Aug, 1974; No. 16, Aug, 1976 - No. 29, Oct, 1978
Marvel Comics Group

1-Andru/Wood-a; origin Kull	1.00	3.00	6.00
2,3	.50	1.50	3.00
4,5	.40	1.20	2.40
6-10	.30	.90	1.80
11-15-Ploog-a	.30	.80	1.60
16-29		.40	.80

NOTE: *No. 1,2,7-9,11 are based on Robert E. Howard stories.* ***Alcala*** *inks-17-20; c-24.* ***Ditko*** *a-12r, 15r.* ***Gil Kane*** *c-21.* ***Ploog*** *c-11-13.* ***Severin*** *a-2-9.* ***Starlin*** *c-14.*

KUNG FU (See Deadly Hands of . . ., & Master of . . .)

KUNG FU FIGHTER (See Richard Dragon . . .)

LABOR IS A PARTNER
1949 (32 pgs. in color; paper cover)
Catechetical Guild Educational Society

nn-Anti-communism	30.00	80.00	160.00
Confidential Preview-(B&W, 8½x11'', saddle stitched)-only one known copy; text varies from color version, advertises next book on secularism (If the Devil Would Talk)	35.00	100.00	200.00

LAD: A DOG
1961 - No. 2, July-Sept, 1962
Dell Publishing Co.

4-Color 1303 (movie)	1.00	3.00	6.00
2	.85	2.50	5.00

LADY AND THE TRAMP (See 4-Color No. 629,634, & Movie Classics and Comics)

LADY AND THE TRAMP IN "BUTTER LATE THAN NEVER"
1955 (14 pgs.) (Walt Disney)
American Dairy Association (Premium)

	2.00	6.00	12.00

LADY BOUNTIFUL
1917 (10¼x13½''; 24 pgs.; B&W; cardboard cover)
Saalfield Publ. Co./Press Publ. Co.

by Gene Carr; 2 panels per page	4.00	12.00	24.00

LADY COP (See First Issue Special)

LADY LUCK (Formerly Smash No. 1-85)
Dec, 1949 - No. 90, Aug, 1950
Quality Comics Group

86(No.1)	17.00	50.00	90.00
87-90	14.00	40.00	70.00

LAFF-A-LYMPICS (See The Funtastic World of Hanna-Barbera)
Mar, 1978 - No. 13, Mar, 1979
Marvel Comics Group

	Good	Fine	Mint
1		.30	.60
2-13		.25	.50

LAFFY-DAFFY COMICS
Feb, 1945 - No. 2, March, 1945
Rural Home Publ. Co.

1,2	.85	2.50	5.00

LANA (Little Lana & True Life Tales No. 8 on?)
Aug, 1948 - No. 7, Aug, 1949
Marvel Comics (MjMC)

1	2.50	7.00	14.00
2-Kurtzman's "Hey Look"	3.00	8.00	16.00
3-7	1.50	4.00	8.00

LANCELOT & GUINEVERE (See Movie Classics)

LANCELOT LINK, SECRET CHIMP (TV)
April, 1971 - No. 8, Feb, 1973
Gold Key

1-Photo-c	.50	1.50	3.00
2-8	.35	1.00	2.00

LANCE O'CASEY (See Mighty Midget Comics)
Spring, 1946 - No. 3, Fall, 1946; No. 4, Summer, 1948
Fawcett Publications

1	4.00	12.00	24.00
2-4	3.00	8.00	16.00

LANCER (TV)
Feb, 1969 - No. 3, Sept, 1969
Gold Key

1	1.00	3.00	6.00
2,3	.70	2.00	4.00

LAND OF THE GIANTS (TV)
Nov, 1968 - No. 5, Sept, 1969
Gold Key

1-Bondage photo-c	1.00	3.00	6.00
2-5	.70	2.00	4.00

LAND OF THE LOST COMICS (Radio)
July-Aug, 1946 - No. 9, Spring, 1948
E. C. Comics

1	10.00	30.00	60.00
2-9	7.00	20.00	40.00

LAND UNKNOWN, THE (See 4-Color No. 845)

LARAMIE (TV)
Aug, 1960 - July, 1962
Dell Publishing Co./Gold Key

4-Color 1125,1223,1284	1.00	3.00	6.00
01-418-207(Gold Key?)	.85	2.50	5.00

LAREDO (TV)
June, 1966
Gold Key

1 (10179-606)	.85	2.50	5.00

LARGE FEATURE COMIC (Continuation of Black & White)
1941 - 1943 (B&W interior; 8½x11-3/8'' with thin slick color cover; 52 pages)
Dell Publishing Co.

25-Smilin' Jack	14.00	40.00	80.00
26-Smitty	8.00	22.00	45.00
27-Terry & the Pirates	20.00	60.00	120.00
28-Grin & Bear It	5.00	14.00	28.00
29-Moon Mullins	7.00	20.00	40.00
30-Tillie the Toiler	6.00	18.00	36.00

LARGE FEATURE COMIC (continued)

	Good	Fine	Mint
1-Peter Rabbit by Cady	25.00	70.00	140.00
2-Winnie Winkle	6.00	18.00	36.00
3-Dick Tracy	30.00	80.00	160.00
4-Tiny Tim	12.00	35.00	70.00
5-Toots & Casper	5.00	14.00	28.00
6-Terry & the Pirates	20.00	60.00	120.00
7-Pluto Saves the Ship (Disney) written by Carl Barks, Jack Hannah, & Nick George	70.00	180.00	360.00
8-Bugs Bunny ('42)	55.00	160.00	320.00
9-Bringing Up Father	5.00	15.00	30.00
10-Popeye (Thimble Theatre)	20.00	60.00	120.00
11-Barney Google & Snuffy Smith	8.00	25.00	50.00
12-Private Buck	5.00	14.00	28.00

NOTE: *Above rarely found in fine or mint condition.*

LARRY DOBY, BASEBALL HERO
1950 (Cleveland Indians)
Fawcett Publications

	Good	Fine	Mint
nn-Bill Ward-a	10.00	30.00	60.00

LARS OF MARS
May-June, 1951 - No. 11, July-Aug, 1951
Ziff-Davis Publishing Co.

	Good	Fine	Mint
10-Origin; Anderson-a(3) in each	14.00	40.00	80.00
11-Painted-c	14.00	40.00	80.00

LASH LARUE WESTERN
June, 1949 - No. 46, Jan, 1954
Fawcett Publications

	Good	Fine	Mint
1	14.00	40.00	80.00
2-5	8.00	24.00	48.00
6-10: 7-Drug mention	5.50	16.00	32.00
11-20: 15-Drug mention	3.50	10.00	20.00
21-46: 31-Drug mention	3.00	8.00	16.00

LASH LARUE WESTERN
No. 47, 1954 - No. 84, June, 1961
Charlton Comics

	Good	Fine	Mint
47-66,69,70	1.20	3.50	7.00
67,68-(68 pgs.)	1.50	4.00	8.00
71-84	.85	2.50	5.00

LASSIE (M-G-M's. . . No. 1-36)
Oct-Dec, 1950 - No. 70, July, 1969
Dell Publishing Co./Gold Key No. 59 (10/62) on

	Good	Fine	Mint
1	2.00	6.00	12.00
2-10	1.00	3.00	6.00
11-19: 12-Rocky Langford (Lassie's master) marries Gerry Lawrence. 15-1st app. Timbu	.85	2.50	5.00
20-22-Matt Baker-a	1.50	4.00	8.00
23-40: 33-Robinson-a. 39-1st app. Timmy as Lassie picks up her TV family	.50	1.50	3.00
41-70: 63-Last Timmy. 64-r-/No. 19. 65-Forest Ranger Corey Stuart begins, ends No. 69. 70-Forest Rangers Bob Ericson & Scott Turner app. (Lassie's new masters)	.35	1.00	2.00
11193(1979-Golden Press)-224 pgs.; $1.95	.50	1.50	3.00
The Adventures of. . .(Red Heart Dog Food giveaway, 1949)	3.00	8.00	16.00
Kite Fun Book('73)-Pacific Gas & Elect. Co., Sou. Calif. Edison & Florida Power & Light(16 pgs.; 5x7'')	2.00	6.00	12.00

(See March of Comics No. 210,217,230,254,266,278,296,308,324, 334,346,358,370,381,394,411)

LAST HUNT, THE (See 4-Color No. 678)

LAST OF THE COMANCHES
1953 (Movie)
Avon Periodicals

	Good	Fine	Mint
nn-Kinstler c/a, 21pgs.; Ravielli-a	6.00	18.00	36.00

LAST OF THE ERIES, THE (See American Graphics)

LAST OF THE FAST GUNS, THE (See 4-Color No. 925)

LAST OF THE MOHICANS (See King Classics)

LAST TRAIN FROM GUN HILL (See 4-Color No. 1012)

LATEST ADVENTURES OF FOXY GRANDPA (See Foxy. . .)

LATEST COMICS (Super Duper No. 3?)
March, 1945
Spotlight Publ./Palace Promotions (Jubilee)

	Good	Fine	Mint
1-Super Duper	1.00	3.00	6.00
2-Bee-29 (no date)	1.00	3.00	6.00

LAUGH COMICS (Formerly Black Hood No. 1-19) (Laugh No. 226 on)
No. 20, Fall, 1946 - Present
Archie Publications (Close-Up)

	Good	Fine	Mint
20-Archie & Katy Keene begin	20.00	60.00	120.00
21-23,25	10.00	30.00	60.00
24-''Pipsy'' by Kirby, 6 pgs.	11.00	32.00	64.00
26-30	6.00	18.00	36.00
31-40	4.00	12.00	24.00
41-70: 41,67-Debbi by Bill Woggon	3.00	8.00	16.00
71-100	2.00	5.00	10.00
101-126	1.00	3.00	6.00
127,129-131,133,135,140-142,144-Jaguar app.; The Fly-No. 129	1.00	3.00	6.00
128,132,134,136,137,139-Fly app.	1.00	3.00	6.00
138-Flyman & Flygirl app.	1.00	3.00	6.00
143-Flygirl app.	1.00	3.00	6.00
145-160	.70	2.00	4.00
161-165,167-180	.40	1.20	2.40
166-Beatles-c	.50	1.50	3.00
181-220		.60	1.20
221-260		.40	.80
261-368		.30	.60

NOTE: *Josie app.-No. 145, 160, 164. Katy Keene app.-No. 20, 21, 41, 47, 49, 52, 54-56, 59, 65, 67, 82, 85, 88-90, 93, 95, 99-103, 106, 107, 110, 111, 113, 114, 116, 118, 119, 121, 122, 124, 130.*

LAUGH COMICS DIGEST
8/74; No. 2, 9/75; No. 3, 3/76 - Present (160 pgs.)
Archie Publications (Close-Up No. 1, 3 on)

	Good	Fine	Mint
1-Adams-a	.35	1.00	2.00
2,7,8,19-Adams-a		.60	1.20
3-6,9,10		.40	.80
11-18,20-24,26,28-37		.30	.60
25,27-Katy Keene, The Jaguar stories		.40	.80

LAUGH COMIX (Formerly Top Notch Laugh; becomes Suzie No. 49 on)
No. 46, Summer, 1944 - No. 48, Winter, 1944-45
MLJ Magazines

	Good	Fine	Mint
46-48-Wilbur & Suzie	3.50	10.00	20.00

LAUGH-IN MAGAZINE (Magazine)
Oct, 1968 - No. 12, Oct, 1969 (50 cents) (Satire)
Laufer Publ. Co.

	Good	Fine	Mint
V1No.1	.50	1.50	3.00
2-12	.30	.80	1.60

LAUREL & HARDY (See March of Comics No. 302,314)

LAUREL AND HARDY (. . .Comics)
March, 1949 - No. 28, 1951
St. John Publishing Co.

	Good	Fine	Mint
1	10.00	28.00	56.00
2,3	5.00	14.00	28.00
4-10	3.00	8.00	16.00
11-28	2.00	6.00	12.00

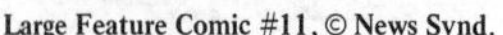
Large Feature Comic #11, © News Synd.

Lassie #2, © DELL

Laugh Comics #41, © AP

Law Against Crime #3, © STAR

Leading Comics #3, © DC

Legend Of Jesse James #1, © GK

LAUREL AND HARDY (TV)
Oct, 1962 - No. 4, Sept-Nov, 1963
Dell Publishing Co.

	Good	Fine	Mint
12-423-210 (8-10/62)	1.50	4.00	8.00
2-4 (Dell)	1.00	3.00	6.00

LAUREL AND HARDY
Jan, 1967 - No. 2, Oct, 1967 (Larry Harmon's)
Gold Key

	Good	Fine	Mint
1,2	.85	2.50	5.00

LAUREL AND HARDY (. . . Comics)
July-Aug, 1972 (50 Cents, Digest) (Larry Harmon's)
National Periodical Publications

	Good	Fine	Mint
1	.35	1.00	2.00

LAW AGAINST CRIME (Law-Crime on cover)
April, 1948 - No. 3, Aug, 1948
Essenkay Publishing Co.

	Good	Fine	Mint
1-(No.1-3: ½ funny animal, ½ crime)-L. B. Cole electrocution-c/a	14.00	40.00	80.00
2-L. B. Cole c/a	10.00	30.00	60.00
3-L. B. Cole c/a; used in **SOTI**, pg. 180,181 & illo-''The wish to hurt or kill couples in lovers' lanes;'' reprinted in All-Famous Crime No. 9	15.00	45.00	90.00

LAWBREAKERS (. . . Suspense Stories No. 9 on)
Mar, 1951 - No. 9, Oct-Nov, 1952 (two No. 9's)
Law and Order Magazines (Charlton Comics)

	Good	Fine	Mint
1	3.00	9.00	18.00
2,3,5,6,8,9	1.50	4.50	9.00
4-''White Death'' junkie story	3.50	10.00	20.00
7-''The Deadly Dopesters'' drug story	3.00	9.00	18.00

LAWBREAKERS ALWAYS LOSE!
Spring, 1948 - No. 10, Oct, 1949
Marvel Comics (CBS)

	Good	Fine	Mint
1-Kurtzman-a, 2 pgs.	5.50	16.00	32.00
2-5	2.50	7.00	14.00
6(2/49)-Has editorial defense against charges of Dr. Wertham	3.00	9.00	18.00
7-Used in **SOTI**, illo-''Comic-book philosophy;''	6.00	18.00	36.00
8-10	1.20	3.50	7.00

LAWBREAKERS SUSPENSE STORIES (Formerly Lawbreakers; Strange Suspense Stories No. 16 on)
No. 9, Mar, 1953 - No. 15, Nov, 1953
Capitol Stories/Charlton Comics

	Good	Fine	Mint
9,10,12-14	2.00	6.00	12.00
11-Severed tongues c/story & woman negligee scene	10.00	28.00	56.00
15-Acid-in-face c/story; hands dissolved in acid story	5.00	15.00	30.00

LAW-CRIME (See Law Against Crime)

LAWMAN (TV)
1958 - No. 11, Apr-June, 1962
Dell Publishing Co.

	Good	Fine	Mint
4-Color 970,1035('58-60)	1.00	3.00	6.00
3(2-4/60)-Toth-a	2.00	6.00	12.00
4-11	.70	2.00	4.00

LAWRENCE (See Movie Classics)

LEADING COMICS (. . . Screen Comics No. 42 on)
Winter, 1941-42 - No. 41, 1948
National Periodical Publications

	Good	Fine	Mint
1-Origin The Seven Soldiers of Victory; Crimson Avenger, Green Arrow & Speedy, Shining Knight, The Vigilante, Star Spangled Kid & Stripsey begin	60.00	180.00	360.00
2-Meskin-a	30.00	90.00	180.00
3	22.00	65.00	130.00
4,5	20.00	55.00	110.00
6-10	14.00	40.00	85.00
11-14(Spring, 1945)	11.00	32.00	65.00
15-Content change to funny animal	2.00	5.00	10.00
16-22,24-30	1.50	4.00	8.00
23-1st app. Peter Porkchops	3.00	8.00	16.00
31,32,34-41	1.00	3.00	6.00
33-(Scarce)	3.00	8.00	16.00

LEADING SCREEN COMICS (Formerly Leading Comics)
No. 42, 1949 - No. 77, Aug-Sept, 1955
National Periodical Publications

	Good	Fine	Mint
42-77	1.00	3.00	6.00

NOTE: ***Mayer*** *a-75(3).* ***Post*** *a-34.*

LEATHERNECK THE MARINE (See Mighty Midget Comics)

LEAVE IT TO BEAVER (TV)
1958 - May-July, 1962
Dell Publishing Co.

	Good	Fine	Mint
4-Color 912,999,1103,1191,1285, 01-428-207	1.00	3.00	6.00

LEAVE IT TO BINKY (Binky No. 72 on) (See Super DC Giant and Showcase)
2-3/48 - No. 60, 12-1/58; No. 61, 6-7/68 - No. 71, 2-3/70
National Periodical Publications

	Good	Fine	Mint
1	5.50	16.00	32.00
2-5	3.00	8.00	16.00
6-10	2.00	6.00	12.00
11-20	1.50	4.00	8.00
21-28,30-60	.85	2.50	5.00
29-Used in **POP**, pg. 78	2.00	6.00	12.00
61-71	.45	1.30	2.60

LEE HUNTER, INDIAN FIGHTER (See 4-Color No. 779,904)

LEFT-HANDED GUN, THE (See 4-Color No. 913)

LEGEND OF CUSTER, THE (TV)
January, 1968
Dell Publishing Co.

	Good	Fine	Mint
1	.85	2.50	5.00

LEGEND OF JESSE JAMES, THE (TV)
February, 1966
Gold Key

	Good	Fine	Mint
10172-602	.85	2.50	5.00

LEGEND OF LOBO, THE (See Movie Comics)

LEGEND OF YOUNG DICK TURPIN, THE (TV)
May, 1966 (Disney TV episode)
Gold Key

	Good	Fine	Mint
1 (10176-605)	1.00	3.00	6.00

LEGENDS OF DANIEL BOONE, THE
Oct-Nov, 1955 - No. 8, Dec-Jan, 1956-57
National Periodical Publications

	Good	Fine	Mint
1 (Scarce)	5.50	16.00	32.00
2-8 (Scarce)	3.00	8.00	16.00

LEGION OF MONSTERS (Magazine)
September, 1975 (black & white)
Marvel Comics Group

	Good	Fine	Mint
1-Origin & 1st app. Legion of Monsters; Adams-c; Morrow-a; origin & only app. The Manphibian	.40	1.20	2.40

LEGION OF SUPER-HEROES (See Action, Adventure, All New Collectors Ed., Limited Collectors Ed., Superboy, & Superman)
Feb, 1973 - No. 4, July-Aug, 1973
National Periodical Publications

LEGION OF SUPER-HEROES (continued) Good Fine Mint
1-Legion & Tommy Tomorrow reprints begin .85 2.50 5.00
2-4 .35 1.00 2.00

LEGION OF SUPER-HEROES (Formerly Superboy)
No. 259, Jan, 1980 - Present
DC Comics

259(No.1)-Superboy leaves Legion .50 1.00
260-264,266-270 .40 .80
265-Contains 28pg. insert 'Superman & the TR5-80 Computer' .40 .80
271-282: 272-Blok joins; origin; 20pg. insert-Dial 'H' For Hero. 277-Intro Reflecto. 280-Superboy re-joins legion .30 .60
NOTE: ***Aparo** c-282. **Austin** c-268i. **Ditko** a-267, 268, 272, 274, 276, 281. **Infantino** a-272p. **Perez** c-268p, 277p-281p. **Starlin** a-265. **Staton** a-259p, 260p, 280.*

LENNON SISTERS LIFE STORY, THE (See 4-Color No. 951,1014)

LEO THE LION
No date (10 cents)
I. W. Enterprises

1-Reprint .50 1.50 3.00

LEROY
Nov, 1949 - 1950
Standard Comics

1 1.00 3.00 6.00
2-Frazetta text illo. 2.00 5.00 10.00
3-6: 3-Lubbers-a .70 2.00 4.00

LET'S PRETEND
May-June, 1950 - No. 3, Sept-Oct, 1950
D. S. Publishing Co.

1 3.00 9.00 18.00
2,3 2.00 5.00 10.00

LET'S READ THE NEWSPAPER
1974
Charlton Press

Features Quincy by Ted Sheares .30 .60

LET'S TAKE A TRIP (TV) (CBS TV Presents)
Spring, 1958
Pines

1-Marv Levy c/a .70 2.00 4.00

LETTERS TO SANTA (See March of Comics No. 228)

LIBERTY COMICS (Miss Liberty No. 1)
1945 - 1946 (MLJ reprints)
Green Publishing Co.

4 4.00 12.00 24.00
10-Hangman & Boy Buddies app.; Suzie & Wilbur begin; reprint of Hangman No. 8 4.00 12.00 24.00
11(V2No.2, 1/46)-Wilbur in women's clothes 9.00 25.00 50.00
12-Black Hood & Suzie app. 3.50 10.00 20.00
14,15-Patty of Airliner & Leonard Star in both 2.00 6.00 12.00

LIBERTY GUARDS
No date (1946?)
Chicago Mail Order

nn-Reprints Man of War No. 1 with cover of Liberty Scouts No. 1; Gustavson-c 9.00 25.00 50.00

LIBERTY SCOUTS (See Man of War & Liberty Guards)
June, 1941 - No. 3, Fall, 1941
Centaur Publications

2(No.1)-Origin The Fire-Man, Man of War; Vapo-Man & Liberty Scouts begin; Gustavson-c/a 25.00 75.00 160.00
3(No.2): Gustavson-c/a 20.00 60.00 120.00

LIDSVILLE (TV)
Oct, 1972 - No. 5, Oct, 1973
Gold Key
Good Fine Mint
1 .85 2.50 5.00
2-5 .35 1.00 2.00

LIEUTENANT, THE (TV)
April-June, 1964
Dell Publishing Co.

1 .70 2.00 4.00

LT. ROBIN CRUSOE, U.S.N. (See Movie Comics and Walt Disney Showcase No. 26)

LIFE OF CHRIST, THE
1949 (100 pages) (35 cents)
Catechetical Guild Educational Society

301-Reprints from Topix(1949)-V5No.11,12 4.00 12.00 24.00

LIFE OF CHRIST VISUALIZED
1942 - 1943
Standard Publishers

1-3: All came in cardboard case 3.00 8.00 16.00

LIFE OF CHRIST VISUALIZED
1946? (48 pgs. in color)
The Standard Publ. Co.

1.00 3.00 6.00

LIFE OF ESTHER VISUALIZED
1947 (48 pgs. in color)
The Standard Publ. Co.

2062 1.00 3.00 6.00

LIFE OF JOSEPH VISUALIZED
1946 (48 pgs. in color)
The Standard Publ. Co.

1054 1.00 3.00 6.00

LIFE OF PAUL (See The Living Bible)

LIFE OF RILEY, THE (See 4-Color No. 917)

LIFE OF THE BLESSED VIRGIN
1950 (68 pages) (square binding)
Catechetical Guild (Giveaway)

nn-Contains "The Woman of the Promise" & "Mother of Us All" rebound 4.00 12.00 24.00

LIFE'S LIKE THAT
1945 (68 pgs.; B&W; 25 cents)
Croyden Publ. Co.

nn-Newspaper Sunday strip reprints by Neher 1.50 4.00 8.00

LIFE'S LITTLE JOKES
No date (1924) (52 pgs.; B&W)
MS Publ. Co.

By Rube Goldberg 7.00 20.00 40.00

LIFE STORIES OF AMERICAN PRESIDENTS
November, 1957 (25 cents)
Dell Publishing Co.

1-Buscema-a 3.00 8.00 16.00

LIFE STORY
April, 1949 - V8No.45, Feb?, 1953
Fawcett Publications

V1No.1 3.00 8.00 16.00
2-6 1.20 3.50 7.00
V2No.7-12: 9,12-photo-c 1.00 3.00 6.00
V3No.13-Wood-a 5.00 15.00 30.00

Legion Of Super Heroes #259, © DC

Let's Take A Trip #1, © PINE

Liberty Comics #11, © Green

Life With Archie #47, © AP

Lightning Comics V3#1, © ACE

Linda Carter #5, © MCG

LIFE STORY (continued)

	Good	Fine	Mint
V3No.14-18, V4No.19-21,23,24	.85	2.50	5.00
V4No.22-Photo-c; drug use story	1.00	3.00	6.00
V5No.25-30, V6No.31-36	.70	2.00	4.00
V7No.37,39-42, V8No.44,45	.50	1.50	3.00
V7No.38, V8No.43-Evans-a	1.50	4.00	8.00

NOTE: ***Powell*** *a-13,23,26,28,30,32.*

LIFE WITH ARCHIE
Sept, 1958 - Present
Archie Publications

	Good	Fine	Mint
1	8.00	24.00	48.00
2	4.00	12.00	24.00
3-5	2.50	7.00	14.00
6-10	2.00	5.00	10.00
11-25	1.00	3.00	6.00
26-41	.70	2.00	4.00
42-45: 42-Pureheart begins	.35	1.00	2.00
46-Origin Pureheart	.35	1.00	2.00
47-50: 50-United Three begin	.30	.90	1.80
51-59-Pureheart ends		.60	1.20
60-100: 60-Archie band begins		.50	1.00
101-150		.40	.80
151-219		.30	.60

LIFE WITH MILLIE (Formerly A Date With Millie) (Modeling With Millie No. 21 on)
No. 8, Dec, 1960 - No. 20, Dec, 1962

	Good	Fine	Mint
8-10	1.00	3.00	6.00
11-20	.70	2.00	4.00

LIFE WITH SNARKY PARKER (TV)
August, 1950
Fox Features Syndicate

	Good	Fine	Mint
1	3.00	9.00	18.00

LIGHT IN THE FOREST (See 4-Color No. 891)

LIGHTNING COMICS (Formerly Sure-Fire No. 1-3) (No V3No.2)
No. 4, Dec, 1940 - No. 13(V3No.1), June, 1942
Ace Magazines

	Good	Fine	Mint
4	12.00	35.00	70.00
5,6: 6-Dr. Nemesis begins	10.00	30.00	60.00
V2No.1-6: 2-''Flash Lightning'' becomes ''Lash. . .''	9.00	25.00	50.00
V3No.1-Intro. Lightning Girl & The Sword	9.00	25.00	50.00

LI'L (See Little)

LILY OF THE ALLEY IN THE FUNNIES
No date (1920's?) (10¼x15½''; 28 pgs. in color)
Whitman Publishers

	Good	Fine	Mint
W936 - by T. Burke	4.00	12.00	24.00

LIMITED COLLECTORS' EDITION (See Famous 1st Edition & Rudolph the Red Nosed Reindeer; becomes All-New Collectors' Edition)
(No.21-34,51-59: 84 pgs.; No.35-41: 68 pgs.; No.42-50: 60 pgs.)
C-21, Summer, 1973 - Present ($1.00) (10x13½'')
National Periodical Publications/DC Comics

	Good	Fine	Mint
nn(C-20)-Rudolph	.30	.80	1.60
C-21: Shazam; Captain Marvel Jr. reprint by Raboy	.35	1.00	2.00
C-22: Tarzan; complete origin reprinted from No. 207-210; all Kubert	.50	1.50	3.00
C-23: House of Mystery; Wrightson, Adams, Wood, Toth, Orlando-a	.35	1.00	2.00
C-24: Rudolph	.30	.80	1.60
C-25: Batman; Adams-c/a	.50	1.50	3.00
C-27: Shazam	.35	1.00	2.00
C-29: Tarzan; reprints ''Return of Tarzan'' from No. 219-223 by Kubert	.50	1.50	3.00
C-31: Superman; origin-r; Adams-a	.50	1.50	3.00
C-32: Ghosts (new-a)	.30	.80	1.60
C-33: Rudolph (new-a)	.30	.80	1.60
C-34: Xmas with the Super-Heroes; unpublished Angel & Ape story by Oksner & Wood	.35	1.00	2.00
C-35: Shazam; cover features TV's Captain Marvel, Jackson Bostwick	.30	.80	1.60
C-36: The Bible; all new adaptation beginning with Genesis by Kubert, Redondo & Mayer	.70	2.00	4.00
C-37: Batman; r-1946 Sundays	.35	1.00	2.00
C-38: Superman; 1 pg. Adams	.35	1.00	2.00
C-39: Secret Origins/Super Villains; Adams-a(r)	.70	2.00	4.00
C-40: Dick Tracy by Gould featuring Flattop; newspaper-r from 12/21/43 - 5/17/44	.70	2.00	4.00
C-41: Super Friends; Toth-c/a	.40	1.20	2.40
C-42: Rudolph	.25	.70	1.40
C-43: Christmas with the Super-Heroes; Wrightson, S&K, Adams-a	.50	1.50	3.00
C-44: Batman; Adams-r; painted-c	.35	1.00	2.00
C-45: Secret Origins/Super Villains; Flash-r/105	.35	1.00	2.00
C-46: Justice League of America; 3 pg. Toth-a	.50	1.50	3.00
C-47: Superman Salutes the Bicentennial (Tomahawk interior); 2 pgs. new-a		.60	1.20
C-48: The Superman-Flash Race; 6 pgs. Adams-a	.40	1.20	2.40
C-49: Superboy & the Legion of Super-Heroes	.35	1.00	2.00
C-50: Rudolph		.60	1.20
C-51: Batman; Adams-c/a	.35	1.00	2.00
C-52: The Best of DC; Adams-c/a; Toth, Kubert-a	.30	.80	1.60
C-57: Welcome Back, Kotter-r(5/78)		.50	1.00
C-59: Batman's Strangest Cases; Adams, Wrightson-r; Adams/Wrightson-c		.50	1.00

NOTE: *All-r with exception of some special features and covers.* ***Aparo*** *c-37.* ***Giordano*** *a-39, 45.* ***Infantino*** *a-25, 39, 44, 45, 52.*

LINDA (Phantom Lady No. 5 on)
Apr-May, 1954 - No. 4, Oct-Nov, 1955
Ajax-Farrell Publ. Co.

	Good	Fine	Mint
1-Kamen-a	4.00	12.00	24.00
2-4-Kamen-a; 2-Lingerie panel	3.50	10.00	20.00

LINDA CARTER, STUDENT NURSE
Sept, 1961 - No. 9, Jan, 1963
Atlas Comics (AMI)

	Good	Fine	Mint
1	.50	1.50	3.00
2-9	.35	1.00	2.00

LINDA LARK
Oct-Dec, 1961 - No. 8, Aug-Oct, 1963
Dell Publishing Co.

	Good	Fine	Mint
1	.50	1.50	3.00
2-8	.40	1.20	2.40

LINUS, THE LIONHEARTED (TV)
September, 1965
Gold Key

	Good	Fine	Mint
1 (10155-509)	.85	2.50	5.00

LION, THE (See Movie Comics)

LION OF SPARTA (See Movie Classics)

LIPPY THE LION AND HARDY HAR HAR (TV)
March, 1963 (Hanna-Barbera)
Gold Key

	Good	Fine	Mint
1 (10049-303)	.85	2.50	5.00

LI'L ABNER (See Comics on Parade)
1939 - 1940
United Features Syndicate

	Good	Fine	Mint
Single Series 4 ('39)	14.00	40.00	80.00

LI'L ABNER (continued)

	Good	Fine	Mint
Single Series 18 ('40) (No. 18 on inside, No. 2 on cover)	12.00	36.00	72.00

LI'L ABNER (Al Capp's) (See Oxydol-Dreft)
No. 61, Dec, 1947 - No. 97, Jan, 1955
Harvey Publ. No. 61-69 (2/49)/Toby Press No. 70 on

	Good	Fine	Mint
61(No.1)-Wolverton-a	7.00	20.00	40.00
62-65	5.00	14.00	28.00
66,67,69,70	3.50	10.00	20.00
68-Full length Fearless Fosdick story	5.00	14.00	28.00
71-74,76,80	3.00	8.00	16.00
75,77-79,86,91-All with Kurtzman art; 91 reprints No. 77	4.00	12.00	24.00
81-85,87-90,92-94,96,97: 93-reprints No. 71	2.00	6.00	12.00
95-Full length Fearless Fosdick story	3.50	10.00	20.00
. . . & the Creatures from Drop-Outer Space (Giveaway)(nn)	2.50	7.00	14.00
. . . Joins the Navy (1950) (Toby Press Premium)	2.50	7.00	14.00
. . . by Al Capp Giveaway (Circa 1955, no date)	2.50	7.00	14.00

NOTE: ***Powell** a-61.*

LI'L ABNER
1951
Toby Press

	Good	Fine	Mint
1	2.50	7.00	14.00

LI'L ABNER'S DOGPATCH (See Al Capp's . . .)

LITTLE AL OF THE F.B.I.
No. 10, 1950 (no month) - No. 11, Apr-May, 1951
Ziff-Davis Publications (Saunders painted covers)

	Good	Fine	Mint
10(1950)	1.50	4.50	9.00
11(1951)-Morphine drug mention story	3.00	8.00	16.00

LITTLE AL OF THE SECRET SERVICE
1950 - No. 10, 1951 (Saunders painted covers)
Ziff-Davis Publications

	Good	Fine	Mint
1	2.00	6.00	12.00
2-9	1.50	4.50	9.00
10-Spanking panel	3.50	10.00	20.00

LITTLE AMBROSE
September, 1958
Archie Publications

	Good	Fine	Mint
1	3.50	10.00	20.00

LITTLE ANGEL
No. 5, Sept, 1954; No. 6, Sept, 1955 - No. 16, Sept, 1959
Standard (Visual Editions)/Pines

	Good	Fine	Mint
5-16	.70	2.00	4.00

LITTLE ANNIE ROONEY
1935 (48 pgs.; B&W dailies) (25 cents)
David McKay Publications

	Good	Fine	Mint
Book 1-Daily strip-r by Darrell McClure	7.00	20.00	40.00

LITTLE ANNIE ROONEY
1938; Aug, 1948 - No. 3, Oct, 1948
David McKay/St. John/Standard

	Good	Fine	Mint
Feature Book 11 (McKay, 1938)	10.00	30.00	60.00
1 (St. John)	3.00	8.00	16.00
2,3	2.00	6.00	12.00

LITTLE ARCHIE (The Adventures of No.?-on . . .)
1956 - Present (Giants No. 3-84)
Archie Publications

	Good	Fine	Mint
1	10.00	28.00	56.00
2	5.50	16.00	32.00
3-5	3.50	10.00	20.00
6-10	3.00	8.00	16.00
11-20	2.00	5.00	10.00
21-40: Little Pureheart begins No. 40, ends No. 42,44	1.00	3.00	6.00
41-80: 42-Intro. The Little Archies. 59-Little Sabrina begins	.40	1.20	2.40
81-100		.40	.80
101-172		.30	.60
. . . In Animal Land 1('57)	3.00	8.00	16.00
. . . In Animal Land 17(Winter, 1957-58)-19(Summer,'58)-Formerly Li'l Jinx	2.50	7.00	14.00

LITTLE ARCHIE COMICS DIGEST ANNUAL
Oct, 1977 - Present (Digest) (192 pages)
Archie Publications

	Good	Fine	Mint
1(10/77)-Reprints		.60	1.20
2(4/78)-Adams-a		.30	.60
3(11/78)-The Fly reprints by S&K; Adams-a		.30	.60
4(4/79), 5(10/79), 6(4/80), 7(10/80)		.25	.50

LITTLE ARCHIE MYSTERY
Aug, 1963 - No. 2, Oct, 1963
Archie Publications

	Good	Fine	Mint
1 (Scarce)	4.00	12.00	24.00
2	3.00	8.00	16.00

LITTLE ASPIRIN (See Wisco)
July, 1949 - No. 3, Dec, 1949 (52 pages)
Marvel Comics (CnPC)

	Good	Fine	Mint
1-Kurtzman-a, 4 pgs.	4.00	12.00	20.00
2-Kurtzman-a, 4 pgs.	3.00	8.00	14.00
3-No Kurtzman	1.00	3.00	6.00

LITTLE AUDREY (See Harvey Hits No. 11,19)
April, 1948 - No. 24, June, 1952
St. John Publ.

	Good	Fine	Mint
1	12.00	35.00	70.00
2-5	5.50	16.00	32.00
6-10	3.50	10.00	32.00
11-20	2.00	5.00	10.00
21-24	1.00	3.00	6.00

LITTLE AUDREY
No. 25, Aug, 1952 - No. 53, April, 1957
Harvey Publications

	Good	Fine	Mint
25	3.00	8.00	16.00
26-30	1.50	4.00	8.00
31-40	1.00	3.00	6.00
41-53	.85	2.50	5.00

NOTE: *Richie Rich appears in No. 25-30?*

LITTLE AUDREY (. . . Yearbook)
1950 (260 pages) (50 cents)
St. John Publishing Co.

Contains 8 complete 1949 comics rebound; Casper, Alice in Wonderland, Little Audrey, Abbott & Costello, Pinocchio, Moon Mullins, Three Stooges (from Jubilee), Little Annie Rooney app. (Rare)

	Good	Fine	Mint
	30.00	90.00	180.00

(Also see All Good & Treasury of Comics)

NOTE: *This book contains remaindered St. John comics; many variations possible.*

LITTLE AUDREY (See Playful . . .)

LITTLE AUDREY & MELVIN (Audrey & . . . No. 62)
May, 1962 - No. 61, Dec, 1973
Harvey Publications

	Good	Fine	Mint
1	5.50	16.00	32.00

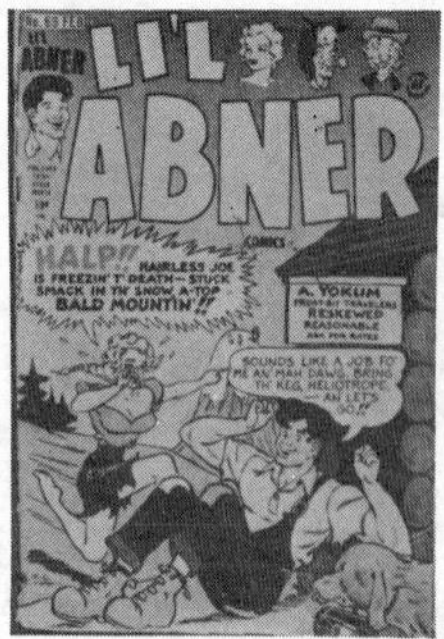

Li'l Abner #69, © UFS

Little Annie Rooney #1, © DMP

Little Audrey #8, © STJ

Little Beaver #5, © KING

Little Dot #7, © HARV

Little Eva #3, © STJ

LITTLE AUDREY & MELVIN (continued)

	Good	Fine	Mint
2-5	3.00	8.00	16.00
6-10	2.00	5.00	10.00
11-20	1.00	3.00	6.00
21-40	.70	2.00	4.00
41-61	.40	1.20	2.40

LITTLE AUDREY TV FUNTIME
Sept, 1962 - No. 33, Oct, 1971
Harvey Publications

	Good	Fine	Mint
1-Richie Rich app.	3.50	10.00	20.00
2,3: Richie Rich app.	2.00	6.00	12.00
4,5	1.75	5.00	10.00
6-10	.85	2.50	5.00
11-20	.50	1.50	3.00
21-33	.35	1.00	2.00

LITTLE BAD WOLF (See 4-Color No. 403,473,564, Walt Disney Showcase No. 21 and Wheaties)

LITTLE BEAVER
1948 - No. 8, Jan, 1953
Dell Publishing Co.

	Good	Fine	Mint
4-Color 211('48)	2.00	5.00	10.00
4-Color 267,294,332	1.20	3.50	7.00
4-Color 483,529	1.00	3.00	6.00
4-Color 612,660,695,744,817,870	.70	2.00	4.00
3(10/51)-8	.70	2.00	4.00

LITTLE BIT
March, 1949 - No. 2, 1949
Jubilee/St. John Publishing Co.

	Good	Fine	Mint
1,2	.85	2.50	5.00

LITTLE DOT (See Tastee-Freez Comics, Li'l Max, Humphrey, and Sad Sack)
9/53 - No. 150, 7/73; No. 151, 9/73 - No. 164, 4/76
Harvey Publications

	Good	Fine	Mint
1-Intro. & 1st app. Richie Rich & Little Lotta	50.00	150.00	280.00
2	30.00	80.00	140.00
3	17.00	50.00	80.00
4	12.00	36.00	60.00
5-Origin Little Dot's Dress	14.00	40.00	70.00
6-Richie Rich, Little Lotta, & Little Dot all on cover; 1st Richie Rich cover featured	14.00	40.00	70.00
7-10	5.00	15.00	30.00
11-20	4.00	12.00	24.00
21-40	2.00	6.00	12.00
41-60	1.00	3.00	6.00
61-80	.70	2.00	4.00
81-100	.45	1.30	2.60
101-130	.35	1.00	2.00
131-164		.50	1.00

NOTE: *Richie Rich & Little Lotta in all.*

LITTLE DOT DOTLAND (Dot Dotland No. 62)
July, 1962 - No. 61, Dec, 1973; No. 62, Sept, 1974
Harvey Publications

	Good	Fine	Mint
1-Richie Rich begins	4.00	12.00	24.00
2,3	2.00	6.00	12.00
4,5	2.00	5.00	10.00
6-10	1.75	5.00	8.00
11-20	1.00	3.00	6.00
21-30	.50	1.50	3.00
31-62	.30	.80	1.60

LITTLE DOT'S UNCLES & AUNTS (See Harvey Hits No. 4,13,24)
May, 1962 - No. 52, April, 1974
Harvey Publications

	Good	Fine	Mint
1-Richie Rich begins	4.00	12.00	24.00
2,3	2.00	6.00	12.00
4,5	2.00	5.00	10.00
6-10	1.50	4.00	8.00
11-20	1.00	3.00	6.00
21-30	.50	1.50	3.00
31-52	.30	.80	1.60

LITTLE EVA
May, 1952 - No. 31, Nov, 1956
St. John Publishing Co.

	Good	Fine	Mint
1	4.00	12.00	24.00
2-5	2.00	6.00	12.00
6-10	1.00	3.00	6.00
11-31	.85	2.50	5.00
3-D 1,2(10/53-11/53)(25 cents)	6.00	18.00	36.00
I.W. Reprint No. 1-3,6-8	.30	.90	1.80
Super Reprint No. 10,12('63),14,16,18('64)	.30	.90	1.80

LITTLE FIR TREE, THE
1942 (8½x11'') (12 pgs. with cover)
W. T. Grant Co. (Christmas giveaway)

8 pg. Kelly-a reprint/Santa Claus Funnies not signed.
(One copy sold for $300.00 in 1977)

LI'L GENIUS (Summer Fun No. 54 on) (See Blue Bird)
1954 - No. 52, Jan, 1965; No. 53, Oct, 1965
Charlton Comics

	Good	Fine	Mint
1	1.50	4.00	8.00
2-16,19,20	.70	2.00	4.00
17-(68 pgs.)	.85	2.50	5.00
18-(100 pgs., 10/58)	1.00	3.00	6.00
21-53	.40	1.20	2.40

LI'L GHOST
Feb, 1958 - No. 3, Mar, 1959
St. John Publishing Co./Fago No. 2 on

	Good	Fine	Mint
1(St. John)	1.50	4.00	8.00
1(Fago)	1.00	3.00	6.00
2,3	.70	2.00	4.00

LITTLE GIANT COMICS
July, 1938 - No. 3, Oct, 1938 (132 pgs.) (6¾x4½'')
Centaur Publications

	Good	Fine	Mint
1-3-B&W with color-c	10.00	28.00	56.00

LITTLE GIANT DETECTIVE FUNNIES
Oct, 1938 - No. 3, Feb, 1939 (132 pgs.) (6¾x4½'')
Centaur Publications

	Good	Fine	Mint
1	10.00	28.00	56.00
2,3	6.00	18.00	36.00
4(1/39)-B&W; no-c; 36 pgs., 6½x9½''; Eisner-r	6.00	18.00	36.00

LITTLE GIANT MOVIE FUNNIES
Aug, 1938 - No. 2, Oct, 1938 (132 pgs.) (6¾x4½'')
Centaur Publications

	Good	Fine	Mint
1-Ed Wheelan's ''Minute Movies''-r	10.00	28.00	56.00
2-Ed Wheelan's ''Minute Movies''-r	6.00	18.00	36.00

LITTLE GROUCHO (. . . Grouchy No. 2) (See Tippy Terry)
Feb-Mar, 1955 - No. 2, June-July, 1955
Reston Publ. Co.

	Good	Fine	Mint
16, 1	.85	2.50	5.00
2(6-7/55)	.70	2.00	4.00

LITTLE HIAWATHA (See 4-Color No. 439,787,901,988)

LITTLE IKE
April, 1953 - No. 4, Oct, 1953
St. John Publishing Co.

	Good	Fine	Mint
1	1.50	4.00	8.00
2-4	1.00	3.00	6.00

LITTLE IODINE (See Giant Comic Album)
April, 1949 - No. 57, July-Sept, 1962
Dell Publishing Co.

	Good	Fine	Mint
4-Color 224,257	3.00	8.00	16.00
1(3-5/50)	3.00	8.00	16.00
2-10	1.00	3.00	6.00
11-20	.85	2.50	5.00
21-30	.70	2.00	4.00
31-40	.40	1.20	2.40
41-57	.30	.80	1.60

LITTLE JACK FROST
1951
Avon Periodicals

	Good	Fine	Mint
1	3.00	8.00	16.00

LI'L JINX (Formerly Ginger?) (Little Archie in Animal Land No. 17)
No. 11(No.1), Nov, 1956 - No. 16, Sept, 1957
Archie Publications

	Good	Fine	Mint
11-16	2.50	7.00	14.00

LI'L JINX (See Archie Giant Series Magazine)

LI'L JINX CHRISTMAS BAG (See Archie Giant Series Mag. No. 195, 206,219)

LI'L JINX GIANT LAUGH-OUT
No. 33, Sept, 1971 - No. 43, Nov, 1973 (52 pgs.)
Archie Publications

	Good	Fine	Mint
33-43	.35	1.00	2.00

(See Archie Giant Series Mag. No. 176,185)

LITTLE JOE (See 4-Color No. 1)

LITTLE JOE
1953
St. John Publishing Co.

	Good	Fine	Mint
1	.85	2.50	5.00

LITTLE JOHNNY & THE TEDDY BEARS
1907 (10x14'') (32 pgs. in color)
Reilly & Britton Co.

	Good	Fine	Mint
By J. R. Bray	10.00	30.00	60.00

LI'L KIDS
8/70 - No. 2, 10/70; No. 3, 11/71 - No. 12, 6/73
Marvel Comics Group

	Good	Fine	Mint
1	.35	1.00	2.00
2-12: 10,11-Calvin app.		.50	1.00

LITTLE KING (See 4-Color No. 494,597,677)

LITTLE KLINKER
1960 (20 pgs.) (slick cover)
Little Klinker Ventures (Montgomery Ward Giveaway)

	Good	Fine	Mint
		1.00	2.00

LITTLE LANA (Formerly Lana)
No. 8, Nov, 1949 - No. 9, Mar, 1950
Marvel Comics (MjMC)

	Good	Fine	Mint
8,9	1.20	3.50	7.00

LITTLE LENNY
June, 1949 - No. 3, Nov, 1949
Marvel Comics (CDS)

	Good	Fine	Mint
1	1.20	3.50	7.00
2,3	.85	2.50	5.00

LITTLE LIZZIE
June, 1949 - No. 5, April, 1950; Sept, 1953
Marvel Comics (PrPI)/Atlas (OMC)

	Good	Fine	Mint
1	1.20	3.50	7.00
2-5 (3-5 exist?)	.85	2.50	5.00
1 (1953)	.70	2.00	4.00

LITTLE LOTTA (See Harvey Hits No. 10)
11/1955 - No. 110, 11/1973; No. 111, 9/1974 - No. 121, 5/1976
Harvey Publications

	Good	Fine	Mint
1-Richie Rich & Little Dot begin	14.00	40.00	80.00
2,3	7.00	20.00	40.00
4,5	4.00	12.00	24.00
6-10	3.00	9.00	18.00
11-20	2.00	5.00	10.00
21-40	1.50	4.00	8.00
41-60	1.00	3.00	6.00
61-80	.50	1.50	3.00
81-100	.30	.80	1.60
101-121		.50	1.00

LITTLE LOTTA FOODLAND
September, 1963 - No. 29, Oct, 1972
Harvey Publications

	Good	Fine	Mint
1	4.00	12.00	24.00
2,3	2.50	7.00	14.00
4,5	2.00	6.00	12.00
6-10	1.50	4.50	9.00
11-20	1.00	3.00	6.00
21-29	.70	2.00	4.00

LITTLE LULU (Marge's. . .)
June, 1945 - No. 164, July-Sept, 1962; No. 165, Oct, 1962 - Present
Dell Publishing Co./Gold Key 165-257/ Whitman 258 on

	Good	Fine	Mint
4-Color 74('45)	80.00	180.00	340.00
4-Color 97('46)	40.00	90.00	160.00
(Above two books done entirely by John Stanley - cover, pencils, and inks.)			
4-Color 110('46)-1st Alvin Story Telling Time	20.00	55.00	110.00
4-Color 115	20.00	55.00	110.00
4-Color 120, 131	18.00	45.00	90.00
4-Color 139('47),146,158	14.00	40.00	80.00
4-Color 165-Smokes doll hair & has wild hallucinations	18.00	45.00	90.00
1(1948)	50.00	120.00	240.00
2	25.00	60.00	120.00
3-5	14.00	40.00	80.00
6-10	10.00	30.00	60.00
11-20	8.00	24.00	48.00
21-30: 26-Reprints F.C. 110	5.50	16.00	32.00
31-38,40	4.00	12.00	24.00
39-Intro. Witch Hazel in ''That Awful Witch Hazel''	5.50	16.00	32.00
41-60: 45-2nd Witch Hazel app. 49-Gives Stanley & others credit	3.50	10.00	20.00
61-80: 80-Intro. Little Itch (2/55)	3.00	8.00	16.00
81-100	2.00	5.00	10.00
101-130	1.50	4.00	8.00
131-164,167-170; 165 & 166 listed below as Giant issues	1.00	3.00	6.00
171-205	.70	2.00	4.00
206-Last issue to carry Marge's name	.35	1.00	2.00
207-220	.30	.80	1.60
221-250: 241-Stanley-r		.50	1.00
251-261: 256-Stanley-r		.30	.60
. . .& Alvin Story Telling Time 1(3/59)-r/No. 2,5,3,11,30, 10,21,17,8,14,16	4.00	12.00	24.00
. . .& Her Friends 4(3/56)-100 pgs.	3.50	10.00	20.00
. . .& Her Special Friends 3(3/55)-100 pgs.	3.50	10.00	20.00
. . .& Tubby at Summer Camp 5(1957)	3.50	10.00	20.00
. . .& Tubby at Summer Camp 2(10/58)	3.50	10.00	20.00
. . .& Tubby Halloween Fun 6(1957)	2.50	7.00	14.00

Little Klinker nn

Little Lulu #2, © WEST

Little Lulu #39, © WEST

L.L. & Tuby In Alaska #1, © WEST

Little Miss Muffet #13, © KING

L.O.A., Popped Wheat, © News Synd.

LITTLE LULU (continued)

	Good	Fine	Mint
...& Tubby Halloween Fun 2(1958)	2.50	7.00	14.00
...& Tubby Halloween Fun 23(1959)(Dell Giant)	4.00	12.00	24.00
...& Tubby in Alaska 1(7/59)	3.50	10.00	20.00
...& Tubby in Australia 42(1961)	2.50	7.00	14.00
...& Tubby in Hawaii 29(4/60)	3.50	10.00	20.00
...& Tubby in Japan (12 cents)(5-7/62) 01476-207	2.50	7.00	14.00
...& Witch Hazel Halloween Fun 36(1960)	3.00	9.00	18.00
...& Witch Hazel Trick & Treat 50(1961)	3.00	9.00	18.00
...Christmas Diary 166(1962-63)(G. K.)	2.50	7.00	14.00
...in Paris 165(1962-G.K.)	2.50	7.00	14.00
...on Vacation 1(1954)-r-/4C-110,14,4C-146,5,4C-97,4, 4C-158,3,1	7.00	20.00	40.00
...Summer Camp 1('67-G.K.) '57-58-r	1.50	4.00	8.00
...Summer Camp 2 (Exist?)	1.50	4.00	8.00
...Trick & Treat 1 (12 cents)(12/62-Gold Key)	2.50	7.00	14.00
...Tubby Annual 1(1953)-r-4-Color No. 165,4C-74,4C-146, 4C-97,4C-158,4C-139,4C-131	12.00	35.00	70.00
...Tubby Annual 2(1954)-r/4C-139,6,4C-115,4C-74,5, 4C-97,3,4C-146,18	10.00	30.00	60.00

NOTE: *All Giants by **Stanley** except Christmas Diary No. 166 and In Paris No. 165. r-179, 189-91, 193, 195, 220, 254, 255.*

LITTLE LULU (See Golden Comics Digest No. 19,23,27,29,33,36,40, 43,46 & March of Comics No. 251,267,275,293,307,323,335,349, 355,369,385,406,417)

LITTLE MARY MIXUP (See Single Series No. 10,26)

LITTLE MAX COMICS (Joe Palooka's Pal)
Oct, 1949 - No. 73, Nov, 1961
Harvey Publications

	Good	Fine	Mint
1-Infinity-c; Little Dot begins	7.00	20.00	40.00
2,3-Little Dot app.	3.50	10.00	20.00
4-10: 5-Little Dot app.	1.50	4.00	8.00
11-20	.85	2.50	5.00
21-72	.60	1.80	3.60
73-Richie Rich app.	.85	2.50	5.00

LI'L MENACE
Dec, 1958 - No. 3, May, 1959
Fago Magazine Co.

	Good	Fine	Mint
1-Peter Rabbit app.	.85	2.50	5.00
2-Peter Rabbit (Vincent Fago's)	.70	2.00	4.00
3	.35	1.00	3.00

LITTLE MISS MUFFET
Dec, 1948 - No. 13, March, 1949
Standard Comics/King Features Synd.

	Good	Fine	Mint
11-13-Strip reprints; Fanny Cory-a	1.50	4.00	8.00

LITTLE MISS SUNBEAM COMICS
June-July, 1950 - No. 4, Dec-Jan, 1950-51
Magazine Enterprises/Quality Bakers of America

	Good	Fine	Mint
1	3.00	8.00	16.00
2-4	2.50	7.00	14.00
Bread Giveaway 1-4(Quality Bakers, 1949-50)-14 pgs. each	1.50	4.00	8.00
Bread Giveaway (1957)	1.00	3.00	6.00

LITTLE MONSTERS, THE
Nov, 1964 - No. 44, Feb, 1978
Gold Key

	Good	Fine	Mint
1	.85	2.50	5.00
2-10	.50	1.50	3.00
11-20	.30	.80	1.60
21-44: 20,34-39,43-reprints		.40	.80

LITTLE NEMO (See Cocomalt, Future Comics, Help, Jest, Kayo, Punch, Red Seal, & Superworld; most by Winsor McCay Jr., son of famous artist) (Other McCay books: see Little Sammy Sneeze & Dreams of the Rarebit Fiend)

LITTLE NEMO (...in Slumberland)
1906, 1909 (Sunday strip reprints in color) (cardboard covers)
Doffield & Co.(1906)/Cupples & Leon Co.(1909)

	Good	Fine	Mint
1906-11x16½'' in color by Winsor McCay; 30 pgs. (Very Rare)	120.00	300.00	600.00
1909-10x14'' in color by Winsor McCay (Very Rare)	100.00	250.00	500.00

LITTLE NEMO (...in Slumberland)
1945 (28 pgs.; 11x7¼''; B&W)
McCay Features/Nostalgia Press('69)

	Good	Fine	Mint
Reprints from 1905 & 1911 by Winsor McCay	3.00	8.00	16.00
1969-70 (exact reprint)	1.50	4.00	8.00

LITTLE ORPHAN ANNIE (See Merry Christmas..., Nickel Books, & Super Book No. 11,23)

LITTLE ORPHAN ANNIE (See Treasury Box of...)
1926 - 1934 (Daily strip reprints) (7x8¾'') (B&W)
Cupples & Leon Co.

(Hardcover Editions, 100 pages)

	Good	Fine	Mint
1(1926)-Little Orphan Annie	10.00	30.00	60.00
2('27)-In the Circus	7.00	20.00	40.00
3('28)-The Haunted House	7.00	20.00	40.00
4('29)-Bucking the World	7.00	20.00	40.00
5('30)-Never Say Die	7.00	20.00	40.00
6('31)-Shipwrecked	7.00	20.00	40.00
7('32)-A Willing Helper	5.50	16.00	32.00
8('33)-In Cosmic City	5.50	16.00	32.00
9('34)-Uncle Dan	7.00	20.00	40.00

NOTE: *Hardcovers with dust jackets are worth 20-50 percent more; the earlier the book, the higher the percentage. Each book reprints dailies from the previous year.*

LITTLE ORPHAN ANNIE
1937 - 1948
David McKay Publ./Dell Publishing Co.

	Good	Fine	Mint
Feature Book(McKay) 7-('37) (Very Rare)	70.00	180.00	360.00
4-Color 12(1941)	17.00	50.00	100.00
4-Color 18('43)-Flag-c	14.00	40.00	80.00
4-Color 52('44)	8.00	24.00	48.00
4-Color 76('45)	7.00	20.00	40.00
4-Color 107('46)	5.00	15.00	30.00
4-Color 152('47)	4.00	12.00	24.00
4-Color 206('49)	3.50	10.00	20.00
1(3-5/48)	10.00	30.00	60.00
2,3	5.00	15.00	30.00
Junior Commandos Giveaway(same cover as 4-Color No. 18, K.K. Publ.(Big Shoe Store); same back cover as '47 Popped Wheat giveaway; 16 pgs.	14.00	40.00	80.00
Popped Wheat Giveaway('47)-16 pgs. full color; '38,'40 reprints	.85	2.50	5.00
Quaker Giveaway(1940)	6.00	18.00	36.00
Quaker Giveaway(Full color-20 pgs., 1941); ''LOA and the Rescue,'' ''LOA and the Kidnappers,'' '' Advs. of LOA'' each....	5.00	15.00	30.00
Sparkies Giveaway(Full color-20 pgs., 1942); ''LOA and Mr. Grudge'' and ''LOA and the Great Am''	3.50	10.00	20.00

LI'L PALS
Sept, 1972 - No. 5, May, 1973
Marvel Comics Group

	Good	Fine	Mint
1-5		.30	.60

LI'L PAN
No. 6, Dec-Jan, 1947 - No. 8, Apr-May, 1947
Fox Features Syndicate

	Good	Fine	Mint
6-8	1.00	3.00	6.00

LITTLE PEOPLE (See 4-Color No. 485,573,633,692,753,809,868, 908,959,1024,1062)

LITTLE RASCALS (See 4-Color No. 674,778,825,883,936,974,1030, 1079,1137,1174,1224,1297)

LI'L RASCAL TWINS (Formerly Nature Boy)
1957 - No. 17, March, 1959
Charlton Comics

	Good	Fine	Mint
6-17-Li'l Genius & Tomboy	.40	1.20	2.40

LITTLE ROQUEFORT
June, 1952 - No. 9, Oct, 1953; No. 10, Summer, 1958
St. John Publishing Co./Pines No. 10

	Good	Fine	Mint
1	1.50	4.00	8.00
2-10	.85	2.50	5.00

LITTLE SAD SACK (See Harvey Hits No. 73,76,79,81,83)
Oct, 1964 - No. 19, Nov, 1967
Harvey Publications

	Good	Fine	Mint
1-Richie Rich app. cover only	1.50	4.00	8.00
2-19	.35	1.00	2.00

LITTLE SAMMY SNEEZE
1905 (28 pgs. in color; 11x16½'')
New York Herald Co.

	Good	Fine	Mint
By Winsor McCay (Rare)	150.00	400.00	600.00

NOTE: *Rarely found in fine to mint condition.*

LITTLE SCOUTS
1951 - No. 587, Oct, 1954
Dell Publishing Co.

	Good	Fine	Mint
4-Color No. 321 ('51)	.85	2.50	5.00
2(10-12/51) - 6(10-12/52)	.50	1.50	3.00
4-Color No. 462,506,550,587	.50	1.50	3.00

LITTLE SPUNKY
No date (1963?) (10 cents)
I. W. Enterprises

	Good	Fine	Mint
1-Reprint	.30	.80	1.60

LITTLE STOOGES, THE (The Three Stooges' Sons)
Sept, 1972 - No. 7, Mar, 1974
Gold Key

	Good	Fine	Mint
1-Norman Maurer cover/stories in all	.30	.80	1.60
2-7		.50	1.00

LITTLEST OUTLAW (See 4-Color No. 609)

LITTLEST SNOWMAN, THE
1956; Dec-Feb, 1964
Dell Publishing Co./Gold Key

	Good	Fine	Mint
4-Color No. 755,864	.70	2.00	4.00
1(1964)(Gold Key)	.70	2.00	4.00

LI'L TOMBOY (Formerly Fawcett's Funny Animals)
V14No.93, March, 1957 - No. 108, May, 1959 (No. 92 exist?)
Charlton Comics

	Good	Fine	Mint
V14No.93 - No. 108	.50	1.50	3.00

LI'L WILLIE (Formerly Willie Comics)
July, 1949 - No. 21, Aug-Sept, 1949
Marvel Comics (MgPC)

	Good	Fine	Mint
20,21	.85	2.50	5.00

LIVE IT UP
1973, 1976 (39-49 cents)
Spire Christian Comics (Fleming H. Revell Co.)

	Good	Fine	Mint
nn		.50	1.00

LIVING BIBLE, THE
Fall, 1945 - No. 3, Spring, 1946
Living Bible Corp.

	Good	Fine	Mint
1-Life of Paul	5.00	15.00	30.00
2-Joseph & His Brethren	3.50	10.00	20.00
3-Chaplains of War (classic-c)	5.00	15.00	30.00

NOTE: *All have* ***L. B. Cole*** *-c.*

LOBO
Dec, 1965 - No. 2, Oct, 1966
Dell Publishing Co.

	Good	Fine	Mint
1,2	.70	2.00	4.00

LOCO (Magazine) (Satire)
Aug, 1958 - V1No.3, Jan, 1959
Satire Publications

	Good	Fine	Mint
V1No.1-Chic Stone-a	.85	2.50	5.00
V1No.2,3-Severin-a, 2 pgs. Davis; 3-Heath-a	.50	1.50	3.00

LOGAN'S RUN
Jan, 1977 - No. 7, July, 1977
Marvel Comics Group

	Good	Fine	Mint
1	.30	.80	1.60
2-7: 6-Gulacy-c; Thanos-a		.40	.80

LOIS LANE (See Superman's Girlfriend . . .)

LOLLY AND PEPPER
1957 - July, 1962
Dell Publishing Co.

	Good	Fine	Mint
4-Color 832,940,978,1086,1206	.70	2.00	4.00
01-459-207	.70	2.00	4.00

LOMAX (See Police Action)

LONE EAGLE (The Flame No. 5 on)
Apr-May, 1954 - No. 4, Oct-Nov, 1954
Ajax/Farrell Publications

	Good	Fine	Mint
1	2.00	6.00	12.00
2-4: 2-Bondage-c	1.00	3.00	6.00

LONELY HEART (Dear Heart No. 15 on)
No. 9, March, 1955 - No. 14, Feb, 1956
Ajax/Farrell Publ. (Excellent Publ.)

	Good	Fine	Mint
9-Kamenesque-a; lingerie panel	1.50	4.00	8.00
10-14	1.00	3.00	6.00

LONE RANGER, THE (See March of Comics No. 165,174,193,208, 225,238,310,322,338,350, Feature Book No. 21,24(McKay), and Aurora)

LONE RANGER, THE
1939 - 1947
Dell Publishing Co.

	Good	Fine	Mint
Black & White 3('39)-Heigh-Yo Silver; text with ill. by Robert Weisman	30.00	90.00	200.00
Black & White 7('39)-Ill. by Henry Valleley; Hi-Yo Silver the Lone Ranger to the Rescue	50.00	140.00	280.00
4-Color 82('45)	12.00	35.00	70.00
4-Color 98('45),118('46)	10.00	30.00	60.00
4-Color 125('46),136('47)	7.00	20.00	40.00
4-Color 151,167('47)	5.50	16.00	32.00

LONE RANGER COMICS, THE (10 cents)
1939(inside), 1938 on-c) (68 pgs. in color) (Regular size)
Lone Ranger, Inc. (Ice cream mail order)

	Good	Fine	Mint
(Scarce)-not by Valleley	50.00	140.00	240.00

LONE RANGER, THE (No. 1-37: strip reprints)
Jan-Feb, 1948 - No. 145, May-July, 1962
Dell Publishing Co.

	Good	Fine	Mint
1	20.00	60.00	120.00
2	14.00	40.00	80.00
3-7,9,10	8.00	24.00	48.00
8-Origin retold	10.00	30.00	60.00

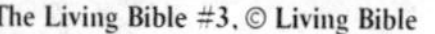

The Living Bible #3, © Living Bible

Logan's Run #4, © MCG

The Lone Ranger #8, © The Lone Ranger

The Lone Ranger #37, © The Lone Ranger

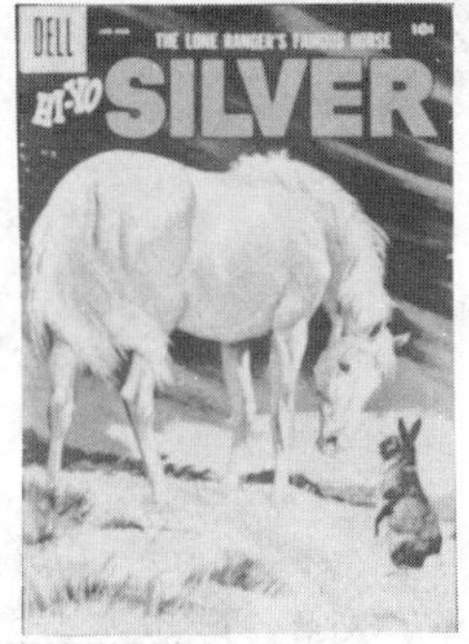

L.R.'s F.H. Hi-Yo Silver #21, © The Lone Ranger

Looney Tunes #24, © L. Schlesinger

LONE RANGER (continued)

	Good	Fine	Mint
11-"Young Hawk" Indian boy serial begins, ends 145	5.50	16.00	32.00
12-20	5.50	16.00	32.00
21,22,24-30	5.00	14.00	28.00
23-Origin retold	7.00	20.00	40.00
31-37-Last newspaper-r issue; new outfit	3.50	10.00	20.00
38-60	2.50	7.00	14.00
61-80: 71-Blank inside-c	2.00	5.00	10.00
81-111	1.50	4.00	8.00
112-1st Clayton Moore-c	5.00	14.00	28.00
113-117	2.50	7.00	14.00
118-Origin Lone Ranger, Tonto, & Silver retold; Special anniversary issue	5.00	14.00	28.00
119-145: 139-Last issue by Fran Striker	2.50	7.00	14.00
Cheerios Giveaways 1-"The Lone Ranger, His Mask & How He Met Tonto." 2-"The Lone Ranger & the Story of Silver" (1954) each....	4.00	12.00	24.00
Doll Giveaway(Gabriel Ind.)(1973, 3¼x5")	.50	1.50	3.00
...Golden West 3('55, 100 pgs.)	3.00	8.00	16.00
How the L. R. Captured Silver Book(1936)-Silvercup Bread giveaway	20.00	60.00	120.00
...In Milk for Big Mike(1955, Dairy Association giveaway)	3.50	10.00	20.00
Merita Bread giveaway('54; 16 pgs.; 5x7¼")-"How to Be a L. R. Health & Safety Scout"	3.50	10.00	20.00
...Movie Story('56; 100 pgs.)-Origin Lone Ranger in text	7.00	20.00	40.00
Western Treasury 1('53)-Origin of Lone Ranger	5.00	15.00	30.00
Western Treasury 2('54) (Becomes Golden West 3)	3.50	10.00	20.00

LONE RANGER, THE
9/64 - No. 16, 12/69; No. 17, 11/72; No. 18, 9/74 - No. 28, 3/77
Gold Key

	Good	Fine	Mint
1-Retells origin	1.00	3.00	6.00
2-17: Small Bear reprints in No. 6-12	.70	2.00	4.00
18-28	.35	1.00	2.00
Golden West 1(30029-610)-Giant, 10/66-reprints most Golden West No. 3	1.00	3.00	6.00

LONE RANGER'S COMPANION TONTO, THE
No. 2, Feb-Apr, 1951 - No. 33, Nov, 1958
Dell Publishing Co.

	Good	Fine	Mint
4-Color 312(1951)	3.50	10.00	20.00
2,3	2.00	5.00	10.00
4-10	1.50	4.00	8.00
11-20	1.00	3.00	6.00
21-33	.85	2.50	5.00

(See Aurora Comic Booklets)

LONE RANGER'S FAMOUS HORSE HI-YO SILVER, THE
No. 3, July-Sept, 1952 - No. 36, Oct, 1960
Dell Publishing Co.

	Good	Fine	Mint
4-Color 369-Silver's origin as told by The L.R.	2.00	5.00	10.00
4-Color 392	2.00	5.00	10.00
3-10	1.00	3.00	6.00
11-36	.85	2.50	5.00

LONE RIDER
April, 1951 - No. 26, July, 1955
Ajax/Farrell Publications

	Good	Fine	Mint
1	2.00	5.00	10.00
2-5: 2-Kamenish-a	.85	2.50	5.00
6-10	.70	2.00	4.00
11-26: 21-3-D effect-c	.50	1.50	3.00

LONG BOW (...Indian Boy)
1951 - 1953
Fiction House Magazines (Real Adventures Publ.)

	Good	Fine	Mint
1	2.00	6.00	12.00
2-9	1.20	3.50	7.00

LONGEST DAY (See Movie Classics)

LONG JOHN SILVER & THE PIRATES (Formerly Terry & the Pirates)
No. 30, Aug, 1956 - No. 32, March, 1957
Charlton Comics

	Good	Fine	Mint
30-32	.85	2.50	5.00

LOONEY TUNES & MERRIE MELODIES COMICS ("Looney Tunes" No. 166 (8/55) on)
1941 - No. 246, July-Sept, 1962
Dell Publishing Co.

	Good	Fine	Mint
1-Porky Pig, Bugs Bunny, Elmer Fudd begin	90.00	250.00	500.00
2,3	50.00	140.00	280.00
4-Kandi the Cave Kid by Walt Kelly; also in No. 5,6,8,11,15	35.00	100.00	200.00
5	17.00	50.00	100.00
6-10	14.00	40.00	80.00
11-25: 20-Pat, Patsy & Pete by Kelly in No. 20-25	10.00	30.00	60.00
26-30	7.00	20.00	40.00
31-40	5.00	15.00	30.00
41-50	3.00	8.00	16.00
51-60	2.00	6.00	12.00
61-80	1.20	3.50	7.00
81-100	.85	2.50	5.00
101-150	.50	1.50	3.00
151-200	.40	1.20	2.40
201-246	.30	.80	1.60

LOONEY TUNES (2nd Series)
April, 1975 - Present
Gold Key

	Good	Fine	Mint
1		.40	.80
2-35: Reprints-No. 4,9-12,14,15		.20	.40

LOONY SPORTS (Magazine)
Spring, 1975 (68 pages)
3-Strikes Publishing Co.

	Good	Fine	Mint
1-Sports satire	.30	.80	1.60

LOOY DOT DOPE (See Single Series No. 13)

LORD JIM (See Movie Comics)

LORNA THE JUNGLE GIRL (...Jungle Queen No. 1-5)
June, 1953 - No. 26, Aug, 1957
Atlas Comics (OMC No.1-11/NPI No.12-26)

	Good	Fine	Mint
1	5.00	15.00	30.00
2-5: 2-Intro. & 1st app. Greg Knight	3.50	10.00	20.00
6-15	3.00	8.00	16.00
16,17,19-26: 23,26-Everett-c	2.00	6.00	12.00
18-Williamson/Colleta-c	3.50	10.00	20.00

LOST IN SPACE (Space Family Robinson..., on Space Station One)
(Formerly Space Family Robinson, see Gold Key Champion)
No. 37, 10/73 - No. 54, 11/78; No. 55, 3/81 - Present
Gold Key

	Good	Fine	Mint
37-58: Reprints-No. 49,50,55		.30	.60

LOST WORLD, THE (See 4-Color No. 1145)

LOST WORLDS
No. 5, Oct, 1952 - No. 6, Dec, 1952
Standard Comics

	Good	Fine	Mint
5-"Alice in Terrorland" by Toth; J. Katz-a	6.00	18.00	36.00
6-Toth-a	4.00	12.00	24.00

LOTS 'O' FUN COMICS
1940's? (5 cents) (heavy stock; blue covers)
Robert Allen Co.

LOTS 'O' FUN COMICS (continued)

nn-Contents can vary; Felix, Planet Comics known; contents would determine value. Similar to Up-To-Date Comics. Remainders - re-packaged.

LOU GEHRIG (See The Pride of the Yankees)

LOVE ADVENTURES (Actual Confessions No. 13)
Oct, 1949 - No. 12, Aug, 1952
Marvel/Atlas Comics (MPI)

	Good	Fine	Mint
1	2.00	6.00	12.00
2-Powell-a	1.50	4.00	8.00
3-8,10-12: 8-Robinson-a	.85	2.50	5.00
9-Everett-a	1.50	4.00	8.00

LOVE AND MARRIAGE
March, 1952 - No. 16, Sept, 1954
Superior Comics Ltd.

	Good	Fine	Mint
1	3.00	8.00	16.00
2-16	1.50	4.00	8.00
I.W. Reprint No. 1,2,8,11,14	.30	.80	1.60
Super Reprint No. 10('63),15,17('64)	.30	.80	1.60

NOTE: *All issues have Kamenish art.*

LOVE AND ROMANCE
Sept, 1971 - No. 24, Sept, 1975
Charlton Comics

	Good	Fine	Mint
1		.30	.60
2-24		.15	.30

LOVE AT FIRST SIGHT
Oct, 1949 - No. 42, Aug, 1956
Ace Magazines (RAR Publ. Co./Periodical House)

	Good	Fine	Mint
1	3.00	8.00	16.00
2-10	1.50	4.00	8.00
11-42: 26-Anne Brewster-a	.70	2.00	4.00
6(1960)		.40	.80

LOVE BUG, THE (See Movie Comics)

LOVE CLASSICS
Nov, 1949 - No. 2, Jan, 1950
A Lover's Magazine/Marvel Comics

	Good	Fine	Mint
1,2: 2-Virginia Mayo photo-c	2.50	7.00	14.00

LOVE CONFESSIONS
Oct, 1949 - No. 54, Dec, 1956 (some issues: photo covers)
Quality Comics Group

	Good	Fine	Mint
1-Ward c/a, 9 pgs; Gustavson-a	12.00	35.00	70.00
2-Gustavson-a	4.00	12.00	24.00
3	3.00	8.00	16.00
4-Crandall-a	4.00	12.00	24.00
5-Ward-a, 7 pgs.	5.00	14.00	28.00
6,7,9	1.50	4.00	8.00
8-Ward-a	4.00	12.00	24.00
10-Ward-a(2)	4.00	12.00	24.00
11-13,15,16,18,20	1.50	4.00	8.00
14,17,19,22-Ward-a; 17-Faith Dominique photo-c	3.50	10.00	20.00
21,23-38,40-44	.85	2.50	5.00
39-Matt Baker-a	1.50	4.00	8.00
45-Ward-a	2.00	5.00	10.00
46-48,50-54	.70	2.00	4.00
49-Baker c/a	2.50	7.00	14.00

LOVE DIARY
July, 1949 - No. 47, 1954
Our Publishing Co./Toytown/Patches

	Good	Fine	Mint
1-Krigstein-a	4.00	12.00	24.00
2,3-Krigstein & Mort Leav-a in each	3.00	8.00	16.00
4-8	1.00	3.00	6.00
9,10-Everett-a	1.50	4.00	8.00
11-20	1.00	3.00	6.00
21-47	.70	2.00	4.00

LOVE DIARY
September, 1949
Quality Comics Group

	Good	Fine	Mint
1-Ward-c, 9 pgs.	9.00	25.00	50.00

LOVE DIARY
July, 1958 - No. 102, Dec, 1976
Charlton Comics

	Good	Fine	Mint
1	.85	2.50	5.00
2-5,7-10	.40	1.20	2.40
6-Torres-a	.85	2.50	5.00
11-20: 16,20-Leav-a		.60	1.20
21-102: 45-Leav-a		.20	.40

NOTE: *Photo c-10, 20.*

LOVE DOCTOR (See Dr. Anthony King. . .)

LOVE DRAMAS (True Secrets No. 3 on?)
Oct, 1949 - No. 2, Jan, 1950
Marvel Comics (IPS)

	Good	Fine	Mint
1-Jack Kamen-a	4.00	12.00	24.00
2	2.50	7.00	14.00

LOVE EXPERIENCES (Challenge of the Unknown No. 6)
10/49 - No. 5, 1950; No. 6, 4/51 - No. 35, 12/55
Ace Periodicals (A.A. Wyn/Periodical House)

	Good	Fine	Mint
1	2.00	6.00	12.00
2-5	1.00	3.00	6.00
6-10	.70	2.00	4.00
11-35: 15,20,30-Photo-c	.35	1.00	2.00

NOTE: ***Anne Brewster** a-15.*

LOVE EXPRESSIONS
1949?
Ace Magazines

	Good	Fine	Mint
1	2.00	6.00	12.00

LOVE JOURNAL
No. 10, Oct, 1951 - No. 25, July, 1954
Our Publishing Co.

	Good	Fine	Mint
10	1.50	4.00	8.00
11-25	1.00	3.00	6.00

LOVELAND
Nov, 1949 - 1950
Mutual Mag./Eye Publ. (Atlas)

	Good	Fine	Mint
1,2: 1-Photo-c	1.50	4.00	8.00

LOVE LESSONS
Oct, 1949 - No. 5, June, 1950
Harvey Comics/Key Publ. No. 5

	Good	Fine	Mint
1-Same cover as Love Letters 1	2.00	6.00	12.00
2-5: 2-Powell-a	1.50	4.00	8.00

LOVE LETTERS
1949
Harvey Comics

	Good	Fine	Mint
1-Cover-r as Love Lessons 1	2.50	7.00	14.00

LOVE LETTERS
Nov, 1949 - No. 51, Dec, 1956
Quality Comics Group

	Good	Fine	Mint
1-Ward-c, Gustavson-a	7.00	20.00	40.00
2-Ward-c, Gustavson-a	6.00	18.00	36.00
3-Gustavson-a	4.00	12.00	24.00
4-Ward-a, 9 pgs.	6.00	18.00	36.00
5-8,10	1.50	4.00	8.00

Love & Marriage #6, © SUPR

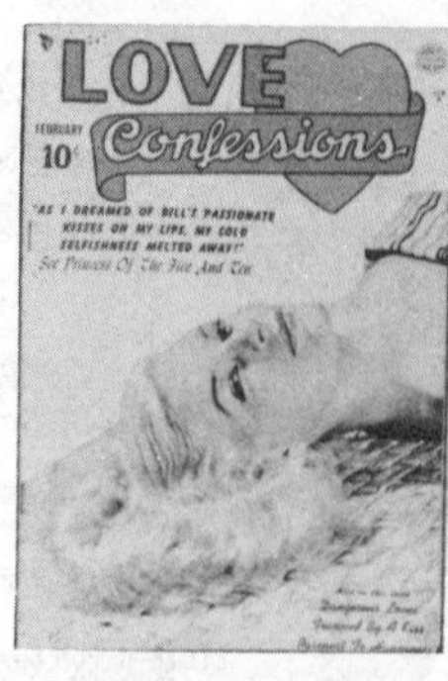

Love Confessions #3, © QUA

Love Journal #10, © Our Publ.

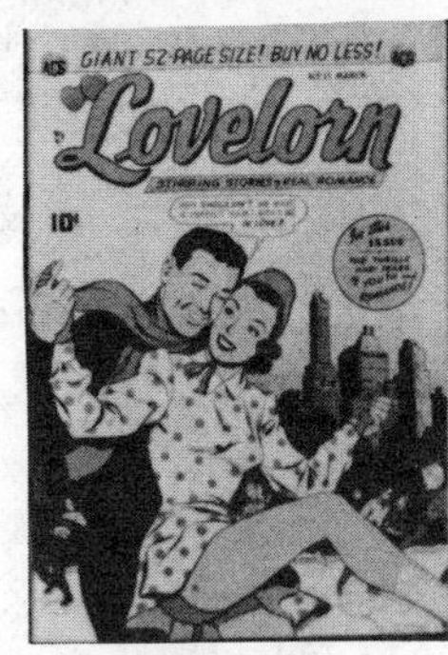

Lovelorn #11, © ACG

Love Problems & Advice #4, © HARV

Love Secrets #37, © QUA

LOVE LETTERS (continued)

	Good	Fine	Mint
9-One pg. Ward-''Be Popular with the Opposite Sex''; Robert Mitchum photo-c	3.00	8.00	16.00
11-Ward-r/Broadway Romances 2 & retitled	3.00	8.00	16.00
12-15,18-20	1.00	3.00	6.00
16,17-Ward-a; 17-Jane Russell photo-c	3.50	10.00	20.00
21-27,29,32-42,44-48	.85	2.50	5.00
28-Ward-a(p)	3.00	8.00	16.00
30,31-Ward-a	2.50	7.00	14.00
43-Baker-c	2.00	6.00	12.00
49,50-Baker-a	2.50	7.00	14.00
51-Baker-c	2.00	6.00	12.00

NOTE: *Photo-c on most 3-28.*

LOVE LIFE
1951
P. L. Publishing Co.

	Good	Fine	Mint
1	2.00	6.00	12.00

LOVELORN (Confessions of the Lovelorn No. 52 on)
Aug-Sept, 1949 - No. 51, July, 1954
American Comics Group (Michel Publ./Regis Publ.)

	Good	Fine	Mint
1	2.00	6.00	12.00
2-10	1.00	3.00	6.00
11-20,22-48: 18-Drucker-a, 2pgs.	.50	1.50	3.00
21-Prostitution story	1.50	4.00	8.00
49-51-Has 3-D effect	3.00	9.00	18.00

LOVE MEMORIES
1949 (no month) - No. 4, July, 1950
Fawcett Publications

	Good	Fine	Mint
1	3.00	8.00	16.00
2-4	1.50	4.00	8.00

LOVE MYSTERY
June, 1950 - No. 3, Oct, 1950
Fawcett Publications

	Good	Fine	Mint
1,2-Photo-c; George Evans-a each	5.00	15.00	30.00
3-Powell-a	4.00	12.00	24.00

LOVE PROBLEMS
1949 (132 pages)
Fox Features Syndicate

nn-See Fox Giants. Contents can vary and determines price.

LOVE PROBLEMS AND ADVICE ILLUSTRATED (Becomes Romance Stories of True Love)
June, 1949 - No. 6, Apr, 1950; No. 7, Jan, 1951 - No. 44, Mar, 1957
McCombs/Harvey Publ./Home Comics

	Good	Fine	Mint
V1No.1	3.00	8.00	16.00
2-10	1.00	3.00	6.00
11-13,15-37,39-44	.70	2.00	4.00
14-Rape scene	.85	2.50	5.00
38-S&K-c	1.50	4.00	8.00

NOTE: ***Powell** a-1,2,7-14,17-25,28,29,33,40,41. No. 3 has True Love. . on inside.*

LOVE ROMANCES (Formerly Ideal No. 5?)
No. 6, May, 1949 - No. 106, July, 1963
Timely/Marvel/Atlas(TCI No. 7-71/Male No. 72-106)

	Good	Fine	Mint
6	1.50	4.00	8.00
7,9-20: 9-12-Photo-c	1.00	3.00	6.00
8-Kubert-a	3.00	8.00	16.00
21,24-Krigstein-a	2.50	7.00	14.00
22,23,25-35,37,39,40	.70	2.00	4.00
36,38-Krigstein-a	2.00	5.00	10.00
41-43,46-48,50-56,58-74	.50	1.50	3.00
44-lingerie panel	.60	1.80	3.60
45,57-Matt Baker-a	1.50	4.00	8.00
49-Toth-a, 6 pgs.	2.00	5.00	10.00
75,77,82-Matt Baker-a	1.50	4.00	8.00
76,78-81,84,86-95,97,100-104	.40	1.20	2.40
83-Kirby-c, Severin-a	1.20	3.50	7.00
85,96-Kirby c/a	1.20	3.50	7.00
98-Kirby-a(4)	3.00	8.00	16.00
99,105,106-Kirby-a	1.20	3.50	7.00

NOTE: ***Anne Brewster** a-72. **Colletta** c-80. **Kirby** c-80, 85, 88. **Robinson** a-29.*

LOVERS (Formerly Blonde Phantom)
No. 23, May, 1949 - No. 85, June, 1957
Marvel Comics No. 23,24/Atlas No. 25 on (ANC)

	Good	Fine	Mint
23	1.50	4.00	8.00
24-Tothish plus Robinson-a; photo-c	1.50	4.00	8.00
25,30-Kubert-a; 7, 10 pgs.	2.50	7.00	14.00
26-29,31-36,39,40	.85	2.50	5.00
37,38-Krigstein-a	2.50	7.00	14.00
41-Everett-a(2)	1.50	4.00	8.00
42,44-64: 59-Colletta-a	.50	1.50	3.00
43-1pg. Frazetta ad	1.00	3.00	6.00
65,85-Baker-a	1.50	4.00	8.00
66,68-84	.40	1.20	2.40
67-Toth-a	2.00	5.00	10.00

NOTE: ***Powell** a-27.*

LOVERS' LANE
Oct, 1949 - No. 41, June, 1954
Lev Gleason Publications

	Good	Fine	Mint
1	2.00	6.00	12.00
2,3,5-10	.85	2.50	5.00
4-Fuje-a, 9 pgs.	.85	2.50	5.00
11-19: 19-Photo-c	.50	1.50	3.00
20-Frazetta 1 pg. ad	1.00	3.00	6.00
21-38,40,41	.50	1.50	3.00
39-Story narrated by Frank Sinatra	1.00	3.00	6.00

NOTE: ***Fuje**-c on many issues.*

LOVE SCANDALS
Feb, 1950 - No. 5, Oct, 1950 (No. 4,5 - photo covers)
Quality Comics Group

	Good	Fine	Mint
1-Ward c/a, 9 pgs.	9.00	25.00	50.00
2,3	3.00	9.00	18.00
4-Ward c/a, 18 pgs; Gil Fox-a	9.00	25.00	50.00
5-C. Cuidera-a	3.00	9.00	18.00

LOVE SECRETS
Oct, 1949 - No. 56, Dec, 1956
Quality Comics Group

	Good	Fine	Mint
1	4.00	12.00	24.00
2-10	1.50	4.00	8.00
11-33,35-39	1.00	3.00	6.00
34,45-Ward-a	3.00	8.00	16.00
40-Matt Baker-c	2:00	6.00	12.00
41-44,47-50,53,54	.85	2.50	5.00
46-Baker, Ward-a	2.00	6.00	12.00
51,52-Ward(r)-(No. 52/Love Confessions No. 17)	1.50	4.00	8.00
55,56-Baker-a; cover-No. 56	1.50	4.00	8.00

LOVE SECRETS
No. 2, Jan, 1950
Atlas Comics(IPC)

	Good	Fine	Mint
2	1.00	3.00	6.00

LOVE STORIES
No. 6, 1950 - No. 18, Aug, 1954
Fox Features Syndicate/Star Publ. No. 13 on

	Good	Fine	Mint
6,8-Wood-a	6.00	18.00	36.00
7,9-12	2.50	7.00	14.00
13-18-L. B. Cole-a	3.00	9.00	18.00

LOVE STORIES (Formerly Heart Throbs)
No. 147, Nov, 1972 - No. 152, Oct-Nov, 1973

LOVE STORIES (continued)
National Periodical Publications

	Good	Fine	Mint
147-152		.20	.40

LOVE STORIES OF MARY WORTH (See Harvey Hits No. 55)
Sept, 1949 - No. 5, May, 1950
Harvey Publications

	Good	Fine	Mint
1-1940's newspaper reprints-No. 1-4	3.00	8.00	16.00
2,4,5	2.00	6.00	12.00
3-Kamen/Baker-a?	2.00	6.00	12.00

LOVE TALES (Formerly The Human Torch No. 35)
No. 36, May, 1949 - No. 75, Sept, 1957
Marvel/Atlas Comics (ZPC No. 36-50/MMC No. 67-75)

	Good	Fine	Mint
36	1.20	3.50	7.00
37-44,46-50: 41-Photo-c	.70	2.00	4.00
45-Powell-a	1.00	3.00	6.00
51,69-Everett-a	1.20	3.50	7.00
52-Krigstein-a	2.00	5.00	10.00
53-68,70-75	.50	1.50	3.00

LOVE, 10 STORIES
July, 1955
Charlton Comics

	Good	Fine	Mint
6	.40	1.20	2.40

LOVE THRILLS
1950 (132 pages)
Fox Features Syndicate

nn-See Fox Giants. Contents can vary and determines price.

LOVE TRAILS
Dec, 1949 - No. 2, Feb, 1950 (52 pgs.)
A Lover's Magazine (CDS)(Marvel)

	Good	Fine	Mint
1,2	2.00	6.00	12.00

LOWELL THOMAS' HIGH ADVENTURE (See 4-Color No. 949,1001)

LT. (See Lieutenant)

LUCKY COMICS
Jan, 1944; No. 2, Summer, 1945 - No. 5, Summer, 1946
Consolidated Magazines

	Good	Fine	Mint
1-Lucky Starr, Bobbie	2.50	7.00	14.00
2-5	1.20	3.50	7.00

LUCKY DUCK
No. 5, Jan, 1953 - No. 8, Sept, 1953
Standard Comics (Literary Ent.)

	Good	Fine	Mint
5-8-Irving Spector-a	1.20	3.50	7.00

LUCKY FIGHTS IT THROUGH (Also see The K. O. Punch)
1949 (16 pgs. in color; paper cover) (Giveaway)
Educational Comics

	Good	Fine	Mint
(Very Rare)-1st Kurtzman work for E. C.; V.D. prevention	150.00	400.00	700.00

(Prices vary widely on this book)

NOTE: *Subtitled "The Story of That Ignorant, Ignorant Cowboy." Prepared for Communications Materials Center, Columbia University.*

LUCKY "7" COMICS
1944 (No date listed)
Howard Publishers Ltd.

	Good	Fine	Mint
1-Congo Raider, Punch Powers; bondage-c	5.00	15.00	30.00

LUCKY STAR
1950 - No. 7, 1951; No. 8, 1953 - No. 14, 1955 (5x7¼"; full color)
Nation Wide Publ. Co.

	Good	Fine	Mint
1-Jack Davis-a	3.00	8.00	16.00
2,3-(52 pgs.)-Jack Davis-a	2.50	7.00	14.00
4-7-(52 pgs.)	2.00	5.00	10.00
8-14-(36 pgs.)	1.50	4.00	8.00
Given away with Lucky Star Western Wear by the Juvenile Mfg. Co.	1.50	4.00	8.00

LUCY SHOW, THE (TV)
June, 1963 - No. 5, June, 1964
Gold Key

	Good	Fine	Mint
1	1.00	3.00	6.00
2-5	.50	1.50	3.00

LUCY, THE REAL GONE GAL (Meet Miss Pepper No. 5 on)
June, 1953 - No. 4, Dec, 1953
St. John Publishing Co.

	Good	Fine	Mint
1-4: 3-Drucker-a	1.50	4.00	8.00

LUDWIG BEMELMAN'S MADELEINE & GENEVIEVE (See 4-Color No. 796)

LUDWIG VON DRAKE (Walt Disney)
Nov-Dec, 1961 - No. 4, June-Aug, 1962
Dell Publishing Co.

	Good	Fine	Mint
1	.70	2.00	4.00
2-4	.40	1.20	2.40
. . . Fish Stampede (15 pgs.; 1962; Fritos giveaway)	.70	2.00	4.00

LUKE CAGE (See Hero for Hire)

LUKE SHORT'S WESTERN STORIES
April, 1954 - 1958
Dell Publishing Co.

	Good	Fine	Mint
1 (4/54)	1.50	4.00	8.00
4-Color 580(8/54), 2(10/54)	1.00	3.00	6.00
4-Color 651-Kinstler-a	1.20	3.50	7.00
4-Color 739,771,807,875,927	1.00	3.00	6.00
4-Color 848	1.50	4.00	8.00

LUNATICKLE (Magazine) (Satire)
Feb, 1956 - No. 2, Apr, 1956
Whitstone Publ.

	Good	Fine	Mint
1,2-Kubert-a	1.50	4.50	9.00

LYNDON B. JOHNSON
March, 1965
Dell Publishing Co.

	Good	Fine	Mint
12-445-503	1.50	4.00	8.00

MACHINE MAN (Also see 2001 . . .)
April, 1978 - No. 9, Dec, 1978; No. 10, Aug, 1979 - No.19, 1980
Marvel Comics Group

	Good	Fine	Mint
1	.30	.80	1.60
2-5		.40	.80
6-18		.30	.60
19-Wendigo, Alpha Force-ties into X-Men No. 140		.60	1.20

NOTE: ***Ditko*** *a-10-19; c-10-13, 15-17.* ***Kirby*** *a-all; c-1-5, 7-9.* ***Simonson*** *c-6.*

MACKENZIE'S RAIDERS (See 4-Color No. 1093)

MACO TOYS COMIC
1959 (36 pages; full color) (Giveaway)
Maco Toys/Charlton Comics

	Good	Fine	Mint
1-All military stories featuring Maco Toys	1.00	3.00	6.00

MAD
Oct-Nov, 1952 - Present (No. 24 on, magazine format)
(Kurtzman editor No. 1-28, Feldstein No. 29 on)
E. C. Comics

	Good	Fine	Mint
1-Wood, Davis, Elder start as regulars	60.00	160.00	300.00

Lucky Duck #6, © STD

Ludwig Von Drake #3, © WDP

Machine Man #1, © MCG

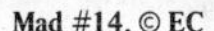
Mad #14, © EC

Mad #35, © EC

Madhouse #97, © AP

MAD (continued)

	Good	Fine	Mint
2-Davis-c	30.00	80.00	150.00
3	18.00	50.00	90.00
4-Marijuana story "Flob Was a Slob" by Davis	15.00	40.00	74.00
5-Low distribution; Elder-c	50.00	120.00	240.00
6-10	10.00	30.00	56.00
11-Wolverton-a	10.00	30.00	56.00
12-15	7.00	20.00	40.00
16-23(5/55): 22-all by Elder. 23-Special announcement of cancellation	5.50	16.00	32.00
24(7/55)-1st magazine issue (25 cents); Kurtzman logo & border on-c	12.00	35.00	70.00
25-Jaffee starts as regular writer	5.50	16.00	32.00
26	4.00	12.00	24.00
27-Davis-c; Jaffee starts as story artist; new logo	4.00	12.00	24.00
28-Elder-c; Heath back-c; last issue edited by Kurtzman; (three cover variations exist with different wording on contents banner on lower right of cover; value of each the same)	4.00	12.00	24.00
29-Wood-c; Kamen-a; Don Martin starts as regular; Feldstein editing begins	4.00	12.00	24.00
30-1st A. E. Neuman cover by Mingo; Crandall inside-c; last Elder art; Bob Clarke starts as regular	5.00	15.00	30.00
31-Freas starts as regular; last Davis art until No. 99	3.50	10.00	30.00
32-Orlando, Drucker, Woodbridge start as regulars; Wood back-c	3.50	10.00	20.00
33-Orlando back-c	3.50	10.00	20.00
34-Berg starts as regular	3.00	8.00	16.00
35-Mingo wraparound-c; Crandall-a	3.00	8.00	16.00
36-40	2.00	6.00	12.00
41-50	1.75	5.00	10.00
51-60: 60-Two Clarke-c; Prohias starts as regular	1.00	3.00	6.00
61-70: 64-Rickard starts as regular. 68-Martin-c	.85	2.50	5.00
71-80: 76-Aragones starts as regular	.85	2.50	5.00
81-90: 86-1st Fold-in. 89-One strip by Walt Kelly. 90-Frazetta back-c	.70	2.00	4.00
91-100: 91-Jaffee starts as story artist. 99-Davis-a resumes	.40	1.20	2.40
101-120: 101-Infinity-c. 105-Batman TV show take-off. 106-Frazetta back-c	.35	1.00	2.00
121-140: 130-Torres starts as regular. 122-Drucker & Mingo-c. 128-Last Orlando. 135,139-Davis-c	.30	.80	1.60
141-170: 165-Martin-c. 169-Drucker-c		.50	1.00
171-200: 173,178-Davis-c. 176-Drucker-c. 182-Bob Jones starts as regular. 186-Star Trek take-off. 187-Harry North starts as regular. 196-Star Wars take-off		.40	.80
201-214: 203-Star Wars take-off. 204-Hulk TV show take-off. 208-Superman movie take-off		.30	.60

NOTE: ***Jules Feiffer*** *a(r)-42.* ***Freas****-most-c and back covers-40-74.* ***Heath*** *a-14, 27.* ***Kamen*** *a-29.* ***Krigstein*** *a-12, 17, 24, 26.* ***Kurtzman*** *c-1, 3, 4, 6-10, 13, 14, 16, 18.* ***Mingo*** *c-30-37, 75-111.* ***John Severin*** *a-1-6, 9, 10.* ***Wolverton*** *c-11; a-11, 17, 29, 31, 36, 40, 82, 137.* ***Wood*** *a-24-45, 59; c-26, 29.*

MAD (See . . . Follies, . . . Special, More Trash from . . . , and The Worst from . . .)

MAD ABOUT MILLIE
April, 1969 - No. 17, Dec, 1970
Marvel Comics Group

	Good	Fine	Mint
1-Giant issue		.60	1.20
2-17		.30	.60
Annual 1(11/71)		.40	.80

MADAME XANADU
July, 1981 - Present (No ads; $1.00; 32 pgs.)
DC Comics

	Good	Fine	Mint
1-Marshall Rogers-a(25 pgs.); Kaluta-c/a(2 pgs.); pin-up of Madame Xanadu		.60	1.20

MAD FOLLIES (Special)
1963 - No. 7, 1969
E. C. Comics

	Good	Fine	Mint
nn(1963)-Paperback book covers	4.00	12.00	24.00
2(1964)-Calendar	3.00	8.00	16.00
3(1965)-Mischief Stickers	1.75	5.00	10.00
4(1966)-Mobile; reprints Frazetta back-c/Mad No. 90	2.00	6.00	12.00
5(1967)-Stencils	1.75	5.00	10.00
6(1968)-Mischief Stickers	1.50	4.00	8.00
7(1969)-Nasty Cards	1.50	4.00	8.00

NOTE: ***Clarke*** *c-4.* ***Mingo*** *c-1-3.* ***Orlando*** *a-5.*

MAD HATTER, THE (Costume Hero)
Jan-Feb, 1946 - No. 2, Sept-Oct, 1946
O. W. Comics Corp.

	Good	Fine	Mint
1-Freddy the Firefly begins; Giunta-a	10.00	30.00	60.00
2-Has ad for E.C.'s Animal Fables No. 1	8.00	24.00	48.00

MADHOUSE
1954; June, 1957 - No. 4, Dec?, 1957
Ajax/Farrell Publ. (Excellent Publ./4-Star)

	Good	Fine	Mint
1(1954)	5.00	14.00	28.00
2,3	2.50	7.00	14.00
4-Surrealistic-c	3.50	10.00	20.00
1(1957)	2.00	5.00	10.00
2-4	1.20	3.50	7.00

MADHOUSE (Formerly Madhouse Glads)
No. 95, Sept, 1974 - No. 97, Jan, 1975; No. 98, Aug, 1975 - Present
Red Circle Productions/Archie Publications

	Good	Fine	Mint
95-Horror stories through No. 97		.60	1.20
96-Jones-a		.60	1.20
97-Intro. Henry Hobson; Morrow, Thorne-a		.40	.80
98-122-Satire/humor stories		.30	.60
Annual 8(1970-71)- 12(1974-75)-Formerly Madhouse Ma-ad Annual		.40	.80
. . . Comics Digest 1(1975-76)- 6(1977-79)		.50	1.00

NOTE: ***McWilliams*** *a-97.* ***Morrow*** *c-95-97. See Archie Comics Digest No. 1, 13.*

MADHOUSE GLADS (Formerly Madhouse Ma-ad; Madhouse No. 95 on)
No. 75, Oct, 1970 - No. 94, Aug, 1974 (No. 78-92: 52 pgs.)
Archie Publications

	Good	Fine	Mint
75		.25	.50
76-94		.20	.40

MADHOUSE MA-AD (. . . Jokes No. 67-70; . . . Freak-Out No. 71-74) (Formerly Archie's Madhouse) (Becomes Madhouse Glads No. 75 on)
No. 67, April, 1969 - No. 74, Sept, 1970
Archie Publications

	Good	Fine	Mint
67-74		.25	.50
. . . Annual 7(1969-70)-Formerly Archie's Madhouse Annual; becomes Madhouse Annual		.30	.60

MAD MONSTER PARTY (See Movie Classics)

MAD SPECIAL (. . . Super Special)
Fall, 1970 - Present (84 - 116 pages)
E. C. Publications, Inc.

	Good	Fine	Mint
Fall 1970(No.1)-Bonus-Voodoo Doll; contains 17 pgs. new material	2.00	6.00	12.00
Spring 1971(No.2)-Wall Nuts; 17 pgs. new material	1.50	4.00	8.00
3-Protest Stickers	1.50	4.00	8.00
4-8: 4-Mini Posters. 5-Mad Flag. 7-Presidential candidate posters, Wild Shocking Message posters. 8-TV Guise	1.00	3.00	6.00

MAD SPECIAL (continued)

	Good	Fine	Mint
9(1972)-Contains Nostalgic Mad No. 1 (28 pgs.)	1.00	3.00	6.00
10,11,13: 10-Nonsense Stickers (Don Martin). 11-33⅓ RPM record. 13-Sickie Stickers; 3 pgs. new Wolverton	1.00	3.00	6.00
12-Contains Nostalgic Mad No. 2 (36 pgs.); Davis, Wolverton-a	1.00	3.00	6.00
14-Vital Message posters & Art Depreciation paintings	.70	2.00	4.00
15-Contains Nostalgic Mad No. 3 (28 pgs.)	1.00	3.00	6.00
16,17,19,20: 16-Mad-hesive Stickers. 17-Don Martin posters. 20-Martin Stickers	.55	1.60	3.20
18-Contains Nostalgic Mad No. 4 (36 pgs.)	.70	2.00	4.00
21,24-Contains Nostalgic Mad No. 5 (28 pgs.) & No. 6 (28 pgs.)	.55	1.60	3.20
22,23,25-27,29,30: 22-Diplomas. 23-Martin Stickers. 25-Martin Posters. 26-33⅓ RPM record. 27-Mad Shock-Sticks. 29-Mad Collectable-Correctable Posters. 30-The Movies	.40	1.20	2.40
28-Contains Nostalgic Mad No. 7 (36 pgs.)	.55	1.60	3.20

NOTE: *No. 28-30: no number on cover.* ***Mingo*** *c-9, 11, 15, 19, 23.*

MAD'S SERGIO ARAGONES ON PARADE
1979 (160 pgs.)
E. C. Publications

	Good	Fine	Mint
1		.75	1.50

MAGIC AGENT (See Unknown Worlds)
Jan-Feb, 1961 - No. 3, May-June, 1961
American Comics Group

	Good	Fine	Mint
1-Origin & 1st app. John Force	.40	1.20	2.40
2,3	.30	.80	1.60

MAGIC COMICS
Aug, 1939 - No. 123, Nov-Dec, 1949
David McKay Publications

	Good	Fine	Mint
1-Mandrake the Magician, Henry, Popeye (not by Segar), Blondie, Barney Baxter, Secret Agent X-9 (not by Raymond), Bunky by Billy DeBeck & Thornton Burgess text stories illustrated by Harrison Cady begin	30.00	80.00	160.00
2	14.00	40.00	80.00
3	12.00	30.00	70.00
4	10.00	28.00	56.00
5	8.00	24.00	48.00
6-10	6.00	18.00	36.00
11-16,18-20	5.00	15.00	30.00
17-The Lone Ranger begins	5.50	16.00	32.00
21-30	4.00	12.00	24.00
31-40	3.00	9.00	18.00
41-50	2.75	8.00	16.00
51-60	2.00	6.00	12.00
61-70	1.50	4.00	8.00
71-100	1.20	3.50	7.00
101-106,109-123	1.00	3.00	6.00
107,108-Flash Gordon in each, not by Raymond	3.00	8.00	16.00

MAGICA DE SPELL (See Walt Disney Showcase No. 30)

MAGIC OF CHRISTMAS AT NEWBERRYS, THE
1967 (20 pgs.; slick cover; B&W inside)
E. S. London (Giveaway)

	Good	Fine	Mint
		.60	1.20

MAGIC SWORD, THE (See Movie Classics)

MAGILLA GORILLA (TV) (Hanna-Barbera)
May, 1964 - No. 10, Dec, 1968
Gold Key

	Good	Fine	Mint
1	.85	2.50	5.00
2,4-10	.50	1.50	3.00
3-Vs. Yogi Bear for President	.50	1.50	3.00

MAGILLA GORILLA (TV)
Nov, 1970 - No. 5, July, 1971 (Hanna-Barbera)
Charlton Comics

	Good	Fine	Mint
1-5	.50	1.50	3.00

MAGNUS, ROBOT FIGHTER (. . . 4000 A.D.)
Feb, 1963 - No. 46, Jan, 1977
Gold Key

	Good	Fine	Mint
1-Origin Magnus; Aliens series begins	5.50	16.00	32.00
2,3	3.00	8.00	16.00
4-10	1.50	4.00	8.00
11-20	1.00	3.00	6.00
21,22,24-28: 22-Reprints origin from No. 1. 28-Last new material issue; Aliens series ends	.50	1.50	3.00
23-Exists with two different prices, 12 cents and 15 cents	.50	1.50	3.00
29-41,43,45,46-Reprints	.30	.80	1.60
42,44-New material		.50	1.00

NOTE: ***Russ Manning*** *a-1-22, 28, 29-43(r).*

MAID OF THE MIST (See American Graphics)

MAJOR HOOPLE COMICS
1942
Nedor Publications

	Good	Fine	Mint
1-Mary Worth, Phantom Soldier by Moldoff app.	6.00	18.00	36.00

MAJOR INAPAK THE SPACE ACE
1951 (20 pages) (Giveaway)
Magazine Enterprises (Inapac Foods)

	Good	Fine	Mint
1-Bob Powell-a	.30	.80	1.60

NOTE: *Many warehouse copies surfaced in 1973.*

MAJOR VICTORY COMICS
1944 - No. 3, Summer, 1945
H. Clay Glover/Service Publ./Harry 'A' Chesler

	Good	Fine	Mint
1-Origin Major Victory by C. Sultan (reprint from Dynamic No. 1); Spider Woman 1st app.	10.00	30.00	60.00
2-Dynamic Boy app.	7.00	20.00	40.00
3-Rocket Boy app.	5.50	16.00	32.00

MALTESE FALCON (See Feature Book No. 48 (McKay))

MALU IN THE LAND OF ADVENTURE
1964
I. W. Enterprises

	Good	Fine	Mint
1-Reprints Avon's Slave Girl Princess No. 1; Severin-c	5.00	14.00	28.00

MAMMOTH COMICS
1937 (84 pages) (Black & White, 8½x11½'')
Whitman Publishing Co.(K. K. Publications)

	Good	Fine	Mint
1-Terry & the Pirates, Dick Tracy, Little Orphan Annie, Wash Tubbs, & other reprints	35.00	100.00	200.00

MAMMY YOKUM & THE GREAT DOGPATCH MYSTERY
1951 (Giveaway)
Toby Press

	Good	Fine	Mint
Li'l Abner	4.00	12.00	24.00

MAN-BAT (Also see Detective No. 400, Brave & the Bold, and Batman Family)
Dec-Jan, 1975-76 - No. 2, Feb-Mar, 1976
National Periodical Publications

	Good	Fine	Mint
1-Ditko-a	.30	.90	1.80
2		.45	.90

Magic Comics #100, © DMP

Magnus Robot Fighter #8, © GK

Mammoth Comics #1, © WHIT

Mandrake The Magician #2, © KING

Man In Black #2, © HARV

Many Ghosts Of Dr. Graves #45, © CC

MAN COMICS
Dec, 1949 - No. 28, Sept, 1953
Marvel/Atlas Comics (NPI)

	Good	Fine	Mint
1-Tuska-a	2.00	5.00	10.00
2-5: 2-Tuska-a	1.00	3.00	6.00
6-13,15	.70	2.00	4.00
14-Krenkel (3pgs.), Berg, Pakula-a	1.50	4.00	8.00
16-21,23-28	.55	1.60	3.20
22-Krigstein-a	2.50	7.00	14.00

NOTE: ***Berg** a-15. **Colan** a-21. **Everett** c-25. **Heath** a-11. Kubertish a-by **Bob Brown**-3. **Maneely** c-11.*

MANDRAKE THE MAGICIAN (See Feature Book No. 18,19,23,46,52, 55)

MANDRAKE THE MAGICIAN (See Comics Hits No. 53)
1956; Sept, 1966 - No. 10, Nov, 1967
Dell Publishing Co./King Comics

	Good	Fine	Mint
4-Color 752('56)	2.00	6.00	12.00
1(King)-Begin S.O.S. Phantom series, ends No. 3	.70	2.00	4.00
2-5: 4-Girl Phantom app. 5-Brick Bradford app., also No. 6	.55	1.60	3.20
6,7,9: 7-Origin Lothar. 9-Brick Bradford app.	.35	1.00	2.00
8-Jeff Jones-a	.85	2.50	5.00
10-Rip Kirby app.; 14 pgs. art by Raymond	1.50	4.00	8.00

MANDRAKE THE MAGICIAN GIANT COMIC ALBUM
1972 (48 pgs.; 11x14''; B&W; cardboard covers)
Modern Promotions

	Good	Fine	Mint
nn-Strip reprints by Lee Falk	1.50	4.00	8.00

MAN FROM ATLANTIS, THE
Feb, 1978 - No. 7, Aug, 1978
Marvel Comics Group

	Good	Fine	Mint
1-(80 pgs.; $1.00)-Buscema-c; origin story		.50	1.00
2-7		.40	.80

MAN FROM U.N.C.L.E., THE (TV)
Feb, 1965 - No. 22, April, 1969 (All photo covers)
Gold Key

	Good	Fine	Mint
1	1.00	3.00	6.00
2	.50	1.50	3.00
3-10: 7-Jet Dream begins	.30	.80	1.60
11-22: 21,22-Reprints		.50	1.00

MAN FROM WELLS FARGO (TV)
July, 1962
Dell Publishing Co.

	Good	Fine	Mint
4-Color 1287, 01-495-207	1.00	3.00	6.00

MANHUNT! (Becomes Red Fox No. 15 on)
Oct, 1947 - No. 14, 1953
Magazine Enterprises

	Good	Fine	Mint
1-Red Fox by L. B. Cole, Undercover Girl by Whitney, Space Ace begin; negligee panels	14.00	40.00	70.00
2-Electrocution-c	10.00	30.00	60.00
3-5	10.00	28.00	50.00
6-Bondage-c by Whitney	10.00	28.00	50.00
7-9: 7-Space ace ends. 8-Trail Colt begins	7.00	20.00	36.00
10-G. Ingels-a	8.00	24.00	40.00
11(8/48)-Frazetta-a, 7 pgs.; The Duke, Scotland Yard begin	17.00	50.00	80.00
12	5.00	14.00	28.00
13(A-1 63)-Frazetta, r-/Trail Colt No. 1, 7 pgs.	12.00	35.00	70.00
14(A-1 77)-Classic bondage-c; last L. B. Cole Red Fox; Ingels-a	7.00	20.00	40.00

NOTE: ***Guardineer** a-1-5; c-8. **Whitney** a-2-14; c-1-6, 10. Red Fox by **L. B. Cole**-No. 1-14. No. 15 was advertised but came out as Red Fox No. 15.*

MANHUNTER (See First Issue Special)

MAN IN BLACK (See Thrill-O-Rama) (Also see Front Page and Strange Story Comics)
Sept, 1957 - 1958
Harvey Publications

	Good	Fine	Mint
1-Bob Powell c/a	5.00	14.00	28.00
2-5: Powell c/a	3.50	10.00	20.00

MAN IN FLIGHT (See 4-Color No. 836)

MAN IN SPACE (See Dell Giant No. 27 & 4-Color No. 716,954)

MAN OF PEACE, POPE PIUS XII
1950 (See Pope Pius XII. . & Topix V2No.8)
Catechetical Guild

	Good	Fine	Mint
	5.00	14.00	28.00

MAN OF WAR (See Liberty Scouts & Liberty Guards)
Nov, 1941 - No. 2, Jan, 1942
Centaur Publications

	Good	Fine	Mint
1-The Fire-Man, Man of War, The Sentinel, & Vapo-Man begin; Gustavson-c/a; Flag-c	25.00	75.00	160.00
2-The Ferret app.; Gustavson-c/a	22.00	65.00	135.00

MAN O' MARS
1953; 1964
Fiction House Magazines

	Good	Fine	Mint
1-Space Rangers	8.00	24.00	48.00
I.W. Reprint No. 1/Man O'Mars No. 1; Murphy Anderson-a	3.00	8.00	16.00

MAN-THING, THE (See Fear)
Jan, 1974 - No. 22, Oct, 1975; Nov, 1979 - V2No. 11, July, 1981
Marvel Comics Group

	Good	Fine	Mint
1-Howard the Duck app. (2nd anywhere); origin retold	1.50	4.50	9.00
2-4	.70	2.00	4.00
5-Ploog-a	.50	1.50	3.00
6-Drug propaganda story	.40	1.10	2.20
7-11-Ploog-a	.40	1.10	2.20
12-20		.60	1.20
21-Origin by Mooney		.50	1.00
22-Howard the Duck cameo		.60	1.20
V2No.1(1979)	.30	.80	1.60
2-11: 6-Golden-c		.40	.80
Giant Size 1(8/74)-Ploog c/a	.40	1.10	2.20
Giant Size 2,3	.30	.80	1.60
Giant Size 4-Howard the Duck by Brunner; Ditko-a(r)	2.00	6.00	12.00
Giant Size 5-Howard the Duck by Brunner	1.50	4.50	9.00

NOTE: ***Alcala** a-14, Giant Size 3. **Brunner** c-1, Giant Size 4. **Ditko** a-Gnt. Size 1r, 4r. **Kirby** a-Gnt. Size 1r. **Mooney** a-1, 2p, 3, 18, 20-22. **Ploog** Man-Thing-5-11; c-5, 6, 8, 9, 11.*

MAN WITH THE X-RAY EYES, THE (See X, . . . under Movie Comics)

MANY GHOSTS OF DR. GRAVES, THE
May, 1967 - No. 60, Dec, 1976; No. 61, Sept, 1977 - No. 62, Oct, 1977; No. 63, Feb, 1978 - No. 65, April, 1978
Charlton Comics

	Good	Fine	Mint
1	.40	1.20	2.40
2-10		.50	1.00
11-20		.40	.80
21-44		.30	.60
45-1st Newton comic book work	.35	1.00	2.00
46,48,50-65		.30	.60
47,49-Newton-a		.40	.80

NOTE: ***Ditko** a-1, 7, 9, 11-13, 15-18, 20-22, 24, 26, 35, 37, 38, 40-44, 47, 48, 51-54, 58, 60r, 61r, 63-65r; c-No. 11-13, 16-18, 22, 24, 26-35, 38, 40, 55, 58, 63-65. **Newton** c-49, 52. **Sutton** c/a-42.*

MANY LOVES OF DOBIE GILLIS (TV)
May-June, 1960 - No. 26, Oct, 1964
National Periodical Publications

M.L.O Dobie Gillis #1, © DC

March Of Comics #5, © Walter Lantz

March Of Comics #23, © J. Gruelle

MANY LOVES OF DOBIE GILLIS (continued)	**Good**	**Fine**	**Mint**
1	3.50	10.00	20.00
2-5	2.00	5.00	10.00
6-10	1.00	3.00	6.00
11-26	.85	2.50	5.00

MARAUDER'S MOON (See 4-Color No. 848)

MARCH OF COMICS (Boys' and Girls'. . .)
1946 - Present (No. 1-4: No No.'s)
(K.K. Giveaway) (Founded by Sig Feuchtwanger)
K. K. Publications/Western Publishing Co.

Early issues were full size, 32 pages, and were printed with and without an extra cover of slick stock, just for the advertiser. The binding was stapled if the slick cover was added; otherwise, the pages were glued together at the spine. 1948 - 1951 issues were full size, 24 pages, pulp covers. Starting in 1952 they were half-size and 32 pages with slick covers. 1959 and later issues had only 16 pages plus covers. 1952 -1959 issues read oblong; 1960 and later issues read upright.

	Good	Fine	Mint
1(nn)(1946)-Goldilocks; Kelly back-c	20.00	60.00	120.00
2(nn)(1946)-How Santa Got His Red Suit; Kelly-a(11 pgs.) Copyright 1944	20.00	60.00	120.00
3(nn)(1947)-Our Gang (Walt Kelly)	40.00	110.00	220.00
4(nn)Donald Duck by Carl Barks, ''Maharajah Donald,'' 28 pgs.; Kelly-c?	500.00	1200.00	2400.00
5-Andy Panda	12.00	36.00	72.00
6-Popular Fairy Tales; Kelly-c; Noonan-a(2)	17.00	50.00	100.00
7-Oswald the Rabbit; Kelly-c?	17.00	50.00	100.00
8-Mickey Mouse, 32 pgs.	60.00	150.00	300.00
9-The Story of the Gloomy Bunny	8.00	24.00	48.00
10-Out of Santa's Bag	7.00	20.00	40.00
11-Fun With Santa Claus	5.50	16.00	32.00
12-Santa's Toys	5.50	16.00	32.00
13-Santa's Surprise	5.50	16.00	32.00
14-Santa's Candy Kitchen	5.50	16.00	32.00
15-Hip-It-Ty Hop & the Big Bass Viol	5.50	16.00	32.00
16-Woody Woodpecker (1947)	8.00	24.00	48.00
17-Roy Rogers (1948)	14.00	40.00	80.00
18-Popular Fairy Tales	10.00	28.00	56.00
19-Uncle Wiggily	7.00	20.00	40.00
20-Donald Duck by Carl Barks, ''Darkest Africa,'' 22 pgs.; Kelly-c	325.00	800.00	1600.00
21-Tom and Jerry	7.00	20.00	40.00
22-Andy Panda	7.00	20.00	40.00
23-Raggedy Ann; Kerr-a	10.00	30.00	60.00
24-Felix the Cat, 1932 daily strip reprints by Otto Messmer	13.00	38.00	76.00
25-Gene Autry	12.00	35.00	70.00
26-Our Gang; Walt Kelly	17.00	50.00	100.00
27-Mickey Mouse	35.00	85.00	170.00
28-Gene Autry	12.00	35.00	70.00
29-Easter Bonnet Shop	4.00	12.00	24.00
30-Here Comes Santa	3.50	10.00	20.00
31-Santa's Busy Corner	3.50	10.00	20.00
32-No book produced			
33-A Christmas Carol	3.50	10.00	20.00
34-Woody Woodpecker	5.50	16.00	32.00
35-Roy Rogers (1948)	11.00	32.00	64.00
36-Felix the Cat(1949)-by Messmer; daily strip reprints	11.00	32.00	64.00
37-Popeye	10.00	30.00	60.00
38-Oswald the Rabbit	5.50	16.00	32.00
39-Gene Autry	11.00	32.00	64.00
40-Andy and Woody	5.50	16.00	32.00
41-Donald Duck by Carl Barks, ''Race to the South Seas,'' 22 pgs.; Kelly-c	240.00	600.00	1200.00
42-Porky Pig	5.50	16.00	32.00
43-Henry	3.50	10.00	20.00
44-Bugs Bunny	5.50	16.00	32.00
45-Mickey Mouse	30.00	70.00	140.00
46-Tom and Jerry	5.50	16.00	32.00
47-Roy Rogers	11.00	32.00	64.00
48-Greetings from Santa	3.00	8.00	16.00
49-Santa Is Here	3.00	8.00	16.00
50-Santa's Workshop (1949)	3.00	8.00	16.00
51-Felix the Cat (1950) by Messmer	10.00	28.00	56.00
52-Popeye	8.00	24.00	48.00
53-Oswald the Rabbit	5.50	16.00	32.00
54-Gene Autry	10.00	28.00	56.00
55-Andy and Woody	5.00	14.00	28.00
56-Donald Duck-not by Barks; Barks art on back-c	20.00	60.00	120.00
57-Porky Pig	5.00	14.00	28.00
58-Henry	3.00	8.00	16.00
59-Bugs Bunny	5.00	14.00	28.00
60-Mickey Mouse	17.00	50.00	100.00
61-Tom and Jerry	4.00	12.00	24.00
62-Roy Rogers	10.00	28.00	56.00
63-Welcome Santa	3.00	8.00	16.00
64-Santa's Helpers	3.00	8.00	16.00
65-Jingle Bells (1950)	3.00	8.00	16.00
66-Popeye (1951)	7.00	20.00	40.00
67-Oswald the Rabbit	3.50	10.00	20.00
68-Roy Rogers	9.00	25.00	50.00
69-Donald Duck-not Barks	15.00	45.00	90.00

March Of Comics #41, © WDP

March Of Comics #60, © WDP

March Of Comics #69, © WDP

March Of Comics #78, © Gene Autry

March Of Comics #125, © ERB

March Of Comics #203, © Walter Lantz

MARCH OF COMICS (continued)	Good	Fine	Mint
70-Tom and Jerry	3.50	10.00	20.00
71-Porky Pig	3.50	10.00	20.00
72-Krazy Kat	5.50	16.00	32.00
73-Roy Rogers	9.00	25.00	50.00
74-Mickey Mouse (1951)	11.00	32.00	64.00
75-Bugs Bunny	3.50	10.00	20.00
76-Andy and Woody	3.50	10.00	20.00
77-Roy Rogers	7.00	20.00	40.00
78-Gene Autry(1951)-Last regular size issue	7.00	20.00	40.00
79-Andy Panda (1952)-5x7'' size	2.50	7.00	14.00
80-Popeye	5.50	16.00	32.00
81-Oswald the Rabbit	3.00	8.00	16.00
82-Tarzan	8.00	24.00	48.00
83-Bugs Bunny	3.00	8.00	16.00
84-Henry	2.00	6.00	12.00
85-Woody Woodpecker	2.00	6.00	12.00
86-Roy Rogers	5.00	15.00	30.00
87-Krazy Kat	4.00	12.00	24.00
88-Tom and Jerry	2.00	6.00	12.00
89-Porky Pig	2.00	6.00	12.00
90-Gene Autry	5.00	15.00	30.00
91-Roy Rogers & Santa	5.00	15.00	30.00
92-Christmas with Santa	2.00	6.00	12.00
93-Woody Woodpecker (1953)	2.00	6.00	12.00
94-Indian Chief	3.50	10.00	20.00
95-Oswald the Rabbit	2.00	6.00	12.00
96-Popeye	4.00	12.00	24.00
97-Bugs Bunny	2.00	6.00	12.00
98-Tarzan	7.00	20.00	40.00
99-Porky Pig	2.00	6.00	12.00
100-Roy Rogers	4.00	12.00	24.00
101-Henry	2.00	5.00	10.00
102-Tom Corbett	6.00	18.00	36.00
103-Tom and Jerry	2.00	5.00	10.00
104-Gene Autry	4.00	12.00	24.00
105-Roy Rogers	4.00	12.00	24.00
106-Santa's Helpers	2.00	5.00	10.00
107-Santa's Christmas Book - not published			
108-Fun with Santa (1953)	2.00	5.00	10.00
109-Woody Woodpecker (1954)	1.50	4.00	8.00
110-Indian Chief	2.00	6.00	12.00
111-Oswald the Rabbit	1.50	4.00	8.00
112-Henry	1.00	3.00	6.00
113-Porky Pig	1.50	4.00	8.00
114-Tarzan (Russ Manning)	7.00	20.00	40.00
115-Bugs Bunny	2.00	5.00	10.00
116-Roy Rogers	4.00	12.00	24.00
117-Popeye	3.50	10.00	20.00
118-Flash Gordon	8.00	24.00	48.00
119-Tom and Jerry	1.50	4.00	8.00
120-Gene Autry	4.00	12.00	24.00
121-Roy Rogers	4.00	12.00	24.00
122-Santa's Surprise (1954)	1.20	3.50	7.00
123-Santa's Christmas Book	1.20	3.50	7.00
124-Woody Woodpecker (1955)	1.20	3.50	7.00
125-Tarzan	5.50	16.00	32.00
126-Oswald the Rabbit	1.20	3.50	7.00
127-Indian Chief	1.50	4.00	8.00
128-Tom and Jerry	1.20	3.50	7.00
129-Henry	1.00	3.00	6.00
130-Porky Pig	1.20	3.50	7.00
131-Roy Rogers	4.00	12.00	24.00
132-Bugs Bunny	1.20	3.50	7.00
133-Flash Gordon	6.00	18.00	36.00
134-Popeye	3.00	8.00	16.00
135-Gene Autry	3.50	10.00	20.00
136-Roy Rogers	3.50	10.00	20.00
137-Gifts from Santa	1.00	3.00	6.00
138-Fun at Christmas (1955)	1.00	3.00	6.00
139-Woody Woodpecker (1956)	1.20	3.50	7.00
140-Indian Chief	1.50	4.00	8.00

	Good	Fine	Mint
141-Oswald the Rabbit	1.20	3.50	7.00
142-Flash Gordon	5.50	16.00	32.00
143-Porky Pig	1.20	3.50	7.00
144-Tarzan (Russ Manning)	5.50	16.00	32.00
145-Tom and Jerry	1.00	3.00	6.00
146-Roy Rogers	3.50	10.00	20.00
147-Henry	.85	2.50	5.00
148-Popeye	3.00	8.00	16.00
149-Bugs Bunny	1.20	3.50	7.00
150-Gene Autry	3.50	10.00	20.00
151-Roy Rogers	3.50	10.00	20.00
152-The Night Before Christmas	1.00	3.00	6.00
153-Merry Christmas (1956)	1.00	3.00	6.00
154-Tom and Jerry (1957)	1.00	3.00	6.00
155-Tarzan	5.50	16.00	32.00
156-Oswald the Rabbit	1.00	3.00	6.00
157-Popeye	2.00	6.00	12.00
158-Woody Woodpecker	1.00	3.00	6.00
159-Indian Chief	1.50	4.00	8.00
160-Bugs Bunny	1.20	3.50	7.00
161-Roy Rogers	3.00	8.00	16.00
162-Henry	.85	2.50	5.00
163-Rin Tin Tin	1.50	4.00	8.00
164-Porky Pig	1.00	3.00	6.00
165-The Lone Ranger	3.50	10.00	20.00
166-Santa and His Reindeer	1.00	3.00	6.00
167-Roy Rogers and Santa	3.00	8.00	16.00
168-Santa's Workshop (1957)	1.00	3.00	6.00
169-Popeye (1958)	2.00	6.00	12.00
170-Indian Chief	1.50	4.00	8.00
171-Oswald the Rabbit	1.00	3.00	6.00
172-Tarzan	4.00	12.00	24.00
173-Tom and Jerry	1.00	3.00	6.00
174-The Lone Ranger	3.50	10.00	20.00
175-Porky Pig	1.00	3.00	6.00
176-Roy Rogers	3.00	8.00	16.00
177-Woody Woodpecker	1.00	3.00	6.00
178-Henry	1.00	3.00	6.00
179-Bugs Bunny	1.00	3.00	6.00
180-Rin Tin Tin	1.00	3.00	6.00
181-Happy Holiday	.85	2.50	5.00
182-Happi Tim	1.20	3.50	7.00
183-Welcome Santa (1958)	.85	2.50	5.00
184-Woody Woodpecker (1959)	.85	2.50	5.00
185-Tarzan	4.00	12.00	24.00
186-Oswald the Rabbit	.85	2.50	5.00
187-Indian Chief	1.50	4.00	8.00
188-Bugs Bunny	.85	2.50	5.00
189-Henry	.85	2.50	5.00
190-Tom and Jerry	.85	2.50	5.00
191-Roy Rogers	3.00	8.00	16 00
192-Porky Pig	.85	2.50	5.00
193-The Lone Ranger	3.50	10.00	20.00
194-Popeye	2.00	5.00	10.00
195-Rin Tin Tin	1.50	4.00	8.00
196-Sears Special - not published			
197-Santa Is Coming	.70	2.00	4.00
198-Santa's Helpers (1959)	.70	2.00	4.00
199-Huckleberry Hound (1960)	.70	2.00	4.00
200-Fury	.70	2.00	4.00
201-Bugs Bunny	.70	2.00	4.00
202-Space Explorer	1.50	4.00	8.00
203-Woody Woodpecker	.70	2.00	4.00
204-Tarzan	3.00	8.00	16.00
205-Mighty Mouse	1.50	4.00	8.00
206-Roy Rogers	3.00	8.00	16.00
207-Tom and Jerry	.70	2.00	4.00
208-The Lone Ranger	3.50	10.00	20.00
209-Porky Pig	.70	2.00	4.00
210-Lassie	1.00	3.00	6.00
211-Sears Special - not published			

MARCH OF COMICS (continued)	Good	Fine	Mint
212-Christmas Eve	.70	2.00	4.00
213-Here Comes Santa (1960)	.70	2.00	4.00
214-Huckleberry Hound (1961)	.50	1.50	3.00
215-Hi Yo Silver	2.00	6.00	12.00
216-Rocky & His Friends	.85	2.50	5.00
217-Lassie	.85	2.50	5.00
218-Porky Pig	.70	2.00	4.00
219-Journey to the Sun	1.50	4.00	8.00
220-Bugs Bunny	.70	2.00	4.00
221-Roy and Dale	2.00	6.00	12.00
222-Woody Woodpecker	.70	2.00	4.00
223-Tarzan	3.50	10.00	20.00
224-Tom and Jerry	.70	2.00	4.00
225-The Lone Ranger	2.00	6.00	12.00
226-Christmas Treasury (1961)	.70	2.00	4.00
227-Sears Special - not published?			
228-Letters to Santa (1961)	.70	2.00	4.00
229-The Flintstones (1962)	.70	2.00	4.00
230-Lassie	.85	2.50	5.00
231-Bugs Bunny	.70	2.00	4.00
232-The Three Stooges	1.50	4.00	8.00
233-Bullwinkle	1.50	4.00	8.00
234-Smokey the Bear	.50	1.50	3.00
235-Huckleberry Hound	.50	1.50	3.00
236-Roy and Dale	2.00	5.00	10.00
237-Mighty Mouse	1.00	3.00	6.00
238-The Lone Ranger	2.00	6.00	12.00
239-Woody Woodpecker	.70	2.00	4.00
240-Tarzan	3.50	10.00	20.00
241-Santa Claus Around the World	.70	2.00	4.00
242-Santa's Toyland (1962)	.70	2.00	4.00
243-The Flintstones (1963)	.70	2.00	4.00
244-Mister Ed	.50	1.50	3.00
245-Bugs Bunny	.70	2.00	4.00
246-Popeye	1.00	3.00	6.00
247-Mighty Mouse	1.00	3.00	6.00
248-The Three Stooges	1.50	4.00	8.00
249-Woody Woodpecker	.50	1.50	3.00
250-Roy and Dale	2.00	5.00	10.00
251-Little Lulu by Stanley	10.00	30.00	60.00
252-Tarzan	2.50	7.00	14.00
253-Yogi Bear	.50	1.50	3.00
254-Lassie	.85	2.50	5.00
255-Santa's Christmas List	.70	2.00	4.00
256-Christmas Party (1963)	.70	2.00	4.00
257-Mighty Mouse	1.00	3.00	6.00
258-The Sword in the Stone (Disney)	3.50	10.00	20.00
259-Bugs Bunny	.70	2.00	4.00
260-Mister Ed	.50	1.50	3.00
261-Woody Woodpecker	.70	2.00	4.00
262-Tarzan	3.00	8.00	16.00
263-Donald Duck-not Barks	3.50	10.00	20.00
264-Popeye	1.00	3.00	6.00
265-Yogi Bear	.50	1.50	3.00
266-Lassie	.85	2.50	5.00
267-Little Lulu	7.00	20.00	40.00
268-The Three Stooges	1.00	3.00	6.00
269-A Jolly Christmas	.70	2.00	4.00
270-Santa's Little Helpers	.70	2.00	4.00
271-The Flintstones (1965)	.50	1.50	3.00
272-Tarzan	2.50	7.00	14.00
273-Bugs Bunny	.70	2.00	4.00
274-Popeye	1.00	3.00	6.00
275-Little Lulu	5.50	16.00	32.00
276-The Jetsons	.85	2.50	5.00
277-Daffy Duck	.50	1.50	3.00
278-Lassie	.85	2.50	5.00
279-Yogi Bear	.50	1.50	3.00
280-The Three Stooges	.50	1.50	3.00
281-Tom and Jerry	.40	1.20	2.40

	Good	Fine	Mint
282-Mister Ed	.40	1.20	2.40
283-Santa's Visit	.70	2.00	4.00
284-Christmas Parade (1965)	.70	2.00	4.00
285-Astro Boy	1.50	4.00	8.00
286-Tarzan	2.50	7.00	14.00
287-Bugs Bunny	.40	1.20	2.40
288-Daffy Duck	.40	1.20	2.40
289-The Flintstones	.50	1.50	3.00
290-Mister Ed	.40	1.20	2.40
291-Yogi Bear	.40	1.20	2.40
292-The Three Stooges	1.00	3.00	6.00
293-Little Lulu	3.50	10.00	20.00
294-Popeye	1.00	3.00	6.00
295-Tom and Jerry	.35	1.00	2.00
296-Lassie	.70	2.00	4.00
297-Christmas Bells	1.00	3.00	6.00
298-Santa's Sleigh (1966)	1.00	3.00	6.00
299-The Flintstones (1967)	.35	1.00	2.00
300-Tarzan	2.50	7.00	14.00
301-Bugs Bunny	.40	1.20	2.40
302-Laurel and Hardy	1.00	3.00	6.00
303-Daffy Duck	.35	1.00	2.00
304-The Three Stooges	1.00	3.00	6.00
305-Tom and Jerry	.35	1.00	2.00
306-Daniel Boone	1.00	3.00	6.00
307-Little Lulu	3.50	10.00	20.00
308-Lassie	.70	2.00	4.00
309-Yogi Bear	.35	1.00	2.00
310-The Lone Ranger	2.00	6.00	12.00
311-Santa's Show	.70	2.00	4.00
312-Christmas Album (1967)	.70	2.00	4.00
313-Daffy Duck (1968)	.35	1.00	2.00
314-Laurel and Hardy	1.00	3.00	6.00
315-Bugs Bunny	.40	1.20	2.40
316-The Three Stooges	1.00	3.00	6.00
317-The Flintstones	.40	1.20	2.40
318-Tarzan	2.00	6.00	12.00
319-Yogi Bear	.35	1.00	2.00
320-Space Family Robinson	2.00	5.00	10.00
321-Tom and Jerry	.35	1.00	2.00
322-The Lone Ranger	2.00	6.00	12.00
323-Little Lulu-not Stanley	2.50	7.00	14.00
324-Lassie	.70	2.00	4.00
325-Fun with Santa	.50	1.50	3.00
326-Christmas Story (1968)	.50	1.50	3.00
327-The Flintstones (1969)	.40	1.20	2.40
328-Space Family Robinson	2.00	5.00	10.00
329-Bugs Bunny	.40	1.20	2.40
330-The Jetsons	.50	1.50	3.00
331-Daffy Duck	.35	1.00	2.00
332-Tarzan	2.00	6.00	12.00
333-Tom and Jerry	.35	1.00	2.00
334-Lassie	.50	1.50	3.00
335-Little Lulu	2.50	7.00	14.00
336-The Three Stooges	1.00	3.00	6.00
337-Yogi Bear	.35	1.00	2.00
338-The Lone Ranger	2.00	6.00	12.00
339-(Did not come out)			
340-Here Comes Santa (1969)	.50	1.50	3.00
341-The Flintstones	.35	1.00	2.00
342-Tarzan	2.00	6.00	12.00
343-Bugs Bunny	.35	1.00	2.00
344-Yogi Bear	.35	1.00	2.00
345-Tom and Jerry	.35	1.00	2.00
346-Lassie	.50	1.50	3.00
347-Daffy Duck	.35	1.00	2.00
348-The Jetsons	.50	1.50	3.00
349-Little Lulu-not Stanley	1.50	4.00	8.00
350-The Lone Ranger	2.00	5.00	10.00
351-Beep-Beep, the Road Runner	.40	1.20	2.40

March Of Comics #237, © MGM

March Of Comics #285, © GK

March Of Comics #328, © GK

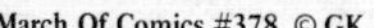
March Of Comics #378, © GK

March Of Comics #439, © WEST

March Of Crime nn, © FOX

MARCH OF COMICS (continued)	Good	Fine	Mint
352-Space Family Robinson	2.00	5.00	10.00
353-Beep-Beep, the Road Runner (1971)	.40	1.20	2.40
354-Tarzan (1971)	2.00	5.00	10.00
355-Little Lulu-not Stanley	1.50	4.00	8.00
356-Scooby Doo, Where Are You?	.40	1.20	2.40
357-Daffy Duck & Porky Pig	.40	1.20	2.40
358-Lassie	.50	1.50	3.00
359-Baby Snoots	.50	1.50	3.00
360-H. R. Pufnstuf (TV)	.40	1.20	2.40
361-Tom and Jerry	.35	1.00	2.00
362-Smokey the Bear	.35	1.00	2.00
363-Bugs Bunny & Yosemite Sam	.35	1.00	2.00
364-The Banana Splits	.35	1.00	2.00
365-Tom and Jerry (1972)	.35	1.00	2.00
366-Tarzan	2.00	5.00	10.00
367-Bugs Bunny & Porky Pig	.35	1.00	2.00
368-Scooby Doo (4/72)	.35	1.00	2.00
369-Little Lulu-not Stanley	1.00	3.00	6.00
370-Lassie	.50	1.50	3.00
371-Baby Snoots	.50	1.50	3.00
372-Smokey the Bear	.35	1.00	2.00
373-The Three Stooges	.70	2.00	4.00
374-Wacky Witch	.35	1.00	2.00
375-Beep-Beep & Daffy Duck	.35	1.00	2.00
376-The Pink Panther (1972)	.35	1.00	2.00
377-Baby Snoots (1973)	.50	1.50	3.00
378-Turok, Son of Stone	2.00	5.00	10.00
379-Heckle & Jeckle New Terrytoons		.50	1.00
380-Bugs Bunny & Yosemite Sam		.50	1.00
381-Lassie		.60	1.20
382-Scooby Doo, Where Are You?	.30	.80	1.60
383-Smokey the Bear		.50	1.00
384-Pink Panther		.50	1.00
385-Little Lulu	1.00	3.00	6.00
386-Wacky Witch		.40	.80
387-Beep-Beep & Daffy Duck		.40	.80
388-Tom and Jerry (1973)		.40	.80
389-Little Lulu-not Stanley	1.00	3.00	6.00
390-Pink Panther		.40	.80
391-Scooby Doo		.40	.80
392-Bugs Bunny & Yosemite Sam		.40	.80
393-New Terrytoons (Heckle & Jeckle)		.60	1.20
394-Lassie		.60	1.20
395-Woodsy Owl		.40	.80
396-Baby Snoots	.40	1.20	2.40
397-Beep-Beep & Daffy Duck		.40	.80
398-Wacky Witch		.40	.80
399-Turok, Son of Stone	.70	2.00	4.00
400-Tom and Jerry		.40	.80
401-Baby Snoots (1975) (Reprints No. 371)	.40	1.20	2.40
402-Daffy Duck (Reprints No. 313)		.40	.80
403-Bugs Bunny (Reprints No. 343)		.40	.80
404-Space Family Robinson (Reprints No. 328)	1.50	4.00	8.00
405-Cracky		.40	.80
406-Little Lulu (Reprints No. 355)	1.00	3.00	6.00
407-Smokey the Bear (Reprints No. 362)		.40	.80
408-Turok, Son of Stone	1.50	4.00	8.00
409-Pink Panther		.40	.80
410-Wacky Witch		.40	.80
411-Lassie (Reprints No. 324)		.50	1.00
412-New Terrytoons (1975)		.40	.80
413-Daffy Duck (1976)(Reprints No. 331)		.40	.80
414-Space Family Robinson (Reprints No. 328)	1.00	3.00	6.00
415-Bugs Bunny (Reprints No. 329)		.40	.80
416-Road Runner (Reprints No. 353)		.40	.80
417-Little Lulu (Reprints No. 323)	.70	2.00	4.00
418-Pink Panther (Reprints No. 384)		.40	.80
419-Baby Snoots (Reprints No. 377)		.50	1.00
420-Woody Woodpecker		.40	.80

	Good	Fine	Mint
421-Tweety & Sylvester		.40	.80
422-Wacky Witch (Reprints No. 386)		.40	.80
423-Little Monsters		.40	.80
424-Cracky (12/76)		.30	.60
425-Daffy Duck		.30	.60
426-Underdog		.30	.60
427-Little Lulu	.70	2.00	4.00
428-Bugs Bunny		.30	.60
429-The Pink Panther		.30	.60
430-Beep-Beep, the Road Runner		.30	.60
431-Baby Snoots		.40	.80
432-Lassie		.40	.80
433-Tweety & Sylvester		.30	.60
434-Wacky Witch		.30	.60
435-New Terrytoons		.30	.60
436-Wacky Advs. of Cracky		.30	.60
437-Daffy Duck		.30	.60
438-Underdog		.30	.60
439-Little Lulu		.40	.80
440-Bugs Bunny		.30	.60
441-The Pink Panther		.30	.60
442-Beep-Beep, the Road Runner		.30	.60
443-Baby Snoots		.40	.80
444-Tom and Jerry		.30	.60
445-Tweety and Sylvester		.30	.60
446-Wacky Witch		.30	.60
447-Mickey Mouse		.40	.80
448-Cracky		.20	.40
449-Pink Panther		.20	.40
450-Baby Snoots		.20	.40
451-Tom and Jerry		.20	.40
452-Bugs Bunny		.20	.40
453-Popeye		.20	.40
454-Woody Woodpecker		.20	.40
455-Beep-Beep, the Road Runner		.20	.40
456-Little Lulu		.30	.60
457-Tweety & Sylvester		.20	.40
458-Wacky Witch		.20	.40
459-Mighty Mouse		.20	.40
460-Daffy Duck		.20	.40
461-The Pink Panther		.20	.40
462-Baby Snoots		.20	.40
463-Tom and Jerry		.20	.40
464-Bugs Bunny		.20	.40
465-Popeye		.20	.40
466-Woody Woodpecker		.20	.40
467-Underdog		.20	.40
468-Little Lulu		.30	.60
469-Tweety & Sylvester		.20	.40
470-Wacky Witch		.20	.40
471-Mighty Mouse		.20	.40
472-Heckle & Jeckle		.20	.40
473-Pink Panther		.20	.40
474-Baby Snoots		.20	.40
475-			
476-			
477-Popeye		.20	.40
478-Woody Woodpecker		.20	.40
479-Underdog		.20	.40
480-Tom and Jerry		.20	.40
481-Tweety and Sylvester		.20	.40
482-Wacky Witch		.20	.40

MARCH OF CRIME (My Love Affair No. 1-6)
1949 (132 pgs.); No. 7, 7/50 - No. 2, 9/50; No. 3, 9/51
Fox Features Syndicate

	Good	Fine	Mint
nn(1949)(132 pgs.)-See Fox Giants. Contents can vary and determines price.			
7(No.1)(7/50)-Wood-a	8.00	24.00	48.00
2(9/50)-Wood-a	8.00	24.00	48.00
3(9/51)	3.50	10.00	20.00

MARCO POLO
1962 (Movie classic)
Charlton Comics

	Good	Fine	Mint
nn (Scarce)	6.00	18.00	36.00

MARGARET O'BRIEN, THE ADVENTURES OF
1947 (20 pgs. in color; slick cover; regular size) (Premium)
Bambury Fashions (Clothes)

In "The Big City"-movie adaptation (Scarce)	7.00	20.00	40.00

MARGIE (See My Little. . .)

MARGIE (TV)
Mar-May, 1962 - No. 2, July-Sept, 1962
Dell Publishing Co.

4-Color 1307, 2	.85	2.50	5.00

MARGIE COMICS (Formerly Comedy) (Reno Browne No. 50 on)
No. 35, Winter, 1946-47 - No. 49, 1949
Marvel Comics (ACI)

35-38,42,45,47-49	1.00	3.00	6.00
39,41,43,44,46-Kurtzman's "Hey Look"	1.50	4.50	9.00
40-Three "Hey Looks," three "Giggles & Grins" by Kurtzman	2.00	6.00	12.00

MARINES (See Tell It to the. . .)

MARINES ATTACK
Aug, 1964 - No. 9, Feb, 1966
Charlton Comics

1		.40	.80
2-9		.30	.60

MARINES AT WAR (Tales of the Marines No. 4)
No. 5, April, 1957 - No. 7, Aug, 1957
Atlas Comics (OPI)

5-7	.50	1.50	3.00

NOTE: ***Berg*** *a-5.* ***Colan*** *a-5.* ***Drucker*** *a-5.* ***Maneely*** *a-5.* ***Orlando*** *a-7.* ***Severin*** *c-5.*

MARINES IN ACTION
June, 1955 - No. 14, Sept, 1957
Atlas News Co.

1-Rock Murdock, Boot Camp Brady begin	1.20	3.50	7.00
2-14	.70	2.00	4.00

NOTE: ***Berg*** *a-8, 9, 11, 14.* ***Heath*** *c-9.* ***Severin*** *c-8, 14.*

MARINES IN BATTLE
Aug, 1954 - No. 25, Sept, 1958
Atlas Comics (ACI No. 1-12/WPI No. 13-25)

1-Heath-c; Iron Mike McGraw by Heath; history of U.S. Marine Corps. begins	2.00	6.00	12.00
2-6,8-10	1.00	3.00	6.00
7-Six pg. Kubert/Moskowitz-a	2.00	5.00	10.00
11-16,18,20-22,24	.70	2.00	4.00
17-Williamson-a, 3 pgs.	3.00	9.00	18.00
19-Davis, Colan-a	2.00	5.00	10.00
23-Crandall-a; Mark Murdock app.	2.00	5.00	10.00
25-Torres-a	2.00	5.00	10.00

NOTE: ***Berg*** *a-22.* ***Everett*** *a-4; c-21.* ***Orlando*** *a-14.* ***Powell*** *a-16.*

MARINE WAR HEROES (Charlton Premiere No. 19)
Jan, 1964 - No. 18, Mar, 1967
Charlton Comics

1		.40	.80
2-18		.30	.60

NOTE: ***Montes/Bache*** *a-1,14,18; c-1.*

MARK OF ZORRO (See 4-Color No. 228)

MARK STEEL
1967, 1968, 1972 (24 pgs.) (Color)
American Iron & Steel Institute (Giveaway)

	Good	Fine	Mint
1967,1968-"Journey of Discovery with. . ."; Neal Adams art	1.00	3.00	6.00
1972-". . . Fights Pollution;" Adams-a	.70	2.00	4.00

MARK TRAIL
Oct, 1955 - No. 5, Summer, 1958
Standard Magazines (Hall Syndicate)

1-Sunday strip-r	2.00	6.00	12.00
2-5	1.20	3.50	7.00
. . . Adventure Book of Nature 1(Summer, 1958; Pines)-100 pg. Giant; contains 78 Sunday strip-r	3.00	8.00	16.00

MARMADUKE MONK
No date; 1963 (10 cents)
I. W. Enterprises/Super Comics

1-I.W. Reprint		.60	1.20
14-(Super Reprint)(1963)		.60	1.20

MARMADUKE MOUSE
Spring, 1946 - No. 65, Dec, 1956
Quality Comics Group (Arnold Publ.)

1	2.50	7.00	14.00
2-30	1.20	3.50	7.00
31-65	.70	2.00	4.00
Super Reprint No. 14(1963)		.60	1.20

MARS & BEYOND (See 4-Color No. 866)

M.A.R.S. PATROL TOTAL WAR (Total War No. 1,2)
No. 3, Sept, 1966 - No. 10, Aug, 1969
Gold Key

3-Wood-a	1.00	3.00	6.00
4-10	.70	2.00	4.00

MARTHA WAYNE (See The Story of. . .)

MARTIN KANE (Formerly My Secret Affair)
No. 4, June, 1950 - No. 2, Aug, 1950
Fox Features Syndicate (Hero Books)

4(No.1)-Wood-c/a(2); used in **SOTI**, pg. 160; 1 pg. opium drug mention story	8.00	24.00	48.00
2-Orlando-a, 5pgs; Wood-a(2)	5.50	16.00	32.00

MARTY MOUSE
No date (1958?) (10 cents)
I. W. Enterprises

1-Reprint		.60	1.20

MARVEL ADVENTURE
Dec, 1975 - No. 6, Oct, 1976
Marvel Comics Group

1-Daredevil-r		.40	.80
2-6		.25	.50

MARVEL BOY (Astonishing No. 3 on)
Dec, 1950 - No. 2, Feb, 1951
Marvel Comics (20CC)

1-Origin Marvel Boy by Russ Heath	14.00	40.00	80.00
2-Everett-a	11.00	32.00	64.00

MARVEL CHILLERS
Oct, 1975 - No. 7, Oct, 1976
Marvel Comics Group

1-Intro. Modred the Mystic		.50	1.00
2,3-Tigra, the Were-Woman begins (origin) No. 3, ends No. 7		.40	.80
4,5,7: 7-Kirby-c		.40	.80
6-Byrne-a	.30	.90	1.80

Margie Comics #49, © MCG

M.A.R.S. Patrol #3, © GK

Marvel Chillers #6, © MCG

Marvel Comics #1, © MCG

Marvel Family #64, © FAW

Marvel Feature (1st) #4, © MCG

MARVEL CLASSICS COMICS (Also see Pendulum Ill. Class.)
1976 - No. 36, Dec, 1978
Marvel Comics Group

	Good	Fine	Mint
1-Dr. Jekyll and Mr. Hyde; Redondo-a		.30	.60
2-Time Machine; Nino-a		.30	.60
3-Hunchback of Notre Dame		.30	.60
4-20,000 Leagues Under the Sea, 5-Black Beauty, 6-Gulliver's Travels, 7-Tom Sawyer, 8-Moby Dick-Nino art, 9-Dracula-Redondo story, 10-Red Badge of Courage each....		.30	.60
11-Mysterious Island, 12-The Three Musketeers-Nino art, 13-Last of the Mohicans, 14-War of the Worlds, 15-Treasure Island, 16-Ivanhoe, 17-The Count of Monte Cristo, 18-The Odyssey, 19-Robinson Crusoe, 20-Frankenstein each....		.30	.60
21-Master of the World, 22-Food of the Gods, 23-The Moonstone, 24-She, 25-The Invisible Man, 26-The Illiad-Buscema cover, 27-Kidnapped, 28-The Pit and the Pendulum, 29-Prisoner of Zenda, 30-Arabian Nights, 31-First Man in the Moon, 32-White Fang, 33-The Prince and the Pauper, 34-Robin Hood, 35-Alice in Wonderland, 36-A Christmas Carol each....		.30	.60

NOTE: *__Golden__ a-28. __Nino__ a-2, 8, 12. No. 1-12 were reprinted from Pendulum Ill. Classics*

MARVEL COLLECTORS' ITEM CLASSICS (Marvel's Greatest No. 23 on)
1965 - No. 22, Aug, 1969
Marvel Comics Group

	Good	Fine	Mint
1	1.50	4.00	8.00
2-4	.60	1.80	3.60
5-10	.40	1.20	2.40
11-22	.30	.80	1.60

NOTE: *All reprints; __Ditko, Kirby__ art in all.*

MARVEL COMICS (Marvel Mystery No. 2 on)
October, November, 1939
Timely Comics (Funnies, Inc.)

NOTE: The first issue was originally dated October 1939. Most copies have a black circle stamped over the date (on cover and inside) with "November" printed over it. However, some copies do not have the November overprint and could have a higher value. Most No. 1's have printing defects, i.e., tilted pages which caused trimming into the panels usually on right side and bottom. Covers exist with and without gloss finish

	Good	Fine	Mint
1-Origin Sub-Mariner by Bill Everett(1st newsstand app.); 1st 8 pgs. reprinted from Motion Picture Funnies Weekly No. 1; Human Torch by Carl Burgos, Kazar the Great, & Jungle Terror (only app.); intro. The Angel, The Masked Raider (ends No. 12); cover by sci/fi pulp illustrator Frank R. Paul	2800.00	7500.00	16,000.00

(Prices vary widely on this book)

MARVEL COMICS SUPER SPECIAL (Also see Howard the Duck No. 12) (Magazine) ($1.50)
September, 1977 - Present (No No. 7)
Marvel Comics Group

	Good	Fine	Mint
1-Kiss, 40 pgs. comics plus photos & features; Simonson-a(p)	.85	2.50	5.00
2-Conan (3/78)	.50	1.50	3.00
3-Close Encounters of the Third Kind (6/78); Simonson-a	.40	1.20	2.40
4-The Ultimate Beatles Book (8/78)	.35	1.10	2.20
5-Kiss (12/78)	.35	1.10	2.20
6-Jaws II (12/78)	.30	.90	1.80
7-Published in Britain only-Sgt. Pepper's Lonely Hearts Club Band			
8-Battlestar Galactica-tabloid size	.30	.90	1.80
8-Battlestar Galactica publ. in reg. magazine format; low distribution ($1.50)8½x11"	1.00	3.00	6.00
9-Conan	.30	.90	1.80
10-Star Lord	.30	.90	1.80
10-13-Weirdworld begins No. 11; 25 copy special press run of each with gold seal and signed by artists (Proof quality), Spring-June, 1979	10.00	30.00	60.00
11-Weirdworld (regular issue)	.80	2.30	4.60
12-Weirdworld (regular issue)	.50	1.50	3.00
13-Weirdworld (regular issue)	.35	1.10	2.20
14-Adapts movie 'Meteor'	.30	.80	1.60
15-Star Trek with photos & pin-ups($1.50)	.30	.80	1.60
15-with $2.00 price(scarce); the price was changed at tail end of a 200,000 press run	.80	2.30	4.60
16-'Empire Strikes Back'-Williamson-a	.30	.80	1.60
17-Xanadu	.30	.80	1.60
18-Raiders of the Lost Ark	.30	.80	1.60
19-For Your Eyes Only (James Bond)	.30	.80	1.60
20-Dragon Slayer	.30	.80	1.60

NOTE: *__J. Buscema__ a-1, 2, 9, 11-13, 18p; c-11(part), 12. __Chaykin__ a-9, 19; c-18, 19.*

MARVEL DOUBLE FEATURE
Dec, 1973 - No. 21, Mar, 1977
Marvel Comics Group

	Good	Fine	Mint
1-Captain America & Iron Man-r begin	.30	.80	1.60
2-5		.40	.80
6-21: 18-Kirby-c		.40	.80

MARVEL FAMILY (Also see Captain Marvel No. 18)
Dec, 1945 - No. 89, Jan, 1954
Fawcett Publications

	Good	Fine	Mint
1-Origin Captain Marvel, Captain Marvel Jr., Mary Marvel, & Uncle Marvel retold; Black Adam origin & 1st app.	40.00	110.00	225.00
2	20.00	60.00	120.00
3	17.00	50.00	100.00
4,5	10.00	30.00	60.00
6-10: 7-Shazam app.	8.00	24.00	48.00
11-20	5.50	16.00	32.00
21-30	4.00	12.00	24.00
31-40	3.50	10.00	20.00
41-50	3.00	8.00	16.00
51-77,79,80,82-89	2.50	7.00	14.00
78,81-Used in **POP**, pgs. 92,93	3.00	8.00	16.00

MARVEL FEATURE (See Marvel Two-In-One)
Dec, 1971 - No. 12, Nov, 1973 (No. 1,2: 25 cents)
Marvel Comics Group

	Good	Fine	Mint
1-Origin The Defenders; Sub-Mariner, The Hulk & Dr. Strange; G.A. Sub-Mariner-r, Adams-c	2.00	6.00	12.00
2-G.A. Sub-Mariner-r	1.00	3.00	6.00
3-Defender series ends	1.00	3.00	6.00
4-Begin Ant-Man series	.30	.80	1.60
5-7	.30	.80	1.60
8-Origin The Wasp; Starlin-a; (r)	.30	.80	1.60
9,10-Last Ant-Man	.30	.80	1.60
11,12-Thing team-ups; Starlin-a	.30	.80	1.60

MARVEL FEATURE (Also see Red Sonja)
Nov, 1975 - No. 7, Nov, 1976
Marvel Comics Group

	Good	Fine	Mint
1-Red Sonja begins; Adams r/Savage Sword of Conan No. 1	.30	.80	1.60
2-7		.50	1.00

MARVEL MINI-BOOKS
1966 (50 pgs.; 5/8''x7/8'') (6 different issues)
Marvel Comics Group (Smallest comics ever published)

	Good	Fine	Mint
Captain America, Spider-Man, Sgt. Fury, Hulk, Thor	1.00	3.00	6.00
Millie the Model	.70	2.00	4.00

NOTE: *Each came in six different color covers.*

MARVEL MOVIE PREMIERE (Magazine)
Sept, 1975 (One Shot) (Black & White)
Marvel Comics Group

	Good	Fine	Mint
1-Burroughs "The Land That Time Forgot" adaptation	.40	1.20	2.40

MARVEL MYSTERY COMICS (Formerly Marvel Comics) (Marvel Tales No. 93 on)
No. 2, Dec, 1939 - No. 92, June, 1949
Timely Comics/Marvel Comics

	Good	Fine	Mint
2-American Ace begins, ends No. 3; Human Torch by Burgos, Sub-Mariner by Everett continues; new logo taken from a Marvel pulp begins	475.00	1400.00	2800.00
3-Angel by Gustavson begins	275.00	800.00	1600.00
4-Intro. Electro, the Marvel of the Age (ends No. 19), The Ferret, Mystery Detective (ends No. 9); bondage-c	240.00	700.00	1400.00
5	400.00	1200.00	2400.00
6,7: 7-Bondage-c	140.00	420.00	850.00
8-Human Torch & Sub-Mariner battle	175.00	500.00	1000.00
9-(Scarce)-Human Torch & Sub-Mariner battle	225.00	650.00	1300.00
10-Human Torch & Sub-Mariner battle, conclusion; Terry Vance, the Schoolboy Sleuth begins, ends No. 57	120.00	320.00	640.00
11,12: 12-Kirby-c	75.00	200.00	400.00
13-Intro. & 1st app. The Vision by S&K	95.00	250.00	500.00
14-16	60.00	150.00	300.00
17-Human Torch/Sub-Mariner x-over	60.00	150.00	300.00
18,19	55.00	140.00	280.00
20-Origin The Angel in text	50.00	130.00	260.00
21-Intro. & 1st app. The Patriot; not in No. 46-48	45.00	120.00	240.00
22-25: 23-Last Gustavson Angel; origin The Vision in text. 24-Injury-to-eye story	40.00	100.00	200.00
26-30: 27-Kazar ends; last S&K Vision. 28-Jimmy Jupiter in the Land of Nowhere begins, ends No. 48. 29-Bondage-c	35.00	90.00	180.00
31-33,35-40	30.00	80.00	160.00
34-Everett, Burgos, Martin Goodman, Funnies, Inc. office appear in story	35.00	90.00	180.00
41-48-Last Vision & Flag-c	28.00	70.00	140.00
49-Origin Miss America	40.00	100.00	200.00
50-60: 50-Mary becomes Miss Patriot. 53-Bondage-c	25.00	70.00	140.00
61-70; 63-The Villainess Cat-Woman only app.	20.00	60.00	120.00
71-75: 74-Last Patriot. 75-Young Allies begin	20.00	60.00	120.00
76-81: 76-10 Chapter Miss America serial begins, ends No. 85. 79-Last Angel. 81-Capt. America app.	20.00	60.00	120.00
82-Origin Namora; Captain America app.	30.00	85.00	180.00
83,85: 83-Last Young Allies. 85-Last Miss America	20.00	60.00	120.00
84-Blonde Phantom begins; Captain America app.	25.00	70.00	140.00
86,87,89-Captain America app. in all. Sungirl in No. 89. 87-Last Toro	20.00	60.00	120.00
88-Golden Girl, Namora, & Sungirl x-over; Captain America app.	25.00	70.00	140.00
90,91: Capt. America app. in both. 91-Venus app., Blonde Phantom & Sub-mariner end	20.00	60.00	120.00
92-Origin Human Torch retold; Captain America app.; no Sub-Mariner; The Witness app.	30.00	90.00	200.00
(Rare) 132 Pg. issue, B&W, 25 cents (1943-44)-printed in N. Y.; square binding, blank inside covers; has Marvel No. 33-c in color; contains 2 Capt. America & 2 Marvel Mystery Comics-r	100.00	300.00	600.00

NOTE: ***Everett*** *c-7-9, 27.* ***Schomburg*** *c-33, 35, 53.*

MARVEL PREMIERE
April, 1972 - Present
Marvel Comics Group

	Good	Fine	Mint
1-Origin Warlock by Gil Kane/Adkins; origin Center-Earth	1.00	3.00	6.00
2-Warlock ends; Kirby Yellow Claw-r	.70	2.00	4.00
3-Dr. Strange series begins, Smith-a(p)	1.20	3.50	7.00
4-Smith-a	.70	2.00	4.00
5-7,9,10: 10-Death of the Ancient One	.30	.90	1.80
8-Starlin-a(p)	.35	1.10	2.20
11-14: 11-Origin-r by Ditko. 14-Intro. God; last Dr. Strange	.30	.80	1.60
15-Iron Fist begins (origin), ends 25	.80	2.30	4.60
16-20		.60	1.20
21-24,26-28: 26-Hercules app. 27-Satana app. 28-Legion of Monsters		.50	1.00
25-Byrne's 1st Iron Fist	.40	1.20	2.40
29-Liberty Legion; retells origins of Red Raven, Thin Man, The Whizzer, Miss America, Blue Diamond		.50	1.00
30-Liberty Legion		.50	1.00
31-Woodgod		.50	1.00
32-Monark Starstalker		.50	1.00
33,34-Solomon Kane		.50	1.00
35-Origin, 1st app. 3-D Man		.50	1.00
36,37-(3-D Man)	.40	1.20	2.40
38-Weirdworld; Nino/Ploog-a		.60	1.20
39,40-Torpedo		.50	1.00
41-46,49,50: 41-Seeker 3000, 42-Tigra, 43-Paladin, 44-The Jack of Hearts, 45-Man-Wolf, 46-God War/Man-Wolf, 49-The Falcon, 50-Alice Cooper		.40	.80
47,48-Byrne-a; 47-Origin new Ant-Man. 48-Ant-Man	.35	1.10	2.20
51-56: 51-53-Black Panther, 54-Caleb Hammer, 55-Wonder Man, 56-Dominic Fortune, 57-60-Dr. Who		.40	.80
57-Dr. Who	.30	.90	1.80
58-60-Dr. Who		.60	1.20
61-Star Lord		.60	1.20

NOTE: ***Adams*** *a-10-14i.* ***Austin*** *a-56; c-56, 58.* ***Brunner*** *a-4, 6, 9-14; c-9-14.* ***Byrne*** *a-47, 48.* ***Chaykin*** *a-32-34, 56; c-32, 33, 56.* ***Kirby*** *c-26, 29-31, 35.* ***McWilliams*** *a-25i.* ***Miller*** *c-58p.* ***Nino*** *a-38i.* ***Ploog*** *c-5-7.* ***Russell*** *a-7p.* ***Simonson*** *a-60; c-57.* ***Starlin*** *c-8.*

MARVEL PRESENTS
October, 1975 - No. 12, Aug, 1977
Marvel Comics Group

	Good	Fine	Mint
1-Bloodstone app.	.30	.80	1.60
2-Bloodstone app; Kirby-c		.50	1.00
3-Guardians of the Galaxy		.50	1.00
4-7,9,11,12		.40	.80
8-Reprints Silver Surfer No. 2		.40	.80
10-Starlin-a(p)		.40	.80

MARVEL PREVIEW (Magazine)
1975 - Present (B&W) ($1.00)
Marvel Comics Group

	Good	Fine	Mint
1-Man Gods From Beyond the Stars; Adams-a(i) & cover; Nino-a	.70	2.00	4.00
2-Origin The Punisher & 1st app. Dominic Fortune; Morrow-c	.45	1.30	2.60
3-Blade the Vampire Slayer	.35	1.00	2.00
4-Star-Lord & Sword in the Star (origins & 1st app.)	.85	2.50	5.00
5,6-Sherlock Holmes	.60	1.80	3.60
7-9: 7-Satana, Sword in the Star app., 8-Legion of Monsters, 9-Man-God; origin Star Hawk-ends No. 20.	.30	.90	1.80
10-Thor the Mighty; Starlin-a	.40	1.20	2.40
11-Star-Lord; Byrne-a	.40	1.20	2.40
12-20: 12-Haunt of Horror, 16-Detectives, 17-Black Mark by G. Kane, 18-Star-Lord, 19-Kull	.25	.70	1.40
21,22: 21-Moon Knight; Ditko-a, 22-King Arthur	.25	.70	1.40
23-Miller-a; Bizarre Advs.	.35	1.00	2.00
24, 25-Lethal Ladies-Golden-a, 26, 27	.25	.70	1.40

NOTE: ***Austin*** *a-25i.* ***Buscema*** *a-22, 23, 27p.* ***Byrne*** *a-10, 11.* ***Chaykin*** *a-2, 20r; c-20.* ***Golden*** *a-25p.* ***Gulacy*** *c-24, 25, 27.* ***Infantino*** *a-14.* ***Miller*** *a-23.* ***Morrow*** *c-2-4.* ***Perez*** *a-20, 27p.* ***Ploog*** *a-8.* ***Rogers***

Marvel Mystery Comics #3, © MCG

Marvel Mystery Comics #23, © MCG

Marvel Premiere #36, © MCG

Marvel Spectacular #1, © MCG

Marvel Spotlight #2, © MCG

Marvel Super Heroes #14, © MCG

MARVEL PREVIEW (continued)
a-25p. ***Starlin*** *c-13, 14.*

MARVEL'S GREATEST COMICS (Marvel Coll. Item Classics No. 1-22)
No. 23, Oct, 1969 - No. 96, Jan, 1981
Marvel Comics Group

	Good	Fine	Mint
23,24-Dr. Strange, Fantastic Four, Iron Man, Watcher		.50	1.00
25-28-Capt. America, Dr. Strange, Iron Man, Fantastic Four		.50	1.00
29-34		.50	1.00
35-37-Silver Surfer-r/Fantastic Four No. 48-50		.40	.80
38-60-Fantastic Four-r		.40	.80
61-96: 75,80-Kirby-c		.30	.60

NOTE: ***Buscema*** *a-85-92r; c-87-92r.* ***Ditko*** *a-23-28r.* ***Kirby*** *reprints in all.*

MARVELS OF SCIENCE
March, 1946 - No. 4, June, 1946
Charlton Comics

	Good	Fine	Mint
1-(1st Charlton comic)	3.50	10.00	20.00
2-4	2.00	5.00	10.00

MARVEL SPECIAL EDITION (Also see Special Collectors' Edition)
1975 - Present (84 pgs.) (Oversized)
Marvel Comics Group

	Good	Fine	Mint
1-Spider-Man(r); Ditko-a(r)	.50	1.50	3.00
1-Star Wars (1977); r-Star Wars No. 1-3	.50	1.50	3.00
1-Close Encounters-movie	.40	1.20	2.40
2-Star Wars (1978); r-Star Wars No. 4-6	.40	1.20	2.40
3-Star Wars (1978); r-Star Wars No. 1-6	.40	1.20	2.40

NOTE: ***Chaykin*** *c/a-1(1977), 2, 3.*

MARVEL SPECTACULAR
Aug, 1973 - No. 19, Nov, 1975
Marvel Comics Group

	Good	Fine	Mint
1-Thor-r begin by Kirby	.30	.80	1.60
2-19		.40	.80

MARVEL SPOTLIGHT
11/71 - No. 33, 4/77; 7/79 - V2No. 11, 3/81
Marvel Comics Group

	Good	Fine	Mint
1-Origin Red Wolf; Wood inks, Adams-c	.70	2.00	4.00
2-(Giant)-Venus-r by Everett; origin Werewolf by Ploog; Adams-c	.50	1.50	3.00
3,4-Werewolf ends No. 4	.35	1.10	2.20
5-Origin Ghost Rider	1.50	4.00	8.00
6-8-Last Ploog issue	.50	1.50	3.00
9-11-Last Ghost Rider	.30	.80	1.60
12-Origin The Son of Satan (begins series)	.30	.80	1.60
13-20		.50	1.00
21-27: 25-Sinbad. 26-Scarecrow. 27-Sub-Mariner		.40	.80
28,29-Moon Night app.	.35	1.00	2.00
30-The Warriors Three		.40	.80
31-Nick Fury app.		.40	.80
32-Intro/partial origin Spider-Woman	.70	2.00	4.00
33-Deathlok		.40	.80
V2No.1-4: Capt. Marvel; No. 1-Capt. Marvel story continues from Capt. Marvel No. 62.		.30	.60
5-10: 5-Dragon Lord, 6,7-Star Lord, 8-Capt. Marvel, 9-11-Capt. Universe app.		.30	.60

NOTE: ***Austin*** *c-V2No.2i, 8.* ***Buscema*** *a-30.* ***Ditko*** *a-4, 5, 10-12, V2No.9-11; c-4, 5, 9, V2No.9-11.* ***Kirby*** *c-29.* ***McWilliams*** *a-20i.* ***Miller*** *a-V2No.8p; c-V2No.2p, 5, 7, 9p.* ***Mooney*** *a-8, 10i, 14-17, 24.* ***Ploog*** *a-2-8; c-2-9.* ***Sutton*** *a-6, 7.*

MARVEL SUPER ACTION (Magazine)
January, 1976 (One Shot) (76 pgs.; black & white)
Marvel Comics Group

	Good	Fine	Mint
1-Origin & 2nd app. Dominic Fortune; The Punisher app., Weird World & The Huntress; Evans & Ploog-a	1.00	3.00	6.00

MARVEL SUPER-ACTION
May, 1977 - No. 37, Nov, 1981
Marvel Comics Group

	Good	Fine	Mint
1-Capt. America-r by Kirby begin		.40	.80
2-5: 4-Marvel Boy-r(origin)		.40	.80
6-10,12,13: 14-Avengers-r		.40	.80
11-C. A. origin-r/C. A. No. 109		.40	.80
14-38-Avengers-r		.30	.60

NOTE: ***Buscema*** *c-18-20, 22, 35-37.* ***Everett*** *a-4.* ***Heath*** *a-4.* ***Smith*** *a-27r, 28r.*

MARVEL SUPER HEROES (Fantasy Masterpieces No. 1-11)
(Also see Giant Size Super Heroes)
No. 12, 12/67 - No. 31, 11/71; No. 32, 9/72 - No. 106, Feb, 1982
Marvel Comics Group

	Good	Fine	Mint
12-Origin & 1st app. Capt. Marvel of the Kree; G.A. Torch, Destroyer, Capt. America, Black Knight, Sub-Mariner-r	.85	2.50	5.00
13-G.A. Black Knight, Torch, Vision, Capt. America, Sub-Mariner-r; Capt. Marvel app.	.40	1.20	2.40
14-G.A. Sub-Mariner, Torch, Mercury, Black Knight, Capt. America reprints; Spider-Man app.	.40	1.20	2.40
15-Black Bolt cameo in Medusa; G.A. Black Knight, Sub-Mariner, Black Marvel, Capt. America-r	.40	1.20	2.40
16-Origin & 1st app. Phantom Eagle; G.A. Torch, Capt. America, Black Knight, Patriot, Sub-Mariner-r		.50	1.00
17-Origin Black Knight; G.A. Torch, Sub-Mariner, All-Winners Squad reprints		.50	1.00
18-Origin Guardians of the Galaxy; G.A. Sub-Mariner, All-Winners Squad-r	.40	1.20	2.40
19-G.A. Torch, Marvel Boy, Black Knight, Sub-Mariner-r; Smith-c(p) Tuska-a(r)		.50	1.00
20-G.A. Sub-Mariner, Torch, Capt. America-r; Dr. Doom app.		.50	1.00
21-1st all-r ish; Avengers, Sub-Mariner, Hulk, X-Men app.		.50	1.00
22-Daredevil & X-Men-r		.50	1.00
23-X-Men & Daredevil-r; new Watcher story		.50	1.00
24-Daredevil & X-Men-r		.50	1.00
25-27-Hulk, X-Men & Daredevil-r		.50	1.00
28-Daredevil & Iron Man-r; Iron Man origin retold		.50	1.00
29-31-Iron Man & Daredevil-r; 31-Last Giant issue		.50	1.00
32-40-All Sub-Mariner/Hulk-r		.40	.80
41-46,48-50		.40	.80
47-Starlin-c		.40	.80
51-55		.40	.80
56-61-Hulk-r begin		.40	.80
62-106		.30	.60

NOTE: ***Austin*** *a-104.* ***Everett*** *a-14,15(i); c-85(r). New* ***Kirby*** *c-22, 27.*

MARVEL SUPER HEROES SPECIAL
October, 1966
Marvel Comics Group

	Good	Fine	Mint
1-Reprints origin Daredevil; G.A. Sub-Mariner & Torch app.	1.00	3.00	6.00

MARVEL SUPER SPECIAL (See Marvel Comics Super . . .)

MARVEL TALES (Marvel Mystery No. 1-92)
No. 93, Aug, 1949 - No. 159, Aug, 1957
Marvel/Atlas Comics (MCI)

	Good	Fine	Mint
93	10.00	30.00	60.00
94-Everett-a	10.00	30.00	60.00
95,99-101,103,105	5.00	14.00	28.00
96-Bondage-c	5.50	16.00	32.00
97-Sun Girl, 2 pgs; Kirby-a	8.00	24.00	48.00
98-Krigstein-a	5.50	16.00	32.00
102-Wolverton-a "The End of the World," 6 pgs.	20.00	60.00	120.00
104-Wolverton-a "Gateway to Horror," 6 pgs; Heath-c	17.00	50.00	100.00
106,107-Krigstein-a	5.50	16.00	32.00

MARVEL TALES (continued)

	Good	Fine	Mint
108-121,123-131-Last pre-code issue; 120-Jack Katz-a	3.00	8.00	16.00
122-Krigstein, Kubert-a	5.00	14.00	28.00
132,133,135-141,143	2.00	6.00	12.00
134-Krigstein, Kubert-a	3.50	10.00	20.00
142-Krigstein-a	3.00	9.00	18.00
144-Williamson/Krenkel-a, 3 pgs.	3.50	10.00	20.00
145,147-Ditko-a	2.00	6.00	12.00
146,148-151,153-155,158	1.50	4.00	8.00
152-Wood, Morrow-a	3.00	8.00	16.00
156-Torres-a	2.00	6.00	12.00
157,159-Krigstein-a	3.50	10.00	20.00

NOTE: ***Colan** a-105, 107. **Sid Check** a-147. **Drucker** a-127, 135, 146, 150. **Everett** a-98, 104, 106, 108(2), 131, 151, 153; c-111, 117, 127, 143, 148-151, 153. **Heath** c-105, 130. **Gil Kane** a-117. **Maneely** a-126. **Mooney** a-114. **Morrow** a-150, 152, 156. **Orlando** a-149, 151, 157. **Pakula** a-144. **Powell** a-136, 137, 150, 154. **Rico** a-99. **Sekowsky** a-96. **Whitney** a-107. **Wildey** a-126, 138.*

MARVEL TALES
1964 - Present (No. 1-32, 72 pgs.)
Marvel Comics Group

	Good	Fine	Mint
1-Origin Spider-Man, Hulk, Ant/Giant Man, Iron Man, Thor, & Sgt. Fury; all-r	5.00	15.00	30.00
2-Origin X-Men, Dr. Strange, Avengers-r	2.50	7.00	14.00
3	1.00	3.00	6.00
4,5	.50	1.50	3.00
6-12,14,15	.40	1.20	2.40
13-Reprints origin Marvel Boy from Marvel Boy No. 1	.40	1.20	2.40
16-23: Last 68 pg. issue		.50	1.00
24-30		.50	1.00
31-70: 63-Mooney-a		.40	.80
71-74,76-97		.40	.80
75-Origin Spider-Man-r		.40	.80
98-Death of Gwen Stacy-r/Amazing Spider-Man No. 121		.60	1.20
99-Death Green Goblin		.60	1.20
100-(60 cent size)issues		.40	.80
101-136-All Spider-Man-r		.30	.60
137-Dr. Strange-r begin		.30	.60

NOTE: *No. 1-32 are reprints. **Austin** a-100i. **Ditko** a-1-30, 83, 100. **G. Kane** a-71, 81, 100, 101; c-125-127p, 130p. **Mooney** a-103(i)r. **Nasser** a-100p.*

MARVEL TEAM-UP
March, 1972 - Present
Marvel Comics Group

	Good	Fine	Mint
1-Spider-Man, Human Torch	3.00	9.00	18.00
2-SpM/Hulk, 3-SpM/H-T	2.00	5.00	10.00
4-SpM/X-Men	1.00	3.00	6.00
5-10: 5-SpM/Vision. 6-SpM/Thing. 7-SpM/Thor. 8-SpM/The Cat. 9-SpM/Iron Man. 10-SpM/Torch	.80	2.30	4.60
11-20: 11-SpM/Inhumans. 12-SpM/Werewolf. 13-SpM/Capt. America. 14-SpM/Sub-Mariner. 15-SpM/Ghost Rider (new.). 16-SpM/Capt. Marvel. 17-SpM/Mr. Fantastic. 18-H-T/Hulk. 19-SpM/Ka-Zar. 20-SpM/Black Panther	.50	1.50	3.00
21-30: 21-SpM/Dr. Strange. 22-SpM/Hawkeye. 23-H-T/Iceman. 24-SpM/Brother Voodoo. 25-SpM/Daredevil. 26-H-T/Thor. 27-SpM/Hulk. 28-SpM/Hercules. 29-H-T/Iron Man. 30-SpM/Falcon	.35	1.00	2.00
31-40: 31-SpM/Iron Fist. 32-H-T/Son of Satan. 33-SpM/Nighthawk. 34-SpM/Valkyrie. 35-H-T/Dr. Strange. 36-SpM/Frankenstein. 37-SpM/Man-Wolf. 38-SpM/Beast. 39-SpM/H-T. 40-SpM/Sons of the tiger/H-T	.30	.80	1.60
41-50: 41-SpM/Scarlet Witch. 42-SpM/The Vision. 43-SpM/Dr. Doom; retells origin. 44-SpM/Moondragon. 45-SpM/Killraven. 46-SpM/Deathlok. 47-SpM/Thing. 48-SpM/Iron Man. 49,50-SpM/Dr. Strange/Iron Man		.60	1.20
51,52,56-58: 51-SpM/Dr. Strange/Iron Man. 52-SpM/Capt. America. 56-SpM/Daredevil. 57-SpM/Black Widow. 58-SpM/Ghost Rider		.50	1.00
53-SpM/Woodgod/Hulk; new X-Men app., 1st by Byrne	2.00	5.00	10.00
54,55,59,60: 54-SpM/Woodgod/Hulk. 55-SpM/Warlock. 59-SpM/Yellowjacket/The Wasp. 60-SpM/The Wasp-All Byrne-a	.50	1.50	3.00
61-70: 61-SpM/H-T. 62-SpM/Ms. Marvel. 63-SpM/Iron Fist. 64-SpM/Daughters of the Dragon. 65-SpM/Capt. Britain (1st U.S. app.). 66-SpM/Capt. Britain. 67-SpM/Tigra. 68-SpM/Man-Thing. 69-SpM/Havock. 70-SpM/Thor-All Bryne-a	.35	1.10	2.20
71,72,76: 71-SpM/Falcon. 72-SpM/Iron Man. 76-SpM/Dr. Strange/Ms. Marvel. Byrne-c	.30	.80	1.60
73,74,77,78,80: 73-SpM/Daredevil. 74-SpM/Not Ready for Prime Time Players. 77-Dr. Strange/SpM. 78-SpM/Wonder-man. 80-Dr. Strange/SpM		.40	.80
75,79: 75-SpM/Power Man. 79-SpM/Mary Jane Watson as Red Sonja. Both Byrne-a(p)	.35	1.10	2.20
81-90: 81-SpM/Santana. 82-SpM/Black Widow. 83-SpM/Nick Fury. 84-SpM/Shang-Chi. 85-SpM/Black Widow. 86-SpM/Guardians of the Galaxy. 87-SpM/Black Panther. 88-SpM/The Invisible Girl. 89-SpM/Nightcrawler. 90-SpM/Beast		.30	.60
91-99: 91-SpM/Ghost Rider. 92-SpM/Hawkeye. 93-SpM/Werewolf by Night. 94-SpM vs. The Shroud. 95-SpM/Nick Fury/Shield; intro. Mockingbird. 96-SpM/Howard The Duck. 97-Spider-Woman/Hulk. 98-SpM/Black Widow. 99-SpM/Machine Man		.30	.60
100-SpM/Fantastic-4(Double size); origin Storm; X-Men x-over Miller-a/c(p); Byrne-a	.35	1.10	2.20
101-111: 101-SpM/Nighthawk(Ditko-a). 102-SpM/Doc Samson 103-SpM/Ant-Man. 104-Hulk/Ka-Zar. 105-Hulk/Powerman/Iron Fist. 106-SpM/Capt. America. 107-SpM/She-Hulk. 108-SpM/Paladin. 109-SpM/Paladin/Dazzler. 110-Iron Man/SpM. 111-SpM/DevilSlayer		.30	.60
Annual 1(1976)-New X-Men app; Byrne-a.	2.00	5.00	10.00
Annual 2(12/79)-SpM/Hulk		.50	1.00
Annual 3(11/80)-Hulk/Power Man/Machine Man/Iron Fist		.50	1.00
Annual 4(10/81)-SpM/Daredevil/Moon Knight/Power Man/Iron Fist Miller-a/c(p)		.50	1.00

NOTE: ***Austin** a-79i; c-76i, 79i, 112i. **Buckler** a-89p; c-82, 83, 89p. **Byrne** a-53-55, 59-70, 75p, 76p, 79p, 100, Annual 1; c-68p, 72p, 75, 76p, 79p. **Chaykin** a-76p, 77. **Ditko** a-101. **Infantino** a-93, 97. **Kane** a-4-6, 13, 14, 16-19, 23. **Layton** c-72i. **Leialoha** a-82-85i; c-83i, 84. **Miller** c-99p. **Simonson** c-99i. **Starlin** c-27. "H-T" means Human Torch; "SpM" means Spider-Man; "S-M" means Sub-Mariner.*

MARVEL TREASURY EDITION ($1.50)
Sept, 1974 - Present (100 pgs.; oversized)
Marvel Comics Group

	Good	Fine	Mint
1-Spider-Man-r by Ditko	.85	2.50	5.00
2-Fantastic Four, Silver Surfer; Kirby-a	.50	1.50	3.00
3-The Mighty Thor	.50	1.50	3.00
4-Conan; Smith-r, Smith-c	.85	2.50	5.00
5-The Hulk (origin)	.50	1.50	3.00
6-Doctor Strange; Brunner c/a; Ditko-a(r); Adams-a(i)(r)	.35	1.10	2.20
7-Avengers; Kirby-c	.40	1.20	2.40
8-Christmas stories; Spider-Man, Hulk, Nick Fury	.35	1.10	2.20
9-Giant; Super-hero Team-up	.35	1.10	2.20
10-Thor-r; Kirby-a	.35	1.10	2.20
11-Fantastic Four-r; Kirby-a	.30	.80	1.60
12-Mostly-r/Howard the Duck No. 1	.35	1.10	2.20
13-Giant Super-hero Holiday Grab-Bag	.30	.80	1.60
14-Spider-Man	.35	1.10	2.20

Marvel Tales #109(1st), © MCG

Marvel Tales #98(2nd), © MCG

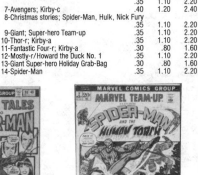

Marvel Team-Up #2, © MCG

Marvel Triple Action #17, © MCG

Marvel Two-In-One #2, © MCG

Mary Marvel #25, © FAW

MARVEL TREASURY EDITION (continued)

	Good	Fine	Mint
15-Conan; Smith, Buscema, Adams-a(r)	.60	1.80	3.60
16-Giant; Super-hero Team-up; The Defenders; origin of The Defenders & Valkyrie	.30	.80	1.60
17-The Hulk	.30	.80	1.60
18-Marvel Team-up; Spider-Man's 1st team-ups with the X-Men, Werewolf By Night, Ghost Rider, Iron Fist; all-r	.35	1.00	2.00
19-Conan the Barbarian by Buscema; (r)	.30	.80	1.60
20-Hulk-r	.30	.80	1.60
21-Fantastic Four-r	.30	.80	1.60
22-Spider-Man-r	.30	.80	1.60
23-Conan-r	.35	1.00	2.00
24-Rampaging Hulk	.30	.80	1.60
25-Spider-Man vs. The Hulk	.30	.80	1.60
26-The Hulk	.30	.80	1.60
27-Spider-Man	.30	.80	1.60
28-Spider-Man/Superman; Buscema-c/a	.30	.80	1.60

NOTE: *Reprints-2,3,5,7-9,13,14,16,17.*

MARVEL TREASURY OF OZ (See MGM's Marvelous . . .)
1975 (oversized) ($1.50)
Marvel Comics Group

	Good	Fine	Mint
1-The Marvelous Land of Oz; Alcala & Buscema-a; movie adaptation	.40	1.20	2.40

MARVEL TREASURY SPECIAL
1974; 1976 (84 pgs.; oversized) ($1.50)
Marvel Comics Group

	Good	Fine	Mint
Vol. 1-Spider-Man, Torch, Sub-Mariner, Avengers "Giant Superhero Holiday Grab-Bag;" Smith-a	.70	2.00	4.00
Vol. 1-Capt. America's Bicentennial Battles (6/76)-Kirby-a; Smith inks, 11 pgs.	.70	2.00	4.00

MARVEL TRIPLE ACTION
2/72 - No. 24, 3/75; No. 25, 8/75 - No. 47, 4/79
Marvel Comics Group

	Good	Fine	Mint
1-Giant	.40	1.20	2.40
2-4		.50	1.00
5,6,8-10		.40	.80
7-Starlin-c		.50	1.00
11-15,17-20		.40	.80
16-Wood inks		.40	.80
21-30		.40	.80
31-47		.40	.80
Giant-Size 1(5/75)		.40	.80
Giant-Size 2(7/75)		.40	.80

NOTE: *Fantastic Four reprints-No. 1-4; Avengers reprints-No. 5 on.* **Ditko** *a-1r, 2r; c-47.*

MARVEL TWO-IN-ONE
January, 1974 - Present
Marvel Comics Group

	Good	Fine	Mint
1-Thing team-ups begin	2.00	5.00	10.00
2-4: 2-Warlock app.	.85	2.50	5.00
5-Guardians of the Galaxy	.85	2.50	5.00
6-Starlin-c	.70	2.00	4.00
7-10	.70	2.00	4.00
11-20	.50	1.50	3.00
21-28,31-40	.30	.80	1.60
29,30-Spider-Woman app.	.30	.90	1.80
41,42,44-49: 41-Storm app.		.50	1.00
43,50,53-55-Byrne-a	.35	1.10	2.20
51-Miller-a(p)	.35	1.00	2.00
52-Moon Knight app.		.50	1.00
56-Byrne-c	.30	.80	1.60
57-71: 60-Intro. Impossible Woman. 61-63-Warlock app.		.40	.80
72-82		.30	.60
Annual 1(6/76)-Liberty Legion x-over	.30	.80	1.60
Annual 2(2/77)-Starlin c/a; Thanos dies	.70	2.00	4.00
Annual 3(7/78)-Nova app.		.50	1.00
Annual 4(9/79)-The Thing/Black Bolt		.50	1.00
Annual 5(9/80)-The Thing/Hulk		.40	.80
Annual 6(10/81)-The Thing/Ka-Zar; American Eagle debut		.40	.80

NOTE: **Austin** *c-54-58i, 61i.* **John Buscema** *a-30,45; c-30p.* **Byrne** *a-43, 50, 53-55p; c-53, 56.* **Gil Kane** *a-1,2.* **Kirby** *c-10, 12, 20, 22, 25, 27.* **Marcos** *a-52i.* **Mooney** *a-38i.* **Perez** *a-56-58p, 60p, 64p, 65p; c-51, 52, 54-58p, 61p, 62i-66i.* **Simonson** *c-43i; Annual 6i.* **Starlin** *c-Annual 1.*

MARVIN MOUSE
September, 1957
Atlas Comics (BPC)

	Good	Fine	Mint
1-Everett/Maneely-a	2.00	5.00	8.00

MARY JANE & SNIFFLES (See 4-Color No. 402,474)

MARY MARVEL COMICS (Monte Hale No. 29 on) (Also see Captain Marvel No. 18, Marvel Family, & Shazam)
Dec, 1945 - No. 28, Sept, 1948
Fawcett Publications

	Good	Fine	Mint
1	35.00	100.00	200.00
2	17.00	50.00	100.00
3	12.00	35.00	70.00
4	10.00	28.00	56.00
5-7	8.00	22.00	44.00
8-Bulletgirl x-over in Mary Marvel	8.00	22.00	44.00
9,10	5.00	15.00	30.00
11-20	4.00	12.00	24.00
21-28	3.50	10.00	20.00

MARY POPPINS (See Walt Disney Showcase No. 17 & Movie Comics)

MARY'S GREATEST APOSTLE (St. Louis Grignion de Montfort)
No date (16 pages; paper cover)
Catechetical Guild (Topix) (Giveaway)

	Good	Fine	Mint
	2.50	7.00	14.00

MARY WORTH (See Love Stories of . . . & Comic Hits)
March, 1956
Argo

	Good	Fine	Mint
1	2.50	7.00	14.00

MASK COMICS
Feb-Mar, 1945 - No. 2, Apr-May, 1945; No. 2, Fall, 1945
Rural Home Publications

	Good	Fine	Mint
1-Classic L. B. Cole Satan-c/a	60.00	170.00	340.00
2-(Scarce)Classic L. B. Cole Satan-c; Black Rider, The Boy Magician, & The Collector app.	30.00	80.00	160.00
2(Fall, 1945)-No publ.-same as regular No. 2; L. B. Cole-c	17.00	50.00	100.00

NOTE: *No. 2 sold over 1,000,000 copies on the stands.*

MASKED BANDIT, THE
1952
Avon Periodicals

	Good	Fine	Mint
nn-Kinstler-a	7.00	20.00	40.00

MASKED MARVEL
Sept, 1940 - No. 3, Dec, 1940
Centaur Publications

	Good	Fine	Mint
1-The Masked Marvel begins	25.00	70.00	150.00
2,3: 2-Gustavson, Tarpe Mills-a	15.00	45.00	90.00

MASKED RAIDER, THE (Billy The Kid No. 9 on; Frontier Scout, Daniel Boone No. 10-13; See Blue Bird)
6/55 - No. 8, 1956; No. 14, 1956 - No. 30, 6/61
Charlton Comics

	Good	Fine	Mint
1	1.20	3.50	7.00
2-8: 8-Billy The Kid app.	.70	2.00	4.00
14,16-30: 22-Rocky Lane app.	.35	1.00	2.00
15-Williamson-a, 7 pgs.	2.00	6.00	12.00

MASKED RANGER
April, 1954 - No. 9, Aug, 1955
Premier Magazines

	Good	Fine	Mint
1-Woodbridge-a; Check-a(2)	4.00	12.00	24.00
2,3-Crimson Avenger app.	2.00	5.00	10.00
4-8-All Woodbridge-a	3.00	8.00	16.00
9-Torres-a	3.50	10.00	20.00

NOTE: ***Woodbridge** c/a-1,4-8.*

MASK OF DR. FU MANCHU, THE (See Dr. Fu Manchu)
1951
Avon Periodicals

	Good	Fine	Mint
1-Wood c/a, 26 pgs.	125.00	300.00	550.00

MASQUE OF THE RED DEATH (See Movie Classics)

MASTER COMICS
Mar, 1940 - No. 133, Apr, 1953 (No. 1-6: oversized issues)
Fawcett Publications

	Good	Fine	Mint
1-Origin Masterman; The Devil's Dagger, El Carim, Master of Magic, Rick O'Say, Morton Murch, White Rajah, Shipwreck Roberts, Frontier Marshall, Streak Sloan, Mr. Clue begin (all features end No. 6)	100.00	280.00	560.00
2	50.00	140.00	280.00
3-5	25.00	75.00	150.00
6-Last Masterman	20.00	60.00	120.00
7-(10/40)-Bulletman, Zorro, the Mystery Man (ends No. 22), Lee Granger, Jungle King, & Buck Jones begin; only app. The War Bird & Mark Swift & the Time Retarder	50.00	130.00	260.00
8-The Red Gaucho (ends No. 13), Captain Venture (ends No. 22) & The Planet Princess begin	22.00	65.00	130.00
9,10: 10-Lee Granger ends	20.00	55.00	110.00
11-Origin Minute-Man	40.00	120.00	240.00
12	25.00	75.00	150.00
13-Origin Bulletgirl	40.00	110.00	220.00
14-16: 14-Companions Three begins, ends No. 31	22.00	65.00	130.00
17-20: 17-Raboy-a on Bulletman begins	25.00	75.00	150.00
21-(Scarce)-Captain Marvel x-over in Bulletman; Capt. Nazi origin	150.00	370.00	750.00
22-Captain Marvel Jr. x-over in Bulletman; Capt. Nazi app; bondage-c	100.00	280.00	580.00
23-Captain Marvel Jr. begins, vs. Capt. Nazi	80.00	220.00	450.00
24,25,29	25.00	75.00	150.00
26-28,30-Captain Marvel Jr. vs. Capt. Nazi. 30-Flag-c	25.00	75.00	150.00
31,32: 32-Last El Carim & Buck Jones; Balbo, the Boy Magician intro. in El Carim	17.00	50.00	100.00
33-Balbo, the Boy Magician (ends No. 47), Hopalong Cassidy (ends No. 49) begins	17.00	50.00	100.00
34-Capt. Marvel Jr. vs. Capt. Nazi	17.00	50.00	100.00
35	17.00	50.00	100.00
36-40: 40-Flag-c	15.00	45.00	90.00
41-Bulletman, Capt. Marvel Jr. & Bulletgirl x-over in Minute-Man; only app. Crime Crusaders Club (Capt. Marvel Jr., Minute-Man, Bulletman & Bulletgirl)-only team in Fawcett Comics	17.00	50.00	100.00
42-47,49: 47-Hitler becomes Corpl. Hitler Jr. 49-Last Minute-Man	9.50	28.00	56.00
48-Intro. Bulletboy; Capt. Marvel cameo in Minute-Man	10.00	30.00	60.00
50-Radar, Nyoka the Jungle Girl begin; Capt. Marvel x-over in Radar; origin Radar	6.00	18.00	36.00
51-58	4.00	12.00	24.00
59-62: Nyoka serial ''Terrible Tiara'' in all; 61-Capt. Marvel Jr. 1st meets Uncle Marvel	5.00	14.00	28.00
63-80	3.50	10.00	20.00
81-100: 88-Hopalong Cassidy begins (ends No. 94). 95-Tom Mix begins (ends No. 133)	3.00	9.00	18.00
101-106-Last Bulletman	2.50	7.00	14.00
107-131	2.00	6.00	12.00
132-B&W and color illos in **POP**	3.50	10.00	20.00
133	4.00	12.00	24.00

NOTE: ***Mac Raboy** a-15-39, 40 in part, 42; c-21-49, 52, 54, 56, 58, 59.*

MASTER DETECTIVE
1964 (Reprint)
Super Comics

	Good	Fine	Mint
10,17,18: 17-Young King Cole; McWilliams-a	.40	1.20	2.40

MASTER OF KUNG FU (Formerly Special Marvel Edition)
No. 17, April, 1974 - Present
Marvel Comics Group

	Good	Fine	Mint
17-Starlin-a; intro Black Jack Tarr	.50	1.50	3.00
18-20: 19-Man-Thing app.	.35	1.00	2.00
21-23,25-30	.30	.90	1.80
24-Starlin, Simonson-a	.30	.90	1.80
31-40: 33-1st Leikowee		.50	1.00
41-53,55-60: 53-Reprints 20		.40	.80
54-Starlin-c		.40	.80
61-99: 91-Drug mention		.40	.80
100-(Double size)	.30	.90	1.80
101-107		.30	.60
Giant Size 1(9/74)-Russell-a	.35	1.10	2.20
Giant Size 2-r/Yellow Claw No. 1	.30	.80	1.60
Giant Size 3,4(6/75)-r-/2 Kirby stories/Yellow Claw	.30	.80	1.60
Annual 1(4/76)-Iron Fist	.30	.80	1.60

NOTE: ***Gulacy** a-18-20, 22, 25, 29-31, 33-35, 39, 40, 42-50, Giant Size No. 1, 2; c-51, 55, 64, 67.*

MASTERS OF TERROR (Magazine)
July, 1975 - No. 2, 1975 (Black & White) (All Reprints)
Marvel Comics Group

	Good	Fine	Mint
1-Brunner, Smith-a; Morrow-c; Adams-a(i)(r); Starlin-a(p) Gil Kane-a	.35	1.00	2.00
2-Reese, Kane, Mayerik-a	.25	.70	1.40

MASTER OF THE WORLD (See 4-Color No. 1157)

MATT SLADE GUNFIGHTER (Stories of Romance & Kid Slade Gunfighter No. 5 on?)
May, 1956 - No. 4, Nov, 1956
Atlas Comics (SPI)

	Good	Fine	Mint
1-Williamson/Torres-a	4.00	12.00	24.00
2-Williamson-a	3.50	10.00	20.00
3,4	2.00	5.00	10.00

MAUD
1906 (32 pgs. in color; 10x15½'') (cardboard covers)
Frederick A. Stokes Co.

	Good	Fine	Mint
By Fred Opper	10.00	30.00	60.00

MAVERICK (TV)
1958 - No. 19, Apr-June, 1962
Dell Publishing Co.

	Good	Fine	Mint
4-Color 892,930,945,962,980,1005	1.20	3.50	7.00
7(10-12/59)-19	1.00	3.00	6.00

MAVERICK MARSHAL
Nov, 1958 - No. 7, May, 1960
Charlton Comics

	Good	Fine	Mint
1	.60	1.80	3.60
2-7	.35	1.00	2.00

MAX BRAND (See Silvertip)

Masked Ranger #7, © PG

Master Comics #37, © FAW

Master Of Kung-Fu #17, © MCG

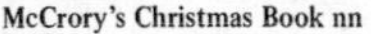
McCrory's Christmas Book nn

MD #1, © WMG

Menace #8, © MCG

MAYA (See Movie Classics)
March, 1968
Gold Key

	Good	Fine	Mint
1 (10218-803)(TV)	.70	2.00	4.00

MAZIE (. . . & Her Friends) (See Tastee-Freez)
1953 - 1958
Mazie Comics(Magazine Publ.)/Harvey Publ.

1	.85	2.50	5.00
2-10	.50	1.50	3.00
11-28		.50	1.00

MAZIE
1950 - 1951 (5 cents) (5x7¼''-miniature)
Nation Wide Publishers

1-7	.35	1.00	2.00

McCRORY'S CHRISTMAS BOOK
1955 (36 pgs.; slick cover)
Western Printing Co. (McCrory Stores Corp. giveaway)

	1.50	4.00	8.00

McCRORY'S TOYLAND BRINGS YOU SANTA'S PRIVATE EYES
1956 (16 pgs.)
Promotional Publ. Co. (Giveaway)

Has 9 pg. story plus 7 pg. toy ads	1.00	3.00	6.00

McCRORY'S WONDERFUL CHRISTMAS
1954 (20 pgs.; slick cover)
Promotional Publ. Co. (Giveaway)

	1.50	4.00	8.00

McHALE'S NAVY (TV) (See Movie Classics)
May-July, 1963 - No. 3, Nov-Jan, 1963-64
Dell Publishing Co.

1-3	.85	2.50	5.00

McKEEVER & THE COLONEL (TV)
Feb-Apr, 1963 - No. 3, Aug-Oct, 1963
Dell Publishing Co.

1-3	.85	2.50	5.00

McLINTOCK (See Movie Comics)

MD
Apr-May, 1955 - No. 5, Dec-Jan, 1955-56
E. C. Comics

1-Not approved by code	5.50	16.00	32.00
2-5	4.00	12.00	24.00

NOTE: ***Crandall, Evans, Ingels, Orlando*** *art in all issues;* ***Craig*** *c-1-5.*

MEDAL FOR BOWZER, A
No date (1948-50?)
Will Eisner Giveaway

Eisner-c/script	6.00	18.00	36.00

MEDAL OF HONOR COMICS
Spring, 1946
A. S. Curtis

1	2.50	7.00	14.00

MEET ANGEL (Formerly Angel & the Ape)
No. 7, Nov-Dec, 1969
National Periodical Publications

7-Wood a(i)		.50	1.00

MEET CORLISS ARCHER (My Life No. 4 on)
March, 1948 - No. 3, July, 1948
Fox Features Syndicate

1-Feldstein c/a	17.00	50.00	100.00
2-Feldstein-c only	14.00	40.00	80.00
3-Part Feldstein-c only	10.00	30.00	60.00

NOTE: *No. 1-3 used in* ***Seduction of the Innocent****, pg. 39.*

MEET HERCULES (See Three Stooges)

MEET HIYA A FRIEND OF SANTA CLAUS
1949 (18 pgs.?) (paper cover)
Julian J. Proskauer (Giveaway)

	Good	Fine	Mint
	2.50	7.00	14.00

MEET MERTON
1954 - No. 4, June, 1954
Toby Press

1-Dave Berg-a	.85	2.50	5.00
2-4-Dave Berg-a	.70	2.00	4.00
I.W. Reprint No. 9		.50	1.00
Super Reprint No. 11('63), 18		.40	.80

MEET MISS BLISS
May, 1955 - No. 3, Sept, 1955
Atlas Comics (LMC)

1	2.00	5.00	10.00
2,3	1.20	3.50	7.00

MEET MISS PEPPER (Formerly Lucy . . .)
No. 5, April, 1954 - No. 6, June, 1954
St. John Publishing Co.

5-Kubert/Maurer-a	8.00	24.00	48.00
6-Kubert-a	7.00	20.00	40.00

MEET THE NEW POST GAZETTE SUNDAY FUNNIES
3/12/49 (16 pgs.; paper covers)
Commercial comics (insert in newspaper)
Pittsburgh Post Gazette

Dick Tracy by Gould, Gasoline Alley, Terry & the Pirates, Brenda Starr, Buck Rogers by Yager, The Gumps, Peter Rabbit by Fago, Superman, Funnyman by Siegel & Shuster, The Saint, Archie, & others done especially for this book. Sold in 1978 . . . . $500.00

MEL ALLEN'S SPORTS COMICS
No. 5, Nov, 1949 - No. 6, Jan, 1950?
Standard Comics

5(No. 1 on inside)-Tuska-a	2.00	6.00	12.00
6	1.50	4.00	8.00

MELVIN MONSTER
Apr-June, 1965 - No. 10, Oct, 1969 (No No. 6)
Dell Publishing Co.

1-by John Stanley	3.00	9.00	18.00
2-5,7-10-All by Stanley	2.00	6.00	12.00

MELVIN THE MONSTER (Dexter the Demon No. 6 on)
July, 1956 - No. 6, July, 1957
Atlas Comics (HPC)

1-6	.85	2.50	5.00

MENACE
March, 1953 - No. 11, May, 1954
Atlas Comics (HPC)

1-Everett-a	4.00	12.00	24.00
2-4-Everett-a	2.00	6.00	12.00
5-Origin & 1st app. The Zombie by Everett (reprinted in Tales of Zombie No. 1)(7/53)	3.00	9.00	18.00
6,7,10,11: 10-H-Bomb panels	1.50	4.50	9.00
8-End of world story	1.50	4.50	9.00
9-Everett-a r-in Vampire Tales No. 1	2.50	7.00	14.00

NOTE: ***Everett*** *c-1-3,5.* ***Heath*** *a-1-5,7,8; c-10.* ***Katz*** *a-11.* ***Powell*** *a-11.* ***Shelly*** *a-10.*

MEN AGAINST CRIME (Hand of Fate No. 8 on) (Also see Mr. Risk)
1950 - No. 7, Oct, 1951
Ace Magazines

1	2.00	6.00	12.00
2-7: 2,3-Mr. Risk app.	1.50	4.00	8.00

MEN FROM PACIFIC PLANTRONICS, THE (See Business Week . . .)

MEN, GUNS, & CATTLE (See Classics Special)

MEN IN ACTION (Battle Brady No. 10 on)
April, 1952 - No. 9, Dec, 1952
Atlas Comics (IPS)

	Good	Fine	Mint
1	2.00	6.00	12.00
2-6,8,9	1.20	3.50	7.00
7-Krigstein-a	3.00	8.00	16.00

MEN IN ACTION
1957 - 1958
Ajax/Farrell Publications

1	1.50	4.00	8.00
2-9	.85	2.50	5.00

MEN INTO SPACE (See 4-Color No. 1083)

MEN OF BATTLE (See New . . .)

MEN OF COURAGE
1949
Catechetical Guild

Contains bound Topix comics-V7No.2,4,6,8,10,16,18,20	3.00	9.00	18.00

MEN OF WAR
August, 1977 - No. 26, March, 1980
DC Comics, Inc.

1-Origin Gravedigger, cont'd. in No. 2		.40	.80
2-26		.30	.60

NOTE: ***Chaykin*** *a-9, 10, 12-14, 19, 20.* ***Evans*** *c-25.* ***Kubert*** *c-2-13, 16-26.*

MEN'S ADVENTURES (Formerly True Adventures)
No. 4, Aug, 1950 - No. 28, July, 1954
Marvel/Atlas Comics (CCC)

4(No.1)	3.00	8.00	16.00
5-10	1.50	4.00	8.00
11-20	1.00	3.00	6.00
21,22,24-26	.85	2.50	5.00
23-Crandall-a	2.50	7.00	14.00
27,28-Captain America, Human Torch, & Sub-Mariner app. in each	13.00	38.00	76.00

NOTE: ***Berg*** *a-16.* ***Burgos*** *c-27.* ***Everett*** *a-10, 22, 25, 28; c-21, 22.* ***Mac Pakula*** *a-25.* ***Powell*** *a-27. Adventure-No. 4-10; War-No. 11-20; Horror-No. 21-26.*

MEN WHO MOVE THE NATION
(Giveaway) (Black & White)

Neal Adams-a	2.00	5.00	10.00

MERLIN JONES AS THE MONKEY'S UNCLE (See Movie Comics and The Misadventures of . . . under Movie Comics)

MERRILL'S MARAUDERS (See Movie Classics)

MERRY CHRISTMAS (See Donald Duck . . . , Dell Giant No. 39, & March of Comics No. 153)

MERRY CHRISTMAS, A
1948 (nn) (Giveaway)
K. K. Publications (Child Life Shoes)

	3.00	8.00	16.00

MERRY CHRISTMAS
1956 (7¼x5¼'')
K. K. Publications (Blue Bird Shoes Giveaway)

	1.00	3.00	6.00

MERRY CHRISTMAS
1969 (25 cents) (28 pgs.; slick cover)
Gilberton Co.

	Good	Fine	Mint
	.35	1.00	2.00

MERRY CHRISTMAS FROM MICKEY MOUSE
1939 (16 pgs.) (Color & B&W)
K. K. Publications (Shoe store giveaway)

Donald Duck & Pluto app.; text with art (Rare)	80.00	240.00	400.00

MERRY CHRISTMAS FROM SEARS TOYLAND
1939 (16 pgs.) (In color)
Sears Roebuck Giveaway

Dick Tracy, Little Orphan Annie, The Gumps, Terry & the Pirates	15.00	45.00	90.00

MERRY COMICS
December, 1945
Carlton Publishing Co.

nn-Boogeyman app.	1.50	4.00	8.00

MERRY COMICS
1947
Four Star Publications

1	1.50	4.00	8.00

MERRY-GO-ROUND COMICS
1944 (132 pgs.; 25 cents); 1946; Sept-Oct, 1947
LaSalle Publ. Co./Croyden Publ./Rotary Litho.

nn(1944)(LaSalle)	3.00	8.00	16.00
21	1.20	3.50	7.00
1(1946)(Croyden)	.85	2.50	5.00
V1No.1(9-10/47; 52 pgs.)(Rotary Litho. Co. Ltd., Canada)	.85	2.50	5.00

MERRY MAILMAN
1955
Charlton Comics

1 (Exist?)	1.20	3.50	7.00

MERRY MOUSE
June, 1953 - No. 4, Jan-Feb, 1954
Avon Periodicals

1-4	1.20	3.50	7.00

METAL MEN (See Brave & the Bold, DC Comics Presents, and Showcase)
4-5/63 - No. 41, 12-1/69-70; No. 42, 2-3/73 - No. 44, 7-8/73; No. 45, 4-5/76 - No. 56, 2-3/78
National Periodical Publications/DC Comics

1	3.00	9.00	18.00
2	1.50	4.50	9.00
3-5	1.00	3.00	6.00
6-10	.75	2.20	4.40
11-26	.50	1.50	3.00
27-Origin Metal Men	.50	1.50	3.00
28-41(1970)	.30	.80	1.60
42-44(1973)-Reprints		.30	.60
45('76)-49-Simonson-a in all		.50	1.00
50-56: 54,55-Green Lantern x-over		.40	.80

NOTE: ***Aparo*** *c-53.* ***Kane*** *a/c-30,31.* ***Staton*** *a-50p, 51-56.* ***Simonson*** *c-50.*

METAMORPHO (See Action, Brave & the Bold, First Issue Special, & World's Finest)
July-Aug, 1965 - No. 17, Mar-Apr, 1968
National Periodical Publications

1	2.00	5.00	10.00
2-5	.85	2.50	5.00
6-9	.50	1.50	3.00
10-Origin & 1st app. Element Girl (1-2/67)	.50	1.50	3.00

Men Of War #1, © DC

Metal Men #2, © DC

Metamorpho #5, © DC

Mickey Finn #1, © McNaught Synd.

M.M. Four Color #268, © WDP

M.M. & Goofy Explore Energy nn, © WDP

METAMORPHO (continued)

	Good	Fine	Mint
11-17	.30	.80	1.60

NOTE: ***Ramona Fraden** a-1-4. **Orlando** a-5, 6; c-5-9, 11. **Sal Trapani** a-7-16.*

METEOR COMICS
November, 1945
L. L. Baird (Croyden)

	Good	Fine	Mint
1-Captain Wizard, Impossible Man, Race Wilkins app.; origin Baldy Bean, Capt. Wizard's sidekick; Bare-breasted mermaids story	5.50	16.00	32.00

MGM'S MARVELOUS WIZARD OF OZ
November, 1975 (84 pgs.; oversize) ($1.50)
Marvel Comics Group/National Periodical Publications

	Good	Fine	Mint
1-Adaptation of MGM's movie (See Marvel Treasury of...)	.70	2.00	4.00

M.G.M's MOUSE MUSKETEERS (Formerly The Two Mouseketeers)
Jan, 1956 - 1962
Dell Publishing Co.

	Good	Fine	Mint
4-Color 670,711,728,764	.50	1.50	3.00
8-21(4/57-3-5/60)	.35	1.00	2.00
4-Color 1135,1175,1290	.50	1.50	3.00

MICKEY AND DONALD IN VACATIONLAND (See Dell Giant No. 47)

MICKEY & THE BEANSTALK (See Story Hour Series)

MICKEY & THE SLEUTH (See Walt Disney Showcase No. 38,39)

MICKEY FINN
1942 - V3No. 2, May, 1952
McNaught Syndicate No. 5 on (Columbia)/Headline V3No.2

	Good	Fine	Mint
1	4.50	13.00	26.00
2	2.50	7.00	14.00
3-Charlie Chan app.	2.00	5.00	10.00
4	1.50	4.00	8.00
5-15(1949), V3No.1,2(1952)	.85	2.50	5.00

MICKEY MOUSE
1931 - 1934 (52 pgs.; 10x9¾''; cardboard covers)
David McKay Publications

	Good	Fine	Mint
1(1931)	80.00	240.00	400.00
2(1932)	60.00	180.00	300.00
3(1933)-All color Sunday reprints; page No.'s 5-17, 32-48 reissued in Whitman No. 948	120.00	350.00	600.00
4(1934)	50.00	150.00	280.00

NOTE: *Each book reprints strips from previous year - dailies in black and white in No. 1,2,4; Sundays in color in No. 3. Later reprints exist; i.e., No. 2 (1934).*

MICKEY MOUSE
1933 (Copyright date, printing date unknown)
(30 pages; 10x8¾''; cardboard covers)
Whitman Publishing Co.

	Good	Fine	Mint
948-(1932 Sunday strips in color)	90.00	250.00	400.00

NOTE: Some copies were bound with a second front cover upside-down instead of the regular back cover; both covers have the same art, but different right and left margins.

NOTE: *The above book is an exact, but abbreviated reissue of David McKay No. 3 but with ½-inch of border trimmed from the top and bottom.*

MICKEY MOUSE (See The Best of Walt Disney Comics, Cheerios giveaways, 40 Big Pages..., Merry Christmas From..., The New..., and Wheaties)

MICKEY MOUSE (...Secret Agent No. 107-109; Walt Disney's... No. 148-205?)
1941 - Present
Dell Publ. Co./Gold Key No. 85(11/62)-204/Whitman No. 205 on

	Good	Fine	Mint
4-Color 16(1941)-1st M.M. comic book-''vs. the Phantom Blot'' by Gottfredson	300.00	800.00	1600.00
(Prices vary widely on this book)			
4-Color 27(1943)-''7 Colored Terror''	50.00	120.00	240.00
4-Color 79(1945)-By Carl Barks (1 story)	70.00	170.00	340.00
4-Color 116(1946)	10.00	28.00	56.00
4-Color 141(1947)	10.00	28.00	56.00
4-Color 157('47),170,181,194('48)	8.00	22.00	44.00
4-Color 214('49),231,248,261	5.00	15.00	30.00
4-Color 268-Reprints/WDC&S No. 22-24 by Gottfredson (''Surprise Visitor'')	5.00	15.00	30.00
4-Color 279,286,296	4.00	12.00	24.00
4-Color 304,313(No.1),325(No.2),334	3.50	10.00	20.00
4-Color 343,352,362,371,387	3.00	8.00	16.00
4-Color 401,411,427('52)	2.00	6.00	12.00
4-Color 819-M.M. in Magicland	1.50	4.00	8.00
4-Color 1057,1151,1246(1959-61)-Album	1.00	3.00	6.00
28(12-1/52-53)-32,34	1.00	3.00	6.00
33-(Exists with 2 dates, 10-11/53 & 12-1/54)	1.00	3.00	6.00
35-46,48-50	.85	2.50	5.00
47-Story swipe-'The Rare Stamp Search'/4-Color 422-'The Gilded Man'	1.00	3.00	6.00
51-80	.70	2.00	4.00
81-99: 93,95-titled ''Mickey Mouse Club Album''	.55	1.60	3.20
100-105: Reprints 4-Color 427,194,279,170,343,214 in that order	1.00	3.00	6.00
106-130	.35	1.00	2.00
131-146		.50	1.00
147-Reprints ''The Phantom Fires'' from WDC&S 200-202	1.00	3.00	6.00
148-Reprints ''The Mystery of Lonely Valley'' from WDC&S 208-210	1.00	3.00	6.00
149-158		.40	.80
159-Reprints ''The Sunken City'' from WDC&S 205-207	.85	2.50	5.00
160-170: 162-170-r		.40	.80
171-178,180-200		.30	.60
179-(52 pgs.)		.40	.80
201-210		.30	.60
Album 01-518-210(Dell), 1(10082-309)(9/63-Gold Key)	.35	1.00	2.00
Almanac 1('57)-Barks-a, 8pgs.	7.00	20.00	40.00
...& Goofy ''Bicep Bungle''(1952, 14 pgs.) Fritos giveaway	2.00	6.00	12.00
...& Goofy Explore Business(1978)		.40	.80
...& Goofy Explore Energy(1976-1978) 36 pgs.; Exxon Giveaway in color; regular size		.40	.80
...& Goofy Explore Energy Conservation(1976-1978)-Exxon		.40	.80
Birthday Party 1('53)(25th Anniversary)-Reprints entire 48 pgs. of Gottfredson's ''M.M. in Love Trouble'' from WDC&S 36-39. Quality equal to original. Also reprints one story each from 4-Color 27,79, & 181 plus 6 panels of highlights in the career of Mickey Mouse	12.00	35.00	70.00
Club 1(1/64-G.K.)(TV)	.85	2.50	5.00
Club Fun Book 11190(Golden Press, $1.95, 224pgs, 1977)	.40	1.20	2.40
Club Parade 1(12/55)-Reprints 4-Color 16 with some art redrawn & recolored with night scenes turned into day; quality much poorer than original	10.00	28.00	56.00
In Fantasy Land 1('57)	2.00	5.00	10.00
In Frontier Land 1('56)-M.M. Club issue	2.00	5.00	10.00
Mini Comic 1(1976)(3¼x6½'')-Reprints 158		.30	.60
Surprise Party 1(30037-901, G.K.)(1/69)-40th Anniversary	2.00	5.00	10.00

MICKEY MOUSE BOOK
1930 (2 printings, 16pgs., paperbound)
Bibo & Lang

Very first Disney book; origin of Mickey Mouse (1st Printing);

MICKEY MOUSE BOOK (continued)	Good	Fine	Mint
cartoons, songs, games	150.00	400.00	800.00

MICKEY MOUSE CLUB MAGAZINE (See Walt Disney . . .)

MICKEY MOUSE CLUB SPECIAL (See The New Mickey Mouse . . .)

MICKEY MOUSE MAGAZINE
V1No.1, Jan, 1933 - V1No.9, Sept, 1933
No. 1-3 published by Kamen-Blair (Kay Kamen, Inc.)
Walt Disney Productions

(Scarce)-Distributed by leading stores through their local theatres. First few issues had 5 cents listed on cover, later ones had no price.

	Good	Fine	Mint
V1No.1	120.00	300.00	600.00
2-9	60.00	150.00	300.00

MICKEY MOUSE MAGAZINE
V1No.1, Nov, 1933 - V2No.12, Oct, 1935
Mills giveaways issued by different dairies
Walt Disney Productions

	Good	Fine	Mint
V1No.1	20.00	60.00	120.00
2-12	10.00	30.00	60.00
V2No.1-12	8.00	24.00	48.00

MICKEY MOUSE MAGAZINE (Becomes Walt Disney's Comics & Stories) (No V3No. 1)
Summer, 1935 - V5No.12, Sept, 1940
K. K. Publications

	Good	Fine	Mint
V1No.1-John Stanley c/a	100.00	275.00	550.00
2	50.00	150.00	300.00
3	30.00	80.00	160.00
4-6	20.00	60.00	120.00
7-9	17.00	50.00	100.00
10-12	14.00	40.00	80.00
V2No.1-9,11-13: Gottfredson Mickey Mouse (B&W) reprints begin No.?	12.00	35.00	70.00
10-1st Mickey Mouse in four color	12.00	35.00	70.00
V3No.2-12	12.00	35.00	70.00
V4No.1-12	12.00	35.00	70.00
V5No.1-8	17.00	50.00	100.00
9-Regular comic book size begins	35.00	100.00	200.00
10,11	40.00	120.00	240.00
12-(Rare)-The transition issue that changed the magazine into a comic book; strip-r	200.00	450.00	900.00
V4No.1 (Giveaway)	12.00	35.00	70.00

NOTE: *No. 1-9 sold 150,000 copies per month; No. 10 on sold 500,000 per month.*

MICKEY MOUSE MARCH OF COMICS
1947 - 1951 (Giveaway)
K. K. Publications

	Good	Fine	Mint
8(1947)-32 pgs.	60.00	150.00	300.00
27(1948)	35.00	85.00	170.00
45(1949)	30.00	70.00	140.00
60(1950)	17.00	50.00	100.00
74(1951)	11.00	32.00	64.00

MICKEY MOUSE SUMMER FUN (Summer Fun No. 2)
1958
Dell Publishing Co.

	Good	Fine	Mint
1	3.00	8.00	16.00

MICKEY MOUSE'S SUMMER VACATION (See Story Hour Series)

MICROBOTS, THE
December, 1971 (One Shot)
Gold Key

	Good	Fine	Mint
1 (10271-112)		.50	1.00

MICRONAUTS, THE
January, 1979 - Present
Marvel Comics Group

	Good	Fine	Mint
1	.85	2.50	5.00
2-5	.40	1.20	2.40
6-10: 7-Manthing app. 8-1st app. Capt. Universe. 9-1st app. Cilicia	.30	.90	1.80
11-20: 13-1st app. Jasmine. 15-17-Fantastic-4 app. 17-Death of Jasmine. 20-Ant-Man app.	.25	.70	1.40
21-30: 21-Microverse series begins. 25-Origin Baron Karza. 25-29-Nick Fury app. 27-Death of Biotron		.50	1.00
31-34,36,38-40: Dr. Strange app. No. 31,34,35		.30	.60
35-Double size		.40	.80
37-X-Men app.		.40	.80
nn-Reprints No.1-3; blank UPC; diamond on top		.30	.60
Annual 1(12/79)-Ditko c/a	.30	.90	1.80
Annual 2(10/80)-Ditko c/a		.60	1.20

NOTE: *No. 39-on distributed only through comic shops.* ***Adams*** *c-7i.* ***Chaykin*** *a-13-18.* ***Cockrum*** *c-1.* ***Golden*** *a-1-12; c-2-23, 24p, 25p.* ***Layton*** *c-33-36.*

MIDGET COMICS (Fighting Indian Stories)
Feb, 1950 - No. 2, Apr, 1950 (5-3/8''x7-3/8'')
St. John Publishng Co.

	Good	Fine	Mint
1-Matt Baker-c	2.00	6.00	12.00
2-Tex West, Cowboy Marshal	1.20	3.50	7.00

MIDNIGHT
April, 1957 - No. 6, June, 1958
Ajax/Farrell Publ. (Four Star Comic Corp.)

	Good	Fine	Mint
1-Reprints from Voodoo & Strange Fantasy with some changes	2.00	6.00	12.00
2-5	1.00	3.00	6.00
6-Baker-r/Phantom Lady	2.00	6.00	12.00

MIDNIGHT MYSTERY
Jan-Feb, 1961 - No. 7, Oct, 1961
American Comics Group

	Good	Fine	Mint
1	1.50	4.00	8.00
2-7	.85	2.50	5.00

MIDNIGHT TALES
Dec, 1972 - No. 18, May, 1976
Charlton Press

	Good	Fine	Mint
V1No.1		.60	1.20
2-10,15-18		.40	.80
11-14-Newton-a		.40	.80
12,17(Modern Comics reprint, 1977)		.15	.30

NOTE: ***Adkins*** *a-12,13p.* ***Howard*** *(Wood imitator) a-1-12, 14, 15, 17, 18; c-1-18.* ***Staton*** *a-8, 9, 13i.* ***Sutton*** *a-9*

MIGHTY ATOM (. . . & the Pixies No. 6) (Formerly The Pixies No. 1-5)
No. 6, 1949; Nov, 1957 - No. 6, Aug-Sept, 1958
Magazine Enterprises

	Good	Fine	Mint
6(1949-M.E.)-no month (1st Series)	1.50	4.00	8.00
1-6(2nd Series)-Pixies-r	.70	2.00	4.00
I.W. Reprint No. 1(no date)	.30	.90	1.80
Giveaway(1959, Whitman)-Evans-a	1.50	4.00	8.00

MIGHTY BEAR (Formerly Fun Comics, Mighty Ghost No. 4)
No. 13, Jan, 1954 - No. 14, Mar, 1954; 9/57 - No. 2, 11/57
Star Publ. No. 13,14/Ajax-Farrell (Four Star)

	Good	Fine	Mint
13,14-L. B. Cole-c	3.00	8.00	16.00
1,2(1957)Four Star (Ajax)	.70	2.00	4.00

MIGHTY COMICS (. . . Presents) (Formerly Flyman)
No. 40, Nov, 1966 - No. 50, Oct, 1967
Radio Comics (Archie)

	Good	Fine	Mint
40-Web	.85	2.00	4.00
41-Shield, Black Hood	.50	1.50	3.00
42-Black Hood	.50	1.50	3.00
43-Shield & Web	.50	1.50	3.00

Mickey Mouse Mag. V5#11, © WDP

Micronauts #1, © MCG

Midget Comics #2, © STJ

Mighty Crusaders #2, © AP

Mighty Mouse #1(Timely), © MGM

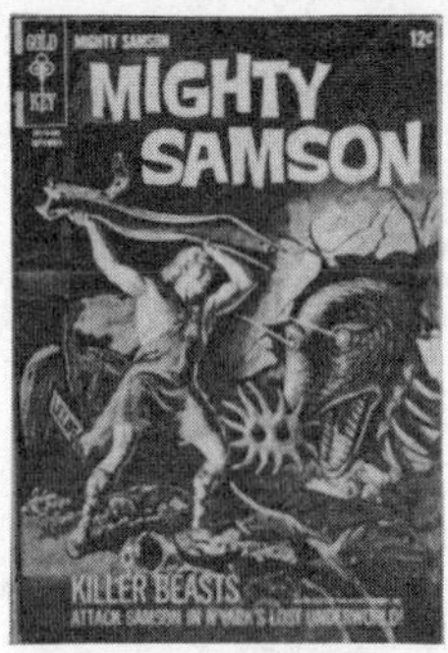

Mighty Samson #7, © GK

MIGHTY COMICS (continued)

	Good	Fine	Mint
44-Black Hood, Steel Sterling & The Shield	.50	1.50	3.00
45-Shield & Hangman; origin Web retold	.50	1.50	3.00
46-Steel Sterling & Web	.50	1.50	3.00
47-Black Hood & Mr. Justice	.50	1.50	3.00
48-Shield & Hangman; Wizard x-over in Shield	.50	1.50	3.00
49-Steel Sterling & Fox; Black Hood x-over in Steel Sterling	.50	1.50	3.00
50-Black Hood & Web; Inferno x-over in Web	.50	1.50	3.00

MIGHTY CRUSADERS, THE
Nov, 1965 - No. 7, Oct, 1966
Mighty Comics Group (Radio Comics) (Archie)

	Good	Fine	Mint
1-Origin The Shield	1.50	4.00	8.00
2-Origin Comet	1.00	3.00	6.00
3-Origin Fly-Man	.70	2.00	4.00
4-Fireball, Inferno, Firefly, Web, Fox, Bob Phantom, Blackjack, Hangman, Zambini, Kardak, Steel Sterling, Mr. Justice, Wizard, Capt. Flag, Jaguar x-over	.85	2.50	5.00
5-Intro. Ultra-Men (Fox, Web, Capt. Flag) & Terrific Three (Jaguar, Mr. Justice, Steel Sterling)	.70	2.00	4.00
6,7: 7-Steel Sterling feature; origin Fly-Girl	.70	2.00	4.00

MIGHTY GHOST (Formerly Mighty Bear)
No. 4, June, 1958
Ajax/Farrell Publ.

	Good	Fine	Mint
4	.70	2.00	4.00

MIGHTY HERCULES, THE (TV)
July, 1963 - No. 2, Nov, 1963
Gold Key

	Good	Fine	Mint
1,2(10072-307,311)	1.00	3.00	6.00

MIGHTY HEROES, THE (TV) (Funny)
Mar, 1967 - No. 4, July, 1967
Dell Publishing Co.

	Good	Fine	Mint
1-Reprints 1957 Heckle & Jeckle	.35	1.00	2.00
2,3		.40	.80
4-Two 1958 Mighty Mouse reprints		.60	1.20

MIGHTY MARVEL WESTERN, THE
10/68 - No. 46, 9/76 (No. 1-14: 68 pgs.; No. 15,16: 52 pgs.)
Marvel Comics Group

	Good	Fine	Mint
1-Begin Kid Colt, Rawhide Kid, Two-Gun Kid-r		.40	.80
2-10		.30	.60
11-20		.30	.60
21-30: 24-Kid Colt-r end. 25-Matt Slade-r begin		.30	.60
31,33-36,38-46: 31-Baker-r		.30	.60
32-Origin-r/Ringo Kid No. 23; Williamson-r/Kid Slade No.7		.30	.60
37-Williamson, Kirby-r/Two-Gun Kid 51		.30	.60

NOTE: *No. 21-24* ***Jack Davis*** *reprints.* ***Kirby*** *reprints-No. 1-3,6,9,12, 14,16,26,29,32,36,41,43,44; cover-No. 29. No Matt Slade-No. 43.*

MIGHTY MIDGET COMICS, THE (Miniature)
No date; circa 1942-1943 (36 pages) (Approx. 5x4'')
(Black & White & Red) (Sold 2 for 5 cents)
Samuel E. Lowe & Co.

	Good	Fine	Mint
Bulletman No. 11(1943)-Reprints cover/Bulletman No. 3	2.00	6.00	12.00
Captain Marvel No. 11(16pp)-two stories	2.00	6.00	12.00
Captain Marvel No. 11 (2 issues; one issue has ad on back for Captain Marvel comics & is believed to be the small comic glued to cover of Capt. Marvel No. 20)-Golden Arrow, Spysmasher, Ibis, Lance O'Casey x-over	2.00	6.00	12.00
Captain Marvel Jr. No. 11	2.00	6.00	12.00
Golden Arrow No. 11	1.00	3.00	6.00
Ibis the Invincible No. 11(1942)-Reprints cover/Ibis No. 1	2.00	6.00	12.00
Spy Smasher No. 11(1942)	2.00	6.00	12.00

NOTE: *The above books came in a box called ''box full of books'' and was distributed with other Samuel Lowe puzzles, paper dolls, coloring books, etc. They are not titled Mighty Midget Comics. All have a war bond seal on back cover. These books came in a ''Mighty Midget'' counter display rack.*

	Good	Fine	Mint
Balbo, the Boy Magician No. 12	1.50	4.00	8.00
Bulletman No. 12	2.00	6.00	12.00
Commando Yank No. 12	1.50	4.00	8.00
Dr. Voltz the Human Generator	1.00	3.00	6.00
Lance O'Casey No. 12	1.00	3.00	6.00
Leatherneck the Marine	1.00	3.00	6.00
Minute Man No. 12	2.00	6.00	12.00
Mister Q	1.00	3.00	6.00
Mr. Scarlet & Pinky No. 12	2.00	6.00	12.00
Pat Wilton & His Flying Fortress	1.00	3.00	6.00
The Phantom Eagle No. 12	1.50	4.00	8.00
Tornado Tom; reprints from Cyclone No. 1-3; origin	1.50	4.00	8.00

MIGHTY MOUSE (See Adventures of . . ., Dell Giant No. 43, Giant Comics Edition, March of Comics No. 205,237,247,257,471, Oxydol-Dreft, Paul Terry's, & Terry-Toons Comics)

MIGHTY MOUSE (1st Series)
Fall, 1946 - No. 4, Summer, 1947
Timely/Marvel Comics

	Good	Fine	Mint
1	14.00	40.00	80.00
2-4	10.00	30.00	60.00

MIGHTY MOUSE (2nd Series) (Paul Terry's. . . No. 63-71)
Aug, 1947 - No. 67, 11/55; No. 68, 3/56 - No. 83, 6/59
St. John Publishing Co./Pines No. 68 (3/56) on

	Good	Fine	Mint
5(No.1)	5.50	16.00	32.00
6-10	3.50	10.00	20.00
11-19	2.00	6.00	12.00
20-25-(52 pgs.)	2.00	6.00	12.00
20-25-(36 pg. editions)	1.75	5.00	10.00
26-37	1.50	4.00	8.00
38-45-(100 pgs.)	3.00	8.00	16.00
46-83: 82-Infinity-c	1.00	3.00	6.00
Album 1(10/52)-100 pgs.	5.50	16.00	32.00
Album 2(11/52-St. John) - 3(12/52) (100 pgs.)	4.00	12.00	24.00
Fun Club Magazine 1(Fall, 1957-Pines)	3.50	10.00	20.00
Fun Club Magazine 2-6(Winter, 1958-Pines)	2.00	6.00	12.00
3-D 1-(1st printing-9/53)(St. John)-stiff covers	10.00	30.00	60.00
3-D 1-(2nd printing-10/53)-slick, glossy covers, slighty smaller	8.00	24.00	48.00
3-D 2(11/53), 3(12/53)-(St. John)	7.00	20.00	40.00

MIGHTY MOUSE (TV)(3rd Series)(Formerly Advs. of Mighty Mouse)
No. 161, Oct, 1964 - No. 172, Oct, 1968
Gold Key

	Good	Fine	Mint
161(10/64)-165(9/65)-(Becomes Advs. of. . . No. 166 on)	1.50	4.00	8.00
166(3/66)-172	1.00	3.00	6.00

MIGHTY MOUSE ADVENTURES (Advs. of. . . No. 2 on, 1st Series)
November, 1951
St. John Publishing Co.

	Good	Fine	Mint
1	8.00	24.00	48.00

MIGHTY MOUSE ADVENTURE STORIES
1953 (384 pgs.) (50 Cents)
St. John Publishing Co.

	Good	Fine	Mint
Rebound issues	7.00	20.00	40.00

MIGHTY SAMSON (Also see Gold Key Champion)
7/64 - No.20, 11/69?; No.21, 8/72; No.22, 12/73 - No.31, 3/76
Gold Key

	Good	Fine	Mint
1-Origin	.70	2.00	4.00
2-5	.35	1.00	2.00
6-10: 7-Tom Morrow begins, ends No. 20	.25	.70	1.40

MIGHTY SAMSON (continued)

	Good	Fine	Mint
11-20		.50	1.00
21-31: 21,22-Reprints		.40	.80

MIGHTY THOR (See Thor)

MIKE BARNETT, MAN AGAINST CRIME
1952
Fawcett Publications

	Good	Fine	Mint
1	2.50	7.00	14.00
2-4,6	2.00	6.00	12.00
5-''Market for Morphine'' cover/story	4.00	12.00	24.00

MIKE SHAYNE PRIVATE EYE
Nov-Jan, 1962 - No. 3, Sept-Nov, 1962
Dell Publishing Co.

	Good	Fine	Mint
1	1.20	3.50	7.00
2,3	.85	2.50	5.00

MILITARY COMICS (Becomes Modern No. 44 on)
Aug, 1941 - No. 43, Oct, 1945
Quality Comics Group

	Good	Fine	Mint
1-Origin Blackhawk by C. Cuidera, Miss America, The Death Patrol by Jack Cole (also No. 2-7,27-30), & The Blue Tracer by Guardineer; X of the Underground, The Yankee Eagle, Q-Boat & Shot & Shell, Archie Atkins, Loops & Banks by Bud Ernest (Bob Powell) (ends No. 13) begin	175.00	430.00	860.00
2-Secret War News begins (by McWilliams No. 2-16); Cole-a	80.00	210.00	420.00
3-Origin Chop Chop	55.00	145.00	290.00
4	50.00	125.00	250.00
5-The Sniper begins; Miss America in costume No. 4-7	40.00	105.00	210.00
6-9: 8-X of the Underground begins (ends No. 13). 9-The Phantom Clipper begins (ends No. 16)	25.00	75.00	150.00
10-Classic Eisner-c	32.00	85.00	170.00
11	20.00	60.00	120.00
12-Blackhawk by Crandall begins, ends No. 22	30.00	80.00	160.00
13-15: 14-Private Dogtag begins (ends No. 83)	20.00	60.00	120.00
16-20: 16-Blue Tracer ends. 17-P.T. Boat begins	14.00	40.00	80.00
21-31: 22-Last Crandall Blackhawk. 27-Death Patrol revived. 31-Drug story	12.00	35.00	70.00
32-43	10.00	30.00	60.00

NOTE: ***Berg** a-6. **J. Cole** a-29-32. **Crandall** a-12-22; c-13-22. **Eisner** c-1, 9, 10. **Ward** Blackhawk-30, 31(15 pgs. each); c-29, 30.*

MILITARY WILLY
1907 (14 pgs.; ½ in color (every other page)) (regular comic book format)(7x9½'')(stapled)
J. I. Austen Co.

	Good	Fine	Mint
By F. R. Morgan	8.00	24.00	48.00

MILLIE, THE LOVABLE MONSTER
Sept-Nov, 1962 - No. 6, Jan, 1973
Dell Publishing Co.

	Good	Fine	Mint
12-523,211, 2(8-10/63)	.85	2.50	5.00
3(8-10/64), 4(7/72), 5(10/72), 6(1/73)	.50	1.50	3.00

NOTE: ***Woggon** a-3-6; c-3-6. 4 reprints 1; 5 reprints 2; 6 reprints 3.*

MILLIE THE MODEL (See Modeling With . . ., A Date With . . ., and Life With . . .)
1945 - No. 207, December, 1973
Marvel/Atlas/Marvel Comics (SPI/Male/VPI)

	Good	Fine	Mint
1	10.00	30.00	60.00
2	5.00	14.00	28.00
3-7	2.50	7.00	14.00
8,10-Kurtzman's ''Hey Look''	3.00	8.00	16.00
9-Powerhouse Pepper by Wolverton, 4 pgs.	5.50	16.00	32.00
11-Kurtzman-a	2.00	6.00	12.00
12,15,17-30	1.00	3.00	6.00
13,14,16-Kurtzman's ''Hey Look''	1.50	4.00	8.00
31-60	.50	1.50	3.00
61-100	.25	.70	1.40
101-106,108-207: 192-(52 pgs.)		.50	1.00
107-Jack Kirby app. in story		.40	.80
Annual 1(1962)	1.00	3.00	6.00
Annual 2-10(1963-11/71)	.70	2.00	4.00
Queen-Size 11(9/74), 12(1975)	.35	1.00	2.00

MILT GROSS FUNNIES
Aug, 1947 - No. 2, Sept, 1947
Rotary Lithograph Co.

	Good	Fine	Mint
1,2	2.50	7.00	14.00

MILTON THE MONSTER & FEARLESS FLY (TV)
May, 1966
Gold Key

	Good	Fine	Mint
1 (10175-605)	.85	2.50	5.00

MINUTE MAN (See Mighty Midget Comics)
1941 - No. 3, Spring, 1942
Fawcett Publications

	Good	Fine	Mint
1	40.00	110.00	225.00
2,3	25.00	75.00	150.00

MINUTE MAN
No date (B&W; 16 pgs.; paper cover blue & red)
Sovereign Service Station giveaway

	Good	Fine	Mint
American history	1.00	3.00	6.00

MINUTE MAN ANSWERS THE CALL, THE
1942 (4 pages)
By M. C. Gaines (War Bonds giveaway)

	Good	Fine	Mint
Sheldon Moldoff-a	3.50	10.00	20.00

MIRACLE COMICS
Feb, 1940 - No. 4, March, 1941
Hillman Periodicals

	Good	Fine	Mint
1-Sky Wizard, Master of Space, Dash Dixon, Man of Might, Dusty Doyle, Pinkie Parker, The Kid Cop, K-7, Secret Agent, The Scorpion, & Blandu, Jungle Queen begin; Masked Angel only app.	15.00	45.00	100.00
2-4: 3-Bill Colt, the Ghost Rider begins. 4-The Veiled Prophet & Bullet Bob app.	12.00	35.00	75.00

MIRACLE OF THE WHITE STALLIONS, THE (See Movie Comics)

MIRTH OF A NATION
1941 (Small size, 10 Cents) (Gags)
William Wise & Co. (Harry 'A' Chesler)

	Good	Fine	Mint
1-5-Art by Harry 'A' Chesler, Jr. plus a strip called Private Chesler	2.00	5.00	10.00

MISADVENTURES OF MERLIN JONES, THE (See Movie Comics & Merlin Jones as the Monkey's Uncle under Movie Comics)

MISCHIEVOUS MONKS OF CROCODILE ISLE, THE
1908 (8½x11½''; 4 pgs. in color; 12 pgs.)
J. I. Austen Co., Chicago

	Good	Fine	Mint
By F. R. Morgan; reads longwise	4.00	12.00	24.00

MISS AMERICA COMICS (Miss America Mag. No. 2 on)
1944 (One Shot)
Marvel Comics (MAP)

	Good	Fine	Mint
1	30.00	90.00	180.00

MISS AMERICA MAGAZINE (Formerly Miss America) (Miss America No. 52 on)
V1No.2, Nov, 1944 - No. 93, Nov, 1958

Military Comics #24, © QUA

Miracle Comics #4, © HILL

Mirth Of A Nation #1, © WHW

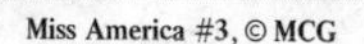
Miss America #3, © MCG

Mr. & Mrs. nn, © WHIT

Mister Miracle #9, © DC

MISS AMERICA MAGAZINE (continued)
Miss America Publ. Corp./Marvel/Atlas (MAP)

	Good	Fine	Mint
V1No.2: Photo cover of teenage girl in Miss America costume; Miss America, Patsy Walker (intro.) comic stories plus movie reviews & stories; intro. Buzz Baxter & Hedy Wolfe	40.00	100.00	180.00
3-5-Miss America & Patsy Walker stories	12.00	32.00	56.00
6-Patsy Walker only	2.00	5.00	10.00
V2No.1(4/45)-6(9/45)-Patsy Walker continues	1.20	3.50	7.00
V3No.1(10/45)-6(4/46)	1.20	3.50	7.00
V4No.1(5/46)-6(10/46), V5No.1(11/46)-6(4/47), V6No.1(5/47)-3(7/47)	1.00	3.00	6.00
V7No.1(8/47)-23(6/49)	.85	2.50	5.00
V7No.24(7/49)-Kamen-a	1.00	3.00	6.00
V7No.25(8/49)-44?, VII,nn(5/52)	.85	2.50	5.00
V1,nn(7/52)-V1,nn(1/53)(No.46-49)	.85	2.50	5.00
V7No.50(Spring '53)-V7No.54(7/53)	.70	2.00	4.00
55-93	.70	2.00	4.00

MISS BEVERLY HILLS OF HOLLYWOOD
Mar-Apr, 1949 - No. 11, Oct-Nov, 1950
National Periodical Publications

	Good	Fine	Mint
1	9.00	25.00	50.00
2-11 (10, 11 Exist?)	7.00	20.00	40.00

MISS CAIRO JONES
1945
Croyden Publishers

	Good	Fine	Mint
1-Bob Oksner daily newspaper reprints (1st strip story)	7.00	20.00	40.00

MISS FURY COMICS (Newspaper strip reprints)
Winter, 1942-43 - No. 8, Winter, 1946
Timely Comics

	Good	Fine	Mint
1-Origin Miss Fury by Tarpe' Mills (68 pgs.) in costume w/pin-ups	130.00	360.00	720.00
2-(60 pgs.)-In costume w/pin-ups	60.00	160.00	320.00
3-(60 pgs.)-In costume w/pin-ups	45.00	125.00	250.00
4-(52 pgs.)-Costume, 2 pgs. w/pin-ups	40.00	105.00	210.00
5-(52 pgs.)-In costume w/pin-ups	35.00	90.00	180.00
6-(52 pgs.)-Not in costume in inside stories, w/pin-ups	24.00	60.00	120.00
7,8-(36 pgs.)-In costume 1 pg. each, no pin-ups	24.00	60.00	120.00

MISSION IMPOSSIBLE (TV)
May, 1967 - No. 5, Oct, 1969 (No. 1-3 have photo-c)
Dell Publishing Co.

	Good	Fine	Mint
1	1.00	3.00	6.00
2-5	.85	2.50	5.00

MISS LIBERTY (Becomes Liberty)
1945 (MLJ reprints)
Burten Publishing Co.

	Good	Fine	Mint
1-The Shield & Dusty, The Wizard, & Roy, the Super Boy app.; r-/Shield-Wizard No. 13	8.00	24.00	48.00

MISS MELODY LANE OF BROADWAY
Feb-Mar, 1950 - No. 4, Sept-Oct, 1950
National Periodical Publications

	Good	Fine	Mint
1	9.00	25.00	50.00
2-4 (4-Exist?)	7.00	20.00	40.00

MISS PEACH
Oct-Dec, 1963; 1969
Dell Publishing Co.

	Good	Fine	Mint
1-John Stanley-a	2.50	7.00	14.00
. . . Tells You How to Grow(1969; 25 cents)-Mell Lazarus-a; also given away (36 pgs.)	2.00	5.00	10.00

MISS PEPPER (See Meet Miss Pepper)

MISS SUNBEAM (See Little Miss. . .)

MISS VICTORY (See Holyoke One-Shot No. 3)
1945
Holyoke Publishing Co. (Tem)

	Good	Fine	Mint
1	7.00	20.00	40.00
2	5.50	16.00	32.00

MR. & MRS.
1922 (52, 28 pgs.) (9x9½'', cardboard-c)
Whitman Publishing Co.

	Good	Fine	Mint
By Briggs (B&W, 52pgs.)	4.00	12.00	24.00
28 page edition-(9x9½'')-Reprints Sunday strips in full color	12.50	25.00	50.00

MR. & MRS. BEANS (See Single Series No. 11)

MR. & MRS. J. EVIL SCIENTIST
Nov, 1963 - No. 6, Oct, 1966 (Hanna-Barbera)
Gold Key

	Good	Fine	Mint
1	.85	2.50	5.00
2-6	.50	1.50	3.00

MR. ANTHONY'S LOVE CLINIC
Nov, 1949 - No. 5, Apr-May, 1950
Hillman Periodicals

	Good	Fine	Mint
1-Photo-c	2.00	6.00	12.00
2-5	1.20	3.50	7.00

MR. DISTRICT ATTORNEY
Jan-Feb, 1948 - No. 67, Jan-Feb, 1959
National Periodical Publications

	Good	Fine	Mint
1	8.00	24.00	48.00
2-10	3.50	10.00	20.00
11-20	2.00	6.00	12.00
21-40	2.00	5.00	10.00
41-67	1.00	3.00	6.00

MR. DISTRICT ATTORNEY (See 4-Color No. 13)

MISTER ED, THE TALKING HORSE (TV)
Mar-May, 1962 - No. 6, Feb, 1964
Dell Publishing Co./Gold Key

	Good	Fine	Mint
4-Color 1295	1.00	3.00	6.00
1(11/62)-6 (Gold Key)	.50	1.50	3.00

(See March of Comics No. 244,260,282,290)

MR. MAGOO (TV) (The Nearsighted. . ., . . . & Gerald McBoing Boing 1954 issues; formerly Gerald. . .)
No. 6, Nov-Jan, 1953-54; 1963 - 1965
Dell Publishing Co.

	Good	Fine	Mint
6	1.20	3.50	7.00
4-Color 561,602('54)	1.20	3.50	7.00
4-Color 1235,1305('61)	.70	2.00	4.00
3-5(9-11/63)	.50	1.50	3.00
4-Color 1235(12-536-505)(3-5/65)-2nd Printing	.50	1.50	3.00

MISTER MIRACLE (See Brave & the Bold & Cancelled Comic Caval.)
3-4/71 - No. 18, 2-3/74; No. 19, 9/77 - No. 25, 8-9/78
National Periodical Publications/DC Comics

	Good	Fine	Mint
1	.75	2.20	4.40
2	.50	1.50	3.00
3	.40	1.20	2.40
4-Boy Commando reprints begin	.35	1.10	2.20
5-Young Scott Free begins	.35	1.10	2.20
6-8	.35	1.10	2.20
9-Origin Mr. Miracle	.35	1.10	2.20
10-14,16,17	.30	.80	1.60
15-Origin Shilo Norman	.30	.90	1.80
18-Barda & Scott Free wed; New Gods app.	.30	.80	1.60

MISTER MIRACLE (continued)

	Good	Fine	Mint
19-Adams part(i); Rogers-a(p)	.30	.90	1.80
20-22-Rogers-a(p)		.60	1.20
23-25-Golden-a(p)		.30	.60

NOTE: ***Golden*** *c-25.* ***Heath*** *a-24,25; c-25.* ***Kirby*** *a/c-1-18.* ***Rogers*** *c-19-24. 4-8 contain* ***Simon & Kirby*** *Boy Commando reprints from Detective 82,76, Boy Commandos 1,3, Detective 64 in that order.*

MR. MIRACLE (See Holyoke One-Shot No. 4)

MR. MUSCLES (Formerly Blue Beetle No. 18-21)
No. 22, Mar, 1956 - No. 23, May-June, 1956
Charlton Comics

	Good	Fine	Mint
22,23	1.00	3.00	6.00

MISTER MYSTERY
Sept, 1951 - No. 19, Oct, 1954
Mr. Publ. (Media Publ.) No. 1-3/SPM Publ./Stanmore (Aragon)

	Good	Fine	Mint
1-Kurtzman horror story swiped	8.00	24.00	48.00
2,3-Kurtzman story swipe	7.00	20.00	40.00
4,6: Bondage-c; 6-Torture	7.00	20.00	40.00
5,8,10	5.50	16.00	32.00
7-''The Brain Bats of Venus'' by Wolverton; partially re-used in Weird Tales of the Future No. 7	40.00	100.00	200.00
9-Nostrand-a	5.50	16.00	32.00
11-Wolverton ''Robot Woman'' story/Weird Mysteries No. 2, cut up, rewritten & partially redrawn	17.00	50.00	100.00
12-Classic injury to eye-c	20.00	60.00	120.00
13,14,17,19	3.50	10.00	20.00
15-''Living Dead'' junkie story	5.50	16.00	32.00
16-Bondage-c; drug story	5.50	16.00	32.00
18-''Robot Woman'' by Wolverton reprinted from Weird Mysteries No. 2; bondage-c	14.00	40.00	80.00

NOTE: ***Andru*** *c/a-1, 2.* ***Bailey*** *c-10-19(most).*

MISTER Q (See Mighty Midget Comics)

MR. RISK (Formerly All Romances) (See Men Against Crime)
No. 7, Oct, 1950 - No. 2, Dec, 1950
Ace Magazines

	Good	Fine	Mint
7,2	.85	2.50	5.00

MR. SCARLET & PINKY (See Mighty Midget Comics)

MR. UNIVERSE
1951
Mr. Publications Media Publ. (Stanmore, Aragon)

	Good	Fine	Mint
1-Drug mention story	5.00	14.00	28.00
2-'Jungle That Time Forgot', 24pg. story	3.50	10.00	20.00
3-Marijuana story	3.50	10.00	20.00
4,5-''Goes to War''	2.00	5.00	10.00

MITZI COMICS (. . . Boy Friend No. 2 on?)
Spring, 1948 - No. 4, Winter, 1948
Timely Comics

	Good	Fine	Mint
1-Kurtzman's ''Hey Look'' plus 3 pgs. ''Giggles 'n' Grins''	3.00	8.00	16.00
2-4	1.50	4.00	8.00

MITZI'S BOY FRIEND (Becomes Mitzi's Romances)
No. 2, June, 1948 - No. 7, April, 1949
Marvel Comics

	Good	Fine	Mint
2-7	.85	2.50	5.00

MITZI'S ROMANCES (Formerly Mitzi's Boy Friend)
No. 8, June, 1949 - No. 10, Dec, 1949
Timely/Marvel Comics

	Good	Fine	Mint
8-10	.85	2.50	5.00

MOBY DICK (See 4-Color No. 717, Feature Presentations No. 6, and King Classics)

MOBY DUCK (See W. D. Showcase No. 2,11, Donald Duck No. 112)
10/67 - No. 11, 10/70; No. 12, 1/74 - No. 30, 2/78
Gold Key (Disney)

	Good	Fine	Mint
1	.85	2.50	5.00
2-5	.60	1.80	3.60
6-11	.30	.90	1.80
12-30: 21,30-r		.50	1.00

MODEL FUN (With Bobby Benson)
No. 3, Winter, 1954-55 - No. 5, July, 1955
Harle Publications

	Good	Fine	Mint
3-5-Bobby Benson	1.00	3.00	6.00

MODELING WITH MILLIE (Formerly Life With Millie)
No. 21, Feb, 1963 - No. 54, June, 1967
Atlas/Marvel Comics Group (Male Publ.)

	Good	Fine	Mint
21-30		.60	1.20
31-54		.30	.60

MODERN COMICS (Military No. 1-43)
No. 44, Nov, 1945 - No. 102, Oct, 1950
Quality Comics Group

	Good	Fine	Mint
44	10.00	30.00	56.00
45-52: 49-1st app. Fear, Lady Adventuress	8.00	24.00	48.00
53-Torchy by Ward begins (9/46)	14.00	40.00	80.00
54-60: 55-J. Cole-a	9.00	25.00	50.00
61-77,79,80: 73-J. Cole-a	7.00	20.00	40.00
78-1st app. Madame Butterfly	9.00	25.00	50.00
81-101: 82,83-One pg. J. Cole-a	6.00	18.00	36.00
102-(Scarce)-J. Cole-a; some issues have Spirit by Eisner	8.00	24.00	48.00

NOTE: ***Crandall*** *Blackhawk-No. 46-51, 54, 56.* ***Gustavson*** *a-47.* ***Ward*** *Blackhawk-No. 52, 53, 55 (15 pgs. each). Torchy in No. 53-102; by* ***Ward*** *only in No. 53-89(9/49).*

MODERN LOVE
June-July, 1949 - No. 8, Aug-Sept, 1950
E. C. Comics

	Good	Fine	Mint
1	30.00	80.00	175.00
2-Craig/Feldstein-c	25.00	70.00	140.00
3	17.00	50.00	115.00
4-6 (Scarce)	30.00	80.00	170.00
7,8	17.00	50.00	115.00

NOTE: ***Feldstein*** *a-in most issues.* ***Ingels*** *a-1, 2, 4-7.* ***Wood*** *a-7. (Canadian reprints known; see Table of Contents.)*

MOD LOVE
1967 (36 pages) (50 cents)
Western Publishing Co.

	Good	Fine	Mint
1	.85	2.50	5.00

MODNIKS, THE
Aug, 1967 - No. 2, Aug, 1970
Gold Key

	Good	Fine	Mint
10206-708(No.1), 2	.50	1.50	3.00

MOD SQUAD (TV)
Jan, 1969 - No. 8, April, 1971
Dell Publishing Co.

	Good	Fine	Mint
1	.85	2.50	5.00
2-8: 8 reprints No. 2	.50	1.50	3.00

MOD WHEELS
March, 1971 - No. 19, Jan, 1976
Gold Key

	Good	Fine	Mint
1	.85	2.50	5.00
2-19: 11,15-Extra 16pgs. ads	.50	1.50	3.00

MOE & SHMOE COMICS
Spring, 1948 - No. 2, Summer, 1948
O. S. Publ. Co.

Mister Mystery #15, © Aragon

Modern Comics #102, © QUA

Modern Love #3, © WMG

Monster Hunters #1, © CC

Monte Hale Western #59, © FAW

Monty Hall #5, © TOBY

MOE & SHMOE COMICS (continued)

	Good	Fine	Mint
1	1.50	4.00	8.00
2	1.00	3.00	6.00

MOLLY MANTON'S ROMANCES (My Love No. 3)
Sept, 1949 - No. 2, Nov, 1949
Marvel Comics

	Good	Fine	Mint
1	2.00	6.00	12.00
2	1.50	4.00	8.00

MOLLY O'DAY (Super Sleuth)
February, 1945 (1st Avon comic)
Avon Periodicals

	Good	Fine	Mint
1-Molly O'Day, The Enchanted Dagger by Tuska (reprint/Yankee No. 1), Capt'n Courage, Corporal Grant app.	22.00	65.00	140.00

MONKEES, THE (TV)
March, 1967 - No. 17, Oct, 1969 (No. 1-4,6,7 have photo-c)
Dell Publishing Co.

	Good	Fine	Mint
1	1.50	4.00	8.00
2-17: 17 reprints No. 1	1.00	3.00	6.00

MONKEY & THE BEAR, THE
Sept, 1953 - No. 3, Jan, 1954
Atlas Comics (ZPC)

	Good	Fine	Mint
1-3	.80	2.40	4.80

MONKEYSHINES COMICS (Ernie No. 24? on)
Summer, 1944 - No. 23?, 1949
Ace Periodicals/Publishers Specialists/Current Books

	Good	Fine	Mint
1	1.50	4.00	8.00
2-10	1.00	3.00	6.00
11-23	.70	2.00	4.00

MONKEY SHINES OF MARSELEEN
1909 (11½x17'') (28 pages in two colors)
Cupples & Leon Co.

	Good	Fine	Mint
By Norman E. Jennett	7.00	20.00	40.00

MONKEY'S UNCLE, THE (See Movie Comics under Merlin Jones as the . . .)

MONROES, THE (TV)
April, 1967
Dell Publishing Co.

	Good	Fine	Mint
1-Photo-c	.70	2.00	4.00

MONSTER
1953
Fiction House Magazines

	Good	Fine	Mint
1-Dr. Drew by Grandenetti; reprint from Rangers Comics	7.00	20.00	40.00
2	5.50	16.00	32.00

MONSTER CRIME COMICS (Also see Crime Must Stop)
October, 1952
Hillman Periodicals

	Good	Fine	Mint
1 (Scarce)	20.00	60.00	130.00

MONSTER HOWLS (Magazine)
December, 1966 (Satire) (35 cents) (68 pgs.)
Humor-Vision

	Good	Fine	Mint
1	.80	2.40	4.80

MONSTER HUNTERS
8/75 - No. 9, 1/77; No. 10, 10/77 - No. 18, 2/79
Charlton Comics

	Good	Fine	Mint
1-Howard-a, Newton-c		.40	.80
2-Ditko-a		.40	.80
3-11		.30	.60
12,13,15-18-All reprints		.25	.50
14-Special all-Ditko issue		.50	1.00
1,2(Modern Comics reprints, 1977)		.15	.30

NOTE: ***Ditko*** *a-6, 8, 10, 13-15r, 18r; c-13-15, 18.* ***Sutton*** *a-2, 4; c-2, 4.*

MONSTER OF FRANKENSTEIN (See Frankenstein)

MONSTERS ON THE PROWL (Chamber of Darkness No. 1-8)
No. 9, 2/71 - No. 27, 11/73; No. 28, 6/74 - No. 30, 10/74
Marvel Comics Group (No. 13,14: 52 pgs.)

	Good	Fine	Mint
9-Smith inks	.40	1.20	2.40
10-13,15		.40	.80
14,17-30-All reprints		.40	.80
16-Kull app.	.50	1.50	3.00

NOTE: ***Ditko*** *a-9r, 14r, 16r.* ***Kirby*** *r-10-17, 21, 23, 25, 27, 28, 30; c-9, 25.* ***Kirby/Ditko*** *r-14, 16-20, 22, 24, 26, 29.* ***Marie/John Severin*** *a-16(Kull). 9-13, 15-contain one new story. Woodish art by* ***Reese****-11.*

MONSTERS UNLEASHED (Magazine)
July, 1973 - No. 11, April, 1975 (B&W)
Marvel Comics Group

	Good	Fine	Mint
1-Morrow-c; Reese-a	.50	1.50	3.00
2-The Frankenstein Monster begins; Brunner-r; Boris-c	.35	1.00	2.00
3-Adams-c; The Man-Thing begins (origin reprint by Morrow); Adams, G. Kane-a; Davis-r	.40	1.20	2.40
4-Intro. Satana, the Devil's daughter; Krigstein-r; Buscema-a	.40	1.20	2.40
5-Man-Thing app.	.35	1.10	2.20
6-Ploog-a; Frankenstein app.	.35	1.10	2.20
7-Williamson-a(r)	.35	1.10	2.20
8-Adams-a(r)	.30	.90	1.80
9-1st app. Wendigo	.70	2.00	4.00
10	.30	.80	1.60
11(Annual 1)(Summer,'75)-Brunner-c; Kane, Adams-a	.30	.80	1.60

MONTANA KID, THE (See Kid Montana)

MONTE HALE WESTERN (Mary Marvel No. 1-28)
No. 29, Oct, 1948 - No. 88, 1955
Fawcett Publications/Charlton No. 81? on

	Good	Fine	Mint
29(No.1)	8.00	24.00	48.00
30-40	4.00	12.00	24.00
41-50	3.50	10.00	20.00
51-86,88	2.50	7.00	14.00
87-Wolverton-r	3.50	10.00	20.00

MONTY HALL OF THE U.S. MARINES (See With the Marines . . .)
Aug, 1951 - No. 11, 1953
Toby Press

	Good	Fine	Mint
1	3.00	9.00	18.00
2-5	2.50	7.00	14.00
6-11	2.00	5.00	10.00

NOTE: *3-5 full page pin-ups (Pin-Up Pete) by* ***Jack Sparling*** *in No. 1-8,11 at least.*

A MOON, A GIRL . . . ROMANCE (Becomes Weird Fantasy No. 13 on; formerly Moon Girl No. 1-8)
No. 9, Sept-Oct, 1949 - No. 12, Mar-Apr, 1950
E. C. Comics

	Good	Fine	Mint
9-Moon Girl cameo	40.00	115.00	230.00
10,11	30.00	90.00	180.00
12-(Scarce)	40.00	120.00	240.00

NOTE: ***Feldstein, Ingels*** *art in all. Canadian reprints known; see Table of Contents.*

MOON GIRL AND THE PRINCE (No. 1) (Moon Girl No. 2-6; Moon Girl Fights Crime No. 7,8; becomes A Moon, A Girl, Romance No. 9 on)
Fall, 1947 - No. 8, Summer, 1949
E. C. Comics (Also see Happy Houlihans)

	Good	Fine	Mint
1-Origin Moon Girl	35.00	105.00	210.00

MOON GIRL AND THE PRINCE (continued)	Good	Fine	Mint
2	25.00	75.00	150.00
3,4-Moon Girl vs. a vampire No. 4	20.00	55.00	110.00
5-E.C.'s 1st horror story, "Zombie Terror"	50.00	140.00	280.00
6-8 (Scarce)	25.00	75.00	150.00

NOTE: *No. 2 & No. 3 are 52 pgs., No. 4 on, 36 pgs. Canadian reprints known; see Table of Contents.*

MOON KNIGHT (Also See Werewolf by Night No. 32)
November, 1980 - Present
Marvel Comics Group

	Good	Fine	Mint
1-Origin-resumed in No. 4	.40	1.20	2.40
2-5: 4-Intro Midnight Man		.60	1.20
6-15		.40	.80

NOTE: ***Miller*** *c-12p. No. 14-on will be distributed only through nostalgia shops.*

MOON MULLINS
1927 - 1933 (52 pgs.) (daily B&W strip reprints)
Cupples & Leon Co.

	Good	Fine	Mint
Series 1('27)-By Willard	10.00	28.00	56.00
Series 2('28), Series 3('29), Series 4('30)	7.00	20.00	40.00
Series 5('31), 6('32), 7('33)	5.00	15.00	30.00
Big Book 1('30)-B&W	12.00	35.00	70.00

MOON MULLINS (See Superbook No. 3)
1941 - 1945
Dell Publishing Co.

	Good	Fine	Mint
4-Color 14(1941)	8.00	24.00	48.00
Large Feature Comic 29(1941)	7.00	20.00	40.00
4-Color 31(1943)	6.00	18.00	36.00
4-Color 81(1945)	3.50	10.00	20.00

MOON MULLINS
Dec-Jan, 1947-48 - No. 8, 1949 (52 pgs.)
Michel Publ. (American Comics Group)

	Good	Fine	Mint
1-Willard-r, alternating Sunday & daily newspaper reprints	3.00	9.00	18.00
2-7-Willard-r	2.00	5.00	10.00
8-Willard-r, Milt Gross	2.50	7.00	14.00

MOON PILOT (See 4-Color No. 1313)

MOON-SPINNERS, THE (See Movie Comics)

MOPSY (See TV Teens & Pageant of Comics)
Feb, 1948 - No. 19, Sept, 1953
St. John Publ. Co.

	Good	Fine	Mint
1-Partial reprints; also reprints "Some Punkins" by Neher	3.50	10.00	20.00
2-10(1953)	2.00	6.00	12.00
11-19	1.75	5.00	10.00

MORE FUN COMICS (Formerly New Fun No. 1-6)
No. 7, Jan, 1936 - No. 127, Nov-Dec, 1947
National Periodical Publications

	Good	Fine	Mint
7(1/36)-Oversized, paper-c; 1 pg. Kelly-a	40.00	100.00	200.00
8(2/36)-Oversized, slick-c; 1 pg. Kelly-a	40.00	100.00	200.00
9(3-4/36)-Paper-c(Very Rare)	45.00	110.00	220.00
10,11(7/36)-Last henri Duval by Siegel & Shuster(Paper-c)	30.00	80.00	160.00
12(8/36)-Slick-c begin	25.00	70.00	140.00
V2No.1(9/36, No.13)	30.00	80.00	160.00
2(10/36, No.14)-Dr. Occult in costume (Superman prototype) begins, ends No. 17	30.00	80.00	160.00
V2No.3(11/36, No.15), 16(V2No.4), 17(V2No.5)-Cover numbering begins No. 16	20.00	60.00	120.00
18-20(V2No.8, 5/37)	15.00	44.00	76.00
21(V2No.9)-24(V2No.12, 9/37)	11.00	32.00	64.00
25(V3No.1, 10/37)-27(V3No.3, 12/37)	11.00	32.00	64.00
28-30: 30-1st non-funny cover	11.00	32.00	64.00
31-35: 32-Last Dr. Occult	10.00	28.00	56.00
36-40: 36-The Masked Ranger begins, ends No. 41	8.00	24.00	48.00
41-50	7.00	20.00	40.00
51-1st app. The Spectre (in costume) in one panel ad at end of Buccaneer story	20.00	60.00	120.00
52-Origin The Spectre (out of costume), Part 1 by Bernard Baily; last Wing Brady (Rare)	700.00	2100.00	4500.00
53-Origin The Spectre (out of costume), Part 2; Capt. Desmo begins (Scarce)	500.00	1500.00	3000.00
(Prices vary widely on above two books)			
54-The Spectre in costume; last King Carter	175.00	475.00	1000.00
55-(Scarce)-Dr. Fate begins (Intro & 1st app.); last Bulldog Martin	130.00	380.00	800.00
56-60: 56-Congo Bill begins	75.00	220.00	460.00
61-66: 63-Last St. Bob Neal. 64-Lance Larkin begins	60.00	160.00	340.00
67-(Scarce)-Origin Dr. Fate; last Congo Bill & Biff Bronson	80.00	230.00	470.00
68-70: 68-Clip Carson begins. 70-Last Lance Larkin	50.00	135.00	275.00
71-(Scarce)-Origin & 1st app. Johnny Quick	65.00	190.00	400.00
72-Dr. Fate's new helmet; last Sgt. Carey, Sgt. O'Malley & Captain Desmo	40.00	115.00	235.00
73-(Rare)-Origin & 1st app. Aquaman; intro. Green Arrow & Speedy	110.00	320.00	675.00
74-80: 76-Last Clip Carson; Johnny Quick by Meskin begins, ends No. 97	40.00	115.00	235.00
81-88: 87-Last Radio Squad	30.00	85.00	175.00
89-Origin Green Arrow & Speedy Team-up	32.00	95.00	200.00
90-99: 93-Dover & Clover begin. 97-Kubert-a. 98-Last Dr. Fate	17.00	50.00	100.00
100	20.00	60.00	120.00
101-Origin & 1st app. Superboy; last Spectre issue	180.00	480.00	1000.00
102-2nd Superboy	35.00	100.00	200.00
103-3rd Superboy	25.00	75.00	150.00
104-107: 107-Last Johnny Quick & Superboy	20.00	60.00	120.00
108-120: 108-Genius Jones begins	3.50	10.00	20.00
121-124,126: 121-123-Kellyish-c by Post	3.00	8.00	16.00
125-Superman on cover	15.00	45.00	90.00
127-(Scarce)-Post c/a	10.00	28.00	56.00

NOTE: *Cover features: The Spectre-No. 52-55, 57-60, 62-67. Dr. Fate-No. 55, 56, 61, 68-76. The Green Arrow & Speedy-No. 77-85, 88-97, 99, 101; w/Dover & Clover-No. 98, 103. Johnny Quick-No. 86, 87, 100. Superboy-No. 101-107; w/Dover & Clover-No. 102-107. Genius Jones-No. 108-127.* ***Moldoff*** *c-51.*

MORE SEYMOUR (See Seymour My Son)
October, 1963
Archie Publications

	Good	Fine	Mint
1	1.50	4.00	8.00

MORE TRASH FROM MAD (Annual)
1958 - No. 12, 1969
E. C. Comics

	Good	Fine	Mint
nn(1958)-8 pgs. color Mad reprint from No. 20	5.50	16.00	32.00
2(1959)-Market Product Labels	4.00	12.00	24.00
3(1960)-Text book covers	3.50	10.00	20.00
4(1961)-Sing Along with Mad booklet	3.00	8.00	16.00
5(1962)-Window Stickers; reprint from Mad No. 39	2.00	6.00	12.00
6(1963)-TV Guise booklet	3.50	8.00	16.00
7(1964)-Alfred E. Neuman commemorative stamps	1.50	4.00	8.00
8(1965)-Life size poster-A. E. Neuman	1.50	4.00	8.00

Moon Mullins #1, © N.Y. News Synd.

Mopsy #11, © STJ

More Fun Comics #72, © DC

Morlock 2001 #3, © ATLAS

Motion Picture Comics #111, © FAW

Motion Picture Funnies Weekly #1, © MCG

MORE TRASH FROM MAD (continued) — Good / Fine / Mint
9,10(1966-67)-Mischief Sticker 1.50 4.00 8.00
11(1968)-Campaign poster & bumper sticker 1.50 4.00 8.00
12(1969)-Pocket medals 1.50 4.00 8.00
NOTE: ***Kelly Freas*** *c-1, 2, 4.* ***Mingo*** *c-3, 5-9, 12.*

MORGAN THE PIRATE (See 4-Color No. 1227)

MORLOCK 2001 (. . . & the Midnight Men No. 3)
Feb, 1975 - No. 3, July, 1975
Atlas/Seaboard Publ.

1-Origin & 1st app. .50 1.00
2 .30 .60
3-Ditko/Wrightson-a; origin The Midnight Man & The Midnight Men .60 1.20

MORTIE (Mazie's Friend)
Dec, 1952 - No. 4, June, 1953?
Magazine Publishers/Harvey Publications

1 .80 2.40 4.80
2,4 (No. 5,6 exist?) .50 1.50 3.00

MORTY MEEKLE (See 4-Color No. 793)

MOSES & THE TEN COMMANDMENTS
1957 (100 pages) (25 cents & 30 cents)
Dell Publishing Co.

1-Not based on movie; Dell's adaptation; Sekowsky-a 2.50 7.00 14.00

MOTHER GOOSE (See Christmas With Mother Goose & 4-Color No. 41,59,68,862)

MOTHER OF US ALL
1950? (32 pgs.)
Catechetical Guild Giveaway

2.00 6.00 12.00

MOTION PICTURE COMICS (See Fawcett Movie Comics)
1950 - No. 114, Jan, 1953
Fawcett Publications

101-''Vanishing Westerner''-Monte Hale (1950) 10.00 30.00 60.00
102-''Code of the Silver Sage''-Rocky Lane (1/51) 8.00 24.00 48.00
103-''Covered Wagon Raid''-Rocky Lane (3/51) 8.00 24.00 48.00
104-''Vigilante Hideout''-Rocky Lane (5/51) 8.00 24.00 48.00
105-''Red Badge of Courage''-Audie Murphy; Bob Powell-a (7/51) 14.00 40.00 80.00
106-''The Texas Rangers''-George Montgomery (9/51) 12.00 35.00 70.00
107-''Frisco Tornado''-Rocky Lane (11/51) 8.00 24.00 48.00
108-''Mask of the Avenger''-John Derek 8.00 24.00 48.00
109-''Rough Rider of Durango''-Rocky Lane 8.00 24.00 48.00
110-''When Worlds Collide''-George Evans-a (1951); Williamson & Evans drew themselves in story; (Also see Famous Funnies No. 72-88) 30.00 90.00 200.00
111-''The Vanishing Outpost''-Lash LaRue 10.00 28.00 56.00
112-''Brave Warrior''-Jon Hall & Jay Silverheels 7.00 20.00 40.00
113-''Walk East on Beacon''-George Murphy; Shaffenberger-a 6.00 18.00 36.00
114-''Cripple Creek''-George Montgomery (1/53) 7.00 20.00 40.00

MOTION PICTURE FUNNIES WEEKLY (Amazing Man No. 5 on?)
1939 (36 pgs.)(Giveaway)(Black & White)
No month given; last panel in Sub-Mariner story dated 4/39
(Also see Colossus, Green Giant & Invaders No. 20)
First Funnies, Inc.

1-Origin & 1st printed app. Sub-Mariner by Bill Everett (8 pgs.); Fred Schwab-c; reprinted in Marvel Mystery No. 1 with color added over the craft tint which was used to shade the black & white version; Spy Ring, American Ace (reprinted in Marvel Mystery No. 3) app. (Rare)-only seven (7) known copies
$2500.00 — $6000.00

NOTE: The only seven known copies (with an eighth suspected) were discovered in 1974 in the estate of the deceased publisher. Covers only to issues No. 2-4 were also found which evidently were printed in advance along with No. 1. No. 1 was to be distributed only through motion picture movie houses. However, it is believed that only advanced copies were sent out and the motion picture houses not going for the idea. Possible distribution at local theaters in Boston suspected. The last panel of Sub-Mariner contains a rectangular box with ''Continued Next Week'' printed in it. When reprinted in Marvel Mystery, the box was left in with lettering omitted.

MOUNTAIN MEN (See Ben Bowie)

MOUSE MUSKETEERS (See M.G.M.'s...)

MOUSE ON THE MOON, THE (See Movie Classics)

MOVIE CLASSICS
Jan, 1953 - Dec, 1969
Dell Publishing Co.

(Before 1962, most movie adaptations were part of the 4-Color Series)

	Good	Fine	Mint
Around the World Under the Sea 12-030-612 (12/66)	1.00	3.00	6.00
Bambi 3(4/56)-Disney; r-/4-Color 186	1.00	3.00	6.00
Battle of the Bulge 12-056-606 (6/66)	1.00	3.00	6.00
Beach Blanket Bingo 12-058-509	3.00	8.00	16.00
Bon Voyage 01-068-212 (12/62)-Disney	.85	2.50	5.00
Castilian, The 12-110-401	.85	2.50	5.00
Cat, The 12-109-612 (12/66)	.85	2.50	5.00
Cheyenne Autumn 12-112-506 (4-6/65)	2.00	5.00	10.00
Circus World, Samuel Bronston's 12-115-411; John Wayne app.	1.00	3.00	6.00
Countdown 12-150-710 (10/67); James Caan photo-c	.85	2.50	5.00
Creature, The 1 (12-142-302) (12-2/62-63)	1.50	4.00	8.00
Creature, The 12-142-410 (10/64)	1.00	3.00	6.00
David Ladd's Life Story 12173-212 (10-12/62)	2.00	5.00	10.00
Die, Monster, Die 12-175-603 (3/66)	1.50	4.00	8.00
Dirty Dozen 12-180-710 (10/67)	1.20	3.50	7.00
Dr. Who & the Daleks 12-190-612 (12/66)	2.00	5.00	10.00
Dracula 12-231-212 (10-12/62)	1.50	4.00	8.00
El Dorado 12-240-710 (10/67)-John Wayne	3.00	8.00	16.00
Ensign Pulver 12-257-410 (8-10/64)	1.20	3.50	7.00
Frankenstein 12-283-305 (3-5/63)	1.50	4.00	8.00
Great Race, The 12-299-603 (3/66)	1.00	3.00	6.00
Hallelujah Trail, The 12-307-602 (2/66) (Shows 1/66 inside)	2.00	6.00	12.00
Hatari 12-340-301 (1/63)-John Wayne	2.00	5.00	10.00
Horizontal Lieutenant, The 01-348-210 (10/62)	1.20	3.50	7.00
Incredible Mr. Limpet, The 12-370-408	1.20	3.50	7.00
Jack the Giant Killer 12-374-301 (1/63)	3.00	8.00	16.00
Jason & the Argonauts 12-376-310 (8-10/63)	3.00	8.00	16.00
Lady and the Tramp 1 (6/55-Giant, 100 pgs.)-Disney	.85	2.50	5.00
Lancelot & Guinevere 12-416-310 (10/63)	1.20	3.50	7.00
Lawrence 12-426-308 (8/63)-Story of Lawrence of Arabia; movie ad on back-c; not exactly like movie	1.50	4.00	8.00
Lion of Sparta 12-439-301 (1/63)	1.00	3.00	6.00
Longest Day, The ('62)	1.50	4.00	8.00
Mad Monster Party 12-460-801 (9/67)	2.00	6.00	12.00
Magic Sword, The 01-496-209 (9/62)	2.00	6.00	12.00
Masque of the Red Death 12-490-410 (8-10/64)	2.00	5.00	10.00
Maya 12-495-612 (12/66)	1.50	4.00	8.00
McHale's Navy 12-500-412 (10-12/64)	1.20	3.50	7.00
Merrill's Marauders 12-510-301 (1/63)	1.00	3.00	6.00

MOVIE CLASSICS (continued) — Good / Fine / Mint

Mouse on the Moon, The 12-530-312 (10/12/63) 1.20 3.50 7.00
Mummy, The 12-537-211 (9-11/62) 2 different back-c issues 1.50 4.00 8.00
Music Man, The 12-538-301 (1/63) 1.20 3.50 7.00
Naked Prey, The 12-545-612 (12/66) 2.00 5.00 10.00
Night of the Grizzly, The 12-558-612 (12/66) 1.50 4.00 8.00
None But the Brave 12-565-506 (4-6/65) .85 2.50 5.00
Operation Bikini 12-597-310 (10/63) 1.00 3.00 6.00
Operation Crossbow 12-590-512 (10-12/65) .85 2.50 5.00
Peter Pan Treasure Chest 1 (1/53, 212pgs.)-Disney; contains movie adaptation plus other stories 14.00 40.00 80.00
Prince & the Pauper, The 01-654-207 (5-7/62)-Disney 1.50 4.00 8.00
Raven, The 12-680-309 (9/63) 1.50 4.00 8.00
Ring of Bright Water 01-701-910 (10/69) (inside shows No. 12-701-909) .85 2.50 5.00
Runaway, The 12-707-412 (10-12/64) .85 2.50 5.00
Santa Claus Conquers the Martians 12-725-603 (3/66); another version given away with a Golden Record, SLP 170, nn, no price ('66) 2.00 6.00 12.00
Six Black Horses 12-750-301 (1/63) 1.50 4.00 8.00
Ski Party 12-743-511 (9-11/65) 2.00 6.00 12.00
Sleeping Beauty 1 (1959-Giant, 100 pgs.)-Disney 4.00 12.00 24.00
Smoky 12-746-702 (2/67) .85 2.50 5.00
Sons of Katie Elder 12-748-511 (9-11/65); John Wayne app. 2.00 6.00 12.00
Sword of Lancelot (1963) 2.50 7.00 14.00
Tales of Terror 12-793-302 (2/63) 1.00 3.00 6.00
Taras Bulba (1962) 5.50 16.00 32.00
Three Stooges Meet Hercules 01828-208 (8/62) 2.50 7.00 14.00
Tomb of Ligeia 12-830-506 (4-6/65) 1.20 3.50 7.00
Treasure Island 01-845-211 (7-9/62)-Disney; reprints 4-Color 624 .85 2.50 5.00
Twice Told Tales (Nathaniel Hawthorne) 12-840-401 (11-1/63-64) 1.00 3.00 6.00
Two on a Guillotine 12-850-506 (4-6/65) 1.00 3.00 6.00
Universal Presents-Dracula-The Mummy & other stories 02-530-311 (9-11/63-Giant, 84 pgs.)-reprints Dracula No. 12-231-212, The Mummy No. 12-537-211, & part of Ghost Stories No. 1 1.75 5.00 10.00
Valley of Gwangi 01-880-912 (12/69) 2.00 6.00 12.00
War Gods of the Deep 12-900-509 (7-9/65) .85 2.50 5.00
War Wagon, The 12-533-709 (9/67); John Wayne app. 1.50 4.00 8.00
Who's Minding the Mint? 12-924-708 (8/67) 1.00 3.00 6.00
Wolfman, The 12-922-308 (6-8/63) 1.20 3.50 7.00
Wolfman, The 1 (12-922-410)(8-10/64)-2nd printing; reprints No. 12-922-308 1.00 3.00 6.00
Zulu 12-950-410 (8-10/64) 2.00 5.00 10.00

MOVIE COMICS (See Fawcett Movie Comics)

MOVIE COMICS
April, 1939 - No. 6, Sept, 1939
National Periodical Publications/Picture Comics

1-''Gunga Din,'' ''Son of Frankenstein,'' ''The Great Man Votes,'' ''Fisherman's Wharf,'' & ''Scouts to the Rescue'' part 1; Wheelan ''Minute Movies'' begin 70.00 200.00 400.00
2-''Stagecoach,'' ''The Saint Strikes Back,'' ''King of the Turf,'' ''Scouts to the Rescue'' part 2, ''Arizona Legion'' 50.00 140.00 280.00
3-''East Side of Heaven,'' ''Mystery in the White Room,'' ''Four Feathers,'' ''Mexican Rose'' with Gene Autry, ''Spirit of Culver,'' ''Many Secrets,'' ''The Mikado'' 45.00 130.00 260.00
4-''Captain Fury,'' Gene Autry in ''Blue Montana Skies,'' ''Streets of N. Y.'' with Jackie Cooper, ''Oregon Trail'' part 1 with Johnny Mack Brown, ''Big Town Czar'' with Barton MacLane, & ''Star Reporter'' with Warren Hull 40.00 120.00 240.00
5-''Man in the Iron Mask,'' ''Five Came Back,'' Wolf Call,'' ''The Girl & the Gambler,'' ''The House of Fear,'' ''The Family Next Door,'' ''Oregon Trail'' part 2 40.00 120.00 240.00
6-''The Phantom Creeps,'' ''Chumps at Oxford,'' & ''The Oregon Trail'' part 3 50.00 140.00 280.00

NOTE: *Above books contain many original movie stills with dialogue from movie scripts.*

MOVIE COMICS
Dec, 1946 - 1947
Fiction House Magazines

1-Big Town & Johnny Danger begin; Celardo-a 11.00 32.00 64.00
2-''White Tie & Tails'' with William Bendix; Mitzi of the Movies begins by Matt Baker, ends No. 4 10.00 30.00 60.00
3-Andy Hardy 10.00 30.00 60.00
4-Mitzi In Hollywood by Matt Baker 14.00 40.00 80.00

MOVIE COMICS
Oct, 1962 - March, 1972
Gold Key/Whitman

Alice in Wonderland 10144-503 (3/65)-Disney; partial reprint of 4-Color 331 1.00 3.00 6.00
Aristocats, The 1 (30045-103)(3/71)-Disney; with pull-out poster (25 cents) 1.00 3.00 6.00
Bambi 1 (10087-309)(9/63)-Disney; reprints 4-Color 186 1.00 3.00 6.00
Bambi 2 (10087-607)(7/66)-Disney; reprints 4-Color 186 1.00 3.00 6.00
Beneath the Planet of the Apes 30044-012 (12/70)-with pull-out poster 1.50 4.50 9.00
Big Red 10026-211 (11/62)-Disney .70 2.00 4.00
Big Red 10026-503 (3/65)-Disney; reprints 10026-211 .70 2.00 4.00
Blackbeard's Ghost 10222-806 (6/68)-Disney 1.20 3.50 7.00
Buck Rogers Giant Movie Edition 11296 (Whitman), 02489 (Marvel)-2 formats; 1979; tabloid size; $1.50; adaptation of movie; Bolle, McWilliams-a .30 .80 1.60
Bullwhip Griffin 10181-706 (3/67)-Disney 1.20 3.50 7.00
Captain Sindbad 10077-309 (9/63)-Manning-a 2.00 6.00 12.00
Chitty Chitty Bang Bang 1 (30038-902)(2/69)-with pull-out poster 1.50 4.00 8.00
Cinderella 10152-508 (8/65)-Disney; reprints 4-Color 786 1.00 3.00 6.00
Darby O'Gill & the Little People 10251-001(1/70)-Disney; reprints 4-Color 1024 (Toth) 2.00 5.00 10.00
Dumbo 1 (10090-310)(10/63)-Disney; reprints 4-Color 668 .85 2.50 5.00
Emil & the Detectives 10120-502 (2/65)-Disney 1.75 5.00 10.00
Escapade in Florence 1 (10043-301)(1/63)-Disney; starring Annette 2.00 6.00 12.00
Fall of the Roman Empire 10118-407 (7/64); Sophia Loren photo-c 1.00 3.00 6.00
Fantastic Voyage 10178-702 (2/67)-Wood/Adkins-a 1.50 4.50 9.00
55 Days at Peking 10081-309 (9/63) 1.50 4.00 8.00
Fighting Prince of Donegal, The 10193-701 (1/67)-Disney 1.00 3.00 6.00
First Men in the Moon 10132-503 (3/65) 1.50 4.00 8.00
Gay Purr-ee 30017-301(1/63, 84pgs.) 1.00 3.00 6.00
Gnome Mobile, The 10207-710 (10/67)-Disney 1.00 3.00 6.00
Goodbye, Mr. Chips 10246-006 (6/70) 1.20 3.50 7.00
Happiest Millionaire, The 10221-804 (4/68)-Disney .70 2.00 4.00

War Gods Of The Deep, © DELL

Beneath The Planet O.T. Apes, © GK

Goodbye Mr. Chips, © GK

The Love Bug, © WDP

Swiss Family Robinson, © WDP

Ms. Marvel #5, © MCG

MOVIE COMICS (continued)	**Good**	**Fine**	**Mint**
Hey There, It's Yogi Bear 10122-409 (9/64)-Hanna-Barbera	.70	2.00	4.00
Horse Without a Head, The 10109-401 (1/64)-Disney	1.00	3.00	6.00
How the West Was Won 10074-307 (7/63)	2.00	5.00	10.00
In Search of the Castaways 10048-303 (3/63)-Disney; Haley Mills	1.50	4.00	8.00
Jungle Book, The 1 (6022-801)(1/68-Whitman)-Disney; large size (10x13½''); 59 cents	1.00	3.00	6.00
Jungle Book, The 1 (30033-803)(3/68)-Disney; same contents as Whitman No. 1	.70	2.00	4.00
Kidnapped 10080-306 (6/63)-Disney; reprints 4-Color 1101	.70	2.00	4.00
King Kong 30036-809(9/68-68 pgs.)-painted-c	2.00	6.00	12.00
King Kong nn-Whitman Treasury($1.00,68pgs.,1968), same cover as Gold Key issue	.50	1.50	3.00
Lady and the Tramp 10042-301 (1/63)-Disney; r-4-Color 629	.70	2.00	4.00
Lady and the Tramp 1 (1967-Giant; 25 cents)-Disney; r-part of Dell No. 1	.70	2.00	4.00
Lady and the Tramp 2 (10042-203)(3/72)-Disney; r-4-Color 629	.70	2.00	4.00
Legend of Lobo, The 1 (10059-303)(3/63)-Disney	.70	2.00	4.00
Lt. Robin Crusoe, U.S.N. 10191-610 (10/66)-Disney	.70	2.00	4.00
Lion, The 10035-301 (1/63)	.70	2.00	4.00
Lord Jim 10156-509 (9/65)	.85	2.50	5.00
Love Bug, The 10237-906 (6/69)-Disney	1.00	3.00	6.00
Mary Poppins 10136-501 (1/65)-Disney	1.00	3.00	6.00
Mary Poppins 30023-501 (1/65-68 pgs.)-Disney	2.00	6.00	12.00
McLintock 10110-403 (3/64); John Wayne app.	1.50	4.00	8.00
Merlin Jones as the Monkey's Uncle 10115-510 (10/65)-Disney	1.00	3.00	6.00
Miracle of the White Stallions, The 10065-306 (6/63)-Disney	.70	2.00	4.00
Misadventures of Merlin Jones, The 10115-405 (5/64)-Disney	.70	2.00	4.00
Moon-Spinners, The 10124-410 (10/64)-Disney; Haley Mills	1.00	3.00	6.00
Mutiny on the Bounty 1 (10040-302)(2/63)	1.00	3.00	6.00
Nikki, Wild Dog of the North 10141-412 (12/64)-Disney; reprints 4-Color 1226	.70	2.00	4.00
Old Yeller 10168-601 (1/66)-Disney; reprints 4-Color 869	.60	1.80	3.60
One Hundred & One Dalmations 1 (10247-002) (2/70)-Disney; reprints 4-Color 1183	.85	2.50	5.00
Peter Pan 1 (10086-309)(9/63)-Disney; reprints 4-Color 442	.70	2.00	4.00
Peter Pan 2 (10086-909)(9/69)-Disney; reprints 4-Color 442	.70	2.00	4.00
P.T. 109 10123-409 (9/64)-John F. Kennedy	1.50	4.00	8.00
Rio Conchos 10143-503(3/65)	1.00	3.00	6.00
Robin Hood 10163-506 (6/65)-Disney; reprints 4-Color 413	.60	1.80	3.60
Shaggy Dog & the Absent-Minded Professor 30032-708 (8/67-Giant, 68 pgs.)-Disney; reprints 4-Color 985,1199	1.20	3.50	7.00
Sleeping Beauty 1 (30042-009)(9/70)-Disney; reprints 4-Color 973; with pull-out poster	.70	2.00	4.00
Snow White & the Seven Dwarfs 1 (10091-310)(10/63)-Disney; reprints 4-Color 382	.85	2.50	5.00
Snow White & the Seven Dwarfs 10091-709 (9/67)-Disney; reprints 4-Color 382	.70	2.00	4.00
Son of Flubber 1 (10057-304)(4/63)-Disney; sequel to ''The Absent-Minded Professor''	1.00	3.00	6.00
Summer Magic 10076-309 (9/63)-Disney; Haley Mills; Manning-a	2.50	7.00	14.00
Swiss Family Robinson 10236-904 (4/69)-Disney; reprints 4-Color 1156	.70	2.00	4.00
Sword in the Stone, The 30019-402 (2/64-Giant, 84 pgs.)-Disney	1.20	3.50	7.00
That Darn Cat 10171-602 (2/66)-Disney	.85	2.50	5.00
Those Magnificent Men in Their Flying Machines 10162-510 (10/65)	.85	2.50	5.00
Three Stooges in Orbit 30016-211 (11/62-Giant, 32 pgs.)-All photos from movie	2.50	7.00	14.00
Tiger Walks, A 10117-406 (6/64)-Disney; Torres-a	1.20	3.50	7.00
Toby Tyler 10142-502 (2/65)-Disney; reprints 4-Color 1092	.70	2.00	4.00
Treasure Island 1 (10200-703)(3/67)-Disney; reprints 4-Color 624	.70	2.00	4.00
20,000 Leagues Under the Sea 1 (10095-312)(12/63)-Disney; reprints 4-Color 614	.70	2.00	4.00
Wonderful Adventures of Pinocchio, The 1 (10089-310)(10/63)-Disney; reprints 4-Color 545	.70	2.00	4.00
Wonderful Adventures of Pinocchio, The 10089-109 (9/71)-Disney; reprints 4-Color 545	.70	2.00	4.00
Wonderful World of the Brothers Grimm 1 (10008-210)(10/62)	2.00	5.00	10.00
X, the Man with the X-Ray Eyes 10083-309 (9/63)	2.00	5.00	10.00
Yellow Submarine 35000-902 (2/69-Giant, 68 pgs.)-with pull-out poster; The Beatles cartoon movie	7.00	20.00	30.00

MOVIE LOVE (See Personal Love)
Feb, 1950 - No. 22, Aug, 1953
Famous Funnies

	Good	Fine	Mint
1	3.00	8.00	16.00
2-7,9	2.00	5.00	10.00
8-Williamson/Frazetta-a, 6 pgs.	25.00	75.00	150.00
10-Frazetta-a, 6 pgs. (Rare)	30.00	90.00	180.00
11-16	2.00	5.00	10.00
17-One pg. Frazetta ad	3.00	8.00	16.00
18-22	1.50	4.50	9.00

NOTE: *Each issue has a full-length movie adaptation with photo covers.*

MOVIE THRILLERS
1949
Magazine Enterprises

	Good	Fine	Mint
1-''Rope of Sand'' with Burt Lancaster	10.00	30.00	60.00

MOVIE TOWN ANIMAL ANTICS (Formerly Animal Antics; Raccoon Kids No. 52 on)
No. 24, Jan-Feb, 1950 - No. 51, July-Aug, 1954
National Periodical Publications

	Good	Fine	Mint
24-51-Raccoon Kids continue	1.20	3.50	7.00

NOTE: ***Sheldon Mayer*** *a-37,40,44,47.*

MOVIE TUNES (Frankie No. 4 on) (Also see Animated . . .)
Spring, 1946 - No. 3, Fall, 1946
Marvel Comics (MgPC)

	Good	Fine	Mint
1-Super Rabbit	2.00	6.00	12.00
2,3-Super Rabbit	1.50	4.00	8.00

MOWGLI JUNGLE BOOK (See 4-Color No. 487,582,620)

MR. (See Mister)

MS. MARVEL
Jan, 1977 - No. 23, Apr, 1979
Marvel Comics Group

	Good	Fine	Mint
1-Buscema-a	.30	.80	1.60
2-Origin		.50	1.00
3-5: 5-Vision app.		.40	.80
6-23: 20-New costume		.40	.80

NOTE: ***Buscema*** *a-1-3; c-2, 4, 7, 8, 15.* ***Gil Kane*** *c-8.* ***Starlin*** *c-12.*

MUGGSY MOUSE
1951 - 1953; 1963
Magazine Enterprises

	Good	Fine	Mint
1(A-1 33), 2(A-1 36), 3(A-1 39), 4(A-1 95), 5(A-1 99)	.70	2.00	4.00
Super Reprint No. 14(1963)	.30	.80	1.60
I.W. Reprint No. 1,2 (no date)	.30	.80	1.60

MUGGY-DOO, BOY CAT
July, 1953 - No. 4, Jan, 1954
Standard Publications

1-Art by Irving Spector	1.50	4.00	8.00
2-4	.85	2.50	5.00
Super Reprint No. 12('63), 16('64)		.50	1.00

MUMMY, THE (See Movie Classics)

MUNSTERS, THE (TV)
Jan, 1965 - No. 16, Jan, 1968
Gold Key

1 (10134-501)	1.00	3.00	6.00
2-5	.70	2.00	4.00
6-16	.50	1.50	3.00

MURDER, INCORPORATED (My Private Life No. 16 on)
1/48 - No. 15, 12/49; (2 No.9's); 6/50 - No. 3, 8/51
Fox Features Syndicate

1 (1st Series)	8.00	24.00	48.00
2-Transvestite, electrocution story	4.50	15.00	30.00
3-7,9(4/49),10(5/49),11-13,15	4.00	12.00	24.00
8-Used in **SOTI**, pg. 160	7.00	20.00	40.00
9(3/49)-Possible use in **SOTI**, pg. 145; r-Blue Beetle No. 56('48)	6.00	18.00	36.00
14-Narcotics racket mentioned	4.00	12.00	24.00
5(6/50)(2nd Series)-Formerly My Desire	3.00	9.00	18.00
2(8/50)	1.50	4.00	8.00
3(8/51)-Used in **POP**, pg. 81; drug story; Rico-a	4.00	12.00	24.00

MURDEROUS GANGSTERS
July, 1951 - No. 4, June, 1952
Avon Periodicals/Realistic No. 3 on

1-Pretty Boy Floyd, Leggs Diamond; 1 pg. Wood	10.00	30.00	60.00
2-Baby Face Nelson; 1 pg. Wood; cocaine drug mention story	7.00	20.00	40.00
3	5.50	16.00	32.00
4-''Murder by Needle'' drug story	7.00	20.00	40.00

MURDER TALES (Magazine)
V1No.10, Nov, 1970 - V1No.11, Jan, 1971 (52 pages)
World Famous Publications

V1No.10-One pg. Frazetta ad	.60	1.80	3.60
11-Guardineer-r; bondage-c	.30	.90	1.80

MUSHMOUSE AND PUNKIN PUSS (TV)
September, 1965 (Hanna-Barbera)
Gold Key

1 (10153-509)	.85	2.50	5.00

MUSIC MAN, THE (See Movie Classics)

MUTINY (Stormy Tales of Seven Seas)
Oct, 1954 - No. 3, Feb, 1955
Aragon Magazines

1	3.00	8.00	16.00
2,3: 2-Capt. Mutiny. 3-Bondage-c	1.50	4.00	8.00

MUTINY ON THE BOUNTY (See Movie Comics)

MUTT & JEFF (. . . Cartoon, The) (See Xmas Comics)
1910 - 1914 (5¾x15½'') (Hardcover-B&W)
Ball Publications

	Good	Fine	Mint
1(1910)	15.00	45.00	90.00
2(1911), 3(1912)	12.00	35.00	70.00
4(1913) (Scarce)	14.00	40.00	80.00
5(1914) (Rare)	15.00	45.00	90.00

NOTE: *Cover variations exist showing Mutt & Jeff reading various newspapers; i.e., The Oregon Journal, The American, and The Detroit News. Reprinting of each issue began soon after publication. No. 5 may not have been reprinted. Values listed include the reprints.*

MUTT & JEFF
1916 - 1933? (B&W dailies) (9½x9½''; stiff cover; 52 pgs.)
Cupples & Leon Co.

6-22-By Bud Fisher	7.00	20.00	40.00

(NOTE: *Later issues are somewhat rarer.)*

nn(1920)-(Advs. of. . .) 16x11''; 20 pgs.; reprints 1919 Sunday strips	15.00	45.00	90.00
Big Book nn(1926, 144pgs., hardcovers)	12.00	35.00	70.00
w/dust jacket. . . .	20.00	60.00	120.00
Big Book 1(1928)-Thick book (hardcovers)	12.00	35.00	70.00
w/dust jacket. . . .	20.00	60.00	120.00
Big Book 2(1929)-Thick book (hardcovers)	12.00	35.00	70.00
w/dust jacket. . . .	20.00	60.00	120.00

NOTE: *The Big Books contain three previous issues rebound.*

MUTT & JEFF
1921 (9x15'')
Embee Publ. Co.

Sunday strips in color (Rare)	25.00	70.00	140.00

MUTT AND JEFF
Summer, 1939 (no date) - No. 148, Nov, 1965
All American/National 1-103 (6/58)/Dell 104-115 (10-12/59)/
Harvey 116 (2/60)-148

1(nn)-Lost Wheels	30.00	80.00	160.00
2(nn)-Charging Bull (Summer 1940, no date)	14.00	40.00	80.00
3(nn)-Bucking Broncos (Summer 1941, no date)	10.00	30.00	60.00
4(Winter,'41), 5(Summer,'42)	8.00	23.00	46.00
6-10	5.00	14.00	28.00
11-20	3.00	8.00	16.00
21-30	1.50	4.00	8.00
31-75-Last Fisher issue	.85	2.50	5.00
76-100	.70	2.00	4.00
101-148: 117,118,120-131-Richie Rich app.	.70	2.00	4.00
. . .Jokes 1-3(8/60-61, Harvey)-84 pgs.; Richie Rich in all	.85	2.50	5.00
. . . New Jokes 1-4(10/63-1965, Harvey)-68 pgs.; Richie Rich in all; Stumbo in No. 1	.70	2.00	4.00

NOTE: *Issues 1-74 by* ***Bud Fisher****. 86 on by* ***Al Smith****. Issues from 1963 on have* ***Fisher*** *reprints. Clarification: early issues signed by Fisher are mostly drawn by Smith.*

MY BROTHERS' KEEPER
1973 (36 pages) (35-49 cents)
Spire Christian Comics (Fleming H. Revell Co.)

nn		.50	1.00

MY CONFESSIONS (My Confession No. 7; formerly Western True Crime; A Spectacular Features Magazine No. 11 on)
No. 7, Aug, 1949 - No. 10, Jan-Feb, 1950
Fox Features Syndicate

7-Wood-a, 10 pgs.	6.00	18.00	36.00
8-Wood-a, 18 pgs.	6.00	18.00	36.00
9,10	2.50	7.00	14.00

MY DATE COMICS
July, 1947 - V1No.4, Jan, 1948 (1st Romance comic)
Hillman Periodicals

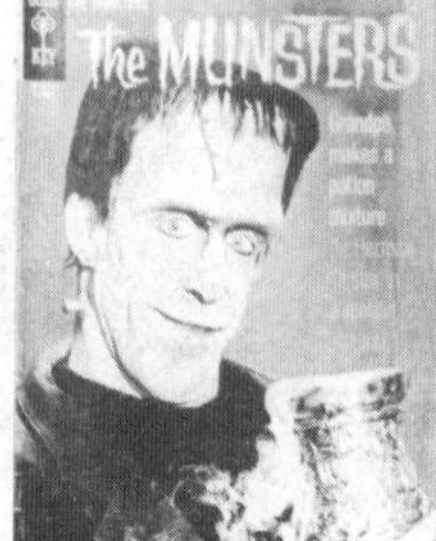

The Munsters #4, © GK

Murder Incorporated #2, © FOX

Mutt & Jeff #6, © Ball Synd.

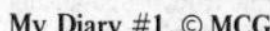
My Diary #1, © MCG

My Favorite Martian #9, © GK

My Great Love #1, © FOX

MY DATE COMICS (continued)

	Good	Fine	Mint
1-S&K-c/a	6.00	18.00	36.00
2-4-S&K, Dan Barry-a	5.00	14.00	28.00

MY DESIRE (Formerly Jo-Jo) (Murder, Inc. No. 5 on)
No. 30, Aug, 1949 - No. 4, April, 1950
Fox Features Syndicate

	Good	Fine	Mint
30,31(No.1,2)	3.00	8.00	16.00
32(12/49)-Wood-a	6.00	18.00	36.00
3,4	2.50	7.00	14.00
31 (Canadian edition)	1.50	4.00	8.00

MY DIARY
Dec, 1949 - No. 2, Mar, 1950
Marvel Comics (A Lovers Mag.)

	Good	Fine	Mint
1,2	2.50	7.00	14.00

MY DOG TIGE (Buster Brown's Dog)
1957 (Giveaway)
Buster Brown Shoes

	Good	Fine	Mint
	2.00	5.00	10.00

MY EXPERIENCE (Formerly All Top; Judy Canova No. 23 on)
No. 19, Sept, 1949 - No. 22, Mar, 1950
Fox Features Syndicate

	Good	Fine	Mint
19-Wood-a	6.00	18.00	36.00
20	2.50	7.00	14.00
21-Wood-a(2)	9.00	25.00	50.00
22-Wood-a, 9 pgs.	6.00	18.00	36.00

MY FAVORITE MARTIAN (TV)
Jan, 1964 - No. 9, Oct, 1966 (No. 1,3-9 have photo-c)
Gold Key

	Good	Fine	Mint
1-Russ Manning-a	1.50	4.00	8.00
2-9	.70	2.00	4.00

MY FRIEND IRMA (Radio/TV) (Formerly Western Life Romances)
No. 3, June, 1950 - No. 47, Dec, 1954; No. 48, Feb, 1955
Marvel/Atlas Comics (BFP)

	Good	Fine	Mint
3	1.50	4.00	8.00
4-Kurtzman-a, 10 pgs.	5.00	14.00	28.00
5-''Egghead Doodle'' by Kurtzman, 4 pgs.	3.50	10.00	20.00
6,8-10	.70	2.00	4.00
7-One pg. Kurtzman	1.20	3.50	7.00
11,13-20	.60	1.80	3.60
12-Silhoutted nudity	1.00	3.00	6.00
21,22,24-48	.60	1.80	3.60
23-One pg. Frazetta	1.00	3.00	6.00

MY GIRL PEARL
4/55 - No. 6, 9/57; No. 7, 8/60 - No. 16, 2/62
Atlas Comics

	Good	Fine	Mint
1	1.50	4.00	8.00
2-16	.85	2.50	5.00

MY GREATEST ADVENTURE (Doom Patrol No. 86 on)
Jan-Feb, 1955 - No. 85, Feb, 1964
National Periodical Publications

	Good	Fine	Mint
1-Before CCA	15.00	45.00	100.00
2-5	9.00	25.00	48.00
6-10	3.50	10.00	20.00
11-16,19,22-27,29,30	2.50	7.00	14.00
17,18-Kirby c/a-18	3.50	10.00	20.00
20,21,28-Kirby-a	3.00	8.00	16.00
31-57,59	1.00	3.00	6.00
58,60,61,77-Toth-a	1.50	4.50	9.00
62-76,78,79	.50	1.50	3.00
80-(6/63)-Intro/origin Doom Patrol; origin Robotman, Negative Man, & Elasti-Girl	1.50	4.50	9.00
81,85-Toth-a	.85	2.50	5.00
82-84	.50	1.50	3.00

NOTE: ***Anderson** a-42. **Moreira** a-23, 27.*

MY GREATEST THRILLS IN BASEBALL
(16 pg. Giveaway)
Mission of California

	Good	Fine	Mint
By Mickey Mantle	4.00	12.00	24.00

MY GREAT LOVE
Oct, 1949 - No. 4, Apr, 1950
Fox Features Syndicate

	Good	Fine	Mint
1	3.50	10.00	20.00
2-4	2.50	7.00	14.00

MY INTIMATE AFFAIR (Inside Crime No. 3)
Mar, 1950 - No. 2, May, 1950
Fox Features Syndicate

	Good	Fine	Mint
1	3.50	10.00	20.00
2	2.50	7.00	14.00

MY LIFE (Meet Corliss Archer No. 1-3)
No. 4, Sept, 1948 - No. 15, July, 1950
Fox Features Syndicate

	Good	Fine	Mint
4-Used in **SOTI**, pg. 39; Kamen/Feldstein-a	12.00	36.00	72.00
5-Kamen-a	6.00	18.00	36.00
6-Kamen/Feldstein-a	6.00	18.00	36.00
7-Wash cover	4.00	12.00	24.00
8,9,11-15	2.50	7.00	14.00
10-Wood-a	6.00	18.00	36.00

MY LITTLE MARGIE (TV)
1954 - No. 54, Nov, 1964
Charlton Comics

	Good	Fine	Mint
1	1.50	4.00	8.00
2-19: 8,9-Infinity-c	.85	2.50	5.00
20-(100 page ish)	1.50	4.00	8.00
21-53	.35	1.00	2.00
54-Beatles on cover; lead story spoofs the Beatle haircut craze of the 1960's	2.00	6.00	12.00

MY LITTLE MARGIE'S BOY FRIENDS
1955 - 1961
Charlton Comics

	Good	Fine	Mint
1-Has several Archie swipes	1.20	3.50	7.00
2-10	.70	2.00	4.00
11-20	.50	1.50	3.00
21-38		.60	1.20

MY LITTLE MARGIE'S FASHIONS
Feb, 1959 - No. 5, 1959
Charlton Comics

	Good	Fine	Mint
1	2.00	6.00	12.00
2-5	1.00	3.00	6.00

MY LOVE (Formerly Molly Manton's Romances No. 1 & 2)
July, 1949 - No. 4, March, 1950
Marvel Comics (CDS)

	Good	Fine	Mint
1(7/49)(becomes Blaze the Wonder Collie No. 2)	1.50	4.00	8.00
3(1/50), 4	.85	2.50	5.00

MY LOVE
Sept, 1969 - No. 39, Mar, 1976
Marvel Comics Group

	Good	Fine	Mint
1-9		.30	.60
10-Williamson-r/My Own Romance No. 71; Kirby-a		.60	1.20
11-20: 14-Morrow-a		.20	.40
21,22,24-39: 38,39-Reprints		.20	.40
23-Steranko-r/Our Love Story No. 5		.30	.60
Special(12/71)		.30	.60

MY LOVE AFFAIR (March of Crime No. 7)
July, 1949 - No. 6, May, 1950

MY LOVE AFFAIR (continued)
Fox Features Syndicate

	Good	Fine	Mint
1	4.00	12.00	24.00
2,4	2.50	7.00	14.00
3,5,6-Wood-a	6.00	18.00	36.00

MY LOVE LIFE (Formerly Zegra)
No. 6, June, 1949 - No. 13, Aug, 1950
Fox Features Syndicate

6-Kamen/Feldstein-a 5.00 15.00 30.00
7-13 2.50 7.00 14.00

MY LOVE MEMOIRS (Formerly Women Outlaws; Hunted No. 13 on)
No. 9, Nov, 1949 - No. 12, May, 1950
Fox Features Syndicate

9,11,12-Wood-a 6.00 18.00 36.00
10 2.50 7.00 14.00

MY LOVE SECRET (Formerly Phantom Lady) (Animal Crackers No.31)
No. 24, June, 1949 - No. 30, June, 1950; 1954
Fox Features Syndicate/M. S. Distr.

24-Kamen/Feldstein-a 5.00 15.00 30.00
25-Possible caricature of Wood on the cover? 3.00 8.00 16.00
26,28-Wood-a 6.00 18.00 36.00
27,29,30: 30-photo-c 2.50 7.00 14.00
53-(Reprint, M.S. Distr.) 1954? no date given; formerly Western Thrillers No. 52 (Crimes by Women No. 54) 1.50 4.00 8.00

MY LOVE STORY (Hoot Gibson Western No. 5 on)
Sept, 1949 - No. 4, Mar, 1950
Fox Features Syndicate

1 4.00 12.00 24.00
2 2.50 7.00 14.00
3,4-Wood-a 6.00 18.00 36.00

MY LOVE STORY
April, 1956 - No. 9, Aug, 1957
Atlas Comics (GPS)

1-Colletta-a(2) 1.50 4.00 8.00
2,4-9 .60 1.80 3.60
3-Matt Baker-a 1.50 4.00 8.00
NOTE: ***Colletta*** *art in most.*

MY ONLY LOVE
July, 1975 - No. 9, Nov, 1976
Charlton Comics

1,2,4-9 .20 .40
3-Toth-a .40 .80

MY OWN ROMANCE (Formerly My Romance; Teen-Age Romance No. 77 on)
No. 3, Feb, 1949 - No. 76, July, 1960
Marvel/Atlas (MjPC/RCM No. 3-59/ZPC No. 60-76)

3-5 1.50 4.00 8.00
6-20: 14-Powell-a .70 2.00 4.00
21-70,72-76 .60 1.80 3.60
71-Williamson-a 4.00 12.00 24.00
NOTE: ***Coletta*** *a-45(2), 50; c-50.* ***Romita*** *a-36.*

MY PAST (. . . Confessions) (Formerly Western Thrillers)
No. 8, Oct, 1949 - No. 11, April, 1950 (Crimes Inc. No. 12)
Fox Features Syndicate

8-10 2.50 7.00 14.00
11-Wood-a 6.00 18.00 36.00

MY PERSONAL PROBLEM
Nov, 1955 - No. 3, Sept, 1956; Oct, 1957 - 1958
Ajax/Farrell/Steinway Comic

1-3 1.50 4.00 8.00
1(10/57), 2('58)-Steinway .70 2.00 4.00

MY PRIVATE LIFE (Formerly Murder, Inc.)
No. 16, Feb, 1950
Fox Features Syndicate

16 3.00 8.00 16.00

MY REAL LOVE
No. 5, June, 1952
Standard Comics

5-Toth-a, 3 pgs.; photo-c 3.50 10.00 20.00

MYRA NORTH (See 4-Color No. 3)

MY ROMANCE (My Own Romance No. 3 on)
Sept, 1948 - No. 3, Jan, 1949
Marvel Comics (RCM)

1 3.00 8.00 16.00
2,3 1.50 4.00 8.00

MY ROMANTIC ADVENTURES (Formerly Romantic Adventures)
No. 68, Aug, 1956 - No. 138, Mar, 1964
American Comics Group

68-85 .70 2.00 4.00
86-Three pg. Williamson-a (2/58) 3.50 8.00 16.00
87-138 .35 1.00 2.00
NOTE: ***Whitney*** *art in most.*

MY SECRET
Aug, 1949 - No. 3, Oct, 1949
Superior Comics, Ltd.

1 3.00 8.00 16.00
2,3 2.00 6.00 12.00

MY SECRET AFFAIR (Martin Kane No. 4)
Dec, 1949 - No. 3, April, 1950
Hero Book (Fox Features Syndicate)

1-Harrison/Wood-a, 10 pgs. 7.00 20.00 40.00
2-Wood-a (poor) 5.00 14.00 28.00
3-Wood-a 6.00 18.00 36.00

MY SECRET CONFESSION
September, 1955
Sterling Comics

1-Sekowsky-a 1.50 4.00 8.00

MY SECRET LIFE (Formerly Western Outlaws; Romeo Tubbs No. 26 on)
No. 22, July, 1949 - No. 27, May, 1950
Fox Features Syndicate

22 2.50 7.00 14.00
23,26-Wood-a, 6 pgs. 6.00 18.00 36.00
24,25,27 2.00 5.00 10.00
NOTE: *The title was changed to Romeo Tubbs after No. 25 even though No. 26 & 27 did come out.*

MY SECRET LIFE (Formerly Young Lovers; Sue and Sally Smith No. 48 on)
No. 19, Aug, 1957 - No. 47, 1962
Charlton Comics

19-47 .30 .60

MY SECRET MARRIAGE
May, 1953 - No. 24, July, 1956
Superior Comics, Ltd.

1 2.50 7.00 14.00
2-24 1.50 4.00 8.00
I.W. Reprint No. 9 .30 .90 1.80
NOTE: *Many issues contain Kamenish art.*

My Love Affair #1, © FOX

My Romance #3, © MCG

My Secret Marriage #17, © SUPR

Mysteries Weird & Strange #10, © SUPR

Mysterious Stories #3, © PM

Mystery In Space #2, © DC

MY SECRET ROMANCE (A Star Presentation No. 3)
Jan, 1950 - No. 2, March, 1950
Hero Book (Fox Features Syndicate)

	Good	Fine	Mint
1-Wood-a	7.00	20.00	40.00
2-Wood-a	6.00	18.00	36.00

MY SECRET STORY (Sabu No. 30 on)
No. 26, Oct, 1949 - No. 29, April, 1950
Fox Features Syndicate

	Good	Fine	Mint
26-29	2.50	7.00	14.00

MYSTERIES (. . . Weird & Strange)
May, 1953 - No. 11, Jan, 1955
Superior/Dynamic Publ. (Randall Publ. Ltd.)

	Good	Fine	Mint
1	3.50	10.00	20.00
2-A-Bomb blast story	2.00	6.00	12.00
3-9,11	1.50	4.00	8.00
10-Kamenish c/a r-/Strange Mysteries No. 2; cover from a panel in S.M. No. 2	4.00	12.00	24.00

MYSTERIES OF SCOTLAND YARD (See A-1 Comics No. 121)

MYSTERIES OF UNEXPLORED WORLDS (See Blue Bird) (Son of Vulcan V2No.49 on)
Aug, 1956 - No. 48, Sept, 1965
Charlton Comics

	Good	Fine	Mint
1-Ditko-a	4.00	12.00	24.00
2-No Ditko	1.50	4.00	8.00
3-6,8,9-Ditko-a	2.50	7.00	14.00
7-(68 pg. ish); Ditko-a	3.50	10.00	20.00
10-Ditko-c/a(4)	3.00	8.00	16.00
11-Ditko-c/a(3)-signed J. Kotdi	2.00	6.00	12.00
12,19,21-24,26-Ditko-a	2.00	5.00	10.00
13-18,20	.80	2.40	4.80
25,27-30	.70	2.00	4.00
31-45	.40	1.20	2.40
46-Son of Vulcan origin & series begins	.70	2.00	4.00
47,48	.50	1.50	3.00

NOTE: ***Ditko** c-3-6 9-11, 19, 21-24.*

MYSTERIOUS ADVENTURES
March, 1951 - No. 25, Aug, 1955
Story Comics

	Good	Fine	Mint
1	6.00	18.00	36.00
2	3.50	10.00	20.00
3,4,6,9,10	3.00	8.00	16.00
5-Bondage-c	3.50	10.00	20.00
7-Eye injury panel	3.00	8.00	16.00
8-Eyeball story	3.00	8.00	16.00
11(12/52)-Used in **SOTI**, pg. 84.	5.00	15.00	30.00
12-Dismemberment, eyes ripped out	5.00	15.00	30.00
13-Eye injury panel	5.00	15.00	30.00
14,18,19	2.00	6.00	12.00
15-Violence; beheading, acid in face, face carved with knife	5.00	15.00	30.00
16-Violence, dismemberment, injury to eye	5.00	15.00	30.00
17-Violence, dismemberment	5.00	15.00	30.00
20-Violence, head split open, fried body organs-used by Wertham in the Senate hearings	5.00	15.00	30.00
21-Blood drainage story, hanging panels, intestines pulled out; bondage/beheading-c	4.50	13.00	26.00
22-'Cinderella' parody	2.50	7.00	14.00
23-Disbrow-a	3.00	9.00	18.00
24,25	2.00	6.00	12.00

NOTE: *Tothish art by **Ross Andru**-No. 22, 23. **Bache** a-8. **Cameron** a-6, 7. **Hollingsworth** a-3-8, 12. **Schaffenberger** a-25. **Wildey** a-17.*

MYSTERIOUS ISLAND (See 4-Color No. 1213)

MYSTERIOUS ISLE
Nov-Jan, 1964 (Jules Verne)
Dell Publishing Co.

	Good	Fine	Mint
1	1.00	3.00	6.00

MYSTERIOUS STORIES (Horror From the Tomb No. 1)
Dec-Jan, 1954-1955 - No. 7, Dec, 1955
Premier Magazines

	Good	Fine	Mint
2-Woodbridge-c	3.50	10.00	20.00
3-Woodbridge c/a	3.50	10.00	20.00
4-7: 6-Woodbridge-c	2.50	7.00	14.00

MYSTERIOUS SUSPENSE
October, 1968
Charlton Comics

	Good	Fine	Mint
1-The Question app. by Ditko	2.00	5.00	10.00

MYSTERIOUS TRAVELER (See Tales of the . . .)

MYSTERIOUS TRAVELER COMICS (Radio)
Nov, 1948 - No. 4, 1949
Trans-World Publications

	Good	Fine	Mint
1-Powell-c/a(2); Poe adaptation, 'Tell Tale Heart'	7.00	20.00	40.00
2-4	5.00	14.00	28.00

MYSTERY COMICS
1944 - No. 4, 1944
Better Publications

	Good	Fine	Mint
1-The Magnet, The Silver Knight, Brad Spencer, Wonderman, Dick Devins, King of Futuria, & Zudo the Jungle Boy begin	17.00	50.00	100.00
2	12.00	35.00	70.00
3-Lance Lewis, Space Detective begins	10.00	30.00	60.00
4	10.00	30.00	60.00

MYSTERY COMICS DIGEST
March, 1972 - No. 26, Oct, 1975
Gold Key

	Good	Fine	Mint
1-Ripley's; reprint of Ripley's No. 1; origin Ra-Ka-Tep the Mummy; Wood-a	1.00	3.00	6.00
2-Boris Karloff; Wood-a; 1st app. Werewolf Count Wulfstein	.50	1.50	3.00
3-Twilight Zone; Crandall, Toth & George Evans-a; 1st app. Tragg & Simbar the Lion Lord; 2 Crandall/Frazetta-a r-Twilight Zone No. 1	.50	1.50	3.00
4-Ripley's Believe It or Not; 1st app. Baron Tibor, the Vampire	.40	1.20	2.40
5-Boris Karloff Tales of Mystery; 1st app. Dr. Spektor	.40	1.20	2.40
6-Twilight Zone; 1st app. U.S. Marshal Reid & Sir Duane	.40	1.20	2.40
7-Ripley's Believe It or Not; origin The Lurker in the Swamp; 1st app. Duroc	.30	.80	1.60
8-Boris Karloff Tales of Mystery	.30	.80	1.60
9-Twilight Zone; Williamson, Crandall, McWilliams-a; 2nd Tragg app.	.50	1.50	3.00
10,13-Ripley's Believe It or Not		.60	1.20
11,14-Boris Karloff Tales of Mystery. 14-1st app. Xorkon		.50	1.00
12,15-Twilight Zone		.50	1.00
16,19,22,25-Ripley's Believe It or Not		.50	1.00
17-Boris Karloff Tales of Mystery; Williamson-r	.30	.90	1.80
18,21,24-Twilight Zone		.50	1.00
20,23,26-Boris Karloff Tales of Mystery		.50	1.00

NOTE: *Dr. Spektor app.-No. 5,10-12,21. Durak app.-No. 15. Duroc app.-No. 14 (later called Durak). King George 1st app.-No. 8.*

MYSTERY IN SPACE
Apr-May, 1951 - No. 110, Sept, 1966; (No. 1-4: 52 pgs.)
No. 111, Aug, 1980 - No. 117, March, 1981
National Periodical Publications

	Good	Fine	Mint
1-Frazetta-a, 8 pgs.; Knights of the Galaxy begins, ends No. 8	70.00	200.00	400.00
2	30.00	90.00	180.00
3	25.00	70.00	140.00
4,5	14.00	40.00	80.00
6-10: 7-Toth-a	9.00	25.00	50.00

MYSTERY IN SPACE (continued)

	Good	Fine	Mint
11-15: 13-Toth-a	7.00	21.00	42.00
16-18,20-25: Interplanetary Insurance feature by Infantino in all. 24-Last precode issue	6.00	18.00	36.00
19-Virgil Finley-a	9.00	25.00	50.00
26-Space Cabbie begins	4.00	12.00	24.00
27-34,36-40	4.00	12.00	24.00
35-Kubert-a	5.00	14.00	28.00
41-51: 47-Space Cabbie feature ends	2.50	7.00	14.00
52-All Gil Kane issue	3.00	8.00	16.00
53-1st Adam Strange app.	20.00	60.00	130.00
54	10.00	28.00	60.00
55	6.00	18.00	40.00
56-60	5.00	15.00	32.00
61-70: 61-1st app. Adam Strange foe Ulthoon. 62-1st app. A.S. foe Motan. 63-Origin Vandor. 66-Star Rovers begin. 68-Origin Dust Devil	3.00	9.00	18.00
71-74,76-80	2.00	6.00	12.00
75-JLA x-over in Adam Strange	2.50	7.00	14.00
81-86	1.20	3.50	7.00
87-90-Hawkman in all	.80	2.30	4.60
91-102: 91-End Infantino art on Adam Strange. 92-Space Ranger begins. 94,98-Adam Strange/Space Ranger team-up. 102-Adam Strange ends	.35	1.10	2.20
103-Origin Ultra, the Multi-Alien; Space Ranger ends	.35	1.10	2.20
104-110(9/66)	.30	.80	1.60
111(9/80)-117		.30	.60

NOTE: ***Anderson*** *a-2, 4, 8-10, 12-17, 19, 45-48, 51, 57, 61-64, 70, 76, 87-98; c-9, 10, 15-25, 87, 89, 105-108, 110.* ***Aparo*** *a-111.* ***Craig*** *a-114, 116.* ***Ditko*** *a-111, 114-116.* ***Drucker*** *a-13, 14.* ***Golden*** *a-113.* ***Infantino*** *a-1-8, 11, 14-25, 27-46, 48, 49, 51, 53-91, 103, 117; c-60-86, 88, 90, 91, 105, 107.* ***Gil Kane*** *a-100-102; c-52, 101.* ***Kubert*** *a-113; c-111-15.* ***Newton*** *a-117.* ***Rogers*** *a-111.* ***Simon & Kirby*** *a-4(2 pgs.).* ***Starlin*** *c-116.* ***Sutton*** *a-112.*

MYSTERY MEN COMICS
Aug, 1939 - No. 31, Feb, 1942
Fox Features Syndicate

	Good	Fine	Mint
1-Intro. & 1st app. The Blue Beetle, The Green Mask, Rex Dexter of Mars by Briefer, Zanzibar by Tuska, Lt. Drake, D-13-Secret Agent by Powell, Chen Chang, WingTurner, & Captain Denny Scott; bondage-c	60.00	180.00	375.00
2-Opium story	35.00	100.00	200.00
3	30.00	80.00	160.00
4-Capt. Savage begins	25.00	70.00	140.00
5	18.00	54.00	110.00
6-8: 7,8-Bondage-c	17.00	50.00	100.00
9-The Moth begins	14.00	40.00	80.00
10-Wing Turner by Kirby	12.00	36.00	72.00
11-Intro. Domino	10.00	30.00	60.00
12,13,15-18	8.00	24.00	48.00
14-Intro. Lynx & sidekick Blackie	10.00	30.00	60.00
19-Intro. & 1st app. Miss X (ends No. 21)	10.00	30.00	60.00
20-25	8.00	24.00	48.00
26-The Wraith begins	8.00	24.00	48.00
27-31	8.00	24.00	48.00

NOTE: ***Cuidera*** *a-22.* ***Lou Fine*** *c-1-5,8,9.* ***Simon*** *c-10, 12.* ***Tuska*** *a-22.*

MYSTERY TALES
March, 1952 - No. 54, Aug, 1957
Atlas Comics (20CC)

	Good	Fine	Mint
1	6.00	18.00	36.00
2-Krigstein-a	3.50	10.00	20.00
3-10: 6-A-Bomb panel. 10-Gil Kane-a	2.50	7.00	14.00
11-19	1.50	4.50	9.00
20-Torres-a; last precode issue	2.50	7.00	14.00
21-27,29-35,37,38,41-43,49	1.00	3.00	6.00
28-Jack Katz-a	1.50	4.50	9.00
36,39-Krigstein-a	3.00	8.00	16.00
40-Ditko-a	2.00	5.00	10.00
44,48,51-Williamson-a; with Mayo 44,51	3.50	10.00	20.00
45-Ditko-a	2.00	5.00	10.00
46-Williamson/Krenkel-a	3.50	10.00	20.00
47-Crandall, Powell-a	2.50	7.00	14.00
50-Torres, Morrow-a	2.50	7.00	14.00
52,53	1.00	3.00	6.00
54-Crandall, Check-a	2.00	5.00	10.00

NOTE: ***Colan*** *a-3.* ***Everett*** *a-2, 28, 29, 33, 35, 43; c-9-11, 14, 38, 46, 48-51, 53.* ***Heath*** *a-3; c-3, 15, 26.* ***Kinstler*** *a-15.* ***Maneely*** *c-31.* ***Orlando*** *a-51.* ***Pakula*** *a-3.* ***Powell*** *a-21, 29, 37, 38, 48.* ***Robinson*** *a-7p,42.* ***Wildey*** *a-37. 26-No code on cover.*

MYSTERY TALES
1964
Super Comics

	Good	Fine	Mint
Super Reprint No. 16,17('64)	.50	1.50	3.00
Super Reprint No. 18-Kubert art/Strange Terrors No. 4	.50	1.50	3.00

MYSTIC (3rd Series)
March, 1951 - No. 61, Aug, 1957
Marvel/Atlas Comics (CSI)

	Good	Fine	Mint
1	6.00	18.00	36.00
2	3.00	9.00	18.00
3,5,7-10	2.00	6.00	12.00
4-"The Devil Birds" by Wolverton, 6 pgs.	17.00	50.00	100.00
6-"The Eye of Doom" by Wolverton, 7 pgs.	17.00	50.00	100.00
11-20	2.00	5.00	10.00
21-25,27-30,32-35-Last pre-code issue	1.50	4.00	8.00
26-Atomic War, severed head stories	2.00	5.00	10.00
31-Sid Check-a	2.00	5.00	10.00
36-51,53-55,57,61	1.00	3.00	6.00
52-Wood & Crandall-a	4.00	12.00	24.00
56-Severin-c, Powell-a	1.20	3.50	7.00
58,59-Krigstein-a	3.00	8.00	16.00
60-Williamson/Mayo-a, 4 pgs.	3.50	10.00	20.00

NOTE: ***Andru*** *a-25.* ***Check*** *a-60.* ***Colan*** *a-7.* ***Drucker*** *a-46, 52, 56.* ***Everett*** *a-8, 9, 17, 40, 44, 53, 57-59; c-18, 24p, 42, 47, 49, 53-55, 58, 61.* ***Heath*** *a-10; c-10, 25.* ***Infantino*** *a-12.* ***Kane*** *a-1,8.* ***Jack Katz*** *a-31, 33.* ***Maneely*** *a-58; c-29, 31.* ***Moldoff*** *a-29.* ***Morrow*** *a-51.* ***Orlando*** *a-57, 61.* ***Powell*** *a-55.* ***Robinson*** *a-5.* ***Sekowsky*** *a-1, 2, 4, 5.* ***Whitney*** *a-33. Canadian reprints known-title 'Startling'.*

MYSTICAL TALES
June, 1956 - No. 8, Aug, 1957
Atlas Comics (EPI)

	Good	Fine	Mint
1-Everett c/a	5.00	14.00	28.00
2-4-Crandall-a	3.50	10.00	20.00
5-Williamson-a, 4 pgs.	4.00	12.00	24.00
6-Torres, Krigstein-a	3.50	10.00	20.00
7-Torres, Orlando-a	3.00	8.00	16.00
8-Krigstein, Check-a	3.50	10.00	20.00

NOTE: ***Everett*** *c-4, 6, 7.* ***Orlando*** *a-1, 2.* ***Powell*** *a-1, 4.*

MYSTIC COMICS (1st Series)
March, 1940 - No. 10, Aug, 1942
Timely Comics

	Good	Fine	Mint
1-Origin The Blue Blaze, The Dynamic Man, & Flexo the Rubber Man; Zephyr Jones, 3X's & Deep Sea Demon app.; The Magician begins	240.00	600.00	1200.00
2-The Invisible Man & Master Mind Excello begin; Space Rangers, Zara of the Jungle, Taxi Taylor app; bondage-c	110.00	310.00	620.00
3-Origin Hercules, who last appears in No. 4	90.00	250.00	500.00
4-Origin The Thin Man & The Black Widow; Merzak the Mystic app.; last Flexo, Dynamic Man, Invisible Man & Blue Blaze. (Some			

Mystery Men Comics #4, © FOX

Mystery Tales #51, © MCG

Mystic #23, © MCG

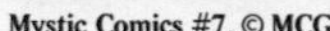
Mystic Comics #7, © MCG

Nancy & Sluggo #17, © UFS

National Comics #10, © QUA

MYSTIC COMICS (continued) — Good / Fine / Mint

issues have date sticker on cover) 100.00 300.00 625.00
5-Origin The Black Marvel, The Blazing Skull, The Sub-Earth Man, Super Slave & The Terror; The Moon Man & Black Widow app. 95.00 280.00 575.00
6-Origin The Challenger & The Destroyer 80.00 230.00 480.00
7-The Witness begins (origin); origin Davey & the Demon; last Black Widow; Simon & Kirby-c 60.00 180.00 375.00
8 50.00 145.00 300.00
9-Gary Gaunt app.; last Black Marvel, Mystic & Blazing Skull; bondage-c 50.00 145.00 300.00
10-Father Time, World of Wonder, & Red Skeleton app.; last Challenger & Terror 50.00 145.00 300.00

MYSTIC COMICS (2nd Series)
Oct, 1944 - No. 4, Winter, 1944-45
Timely Comics

1-The Angel, The Destroyer, The Human Torch, Terry Vance the Schoolboy Sleuth, & Tommy Tyme begin 30.00 80.00 160.00
2,3: 2-Last Human Torch & Terry Vance. 3-Last Angel (two stories) & Tommy Tyme 20.00 60.00 130.00
4-The Young Allies app. 15.00 45.00 100.00

MY STORY (. . . True Romances in Pictures No. 5,6) (Formerly Zago)
No. 5, May, 1949 - No. 12, Aug, 1950
Hero Books (Fox Features Syndicate)

5-Kamen/Feldstein-a 5.00 15.00 30.00
6-8,11,12 2.50 7.00 14.00
9,10-Wood-a 6.00 18.00 36.00

MY TRUE LOVE (Frank Buck No. 70 on)
No. 65, July, 1949 - No. 69, March, 1950
Fox Features Syndicate

65-69 3.00 8.00 12.00

NAKED PREY, THE (See Movie Classics)

NAMORA
Fall, 1948 - No. 3, Dec, 1948
Marvel Comics

1-Sub-Mariner x-over in Namora; Everett-a 30.00 90.00 190.00
2-The Blonde Phantom app. in Sub-Mariner story; Everett-a 25.00 70.00 150.00
3-Sub-Mariner app.; Everett-a 20.00 60.00 125.00

NANCY AND SLUGGO
1949 - No. 23, 1954
United Features Syndicate

16(No.1) 1.20 3.50 7.00
17-23 .85 2.50 5.00

NANCY & SLUGGO (Nancy No. 146-173; formerly Sparkler Comics)
No. 121, Apr, 1955 - No. 192, Oct, 1963
St. John/Dell No. 146-187/Gold Key No. 188 on

121(4/55)-145(7/57)-St. John .85 2.50 5.00
146(9/57)-Peanuts begins, ends No. 192 (Dell) .70 2.00 4.00
147-161 (Dell) .70 2.00 4.00
162-180-John Stanley-a 1.20 3.50 7.00
181-187(3-4/62)(Dell) .70 2.00 4.00
188(10/62)-192 (G.Key) .70 2.00 4.00
4-Color 1034-Summer Camp .70 2.00 4.00
. . . Travel Time 1('58-Dell)(25 cents) 1.50 4.00 8.00
(See Dell Giant No. 34,45)

NANNY AND THE PROFESSOR (TV)
Aug, 1970 - No. 2, Oct, 1970
Dell Publishing Co.

1(01-546-008), 2 .70 2.00 4.00

NAPOLEON (See 4-Color No. 526)

NAPOLEON & SAMANTHA (See Walt Disney Showcase No. 10)

NAPOLEON & UNCLE ELBY (See Clifford Bride's . . .)
1942 (68 pages) (One Shot)
Eastern Color Printing Co. — Good / Fine / Mint

1 6.00 18.00 36.00
1945-American Book-Strafford Press (128 pgs.) (8x10½''-B&W reprints; hardcover) 4.00 12.00 24.00

NAPOLEON & UNCLE ELBY
1954
Dell Publishing Co.

1(Exist?) .50 1.50 3.00

NATIONAL COMICS
July, 1940 - No. 75, Nov, 1949
Quality Comics Group

1-Origin Uncle Sam & sidekick Buddy by Eisner, & Merlin the Magician (ends No. 26); Cyclone, Wonder Boy (ends No. 26), Kid Patrol, Sally O'Neal Policewoman, Pen Miller (ends No. 22), Kid Dixon, Prop Powers (ends No. 26), & Paul Bunyan (ends No. 22) begin 120.00 350.00 750.00
2 60.00 170.00 360.00
3-Last Eisner Uncle Sam 50.00 130.00 275.00
4-Last Cyclone 30.00 85.00 175.00
5-Quick Silver begins; origin Uncle Sam; bondage-c 35.00 110.00 225.00
6-11: 8-Jack & Jill begins (ends No. 22). 9-Flag-c 28.00 80.00 160.00
12,17-22 15.00 50.00 100.00
13-16-Lou Fine-a 25.00 70.00 150.00
23-The Unknown & Destroyer 171 begin 17.00 50.00 100.00
24-26,28,30 14.00 40.00 80.00
27-G-2 the Unknown begins (ends No. 46) 14.00 40.00 80.00
29-Origin The Unknown 14.00 40.00 80.00
31-33: 33-Chic Carter begins (ends No. 47) 10.00 30.00 60.00
34-40: 35-Last Kid Patrol 7.00 20.00 40.00
41-47,49,50: 42-The Barker begins 5.50 16.00 32.00
48-Origin The Whistler 5.50 16.00 32.00
51-Sally O'Neil by Ward, 8 pgs. (12/45) 8.00 24.00 48.00
52-60 4.00 12.00 24.00
61-67: 67-Format change; Quicksilver app. 3.00 9.00 18.00
68-75: The Barker ends 2.00 5.00 10.00

NOTE: ***Cole*** *Quicksilver-13; c-46.* ***Crandall*** *Uncle Sam-11-13 (with* ***Fine****), 25, 26; c-24-26, 30-33.* ***Crandall*** *Paul Bunyan-10-13.* ***Fine*** *Uncle Sam-13 (w/****Crandall****), 17, 18; c-1-14, 16, 18, 21.* ***Guardineer*** *Quicksilver-27.* ***Gustavson*** *Quicksilver-14-26.* ***McWilliams*** *a-23-28, 55, 57.*

NATIONAL CRUMB, THE (Magazine-Size)
August, 1975 (52 pages) (Satire)
Mayfair Publications

1 .50 1.50 3.00

NATIONAL VELVET (TV)
May-July, 1961 - March, 1963
Dell Publishing Co./Gold Key

4-Color 1195,1312 .85 2.50 5.00
01556-207,210 .85 2.50 5.00
1(12/62), 2(3/63)-Gold Key .85 2.50 5.00

NATURE BOY (Formerly Danny Blaze; Li'l Rascal Twins No. 6 on)
No. 3, March, 1956 - No. 5, Feb, 1957
Charlton Comics

3-Origin; Blue Beetle story; Buscema-a 5.50 16.00 32.00
4,5 4.00 12.00 24.00

NOTE: ***Buscema*** *a-5.* ***Powell*** *a-4.*

NATURE OF THINGS (See 4-Color No. 727,842)

NAVY ACTION (Sailor Sweeney No. 12-14)
Aug, 1954 - No. 11, Apr, 1956; No. 15, 1/57 - No. 18, 8/57
Atlas Comics (CDS)

1-Powell-a 2.50 7.00 14.00

NAVY ACTION (continued)

	Good	Fine	Mint
2-11	1.20	3.50	7.00
15-18	.85	2.50	5.00

NOTE: ***Berg** a-9.* ***Drucker** a-7,17.*

NAVY COMBAT
June, 1955 - No. 20, Oct, 1958
Atlas Comics (MPI)

	Good	Fine	Mint
1-Torpedo Taylor begins by D. Heck	2.00	6.00	12.00
2-10	1.00	3.00	6.00
11-13,15,16,18-20	.85	2.50	5.00
14-Torres-a	2.00	6.00	12.00
17-Williamson-a, 4 pgs.	3.00	8.00	16.00

NOTE: ***Berg** a-10,11.* ***Drucker** a-7.* ***Everett** a-3,20; c-10,15.* ***Pakula** a-7.*

NAVY HEROES
1945
Almanac Publishing Co.

	Good	Fine	Mint
1-Heavy in propaganda	2.00	6.00	12.00

NAVY: HISTORY & TRADITION
1958 - 1961 (nn) (Giveaway)
Stokes Walesby Co./Dept. of Navy

	Good	Fine	Mint
1772-1778, 1778-1782, 1782-1817, 1817-1865, 1865-1936, 1940-1945	2.00	6.00	12.00
1861: Naval Actions of the Civil War: 1865	2.00	6.00	12.00

NAVY PATROL
May, 1955 - No. 4, Nov, 1955
Key Publications

	Good	Fine	Mint
1	2.00	5.00	10.00
2-4	.85	2.50	5.00

NAVY TALES
Jan, 1957 - No. 4, July, 1957
Atlas Comics (CDS)

	Good	Fine	Mint
1-Everett-c; Berg, Powell-a	2.00	6.00	12.00
2-Williamson/Mayo-a, 5 pgs. plus Crandall-a	4.00	11.00	22.00
3,4: 3-Krigstein-a. 4-Crandall-a	2.00	6.00	12.00

NAVY TASK FORCE
Feb, 1954 - No. 8, April, 1956
Stanmor Publications/Aragon Mag. No. 4-8

	Good	Fine	Mint
1	1.50	4.00	8.00
2-8	.85	2.50	5.00

NAVY WAR HEROES
Jan, 1964 - No. 7, Mar-Apr, 1965
Charlton Comics

	Good	Fine	Mint
1		.40	.80
2-7		.30	.60

NAZA (Stone Age Warrior)
Nov-Jan, 1964 - No. 9, March, 1966
Dell Publishing Co.

	Good	Fine	Mint
1 (12-555-401)	.85	2.50	5.00
2-9	.60	1.80	3.60

NEBBS, THE
1928 (Daily B&W strip reprints; 52 pages)
Cupples & Leon Co.

	Good	Fine	Mint
By Sol Hess; Carlson-a	3.50	10.00	20.00

NEBBS, THE
1941 - 1945
Dell Publishing Co./Croyden Publishers

	Good	Fine	Mint
Black & White 23(1941)	5.00	15.00	30.00
1(1945)-Reprints	2.00	5.00	10.00

NEGRO (See All-Negro)

NEGRO HEROES (Reprints from True, Real Heroes, & Calling All Girls)
Spring, 1947 - No. 2, Summer, 1948
Parents' Magazine Institute

	Good	Fine	Mint
1	17.00	50.00	100.00
2 (Scarce)	30.00	80.00	160.00

NEGRO ROMANCE (Negro Romances No. 4?)
June, 1950 - No. 3, Oct, 1950
Fawcett Publications

	Good	Fine	Mint
1-Evans-a	50.00	140.00	280.00
2,3	35.00	100.00	200.00

NEGRO ROMANCES (Formerly Negro Romance?; Romantic Secrets No. 5 on?)
No. 4, May, 1955
Charlton Comics

	Good	Fine	Mint
4-Reprints Fawcett No. 2	25.00	70.00	140.00

NELLIE THE NURSE
1945 - No. 36, Oct, 1952; 1957
Marvel/Atlas Comics (SPI/LMC)

	Good	Fine	Mint
1	4.50	13.00	26.00
2-4	2.00	6.00	12.00
5-Kurtzman's "Hey Look"	3.00	8.00	16.00
6-8,10	1.50	4.00	8.00
9-Wolverton-a, 1 pg.	2.00	5.00	10.00
11,14-16,18-Kurtzman's "Hey Look"	2.50	7.00	14.00
12-"Giggles 'n' Grins" by Kurtzman	1.50	4.00	8.00
13,17,19-27,29-36	.70	2.00	4.00
28-Kurtzman's Rusty reprint	1.50	4.00	8.00
1('57)-Leading Mag. (Atlas)	.50	1.50	3.00

NELLIE THE NURSE (See 4-Color No. 1304)

NEUTRO
January, 1967
Dell Publishing Co.

	Good	Fine	Mint
1	.70	2.00	4.00

NEVADA (See Zane Grey's Stories of the West No. 1)

NEVER AGAIN (War stories; becomes Soldier & Marine V2No.9)
Aug, 1955 - No. 8, July, 1956
Charlton Comics

	Good	Fine	Mint
1	3.00	8.00	12.00
2-8	2.50	5.00	7.50

NEW ADVENTURE COMICS (Formerly New Comics; becomes Adventure Comics No. 32 on)
V1No.12, Jan, 1937 - No. 31, Oct, 1938
National Periodical Publications

	Good	Fine	Mint
V1No.12-Federal Men by Siegel & Shuster continues	22.00	65.00	140.00
V2No.1(2/37, No.13)	17.00	50.00	115.00
14(V2No.2)-20(V2No.8): 15-1st Adventure logo. 16-1st Shuster-c; 1st non-funny cover. 17-Nadir, Master of Magic begins, ends No. 30	17.00	50.00	115.00
21(V2No.9),22(V2No.10, 2/37)	12.00	35.00	75.00
23-31	12.00	35.00	75.00

NEW ADVENTURE OF SNOW WHITE AND THE SEVEN DWARFS, A
(See Snow White Bendix Giveaway)

NEW ADVENTURES OF CHARLIE CHAN, THE
May-June, 1958 - No. 6, Mar-Apr, 1959
National Periodical Publications

	Good	Fine	Mint
1	5.50	16.00	32.00
2-6-Sid Greene-a	3.00	8.00	16.00

NEW ADVENTURES OF HUCK FINN, THE (TV)
September, 1968 (Hanna-Barbera)

Navy Action #16, © MCG

Nellie The Nurse #21, © MCG

New Adventure Comics V2#1, © DC

N.A. Of Superboy #1, © DC

New Funnies #70, © DELL

New Gods #4, © DC

NEW ADVS. OF HUCK FINN (continued)
Gold Key

	Good	Fine	Mint
1-''The Curse of Thut''	.70	2.00	4.00

NEW ADVENTURES OF PETER PAN (Disney)
1953 (36 pgs.; 5x7¼'') (Admiral giveaway)
Western Publishing Co.

	Good	Fine	Mint
	4.00	12.00	24.00

NEW ADVENTURES OF PINOCCHIO
Oct-Dec, 1962 - No. 3, 1963
Dell Publishing Co.

	Good	Fine	Mint
12-562-212	2.00	5.00	10.00
2,3	1.00	3.00	6.00

NEW ADVENTURES OF ROBIN HOOD (See Robin Hood)

NEW ADVENTURES OF SHERLOCK HOLMES (See 4-Color No. 1169, 1245)

NEW ADVENTURES OF SUPERBOY, THE
Jan, 1980 - Present
DC Comics

	Good	Fine	Mint
1		.60	1.20
2-5		.50	1.00
6-10		.40	.80
11-24: 15-Superboy gets new parents		.30	.60

NOTE: *Schaffenberger c-1p. Starlin a-7.*

NEW ADVENTURES OF THE PHANTOM BLOT, THE (See Phantom Blot, The)

NEW BOOK OF COMICS
1936; Spring, 1938 (100 pgs.) (Reprints)
National Periodical Publications

	Good	Fine	Mint
1(Rare)-Contains r-New Comics, New Fun & More Fun; Moldoff-a	40.00	120.00	240.00
2-Dr. Occult by Siegel & Shuster(in costume-a Superman prototype); No. 1 & 2 r-/New Comics & More Fun	30.00	80.00	160.00

NEW COMICS (New Adventure No. 12 on)
Dec, 1935 - No. 11, Dec, 1936 (No. 1-6, soft cover)
National Periodical Publications

	Good	Fine	Mint
V1No.1-Billy the Kid, Sagebrush 'n' Cactus, Jibby Jones, Needles, The Vikings, Sir Loin of Beef, Now-When I Was a Boy, & other 1-2 pg. strips; 2 pgs. Kelly art(1st)-(Gulliver's Travels)	150.00	400.00	850.00
2-Federal Men by Siegel & Shuster begins	70.00	200.00	425.00
3-6	40.00	110.00	225.00
7-11	25.00	70.00	140.00

NOTE: *No. 1-6 rarely occur in mint condition.*

NEW FUN COMICS (More Fun No. 7 on)
Feb, 1935 - No. 6, Oct, 1935 (Large size, No. 3-6-slick covers)
National Periodical Publications

	Good	Fine	Mint
V1No.1 (1st DC comic)-Paper-c	175.00	450.00	900.00
2(3/35)-(Very Rare)-Paper-c	90.00	260.00	550.00
3-5(8/35)	50.00	150.00	325.00
6(10/35)-1st Dr. Occult by Siegel & Shuster(Leger & Reuths); Walt Kelly-a, 1 pg.; last ''New Fun'' title. ''New Comics'' No. 1 begins in Dec. which is reason for title change to More Fun; Henri Duval (ends No. 9) by Siegel & Shuster begins	80.00	220.00	450.00

NEW FUNNIES (The Funnies, No. 1-64; Walter Lantz . . ., No. 109 on; No. 259,260,272,273-New TV . . .; No. 261-271-TV Funnies)
No. 65, July, 1942 - No. 288, Mar-Apr, 1962
Dell Publishing Co.

	Good	Fine	Mint
65(No.1)-Andy Panda, Raggedy Ann, Oswald the Rabbit, & Li'l Eight Ball begin	40.00	100.00	200.00
66-70: 67-Billy & Bonnie Bee by Frank Thomas begins. 69-2pg. Kelly-a	14.00	40.00	80.00
71,74-Brownies by Kelly	10.00	30.00	60.00
72,73,75: 72-Kelly illos	8.00	24.00	48.00
76-Andy Panda (Carl Barks & Pabian art); Brownies by Kelly; Woody Woodpecker app. in Oswald story	80.00	200.00	400.00
77-Brownies by Kelly	9.00	25.00	50.00
78,79-Andy Panda in a World of Real People ends, becomes all funny animal	7.00	20.00	40.00
80-82	7.00	20.00	40.00
83-85-Kelly text illos	6.00	18.00	36.00
86-90	3.00	8.00	16.00
91-100	2.00	5.00	10.00
101-120	1.20	3.50	7.00
121-150	.60	1.80	3.60
151-200: 182-Origin & 1st app. Nuthead & Splinter	.40	1.20	2.40
201-288		.60	1.20

NOTE: *Early issues written by **John Stanley**.*

NEW GODS, THE (Orion of. . . No. 2,3; Return of. . ., No. 12 on) (See Adventure, First Issue Spec., & Super-Team Family)
2-3/71 - No. 11, 10-11/72; No. 12, 7/77 - No. 19, 7-8/78
National Periodical Publications/DC Comics

	Good	Fine	Mint
1	1.00	3.00	6.00
2	.70	2.00	4.00
3,4-Origin Manhunter reprinted in No. 4	.50	1.50	3.00
5-8: 5-Young Gods feature. 7-Origin Orion. 7,8-Young Gods app.	.40	1.20	2.40
9-11	.35	1.10	2.20
12-14,16-19-Newton/Atkins-a		.50	1.00
15		.40	.80

NOTE: *No. 4-9 contain Manhunter reprints by **Simon & Kirby** from Adventure No. 73,74,75,76,77,78 in that order. **Kirby** c/a-1-11. **Starlin** c-17. **Staton** c-19.*

NEW HEROIC (See Heroic)

NEWLYWEDS
1907; 1917 (cardboard covers)
Saalfield Publ. Co.

	Good	Fine	Mint
. . .'& Their Baby' by McManus; Saalfield, 1907, 13x10'', 57pgs. daily strips in full color	20.00	50.00	100.00
. . .'& Their Baby's Comic Pictures, The', by McManus, Saalfield, 1917, 14x10'', 22pgs, oblong, cardboard covers. Reprints 'Newlyweds' (Baby Snookums strips) mainly from 1916; blue cover; says for painting and crayoning, but some pages in color. (Scarce)	14.00	40.00	80.00

NEW MEN OF BATTLE, THE
1949 (nn) (Cardboard covers)
Catechetical Guild

	Good	Fine	Mint
nn(V8No.1-V8No.6)-192 pgs.; contains 6 issues of Topix rebound	2.00	6.00	12.00
nn(V8No.7-V8No.11)-160 pgs.; contains 5 issues of Topix	2.00	6.00	12.00

NEW MICKEY MOUSE CLUB FUN BOOK, THE
October, 1977 ($1.95) (224 pgs.; cardboard covers)
Golden Press

	Good	Fine	Mint
11190-Reprints/Silly Symphonies No. 2,3,7,8, Mickey Mouse No. 92,100, 4-Color No. 614,842, & Mickey Mouse Club Magazine No. 1	.50	1.50	3.00

NEW PEOPLE, THE (TV)
Jan, 1970 - No. 2, May, 1970
Dell Publishing Co.

	Good	Fine	Mint
1,2	.70	2.00	4.00

NEW ROMANCES
No. 5, May, 1951 - No. 20, Feb, 1954
Standard Comics

	Good	Fine	Mint
5-9	1.50	4.00	8.00
10,11,14,16,17-Toth-a	3.00	9.00	18.00

NEW ROMANCES (continued) — Good / Fine / Mint

12,13,15,18-20 .85 2.50 5.00

NOTE: ***Celardo** a-9.* ***Moreira** a-6.* ***Tuska** a-7,20.*

NEW TEEN TITANS, THE (See DC Comics Presents No. 26)
November, 1980 - Present
DC Comics

	Good	Fine	Mint
1-Robin, Kid Flash, Wonder Girl, The Changeling, Starfire, The Raven, Cyborg begin; partial origin	2.50	7.50	15.00
2	1.50	4.00	8.00
3-Origin Starfire; Intro The Fearsome 5	1.00	3.00	6.00
4-Origin continues; J.L.A. app.	1.00	3.00	6.00
5-10: 6-Raven origin. 7-Cyborg origin. 8-Origin Kid Flash retold. 10-Origin Changeling retold	.50	1.50	3.00
11-14	.25	.75	1.50

NOTE: ***Perez** a-1-4p, 6-14p; c-1-13, 14p..*

NEW TERRYTOONS (TV)
6-8/60 - No. 8, 3-5/62; 10/62 - No. 54, 1/79
Dell Publishing Co./Gold Key

	Good	Fine	Mint
1('60-Dell)-Deputy Dawg begins	1.50	4.00	8.00
2-8('62)	.70	2.00	4.00
1(30010-210)(3/62-G.Key, 84 pgs.)-Heckle & Jeckle begins	.35	1.00	2.00
2(30010-301)-84 pgs.(Exist?)		.60	1.20
3-16		.40	.80
17-54		.30	.60

NOTE: *Reprints: No. 4-12,38,40,47. (See March of Comics No. 393, 412)*

NEW TESTAMENT STORIES VISUALIZED
1946 - 1947
Standard Publishing Co.

''New Testament Heroes—Acts of Apostles Visualized, Book I''
''New Testament Heroes—Acts of Apostles Visualized, Book II''
''Parables Jesus Told'' Set.... 10.00 30.00 60.00

NOTE: *All three are contained in a cardboard case, illustrated on front and info about the set.*

NEW TV FUNNIES (See New Funnies)

NEW YORK GIANTS (See Thrilling True Story of the Baseball Giants)

NEW YORK STATE JOINT LEGISLATIVE COMMITTEE TO STUDY THE PUBLICATION OF COMICS, THE
1951
N. Y. State Legislative Document

This document was referenced by Wertham for **Seduction of the Innocent**. Contains numerous repros from comics showing violence, sadism, torture, and sex.

NEW YORK WORLD'S FAIR
1939, 1940 (100 pages) (Cardboard covers)
National Periodical Publications

	Good	Fine	Mint
1939-Scoop Scanlon, Superman, Sandman, Zatara, Slam Bradley, Ginger Snap by Bob Kane begin	150.00	435.00	875.00
1940-Batman, Hourman, Johnny Thunderbolt app.	90.00	250.00	510.00

NOTE: The 1939 edition was published at 25 cents. Since all other comics were 10 cents, it didn't sell. Remaining copies were repriced with 15 cents stickers placed over the 25 cents price. Four variations on the 15 cents stickers known. It was advertised in other DC comics at 25 cents. Everyone who sent a quarter through the mail for it received a free Superman No. 1 or No. 2 to make up the dime difference. The 1940 edition was priced at 15 cents.

NICKEL COMICS
1938 (Pocket size - 7½x5½'') (132 pages)
Dell Publishing Co.

	Good	Fine	Mint
1-''Bobby & Chip'' by Otto Messmer, Felix the Cat artist. Contains some English reprints	14.00	40.00	80.00

NICKEL COMICS
May, 1940 - No. 8, Aug, 1940 (36 pgs.) (Bi-Weekly) (5 cents)
Fawcett Publications

	Good	Fine	Mint
1-Origin Bulletman	55.00	160.00	320.00
2	30.00	90.00	170.00
3	25.00	70.00	130.00
4-The Red Gaucho begins	20.00	60.00	120.00
5-8: 5-Bondage-c	17.00	50.00	100.00

NOTE: *Covers on some issues by **C. C. Beck**. **Jack Binder** cover-No.1.*

NICK FURY, AGENT OF SHIELD (See Shield)
June, 1968 - No. 18, March, 1971
Marvel Comics Group

	Good	Fine	Mint
1	1.50	4.00	8.00
2,3	1.00	3.00	6.00
4-Origin retold	.85	2.50	5.00
5-Steranko c/a	.85	2.50	5.00
6,7-Steranko-c	.70	2.00	4.00
8-11: 9-Hate Monger begins (ends No. 11). 11-Smith-c	.35	1.10	2.20
12-Smith c/a	.55	1.60	3.20
13-15	.30	.80	1.60
16-18-All reprints; 52 pgs.		.50	1.00

NOTE: ***Craig** a-10i.* ***Kirby** a-18r.* ***Steranko** a-1-3, 5; c-1-7.*

NICK HALIDAY
May, 1956
Argo

	Good	Fine	Mint
1-Daily & Sunday strip-r by Petree	2.50	7.00	14.00

NIGHT BEFORE CHRISTMAS, THE (See March of Comics No. 152)

NIGHTINGALE, THE
1948 (14pgs., 7¼x10¼'', ½B&W) (10 cents)
Henry H. Stansbury Once-A-Time Press, Inc.

(Very Rare)-low distribution; distributed to Weschester county & Bronx, N.Y. only; used in **Seduction of the Innocent**, pg. 312,313 as the 1st and only ''good'' comic book ever published; ill. by Dong Kingman; 1,500 words of text, printed on high quality paper & no word balloons. Copyright registered 10/22/48, distributed week of 12/5/48. (by Hans Christian Andersen) Estimated value... 100.00

NIGHTMARE
Summer, 1952 - No. 2, Fall, 1952; No. 3,4, 1953
Ziff-Davis (Approved Comics)/St. John No. 3,4

	Good	Fine	Mint
1-1pg. Kinstler-a	8.00	24.00	48.00
2-Kinstler-a-Poe's ''Pit & the Pendulum;''	5.50	18.00	36.00
3-Kinstler-a	5.50	16.00	32.00
4	5.00	14.00	28.00

NOTE: *All have painted covers.*

NIGHTMARE (Formerly Weird Horrors No. 1-9) (Amazing Ghost Stories No. 14 on)
No. 10, Dec, 1953 - No. 13, Aug, 1954
St. John Publishing Co.

	Good	Fine	Mint
10-Reprints Ziff-Davis Weird Thrillers No. 2 with new Kubert-c plus 2 pgs. Kinstler, & Toth-a	10.00	27.00	54.00
11-Krigstein-a	6.00	18.00	36.00
12-Kubert bondage-c; adaptation of Poe's 'The Black Cat;' Cannibalism story	4.50	13.00	26.00
13-Reprints Z-D Weird Thrillers No. 3 with new cover; Powell-a(2), Tuska-a	3.00	9.00	18.00

NOTE: ***Anderson** a-10, 11.* ***Colan** a-10.*

NIGHTMARE (Magazine)
Dec, 1970 - No. 23, Feb, 1975 (B&W) (68 pages)
Skywald Publishing Corp.

	Good	Fine	Mint
1-Everett-a	.50	1.50	3.00
2-5	.35	1.10	2.20
6-Kaluta-a	.50	1.50	3.00

New Teen Titans #3, © DC

Nick Fury #7, © MCG

Nightmare #11, © STJ

Noman #2, © TC

Not Brand Echh #4, © MCG

Nova #20, © MCG

NIGHTMARE (continued)

	Good	Fine	Mint
7,9,10	.35	1.10	2.20
8-Features E. C. movie ''Tales From the Crypt;'' reprints some E. C. comics panels	1.00	3.00	6.00
11-20		.40	.80
21-(1974 Summer Special)-Kaluta-a	.30	.90	1.80
22-Tomb of Horror issue		.50	1.00
23-(1975 Winter Special)		.50	1.00
Annual 1(1972)	.30	.80	1.60
Winter Special 1(1973)	.30	.80	1.60
Yearbook-nn(1974)		.50	1.00

NOTE: ***Adkins*** *a-5.* ***Boris*** *c-2, 5.* ***Everett*** *a-5.* ***Jones*** *a-6, 21; c-6.* ***Wildey*** *a-6, '74 Yearbook.* ***Wrightson*** *a-9.*

NIGHTMARE & CASPER (See Harvey Hits No. 71) (Casper & Nightmare No. 6 on)
Aug, 1963 - No. 5, Aug, 1964 (25 cents)
Harvey Publications

	Good	Fine	Mint
1	5.50	16.00	32.00
2-5	2.50	7.00	14.00

NIGHTMARES (See Do You Believe in . . .)

NIGHT NURSE
Nov, 1972 - No. 4, May, 1973
Marvel Comics Group

	Good	Fine	Mint
1-4		.50	1.00

NIGHT OF MYSTERY
1953 (no month) (One Shot)
Avon Periodicals

	Good	Fine	Mint
nn-1pg. Kinstler-a, Hollingsworth-c	7.00	20.00	40.00

NIGHT OF THE GRIZZLY, THE (See Movie Classics)

NIGHT RIDER
Oct, 1974 - No. 6, Aug, 1975
Marvel Comics Group

	Good	Fine	Mint
1		.50	1.00
2-6		.30	.60

NOTE: *No. 1-6 reprints Ghost Rider No. 1-6.*

NIKKI, WILD DOG OF THE NORTH (See 4-Color No. 1226 & Movie Comics)

1984 (Magazine) (1994 No. 11 on)
June, 1978 - No. 10, Jan, 1980 ($1.50)
Warren Publishing Co.

	Good	Fine	Mint
1	.50	1.50	3.00
2-10	.30	.90	1.80

NOTE: ***Alacla*** *a-1-3.* ***Corben*** *a-1-8; c-1,2.* ***Nino*** *a-1-10, 20(2).* ***Thorne*** *a-7-10.* ***Wood*** *a-1, 2, 5i.*

1994 (Formerly 1984) (Magazine)
No. 11, Feb, 1980 - Present
Warren Publishing Co.

	Good	Fine	Mint
11-20	.30	.80	1.60

NOTE: ***Nino*** *a-11-21; c-21.* ***Redondo*** *c-20.* ***Thorne*** *a-11-14, 17-21.*

NIPPY'S POP
1917 (Sunday strip reprints-B&W) (10½x13½'')
The Saalfield Publishing Co.

	Good	Fine	Mint
32 pages	3.50	10.00	20.00

NOAH'S ARK
1973 (35-49 Cents)
Spire Christian Comics/Fleming H. Revell Co.

	Good	Fine	Mint
By Al Hartley		.40	.80

NOMAN
Nov, 1966 - No. 2, March, 1967
Tower Comics

	Good	Fine	Mint
1-Wood/Williamson-c; Lightning begins; Dynamo cameo; Kane-a(p)	.85	2.50	5.00
2-Wood-c only; Dynamo x-over; Whitney-a-No. 1,2	.70	2.00	4.00

NONE BUT THE BRAVE (See Movie Classics)

NOODNIK COMICS (See Pinky the Egghead)
1953; No. 2, Feb, 1954 - No. 5, Aug, 1954
Comic Media/Mystery/Biltmore

	Good	Fine	Mint
3-D(1953-Comic Media)(No.1)	8.00	24.00	48.00
2-5	1.20	3.50	7.00

NORTH TO ALASKA (See 4-Color No. 1155)

NORTHWEST MOUNTIES (Also see Approved Comics)
Oct, 1948 - No. 4, July, 1949
Jubilee Publications/St. John

	Good	Fine	Mint
1-Rose of the Yukon by Matt Baker; Walter Johnson-a	9.00	25.00	50.00
2-Baker-a; Ventrilo app.	8.00	22.00	44.00
3-Bondage-c, Baker-a; Sky Chief, K-9 app.	9.00	25.00	50.00
4-Baker-c, 2 pgs.; Blue Monk app; 2pg. opium story	8.00	22.00	44.00

NO SLEEP 'TIL DAWN (See 4-Color No. 831)

NOT BRAND ECHH
Aug, 1967 - No. 13, May, 1969 (No. 9-13: 68 pages)
Marvel Comics Group

	Good	Fine	Mint
1	1.50	4.00	8.00
2-4: 3-Origin Thor, Hulk & Capt. America; Beatles, Alfred E. Neuman cameo. 4-X-Men app.	.85	2.50	5.00
5-Origin & intro. Forbush Man	.70	2.00	4.00
6-8: 7-Origin Fantastic-4 & Superman; Nixon/Reagan cameo. 8-Beatles cameo	.70	2.00	4.00
9-13-All Giants. 9-Beatles cameo. 10-All-r; The Old Witch, Crypt Keeper & Vault Keeper cameos. 12,13-Beatles cameo, Avengers satire No. 12	.35	1.00	2.00

NOTE: ***Kirby*** *a-1,3,5-7,10; c-1. Archie satire-No. 9.*

NO TIME FOR SERGEANTS (TV)
July, 1958 - No. 3, Aug-Oct, 1965
Dell Publishing Co.

	Good	Fine	Mint
4-Color 914 (Movie)	1.20	3.50	7.00
1(2-4/65)-3 (TV)	.70	2.00	4.00

NOVA
Sept, 1976 - No. 25, May, 1979
Marvel Comics Group

	Good	Fine	Mint
1-Origin	.85	2.50	5.00
2,3	.40	1.20	2.40
4-Thor app.	.30	.80	1.60
5-Marvel Gang app.		.50	1.00
6-10		.50	1.00
11,13,14,19		.40	.80
12-Spider-Man x-over		.40	.80
15-18-Nick Fury & Shield app.		.40	.80
20-Reveals I.D. to family		.40	.80
21-25: 21,22-The Comet (MLJ) app.; Nova reveals I.D. to family		.40	.80

NOTE: ***Austin*** *c-21i.* ***John Buscema*** *a-1p, 2, 21; c-1p, 2, 15.* ***Infantino*** *a-15-20, 22, 23; c-17-20, 21p.* ***Kirby*** *c-5, 7.*

NOW AGE ILLUSTRATED (See Pendulum Ill. Classics)

NUKLA
Oct-Dec, 1965 - No. 4, Sept, 1966
Dell Publishing Co.

	Good	Fine	Mint
1-Origin Nukla	.85	2.50	5.00
2,3	.50	1.50	3.00
4-Ditko-a	.70	2.00	4.00

NURSE BETSY CRANE (Formerly Teen Secret Diary)
Aug, 1961 - No. 27, Mar, 1964
Charlton Comics

	Good	Fine	Mint
V2No.12-27		.50	1.00

NURSE HELEN GRANT (See The Romances of. . .)

NURSE LINDA LARK (See Linda Lark)

NURSERY RHYMES
1950 - No. 10, July-Aug, 1951
Ziff-Davis Publ. Co. (Approved Comics)

	Good	Fine	Mint
2	3.00	8.00	16.00
3-10: 10-Howie Post-a	2.00	5.00	10.00

NURSES, THE (TV)
April, 1963 - No. 3, Oct, 1963
Gold Key

	Good	Fine	Mint
1	.70	2.00	4.00
2,3	.50	1.50	3.00

NUTRA-CHILD (Also see World's Greatest Super Heroes)
December, 1976 (8x8'')
Vitamin Giveaway

	Good	Fine	Mint
Neal Adams c/a	.30	.80	1.60

NUTS! (Satire)
March, 1954 - No. 5, Nov, 1954
Premiere Comics Group

	Good	Fine	Mint
1	4.00	12.00	24.00
2,4,5: 5-Capt. Marvel parody	3.00	9.00	18.00
3-Drug ''reefers'' mentioned	4.00	12.00	24.00

NUTS (Magazine) (Satire)
Feb, 1958 - No. 2, April, 1958
Health Knowledge

	Good	Fine	Mint
1	2.00	6.00	12.00
2	1.50	4.00	8.00

NUTS & JOLTS (See Black & White No. 22)

NUTSY SQUIRREL (Formerly Hollywood Funny Folks)
No. 61, 9-10/54 - No. 69, 1-2/56; No. 70, 8-9/56 - No. 71, 10-11/56; No. 72, 11/57
National Periodical Publications

	Good	Fine	Mint
61-72	.70	2.00	4.00

NUTTY COMICS
Winter, 1946
Fawcett Publications

	Good	Fine	Mint
1-Capt. Kidd story; 1pg. Wolverton-a	5.00	15.00	30.00

NUTTY COMICS
1945 - No. 8, June-July, 1947
Harvey Publications (Home Comics)

	Good	Fine	Mint
nn-Helpful Hank, Bozo Bear & others	1.00	3.00	6.00
2-4	.80	2.30	4.60
5-8: 5-Rags Rabbit begins	.80	2.30	4.60

NUTTY LIFE
No. 2, Summer, 1946
Fox Features Syndicate

	Good	Fine	Mint
2	2.00	6.00	12.00

NYOKA, THE JUNGLE GIRL (Formerly Jungle Girl)
No. 2, Winter, 1945 - No. 77, June, 1953
Fawcett Publications

	Good	Fine	Mint
2	20.00	60.00	120.00
3	12.00	35.00	70.00
4,5-Bondage-c both	9.00	25.00	50.00
6-10	7.00	20.00	40.00
11,13,14,17,18-Krigstein-a	8.00	24.00	48.00
12,15,16,19,20	6.00	18.00	36.00
21-30	4.00	12.00	24.00
31-40	3.00	8.00	16.00
41-50	2.50	7.00	14.00
51-60	2.00	6.00	12.00
61-77	1.50	4.00	8.00

NYOKA, THE JUNGLE GIRL (Space Adventures No. 23 on?; also see Zoo Funnies)
No. 9,10; No. 11, May, 1955 - No. 22, Nov, 1957
Charlton Comics

	Good	Fine	Mint
9-22	1.50	4.00	8.00

OAKEY DOAKES
July, 1942 (One Shot)
Eastern Color Printing Co.

	Good	Fine	Mint
1	8.00	24.00	48.00

OAKLAND PRESS FUNNYBOOK, THE
9/17/78 - Present (16 pgs.) (Weekly)
(Full color in comic book form)
The Oakland Press

	Good	Fine	Mint
Contains Tarzan by Manning, Marmaduke, Bugs Bunny, etc. (low distribution)	.30	.80	1.60

OBIE
1953 (6 cents)
Store Comics

	Good	Fine	Mint
1	.70	2.00	4.00

OCCULT FILES OF DOCTOR SPEKTOR, THE
May, 1973 - No. 24, Feb, 1977
Gold Key

	Good	Fine	Mint
1-1st app. Lakota; Baron Tibor begins	.30	.90	1.80
2-5: 3-Ra-Ka-Tep, the Mummy begins. 4-Intro. Elliott Kane; Duroc (later called Durak) app. 5-Hyde begins; 1st app. Count Dracula		.60	1.20
6-10: 6-Origin Simbar, the Lion Lord; 1st app. Frankenstein Monster. 7-Flashbacks to Tragg No. 8 & Dagar No. 1; establishes blood-link between Tragg, Dagar, & Spektor. 8-1st app. Cindy Bask (Kane's girlfriend). 9-Kareena app. 10-Origin Dark Gods		.50	1.00
11-13: 11-1st app. Spektor as Werewolf. 12-1st app. Dr. Tong & Lu-Sai		.50	1.00
14-Dr. Solar app.		.50	1.00
15-17: 15-Baron Tibor dies. 16-Durak app. 17-1st app. Anne Sara, Spektor's cousin		.40	.80
18-22,24		.40	.80
23-Dr. Solar cameo		.30	.60
9(Modern Comics reprint, 1977)		.15	.30

NOTE: *Also see Dan Curtis, Golden Comics Digest 33, Mystery Comics Digest 5, & Spine Tingling Tales.*

ODELL'S ADVENTURES IN 3-D (See Adventures in. . .)

OFFICIAL SOUPY SALES COMIC (See Soupy Sales)

OFFICIAL TRUE CRIME CASES (Formerly All-Winner No. 21; All-True Crime Cases No. 26 on)
No. 22, Spring, 1947 - No. 25, Winter, 1947-48
Timely/Marvel (OCI)

	Good	Fine	Mint
22-25: 24-Burgos-a	2.00	5.00	10.00

O.G. WHIZ
2/71 - No. 6, 5/72; No. 7, 5/78 - No. 11, 1/79
Gold Key

	Good	Fine	Mint
1,2-John Stanley script, pencils, inks, & lettering	3.00	8.00	16.00
3-6(1972)	1.50	4.00	8.00
7-11(1978-1979): 11-Reprints	.35	1.00	3.00

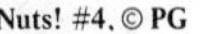
Nuts! #4, © PG

Nyoka #4, © FAW

O.F.O. Dr. Spektor #14, © GK

Oklahoma Kid #1, © AJAX

Omac #8, © DC

Omega The Unknown #2, © MCG

OH, BROTHER! (Teen Comedy)
Jan, 1953 - No. 5, Oct, 1953
Stanhall Publ./Trojan/Standard No. 5

	Good	Fine	Mint
1	.85	2.50	5.00
2-5	.70	2.00	4.00

OH SUSANNA (See 4-Color No. 1105)

OKAY COMICS
July, 1940
United Features Syndicate

	Good	Fine	Mint
1-Captain & the Kids & Hawkshaw the Detective reprints	8.00	24.00	48.00

OK COMICS
July, 1940 - No. 2, Oct, 1940
United Features Syndicate

	Good	Fine	Mint
1-Little Giant, Phantom Knight, Sunset Smith, & The Teller Twins begin	12.00	35.00	75.00
2 (Rare)-Origin Mister Mist	12.00	35.00	75.00

OKLAHOMA KID
June, 1957 - No. 4, 1958
Ajax/Farrell Publ.

	Good	Fine	Mint
1	2.00	5.00	10.00
2-4	.85	2.50	5.00

OKLAHOMAN, THE (See 4-Color No. 820)

OLD GLORY COMICS
1944 (Giveaway)
Chesapeake & Ohio Railway

	Good	Fine	Mint
Capt. Fearless reprint	2.50	7.00	14.00

OLD IRONSIDES (See 4-Color No. 874)

OLD YELLER (See 4-Color No. 869, Movie Comics, and Walt Disney Showcase No. 25)

OMAC (One Man Army, . . . Corps. No. 4 on)
Sept-Oct, 1974 - No. 8, Nov-Dec, 1975
National Periodical Publications

	Good	Fine	Mint
1-Origin		.60	1.20
2-8: 8-2pg. Adams ad		.30	.60

NOTE: ***Kirby*** *a-1-8; c-1-7.* ***Kubert*** *c-8. See Kamandi No. 59 & Cancelled Comic Cavalcade.*

O'MALLEY AND THE ALLEY CATS
April, 1971 - No. 9, Jan, 1974 (Disney)
Gold Key

	Good	Fine	Mint
1	.50	1.50	3.00
2-9	.30	.80	1.60

OMEGA THE UNKNOWN
March, 1976 - No. 10, Oct, 1977
Marvel Comics Group

	Good	Fine	Mint
1	.30	.80	1.60
2-10: 2-Hulk app.		.40	.80

ONE HUNDRED AND ONE DALMATIANS (See 4-Color No. 1183, Movie Comics, and Walt Disney Showcase No. 9)

100 PAGES OF COMICS
1937 (Stiff covers)
Dell Publishing Co.

	Good	Fine	Mint
101(Found on back cover)-Alley Oop, Wash Tubbs, Capt. Easy, Og Son of Fire, Apple Mary, Tom Mix, Dan Dunn, Tailspin Tommy, Doctor Doom	25.00	75.00	150.00

100-PAGE SUPER SPECTACULAR (See DC. . .)

$1,000,000 DUCK (See Walt Disney Showcase No. 5)

ONE MILLION YEARS AGO (Tor No. 2 on)
September, 1953
St. John Publishing Co.

	Good	Fine	Mint
1-Origin; Kubert-a	20.00	60.00	120.00

ONE SHOT (See 4-Color. . .)

1001 HOURS OF FUN
1942 (52 pgs.; 11¼x8-3/8'')(Like Large Feature Comics)
Dell Publishing Co.

	Good	Fine	Mint
Puzzles & games; by A. W. Nugent	5.00	15.00	30.00

ON STAGE (See 4-Color No. 1336)

ON THE AIR
1947 (Giveaway) (paper cover)
NBC Network Comic

	Good	Fine	Mint
(Rare)	5.00	15.00	30.00

ON THE DOUBLE (See 4-Color No. 1232)

ON THE LINKS
December, 1926 (48 pages) (9x10'')
Associated Feature Service

	Good	Fine	Mint
Daily strip-r	5.00	14.00	28.00

ON THE ROAD WITH ANDRAE CROUCH
1973, 1977 (39 cents)
Spire Christian Comics (Fleming H. Revell)

	Good	Fine	Mint
nn		.50	1.00

ON THE SPOT (Pretty Boy Floyd. . .)
Fall, 1948
Fawcett Publications

	Good	Fine	Mint
nn-Bondage-c	7.00	20.00	40.00

OPERATION BIKINI (See Movie Classics)

OPERATION BUCHAREST (See The Crusaders)

OPERATION CROSSBOW (See Movie Classics)

OPERATION PERIL
Oct-Nov, 1950 - 1953
American Comics Group (Michel Publ.)

	Good	Fine	Mint
1-Time Travelers, Danny Danger (by Leonard Starr) & Typhoon Tyler (by Ogden Whitney) begin	3.50	10.00	20.00
2-5: 3-Horror story	2.50	7.00	14.00
6-12-Last Time Travelers; change to war format	2.00	5.00	10.00
13-16	1.50	4.00	8.00

NOTE: ***Whitney*** *a-1,2,8-10; c-1,8,9.*

ORAL ROBERTS' TRUE STORIES (Junior Partners No. 120 on)
1956 (no month) - No. 119, 7/59 (15 cents)(No No., 102: 25 cents)
TelePix Publ. (Oral Roberts' Evangelistic Assoc./Healing Waters)

	Good	Fine	Mint
V1No.1(1956)-(Not code approved)-''The Miracle Touch''	4.00	12.00	24.00
102-(only issue approved by code)(10/56)	3.00	8.00	16.00
103-119: 115-(114 on inside)	1.50	4.00	8.00

NOTE: *Also see Happiness & Healing For You.*

ORANGE BIRD, THE
No date (1980) (36 pgs.; in color; slick cover)
Walt Disney Educational Media Co.

	Good	Fine	Mint
Included with educational kit on foods		.30	.60

ORIGINAL SWAMP THING SAGA, THE (See DC Spec. Series No.2,14)

OSCAR (Formerly Animated Funny Comic Tunes; Awful. . .No. 12 on)
No. 24, Spring, 1947 - No. 11, June, 1949
Marvel Comics

	Good	Fine	Mint
24(1947)	1.20	3.50	7.00
25(9/47)-Wolverton-a plus Kurtzman's ''Hey Look''	4.00	12.00	24.00
3-9,11	.85	2.50	5.00
10-Kurtzman's ''Hey Look''	2.50	7.00	14.00

OSWALD THE RABBIT
1943 - 1962 (Walter Lantz)
Dell Publishing Co.

	Good	Fine	Mint
4-Color 21(1943)	14.00	40.00	80.00
4-Color 39(1943)	10.00	30.00	60.00
4-Color 67(1944)	7.00	20.00	40.00
4-Color 102(1946)-Kelly-a, 1 pg.	7.00	20.00	40.00
4-Color 143,183	3.00	8.00	16.00
4-Color 225,273	2.00	5.00	10.00
4-Color 315,388	1.00	3.00	6.00
4-Color 458,507,549,593	.70	2.00	4.00
4-Color 623,697,792,894,979,1268	.50	1.50	3.00

OSWALD THE RABBIT (See March of Comics No. 7,38,53,67,81,95, 111,126,141,156,171,186, & Super Book No. 8,20)

OUR ARMY AT WAR (Sgt. Rock No. 302 on)
Aug, 1952 - No. 301, Feb, 1977
National Periodical Publications

	Good	Fine	Mint
1	20.00	60.00	120.00
2	9.00	27.00	54.00
3	9.00	27.00	54.00
4-Krigstein-a	10.00	30.00	60.00
5-7	5.00	14.00	28.00
8-10-Krigstein-a	5.50	16.00	32.00
11,14-Krigstein-a	5.50	16.00	32.00
12,15-20	3.50	10.00	20.00
13-Krigstein c/a	5.50	16.00	32.00
21-30	3.00	8.00	16.00
31-40	2.00	6.00	12.00
41-60	1.75	5.00	10.00
61-70	1.00	3.00	6.00
71-80	.85	2.50	5.00
81-1st Sgt. Rock app. by Andru & Esposito in Easy Co. story	14.00	40.00	80.00
82-Sgt. Rock cameo in Easy Co. story (6 panels)	5.00	15.00	30.00
83-1st Kubert Sgt. Rock	8.00	24.00	48.00
84,86-90	3.00	9.00	18.00
85-1st app. & origin Ice Cream Soldier	2.75	8.00	20.00
91-All Sgt. Rock issue	3.50	10.00	20.00
92-100	1.20	3.50	7.00
101-120: 103-1st app. Bulldozer & Zack. 113-1st app. Jackie Johnson. 120-1st app. Wildman	1.00	3.00	6.00
121-127,129-150: 135-1st app. Canary. 139-1st app. Little Sure Shot	.70	2.00	4.00
128-Training & origin Sgt. Rock	1.00	3.00	6.00
151-Intro. Enemy Ace by Kubert	1.00	3.00	6.00
152-157,159-163,165-170: 153,155-Enemy Ace stories. 157-Two pg. pin-up. 162,163-Viking Prince x-over in Sgt. Rock	.80	2.40	4.80
158-1st app. & origin Iron Mator(1965)	1.00	3.00	6.00
164-Giant G-19	1.00	3.00	6.00
171-176,178-181	.30	.80	1.60
177-(80 pg. Giant G-32)	.35	1.00	2.00
182,183,186-Adams-a; 186-Origin retold	.80	2.40	4.80
184,185,187-189,191-199: 189-Intro. The Teen-age Underground Fighters of Unit 3		.50	1.00
190-(80 pg. Giant G-44)	.30	.80	1.60
200-12 pg. Rock story told in verse; Evans-a		.50	1.00
201-Krigstein-r/No. 14		.50	1.00
202,206-215		.40	.80
203-(80 pg. Giant G-56)-All-r, no Sgt. Rock		.60	1.20
204,205-All-r, no Sgt. Rock		.40	.80
216-(80 pg. Giant G-68)		.60	1.20
217-228		.40	.80
229-(80 pg. Giant G-80)		.60	1.20
230-234,236-239		.30	.60
235,241-Toth-a		.50	1.00
240-Adams-a	.30	.80	1.60
242-(50 cents ish. DC-9)-Kubert-c	.30	.80	1.60
243-248,250-253		.30	.60
249-Wood-a		.60	1.20
254-Toth-a		.40	.80
255-301		.30	.60

NOTE: ***Alcala** a-251. **Drucker** a-27, 67, 68, 79, 82, 83, 96, 164, 177, 203, 212, 244, 269, 275, 280. **Evans** a-165-175, 200, 266, 269, 270, 274, 276, 278, 280. **Kubert** a-38,59, 67, 68 & most issues from 83 on. Medal of Honor by **Maurer**-233, 237, 239, 240, 280, 284, 288, 290, 291, 295. U.S.S. Stevens by **Glanzman**-218, 220, 222, 223, 225, 227, 230-232, 238, 240, 241, 244, 247, 248, 256-259, 261, 265-267, 271, 282, 283, 298.*

OUR FIGHTING FORCES
Oct-Nov, 1954 - No. 181, Sept-Oct, 1978
National Periodical Publications/DC Comics

	Good	Fine	Mint
1-Grandenetti c/a	15.00	45.00	90.00
2	8.00	24.00	48.00
3-Kubert c	7.00	20.00	40.00
4,5	5.00	14.00	28.00
6-9	3.50	10.00	20.00
10-Wood-a	6.00	18.00	36.00
11-20	2.50	7.00	14.00
21-30	2.00	5.00	10.00
31-40	1.50	4.00	8.00
41-44	1.00	3.00	6.00
45-Gunner & Sarge begin (ends No. 94)	7.00	20.00	40.00
46-50	.70	2.00	4.00
51-90	.55	1.60	3.20
91-100: 95-Devil-Dog begins, ends No. 98. 99-Capt. Hunter begins, ends No. 106	.35	1.00	2.00
101-122: 106-Hunters Hellcats begin. 116-Mlle. Marie app. 121-Intro. Heller		.50	1.00
123-Losers (Capt. Storm, Gunner/Sarge, Johnny Cloud) begin		.40	.80
124-133,135-145		.30	.60
134,146-Toth-a		.30	.60
147-181		.30	.60

NOTE: ***Adams** c-147. **Drucker** a-39, 42, 43. **Evans** a-149, 165-173(Losers), 177-181. **Heath** a-2, 16, 18. **Infantino** a-135. **Kirby** a-151-162; c-152-159. **Kubert** art in many issues. **Redondo** a-166. Medal of Honor by **Maurer**-No. 135. U.S.S. Stevens by **Glanzman**-No. 125-128, 134, 138-141, 143, 144.*

OUR FIGHTING MEN IN ACTION
1957 - 1958
Ajax/Farrell Publ. (Four Star Comic Corp.)

	Good	Fine	Mint
1	1.20	3.50	7.00
2-6: 3-Kiefer-a	.85	2.50	5.00

OUR FLAG COMICS
Aug, 1941 - No. 5, April, 1942
Ace Magazines

	Good	Fine	Mint
1-Captain Victory, The Unknown Soldier & The Three Cheers begin	50.00	140.00	280.00
2-Origin The Flag	25.00	70.00	140.00
3-5: 4-Intro & 1st app. Mr. Risk	20.00	60.00	120.00

NOTE: ***Anderson** a-4.*

OUR GANG COMICS (With Tom & Jerry No. 39-59; becomes Tom & Jerry No. 60 on)
Sept-Oct, 1942 - No. 59, June, 1949
Dell Publishing Co.

	Good	Fine	Mint
1-Our Gang & Barney Bear by Kelly, Tom & Jerry, Pete Smith, Flip & Dip, The Milky Way begin	80.00	200.00	400.00
2	40.00	100.00	200.00
3-5	30.00	70.00	140.00
6-Bumbazine & Albert only app. by Kelly	50.00	120.00	240.00
7-No Kelly story	15.00	45.00	90.00
8-Benny Burro begins by Barks	40.00	110.00	220.00

Our Army At War #3, © DC

Our Fighting Forces #27, © DC

Our Gang Comics #7, © DELL

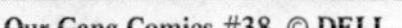
Our Gang Comics #38, © DELL

Outer Space #20, © CC

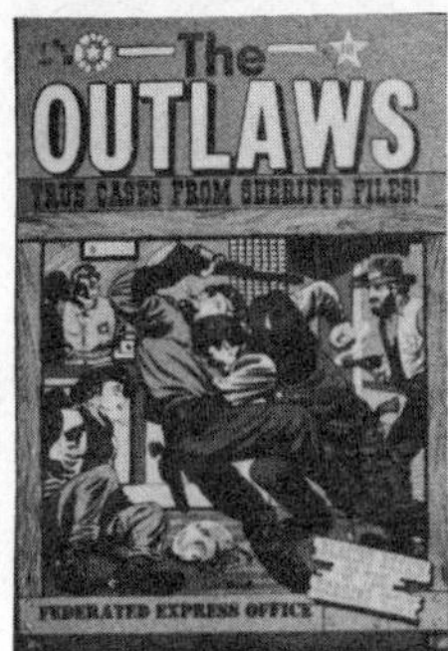

The Outlaws #10, © STAR

OUR GANG COMICS (continued)

	Good	Fine	Mint
9-Barks-a(2): Benny Burro & Happy Hound; no Kelly story	30.00	90.00	180.00
10-Benny Burro by Barks	25.00	70.00	140.00
11-1st Barney Bear & Benny Burro by Barks; Happy Hound by Barks	25.00	70.00	140.00
12-20	14.00	40.00	80.00
21-30	10.00	28.00	56.00
31-36-Last Barks issue	6.00	18.00	36.00
37,39,40	2.00	5.00	10.00
38-Opium drug story	2.00	6.00	12.00
41-50	1.50	4.00	8.00
51-57	1.20	3.50	7.00
58,59-No Kelly art or Our Gang story	.85	2.50	5.00

NOTE: *No. 31-36 contain **Barks** art in part only. **Barks** did not write Barney Bear stories No. 30-34. (See March of Comics No. 3,26)*

OUR LADY OF FATIMA
3/11/55 (15 cents) (36 pages)
Catechetical Guild Educational Society

	Good	Fine	Mint
395	3.00	8.00	16.00

OUR LOVE (Romantic Affairs No. 3)
1949 - No. 2, Jan, 1950
Marvel Comics (SPC)

	Good	Fine	Mint
1	3.00	8.00	16.00
2	1.50	4.00	8.00

OUR LOVE STORY
Oct, 1969 - No. 38, Feb, 1976
Marvel Comics Group

	Good	Fine	Mint
1	.50	1.50	3.00
2-4,6-13: 9-J. Buscema-a		.50	1.00
5-Steranko-a	1.00	3.00	6.00
14-New story by Gary Fredrich & Tarpe' Mills	.50	1.50	3.00
15-38		.20	.40

OUR MISS BROOKS (See 4-Color No. 751)

OUR SECRET
1950 - No. 8, Aug, 1950
Superior Comics Ltd.

	Good	Fine	Mint
4-8	2.00	6.00	12.00

OUTBURSTS OF EVERETT TRUE
1921 (32 pages) (B&W)
Saalfield Publ. Co.

	Good	Fine	Mint
1907 (2-panel strips reprint)	6.00	18.00	36.00

OUTER LIMITS, THE (TV)
Jan-Mar, 1964 - No. 18, Oct, 1969
Dell Publishing Co.

	Good	Fine	Mint
1	1.00	3.00	6.00
2	.70	2.00	4.00
3-10	.55	1.60	3.00
11-18: 17 reprints No. 1; 18-No. 2	.30	.80	1.60

OUTER SPACE (Formerly This Mag. Is Haunted, 2nd Series)
May, 1958 - No. 25, Dec, 1959
Charlton Comics

	Good	Fine	Mint
17-Williamson/Wood style art; not by them; (Sid Check?)	2.00	6.00	12.00
18-20-Ditko-a	2.00	6.00	12.00
21-25: 21-Ditko-c	1.50	4.00	8.00
V2No.1(11/68)-Ditko-c/a	1.00	3.00	6.00
V3No.2-Ditko-c	.70	2.00	4.00

OUTLAW (See Return of the. . .)

OUTLAW FIGHTERS
Aug, 1954 - No. 5, April, 1955
Atlas Comics (IPC)

	Good	Fine	Mint
1	2.00	6.00	12.00
2-5: 5-Heath-a, 7pgs.	1.50	4.00	8.00

OUTLAW KID, THE (1st Series)
Sept, 1954 - No. 19, Sept, 1957
Atlas Comics (CCC No. 1-11/EPI No. 12-29)

	Good	Fine	Mint
1-Black Rider app.	3.00	9.00	18.00
2-7,9: 2-Black Rider app.	1.50	4.00	8.00
8-Williamson/Woodbridge-a, 4 pgs.	3.00	10.00	20.00
10-Williamson-a	3.50	10.00	20.00
11-17,19	1.20	3.50	7.00
18-Williamson-a	3.00	8.00	16.00

NOTE: ***Berg** a-13. **Wildey** a-1, 4, 5, 7, 8, 10, 11, 13-18.*

OUTLAW KID, THE (2nd Series)
Aug, 1970 - No. 30, Oct, 1975
Marvel Comics Group

	Good	Fine	Mint
1,2-Reprints; Wildey-a		.40	.80
3-Williamson-a(r)		.40	.80
4-8		.30	.60
9-Williamson-a(r)		.40	.80
10-Origin Outlaw Kid; new material begins		.25	.50
11,12-Bounty Hawk cameo 11, x-over in 12		.25	.50
13-16-Last new material		.25	.50
17-26,29,30		.25	.50
27-Origin-r/No. 10		.25	.50
28-Williamson-r		.25	.50

NOTE: ***Berg** a-7. **Gil Kane** c-10, 11, 15. **Wildey** a-3, 6, 7, 19, 21, 22, 26.*

OUTLAWS
Feb-Mar, 1948 - No. 9, June-July, 1949
D. S. Publishing Co.

	Good	Fine	Mint
1	6.00	18.00	36.00
2-Ingels-a	7.00	20.00	40.00
3,5,6: 3-Not Frazetta	3.00	8.00	16.00
4-Orlando-a	5.00	14.00	28.00
7,8-Ingels-a in each	6.00	18.00	36.00
9-(Scarce)-Frazetta-a, 7 pgs.	17.00	50.00	100.00

NOTE: *No. 3 was printed in Canada with **Frazetta** art "Prairie Jinx," 7 pgs. **McWilliams** a-6.*

OUTLAWS THE (Formerly Western Crime Cases?)
No. 10, May, 1952 - No. 13, Sept, 1953; No. 14, April, 1954
Star Publishing Co.

	Good	Fine	Mint
10-14-L. B. Cole-c. 14-Kamen, Feldstein-a	3.00	8.00	16.00

OUTLAWS OF THE WEST (Formerly Cody of the Pony Express No. 10)
No. 11, 7/57 - No. 81, 5/70; No. 82, 7/79 - No. 88, 1980
Charlton Comics

	Good	Fine	Mint
11-13,15-17,19,20	.80	2.40	4.80
14-(68 pgs.)(15 cents)	1.00	3.00	6.00
18-Ditko-a	2.00	5.00	10.00
21-50	.35	1.10	2.20
51-70: 54-Kid Montana app. 64-Captain Doom begins (1st app.)		.40	.80
71-81: 73-Origin & 1st app. The Sharp Shooter, last app. No. 74. 75-Last Capt. Doom. 80,81-Ditko-a		.40	.80
82-88		.30	.60
64(Modern Comics reprint, 1977)		.15	.30

OUTLAWS OF THE WILD WEST
1952 (132 pages) (25 cents)
Avon Periodicals

	Good	Fine	Mint
1-Wood back-c; Kubert-a (3 Jesse James-r)	8.00	24.00	48.00

OUT OF SANTA'S BAG (March of Comics No. 10)

OUT OF THE NIGHT (The Hooded Horseman No. 18 on)
Feb-Mar, 1952 - No. 17, Oct-Nov, 1954
American Comics Group (Creston/Scope)

	Good	Fine	Mint
1-Williamson-a, 9 pgs.; Torres-a	12.00	35.00	70.00

OUT OF THE NIGHT (continued)

	Good	Fine	Mint
2-Williamson-a, 5 pgs.	10.00	28.00	56.00
3,5-10	2.00	6.00	12.00
4-Williamson-a, 7 pgs.	10.00	28.00	56.00
11,12,14-17	1.50	4.50	9.00
13-Nostrand-a	2.00	6.00	12.00

NOTE: ***Landau** a-14,16,17. **Shelly** a-12.*

OUT OF THE PAST A CLUE TO THE FUTURE
1946? (16 pages) (paper cover)
E. C. Comics (Public Affairs Comm.)

Based on public affairs pamphlet-''What Foreign Trade Means to You''	5.50	16.00	32.00

OUT OF THE SHADOWS
No. 5, July, 1952 - No. 14, Aug, 1954
Standard Comics/Visual Editions

5,6,14-Toth-a; Moreira, Tuska-a, No. 5	3.50	10.00	20.00
7-Jack Katz-a(2)	2.00	6.00	12.00
8	2.00	5.00	10.00
9-Crandall-a(2)	3.50	10.00	20.00
10,11-Toth-a, 3(p),2 pgs.	2.00	6.00	12.00
12-Toth-a(2)	4.00	12.00	24.00
13-Cannabalism story	2.00	6.00	12.00

NOTE: ***Katz** a-6(2), 7(2), 11. **Sekowsky** a-10, 13.*

OUT OF THIS WORLD
June, 1950 (One Shot)
Avon Periodicals

1-Kubert-a(2) (one reprint/Eerie No. 1-'47) plus Crom the Barbarian by Giunta (origin)	30.00	90.00	180.00

OUT OF THIS WORLD ADVENTURES (Pulp)
July, 1950 - No. 2, Dec, 1950; No. 2, April, 1951
Avon Periodicals

1-Has Avon's Out of This World No. 1 comic insert	10.00	30.00	60.00
2-Has Avon's Strange Worlds No. 1; used in **SOTI**, pg. 120; describes the pulp with comic insert	9.00	25.00	50.00
2(4/51)-Has Avon's Flying Saucers No. 1	12.00	35.00	70.00

NOTE: *Comic book inserts can vary.*

OUT OF THIS WORLD
Oct, 1956 - No. 16, Dec-Jan, 1960
Charlton Comics

1	3.50	10.00	20.00
2	2.00	5.00	10.00
3-6-Ditko-a(4) each	5.00	14.00	28.00
7,8-(68 pgs.; 15 cents)-Ditko-a(4) each	4.00	12.00	24.00
9-12,16-Ditko-a	3.00	8.00	16.00
13-15	1.00	3.00	6.00

NOTE: ***Ditko** c-3-7,11,16.*

OUT OUR WAY WITH WORRY WART (See 4-Color No. 680)

OUTSIDERS, THE (See First Issue Special)

OUTSTANDING AMERICAN WAR HEROES
1944 (16 pgs.) (paper cover)
The Parents' Institute

nn-Reprints from True Comics	2.50	7.00	14.00

OVERSEAS COMICS (Also see G.I. & Jeep Comics)
1944 (7¼x10¼''; 16 pgs. in color)
Giveaway (Distributed to U.S. armed forces)

23-65-Bringing Up Father, Popeye, Joe Palooka, Dick Tracy, Superman, Gasoline Alley, Buz Sawyer, Li'l Abner, Blondie, Terry & the Pirates, Out Our Way	3.00	8.00	16.00

OWL, THE
April, 1967; No. 2, April, 1968
Gold Key

	Good	Fine	Mint
1,2	.50	1.50	3.00

OXYDOL-DREFT
1950 (Set of 6 pocket-size giveaways; distributed through the mail as a set) (Scarce)
Oxydol-Dreft

1-Li'l Abner, 2-Daisy Mae, 3-Shmoo	4.00	12.00	24.00
4-John Wayne; Williamson/Frazetta-c from John Wayne No. 3	4.00	12.00	24.00
5-Archie	4.00	12.00	24.00
6-Terrytoons Mighty Mouse	4.00	12.00	24.00

NOTE: *Set is worth more with original envelope.*

OZ (See MGM's Marvelous . . . & Marvel Treasury . . .)

OZARK IKE
Feb, 1948; Nov, 1948 - No. 24, Dec, 1951; No. 25, Sept, 1952
Dell Publishing Co./Standard Comics

4-Color 180(1948-Dell)	4.00	12.00	24.00
B11, B12	3.50	10.00	20.00
13-15	3.50	10.00	20.00
16-25	3.00	8.00	16.00

OZZIE & BABS (TV Teens No. 14 on)
1947 - No. 13, Fall, 1949
Fawcett Publications

1	2.00	6.00	12.00
2-13	1.20	3.50	7.00

OZZIE & HARRIET (See The Adventures of . . .)

PADRE OF THE POOR
No date (16 pgs.) (paper cover)
Catechetical Guild Giveaway

	2.50	7.00	14.00

PAGEANT OF COMICS (See Jane Arden & Mopsy)
Sept, 1947 - No. 2, Oct, 1947
Archer St. John

1-Mopsy strip-r	3.00	9.00	18.00
2-Jane Arden strip-r	3.00	9.00	18.00

PANCHO VILLA
1950
Avon Periodicals

nn-Kinstler-c	8.00	24.00	48.00

PANHANDLE PETE AND JENNIFER (TV)
July, 1951 - No. 3, Nov, 1951
J. Charles Laue Publishing Co.

1-3	1.50	4.00	8.00

PANIC (Companion to Mad)
Feb-Mar, 1954 - No. 12, Dec-Jan, 1955-56
E. C. Comics

1-Elder draws entire E. C. staff	7.00	20.00	36.00
2	5.50	16.00	28.00
3-Kelly parody; reefer mention	4.00	12.00	20.00
4-Infinity-c	4.00	12.00	20.00
5-12	3.00	10.00	18.00

NOTE: ***Davis** a-1-12; c-12. **Elder** a-1-12. **Feldstein** c-1-3,5. **Kamen** a-1. **Orlando** a-1-9. **Wolverton** c-4, panel-3. **Wood** a-2-9, 11, 12.*

PANIC (Magazine) (Satire)
7/58 - No. 6, 7/59; V2No.10, 12/65 - V2No.12, 1966
Panic Publications

1	1.00	3.00	6.00
2-6	.85	2.50	5.00
V2No.10-12: Reprints earlier issues	.40	1.20	2.40

Out Of The Night #5, © ACG

Out Of This World #14, © CC

Panic #3, © WMG

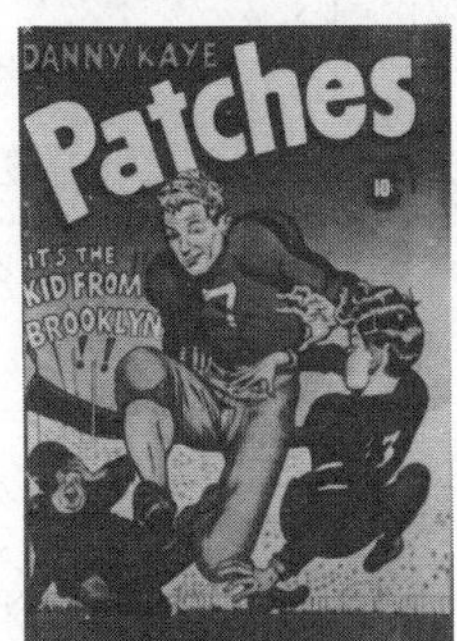

Patches #5, © RH

Patsy Walker #26, © MCG

Paul Terry's Comics #89, © MGM

PANIC (continued)

NOTE: ***Davis** a-3(2 pgs.), 4, 5, 10; c-10. **Elder** a-5. **Powell** a-V2No.10. **Torres** a-1-5.*

PARADE (See Hanna-Barbera. . .)

PARADE COMICS (Frisky Animals on Parade No. 2 on)
Sept, 1957
Ajax/Farrell Publ. (World Famous Publ.)

	Good	Fine	Mint
1	.85	2.50	5.00

NOTE: *Cover title: Frisky Animals on Parade.*

PARADE OF PLEASURE
1954 (192 pgs.) (Hardback book)
Derric Verschoyle Ltd., London, England

By Geoffrey Wagner. Contains section devoted to the censorship of American comic books with illustrations in color and black and white. (Also see **Seduction of the Innocent**). Distributed in USA by

Library Publishers, N. Y.	25.00	70.00	120.00
with dust jacket. . . .	35.00	100.00	180.00

PARAMOUNT ANIMATED COMICS (Also see Comics Hits No. 60)
Feb, 1953 - No. 22, July, 1956
Harvey Publications

1-Baby Huey, Herman & Katnip, Buzzy the Crow begin	8.00	24.00	48.00
2-6	4.00	12.00	24.00
7-Baby Huey becomes permanent cover feature; cover title becomes Baby Huey with No. 9	8.00	24.00	48.00
8-10	3.50	10.00	20.00
11-22	2.50	7.00	14.00

PARENT TRAP, THE (See 4-Color No. 1210)

PAROLE BREAKERS
Dec, 1951 - No. 3, July, 1952
Avon Periodicals/Realistic

1(No.2 on inside)-Drug mention story; c-/Avon paperback 283	10.00	28.00	56.00
2-Kubert-a; c-/Avon paperback 114	8.00	24.00	48.00
3-Kinstler-c	7.00	20.00	40.00

PARTRIDGE FAMILY, THE (TV)
March, 1971 - No. 21, Dec, 1973
Charlton Comics

1	.70	2.00	4.00
2-4,6-21	.50	1.50	3.00
5-Partridge Family Summer Special (52 pgs.); The Shadow, Lone Ranger, Charlie McCarthy, Flash Gordon, Hopalong Cassidy, Gene Autry & others app.	.55	1.60	3.20

PASSION, THE
1955
Catechetical Guild

394	3.50	10.00	20.00

PAT BOONE (Also see Superman's Girlfriend Lois Lane No. 9)
Sept-Oct, 1959 - No. 5, May-Jun, 1960
National Periodical Publications

1	7.00	20.00	40.00
2-5	4.00	12.00	24.00

PATCHES
Mar-Apr, 1945 - No. 11, Nov, 1947
Rural Home/Patches Publ. (Orbit)

1-L. B. Cole-c	6.00	18.00	36.00
2-11: 5-L.B. Cole-c	3.00	9.00	18.00

PATORUZU (See Adventures of. . .)

PATSY & HEDY
1952 - No. 110, Feb, 1967
Atlas Comics/Marvel (GPI/Male)

	Good	Fine	Mint
1	4.00	12.00	24.00
2-10	2.00	5.00	10.00
11-20	1.00	3.00	6.00
21-50	.70	2.00	4.00
51-110: 88-Lingerie panel	.30	.80	1.60
Annual 1('63)	1.50	4.00	8.00

PATSY & HER PALS
May, 1953 - No. 29, Aug, 1957
Atlas Comics (PPI)

1	3.50	10.00	20.00
2	2.00	5.00	10.00
3-10	1.50	4.00	8.00
11-29: 24-Everett-c	.85	2.50	5.00

PATSY WALKER (Also see Girls' Life & Miss America Magazine)
1945 (no month) - No. 124, Dec, 1965
Marvel/Atlas Comics (BPC)

1	10.00	30.00	60.00
2	5.50	16.00	32.00
3-10	4.00	12.00	24.00
11,12,15,16,18,23,24,26-29	2.00	6.00	12.00
13,14,17,19-22-Kurtzman's "Hey Look"	4.00	12.00	24.00
25-Rusty by Kurtzman	3.50	10.00	20.00
30-60	.85	2.50	5.00
61-100	.35	1.00	2.00
101-124		.40	.80
Fashion Parade 1('66)-68 pgs.	.85	2.50	5.00

PAT THE BRAT (Adventures of Pipsqueak No. 35 on)
June, 1953; Summer, 1955 - No. 34, Sept, 1959
Archie Publications (Radio)

nn(6/53)	4.00	12.00	24.00
1(Summer, 1955)	3.00	8.00	16.00
2-10	1.50	4.00	8.00
11-34	1.00	3.00	6.00

PAT THE BRAT COMICS DIGEST MAGAZINE
October, 1980 - Present
Archie Publications

1		.50	1.00

PATTY POWERS (Formerly Two-Gun Western?)
No. 4, Feb, 1956 - No. 7, Oct, 1956
Atlas Comics

4-7	.85	2.50	5.00

PAT WILTON (See Mighty Midget Comics)

PAUL
1978 (49 cents)
Spire Christian Comics (Fleming H. Revell Co.)

		.40	.80

PAULINE PERIL (See The Close Shaves of. . .)

PAUL REVERE'S RIDE (See 4-Color No. 822)

PAUL TERRY'S ADVENTURES OF MIGHTY MOUSE (See Adventures of. . .)

PAUL TERRY'S COMICS (Formerly Terry-Toons Comics; becomes Adventures of Mighty Mouse No. 126 on)
No. 85, Mar, 1951 - No. 125, May, 1955
St. John Publishing Co.

85,86-Same as Terry-Toons No. 85, & 86 with only a title change	2.00	5.00	10.00
87-100	1.50	4.00	8.00
101-104,106-125-Mighty Mouse	1.00	3.00	6.00
105-Giant Comics Edition, 100pgs. (9/53)	2.00	6.00	12.00

PAUL TERRY'S HOW TO DRAW FUNNY CARTOONS
1940's (14 pages) (Black & White)

PAUL TERRY'S HOW TO... (continued)
Terrytoons, Inc. (Giveaway)

	Good	Fine	Mint
Heckle & Jeckle, Mighty Mouse, etc.	4.00	12.00	24.00

PAUL TERRY'S MIGHTY MOUSE (See Mighty Mouse)

PAUL TERRY'S MIGHTY MOUSE ADVENTURE STORIES
1953 (384 pgs.) (50 cents) (cardboard covers)
St. John Publishing Co.

	Good	Fine	Mint
nn	12.00	35.00	75.00

PAWNEE BILL
Feb, 1951 - No. 3, July, 1951
Story Comics

	Good	Fine	Mint
1	2.00	6.00	12.00
2,3: 3-Origin Golden Warrior; Cameron-a	1.00	3.00	6.00

PAY-OFF (This Is the..., ...Crime, ...Detective Stories)
July-Aug, 1948 - No. 5, Mar-Apr, 1949 (52 pages)
D. S. Publishing Co.

	Good	Fine	Mint
1	2.00	6.00	12.00
2-5	1.50	4.50	9.00

PEACEMAKER, THE
Mar, 1967 - No. 5, Nov, 1967
Charlton Comics

	Good	Fine	Mint
1-Fightin' Five begins	.30	.90	1.80
2,3,5		.60	1.20
4-Origin The Peacemaker	.30	.80	1.60
1,2(Modern Comics reprint, 1978)		.15	.30

PEANUTS (Charlie Brown) (See Nancy & Sluggo)
Feb, 1958 - No. 13, Apr-Jun, 1962; May, 1963 - No. 4, Feb, 1964
Dell Publishing Co./Gold Key

	Good	Fine	Mint
4-Color 878,969,1015('59)	2.00	6.00	12.00
4(2-4/60)	1.50	4.00	8.00
5-13	1.00	3.00	6.00
1 (Gold Key)	1.00	3.00	6.00
2-4	.85	2.50	5.00
1(1953-54)-Reprints United Features' Strange As It Seems, Willie, Fernand	3.50	10.00	20.00

PEBBLES & BAMM BAMM (TV)
Jan, 1972 - No. 36, Dec, 1976 (Hanna-Barbera)
Charlton Comics

	Good	Fine	Mint
1	.85	2.50	5.00
2-36	.50	1.50	3.00

PEBBLES FLINTSTONE (TV)
Sept, 1963 (Hanna-Barbera)
Gold Key

	Good	Fine	Mint
1 (10088-309)	.85	2.50	5.00

PECKS BAD BOY & COUSIN CYNTHIA
1907 - 1908 (Strip reprints) (11¼x15¾'')
Thompson of Chicago (by Walt McDougal)

	Good	Fine	Mint
...& Cousin Cynthia(1907)-In color	10.00	30.00	60.00
...& His Chums(1908)-Hardcover; in full color; 16 pgs.	10.00	30.00	60.00
Advs. of...in Pictures(1908)-In color; Stanton & Van V. Liet Co.	10.00	30.00	60.00

PEDRO (Also see Romeo Tubbs)
No. 18, June, 1950 - No. 2, Aug, 1950?
Fox Features Syndicate

	Good	Fine	Mint
18(No.1)-Wood c/a(p)	7.00	20.00	40.00
2-Wood-a?	6.00	18.00	36.00

PEE-WEE PIXIES (See The Pixies)

PENALTY (See Crime Must Pay the...)

PENDULUM ILLUSTRATED BIOGRAPHIES
1979 (B&W)
Pendulum Press

19-355x-George Washington/Thomas Jefferson, 19-3495-Charles Lindbergh/Amelia Earhart, 19-3509-Harry Houdini/Walt Disney, 19-3517-Davy Crockett/Daniel Boone-Redondo-a, 19-3525-Elvis Presley/Beatles, 19-3533-Benjamin Franklin/Martin Luther King Jr, 19-3541-Abraham Lincoln/Franklin D. Roosevelt, 19-3568-Marie Curie/Albert Einstein-Redondo-a, 19-3576-Thomas Edison/Alexander Graham Bell-Redondo-a, 19-3584-Vince Lombardi/Pele, 19-3592-Babe Ruth/Jackie Robinson, 19-3606-Jim Thorpe/Althea Gibson

Softback	1.50
Hardback	4.50

NOTE: *Above books still available from publisher.*

PENDULUM ILLUSTRATED CLASSICS (Now Age Illustrated)
1973 - 1978 (62pp, B&W, 5-3/8x8'') (Also see Marvel Classics)
Pendulum Press

64-100x(1973)-Dracula-Redondo art, 64-131x-The Invisible Man-Nino art, 64-0968-Dr Jekyll and Mr Hyde-Redondo art, 64-1005-Black Beauty, 64-1010-Call of the Wild, 64-1020-Frankenstein, 64-1025-Hucklebury Finn, 64-1030-Moby Dick-Nino-a, 64-1040-Red Badge of Courage, 64-1045-The Time Machine-Nino-a, 64-1050-Tom Sawyer, 64-1055-Twenty Thousand Leagues Under the Sea, 64-1069-Treasure Island, 64-1328(1974)-Kidnapped, 64-1336-Three Musketeers-Nino art, 64-1344-A Tale of Two Cities, 64-1352-Journey to the Center of the Earth, 64-1360-The War of the Worlds-Nino-a, 64-1379-The Greatest Advs of Sherlock Holmes-Redondo art, 64-1387-Mysterious Island, 64-1395-Hunchback of Notre Dame, 64-1409-Helen Keller-story of my life, 64-1417-Scarlet Letter, 64-1425-Gulliver's Travels, 64-2618(1977)-Around the World in Eighty Days, 64-2626-Captains Courageous, 64-2634-Connecticut Yankee, 64-2642-The Hound of the Baskervilles, 64-2650-The House of Seven Gables, 64-2669-Jane Eyre, 64-2677-The Last of the Mohicans, 64-2685-The Best of O'Henry, 64-2693-The Best of Poe-Redondo-a, 64-2707-Two Years Before the Mast, 64-2715-White Fang, 64-2723-Wuthering Heights, 64-3126(1978)-Ben Hur-Redondo art, 64-3134-A Christmas Carol, 64-3142-The Food of the Gods, 64-3150-Ivanhoe, 64-3169-The Man in the Iron Mask, 64-3177-The Prince and the Pauper, 64-3185-The Prisoner of Zenda, 64-3193-The Return of the Native, 64-3207-Robinson Crusoe, 64-3215-The Scarlet Pimpernal, 64-3223-The Sea Wolf, 64-3231-The Swiss Family Robinson, 64-3851-Billy Budd, 64-386x-Crime and Punishment, 64-3878-Don Quixote, 64-3886-Great Expectations, 64-3894-Heidi, 64-3908-The Iliad, 64-3916-Lord Jim, 64-3924-The Mutiny on Board H.M.S. Bounty, 64-3932-The Odyssey, 64-3940-Oliver Twist, 64-3959-Pride and Prejudice, 64-3967-The Turn of the Screw

Softback	1.45
Hardback	4.50

NOTE: *All of the above books can be ordered from the publisher; some were reprinted as Marvel Classic Comics No. 1-12.*

PENDULUM ILLUSTRATED ORIGINALS
1979 (in color)
Pendulum Press

	Good	Fine	Mint
94-4254-Solarman: The Beginning	.30	.80	1.60

PENNY
1947 - 1949
Avon Periodicals

	Good	Fine	Mint
1-Photo & biography of creator; newspaper reprints	2.50	7.00	14.00
2-6	1.50	4.00	8.00

PEP COMICS
Jan, 1940 - Present
MLJ Magazines/Archie Publications No. 57 on

1-Intro. The Shield by Irving Novick (1st patriotic hero); origin The Comet by Jack Cole, The Queen of Diamonds & Kayo Ward; The

Peanuts #6, © UFS

Penny #1, © AVON

Pep Comics #1, © MLJ

Pep Comics #36, © MLJ

Perfect Crime #25, © Cross Publ.

Perfect Love #3, © ZD

PEP COMICS (continued)

	Good	Fine	Mint
Rocket, The Press Guardian (The Falcon No. 1 only), Sergeant Boyle, Fu Chang, & Bentley of Scotland Yard	100.00	260.00	550.00
2-Origin The Rocket	50.00	125.00	265.00
3	30.00	85.00	190.00
4-Wizard cameo	28.00	80.00	170.00
5-Wizard cameo in Shield story	25.00	70.00	150.00
6-10: 6-Transvestite story in Sgt. Boyle. 8-Last Cole Comet, no Cole art in No. 6,7	20.00	55.00	115.00
11-Dusty, Shield's sidekick begins; last Press Guardian, Fu Chang	17.00	50.00	110.00
12-Origin Fireball; last Rocket & Queen of Diamonds; bondage-c	25.00	70.00	150.00
13-15: 15-Bondage-c	17.00	50.00	110.00
16-Origin Madam Satan	25.00	70.00	150.00
17-Origin The Hangman; death of The Comet	60.00	175.00	360.00
18-20-Last Fireball	16.00	48.00	96.00
21-Last Madam Satan	16.00	48.00	96.00
22-Intro. & 1st app. Archie, Betty, & Jughead(12/41); (also see Jack-pot)	150.00	400.00	800.00
(Prices vary widely on this book.)			
23-25,27-29	17.00	50.00	100.00
26-1st app. Veronica Lodge	20.00	60.00	120.00
30-Capt. Commando begins	11.00	33.00	66.00
31-35,37-40: 31-Bondage-c. 34-Bondage/Hypo-c	9.00	25.00	50.00
36-1st Archie-c	15.00	45.00	90.00
41-47: 47-Last Hangman issue. 41 on are all Archie-c	8.00	22.00	44.00
48-Black Hood begins(5/44); ends No. 51,59,60	6.00	18.00	36.00
49-58,60: 52-Suzie begins. 56-Last Capt. Commando; lingerie panel. 60-Katy Keene begins	4.00	12.00	24.00
59-Black Hood not in costume; spanking & lingerie panels; Archie dresses as his aunt; Suzie ends	4.00	12.00	24.00
61,63-65-Last Shield; 63-Drug story	4.00	12.00	24.00
62-1st app. Li'l Jinx	6.00	18.00	36.00
66-70: 66-G-Man Club becomes Archie Club (2/48)	3.00	8.00	16.00
71-80	2.00	6.00	12.00
81-100	1.50	4.00	8.00
101-120	1.00	3.00	6.00
121-149	.70	2.00	4.00
150,152,157,159-Jaguar stories in all	.60	1.80	3.60
151,154,160-The Fly stories in all	.60	1.80	3.60
153,155,156,158-Flygirl stories in all	.60	1.80	3.60
161-167,169-195,197-200	.35	1.10	2.20
168-Jaguar app.	.50	1.50	3.00
196-Beatles on cover	.60	1.80	3.60
201-240		.50	1.00
241-300		.40	.80
301-379		.30	.60

NOTE: ***Schomburg** c-38. Katy Keene by **Bill Woggon** in many issues. **Bob Wood** a-6.*

PEPE (See 4-Color No. 1194)

PERCY & FERDIE
1921 (52 pages) (B&W dailies, 10x10'', cardboard-c)
Cupples & Leon Co.

	Good	Fine	Mint
By H. A. MacGill	5.00	14.00	28.00

PERFECT CRIME, THE
Oct, 1949 - 1953
Cross Publications

	Good	Fine	Mint
1-Powell-a(2)	3.00	9.00	18.00
2-7,9,10: 7-Steve Duncan begins, ends No. 30	2.50	7.00	14.00
8-Heroin drug story	5.00	14.00	28.00
11-Used in **SOTI**, pg. 159; bondage-c	5.00	14.00	28.00
12-14	1.50	4.50	9.00
15-''The Most Terrible Menace''-2 pg. drug editorial; narcotics mentioned story	3.50	10.00	20.00
16,17,19-25,27-29,31-33	1.20	3.50	7.00
18-Drug cover, heroin drug propaganda story, plus 2 pg. drug editorial	5.00	15.00	30.00
26-Graphic drug cover with hypodermic; drug propaganda story	6.00	18.00	36.00
30-Classic strangulation cover	5.00	14.00	28.00

NOTE: ***Powell** a-No. 1,2,4. **Wildey** a-1,5.*

PERFECT LOVE
No. 2, Oct-Nov, 1951 - No. 10, Dec, 1953
Ziff-Davis(Approved Comics)/St. John No. 9 on

	Good	Fine	Mint
2	2.50	7.00	14.00
3,6,7,9,10	2.00	5.00	10.00
4-Kinstler-a	2.00	6.00	12.00
5-Woodbridge-a?	2.00	5.00	10.00
8-Kinstler-a	2.00	6.00	12.00

PERRI (See 4-Color No. 847)

PERRY MASON (See Feature Book No. 49,40 (McKay))

PERRY MASON MYSTERY MAGAZINE (TV)
June-Aug, 1964 - No. 2, Oct-Dec, 1964
Dell Publishing Co.

	Good	Fine	Mint
1,2	1.00	3.00	6.00

PERSONAL LOVE (Also see Movie Love)
Jan, 1950 - No. 33, June, 1955
Famous Funnies

	Good	Fine	Mint
1	4.00	12.00	24.00
2-7,9,10: 5-Everett-a	2.50	7.00	14.00
8-Kinstler-a, 7pgs.	3.00	8.00	16.00
11-Toth-a	4.50	13.00	26.00
12-15,18-23	2.00	5.00	10.00
16,17-One pg. Frazetta	3,00	8.00	16.00
24,25,27,28-Frazetta-a in all-8,7,8 & 6 pgs. each; 24-Everett-a	30.00	70.00	140.00
26,29-31,33	1.50	4.00	8.00
32-Classic Frazetta-a, 8 pgs.	50.00	125.00	250.00

PERSONAL LOVE (Young Love V3No.3 on)
V1No.1, Sept, 1957 - V3No.2, Nov-Dec, 1959
Prize Publ. (Headline)

	Good	Fine	Mint
V1No.1	1.25	2.50	5.00
2-6(7-8/58)	.60	1.20	2.40
V2No.1(9-10/58)-V2No.6(7-8/59)	.50	1.00	2.00
V3No.1-2	.30	.60	1.20

NOTE: *Photo covers on most issues.*

PETER COTTONTAIL
Jan, 1954; Feb, 1954 - No. 2, Mar, 1954
Key Publications

	Good	Fine	Mint
1(1/54)-Not 3-D	3.00	6.00	12.00
1(2/54)-(3-D); written by Bruce Hamilton	10.00	20.00	40.00
2-Reprints 3-D No. 1 but not in 3-D	2.50	5.00	10.00

PETER GUNN (See 4-Color No. 1087)

PETER PAN (See New Adventures of . . ., 4-Color No. 442,446,926, and Movie Classics & Comics)

PETER PAN TREASURE CHEST (See Movie Classics)

PETER PANDA
Aug-Sept, 1953 - No. 31, Aug-Sept, 1958
National Periodical Publications

	Good	Fine	Mint
1	9.00	18.00	36.00
2-10	4.00	8.00	16.00
11-31	1.50	3.00	6.00

PETER PARKER (See The Spectacular Spider-Man)

PETER PAT (See Single Series No. 8)

PETER PAUL'S 4 IN 1 JUMBO COMIC BOOK
No date (1953)
Capitol Stories

	Good	Fine	Mint
1-Contains 4 comics bound; Space Adventures, Space Western, Crime & Justice, Racket Squad in Action	8.00	24.00	48.00

PETER PENNY AND HIS MAGIC DOLLAR
1947 (16 pgs.; paper cover; regular size)
American Bankers Association, N. Y. (Giveaway)

	Good	Fine	Mint
nn-(Scarce)-Used in **SOTI**, pg. 310, 311	3.50	10.00	20.00
Another version (7¼x11'')-redrawn, 16 pgs., paper-c	3.50	10.00	20.00

PETER PIG
No. 5, May, 1953 - No. 6, Aug, 1953
Standard Comics

	Good	Fine	Mint
5,6	.85	2.50	5.00

PETER PORKCHOPS
Nov-Dec, 1949 - No. 61, Sept-Nov, 1959; No. 62, Oct-Dec, 1960
National Periodical Publications

	Good	Fine	Mint
1	6.00	18.00	36.00
2-10	3.00	8.00	16.00
11-30	1.50	4.00	8.00
31-62: 36-Sheldon Mayer-a	.85	2.50	5.00

PETER POTAMUS (TV)
January, 1965 (Hanna-Barbera)
Gold Key

	Good	Fine	Mint
1	.85	2.50	5.00

PETER RABBIT (See Large Feature Comic No. 1)

PETER RABBIT
1922 - 1923 (9¼x6¼'') (paper cover)
John H. Eggers Co. The House of Little Books Publishers

	Good	Fine	Mint
B1-B4-(Rare)-(Set of 4 books which came in a cardboard box)-Each book reprints ½ of a Sunday page per page and contains 8 B&W and 2 color pages; by Harrison Cady each....	17.00	50.00	100.00

PETER RABBIT (Adventures of...)
1947 - No. 34, Aug-Sept, 1956
Avon Periodicals

	Good	Fine	Mint
1(1947)-Reprints 1943-44 Sunday strips; contains a biography & drawing of Cady	17.00	50.00	100.00
2-6(1949)-Last Cady issue	14.00	40.00	80.00
7-10(1950-51)	2.50	7.00	14.00
11(11/51)-34('56)-Avon's character	1.50	4.00	8.00
...Easter Parade (Giant)	5.00	15.00	30.00
...Jumbo Book(1954-Giant Size, 25 cents)-6 pgs.; Jesse James by Kinstler	10.00	28.00	56.00

PETER RABBIT
1958
Fago Magazine Co.

	Good	Fine	Mint
1	2.00	6.00	12.00

PETER, THE LITTLE PEST (No. 4 titled Petey)
Nov, 1969 - No. 4, May, 1970
Marvel Comics Group

	Good	Fine	Mint
1	.35	1.00	2.00
2-4-Reprints Dexter the Demon & Melvin the Monster		.50	1.00

PETER WHEAT (The Adventures of...)
1948 - 1956? (16 pgs. in color) (paper covers)
Bakers Associates Giveaway

	Good	Fine	Mint
nn(No.1)-States on last page, end of 1st Adventure of...; Kelly-a	20.00	60.00	120.00
nn(4 issues)-Kelly-a	14.00	40.00	80.00
6-10-All Kelly-a	11.00	32.00	64.00
11-20-All Kelly-a	9.00	25.00	50.00
21-30-All Kelly-a	7.00	20.00	40.00
31-40	5.00	15.00	30.00
41-66	4.50	13.00	26.00

NOTE: ***Al Hubbard** art No. 34? on; written by Del Connell.*

PETER WHEAT FUN BOOK
1952 (32 pgs.; paper cover; B&W w/some color) (8¼x10¾'')
Bakers Associates

	Good	Fine	Mint
Contains cut-outs, puzzles, games, magic, & pages to color	7.00	20.00	40.00

PETER WHEAT NEWS
1948 - No. 30, 1949 (4 pgs. in color)
Bakers Associates

	Good	Fine	Mint
Vol. 1-All have 2 pgs. Peter Wheat by Kelly	17.00	50.00	100.00
2-10	12.00	35.00	70.00
11-20	6.00	18.00	36.00
21-30	3.50	10.00	20.00

NOTE: *Early issues have no date & Kelly art.*

PETE THE PANIC
November, 1955? (mid 1950s)
Stanmor Publications

	Good	Fine	Mint
nn	1.00	3.00	4.50

PETEY (See Peter, the Little Pest)

PETTICOAT JUNCTION (TV)
Oct-Dec, 1964 - No. 5, Oct-Dec, 1965
Dell Publishing Co.

	Good	Fine	Mint
1	.85	2.50	5.00
2-5: 5-Photo-c	.50	1.50	3.00

PETUNIA (See 4-Color No. 463)

PHANTASMO (See Black & White No. 18)

PHANTOM, THE
1939 - 1949
David McKay Publishing Co.

	Good	Fine	Mint
Feature Book 20,22	25.00	75.00	150.00
Feature Book 39	14.00	40.00	80.00
Feature Book 53,56,57	10.00	30.00	60.00

PHANTOM, THE (See Ace Comics, Eat Right to Work..., Future Comics, Comics Hits No. 51,56 & Harvey Hits No. 1,6,12,15,26,36, 44,48)

PHANTOM, THE (No No.29) (Also see Comics Reading Library)
Nov, 1962 - No. 17, July, 1966; No. 18, Sept, 1966 - No. 28, Dec, 1967; No. 30, Feb, 1969 - No. 74, Jan, 1977
Gold Key (No.1-17)/King (No.18-28)/Charlton (No.30 on)

	Good	Fine	Mint
1-Manning-a	1.50	4.00	8.00
2-King, Queen & Jack begins, ends No. 11	.70	2.00	4.00
3-5	.55	1.60	3.20
6-10	.45	1.30	2.60
11-17: 12-Track Hunter begins	.40	1.20	2.40
18-Flash Gordon begins; Wood-a	.80	2.40	4.80
19,20-Flash Gordon ends	.55	1.60	3.20
21-24,26,27: 21-Mandrake begins. 26-Brick Bradford app.	.40	1.20	2.40
25-Jeff Jones-a; 1 pg. Williamson ad	.55	1.60	3.20
28(nn)-Brick Bradford app.	.50	1.50	3.00
30-40: 36,39-Ditko-a	.35	1.00	2.00
41-66: 62-Bolle-c	.25	.70	1.40
67-71,73,74-Newton c/a; 67-Origin retold	.25	.70	1.40
72		.50	1.00

PHANTOM BLOT, THE (No. 1 titled New Adventures of...)
Oct, 1964 - No. 7, Nov, 1966 (Disney)

Peter Rabbit #22, © AVON

Peter Wheat #9, © Bakers Assoc.

The Phantom #18, © KING

Phantom Lady #22, © FOX

Phantom Stranger #33, © DC

Pictorial Romances #22, © STJ

PHANTOM BLOT (continued)
Gold Key

	Good	Fine	Mint
1	1.00	3.00	6.00
2-1st Super Goof	.70	2.00	4.00
3-7	.50	1.50	3.00

PHANTOM EAGLE (See Mighty Midget Comics)

PHANTOM LADY (1st Series) (My Love Secret No. 24 on) (Also see All Top, Daring Adventures, Jungle Thrills, and Wonder Boy)
Aug, 1947 - No. 23 April, 1949
Fox Features Syndicate

	Good	Fine	Mint
13(No.1)-Phantom Lady by Matt Baker begins; The Blue Beetle app.	90.00	250.00	500.00
14(No.2)	60.00	160.00	320.00
15-Drug use story	50.00	130.00	260.00
16-Negligee-c, panels	50.00	130.00	260.00
17-Classic bondage cover; used in **SOTI**, illo-''Sexual stimulation by combining 'headlights' with the sadist's dream of tying up a woman''	150.00	450.00	800.00
18,19	40.00	110.00	220.00
20-23: 23-Bondage-c	30.00	90.00	180.00

NOTE: ***Matt Baker*** *c/a in all.*

PHANTOM LADY (2nd Series) (See Terrific Comics) (Formerly Linda)
Dec-Jan, 1955 - No. 4, June, 1955
Ajax/Farrell Publ.

	Good	Fine	Mint
V1No.5(No.1)-by Matt Baker	17.00	50.00	100.00
V1No.2-4-Red Rocket in No. 3,4	12.00	35.00	70.00

PHANTOM PLANET, THE (See 4-Color No. 1234)

PHANTOM STRANGER, THE (1st Series)
Aug-Sept, 1952 - No. 6, June-July, 1953
National Periodical Publications

	Good	Fine	Mint
1 (Scarce)	25.00	70.00	150.00
2-6 (Scarce)	15.00	45.00	100.00

PHANTOM STRANGER, THE (2nd Series) (See Showcase)
May-June, 1969 - No. 41, Feb-Mar, 1976
National Periodical Publications

	Good	Fine	Mint
1	1.00	3.00	6.00
2,3,5-10	.40	1.20	2.40
4-Adams-a	1.00	3.00	6.00
11-19: Last 25 cents issue. 15-Toth-a(r). 17-Cassandra Craft begins		.60	1.20
20-22: 22-Dark Circle begins		.50	1.00
23-Spawn of Frankenstein begins by Kaluta, ends No. 25	.35	1.10	2.20
24,25	.30	.90	1.80
26-30		.60	1.20
31-The Black Orchid begins		.50	1.00
32,35,36-Black Orchid by Redondo		.50	1.00
33-Deadman app.		.40	.80
34,37,38: 34-New Dr. 13 story		.30	.60
39-41-Deadman in all		.30	.60

NOTE: ***Adams*** *c-3-19.* ***Aparo*** *a-11, 15-17, 19-26; c-20-24, 33.* ***Dezuniga*** *a-15, 16, 19-22, 31, 34.* ***Grell*** *a-33.* ***Kaluta*** *a-23-25; c-26.* ***Meskin*** *r-15, 16, 18.* ***Sparling*** *a-20.* ***Starr*** *a-17. Black Orchid by* ***Carrilo****-38-41. Dr. 13 solo in-13, 18, 20. Frankenstein by* ***Kaluta****-23-25; by* ***Baily****-27-30. No Black Orchid-33,34.*

PHANTOM WITCH DOCTOR
1952
Avon Periodicals

	Good	Fine	Mint
1-Kinstler-c, 7 pgs.	14.00	40.00	80.00

PHANTOM ZONE, THE
January, 1982 - Present
DC Comics

	Good	Fine	Mint
1-Superman app.		.30	.60

PHIL RIZZUTO (Baseball Hero)
1951 (New York Yankees)
Fawcett Publications

	Good	Fine	Mint
nn	8.00	24.00	48.00

PHOENIX
Jan, 1975 - No. 4, Oct, 1975
Atlas/Seaboard Publ.

	Good	Fine	Mint
1-Origin		.40	.80
2,3: 3-Origin & only app. The Dark Avenger		.30	.60
4-New origin/costume The Protector (formerly Phoenix)		.30	.60

NOTE: ***Infantino*** *appears in No. 1,2.*

PICNIC PARTY (Walt Disney's) (Vacation Parade No. 1-5)
1955 - 1957
Dell Publishing Co.

	Good	Fine	Mint
6,7-Uncle Scrooge	2.00	5.00	10.00
8-Carl Barks-a, 6pgs.	5.00	14.00	28.00

PICTORIAL CONFESSIONS (Pictorial Romances No. 4 on)
Sept, 1949 - No. 3, Dec, 1949
St. John Publishing Co.

	Good	Fine	Mint
1-Baker-c/a(3)	8.00	23.00	46.00
2-Baker-a; photo-c	4.00	12.00	24.00
3-Kubert, Baker-a; part Kubert-c	6.00	18.00	36.00

PICTORIAL LOVE STORIES (Formerly Tim McCoy)
No. 22, Oct, 1949 - No. 26, July, 1950
Charlton Comics

	Good	Fine	Mint
22-26-''Me-Dan Cupid'' in all	4.00	12.00	24.00

PICTORIAL LOVE STORIES
October, 1952
St. John Publishing Co.

	Good	Fine	Mint
1-Baker c/a	8.00	23.00	46.00

PICTORIAL ROMANCES (Formerly Pictorial Confessions)
No. 4, Jan, 1950 - No. 24, Mar, 1954
St. John Publishing Co.

	Good	Fine	Mint
4,5,10-All Matt Baker issues	5.00	15.00	30.00
6-9,12,13,15,16-Baker-c, 2-3 stories	4.00	12.00	24.00
11-Baker c/a(3); Kubert-a	5.00	15.00	30.00
14,21-24-Baker-c/a each	3.00	9.00	18.00
17-20(7/53)-100 pgs. each; Baker-c/a	5.00	14.00	28.00

NOTE: ***Matt Baker*** *art in most issues.* ***Estrada*** *a-19(2).*

PICTURE NEWS (Dick Quick No. 10 on)
Jan, 1946 - No. 9, Sept, 1946
Lafayette Street Corp.

	Good	Fine	Mint
1-Milt Gross begins, ends No. 6; 4 pg. Kirby-a; A-Bomb-c	5.00	15.00	30.00
2-5	1.50	4.00	8.00
6-9	1.00	3.00	6.00

PICTURE PARADE (Picture Progress No. 5 on)
Sept, 1953 - V1No.4, Dec, 1953 (28 pages)
Gilberton Corp.

	Good	Fine	Mint
V1No.1-Andy's Atomic Adventures, 2-Around the World with the United Nations, 3-Adventures of the Lost One(The Amer. Indian), 4-A Christmas Adventure	2.00	6.00	12.00

PICTURE PROGRESS (Formerly Picture Parade)
V1No.5, Jan, 1954 - V3No.2, Oct, 1955 (28-36 pgs.)
Gilberton Corp.

	Good	Fine	Mint
V1No.5-News in Review 1953, 6-The Birth of America, 7-The Four Seasons, 8-Paul Revere's Ride, 9-The Hawaiian Islands(5/54), V2No.1-The Story of Flight(9/54), 2-Vote for Crazy River(The Meaning of Elections), 3-Louis Pasteur, 4-The Star Spangled Banner, 5-News in Review 1954, 6-Alaska: The Great Land, 7-Life in the Circus, 8-The Time of the Cave Man, 9-Summer Fun(5/55) each....	.70	2.00	4.00

V3No.1-The Man Who Discovered America, 2-The Lewis & Clark Ex-

PICTURE PROGRESS (continued) — Good / Fine / Mint
pedition each.... .70 2.00 4.00

PICTURE SCOPE JUNGLE ADVENTURES
1954 (36 pgs.) (Says 3-D on cover, but not 3-D)
Star Publishing Co.

nn-Disbrow-a/script; L.B. Cole-c 8.00 24.00 48.00

PICTURE STORIES FROM AMERICAN HISTORY
1945 - 1947 (68 - 52 pages)
National/All-American/E. C. Comics

1 4.00 12.00 24.00
2-4 3.00 9.00 18.00

PICTURE STORIES FROM SCIENCE
Spring, 1947 - No. 2, Fall, 1947
E. C. Comics

1,2 5.00 15.00 30.00

PICTURE STORIES FROM THE BIBLE
Fall, 1942-43 & 1944-46
National/All-American/E. C. Comics

1-4('42-Fall,'43)-Old Testament (DC) 4.00 12.00 24.00
Complete Old Testament Edition, 232 pgs. (1943-DC); contains No. 1-4 7.00 20.00 40.00
Complete Old Testament Edition (1945-publ. by Bible Pictures Ltd.)-232 pgs., hardbound, in color with dust jacket 7.00 20.00 40.00

NOTE: *Both Old and New Testaments published in England by Bible Pictures Ltd. in hardback, 1943, in color, 376 pages.*

1,2(Old Testament reprints in comic book form)(E.C.)-52 pgs. 4.00 12.00 24.00
1-3(New Testament)(1944-46-DC)-52 pgs. each 4.00 12.00 24.00
The Complete Life of Christ Edition(1945)-Contains No. 1 & 2 of the New Testament Edition 5.00 14.00 28.00
Complete New Testament Edition(1946-E.C.)-144 pgs.; contains No. 1-3 5.50 16.00 32.00
1(New Testament reprint in comic book form)(E.C.)-52 pgs. 3.00 8.00 16.00

PICTURE STORIES FROM WORLD HISTORY
Spring, 1947 - No. 2, Summer, 1947 (52, 48 pgs.)
E. C. Comics

1,2 4.00 12.00 24.00

PINHEAD & FOODINI (TV) (Also see The Great Foodini)
July, 1951 - No. 4, Jan, 1952
Fawcett Publications

1 3.00 8.00 16.00
2-4(No. 4-Exist?) 2.00 6.00 12.00

PINK LAFFIN
1922 (9x12'') (strip reprints)
Whitman Publishing Co.

...the Lighter Side of Life, ...He Tells 'Em, ...and His Family, ...Knockouts — art by Ray Gleason (All Rare) each.... 6.00 16.00 32.00

PINK PANTHER, THE (TV)
April, 1971 - Present
Gold Key

1-The Inspector begins .85 2.50 5.00
2-10 .50 1.50 3.00
11-30: Warren Tufts-a No. 16 on .35 1.00 2.00
31-77: Reprints-No. 37,72 .40 .80
Kite Fun Book(1972)-16 pgs.; Sou. Calif. Edison Co. giveaway .50 1.50 3.00
Mini-Comic No. 1(1976)(3¼x6½'') .25 .50

NOTE: *Pink Panther began as a movie cartoon. (See Golden Comics Digest No. 38,45 and March of Comics No. 376,384,390,409,473)*

PINKY LEE (See The Adventures of...)

PINKY THE EGGHEAD
1963 (Reprints from Noodnik)
I. W./Super Comics

Good / Fine / Mint
I.W. Reprint No. 1,2 (no date) .60 1.20
Super Reprint No. 14 .60 1.20

PINOCCHIO (See 4-Color No. 92,252,545,1203, Movie Comics under Wonderful Advs. of..., & World's Greatest Stories No. 2, New Advs. of...)

PINOCCHIO
1940 (10 pages) (linen-like paper)
Montgomery Ward Co. (Giveaway)

10.00 30.00 60.00

PINOCCHIO LEARNS ABOUT KITES (Also see Donald Duck & Brer Rabbit) (Disney)
1954 (8 pages) (Premium)
Pacific Gas & Electric Co./Florida Power & Light

20.00 60.00 120.00

PIN-UP PETE (Also see Monty Hall... & Great Lover Romances)
1952
Toby Press

1-Jack Sparling pin-ups 6.00 18.00 36.00

PIONEER MARSHAL (See Fawcett Movie Comics)

PIONEER PICTURE STORIES
Dec, 1941 - No. 9, Dec, 1943
Street & Smith Publications

1 3.00 9.00 18.00
2-9 2.00 6.00 12.00

PIONEER WEST ROMANCES (Firehair No. 1,2,7-11)
No. 3, Summer, 1949 - No. 6, Winter, 1949-50
Fiction House Magazines

3-6-Firehair continues 3.50 10.00 20.00

PIPSQUEAK (See The Adventures of...)

PIRACY
Oct-Nov, 1954 - No. 7, Oct-Nov, 1955
E. C. Comics

1-Williamson/Torres-a 14.00 40.00 70.00
2-Williamson/Torres-a 10.00 30.00 56.00
3-7 8.00 24.00 44.00

NOTE: ***Crandall*** *a-in all; c-2-4.* ***Davis*** *a-1, 2, 6.* ***Evans*** *a-3-7; c-7.* ***Ingels*** *a-3-7.* ***Krigstein*** *a-3-5, 7; c-5, 6.* ***Wood*** *a-1, 2; c-1.*

PIRANA (See Thrill-O-Rama No. 2,3)

PIRATE OF THE GULF, THE (See Superior Stories No. 2)

PIRATES COMICS
Feb-Mar, 1950 - No. 4, Aug-Sept, 1950
Hillman Periodicals

1 2.00 5.00 10.00
2-4: 3,4-Berg-a 1.50 4.00 8.00

PIUS XII MAN OF PEACE
No date (12 pgs.; 5½x8½'') (B&W)
Catechetical Guild Giveaway

3.00 8.00 16.00

PIXIE & DIXIE & MR. JINKS (TV)
July-Sept, 1960 - Feb, 1963 (Hanna-Barbera)
Dell Publishing Co./Gold Key

4-Color 1112,1196,1264 .70 2.00 4.00
01-631-207 (Dell) .70 2.00 4.00

P.S. From World History #2, © WMG

Pioneer West Romances #4, © FH

Piracy #2, © WMG

Planet Comics #8, © FH

Plastic Man #42, © QUA

Plop! #5, © DC

PIXIE & DIXIE & MR. JINKS (continued)

	Good	Fine	Mint
1(2/63-G.K.)	.70	2.00	4.00

PIXIE PUZZLE ROCKET TO ADVENTURELAND
November, 1952
Avon Periodicals

	Good	Fine	Mint
1	3.50	10.00	20.00

PIXIES, THE (Advs. of . . .) (Mighty Atom No. 6 on)
Winter, 1946 - No. 4, 1947; No. 5, 1948
Magazine Enterprises

	Good	Fine	Mint
1-Mighty Atom	2.00	6.00	12.00
2-5-Mighty Atom	1.00	3.00	6.00
I.W. Reprint No. 1(1958), 8-(Pee-Wee Pixies), 10-I.W. on cover, Super on inside	.40	1.20	2.40

PLANET COMICS
Jan, 1940 - No. 73, Winter, 1953
Fiction House Magazines

	Good	Fine	Mint
1-Origin Auro, Lord of Jupiter; Flint Baker & The Red Comet begin; Eisner/Fine-c	150.00	450.00	900.00
2-(Scarce)	90.00	250.00	500.00
3-Eisner-c	80.00	220.00	440.00
4-Gale Allen and the Girl Squadron begins	65.00	180.00	375.00
5,6-(Scarce)	55.00	160.00	325.00
7-11	45.00	130.00	275.00
12-The Star Pirate begins	45.00	130.00	275.00
13-15: 13-Reff Ryan begins. 15-Mars, God of War begins	40.00	110.00	225.00
16-20,22	35.00	100.00	200.00
21-The Lost World & Hunt Bowman begin	40.00	110.00	225.00
23-25	30.00	90.00	190.00
26-The Space Rangers begin	30.00	90.00	190.00
27-30	25.00	75.00	150.00
31-35: 33-Origin Star Pirates Wonder Boots, reprinted in No. 52. 35-Mysta of the Moon begins	20.00	60.00	125.00
36-45: 41-New origin of "Auro, Lord of Jupiter." 42-Last Gale Allen. 43-Futura begins	20.00	60.00	125.00
46-52,54-60	14.00	40.00	90.00
53-Used in **SOTI**, pg. 32	15.00	45.00	100.00
61-64	10.00	28.00	60.00
65-68,70: 65-70-All partial reprints of earlier issues; 65-Drug story	9.00	25.00	56.00
69-Used in **POP**, pgs. 101,102	11.00	32.00	70.00
71-73-No series stories	8.00	22.00	50.00
I.W. Reprint No. 1(no date)-reprints No. 70, which reprints part of No. 41	3.00	8.00	16.00
I.W. Reprint No. 8 (reprints No. 72), 9-Reprints No. 73	3.00	8.00	16.00

NOTE: No. 33-38,40-51-Star Pirate by ***Anderson***. ***Fine*** *c-2, 5,* ***Evans*** *a-50-64(Lost World).* ***Ingels*** *a-24-31, 56-61 (Auro, Lord of Jupiter). Mysta of the Moon by* ***Maurice Whitman****-51, 52; by* ***Matt Baker****-53-59. Star Pirate by* ***Tuska****-30; by* ***M. Whitman****-54-56.*

PLANET OF THE APES (Magazine)
Aug, 1974 - No. 29, Feb, 1977 (B&W) (Based on movies)
Marvel Comics Group

	Good	Fine	Mint
1-Ploog-a	.50	1.50	3.00
2-Ploog-a	.40	1.20	2.40
3-10	.30	.80	1.60
11-20		.60	1.20
21-29		.50	1.00

NOTE: ***Alcala*** *a-7-11, 17-22, 24.* ***Ploog*** *a-1-8, 11, 13, 14, 19.* ***Sutton*** *a-12, 15, 17, 19, 20, 23, 24.*

PLANET OF VAMPIRES
Feb, 1975 - No. 3, June, 1975
Seaboard Publications (Atlas)

	Good	Fine	Mint
1-Adams-c(i); 1st Broderick c(p)/a		.50	1.00
2-Adams-c, 3-Heath-a		.40	.80

PLASTIC MAN (Also see Police)
1943 - No. 64, Nov, 1956
Vital Publ. No. 1,2/Quality Comics No. 3 on

	Good	Fine	Mint
nn(No.1)-"The Game of Death;" Jack Cole-a begins; ends-No. 64?	80.00	210.00	420.00
nn(No.2)-"The Gay Nineties Nightmare"	50.00	140.00	280.00
3	30.00	90.00	185.00
4	25.00	72.00	150.00
5	21.00	62.00	130.00
6-10	15.00	45.00	95.00
11-20	12.00	34.00	70.00
21-30	9.00	26.00	60.00
31-39	7.00	20.00	45.00
40-Used in **POP**, pg. 91	8.00	22.00	50.00
41-64	6.00	18.00	38.00
Super Reprint 11('63), 16 (reprints 21, Cole-a), 18('64-Spirit app. by Eisner/Police 95)	2.00	6.00	12.00

PLASTIC MAN (See Brave & the Bold and DC Special No. 15)
11-12/66 - No. 10, 5-6/68; No. 11, 2-3/76 - No. 20, 10-11/77
National Periodical Publications/DC Comics

	Good	Fine	Mint
1-Gil Kane-c	1.20	3.50	5.25
2-5('68): 4-Infantino-c	.85	2.50	3.75
6-10('68)	.70	2.00	3.00
11('76)-20	.40	1.20	1.80

PLAYFUL LITTLE AUDREY (Also see Little Audrey No. 25)
June, 1957 - No. 121, April, 1976
Harvey Publications

	Good	Fine	Mint
1	10.00	30.00	60.00
2-5	5.00	15.00	30.00
6-10	3.50	10.00	20.00
11-20	2.00	5.00	10.00
21-40	1.50	4.00	8.00
41-60	.85	2.50	5.00
61-80	.45	1.30	2.60
81-99	.30	.90	1.80
100	.45	1.30	2.60
101-121	.30	.80	1.60
Clubhouse 1('63)	1.50	4.00	6.00

PLOP!
Sept-Oct, 1973 - No. 24, Nov-Dec, 1976
National Periodical Publications

	Good	Fine	Mint
1-Wrightson-a		.60	1.20
2-4		.50	1.00
5-Wrightson-a		.60	1.20
6-10		.50	1.00
11-20: 18-Nixon satire		.40	.80
21-24-Giant Size, 52 pgs.		.30	.60

NOTE: ***Alcala*** *a-1-3.* ***Anderson*** *a-5.* ***Ditko*** *a-16.* ***Orlando*** *a-21, 22; c-21.* ***Toth*** *a-11.* ***Wolverton*** *a-4(1 pg.), 22; c-1-12, 14, 17.* ***Wood*** *a-14, 16, 18-24; c-13, 15, 16, 18, 19.*

PLUTO (See Cheerios Premiums & Walt Disney Showcase No. 4,7, 13,20,23)
1942 - 1961 (Walt Disney)
Dell Publishing Co.

	Good	Fine	Mint
Large Feature Comic 7(1942)	70.00	180.00	360.00
4-Color 429,509	1.20	3.50	7.00
4-Color 595,654	.70	2.00	4.00
4-Color 736,853,941,1039,1143,1248	.60	1.80	3.60

POCAHONTAS
1941 - No. 2, 1942
Pocahontas Fuel Company

	Good	Fine	Mint
nn(No.1), 2	4.00	12.00	24.00

POCKET COMICS
Aug, 1941 - No. 4, Jan, 1942 (Pocket size; 100 pgs.)
Harvey Publications

1-Origin The Black Cat, Cadet Blakey the Spirit of '76, The Phantom Sphinx, The Red Blazer, & The Zebra; Phantom Ranger, British

POCKET COMICS (continued) — Good / Fine / Mint

Agent No. 99, Spin Hawkins, Satan, Lord of Evil begin — 20.00 60.00 140.00
2 — 14.00 40.00 90.00
3,4 — 10.00 30.00 70.00

POGO PARADE (Annual)
1953 (100 pages)
Dell Publishing Co.

1-Kelly-a (reprints Pogo from Animal Comics in this order: No. 11, 13,21,14,27,16,23,9,18,15,17) — 17.00 50.00 100.00

POGO POSSUM (Also see Animal Comics & Special Delivery)
1949 - 1954
Dell Publishing Co.

4-Color 105(1946)-Kelly-a — 40.00 120.00 240.00
4-Color 148-Kelly-a — 35.00 100.00 200.00
1-Kelly art in all — 30.00 85.00 170.00
2 — 14.00 40.00 80.00
3-5 — 10.00 30.00 60.00
6-10: 10-Infinity-c — 8.00 24.00 48.00
11-16 — 7.00 20.00 40.00

NOTE: *No. 1-4,9-13: 52 pgs.; No. 5-8,14-16: 36 pgs.*

POLICE ACTION
Jan, 1954 - No. 7, Nov, 1954
Atlas News Co.

1 — 2.00 6.00 12.00
2-7: 7-Powell-a — 1.50 4.00 8.00

POLICE ACTION
Feb, 1975 - No. 3, June, 1975
Atlas/Seaboard Publ.

1-Lomax, N.Y.P.D., Luke Malone begin; McWilliams-a; bondage-c — .40 .80
2,3: 2-Origin Luke Malone, Manhunter — .30 .60

NOTE: ***McWilliams** a-3. **Ploog** art in all. **Thorne** c-3.*

POLICE AGAINST CRIME
April, 1954 - No. 9, Aug, 1955
Premiere Magazines

1-Disbrow-a; extreme violence - man's face slashed with knife; Hollingsworth-a — 3.00 8.00 16.00
2-9 — 2.00 5.00 10.00

POLICE BADGE NO. 479 (Spy Thrillers No. 1-4)
No. 5, Sept, 1955
Atlas Comics (CPI)

5 — 1.20 3.50 7.00

POLICE CASE BOOK (See Giant Comics Editions)

POLICE CASES (See Authentic. . . & Record Book of. . .)

POLICE COMICS
Aug, 1941 - No. 127, Oct, 1953
Quality Comics Group (Comic Magazines)

1-Origin Plastic Man by Jack Cole, The Human Bomb by Gustavson, & No. 711; intro. Chic Carter by Eisner, The Firebrand by R. Crandall, The Mouthpiece, Phantom Lady, & The Sword — 200.00 500.00 1025.00
2-Plastic Man smuggles opium — 100.00 260.00 540.00
3 — 70.00 200.00 420.00
4 — 60.00 180.00 375.00
5-Plastic Man forced to smoke marijuana — 60.00 180.00 375.00
6,7 — 55.00 155.00 325.00
8-Origin Manhunter — 60.00 180.00 375.00
9,10 — 50.00 140.00 300.00
11-The Spirit strip reprints begin by Eisner(Origin-strip No. 1) — 100.00 260.00 540.00
12-Intro. Ebony — 50.00 140.00 300.00
13-Intro. Woozy Winks; last Firebrand — 50.00 140.00 300.00
14-19: 15-Last No. 711; Destiny begins — 30.00 90.00 200.00
20-The Raven x-over in Phantom Lady; features Jack Cole himself — 30.00 90.00 200.00
21,22-Raven & Spider Widow x-over in Phantom Lady No. 21, cameo in Phantom Lady No. 22 — 25.00 70.00 150.00
23-30: 23-Last Phantom Lady. 24-Chic Carter becomes The Sword, only issue. 24-26-Flatfoot Burns by Kurtzman in all — 19.00 55.00 125.00
31-41-Last Spirit reprint by Eisner — 14.00 40.00 90.00
42,43-Spirit reprint by Eisner/Fine — 10.00 30.00 70.00
44-Spirit reprints begin by Fine, end No. 88,90,92 — 9.50 28.00 60.00
45-50-(No.50 on-c, No.49 on inside)(1/46) — 9.50 28.00 60.00
51-60: 58-Last Human Bomb — 6.00 18.00 40.00
61,62,64-88 — 6.00 18.00 40.00
63-(Some issues have No.65 printed on cover, but No.63 on inside) Kurtzman-a, 6pgs. — 6.00 18.00 40.00
89,91,93-No Spirit — 5.50 16.00 35.00
90,92-Spirit by Fine — 6.00 18.00 40.00
94-102: Spirit by Eisner in all; 101-Last Manhunter. 102-Last Spirit & Plastic Man by Jack Cole — 8.00 22.00 50.00
103-Content change to crime - Ken Shannon — 4.50 13.00 28.00
104-111,114-127-Crandall-a most issues — 4.00 11.00 24.00
112-Crandall-a; drug mention story — 4.00 11.00 24.00
113-Crandall-c/a(2), 9 pgs. each — 3.00 9.00 20.00

NOTE: *Most Spirit stories signed by **Eisner** are not by him; all are reprints. **Cole** c-20, 24-26, 28, 29, 31, 36-38. **Crandall** Firebrand-1-8. Spirit by **Eisner** 1-41, 94-102; by **Eisner/Fine**-42, 43; by **Fine**-44-88, 90, 92. 109-Bondage-c.*

POLICE LINE-UP
Aug, 1951 - No. 4, July, 1952
Realistic Comics/Avon Periodicals

1-Wood-a, 1 pg. plus part-c; spanking panel-r/Saint No. 5 — 8.00 24.00 48.00
2-Classic story "The Religious Murder Cult," drugs, perversion r-/Saint No. 5; c-/Avon paperback 329 — 7.00 20.00 40.00
3-Kubert-a(r)/part-c, Kinstler-a; drug mention story — 5.50 16.00 32.00
4-Kinstler-a — 5.50 16.00 32.00

POLICE THRILLS
1954
Ajax/Farrell Publications

1 — 2.00 5.00 10.00

POLICE TRAP (Public Defender in Action No. 7 on)
Aug-Sept, 1954 - No. 6, Sept, 1955
Mainline No. 1-4 (Prize)/Charlton No. 5,6

1-S&K covers-all issues — 3.00 9.00 18.00
2,3 — 2.00 5.00 10.00
4-S&K-c — 1.20 3.50 7.00
5,6-S&K-c/a — 3.50 10.00 20.00

POLICE TRAP
No. 11, 1963; No. 16-18, 1964
Super Comics

Reprint No. 11,16-18 — .50 1.50 3.00

POLL PARROT
Poll Parrot Shoe Store/International Shoe
1950 - 1951; 1959 - 1962
K. K. Publications (Giveaway)

1-4('50)-Howdy Doody — 1.20 3.50 7.00
2('59)-16('61): 2-The Secret of Crumbley Castle. 5-Bandit Busters. 8-Mixed Up Mission('60). 10-The Frightful Flight. 11-Showdown at Sunup. 13-. . .and the Runaway Genie. 14-Bully for You. 16-. . .& the Rahah's Ruby('62). — .50 1.50 3.00

Pogo Possum #4, © Walt Kelly

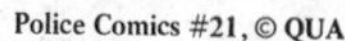
Police Comics #21, © QUA

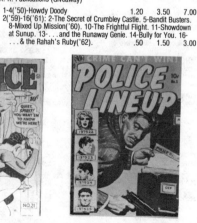

Police Line-Up #1, © AVON

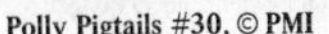
Polly Pigtails #30, © PMI

Popeye #3, © KING

Popular Comics #26, © DELL

POLLY & HER PALS (See Comic Monthly No. 1)

POLLYANNA (See 4-Color No. 1129)

POLLY PIGTAILS (Girls' Fun & Fashion Mag. No. 44 on)
Jan, 1946 - V4No.43, Oct-Nov, 1949
Parents' Magazine Institute/Polly Pigtails

	Good	Fine	Mint
1-Infinity-c	2.50	7.00	14.00
2-5	1.20	3.50	7.00
6-10	1.00	3.00	6.00
11-30	.85	2.50	5.00
31-43	.70	2.00	4.00

PONYTAIL
7-9/62 - No. 12, 10-12/65; No. 13, 11/69 - No. 20, 1/71
Dell Publishing Co./Charlton No. 13 on

	Good	Fine	Mint
nn(No.1)	.50	1.50	3.00
2-12	.30	.80	1.60
13-20		.50	1.00

POP COMICS (7 cents)
1955 (36 pgs.; 5x7''; in color)
Modern Store Publ.

	Good	Fine	Mint
1-Funny animal	.40	1.20	2.40

POPEYE (See Comic Album No. 7,11,15, Comics Reading Libraries, Eat Right to Work . . ., Giant Comic Album & March of Comics No. 37, 52,66,80,96,117,134,148,157,169,194,246,264,274,294,477)

POPEYE (See Thimble Theatre)
1935 (25 cents; 52 pgs.; B&W) (By Segar)
David McKay Publications

	Good	Fine	Mint
1-Daily strip serial reprints-''The Gold Mine Thieves''	40.00	100.00	200.00
2-Daily strip-r	30.00	80.00	160.00

NOTE: *Popeye first entered Thimble Theatre in 1929.*

POPEYE
1937 (8-3/8''x9-3/8'') (cardboard covers)
(All color drawings plus text taken from Segar; probably not by him)
Whitman Publishing Co.

	Good	Fine	Mint
. . . Borrows a Baby Nurse (72 pgs.)			
. . . & His Jungle Pet (72 pgs.) each. . . .	14.00	40.00	80.00
. . . Goes Duck Hunting (28 pgs.)			
Wimpy Tricks Popeye & Rough-House (28 pgs.)			
. . . Plays Nursemaid to Sweet Pea (28 pgs.)			
. . . Calls on Olive Oyl (28 pgs.) each. . . .	10.00	30.00	60.00

POPEYE
1937 - 1939 (All by Segar)
David McKay Publications

	Good	Fine	Mint
Feature Book nn (100 pgs.) (Very Rare)	200.00	600.00	1200.00
Feature Book 2 (52 pgs.)	40.00	120.00	240.00
Feature Book 3 (100 pgs.)-Thought to be a reprint of the nn issue with a new-c	35.00	100.00	200.00
Feature Book 5,10 (76 pgs.)	25.00	70.00	140.00
Feature Book 14 (76 pgs.) (Scarce)	40.00	120.00	240.00

POPEYE (Strip reprints through 4-Color No. 70)
1941 - 1947; No. 1, 2-4/48 - No. 65, 7-9/62; No. 66, 10/62 - No. 80, 5/66; No. 81, 8/66 - No. 92, 12/67; No. 94, 2/69 - No. 138, 1/77; No. 139, 5/78 - Present (no No. 93,160,161)
Dell No. 1-65/Gold Key No. 66-80/King No. 81-92/Charlton No. 94-138/Gold Key No. 139-155/Whitman No. 156 on

	Good	Fine	Mint
Black & White 24('41)-Half by Segar	30.00	80.00	160.00
4-Color 25('41)-by Segar	30.00	80.00	160.00
Large Feature Comic 10('43)	20.00	60.00	120.00
4-Color 17('43)-by Segar	20.00	60.00	120.00
4-Color 26('43)-by Segar	17.00	50.00	100.00
4-Color 43('44)	10.00	30.00	60.00
4-Color 70('45)-Title: . . . & Wimpy	8.00	24.00	48.00
4-Color 113('46-original strips begin),127,145('47),168	3.50	10.00	20.00
1(2-4/48)(Dell)	10.00	30.00	60.00
2	5.00	15.00	30.00
3-10	4.00	12.00	24.00
11-20	3.00	8.00	16.00
21-40	2.00	6.00	12.00
41-45,47-50	1.50	4.00	8.00
46-Origin Swee' Pee	2.00	6.00	12.00
51-60	1.00	3.00	6.00
61-65,68-80	.70	2.00	4.00
66,67-both 84 pgs.	1.00	3.00	6.00
81-92,94-100	.30	.90	1.80
101-143,145-159,162-165		.40	.80
144-50th Anniversary issue	.30	.80	1.60

NOTE: *Reprints-No. 145,147,149,151,153,155.*

	Good	Fine	Mint
Bold Detergent giveaway (Same as regular issue No. 94)		.60	1.20
. . . Kite Fun Book (PG&E, 1977)	.80	2.40	4.80

POPEYE
1972 - 1974 (36 pgs. in color)
Charlton (King Features) (Giveaway)

	Good	Fine	Mint
E-1 to E-15 (Educational comics)		.40	.80
nn-Popeye Gettin' Better Grades-4 pgs. used as intro. to above giveaways (in color)		.40	.80

POPEYE CARTOON BOOK
1934 (36 pgs. plus cover)(8½x13'')(cardboard covers)
The Saalfield Publ. Co.

	Good	Fine	Mint
2095-(Rare)-1933 strip reprints in color by Segar; each page contains a vertical half of a Sunday strip, so the continuity reads row by row completely across each double page spread. If each page is read by itself, the continuity makes no sense. Each double page spread reprints one complete Sunday page (from 1933).	90.00	230.00	460.00
12 Page Version	40.00	120.00	240.00

POPPO OF THE POPCORN THEATRE
10/29/55 - 1956 (published weekly)
Fuller Publishing Co. (Publishers Weekly)

	Good	Fine	Mint
1	2.00	5.00	10.00
2-13	1.00	3.00	6.00

NOTE: *By **Charles Biro**. 10 cents cover price, given away by supermarkets such as IGA.*

POP-POP COMICS
No date (Circa 1945)
R. B. Leffingwell Co.

	Good	Fine	Mint
1	1.00	3.00	6.00

POPSICLE PETE FUN BOOK
1947, 1948
Joe Lowe Corp.

	Good	Fine	Mint
nn-36 pgs. in color; Sammy 'n' Claras, The King Who Couldn't Sleep & Popsicle Pete stories, games, cut-outs	4.00	12.00	24.00
Adventure Book ('48)	3.50	10.00	20.00

POPULAR COMICS
Feb, 1936 - No. 145, July-Sept, 1948
Dell Publishing Co.

	Good	Fine	Mint
1-Terry & the Pirates, Gasoline Alley, Dick Tracy, Moon Mullins, The Gumps begin (all strip-r)	40.00	120.00	240.00
2	20.00	60.00	120.00
3	15.00	45.00	90.00
4,5	12.00	35.00	70.00
6-10	8.00	24.00	48.00
11-20	7.00	20.00	40.00
21-27-Last Terry & the Pirates & Little Orphan Annie	7.00	20.00	40.00

POPULAR COMICS (continued)

	Good	Fine	Mint
28-37	5.50	16.00	32.00
38-43-Tarzan in all	8.00	24.00	48.00
44,45	4.00	12.00	24.00
46-Origin Martan, the Marvel Man	5.00	14.00	28.00
47-50	4.00	12.00	24.00
51-Origin The Voice (The Invisible Detective) strip begins	5.00	14.00	28.00
52-59	4.00	12.00	24.00
60-Origin Professor Supermind and Son	5.00	14.00	28.00
61,62,64-71	4.00	12.00	24.00
63-Smilin' Jack begins	4.00	12.00	24.00
72-The Owl & Terry & the Pirates begin; Smokey Stover reprints begin	4.00	12.00	24.00
73-75	4.00	12.00	24.00
76-78-Capt. Midnight in all	5.00	14.00	28.00
79-86-Last Owl	4.00	12.00	24.00
87-100: 98-Felix the Cat, Smokey Stover-r begin	3.00	9.00	18.00
101-130	2.50	7.00	14.00
131-145	2.00	6.00	12.00

POPULAR FAIRY TALES (See March of Comics No. 6,18)

POPULAR ROMANCE
No. 5, Dec, 1949 - No. 29, 1954
Better-Standard Publications

	Good	Fine	Mint
5-7,9	2.00	5.00	10.00
8-Tuska-a	2.50	7.00	14.00
10-Wood-a, 2 pgs.	3.00	8.00	16.00
11,12,14-21,28,29	1.50	4.00	8.00
13-Severin/Elder-a, 3 pgs.	1.50	4.00	8.00
22-27-Toth-a	3.50	10.00	20.00

NOTE: *All have photo-c.* ***Tuska*** *art in most issues.*

POPULAR TEEN-AGERS (Secrets of Love) (Formerly School Day Romances)
Sept, 1950 - No. 23, Nov, 1954
Star Publications

	Good	Fine	Mint
5-8-Toni Gay, Honey Bunn, etc.; all have L. B. Cole-c; 6-Negligee panels	8.00	24.00	48.00
9-(. . . Romances; change to romance format)	3.50	10.00	20.00
10-(. . . Secrets of Love)	3.50	10.00	20.00
11,16,18,19,22,23	3.00	8.00	16.00
12,13,17,20,21-Disbrow-a	3.50	10.00	20.00
14-Harrison/Wood-a; 2 spanking scenes	8.00	24.00	48.00
15-Wood?, Disbrow-a	8.00	24.00	48.00

NOTE: *All have* ***L. B. Cole*** *covers.*

PORE LI'L MOSE
1902 (30 pgs.; 10½x15''; in full color)
New York Herald Publ. by Grand Union Tea
Cupples & Leon Co.

	Good	Fine	Mint
By R. F. Outcault; 1 pg. strips about early Negroes	30.00	80.00	160.00

PORKY PIG (. . & Bugs Bunny No. 40-69)
1942 - Present
Dell Publishing Co./Gold Key No. 1-93/Whitman No. 94 on

	Good	Fine	Mint
4-Color 16(1942)	30.00	80.00	160.00
4-Color 48(1944)-Carl Barks-a	90.00	220.00	440.00
4-Color 78(1945)	7.00	20.00	40.00
4-Color 112(1946)	5.00	14.00	28.00
4-Color 156,182,191('49)	3.50	10.00	20.00
4-Color 226,241('49),260,271,277,284,295('50)	2.50	7.00	14.00
4-Color 303,311,322,330	1.50	4.00	8.00
4-Color 342,351,360,370,385,399('52),410,426	.85	2.50	5.00
25-30	.40	1.20	2.40
31-50	.30	.80	1.60
51-81(3-4/62)		.50	1.00
1(1/65-G.K.)(2nd Series)	.30	.80	1.60
2,4,5-Reprints 4-Color 226,284 & 271 in that order	.30	.80	1.60
3,6-10		.40	.80
11-50		.30	.60
51-103		.25	.50

NOTE: *Reprints-No. 12,13,15,22,27,67,69-74,76,78.*

PORKY PIG (See March of Comics No. 42,57,71,89,99,113,130, 143,164,175,192,209,218,367, and Super Book No. 6,18,30)

PORKY'S BOOK OF TRICKS
1942 (48 pages) (8½x5½'')
K. K. Publications (Giveaway)

	Good	Fine	Mint
7 pg. comic story, text stories, plus games & puzzles	20.00	60.00	120.00

POST GAZETTE (See Meet the New. . .)

POWDER RIVER RUSTLERS (See Fawcett Movie Comics)

POWER COMICS
1944 - 1945
Holyoke Publ. Co./Narrative Publ.

	Good	Fine	Mint
1-L. B. Cole-c	10.00	30.00	60.00
2-4: 2-Dr. Mephisto begins. 3,4-L. B. Cole-c; Miss Espionage app. each	8.00	24.00	48.00

POWERHOUSE PEPPER COMICS (See Gay Comics)
No. 1, 1943; No. 2, May, 1948 - No. 5, Nov, 1948
Marvel Comics (20CC)

	Good	Fine	Mint
1-Wolverton-a	35.00	110.00	225.00
2-4-All by Wolverton	25.00	70.00	140.00
5-(Scarce)-Wolverton-a	30.00	85.00	170.00

POWER MAN (Formerly Hero for Hire)
No. 17, Feb, 1974 - Present
Marvel Comics Group

	Good	Fine	Mint
17-20: 17-Iron Man app.	.30	.80	1.60
21-30		.50	1.00
31-Part Adams inks	.30	.80	1.60
32-44: 36-Reprint		.40	.80
45-Starlin-c		.40	.80
46,47		.40	.80
48-50-Byrne-a; 50-Iron Fist joins Cage	.35	1.10	2.20
51-56,58-60: 58-Drug mention; intro El Aquila		.40	.80
57-New X-Men app.	.70	2.00	4.00
61-74,76		.30	.60
75-Double size; Larkin painted-c		.40	.80
Giant-Size 1('75)	.30	.80	1.60
Annual 1(11/76)		.50	1.00

NOTE: ***Byrne*** *a-48-50.* ***Layton*** *c-56-59.* ***Leiahola*** *a-60i.* ***Miller*** *c-70-74.* ***Nino*** *a-42i, 43.*

POW MAGAZINE (Bob Sproul's) (Satire Magazine)
Aug, 1966 - No. 3, Feb, 1967 (30 cents)
Humor-Vision

	Good	Fine	Mint
1-3: 2-Jones-a. 3-Wrightson-a	.85	2.50	5.00

PREHISTORIC WORLD (See Classics Special)

PREMIERE (See Charlton Premiere)

PRETTY BOY FLOYD (See On the Spot)

PREZ (See Cancelled Comic Cavalcade & Supergirl No. 10)
Aug-Sept, 1973 - No. 4, Feb-Mar, 1974
National Periodical Publications

	Good	Fine	Mint
1-Origin		.30	.60
2-4		.25	.50

Popular Comics #45, © DELL

Popular Teen-Agers #5, © STAR

Power Man #57, © MCG

Prison Break! #2, © AVON

Prize Comics #4, © PRIZE

Prize Comics Western #98, © PRIZE

PRIDE AND THE PASSION, THE (See 4-Color No. 824)

PRIDE OF THE YANKEES, THE
1949 (The Life of Lou Gehrig)
Magazine Enterprises

	Good	Fine	Mint
nn-Ogden Whitney-a	10.00	30.00	60.00

PRIMUS (TV)
Feb, 1972 - No. 7, Oct, 1972
Charlton Comics

	Good	Fine	Mint
1-5,7-Staton-a in all	.35	1.00	2.00
6-Drug propaganda story	.35	1.00	2.00

PRINCE & THE PAUPER, THE (See Movie Classics)

PRINCE VALIANT (See Comics Reading Libraries, Feature Book No. 26, McKay)

PRINCE VALIANT (See 4-Color No. 567,650,699,719,788,849,900)

PRISCILLA'S POP (See 4-Color No. 569,630,704,799)

PRISON BARS (See Behind . . .)

PRISON BREAK!
Sept, 1951 - No. 5, Sept, 1952
Avon Periodicals/Realistic No. 4 on

	Good	Fine	Mint
1-Wood-c & 1 pg.; has r-/Saint No. 7 retitled Michael Strong Private Eye	10.00	30.00	60.00
2-Wood-c/Kubert-a plus 2 pgs. Wood-a	8.00	24.00	48.00
3-Orlando, Check-a; c-/Avon paperback 179	7.00	20.00	40.00
4,5: Kinstler-c. 5-Infantino-a	6.00	18.00	36.00

PRISON RIOT
1952
Avon Periodicals

	Good	Fine	Mint
1-Marijuana Murders-1 pg. text; Kinstler-c	8.00	24.00	48.00

PRISON TO PRAISE
1974
Logos International

	Good	Fine	Mint
True story of Merlin R. Corothers		.30	.60

PRIVATE BUCK (See Large Feature Comic No. 12 and Black & White No. 21)

PRIVATE EYE
Jan, 1951 - No. 8, March, 1952
Atlas Comics (MCI)

	Good	Fine	Mint
1	2.50	7.00	14.00
2-V. Henkel c/a; drug use story	2.00	5.00	10.00
3-6,8: 8-Rocky Jorden . . .	2.00	5.00	10.00
7-Drugs/cocaine mentioned	2.50	7.00	14.00

PRIVATE EYE (See Mike Shayne . . .)

PRIVATE SECRETARY
Dec-Feb, 1962-63 - No. 2, Mar-May, 1963
Dell Publishing Co.

	Good	Fine	Mint
1,2	.85	2.50	5.00

PRIVATE STRONG (See The Double Life of . . .)

PRIZE COMICS (. . . Western No. 69 on) (Also see Treasure Comics)
March, 1940 - No. 68, Feb-Mar, 1948
Prize Publications

	Good	Fine	Mint
1-Origin Power Nelson, The Futureman & Jupiter, Master Magician; Ted O'Neal, Secret Agent M-11, Jaxon of the Jungle, Bucky Brady & Storm Curtis begin	30.00	85.00	190.00
2-The Black Owl begins	17.00	50.00	100.00
3,4	14.00	40.00	80.00
5,6: Dr. Dekkar, Master of Monsters app. in each	10.00	30.00	60.00
7-Black Owl by S&K; origin/1st app. Dr. Frost & Frankenstein; The Green Lama, Capt. Gallant, The Great Voodini & Twist Turner begin; Kirby-c	30.00	80.00	160.00
8,9-Black Owl & Ted O'Neil by S&K	14.00	40.00	80.00
10,12,14-20	10.00	30.00	60.00
11-Origin Bulldog Denny	10.00	30.00	60.00
13-Origin Yank & Doodle	14.00	40.00	80.00
21-24	5.50	16.00	32.00
25-30	5.00	14.00	28.00
31-33	3.50	10.00	20.00
34-Origin Airmale, Yank & Doodle, & The Black Owl	4.00	12.00	24.00
35-40: 35-Flying Fist & Bingo begin. 37-Intro. Stampy, Airmale's sidekick	3.00	8.00	16.00
41-50: 45-Yank & Doodle learn Black Owl's I.D. (their father). No. 48-Prince Ra begins.	2.50	7.00	14.00
51-62,64-68: 55-No Frankenstein. 64-Black Owl retires	2.00	5.00	10.00
63-Simon & Kirby c/a	3.50	10.00	20.00

PRIZE COMICS WESTERN (Prize No. 1-68)
No. 69(V7No.2), Apr-May, 1948 - No. 119, Nov-Dec, 1956
Prize Publications (Feature)

	Good	Fine	Mint
69(V7No.2)	3.00	8.00	16.00
70-73,76,78,83,84	2.00	6.00	12.00
74,79-Kurtzman-a	4.00	12.00	24.00
75,80,81,87-91,93,96-99,110,111-Severin/Elder stories each (2-3)	2.50	7.00	14.00
77-Photo-c; Bailey story of film 'Streets of Laredo'	2.50	7.00	14.00
82-1st app. The Preacher by Mart Bailey; three Severin/Elder-a	2.50	7.00	14.00
85-American Eagle by John Severin begins (1-2/50)	5.00	14.00	28.00
86,94,95,101-105	2.00	6.00	12.00
92-One pg. dope ad	3.00	8.00	16.00
100	2.50	7.00	14.00
106-108,112	2.00	5.00	10.00
109-Severin/Williamson-a	3.50	10.00	20.00
113-Williamson/Severin-a(2)	4.00	12.00	24.00
114-119: Drifter series in all; by Mort Meskin 114-118	1.20	3.50	7.00

NOTE: ***Kirby** c-63, 75, 83. **Severin & Elder** c-98. **Severin** a-72, 75, 83-86, 96, 97, 100-105; c-most 85-109.*

PRIZE MYSTERY
May, 1955 - No. 3, 1955
Key Publications

	Good	Fine	Mint
1	1.50	4.00	8.00
2,3	1.00	3.00	6.00

PROFESSIONAL FOOTBALL (See Charlton Sport Library)

PSYCHO (Magazine)
Jan, 1971 - No. 24, Mar, 1975 (68 pgs.; B&W) (no No.22?)
Skywald Publishing Corp.

	Good	Fine	Mint
1-All reprints	.35	1.10	2.20
2-Origin & 1st app. The Heap, & Frankenstein series by Adkins	.30	.90	1.80
3-10	.30	.80	1.60
11-21,23		.50	1.00
24-1975 Winter Special		.60	1.20
Annual 1('72)	.30	.80	1.60
Fall Special('74)		.60	1.20
Yearbook(1974-nn)		.60	1.20

NOTE: ***Boris** c-3, 5. **Buckler** a-4 ,5. **Everett** a-3, 4, 6. **Jones** a-4, 6; c-12. **Kaluta** a-13. **Katz/Buckler** a-3. **Morrow** a-1. **Reese** a-5. **Sutton** a-3. **Wildey** a-5.*

PSYCHOANALYSIS
Mar-Apr, 1955 - No. 4, Sept-Oct, 1955
E. C. Comics

	Good	Fine	Mint
1-All Kamen; not approved by code	5.50	16.00	32.00

PSYCHOANALYSIS (continued)

	Good	Fine	Mint
2-4-Kamen-a in all	4.00	12.00	24.00

P.T. 109 (See Movie Comics)

PUBLIC DEFENDER IN ACTION (Formerly Police Trap)
No. 7, Mar, 1956 - No. 12, 1957
Charlton Comics

7-12	.85	2.50	5.00

PUBLIC ENEMIES
1948 - 1949
D. S. Publishing Co.

1	3.50	10.00	20.00
2-Used in **SOTI**, pg. 95	5.50	16.00	32.00
3-5	2.50	7.00	14.00
6,8,9	2.00	6.00	12.00
7-McWilliams-a; Injury to eye	2.50	7.00	14.00

PUDGY PIG
Sept, 1958 - No. 2, Nov, 1958
Charlton Comics

1,2	.50	1.50	3.00

PUNCH & JUDY COMICS
1944 - V3No.9, Dec, 1951
Hillman Periodicals

V1No.1-(60 pgs.)	3.00	8.00	16.00
2-12(7/46)	1.50	4.00	8.00
V2No.1,3-9	1.00	3.00	6.00
V2No.2,10-12, V3No.1-Kirby-a(2) each	5.50	16.00	32.00
V3No.2-Kirby-a	5.00	14.00	28.00
3-9	.85	2.50	5.00

PUNCH COMICS
Dec, 1941 - No. 26, Dec, 1947
Harry 'A' Chesler

1-Mr. E, The Sky Chief, Hale the Magician, Kitty Kelly begin	15.00	45.00	100.00
2-Captain Glory app.	8.00	24.00	48.00
3	7.00	20.00	40.00
4	5.50	16.00	32.00
5	5.00	14.00	28.00
6-8	4.00	12.00	24.00
9-Rocketman & Rocket Girl & The Master Key begin	5.00	14.00	28.00
10-Sky Chief app.	4.00	12.00	24.00
11,12: 11-Sky Chief app.; Fineish art by Sultan. 12-Rocket Boy & Capt. Glory app; Skull-c.	3.50	10.00	20.00
13-17,19	3.50	10.00	20.00
18-Bondage-c; hypodermic panels	4.00	12.00	24.00
20-Unique cover with bare-breasted women	8.00	24.00	48.00
21-Hypo needle story	3.50	10.00	20.00
22-26: 22,23-Little Nemo-not by McCay	3.00	8.00	16.00

PUPPET COMICS
Spring, 1946
George W. Dougherty Co.

1,2	2.50	7.00	10.50

PUPPETOONS (See George Pal's . . .)

PURE OIL COMICS (Also see Salerno Carnival of Comics, 24 Pages of Comics, & Vicks Comics)
Late 1930's (24 pgs.; regular size) (paper cover)
Pure Oil Giveaway

nn-Contains 1-2 pg. strips; i.e., Hairbreadth Harry, Skyroads, Buck Rogers by Calkins & Yager, Olly of the Movies, Napoleon, S'Matter Pop, etc.	20.00	60.00	120.00
Also a 16 pg. 1938 giveaway with Buck Rogers	17.00	50.00	100.00

PURPLE CLAW, THE (Also see Tales of Horror)
Jan, 1953 - No. 3, May, 1953
Minoan Publishing Co./Toby Press

	Good	Fine	Mint
1-Origin	3.50	10.00	20.00
2,3: 1-3 r-in Tales of Horror No. 9-11	3.00	8.00	16.00
I.W. Reprint No. 8-Reprints No. 1	.80	2.40	4.80

PUSSYCAT (See The Adventures of . . .)

PUZZLE FUN COMICS (Also see Jingle Jangle)
Spring, 1946 - No. 2, Summer, 1946;
George W. Dougherty Co.

1(1946)	5.00	15.00	30.00
2	4.00	12.00	24.00

NOTE: *No. 1,2('46) each contain a* ***George Carlson*** *cover plus a 6 pg. story "Alec in Fumbleland;" also many puzzles in each.*

QUAKER OATS (Also see Cap'n Crunch)
1965 (Giveaway) (2½x5½") (16 pages)
Quaker Oats Co.

"Plenty of Glutton," "Lava Come-Back," "Kite Tale," "A Witch in Time"		.50	1.00

QUEEN OF THE WEST, DALE EVANS
July, 1953 - No. 22, Jan, 1959
Dell Publishing Co.

4-Color 479('53)	2.00	6.00	12.00
4-Color 528('54)	2.00	5.00	10.00
3(4-6/54)-Toth-a	3.00	8.00	16.00
4-Toth, Manning-a	3.00	8.00	16.00
5-10-Manning-a	2.50	7.00	14.00
11,19,21-No Manning	1.20	3.50	7.00
12-18,20,22-Manning-a	2.00	5.00	10.00

QUENTIN DURWARD (See 4-Color No. 672)

QUESTAR ILLUSTRATED SCIENCE FICTION CLASSICS
1977 (224 pgs.) ($1.95)
Golden Press

11197-Stories by Asimov, Sturgeon, Silverberg & Niven; Starstream-r	.50	1.50	3.00

QUESTION, THE (See Mysterious Suspense)

QUICK-DRAW McGRAW (TV) (Hanna-Barbera)
12-2/60 - No. 11, 7-9/62; No. 12, 11/62 - No. 15, 6/69
Dell Publishing Co./Gold Key No. 12 on

4-Color 1040	.50	1.50	3.00
2(4-6/60)-6	.35	1.00	2.00
7-11		.60	1.20
12-15-All titled "Quick-Draw McGraw Fun-Type Roundup;" 12,13-(84 pgs.)	.35	1.00	2.00

(See Whitman Comic Books)

QUICK-DRAW McGRAW (TV)
Nov, 1970 - No. 8, Jan, 1972 (Hanna-Barbera)
Charlton Comics

1-8		.40	.80

QUICK-TRIGGER WESTERN (Formerly Cowboy Action)
No. 12, May, 1956 - No. 19, Sept, 1957
Atlas Comics (ACI No. 12/WPI No. 13-19)

12-Baker-a	2.00	6.00	12.00
13-Williamson-a, 5 pgs.	3.50	10.00	20.00
14-Everett, Crandall, Torres, Heath-c/a	3.00	8.00	16.00
15-Torres, Crandall-a	2.00	6.00	12.00
16-Orlando, Kirby-a	1.75	5.00	10.00
17-Crandall-a	1.50	4.00	8.00
18-Baker-a	1.50	4.00	8.00
19	.85	2.50	5.00

NOTE: ***Morrow*** *a-18.* ***Severin*** *c-13,16,17.*

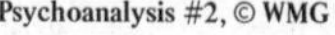
Psychoanalysis #2, © WMG

Public Enemies #5, © DS

Quick-Trigger Western #12, © MCG

Racket Squad In Action #11, © CC

Raggedy Ann & Andy #4, © J. Gruelle

Ragman #4, © DC

QUINCY (See Comics Reading Libraries)

RACCOON KIDS, THE (Formerly Movietown Animal Antics)
No. 52, Sept-Oct, 1954 - No. 64, Nov, 1957
National Periodical Publications (Arleigh No. 63,64)

	Good	Fine	Mint
52-64: 62-Doodles Duck by Mayer	1.00	3.00	6.00

RACE FOR THE MOON
March, 1958 - No. 3, Nov, 1958
Harvey Publications

	Good	Fine	Mint
1-Powell-a; ½-pg. S&K-a; c-from Galaxy Science Fiction pulp (5/53)	4.00	12.00	24.00
2-Kirby/Williamson c(r)/a(3)	10.00	30.00	60.00
3-Kirby/Williamson c/a(4)	12.00	36.00	72.00

RACKET SQUAD IN ACTION
May-June, 1952 - No. 29, March, 1958
Capitol Stories/Charlton Comics

	Good	Fine	Mint
1	3.50	10.00	20.00
2	2.00	5.00	10.00
3-4,6-Dr. Neff, Ghost Breaker app.	2.00	6.00	12.00
5-Dr. Neff, Ghost Breaker app; headlights-c	2.00	6.00	12.00
7-10	1.50	4.00	8.00
11-Ditko c/a	3.00	8.00	16.00
12-Ditko explosion-c (classic); Shuster-a(2); Ditko-a	7.00	20.00	40.00
13-Shuster c/a; Ditko-a; acid in woman's face shown	2.50	7.00	14.00
14-"Shakedown"-marijuana story	4.00	12.00	24.00
15-28	1.50	4.00	8.00
29-(68 pgs.)(15 cents)	1.50	4.00	8.00

RADIANT LOVE (Formerly Daring Love No. 1)
No. 2, Dec, 1953 - No. 6, Aug, 1954
Gilmor Magazines

	Good	Fine	Mint
2-6	1.50	4.00	8.00

RAGGEDY ANN AND ANDY (See March of Comics No. 23)
1942 - No. 39, Aug, 1949; 1955 - No. 4, Mar, 1966
Dell Publishing Co.

	Good	Fine	Mint
4-Color 5(1942)	15.00	45.00	90.00
4-Color 23(1943)	23.00	38.00	76.00
4-Color 45(1943)	10.00	28.00	56.00
4-Color 72(1945)	8.00	24.00	48.00
1(6/46)-Billy & Bonnie Bee by Frank Thomas	10.00	30.00	60.00
2,3: 3-Egbert Elephant by Dan Noonan begins	6.00	18.00	36.00
4-10	5.00	14.00	28.00
11-20	3.00	9.00	18.00
21-Alice In Wonderland cover/story	3.00	9.00	18.00
22-39, 4-Color 262	2.50	7.00	14.00
4-Color 306,354,380,452,533	2.00	6.00	12.00
Giant 1('55)-Tales From...	3.00	9.00	18.00
1(10-12/64-Dell)	.85	2.50	5.00
2,3(10-12/65), 4(3/66)	.50	1.50	3.00

NOTE: ***Kelly** art ("Animal Mother Goose")-No. 1-34, 36, 37; c-28. Peterkin Pottle by **John Stanley** in-32-38.*

RAGGEDY ANN AND ANDY
Dec, 1971 - No. 6, Sept, 1973
Gold Key

	Good	Fine	Mint
1	.50	1.50	3.00
2-6	.30	.80	1.60

RAGGEDY ANN & THE CAMEL WITH THE WRINKLED KNEES (See Dell Jr. Treasury No. 8)

RAGMAN (See Batman Family No. 20 & Cancelled Comic Cavalcade)
Aug-Sept, 1976 - No. 5, June-July, 1977
National Periodical Publications

	Good	Fine	Mint
1-Origin	.30	.90	1.80
2-Origin; Kubert-c		.60	1.20
3-5: 4-Drug story		.40	.80

NOTE: ***Kubert** a-4 ,5; c-1-5. **Redondo** studios-a-1-5*

RAGS RABBIT (See Harvey Hits No. 2 & Tastee Freez)
1951 - No. 18, March, 1954
Harvey Publications

	Good	Fine	Mint
11-18	.85	2.50	5.00

RAIDERS OF THE LOST ARK
Sept, 1981 - Present (Movie adaptation)
Marvel Comics Group

	Good	Fine	Mint
1		.60	1.20
2,3: 3-Final chapter of movie adapt.		.40	.80

NOTE: ***Buscema** a(p)-1-3; c(p)-1.*

RALPH KINER, HOME RUN KING
1950 (Pittsburgh Pirates)
Fawcett Publications

	Good	Fine	Mint
nn	8.00	24.00	48.00

RAMAR OF THE JUNGLE
1954 - No. 5, Sept, 1956
Toby Press No. 1/Charlton No. 2 on

	Good	Fine	Mint
1	3.50	10.00	20.00
2-5 (6,7 exist?)	3.00	8.00	16.00

RAMPAGING HULK, THE (Magazine) (The Hulk No. 10 on)
Jan, 1977 - No. 10, Sept, 1978
Marvel Comics Group

	Good	Fine	Mint
1-Bloodstone featured	.70	2.00	4.00
2-Old X-Men app; origin old & new X-Men in text	.50	1.50	3.00
3-10: 10-1st full color issue	.40	1.20	2.40

NOTE: ***Alcala** a-1-4i, 8i. **Buscema** a-1. **Nino** a-4i. **Simonson** a-1-3p. **Starlin** a-4(w/**Nino**), 7; c-4, 5, 7.*

RANGE BUSTERS
Sept, 1950 - No. 8, 1951
Fox Features Syndicate

	Good	Fine	Mint
1	3.00	9.00	18.00
2-8	2.00	5.00	10.00

RANGE BUSTERS (Formerly Cowboy Love?; Wyatt Earp, Frontier Marshall No. 11 on)
No. 8, May, 1955 - No. 10, Sept, 1955
Charlton Comics

	Good	Fine	Mint
8-10	.85	2.50	5.00

RANGELAND LOVE
Dec, 1949 - No. 2, Mar, 1950
Atlas Comics (CDS)

	Good	Fine	Mint
1,2	2.50	7.00	14.00

RANGER, THE (See 4-Color No. 255)

RANGE RIDER (See Flying A's...)

RANGE RIDER, THE (See 4-Color No. 404)

RANGE ROMANCES
Dec, 1949 - No. 5, Aug, 1950
Comic Magazines (Quality Comics)

	Good	Fine	Mint
1-Gustavson-c/a	9.00	25.00	50.00
2-Crandall-c/a; "spanking" scene	10.00	30.00	60.00
3-Crandall, Gustavson-a	6.00	18.00	36.00
4-Crandall-a	5.50	16.00	32.00
5-Gustavson-a; Crandall-a(p)	6.00	18.00	36.00

RANGERS COMICS (...of Freedom No. 1-7)
Oct, 1941 - No. 69, Winter, 1952-53
Fiction House Magazines (Flying stories)

	Good	Fine	Mint
1-Intro. Ranger Girl & The Rangers of Freedom; ends No. 4, cover app. only-No. 5	30.00	90.00	190.00

RANGERS COMICS (continued)

	Good	Fine	Mint
2	20.00	60.00	120.00
3	17.00	50.00	100.00
4,5	10.00	30.00	60.00
6,7-Sky Rangers begin No. 7?	9.00	25.00	50.00
8-12-Commando Rangers begin-No. 11	8.00	24.00	46.00
13-Commando Ranger begins-not same as Comm. Rangers	8.00	24.00	46.00
14-21: 21-Firehair begins	7.00	20.00	40.00
22-30: 23-Kazanda begins, ends No. 28. 28-Origin Tiger Man. 30-Crusoe Island begins, ends No. 40	6.00	18.00	36.00
31-40: 33-Lingerie, hypodermic panels. 38-Drug story. 39-Lingerie panels	5.00	15.00	30.00
41-46	4.00	12.00	24.00
47-56-''Eisnerish'' Dr. Drew by Grandenetti	5.00	15.00	30.00
57-60-Straight Dr. Drew by Grandenetti	3.50	10.00	20.00
61,62,64-66: 64-Suicide Smith begins	3.00	9.00	18.00
63-Used in **POP**, pgs. 85, 99	3.50	10.00	20.00
67-69: 67-The Space Rangers begin, end No. 69	3.00	9.00	18.00

NOTE: *A very large percentage of above have bondage, discipline, etc. covers. Firehair art by* ***Lee Elias****-No. 21-28; by* ***Bob Lubbers****-No. 30-38. Glory Forbes by* ***Matt Baker****-No. 36-38. ''I Confess'' by* ***Evans****-No. 47-52. Tiger Man art by* ***John Celardo****-No. 36-39; by* ***Evans****-No. 40-45, 48, 52. Werewolf Hunter by* ***Evans****-No. 39.* ***Moreira*** *a-45.* ***Tuska*** *a-16,22.*

RANGO (TV)
August, 1967
Dell Publishing Co.

	Good	Fine	Mint
1	.70	2.00	4.00

RATFINK (See Frantic & Zany)
October, 1964
Canrom, Inc.

	Good	Fine	Mint
1-Woodbridge-a	.70	2.00	4.00

RAT PATROL, THE (TV)
March, 1967 - No. 6, Oct, 1969
Dell Publishing Co.

	Good	Fine	Mint
1	.85	2.50	5.00
2-6	.50	1.50	3.00

RAVEN, THE (See Movie Classics)

RAWHIDE (TV)
Sept-Nov, 1959 - June-Aug, 1962; July, 1963 - No. 2, Jan, 1964
Dell Publishing Co./Gold Key

	Good	Fine	Mint
4-Color 1028,1097,1160,1202,1261,1269	1.00	3.00	6.00
01-684-208(8/62-Dell)	1.00	3.00	6.00
1(10071-307, G.K.), 2	.70	2.00	4.00

NOTE: *All have Clint Eastwood photo-c.*

RAWHIDE KID
3/55 - No. 16, 9/57; No. 17, 8/60 - No. 151, 5/79
Atlas/Marvel Comics (CnPC No. 1-16/AMI No. 17-30)

	Good	Fine	Mint
1	10.00	28.00	60.00
2	5.00	15.00	30.00
3-5	3.50	10.00	20.00
6,8-10	2.00	6.00	12.00
7-Williamson-a, 4 pgs.	3.50	10.00	20.00
11-15	1.75	5.00	10.00
16-Torres-a	2.00	6.00	12.00
17-Origin by J. Kirby	3.00	8.00	16.00
18-22,24-30	.85	2.50	5.00
23-Origin by J. Kirby	2.00	6.00	12.00
31,32,36-44: 40-Two-Gun Kid x-over. 42-1st Larry Lieber issue	.70	2.00	4.00
33-35-Davis-a. 35-Intro & death of The Raven	1.00	3.00	6.00
45-Origin retold	1.50	4.00	8.00
46-Toth-a	1.50	4.00	8.00
47-70: 50-Kid Colt x-over. 64-Kid Colt story. 66-Two-Gun Kid story. 67-Kid Colt story	.30	.80	1.60
71-78		.50	1.00
79-Williamson-a r-/Kid Colt No. 59, 4 pgs.		.60	1.20
80-85		.30	.60
86-Origin-r; Williamson-a r-/Ringo Kid No. 13, 4 pgs.		.60	1.20
87-91,93,94: 89,90-Kid Colt x-over		.40	.80
92-52pgs.; all Kirby issue		.40	.80
95-Williamson-r		.40	.80
96-99,101-110: 105-Western Kid-r		.40	.80
100-Origin retold & expanded		.40	.80
111-Williamson-r		.40	.80
112-115-Last new story		.40	.80
116-151		.30	.60
Special 1(9/71)-Reprints		.40	.80

NOTE: ***Davis*** *a-125r.* ***Everett*** *a-65, 66, 88.* ***G. Kane*** *c-101.* ***Kirby*** *a-17-32, 34, 42, 43, 84, 86, 109r, 112r, 137r, No.1(Special); c-17-35, 40, 41, 43-47, 137.* ***McWilliams*** *a-41.* ***Torres*** *a-99r.* ***Whitney*** *a-66.*

REAL ADVENTURE COMICS (Action Adventure No. 2 on)
April, 1955
Gillmore Magazines

	Good	Fine	Mint
1	.85	2.50	5.00

REAL CLUE CRIME STORIES (Formerly Clue)
June, 1947 - V8No.3, May, 1953
Hillman Periodicals

	Good	Fine	Mint
V2No.4(No.1)-S&K c/a(3); Dan Barry-a	6.00	18.00	36.00
5-7-S&K c/a(3-4); 7-Iron Lady app.; drug mention story	5.00	15.00	30.00
8-12	1.50	4.00	8.00
V3No.1-8,10-12, V4No.1-8,11,12	1.20	3.50	7.00
9-Used in **SOTI**, pg. 102	3.50	10.00	20.00
V4No.9,10(?)-Krigstein-a	2.50	7.00	14.00
V5No.1-5,7,8,10,12	.70	2.00	4.00
6,9,11-Krigstein-a	2.00	5.00	10.00
V6No.1,3-5,8,9,11	.70	2.00	4.00
2-Kinstler-a	.85	2.50	5.00
V6No.6,7,10,12-Krigstein-a	1.50	4.00	8.00
V7No.1-3,5,7-11, V8No.1-3	.70	2.00	4.00
4,12-Krigstein-a	1.50	4.00	8.00
6-McWilliams-a; 1 pg. Frazetta ad	.85	2.50	5.00

NOTE: ***Infantino*** *a-V2No. 8.* ***Kinstler*** *a-V7No.12.* ***Powell*** *a-V4No.11, 12.*

REAL EXPERIENCES (Formerly Tiny Tessie)
No. 25, January, 1950
Atlas Comics (20CC)

	Good	Fine	Mint
25	.70	2.00	4.00

REAL FACT COMICS
Mar-Apr, 1946 - No. 21, July-Aug, 1949
National Periodical Publications

	Good	Fine	Mint
1-S&K-a	7.00	20.00	40.00
2-S&K-a	4.00	12.00	24.00
3	2.00	6.00	12.00
4-''Just Imagine'' begins by Virgil Finley, ends No. 12 (2 pgs. ea.)	3.50	10.00	20.00
5-Batman/Robin-c; 5pg. story about creation of Batman & Robin	10.00	30.00	60.00
6-Origin & 1st app. Tommy Tomorrow; Flag-c	14.00	40.00	80.00
7-(No. 6 on inside)	2.00	6.00	12.00
8-2nd app. Tommy Tomorrow	8.00	24.00	48.00
9-S&K-a	3.50	10.00	20.00
10-Vigilante by Meskin	3.50	10.00	20.00
11,12: 11-Kinstler-a	2.00	6.00	12.00

Rangers Comics #33, © FH

Rawhide Kid #33, © MCG

Real Clue Crime Stories V5#6, © HILL

Realistic Romances #5, © AVON

Real Screen Comics #3, © DC

Reap The Wild Wind nn, © Paramount

REAL FACT COMICS (continued)

	Good	Fine	Mint
13-Tommy Tomorrow cover/story	7.00	20.00	40.00
14,15,17-19	2.00	5.00	10.00
16-Tommy Tomorrow app.; 1st Planeteers app.?	7.00	20.00	40.00
20-Kubert-a	4.00	12.00	24.00
21-Kubert-a, 2 pgs.	2.00	6.00	12.00

REAL FUN OF DRIVING!!, THE
1965, 1967 (Regular size)
Chrysler Corp.

Shaffenberger-a, 12pgs.	.50	1.50	3.00

REAL FUNNIES
Jan, 1943
Nedor Publishing Co.

1	2.50	7.00	14.00
2,3	1.50	4.00	8.00

REAL HEROES COMICS
Sept, 1941 - No. 16, Oct, 1946
Parents' Magazine Institute

1	3.00	8.00	16.00
2-10	2.00	5.00	10.00
11-16: 13-Kiefer-a	1.00	3.00	6.00

REAL HIT
1944 (Savings Bond premium)
Fox Features Publications

1-Blue Beetle-r	3.50	10.00	20.00

REALISTIC ROMANCES
July-Aug, 1951 - No. 17, Aug-Sept, 1954
Realistic Comics/Avon Periodicals

1-Kinstler-a; c-/Avon paperback 211	6.00	18.00	36.00
2-4	3.00	8.00	16.00
5,6,8-Kinstler-a	3.00	9.00	18.00
7-Evans-a?; c-/Avon paperback 360	3.50	10.00	20.00
9,10	3.00	8.00	16.00
11-15,17	2.00	6.00	12.00
16-Kinstler marijuana story-r/Romantic Love No. 6	5.00	15.00	30.00
I.W. Reprint No. 8,9	.45	.90	1.80

NOTE: ***Astarita** a-2-4,7,8.*

REAL LIFE COMICS
Sept, 1941 - No. 59, Sept, 1952
Nedor/Better/Standard Publ./Pictorial Magazine No. 13

1	6.00	18.00	36.00
2	3.00	9.00	18.00
3-Hitler cover	4.00	12.00	24.00
4-10	1.50	4.00	8.00
11-20	1.20	3.50	7.00
21-43,45-49	1.00	3.00	6.00
44-Ward, Guardineer-a	3.50	10.00	20.00
50,52-Frazetta-a, 5&4 pgs; 52-Severin/Elder-a	7.00	20.00	40.00
51,53-57: Severin/Elder-a in each	2.00	6.00	12.00
58-Severin/Elder-a(2)	2.50	7.00	14.00
59-1pg. Frazetta; Severin/Elder-a	1.50	4.00	8.00

NOTE: *Some issues had two titles.* ***Schomburg** c-21, 44.*

REAL LIFE SECRETS (Challange of the Unknown No. 6?)
Sept, 1949 - No. 5, May, 1950
Ace Periodicals

1	2.00	6.00	12.00
2-5	1.00	3.00	6.00

REAL LIFE STORY OF FESS PARKER (Magazine)
1955
Dell Publishing Co.

1	3.00	9.00	18.00

REAL LIFE TALES OF SUSPENSE (See Suspense)

REAL LOVE (Formerly Hap Hazard)
No. 25, April, 1949 - No. 76, Nov, 1956
Ace Periodicals (A. A. Wyn)

	Good	Fine	Mint
25,26	1.50	4.00	8.00
27-L. B. Cole-a	3.00	9.00	18.00
28-35	.85	2.50	5.00
36-76: 61-Photo-c	.70	2.00	4.00

REAL McCOYS, THE (TV)
1960 - 1962
Dell Publishing Co.

4-Color 1071,1193,1265	1.00	3.00	6.00
4-Color 1134-Toth-a	2.50	7.00	14.00
01689-207 (5-7/62)	.70	2.00	4.00

REAL SCREEN COMICS (No. 1 titled Real Screen Funnies; TV Screen Cartoons No. 129-138)
Spring, 1945 - No. 128, May-June, 1959
National Periodical Publications

1-The Fox & the Crow begin	30.00	90.00	180.00
2	14.00	40.00	80.00
3-5	8.00	24.00	48.00
6-10	5.50	16.00	32.00
11-20	4.00	12.00	24.00
21-30	3.00	8.00	16.00
31-50	2.00	6.00	12.00
51-100	1.50	4.00	8.00
101-128	1.00	3.00	6.00

REAL SECRETS
Sept, 1949 - No. 5, May, 1950
Ace Periodicals

1	2.00	5.00	10.00
2-5	1.20	3.50	7.00

REAL SPORTS COMICS
Oct-Nov, 1948
Hillman Periodicals

1-12 pg. Powell-a	3.50	10.00	20.00

REAL WESTERN HERO (Formerly Wow No. 1-69; becomes Western Hero No. 76 on)
No. 70, Sept, 1948 - No. 75, March, 1949
Fawcett Publications

70(No.1)-Featuring Tom Mix, Gabby Hayes, Monte Hale, & Hopalong Cassidy	7.00	20.00	40.00
71-75	3.50	10.00	20.00

REAL WEST ROMANCES
Apr-May, 1949 - V2No.1, Apr-May, 1950
Crestwood Publishing Co./Prize Publ.

V1No.1-S&K-a(p)	4.00	12.00	24.00
2-Spanking panel	3.00	8.00	16.00
3-Kirby-a(p) only	2.50	7.00	14.00
4-7-S&K-a	3.00	8.00	16.00
V2No.1-Kirby-a(p)	2.50	7.00	14.00

NOTE: ***Meskin** a-V1No.5.* ***Severin & Elder** a-V1No.3-6, V2No.1.* ***Leonard Starr** a-1-3.*

REAP THE WILD WIND
1942 (4 pgs.; paper cover; full color; 7½x10½'')
Paramount Pictures (Giveaway)

nn-Preview of movie; line art with color photos	4.00	12.00	24.00

REBEL, THE (See 4-Color No. 1076,1138,1207,1262)

RECORD BOOK OF FAMOUS POLICE CASES
1949 (132 pages) (25 cents)
St. John Publishing Co.

nn-Kubert-a(3) r-/Son of Sinbad; Matt Baker-c	9.00	25.00	50.00

RED ARROW
1951 - No. 3, Oct, 1951
P. L. Publishing Co.

	Good	Fine	Mint
1	1.50	4.00	8.00
2,3	.85	2.50	5.00

RED BALL COMIC BOOK
1947 (Red Ball Shoes giveaway)
Parents' Magazine Institute

Reprints from True Comics	1.00	3.00	6.00

RED BAND COMICS
Feb, 1945 - No. 4, May, 1945
Enwil Associates

1	3.50	10.00	20.00
2-Origin Boogeyman & Santanas	3.00	8.00	16.00
3,4-Captain Wizard app. in both; identical contents in each	3.00	8.00	16.00

RED CIRCLE COMICS
Jan, 1945 - No. 4, April, 1945
Rural Home Publications (Enwil)

1-The Prankster & Red Riot begin	4.00	12.00	24.00
2-4-Starr-a	3.00	8.00	16.00
4-Variations exist; Woman Outlaws & Dorothy Lamour known ('50's-r)	3.00	8.00	16.00

RED CIRCLE SORCERY (Chilling Advs. in Sorcery No. 1-5)
No. 6, Apr, 1974 - No. 11, Feb, 1975
Red Circle Productions (Archie)

6-11		.40	.80

NOTE: ***Chaykin** a-6, 10. **B. Jones** a-7. **McWilliams** a-10. **Morrow** a-5-8, 10, 11; c-6-11. **Thorne** a-8, 10. **Toth** a-7p?, 8, 9. **Wood** a-10.*

RED DRAGON (1st Series) (Trail Blazers No. 1-4)
No. 5, Jan, 1943 - No. 9, Jan, 1944
Street & Smith Publications

5-Origin Red Rover, the Crimson Crimebuster; Rex King, Man of Adventure, Captain Jack Commando, & The Minute Man begin	14.00	40.00	80.00
6-Origin The Black Crusader & Red Dragon (3/43)	10.00	30.00	60.00
7	8.00	24.00	48.00
8-The Red Knight app.	8.00	24.00	48.00
9-Origin Chuck Magnon, Immortal Man	8.00	24.00	48.00

RED DRAGON (2nd Series)
Nov, 1947 - No. 6, Jan, 1949; No. 7, July, 1949
Street & Smith Publications

1-Red Dragon begins; Elliman, Nigel app.; Ed Cartier-a	14.00	40.00	80.00
2-Cartier-c	10.00	30.00	60.00
3,4: 3-Elliman, Nigel app. 4-Cartier c/a	8.00	24.00	48.00
5-7: 5,7-Maneely-a	7.00	20.00	40.00

NOTE: ***Powell** a-1-5,7; c-3,5.*

REDDY GOOSE
No. 2, Jan, 1959 - No. 16, July, 1962 (Giveaway)
International Shoe Co. (Western Printing)

2-16	.30	.80	1.60

REDDY KILOWATT (5 cents) (Also see Story of Edison)
1946 - No. 2, 1947; 1956 - 1960 (no month) (16 pgs.; paper cover)
Educational Comics (E. C.)

	Good	Fine	Mint
1-Reddy Made Magic	12.00	35.00	70.00
2-Edison, the Man Who Changed the World (¾'' smaller than No. 1)	12.00	35.00	70.00
...Comic Book 2 (1958)-''Wizard of Light,'' 16 pgs.	5.50	16.00	32.00
...Comic Book 3 (1956)-''The Space Kite,'' 8 pgs.; Orlando story; regular size	5.50	16.00	32.00
...Comic Book 3 (1960)-''The Space Kite,'' 8 pgs.; Orlando story; regular size	5.00	14.00	28.00

NOTE: *Several copies surfaced in 1979.*

REDDY MADE MAGIC
1956 (16 pages) (paper cover)
Educational Comics (E. C.)

1-Reddy Kilowatt reprints (splash panel changed)	8.00	24.00	48.00

REDEYE (See Comics Reading Libraries)

RED EAGLE (See Feature Book No. 16, McKay)

RED FOX (Manhunt No. 1-14)
1954
Magazine Enterprises

15(A-1 108)-Undercover Girl by Powell; Red Fox by L. B. Cole (cover also); r-from Manhunt	5.00	15.00	30.00

RED GOOSE COMIC SELECTIONS (See Comic Selections)

RED HAWK (See A-1 Comics No. 90)

RED ICEBERG, THE
1960 (10 cents)
Impact Publ. (Catechetical Guild)

(Rare)-Communist propaganda	60.00	170.00	340.00
2nd version - different back-c	70.00	190.00	380.00

NOTE: *This book was the Guild's last anti-communist propaganda book and had very limited circulation. 3 - 4 copies surfaced in 1979 from the defunct publisher's files.*

RED MASK (Formerly Tim Holt)
No. 42, June-July, 1954 - No. 54, 1957
Magazine Enterprises

42-Ghost Rider continues, ends No. 50; Black Phantom continues, ends No. 50,54; 3-D effect stories	4.00	12.00	24.00
43-50	3.00	8.00	16.00
51-1st app. The Presto Kid	3.00	8.00	16.00
52-Origin The Presto Kid	3.00	8.00	16.00
53,54	3.00	8.00	16.00
I.W. Reprint No. 1 (r-/No.52), 2,3 (r-/No.51), 8 (no date; Kinstler-c	.80	2.40	4.80

NOTE: ***Borth** art in all.*

RED MOUNTAIN FEATURING QUANTRELL'S RAIDERS
1952 (Movie) (Also see Jesse James No. 28)
Avon Periodicals

Alan Ladd; Kinstler c/a	10.00	30.00	60.00

RED RABBIT
Jan, 1947 - No. 22, Aug-Sept, 1951
Dearfield Comic/J. Charles Laue Publ. Co.

1	2.00	6.00	12.00
2-10	1.50	4.00	8.00
11-22	.85	2.50	5.00

RED RAVEN COMICS (Human Torch No. 2 on) (Also see Sub-Mariner No. 26, 2nd Series)
August, 1940
Timely Comics

1-Origin Red Raven; Comet Pierce & Mercury by Kirby, The Human Top & The Eternal Brain; intro. Magar, the Mystic & only app.; Kirby-c	500.00	1200.00	2000.00

(Prices vary widely on this book)

RED RYDER COMICS (Hi Spot No. 2)
No. 1, Sept, 1940; No. 3, Aug, 1941 - No. 151, Apr, 1957
Hawley Publ. No. 1-4/Dell Publishing Co. No. 5 on

Red Band Comics #3, © Enwil Assoc.

Red Circle Comics #3, © RH

Red Circle Sorcery #6, © AP

Red Ryder #42, © KING

Redskin #6, © YM

Red Sonja #14, © MCG

RED RYDER COMICS (continued)

	Good	Fine	Mint
1-Red Ryder strip reprints by Harmon; 1st meeting of Red & Little Beaver	55.00	140.00	280.00
3-(Scarce)-Alley Oop, Freckles & His Friends, Dan Dunn, Capt. Easy, King of the Royal Mtd., Red Ryder strip-r begin	30.00	75.00	150.00
4,5	15.00	45.00	90.00
6-10	12.00	35.00	70.00
11-20	8.00	23.00	46.00
21-32-Last Alley Oop, Dan Dunn, Capt. Easy, Freckles	5.00	15.00	30.00
33-40	3.00	10.00	20.00
41-46-Last Red Ryder strip-r	2.50	7.00	14.00
47-60-New stories on Red Ryder begin	2.00	6.00	12.00
61-80: 73-Last King of the Royal Mtd. strip-r by Jim Gary	2.00	5.00	10.00
81-100	1.50	4.00	8.00
101-120	1.20	3.50	7.00
121-144	1.00	3.00	6.00
145-Title changed to Red Ryder Ranch Magazine with photos	.85	2.50	5.00
146-148	.85	2.50	5.00
149-151-Title changed to Red Ryder Ranch Comics	.85	2.50	5.00
4-Color 916	1.50	4.00	8.00
Red Ryder Victory Patrol-Superbook No. 2(1943)-Giveaway; reprints No. 43,44	8.00	24.00	48.00
Wells Lamont Corp. giveaway (1950)-16 pgs. in color; regular size; paper-c; 1941-r	15.00	45.00	90.00

NOTE: ***Fred Harmon** a-1-99; c-1-98, 107, 118. Photo c-99-101, 105, 108-117. No. 119-painted covers begin (not by Harmon).*

RED RYDER PAINT BOOK
1941 (148 pages) (8½x11½'')
Whitman Publishing Co.

	Good	Fine	Mint
Reprints 1940 daily strips	10.00	30.00	60.00

RED SEAL
10/45 - No. 18, 10/46; No. 19, 6/47 - No. 22, 12/47
Harry 'A' Chesler/Superior Publ. No. 19 on

	Good	Fine	Mint
14-The Black Dwarf begins; Little Nemo app; bondage/hypo-c; Tuska-a	7.00	20.00	40.00
15-Drug mention, torture story	6.00	18.00	36.00
16-Used in **SOTI**, pg. 181, illo-''Outside the forbidden pages of de Sade, you find draining a girl's blood only in children's comics;'' drug club story r-later in Crime Reporter No. 1; Veiled Avengers & Barry Kuda app; Tuska-a	14.00	40.00	80.00
17-Lady Satan, Yankee Girl & Sky Chief app; Tuska-a	6.00	18.00	36.00
18,20-Lady Satan & Sky Chief app.	6.00	18.00	36.00
19-No Black Dwarf-on cover only; Zor, El Tigre app.	5.00	15.00	30.00
21-Lady Satan & Black Dwarf app.	5.00	15.00	30.00
22-Zor, Rocketman app.	5.00	15.00	30.00

REDSKIN (Famous Western Badmen No. 13 on)
Sept, 1950 - No. 12, Oct, 1952
Youthful Magazines

	Good	Fine	Mint
1	2.00	6.00	12.00
2-12: 6,12-Bondage-c	1.50	4.00	8.00

RED SONJA (Also see Conan No. 23 & Marvel Feature)
Jan, 1977 - No. 15, May, 1979
Marvel Comics Group

	Good	Fine	Mint
1-All Frank Thorne-c/a	.35	1.10	2.20
2-5	.30	.80	1.60
6-10		.40	.80
11,14,15		.30	.60
12,13-J. Buscema-a		.40	.80

NOTE: ***Brunner** c-12-14.*

RED WARRIOR
Jan, 1951 - No. 6, Dec, 1951
Marvel/Atlas Comics (TCI)

	Good	Fine	Mint
1-Tuska-a	2.00	6.00	12.00
2-6	1.50	4.00	8.00

RED WOLF
May, 1972 - No. 9, Sept, 1973
Marvel Comics Group

	Good	Fine	Mint
1-Kane/Severin-c		.40	.80
2-9: 9-Origin sidekick, Lobo (wolf)		.30	.60

REFORM SCHOOL GIRL!
1951
Realistic Comics

	Good	Fine	Mint
nn-Used in **SOTI**, pg. 358, & cover ill. with caption ''Comic books are supposed to be like fairy tales''	175.00	500.00	900.00

(Prices vary widely on this book)

NOTE: *The cover and title originated from a digest-sized book published by Diversey Publishing Co. of Chicago in 1948. The original book ''House of Fury,'' Doubleday, came out in 1941. The girl's real name which appears on the cover of the digest and comic is Marty Collins, Canadian model and ice skating star who posed for this special color photograph for the Diversey novel.*

REGGIE (Formerly Archie's Rival. . .; Reggie & Me No. 19 on)
No. 15, Sept, 1963 - No. 18, Nov, 1965
Archie Publications

	Good	Fine	Mint
15(9/63), 16(10/64)	2.00	6.00	12.00
17(8/65), 18(11/65)	2.00	6.00	12.00

NOTE: *Cover title No. 15,16 is Archie's Rival. . . .*

REGGIE AND ME (Formerly Reggie)
No. 19, Aug, 1966 - Present (No. 50-68: 52 pgs.)
Archie Publications

	Good	Fine	Mint
19-23-Evilheart app.; with Pureheart No. 22	.85	2.50	5.00
24-50	.30	.90	1.80
51-126		.30	.60

REGGIE'S JOKES (See Reggie's Wise Guy Jokes)

REGGIE'S WISE GUY JOKES
Aug, 1968 - Present (No. 5 on are Giants)
Archie Publications

	Good	Fine	Mint
1	.80	2.40	4.80
2-4	.40	1.20	2.40
5-28 (All Giants)		.40	.80
29-55		.30	.60

REGISTERED NURSE
Summer, 1963
Charlton Comics

	Good	Fine	Mint
1-Reprints Nurse Betsy Crane & Cynthia Doyle	.30	.80	1.60

REG'LAR FELLERS (See Treasure Box of. . .)
1921 - 1929
Cupples & Leon Co./MS Publishng Co.

	Good	Fine	Mint
1(1921)-52 pgs. B&W dailies (Cupples & Leon)	5.50	16.00	32.00
1925, 48 pgs. B&W dailies (MS Publ.)	5.50	16.00	32.00
Softcover (1929, nn, 36 pgs.)	5.50	16.00	32.00
Hardcover (1929)-B&W reprints, 96 pgs.	7.00	20.00	40.00

REG'LAR FELLERS
No. 5, Nov, 1947 - No. 6, Mar, 1948
Visual Editions (Standard)

	Good	Fine	Mint
5,6	2.00	6.00	9.00

REG'LAR FELLERS HEROIC (See Heroic)

RELUCTANT DRAGON, THE (See 4-Color No. 13)

REMEMBER PEARL HARBOR
1942 (68 pages)

REMEMBER PEARL HARBOR (continued)
Street & Smith Publications

	Good	Fine	Mint
nn	7.00	20.00	40.00

RENO BROWNE, HOLLYWOOD'S GREATEST COWGIRL (Formerly Margie; Apache Kid No. 53 on)
No. 50, April, 1950 - No. 52, Sept, 1950
Marvel Comics (MPC)

	Good	Fine	Mint
50-52	3.00	9.00	18.00

REPTILICUS (Reptisaurus No. 3 on)
Aug, 1961 - No. 2, Oct, 1961
Charlton Comics

	Good	Fine	Mint
1 (Movie), 2	1.20	3.50	7.00

REPTISAURUS THE TERRIBLE (Reptilicus No. 1,2)
Jan, 1962 - No. 8, Dec, 1962; Summer, 1963
Charlton Comics

	Good	Fine	Mint
V2No.3-8	.85	2.50	5.00
Special Edition 1 (1963)	.85	2.50	5.00

RESCUERS, THE (See Walt Disney Showcase No. 40)

RESTLESS GUN, THE (See 4-Color No. 934,986,1045,1089,1146)

RETURN OF GORGO, THE (Formerly Gorgo's Revenge)
No. 2, Summer, 1963 - No. 3, Fall, 1964
Charlton Comics

	Good	Fine	Mint
2,3-Ditko-a	2.00	5.00	10.00

RETURN OF KONGA, THE (Konga's Revenge No. 2 on)
1962
Charlton Comics

	Good	Fine	Mint
nn	1.50	4.00	8.00

RETURN OF THE OUTLAW
Feb, 1953 - No. 11, 1955
Toby Press (Minoan)

	Good	Fine	Mint
1-Billy the Kid	1.50	4.00	8.00
2-11	.85	2.50	5.00

REVEALING LOVE STORIES
1950 (132 pages)
Fox Features Syndicate

nn-See Fox Giant. Contents can vary and determines price.

REVEALING ROMANCES
Sept, 1949 - No. 6, Aug, 1950
Ace Magazines

	Good	Fine	Mint
1	1.50	4.00	8.00
2-6	.85	2.50	5.00

REX ALLEN COMICS (Also see 4-Color No. 877)
No. 2, Sept, 1951 - No. 31, Dec-Jan, 1958-59
Dell Publishing Co.

	Good	Fine	Mint
4-Color 316(No.1)(1951)	3.00	8.00	16.00
2-10	2.00	5.00	10.00
11-20	1.50	4.00	8.00
21-23,25-31	1.00	3.00	6.00
24-Toth-a	2.50	7.00	14.00

NOTE: ***Manning** a-20,27-30.*

REX DEXTER OF MARS
Fall, 1940
Fox Features Syndicate

	Good	Fine	Mint
1-Rex Dexter, Patty O'Day, & Zanzibar app.; Briefer-a	35.00	100.00	200.00

REX HART (Formerly Blaze Carson; Whip Wilson No. 9 on)
No. 6, Aug, 1949 - No. 8, Feb, 1950
Timely/Marvel Comics (USA)

	Good	Fine	Mint
6-Black Rider app.	3.00	9.00	18.00
7,8: 8-Blaze the Wonder Collie app. in text	2.50	7.00	14.00

REX MORGAN, M.D. (Also see Harvey Comics Library)
Dec, 1955 - No. 3, 1956
Argo Publ.

	Good	Fine	Mint
1-Reprints Rex Morgan daily newspaper strips & daily panel reprints of "These Women" by D'Alessio & "Timeout" by Jeff Keate	2.50	7.00	14.00
2,3	1.50	4.00	8.00

REX THE WONDER DOG (See The Adventures of. . .)

RHUBARB, THE MILLIONAIRE CAT (See 4-Color No. 423,466,563)

RIBTICKLER (Also see Everybody's Comics)
1945 - No. 9, Aug, 1947; 1957 - 1959
Fox Features Synd./Green Publ. (1957)/Norlen (1959)

	Good	Fine	Mint
nn(1945)-Chicago Nite Life News; Marvel Mutt app. (194 pgs.; 50 cents)	3.00	8.00	16.00
1	1.00	3.00	6.00
2-9: 7-Cosmo Cat app.	.80	2.40	4.80
3,7,8 (Green Publ.-1957)	.40	1.20	2.40
3,7,8 (Norlen Mag.-1959)	.35	1.00	2.00

RICHARD DRAGON, KUNG-FU FIGHTER (See Brave & the Bold)
Apr-May, 1975 - No. 18, Nov-Dec, 1977
National Periodical Publications/DC Comics

	Good	Fine	Mint
1		.45	.90
2-Starlin-a		.45	.90
3-Kirby c/a		.45	.90
4-8-Wood inks		.40	.80
9-18		.30	.60

RICHARD THE LION-HEARTED (See Ideal a Classic. . .)

RICHIE RICH (See Harvey Collectors Comics, Harvey Hits, Little Dot, Little Lotta, Little Sad Sack, Mutt & Jeff, Super Richie, and 3-D Dolly)

RICHIE RICH (. . .the Poor Little Rich Boy) (See Harvey Hits No. 3,9)
Nov, 1960 - Present
Harvey Publications

	Good	Fine	Mint
1-(See Little Dot for 1st app.)	90.00	250.00	440.00
2	40.00	100.00	180.00
3-5	20.00	60.00	120.00
6-10	12.00	35.00	70.00
11-20	5.00	15.00	30.00
21-40	2.50	7.50	15.00
41-60	2.00	5.00	10.00
61-80	1.00	3.00	6.00
81-100	.50	1.50	3.00
101-120	.40	1.20	2.40
121-140	.35	1.00	2.00
141-160: 145,149-Infinity-c	.30	.90	1.80
161-180	.25	.70	1.40
181-200		.45	.90
201-208		.30	.60

RICHIE RICH AND BILLY BELLHOPS
October, 1977 (One Shot) (52pgs.)
Harvey Publications

	Good	Fine	Mint
1	.35	1.10	2.20

RICHIE RICH AND CADBURY
10/77; No. 2, 9/78 - Present (50 cents) (No. 1-10, 52pgs.)
Harvey Publications

	Good	Fine	Mint
1	.35	1.10	2.20
2-5	.30	.80	1.60
6-10		.50	1.00
11-20		.40	.80

RICHIE RICH AND CASPER

Return Of Gorgo #2, © CC

Ribtickler #2, © FOX

Richie Rich #4, © HARV

RICHIE RICH AND CASPER (continued)
Aug, 1974 - Present
Harvey Publications

	Good	Fine	Mint
1	.90	2.60	5.40
2-5	.45	1.30	2.60
6-10		.60	1.20
11-20		.50	1.00
21-40		.40	.80
41		.30	.60

RICHIE RICH AND DOLLAR THE DOG
Sept, 1977 - Present (50 cents) (No. 1-10, 52pgs.)
Harvey Publications

	Good	Fine	Mint
1	.35	1.10	2.20
2-5	.30	.80	1.60
6-20		.40	.80

RICHIE RICH AND DOT
October, 1974 (One Shot)
Harvey Publications

	Good	Fine	Mint
1	1.00	3.00	6.00

RICHIE RICH AND GLORIA
Sept, 1977 - Present (50 cents) (No. 1-11, 52pgs.)
Harvey Publications

	Good	Fine	Mint
1	.40	1.20	2.40
2-5		.60	1.20
6-21		.40	.80

RICHIE RICH AND HIS GIRLFRIENDS
April, 1979 - Present
Harvey Publications

	Good	Fine	Mint
1	.30	.80	1.60
2-10		.45	.90
11		.30	.60

RICHIE RICH AND HIS MEAN COUSIN REGGIE
April, 1979 - No. 6, 1980 (50 cents) (No. 1,2-52pgs.)
Harvey Publications

	Good	Fine	Mint
1		.60	1.20
2-5		.45	.90
6		.30	.60

RICHIE RICH AND JACKIE JOKERS
Nov, 1973 - Present
Harvey Publications

	Good	Fine	Mint
1	1.50	4.00	8.00
2-5	.70	2.00	4.00
6-10	.35	1.00	2.00
11-20		.60	1.20
21-40		.45	.90
41-45		.30	.60

RICHIE RICH BANK BOOKS
Oct, 1972 - Present
Harvey Publications

	Good	Fine	Mint
1	2.00	5.00	10.00
2-5	.85	2.50	5.00
6-10	.50	1.50	3.00
11-20	.35	1.00	2.00
21-30	.30	.80	1.60
31-40		.50	1.00
41-54		.30	.60

RICHIE RICH BEST OF THE YEARS
Oct, 1977 - Present (Digest) (128 pages)
Harvey Publications

	Good	Fine	Mint
1(10/77)-Reprints, No. 2(10/78)-Reprints, No. 3(6/79-75 cents)	.30	.80	1.60
4,5(11/79, 3/80-95 cents)		.40	.80

RICHIE RICH BILLIONS
Oct, 1974 - Present (35-50 cents) (No. 1-33, 52pgs.)
Harvey Publications

	Good	Fine	Mint
1	1.50	4.00	8.00
2-5	.70	2.00	4.00
6-10	.50	1.50	3.00
11-20		.60	1.20
21-30		.45	.90
31-43		.30	.60

RICHIE RICH CASH
Sept, 1974 - Present
Harvey Publications

	Good	Fine	Mint
1	1.50	4.00	8.00
2-5	.70	2.00	4.00
6-10	.35	1.00	2.00
11-20		.60	1.20
21-30		.45	.90
31-43		.30	.60

RICHIE RICH, CASPER & WENDY NATIONAL LEAGUE
June, 1976 (52 pages)
Harvey Publications

	Good	Fine	Mint
1	.70	2.00	3.00

RICHIE RICH COLLECTORS COMICS (See Harvey Coll. Comics)

RICHIE RICH DIAMONDS
Aug, 1972 - Present (35-50 cents) (No. 1-12,23-45, 52pgs.)
Harvey Publications

	Good	Fine	Mint
1	2.00	6.00	12.00
2-5	1.00	3.00	6.00
6-10	.50	1.50	3.00
11-20	.35	1.00	2.00
21-30		.60	1.20
31-40		.50	1.00
41-50		.40	.80
51-55		.30	.60

RICHIE RICH DIGEST STORIES
Oct, 1977 - Present (Digest) (132 pages) (75-95 cents)
Harvey Publications

	Good	Fine	Mint
1-Reprints	.30	.80	1.60
2-12		.40	.80

RICHIE RICH DIGEST WINNERS
Dec, 1977 - Present (Digest) (132 pages) (75-95 Cents)
Harvey Publications

	Good	Fine	Mint
1	.30	.80	1.60
2-11		.40	.80

RICHIE RICH DOLLARS & CENTS
Aug, 1963 - Present (25-50 cents) (No. 1-61,72-94, 52pgs.)
Harvey Publications

	Good	Fine	Mint
1	8.00	24.00	48.00
2	4.00	12.00	24.00
3-5	2.50	7.00	14.00
6-10	2.00	5.00	10.00
11-20	1.50	4.00	8.00
21-30	.85	2.50	5.00
31-50	.50	1.50	3.00
51-70	.30	.80	1.60
71-90 (Early issues are reprints)		.45	.90
91-104		.30	.60

RICHIE RICH FORTUNES
Sept, 1971 - Present (No. 1-17, 52pgs.)
Harvey Publications

	Good	Fine	Mint
1	2.00	6.00	12.00
2-5	1.00	3.00	6.00
6-10	.80	2.30	4.60
11-20	.50	1.50	3.00
21-30	.35	1.00	2.00
31-40		.50	1.00
41-59		.30	.60

RICHIE RICH GEMS
Sept, 1974 - Present
Harvey Publications

	Good	Fine	Mint
1	1.50	4.00	8.00
2-5	.70	2.00	4.00
6-10	.50	1.50	3.00
11-20	.30	.90	1.80
21-30		.45	.90
31-38		.30	.60

RICHIE RICH GOLD AND SILVER
Sept, 1975 - Present (No. 1-27, 52pgs.)
Harvey Publications

	Good	Fine	Mint
1	1.00	3.00	6.00
2-5	.50	1.50	3.00
6-10	.30	.80	1.60
11-20		.45	.90
21-37		.30	.60

RICHIE RICH HOLIDAY DIGEST MAGAZINE
January, 1980 - Present
Harvey Publications

	Good	Fine	Mint
1,2		.50	1.00

RICHIE RICH INVENTIONS
Oct, 1977 - Present (No. 1-11, 52pgs.)
Harvey Publications

	Good	Fine	Mint
1	.35	1.10	2.20
2-5	.30	.80	1.60
6-10		.45	.90
11-21		.30	.60

RICHIE RICH JACKPOTS
Oct, 1972 - Present (No. 41-43, 52pgs.)
Harvey Publications

	Good	Fine	Mint
1	2.00	5.00	10.00
2-5	.85	2.50	5.00
6-10	.50	1.50	3.00
11-20	.30	.90	1.80
21-30		.60	1.20
31-50		.45	.90
51-54		.30	.60

RICHIE RICH MEETS TIMMY TIME
Sept, 1977 (50 Cents) (One Shot) (52 pages)

RICHIE RICH MEETS TIMMY TIME (cont'd.)
Harvey Publications

	Good	Fine	Mint
1	.40	1.20	2.40

RICHIE RICH MILLION DOLLAR DIGEST
October, 1980 - Present
Harvey Publications

	Good	Fine	Mint
1-5		.50	1.00

RICHIE RICH MILLIONS
9/61; No. 2, 9/62 - Present (No. 1-66,52-68pgs.; 85-97, 52pgs.)
Harvey Publications

	Good	Fine	Mint
1	9.00	27.00	54.00
2	5.00	14.00	28.00
3-10	3.50	10.00	20.00
11-20	2.00	5.00	10.00
21-30	1.00	3.00	6.00
31-40	.80	2.30	4.60
41-50	.50	1.50	3.00
51-70	.35	1.00	2.00
71-90	.30	.80	1.60
91-100 (Early issues are reprints)		.45	.90
101-108		.30	.60

RICHIE RICH MONEY WORLD
Sept, 1972 - Present
Harvey Publications

	Good	Fine	Mint
1	2.00	6.00	12.00
2-5	1.00	3.00	6.00
6-10: 9,10-R. Rich mistakenly named Little Lotta on covers	.50	1.50	3.00
11-20	.35	1.10	2.20
21-30		.60	1.20
31-50		.45	.90
51-54		.30	.60

RICHIE RICH PROFITS
Oct, 1974 - Present
Harvey Publications

	Good	Fine	Mint
1	2.00	5.00	10.00
2-5	.80	2.30	4.60
6-10	.50	1.50	3.00
11-20	.35	1.00	2.00
21-30		.45	.90
31-43		.30	.60

RICHIE RICH RICHES
July, 1972 - Present (No. 1-13, 41-45, 52pgs.)
Harvey Publications

	Good	Fine	Mint
1	2.00	5.00	10.00
2-5	.85	2.50	5.00
6-10	.50	1.50	3.00
11-20	.30	.80	1.60
21-40		.45	.90
41-55		.30	.60

RICHIE RICH SUCCESS STORIES
Nov, 1964 - Present (No. 1-56, 67-90, 52pgs.)
Harvey Publications

	Good	Fine	Mint
1	7.00	20.00	40.00
2-5	3.00	9.00	18.00
6-10	2.00	6.00	12.00
11-30	1.00	3.00	6.00
31-50	.50	1.50	3.00
51-70	.30	.90	1.80
71-90 (Early issues are reprints)		.45	.90
91-96		.30	.60

RICHIE RICH VACATIONS DIGEST
Nov, 1977; No. 2, Oct, 1978 - Present (Digest) (132 pgs.)
Harvey Publications

	Good	Fine	Mint
1-Reprints	.30	.80	1.60
2-7		.50	1.00

RICHIE RICH VAULTS OF MYSTERY
Nov, 1974 - Present
Harvey Publications

	Good	Fine	Mint
1	1.50	4.00	8.00
2-10	.70	2.00	4.00
11-20	.30	.90	1.80
21-30		.60	1.20
31-42		.30	.60

RICHIE RICH ZILLIONZ
Oct, 1976 - Present (68 pages) (No. 1-4, 68pgs.; No. 5-18, 52pgs.)
Harvey Publications

	Good	Fine	Mint
1	1.00	3.00	6.00
2-5	.50	1.50	3.00
6-10	.35	1.00	2.00
11-20		.50	1.00
21-29		.30	.60

RICKY
September, 1953
Standard Comics (Visual Editions)

	Good	Fine	Mint
5	.60	1.80	3.60

RICKY NELSON (TV)
1959 - No. 5, Oct-Dec, 1961
Dell Publishing Co.

	Good	Fine	Mint
4-Color 956,998	2.50	7.00	14.00
4-Color 1115,1192-Manning-a	3.00	8.00	16.00
5	1.50	4.00	8.00

RIDER, THE (Frontier Trail No. 6)
March, 1957 - No. 5, 1958
Ajax/Farrell Publ. (Four Star Comic Corp.)

	Good	Fine	Mint
1	1.50	4.00	8.00
2-5	.85	2.50	5.00

RIFLEMAN, THE (TV)
7-9/59 - No. 12, 7-9/62; No. 13, 11/62 - No. 20, 9/64
Dell Publ. Co./Gold Key No. 13 on

	Good	Fine	Mint
4-Color 1009, No. 2	1.75	5.00	10.00
3-Four pgs. Toth-a	2.00	6.00	12.00
4,5,7-10	1.00	3.00	6.00
6-Toth-a	1.50	4.00	8.00
11-20	.70	2.00	4.00

RIMA, THE JUNGLE GIRL
Apr-May, 1974 - No. 7, Apr-May, 1975
National Periodical Publications

	Good	Fine	Mint
1-Origin, part 1	.35	1.00	2.00
2,3-Origin, part 2,3	.25	.70	1.40
4-Origin, conclusion		.50	1.00
5-7: 7-Origin & only app. Space Marshal		.40	.80

NOTE: ***Kubert*** *c-1-7.* ***Nino*** *a-1-5.* ***Redondo*** *a-1-6.*

RING OF BRIGHT WATER (See Movie Classics)

RINGO KID, THE (2nd Series)
1/70 - No. 23, 11/73; No. 24, 11/75 - No. 30, 11/76
Marvel Comics Group

	Good	Fine	Mint
1(1970)-Williamson-a r-from No. 10, 1956		.60	1.20
2-19,21-30		.30	.60
20-Williamson-r/No. 1		.30	.60

NOTE: ***Wildey*** *a-13r.*

RINGO KID WESTERN, THE (1st Series)
Aug, 1954 - No. 21, Sept, 1957
Atlas Comics (HPC)/Marvel Comics

The Rider #1, © AJAX

The Rifleman #13, © DELL

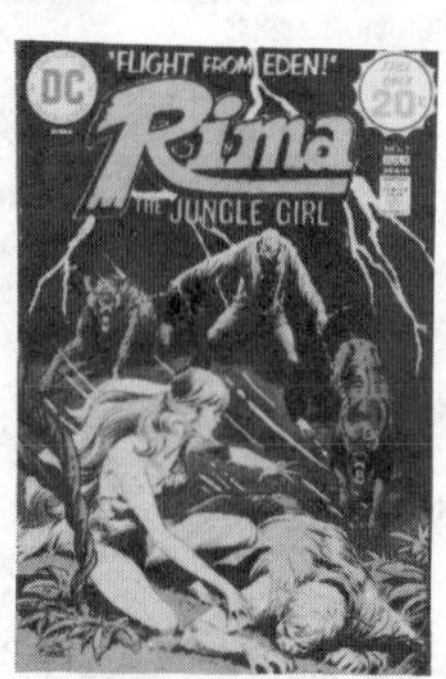

Rima #2, © DC

Rin Tin Tin #31, © DELL

Ripley's B.I.O.N. #53, © GK

Rivets #1, © Argo

RINGO KID WESTERN (continued)

	Good	Fine	Mint
1-Maneely, Sinnott-a	3.00	9.00	18.00
2-5: 2-Black Rider app.	1.50	4.00	8.00
6-8-Severin-c/a(3) each	2.00	6.00	12.00
9,11,14-21	1.00	3.00	6.00
10,13-Williamson-a, 4 pgs.	3.00	8.00	16.00
12-Orlando-a, 4 pgs.	1.50	4.00	8.00

NOTE: ***Maneely** a-15; c-15. **Wildey** a-16,17.*

RIN TIN TIN (See March of Comics No. 163,180,195)

RIN TIN TIN (TV) (. . . & Rusty No. 18 on)
Nov, 1952 - No. 38, May-July, 1961; 1963
Dell Publishing Co./Gold Key

	Good	Fine	Mint
4-Color 434,476,523	1.20	3.50	7.00
4(6-8/54)-10	.85	2.50	5.00
11-38: 31,33-Photo-c	.70	2.00	4.00
1(11/63-G.K.) . . . & Rusty	.50	1.50	3.00

RIO BRAVO (See 4-Color No. 1018)

RIO CONCHOS (See Movie Comics)

RIOT (Satire)
Apr, 1954 - No. 3, Aug, 1954; No. 4, Feb, 1956 - No. 6, June, 1956
Atlas Comics (ACI No. 1-5/WPI No. 6)

	Good	Fine	Mint
1-Russ Heath-a	3.50	10.00	20.00
2-Li'l Abner satire by Post	2.50	7.00	14.00
3,5	2.50	7.00	14.00
4-Infinity-c; Marilyn Monroe '7 Year Itch' movie satire	2.50	7.00	14.00
6-Lorna of the Jungle satire by Everett	2.50	7.00	14.00

NOTE: ***Everett** a-4, 6. **Maneely** a-2,4. **Severin** a-4-6.*

RIPCORD (See 4-Color No. 1294)

RIP HUNTER TIME MASTER (See Showcase)
Mar-Apr, 1961 - No. 29, Nov-Dec, 1965
National Periodical Publications

	Good	Fine	Mint
1	4.00	12.00	24.00
2	2.00	6.00	12.00
3-5	1.40	4.00	8.00
6,7-Toth-a in each	1.50	4.50	9.00
8-15	1.00	3.00	6.00
16-29: 29-G. Kane-c	.50	1.50	3.00

RIP KIRBY (See Feature Book No. 51,54, Comics Hits No.57, & Street Comix)

RIPLEY'S BELIEVE IT OR NOT!
Sept, 1953 - No. 4, March, 1954
Harvey Publications

	Good	Fine	Mint
1	3.50	10.00	20.00
2-4	2.00	6.00	12.00
J. C. Penney giveaway (1948)	3.00	8.00	16.00

RIPLEY'S BELIEVE IT OR NOT! (Formerly True War Stor. No.1(No.3))
No. 4, April, 1967 - No. 94, Feb, 1980
Gold Key

	Good	Fine	Mint
4-McWilliams-a	.50	1.50	3.00
5-Subtitled "True War Stories;" Evans-a	.40	1.20	2.40
6-9: 6-McWilliams-a. 8-Orlando-a	.35	1.10	2.20
10-Evans-a(2)	.40	1.20	2.40
11-14,16-20	.30	.80	1.60
15-Evans-a	.35	1.00	2.00
21,26,28,29		.40	.80
22-25,30-Evans-a		.60	1.20
27-Evans-a(2)	.30	.80	1.60
31-Evans-a(3)	.30	.80	1.60
32-38		.40	.80
39-Crandall-a		.60	1.20
40-Evans-a(2)		.60	1.20
41-60		.30	.60
61-73,84-94		.25	.50
74-83-(52 pgs.)		.30	.60

	Good	Fine	Mint
Story Digest Mag. 1(6/70)-4¾x6½"		.40	.80

NOTE: *Reprints-No. 74,77-84,87,91,93.*

RIPLEY'S BELIEVE IT OR NOT! (See Mystery Comics Digest No. 1,4, 7,10,13,16,19,22,25)

RIPLEY'S BELIEVE IT OR NOT TRUE GHOST STORIES (Becomes . . . True War Stories) (See Dan Curtis)
June, 1965 - No. 2, July, 1965
Gold Key

	Good	Fine	Mint
1-Williamson, Wood & Evans-a	1.50	4.00	8.00
2-Orlando, McWilliams-a	.70	2.00	4.00
Mini-Comic 1(1976-3¼x6½")		.30	.60
11186(1977)-Golden Press; 224 pgs. ($1.95)-Reprints	.50	1.50	3.00
11401(3/79)-Golden Press; 96 pgs. ($1.00)		.60	1.20

RIPLEY'S BELIEVE IT OR NOT TRUE WAR STORIES (Formerly . . . True Ghost Stories; becomes Ripley's Believe It or Not No. 4 on)
August, 1965
Gold Key

	Good	Fine	Mint
1(No.3)-Williamson-a	.70	2.00	4.00

RIPLEY'S BELIEVE IT OR NOT! TRUE WEIRD
June, 1966 - No. 2, Aug, 1966 (B&W Magazine)
Ripley Enterprises

	Good	Fine	Mint
1,2-Comic stories & text	.40	1.20	2.40

RIVETS (See 4-Color No. 518)

RIVETS (A dog)
Jan, 1956 - No. 3, May, 1956
Argo Publ.

	Good	Fine	Mint
1-Reprints Sunday & daily newspaper strips	1.20	3.50	7.00
2,3	.85	2.50	5.00

ROAD RUNNER, THE (See Beep Beep . . .)

ROBIN (See Aurora)

ROBIN HOOD (See 4-Color No. 413,669, King Classics, Movie Comics, The Advs. of. . . , & New Advs. of. . .)

ROBIN HOOD (. . . & His Merry Men, The Illustrated Story of. . .) (See Classic Comics No. 7)

ROBIN HOOD (New Adventures of. . .)
1952 (36 pages) (5x7¼")
Walt Disney Productions (Flour giveaways)

	Good	Fine	Mint
"New Adventures of Robin Hood," "Ghosts of Waylea Castle," & "The Miller's Ransom" each. . . .	1.50	4.00	8.00

ROBIN HOOD (Adventures of. . . No. 8)
No. 52, Nov, 1955 - No. 7, Sept, 1957
Magazine Enterprises (Sussex Publ. Co.)

	Good	Fine	Mint
52-Origin Robin Hood & Sir Gallant of the Round Table	1.50	4.00	8.00
53, 3-7	1.00	3.00	6.00
I.W. Reprint No. 1,2 (reprints No. 4), 9 (reprints No. 52)(1963)	.40	1.20	2.40
Super Reprint No. 10 (reprints No. 53 or 3), 11,15 (reprints No. 5), 17(1964)	.40	1.20	2.40

NOTE: ***Bolle** a-in all. **Powell** a-6,7.*

ROBIN HOOD (. . . Western Tales)
No date (Circa 1955) 20 pages
Shoe Store Giveaway (Robin Hood Stores)

	Good	Fine	Mint
1-7-Reed Crandall-a	2.50	7.00	14.00

ROBIN HOOD (Not Disney)
May-July, 1963 - No. 7, Nov-Jan, 1964-65
Dell Publishing Co.

	Good	Fine	Mint
1	.50	1.50	3.00
2-7	.30	.80	1.60

ROBIN HOOD ($1.50)
1973 (Disney) (8½x11"; cardboard covers) (52 pages)
Western Publishing Co.

	Good	Fine	Mint
96151-"Robin Hood," based on movie, 96152-"The Mystery of Sherwood Forest," 96153-"In King Richard's Service," 96154-"The Wizard's King" each....	.70	2.00	4.00

ROBIN HOOD AND HIS MERRY MEN (Formerly Danger & Adv.)
No. 28, April, 1956 - No. 38, Aug, 1958
Charlton Comics

	Good	Fine	Mint
28-37	.70	2.00	4.00
38-Ditko-a, 5 pgs.	1.50	4.00	8.00

ROBIN HOOD TALES (National Periodical No. 7 on)
Feb, 1956 - No. 6, Nov-Dec, 1956
Quality Comics Group (Comic Magazines)

	Good	Fine	Mint
1	2.00	6.00	12.00
2-5-Matt Baker-a	3.00	8.00	16.00
6	1.20	3.50	7.00
Frontier Days giveaway (1956)	1.20	3.50	7.00

ROBIN HOOD TALES (Continued from Quality)
No. 7, Jan-Feb, 1957 - No. 14, Mar-Apr, 1958
National Periodical Publications

	Good	Fine	Mint
7-14	3.00	8.00	16.00

ROBINSON CRUSOE (Also see King Classics)
Nov-Jan, 1964
Dell Publishing Co.

	Good	Fine	Mint
1	.50	1.50	3.00

ROBOTMEN OF THE LOST PLANET (Also see Space Thrillers)
1952
Avon Periodicals

	Good	Fine	Mint
1-3pg. Kinstler-a	60.00	170.00	340.00

ROB ROY (See 4-Color No. 544)

ROCK AND ROLLO (Formerly T.V. Teens)
V2No.14, Oct, 1957 - No. 19, 1958
Charlton Comics

	Good	Fine	Mint
14-19	.50	1.50	3.00

ROCKET COMICS
Mar, 1940 - No. 3, May, 1940
Hillman Periodicals

	Good	Fine	Mint
1-Rocket Riley & Red Roberts, Phantom Ranger, The Steel Shark, Electro Man, The Defender, Man With a Thousand Faces begin	30.00	80.00	160.00
2,3	14.00	40.00	80.00

ROCKET KELLY
1944; Fall, 1945 - No. 5, 1947
Fox Features Syndicate

	Good	Fine	Mint
nn (1944)	3.00	8.00	16.00
1	3.00	8.00	16.00
2-5: 2-The Puppeteer app. (costumed hero)	2.00	6.00	12.00

ROCKETMAN
June, 1952
Ajax/Farrell Publications

	Good	Fine	Mint
1-Rocketman & Cosmo	7.00	20.00	40.00

ROCKETS AND RANGE RIDERS
1957 (16 pages) (Giveaway)
Richfield Oil Corp.

	Good	Fine	Mint
Toth-a	6.00	18.00	36.00

ROCKET SHIP X
September, 1951
Fox Features Syndicate

	Good	Fine	Mint
1	15.00	45.00	90.00

ROCKET TO ADVENTURE LAND (See Pixie Puzzle...)

ROCKET TO THE MOON
1951
Avon Periodicals

	Good	Fine	Mint
nn-Orlando c/a; adapts Otis Aldebert Kline's "Maza of the Moon"	60.00	160.00	320.00

ROCK HAPPENING
1969
Harvey Publications

	Good	Fine	Mint
1,2	.50	1.50	3.00

ROCKY AND BULLWINKLE KITE FUN BOOK
1963; 1970 (8 pgs.; 16 pgs.) (soft cover) (Giveaway)
Pacific Gas & Electric Co./Southern Calif. Edison

	Good	Fine	Mint
nn(1963)(PG&E)-8 pgs.	1.50	4.00	8.00
nn(1970)(SCEC)-16 pgs.	1.00	3.00	6.00

ROCKY AND HIS FIENDISH FRIENDS (TV)
Oct, 1962 - No. 5, Sept, 1963 (Jay Ward)
Gold Key

	Good	Fine	Mint
1-3 (84 pgs.)	.85	2.50	5.00
4,5 (Regular size)	.50	1.50	3.00

ROCKY AND HIS FRIENDS (See 4-Color No. 1128,1152,1166,1208, 1275,1311 and March of Comics No. 216)

ROCKY JONES SPACE RANGER (See Space Adventures No. 15-18)

ROCKY LANE WESTERN (See Black Jack)
May, 1949 - No. 87, Nov, 1959
Fawcett Publications/Charlton No. 55 on

	Good	Fine	Mint
1	8.00	24.00	48.00
2	5.50	16.00	32.00
3-10	4.00	12.00	24.00
11-20	3.00	8.00	16.00
21-30	2.50	7.00	14.00
31-50	2.00	6.00	12.00
51-78,80-87	2.00	5.00	10.00
79-Giant edition, 68 pgs.	3.00	8.00	16.00

ROD CAMERON WESTERN
Feb, 1950 - No. 20, April, 1953
Fawcett Publications

	Good	Fine	Mint
1	8.00	24.00	48.00
2	4.00	12.00	24.00
3-10	3.50	10.00	20.00
11-20	3.00	8.00	16.00

RODEO RYAN (See A-1 Comics No. 8)

ROGER BEAN, R. G. (Regular Guy)
1915 - 1917 (34 pgs.; B&W; 4¾x16"; cardboard covers)
(No. 1 & 4 bound on side, No. 3 bound at top)
The Indiana News Co.

	Good	Fine	Mint
1-By Chic Jackson	4.00	12.00	24.00
2-4	3.00	9.00	18.00

ROGER DODGER (Also in Exciting No. 57 on)
No. 5, Aug, 1952
Standard Comics

	Good	Fine	Mint
5	.70	2.00	4.00

ROLY POLY COMIC BOOK
1945 - 1946 (MLJ reprints)
Green Publishing Co.

	Good	Fine	Mint
1-Red Rube & Steel Sterling begin	5.00	15.00	30.00
6-The Blue Circle & The Steel Fist app.	3.00	9.00	18.00

Robin Hood & His M.M. #36, © CC

Rocky Lane Western #6, © FAW

Rod Cameron Western #14, © FAW

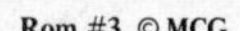
Rom #3, © MCG

Romantic Love #11, © AVON

Romantic Marriage #6, © ZD

ROLY POLY COMIC BOOK (continued)

	Good	Fine	Mint
10-Origin Red Rube retold; Steel Sterling story (Zip No. 41)	3.50	10.00	20.00
11,12,14-The Black Hood in all	3.50	10.00	20.00
15-The Blue Circle & The Steel Fist app.; cover exact swipe from Fox Blue Beetle No. 1	17.00	40.00	80.00

ROM
December, 1979 - Present
Marvel Comics Group

	Good	Fine	Mint
1-Based on a Parker Bros. toy-origin	.50	1.50	3.00
2	.30	.80	1.60
3-5		.60	1.20
6-10		.50	1.00
11-16,19-24		.40	.80
17,18-X-Men app.	.35	1.00	2.00
25-Double size		.40	.80

NOTE: ***Austin*** *c-3i.* ***Golden*** *c-6-12, 19.* ***Layton*** *c-15.* ***Miller*** *c-3p.*

ROMANCE (See True Stories of . . .)

ROMANCE AND CONFESSION STORIES (See Giant Comics Edition)

ROMANCE DIARY
December, 1949 - No. 2, March, 1950
Marvel Comics (CDS)(CLDS)

	Good	Fine	Mint
1,2	2.50	7.50	15.00

ROMANCE OF FLYING, THE
1941-42 (World War II photos)
David McKay Publications

	Good	Fine	Mint
nn-Illustration with text; 8 pgs. of photos of The Doolittle Tokyo Raiders	3.50	10.00	20.00

ROMANCES OF MOLLY MANTON (See Molly Manton)

ROMANCES OF NURSE HELEN GRANT, THE
August, 1957
Atlas Comics (VPI)

	Good	Fine	Mint
1	.85	2.50	5.00

ROMANCES OF THE WEST
Nov, 1949 - No. 2, Mar, 1950
Marvel Comics (SPC)

	Good	Fine	Mint
1-Movie photo of Calamity Jane & Sam Bass	3.50	10.00	20.00
2	3.00	8.00	16.00

ROMANCE STORIES OF TRUE LOVE (Formerly Love Problems & Advice)
No. 45, 5/57 - No. 50, 3/58; No. 51, 9/58 - No. 52, 11/58
Harvey Publications

	Good	Fine	Mint
45-51	.85	2.50	5.00
52-Matt Baker-a	2.00	5.00	10.00

NOTE: ***Powell*** *a-45,46,48-50.*

ROMANCE TALES
No. 7, Oct, 1949 - No. 9, March, 1950
Marvel Comics (CDS)

	Good	Fine	Mint
7-9	1.50	4.00	8.00

ROMANCE TRAIL
July-Aug, 1949 - No. 7, July-Aug, 1950
National Periodical Publications

	Good	Fine	Mint
1-Kinstler-a	5.50	16.00	32.00
2-Kinstler-a	3.00	8.00	16.00
3-7	2.50	7.00	14.00

ROMAN HOLIDAYS, THE (TV)
Feb, 1973 - No. 4, Nov, 1973 (Hanna-Barbera)
Gold Key

	Good	Fine	Mint
1-4	.85	2.50	5.00

ROMANTIC ADVENTURES (My . . . No. 49-67, covers only)
Mar-Apr, 1949 - No. 67, July, 1956 (My . . . No. 68 on)
American Comics Group (B&I Publ. Co.)

	Good	Fine	Mint
1	3.00	8.00	16.00
2	1.50	4.00	8.00
3-10	.85	2.50	5.00
11-20	.55	1.60	3.20
21-67: 40-Shelly-a	.40	1.20	2.40

NOTE: ***Whitney*** *art in many issues.*

ROMANTIC AFFAIRS (Formerly Our Love?)
No. 3, March, 1950
Marvel Comics (Select Publications)

	Good	Fine	Mint
3-Photo-c	1.50	4.00	8.00

ROMANTIC CONFESSIONS
Oct, 1949 - V3No.1, April-May, 1953
Hillman Periodicals

	Good	Fine	Mint
V1No.1-McWilliams-a	2.50	7.00	14.00
V1No.2-12: 2-Briefer-a; negligee panels	1.20	3.50	7.00
V2No.1,2,4-8,10-12	.85	2.50	5.00
V2No.3-Krigstein-a	2.50	7.00	14.00
V2No.9-One pg. Frazetta ad	1.20	3.50	7.00
V3No.1	.70	2.00	4.00

NOTE: ***McWilliams*** *a-V2No.2.*

ROMANTIC HEARTS
Mar, 1951 - No. 9, Aug, 1952; July, 1953 - No. 12, July, 1955
Story Comics/Master/Merit Pubs.

	Good	Fine	Mint
1(3/51) (1st Series)	2.50	7.00	14.00
2-9	1.20	3.50	7.00
1(3/53) (2nd Series)	1.20	3.50	7.00
2-12	.70	2.00	4.00

ROMANTIC LOVE
No. 4, June, 1950
Quality Comics Group

	Good	Fine	Mint
4 (6/50)	1.50	4.00	8.00
I.W. Reprint No. 2,3,8		.60	1.20

ROMANTIC LOVE
Sept-Oct, 1949 - No. 23, Sept-Oct, 1954
Avon Periodicals/Realistic

	Good	Fine	Mint
1-c-/Avon paperback 252	6.00	18.00	36.00
2-4: 3-Painted-c	3.50	10.00	20.00
5-c-/paperback Novel Library 34	4.00	12.00	24.00
6-''Thrill Crazy''-marijuana story; c-/Avon paperback 207; Kinstler-a	6.00	18.00	36.00
7,8: 8-Astarita-a(2)	3.50	10.00	20.00
9-c-/paperback/Novel Library 41; Kinstler-a	4.00	12.00	24.00
10-c-/Avon paperback 212	4.00	12.00	24.00
11-c-/paperback Novel Library 17; Kinstler-a	4.00	12.00	24.00
12-c-/paperback Novel Library 13	4.00	12.00	24.00
13-19,21,22	3:50	10.00	20.00
20-Kinstler-c/a	3.50	10.00	20.00
23-Kinstler-c	3.00	9.00	18.00
nn(1-3/53)(Realistic-r)	2.50	7.00	14.00

NOTE: ***Astarita*** *a-7,10,11.*

ROMANTIC MARRIAGE (Cinderella Love No. 25 on)
Nov-Dec, 1950 - No. 24, Sept, 1954
Ziff-Davis/St. John No. 13 on

	Good	Fine	Mint
1-Photo-c	3.50	10.00	20.00
2-10: 7-Photo-c	2.00	5.00	10.00
11-22,24	1.50	4.00	8.00
23-Baker-c	2.00	5.00	10.00

ROMANTIC PICTURE NOVELETTES
1946
Magazine Enterprises

	Good	Fine	Mint
1-Mary Worth-r	6.00	18.00	36.00

ROMANTIC SECRETS (Becomes Time For Love)
Sept, 1949 - No. 38, 1/53; No. 5, 10/55 - No. 51, 9/64

ROMANTIC SECRETS (continued)
Fawcett/Charlton Comics No. 5 (10/55) on

	Good	Fine	Mint
1	3.00	8.00	16.00
2,3	1.50	4.00	8.00
4,9-Evans-a	2.00	5.00	10.00
5(Charlton; formerly Negro Romances No. 4?)	1.20	3.50	7.00
6-8,10	1.20	3.50	7.00
11-23	.85	2.50	5.00
24-Evans-a	1.50	4.00	8.00
25-31,33-38	.60	1.80	3.60
32-Drug mention story	3.00	8.00	16.00
5(10/55)-51('64)-Charlton		.40	.80

NOTE: ***Powell** a-5,7,10,12,16,17,20,26,29,33,34,36,37.*

ROMANTIC STORY
Nov, 1949 - No. 130, Nov, 1973
Fawcett/Charlton Comics

	Good	Fine	Mint
1	3.00	8.00	16.00
2-5	1.50	4.00	8.00
6-14,16-20: 8-Photo-c	1.20	3.50	7.00
15-Evans-a	2.00	5.00	10.00
21-39,41-50: 21-Toth-a?	.85	2.50	5.00
40-(100 pgs.)	2.00	6.00	12.00
51-56,58-80	.35	1.00	2.00
57-Hypo needle story	.40	1.20	2.40
81-130		.40	.80

NOTE: ***Powell** a-7,8,16,20,30.*

ROMANTIC THRILLS
1950 (Giant) (132 pages)
Fox Features Syndicate

nn-See Fox Giants. Contents may vary and determines price.

ROMANTIC WESTERN
Winter, 1949 - No. 3, June, 1950
Fawcett Publications

	Good	Fine	Mint
1	4.00	12.00	24.00
2-Williamson, McWilliams-a	7.00	20.00	40.00
3	2.00	6.00	12.00

ROMEO TUBBS (Formerly My Secret Life)
No. 26, 5/50 - No. 28, 7/50; No. 1, 1950; No. 27, 12/52
Fox Features Syndicate/Green Publ. Co. No. 27

	Good	Fine	Mint
26-28, 1	2.50	7.50	15.00
27-Contains Pedro on inside; Wood-a	5.00	14.00	28.00

RONALD McDONALD
Sept, 1970 - No. 4, March, 1971
Charlton Press (King Features Synd.)

	Good	Fine	Mint
1		.20	.40
2-4		.15	.30

ROOK
November, 1979 - Present
Warren Publications

	Good	Fine	Mint
1-Nino-a		.40	.80
2-7: 6,7-Alcala-a		.30	.60

ROOKIE COP (Formerly Crime and Justice)
Nov, 1955 - No. 33, Aug, 1957
Charlton Comics

	Good	Fine	Mint
27-33	.85	2.50	5.00

ROOM 222 (TV)
Jan, 1970 - No. 4, Jan, 1971
Dell Publishing Co.

	Good	Fine	Mint
1,2,4: 4 reprints No. 1	.70	2.00	4.00
3-Marijuana story	.85	2.50	5.00

ROOTIE KAZOOTIE (See 3-D-ell)
1952 - 1954
Dell Publishing Co.

	Good	Fine	Mint
4-Color 415,459,502	1.20	3.50	7.00
4(4-6/54)-6(10-12/54)	1.00	3.00	5.00

ROUND THE WORLD GIFT
No date (mid 1940's) (4 pages)
National War Fund (Giveaway)

	Good	Fine	Mint
	10.00	30.00	60.00

ROUNDUP (Western Crime)
July-Aug, 1948 - No. 5, Mar-Apr, 1949
D. S. Publishing Co.

	Good	Fine	Mint
1-1pg. Frazetta on 'Mystery of the Hunting Lodge'?; Ingels-a?	3.00	9.00	18.00
2-Marijuana drug mention story	2.50	10.00	20.00
3-5	2.00	6.00	12.00

ROY CAMPANELLA, BASEBALL HERO
1950
Fawcett Publications

	Good	Fine	Mint
nn	8.00	24.00	48.00

ROY ROGERS (See March of Comics No. 17,35,47,62,68,73,77, 86,91,100,105,116,121,131,136,146,151,161,167,176,191,206, 221,236,250)

ROY ROGERS AND TRIGGER
April, 1967
Gold Key

	Good	Fine	Mint
1-Reprints	.70	2.00	4.00

ROY ROGERS COMICS
1944 - 1948
Dell Publishing Co.

	Good	Fine	Mint
4-Color 38 (1944)	25.00	70.00	140.00
4-Color 63 (1945)	15.00	45.00	90.00
4-Color 86,95 (1945)	11.00	32.00	64.00
4-Color 109 (1946)	8.00	24.00	48.00
4-Color 117,124,137,144	5.50	16.00	32.00
4-Color 153,160,166,177	4.00	12.00	24.00

ROY ROGERS COMICS (See Trigger)
Jan, 1948 - No. 145, Sept-Oct, 1961
Dell Publishing Co.

	Good	Fine	Mint
1-Chuck Wagon Charlies Tales begin (not in 20-46)	14.00	40.00	80.00
2	8.00	24.00	48.00
3-5	5.50	16.00	32.00
6-10	4.00	12.00	24.00
11-20: 20-Trigger feature begins, ends No. 46	3.50	10.00	20.00
21-40	2.50	7.00	14.00
41-55: 55-Last ish. w/back-c picture	2.00	6.00	12.00
56,59-63,65-70	2.00	6.00	12.00
57-Heroin drug propaganda story	3.00	8.00	16.00
58,64-Drug mention story	2.00	6.00	12.00
71-91	1.50	4.00	8.00
92-Title changed to Roy Rogers and Trigger (8/55)	1.50	4.00	8.00
93-110,112-118	1.50	4.00	8.00
111,119-124-Toth-a	3.00	8.00	16.00
125-131,145	1.50	4.00	8.00
132-144-Manning-a	2.00	5.00	10.00
. . . & the Man From Dodge City (Dodge giveaway, 16 pgs., 1954)-Frontier, Inc. (5x7¼'')	4.00	12.00	24.00
. . . Riders Club Comics (1952; 16 pgs.)	5.00	14.00	28.00

NOTE: ***Buscema** a-2 each-74-108. **Manning** a-123, 124, 132-144. **Marsh** a-110.*

Romantic Story #29, © FAW

Roundup #3, © DS

Roy Rogers Comics #57, © Roy Rogers

Rugged Action #1, © MCG

Rulah #22, © FOX

Saddle Romances #9, © WMG

ROY ROGERS' TRIGGER
No. 2, Sept-Nov, 1951 - No. 17, June-Aug, 1955
Dell Publishing Co.

	Good	Fine	Mint
4-Color 329 (5/51)-Photo-c	2.50	7.00	14.00
2-5	2.00	5.00	10.00
6-17	1.00	3.00	6.00

RUDOLPH, THE RED NOSED REINDEER (See Limited Collectors Edition No. 33,50)

RUDOLPH, THE RED NOSED REINDEER
1939 (2,400,000 copies printed)
Montgomery Ward (Giveaway)

	Good	Fine	Mint
Paper cover - 1st app. in print; written by Robert May; ill. by Denver Gillen	9.00	25.00	50.00
Hardcover version	10.00	30.00	60.00

RUDOLPH, THE RED NOSED REINDEER
1950 - No. 13, Winter, 1963-64; 1972-73
(Issues are not numbered) (15 different issues known)
National Periodical Publications

	Good	Fine	Mint
1950 issues	2.50	7.00	14.00
1951-54 issues	2.00	6.00	12.00
1955-63 issues	1.50	4.00	8.00
1972, C-24(1973)-80 pgs.; oversized 10x13½"	.40	1.20	2.40

NOTE: *The 1962-63 issues are 84 pages.*

RUFF & REDDY (TV)
Sept, 1958 - No. 12, Jan-Mar, 1962 (Hanna-Barbera)
Dell Publishing Co./Gold Key

	Good	Fine	Mint
4-Color 937,981,1038	.85	2.50	5.00
4(1-3/60)-12	.70	2.00	4.00

NOTE: *Existence of No. 1 (1966-Gold Key) suspected.*

RUGGED ACTION (Strange Stories of Suspense No. 5 on)
Dec, 1954 - No. 4, June, 1955
Atlas Comics (CSI)

	Good	Fine	Mint
1	2.00	6.00	12.00
2-4	1.00	3.00	6.00

RULAH JUNGLE GODDESS (Formerly Zoot; I Loved No. 28 on) (Also see Terrors of the Jungle)
No. 17, Aug, 1948 - No. 27, June, 1949
Fox Features Syndicate

	Good	Fine	Mint
17	17.00	50.00	100.00
18-20	14.00	40.00	80.00
21-Used in **SOTI**, pg. 388,389	17.00	50.00	100.00
22-Used in **SOTI**, pg. 22,23	14.00	40.00	80.00
23-27	10.00	30.00	60.00

NOTE: ***Kamen*** *c-17-19,21,22.*

RUNAWAY, THE (See Movie Classics)

RUN BABY RUN
1974 (39 cents)
Logos International

	Good	Fine	Mint
By Tony Tallarico from Nicky Cruz's book		.30	.60

RUN, BUDDY, RUN (TV)
June, 1967
Gold Key

	Good	Fine	Mint
1 (10204-706)	.70	2.00	4.00

RUSTY (Formerly Kid Movie Comics; The Kelleys No. 23 on)
No. 12, Apr, 1947 - No. 22, Sept, 1949
Marvel Comics (HPC)

	Good	Fine	Mint
12	1.50	4.00	8.00
13	1.00	3.00	6.00
14-Wolverton's Powerhouse Pepper (4 pgs.) plus Kurtzman's "Hey Look"	5.00	14.00	28.00
15-17-Kurtzman's "Hey Look"	4.00	12.00	24.00
18,19	.85	2.40	5.00
20-Kurtzman, 5 pgs.	4.00	12.00	24.00
21,22-Kurtzman, 17 & 22 pgs.	6.00	18.00	36.00

RUSTY, BOY DETECTIVE
Mar, 1955 - No. 5, Nov, 1955
Good Comics/Lev Gleason

	Good	Fine	Mint
1-Bob Wood, Carl Hubbell-a begins	1.50	4.00	8.00
2-5	1.00	3.00	6.00

RUSTY DUGAN (See Holyoke One-Shot No. 2)

RUSTY RILEY (See 4-Color No. 418,451,486,554)

SAARI, THE JUNGLE GODDESS
November, 1951
P. L. Publishing Co.

	Good	Fine	Mint
1	8.00	24.00	48.00

SABOTAGE (See The Crusaders)

SABRINA'S CHRISTMAS MAGIC (See Archie Giant Series Mag. No. 196,207,220,231,243,455,467,479,491,503)

SABRINA, THE TEEN-AGE WITCH (TV) (See Archie's TV Laugh-Out)
April, 1971 - Present (Giants No. 1-17)
Archie Publications

	Good	Fine	Mint
1	1.50	4.00	8.00
2-5: 3,4-Archie's Group x-over	1.00	3.00	6.00
6-10	.40	1.20	2.40
11-20	.35	1.00	2.00
21-40		.50	1.00
41-64		.30	.60

SABU, "ELEPHANT BOY" (Formerly My Secret Story)
No. 30, June, 1950 - No. 2, Aug, 1950
Fox Features Syndicate

	Good	Fine	Mint
30(No.1)-Wood-a	6.00	18.00	36.00
2-Photo-c; Kamen-a	5.00	14.00	28.00

SACRAMENTS, THE
October, 1955 (25 cents)
Catechetical Guild Educational Society

	Good	Fine	Mint
304	2.00	6.00	12.00

SAD CASE OF WAITING ROOM WILLIE, THE
1950? (no date) (14 pgs. in color; paper covers; regular size)
American Visuals Corp. (For Baltimore Medical Society)

	Good	Fine	Mint
By Will Eisner	10.00	30.00	60.00

SADDLE JUSTICE (Happy Houlihans No. 1,2; becomes Saddle Romances No. 9 on)
No. 3, Spring, 1948 - No. 8, Sept-Oct, 1949
E. C. Comics

	Good	Fine	Mint
3-The first E. C. by Bill Gaines to break away from M. C. Gaines' old Educational Comics format. Craig, Feldstein, H. C. Kiefer, & Stan Asch-a	20.00	60.00	120.00
4-1st Graham Ingels E. C.-a	20.00	60.00	120.00
5-8-Ingels-a in all	17.00	50.00	100.00

NOTE: ***Craig*** *and* ***Feldstein*** *art in most issues. Canadian reprints known; see Table of Contents.*

SADDLE ROMANCES (Saddle Justice No. 3-8; continued as Weird Science No. 12 on)
No. 9, Nov-Dec, 1949 - No. 11, Mar-Apr, 1950
E. C. Comics

	Good	Fine	Mint
9-Ingels-a	17.00	50.00	110.00
10-Wood's 1st work at E. C.; Ingels-a	20.00	60.00	130.00
11-Ingels-a	20.00	60.00	130.00

NOTE: *Canadian reprints known; see Table of Contents.*

SADIE SACK (See Harvey Hits No. 93)

SAD SACK AND THE SARGE

SAD SACK AND THE SARGE (continued)
Sept, 1957 - Present
Harvey Publications

	Good	Fine	Mint
1	5.00	14.00	28.00
2-10	2.00	5.00	10.00
11-20	1.00	3.00	6.00
21-50	.40	1.20	2.40
51-100		.50	1.00
101-151		.25	.50

SAD SACK COMICS (See Tastee Freez & Harvey Hits No. 8)
Sept, 1949 - Present
Harvey Publications

	Good	Fine	Mint
1-Infinity-c; Little Dot begins	14.00	40.00	80.00
2,3: 2-Flying Fool by Powell	5.50	16.00	32.00
4-10	3.00	8.00	16.00
11-30	2.00	5.00	10.00
31-50	.85	2.50	5.00
51-100	.40	1.20	2.40
101-150		.50	1.00
151-283		.25	.50
3-D 1 (1/54-titled ''Harvey 3-D Hits'')	7.00	20.00	40.00
Armed Forces Complimentary copies, HD No. 2-16,19,22-25,28,29 (1956-59),31-39('61),40('62)	.40	1.20	2.40

SAD SACK FUN AROUND THE WORLD
1974 (no month)
Harvey Publications

	Good	Fine	Mint
1-About Great Britain		.40	.80

SAD SACK GOES HOME
1951 (16 pgs. in color)
Harvey Publications

	Good	Fine	Mint
nn-by George Baker	3.50	10.00	20.00

SAD SACK LAUGH SPECIAL
Winter, 1958-59 - No. 93, Feb, 1977
Harvey Publications

	Good	Fine	Mint
1	3.00	8.00	16.00
2-10	1.50	4.00	8.00
11-30	.70	2.00	4.00
31-50	.40	1.20	2.40
51-93		.50	1.00

SAD SACK NAVY, GOBS 'N' GALS
Aug, 1972 - No. 8, Oct, 1973
Harvey Publications

	Good	Fine	Mint
1		.50	1.00
2-8		.30	.60

SAD SACK'S ARMY LIFE (See Harvey Hits No. 17,22,28,32,39,43, 47,51,55,58,61,64,67,70)

SAD SACK'S ARMY LIFE (. . . Parade No. 1-57, . . . Today No. 58 on)
Oct, 1963 - No. 60, Nov, 1975; No. 61, May, 1976
Harvey Publications

	Good	Fine	Mint
1	2.00	6.00	12.00
2-10	1.00	3.00	6.00
11-20	.40	1.20	2.40
21-40		.50	1.00
41-61		.30	.60

SAD SACK'S FUNNY FRIENDS (See Harvey Hits No. 75)
Dec, 1955 - No. 75, Oct, 1969
Harvey Publications

	Good	Fine	Mint
1	3.50	10.00	20.00
2-10	2.00	5.00	10.00
11-20	.85	2.50	5.00
21-30	.40	1.20	2.40
31-50		.50	1.00
51-75		.30	.60

SAD SACK'S MUTTSY (See Harvey Hits No. 74,77,80,82,84,87,89, 92,96,99,102,105,108,111,113,115,117,119,121)

SAD SACK USA (. . . Vacation No. 8)
Nov, 1972 - No. 7, Nov, 1973; No. 8, Oct, 1974
Harvey Publications

	Good	Fine	Mint
1		.50	1.00
2-8		.25	.50

SAD SACK WITH SARGE & SADIE
Sept, 1972 - No. 8, 1973
Harvey Publications

	Good	Fine	Mint
1		.50	1.00
2-8		.25	.50

SAD SAD SACK WORLD
Oct, 1964 - No. 46, Dec, 1973
Harvey Publications

	Good	Fine	Mint
1	.85	2.50	5.00
2-10	.40	1.20	2.40
11-46		.50	1.00

SAGA OF BIG RED, THE
Sept, 1976 ($1.25) (In color)
Omaha World-Herald

	Good	Fine	Mint
nn-by Win Mumma; story of the Nebraska Cornhuskers (sports)	.30	.80	1.60

SAILOR SWEENEY (Navy Action No. 1-11, 15 on)
No. 12, July, 1956 - No. 14, Nov, 1956
Atlas Comics (CDS)

	Good	Fine	Mint
12-14: 12-Shores-a. 13-Severin-c	1.50	4.00	6.00

SAINT, THE
Aug, 1947 - No. 12, Mar, 1952
Avon Periodicals

	Good	Fine	Mint
1-Kamen bondage c/a	20.00	60.00	120.00
2-4	10.00	30.00	60.00
5-Everett-a; spanking panel	12.00	35.00	70.00
6-Miss Fury app., 14 pgs.	15.00	45.00	90.00
7-c-/Avon paperback 118	7.00	20.00	40.00
8,9(12/50): Saint strip-r in No. 8-12; 9-Kinstler-c	7.00	20.00	40.00
10-Wood-a, 1 pg; c-/Avon paperback 289	6.00	18.00	36.00
11	5.00	14.00	28.00
12-c-/Avon paperback 123	5.50	16.00	32.00

NOTE: *Lucky Dale, Girl Detective in No. 1,4,6.*

SALERNO CARNIVAL OF COMICS (Also see Pure Oil Comics, 24 Pages of Comics, & Vicks Comics)
Late 1930s (16 pgs.) (paper cover) (Giveaway)
Salerno Cookie Co.

	Good	Fine	Mint
nn-Color reprints of Calkins' Buck Rogers & Skyroads, plus other strips from Famous Funnies.	20.00	60.00	120.00

SAM HILL PRIVATE EYE
1950 - No. 7, 1951
Close-Up

	Good	Fine	Mint
1-Negligee panel	3.00	8.00	16.00
2,3,6,7	1.50	4.00	8.00
4,5-Drug mention story	2.00	5.00	10.00

SAMSON (1st Series) (Capt. Aero No. 7 on)
Fall, 1940 - No. 6, Sept, 1941
Fox Features Syndicate

	Good	Fine	Mint
1-Will Eisner-a	25.00	70.00	150.00
2	15.00	45.00	95.00
3-Navy Jones app; Simon-c.	10.00	30.00	65.00
4-Yarko the Great, Master Magician by Eisner begins; Fine-c?	9.00	25.00	56.00

Sad Sack #1, © HARV

The Saint #4, © AVON

Salerno Carnival Of Comics nn, © KING

Samson #12, © AJAX

Sandman #3, © DC

Santa Claus Funnies-Grant Giveaway

SAMSON (continued)

	Good	Fine	Mint
5	9.00	25.00	56.00
6-Origin The Topper	9.00	25.00	56.00

SAMSON (2nd Series) (See Spectacular Features Magazine)
No. 12, April, 1955 - No. 14, Aug, 1955
Ajax/Farrell Publications (Four Star)

12-14: Wonder Boy in No. 12,13; Rocket Man in No. 13 — 2.00 6.00 12.00

SAMSON (See Mighty Samson)

SAMSON & DELILAH (See A Spectacular Feature Magazine)

SAMUEL BRONSTON'S CIRCUS WORLD (See Movie Comics under Circus World)

SANDMAN, THE
Winter, 1974; No. 2, Apr-May, 1975 - No. 6, Dec-Jan, 1975-76
National Periodical Publications

	Good	Fine	Mint
1-Kirby-a		.40	.80
2,3-Chua-a in each		.30	.60
4-6: 6-Kirby/Wood c/a		.30	.60

NOTE: ***Kirby** a-4-6; c-1-5.*

SANDS OF THE SOUTH PACIFIC
January, 1953
Toby Press

1 (Scarce) — 4.00 12.00 24.00

SANTA AND HIS REINDEER (See March of Comics No. 166)

SANTA AND POLLYANNA PLAY THE GLAD GAME
1960 (15 pages) (Disney giveaway)
Sales Promotion

1.00 3.00 6.00

SANTA AND THE ANGEL (See 4-Color No. 259 & Dell Jr. Treasury No. 7)

SANTA & THE BUCCANEERS
1959
Promotional Publ. Co. (Giveaway)

Reprints 1952 Santa & the Pirates — .50 1.50 3.00

SANTA & THE CHRISTMAS CHICKADEE
1974 (20 pgs.)
Murphy's (Giveaway)

.50 1.00

SANTA & THE PIRATES
1952
Promotional Publ. Co. (Giveaway)

Marv Levy c/a — .85 2.50 5.00

SANTA AT THE ZOO (See 4-Color No. 259)

SANTA CLAUS AROUND THE WORLD (See March of Comics No. 241)

SANTA CLAUS CONQUERS THE MARTIANS (See Movie Classics)

SANTA CLAUS FUNNIES
No date (1940s) (Color & B&W; 8x10''; 12pgs., heavy paper)
W. T. Grant Co. (Giveaway)

7.00 20.00 40.00

SANTA CLAUS FUNNIES
1942 - 1962
Dell Publishing Co.

	Good	Fine	Mint
nn(No.1)(1942)-Kelly-a	30.00	70.00	140.00
2(1943)-Kelly-a	20.00	50.00	100.00
4-Color 61(1944)-Kelly-a	15.00	45.00	90.00
4-Color 91(1945)-Kelly-a	12.00	35.00	70.00
4-Color 128('46),175('47)-Kelly-a	10.00	28.00	56.00
4-Color 205,254-Kelly-a	8.00	24.00	48.00
4-Color 302,361	1.50	4.50	9.00
4-Color 525,607,666,756,867	.70	2.00	4.00
4-Color 958,1063,1154,1274	.60	1.80	3.60
1(1952-Dell Giant)(Dan Noonan-**A Christmas Carol** adaptation)	3.00	9.00	18.00

NOTE: *Most issues contain only one **Kelly** story.*

SANTA CLAUS PARADE
1951; 1952; 1955 (25 cents)
Ziff-Davis (Approved Comics)/St. John Publishing Co.

	Good	Fine	Mint
nn(1951-Ziff-Davis)-116 pgs. (Xmas Special)	3.50	10.00	20.00
2(12/52-Ziff-Davis)-100 pgs.; Dave Berg-a	3.00	8.00	16.00
V1No.3(1/66-St. John)-100 pgs.	2.00	6.00	12.00

SANTA IS COMING (See March of Comics No. 197)

SANTA IS HERE (See March of Comics No. 49)

SANTA ON THE JOLLY ROGER
1965
Promotional Publ. Co. (Giveaway)

Marv Levy c/a — .50 1.50 3.00

SANTA! SANTA!
1974 (20 pgs.)
R. Jackson (Montgomery Ward giveaway)

.50 1.00

SANTA'S BUSY CORNER (See March of Comics No. 31)

SANTA'S CANDY KITCHEN (See March of Comics No. 14)

SANTA'S CHRISTMAS BOOK (See March of Comics No. 123)

SANTA'S CHRISTMAS COMICS
December, 1952 (100 pages)
Standard Comics (Best Books)

nn — 3.00 8.00 16.00

SANTA'S CHRISTMAS COMIC VARIETY SHOW
1943 (24 pages)
Sears Roebuck & Co.

Contains puzzles & new comics of Dick Tracy, Little Orphan Annie, Moon Mullins, Terry & the Pirates, etc. — 7.00 20.00 40.00

SANTA'S CHRISTMAS LIST (See March of Comics No. 255)

SANTA'S CHRISTMAS TIME STORIES
No date (late 1940s) (16 pgs.; paper cover)
Premium Sales, Inc. (Giveaway)

2.00 6.00 12.00

SANTA'S CIRCUS
1964 (half-size)
Promotional Publ. Co. (Giveaway)

Marv Levy c/a — .50 1.50 3.00

SANTA'S FUN BOOK
1951, 1952 (regular size, 16 pages, paper-c)
Promotional Publ. Co. (Murphy's giveaway)

2.00 5.00 10.00

SANTA'S HELPERS (See March of Comics No. 64,106,198)

SANTA'S LITTLE HELPERS (See March of Comics No. 270)

SANTA'S NEW STORY BOOK
1949 (16 pgs.; paper cover)
Wallace Hamilton Campbell (Giveaway)

3.00 8.00 16.00

SANTA'S REAL STORY BOOK
1952
W. W. Orris (Giveaway)

2.00 6.00 12.00

SANTA'S RIDE
1959
W. T. Grant Co. (Giveaway)

	Good	Fine	Mint
	1.50	4.00	8.00

SANTA'S RODEO
1964 (half-size)
Promotional Publ. Co. (Giveaway)

Marv Levy-a	.70	2.00	4.00

SANTA'S SECRETS
1951 (16 pgs.; paper cover)
Sam B. Anson Christmas giveaway

	2.00	6.00	12.00

SANTA'S SHOW (See March of Comics No. 311)

SANTA'S SLEIGH (See March of Comics No. 298)

SANTA'S STORIES
1953 (regular size; paper cover)
K. K. Publications (Klines Dept. Store)

Kelly-a	10.00	30.00	60.00

SANTA'S SURPRISE (See March of Comics No. 13)

SANTA'S SURPRISE
1947 (36 pgs.; slick cover)
K. K. Publications (Giveaway)

	3.00	8.00	16.00

SANTA'S TINKER TOTS
1958
Charlton Comics

1-Based on "The Tinker Tots Keep Christmas"	.70	2.00	4.00

SANTA'S TOYLAND (See March of Comics No. 242)

SANTA'S TOYS (See March of Comics No. 12)

SANTA'S TOYTOWN FUN BOOK
1952
Promotional Publ. Co. (Giveaway)

Marv Levy-c	1.00	3.00	6.00

SANTA'S VISIT (See March of Comics No. 283)

SANTA'S WORKSHOP (See March of Comics No. 50,168)

SANTIAGO (See 4-Color No. 723)

SARGE SNORKEL (Beetle Bailey)
Oct, 1973 - No. 17, Dec, 1976
Charlton Comics

1-17		.30	.60

SARGE STEEL (Becomes Secret Agent No. 9 on)
Dec, 1964 - No. 8, Mar-Apr, 1966
Charlton Comics

1-Origin	.30	.80	1.60
2-8		.50	1.00

SAVAGE COMBAT TALES
Feb, 1975 - No. 3, July, 1975
Atlas/Seaboard Publ.

1-Sgt. Stryker's Death Squad begins (origin); McWilliams-c/a		.30	.60
2,3: 2-Toth, McWilliams-a; intro. & only app. Warhawk		.30	.60

SAVAGE RAIDS OF GERONIMO (See Geronimo No. 4)

SAVAGE RANGE (See 4-Color No. 807)

SAVAGE SHE-HULK, THE
Feb, 1980 - No. 25, Feb, 1982
Marvel Comics Group

	Good	Fine	Mint
1-Origin & 1st app.	.30	.80	1.60
2,3		.50	1.00
4,5		.40	.80
6-15		.30	.60
16-25		.25	.50

NOTE: ***Austin*** *c-23i.* ***J. Buscema*** *a-1; c-1, 2.* ***Golden*** *c-8-11.*

SAVAGE SWORD OF CONAN, THE (Magazine)
Aug, 1974 - Present (Black & White)
Marvel Comics Group

1-Smith-r; Buscema/Adams/Krenkel-a; origin Blackmark by Gil Kane(part 1) & Red Sonja (3rd app.)	2.00	6.00	12.00
2-Chaykin/Adams-c	1.00	3.00	6.00
3-Severin/Smith-a; Adams-a	.85	2.50	5.00
4-Adams/Kane-a(r)	.70	2.00	4.00
5-10	.55	1.60	3.20
11-20	.50	1.50	3.00
21-30	.40	1.20	2.40
31-70: 70-Article on movie	.30	.90	1.80
Annual 1('75)-B&W, Smith-r (Conan No. 10,13)	.40	1.20	2.40

NOTE: ***Adams*** *a-14p, 60.* ***Alcala*** *a-2 ,4, 7, 12, 15-20, 23, 24, 28, 59, 67, 69.* ***Boris*** *c-1, 4, 5, 7, 9-12, 15.* ***Brunner*** *a-30; c-8, 30.* ***Buscema*** *a-1-5, 7, 10-12, 15-24, 26-28, 31, 32, 36-43, 45, 47-58p, 60-67p, 70; c-40.* ***Chaykin*** *a-18, 22; c-31.* ***Corbin*** *a-4, 16, 29.* ***Finley*** *a-16.* ***Infantino*** *a-34.* ***Jones*** *a-8.* ***Kaluta*** *a-11, 18; c-3, 4.* ***Gil Kane*** *a-3, 8, 13, 29, 47, 64, 65, 67.* ***Krenkel*** *a-9, 11, 14, 16, 24.* ***Morrow*** *a-7.* ***Newton*** *a-6.* ***Nino*** *a/c-6.* ***Redondo*** *c-48, 50, 52, 56, 57.* ***Simonson*** *a-7, 8, 12, 15-17.* ***Smith*** *a-7, 16, 24.* ***Starlin*** *c-26. No. 8 & 10 contain a Robert E. Howard Conan adaptation.*

SAVAGE TALES (Magazine) (B&W)
May, 1971; No. 2, 10/73; No. 3, 2/74 - No. 12, Summer, 1975
Marvel Comics Group

1-Origin & 1st app. The Man-Thing by Morrow; Conan the Barbarian by Barry Smith, Femizons by Romita begin; Ka-Zar-r	9.00	27.00	54.00
2-Smith, Brunner, Morrow, Williamson, Wrightson-a (reprint/Creatures on the Loose No. 10); King Kull app.	3.00	9.00	18.00
3-Smith, Brunner, Steranko, Williamson-a	2.00	6.00	12.00
4,5-Adams-c; last Conan (Smith-r/No. 4) plus Kane/Adams-a. 5-Brak the Barbarian begins, ends No. 8	1.00	3.00	6.00
6-Ka-Zar begins; Williamson-r; Adams-c	.50	1.50	3.00
7-Buscema/Adams-a	.50	1.50	3.00
8-Shanna, the She-Devil begins, ends No. 10; Adams-c/a; Williamson-r	.50	1.50	3.00
9,11	.40	1.20	2.40
10-Adams-a(i)	.50	1.50	3.00
Annual 1(Summer'75)(No.12 on inside)-Ka-Zar origin by G. Kane; B&W; Smith-r/Astonishing Tales	.40	1.20	2.40

NOTE: ***Boris*** *c-7,10.* ***Fabian*** *c-8.* ***Kaluta*** *c-9.* ***Starlin*** *a-5. Robert E. Howard adaptations-1-4.*

SCAMP (Walt Disney)
May, 1956 - No. 1204, 8-10/61; 11/67 - No. 45, 1/79
Dell Publishing Co./Gold Key

4-Color 703,777,806('57),833	.55	1.60	3.20
5(3-5/58)-10(6-8/59)	.30	.80	1.60
11-16(12-2/61)		.50	1.00
4-Color 1204(1961)	.40	1.20	2.40
1(12/67-G.K.)-Reprints begin	.30	.80	1.60
2(3/69)-10		.40	.80
11-45		.30	.60

NOTE: *New stories-No. 20(in part),22-25,27,29-31,34,36-40,42-45. New covers-No. 11,12,14,15,17-25,27,29-31,34,36-38.*

Sarge Steel #7, © CC

Savage She-Hulk #1, © MCG

Scamp #16, © WDP

Scary Tales #1, © CC

Scorpion #1, © ATLAS

Scribbly #13, © DC

SCAR FACE (See The Crusaders)

SCARECROW, THE (. . . of Romney Marsh No. 1)
April, 1964 - No. 3, Oct, 1965 (Disney TV Show)
Gold Key

	Good	Fine	Mint
10112-404 (No.1)	1.00	3.00	6.00
2,3	.70	2.00	4.00

SCARLET O'NEIL (See Harvey Comics Hits No. 59)

SCARY TALES
Aug, 1975 - No. 9, Jan, 1977; No. 10, Sept, 1977 - Present
Charlton Comics

	Good	Fine	Mint
1-Origin & 1st app. Countess Von Bludd, not in No. 2; Staton-c		.40	.80
2-11: 4-Staton-a		.30	.60
12-30-All reprints		.30	.60
1(Modern Comics reprint, 1977)		.15	.30

NOTE: ***Ditko*** *a-3, 5, 7, 8(2), 11, 12, 14-16r, 18(3)r, 19r, 21r; c-5, 11, 14, 18.* ***Powell*** *a-18r.* ***Staton*** *a-20r; c-20.* ***Sutton*** *c-4.*

SCHOOL DAY ROMANCES (. . . of Teen-Agers No. 4) (Popular Teen-Agers No. 5 on)
Nov-Dec, 1949 - No. 4, May-June, 1950
Star Publications

	Good	Fine	Mint
1-Tony Gayle (later Gay), Gingersnapp begin	5.50	16.00	32.00
2,3	3.50	10.00	20.00
4-Ronald Reagan photo-c	4.00	12.00	24.00

NOTE: *All have* ***L. B. Cole*** *covers.*

SCHWINN BICYCLE BOOK (. . . Bike Thrills, 1959)
1949; 1952; 1959 (10 cents)
Schwinn Bicycle Co.

	Good	Fine	Mint
1949	2.50	7.00	14.00
1952-Believe It or Not type facts; comic format; 32 pgs.	1.50	4.00	8.00
1959	1.00	3.00	6.00

SCIENCE COMICS (1st Series)
Feb, 1940 - No. 8, Sept, 1940
Fox Features Syndicate

	Good	Fine	Mint
1-Origin Dynamo (called Electro in No. 1), The Eagle, & Navy Jones; Marga, the Panther Woman, Cosmic Carson & Perisphere Payne, Dr. Doom begin; bondage/hypo-c	50.00	140.00	300.00
2	30.00	90.00	200.00
3	25.00	75.00	160.00
4-Kirby-a	25.00	75.00	160.00
5-8	15.00	45.00	100.00

NOTE: *Cosmic Carson by* ***Kirby****-No. 4 only.* ***Lou Fine*** *c-1,2 only.*

SCIENCE COMICS (2nd Series)
January, 1946 - No. 5, 1946
Humor Publications

	Good	Fine	Mint
1	2.00	6.00	12.00
2,4,5	1.50	4.00	8.00
3-Feldstein-a, 6 pgs.	3.00	9.00	18.00

SCIENCE COMICS
March, 1951
Export Publication Ent., Toronto, Canada
Distr. in U.S. by Kable News Co.

	Good	Fine	Mint
1-Science adventure stories plus some true science features	1.50	4.00	8.00

SCIENCE FICTION SPACE ADVENTURES (See Space Adventures)

SCOOBY DOO (. . . Where Are You? No. 1-16,26; . . . Mystery Comics No. 17-25,27 on) (TV)
March, 1970 - No. 30, Feb, 1975
Gold Key

	Good	Fine	Mint
1	.70	2.00	4.00
2-5	.50	1.50	3.00
6-10	.35	1.00	2.00
11-20	.30	.80	1.60
21-30		.50	1.00

(See March of Comics No. 356,382,391)

SCOOBY-DOO
Oct, 1977 - No. 9, Feb, 1979
Marvel Comics Group

	Good	Fine	Mint
1		.40	.80
2-9		.30	.60

SCOOBY DOO, WHERE ARE YOU? (TV)
April, 1975 - No. 11, Dec, 1976 (Hanna-Barbera)
Charlton Comics

	Good	Fine	Mint
1	.50	1.50	3.00
2-5	.35	1.00	2.00
6-11		.50	1.00

SCOOP
November, 1941 - 1946
Harry 'A' Chesler (Holyoke)

	Good	Fine	Mint
1-Intro. Rocketman & Rocketgirl; origin The Master Key; Dan Hastings begins; c/a by Charles Sultan	12.00	35.00	70.00
2-Rocket Boy app; Injury to eye story (same as Spotlight No. 3)	9.00	25.00	50.00
3-R-Injury to eye story from No. 2	5.00	15.00	30.00
4-8	4.00	12.00	24.00

SCOOTER (See Swing With . . .)

SCOOTER
April, 1946
Rucker Publ. Ltd. (Canadian)

	Good	Fine	Mint
1	1.00	3.00	5.00

SCORPION, THE
Feb, 1975 - No. 3, July, 1975
Atlas/Seaboard Publ.

	Good	Fine	Mint
1-Intro.; bondage-c		.60	1.20
2-Wrightson, Kaluta, Simonson-a(i)		.40	.80
3		.40	.80

NOTE: ***Chaykin*** *a-1,2.*

SCOTLAND YARD (Inspector Farnsworth of . . .)
1955 - No. 4, March, 1956
Charlton Comics

	Good	Fine	Mint
1	3.00	8.00	16.00
2-4: 2-Tothish-a	2.00	5.00	10.00

SCREAM (. . . Comics) (Andy Comics No. 20 on)
Fall, 1944 - No. 19, April, 1948
Humor Publications/Current Books(Ace Magazines)

	Good	Fine	Mint
1	2.00	6.00	12.00
2-15: 11-Racist humor (Indians)	1.50	4.00	8.00
16-Intro. Lily-Belle	1.50	4.00	8.00
17,19	1.00	3.00	6.00
18-Transvestite, Hypo needle story	1.50	4.50	9.00

SCREAM (Magazine)
Aug, 1973 - No. 11, Feb, 1975 (68 pgs.) (B&W)
Skywald Publishing Corp.

	Good	Fine	Mint
1	.50	1.50	3.00
2-5: 3 (12/73)-No. 3 found on pg. 22	.30	.80	1.60
6-11		.50	1.00

SCRIBBLY
Aug-Sept, 1948 - No. 15, Dec-Jan, 1951-52
National Periodical Publications

	Good	Fine	Mint
1	20.00	60.00	120.00
2-5	10.00	30.00	60.00
6-10	7.00	20.00	40.00
11-15	5.50	16.00	32.00

SCRIBBLY (continued)
NOTE: ***Sheldon Mayer** art in all.*

SEA DEVILS (See DC Special No. 10,19, DC Super-Stars No. 14,17, Limited Collectors Ed. No. 39,45, & Showcase)
Sept-Oct, 1961 - No. 35, May-June, 1967
National Periodical Publications

	Good	Fine	Mint
1	3.00	10.00	20.00
2	2.00	5.00	10.00
3-5	1.00	3.00	6.00
6-10	.70	2.00	4.00
11,12,14-20	.50	1.50	3.00
13-Kubert, Colan-a	.70	2.00	4.00
21,23-35	.35	1.00	2.00
22-Intro. International Sea Devils; origin & 1st app. Capt. X & Man Fish	.35	1.00	2.00

NOTE: ***Heath** a-11; c-1-11,14-16.*

SEA HOUND, THE (Capt. Silver's Log of . . .)
1945 (no month) - No. 4, Jan-Feb, 1946
Avon Periodicals

	Good	Fine	Mint
nn	2.50	7.00	14.00
2-4	2.00	5.00	10.00

SEA HOUND, THE
No. 3, July, 1949 - No. 4, Sept, 1949
Capt. Silver Syndicate

	Good	Fine	Mint
3,4	.85	2.50	5.00

SEA HUNT (TV)
1958 - 10-12/59; No. 4, 1-3/60 - No. 13, 4-6/62
Dell Publishing Co.

	Good	Fine	Mint
4-Color 928,994, 4-13: Manning-a No. 4-6,8-11,13	1.50	4.00	8.00
4-Color 1041-Toth-a	2.00	6.00	12.00

SEARCH FOR LOVE
Feb-Mar, 1950 - No. 2, Apr-May, 1950
American Comics Group

	Good	Fine	Mint
1	2.00	6.00	12.00
2	1.50	4.00	8.00

SEARCHERS (See 4-Color No. 709)

SEARS (See Merry Christmas From . . .)

SEASON'S GREETINGS
1935 (6¼x5¼") (32 pgs. in color)
Hallmark (King Features)

Cover features Mickey Mouse, Popeye, Jiggs & Skippy. "The Night Before Christmas" told one panel per page, each panel by a famous artist featuring their character. Art by Alex Raymond, Gottfredson, Swinnerton, Segar, Chic Young, Milt Gross, Sullivan (Messmer), Herriman, McManus, Percy Crosby & others (22 artists in all)
Estimated value . . . . $300.00 — $500.00

NOTE: *This book is a relatively new listing, and there has been a reported sale for a very high figure. However, an estimated price is listed based on desirability and demand.*

SECRET AGENT (Formerly Sarge Steel)
Oct, 1966 - V2No.10, Oct, 1967
Charlton Comics

	Good	Fine	Mint
V2No.9-Sarge Steel begins	.30	.80	1.60
10-Tiffany Sinn, CIA app. (from Career Girl Romances No. 39)		.40	.80

SECRET AGENT (TV)
Nov, 1966 - No. 2, Jan, 1968
Gold Key

	Good	Fine	Mint
1,2	.85	2.50	5.00

SECRET AGENT X-9
1934 (Book 1: 84 pgs.; Book 2: 124 pgs.) (8x7½")
David McKay Publications

	Good	Fine	Mint
Book 1-Contains reprints of the first 13 weeks of the strip by Alex Raymond; complete except for 2 dailies	40.00	120.00	200.00
Book 2-Contains reprints immediately following contents of Book 1, for 20 weeks by Alex Raymond; complete except for two dailies. Note: Raymond mis-dated the last five strips from June, 1934, and while the dating sequence is confusing, the continuity is correct.	35.00	100.00	160.00

SECRET AGENT X-9 (See Feature Book No. 8, McKay)

SECRET AGENT Z-2 (See Z-2)

SECRET DIARY OF EERIE ADVENTURES
1953 (One Shot) (Giant-100 pgs.)
Avon Periodicals

	Good	Fine	Mint
(Rare) Kubert-a; Hollingsworth-c; Check back-c	90.00	250.00	500.00

SECRET HEARTS
9-10/49 - No. 6, 7-8/50; 7,8, 2-3/52 - No. 154, 9/71
National Periodical Publications (Beverly)(Arleigh No. 50-113)

	Good	Fine	Mint
1	5.50	16.00	32.00
2-10 (No. 7 exist?)	3.00	8.00	16.00
11-20	1.50	4.00	8.00
21-30	1.00	3.00	6.00
31-40	.85	2.50	5.00
41-50	.50	1.50	3.00
51-60	.40	1.20	2.40
61-109		.50	1.00
110-"Reach for Happiness" serial begins, ends No. 138		.50	1.00
111-119,121-133,135-138		.40	.80
120,134-Adams-c	.30	.80	1.60
139,140		.25	.50
141,142-"20 Miles to Heartbreak," Chapter 2 & 3 (See Young Love for Chapter 1 & 4); Toth plus Colletta art		.40	.80
143-148,150-154: 144-Morrow-a. (154-Exist?)		.25	.50
149-Toth-a		.30	.60

SECRET LOVE
1949 (Giant Size, 132 pages)
Fox Features Syndicate

nn-See Fox Giants. Contents can vary & determines price.

SECRET LOVE
12/55 - No. 3, 8/56; 4/57 - No. 5, 2/58; No. 6, 6/58
Ajax-Farrell/Four Star Comic Corp. No. 2 on

	Good	Fine	Mint
1(12/55-Ajax)	1.50	4.00	8.00
2,3	1.00	3.00	6.00
1(4/57-Ajax)	1.00	3.00	6.00
2-6: 5-Bakerish-a	.85	2.50	5.00

SECRET LOVE (See Sinister House of . . .)

SECRET LOVES
Nov, 1949 - No. 6, Sept, 1950
Comic Magazines/Quality Comics Group

	Good	Fine	Mint
1-Ward-c	7.00	20.00	40.00
2-Ward-c	6.00	18.00	36.00
3-Crandall-a	5.00	14.00	28.00
4,6	2.50	7.00	14.00
5-Suggestive art-"Boom Town Babe"	3.50	10.00	20.00

SECRET LOVE STORIES
1949 (132 pages)
Fox Features Syndicate

nn-See Fox Giants. Contents can vary and determines price.

SECRET MISSIONS
February, 1950

Sea Devils #11, © DC

Sea Hunt #7, © DELL

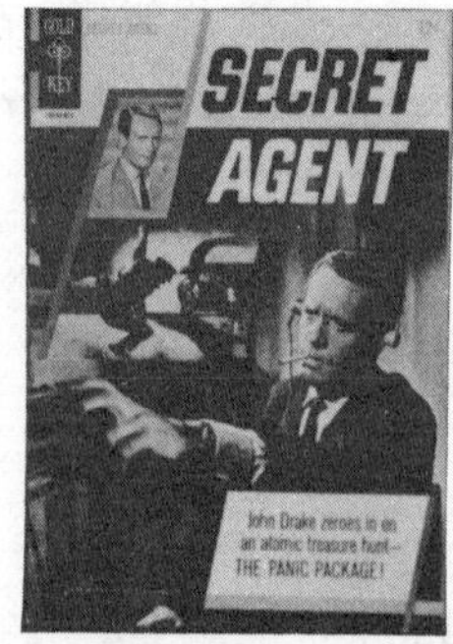

Secret Agent #1, © GK

Secret Origins #2, © DC

S.S. Of Super Villains #1, © DC

Secrets Of Haunted House #26, © DC

SECRET MISSIONS (continued)
St. John Publishing Co.

	Good	Fine	Mint
1-Kubert-c	5.00	15.00	30.00

SECRET MYSTERIES (Formerly Crime Mysteries & Crime Smashers)
No. 16, Nov, 1954 - No. 19, July, 1955
Ribage/Merit Publishing Corp.

	Good	Fine	Mint
16-Horror, Palais-a	2.00	6.00	12.00
17-19-Horror	2.00	6.00	12.00

NOTE: ***L. B. Cole**-a-17p. **Hollingsworth** a-17.*

SECRET ORIGINS (See 80pg. Giants No. 8)
Feb-Mar, 1973 - No. 6, Jan-Feb, 1974; No. 7, Oct-Nov, 1974
National Periodical Publications

	Good	Fine	Mint
1-Origin Superman, Batman, The Ghost, The Flash (Showcase No. 4); Infantino & Kubert-a	.35	1.10	2.20
2-Origin new Green Lantern, the new Atom, & Supergirl; Kane-a	.30	.80	1.60
3-Origin Wonder Woman, Wildcat	.30	.80	1.60
4-Origin Vigilante by Meskin, Kid Eternity		.50	1.00
5-Origin The Spectre	.30	.80	1.60
6-Origin Blackhawk & Legion of Super Heroes	.30	.80	1.60
7-Origin Robin, Aquaman		.50	1.00

SECRET ORIGINS ANNUAL (See 80 Page Giant No. 8)
Aug-Oct, 1961
National Periodical Publications

	Good	Fine	Mint
1('61)-Origin Adam Strange (Showcase No. 17), Green Lantern (G. L. No. 1), Challs (partial/Showcase No. 6, 6 pgs. Kirby art), J'onn J'onzz (Detective No.225), New Flash (Showcase No. 4), Green Arrow (1 pg. text), Superman-Batman team, & Wonder Woman	7.00	20.00	40.00

SECRET ORIGINS OF SUPER-HEROES (See DC Special Series No. 10,19)

SECRET ROMANCE
10/68 - No. 41, 11/76; No. 42, 3/79 - No. 48, 2/80
Charlton Comics

	Good	Fine	Mint
1		.40	.80
2-48: 9-Reese-a		.20	.40

NOTE: *Beyond the Stars app.-No. 9,11,12,14.*

SECRET ROMANCES
April, 1951 - No. 27, July, 1955
Superior Publications Ltd.

	Good	Fine	Mint
1	3.00	9.00	18.00
2-10	2.00	6.00	12.00
11-13,15-18,20-27	1.50	4.00	8.00
14,19-Lingerie panels	2.00	6.00	12.00

SECRET SERVICE (See Kent Blake of the . . .)

SECRET SIX
Apr-May, 1968 - No. 7, Apr-May, 1969
National Periodical Publications

	Good	Fine	Mint
1-Origin	.30	.80	1.60
2-7		.50	1.00

SECRET SOCIETY OF SUPER-VILLAINS
May-June, 1976 - No. 15, June-July, 1978
National Periodical Publications/DC Comics

	Good	Fine	Mint
1-Origin	.35	1.00	2.00
2-5: 2-Re-intro. Capt. Comet		.40	.80
6-15: 9,10-Creeper x-over. 11-Orlando inks. 15-G.A. Atom, Dr. Midnite, & Justice Society app.		.30	.60

NOTE: ***Buckler** a-7-9; c-7-9, 11-13, 15, '77 Special. **Giordano** c-2. **Jones** a-'77 Special. **Marcos** a-2p. **Orlando** a-11i.*

SECRET SOCIETY OF SUPER-VILLAINS SPECIAL (See DC Special Series No. 6)

SECRETS OF HAUNTED HOUSE
4-5/75 - No. 5, 12-1/75-76; No. 6, 6-7/77 - No. 14, 10-11/78; No. 15, 8/79 - Present
National Periodical Publications/DC Comics

	Good	Fine	Mint
1-Nino-a		.50	1.00
2-4: 4-Redondo-a		.30	.60
5-Wrightson-c		.30	.60
6-9,11-25,27-43		.25	.50
10-Golden-a		.50	1.00
26-Rogers-c		.30	.60
Special (3/78)		.30	.60

NOTE: ***Ditko** a-9, 12, 41. **Kaluta** c-11, 14, 16, 29. **Kubert** c-41, 42. **Sheldon Mayer** a-43. **Newton** a-30. **Nino** a-1, 13, 19. **Orlando** c-13, 30, 43. **Redondo** a-29.*

SECRETS OF HAUNTED HOUSE SPECIAL (See DC Spec. Ser. No. 12)

SECRETS OF LIFE (See 4-Color No. 749)

SECRETS OF LOVE (See Popular Teen-Agers . . .)

SECRETS OF LOVE AND MARRIAGE
1956 - V2No.25, June, 1961
Charlton Comics

	Good	Fine	Mint
V2No.1-6	.35	1.00	2.00
V2No.7-9 (All 68 pgs.)		.50	1.00
10-25		.40	.80

SECRETS OF MAGIC (See Wisco)

SECRETS OF SINISTER HOUSE (Sinister House of Secret Love No. 1-4)
No. 5, June-July, 1972 - No. 18, June-July, 1974
National Periodical Publications

	Good	Fine	Mint
5		.40	.80
6,8,9		.30	.60
7-Redondo-a		.40	.80
10-Adams-a(i)	.50	1.50	3.00
11-16,18		.25	.50
17-Toth-r		.30	.60

NOTE: ***Alcala** a-13, 14. **Kaluta** c-7, 11. **Nino** a-8, 11-13. Ambrose Bierce adaptation-No. 14.*

SECRETS OF THE LEGION OF SUPER-HEROES
Jan, 1981 - No. 3, March, 1981
DC Comics

	Good	Fine	Mint
1-Origin of the Legion		.40	.80
2,3		.30	.60

SECRETS OF TRUE LOVE
February, 1958
St. John Publishing Co.

	Good	Fine	Mint
1	1.00	3.00	6.00

SECRETS OF YOUNG BRIDES
No. 5, 9/57 - No. 44, 9/64; 7/75 - No. 9, 11/76
Charlton Comics

	Good	Fine	Mint
5	.30	.90	1.80
6-44: 8-Negligee panel		.40	.80
1-9		.25	.50

SECRET SQUIRREL (TV)
October, 1966 (Hanna-Barbera)
Gold Key

	Good	Fine	Mint
1	.70	2.00	4.00
Florida Power & Light giveaway (1966)	.70	2.00	4.00

SECRET STORY ROMANCES (Becomes True Tales of Love?)
Nov, 1953 - No. 21, Mar, 1956
Atlas Comics (TCI)

	Good	Fine	Mint
1	1.50	4.00	8.00
2-21	.85	2.50	5.00

NOTE: ***Colletta** a-10,14,15,17,21; c-10,14,17.*

SECRET VOICE, THE (See Great American Comics)

SEDUCTION OF THE INNOCENT (Also see N. Y. State Joint Legis. Committee to Study . . .)
1953, 1954 (399 pages) (Hardback)
Rinehart & Co., Inc., N. Y. (Also printed in Canada by Clarke, Irwin & Co. Ltd., Toronto)
Written by Dr. Fredric Wertham

	Good	Fine	Mint
(1st Version)-with bibliographical note intact (several copies got out before the comic publishers forced the removal of this page)		50.00	90.00
with dust jacket. . . .		80.00	150.00
(2nd Version)-		30.00	60.00
with dust jacket. . . .		50.00	90.00
(3rd Version)-Published in England by Kennikat Press, 1954, 399pgs. has bibliographical page		25.00	50.00
1972 r-/of 3rd version; 400pgs w/bibliography page; Kennikat Press		7.50	15.00

NOTE: *Material from this book appeared in the November, 1953(Vol.70, pp50-53,214) issue of the* ***Ladies' Home Journal*** *under the title "What Parents Don't Know About Comic Books." With the release of this book, Dr. Wertham reveals seven years of research attempting to link juvenile delinquency to comic books. Many illustrations showing excessive violence, sex, sadism, and torture are shown. This book was used at the Kefauver Senate hearings which led to the Comics Code Authority. Because of the influence this book had on the comic industry and the collector's interest in it, we feel this listing is justified. Also see* ***Parade of Pleasure.***

SELECT DETECTIVE
Aug-Sept, 1948 - No. 3, Dec-Jan, 1948-49
D. S. Publishing Co.

	Good	Fine	Mint
1-Matt Baker-a	4.00	12.00	24.00
2-Baker, McWilliams-a	3.50	10.00	20.00
3	3.00	8.00	16.00

SENSATIONAL POLICE CASES
1952; 1954
Avon Periodicals

	Good	Fine	Mint
nn-100 pg. issue (1952, 25 cents)-Kubert & Kinstler-a	9.00	25.00	50.00
1 (1954)	4.00	12.00	24.00
2,3,5: 2-Kirbyish-a	3.00	9.00	18.00
4-Reprint/Saint No. 5	3.50	10.00	20.00

SENSATIONAL POLICE CASES
No date (1963?)
I. W. Enterprises

	Good	Fine	Mint
Reprint No. 5-Reprints Prison Break No. 5(1952-Avon); Infantino-a	.80	2.40	4.80

SENSATION COMICS (. . . Mystery No. 110 on)
Jan, 1942 - No. 109, May-June, 1952
National Periodical Publ./All-American

	Good	Fine	Mint
1-Origin Mr. Terrific, Wildcat, The Gay Ghost, & Little Boy Blue; Wonder Woman(cont'd from All Star No. 8), The Black Pirate begin; intro. Justice & Fair Play Club; No. 1 reprinted in Famous First Editions	180.00	500.00	1000.00
2	70.00	200.00	400.00
3	50.00	140.00	280.00
4	40.00	120.00	240.00
5-Intro. Justin, Black Pirate's son	30.00	80.00	160.00
6-10	25.00	70.00	140.00
11-20	19.00	55.00	110.00
21-30	14.00	40.00	80.00
31-33	10.00	30.00	60.00
34-Sargon, the Sorcerer begins, ends No. 36; begins again No. 52	10.00	30.00	60.00
35-40	8.00	24.00	48.00
41-50: 43-The Whip app.	7.00	20.00	40.00
51-60: 56,57-Sargon by Kubert	6.00	18.00	36.00
61-80: 63-Last Mr. Terrific. 65,66-Wildcat by Kubert. 68-Origin Huntress. 73-Bondage-c	5.50	16.00	32.00
81-Used in **SOTI**, pg. 33,34; Krigstein-a	8.00	24.00	48.00
82-90: 83-Last Sargon. 86-The Atom app. 90-Last Wildcat	5.00	14.00	28.00
91-Streak begins by Alex Toth	5.00	14.00	28.00
92,93: 92-Toth-a, 2 pgs.	4.00	12.00	24.00
94-1st all girl issue	6.00	18.00	36.00
95-106: Wonder Woman ends. 99-1st app. Astra, Girl of the Future, ends No. 106	6.00	18.00	36.00
107-(Scarce)-1st mystery issue; Toth-a	10.00	28.00	56.00
108-(Scarce)-J. Peril by Toth(p)	7.00	20.00	40.00
109-(Scarce)-J. Peril by Toth(p)	10.00	28.00	56.00

NOTE: ***Krigstein*** *a-(Wildcat)-81, 84.* ***Moldoff*** *Black Pirate-1-25. Wonder Woman by* ***H. C. Peter****, all issues except No. 17-19, 21.*

SENSATION MYSTERY (Sensation No. 1-109)
No. 110, July-Aug, 1952 - No. 116, July-Aug, 1953
National Periodical Publications

	Good	Fine	Mint
110-114-Johnny Peril continues, ends No. 116	4.00	12.00	24.00
115,116-Toth J. Peril in all	5.00	14.00	28.00

NOTE: ***Anderson*** *a-110, 111, 113, 116.* ***Colan*** *a-114p.* ***Giunta*** *a-112.* ***G. Kane*** *c-112, 113.* ***Infantino*** *a-111, 112, 114, 116; c-116.*

SERGEANT BARNEY BARKER (G. I. Tales No. 4 on)
Aug, 1956 - No. 3, Dec, 1956
Atlas Comics (MCI)

	Good	Fine	Mint
1-Severin-a(4)	3.00	8.00	16.00
2,3-Severin-a(4)	2.00	6.00	12.00

SGT. BILKO (Phil Silvers) (TV)
May-June, 1957 - No. 18, Mar-Apr, 1960
National Periodical Publications

	Good	Fine	Mint
1	4.00	12.00	24.00
2-5	3.00	8.00	16.00
6-18	2.00	5.00	10.00

SGT. BILKO'S PRIVATE DOBERMAN (TV)
June-July, 1958 - No. 11, Feb-Mar, 1960
National Periodical Publications

	Good	Fine	Mint
1	4.00	12.00	24.00
2-5	2.50	7.00	14.00
6-11	1.50	4.00	8.00

SGT. DICK CARTER OF THE U.S. BORDER PATROL (See Holyoke One-Shot)

SGT. FURY (& His Howling Commandos)
May, 1963 - No. 167, Nov, 1981
Marvel Comics Group

	Good	Fine	Mint
1-1st app. Sgt. Fury; Kirby-a	12.00	35.00	70.00
2-Kirby-a	6.25	18.50	35.00
3-5: 3-Reed Richards x-over. 4-Death of Junior Juniper. 5-1st Baron Strucker app.; Kirby-a	2.00	6.00	12.00
6,7-Kirby-a	1.00	3.00	6.00
8-10: 8-Baron Zemo, 1st Percival Pinkerton app. 10-1st app. Capt. Savage (the Skipper)	.85	2.60	5.20
11,12,14-20: 14-1st Blitz Squad. 18-Death of Pamela Hawley	.40	1.20	2.40
13-Captain America app.; Kirby-a	.80	2.40	4.80
21-30: 25-Red Skull app. 27-1st Eric Koenig app., origin Fury's eye patch		.50	1.00
31-40: 34-Origin Howling Commandos. 35-Eric Koeing joins Howlers		.50	1.00
41-60: 43-Bob Hope, Glen Miller app. 44-Flashback-Howlers 1st mission. 51-Roosevelt, Churchill, Stalin app.		.40	.80
61-100: 64-Capt. Savage & Raiders x-over. 76-Fury's Father app. in WWI story. 98-Deadly Dozen x-over. 100-Captain America, Fantastic Four cameos; Stan Lee, Martin Goodman & others app.		.40	.80

Sensation Comics #25, © DC

Sensation Comics #99, © DC

Sgt. Fury #1, © MCG

Sgt. Rock #320, © DC

Shade The Changing Man #2, © DC

The Shadow #3, © DC

SGT. FURY (continued) — Good / Fine / Mint
101-Origin retold .40 .80
102-120: 113-Reprints .30 .60
121-166-Reprints .25 .50
167-Reprints No. 1 .30 .60
Annual 1('65) .50 1.50 3.00
Special 2-7('66-11/71)-Eisenhower app. .50 1.00
NOTE: ***Ditko*** *a-15i.* ***Gil Kane*** *c-37, 96.* ***Kirby*** *a-1-8, 13p, 167p. Special 5; c-1-20, 25, 167p.* ***Severin*** *a-44, 48, 162, 164; inks-49-79; c-162-166.* ***Sutton*** *a-57. Reprints in No. 80, 82, 85, 87, 89, 91, 93, 95, 99, 101, 103, 105, 107, 109, 111.*

SGT. PRESTON OF THE YUKON (TV)
1951 - No. 29, Nov-Jan, 1958-59
Dell Publishing Co.
4-Color 344,373,397('52),419 2.00 5.00 10.00
5(11-1/52-53)-10 1.50 4.00 8.00
11-29: 13-Origin 1.00 3.00 6.00

SERGEANT PRESTON OF THE YUKON
1956 (4 comic booklets) (7x2½'' & 5x2½'')
Giveaways with Quaker Cereals
each...... 3.50 10.00 20.00

SGT. ROCK (Formerly Our Army at War)
No. 302, March, 1977 - Present
National Periodical Publications/DC Comics
302-320: 318-Reprints .40 .80
321-359 .30 .60
NOTE: ***Estrada*** *a-336, 337.* ***Kubert*** *a-328; c-317, 318r-323, 325-333-on.* ***Redondo*** *a-319-322, 325-338.*

SGT. ROCK SPECIAL (See DC Special Series No. 3)

SGT. ROCK SPECTACULAR (See DC Special Series No. 13)

SGT. ROCK'S PRIZE BATTLE TALES (See DC Spec. Series No. 18)
Winter, 1964 (One Shot) (Giant - 80 pgs.)
National Periodical Publications
1-Kubert, Heath-r; new Kubert-c 1.00 3.00 6.00

SEVEN DEAD MEN (See Complete Mystery No. 1)

SEVEN DWARFS (See 4-Color No. 227,382)

SEVEN SEAS COMICS
Apr, 1946 - No. 6, 1947 (no month)
Universal Phoenix Features/Leader No. 6
1-South Sea Girl by Matt Baker, Capt. Cutlass begin 17.00 50.00 80.00
2-6: 3-Six pg. Feldstein-a 14.00 40.00 70.00
NOTE: ***Baker*** *a-1-6; c-3-6.*

1776 (See Charlton Classic Library)

7TH VOYAGE OF SINBAD, THE (See 4-Color No. 944)

77 SUNSET STRIP (TV)
Jan-Mar, 1960 - No. 2, Feb, 1963
Dell Publ. Co./Gold Key
4-Color 1066,1106,1159-Toth-a 2.00 5.00 10.00
4-Color 1211,1263,1291, 01742-209(9/62)-Manning-a in all 1.50 4.00 8.00
1(11/62-G.K.), 2-Manning-a in each 1.00 3.00 6.00

77TH BENGAL LANCERS, THE (See 4-Color No. 791)

SEYMOUR, MY SON (See More Seymour)
September, 1963
Archie Publications (Radio Comics)
1 3.00 8.00 16.00

SHADE, THE CHANGING MAN (See Cancelled Comic Cavalcade)
June-July, 1977 - No. 8, Aug-Sept, 1978
National Periodical Publications/DC Comics
Good / Fine / Mint
1-Ditko c/a in all .50 1.00
2-5 .40 .80
6-8 .30 .60

SHADOW, THE
Aug, 1964 - No. 8, Sept, 1965
Archie Comics (Radio Comics)
1 .70 2.00 4.00
2-8 .35 1.00 2.00

SHADOW, THE
Oct-Nov, 1973 - No. 12, Aug-Sept, 1975
National Periodical Publications
1-Kaluta-a begins .30 .90 1.80
2 .60 1.20
3-Kaluta/Wrightson-a .30 .90 1.80
4,6-Kaluta-a ends .50 1.00
5,7-12: 11-The Avenger (pulp character) x-over .40 .80
NOTE: ***Craig*** *a-10.* ***Cruz*** *a-10-12.* ***Kaluta*** *a-1-4, 6; c-1-4, 6, 10-12.* ***Kubert*** *c-9.* ***Robbins*** *a-5, 7-9.*

SHADOW COMICS
March, 1940 - No. 101, Nov, 1950
Street & Smith Publications
NOTE: *The Shadow first appeared in Fame & Fortune Magazine, 1929, began on radio the same year, and was featured in pulps beginning in 1931.*
V1No.1-Shadow, Doc Savage, Bill Barnes, Nick Carter, Frank Merriwell, Iron Munro, the Astonishing Man begin 60.00 170.00 340.00
2-The Avenger begins, ends No. 6; Capt. Fury only app. 35.00 100.00 170.00
3(No No.-5/40)-Norgil the Magician app. (also No. 9); Doc Savage ends 30.00 80.00 140.00
4,5: 4-The Three Musketeers begins, ends No. 8 30.00 70.00 120.00
6-9: 7-Origin & 1st app. Hooded Wasp & Wasplet; series ends V3No.8 15.00 40.00 70.00
10-Origin The Iron Ghost, ends No. 11; The Dead End Kids begins, ends No. 13 15.00 40.00 70.00
11-Origin The Hooded Wasp & Wasplet retold 15.00 40.00 70.00
12 12.00 32.00 52.00
V2No.1,2(11/41) 10.00 28.00 48.00
3-Origin & 1st app. Supersnipe; series begins 10.00 30.00 50.00
4,5: 4-Little Nemo story 8.00 24.00 46.00
6-9: 6-Blackstone the Magician app. 7.00 20.00 40.00
10-Supersnipe app. 7.00 20.00 40.00
11,12 7.00 20.00 40.00
V3No.1-12: 10-Doc Savage begins, not in V5No.5, V6No.10-12, V8No.4 6.00 18.00 36.00
V4No.1-12 5.00 15.00 30.00
V5No.1-12 5.00 14.00 28.00
V6No.1-8,10-12 5.00 14.00 28.00
9-Intro. Shadow, Jr. 5.00 14.00 28.00
V7No.1-12: 2,5-Shadow, Jr. app.; Powell-a 5.00 14.00 28.00
V8No.1-12-Powell-a 5.00 14.00 28.00
V9No.1-5(No.101) 4.00 12.00 24.00
NOTE: ***Powell*** *art in most issues beginning V6No.11.*

SHADOWS FROM BEYOND (Formerly Unusual Tales)
October, 1966
Charlton Comics
V2No.50 .50 1.00

SHAGGY DOG & THE ABSENT-MINDED PROFESSOR (See 4-Color No. 985 and Movie Comics)

SHANNA, THE SHE-DEVIL
Dec, 1972 - No. 5, Aug, 1973

SHANNA, THE SHE-DEVIL (continued)
Marvel Comics Group

	Good	Fine	Mint
1-Steranko-c; Tuska-a		.60	1.20
2-5: 2-Steranko-c		.40	.80

SHARK FIGHTERS, THE (See 4-Color No. 762)

SHARP COMICS (Slightly large size)
Winter, 1945-46 - V1No.2, Spring, 1946 (52 pgs.)
H. C. Blackerby

V1No.1-Origin Dick Royce Planetarian 5.00 15.00 30.00
2-Origin The Pioneer, Michael Morgan, Dick Royce, Sir Gallagher, Planetarian, Steve Hagen, Weeny and Pop app. 4.75 14.00 28.00

SHARPY FOX
1958; 1963
I. W. Enterprises/Super Comics

1,2-I.W. Reprint(1958) .30 .80 1.60
14-Super Reprint(1963) .30 .80 1.60

SHAZAM (See Giant Comics to Color & Limited Collector's Edition)

SHAZAM! (See World's Finest)
Feb, 1973 - No. 35, May-June, 1978
National Periodical Publications/DC Comics

1-1st app. of original Captain Marvel(origin retold), by C. C. Beck; Captain Marvel Jr. & Mary Marvel x-over .40 .80
2,3,5: 2-Infinity-c; re-intro Mr. Mind & Tawney. 5-Capt. Marvel, Jr.-r .30 .60
4-Origin retold .30 .60
6,7,9,10: 6-G.A.-r; infinity-c. 10-Last Beck ish. .25 .50
8-100 pgs.; reprints Capt. Marvel Jr. by Raboy; origin/C.M. No. 80; origin Mary Marvel/C.M. No. 18 .30 .60
11-Shaffenberger-a begins .25 .50
12-17-All 100 pgs.; 15-Lex Luthor x-over .30 .60
18-24-(regular size) .25 .50
25-1st app. Isis .25 .50
26-30: 27-Kid Eternity app. .25 .50
31-35: 31-Minute Man revived. 34-New look for Capt. Marvel & Capt. Marvel Jr. .25 .50

NOTE: *Reprints-No. 6,7,13-17,21-24.* ***Beck*** *a-1, 4, 5, 13r, 22r; c-1, 4, 5.* ***Giordano*** *a-12.* ***Nasser*** *c-35.* ***Newton*** *a-35.* ***Shaffenberger*** *a-11, 14-20, 25-31, 33i, 35i; c-20, 22, 23, 25, 26, 27i, 28-33, 35i.*

SHEA THEATRE COMICS
No date (1940's) (32 pgs.)
Shea Theatre

Contains Rocket Comics; MLJ cover in mono color 10.00 20.00 30.00

SHEENA, QUEEN OF THE JUNGLE (See 3-D. . .)
Spring, 1942 - No. 18, Winter, 1952-53
Fiction House Magazines

1-Sheena begins 50.00 150.00 300.00
2 25.00 75.00 150.00
3 (1942) 17.00 50.00 100.00
4 (Fall, 1948) 10.00 30.00 60.00
5(Summer'49)-10(Fall,'50) 8.00 24.00 48.00
11-17 7.00 20.00 40.00
18-Used in **POP**, pg. 98 8.00 24.00 48.00
I.W. Reprint No. 9-Reprints No. 17 2.00 5.00 10.00

SHE-HULK (See The Savage She-Hulk)

SHERIFF BOB DIXON'S CHUCK WAGON
November, 1950
Avon Periodicals

1-Kinstler c/a(3) 5.00 14.00 24.00

SHERIFF OF COCHISE, THE
1957 (16 pages) (TV Show)
Mobil Giveaway

	Good	Fine	Mint
Shaffenberger-a	1.00	3.00	6.00

SHERIFF OF TOMBSTONE
Nov, 1958 - No. 17, Sept, 1961
Charlton Comics

V1No.1-Williamson/Severin-c 2.00 6.00 12.00
2-17 .85 2.50 5.00

SHERLOCK HOLMES (See 4-Color No. 1169,1245 & Spect. Stories)

SHERLOCK HOLMES (All New Baffling Advs. of)
1955 - 1956
Charlton Comics

1-Dr. Neff, Ghost Breaker app. (No. 1 only - 36 pgs.) 9.00 25.00 50.00
2 7.00 20.00 40.00

SHERLOCK HOLMES (Also see The Joker)
Sept-Oct, 1975
National Periodical Publications

1-Cruz-a; Simonson-c .60 1.20

SHERRY THE SHOWGIRL
July, 1956 - No. 7, Aug, 1957
Atlas Comics

1 2.00 5.00 10.00
2-7 1.00 3.00 6.00

SHIELD (Nick Fury & His Agents of. . .) (See Nick Fury)
Feb, 1973 - No. 5, Oct, 1973
Marvel Comics Group

1-Steranko-c .50 1.00
2-Steranko-c .40 .80
3-5: 1-5 all contain reprints from Strange Tales No. 146-155. 3-5-Cover-r .40 .80

SHIELD WIZARD COMICS
Summer, 1940 - No. 13, Spring, 1944
MLJ Magazines

1-(V1No.5 on inside)-Origin The Shield by Irving Novick & The Wizard by Ed Ashe, Jr; Flag-c. 60.00 160.00 340.00
2-Origin The Shield retold; intro. Wizard's sidekick, Roy 30.00 85.00 175.00
3,4 19.00 55.00 115.00
5-Dusty, the Boy Detective begins 16.00 46.00 95.00
6-8: 6-Roy the Super Boy begins 12.00 36.00 75.00
9,10 11.00 32.00 65.00
11-13: 13-Bondage-c 9.00 26.00 56.00

SHIP AHOY
November, 1944
Spotlight Publishers

1-L. B. Cole-c 3.50 10.00 20.00

SHMOO (See Al Capp's. . . & Washable Jones &. . .)

SHOCK (Magazine)
(Reprints from horror comics) (Black & White)
May, 1969 - V3No.4, Sept, 1971
Stanley Publications

V1No.1-Cover-r/Weird Tales of the Future No. 7 by Bernard Baily .30 .80 1.60
2-Wolverton-r/Weird Mysteries 5; r-Weird Mystries 7 used in **SOTI**; cover r-/Weird Chills No. 1 .30 .80 1.60
3,5,6 .40 .80
4-Harrison/Williamson-r/Forbidden Worlds No. 6 .60 1.20
V2No.2, V1No.8, V2No.4-6, V3No.1-4 .40 .80

NOTE: ***Disbrow*** *r-V2No.4; bondage covers-V1No.4, V2No.6, V3No.1.*

Shazam #2, © DC

Sheena #17, © FH

Shield Wizard Comics #2, © MLJ

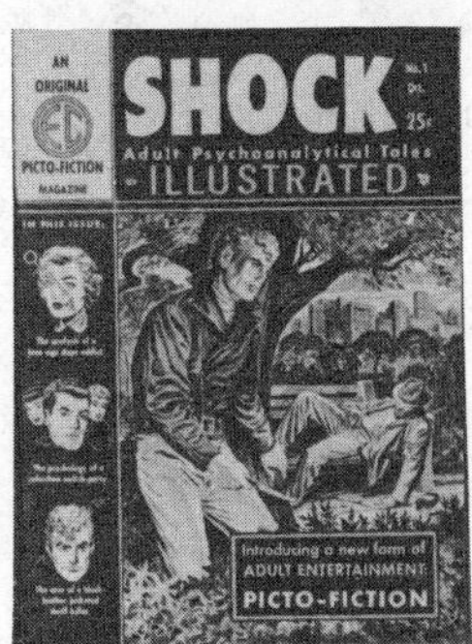

Shock Illustrated #1, © WMG

Shock SuspenStories #10, © WMG

Showcase #28, © DC

SHOCK DETECTIVE CASES (Formerly Crime Fighting Detective)
(Becomes Spook Detective Cases No. 22)
No. 20, Sept, 1952 - No. 21, Nov, 1952
Star Publications

	Good	Fine	Mint
20,21-L. B. Cole-c	4.00	12.00	24.00

NOTE: ***Palais** a-20. No. 21-Fox-r.*

SHOCK ILLUSTRATED (Magazine format)
Sept-Oct, 1955 - No. 3, Spring, 1956
E. C. Comics

1-All by Kamen; drugs, prostitution, wife swapping	3.00	8.00	16.00
2-Williamson-a redrawn from Crime SuspenStories No. 13 plus Ingels, Crandall, & Evans	3.50	10.00	20.00
3-Only 100-200 known copies bound & distr.; Crandall, Evans-a	200.00	500.00	800.00

(Prices vary widely on this book)

SHOCKING MYSTERY CASES (Formerly Thrilling Crime Cases)
No. 50, Sept, 1952 - No. 60, Oct, 1954
Star Publications

50-Disbrow ''Frankenstein'' story	7.00	20.00	40.00
51-Disbrow-a	5.00	14.00	28.00
52-55,57-60	4.00	12.00	24.00
56-Drug use story	5.00	14.00	28.00

NOTE: ***L. B. Cole** covers on all; a-60(2 pgs.). **Hollingsworth** a-52. **Morisi** a-55.*

SHOCKING TALES DIGEST MAGAZINE
Oct, 1981 - Present (95 cents)
Harvey Publications

1-1957-58-r; Powell, Kirby, Nostrand-a		.50	1.00

SHOCK SUSPENSTORIES
Feb-Mar, 1952 - No. 18, Dec-Jan, 1954-55
E. C. Comics

1-Classic Feldstein electrocution-c; Bradbury adaptation	50.00	125.00	250.00
2	30.00	80.00	150.00
3	17.00	50.00	90.00
4-Used in **SOTI**, pg. 387,388	20.00	56.00	100.00
5-7	16.00	48.00	90.00
8-Williamson-a	20.00	56.00	100.00
9-11: 10-Junkie story	14.00	40.00	72.00
12-''The Monkey''-classic junkie cover/story; drug propaganda ish.	15.00	45.00	90.00
13-Frazetta's only solo story for E. C., 7 pgs.	25.00	70.00	120.00
14,16-18	10.00	30.00	56.00
15-Used in 1954 Reader's Digest article, ''For the Kiddies to Read''	10.00	30.00	56.00

NOTE: ***Craig** a-11; c-11. **Crandall** a-9-13, 15-18. **Davis** a-1-5. **Evans** a-7, 8, 14-18; c-16-18. **Feldstein** c-1, 7-9, 12. **Ingels** a-1, 2, 6. **Kamen** a-in all. **Krigstein** a-14, 18. **Orlando** a-1, 3-7, 9, 10, 12, 16, 17. **Wood** a-2-15; c-2-6, 14. No. 16 contains the famous ''Red Dupe'' editorial.*

SHOGUN WARRIORS
Feb, 1979 - No. 20, Sept, 1980
Marvel Comics Group

1-Raydeen, Combatra, & Dangard Ace begin	.40	1.20	2.40
2-5		.60	1.20
6-10		.40	.80
11-20		.30	.60

NOTE: ***Austin** c-11.*

SHOOK UP (Magazine) (Satire)
November, 1958
Dodsworth Publ. Co.

V1No.1	1.00	3.00	6.00

SHORT RIBS (See 4-Color No. 1333)

SHORT STORY COMICS (See Hello Pal, . . .)

SHORTY SHINER
June, 1956 - No. 3, Oct, 1956
Dandy Magazine (Charles Biro)

	Good	Fine	Mint
1	.85	2.50	5.00
2,3	.50	1.50	3.00

SHOTGUN SLADE (See 4-Color No. 1111)

SHOWCASE (See Cancelled Comic Cavalcade)
3-4/56 - No. 93, 9/70; No. 94, 9/77 - No. 104, 9/78
National Periodical Publications/DC Comics

1-Fire Fighters	70.00	175.00	350.00
2-King of the Wild; Kubert-a	22.00	65.00	130.00
3-The Frogmen	19.00	55.00	110.00
4-Origin The Flash (Silver Age) & The Turtle; Kubert-a	175.00	525.00	1100.00
5-Manhunters	14.00	40.00	90.00
6-Origin Challengers by Kirby, partly reprinted in Secret Origins No. 1 & Challengers of the Unknown No. 64,65	40.00	110.00	225.00
7-Challengers by Kirby-r/Challengers of the Unknown No. 75	25.00	75.00	150.00
8-The Flash; origin Capt. Cold	60.00	170.00	340.00
9,10-Lois Lane	25.00	70.00	140.00
11,12-Challengers by Kirby	20.00	55.00	110.00
13-The Flash; origin Mr. Element	50.00	130.00	260.00
14-The Flash; origin Dr. Alchemy, former Mr. Element	50.00	130.00	260.00
15,16-Space Ranger	12.00	35.00	70.00
17-Adam Strange-Origin & 1st app.	30.00	85.00	175.00
18,19-Adam Strange	20.00	55.00	110.00
20,21-Rip Hunter. 21-Sekowsky c/a	6.00	18.00	36.00
22-Origin & 1st app. Silver Age Green Lantern by Gil Kane	50.00	145.00	290.00
23,24-Green Lantern. 23-Nuclear explosion-c	20.00	60.00	120.00
25,26-Rip Hunter by Kubert	4.00	12.00	24.00
27-29-Sea Devils by Heath, c/a	3.50	10.00	20.00
30-Origin Aquaman	4.00	12.00	24.00
31-33-Aquaman	2.50	7.00	14.00
34-Origin & 1st app. Silver Age Atom by Kane	4.00	12.00	24.00
35,36-The Atom by Gil Kane	3.00	9.00	18.00
37-1st app. Metal Men	2.00	6.00	12.00
38-40-Metal Men	1.75	5.00	10.00
41,42-Tommy Tomorrow	1.00	3.00	6.00
43-Dr. No (James Bond); Nodel art; originally done for Classics Ill. Series (appeared as British Classics Ill. No. 158A)	6.00	18.00	36.00
44-Tommy Tomorrow	.85	2.50	5.00
45-Sgt. Rock; Heath-c	1.50	4.00	8.00
46,47-Tommy Tomorrow	.85	2.50	5.00
48,49-Cave Carson	.85	2.50	5.00
50,51-I Spy (Danger Trail reprints by Infantino), Anderson cover inks; King Farady story (not reprint-No. 50)	.85	2.50	5.00
52-Cave Carson	.85	2.50	5.00
53,54-G.I. Joe; Heath-a	.85	2.50	5.00
55,56-Dr. Fate & Hourman	.85	2.50	5.00
57,58-Enemy Ace by Kubert	.85	2.50	5.00
59-Teen Titans	1.50	4.50	9.00
60-The Spectre by Anderson	1.20	2.40	4.80
61,64-The Spectre by Anderson	.70	2.00	4.00
62,63,65-Inferior Five	.35	1.10	2.20
66,67-B'wana Beast		.60	1.20
68,69-Maniaks		.50	1.00
70-Binky		.50	1.00
71-Maniaks		.50	1.00
72-Top Gun (Johnny Thunder-r)-Toth-a		.60	1.20
73-Creeper by Ditko	.85	2.50	5.00
74-Anthro	.30	.80	1.60
75-Hawk & the Dove by Ditko	.60	1.80	3.60

SHOWCASE (continued) | Good | Fine | Mint
76-Bat Lash .40 1.20 2.40
77-Angel & Ape .60 1.20
78-Johnny Double .60 1.20
79-Dolphin; Aqualad origin-r .30 .90 1.80
80-Phantom Stranger-r; Adams-c .50 1.50 3.00
81-Windy & Willy .30 .90 1.80
82-Nightmaster by Grandenetti; Kubert-c .30 .90 1.80
83,84-Nightmaster by Wrightson/Jones/Kaluta in each; Kubert-c
1.50 4.00 8.00
85-87-Firehair; Kubert-a .50 1.50 3.00
88-90-Jason's Quest: 90-Manhunter 2070 app. .50 1.00
91-93-Manhunter 2070; origin-92 .50 1.00
94-Intro/origin new /Doom Patrol & Robotman .60 1.20
95,96-The Doom Patrol. 95-Origin Celsius .50 1.00
97-99-Power Girl; origin-97,98 .40 .80
100-(52 pgs.)-Features most Showcase characters .50 1.00
101-103-Hawkman; Adam Strange x-over .40 .80
104-O.S.S. Spies at War .40 .80

NOTE: ***Anderson** a-50, 55, 56, 60, 61, 64, 101-103i; c-50i, 51i, 55, 56, 60, 61. **Aparo** c-94-96. **Infantino** a/c-4, 8, 13, 14; c-50p, 51p. **Kane** a-22-24, 34-36; c-17-19, 22-24, 31, 34-36, 101-103. **Kirby** c-6, 7, 11, 12. **Kubert** a-2, 4i, 25, 26, 45, 53, 54, 72; c-25, 26, 53, 54, 57, 58, 82-87, 101-104. **Orlando** a/c-62, 63, 97i. **Staton** a-94-100; c-97-100.*

SHOWGIRLS
June, 1957 - No. 4, Dec, 1957
Atlas Comics

1-Millie, Sherry, Chili, Pearl & Hazel begin 2.00 6.00 12.00
2-4 1.50 4.00 8.00

SICK (Magazine) (Satire)
Aug, 1960 - Present
Feature Publ./Headline Publ./Crestwood Publ. Co./Hewfred Publ./ Pyramid Comm./Charlton Publ.

V1No.1-Torres-a 3.00 8.00 16.00
2-5-Torres-a in all 1.50 4.00 8.00
6 1.00 3.00 6.00
V2No.1-8(No.7-14) .70 2.00 4.00
V3No.1-8(No.15-22) .50 1.50 3.00
V4No.1-5(No.23-27) .30 .90 1.80
28-40 .60 1.20
41-137: 45 has No. 44 on cover & No. 45 on inside
.40 .80
Annual 1971 .60 1.20
Annual 2 .60 1.20

NOTE: ***Davis** c/a in most issues of No. 16-27, 30-32, 34, 35. **Simon** a-1-3. **Torres** a-V2No.7, V4No.2. Civil War Blackouts-23, 24.*

SIDESHOW
1949 (One Shot)
Avon Periodicals

1-(Rare)-Similar to Bachelor's Diary 12.00 35.00 80.00

SILK HAT HARRY'S DIVORCE SUIT
1912 (5¾x15½'') (B&W)
M. A. Donoghue & Co.

Newspaper reprints by Tad (Thomas Dorgan) 5.50 16.00 32.00

SILLY PILLY (See Frank Luther's. . .)

SILLY SYMPHONIES (Walt Disney)
Sept, 1952 - 1959 (All Giants)
Dell Publishing Co.

1-Reprints 3 Little Pigs & Mickey Mouse in ''The Brave Little Tailor''
5.00 15.00 30.00
2-Mickey Mouse ''The Sorcerer's Apprentice''
4.00 12.00 24.00
3-(4-Color 71)(not Duck portion), (4-Color 157)
4.00 12.00 24.00

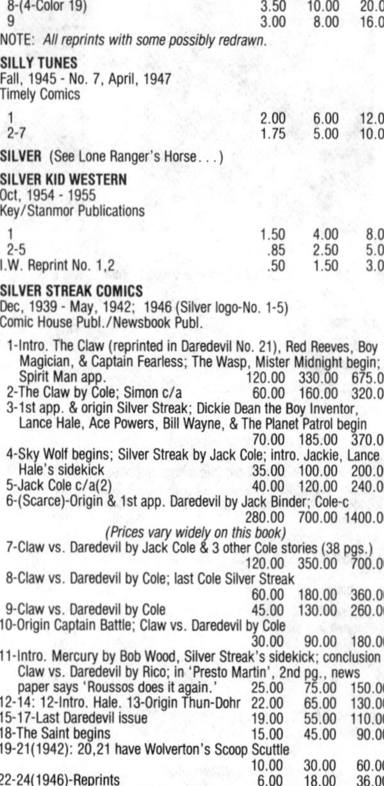

Good | Fine | Mint
4-(4-Color 234) 3.00 8.00 16.00
5-(4-Color Cinderella) 3.00 8.00 16.00
6-Pinocchio (WDC&S 63) & 7 Dwarfs (WDC&S 45)
3.50 10.00 20.00
7-(4-Color 13) 4.00 12.00 24.00
8-(4-Color 19) 3.50 10.00 20.00
9 3.00 8.00 16.00

NOTE: *All reprints with some possibly redrawn.*

SILLY TUNES
Fall, 1945 - No. 7, April, 1947
Timely Comics

1 2.00 6.00 12.00
2-7 1.75 5.00 10.00

SILVER (See Lone Ranger's Horse. . .)

SILVER KID WESTERN
Oct, 1954 - 1955
Key/Stanmor Publications

1 1.50 4.00 8.00
2-5 .85 2.50 5.00
I.W. Reprint No. 1,2 .50 1.50 3.00

SILVER STREAK COMICS
Dec, 1939 - May, 1942; 1946 (Silver logo-No. 1-5)
Comic House Publ./Newsbook Publ.

1-Intro. The Claw (reprinted in Daredevil No. 21), Red Reeves, Boy Magician, & Captain Fearless; The Wasp, Mister Midnight begin; Spirit Man app. 120.00 330.00 675.00
2-The Claw by Cole; Simon c/a 60.00 160.00 320.00
3-1st app. & origin Silver Streak; Dickie Dean the Boy Inventor, Lance Hale, Ace Powers, Bill Wayne, & The Planet Patrol begin
70.00 185.00 370.00
4-Sky Wolf begins; Silver Streak by Jack Cole; intro. Jackie, Lance Hale's sidekick 35.00 100.00 200.00
5-Jack Cole c/a(2) 40.00 120.00 240.00
6-(Scarce)-Origin & 1st app. Daredevil by Jack Binder; Cole-c
280.00 700.00 1400.00
(Prices vary widely on this book)
7-Claw vs. Daredevil by Jack Cole & 3 other Cole stories (38 pgs.)
120.00 350.00 700.00
8-Claw vs. Daredevil by Cole; last Cole Silver Streak
60.00 180.00 360.00
9-Claw vs. Daredevil by Cole 45.00 130.00 260.00
10-Origin Captain Battle; Claw vs. Daredevil by Cole
30.00 90.00 180.00
11-Intro. Mercury by Bob Wood, Silver Streak's sidekick; conclusion Claw vs. Daredevil by Rico; in 'Presto Martin', 2nd pg., news paper says 'Roussos does it again.' 25.00 75.00 150.00
12-14: 12-Intro. Hale. 13-Origin Thun-Dohr 22.00 65.00 130.00
15-17-Last Daredevil issue 19.00 55.00 110.00
18-The Saint begins 15.00 45.00 90.00
19-21(1942): 20,21 have Wolverton's Scoop Scuttle
10.00 30.00 60.00
22-24(1946)-Reprints 6.00 18.00 36.00
nn(11/46)(Newsbook Publ.)-Reprints S.S. story from No. 4-7 plus 2 Captain Fearless stories, all in color; bondage/torture-c
14.00 40.00 80.00

NOTE: ***Jack Cole** a-(Daredevil)-6-10, (Dickie Dean)-3-10, (Pirate Prince)-7, (Silver Streak)-4-8, nn, (Silver Streak cover)-5. **Everett** Red Reed begins No. 20. **Don Rico** Daredevil-11-17. **Simon** Silver Streak-3. **Bob Wood** Silver Streak-9. Claw c-1, 2, 6-8; by **Cole**-6-8.*

SILVER SURFER (See Fantastic Four)
Aug, 1968 - No. 18, Sept, 1970 (No. 1-7: 68 pgs.)
Marvel Comics Group

1-Origin Silver Surfer by John Buscema; Watcher begins(origin), ends No. 7 12.00 35.00 70.00
2 5.50 16.00 32.00

Showcase #100, © DC

Silver Streak Comics #9, © LEV

Silver Surfer #2, © MCG

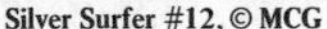
Silver Surfer #12, © MCG

Single Series #22, © UFS

Six Million Dollar Man #1, © CC

SILVER SURFER (continued)

	Good	Fine	Mint
3-1st app. Mephisto	4.00	12.00	24.00
4-Low distribution; Thor app.	7.00	20.00	40.00
5-7-Last giant size. 5-The Stranger app. 6-Brunner inks. 7-Brunner-c	3.00	8.00	16.00
8-10	2.00	6.00	12.00
11-18: 14-Spider-Man x-over. 18-Kirby c/a	1.50	4.00	8.00

SILVERTIP (Max Brand)
1953 - 1958
Dell Publishing Co.

	Good	Fine	Mint
4-Color 491,608,637,667,731,789,898-Kinstler-a	2.00	5.00	10.00
4-Color 572,835	1.20	3.50	7.00

SINBAD, JR. (TV Cartoon)
Sept-Nov, 1965 - No. 3, May, 1966
Dell Publishing Co.

	Good	Fine	Mint
1	.85	2.50	5.00
2,3	.50	1.50	3.00

SINDBAD (See Movie Comics: Capt. Sindbad, and Fantastic Voyages of Sindbad)

SINGING GUNS (See Fawcett Movie Comics)

SINGLE SERIES (Comics on Parade No.30 on) (Also see John Hix. . .)
1938 - 1940
United Features Syndicate

	Good	Fine	Mint
1-Captain & the Kids	14.00	40.00	80.00
2-Broncho Bill (1939)	10.00	30.00	60.00
3-Ella Cinders	10.00	28.00	56.00
4-Li'l Abner (1939)	14.00	40.00	80.00
5-Fritzi Ritz	7.00	20.00	40.00
6-Jim Hardy by Dick Moores	9.00	25.00	50.00
7-Frankie Doodle	7.00	20.00	40.00
8-Peter Pat	7.00	20.00	40.00
9-Strange As It Seems	7.00	20.00	40.00
10-Little Mary Mixup	7.00	20.00	40.00
11-Mr. & Mrs. Beans	5.50	16.00	32.00
12-Joe Jinks	7.00	20.00	40.00
13-Looy Dot Dope	6.00	18.00	36.00
14-Billy Make Believe	6.00	18.00	36.00
15-How It Began (1939)	7.00	20.00	40.00
16-Illustrated Gags (1940)	3.50	10.00	20.00
17-Danny Dingle	5.00	15.00	30.00
18-Li'l Abner	12.00	36.00	72.00
19-Broncho Bill (No. 2 on cover)	8.00	24.00	48.00
20-Tarzan by Hal Foster	70.00	200.00	400.00
21-Ella Cinders (No. 2 on cover)	7.00	20.00	40.00
22-Iron Vic	7.00	20.00	40.00
23-Tailspin Tommy by Hal Forrest	7.00	20.00	40.00
24-Alice in Wonderland	10.00	30.00	60.00
25-Abbie & Slats	8.00	24.00	48.00
26-Little Mary Mixup	7.00	20.00	40.00
27-Jim Hardy by Dick Moores	7.00	20.00	40.00
28-Ella Cinders & Abbie & Slats	7.00	20.00	40.00
1-Captain & the Kids (1939 reprint)	10.00	30.00	60.00
1-Fritzi Ritz (1939 reprint)-2nd edition	6.00	18.00	36.00

NOTE: *Some issues given away at the 1939-40 New York World's Fair (No. 6).*

SINISTER HOUSE OF SECRET LOVE, THE (Secrets of Sinister House No. 5 on)
Oct-Nov, 1971 - No. 4, Apr-May, 1972
National Periodical Publications

	Good	Fine	Mint
1		.60	1.20
2,4		.40	.80
3-Toth-a, 36 pgs.	.30	.80	1.60

SIR LANCELOT (See 4-Color No. 606,775)

SIR WALTER RALEIGH (See 4-Color No. 644)

6 BLACK HORSES (See Movie Classics)

SIX-GUN HEROES
March, 1950 - No. 23, Nov, 1953
Fawcett Publications

	Good	Fine	Mint
1-Rocky Lane, Hopalong Cassidy, Smiley Burnette begin	8.00	24.00	48.00
2	5.50	16.00	32.00
3-10: 6-Lash Larue begins	3.50	10.00	20.00
11-23	3.00	8.00	16.00

SIX-GUN HEROES (Cont'd. from Fawcett) (Becomes Gunmasters No. 84 on)
Jan, 1954 - No. 83, Mar-Apr, 1965
Charlton Comics

	Good	Fine	Mint
V4No.24-46-Tom Mix, Lash Larue	1.50	4.00	8.00
47-Williamson-a, 2 pgs; Torres-a	3.00	8.00	16.00
48,50-61,63-75,82	.85	2.50	5.00
49-Williamson-a, 5 pgs.	3.00	8.00	16.00
62-Origin, 1st app. Gunmaster	.85	2.50	5.00
76-81,83-Gunmaster in all	.35	1.00	2.00
1962 Shoe Store giveaway		.50	1.00

SIXGUN RANCH (See 4-Color No. 580)

SIX-GUN WESTERN
Jan, 1957 - 1958
Atlas Comics (CDS)

	Good	Fine	Mint
1-Crandall-a; two Williamson text illos	3.00	8.00	16.00
2,3,7-Williamson-a in all	3.50	10.00	20.00
4-Woodbridge-a	1.50	4.00	8.00
5,6,8-10	1.00	3.00	6.00
11-Williamson-a (5-11 Exist?)	3.00	8.00	16.00

NOTE: ***Maneely** c-2. **Orlando** a-2. **Pakula** a-2. **Powell** a-3.*

SIX MILLION DOLLAR MAN (Magazine)
June, 1976 - Present (B&W)
Charlton Comics

	Good	Fine	Mint
1-Adams c/a	.35	1.10	2.20
2-Adams-c	.30	.80	1.60
3-8		.60	1.20

SIX MILLION DOLLAR MAN
6/76 - No. 4, 1/77; No. 5, 10/77; No. 6, 2/78 - No. 9, 6/78
Charlton Comics

	Good	Fine	Mint
1-Staton c/a	.30	.80	1.60
2-Adams-c; Staton-a		.50	1.00
3-9		.30	.60

SKATING SKILLS
1957 (36 & 12 pages; 5x7'', two versions) (10 cents)
Custom Comics, Inc.
Chicago Roller Skates

	Good	Fine	Mint
Resembles old ACG cover plus interior art	.40	1.20	2.40

SKEEZIX
1925 - 1928 (Strip reprints) (soft covers) (pictures & text)
Reilly & Lee Co.

	Good	Fine	Mint
. . . and Uncle Walt (1924)-Origin	3.00	15.00	30.00
. . . and Pal (1925)	4.00	12.00	24.00
. . . at the Circus (1926)	4.00	12.00	24.00
. . . & Uncle Walt (1927)	4.00	12.00	24.00
. . . Out West (1928)	4.00	12.00	24.00
Hardback Editions. . .	5.50	16.00	32.00

SKELETON HAND (. . . In Secrets of the Supernatural)
Sept-Oct, 1952 - No. 6, July-Aug, 1953
American Comics Group (B&M Dist. Co.)

	Good	Fine	Mint
1	3.00	9.00	18.00
2-6	2.00	6.00	12.00

SKI PARTY (See Movie Classics)

SKIPPY
1925 (68 pgs.; 8½x11'') (hardcover; in color)
Greenberg Publ.

SKIPPY (continued)

	Good	Fine	Mint
Panel & strips	5.50	16.00	32.00

SKIPPY'S OWN BOOK OF COMICS
1934 (52 pages) (Giveaway)
No publisher listed

	Good	Fine	Mint
nn-(Rare)-Strip-r by Percy Crosby	120.00	300.00	600.00

Published by Max C. Gaines for Phillip's Dental Magnesia to be advertised on the Skippy Radio Show and given away with the purchase of a tube of Phillip's Tooth Paste. This is the first four-color comic book of reprints about one character.

SKULL THE SLAYER
August, 1975 - No. 8, Nov, 1976
Marvel Comics Group

	Good	Fine	Mint
1-Origin; Gil Kane-c		.50	1.00
2-5: 2-Gil Kane-c		.40	.80
6-8: 8-Kirby-c		.40	.80

SKY BLAZERS (Radio)
Sept, 1940 - No. 2, Nov, 1940
Hawley Publications

	Good	Fine	Mint
1-Sky Pirates, Ace Archer, Flying Aces begin	6.00	18.00	36.00
2	4.00	12.00	24.00

SKY KING "RUNAWAY TRAIN"
1964 (16 pages) (regular size)
National Biscuit Co.

	Good	Fine	Mint
	.85	2.50	5.00

SKYMAN (See Big Shot)
1941 - No. 4, 1948
Columbia Comics Group

	Good	Fine	Mint
1-Origin Skyman, The Face app.; Whitney-a	12.00	35.00	70.00
2-Yankee Doodle	6.00	18.00	36.00
3,4	5.00	15.00	30.00

SKY PILOT
1950 (Painted covers by Norman Saunders)
Ziff-Davis Publ. Co.

	Good	Fine	Mint
10,11-Frank Borth-a	2.50	7.00	14.00

SKY RANGER (See Johnny Law. . .)

SKYROCKET
1944
Harry 'A' Chesler

	Good	Fine	Mint
nn-Alias the Dragon, Dr. Vampire, Skyrocket app.	3.50	10.00	20.00

SKY SHERIFF (Breeze Lawson. . .) (Also see Exposed)
Summer, 1948
D. S. Publishing Co.

	Good	Fine	Mint
1-Edmond Goode-a	3.00	9.00	18.00

SLAM BANG COMICS (Western Desperado No. 8)
March, 1940 - No. 7, Sept, 1940
Fawcett Publications

	Good	Fine	Mint
1-Diamond Jack, Mark Swift & The Time Retarder, Lee Granger, Jungle King begin	20.00	60.00	125.00
2	10.00	30.00	65.00
3	9.00	25.00	50.00
4-7: 7-Bondage-c	7.00	20.00	45.00

SLAM BANG COMICS
No date
Post Cereal Giveaway

	Good	Fine	Mint
9-Dynamic Man, Echo, Mr. E, Yankee Boy app.	1.50	4.00	8.00

SLAPSTICK COMICS
No date (1946?) (36 pages)
Comic Magazines Distributors

	Good	Fine	Mint
nn-Firetop feature	3.00	8.00	16.00

SLASH-D DOUBLECROSS
1950 (132 pgs.) (pocket size)
St. John Publishing Co.

	Good	Fine	Mint
Western comics	3.50	10.00	20.00

SLAVE GIRL COMICS (See Malu. . .)
Feb, 1949 - No. 2, Apr, 1949
Avon Periodicals

	Good	Fine	Mint
1	40.00	120.00	240.00
2	30.00	90.00	180.00

SLEEPING BEAUTY (See 4-Color No. 973,984, Movie Classics and Comics)

SLICK CHICK COMICS
1947
Leader Enterprises

	Good	Fine	Mint
1	2.50	7.50	15.00
2,3	2.00	6.00	12.00

SLIM MORGAN (See Wisco)

SLUGGER (of the Little Wise Guys)
April, 1956
Lev Gleason Publications

	Good	Fine	Mint
1	1.00	3.00	6.00

SMASH COMICS (Lady Luck No. 86 on)
Aug, 1939 - No. 85, Oct, 1949
Quality Comics Group

	Good	Fine	Mint
1-Origin Hugh Hazard & His Iron Man, Bozo the Robot, Espionage, Starring Black X by Eisner, & Invisible Justice; Chic Carter & Wings Wendell begin	35.00	100.00	200.00
2-The Lone Star Rider app.	15.00	45.00	90.00
3	10.00	30.00	60.00
4,5	9.00	25.00	50.00
6-12: 12-One pg. Fine	7.00	20.00	40.00
13-Magno begins; last Eisner issue; The Ray app. in full page ad	7.00	20.00	40.00
14-Intro. The Ray by Lou Fine & others	70.00	210.00	450.00
15-17	35.00	100.00	225.00
18-Origin Midnight by Jack Cole	50.00	130.00	280.00
19-22: Last Fine Ray; The Jester begins-No. 22	25.00	70.00	150.00
23,24: 24-The Sword app.; last Chic Carter; Wings Wendall dons new costume No. 24,25	17.00	50.00	115.00
25-Origin Wildfire	18.00	54.00	125.00
26-30	17.00	50.00	105.00
31,32,34: Ray by Rudy Palais; also No. 33	13.00	38.00	76.00
33-Origin The Marksman	14.00	40.00	80.00
35-37	12.00	34.00	68.00
38-The Yankee Eagle begins; last Midnight by Jack Cole	12.00	34.00	68.00
39,40-Last Ray issue	10.00	28.00	56.00
41,43-50	4.50	13.00	26.00
42-Lady Luck begins	5.00	15.00	30.00
51-60: 56-Drug story	3.50	10.00	20.00
61-70	3.00	9.00	18.00
71-85	2.50	7.50	15.00

NOTE: ***Cole** a-(Midnight)-18-38, 68-85; c-38, 60-62, 80. **Crandall** a-(Ray)-23-29, 35-38; c-36, 39, 40, 43, 44, 46. **Fine** a-(Ray)-14, 15, 16(w/**Tuska**), 17-22. **Fuji** Ray story-30. **Guardineer** a-(The Marksman) 39-? **Gustavson** a-4, 6, 7, (The Jester)-22-46; (Magno) 13-21; (Midnight)-39(**Cole** inks). **Kotzky** a-(Espionage)-33-38; c-45, 47. **Powell** a-(Abdul the Arab) 13-24.*

Skull The Slayer #1, © MCG

Sky Sheriff #1, © DS

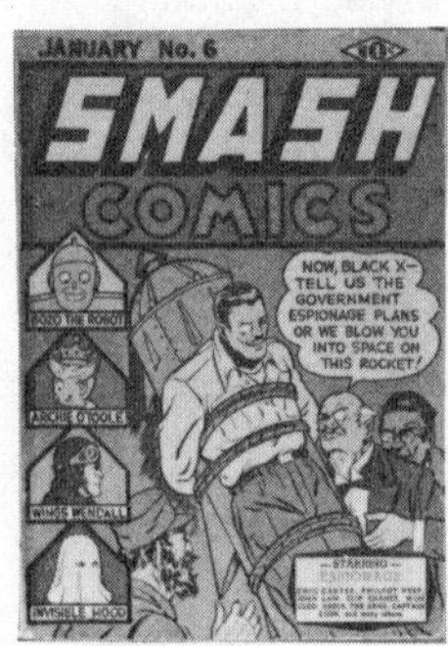

Smash Comics #6, © QUA

Smiley Burnette Western #4, © FAW

Smilin' Jack #1, © N.Y. News Synd.

Snagglepuss #1, © GK

SMASH HIT SPORTS COMICS
Jan, 1949
Essankay Publications

	Good	Fine	Mint
V2No.1-L. B. Cole-c/a	3.00	8.00	16.00

S'MATTER POP?
1917 (44 pgs.; B&W; 10x14''; cardboard covers)
Saalfield Publ. Co.

By Charlie Payne; ½ in full color; pages printed on one side	5.00	14.00	28.00

SMILE COMICS (Also see Gay Comics, Tickle, & Whee)
1955 (52 pages; 5x7¼'') (7 cents)
Modern Store Publ.

1	.50	1.50	3.00

SMILEY BURNETTE WESTERN
March, 1950 - No. 4, Oct, 1950
Fawcett Publications

1	5.50	16.00	32.00
2-4	3.50	10.00	20.00

SMILIN' JACK (See Super Book No. 1,2,7,19)
1941 - No. 8, Oct-Dec, 1949
Dell Publishing Co.

4-Color 5,10 (1940)	17.00	50.00	100.00
Black & White 12,14 (1941)	14.00	40.00	80.00
Large Feature Comic 25 (1941)	14.00	40.00	80.00
4-Color 4 (1942)	17.00	50.00	100.00
4-Color 14 (1943)	14.00	40.00	80.00
4-Color 36,58 (1943-44)	7.00	20.00	40.00
4-Color 80 (1945)	5.00	15.00	30.00
4-Color 149 (1947)	4.00	12.00	24.00
1 (1-3/48)	4.00	12.00	24.00
2-8 (10-12/49)	2.50	7.00	14.00
Popped Wheat Giveaway(1947)-1938 reprints; 16 pgs. in full color	.80	2.40	4.80
Shoe Store Giveaway-1936 reprints; 16 pgs.	3.00	8.00	16.00
Sparked Wheat Giveaway(1942)-16 pgs. in full color	2.00	6.00	12.00

SMILING SPOOK SPUNKY (See Spunky)

SMITTY (See Treasure Box of Famous Comics)
1928 - 1932 (B&W newspaper strip reprints)
(cardboard covers; 9½x9½'', 52 pgs.; 7x8¼'', 36 pgs.)
Cupples & Leon Co.

1928-(96pgs. 7x8¾'')	7.00	20.00	40.00
1928-(Softcover, 36pgs., nn)	8.00	24.00	48.00
1929-At the Ball Game, 1930-The Flying Office Boy, 1931-The Jockey, 1932-In the North Woods....each....	5.50	16.00	32.00
Mid 1930's issue (reprint of 1928 Treasure Box issue)-36 pgs.; 7x8¾''	4.00	12.00	24.00
Hardback Editions (100 pgs., 7x8¼'') with dust jacket each....	8.00	24.00	48.00

SMITTY (See Super Book No. 2, 4)
1940 - No. 7, Aug-Oct, 1949; 1958
Dell Publishing Co.

4-Color 11 (1940)	10.00	28.00	56.00
Large Feature Comic 26 (1941)	8.00	22.00	45.00
4-Color 6 (1942)	7.00	20.00	40.00
4-Color 32 (1943)	4.00	12.00	24.00
4-Color 65 (1945)	3.50	10.00	20.00
4-Color 99 (1946)	3.00	8.00	16.00
4-Color 138 (1947)	2.00	6.00	12.00
1 (11-1/47-48)	2.00	6.00	12.00
2-4 (1949)	1.00	3.00	6.00
5-7	.85	2.50	5.00
4-Color 909	.70	2.00	4.00

SMOKEY BEAR (TV)
Feb, 1970 - No. 13, Mar, 1973
Gold Key

	Good	Fine	Mint
1	.50	1.50	3.00
2-13	.35	1.00	2.00

(See March of Comics No. 362,372,383,407)

SMOKEY STOVER (See Super Book No. 5,17,29)

SMOKEY STOVER FIREFIGHTER OF FOO (See Nickel Books)

SMOKEY STOVER
1942 - 1943
Dell Publishing Co.

4-Color 7 (1942)-Reprints	10.00	30.00	60.00
4-Color 35 (1943)	5.50	16.00	32.00
4-Color 64 (1944)	3.50	10.00	20.00
4-Color 229	1.50	4.00	8.00
4-Color 730,827	1.00	3.00	6.00
General Motors giveaway (1953)	3.00	8.00	16.00
National Fire Protection giveaway('53)-16 pgs., paper-c	3.00	8.00	16.00

SMOKEY THE BEAR
Oct, 1955 - 1961
Dell Publishing Co.

4-Color 653,708,754,818,932	.70	2.00	4.00
4-Color 1016,1119,1214	.50	1.50	3.00
True Story of..., The('60)-U.S. Forest Service giveaway-Publ. by Western Printing Co. (reprinted in '64 & '69)-Reprints 1st 16 pgs. of 4-Color 932	.70	2.00	4.00

(See March of Comics No. 234)

SMOKY (See Movie Classics)

SNAFU (Magazine)
Nov, 1955 - No. 3, Mar, 1956 (B&W)
Atlas Comics (RCM)

1-Heath/Severin-a	3.50	10.00	20.00
2,3-Severin-a	2.50	7.00	14.00

SNAGGLEPUSS (TV)
Oct, 1962 - No. 4, Sept, 1963 (Hanna-Barbera)
Gold Key

1	.85	2.50	5.00
2-4	.50	1.50	3.00

SNAP (Jest No. 10?)
1944
Harry 'A' Chesler

9-Manhunter, The Voice	3.00	8.00	16.00

SNAPPY COMICS
1945
Cima Publ. Co. (Prize Publ.)

1-Airmale app.	1.50	4.00	8.00

SNARKY PARKER (See Life with...)

SNIFFY THE PUP
No. 5, Nov, 1949 - No. 18, Sept, 1953
Standard Publications (Animated Cartoons)

5-Two Frazetta text illos	2.00	6.00	12.00
6-10	.35	1.00	2.00
11-18		.50	1.00

SNOOPER AND BLABBER DETECTIVES (TV) (See Whitman Comic Books)
Nov, 1962 - No. 3, May, 1963 (Hanna-Barbera)
Gold Key

1-3	.70	2.00	4.00

SNOW FOR CHRISTMAS
1957 (16 pages) (Giveaway)
W. T. Grant Co.

	1.20	3.50	7.00

SNOW WHITE (See 4-Color No. 49,227,382 & Movie Comics)

SNOW WHITE AND THE SEVEN DWARFS
1952 (32 pgs.; 5x7¼") (Disney)
Bendix Washing Machines

	Good	Fine	Mint
	4.00	12.00	24.00

SNOW WHITE AND THE 7 DWARFS IN "MILKY WAY"
1955 (16 pgs.) (Disney premium)
American Dairy Association

	Good	Fine	Mint
	4.00	12.00	24.00

SNOW WHITE AND THE SEVEN DWARFS
1957 (small size)
Promotional Publ. Co.

	Good	Fine	Mint
	3.00	8.00	16.00

SNOW WHITE AND THE SEVEN DWARFS
1958 (16 pages) (Disney premium)
Western Printing Co.

	Good	Fine	Mint
"Mystery of the Missing Magic"	3.00	9.00	18.00

SOJOURN ($1.50)
9/77 - No. 2, 1978 (Full tabloid size) (Color & B&W)
White Cliffs Publ. Co.

	Good	Fine	Mint
1-Tor by Kubert, Eagle by Severin, E. V. Race, Private Investigator by Doug Wildey, T. C. Mars by S. Aragones begin plus other strips	.30	.80	1.60
2	.30	.80	1.60

SOLDIER & MARINE COMICS (Fightin' Army No. 16 on)
No. 11, Dec, 1954 - V2No.9, Dec, 1956
Charlton Comics (Toby Press of Conn. V1No.11)

	Good	Fine	Mint
V1No.11(12/54)-13(4/55)	.50	1.50	3.00
V1No.14(6/55), 15	.50	1.50	3.00
V2No.9(Formerly Never Again; Jerry Drummer V2No.10 on)	.50	1.50	3.00

NOTE: ***Bob Powell** a-11.*

SOLDIER COMICS
Jan, 1952 - No. 11, Sept, 1953
Fawcett Publications

	Good	Fine	Mint
1	3.00	8.00	16.00
2-5	1.50	4.00	8.00
6,7,9-11	.85	2.50	5.00
8-Illo. in **POP**	2.00	6.00	12.00

SOLDIERS OF FORTUNE
Feb-Mar, 1951 - No. 13, Feb-Mar, 1953
American Comics Group (Creston Publ. Corp.)

	Good	Fine	Mint
1-Capt. Crossbones by Shelly, Ace Carter, Lance Larsen begin	3.00	9.00	18.00
2-10: 6-Bondage-c	2.00	6.00	12.00
11-13 (War format)	1.00	3.00	6.00

NOTE: ***Shelly** a-1-3, 5. **Whitney** a-6, 8-13; c-1-3, 6. Most issues are 52 pages.*

SOLOMON AND SHEBA (See 4-Color No. 1070)

SONG OF THE SOUTH (See 4-Color No. 693 & Brer Rabbit)

SON OF BLACK BEAUTY (See 4-Color No. 510,566)

SON OF FLUBBER (See Movie Comics)

SON OF SATAN
Dec, 1975 - No. 8, Feb, 1977
Marvel Comics Group

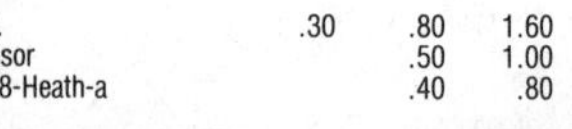

	Good	Fine	Mint
1-Starlin-a(p), 1 pg.	.30	.80	1.60
2-Origin The Possessor		.50	1.00
3-8: 4,5-Russell-a. 8-Heath-a		.40	.80

SON OF SINBAD (Also see Daring Adventures, Abbott & Costello)
February, 1950
St. John Publishing Co.

	Good	Fine	Mint
1-Kubert c/a	20.00	60.00	125.00

SON OF TOMAHAWK (See Tomahawk)

SON OF VULCAN (Mysteries of Unexplored Worlds No. 1-48; Thunderbolt, V3No.51 on)
Nov, 1965 - V2No.50, Jan, 1966
Charlton Comics

	Good	Fine	Mint
49,50	.30	.90	1.80

SONS OF KATIE ELDER (See Movie Classics)

SORCERY (See Chilling Adventures in . . . & Red Circle . . .)

SORORITY SECRETS
July, 1954
Toby Press

	Good	Fine	Mint
1	2.00	5.00	10.00

SOUPY SALES COMIC BOOK (The Official . . .)
1965
Archie Publications

	Good	Fine	Mint
1	2.00	6.00	12.00

SPACE ACE (Jet No. 1; Jet Powers No. 2-4)
1952
Magazine Enterprises

	Good	Fine	Mint
5(A-1 61)-Guardineer-a	7.00	20.00	40.00

SPACE ACTION
June, 1952 - No. 3, Oct, 1952
Ace Magazines (Junior Books)

	Good	Fine	Mint
1	10.00	30.00	60.00
2,3	8.00	24.00	48.00

SPACE ADVENTURES
7/52 - No. 59, 11/64; V3No.60, 10/67; V1No.1, 5/68 - V1No.8, 7/69; No. 9, 5/78 - No. 13, 3/79
Capitol Stories/Charlton Comics

	Good	Fine	Mint
1	5.00	15.00	30.00
2-5	3.00	8.00	16.00
6,8,9	2.50	7.00	14.00
7-Transvestite story	3.50	10.00	20.00
10-Ditko c/a	8.00	24.00	48.00
11-Ditko c/a(2)	8.00	24.00	48.00
12-Ditko-c(Classic)/a	10.00	30.00	60.00
13-Cocaine drug mention story (Fox reprints, 10-11/54); Blue Beetle story	4.00	12.00	24.00
14-Blue Beetle story (Fox reprints, 12-1/54-55)	3.50	10.00	20.00
15,17-19: 15-18-Rocky Jones app.	1.50	4.50	9.00
16-Krigstein, Ditko-a	4.00	12.00	24.00
20-Reprints Fawcett's "Destination Moon"	5.50	16.00	32.00
21,22,24,25,29,31,32-Ditko-a	2.50	7.00	14.00
23-Reprints Fawcett's "Destination Moon"	4.00	12.00	24.00
26,27-Ditko-a(4) each	3.50	10.00	20.00
28,30	1.20	3.50	7.00
33-Origin & 1st app. Captain Atom by Ditko	5.50	16.00	32.00
34-40,42-All Captain Atom by Ditko	2.50	7.00	14.00
41-Ditko-a	1.00	3.00	6.00
43,46-59	.50	1.50	3.00
44,45-Mercury Man in each	.50	1.50	3.00
V3No.60(10/67)-Origin Paul Mann & The Saucers From the Future		.40	.80
1('68)-Ditko-a		.40	.80
2-8('69)-All Ditko-a; Aparo-a-No. 2		.30	.60
9-13('79)-Capt. Atom reprints by Ditko		.30	.60

NOTE: ***Aparo** a-V3No.60. **Ditko** c-9-12, 31. **Shuster** a-11.*

Son Of Satan #1, © MCG

Son Of Vulcan V2#49, © CC

Space Adventures #10, © CC

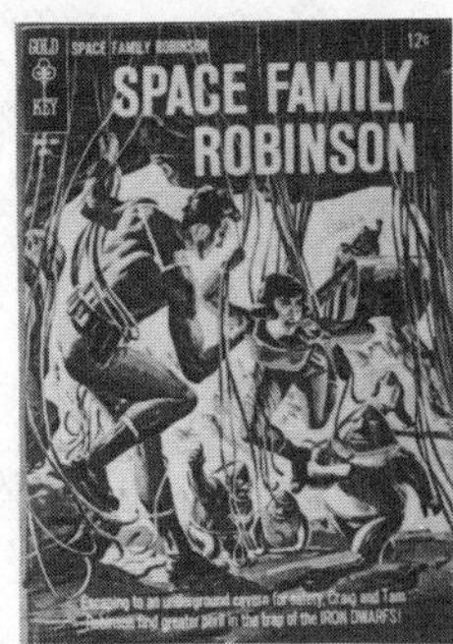

Space Family Robinson #12, © GK

Space 1999 #5, © CC

Space Squadron #5, © MCG

SPACE BUSTERS
Spring/52 - No. 3, Fall/52 (Painted covers by Norman Saunders)
Ziff-Davis Publ. Co.

	Good	Fine	Mint
1-Krigstein-a	14.00	40.00	80.00
2,3: 2-Two pgs. Kinstler-a; bondage-c	10.00	30.00	60.00

NOTE: ***Anderson** a-2.*

SPACE CADET (See Tom Corbett, . . .)

SPACE COMICS
No. 4, Mar-Apr, 1954 - No. 5, May-June, 1954
Avon Periodicals

	Good	Fine	Mint
4,5-Space Mouse, Peter Rabbit, Super Pup, & Merry Mouse app.	1.20	3.50	7.00
I.W. Reprint No. 8(no date)-Space Mouse reprints	.50	1.50	2.25

SPACE DETECTIVE
July, 1951 - No. 4, July, 1952
Avon Periodicals

	Good	Fine	Mint
1-Red Hathway, Space Det. begins, ends No. 4; Wood c/a(3)-23 pgs.; ''Opium Smugglers of Venus'' drug story; Lucky Dale-r/Saint No. 4	60.00	160.00	325.00
2-Tales from the Shadow Squad story; Wood/Orlando-c; Wood inside layouts	25.00	75.00	150.00
3-Kinstler-c	15.00	45.00	90.00
4-Kinstler-a	15.00	45.00	90.00
I.W. Reprint No. 1(reprints No.2), 8(reprints cover No. 1 & part Famous Funnies No. 191)	1.50	4.00	8.00
I.W. Reprint No. 9	1.50	4.00	8.00

SPACE EXPLORER (See March of Comics No. 202)

SPACE FAMILY ROBINSON (. . . Lost in Space No. 15 on) (Lost in Space No. 37 on)
Dec, 1962 - No. 36, Oct, 1969
Gold Key

	Good	Fine	Mint
1-(low distribution)	5.00	15.00	30.00
2(3/63)-Became Lost in Space	3.00	8.00	16.00
3-10: 6-Captain Venture begins	1.50	4.00	8.00
11-20	.70	2.00	4.00
21-36	.35	1.00	2.00

SPACE FAMILY ROBINSON (See March of Comics No. 320,328, 352,404)

SPACE GHOST (TV)
March, 1967 (Hanna-Barbera)
Gold Key

	Good	Fine	Mint
1 (10199-703)	1.00	3.00	6.00

SPACE KAT-ETS (In 3-D)
Dec, 1953 (25 cents)
Power Publishing Co.

	Good	Fine	Mint
1	8.00	24.00	48.00

SPACEMAN
Sept, 1953 - No. 8, Nov, 1954
Atlas Comics (CnPC)

	Good	Fine	Mint
1	5.50	16.00	32.00
2-8	3.50	10.00	20.00

NOTE: ***Everett** c-1,3. **Maneely** c-6.*

SPACE MAN
1962 - No. 8, Mar-May, 1964; No. 9, July, 1972 - No. 10, Oct, 1972
Dell Publishing Co./Gold Key

	Good	Fine	Mint
4-Color 1253 (1-3/62)	1.00	3.00	6.00
2,3	.70	2.00	4.00
4-8	.50	1.50	3.00
9-Reprints No. 1253		.60	1.20
10-Reprints No. 2		.30	.60

SPACE MOUSE (Also see Space Comics)
April, 1953 - No. 5, Apr-May, 1954
Avon Periodicals

	Good	Fine	Mint
1	2.50	7.00	14.00
2-5	1.20	3.50	7.00

SPACE MOUSE (See Comic Album No. 17)
Aug-Oct, 1960 - No. 5, Nov, 1963 (Walter Lantz)
Dell Publishing Co./Gold Key

	Good	Fine	Mint
4-Color 1132,1244	.50	1.50	3.00
1(11/62)-5 (G.K.)	.50	1.50	3.00

SPACE MYSTERIES
1964
I.W. Enterprises

	Good	Fine	Mint
Reprint No. 1,8,9	.50	1.50	3.00

SPACE: 1999
Nov, 1975 - No. 7, Nov, 1976
Charlton Comics

	Good	Fine	Mint
1-Staton-c/a; origin Moonbase Alpha		.60	1.20
2-Staton-a		.50	1.00
3-7: All Byrne-a; c-5	.45	1.25	2.50

SPACE: 1999 (Magazine)
November, 1975 - No. 8, Nov, 1976
Charlton Comics

	Good	Fine	Mint
1-Origin Moonbase Alpha; Morrow c/a	.50	1.50	3.00
2,3-Morrow c/a	.30	.90	1.80
4-8 (No. 7 shows No. 6 on inside)	.30	.80	1.60

SPACE PATROL
Summer/52 - No. 2, Fall/52 (Painted covers by Norman Saunders)
Ziff-Davis Publishing Co.

	Good	Fine	Mint
1-Krigstein-a	17.00	50.00	100.00
2-Krigstein-a	14.00	40.00	80.00

SPACE SQUADRON (Space Worlds No. 6)
June, 1951 - No. 5, Feb, 1952
Marvel/Atlas Comics (ACI)

	Good	Fine	Mint
1	7.00	20.00	40.00
2-5	5.00	15.00	30.00

SPACE THRILLERS
1954 (Giant) (25 cents)
Avon Periodicals

	Good	Fine	Mint
nn-(Scarce)-Robotmen of the Lost Planet; contains 3 rebound comics of The Saint & Strange Worlds. Contents could vary.	70.00	200.00	400.00

SPACE TRIP TO THE MOON (See Space Adventures No. 23)

SPACE WAR (Fightin' Five No. 28 on)
Oct, 1959 - No. 27, Mar, 1964; No. 28, Mar, 1978 - No. 34, 3/79
Charlton Comics

	Good	Fine	Mint
V1No.1	3.00	6.00	12.00
2,3	1.00	3.00	6.00
4,5,8-Ditko c/a	3.00	8.00	16.00
6,10-Ditko-a	2.00	6.00	12.00
7,9,11-27	.85	2.50	5.00
28,29,33,34-Ditko c/a(r)	1.50	4.00	8.00
30-Ditko c/a(r); Staton, Sutton/Wood-a	2.00	5.00	10.00
31-Ditko-c/a; atom-blast-c	2.00	5.00	10.00
32	.30	.90	1.80

NOTE: ***Everett** a-34. **Sutton** a-30, 33.*

SPACE WESTERN (Formerly Cowboy Western Comics; becomes Cowboy Western Comics No. 46 on)
No. 40, Oct, 1952 - No. 45, Aug, 1953
Charlton Comics (Capitol Stories)

	Good	Fine	Mint
40	17.00	40.00	80.00
41,43-45	10.00	30.00	60.00
42-Atom bomb explosion-c	12.00	35.00	70.00

SPACE WORLDS (Space Squadron No. 1-5)
No. 6, April, 1952
Atlas Comics (Male)

	Good	Fine	Mint
6	3.00	8.00	16.00

SPANKY & ALFALFA AND THE LITTLE RASCALS (See The Little Rascals)

SPARKIE, RADIO PIXIE (Big John & Sparkie No. 4)
Winter, 1951 - No. 3, 1952
Ziff-Davis Publ. Co.

	Good	Fine	Mint
1-3	2.00	6.00	12.00

SPARKLE COMICS
Oct-Nov, 1948 - No. 33, Dec-Jan, 1953-54
United Features Syndicate

	Good	Fine	Mint
1-Li'l Abner, Nancy, Captain & the Kids	2.00	6.00	12.00
2-10	1.50	4.00	8.00
11-33	1.00	3.00	6.00

SPARKLE PLENTY (See 4-Color No. 215 & Harvey Com. Libr. No. 2)

SPARKLER COMICS (1st Series)
July, 1940 - No. 2, 1940
United Feature Comic Group

	Good	Fine	Mint
1-Jim Hardy	6.00	18.00	36.00
2-Frankie Doodle	3.00	9.00	18.00

SPARKLER COMICS (2nd Series) (Nancy & Sluggo No. 121 on)
July, 1941 - No. 120, Jan, 1955
United Features Syndicate

	Good	Fine	Mint
1-Origin Sparkman; Tarzan (by Hogarth in all issues), Captain & the Kids, Ella Cinders, Danny Dingle, Dynamite Dunn, Nancy, Abbie & Slats, Frankie Doodle, Broncho Bill begin	30.00	80.00	160.00
2	14.00	40.00	80.00
3	12.00	35.00	70.00
4	10.00	30.00	60.00
5-10	9.00	25.00	50.00
11-13,15-20: 12-Sparkman new costume	7.00	20.00	40.00
14-Hogarth Tarzan-c	10.00	30.00	60.00
21-24,26,27,29,30: 22-Race Riley & the Commandos strips begin, ends No. 44	5.00	15.00	30.00
25,28,31,34,37,39-Tarzan-c by Hogarth	8.00	24.00	48.00
32,33,35,36,38,40	4.00	12.00	24.00
41,43,45,46,48,49	2.50	7.00	14.00
42,44,47,50-Tarzan-c	5.50	16.00	32.00
51,52,54-70: 57-Li'l Abner begins (not in No. 58); Fearless Fosdick app.-No. 58	2.00	6.00	12.00
53-Tarzan-c	5.00	14.00	28.00
71-80	2.00	5.00	10.00
81,82,84-90	1.50	4.00	8.00
83-Tarzan-c; last Li'l Abner	3.00	8.00	16.00
91-96,98-100	1.20	3.50	7.00
97-Origin Casey Ruggles by Warren Tufts	2.00	5.00	10.00
101-107,109-112,114-120	1.00	2.80	5.60
108,113-Toth-a	2.00	6.00	12.00

SPARKLING LOVE
June, 1950; 1953
Avon Periodicals/Realistic (1953)

	Good	Fine	Mint
1(Avon)-Kubert-a	10.00	28.00	56.00
nn(1953)-Reprint; Kubert-a	4.00	12.00	24.00

SPARKLING LOVE STORIES (Pulp magazine)
July, 1950
Avon Periodicals

	Good	Fine	Mint
Contains Avon comic Sparkling Love No. 1	7.00	20.00	40.00

SPARKLING STARS
June, 1944 - No. 33, March, 1948
Holyoke Publishing Co.

	Good	Fine	Mint
1-Hell's Angels	2.50	7.00	14.00
2-10	1.00	3.00	6.00
11-19,21-29,31-33: 24,28,29-Bondage-c	.70	2.00	4.00
20,30-Fangs the Wolf Boy app.	.85	2.50	5.00

SPARKMAN
1945 (One Shot)
United Features Syndicate

	Good	Fine	Mint
1-Origin Sparkman; female torture story	5.50	16.00	36.00

SPARKY WATTS
1942 - 1949
Columbia Comic Group

	Good	Fine	Mint
1(1942)-Skyman & The Face app.	4.00	12.00	24.00
2(1943), 3(1944)	3.00	9.00	18.00
4(1944)-Origin	2.50	7.00	14.00
5(1947)-Skyman app.	2.00	5.00	10.00
6('47),7,8('48),9,10('49)	1.50	4.00	8.00

SPARTACUS (See 4-Color No. 1139)

SPECIAL AGENT (Steve Saunders . . .)
Dec, 1947 - No. 8, Sept, 1949
Parents' Magazine Institute

	Good	Fine	Mint
1	1.00	3.00	6.00
2-8	.85	2.50	5.00

SPECIAL COLLECTORS' EDITION
Dec, 1975 (10¼x13½'')
Marvel Comics Group

	Good	Fine	Mint
1-Kung Fu, Iron Fist & Sons of the Tiger	.40	1.10	2.20

SPECIAL COMICS (Hangman No. 2 on)
Winter, 1941-42
MLJ Magazines

	Good	Fine	Mint
1-Origin The Boy Buddies (Shield & Wizard x-over); death of The Comet; origin The Hangman retold	60.00	170.00	340.00

SPECIAL DELIVERY
1951 (32 pgs.; B&W)
Post Hall Synd. (Giveaway)

Origin of Pogo, Swamp, etc.; 2 pg. biog. on Walt Kelly
(Sold in 1980 for $150.00)

SPECIAL EDITION (See Gorgo, Reptisaurus)

SPECIAL EDITION COMICS
1940 (One Shot)
Fawcett Publications

	Good	Fine	Mint
1-Captain Marvel (came out before Captain Marvel No. 1)	200.00	550.00	1200.00

(Prices vary widely on this book)

SPECIAL MARVEL EDITION (Master of Kung Fu No. 17 on)
Jan, 1971 - No. 16, Feb, 1974
Marvel Comics Group

	Good	Fine	Mint
1-Thor begins (r)		.50	1.00
2-4-Last Thor (r); all Giants		.50	1.00
5-14: Sgt. Fury-r; 11 r-/Sgt. Fury No. 13 (Captain America)		.40	.80
15-Master of Kung Fu begins; Starlin-a; origin & 1st app. Nayland Smith & Dr. Petric	.40	1.20	2.40
16-1st app. Midnight; Starlin-a	.35	1.10	2.20

SPECIAL WAR SERIES
Aug, 1965 - No. 4, Nov, 1965
Charlton Comics

	Good	Fine	Mint
V4No.1-D-Day		.50	1.00
2-Attack!		.40	.80
3-War & Attack		.40	.80
4-Judomaster	.70	2.00	4.00

Sparkler Comics #1(2nd), © UFS

Sparky Watts #1, © CCG

Special Marvel Edition #1, © MCG

Spectacular Spider-Man #27, © MCG

The Spectre #9, © DC

Speed Comics #8, © HARV

SPECTACULAR ADVENTURES (See Adventures)

SPECTACULAR FEATURES MAGAZINE, A (Formerly My Confessions) (Spectacular Features Magazine No. 3)
No. 11, April, 1950 - No. 12, June, 1950
Fox Features Syndicate

	Good	Fine	Mint
11-Samson & Delilah	7.00	20.00	40.00
12-Iwo Jima	5.50	16.00	32.00

SPECTACULAR FEATURES MAGAZINE (Formerly A Spectacular Features Magazine)
No. 3, Aug, 1950
Fox Features Syndicate

	Good	Fine	Mint
3-Drugs/prostitution story	6.00	16.00	24.00

SPECTACULAR SPIDER-MAN, THE (See Marvel Treasury Edition and Marvel Special Edition)

SPECTACULAR SPIDER-MAN, THE (Magazine)
July, 1968 - No. 2, Nov, 1968 (35 cents)
Marvel Comics Group

	Good	Fine	Mint
1-(Black & White)	1.50	4.00	8.00
2-(Color)-Green Goblin app.	1.00	3.00	6.00

SPECTACULAR SPIDER-MAN, THE (Peter Parker)
Dec, 1976 - Present
Marvel Comics Group

	Good	Fine	Mint
1	.70	2.00	4.00
2-5	.30	.80	1.60
6-10		.50	1.00
11-20		.40	.80
21,24-26,29-40: 33-Origin Iguana		.40	.80
22,23-Moon Knight app.	.30	.90	1.80
27-Miller's 1st Daredevil	4.00	12.00	24.00
28-Miller Daredevil	4.00	12.00	24.00
41-59,61		.30	.60
60-Double size; origin retold with new facts revealed		.40	.80
Annual 1 (12/79)		.40	.80
Annual 2 (8/80)-1st app. & origin Rapier		.40	.80
Annual 3 (11/81)-Last Manwolf		.40	.80

NOTE: ***Buckler** a-Annual 1p; c-Annual 1. **Byrne** c-43, 58p. **Cockrum** a-37i; c-22, 27. **Gulacy** c-8. **Layton** c-32. **Miller** c-54p. **Mooney** a(p)-26, 29-34, 36, 37, 39i, Annual 1. **Nasser** c-37p. **Perez** c-10, **Simonson** c-54i.*

SPECTACULAR STORIES MAGAZINE (Formerly A Star Presentation Magazine)
No. 4, July, 1950 - No. 3, Sept, 1950
Fox Features Syndicate (Hero Books)

	Good	Fine	Mint
4-Sherlock Holmes	8.00	24.00	48.00
3-The St. Valentine's Day Massacre	5.50	16.00	32.00

SPECTRE, THE (See Adventure, Showcase, & More Fun)
Nov-Dec, 1967 - No. 10, May-June, 1969
National Periodical Publications

	Good	Fine	Mint
1-Anderson c/a	1.00	3.00	6.00
2-5-Adams c/a; 3-Wildcat x-over	1.00	3.00	6.00
6-8,10: 7-Hourman app.	.50	1.50	3.00
9-Wrightson-a	.70	2.00	4.00

NOTE: ***Anderson** inks-No. 6-8,10.*

SPEED BUGGY (Also see Fun-In No. 12,15)
July, 1975 - No. 9, Nov, 1976 (Hanna-Barbera)
Charlton Comics

	Good	Fine	Mint
1-9		.25	.50

SPEED CARTER SPACEMAN (See Spaceman)

SPEED COMICS (New Speed)
Oct, 1939 - No. 44, 1-2/47 (No.14-16: pocket size, 100 pgs.)
Brookwood Publ./Speed Publ./Harvey Publications

	Good	Fine	Mint
1-Origin Shock Gibson; Ted Parrish, the Man with 1000 Faces begins; Powell-a	35.00	110.00	220.00
2-Powell-a	20.00	60.00	120.00
3	10.00	30.00	60.00
4-Powell-a	8.00	24.00	48.00
5	7.00	20.00	42.00
6-12: 7-Mars Mason begins, ends No. 11. 12-The Wasp begins; Major Colt app. (Capt. Colt No. 12)	7.00	20.00	42.00
13-Intro. Captain Freedom & Young Defenders; Girl Commandos, Pat Parker, War Nurse begins; Major Colt app.	12.00	35.00	70.00
14-16: 15-Pat Parker dons costume, last in costume No. 23; no Girl Commandos	8.00	24.00	48.00
17-Black Cat begins (origin), reprint/Pocket No. 1; not in No. 40,41	17.00	50.00	100.00
18-20	8.00	24.00	48.00
21,22,25-30	7.00	20.00	40.00
23-Origin Girl Commandos	10.00	30.00	60.00
24-Pat Parker Team-up with Girl Commandos	7.00	20.00	40.00
31-44: 35-Bondage-c. 38-Flag-c	5.50	16.00	32.00

NOTE: ***Kubert** a-7-11(Mars Mason), 37, 38, 42-44. **Powell** Shock Gibson-44. **Tuska** a-7.*

SPEED DEMONS (Formerly Frank Merriwell at Yale?; Submarines Attack No. 11 on)
1957 - 1958
Charlton Comics

	Good	Fine	Mint
5-10	.30	.80	1.60

SPEED SMITH THE HOT ROD KING
Spring, 1952
Ziff-Davis Publishing Co.

	Good	Fine	Mint
1-Saunders painted-c	3.00	9.00	18.00

SPEEDY GONZALES (See 4-Color No. 1084)

SPEEDY RABBIT
No date (1958?); 1963
I. W. Enterprises/Super Comics

	Good	Fine	Mint
I.W. Reprint No. 1	.30	.80	1.60
Super Reprint No. 14(1963)	.30	.80	1.60

SPELLBOUND (See The Crusaders)

SPELLBOUND (Tales to Hold You... No. 1, Stories...)
3/52 - No. 23, 6/54; No. 24, 10/55 - No. 34, 6/57
Atlas Comics (ACI No. 1-14/Male No. 15-23/BPC No. 24-34)

	Good	Fine	Mint
1	5.50	16.00	32.00
2-5: 3-Cannibalism story	3.00	8.00	16.00
6-Krigstein-a	3.50	10.00	20.00
7-10	2.00	6.00	12.00
11-16,18-20	1.75	5.00	10.00
17-Krigstein-a	3.50	10.00	20.00
21-24,26-31	1.20	3.50	7.00
25-Orlando-a	1.50	4.00	8.00
32,33-Torres-a	3.50	10.00	20.00
34-Williamson/Mayo-a, 4 pgs.	4.00	12.00	24.00

NOTE: ***Ditko** a-29. **Everett** a-2, 5, 16, 30, 31; c-2, 7, 14, 18, 30. **Heath** a-9, 14; c-3, 20, 21. **Infantino** a-15. **Krigstein** a-6, 17. **Orlando** a-25. **Mac Pakula** a-22. **Powell** a-19, 20, 32. **Romita** a-27.*

SPENCER SPOOK (Formerly Giggle)
No. 100, Mar-Apr, 1955 - No. 101, May-June, 1955
American Comics Group

	Good	Fine	Mint
100,101	.50	1.50	3.00

SPIDER-MAN (See Amazing...)

SPIDER-MAN AND HIS AMAZING FRIENDS
Dec, 1981 - Present
Marvel Comics Group

	Good	Fine	Mint
1-Adapted from original screen play		.30	.60

SPIDER-MAN & THE HULK (Special Edition)

SPIDER-MAN & THE HULK (continued)
June 8, 1980 (20 pgs.)
Chicago Tribune Giveaway (Newspaper network)

	Good	Fine	Mint
	.70	2.00	4.00

SPIDER-WOMAN (Also see Marvel Spotlight No. 32)
April, 1978 - Present (See Marvel Two-In-One)
Marvel Comics Group

	Good	Fine	Mint
1-New origin & mask added	.30	.90	1.80
2-5: 4-Bondage-c		.50	1.00
6-10: 6,8-Bondage-c		.40	.80
11-20: 20-Spider-Man app.		.40	.80
21-36,39-41		.30	.60
37,38-New X-Men x-over; 37-1st Siren	.30	.80	1.60

NOTE: ***Austin** a-37i. **Byrne** c-26. **Infantino** a-1-5, 9-19; c-6-12p.*

SPIDEY SUPER STORIES (Spider-Man)
Oct, 1974 - Present (35 cents) (no ads)
Marvel/Children's TV Workshop

	Good	Fine	Mint
1-(Stories simplified)		.60	1.20
2-5		.40	.80
6-10		.40	.80
11-50: 15-Storm x-over		.30	.60

SPIKE & TYKE (M.G.M.)
Sept, 1953 - No. 1266, Dec-Feb, 1961-62
Dell Publishing Co.

	Good	Fine	Mint
4-Color 499,577,638	.70	2.00	4.00
4(12-2/55-56)-10	.50	1.50	3.00
11-24(12-2/60-61)	.35	1.00	2.00
4-Color 1266	.35	1.00	2.00

SPIN & MARTY (TV) (Walt Disney's)
June, 1956 - No. 1082, Mar-May, 1960
Dell Publishing Co.

	Good	Fine	Mint
4-Color 714,767,808,826	.85	2.50	5.00
5(3-5/58)-10(6-8/59)	.70	2.00	4.00
4-Color 1026,1082	.70	2.00	4.00

SPINE-TINGLING TALES
May, 1975 - No. 4, Jan, 1976
Gold Key

	Good	Fine	Mint
1-Reprints 1st Tragg/Mystery Comics Digest No. 3		.40	.80
2-Origin Ra-Ka-Tep reprint/Mystery Comics Digest No. 1; Dr. Spektor/No. 12		.40	.80
3-All Durak issue; (r)		.40	.80
4-Baron Tibor's 1st app. r-/Mystery Comics Digest No. 4		.40	.80

SPIRIT, THE (Weekly Comic Book)
6/2/40 - 10/5/52 (16 pgs.; 8 pgs.) (no cover) (in color)
(Distributed through various newspapers and other sources)
Will Eisner

NOTE: ***Eisner** script, pencils/inks for the most part from 6/2/40-4/26/42; a few stories assisted by Jack Cole, Fine, Powell and Kotsky.*

	Good	Fine	Mint
6/2/40(No.1)-Origin; reprinted in Police No. 11; Lady Luck (Brenda Banks) by Chuck Mazoujian & Mr. Mystic by S. R. (Bob) Powell begin	75.00	200.00	400.00
6/9/40(No.2)	30.00	75.00	150.00
6/16/40(No.3)-Black Queen app. in Spirit	20.00	55.00	110.00
6/23/40(No.4)-Mr. Mystic receives magical necklace	15.00	45.00	90.00
6/30/40(No.5)	15.00	45.00	90.00
7/7/40(No.6)-Black Queen app. in Spirit	15.00	45.00	90.00
7/14/40(No.7)-8/4/40(No.10)	11.00	32.00	64.00
8/11/40-9/22/40	10.00	30.00	60.00
9/29/40-Ellen drops engagement with Homer Creep	9.00	25.00	50.00
10/6/40-11/3/40	9.00	25.00	50.00
11/10/40-The Black Queen app.	9.00	25.00	50.00
11/17/40, 11/24/40	9.00	25.00	50.00
12/1/40-Ellen spanking by Spirit on cover & inside; Eisner-1st 3 pgs., J. Cole rest	11.00	32.00	64.00
12/8/40-3/9/41	7.00	20.00	40.00
3/16/41-Intro. & 1st app. Silk Satin	11.00	32.00	64.00
3/23/41-6/1/41: 5/11/41-Last Lady Luck by Mazoujian; 5/18/41-Lady Luck by Nick Viscardi begins, ends 2/22/42	7.00	20.00	40.00
6/8/41-2nd app. Satin; Spirit learns Satin is also a British agent	10.00	28.00	56.00
6/15/41-1st app. Twilight	8.00	23.00	46.00
6/22/41-Hitler app. in Spirit	6.00	18.00	36.00
6/29/41-1/25/42,2/8/42	6.00	18.00	36.00
2/1/42-1st app. Duchess	8.00	23.00	46.00
2/15/42-4/26/42-Lady Luck by Klaus Nordling begins 3/1/42	6.00	18.00	36.00
5/3/42-8/16/42-Eisner/Fine/Quality staff assists on Spirit	3.50	10.00	20.00
8/23/42-Satin cover splash; Spirit by Eisner/Fine although signed by Fine	8.00	23.00	46.00
8/30/42,9/27/42-10/11/42,10/25/42-11/8/42-Eisner/Fine/Quality staff assists on Spirit	3.50	10.00	20.00
9/6/42-9/20/42,10/18/42-Fine/Belfi art on Spirit; scripts by Manly Wade Wellman	2.50	7.00	14.00
11/15/42-12/6/42,12/20/42,12/27/42,1/17/43-4/18/43, 5/9/43-8/8/43-Wellman/Woolfolk scripts, Fine pencils, Quality staff inks	2.50	7.00	14.00
12/13/42,1/3/43,1/10/43,4/25/43,5/2/43-Eisner scripts/layouts; Fine pencils, Quality staff inks	3.00	8.00	16.00
8/15/43-Eisner script/layout; pencils/inks by Quality staff	2.00	5.00	10.00
8/22/43-12/12/43-Wellman/Woolfolk scripts, Fine pencils, Quality staff inks; Mr. Mystic by Guardineer-10/10/43-10/24/43	2.00	5.00	10.00
12/19/43-8/13/44-Wellman/Woolfolk/Jack Cole scripts; art by Cole, Fine & Robin King; Last Mr. Mystic-5/14/44	1.50	4.00	8.00
8/22/44-12/16/45-Wellman/Woolfolk scripts; Fine art with unknown staff assists	1.50	4.00	8.00

NOTE: *Scripts/layouts by Eisner, or Eisner/Nordling, Eisner/Mercer or Spranger/Eisner; inks by Eisner or Eisner/Spranger in issues 12/23/45-2/2/47.*

	Good	Fine	Mint
12/23/45-1/13/46	5.00	14.00	28.00
1/20/46-1st postwar Satin app.	6.00	18.00	36.00
1/27/46-3/10/46-Last Lady Luck 3/3/46	5.00	14.00	28.00
3/17/46-Intro. & 1st app. Nylon	6.00	17.00	34.00
3/24/46,3/31/46,4/14/46	5.00	14.00	28.00
4/7/46-2nd app. Nylon	5.00	15.00	30.00
4/21/46-Intro. & 1st app. Mr. Carrion & His Buzzard Pet Julia	8.00	23.00	46.00
4/28/46-5/12/46,5/26/46-6/30/46	5.00	14.00	28.00
5/19/46-2nd app. Mr. Carrion	6.00	17.00	34.00
7/7/46-Intro. & 1st app. Dulcet Tone & Skinny	6.00	18.00	36.00
7/14/46-9/29/46	5.00	14.00	28.00
10/6/46-Intro. & 1st app. P'Gell	6.00	18.00	36.00
10/13/46-11/3/46,11/17/46-11/24/46	5.00	14.00	28.00
11/10/46-2nd app. P'Gell	6.00	17.00	34.00
12/1/46-3rd app. P'Gell	5.00	14.00	28.00
12/8/46-2/2/47	4.50	13.00	26.00

NOTE: *Scripts, pencils/inks by Eisner except where noted in issues 2/9/47-12/19/48.*

	Good	Fine	Mint
2/9/47-7/6/47	4.50	13.00	26.00
7/13/47-''Hansel & Gretel'' fairy tales	6.00	17.00	34.00
7/20/47-Li'l Abner, Daddy Warbucks, Dick Tracy, Fearless Fosdick parody	6.00	17.00	34.00
7/27/47-9/14/47	4.50	13.00	26.00

Spider-Woman #1, © MCG

Spine-Tingling Tales #1, © GK

Spirit Section 6/21/42, © Will Eisner

Spirit Section 2/12/50, © Will Eisner

The Spirit #11, © Will Eisner

The Spirit #2(Harv), © Will Eisner

SPIRIT (continued) — Good / Fine / Mint

9/21/47-Pearl Harbor flashback 4.50 13.00 26.00
9/28/47,10/12/47-11/30/47 4.50 13.00 26.00
10/5/47-"Cinderella" fairy tales 6.00 18.00 36.00
12/7/47-Intro. & 1st app. Powder Pouf 6.00 18.00 36.00
12/14/47-12/28/47 4.50 13.00 26.00
1/4/48-2nd app. Powder Pouf 6.00 17.00 34.00
1/11/48-1st app. Sparrow Fallon; Powder Pouf app. 6.00 17.00 34.00
1/18/48-He-Man ad cover; satire issue 6.00 17.00 34.00
1/25/48-Intro. & 1st app. Castanet 6.00 17.00 34.00
2/1/48-2nd app. Castanet 5.00 14.00 28.00
2/8/48-3/7/48 4.50 13.00 26.00
3/14/48-Only app. Kretchma 5.00 14.00 28.00
3/21/48,3/28/48,4/11/48-4/25/48 4.50 13.00 26.00
4/4/48-Only app. Wild Rice 5.00 14.00 28.00
5/2/48-2nd app. Sparrow 4.50 13.00 26.00
5/9/48-6/27/48,7/11/48,7/18/48 4.50 13.00 26.00
7/4/48-Spirit by Andre Le Blanc 2.50 7.00 14.00
7/25/48-Ambrose Bierce's "The Thing" adaptation classic by Eisner/Grandenetti 8.00 24.00 48.00
8/1/48-8/15/48,8/29/48-9/12/48 4.50 13.00 26.00
8/22/48-Poe's "Fall of the House of Usher" classic by Eisner/Grandenetti 8.00 24.00 48.00
9/19/48-Only app. Lorelei 5.00 14.00 28.00
9/26/48-10/31/48 4.50 13.00 26.00
11/7/48-Only app. Plaster of Paris 6.00 17.00 34.00
11/14/48-12/19/48 4.50 13.00 26.00

NOTE: *Scripts by Eisner or Feiffer or Eisner/Feiffer or Nordling. Art by Eisner with backgrounds by Eisner, Grandenetti, Le Blanc, Stallman, Nordling, Dixon and/or others in issues 12/26/48-4/1/51 except where noted.*

12/26/48-Reprints some covers of 1948 with flashbacks 4.50 13.00 26.00
1/2/49-1/16/49 4.50 13.00 26.00
1/23/49,1/30/49-1st & 2nd app. Thorne 5.00 15.00 30.00
2/6/49-8/14/49 4.50 13.00 26.00
8/21/49,8/28/49-1st & 2nd app. Monica Veto 6.00 17.00 34.00
9/4/49,9/11/49 4.50 13.00 26.00
9/18/49-Love comic cover; has gag love comic ads on inside 7.00 20.00 40.00
9/25/49-Only app. Ice 5.00 15.00 30.00
10/2/49,10/9/40-Autumn News appears & dies in 10/9 ish. 5.00 15.00 30.00
10/16/49-11/27/49,12/18/49,12/25/49 4.50 13.00 26.00
12/4/49,12/11/49-1st & 2nd app. Flaxen 5.00 14.00 28.00
1/1/50-Flashbacks to all of the Spirit girls-Thorne, Ellen, Satin, & Monica 6.00 18.00 36.00
1/8/50-Intro. & 1st app. Sand Saref 10.00 28.00 56.00
1/15/50-2nd app. Saref 8.00 24.00 48.00
1/22/50-2/5/50 4.50 13.00 26.00
2/12/50-Roller Derby ish. 5.00 15.00 30.00
2/19/50-Half Dead Mr. Lox - classic horror 5.00 15.00 30.00
2/26/50-4/23/50,5/14/50,5/28/50,7/23/50-9/3/50 4.50 13.00 26.00
4/30/50-Script/art by Le Blanc with Eisner framing 1.50 4.00 8.00
5/7/50,6/4/50-7/16/50-Abe Kanegson art 1.50 4.00 8.00
5/21/50-Script by Feiffer/Eisner, art by Blaisdell, Eisner framing 1.50 4.00 8.00
9/10/50-P'Gell returns 6.00 17.00 34.00
9/17/50-1/7/51 4.50 13.00 26.00
1/14/51-Life Magazine cover; brief biography of Comm. Dolan, Sand Saref, Silk Satin, P'Gell, Sammy & Willum, Darling O'Shea, & Mr. Carrion & His Pet Buzzard Julia, with pin-ups by Eisner 5.00 15.00 30.00
1/21/51,2/4/51-4/1/51 4.00 12.00 24.00
1/28/51-The Meanest Man in the World classic by Eisner 5.00 15.00 30.00
4/8/51-7/29/51,8/12/51-Last Eisner issue 4.00 12.00 24.00
8/5/51,8/19/51-7/20/52-Not Eisner 1.50 4.00 8.00

Good / Fine / Mint

7/27/52-(Rare)-Denny Colt in Outer Space by Wally Wood; 7 pg. S/F Story of E.C. vintage 80.00 200.00 320.00
8/3/52-(Rare)-"Mission. . . The Moon" by Wood 80.00 200.00 320.00
8/10/52-(Rare)-"A DP On The Moon" by Wood 80.00 200.00 320.00
8/17/52-(Rare)-"Heart" by Wood/Eisner 60.00 160.00 260.00
8/24/52-(Rare)-"Rescue" by Wood 80.00 200.00 320.00
8/31/52-(Rare)-"The Last Man" by Wood 80.00 200.00 320.00
9/7/52-(Rare)-"The Man in The Moon" by Wood 80.00 200.00 320.00
9/14/52-(Rare)-Al Wenzel art 5.00 15.00 30.00
9/21/52-(Rare)-"Denny Colt, Alias The Spirit/Space Report" by Eisner 25.00 60.00 110.00
9/28/52-(Rare)-"Return From The Moon" by Wood 80.00 200.00 320.00
10/5/52-(Rare)-"The Last Story" by Eisner 25.00 60.00 110.00
Large Tabloid pages from 1946 on (Eisner) - Price 30 percent over listed prices.

NOTE: *Spirit sections came out in both large and small format. Some newspapers went to the 8-pg. format months before others. Some printed the pages so they cannot be folded into a small comic book section; these are worth less. (Also see Three Comics & Spiritman).*

SPIRIT, THE (Section)
January 9, 1966
N. Y. Sunday Herald Tribune

New 5-pg. Spirit story by Eisner; 2 pg. article on super-heroes; 2 pgs. color strips (BC, Miss Peach, Peanuts, Wizard of Id) 14.00 40.00 80.00

SPIRIT, THE (1st Series)
1944 - No. 22, Aug, 1950
Quality Comics Group (Vital)

nn(No.1)-"Wanted Dead or Alive" 25.00 75.00 150.00
nn(No.2)-"Crime Doesn't Pay" 17.00 50.00 100.00
nn(No.3)-"Murder Runs Wild" 12.00 36.00 72.00
4,5 10.00 28.00 56.00
6-10 8.00 24.00 48.00
11,17 6.00 18.00 36.00
12-16-Eisner-c 13.00 38.00 76.00
18-21-Strip-r by Eisner; Eisner-c 20.00 60.00 120.00
22-Used by N.Y. Legis. Comm; Classic Eisner-c 40.00 100.00 180.00
Super Reprint No. 11-Reprints Quality Spirit No. 19 by Eisner; Crandall-c 1.50 4.00 8.00
Super Reprint No. 12-Reprints Quality Spirit No. 17 by Fine 1.00 3.00 6.00

SPIRIT, THE (2nd Series)
Spring, 1952 - 1954
Fiction House Magazines

1-Not Eisner 12.00 35.00 70.00
2-Eisner c/a(2) 15.00 45.00 90.00
3-Eisner/Grandenetti-c 10.00 28.00 56.00
4-Eisner/Grandenetti-c; Eisner-a 12.00 35.00 70.00
5-Eisner c/a(4) 15.00 45.00 90.00

SPIRIT, THE
Oct, 1966 - No. 2, Mar, 1967 (Giant Size)
Harvey Publications

1-Eisner-r plus 9 new pgs.(Origin Denny Colt, Take 3, plus 2 filler pages) 4.00 12.00 24.00
2-Eisner-r plus 9 new pgs.(Origin of the Octopus) 3.00 8.00 16.00

SPIRIT, THE (Underground)
Jan, 1973 - No. 2, Sept, 1973 (Black & White)
Kitchen Sink Enterprises (Krupp Comics)

1-New Eisner-c, 4 pgs. new Eisner-a plus-r (titled Crime Convention) 1.00 3.00 6.00

SPIRIT (continued) **Good Fine Mint**

2-New Eisner-c, 4 pgs. new Eisner-a plus-r(titled Meets P'Gell)
1.00 3.00 6.00

SPIRIT, THE (Magazine)
4/74 - No. 16, 1977; No. 17, Winter, 1977 - Present
Warren Publ. Co./Krupp Comic Works No. 17 on

	Good	Fine	Mint
1-Eisner-r begin	.80	2.40	4.80
2-5	.70	2.00	4.00
6-9,11-16: 7-All Ebony ish. 8-Female Foes ish. 12-X-Mas ish.	.40	1.20	2.40
10-Origin	.50	1.40	2.80
17,18(8/78)		.40	.80
19-21-New Eisner-a plus Wood No. 20,21		.40	.80
22,23-Wood-r		.40	.80
Special 1('75)-All Eisner-a	.30	.90	1.80

NOTE: *Covers pencilled/inked by **Eisner** only No. 1-9,12-16; painted by Eisner & Ken Kelly No. 10 & 11; painted by Eisner No. 17-up; one color story reprinted in No. 1-10.*

SPIRITMAN (Also see Three Comics)
No date (1944) (10 cents)
(Triangle Sales Co. ad on back cover)
No publisher listed

2-Two Spirit sections (3/26/44, 4/2/44) bound together; by Lou Fine 10.00 20.00 40.00

SPIRIT WORLD (Magazine)
Fall, 1971 (Black & White)
National Periodical Publications

1-Kirby-a/Adams-c .70 2.00 4.00

SPITFIRE
1944 - 1945 (Female undercover agent)
Malverne Herald (Elliot)(J. R. Mahon)

132,133 3.50 10.00 20.00

SPITFIRE COMICS (Also see Double Up)
Aug, 1941 - No. 2, Oct, 1941 (Pocket size; 100 pgs.)
Harvey Publications

	Good	Fine	Mint
1-Origin The Clown, The Fly-Man, The Spitfire & The Magician From Bagdad	14.00	40.00	80.00
2	10.00	30.00	60.00

SPOOF!
Oct, 1970; No. 2, Nov, 1972 - No. 5, May, 1973
Marvel Comics Group

	Good	Fine	Mint
1-Infinity-c	.30	.80	1.20
2-5		.25	.50

SPOOK (Formerly Shock Detective Cases)
No. 22, Jan, 1953 - No. 30, Oct, 1954
Star Publications

	Good	Fine	Mint
22-Sgt. Spook-r; acid in face story	5.00	15.00	30.00
23,25,27: 27-two Sgt. Spook-r	5.00	15.00	30.00
24-Used in **SOTI**, pg. 182,183-r/Inside Crime 2; Transvestite story	7.00	20.00	40.00
26-Disbrow-a	6.00	17.00	34.00
28,29-Rulah app.; Jo-Jo in No. 29	6.00	17.00	34.00
30-Disbrow c/a(2); only Star-c	6.00	17.00	34.00

NOTE: ***L. B. Cole** covers-all issues; a-28(1pg.). **Disbrow** a-26(2), 28, 29(2), 30(2); No. 30 r-/Blue Bolt Weird Tales No. 114.*

SPOOK COMICS
1946
Baily Publications/Star

1-Mr. Lucifer app. 3.50 10.00 20.00

SPOOKY (The Tuff Little Ghost)
11/55 - 139, 11/73; No. 140, 7/74 - No. 155, 3/77; No. 156, 12/77 - No. 158, 4/78; No. 159, 9/78; No. 160, 10/79; No. 161, 6/80
Harvey Publications

	Good	Fine	Mint
1	11.00	32.00	64.00
2	5.50	16.00	32.00
3-10(1956-57)	3.00	8.00	16.00
11-20(1957-58)	1.50	4.00	8.00
21-40(1958-59)	.70	2.00	4.00
41-60	.50	1.50	3.00
61-80	.35	1.10	2.20
81-100	.30	.90	1.80
101-120	.25	.70	1.40
121-140		.60	1.20
141-160		.45	.90
161-		.30	.60

SPOOKY HAUNTED HOUSE
Oct, 1972 - No. 15, Feb, 1975
Harvey Publications

	Good	Fine	Mint
1	1.00	3.00	6.00
2-5	.50	1.50	3.00
6-10	.30	.80	1.60
11-15		.60	1.20

SPOOKY MYSTERIES
No date (1946) (10 cents)
Your Guide Publ. Co.

nn-Mr. Spooky, Super Snooper, Pinky, Girl Detective app. 2.00 6.00 12.00

SPOOKY SPOOKTOWN
6/62 - No. 52, 12/73; No. 53, 10/74 - No. 66, Dec, 1976
Harvey Publications

	Good	Fine	Mint
1-Casper, Spooky	5.50	16.00	32.00
2-5	3.00	8.00	16.00
6-10	1.50	4.00	8.00
11-20	1.00	3.00	6.00
21-40	.50	1.50	3.00
41-66	.30	.80	1.60

SPORT COMICS (True Sport Picture Stories No. 4 on?)
Oct, 1940(No mo.) - No. 4, Nov, 1941
Street & Smith Publications

	Good	Fine	Mint
1-Life story of Lou Gehrig	6.00	18.00	36.00
2-4	3.50	10.00	20.00

SPORT LIBRARY (See Charlton Sport. . .)

SPORTS ACTION (Formerly Sport Stars)
No. 2, Feb, 1950 - No. 14, Sept, 1952
Marvel/Atlas Comics (ACI No. 2,3/SAI No. 4-14)

	Good	Fine	Mint
2	2.50	7.00	14.00
3-Everett-a	2.50	7.00	14.00
4-11,14	2.00	6.00	12.00
12-Everett-c	2.50	7.00	14.00
13-Krigstein-a	3.00	8.00	16.00

NOTE: *Title may have changed after No. 3, to Crime Must Lose No. 4 on, due to publisher change.*

SPORT STARS
2-3/46 - No. 4, 8-9/46 (½ comic, ½ photo magazine)
Parents' Magazine Institute (Sport Stars)

	Good	Fine	Mint
1-"How Tarzan Got That Way" story of Johnny Weissmuller	4.00	12.00	24.00
2-Baseball greats	3.50	10.00	20.00
3,4	2.50	7.00	14.00

SPORT STARS (Sports Action No. 2)
Nov, 1949
Marvel Comics (ACI)

1-Knute Rockne; painted-c 4.00 12.00 24.00

SPORT THRILLS (Formerly Dick Cole)

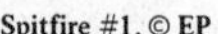
Spitfire #1, © EP

Spook #26, © STAR

Sport Stars #1, © PMI

Spy Fighters #5, © MCG

Spyman #1, © HARV

Stalker #1, © DC

SPORT THRILLS (continued)
No. 11, Nov, 1949 - No. 15, Nov, 1951
Star Publications

	Good	Fine	Mint
11-Dick Cole app.	3.00	9.00	18.00
12-L. B. Cole c/a	3.00	9.00	18.00
13-15-All L. B. Cole-c; 13-Dick Cole app.	3.00	8.00	16.00

SPOTLIGHT
Sept, 1978 - No. 4, Mar, 1979 (Hanna-Barbera)
Marvel Comics Group

	Good	Fine	Mint
1-4		.25	.50

SPOTLIGHT COMICS
Nov, 1944 - No. 3, 1945
Harry 'A' Chesler (Our Army, Inc.)

	Good	Fine	Mint
1-The Black Dwarf, The Veiled Avenger, & Barry Kuda begin; Tuska-c	8.00	24.00	48.00
2	7.00	20.00	40.00
3-Injury to eye story(Same as Scoop No. 3)	7.00	20.00	40.00

SPOTTY THE PUP
No. 3, Dec-Jan, 1953-54
Avon Periodicals

	Good	Fine	Mint
3	1.00	3.00	6.00

SPUNKY (. . . Junior Cowboy) (. . . Comics No. 2 on)
April, 1949 - No. 7, Nov, 1951
Standard Comics

	Good	Fine	Mint
1,2-Text illos by Frazetta	2.50	7.00	14.00
3-7	.85	2.50	5.00

SPUNKY THE SMILING SPOOK
Aug, 1957 - No. 4, May, 1958
Ajax/Farrell (World Famous Comics/Four Star Comic Corp.)

	Good	Fine	Mint
1-Reprints from Frisky Fables	.85	2.50	5.00
2-4	.70	2.00	4.00

SPY AND COUNTERSPY (Spy Hunters No. 3 on)
Aug-Sept, 1949 - No. 2, Oct-Nov, 1949
American Comics Group

	Good	Fine	Mint
1-Origin, 1st app. Jonathan Kent, Counterspy	2.50	7.00	14.00
2	2.00	5.00	10.00

SPY CASES (Formerly The Kellys)
No. 26, Sept, 1950 - No. 19, Oct, 1953
Marvel/Atlas Comics (Hercules Publ.)

	Good	Fine	Mint
26-28(2/51)	2.50	7.00	14.00
4(4/51)-6,8-10	1.50	4.00	8.00
7-Tuska-a	1.50	4.00	8.00
11-19	1.20	3.50	7.00

SPY FIGHTERS
March, 1951 - No. 15, July, 1953
Marvel/Atlas Comics (CSI)

	Good	Fine	Mint
1	2.00	6.00	12.00
2-15	1.20	3.50	7.00

SPY-HUNTERS (Formerly Spy & Counterspy)
No. 3, Dec-Jan, 1949-50 - No. 24, June-July, 1953
American Comics Group

	Good	Fine	Mint
3-Jonathan Kent begins, ends No. 10	2.00	6.00	12.00
4-10: 8-Starr-a	1.50	4.00	8.00
11-15,17-22,24	1.00	3.00	6.00
16-Nine pg. Williamson-a	4.00	12.00	24.00
23-Graphic torture, injury to eye panel	4.00	12.00	24.00

NOTE: ***Whitney*** *a-many issues; c-8, 10, 11, 16.*

SPYMAN (Top Secret Adventures on cover)
Sept, 1966 - No. 3, Feb, 1967
Harvey Publications

	Good	Fine	Mint
1-Steranko-a(p)-1st pro work; 1pg. Adams ad; Tuska c/a, Crandall-a(i)	.50	1.50	3.00
2,3: 2-Steranko-a(p)	.35	1.00	2.00

SPY SMASHER (See Fawcett Miniatures)
1941 - No. 11, Feb, 1943
Fawcett Publications

	Good	Fine	Mint
1-Spy Smasher begins	55.00	160.00	325.00
2	30.00	85.00	175.00
3	25.00	75.00	150.00
4,5	20.00	60.00	120.00
6-11	17.00	50.00	100.00

SPY SMASHER WELL KNOWN COMICS
1944 (12 pgs.; 8½x10½'') (Printed in green)
(paper cover; glued binding)
Bestmaid/Samuel Lowe (Giveaway)

	Good	Fine	Mint
(Scarce)	15.00	45.00	90.00

SPY THRILLERS (Police Badge No. 479 No. 5)
Nov, 1954 - No. 4, May, 1955
Atlas Comics (PrPI)

	Good	Fine	Mint
1	2.00	6.00	12.00
2-4	1.00	3.00	6.00

SQUEEKS
Oct, 1953 - 1954
Lev Gleason Publications

	Good	Fine	Mint
1-Biro-c	1.20	3.50	7.00
2-5: 2,3-Biro-c	.70	2.00	4.00

STALKER
June-July, 1975 - No. 4, Dec-Jan, 1975-76
National Periodical Publications

	Good	Fine	Mint
1-Origin & 1st app; Ditko/Wood-c/a	.30	.80	1.60
2-4		.60	1.20

STAMP COMICS (Stamps. . . on cover)
Oct, 1951 - No. 7, Oct, 1952 (No. 1: 15 cents)
Youthful Magazines/Stamp Comics, Inc.

	Good	Fine	Mint
1('Stamps' on indicia No. 1)	2.50	7.00	14.00
2-6: 3,4-Kiefer, Wildey-a	2.00	6.00	12.00
7-Roy Krenkel, 4 pgs.	3.00	9.00	18.00

NOTE: *Promotes stamp collecting; gives stories behind various commemorative stamps. No. 2, 10 cents printed over 15 cent c-price*

STANLEY & HIS MONSTER (Formerly The Fox & the Crow)
No. 109, Apr-May, 1968 - No. 114, Feb-Mar, 1969
National Periodical Publications

	Good	Fine	Mint
109-114 (113,114 Exist?)	.35	1.00	2.00

STAR COMICS
Feb, 1937 - No. 23 (V2No.7), Aug, 1939 (No. 1-6: large size)
Harry 'A' Chesler/Centaur Publications

	Good	Fine	Mint
V1No.1-Dan Hastings begins	12.00	35.00	80.00
2-5: 5-Little Nemo	9.00	25.00	54.00
6-10	6.00	18.00	42.00
11-15	5.50	16.00	40.00
16-The Phantom Rider begins, ends No. 22	5.50	16.00	40.00
V2No.1(No. 17)	7.00	20.00	48.00
2-7(No. 18-23)	5.50	16.00	36.00

NOTE: ***Burgos*** *a-17-20, 22, 23.* ***Gustavson*** *a-17-23.* ***Tarpe Mills*** *a-17-20, 22, 23.*

STAR FEATURE COMICS
1963
I. W. Enterprises

	Good	Fine	Mint
Reprint No. 9-Stunt-Man Stetson app.	.50	1.50	3.00

STARFIRE
Aug-Sept, 1976 - No. 8, Oct-Nov, 1977
National Periodical Publications/DC Comics

STARFIRE (continued) Good Fine Mint
1-Origin & 1st app; (CCA stamp fell off cover art; so it **was** approved by code) .30 .80 1.60
2-8 .40 .80

STAR HUNTERS (See DC Super Stars No. 16)
Oct-Nov, 1977 - No. 7, Oct-Nov, 1978
National Periodical Publications/DC Comics

1-Newton-a .40 .80
2-6 .30 .60
7-Giant .40 .80
NOTE: ***Buckler** a-5p, 6p; c-5, 6. **Layton** c-3, 5i, 6i. **Nasser** a-3.*

STARK TERROR (Magazine)
Dec, 1970 - No. 5, Aug, 1971 (52 pages) (B&W)
Stanley Publications

1-Bondage, torture-c .50 1.50 3.00
2-4 (Gillmor/Aragon-r) .30 .80 1.60
5 (ACG-r) .60 1.20

STARLET O'HARA IN HOLLYWOOD
Dec, 1948 - No. 4, Sept, 1949
Standard Comics

1 4.00 12.00 24.00
2-4-by Bob Oksner 3.00 8.00 16.00

STARMAN (See Adventure, First Issue Special, Showcase, & Justice League)

STAR PRESENTATION MAGAZINE, A (Formerly My Secret Romance No. 1,2; Spectacular Stories No. 4) (Also see This Is Suspense)
No. 3, May, 1950
Fox Features Syndicate (Hero Books)

3-Dr. Jekyll & Mr. Hyde by Wood & Harrison (reprinted in Startling Terror Tales No. 10); 'The Repulsing Dwarf' by Wood; Wood-c 60.00 150.00 300.00

STAR QUEST COMIX (Warren Presents... on cover)
October, 1978
Warren Publications

1 .50 1.00

STAR RANGER (Cowboy Comics No. 13 on)
Feb, 1937 - No. 12, 1938 (Large size: No. 1-6)
Centaur Publications

1-Ace & Deuce, Air Plunder 12.00 35.00 80.00
2-8,V2No.9-12(small size): 9-Gil Fox, Gustavson-a 6.00 18.00 40.00

STAR RANGER FUNNIES
V1No.15, Oct, 1938 - V2No.2, April, 1939
Centaur Publications

V1No.15-Eisner-a(6pgs.); Gustavson-a 10.00 28.00 60.00
V2No.1,2: 1-Jack Cole-a/c 5.00 15.00 34.00

STARR FLAGG, UNDERCOVER GIRL (See Undercover...)

STARS AND STRIPES COMICS
May, 1941 - No. 6, Dec, 1941
Centaur Publications

2(No.1)-The Shark, The Iron Skull, Aman, The Amazing Man, Mighty Man, Minimidget begin; The Voice & Dash Darwell, the Human Meteor app.; Gustavson Flag-c 30.00 90.00 210.00
3-Origin Dr. Synthe; The Black Panther app. 25.00 70.00 150.00
4-The Stars and Stripes origin 20.00 55.00 120.00
5(No.5 on cover & inside) 14.00 40.00 90.00
5(No.6)-(No.5 on cover, No.6 on inside) 14.00 40.00 90.00
NOTE: ***Gustavson** c-3-6.*

STARSLAYER: THE LOG OF THE JOLLY ROGER
Nov, 1981 - Present
Pacific Comics Good Fine Mint

1-Grell-c/a .50 1.00
2 .50 1.00

STAR SPANGLED COMICS (... War Stories No. 131 on)
Oct, 1941 - No. 130, July, 1952
National Periodical Publications

1-Origin Tarantula; Captain X of the R.A.F., Star Spangled Kid(See Action No. 40) & Armstrong of the Army begin 60.00 170.00 350.00
2 30.00 85.00 175.00
3-5 15.00 45.00 90.00
6-Last Armstrong/Army 12.00 35.00 70.00
7-Origin The Guardian by S&K, & Robotman by Jimmy Thompson; The Newsboy Legion & TNT begin; last Captain X 90.00 250.00 500.00
8-Origin TNT & Dan the Dyna-Mite 50.00 125.00 250.00
9,10 35.00 100.00 200.00
11-17 30.00 80.00 160.00
18-Origin Star Spangled Kid 35.00 100.00 200.00
19-Last Tarantula 30.00 80.00 160.00
20-Liberty Belle begins 30.00 80.00 160.00
21-29-Last S&K issue; 23-Last TNT 20.00 60.00 120.00
30-40 8.00 24.00 48.00
41-50 7.00 20.00 40.00
51-64: Last Newsboy Legion & The Guardian; 53 by S&K 6.00 18.00 36.00
65-Robin begins 7.00 20.00 40.00
66-68,70-80 4.00 12.00 24.00
69-Origin Tomahawk 7.00 20.00 40.00
81-Origin Merry, Girl of 1000 Gimmicks 4.00 12.00 24.00
82-Last Star Spangled Kid 4.00 12.00 24.00
83-Capt. Compass begins, ends No. 130 4.00 12.00 24.00
84,87 (Rare) 6.00 18.00 36.00
85,86,88-99: 91-Federal Men begin, end No. 93. 94-Manhunters Around the World begin, end No. 121 3.50 10.00 20.00
100 5.00 15.00 30.00
101-112,114-121: 114-Retells Robin's origin 3.00 8.00 16.00
113-Frazetta-a, 10 pgs. 13.00 38.00 76.00
122-Ghost Breaker begins (origin), ends No. 130 3.00 8.00 16.00
123-130 2.50 7.00 14.00
NOTE: *Most all issues after No. 29 signed by **Simon & Kirby** are **not** by them.*

STAR SPANGLED WAR STORIES (Star Spangled Comics No. 1-130; The Unknown Soldier No. 205 on) (See Showcase)
No. 131, 8/52 - No. 133, 10/52; No. 3, 11/52 - No. 204, 2-3/77
National Periodical Publications

131(No.1) 10.00 30.00 60.00
132 7.00 20.00 40.00
133-Used in **POP**, Pg. 94 8.00 24.00 48.00
3-5: 4-Devil Dog Dugan app. 5.50 16.00 32.00
6-Evans-a 4.00 12.00 24.00
7-10 3.50 10.00 20.00
11-20 3.00 8.00 16.00
21-30 2.00 6.00 12.00
31-33,35-40 2.00 5.00 10.00
34-Krigstein-a 3.00 9.00 18.00
41-50 1.50 4.00 8.00
51-83 1.20 3.50 7.00
84-Origin Mlle. Marie 2.50 7.00 14.00
85-89-Mlle. Marie in all 1.20 3.50 7.00
90-1st Dinosaur issue 3.00 9.00 18.00
91-100 .85 2.50 5.00
101-120 .60 1.80 3.60
121-133,135-137-Last dinosaur story; Heath Birdman-No. 129,131 .35 1.00 2.00
134,144-Adams-a plus Kubert No. 144 .70 2.00 4.00
138-Enemy Ace begins by Joe Kubert, ends No. 161

Star Hunters #1, © DC

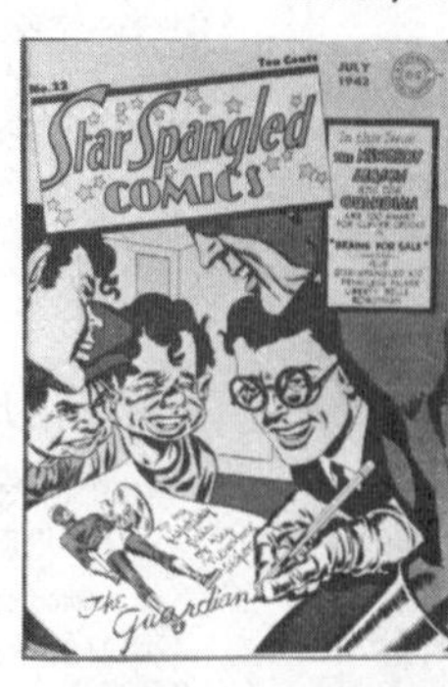

Star Spangled Comics #22, © DC

Star Spangled War Stories #126, © DC

Startling Comics #2, © BP

Startling Terror Tales #12, © STAR

Star Wars #2, © MCG

STAR SPANGLED WAR STORIES (continued) **Good** **Fine** **Mint**

	Good	Fine	Mint
	.50	1.50	3.00
139-143,145-148,152,153,155	.35	1.00	2.00
149,150-Viking Prince by Kubert	.40	1.20	2.40
151-1st Unknown Soldier	.30	.80	1.60
154-Origin Unknown Soldier	.30	.80	1.60
156-1st Battle Album		.40	.80
157-161-Last Enemy Ace		.40	.80
162-180,184-204: 164-Toth-a. 166-The Young Commandos app; 197-Kaluta-a(i)		.30	.60
181-183-Enemy Ace vs. Balloon Buster serial app.		.30	.60

NOTE: ***Anderson*** *a-6; c-120.* ***Chaykin*** *a-167.* ***Drucker*** *a-61, 64, 66, 73-84.* ***John Giunta*** *a-72.* ***Infantino*** *a-19-21, 37, 163r; c-118, 121.* ***Kaluta*** *c-167.* ***Kubert*** *a-6-138(most later issues), 200.* ***Maurer*** *a-160.* ***Simonson*** *a-170.* ***Sutton*** *a-168.* ***Wildey*** *a-161. Suicide Squad in 110, 116-118, 120, 121, 127. U.S.S. Stevens by* ***Glanzman****-171, 172, 174.*

STARSTREAM (Adventures in Science Fiction)
1976 (68 pgs.; cardboard covers) (79 cents)
Whitman/Western Publishing Co.

	Good	Fine	Mint
1-Bolle-a	.30	.80	1.60
2-4-McWilliams & Bolle-a		.60	1.20

STAR STUDDED
1945 (25 cents; 132 pgs.); 1945 (196 pgs.)
Cambridge House/Superior Publishers

	Good	Fine	Mint
1-Captain Combat by Giunta, Ghost Woman, Commandette, & Red Rogue app.	5.50	16.00	32.00
nn-The Cadet, Edison Bell, Hoot Gibson, Jungle Lil (196 pgs.); copies vary - Blue Beetle in some	4.00	12.00	24.00

STAR TEAM
1977 (20 pgs.) (6½x5")
Marvel Comics Group (Ideal Toy Giveaway)

	Good	Fine	Mint
nn		.15	.30

STARTLING COMICS
June, 1940 - No. 53, May, 1948
Better Publications (Nedor)

	Good	Fine	Mint
1-Origin Captain Future, Mystico (By Eisner/Fine), the Wonder Man; The Masked Rider begins; drug use story	35.00	100.00	200.00
2	17.00	50.00	100.00
3	10.00	30.00	60.00
4	9.00	25.00	50.00
5-9	7.00	20.00	40.00
10-Origin & 1st app. The Fighting Yank	20.00	60.00	120.00
11-15	8.00	24.00	48.00
16-Origin The Four Comrades; not in No. 32,35; bondage-c	10.00	28.00	56.00
17-Last Masked Rider & Mystico	6.00	18.00	36.00
18-Origin Pyroman	14.00	40.00	80.00
19	7.00	20.00	40.00
20-The Oracle begins; not in No. 26,28,33,34	7.00	20.00	40.00
21-Origin The Ape, Oracle's enemy	5.00	15.00	30.00
22-30	5.00	15.00	30.00
31-33	5.00	15.00	30.00
34-Origin The Scarab & only app.	7.00	20.00	40.00
35-Hypodermic syringe attacks Fighting Yank in drug story	7.00	20.00	40.00
36-40: 36-Last Four Comrades. 40-Last Capt. Future & Oracle	5.00	15.00	30.00
41-Front Page Peggy begins	5.00	15.00	30.00
42,43-Last Pyroman	5.00	15.00	30.00
44-Lance Lewis, Space Detective begins; Ingels-c	10.00	28.00	56.00
45-Tygra begins (origin)	8.00	24.00	48.00
46-Ingels c/a	8.00	24.00	48.00
47-53: 49-Last Fighting Yank. 50,51-Sea-Eagle app.	5.50	16.00	32.00

NOTE: ***Ingels*** *c-44, 46(Wash).* ***Schomburg (Xela)*** *c-47-53 (airbrush).* ***Tuska*** *c-45? Bondage c-46-49.*

STARTLING TERROR TALES
5/52 - No. 14, 2/53; No. 4, 4/53 - No. 11, 1954
Star Publications

	Good	Fine	Mint
10-(1st Series)-Wood/Harrison-a (r-A Star Presentation No. 3) Disbrow/Cole-c	15.00	45.00	90.00
11-L. B. Cole Spider-c; r-Fox's "A Feat. Presentation No. 5"	7.00	20.00	40.00
12,14	5.00	14.00	28.00
13-Jo-Jo-r; Disbrow-a	3.50	10.00	20.00
4-7,9,11('53-54) (2nd Series)	3.00	9.00	18.00
8-Spanking scene; Palais-a(r)	3.50	10.00	20.00
10-Disbrow-a	4.00	12.00	24.00

NOTE: ***L. B. Cole*** *covers-all issues.* ***Palais*** *a-V2No.11r.*

STAR TREK (TV) (See Dan Curtis)
10/67; No. 2, 6/68; No. 3, 12/68; No. 4, 6/69 - No. 61, 4/79
Gold Key

	Good	Fine	Mint
1	7.00	20.00	40.00
2-5	3.50	10.00	20.00
6-10: 1-9-Photo-c	2.00	6.00	12.00
11-20	1.20	3.50	7.00
21-30	1.00	3.00	6.00
31-40	.50	1.50	3.00
41-61: 52-Drug propaganda story	.25	.70	1.40
...the Enterprise Logs nn(8/76)-Golden Press, 224 pgs. ($1.95) -Reprints No. 1-8 plus 7 pgs. by McWilliams (No. 11185)	1.00	3.00	6.00
...the Enterprise Logs Vol.2('76)-Reprints No. 9-17 (No. 11187)	.85	2.50	5.00
...the Enterprise Logs Vol.3('77)-Reprints No. 18-26 (No. 11188); four pgs. McWilliams	.70	2.00	4.00
Star Trek Vol.4(Winter'77)-Reprints No. 27,28,30-36,38 (No. 11189) plus three pgs. new art	.70	2.00	4.00

NOTE: ***McWilliams*** *a-38,40-57,60. No. 29 reprints No. 1; No. 35 reprints No. 4; No. 37 reprints No. 5; No. 45 reprints No. 7. The tabloids all have photo covers and blank inside covers.*

STAR TREK
April, 1980 - Present
Marvel Comics Group

	Good	Fine	Mint
1-r/Marvel Super Special		.50	1.00
2-10		.40	.80
11-17		.30	.60

NOTE: ***Buscema*** *a-13.* ***Chaykin*** *a-15.* ***Gil Kane*** *a-15.* ***Nasser*** *c/a-7.* ***Simonson*** *c-17.*

STAR WARS (Movie) (Also see Contemporary Motivators & Marvel Special Edition)
July, 1977 - Present
Marvel Comics Group

	Good	Fine	Mint
1-(Regular 30 cents edition)-Price in square w/UPC code	1.50	4.00	8.00
1-(35 cents cover price; limited distribution - 1500 copies?)- Price in square w/UPC code	3.00	8.00	16.00
2-4	.70	2.00	4.00
5-10	.50	1.50	3.00
11-16	.35	1.00	2.00
17-19	.50	1.50	3.00
20-30	.30	.90	1.80
31-37	.30	.80	1.60
38-Golden c/a	.35	1.00	2.00
39-The Empire Strikes Back r-begin, ends No. 44; Williamson c/a	.30	.90	1.80
40-44-Williamson c/a		.45	.90
45-49,51-55		.30	.60
50-(75 cents, 52pgs.) Williamson-a		.50	1.00

1-5-Reprints; has "reprint" in upper lefthand corner of cover or on

STAR WARS (continued) — Good / Fine / Mint
inside or price and number inside a diamond with no date or UPC on cover; 30 cents and 35 cents issues published — .40 / .80
Annual 1 (12/79) — .35 / 1.00 / 2.00

NOTE: ***Austin*** *c-12i-14i, 21i, 38.* ***Byrne*** *c-13p.* ***Chaykin*** *a-1-10; c-1.* ***Infantino*** *a-11-15p, 18-31p, 31-37, 47, 48, 53p, 54p; c-12, 14, 15, 18-31, 31-37, 48.* ***Leialoha*** *inks-2-5.* ***Simonson*** *a-16, 49-54; c-16, 49, 50i, 51-54.* ***Williamson*** *a-39p, 40-44, 46, 50; c-39, 40, 50p.*

STEEL, THE INDESTRUCTIBLE MAN
March, 1978 - No. 5, Oct-Nov, 1978
DC Comics, Inc.

	Good	Fine	Mint
1		.40	.80
2-4		.30	.60
5-Giant		.40	.80

STEVE CANYON (See 4-Color No. 519,578,641,737,804,939,1033, and Comics Hits No. 52)

STEVE CANYON
1959 (96 pgs.; no text; 6¾x9''; hardcover)(B&W inside)
Grosset & Dunlap

	Good	Fine	Mint
100100-Reprints 2 stories from strip (1953, 1957)	3.00	8.00	16.00
100100 (softcover edition)	2.50	7.00	14.00

STEVE CANYON COMICS
Feb, 1948 - No. 6, Dec, 1948 (Strip reprints) No. 4,5-52pgs.
Harvey Publications

	Good	Fine	Mint
1-Origin; has biog of Milton Caniff; Powell-a, 2pgs.; Caniff-a	13.00	38.00	76.00
2-6: Caniff, Powell-a in all	8.00	23.00	46.00
Dept. Store giveaway No. 3(6/48, 36pp)	8.00	23.00	46.00
Strictly for the Smart Birds-16 pgs., 1951; Information Comics Div. (Harvey) Premium	8.00	23.00	46.00

STEVE DONOVAN, WESTERN MARSHAL (TV)
1956
Dell Publishing Co.

	Good	Fine	Mint
4-Color 675,768-Kinstler-a	1.50	4.50	9.00
4-Color 880, 1	1.00	3.00	6.00

STEVE ROPER
April, 1948 - No. 5, Dec, 1948
Famous Funnies

	Good	Fine	Mint
1-Contains 1944 daily newspaper-r	2.00	5.00	10.00
2-5	1.20	3.50	7.00

STEVE SAUNDERS SPECIAL AGENT (See Special Agent)

STEVE SAVAGE (See Captain . . .)

STEVE ZODIAC & THE FIRE BALL XL-5 (TV)
January, 1964
Gold Key

	Good	Fine	Mint
1 (10108-401)	1.50	4.00	8.00

STEVIE
1952 - No. 6, April, 1954
Harvey Magazine Publ./Mazie (Magazine Publ.)

	Good	Fine	Mint
1	1.00	3.00	6.00
2-6	.85	2.50	5.00

STEVIE MAZIE'S BOY FRIEND (See Harvey Hits No. 5)

STONEY BURKE (TV)
June-Aug, 1963 - No. 2, Sept-Nov, 1963
Dell Publishing Co.

	Good	Fine	Mint
1,2	.70	2.00	4.00

STONY CRAIG
1946 (No No.)
Pentagon Publishing Co.

	Good	Fine	Mint
Reprints Bell Syndicate's ''Sgt. Stony Craig'' newspaper strips	2.00	5.00	10.00

STORIES BY FAMOUS AUTHORS ILLUSTRATED (Fast Fiction No.1-5)
Fall, 1950 - No. 13, May, 1951
Seaboard Publ./Famous Authors Ill.

	Good	Fine	Mint
1-Scarlet Pimpernel-Baroness Orczy	5.00	15.00	30.00
2-Capt. Blood-Rafael Sabatini	5.00	15.00	30.00
3-She, by Haggard	7.00	20.00	40.00
4-The 39 Steps-John Buchan	3.50	10.00	20.00
5-Beau Geste-P. C. Wren	3.50	10.00	20.00

NOTE: The above five issues are exact reprints of Fast Fiction No. 1-5 except for the title change and new Kiefer covers on No. 1 and 2. The above 5 issues were released before Famous Authors No. 6.

	Good	Fine	Mint
6-Macbeth, by Shakespeare; Kiefer art (8/50); used in **SOTI**, pg. 22,143.	6.00	18.00	36.00
7-The Window; Kiefer-a	3.50	10.00	20.00
8-Hamlet, by Shakespeare; Kiefer-a	6.00	18.00	36.00
9-Nicholas Nickleby, by Dickens; G. Schrotter-a	3.50	10.00	20.00
10-Romeo & Juliet, by Shakespeare; Kiefer-a	3.50	10.00	20.00
11-Ben-Hur; Schrotter-a	5.00	15.00	30.00
12-La Svengali; Schrotter-a	5.00	15.00	30.00
13-Scaramouche; Kiefer-a	5.00	15.00	30.00

STORIES OF CHRISTMAS
1942 (32 pages; paper cover) (Giveaway)
K. K. Publications

	Good	Fine	Mint
Adaptation of ''A Christmas Carol;'' Kelly story-''The Fir Tree'' Infinity-c	40.00	100.00	200.00

STORIES OF ROMANCE (Formerly Matt Slade Gunfighter?)
No. 5, Mar, 1956 - No. 13, Aug, 1957
Atlas Comics (LMC)

	Good	Fine	Mint
5-13	.85	2.50	5.00

NOTE: ***Coletta*** *a-9(2).* ***Ann Brewster*** *a-13.*

STORMY (See 4-Color No. 537)

STORY HOUR SERIES (Disney)
1948, 1949; 1951-1953 (36 pgs.) (4½x6¼'')
Given away with subscription to Walt Disney's Comics & Stories
Whitman Publishing Co.

	Good	Fine	Mint
nn(1949)-Johnny Appleseed(B&W & color)	2.50	7.00	14.00
nn(1949)-The Three Orphan Kittens(B&W & color)	2.50	7.00	14.00
800-Donald Duck in ''Bringing Up the Boys;'' 1948 Paper Cover	7.00	20.00	40.00
1953	3.00	9.00	18.00
801-Mickey Mouse's Summer Vacation 1948 Paper Cover	4.00	12.00	24.00
1951, 1952 edition	2.00	6.00	12.00
803-Bongo 1948 Paper Cover	3.00	8.00	16.00
804-Mickey and the Beanstalk 1948 Paper Cover	3.50	10.00	20.00

1948 Hard Cover Edition of each . . . . $2.00 - $3.00 more

STORY OF CHECKS, THE
1972 (5th edition)
Federal Reserve Bank of New York

	Good	Fine	Mint
Severin-a	.30	.90	1.80

STORY OF EDISON, THE
1956 (16 pgs.) (Reddy Killowatt)
Educational Comics

	Good	Fine	Mint
Reprint of Reddy Killowatt No. 2(1947)	4.00	12.00	24.00

STORY OF HARRY S. TRUMAN, THE

Steel #3, © DC

Stony Craig nn, © Pentagon Publ.

Stories By Famous Authors #13, © Seaboard

Straight Arrow #5, © ME

Strange Adventures #206, © DC

Strange Fantasy #9, © AJAX

STORY OF HARRY S. TRUMAN (continued)
1948 (16 pgs.) (in color, regular size)
Democratic National Committee (Giveaway)

	Good	Fine	Mint
Gives biography on career of Truman; used in **SOTI**, pg. 311	10.00	28.00	56.00

STORY OF JESUS (See Classics Special)

STORY OF MANKIND, THE (See 4-Color No. 851)

STORY OF MARTHA WAYNE, THE
April, 1956
Argo Publ.

	Good	Fine	Mint
1-Newspaper-r	1.00	3.00	6.00

STORY OF RUTH, THE (See 4-Color No. 1144)

STORY OF THE COMMANDOS, THE (Combined Operations)
1943 (68 pgs.; B&W) (15 cents)
Long Island Independent (Distr. by Gilberton)

	Good	Fine	Mint
nn-All text (no comics); photos & illustrations; ads for Classics Comics on back cover (Rare)	7.00	20.00	40.00

STORY OF THE GLOOMY BUNNY, THE (See March of Comics No. 9)

STRAIGHT ARROW
Feb-Mar, 1950 - No. 55, Mar, 1956
Magazine Enterprises

	Good	Fine	Mint
1-Whitney-a	10.00	30.00	60.00
2-Red Hawk begins by Powell, ends No. 55	5.00	14.00	28.00
3-Frazetta-c	12.00	35.00	70.00
4-10	2.50	7.00	14.00
11-20	1.50	4.00	8.00
21,23-35,37-40	1.20	3.50	7.00
22-Frazetta-c	9.00	25.00	50.00
36-Drug story	3.50	9.00	18.00
41-55	1.50	4.00	8.00

NOTE: ***Powell*** *art in all.*

STRAIGHT ARROW'S FURY (See A-1 Comics No. 119)

STRANGE
March, 1957 - No. 6, May, 1958
Ajax-Farrell Publ. (Four Star Comic Corp.)

	Good	Fine	Mint
1	2.00	6.00	12.00
2-6	1.20	3.50	7.00

STRANGE ADVENTURES
Aug-Sept, 1950 - No. 244, Oct-Nov, 1973 (No. 1-12: 52 pgs.)
National Periodical Publications

	Good	Fine	Mint
1-Adaptation of "Destination Moon;" Kris KL-99 & Darwin Jones begin	40.00	120.00	240.00
2	20.00	60.00	120.00
3-4: 4-Kirby-a	12.00	36.00	72.00
5-8,10: 7-Origin Kris KL-99	10.00	30.00	60.00
9-Intro. & origin Captain Comet (6/51)	30.00	80.00	185.00
11,14-16,20	7.00	20.00	40.00
12,13,17-Toth-a	9.00	25.00	50.00
18,19	6.00	16.00	32.00
21-30	5.00	14.00	28.00
31,34-38	3.50	10.00	20.00
32,33-Krigstein-a	6.00	16.00	32.00
39-Ill. in **SOTI**-"Treating police contemptuously" (top right)	12.00	35.00	70.00
40-49-Last Capt. Comet; not in 45,47,48	3.50	10.00	20.00
50-53-Last pre-code issue	3.00	8.00	16.00
54-70	2.00	5.00	10.00
71-100	1.50	4.00	8.00
101-110: 104-Space Museum begins by Sekowsky	1.00	3.00	6.00
111-116,118-120: 114-Star Hawkins begins, ends No. 185	.85	2.50	5.00
117-Origin Atomic Knights	5.00	15.00	30.00
121-140: 124-Origin Faceless Creature	.70	2.00	4.00
141-160: 159-Star Rovers app. 160-Last Atomic Knights	.35	1.00	2.00
161-179: 161-Last Space Museum. 163-Star Rovers app. 170-Infinity-c. 177-Origin Immortal Man	.30	.90	1.80
180-Origin Animal Man	.35	1.00	2.00
181-186,188-204: 190-Last Animal Man		.60	1.20
187-Origin The Enchantress		.60	1.20
205-Intro & Origin Deadman by Infantino; drug mention story	4.00	12.00	24.00
206-Adams-a begins	2.50	7.50	15.00
207-210	2.00	6.00	12.00
211-216-Last Deadman	1.75	5.00	10.00
217-Adam Strange & Atomic Knights-r begin		.50	1.00
218-225: 222-New Adam Strange story by Gil Kane		.40	.80
226-231(All 68 pgs.): 226-Atomic blast-c. 231-Last Atomic Knights-r		.40	.80
232-236(All 52 pgs.): Star Rovers app.-No. 232-234,236		.30	.60
237-244		.30	.60

NOTE: ***Adams*** *a-206-216, 228, 235; c-207-218, 228, 228, 235.* ***Anderson*** *a-8-52, 94, 96, 97, 99, 115, 117, 119-163, 222, 226; c/r-217-233, 235-239, 241-243.* ***Ditko*** *a-188, 189.* ***Drucker*** *a-42, 43, 45.* ***Finlay*** *a-2, 3, 6, 7, 210r, 229r.* ***Infantino*** *a-10-101, 106-151, 154, 157-163, 180, 190; c/r-197, 199-211, 218-221, 223-244.* ***Kaluta*** *c-238, 240.* ***Gil Kane*** *a-8-116, 124, 125, 130, 138, 146-157, 173-186; 204r, 222r, 227-231r.* ***Kubert*** *a-55(2 pgs.), 226; c-219, 220, 225-227, 232, 234.* ***Morrow*** *c-230.* ***Powell*** *a-4.* ***Mike Sekowsky*** *a-97-162; c-206, 217-219r.* ***Simon & Kirby*** *a-2r (2 pg.)* ***Toth*** *a-8, 12, 13, 17-19.* ***Wood*** *a-154i.* ***Chris KL99*** *in 1-3, 5, 7, 9, 11, 15.* ***Capt. Comet*** *covers-9-14, 17-19, 24, 26, 27, 32-44.*

STRANGE AS IT SEEMS
1932 (64 pgs.; B&W; square binding)
Blue-Star Publishing Co.

	Good	Fine	Mint
1-Newspaper-r	8.00	24.00	48.00

NOTE: *Published with and without No. 1 and price on cover.*

	Good	Fine	Mint
Ex-Lax giveaway(1936,24pgs,5x7",B&W)-McNaught Synd.	2.00	6.00	12.00

STRANGE AS IT SEEMS
1939
United Features Syndicate

	Good	Fine	Mint
Single Series 9, 1,2	7.00	20.00	40.00

STRANGE CONFESSIONS
Jan-Mar, 1952 - No. 4, Fall, 1952
Ziff-Davis Publ. Co. (Approved)

	Good	Fine	Mint
1(Scarce)-Photo-c; Kinstler-a	10.00	30.00	75.00
2,3(Scarce)	6.00	16.00	40.00
4(Scarce)-Reformatory girl story	6.00	16.00	40.00

STRANGE FANTASY
Aug, 1952 - No. 14, Oct-Nov, 1954
Harvey Publ./Ajax-Farrell No. 2 on

	Good	Fine	Mint
1-The Black Cat app.	7.00	20.00	40.00
2(8/52)-Jungle Princess story; no Black Cat; Kamenish-a	3.50	10.00	20.00
2(10/52)-No Black Cat or Rulah; Bakerish, Kamenish-a	4.00	12.00	24.00
3-Rulah story, called Pulah	4.00	12.00	24.00
4-Rocket Man app.	3.50	10.00	20.00
5,6,8,10,12,14	2.00	6.00	12.00
7-Madam Satan/Slave story	3.00	8.00	16.00
9(w/Black Cat), 9(w/Boy's Ranch; S&K-a)	4.00	12.00	24.00
9-Regular issue	2.50	7.00	14.00
11-Jungle story	3.00	8.00	16.00
13-Bondage-c; Rulah (Kolah) story	4.00	12.00	24.00

STRANGE GALAXY (Magazine)
V1No.8, Feb, 1971 - No. 11, Aug, 1971 (B&W)

STRANGE GALAXY (continued)
Eerie Publications

	Good	Fine	Mint
V1No.8-Cover reprinted from Fantastic V19No.3 (2/70) (a pulp)		.60	1.20
9-11		.60	1.20

STRANGE JOURNEY
Sept, 1957 - No. 4, June, 1958 (Farrell reprints)
America's Best (Steinway Publ.) (Ajax/Farrell)

	Good	Fine	Mint
1	3.00	8.00	16.00
2-4	2.00	6.00	12.00

STRANGE LOVE
1950 (132 pages)
Hero Books/Fox Features Syndicate

nn-Photo-c. See Fox Giants. Contents can vary and determines price.

STRANGE MYSTERIES
Sept, 1951 - No. 21, Dec, 1954
Superior/Dynamic Publications

	Good	Fine	Mint
1-Bondage-a	6.00	18.00	36.00
2-All Kamenish-a	4.00	12.00	24.00
3-5	3.00	9.00	18.00
6-8: 6,7-Kamenish-a	2.00	6.00	12.00
9-Bondage 3-D effect-c	2.50	7.00	14.00
10-Used in **SOTI**, pg. 181	3.00	9.00	18.00
11,13-16	1.50	4.50	9.00
12,17,18-Kamenish-a	3.00	9.00	18.00
19-Bakerish-c/a; Kamenish-a	5.00	14.00	28.00
20,21-Kamenish-a	3.50	10.00	20.00

STRANGE MYSTERIES
1963 - 1964
I. W. Enterprises/Super Comics

	Good	Fine	Mint
I.W. Reprint No. 9	.60	1.80	3.60
Super Reprint No. 10-12,15-17('63-'64): No. 12-reprints Tales of Horror No. 5 (3/53) less cover. No. 15,16-reprints The Dead Who Walk	.60	1.80	3.60
Super Reprint No. 18-Reprint of Witchcraft No. 1; Kubert-a	.60	1.80	3.60

STRANGE PLANETS
1958; 1963-64
I. W. Enterprises/Super Comics

	Good	Fine	Mint
I.W. Reprint No. 1(no date)-E. C. Incredible S/F No. 30 plus-c/Strange Worlds No. 3	5.00	14.00	28.00
I.W. Reprint No. 8	1.50	4.00	8.00
I.W. Reprint No. 9-Orlando/Wood-a (Strange Worlds No. 4); c-from Flying Saucers No. 1	4.00	12.00	24.00
Super Reprint No. 10-22 pg. Wood-a from Space Detective No. 1; c-/Attack on Planet Mars	4.00	12.00	24.00
Super Reprint No. 11-25 pg. Wood-a from An Earthman on Venus	7.00	20.00	40.00
Super Reprint No. 12-Orlando-a from Rocket to the Moon	5.00	15.00	30.00
Super Reprint No. 15-Reprints Atlas stories; Heath-a	1.50	4.00	8.00
Super Reprint No. 16-Avon's Strange Worlds No. 6; Kinstler, Check art	2.00	5.00	10.00
Super Reprint No. 17	1.50	4.00	8.00
Super Reprint No. 18-Reprints Daring Adventures; Space Busters, Explorer Joe, The Son of Robin Hood; Krigstein-a	2.00	5.00	10.00

STRANGE SPORTS STORIES (See Brave & the Bold, DC Special, and DC Super Stars No. 10)
Sept-Oct, 1973 - No. 6, July-Aug, 1974
National Periodical Publications

	Good	Fine	Mint
1		.30	.60
2-6: 3-Swan/Anderson-a		.25	.50

STRANGE STORIES FROM ANOTHER WORLD (Unknown World No. 1)
No. 2, Aug, 1952 - No. 5, Feb, 1953
Fawcett Publications

	Good	Fine	Mint
2-5-Saunders painted-c	4.00	12.00	24.00

STRANGE STORIES OF SUSPENSE (Rugged Action No. 1-4)
No. 5, Oct, 1955 - No. 16, Aug, 1957
Atlas Comics (CSI)

	Good	Fine	Mint
5(No.1)	3.00	8.00	16.00
6,9	1.50	4.00	8.00
7-E. C. swipe cover/Vault of Horror No. 32	2.00	6.00	12.00
8-Williamson/Mayo-a; Pakula-a	3.50	10.00	20.00
10-Crandall, Torres, Meskin-a	3.50	10.00	20.00
11,13	1.20	3.50	7.00
12-Torres, Pakula-a	2.00	6.00	12.00
14-Williamson-a	3.00	9.00	18.00
15-Krigstein-a	2.50	7.00	14.00
16-Fox, Powell-a	2.50	7.00	14.00

NOTE: ***Everett*** *a-6, 7, 13; c-9, 11-13.* ***Morrow*** *a-13.*

STRANGE STORY (Also see Front Page)
June-July, 1946 (52 pages)
Harvey Publications

	Good	Fine	Mint
1-The Man in Black Called Fate by Powell	4.50	13.00	26.00

STRANGE SUSPENSE STORIES (Lawbreakers Suspense Stories No. 6-15; This Is Suspense No. 23 on; Captain Atom V1No.78 on)
June, 1952 - No. 5, Feb, 1953; No. 16, Jan, 1954 - No. 77, Oct, 1965; V3No. 1, Oct, 1967 - V1No.9, Sept, 1969 (No. 23-26 Exist?)
Fawcett Publications/Charlton Comics No. 16 on

	Good	Fine	Mint
1-(Fawcett)-Powell, Sekowsky-a	7.00	20.00	40.00
2-5: 2-5-George Evans horror stories	3.50	10.00	20.00
16(1/54)	3.00	8.00	16.00
17,21,23-Last pre-code issue	2.00	6.00	12.00
18,20-Ditko-c/a(2)	4.00	12.00	24.00
19-Ditko electric chair-c; Ditko-a	6.00	16.00	32.00
22(11/54)-Ditko-c/a, Shuster-a	3.50	10.00	20.00
27-30,35,38,40,42-44,46,48,49,53-67	1.20	3.50	7.00
31-33,37,39,41,45,47,50-52-Ditko-a	2.00	5.00	10.00
34-Story of ruthless business man-Wm. B. Gaines; Ditko-c/a	2.50	7.00	14.00
36-(68 pgs.); Ditko-a	4.00	12.00	24.00
68-74	.50	1.50	3.00
75-Origin Captain Atom by Ditko-r/Space Advs.	4.00	12.00	24.00
76,77-Ditko Captain Atom-r/Space Advs.	1.50	4.00	8.00
V3No.1(10/67)-4		.40	.80
V1No.2-9: 2-Ditko-a		.30	.60

NOTE: ***Alascia*** *a-19.* ***Bailey*** *a-1-3; c-5* ***Evans*** *c-3.* ***Shuster*** *a-19, 21.*

STRANGE TALES (Dr. Strange No. 169 on)
6/51 - No. 168, 5/68; No. 169, 9/73 - No. 188, 11/76
Atlas (CCPC No. 1-67/ZPC No. 68-79/VPI No. 80-107)/Marvel No. 108 on

	Good	Fine	Mint
1	50.00	120.00	250.00
2	17.00	50.00	110.00
3-5	14.00	40.00	80.00
6-9	9.50	28.00	56.00
10-Krigstein-a	10.00	30.00	60.00
11-14,16-20	4.00	12.00	24.00
15-Krigstein-a	5.00	14.00	28.00
21,23-27,29-32,34	3.00	9.00	18.00
22-Krigstein-a	3.50	10.00	20.00
28-Jack Katz-a	3.50	10.00	20.00
33-Davis-a	3.50	10.00	20.00
35-41,43,44,46-52,54,55,57,60	2.00	6.00	12.00
42,45,59,61-Krigstein-a	3.00	9.00	18.00
53-Torres, Crandall-a	3.50	10.00	20.00
56-Crandall-a	3.00	9.00	18.00
58,64-Williamson-a in each, with Mayo-No. 58			

Strange Mysteries #19, © SUPR

Strange Suspense Stories #36, © CC

Strange Tales #11, © MCG

Strange Tales #101, © MCG

Str. Tales Of The Unusual #8, © MCG

Strange Worlds #2, © MCG

STRANGE TALES (continued)

	Good	Fine	Mint
	3.50	10.00	20.00
62-Torres-a	2.00	6.00	12.00
63,65,66	1.75	5.00	10.00
67-80-Ditko/Kirby in all	1.75	5.00	10.00
81-90-Ditko/Kirby in all	1.50	4.00	8.00
91-96,98-100-Kirby-a	1.50	4.00	8.00
97-Aunt May app.; Kirby-a	2.00	6.00	12.00
101-Human Torch begins by Jack Kirby (10/62)	14.00	40.00	90.00
102	7.00	20.00	40.00
103-105	6.00	16.00	32.00
106,108,109	3.50	10.00	20.00
107-Human Torch/Sub-Mariner battle	4.00	12.00	24.00
110-Intro Dr. Strange, Ancient One & Wong by Ditko	10.00	30.00	60.00
111	3.00	9.00	18.00
112,113	2.00	5.00	10.00
114-Acrobat disguised as Captain America, 1st app. since the G.A.; intro. & 1st app. Victoria Bentley	2.50	7.00	14.00
115-Origin Dr. Strange	4.00	12.00	24.00
116-120	1.00	3.00	6.00
121-125	.70	2.00	4.00
126-129,131-133: Thing/Torch team-up in all; 126-Intro Clea; last Human Torch-No. 134	.70	2.00	4.00
130-The Beatles cameo	1.20	3.50	7.00
134-Last Human Torch; Wood-a(i)	.70	2.00	4.00
135-Origin Nick Fury, Agent of Shield by Kirby	1.20	3.50	7.00
136-147,149: 146-Last Ditko Dr. Strange who is in consecutive stories since No. 113	.40	1.20	2.40
148-Origin Ancient One	.50	1.50	3.00
150(11/66)-J. Buscema 1st work at Marvel	.40	1.20	2.40
151-1st Marvel work by Steranko (with Kirby)	.50	1.50	3.00
152,153-Kirby/Steranko-a	.40	1.20	2.40
154-158-Steranko-a/script	.40	1.20	2.40
159-Origin Nick Fury; Intro Val; Captain America app; Steranko-a	.50	1.50	3.00
160-162-Steranko-a/scripts; Capt. America app.	.40	1.20	2.40
163-166,168-Steranko-a(p)	.35	1.10	2.20
167-Steranko pen/script; classic cover	.50	1.50	3.00
169,170-Brother Voodoo origin in each; series ends No. 173		.40	.80
171-177: 174-Origin Golem. 177-Brunner-c		.40	.80
178-Warlock by Starlin with covers; origin Warlock & Him	.85	2.50	5.00
179-181-Warlock by Starlin with covers	.50	1.50	3.00
182-188		.30	.60
Annual 1(1962)-Reprints from Str. Tales No. 73,76,78, Tales of Suspense No. 7,9, Tales to Astonish No. 1,6,7, & Journey Into Mystery No. 53,55,59	6.00	18.00	36.00
Annual 2(1963)-Reprints from Str. Tales No. 67, Str. Worlds (Atlas) No. 1-3, World of Fantasy No. 16; Human Torch vs. Spider-Man by Ditko/Kirby; Kirby-c	5.00	15.00	30.00

NOTE: ***Briefer*** *a-17.* ***Colan*** *a-11, 20.* ***Davis*** *c-71.* ***Ditko*** *a-50, 67-146, 175r, 182-188r.* ***Everett*** *a-40-42, 45, 73, 147-152, 164i; c-10, 11, 13, 24, 50, 51, 150, 152.* ***Heath*** *c-20.* ***G. Kane*** *c-170-73.* ***Kirby*** *Human Torch-101-105, 108, 109, 114, 120; Nick Fury (pencils)-135, 141-143; (layouts)-136-140, 144-153; other* ***Kirby*** *a-73, 153; layouts-135-140, 144-153; c-68-70, 72-92, 94, 101-140.* ***Leiber/Fox*** *a-110, 111, 113.* ***Maneely*** *a-42.* ***Moldoff*** *a-20.* ***Orlando*** *a-41, 44, 46, 49, 52.* ***Powell*** *a-42, 44, 49, 131-133, 134p.* ***Robinson*** *a-17.* ***Wildey*** *a-42.* ***Woodbridge*** *a-59. Fantastic Four cameo-101-134. Jack Katz app.-26.*

STRANGE TALES OF THE UNUSUAL
Dec, 1955 - No. 11, Sept, 1957
Atlas Comics (ACI No. 1-4/WPI No. 5-12)

	Good	Fine	Mint
1-Powell-a	4.00	12.00	24.00
2,4,6,8,11	1.20	3.50	7.00
3-Williamson-a, 4 pgs.	4.00	12.00	24.00
5-Crandall, Ditko-a	2.50	7.00	14.00
7-Kirby, Orlando-a	2.00	6.00	12.00
9-Krigstein-a	2.50	7.00	14.00
10-Torres, Morrow-a	2.00	6.00	12.00

NOTE: ***Bailey*** *a-6.* ***Everett*** *a-2, 6; c-6, 11.* ***Orlando*** *a-7.*

STRANGE TERRORS
June, 1952 - No. 7, June, 1953
St. John Publishing Co.

	Good	Fine	Mint
1-Bondage-c; Zombies spelled Zoombies on-c; Finesque-a	6.00	16.00	32.00
2	3.00	8.00	16.00
3-Kubert-a; painted-c	6.00	16.00	32.00
4-Kubert-a (reprinted in Mystery Tales No. 18); Ekgren-c; Fine-esque-a; Jerry Iger caricature	10.00	30.00	60.00
5-Kubert-a	5.00	14.00	28.00
6-Giant, 100 pgs.; Cameron-a (3/53)	7.00	20.00	40.00
7-Giant, 100 pgs.; Kubert c/a	10.00	28.00	60.00

STRANGE WORLD OF YOUR DREAMS
Aug, 1952 - No. 4, Jan-Feb, 1953
Prize Publications

	Good	Fine	Mint
1-Simon & Kirby-a	12.00	35.00	70.00
2,3-Simon & Kirby-a	10.00	28.00	56.00
4-S&K-c; Meskin?-a	9.00	25.00	50.00

STRANGE WORLDS (No. 18 continued from Avon's Eerie No. 1-17)
Nov, 1950 - No. 22, Sept-Oct, 1955
Avon Periodicals

	Good	Fine	Mint
1-Kenton of the Star Patrol by Kubert(Reprint/Eerie No.1-'47); Crom the Barbarian by John Giunta	30.00	80.00	165.00
2-Wood-a; Crom the Barbarian by Giunta; Dara of the Vikings app.; used in **SOTI**, pg. 112; injury to eye panel	30.00	80.00	165.00
3-Wood/Orlando-a (Kenton), Wood/Williamson/Frazetta/Krenkel/Orlando-a (7 pgs.); Malu Slave Girl Princess app.; Kinstler-c	75.00	220.00	450.00
4-Wood c/a (Kenton); Orlando-a; origin The Enchanted Daggar; Sultan-a	25.00	75.00	150.00
5-Orlando/Wood-a (Kenton); Wood-c	20.00	60.00	135.00
6-Kinstler-a(2); Orlando/Wood-c, Check-a	11.00	32.00	70.00
7-Kinstler, Fawcette & Becker/Alascia-a	9.00	25.00	55.00
8-Kubert, Kinstler, Hollingsworth & Lazarus stories; Lazarus-c	10.00	30.00	65.00
9-Kinstler, Fawcette, Alascia-a	9.00	25.00	55.00
10	8.00	22.00	50.00
18-Reprints "Attack on Planet Mars" by Kubert	10.00	28.00	60.00
19-Reprints Avon's Robotmen of the Lost Planet	10.00	28.00	60.00
20-War stories; Wood-c(r)/U.S. Paratroops No. 1	3.00	8.00	16.00
21,22-War stories	3.00	8.00	16.00
I.W. Reprint No. 5-Kinstler-a(r)/Avon's No. 9	1.50	4.00	8.00

STRANGE WORLDS
Dec, 1958 - No. 5, July-Aug, 1959
Marvel Comics (MPI No. 1,2/Male No. 3,5)

	Good	Fine	Mint
1-Kirby & Ditko-a	6.00	18.00	36.00
2-Ditko c/a	4.00	12.00	24.00
3-Kirby-a(2)	4.00	12.00	24.00
4-Williamson-a	6.00	18.00	36.00
5-Ditko-a	3.00	9.00	18.00

NOTE: ***Buscema*** *a-3.* ***Ditko*** *a-1-5; c-2.* ***Kirby*** *a-1, 3; c-1, 3-5.*

STREET COMIX (50 cents)
1973 (36 pgs.; B&W) (20,000 print run)
Street Enterprises/King Features

	Good	Fine	Mint
1-Rip Kirby		.40	.80
2-Flash Gordon		.60	1.20

STRICTLY PRIVATE
1942
Eastern Color Printing Co.

	Good	Fine	Mint
1,2	6.00	18.00	36.00

STRONG MAN (Also see Complimentary Comics)
Mar-Apr, 1955 - No. 4, Sept-Oct, 1955
Magazine Enterprises

	Good	Fine	Mint
1(A-1 130)-Powell-a	5.00	15.00	30.00
2(A-1 132), 3(A-1 134), 4(A-1 139)-Powell-a	4.00	12.00	24.00

STUMBO THE GIANT (See Harvey Hits No. 49,54,57,60,63,66,69, 72,78,88)

STUMBO TINYTOWN
Oct, 1963 - No. 13, Nov, 1966
Harvey Publications

	Good	Fine	Mint
1	8.00	24.00	48.00
2	4.00	12.00	24.00
3-5	3.00	8.00	16.00
6-13	2.00	5.00	10.00

STUNTMAN COMICS
Apr-May, 1946 - No. 2, June-July, 1946; No. 3, Oct-Nov, 1946
Harvey Publications

	Good	Fine	Mint
1-Origin Stuntman by S&K reprinted in Black Cat No. 9	60.00	150.00	300.00
2-S&K-a	30.00	90.00	180.00
3-Small size (5½x8½''; B&W; 32 pgs.); distributed to mail subscribers only; S&K-a; Kid Adonis by S&K reprinted in Green Hornet No. 37. (Sold in San Francisco, 1976 for $700.00)			

(Also see All-New No. 15, Boy Explorers No. 2, & Flash Gordon No. 5)

SUBMARINE ATTACK (Formerly Speed Demons)
No. 11, May, 1958 - No. 60, Feb, 1967
Charlton Comics

	Good	Fine	Mint
11-20	.30	.90	1.80
21-60		.60	1.20

NOTE: ***Montes/Bache** a-38, 40, 41.*

SUB-MARINER (See All-Winners, Blonde Phantom, Daring, Human Torch, Marvel Mystery, Motion Picture Funnies Weekly, & Namora)

SUB-MARINER, THE (2nd Series)
May, 1968 - No. 72, Sept, 1974 (No. 43: 52 pgs.)
Marvel Comics Group

	Good	Fine	Mint
1-Origin Sub-Mariner	2.00	6.00	12.00
2-Triton app.	1.00	3.00	6.00
3-5: 5-1st Tiger Shark	.70	2.00	4.00
6-10: 8-The Thing app.	.50	1.50	3.00
11-13,15-18,20	.40	1.20	2.40
14-Sub-Mariner vs. G.A. Human Torch	.50	1.50	3.00
19-1st app. Sting Ray	.30	.90	1.80
21-30: 26-Red Raven app. 30-Capt. Marvel app.		.60	1.20
31-33,37,39,40: 37-Death of Lady Dorma		.60	1.20
34-Silver Surfer, Hulk app.	.30	.80	1.60
35-Ties into 1st Defenders story; Avengers, Silver Surfer, Hulk app.	.40	1.20	2.40
36-Wrightson inks	.40	1.20	2.40
38-Origin	.40	1.20	2.40
41,42,45,47-49		.50	1.00
43-(52 pgs.)		.50	1.00
44-Sub-Mariner vs. Human Torch		.50	1.00
46-Death of S-M father, Capt. MacKenzie		.50	1.00
50-55,58,60-Everett-a. 50-1st app. Nita, Namor's niece. 52,53-Sunfire app.		.50	1.00
56		.50	1.00
57-All Everett issue		.50	1.00
59-Everett-c	.35	1.10	2.20
61-Last artwork by Everett; 1st 4 pgs. completed by Mortimer; pgs. 5-20 by Mooney	.40	1.20	2.40
62-1st Tales of Atlantis, ends No. 66		.40	.80
63-72		.40	.80
Special 1(1971)	.35	1.10	2.20
Annual 2(1/72)-Everett-a	.30	.80	1.60

NOTE: ***Buscema** a-1-8p. **Chaykin** a-62-64. **Craig** a-19-21i. **Weiss** a-54.*

SUB-MARINER (1st Series) (. . . Comics No. 3 on) (Best Love No. 33 on) (Amazing Mysteries No. 32 on)
Spring, 1941 - No. 32, 7/49; No. 33, 4/54 - No. 42, 10/55
Timely No. 1-32 (MPC)/Atlas No. 33-42 (CCC)

	Good	Fine	Mint
1-The Sub-Mariner by Everett & The Angel begin	280.00	750.00	1600.00
2-Everett-a	120.00	350.00	800.00
3	85.00	235.00	500.00
4-Everett-a, 40 pgs.; 1 pg. Wolverton-a	80.00	225.00	475.00
5	60.00	155.00	320.00
6-10: 9-Wolverton-a, 3 pgs.	40.00	115.00	250.00
11-15: 13-Bondage-c	30.00	80.00	170.00
16-20	26.00	65.00	150.00
21-Last Angel; Everett-a	18.00	52.00	105.00
22-Young Allies app.; Everett-a	18.00	52.00	105.00
23-The Human Torch, Namora x-over	18.00	52.00	105.00
24-Namora x-over	18.00	52.00	105.00
25-The Blonde Phantom begins, ends No. 31; Kurtzman-a; Namora x-over	25.00	70.00	140.00
26,27	20.00	60.00	120.00
28-Namora cover plus story by Everett	20.00	60.00	120.00
29-31: 29-The Human Torch app. 31-Capt. America app.	20.00	60.00	120.00
32-Origin Sub-Mariner	30.00	85.00	180.00
33-Origin Sub-Mariner; The Human Torch app.; Namora x-over in Sub-Mariner, No. 33-42	17.00	50.00	100.00
34,35-Human Torch in each. 34-Bondage-c	14.00	40.00	80.00
36-41: 36,38,39-Namora app.	14.00	40.00	80.00
42-Last issue	15.00	45.00	90.00

NOTE: *Angel by **Gustavson**-No. 1. **Everett** art in all; c-1, 2. **Schomburg** c-10, 14.*

SUE & SALLY SMITH (Formerly My Secret Life)
1963 (Flying Nurses)
Charlton Comics

	Good	Fine	Mint
V2No.48-54		.20	.40

SUGAR & SPIKE
Apr-May, 1956 - No. 98, Oct-Nov, 1971
National Periodical Publications

	Good	Fine	Mint
1 (Scarce)	30.00	90.00	200.00
2	14.00	40.00	80.00
3-5	10.00	30.00	60.00
6-10	7.00	20.00	40.00
11-20	6.00	16.00	32.00
21-29,31-40	2.50	7.00	14.00
30-Scribbly x-over	4.00	12.00	24.00
41-98: 72-Origin & 1st app. Bernie the Brain. 85-68 pgs.; reprints No. 72. No. 96-68 pgs. No. 97,98-52 pgs.	1.00	3.00	6.00

NOTE: *All written and drawn by **Sheldon Mayer**.*

SUGAR BEAR
No date (16 pages) (2½x4½'')
Post Cereal Giveaway

	Good	Fine	Mint
''The Almost Take Over of the Post Office,'' ''The Race Across the Atlantic,'' ''The Zoo Goes Wild'' each. . .		.40	.80

SUGAR BOWL COMICS
May, 1948 - 1949

Sub-Mariner #8(2nd), © MCG

Sub-Mariner #13(1st), © MCG

Sugar & Spike #26, © DC

Summer Fun #2, © WDP

Sun Girl #1, © MCG

Superboy #5, © DC

SUGAR BOWL COMICS (continued)
Famous Funnies

	Good	Fine	Mint
1-Toth-c/a	3.50	10.00	20.00
2,4,5	2.00	5.00	10.00
3-Toth-a	3.00	9.00	18.00

SUGARFOOT (See 4-Color No. 907,992,1059,1098,1147,1209)

SUMMER FUN (Walt Disney's . . .) (Formerly Mickey Mouse . . .)
No. 2, 1959
Dell Publishing Co.

	Good	Fine	Mint
2-Barks-a(2), 24 pgs.	5.00	15.00	30.00

SUMMER FUN (Formerly Li'l Genius; Holiday Surprise No. 55)
No. 54, Oct, 1966 (Giant)
Charlton Comics

	Good	Fine	Mint
54		.30	.60

SUMMER LOVE (Formerly Brides in Love)
V2No.46, Oct, 1965 - V2No.48, Nov, 1968
Charlton Comics

	Good	Fine	Mint
V2No.46-Beatle c/a	1.00	3.00	6.00
47-Beatle story	1.00	3.00	6.00
48	.35	1.00	2.00

SUMMER MAGIC (See Movie Comics)

SUNDANCE (See 4-Color No. 1126)

SUNDANCE KID
June, 1971 - No. 3, Sept, 1971 (52 pages)
Skywald Publications

	Good	Fine	Mint
1-Durango Kid; 2 Kirby Bullseye-r		.60	1.20
2-Swift Arrow, Durango Kid, Bullseye by S&K; Meskin plus 1 pg. origin		.40	.80
3-Durango Kid, Billy the Kid, Red Hawk-r		.30	.60

SUNDAY FUNNIES
1950
Harvey Publications

	Good	Fine	Mint
1	1.50	4.00	8.00

SUN FUN KOMIKS
1939 (Black, white & red)
Sun Publications

	Good	Fine	Mint
1	5.00	15.00	30.00

SUN GIRL
Aug, 1948 - No. 3, Dec, 1948
Marvel Comics

	Good	Fine	Mint
1-Sun Girl begins; Miss America app.	30.00	80.00	170.00
2,3: 2-The Blonde Phantom begins	20.00	55.00	120.00

SUNNY, AMERICA'S SWEETHEART
No. 11, Dec, 1947 - No. 14, June, 1948
Fox Features Syndicate

	Good	Fine	Mint
11-14-Feldstein c/a	17.00	50.00	90.00
I.W. Reprint No. 8-Feldstein-a; r-Fox issue	3.50	10.00	20.00

SUNSET CARSON
Feb, 1951 - No. 4, 1951
Charlton Comics

	Good	Fine	Mint
1	5.00	15.00	30.00
2-4	4.00	12.00	24.00

SUPER ANIMALS PRESENTS PIDGY & THE MAGIC GLASSES
Dec, 1953
Star Publications

	Good	Fine	Mint
3-D 1-L. B. Cole-c	7.00	20.00	40.00

SUPER BOOK OF COMICS
(Omar Bread & Pan-Am Motor Oil Co. giveaways)
1943 - 1946 (32 pgs.; later issues-16 pgs.) (some No.'s repeated)
Dell Publishing Co.

	Good	Fine	Mint
1-Smilin' Jack (Omar)	4.00	12.00	24.00
1-Dick Tracy	10.00	30.00	60.00
2-Red Ryder Victory Patrol	7.00	20.00	40.00
2-King of the Royal Mtd.	5.00	14.00	28.00
2-Smitty	2.50	7.00	14.00
2-Smilin' Jack (Omar)	3.50	10.00	20.00
3-Captain Midnight	8.00	24.00	48.00
3-Terry & the Pirates	8.00	24.00	48.00
3-Moon Mullins	2.00	6.00	12.00
4-Smitty	2.00	6.00	12.00
4-Andy Panda	3.00	8.00	16.00
5-Don Winslow	3.00	8.00	16.00
5-Smokey Stover (Omar)	2.00	6.00	12.00
5-Terry & the Pirates	8.00	24.00	48.00
6-Don Winslow; McWilliams-a	3.50	10.00	20.00
6-King of the Royal Mtd.	5.00	14.00	28.00
6-Porky Pig	3.00	8.00	16.00
7-Dick Tracy	8.00	24.00	48.00
7-Smilin' Jack (Omar)	3.00	8.00	16.00
8-Oswald the Rabbit	2.00	6.00	12.00
9-Alley Oop	6.00	16.00	32.00
9-Terry & the Pirates	6.00	16.00	32.00
10-Elmer Fudd (Omar)	2.00	5.00	10.00
11-Little Orphan Annie	4.00	12.00	24.00
12-Woody Woodpecker	2.00	6.00	12.00
13-Dick Tracy (16 pgs.) (Omar)	8.00	24.00	48.00
14-Bugs Bunny (Omar)	3.00	8.00	16.00
15-Andy Panda	2.00	5.00	10.00
16-Terry & the Pirates	7.00	20.00	40.00
17-Smokey Stover	3.00	8.00	16.00
18-Porky Pig (Omar)	2.00	6.00	12.00
19-Smilin' Jack (Omar)	3.00	8.00	16.00
20-Oswald the Rabbit (Omar)	2.00	6.00	12.00
21-Gasoline Alley (Omar)	4.00	12.00	24.00
22-Elmer Fudd	2.00	5.00	10.00
23-Little Orphan Annie (Omar)	3.50	10.00	20.00
24-Woody Woodpecker (Omar)	1.50	4.00	8.00
25-Dick Tracy	7.00	20.00	40.00
26-Bugs Bunny (Omar)	1.50	4.00	8.00
27-Andy Panda	1.50	4.00	8.00
28-Terry & the Pirates (1946)(Omar)	7.00	20.00	40.00
29-Smokey Stover	2.00	5.00	10.00
30-Porky Pig (Omar)	1.50	4.00	8.00
nn-Bugs Bunny ('48)	1.50	4.00	8.00
nn-Dan Dunn ('39 reprint)	3.00	8.00	16.00
nn-Dick Tracy	5.00	15.00	30.00
nn-Elmer Fudd ('46)	1.50	4.00	8.00
nn-Woody Woodpecker	1.50	4.00	8.00

SUPERBOY (See Adventure, Aurora, DC Comics Presents, DC Super Stars, 80 page Giant No. 10, More Fun, and The New Advs. of . .)

SUPERBOY (. . . & the Legion of Super Heroes with No. 197)
(Becomes The Legion of Super Heroes No. 259 on)
Mar-Apr, 1949 - No. 258, Dec, 1979
National Periodical Publications/DC Comics

	Good	Fine	Mint
1	175.00	450.00	950.00
2-Used in **SOTI**, pg. 35-36,226	70.00	200.00	380.00
3	50.00	140.00	260.00
4,5: 5-Pre-Supergirl tryout	40.00	120.00	220.00
6-10: 8-1st Superbaby. 10-1st app. Lana Lang	30.00	80.00	150.00
11-15	24.00	60.00	120.00
16-20	15.00	40.00	80.00
21-26,28-30	10.00	24.00	48.00
27-Low distribution	12.00	36.00	60.00
31-38: 38-Last pre-code ish.	7.00	20.00	40.00
39-50	6.00	16.00	32.00
51-60	4.00	12.00	24.00
61-67,69,70	3.50	10.00	20.00
68-Origin & 1st app. original Bizarro (10-11/58)	5.50	15.00	30.00

SUPERBOY (continued)	Good	Fine	Mint
71-76,79: 76-1st Supermonkey	1.50	4.00	8.00
77-Pre-Pete Ross tryout	2.00	6.00	12.00
78-Origin Mr. Mxyzptlk & Superboy's costume	3.50	10.00	20.00
80-1st meeting of Superboy & Supergirl (4/60)	1.50	4.00	8.00
81,84,85,87,88,90-92,94-97,99: 89-Intro. Mon-El. 90-Pete Ross learns Superboy's I.D.	1.20	3.50	7.00
82-1st Bizarro Krypto	1.20	3.50	7.00
83-Origin & 1st app. Kryptonite Kid	1.50	4.00	8.00
86(1/61)-4th Legion app; Intro Pete Ross	3.50	10.00	20.00
89(6/61)-Mon-el 1st app.	5.00	15.00	30.00
93(12/61)-10th Legion app; Chameleon Boy app.	2.00	5.00	10.00
98(7/62)-19th Legion app; -Origin & intro. Ultra Boy; Pete Ross joins Legion	2.50	7.00	14.00
100-Ultra Boy app; 1st app. Phantom Zone villains, Dr. Xadu & Erndine. 2 pg. map of Krypton; origin Superboy retold; r-cover of Superman 1; Pete Ross joins Legion	2.00	6.00	12.00
101-103,105-116,118-120: 111-1st app. Mental Emperor(Pa Kent)	.85	2.50	5.00
104-Origin Phantom Zone	1.00	3.00	6.00
117-Legion app.	1.00	3.00	6.00
121-123,127-140: 129-Giant G-22. 131-Legion cameo(statues). 132-1st app. Supremo. 138-Giant G-35	.50	1.50	3.00
(80-pg. Giant G-22,35)	.80	2.30	4.60
124(10/65)-1st app. Insect Queen (Lana Lang)	.70	2.00	4.00
125-Only app. Kid Psycho	.70	2.00	4.00
126-Origin Krypto the Super Dog retold	.70	2.00	4.00
141-146,149-176: 145-Superboy's parents regain their youth. 156,165,174-All Giants G-59,G-71,G-8. 172,173,176-Legion app.	.40	1.10	2.20
(Giants G-59,71,83)	.50	1.50	3.00
147(6/68)-Giant G-47; origin Saturn Girl, Lightning Lad, & Cosmic Boy	.50	1.50	3.00
148-Polar Boy app.	.40	1.10	2.20
177-184,186,187 (All 52 pgs.): 184-Origin Dial H for Hero-r	.30	.80	1.60
185-100 pg. Super Spec. No. 12; Legion app.-c, story (r)	.40	1.10	2.20
188-190: 188-Origin Karkan	.30	.80	1.60
191-196,198,199: 193-Chameleon Boy & Shrinking Violet get new costumes. 195-1st app. Wildfire & Erg; Phantom Girl gets new costume. 196-Last Superboy solo story. 198-Element Lad & Princess Projectra get new costumes	.30	.80	1.60
197-Legion begins; Lightning Lad's new costume	.40	1.10	2.20
200-Bouncing Boy & Duo Damsel marry; Jonn' Jonzz' cameo	.40	1.20	2.40
201,204,206,207,209: 201-Re-intro Erg as Wildfire. 204-Supergirl resigns from Legion. 209-Karate Kid new costume	.25	.70	1.40
202,205-(100 pgs.): 202-Light Lass gets new costume	.35	1.00	2.00
203-Invisible Kid dies	.35	1.00	2.00
208-(68 pgs.)	.30	.90	1.80
210-Origin Karate Kid	.35	1.00	2.00
211-215,217-220: 212-Matter-Eater Lad resigns		.60	1.20
216-1st app. Tyroc who joins Legion in No. 218		.60	1.20
221-230: 226-Intro. Dawnstar. 228-Death of Chemical King.		.50	1.00
231-237,240-242-(all 52 pgs.): 240-Origin Dawnstar		.50	1.00
238-Starlin-c; r-/Adv. No. 359,360		.50	1.00
239(52 pgs.)-Starlin-a(p)		.50	1.00
243-245-(44 pgs.)		.50	1.00
246-249		.40	.80
250,251-Starlin-a(signed Apollo)		.50	1.00
252-259: 253-Intro Blok. 259-Superboy leaves Legion		.40	.80
Annual 1 (6/64)	2.00	5.00	10.00

NOTE: ***Adams** c-143, 145, 146, 148-155, 157-161, 163, 164, 166-168, 172, 173, 175, 176, 178. **Anderson** inks-167-172, 175-184, 186-195, 197, 245; c-169, 174. **Chaykin** a-240p. **Cockrum** a-188. **Ditko** a-257. **Giordano** c-252-56, **Grell** a-203, 207-211, 213, 224; c-207-211, 213-217, 223, 224, 231, 232, 239, 243, 246, 258. **Infantino** c-171. **Nasser** a-222, 225, 226, 230, 231, 233, 236. **Simonson** a-237p. **Staton** a-227, 243-249, 252-258; c-247-251. **Wood** inks-152-155, 157-161. Legion app.-172, 173, 176, 183, 184, 188, 190, 191, 193, 195.*

SUPERBOY SPECTACULAR
1980 (Giant)
DC Comics

	Good	Fine	Mint
1-Distributed only through comic shops; reprints		.60	1.20

SUPER BRAT
January, 1954 - No. 4, July, 1954
Toby Press

	Good	Fine	Mint
1(1954)	.75	2.50	5.00
2-4: 4-Li'l Teevy by Mel Lazarus	.30	1.20	2.40
I.W. Reprint No. 1,2,3,7,8('58)		.40	.80
I.W. (Super) Reprint No. 10('63)		.40	.80

SUPERCAR (TV)
Nov, 1962 - No. 4, Aug, 1963
Gold Key

	Good	Fine	Mint
1	1.50	4.00	8.00
2-4	1.00	3.00	6.00

SUPER CAT (Also see Frisky Animals)
Sept, 1957 - No. 4, May, 1958
Ajax/Farrell Publ. (Four Star Comic Corp.)

	Good	Fine	Mint
1('57-Ajax)(2nd Series)	.50	1.50	3.00
2-4	.35	1.00	2.00

SUPER CIRCUS
January, 1951 - No. 5, 1951
Cross Publishing Co.

	Good	Fine	Mint
1	2.00	5.00	10.00
2-5	1.50	4.00	8.00

SUPER CIRCUS (TV)
March, 1954 - April, 1956
Dell Publishing Co.

	Good	Fine	Mint
4-Color 542,592,694('54-'56)	1.00	3.00	6.00

SUPER COMICS
May, 1938 - No. 121, Feb-Mar, 1949
Dell Publishing Co.

	Good	Fine	Mint
1-Terry & the Pirates, The Gumps, Dick Tracy, Little Orphan Annie, Gasoline Alley, Little Joe, Smilin' Jack begin	40.00	120.00	240.00
2	20.00	60.00	120.00
3	14.00	40.00	80.00
4	12.00	35.00	70.00
5-10	9.00	25.00	50.00
11-20	8.00	22.50	45.00
21-Origin Magic Morro	6.00	18.00	36.00
22-30	6.00	18.00	36.00
31-40	5.00	14.00	28.00
41-50: 43-Terry & the Pirates ends	4.00	12.00	24.00
51-60	3.50	10.00	20.00
61-70	3.00	8.00	16.00
71-80	2.50	7.00	14.00
81-100	2.00	6.00	12.00

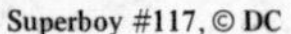
Superboy #117, © DC

Supercar #3, © GK

Super Comics #26, © DELL

Super Friends #1, © DC

Supergirl #8, © DC

Super Heroes #1, © DELL

SUPER COMICS (continued)

	Good	Fine	Mint
101-115-Last Dick Tracy	1.75	5.00	10.00
116-121: 119-121-Terry & the Pirates app.	1.50	4.00	8.00

SUPER COPS, THE
July, 1974 (One Shot)
Red Circle Productions (Archie)

	Good	Fine	Mint
1-Morrow-c/a; drug mention		.30	.60

SUPER CRACKED (See Cracked)

SUPER DC GIANT (25 cents) (No No. 1-12)
No. 13, 9-10/70 - No. 26, 7-8/71; No. 27, Fall, 1976
National Periodical Publications

	Good	Fine	Mint
S-13-Binky	.30	.90	1.80
S-14-Top Guns of the West; Kubert-c; Trigger Twins, Johnny Thunder, Wyoming Kid-r		.60	1.20
S-15-Western comics; Kubert-c; Pow Wow Smith, Vigilante, Buffalo Bill-r		.60	1.20
S-16-Best of the Brave & the Bold; Kubert-a	.30	.90	1.80
S-17-Love 1970	.30	.90	1.80
S-18-Three Mouseketeers; Dizzy Dog, Doodles Duck, Bo Bunny-r		.60	1.20
S-19-Jerry Lewis; Adams-a(i)(3)	.50	1.50	3.00
S-20-House of Mystery; Adams-c; Kirby-a(3)(r)	.30	.80	1.60
S-21-Love 1971		.60	1.20
S-22-Top Guns of the West		.60	1.20
S-23-The Unexpected		.60	1.20
S-24-Supergirl	.30	.80	1.60
S-25-Challengers of the Unknown; all Kirby/Wood-r	.30	.80	1.60
S-26-Aquaman (1971)	.30	.80	1.60
27-Strange Flying Saucer Adventures (Fall, '76)		.60	1.20

SUPER DOOPER
1946 (10 cents) (32 pages) (paper cover)
Able Manufacturing Co.

	Good	Fine	Mint
1-4,6	.85	2.50	5.00
5,7-Capt. Freedom & Shock Gibson	2.00	5.00	10.00

SUPER DUCK COMICS (The Cockeyed Wonder) (See Jolly Jingles)
Fall, 1944 - No. 94, Dec, 1960
MLJ Mag. No. 1-4/Close-Up No. 5 on (Archie)

	Good	Fine	Mint
1-Origin	9.00	25.00	50.00
2-5	4.00	12.00	24.00
6-10	2.50	7.00	14.00
11-20	2.00	5.00	10.00
21,23-40	1.50	4.00	8.00
22-Used in **SOTI**, pg. 35,307,308	3.00	9.00	18.00
41-94	.70	2.00	4.00

SUPER DUPER
1941
Harvey Publications

	Good	Fine	Mint
5-Captain Freedom & Shock Gibson app.	6.00	18.00	36.00
8,11	3.50	10.00	20.00

SUPER DUPER COMICS (Formerly Latest Comics?)
May-June, 1947
F. E. Howard Publ.

	Good	Fine	Mint
3-Mr. Monster app.	1.00	3.00	6.00

SUPER FRIENDS (TV) (Also see Best of DC & Limited Coll. Ed.)
Nov, 1976 - No. 47, Aug, 1981
National Periodical Publications/DC Comics

	Good	Fine	Mint
1-Superman, Batman, Wonder Woman, Aquaman, Robin, Wendy, Marvin & Wonder Dog begin; Orlando-a		.40	.80
2-10: 7-1st app. Wonder Twins		.30	.60
11-47: 14-Origin Wonder Twins		.25	.50

NOTE: ***Schaffenberger*** *a-14, 18, 20; c-18, 20.* ***Staton*** *a-43, 45.*

SUPER FRIENDS SPECIAL, THE
1981 (Giveaway) (no code or price) (no ads)
DC Comics

	Good	Fine	Mint
1		.30	.60

SUPER FUN
January, 1956
Gillmor Magazines

	Good	Fine	Mint
1-Comics, puzzles, cut-outs by A. W. Nugent	.85	2.50	5.00

SUPER FUNNIES (. . . Western Funnies No. 3,4)
Dec, 1953 - No. 4, 1954 (Satire)
Superior Comics Publishers Ltd. (Canada)

	Good	Fine	Mint
1-(3-D)-Dopey Duck	6.00	18.00	36.00
2-Horror & crime satire	1.50	4.00	8.00
3,4-(Western-Phantom Ranger)	1.00	3.00	6.00

SUPERGEAR COMICS
1976 (4 pages in color) (slick paper)
Jacobs Corp. (Giveaway)

	Good	Fine	Mint
(Rare)-Superman, Lois Lane; Steve Lombard app.		.40	.80

NOTE: *500 copies printed, over half destroyed?*

SUPERGIRL (See Action, Adventure, Brave & the Bold, Super DC Giant, Superman Family, & Super-Team Family)
11/72 - No. 9, 12-1/73-74; No. 10, 9-10/74
National Periodical Publications

	Good	Fine	Mint
1-Zatanna begins; ends No. 5	.50	1.50	3.00
2-5: 5-Zatanna origin-r	.30	.80	1.60
6-10: 8-JLA x-over		.40	.80

NOTE: ***Anderson*** *a-5. Zatanna in No. 1-3,5,7(Guest); Prez-No. 10.*

SUPER GOOF (Walt Disney)
Oct, 1965 - Present
Gold Key No. 1-57/Whitman No. 58 on

	Good	Fine	Mint
1	.70	2.00	4.00
2-10	.35	1.00	2.00
11-20		.50	1.00
21-62		.20	.40

NOTE: *Reprints in No. 16,24,28,29,37,38,43,46,56,58.*

SUPER GREEN BERET (Tod Holton . . .)
April, 1967 - No. 2, June, 1967 (68 pages)
Lightning Comics (Milson Publ. Co.)

	Good	Fine	Mint
1,2	.50	1.50	3.00

SUPER HEROES (See Marvel . . . & Giant-Size . . .)

SUPER HEROES
Jan, 1967 - No. 4, June, 1967
Dell Publishing Co.

	Good	Fine	Mint
1-Origin & 1st app. Fab 4	.70	2.00	4.00
2-4	.35	1.00	2.00

SUPER HEROES BATTLE SUPER-GORILLAS (See DC Special No. 16)
Winter, 1976-77 (One Shot)
National Periodical Publications

	Good	Fine	Mint
1-Superman, Batman, Flash stories; Infantino art; all-r		.40	.80

SUPER HEROES PUZZLES AND GAMES
1979 (32 pgs.) (regular size)
General Mills Giveaway (Marvel Comics Group)

	Good	Fine	Mint
Four 2-pg. origin stories of Spider-Man, Captain America, The Hulk, Spider-Woman		.40	.80

SUPERHEROES VS. SUPERVILLAINS
July, 1966 (no month given)
Archie Publications

	Good	Fine	Mint
1-Reprints from Archie Superhero comics	1.00	3.00	6.00

SUPERICHIE (Formerly Super Richie)
No. 5, Oct, 1976 - No. 18, Jan, 1979
Harvey Publications

	Good	Fine	Mint
5-18		.25	.50

SUPERIOR STORIES
May-June, 1955 - No. 4, Nov-Dec, 1955
Nesbit Publishing Co.

	Good	Fine	Mint
1-Invisible Man app.	3.00	8.00	16.00
2-The Pirate of the Gulf by J. H. Ingrahams	2.00	5.00	10.00
3-Wreck of the Grosvenor	2.00	5.00	10.00
4-O'Henry's "The Texas Rangers"	2.50	7.00	14.00

SUPER MAGIC (Super Magician No. 2 on)
May, 1941
Street & Smith Publications

	Good	Fine	Mint
V1No.1-Blackstone the Magician app.; origin & 1st app. Rex King (Black Fury); not Eisner-c	14.00	40.00	80.00

SUPER MAGICIAN COMICS (Super Magic No. 1)
No. 2, Sept, 1941 - V5No.8, Feb-Mar, 1947
Street & Smith Publications

	Good	Fine	Mint
V1No.2-Rex King, Man of Adventure app.	5.00	15.00	30.00
3-Tao-Anwar, Boy Magician begins	4.00	12.00	24.00
4-Origin Transo	3.50	10.00	20.00
5-12: 11-Supersnipe app.	3.50	10.00	20.00
V2No.1-The Shadow app.	2.50	7.00	14.00
2-12: 5-Origin Tigerman. 8-Red Dragon begins	2.00	5.00	10.00
V3No.1-12: 5-Origin Mr. Twilight	2.00	5.00	10.00
V4No.1-12: 11-Nigel Elliman begins	1.50	4.00	8.00
V5No.1-6	1.50	4.00	8.00
7,8-Red Dragon by Cartier	5.00	14.00	28.00

SUPERMAN (See Action Comics, All-New Coll. Ed., All-Star Comics, Best of DC, Brave & the Bold, DC Comics Presents, Giant Comics to Color, Limited Coll. Ed., Taylor's Christmas Tabloid, 3-D . . ., World's Finest Comics & World of Krypton)

SUPERMAN
Summer, 1939 - Present
National Periodical Publications/DC Comics

	Good	Fine	Mint
1(nn)-1st four Action stories reprinted; origin Superman by Siegel & Shuster; has a new 2 pg. origin plus 4 pgs. omitted in Action story	1500.00	4500.00	9000.00
(Prices vary widely on this book)			
2-All daily strip-r	350.00	950.00	2000.00
3-2nd story-r from Action No. 6	250.00	625.00	1300.00
4	160.00	425.00	900.00
5	135.00	330.00	780.00
6,7	100.00	270.00	560.00
8-10: 8-Drug story. 10-1st mention of Daily Planet and Perry White	80.00	215.00	450.00
11-13,15: 13-Jimmy Olsen app.	45.00	130.00	280.00
14-Patriotic Shield-c	50.00	150.00	300.00
16-20	40.00	110.00	235.00
21-23,25	30.00	85.00	180.00
24-Flag-c	35.00	100.00	200.00
26-29: 28-Lois Lane Girl Reporter series begins, ends No. 40,42	25.00	75.00	160.00
30-Origin & 1st app. Mr. Mxyztplk (pronounced "Mix-it-plk"); name later became Mxyzptlk ("Mix-yez-pit-l-ick"); the character was inspired by a combination of the name of Al Capp's Joe Blyfstyk (the little man with the black cloud over his head) & the devilish antics of Bugs Bunny	60.00	170.00	375.00
31,32,34-40	20.00	60.00	135.00
33-(3-4/45)-2nd app. Mxyztplk	25.00	75.00	150.00
41-44,46-50	15.00	45.00	100.00
45-1st app. Lois Lane as Superwoman	18.00	54.00	115.00
51,52	12.00	34.00	72.00
53-Origin Superman retold	30.00	80.00	185.00
54,56-60	12.00	34.00	72.00
55-Used in **SOTI**, pg. 33	14.00	40.00	82.00
61-Origin Superman retold; origin Green Kryptonite (1st Kryptonite story)	17.00	50.00	110.00
62-65,67-70: 62-Orson Wells app.	13.00	34.00	72.00
66-2nd Superbaby story	14.00	38.00	80.00
71-75: 75-Some have No. 74 on-c	11.00	32.00	70.00
72-Giveaway(9-10/51)-(Rare)-Price blackened out; came with banner wrapped around book	12.00	34.00	75.00
76-(Scarce)-Batman x-over; Superman & Batman learn each other's I.D.	30.00	90.00	200.00
77-80	9.00	25.00	55.00
81-Used in **POP**, pg. 88	10.00	30.00	65.00
82-90	8.00	25.00	55.00
91-95: 95-Last pre-code ish.	7.00	20.00	45.00
96-99,101-110	6.00	16.00	34.00
100	17.00	50.00	110.00
111-120	4.00	12.00	24.00
121-130: 127-Origin & 1st app. Titano. 128-Red Kryptonite used (4/59). 129-Intro-origin Lori Lemaris, the Mermaid	3.00	9.00	18.00
131-139: 139-Lori Lemaris app.	2.50	7.00	14.00
140-1st Blue Kryptonite	3.00	9.00	18.00
141,142,144-146,148,150: 146-Superman's life story	2.00	6.00	12.00
143-Superman finds loco weed	2.00	6.00	12.00
147(8/61)-7th Legion app; 1st app. Legion of Super-Villains; intro. Adult Legion	2.50	7.00	14.00
149(11/61)-9th Legion app.-cameo	2.50	7.00	14.00
151,153-154,158-160,163,164: 158-1st app. Flamebird & Nightwing	1.50	4.50	9.00
152(4/62)-15th Legion app.	2.00	5.00	10.00
155(8/62)-20th Legion app; Lightning Man & Cosmic Man, & Adult Legion app.	2.00	5.00	10.00
156,162-Legion app.	2.00	5.00	10.00
157-1st app. Gold Kryptonite; Mon-el app.	2.00	5.00	10.00
161-1st told death of Ma and Pa Kent	2.00	5.00	10.00
165-Saturn Woman cameo	1.40	4.00	8.00
166,168-175,177-180: 169-Last Sally Selwyn. 170-Pres. Kennedy app. 172,173-Legion cameo	1.00	3.00	6.00
167-New origin Brainiac & Brainiac 5; intro Tixarla (Later Luthor's wife)	1.50	4.50	9.00
176-Legion of Super Pets app.	1.20	3.50	7.00
181,182,184-186,188-192,194-196,198,200: 181-1st 2965 story/series. 189-Origin/destruction of Krypton II	.85	2.50	5.00
183(G-18),193(G-31),197(G-36)-All Giants	1.00	3.00	6.00
187(G-23-Giant)-Capt. America app; Shield cameo	1.00	3.00	6.00
199-1st Superman/Flash race	1.00	3.00	6.00
201,203-206,208-211,213-216,218-221,223-226,228-231,234-238: 213-Brainic-5 app.	.50	1.50	3.00
202(G-42),207(G-48),212(G-54),217(G-60),222(G-66),227(G-72), 239(G-84)-All Giants: 207-Legion app.	.70	2.00	4.00
232(Giant, G-78)-All Krypton issue	.70	2.00	4.00
233-1st app. Morgan Edge, Clark Kent switch from newspaper reporter to TV newscaster	.40	1.60	3.20
240-Kaluta-a	.30	.90	1.80
241-244 (52 pgs.)	.40	1.10	2.20
245-DC 100 pg. Super Spec. No. 7; Air Wave, Kid Eternity-r	.50	1.50	3.00
246-248,250,251,253 (All 52 pgs.): 248-World of Krypton story. 253-Finley-a, 2pgs.		.50	1.00
249,254-Adams-a. 249-(52 pgs.); origin & 1st app. Terra-Man by Adams (inks)	.85	2.50	5.00
252-DC 100 pg. Super Spec. No. 13; Ray, Black Condor, Starman, Hawkman, Dr. Fate, Spectre app.; Adams-c	.80	2.40	4.80

Super Magician Comics V2#9, © S&S

Superman #24, © DC

Superman #254, © DC

Superman #300, © DC

Superman Family #194, © DC

Superman's G.F. Lois Lane #79, © DC

SUPERMAN (continued)	Good	Fine	Mint
255-263		.60	1.20
264-1st app. Steve Lombard	.35	1.00	2.00
265-271,273-277,279-283,285-291,293,294,296-299		.50	1.00
272,278,284-All 100 pgs.	.30	.80	1.60
292-Origin Lex Luthor retold		.50	1.00
295-Legion cameo		.50	1.00
300-Retells origin		.60	1.20
301-330: 327-329-(44 pgs.). 330-More facts revealed about I. D.		.40	.80
331-366: 338-The bottled city of Kandor enlarged. 353-Origin Bruce Wayne		.30	.60
Annual 1(10/60)-Reprints 1st Supergirl/Action No. 252; r-/Lois Lane No. 1	10.00	30.00	60.00
Annual 2(1960)-Brainiac, Titano origin-r	7.00	20.00	40.00
Annual 3(1961)	4.00	12.00	24.00
Annual 4(1961)-11th Legion app; 1st Legion origins-text & pictures	3.00	8.00	16.00
Annual 5-All Krypton issue	2.00	6.00	12.00
Annual 6('62)-Legion-r/Adv. No. 247	1.40	4.00	8.00
Annual 7(1963)-Origin-r/Superman-Batman team/Adv. 275; r-1955 Superman dailies	1.50	4.50	9.00
Annual 8('64)	1.40	4.00	8.00
The Amazing World of Superman "Official Metropolis Edition" ($2.00; 14x10½")-Origin retold	1.40	4.00	8.00
Game Giveaway-20pgs., 1966; origin retold	.70	2.00	4.00
Pizza Hut Giveaway(12/77)-Exact-r of No. 97,113	.25	.75	1.50
Radio Shack Giveaway-36pgs. (7/80) 'The Computers That Saved Metropolis;' Starlin-a; included as advertising insert in Action 509, New Advs. of Superboy 7, Legion of Super-Heroes 265, & House of Mystery 282. (All comics were 64 pgs. & 40 cents; all dated 7/80.) Cover of inserts printed on newsprint. Giveaway contains 4 extra pgs. of Radio Shack advertising that inserts do not.	.25	.75	1.50
Radio Shack Giveaway-(7/81) 'Victory by Computer;' Super-Girl guest stars; also the TRS-80 Computer Whiz Kids	.25	.75	1.50
...Special Edition No. 5 (U.S. Navy giveaway, 1945)-52 pgs., regular comic book format	25.00	70.00	140.00
11195(2/79,224pp,$1.95)-Golden Press	.40	1.20	2.40

NOTE: ***Adams*** *a-249i, 254; c-204-208, 210, 212-215, 219, 231, 233-237, 240-243, 249-252, 254, 263, 307, 308, 313, 314, 317.* ***Adkins*** *a-323i.* ***Anderson*** *a-233-270.* ***Wayne Boring*** *art-late 1940's to early 1960's.* ***Buckler*** *c-324-327.* ***Burnley*** *a-252r.* ***Cockrum*** *a-248.* ***Fine*** *a-252r.* ***Infantino*** *a-242, 245; c-199, 216, 238.* ***Kubert*** *c-216.* ***Lopez*** *a-301; c-301, 320, 323, 344.* ***Morrow*** *a-238.* ***Starlin*** *c-355.* ***Staton*** *a-354.*

SUPERMAN & THE GREAT CLEVELAND FIRE (Giveaway)
1948 (4 pages, no cover) (Hospital Fund)
National Periodical Publications

	Good	Fine	Mint
In full color	60.00	140.00	240.00

SUPERMAN COSTUME COMIC
1954 (One Shot) (Came in box w/costume; slick-c)
National Periodical Publications

	Good	Fine	Mint
1-(Rare)	25.00	70.00	150.00

SUPERMAN FAMILY, THE (Formerly Superman's Pal Jimmy Olsen)
No. 164, Apr-May, 1974 - Present
National Periodical Publications/DC Comics

	Good	Fine	Mint
164-Jimmy Olsen, Supergirl, Lois Lane begin	.30	.90	1.80
165-176 (100 - 68 pgs.)		.60	1.20
177-181 (52 pgs.)		.50	1.00
182-$1.00 ish. begin; Marshall Rogers-a; Krypto begins, ends No. 192	.30	.80	1.60
183-193,195-213: 183-Nightwing-Flamebird begins, ends No. 194. 189-Brainiac 5, Mon-El app. 191-Superboy begins, ends No. 198		.60	1.20
194-Rogers-a	.30	.80	1.60

NOTE: ***Adams*** *c-182-185.* ***Anderson*** *a-186i.* ***Buckler*** *c-190, 191.* ***Jones*** *a-191-193.* ***Lopez*** *c-186, 187, 196-198.* ***Orlando*** *a-186i, 187i.* ***Rogers*** *a-182, 194.* ***Schaffenberger*** *a-176, 180, 182, 185, 190-93, 195-98; c-176.* ***Staton*** *a-191-194, 196.* ***Tuska*** *a-207-209.*

SUPERMAN (Miniature)
1953; 1955 - 1956 (3 issues) (No No.'s) (32 pgs.)
The pages are numbered in the 1st issue: 1-32; 2nd: 1A-32A, and 3rd: 1B-32B
National Periodical Publications

	Good	Fine	Mint
No date-Py-Co-Pay Tooth Powder giveaway (8 pgs.; circa late '40's - early '50's)	12.00	35.00	70.00
1-The Superman Time Capsule (Kellogg's Sugar Smacks)(1955)	10.00	28.00	56.00
1A-Duel in Space	8.00	23.00	46.00
1B-The Super Show of Metropolis (also No. 1-32, no B)	8.00	23.00	46.00

NOTE: *Numbering variations exist. Each title could have any combination-No. 1, 1A, or 1B.*

SUPERMAN RECORD COMIC
1966 (Golden Records)
National Periodical Publications

	Good	Fine	Mint
1 (with record)	.80	2.40	4.80
8 (with record)-Record reads origin of Superman from comic; came with iron-on patch, decoder, membership card & button	1.00	3.00	6.00

SUPERMAN'S CHRISTMAS ADVENTURE
1940, 1944 (16 pgs.) (Giveaway)
Distr. by Nehi drinks, Bailey Store, Ivey-Keith Co., Kennedy's Boys Shop, Macy's Store
National Periodical Publications

	Good	Fine	Mint
1(1940)-by Burnley	80.00	200.00	380.00
nn(1944)	60.00	150.00	300.00

SUPERMAN SCRAPBOOK
1940 (10x17")
Saalfield

	Good	Fine	Mint
Contains Sundays No. 135,163-172,198,199 plus origin from Action No. 1	18.00	50.00	100.00

SUPERMAN'S GIRLFRIEND LOIS LANE (See 80 Pg. Giants No. 3,14, Showcase, & Superman Family)

SUPERMAN'S GIRLFRIEND LOIS LANE
3-4/58 - No. 136, 1-2/74; No. 137, 9-10/74
National Periodical Publications

	Good	Fine	Mint
1	40.00	110.00	240.00
2	14.00	40.00	85.00
3	12.00	35.00	70.00
4,5	10.00	28.00	56.00
6-10: 9-Pat Boone app.	6.00	18.00	36.00
11-20: 14-Supergirl x-over	4.00	12.00	24.00
21-30: 23-1st app. Lena Thorul, Lex Luthor's sister. 29-Aquaman, Batman, Green Arrow cameo	2.00	6.00	12.00
31,32,34-46,48-49	1.00	3.00	6.00
33(5/62)-Mon-el app.	2.00	6.00	12.00
47-Legion app.	1.00	3.00	6.00
50-Triplicate Girl, Phantom Girl & Shrinking Violet app.	1.00	3.00	6.00
51-55,57-67,69,70	.40	1.20	2.40
56-Saturn Girl app.	.50	1.50	3.00
68-(Giant G-26)	.50	1.50	3.00
71-76,78	.30	.80	1.60
77-(Giant G-39)	.35	1.00	2.00
79-Adams-c begin, end No. 95,108	.35	1.00	2.00
80-85,87-94: 89-Batman x-over; all Adams-c	.30	.80	1.60
86-(Giant G-51)-Adams-c	.35	1.00	2.00
95-(Giant G-63)-Wonder Woman x-over; Adams-c	.35	1.00	2.00
96-103,106,107,109-111		.40	.80
104-(Giant G-75)	.30	.80	1.60

SUPERMAN'S GIRLFRIEND... (continued) Good Fine Mint

105-Origin & 1st app. The Rose & the Thorn .50 1.00
108-Adams-c .50 1.00
112,114-123 (52 pgs.): 111-Morrow-a. 122-G.A.-r/Superman No. 30. 123-G.A. Batman-r .40 .80
113-(Giant G-87) .60 1.20
124-137: 130-Last Rose & the Thorn. 132-New Zatanna story. 136-Wonder Woman x-over .30 .60
Annual 1(8-10/62) 1.50 4.50 9.00
Annual 2(8-10/63) .85 2.50 5.00

NOTE: ***Anderson** a-134i, 135i. **Buckler** a-118-121. **Infantino** a-116-118p. **Schaffenberger** a-1-28, 30-81.*

SUPERMAN'S PAL JIMMY OLSEN (Superman Family No. 164 on) (See 80 Page Giants)
Sept-Oct, 1954 - No. 163, Feb-Mar, 1974
National Periodical Publications

1 60.00 175.00 375.00
2 25.00 70.00 150.00
3: Last pre-code ish. 15.00 45.00 100.00
4,5 12.00 35.00 70.00
6-10 7.00 20.00 40.00
11-20 5.00 14.00 28.00
21-30 2.50 7.00 14.00
31-40: 31-Origin Elastic Lad. 33-One pg. biography of Jack Larson (TV Jimmy Olsen). 36-Intro Lucy Lane 2.00 5.00 10.00
41-47,49,50: 41-1st J.O. Robot 1.20 3.50 7.00
48-Intro/origin Superman Emergency Squad 1.45 4.00 8.00
51-61,64-69: 57-Olsen marries Supergirl .70 2.00 4.00
62(7/62)-18th Legion app.; Mon-el, Elastic Lad app. .70 2.00 4.00
63(9/62)-Legion of Super-Villains app. .70 2.00 4.00
70-Element Lad app. .70 2.00 4.00
71,74,75,78,80-84,86,89,90: 86-J.O. Robot becomes Congorilla .50 1.50 3.00
72(10/63)-Legion app; Elastic Lad (Olsen) joins .55 1.60 3.20
73-Ultra Boy app. .55 1.60 3.20
76,85-Legion app. .55 1.60 3.20
77-Olsen with Colossal Boy's power & costume; origin Titano retold .55 1.60 3.20
79(9/64)-Titled The Red-headed Beatle of 1000 B.C. .70 2.00 4.00
87-Legion of Super Villains app. .70 2.00 4.00
88-Star Boy app. .55 1.60 3.20
91-94,96-98,101-103,105,107-109 .30 .80 1.60
95(G-25),104(G-38)-Giants .35 1.00 2.00
99-Legion app; Olsen with powers/costumes of Lightning Lad, Sun Boy, & Star Boy .35 1.00 2.00
100-Legion cameo app. .50 1.50 3.00
106-Legion app. .35 1.00 2.00
110-Infinity-c .30 .80 1.60
111,112,114-116,118-121,123-130,132 .50 1.00
113(G-50),122(G-62),131(G-74)-Giants .30 .80 1.60
117-Legion app. .25 .70 1.40
133-Newsboy Legion by Kirby begins .50 1.50 3.00
134-139: 135-G.A. Guardian app. 136-Origin new Guardian .35 1.00 2.00
140-(Giant G-86) .30 .80 1.60
141-Newsboy Legion reprints by S&K begin (52 pg. issues begin) .30 .80 1.60
142-148-Newsboy Legion-r .30 .80 1.60
149,150-G.A. Plastic Man reprint in both; last 52 pg. ish. 150-Last Newsboy Legion .50 .100
151-163 .30 .60

NOTE: *Issues No. 141-148 contain **Simon & Kirby** Newsboy Legion reprints from Star Spangled No. 7,8,9,10,11,12,13,14 in that order. **Adams** c-109-112, 115, 117, 118, 120, 121, 132, 134-136, 146-148. **Anderson** a-129, 130, 132; c-125-128i, 145i. **Kirby** a-133-139, 141-148; c-133, 139, 145p. **Kirby/Adams** c-137, 138, 141-144, 146.*

SUPERMAN SPECTACULAR (See DC Special Series No. 5)

SUPERMAN 3-D (See 3-D...)

SUPERMAN-TIM (Becomes Gene Autry-Tim)
1942 - 1950 (½-size) (B&W Giveaway) Good Fine Mint
Superman-Tim Stores/National Periodical Publications

Issues with a Superman story 15.00 40.00 60.00
Issues with Superman text illos 7.00 20.00 36.00
Issues without Superman 6.00 18.00 30.00

SUPERMAN VS. THE AMAZING SPIDER-MAN
April, 1976 (100 pgs.) ($2.00) (Over-sized)
National Periodical Publications/Marvel Comics Group

1 1.50 4.00 8.00
2 .45 1.25 2.50

SUPERMAN WORKBOOK
1945 (One Shot) (68 pgs.) (B&W)
National Periodical Publ./Juvenile Group Foundation
15.00 40.00 90.00

SUPERMOUSE (...the Big Cheese)
Dec, 1948 - No. 45, Fall, 1958
Standard Comics/Pines No. 13 on (Literary Ent.)

1 8.00 24.00 40.00
2,3,5,6-Text illos by Frazetta in all 4.00 12.00 20.00
4-Two pg. text illos by Frazetta 5.00 15.00 26.00
7-10 1.40 4.00 8.00
11-20: 13-Racist humor (Indians) .70 2.00 4.00
21-45 .35 1.00 2.00
1-Summer Holiday issue (Summer,'57-Pines)-100 pgs. 1.40 4.00 8.00
2-Giant Summer issue (Summer,'58-Pines)-100 pgs. .85 2.50 5.00

SUPER-MYSTERY COMICS
July, 1940 - V8No.6, July, 1949
Ace Magazines

V1No.1-Magno, the Magnetic Man & Vulcan begin 30.00 90.00 190.00
2 17.00 50.00 100.00
3-The Black Spider begins 14.00 40.00 80.00
4-Origin Davy 12.00 36.00 70.00
5-Intro. The Clown 12.00 36.00 70.00
6(2/41) 10.00 30.00 60.00
V2No.1(4/41)-Origin Buckskin 10.00 30.00 60.00
2-6(2/42): 3-The Clown app. 5-Bondage-c 8.00 24.00 48.00
V3No.1(4/42),2: 1-Vulcan & Black Ace begin 7.00 20.00 40.00
3-Intro. The Lancer; Dr. Nemesis & The Sword begin; Kurtzman c/a(2) (Mr. Risk & Paul Revere Jr.) 10.00 30.00 60.00
4-Kurtzman-a 8.00 24.00 48.00
5-Kurtzman-a(2) 8.00 24.00 48.00
6(10/43)-Mr. Risk app.; Kurtzman's Paul Revere Jr. 8.00 24.00 48.00
V4No.1(1/44)-L.B. Cole-a 5.50 16.00 32.00
2-6(4/45) 5.00 14.00 28.00
V5No.1(7/45)-6 4.00 12.00 24.00
V6No.1-6: 3-Torture story. 4-Last Magno. Mr. Risk app. in No. 2,4-6 3.50 10.00 20.00
V7No.1-6, V8No.1-4,6 3.50 10.00 20.00
V8No.5-Meskin, Tuska, Sid Green-a 4.00 12.00 24.00

SUPERNATURAL THRILLERS
12/72 - No. 6, 11/73; No. 7, 7/74 - No. 15, 10/75
Marvel Comics Group

1-It!-Sturgeon adaptation .30 .80 1.60
2-The Invisible Man .30 .80 1.60

Superman's Pal J. Olsen #12, © DC

Super-Mystery Comics V2#4, © ACE

Supernatural Thrillers #2, © MCG

Super Rabbit #1, © MCG

Supersnipe Comics V2#3, © S&S

Suspense Comics #9, © L.B. Cole

SUPERNATURAL THRILLERS (continued)

	Good	Fine	Mint
3-The Valley of the Worm	.40	1.10	2.20
4-Dr. Jekyll & Mr. Hyde		.50	1.00
5-The Living Mummy		.30	.60
6-The Headless Horseman		.30	.60
7-The Living Mummy begins		.30	.60
8-15		.30	.60

NOTE: ***Brunner** c-11. **Ditko** a-8r, 9r. **McWilliams** a-14i. **Steranko** c-1, 2. Robert E. Howard story-No. 3.*

SUPER PUP
No. 4, Mar-Apr, 1954 - No. 5, 1954
Avon Periodicals

4,5	.85	2.50	5.00

SUPER RABBIT (See Comedy Comics & Wisco)
Fall, 1943 - No. 14, Nov, 1948
Timely Comics (CmPl)

1-1pg. Capt. America by Kirby	14.00	40.00	80.00
2,3	4.00	12.00	24.00
4,5,7-10,12-14	2.00	6.00	12.00
6-Origin	3.50	10.00	18.00
11-Kurtzman's "Hey Look"	5.00	14.00	24.00
I.W. Reprint No. 1,2('58),7,10('63)	.70	2.00	4.00

SUPER RICHIE (Superichie No. 5 on)
Sept, 1975 - No. 4, Mar, 1976 (52 pages)
Harvey Publications

1		.40	.80
2-4		.20	.40

SUPERSNIPE COMICS (Army & Navy No. 1-5)
Oct, 1942 - V5No.1, Aug-Sept, 1949 (Also see Shadow Comics)
Street & Smith Publications

V1No.6-Rex King Man of Adventure(costumed hero) by Jack Binder begins; Supersnipe by George Marcoux continues from Army & Navy No. 5; Bill Ward-a	15.00	40.00	70.00
7-12: 9-Doc Savage x-over in Supersnipe. 11-Little Nemo app.	10.00	32.00	56.00
V2No.1-12: 1-Huck Finn by Clare Dwiggins begins, ends V3/5	7.00	20.00	36.00
V3No.1-12: 8-Bobby Crusoe by Dwiggins begins, ends V3/12	6.00	16.00	28.00
V4No.1-12, V5No.1	5.00	14.00	24.00

NOTE: *Doc Savage in some issues.*

SUPERSPOOK (Formerly Frisky Animals on Parade)
1958
Ajax/Farrell Publications

4	1.00	3.00	6.00

SUPER SPY (See Wham)
Oct, 1940 - No. 2, Nov, 1940
Centaur Publications

1-Origin The Sparkler	20.00	60.00	135.00
2	15.00	45.00	90.00

SUPER-TEAM FAMILY
10-11/75 - No. 15, 3-4/78 (No.1-4: 68 pgs.; No.5 on: 52 pgs.)
National Periodical Publications/DC Comics

1-Reprints; Adams, Kane/Wood, Infantino-a	.30	.80	1.60
2,3: 2-The Creeper, Wildcat app.; Adams-a(r). 3-Brunner-c; Wood-a; Adams-a(r); Hawkman-Flash app.		.60	1.20
4-7-Reprints		.40	.80
8-10-Challengers of the Unknown		.40	.80
11-15: 11-Weiss-a; Flash, Supergirl, Atom. 12-Green Lantern, Hawkman, Atom. 13-Aquaman, Capt. Comet, Atom. 14-Wonder Woman, Atom. 15-Flash, New Gods		.30	.60

NOTE: ***Adams** a-1r, 2r. **Estrada** a-2. **Giordano** c-1, 2. **Infantino** a-1r. **Jones** a-14, 15. **G. Kane** a/c-11. **Lopez** c-15. **Wood** a-1i(r).*

SUPER TV HEROES (See Hanna-Barbera. . .)

SUPER-VILLAIN TEAM-UP
8/75 - No. 14, 10/77; No. 15, 11/78; No. 16, 5/79 - No. 17, 6/80
Marvel Comics Group

	Good	Fine	Mint
1-Sub-Mariner app.	.45	1.30	2.60
2-5: 4-Mooney-a		.60	1.20
6-Starlin-c		.50	1.00
7-13		.50	1.00
14-Byrne-c	.30	.80	1.60
15-17		.40	.80
Giant-Size 1(10/74, 68 pgs.)-Craig inks	.30	.90	1.80
Giant-Size 2(7/75, 68 pgs.)-Dr. Doom, Sub-Mariner app.	.30	.80	1.60

NOTE: ***Byrne** c-14. **Cockran** c-11, 12. **Ditko** a-2r. **Everett** a-1p, 3p. **Infantino** a-16.*

SUPER WESTERN COMICS (Buffalo Bill No. 5 on)
Aug, 1950 - No. 4, Mar, 1951
Youthful Magazines

1-Buffalo Bill begins; Powell-a	2.00	5.00	10.00
2-4	1.50	4.00	8.00

SUPER WESTERN FUNNIES (See Super Funnies)

SUPERWORLD COMICS
April, 1940 - No. 3, Aug, 1940
Hugo Gernsback (Komos Publ.)

1-Origin Hip Knox, Super Hypnotist; Mitey Powers & Buzz Allen, the Invisible Avenger, Little Nemo begin; cover by Frank R. Paul	25.00	70.00	140.00
2-Marvo 1,2 Go+, the Super Boy of the Year 2680	20.00	60.00	120.00
3	17.00	50.00	100.00

SURE-FIRE COMICS (Lightning Comics No. 4 on)
June, 1940 - No. 4, Oct, 1940 (Two No. 3's)
Ace Magazines

V1No.1-Origin Flash Lightning; X-The Phantom Fed, Ace McCoy, Buck Steele, Marvo the Magician, The Raven begin	24.00	65.00	140.00
2	16.00	45.00	100.00
3(9/40)	12.00	36.00	80.00
3(No.4)(10/40)-nn on cover, No. 3 on inside	12.00	36.00	80.00

SURF 'N' WHEELS
Nov, 1969 - No. 20, 1972
Charlton Comics

1		.40	.80
2-20?		.25	.50

SURF'TOONS (Magazine)
1965 (50 cents)
Petersen Publishing Co.

1('65)(no month)	.50	1.50	3.00
Many issues, nn's	.30	.80	1.60

SURPRISE ADVENTURES (Formerly Tormented)
Mar, 1955 - No. 5, July, 1955
Sterling Comic Group

3-5: 3,5-Sekowsky-a	.85	2.50	5.00

SUSPENSE COMICS
Dec, 1943 - No. 12, Sept, 1946
Continental Publishing Co.

1-The Grey Mask begins; bondage/torture-c; L. B. Cole-a, 7pgs.	15.00	40.00	90.00
2-Intro. The Mask; Rico, Giunta, L. B. Cole-a, 7pgs.	12.00	32.00	70.00
3-6: 3,5-Schomburg-c	10.00	30.00	60.00
7,9,10	9.50	28.00	56.00
8-Classic L. B. Cole spider-c	25.00	70.00	140.00
11-Classic Devil-c	14.00	40.00	80.00

SUSPENSE COMICS (continued)

	Good	Fine	Mint
12-Drug story; r-No.7-c	12.00	35.00	70.00

NOTE: ***L. B. Cole*** *c-6-12.* ***Larsen*** *a-11.* ***Palais*** *a-10,11.*

SUSPENSE COMICS (Radio) (Real Life Tales of . . . No. 1,2) (Amazing Detective Cases No. 3 on? . . . change to horror)
Dec, 1949 - No. 29, Apr, 1953 (No. 1-8,17-23: 52 pgs.)
Marvel/Atlas Comics (CnPC No. 1-10/BFP No. 11-29)

	Good	Fine	Mint
1-Powell-a; Peter Lorre photo-c	6.00	18.00	36.00
2-Crime stories	2.50	7.00	14.00
3-Change to horror	3.00	9.00	18.00
4,7-17,19-21,23,26-29	2.50	7.00	14.00
5,18,22-Krigstein-a	3.00	9.00	18.00
6-Tuska-a(2)	3.00	8.00	16.00
24-Tuska-a	3.00	8.00	16.00
25-Electric chair c/a	3.50	10.00	20.00

NOTE: ***Briefer*** *a-27.* ***Colan*** *a-8(2), 9.* ***Everett*** *a-5, 6(2), 19, 23, 28; c-21-23.* ***Heath*** *a-5, 6, 8, 10, 12, 14.* ***Palais*** *a-10.* ***Rico*** *a-7-9.* ***Robinson*** *a-29.* ***Sekowsky*** *a-11.* ***Tuska*** *a-5, 6(2), 12; c-12.* ***Whitney*** *a-15, 16, 22.*

SUSPENSE DETECTIVE
June, 1952 - No. 5, Mar, 1953
Fawcett Publications

	Good	Fine	Mint
1-Evans-a, 11 pgs; Bailey c/a	4.00	12.00	24.00
2-Evans-a, 10 pgs.	3.00	8.00	16.00
3	2.50	7.00	14.00
4,5-Bondage-c	3.00	8.00	16.00

NOTE: ***Bailey*** *a-4, 5.* ***Sekowsky*** *a-2, 4, 5.*

SUSPENSE STORIES (See Strange Suspense Stories)

SUZIE COMICS (Formerly Laugh Comics)
Spring, 1945 - No. 100, Aug, 1954
MLJ Mag./Close-Up No. 51 on (Archie)

	Good	Fine	Mint
49	8.00	24.00	48.00
50-55: 50?-Katy Keene begins, ends No. 100	5.00	14.00	28.00
56-65	3.00	8.00	16.00
66-80	2.50	7.00	14.00
81-87,89-100	2.00	6.00	12.00
88-Used in **POP**, pg. 76,77	3.00	8.00	16.00

SUZIE Q. SMITH (See 4-Color No. 323,377,453,553)

SWAMP FOX, THE (See 4-Color No. 1179)

SWAMP FOX, THE
1960 (14 pages) (Canada Dry Premiums)
Walt Disney Productions

	Good	Fine	Mint
Titles: (A)-Tory Masquerade, (B)-Rindau Rampage, (C)-Turnabout Tactics	1.00	3.00	6.00

SWAMP THING (See Brave & the Bold, DC Comics Presents No. 8, & House of Secrets No. 92)
Oct-Nov, 1972 - No. 24, Aug-Sept, 1976; No. 25, 1978
National Periodical Publications/DC Comics

	Good	Fine	Mint
1-c/a by Wrightson begin	1.50	4.00	8.00
2	.85	2.00	4.00
3-Intro. Patchworkman	.50	1.50	3.00
4,5	.40	1.20	2.40
6-10: 7-Batman app. 9-J. Jones-a(i). 10-Last Wrightson issue	.40	1.20	2.40
11-15-Redondo-a	.35	1.00	2.00
16-23-Redondo-a; 23-Swamp Thing reverts back to Dr. Holland	.30	.80	1.60
24,25		.40	.80

(Also see DC Special Series No. 2, 14)

NOTE: ***Carrillo & Chua*** *a-25.*

SWAT MALONE
Sept, 1955
Swat Malone Enterprises

	Good	Fine	Mint
V1No.1-Hy Fleishman-a	2.00	6.00	12.00

SWEENEY (Buz Sawyer's Pal, Roscoe. . .)
1949
Standard Comics

	Good	Fine	Mint
4,5-Crane-a No. 5	2.00	6.00	12.00

SWEE'PEA (See 4-Color No. 219)

SWEETHEART DIARY (Cynthia Doyle No. 66-73)
1949 - 1969
Fawcett Publications/Charlton Comics

	Good	Fine	Mint
1	3.50	10.00	20.00
2,5-10: 6-Photo-c	2.00	5.00	10.00
3,4-Wood-a	6.00	18.00	36.00
11-20	.85	2.50	5.00
21-40	.50	1.50	3.00
41-60	.30	.80	1.60
61-65,74-107		.40	.80

SWEETHEART LOVE STORIES
Oct, 1955
Charlton Comics

	Good	Fine	Mint
32	.30	.80	1.60

SWEETHEARTS (Formerly Captain Midnight)
No. 68, Oct, 1948 - No. 125, Sept, 1954
Fawcett Publications

	Good	Fine	Mint
68	2.50	7.00	14.00
69-80: 72-Baker-a?	1.50	4.00	8.00
81-84,86-93,95-102,104,106-109,111-116,118,119,121,123-125	.85	2.50	5.00
85,94,103,105,110,117-George Evans-a	2.00	5.00	10.00
120-Atom Bomb story	1.00	3.00	6.00
122-Marijuana story	1.00	3.00	6.00

NOTE: *Photo-c-112.*

SWEETHEARTS
V2No.23, May, 1954 - No. 137, Dec, 1973
Charlton Comics

	Good	Fine	Mint
V2No.23-39,41-50: 46-Jimmy Rodgers c/story	.30	.80	1.60
40-Photo-c; Tommy Sands story	.30	.80	1.60
51-137		.25	.50

SWEETHEART SCANDALS
1950 (Giant) (132 pages)
Fox Features Syndicate

nn-See Fox Giants. Contents may vary and determines price.

SWEETIE PIE (See 4-Color No. 1185,1241)

SWEETIE PIE
Dec, 1955 - No. 15, Fall, 1957
Ajax/Pines (Literary Ent.)

	Good	Fine	Mint
1-By Napine Seltzer	.85	2.50	5.00
2-15	.50	1.50	3.00

SWEET LOVE
Sept, 1949 - No. 5, May, 1950
Home Comics (Harvey)

	Good	Fine	Mint
1	2.00	6.00	12.00
2-4: 3-Powell-a	1.50	4.00	8.00
5-Kamen, Powell-a	3.00	8.00	16.00

SWEET ROMANCE
October, 1968
Charlton Comics

	Good	Fine	Mint
1		.40	.80

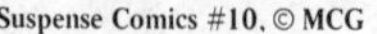
Suspense Comics #10, © MCG

Swamp Thing #2, © DC

Sweethearts #28, © CC

Sword Of Sorcery #2, © DC

Tales Cal. To Drive You Bats #2, © AP

Tales From The Crypt #28, © WMG

SWEET SIXTEEN
Aug-Sept, 1946 - No. 13, Jan, 1948
Parents' Magazine Institute

	Good	Fine	Mint
1-Van Johnson's life story; Dorothy Dare, Queen of Hollywood Stunt Artists begins (in all issues)	3.00	8.00	16.00
2-6,8-11: 6-Dick Haymes story	2.00	5.00	10.00
7-Ronald Reagan's life story	4.00	12.00	24.00
12-Bob Cummings, Vic Damone story	2.00	5.00	10.00
13-Robert Mitchum's life story	2.50	7.00	14.00

SWIFT ARROW
2-4/54 - No. 5, 10-11/54; 4/57 - No. 3, 9/57
Ajax/Farrell Publications

	Good	Fine	Mint
1(1954) (1st Series)	2.00	5.00	10.00
2-5	1.20	3.50	7.00
1 (2nd Series) (Swift Arrow's Gunfighters No. 4)	1.20	3.50	7.00
2,3: 2-Lone Rider begins	.85	2.50	5.00

SWIFT ARROW'S GUNFIGHTERS (Formerly Swift Arrow)
No. 4, Nov, 1957
Ajax/Farrell Publ. (Four Star Comic Corp.)

	Good	Fine	Mint
4	.85	2.50	5.00

SWING WITH SCOOTER
6-7/66 - No. 35, 8-9/71; No. 36, 10-11/72
National Periodical Publications

	Good	Fine	Mint
1	.85	2.50	5.00
2-10	.40	1.20	2.40
11-32,35,36		.60	1.20
33-Interview with David Cassidy		.40	.80
34-Interview with Ron Ely (Doc Savage)		.40	.80

NOTE: ***Orlando*** *a-1-3, 6, 11; c-1, 2, 10, 11, 13. No. 20, 33, 34: 68 pgs.; No. 35: 52 pgs.*

SWISS FAMILY ROBINSON (See 4-Color No. 1156, King Classics, & Movie Comics)

SWORD & THE DRAGON, THE (See 4-Color No. 1118)

SWORD & THE ROSE, THE (See 4-Color No. 505,682)

SWORD IN THE STONE, THE (See March of Comics No. 258 & Movie Comics)

SWORD OF LANCELOT (See Movie Classics)

SWORD OF SORCERY (See Wonder Woman No. 201)
Feb-Mar, 1973 - No. 5, Nov-Dec, 1973
National Periodical Publications

	Good	Fine	Mint
1-Leiber Fafhrd & The Gray Mouser; Adams/Bunkers inks; also No. 2; Kaluta-c	.40	1.20	2.40
2-Wrightson-c(i); Adams-a(i)	.35	1.10	2.20
3,4	.35	1.10	2.20
5-Starlin-a; Conan cameo	.30	.90	1.80

NOTE: ***Chaykin*** *a-1-4; c-1-5.* ***Kaluta*** *a-3i.* ***Simonson*** *a-1i, 3p, 4i, 5p; c-5*

TAFFY
Mar-Apr, 1945 - No. 12, 1948
Rural Home/Orbit Publ.

	Good	Fine	Mint
1-L. B. Cole-c; origin of Wonderworm plus 7 chapter WWII Funny Animal Adv.	3.50	10.00	20.00
2-L. B. Cole-c	3.00	8.00	16.00
3-12: 6-Perry Como c/story. 7-Duke Ellington, 2 pgs.	2.00	5.00	10.00

TAILSPIN
November, 1944
Spotlight Publishers

	Good	Fine	Mint
nn-Firebird app.; L. B. Cole-c	3.00	9.00	18.00

TAILSPIN TOMMY STORY & PICTURE BOOK
1931? (no date) (Color strip reprints) (10½x10'')
McLoughlin Bros.

	Good	Fine	Mint
266-by Forrest	10.00	30.00	60.00

TAILSPIN TOMMY
1932 (100 pages) (hardcover)
Cupples & Leon Co.

	Good	Fine	Mint
(Rare)-B&W strip reprints from 1930 by Hal Forrest & Glenn Claffin	15.00	40.00	80.00

TAILSPIN TOMMY
1937 - 1940
United Features Syndicate/Service Publ. Co.

	Good	Fine	Mint
Single Series 23('40)	7.00	20.00	40.00
Best Seller 1('46)-Service Publ. Co.	4.00	12.00	24.00

TALES CALCULATED TO DRIVE YOU BATS
Nov, 1961 - No. 7, Nov, 1962; 1966
Archie Publications

	Good	Fine	Mint
1	3.00	9.00	18.00
2	1.50	4.50	9.00
3-6	1.20	3.50	7.00
7-Story line change	.70	2.00	4.00
1('66)-25 cents; r-No. 1,2	.80	2.40	4.80

TALES FROM THE CRYPT (Formerly The Crypt of Terror No. 17-19)
No. 20, Oct-Nov, 1950 - No. 46, Feb-Mar, 1955
E. C. Comics

	Good	Fine	Mint
20	50.00	120.00	240.00
21-Kurtzman-r/Haunt of Fear No. 15(1)	35.00	100.00	190.00
22-Moon Girl costume at costume party, one panel	30.00	80.00	150.00
23-25	20.00	60.00	110.00
26-30	16.00	48.00	90.00
31-Williamson-a; B&W and color illos. in **POP**; Kamen draws himself, Gaines, Feldstein, Ingels, Craig & Davis in his story	20.00	60.00	110.00
32,35-39	12.00	34.00	64.00
33-Origin The Crypt Keeper	20.00	60.00	110.00
34-Used in **POP**, pg. 83	12.00	36.00	64.00
40-Used in Senate hearings & in Hartford Cournat anti-comics editorials-1954	12.00	36.00	64.00
41-46: 45-2pgs. showing E.C. staff	11.00	32.00	56.00

NOTE: ***Craig*** *a-20, 22-24; c-20.* ***Crandall*** *a-38, 44.* ***Davis*** *a-23, 24-46; c-29-46.* ***Elder*** *a-37, 38.* ***Evans*** *a-32-34, 36, 40, 41, 43, 46.* ***Feldstein*** *a-20-23; c-21-25, 28.* ***Ingels*** *a-in all.* ***Kamen*** *a-20, 22, 25, 27-31, 33-36, 39, 41-45.* ***Krigstein*** *a-40, 42, 45.* ***Kurtzman*** *a-21.* ***Orlando*** *a-27-30, 35, 37, 39, 46.* ***Wood*** *a-21, 24, 25; c-26, 27. Canadian reprints known; see Table of Contents.*

TALES FROM THE CRYPT (Magazine)
No. 10, July, 1968 (35 cents) (B&W)
Eerie Publications

	Good	Fine	Mint
10-Contains Farrell reprints from 1950's	.30	.80	1.60

TALES FROM THE GREAT BOOK
Feb, 1955 - No. 4, Jan, 1956
Famous Funnies

	Good	Fine	Mint
1	2.00	6.00	12.00
2-4-Lehti-a in all	1.20	3.50	7.00

TALES FROM THE TOMB
Oct, 1962 - No. 2, Dec, 1962
Dell Publishing Co.

	Good	Fine	Mint
1(02-810-210)(Giant)-All stories written by John Stanley	1.50	4.00	8.00
2	1.50	4.00	8.00

TALES FROM THE TOMB (Magazine)
V1No.6, July, 1969 - V6No.6, Dec, 1974 (52 pgs.)
Eerie Publications

	Good	Fine	Mint
V1No.6-8	.30	.80	1.60
V2No.1-3,5,6: 6-Rulah-r		.60	1.20

TALES FROM THE TOMB (continued)

	Good	Fine	Mint
4-LSD story-r/Weird V3No.5	.50	1.50	3.00
V3No.1-Rulah-r	.30	.80	1.60
2-6('70), V4No.1-6('72), V5No.1-6('73), V6No.1-6('74)		.40	.80

TALES OF ASGARD
Oct, 1968 (One Shot) (68 pages)
Marvel Comics Group

	Good	Fine	Mint
1-Thor reprints from Journey into Mystery No. 97-106; new Kirby-c	.50	1.50	3.00

TALES OF DEMON DICK & BUNKER BILL
1934 (78 pgs; 5x10½''; B&W) (hardcover)
Whitman Publishing Co.

	Good	Fine	Mint
793-by Dick Spencer	3.50	10.00	20.00

TALES OF EVIL
Feb, 1975 - No. 3, July, 1975
Atlas/Seaboard Publ.

	Good	Fine	Mint
1		.30	.60
2-Intro. The Bog Beast		.25	.50
3-Origin The Man-Monster		.25	.50

TALES OF GHOST CASTLE
May-June, 1975 - No. 3, Sept-Oct, 1975
National Periodical Publications

	Good	Fine	Mint
1-Two pg. Redondo-a; Aparo-a		.40	.80
2,3: 2-Nino-a		.25	.50

TALES OF HORROR
June, 1952 - No. 13, Oct, 1954
Toby Press/Minoan Publ. Corp.

	Good	Fine	Mint
1	4.00	12.00	24.00
2,12-Myron Fass c/a; torture scenes	2.00	6.00	12.00
3-8,13	2.00	6.00	12.00
9-11-Reprints Purple Claw No. 1-3	3.00	9.00	18.00

NOTE: ***Hollingsworth*** *a-2.*

TALES OF JUSTICE (Formerly Justice)
No. 54, Jul, 1956 - No. 67, Aug, 1957
Atlas Comics (MjMC No. 63-66/Male No. 67)

	Good	Fine	Mint
54-57	2.00	5.00	10.00
58,59-Krigstein-a	2.50	7.00	14.00
60-63,65	.85	2.50	5.00
64-Crandall-a	2.00	5.00	10.00
66-Torres, Orlando-a	2.00	5.00	10.00
67-Crandall-a	2.00	5.00	10.00

NOTE: ***Everett*** *a-60.* ***Orlando*** *a-65,66.* ***Severin*** *c-58.*

TALES OF SUSPENSE (Captain America No. 100 on)
Jan, 1959 - No. 99, March, 1968
Atlas (WPI No. 1,2/Male No. 3-12/VPI No. 13-40)/Marvel No. 41 on

	Good	Fine	Mint
1-Williamson-a, 5 pgs.	25.00	75.00	160.00
2,3	10.00	30.00	65.00
4-Williamson-a, 4 pgs; Kirby/Everett c/a	12.00	32.00	70.00
5-10	5.50	16.00	36.00
11,13-22	3.50	10.00	24.00
12-Crandall-a	4.00	12.00	28.00
23-38	2.00	5.00	12.00
39-Origin & 1st app. Iron Man; 1st Iron Man story-Kirby layouts	50.00	140.00	300.00
40-Iron Man in new armor	20.00	50.00	100.00
41	10.00	30.00	60.00
42-45: 45-Intro. & 1st app. Happy & Pepper	5.00	14.00	28.00
46,47	2.50	7.00	14.00
48-New Iron Man armor	3.00	8.00	16.00
49-51: 50-1st app. Mandarin	1.50	4.50	9.00
52-1st app. The Black Widow	2.00	6.00	12.00
53-Origin The Watcher (5/64); Black Widow app.	1.50	4.50	9.00
54-56	1.20	3.50	7.00
57-1st app./Origin Hawkeye (9/64)	1.20	3.50	7.00
58-Captain America begins (10/64)	1.20	3.50	7.00
59-Iron Man plus Captain America features begin; intro Jarvis, Avenger's butler	.85	2.50	5.00
60,61,64	.60	1.60	3.20
62-Origin Mandarin (2/65)	.70	2.00	4.00
63-Origin Captain America (3/65)	.85	2.50	5.00
65-1st Red Skull (6/65)	.60	1.60	3.20
66-Origin Red Skull	.60	1.60	3.20
67-94,96-99: 69-1st app. Titanium Man. 76-Intro Batroc & Sharon Carter, Agent 13 of Shield. 79-Intro Cosmic Cube. 94-Intro Modok	.60	1.60	3.20
95-Capt. America's i.d. revealed	.60	1.60	3.20

NOTE: ***Craig*** *a-(Iron Man)-99i.* ***Crandall*** *a-12.* ***Davis*** *a-38.* ***Ditko*** *Iron Man-47-49.* ***Ditko/Kirby*** *art in most all issues No. 1-15, 17-49.* ***Gil Kane*** *a-88p, 89-91.* ***Kirby*** *Captain America-59-75, 77-86, 92-99; layouts-69-75, 77; c-58-72, 74, 76, 78, 80, 82, 84, 86, 92, 94, 96.* ***Kirby*** *pencils (Iron Man)-40, 41, 43; c-39-44, 46-56. 98p.* ***Leiber/Fox*** *a-42, 43, 45, 51.* ***Tuska*** *a-70-75p.* ***Wood*** *a-(Iron Man)-71i.*

TALES OF SWORD & SORCERY (See Dagar)

TALES OF TERROR
1952 (no month)
Toby Press Publications

	Good	Fine	Mint
1-Fawcette-c; Ravielli-a	2.00	6.00	12.00

TALES OF TERROR (See Movie Classics)

TALES OF TERROR (Magazine)
Summer, 1964
Eerie Publications

	Good	Fine	Mint
1	1.00	3.00	6.00

TALES OF TERROR ANNUAL
1951 - 1953 (25 cents)
E. C. Comics

	Good	Fine	Mint
nn(1951) (Scarce)	275.00	650.00	1300.00
2(1952)	130.00	325.00	650.00
3(1953)	80.00	225.00	450.00

No. 1 contains three horror and one science fiction comic which came out in 1950. No. 2 contains a horror, crime, and science fiction book which generally had cover dates in 1951, and No. 3 had horror, crime, and shock books that generally appeared in 1952. All E. C. annuals contain four complete books that did not sell on the stands which were rebound in the annual format, minus the covers, and sold from the E. C. office and on the stands in key cities. The contents of each annual may vary in the same year.

TALES OF TERROR ILLUSTRATED (See Terror Ill.)

TALES OF TEXAS JOHN SLAUGHTER (See 4-Color No. 997)

TALES OF THE GREEN BERET
Jan, 1967 - No. 5, Oct, 1969
Dell Publishing Co.

	Good	Fine	Mint
1	.50	1.50	3.00
2-5: 5 reprints No. 1	.35	1.00	2.00

NOTE: ***Glanzman*** *a-1-4.*

TALES OF THE GREEN LANTERN CORPS
May, 1981 - Present
DC Comics

	Good	Fine	Mint
1-Origin of G.L. & the Guardians; Staton-a		.50	1.00
2,3-Staton-a		.30	.60

TALES OF THE INVISIBLE (See Comics Hits No. 59)

TALES OF THE KILLERS (Magazine)
V1No.10, Dec, 1970 - V1No.11, Feb, 1971 (52 pgs.) (B&W)

Tales Of Ghost Castle #1, © DC

Tales Of Suspense #65, © MCG

Tales O.T. Green Lantern Corps #1, © DC

Tales O.T. Myst. Traveler #7, © CC

Tales O.T. Unexpected #85, © DC

Tales To Astonish #18, © MCG

TALES OF THE KILLERS (continued)
World Famous Periodicals

	Good	Fine	Mint
V1No.10-One pg. Frazetta	.80	2.40	4.80
11	.50	1.50	3.00

TALES OF THE MARINES (Devil-Dog Dugan No. 3; Marines at War No. 5 on)
February, 1957
Atlas Comics (OPI)

	Good	Fine	Mint
4-Powell-a	1.20	3.50	7.00

TALES OF THE MYSTERIOUS TRAVELER
Aug, 1956 - No. 13, June, 1959
Charlton Comics

	Good	Fine	Mint
1-Ditko-a?	8.00	24.00	48.00
2	3.00	8.00	16.00
3-6,10-Ditko c/a(3-4)	5.00	14.00	28.00
7,9-Ditko-a(3 & ?)	5.00	14.00	28.00
8,11-Ditko c/a	5.00	14.00	28.00
12,13-Ditko-c only	3.00	8.00	16.00

TALES OF THE PONY EXPRESS (See 4-Color No. 829,942)

TALES OF THE TEXAS RANGERS (Jace Pearson's)
1952 - 1959
Dell Publishing Co.

	Good	Fine	Mint
4-Color 396	2.00	6.00	12.00
2(5-7/53)	1.50	4.00	8.00
3-10	1.50	4.00	8.00
4-Color 648(9/55)	1.50	4.00	8.00
11-22 (No. 21,22-exist?)	1.00	3.00	6.00
4-Color 961-Toth-a	2.00	6.00	12.00
4-Color 1021	1.00	3.00	6.00

TALES OF THE UNEXPECTED (The Unexpected No. 105 on) (See Super DC Giant)
Feb-Mar, 1956 - No. 104, Dec-Jan, 1968
National Periodical Publications

	Good	Fine	Mint
1	14.00	40.00	80.00
2	8.00	24.00	48.00
3-5	5.00	15.00	30.00
6-10	4.00	12.00	24.00
11,12,14,15	2.00	6.00	12.00
13,16-18,21-23: Kirby or S&K-a. 16-Character named 'Thor' with a magic hammer - not like later Thor	3.00	9.00	18.00
19,20,24-39: 24-Cameron-a	1.50	4.00	8.00
40-Space Ranger begins, ends No. 82	6.00	18.00	36.00
41-50	1.00	3.00	6.00
51-70	.70	2.00	4.00
71-100: 91-1st Automan (also in No. 94,97)	.35	1.00	2.00
101-104		.60	1.20

NOTE: ***Adams*** *c-104.* ***Anderson*** *a-50.* ***Bob Kane*** *a-48.* ***Kirby*** *a-12; c-22.* ***Mooney*** *a-40-82(Space Ranger).* ***Moreira*** *a-16, 30?.*

TALES OF THE WEST (See 3-D. . .)

TALES OF THE WIZARD OF OZ (See 4-Color No. 1308)

TALES OF THE ZOMBIE (Magazine)
Aug, 1973 - No. 10, Mar, 1975 (75 cents) (B&W)
Marvel Comics Group

	Good	Fine	Mint
V1No.1-Reprint/Menace No. 5; origin	.50	1.50	3.00
2-Everett biography & memorial	.40	1.10	2.20
3	.30	.80	1.60
V2No.1(No.4)-Photos, text of Bond movie 'Live & Let Die'	.30	.80	1.60
5-7,9,10		.60	1.20
8-Kaluta-a	.30	.80	1.60
Annual 1(Summer,'75)(No.11)-B&W; Everett, Buscema-a	.30	.80	1.60

NOTE: ***Alcala*** *a-7-9.* ***Boris*** *c-1-4.*

TALES OF VOODOO (Magazine)
V1No.11, Nov, 1968 - V7No.6, Nov, 1974
Eerie Publications

	Good	Fine	Mint
V1No.11	.40	1.10	2.20
V2No.1(3/69)-V2No.4(9/69)		.60	1.20
V3No.1-6('70): 4-'Claws of the Cat' redrawn from Climax No. 1		.50	1.00
V4No.1-6('71), V5No.1-6('72), V6No.1-6('73), V7No.1-6('74)		.50	1.00
Annual 1	.50	1.50	3.00

NOTE: *Bondage-c-V1No.10, V2No.4, V3No.4.*

TALES OF WELLS FARGO (See 4-Color No. 876,968,1023,1075, 1113,1167,1215)

TALES TO ASTONISH (The Incredible Hulk No. 102 on)
Jan, 1959 - No. 101, March, 1968
Atlas (MAP No. 1/ZPC No. 2-14/VPI No. 15-42)/Marvel No. 43 on

	Good	Fine	Mint
1-Jack Davis-a	25.00	75.00	160.00
2	12.00	32.00	70.00
3	8.50	25.00	56.00
4	6.00	18.00	40.00
5-Williamson-a, 4 pgs.	8.50	25.00	56.00
6-10	5.00	14.00	30.00
11-20	3.00	9.00	20.00
21-26,28-34	2.00	6.00	12.00
27-1st Antman app. (1/62)	55.00	160.00	335.00
35-2nd Antman; begins series	22.00	65.00	140.00
36	10.00	30.00	60.00
37-40	5.00	15.00	30.00
41-43	2.00	6.00	12.00
44-Origin & 1st app. The Wasp	2.50	7.00	14.00
45-48,50	1.75	5.00	10.00
49-Antman becomes Giant Man	2.00	6.00	12.00
51-60: 52-Origin & 1st app. Black Knight. 59-Giant Man vs. Hulk feat. story. 60-Giant Man & Hulk double feature begins	1.00	3.00	6.00
61-70: 62-1st app. The Leader. 65-New Giant Man costume. 69-Last Giant Man. 70-Sub-Mariner begins	.70	2.00	4.00
71-80	.50	1.50	3.00
81-91: 90-1st app. The Abomination	.40	1.20	2.40
92,93-Silver Surfer app.	1.00	3.00	6.00
94-99	.30	.90	1.80
100,101: 100: Hulk battles Sub-Mariner	.55	1.60	3.20

NOTE: ***Ditko*** *a-in most issues-1-43,45-48.* ***Ditko*** *Hulk-60-67, Giant Man-61.* ***Everett*** *Hulk-78-84, Sub-Mariner-87-91, 94-96; inks-79, 85-91, 94.* ***Kirby*** *a-1-27(most), 35-40, 44, 49-70; layouts-71-84(Hulk); pencils (Sub-Mariner)-82, 83; c-50-70, 73, 75, 77(w/****Romita****), 78(w/****Colan****), 79, 81, 85(all w/****Everett****), 90.* ***Leiber/Fox*** *a-47, 48, 50, 51.* ***Powell*** *Hulk-73, 74, Giant-Man-64,65p.*

TALES TO ASTONISH (2nd Series)
Dec, 1979 - No. 14, Jan, 1981
Marvel Comics Group

	Fine	Mint
V2No.1-Buscema-r from Sub-Mariner No. 1	.40	.80
2-14: Buscema Sub-Mariner-r	.30	.60

TALES TO HOLD YOU SPELLBOUND (See Spellbound)

TALKING KOMICS
1957 (20 pages) (Slick covers)
Belda Record & Publ. Co.

Each comic contained a record that followed the story - much like the Golden Record sets. Known titles: Chirpy Cricket, Lonesome Octopus, Sleepy Santa, Grumpy Shark, Flying Turtle, Happy Grasshopper

	Good	Fine	Mint
with records . . .	.80	2.40	4.80

TALLY-HO COMICS
December, 1944
Swappers Quarterly (Baily Publ. Co.)

	Good	Fine	Mint
nn-Frazetta's 1st work as Giunta's assistant; Man In Black story; violence	17.00	50.00	90.00

TAMMY, TELL ME TRUE (See 4-Color No. 1233)

TARANTULA (See Weird Suspense)

TARAS BULBA (See Movie Classics)

	Good	Fine	Mint

TARGET COMICS (. . . Western Romances No. 106 on)
Feb, 1940 - V10No.3(No. 105), Aug-Sept, 1949
Funnies, Inc./Novelty Publications/Star Publications

	Good	Fine	Mint
V1No.1-Origin & 1st app. Manowar, The White Streak by Burgos; & Bulls-Eye Bill by Everett; City Editor (ends No. 5), High Grass Twins by Jack Cole (ends No. 4), T-Men by Joe Simon (ends No. 9), Rip Rory (ends No. 4), Fantastic Feature Films by Tarpe Mills (ends No. 39), & Calling 2-R (ends No. 14) begin; Marijuana use story	75.00	225.00	500.00
2	40.00	110.00	250.00
3,4	30.00	80.00	180.00
5-Origin The White Streak in text; Space Hawk by Wolverton begins	70.00	180.00	400.00
6-The Chameleon by Everett begins; White Streak origin cont'd. in text	35.00	100.00	220.00
7-Wolverton-c	80.00	220.00	500.00
8,9,12	25.00	70.00	160.00
10-Intro. & 1st app. The Target; Kirby-c	40.00	100.00	220.00
11-Origin The Target & The Targeteers	35.00	90.00	200.00
V2No.1,2: 1-Target by Bob Wood	25.00	60.00	120.00
3,5	15.00	40.00	80.00
4-The Cadet begins	15.00	40.00	80.00
6-10-Red Seal with White Streak in all	15.00	40.00	80.00
11,12	14.00	35.00	70.00
V3No.1-10-Last Wolverton issue	14.00	35.00	70.00
11,12	2.50	7.00	14.00
V4No.1-5,7-12	1.50	4.00	8.00
6-Targetoons by Wolverton, 1 pg.	2.00	5.00	10.00
V5No.1-8	1.25	3.50	7.00
V6No.1-10	.85	2.50	5.00
V7No.1-12, V8No.1-5,7-9,11,12	.85	2.50	5.00
V8No.6-Krigstein-a	1.50	4.00	8.00
10-L. B. Cole-c	4.00	12.00	24.00
V9No.1,3,6,10,12, V10No.2-L.B. Cole-c	4.00	12.00	24.00
V9No.2,4,5,7-9,11, V10No.1,3	.85	2.50	5.00

NOTE: ***Jack Cole*** *a-1-8.* ***Everett*** *c-1-9.* ***Rico*** *a-V7No.10.* ***Simon*** *a-1, 2.* ***Tarpe Mills*** *a-1, 2, 4, 6, V2No. 1.*

TARGET: THE CORRUPTORS (TV)
No. 1306, Mar-May, 1962 - No. 3, 1962
Dell Publishing Co.

	Good	Fine	Mint
4-Color 1306, No. 2,3	1.00	3.00	6.00

TARGET WESTERN ROMANCES (Formerly Target)
No. 106, Oct-Nov, 1949 - No. 107, Dec-Jan, 1949-50
Star Publications

	Good	Fine	Mint
106-Silhouette nudity panel; L. B. Cole-c	4.00	12.00	24.00
107-L. B. Cole-c	3.50	10.00	20.00

TARGITT
March, 1975 - No. 3, July, 1975
Atlas/Seaboard Publ.

	Good	Fine	Mint
1-Origin; Nostrand-a in all		.40	.80
2,3: 2-1st in costume		.25	.50

TARZAN (See Aurora, Comics on Parade, Crackajack Comics, DC 100-Page Super Spec., Famous Feat. Stories 1, Golden Comics Digest No. 4,9, Jeep Comics 1-29, Jungle Tales of . . ., Limited Collectors Edition, Popular Comics, Sparkler, Sport Stars 1, Tip Top, & Top Comics)

TARZAN
1939 - 1947
Dell Publishing Co./United Features Syndicate

	Good	Fine	Mint
Black & White 5('39)-(Scarce)-by Hal Foster; r-1st dailies from 1929	90.00	250.00	500.00
Single Series 20('40)-by Hal Foster	70.00	200.00	400.00
4-Color 134('46)-Marsh-a	25.00	70.00	140.00
4-Color 161('47)-Marsh-a	20.00	60.00	120.00

TARZAN (. . . of the Apes No. 138 on)
1-2/48 - No. 131, 7-8/62; No. 132, 10/62 - No. 206, 2/72
Dell Publishing Co./Gold Key No. 132 on

	Good	Fine	Mint
1-Jesse Marsh-a begins	35.00	100.00	200.00
2	18.00	50.00	100.00
3-5	14.00	38.00	76.00
6-10	10.00	28.00	56.00
11-15: 11-Two Against the Jungle begins, ends No. 24	7.00	20.00	40.00
16-20	6.00	18.00	36.00
21-24,26-30	5.00	14.00	28.00
25-1st "Brothers of the Spear" episode; series ends No. 156,160, 161,196-206	5.00	14.00	28.00
31-40	3.00	8.00	16.00
41-50	2.50	7.00	14.00
51-60: 56-Eight pg. Boy story	2.00	5.00	10.00
61,62,64-70	1.50	4.00	8.00
63-Two Tarzan stories, 1 by Manning	2.00	5.00	10.00
71-100	1.25	3.50	7.00
101-109,111-120	.85	2.50	5.00
110 (Scarce)	1.50	4.00	8.00
121-140	.70	2.00	4.00
141-154	.60	1.80	3.60
155-Origin Tarzan	.85	2.50	5.00
156-177: 157-Bantu, Dog of the Arande begins, ends No. 159, 195. 162-No Manning. 169-Leopard Girl app.	.75	1.50	3.00
178-Tarzan origin reprint/No. 155; Leopard Girl app., also in No. 179,190-193	.30	.90	1.80
179-199,201-206	.30	.90	1.80
200 (Scarce)	.50	1.50	3.00
Story Digest 1(6/70-G.K.)	.50	1.50	3.00

NOTE: *No. 162,165,168,171 are TV issues. No. 1-153-all have* ***Marsh*** *art on Tarzan. No. 154-161,163,164,166,167,172-177 all have* ***Manning*** *art on Tarzan. No. 178,202 have* ***Manning*** *Tarzan reprints. No "Brothers of the Spear" in No. 1-24,157-159,162-195. No. 39-126,128-156 all have* ***Russ Manning*** *art on "Brothers of the Spear;" No. 196-201,203-205 all have* ***Manning*** *B.O.T.S. reprints; No. 25-38,127 all have* ***Jesse Marsh*** *art on B.O.T.S. No. 206 has a* ***Marsh*** *B.O.T.S. reprint.* ***Doug Wildey*** *art-No. 179-187. Many issues have front and back photo covers.*

TARZAN OF THE APES (Continuation of Gold Key series)
No. 207, April, 1972 - No. 258, Feb, 1977
National Periodical Publications

	Good	Fine	Mint
207-Origin Tarzan by Joe Kubert, part 1; John Carter begins (origin); 52 pg. issues thru No. 209	.70	2.00	4.00
208-210: Origin, parts 2-4. 209-Last John Carter. 210-Kubert-a	.40	1.20	2.40
211-Hogarth-a	.30	.80	1.60
212-214: Adaptations from "Jungle Tales of Tarzan." 213-Beyond the Farthest Star begins, ends No. 218		.60	1.20
215-218,224,225-All by Kubert. 215-part Foster-r		.60	1.20
219-223: Adapts "The Return of Tarzan" by Kubert		.60	1.20
226-Manning-a		.50	1.00
227-229		.50	1.00
230-100 pgs.; Kubert, Kaluta-a; Korak begins, ends No. 234; Carson of Venus app.	.30	.80	1.60
231-234: Adapts "Tarzan and the Lion Man;" all 100 pgs.; Rex, the Wonder Dog r-No. 232,233		.60	1.20
235-Last Kubert issue; 100 pgs.		.60	1.20
236,237,239		.40	.80
238-(68 pgs.)		.50	1.00
240-243: Adapts "Tarzan & the Castaways"		.40	.80
244-249		.40	.80
250-256: Adapts "Tarzan the Untamed;" 252,253-r/No. 213			

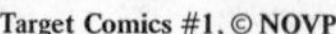
Target Comics #1, © NOVP

Tarzan #28, © ERB

Tarzan Of The Apes #211, © ERB

Tarzan Lord O.T. Jungle #1, © ERB

Teach Ye All Nations nn, © CG

Teen-Age Brides #1, © HARV

TARZAN OF THE APES (continued) — Good / Fine / Mint

	Good	Fine	Mint
		.30	.60
257,258-Kubert-r		.30	.60
Comic Digest 1(Fall,'72)(DC)-50 cents; 160 pgs.; digest size; Kubert-c, Manning-a	.60	1.80	3.60

NOTE: ***Anderson** a-207, 209, 217, 218. **Chaykin** a-216. **Finley** 1(r)-212. **Foster** strip reprints-No. 208, 209, 211, 221. **Infantino** a-230-235. **Kubert** c-207-249, 253. **Lopez** a-251, 255; c-252, 254. **Manning** strip reprints-230-235, 238. **Morrow** a-208. **Nino** a-231-234.*

TARZAN BOOK (The Illustrated . . .)
1929 (80 pages) (7x9")
Grosset & Dunlap

1-(Rare)-Contains 1st B&W Tarzan newspaper comics from 1929. Cloth reinforced spine & dust jacket (50 cents)

	Good	Fine	Mint
with dust jacket. . . .	60.00	150.00	240.00
without dust jacket. . . .	30.00	70.00	120.00
2nd Printing(1934)-76 pgs.; 25 cents; 4 Foster pages dropped; paper spine, circle in lower right cover with 25 cents price. The 25 cents is barely visible on some copies.	15.00	45.00	80.00

1967-House of Greystoke reprint-7x10"; using the complete 300 illustrations/text from the 1929 edition minus the original indicia, foreword, etc. Initial version bound in gold paper & sold for $5.00. Officially titled **Burroughs Biblophile No. 2.** A very few additional copies were bound in heavier blue paper.

	Good	Fine	Mint
Gold binding. . . .	2.00	6.00	12.00
Blue binding. . . .	3.00	8.00	16.00

TARZAN FAMILY (Formerly Korak)
No. 60, Nov-Dec, 1975 - No. 66, Nov-Dec, 1976
(No. 60-62: 68 pgs.; No. 63 on: 52 pgs.)
National Periodical Publications

	Good	Fine	Mint
60-Korak begins; Kaluta-r		.50	1.00
61-65-All Kaluta-r. 62-Foster-r		.40	.80
66		.40	.80

NOTE: *Carson of Venus reprints-60-65. New John Carter-62-64, 65r, 66r. New Korak-60, 62-66. Pellucidar feature-66. **Foster** Sunday r-60('32), 63. **Kaluta** Carson of Venus-60-65. **Kubert** c-60-64. **Manning** strip reprints-60-64. **Morrow** a-66r.*

TARZAN KING OF THE JUNGLE (See Dell Giant No. 37,51)

TARZAN, LORD OF THE JUNGLE
Sept, 1965 (Giant) (soft paper cover) (25 cents)
Gold Key

	Good	Fine	Mint
1-Marsh-r	1.00	3.00	6.00

TARZAN, LORD OF THE JUNGLE
June, 1977 - No. 29, Oct, 1979
Marvel Comics Group

	Good	Fine	Mint
1		.50	1.00
2-Origin by J. Buscema		.40	.80
3-10		.40	.80
11,12-Adams-c inks		.40	.80
13-20		.40	.80
21-29		.25	.50
Annual 1 (10/77)	.30	.80	1.60
Annual 2 (11/78)		.50	1.00
Annual 3 (10/79)		.40	.80

NOTE: ***John Buscema** a-1-18, 22; c-1-19, 22-24. **Buscema** c/a-Annual 1(10/77).*

TARZAN MARCH OF COMICS (See March of Comics No. 82,98,114, 125,144,155,172,185,204,223,240,252,262,272,286,300,318, 332,342,354,366)

TARZAN OF THE APES TO COLOR
1933 (24 pages) (10¾x15¼")
Saalfield

	Good	Fine	Mint
988-(Very Rare)-Contains 1929 daily reprints with some new art by Hal Foster. Two panels blown up large on each page; 25 percent in color; believed to be the only time these panels ever appeared in color.	80.00	220.00	360.00

TARZAN'S JUNGLE ANNUAL
Aug, 1952 - 1958 (25 cents) (Two No. 5's)
Dell Publishing Co.

	Good	Fine	Mint
1	4.00	12.00	24.00
2	3.00	8.00	16.00
3-7: Manning-a-No. 3,5-7	1.50	4.00	8.00

NOTE: *All have **Marsh** art.*

TARZAN'S JUNGLE WORLD (See Dell Giant No. 25)

TASMANIAN DEVIL & HIS TASTY FRIENDS
November, 1962
Gold Key

	Good	Fine	Mint
1-Bugs Bunny & Elmer Fudd x-over	.50	1.50	3.00

TASTEE-FREEZ COMICS
1957 (36 pages) (10 cents) (6 different issues)
Harvey Comics

	Good	Fine	Mint
1-Little Dot, 3-Casper	3.50	10.00	20.00
2-Rags Rabbit, 5-Mazie	2.00	6.00	12.00
4-Sad Sack	2.00	6.00	12.00
6-Dick Tracy	4.00	12.00	24.00

TAYLOR'S CHRISTMAS TABLOID
Mid 1930's, Cleveland, Ohio
Dept. Store Giveaway (Tabloid size; in color)

nn-(Very Rare)-Among the earliest pro work of Siegel & Shuster; one full color page called "The Battle in the Stratosphere," with a pre-Superman look; Shuster art throughout. (Only 1 known copy)
Estimated value. . . . $500.00

TEACH YE ALL NATIONS
No date (16 pages) (paper cover)
Catechetical Guild giveaway

	Good	Fine	Mint
	3.00	8.00	16.00

NOTE: *B&W editor's version(5½x8½") exists; only one known copy.*

TEDDY ROOSEVELT & HIS ROUGH RIDERS
1950
Avon Periodicals

	Good	Fine	Mint
1-Kinstler-c; Palais-a	7.00	20.00	40.00

TEDDY ROOSEVELT ROUGH RIDER (See Classics Special)

TEE AND VEE CROSLEY IN TELEVISION LAND COMICS
1951 (52 pgs.; 8x11"; paper cover; in color)
Crosley Division, Avco Mfg. Corp.

	Good	Fine	Mint
Many stories, puzzles, cut-outs, games, etc.	1.00	3.00	6.00

TEENA
1948 - No. 22, Oct, 1950
Magazine Enterprises/Standard Comics

	Good	Fine	Mint
A-1 No. 11,12,15	1.50	4.00	8.00
20-22 (Standard)	.85	2.50	5.00

TEEN-AGE BRIDES (True Bride's Experiences No. 8)
Aug, 1953 - No. 7, Aug, 1954
Harvey/Home Comics

	Good	Fine	Mint
1	2.00	6.00	12.00
2-7: 1-3,6-Powell-a	1.50	4.00	8.00

TEEN-AGE CONFESSIONS (See Teen Confessions)

TEEN-AGE CONFIDENTIAL CONFESSIONS
July, 1960 - No. 22, 1964
Charlton Comics

	Good	Fine	Mint
1	.40	1.20	2.40
2-22		.50	1.00

TEEN-AGE DIARY SECRETS (Formerly Blue Ribbon Comics) (Becomes Diary Secrets No. 10 on)

TEEN-AGE DIARY SECRETS (continued)
Sept, 1949 - No. 9, Aug, 1950
St. John Publishing Co.

	Good	Fine	Mint
nn(9/49)-oversized issue	6.00	18.00	36.00
6-8-Photo-c; Baker-a (2-3) in each	5.00	14.00	28.00
9-Pocket size	5.00	14.00	28.00

TEEN-AGE DOPE SLAVES (See Harvey Comics Library No. 1)

TEENAGE HOTRODDERS (Top Eliminator No. 25 on)
April, 1963 - No. 24, July, 1967
Charlton Comics

	Good	Fine	Mint
1	.50	1.50	3.00
2-24	.30	.80	1.60

TEEN-AGE LOVE
1950 (132 pages)
Fox Publications (Hero)

nn-See Fox Giants. Contents can vary and determines price.

TEEN-AGE LOVE (Formerly Intimate?)
V2No.4, July, 1958 - No. 96, Dec, 1973
Charlton Comics

	Good	Fine	Mint
V2No.4-9	.30	.80	1.60
10(9/59)-30		.40	.80
31-96: 61&62-Origin Jonnie Love & begin series		.20	.40

TEEN-AGE ROMANCE (Formerly My Own Romance)
No. 77, Sept, 1960 - No. 86, March, 1962
Marvel Comics (ZPC)

	Good	Fine	Mint
77-86	.85	2.50	5.00

TEEN-AGE ROMANCES
Jan, 1949 - No. 60?, 195?
St. John Publ. Co. (Approved Comics)

	Good	Fine	Mint
1-Baker c/a(1)	9.00	25.00	50.00
2-Baker c/a	6.00	18.00	36.00
3-Baker c/a(3)	6.00	18.00	36.00
4-8-Photo-c; Baker-a(2-3) each	5.00	14.00	28.00
9-Baker c/a; Kubert-a	6.00	18.00	36.00
10-12,20-Baker c/a(2-3) each	5.00	14.00	28.00
13-19,21-Complete issues by Baker	6.00	18.00	36.00
22-25-Baker c/a(2-3) each	4.00	12.00	24.00
26-29,31,33,34,36-40-Baker-a	2.50	7.00	14.00
30-No Baker-a	1.25	3.50	7.00
32-Baker c/a, 1pg.	2.00	5.00	10.00
35-Baker c/a, 16pgs.	3.00	8.00	16.00
41-60-Baker-a	2.00	6.00	12.00

TEEN-AGE TALK
1964
I. W. Enterprises

	Good	Fine	Mint
Reprint No. 5,8,9	.30	.80	1.60

TEEN-AGE TEMPTATIONS (Going Steady No. 10 on) (See True Love Pictorial)
Oct, 1952 - No. 9, Aug, 1954
St. John Publishing Co.

	Good	Fine	Mint
1-Baker c/a; has story "Reform School Girl" by Estrada	12.00	36.00	60.00
2-Baker-c	3.00	9.00	18.00
3-7,9-Baker c/a	6.00	18.00	36.00
8-Teenagers smoke reefers; Baker c/a	7.00	20.00	40.00

NOTE: ***Estrada*** *a-1, 4, 5.*

TEEN BEAM (Teen Beat No. 1)
No. 2, Jan-Feb, 1968
National Periodical Publications

	Good	Fine	Mint
2	.70	2.00	4.00

TEEN BEAT (Teen Beam No. 2)
Nov-Dec, 1967
National Periodical Publications

	Good	Fine	Mint
1-Photos & text only	.70	2.00	4.00

TEEN COMICS (Formerly All Teen; Journey Into Unknown Worlds No. 36 on)
No. 21, April, 1947 - No. 35, May, 1950
Marvel Comics (WFP)

	Good	Fine	Mint
21,24,26,28,30-Kurtzman's "Hey Look"	2.00	5.00	10.00
22,23,25,27,29,31-35	1.25	3.50	7.00

TEEN CONFESSIONS
Aug, 1959 - No. 97, Nov, 1976
Charlton Comics

	Good	Fine	Mint
1	2.00	6.00	12.00
2-10	.85	2.50	5.00
11-30	.40	1.20	2.40
31-88,91-97		.50	1.00
89,90-Newton-c		.30	.60

TEENIE WEENIES, THE
1950 - 1951 (Newspaper reprints)
Ziff-Davis Publishing Co.

	Good	Fine	Mint
10,11	3.50	10.00	20.00

TEEN-IN (Tippy Teen)
Summer, 1968 - No. 4, Fall, 1969
Tower Comics

	Good	Fine	Mint
nn(Summer,'68), nn(Spring,'69), 3,4	.70	2.00	4.00

TEEN LIFE (Formerly Young Life)
No. 3, Winter, 1945 - No. 5, Fall, 1945
New Age/Quality Comics Group

	Good	Fine	Mint
3,4: 4-Duke Ellington story	1.00	3.00	6.00
5-Van Johnson, Woody Herman & Jackie Robinson articles	2.00	6.00	12.00

TEEN ROMANCES
1964
Super Comics

	Good	Fine	Mint
15,16-Reprints		.30	.60

TEEN SECRET DIARY (Nurse Betsy Crane No. 12 on)
1959 - No. 11, June, 1961
Charlton Comics

	Good	Fine	Mint
1	.85	2.50	5.00
2-11	.30	.80	1.60
1(1972)		.30	.60

TEEN TALK (See Teen)

TEEN TITANS (See Brave & the Bold, DC Super-Stars No. 1, New Advs. of, and Showcase)
1-2/66 - No. 43, 1-2/73; No. 44, 11/76 - No. 53, 2/78
National Periodical Publications/DC Comics

	Good	Fine	Mint
1-Titans join peace corps; Batman, Flash, Aquaman, Wonder Woman cameos	4.00	12.00	24.00
2	2.00	6.00	12.00
3-5: 4-Speedy app.	1.00	3.00	6.00
6-10	.60	1.80	3.60
11-18: 11-Speedy app.	.40	1.20	2.40
19-Wood-a; Speedy begins as regular	.40	1.20	2.40
20-22: All Adams-a; 21-Hawk & Dove app. 22-Origin Wonder Girl	1.00	3.00	6.00
23-Wonder Girl dons new costume	.35	1.00	2.00
24	.35	1.00	2.00
25-Flash, Aquaman, Batman, Green Arrow, Green Lantern, Superman, & Hawk & Dove guests	.35	1.00	2.00
26-30: 29-Hawk & Dove & Ocean Master app. 30-Aquagirl app.			

Teen-Age Romances #35, © STJ

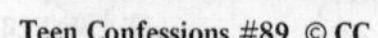
Teen Confessions #89, © CC

Teen Titans #2, © DC

Tell It To The Marines #7, © TOBY

Terror Illustrated #2, © WMG

Terrors Of The Jungle #17, © STAR

TEEN TITANS (continued) — Good / Fine / Mint
.35 1.00 2.00
31-43: 31-Hawk & Dove app. 36,37-Superboy-r. 38-Green Arrow/ Speedy-r; Aquaman/Aqualad story. 39-Hawk & Dove story. (36-39, 52 pgs.) .30 .80 1.60
44-47,49-52: 44-Mal becomes the Guardian. 46-Joker's Daughter begins. 50-Intro. Teen Titans West .50 1.00
48-Intro Bumblebee; Joker's Daughter becomes Harlequin .40 .80
53-Origin retold .40 .80
NOTE: ***Anderson** a-30. **Aparo** a-36. **Buckler** c-46-48, 50-53.*

TEEPEE TIM (Formerly Ha Ha Comics)
No. 100, Feb-Mar, 1955 - No. 102, June-July, 1955
American Comics Group
100-102 .40 .80

TEGRA JUNGLE EMPRESS (Zegra No. 2 on)
August, 1948
Fox Features Syndicate
1-Blue Beetle, Rocket Kelly app.; used in **SOTI**, pg. 31 15.00 35.00 70.00

TELEVISION (TV)

TELEVISION COMICS
No. 5, Feb, 1950 - No. 8, Nov, 1950
Standard Comics (Animated Cartoons)
5(No. 1 on cover)-1st app. Willy Nilly 1.00 3.00 6.00
6-8: 6 has No. 2 on outside .85 2.50 5.00

TELEVISION PUPPET SHOW
1950 - No. 2, Nov, 1950
Avon Periodicals
1,2 3.00 9.00 18.00

TELEVISION TEENS MOPSY (See T.V. Teens)

TELL IT TO THE MARINES
Mar, 1952 - No. 15, July, 1955
Toby Press Publications
1-Lover Leary and His Liberty Belles (with pin-ups), ends No. 5 3.50 10.00 20.00
2-5: 4,5-Photo-c. 4-Transvestism story 2.50 7.00 14.00
6-15: 6-14-Photo-c 1.25 3.50 7.00
I.W. Reprint No. 1,9 .30 .90 1.80
Super Reprint No. 16('64) .30 .90 1.80

TEN COMMANDMENTS (See Moses & the . . . and Classics Special)

TENDER LOVE STORIES
Feb, 1971 - No. 4, July, 1971 (All 52 pgs.) (25 cents)
Skywald Publ. Corp.
1-4 .30 .80 1.60

TENDER ROMANCE (Ideal Romance No. 3 on)
December, 1953 - No. 2, 1954
Key Publications (Gilmour Magazines)
1-Headlight & lingerie panels 3.00 8.00 16.00
2 2.00 6.00 12.00

TENNESSEE JED (Radio)
No date (1945) (16 pgs.; paper cover; regular size) (Giveaway)
Fox Syndicate? (Wm. C. Popper & Co.)
4.00 12.00 24.00

TENNIS (For Speed, Stamina, Strength, Skill)
1956 (16 pgs.) (soft cover) (10 cents)
Tennis Educational Foundation
Derus Productions
Book 1-Endorsed by Gene Tunney, Ralph Kiner, etc. showing how tennis has helped them. 1.50 4.00 8.00

TENSE SUSPENSE
Dec, 1958 - No. 2, Feb, 1959
Fago Publications
Good / Fine / Mint
1,2 1.00 3.00 6.00

TEN STORY LOVE (Formerly a pulp magazine with same title)
V29No.3, June-July, 1951 - V36No.5(No. 210), Sept, 1956
Ace Periodicals
V29No.3(No.166)-6(1/52) .85 2.50 5.00
V30No.1(3/52)-6(9/52), V31No.1(10/52)-6(3/53), V32No.1(4/53)-6(12/53) .50 1.50 3.00
V33, V34No.1-4 .50 1.50 3.00
V34No.5(No.197, 8/54), V34No.6(No.198), V35No.1(No.199)-V35No.6(No.204, 9/55), V36No.1(No.205, 11/55)-V36No.5 (No.210, 9/56) .50 1.50 3.00
NOTE: *Photo-c-V32No.5, V35No.4.*

TEN WHO DARED (See 4-Color No. 1178)

TERRIFIC COMICS
Jan, 1944 - No. 6, Nov, 1944
Continental Publishing Co.
1-Kid Terrific; opium story 8.00 24.00 48.00
2-The Boomerang begins 5.50 16.00 32.00
3,4,6: 3-Diana becomes Boomerang's costumed aide 4.00 12.00 24.00
5-The Reckoner begins; Boomerang & Diana by L. B. Cole & Ed Wheelan's "Comics" McCormick, called the world's No. 1 comic book fan; Schomburg bondage-c 15.00 40.00 80.00
NOTE: ***L. B. Cole** a-1-6.*

TERRIFIC COMICS (Horrific No. 1-13)
No. 14, Dec, 1954 - No. 18, July, 1955
Mystery Publ. (Ajax/Farrell)(Comic Media)
14-Art swipe/Advs. Into Unknown 37 2.00 6.00 12.00
15,16-No Phantom Lady 2.00 6.00 12.00
17,18-Phantom Lady & Wonder Boy 8.00 23.00 46.00
NOTE: ***Palais** a-14.*

TERRIFYING TALES (Terrors of the Jungle No. 4-10)
No. 11, Jan, 1953 - No. 15, Apr, 1954
Novelty-Star Publications
11-Used in **POP**, pgs. 99,100; all Jo-Jo-r 14.00 40.00 80.00
12-All Jo-Jo-r; L. B. Cole splash 14.00 40.00 80.00
13-All Rulah-r; classic devil-c 20.00 60.00 100.00
14-All Rulah reprints 14.00 40.00 80.00
15-Rulah, Zago-r; used in **SOTI**-r/Rulah No. 22 14.00 40.00 80.00
NOTE: *All issues have **L. B. Cole** covers; bondage covers-No. 12-14.*

TERROR ILLUSTRATED (Adult Tales of . . .)
Nov-Dec, 1955 - No. 2, Spring, 1956 (Magazine)
E. C. Comics
1 7.00 20.00 36.00
2 5.00 15.00 28.00
NOTE: ***Craig** a-1. **Crandall** a-1,2; c-1,2. **Evans** a-1, 2. **Ingels** a-1, 2.*

TERRORS OF THE JUNGLE (Terrifying Tales No. 11 on; formerly Jungle Thrills)
No. 17, May, 1952 - No. 10, Sept, 1954
Novelty-Star Publications
17-Reprints Rulah No. 21, used in **SOTI**; L. B. Cole bondage-c 10.00 30.00 60.00
18-Jo-Jo-r 10.00 28.00 50.00
19,20(1952)-Jo-Jo-r; Disbrow-a 10.00 28.00 50.00
21-Jungle Jo, Tangi-r; used in **POP**, pg. 100 & color illos. 12.00 34.00 60.00
4,6,7-Disbrow-a 10.00 28.00 50.00
5,8,10: All Disbrow-a. 5-Jc-Jo-r. 8-Rulah, Jo-Jo-r. 10-Rulah-r 10.00 28.00 50.00
9-Jo-Jo-r; Disbrow-a; Tangi by Orlando 10.00 28.00 50.00
NOTE: ***L. B. Cole** c-all; bondage c-17, 19, 21, 5, 7.*

TERRORS OF THE UNIVERSE
1953
Novelty-Star Publications

	Good	Fine	Mint
8,9-L. B. Cole-c	7.00	20.00	36.00

TERROR TALES (See Beware Terror Tales)

TERROR TALES (Magazine)
V1No.7, 1969 - V6No.6, Dec, 1974; V7No.1, 4/76 - Present
(V1-V6, 52 pgs.; V7 on, 68 pgs.)
Eerie Publications

	Good	Fine	Mint
V1No.7	.30	.80	1.60
V1No.8-11('69): 9-Bondage-c		.60	1.20
V2No.1-6('70), V3No.1-6('71), V4No.1-6('72), V5No.1-6('73), V6No.1-6('74)		.50	1.00
V7No.1,4(no V7No.2), V8No.1-3('77)		.50	1.00
V7No.3-LSD story-r/Weird V3No.5		.50	1.00

TERRY AND THE PIRATES (See Superbook No. 3,5,9,16,28, Super Comics & Merry Christmas . . .)

TERRY AND THE PIRATES
1939 - 1953 (By Milton Caniff)
Dell Publishing Co.

	Good	Fine	Mint
Black & White 2('39)	35.00	100.00	200.00
Black & White 6('39)-1936 dailies	35.00	90.00	180.00
4-Color 9(1940)	30.00	80.00	160.00
Large Feature Comic 27('41), 6('42)	20.00	60.00	120.00
4-Color 44('43)	15.00	45.00	90.00
4-Color 101('45)	10.00	28.00	56.00
Buster Brown Shoes giveaway(1938)-32 pgs.; in color	20.00	60.00	120.00
Canada Dry Premiums-Books No. 1-3(1953-Harvey)-2x5''; 36 pgs.	4.00	12.00	24.00
Family Album(1942)	7.00	20.00	40.00
Gillmore Giveaway('38)-24 pgs.	5.00	14.00	28.00
Popped Wheat Giveaway('38)-Reprints in full color; Caniff-a	.85	2.50	5.00
Shoe Store giveaway('38, 14pp)	2.00	5.00	10.00
Sparked Wheat Giveaway('42)-16 pgs. in full color	4.00	12.00	24.00

TERRY AND THE PIRATES
1941 (16 pgs.; regular size)
Libby's Radio Premium

	Good	Fine	Mint
''Adventure of the Ruby of Genghis Khan'' - Each pg. is a puzzle that must be completed to read the story	7.00	20.00	40.00

TERRY AND THE PIRATES (Long John Silver & the Pirates No. 30 on) (Reprints of daily strips) (Two No. 26's)
No. 3, 4/47 - No. 26, 4/51; No. 26, 6/55 - No. 28, 10/55
Harvey Publications/Charlton No. 26-28

	Good	Fine	Mint
3(No.1)-Boy Explorers by S&K; Terry & the Pirates begin by Caniff	20.00	55.00	110.00
4-S&K Boy Explorers	14.00	35.00	70.00
5-10: 6-10-Powell-a	6.00	18.00	36.00
11-15,17-20: 11-Man in Black app. 12,14-Powell-a	5.00	14.00	28.00
16-Powell-a; girl threatened with red hot poker	5.00	14.00	28.00
21-26(4/51)-Last Caniff issue	4.00	12.00	24.00
26-28('55)(Formerly This Is Suspense)-Not by Caniff	2.50	7.00	14.00

TERRY BEARS COMICS (TerryToons, The . . . No. 4)
June, 1952 - No. 3, Oct, 1952
St. John/Pines No. 4

	Good	Fine	Mint
1-3	1.20	3.50	7.00

TERRY-TOONS COMICS (1st Series) (Becomes Paul Terry's Comics No.85 on; later issues titled ''Paul Terry's . . .) (See Giant Comics Ed.)
Oct, 1942 - No. 86, Feb?, 1951
Timely/Marvel No. 1-59 (7/47)(Becomes Best Western No. 58 on?, Marvel)/St. John No. 60 (8/47) on

	Good	Fine	Mint
1 (Scarce)	20.00	60.00	120.00
2	10.00	30.00	60.00
3-5	7.00	20.00	40.00
6-10	5.00	14.00	28.00
11-20	3.50	10.00	20.00
21-37	2.00	6.00	12.00
38-(Scarce)-1st Mighty Mouse	20.00	60.00	120.00
39	8.00	24.00	48.00
40-49	3.50	10.00	20.00
50-1st app. Heckle & Jeckle	5.00	15.00	30.00
51-60(8/47)	2.50	7.00	14.00
61-84	1.50	4.50	9.00
85,86-Same book as Paul Terry's Comics No. 85,86 with only a title change	1.50	4.50	9.00

TERRY-TOONS COMICS (2nd Series)
June, 1952 - No. 9, Nov, 1953
St. John Publishing Co./Pines

	Good	Fine	Mint
1	2.50	7.00	14.00
2-9	1.50	4.00	8.00
Giant Summer Fun Book 101,102(Summer,'57-Summer,'58)	1.50	4.00	8.00

TERRYTOONS, THE TERRY BEARS (Formerly Terry Bears)
No. 4, Summer, 1958
Pines Comics

	Good	Fine	Mint
4	.85	2.50	5.00

TESSIE THE TYPIST (Tiny Tessie No. 24)
Summer, 1944 - No. 23, Aug, 1949
Timely/Marvel Comics (20CC)

	Good	Fine	Mint
1-Doc Rockblock & others by Wolverton	14.00	40.00	70.00
2-Wolverton's Powerhouse Pepper	6.00	24.00	40.00
3-No Wolverton	2.00	5.00	8.00
4,5,7,8-Wolverton-a	5.50	16.00	28.00
6-Kurtzman's ''Hey Look,'' 2 pgs. Wolverton	7.00	20.00	36.00
9,12-Wolverton's Powerhouse Pepper & Kurtzman's ''Hey Look''	7.00	20.00	36.00
10-Four pgs. Wolverton's Powerhouse Pepper, 1 pg. Kurtzman's ''Hey Look''	7.00	20.00	36.00
11-Eight pgs. Wolverton's Powerhouse Pepper	5.50	16.00	28.00
13-Wolverton's Powerhouse Pepper	5.50	16.00	28.00
14-One pg. Wolverton's Powerhouse Pepper, 2 pgs. Kurtzman's ''Hey Look''	3.50	10.00	16.00
15-18-Kurtzman's ''Hey Look'' plus Giggles 'n' Grins-No. 15	2.50	7.00	12.00
19-Eight pg. Annie Oakley	.85	2.50	5.00
20-23	.70	2.00	4.00

TEXAN, THE (Fightin' Texan No. 16 on)
Aug, 1948 - No. 15, Oct, 1951
St. John Publishing Co.

	Good	Fine	Mint
1-Buckskin Belle	3.00	8.00	16.00
2,3,5,10	1.50	4.00	8.00
4,7,15-Baker c/a	4.00	12.00	24.00
6,9-Baker-c	2.00	5.00	10.00
8,11,13,14-Baker c/a(2-3) each	4.00	12.00	24.00
12-All Matt Baker; Peyote story	5.00	14.00	28.00

NOTE: ***Matt Baker*** *c-6-15.* ***Larsen*** *a-6, 8.* ***Tuska*** *a-1, 2, 8.*

TEXAN, THE (See 4-Color No. 1027,1096)

TEXAS JOHN SLAUGHTER (See 4-Color No. 997,1181)

TEXAS KID
Jan, 1951 - No. 10, July, 1952
Marvel/Atlas Comics (LMC)

Terry & The Pirates #10, © News Synd.

Terry-Toons Comics #38, © MCG

The Texan #14, © STJ

Texas Rangers In Action #20, © CC

Tex Morgan #1, © MCG

The Thing! #5, © CC

TEXAS KID (continued)

	Good	Fine	Mint
1-Tuska-a	3.00	8.00	16.00
2-10: 5-Maneely-c	1.50	4.00	8.00

TEXAS RANGERS, THE (See Superior Stories No. 4 and Tales of. . .)

TEXAS RANGERS IN ACTION (See Blue Bird Comics)
No. 5, July, 1956 - No. 79, Aug, 1970
Charlton Comics

	Good	Fine	Mint
5-10	.50	1.50	3.00
11-Williamson-a(5,5,&8 pgs.); Torres-a	4.00	12.00	24.00
12,14-20	.30	.90	1.80
13-Williamson-a, 5 pgs; Torres-a	3.00	8.00	16.00
21-59	.30	.80	1.60
60-Rileys Rangers begin		.40	.80
61-70: 65-1st app. The Man Called Loco, origin-No. 67		.30	.60
71-79		.25	.50
76(Modern Comics-r, 1977)		.15	.30

TEXAS SLIM (See A-1 Comics No. 2-8,10)

TEX DAWSON, GUN-SLINGER (Gunslinger No. 2 on)
January, 1973
Marvel Comics Group

	Good	Fine	Mint
1-Steranko-c; Williamson-a(r); Tex Dawson-r begin		.40	.80

TEX FARNUM (See Wisco)

TEX FARRELL
Mar-Apr, 1948
D. S. Publishing Co.

	Good	Fine	Mint
1-Shelly-c	3.00	7.00	14.00

TEX GRANGER (Formerly Calling All Boys)
No. 18, June, 1948 - No. 24, Sept, 1949
Parents' Magazine Institute/Commended

	Good	Fine	Mint
18-24	1.00	3.00	6.00

TEX MORGAN
Aug, 1948 - No. 9, Feb, 1950
Marvel Comics (CCC)

	Good	Fine	Mint
1	4.00	12.00	24.00
2-9	2.00	6.00	12.00

TEX RITTER WESTERN
Oct, 1950 - No. 46, May, 1959
Fawcett No. 1-20 (1/54)/Charlton No. 21 on

	Good	Fine	Mint
1	8.00	24.00	48.00
2	6.00	16.00	32.00
3-5	4.00	12.00	24.00
6-10	3.50	10.00	20.00
11-20	2.00	6.00	12.00
21-38,40-46	1.75	5.00	10.00
39-Williamson-c/a (1/58)	4.00	12.00	24.00

TEX TAYLOR (See Wisco)
Sept, 1948 - No. 9, March, 1950
Marvel Comics (HPC)

	Good	Fine	Mint
1	3.50	10.00	20.00
2-9: 9-Photo-c	2.00	6.00	12.00

THAT'S MY POP! GOES NUTS FOR FAIR
1939 (76 pages) (B&W)
Bystander Press

	Good	Fine	Mint
nn-by Milt Gross	5.00	14.00	28.00

THAT DARN CAT (See Movie Comics & Walt Disney Showcase No.19)

THAT THE WORLD MAY BELIEVE
No date (16 pgs.) (Graymoor Friars distr.)
Catechetical Guild Giveaway

	Good	Fine	Mint
	2.00	5.00	10.00

THAT WILKIN BOY (Meet Bingo. . .)
Jan, 1969 - Present
Archie Publications

	Good	Fine	Mint
1	1.50	4.00	8.00
2-10	.70	2.00	4.00
11-26 (last Giant issue)	.35	1.00	2.00
27-48		.50	1.00

T.H.E. CAT (TV)
Oct, 1966 - No. 4, Oct, 1967 (All have photo-c)
Dell Publishing Co.

	Good	Fine	Mint
1	.85	2.50	5.00
2-4	.50	1.50	3.00

THERE'S A NEW WORLD COMING
1973 (35-49 Cents)
Spire Christian Comics/Fleming H. Revell Co.

	Good	Fine	Mint
		.50	1.00

THEY RING THE BELL
1946
Fox Features Syndicate

	Good	Fine	Mint
1	3.50	10.00	20.00

THIEF OF BAGHDAD (See 4-Color No. 1229)

THIMBLE THEATRE STARRING POPEYE
1931, 1932 (52 pgs.; 25 cents; B&W)
Sonnet Publishing Co.

	Good	Fine	Mint
1-Daily strip serial reprints in both by Segar	50.00	130.00	220.00
2	50.00	120.00	200.00

NOTE: *Probably the first Popeye reprint book. Popeye first entered Thimble Theatre in 1929.*

THIMK (Magazine) (Satire)
May, 1958 - No. 6, May, 1959
Counterpart

	Good	Fine	Mint
1	1.50	4.00	8.00
2-6	.85	2.50	5.00

THING!, THE (Blue Beetle No. 18 on)
Feb, 1952 - No. 17, Nov, 1954
Song Hits No. 1/Capitol Stories/Charlton

	Good	Fine	Mint
1	8.00	24.00	48.00
2,4,5	6.00	16.00	32.00
3-Drug mention story	7.00	20.00	40.00
6,8,10	6.00	16.00	32.00
7-Injury to eye-c	10.00	30.00	60.00
9-Used in **SOTI**, pg. 388 & illo-''Stomping on the face is a form of brutality which modern children learn early''	12.00	35.00	70.00
11-Necronomicon story; Nodel & Alascia c/a; Hansel & Gretel parody; Injury-to-eye panel; Check-a	6.00	16.00	32.00
12-''Cinderella'' parody; Ditko c/a(1st)(3-4); lingerie panels	14.00	38.00	76.00
13,15-Ditko c/a(3 & 4)	15.00	45.00	90.00
14-Extreme violence/torture; Rumpelstiltskin story; Ditko c/a(4)	14.00	38.00	76.00
16-Injury to eye panel	8.00	24.00	48.00
17-Ditko-c/a; classic parody-''Through the Looking Glass;'' Powell-a(r)	12.00	35.00	70.00

NOTE: Excessive violence, severed heads, injury to eye are common No. 5 on.

THIRTEEN (. . . Going on 18)
Nov-Jan, 1961-62 - No. 29, Jan, 1971
Dell Publishing Co.

	Good	Fine	Mint
1	2.00	5.00	10.00
2-10	1.50	4.00	8.00
11-29	1.00	3.00	6.00

NOTE: ***John Stanley*** *art/script-No. 3-29.*

THIRTY SECONDS OVER TOKYO
1943 (Movie) (Also see American Library)
David McKay Co.

	Good	Fine	Mint
nn(B&W, text & pictures)	6.00	16.00	32.00

THIS IS SUSPENSE! (Formerly Strange Suspense Stories; Terry and the Pirates No. 26 on)
No. 23, Feb, 1955 - No. 25, 1955
Charlton Comics

	Good	Fine	Mint
23-Wood-a(r)/A Star Presentation No. 3-"Dr. Jekyll & Mr. Hyde"	7.00	20.00	40.00
24-Evans-a	2.00	5.00	10.00
25	1.20	3.50	7.00

THIS IS THE PAYOFF (See Pay-Off)

THIS IS WAR
No. 5, July, 1952 - No. 9, May, 1953
Standard Comics

	Good	Fine	Mint
5,6,9-Toth-a	3.00	8.00	16.00
7,8	1.20	3.50	7.00

THIS IS YOUR LIFE, DONALD DUCK (See 4-Color No. 1109)

THIS MAGAZINE IS CRAZY (Crazy V3No.3 on)
V3No.2, July, 1957 (68 pgs.) (25 cents) (Satire)
Charlton Publ. (Humor Magazines)

	Good	Fine	Mint
V3No.2	.80	2.40	4.80

THIS MAGAZINE IS HAUNTED (Danger and Adventure No. 22 on)
Oct, 1951 - V3No.21, Nov, 1954
Fawcett Publications/Charlton No. 15(2/54) on

	Good	Fine	Mint
1-Evans-a(i?)	7.00	20.00	40.00
2,5-Evans-a	5.50	16.00	32.00
3,4	3.00	9.00	18.00
6-9,11,12,14	2.50	7.00	14.00
10,13-Severed head story	3.00	9.00	18.00
15,20	2.00	6.00	12.00
16-Ditko-c	4.00	12.00	24.00
17-Ditko-c/a(3); blood drainage story	6.00	18.00	36.00
18-Ditko-c/a; E.C. swipe/Haunt of Fear No. 5	6.00	18.00	36.00
19-Injury-to-eye panel; story r-/No.1	4.00	12.00	24.00
21-Ditko-c, Evans-a	4.00	12.00	24.00

NOTE: ***Bailey*** *a-1, 4, 21r/No.1.* ***Powell*** *a-4, 5, 11, 12, 17.* ***Shuster*** *a-19.*

THIS MAGAZINE IS HAUNTED (2nd Series) (Formerly Zaza the Mystic; Outer Space No. 17 on)
V2No.12, July, 1957 - V2No.16, April, 1958
Charlton Comics

	Good	Fine	Mint
V2No.12-16-Ditko c/a in all	4.00	12.00	24.00

THIS MAGAZINE IS WILD (See Wild)

THIS WAS YOUR LIFE (Religious)
1964 (3½x5½") (40 pgs.) (Black, white & red)
Jack T. Chick Publ.

	Good	Fine	Mint
		.40	.80
Another version (5x2¾", 26pgs)	.40	.80	1.20

THOR (Formerly Journey Into Mystery)
March, 1966 - Present
Marvel Comics Group

	Good	Fine	Mint
126	.85	2.50	5.00
127-133,135-140	.50	1.50	3.00
134-Intro High Evolutionary	.80	2.40	4.80
141-145,150: 146-Inhumans begin, end No. 151	.40	1.20	2.40
146,147-Origin The Inhumans	.50	1.50	3.00
148,149-Origin Black Bolt in each; 149-Origin Medusa, Crystal, Maximus, Gorgon, Kornak	.40	1.20	2.40
151-157,159,160	.40	1.20	2.40
158-Reprints origin/No. 83; origin Dr. Blake, concludes No. 159	.60	1.80	3.60
161,163,164,167,170-179-Last Kirby issue	.40	1.20	2.40
162,168,169-Origin Galactus	.45	1.30	2.60
165,166-Warlock(Him) app.	.50	1.50	3.00
180,181-Adams-a	.80	2.40	4.80
182-192,194-199	.30	.90	1.80
193-(52 pgs.); Silver Surfer x-over	.85	2.50	5.00
200	.50	1.50	3.00
201-212,214-226: 225-Intro. Firelord		.60	1.20
213-Starlin-c		.60	1.20
227-230-Buckler-a		.50	1.00
231-250		.40	.80
251-293,295-299,301-314		.40	.80
294-Origin Asgard & Odin		.40	.80
300-End of Asgard; origin of Odin & The Destroyer		.60	1.20
Giant-Size 1('75)		.50	1.00
Special 2(9/66)	.40	1.20	2.40
Special 3,4('67-12/71)(See Journey Into Mystery for No. 1)	.40	1.20	2.40
Annual 5(11/76)		.50	1.00
Annual 6(10/77), 7(9/78)		.40	.80
Annual 8(11/79), 9(11/81)		.40	.80

NOTE: ***Adams*** *c-179-181.* ***Buscema*** *a-178, 182-226, 231-253, 254r, 256-259, 272-278, 283-285, Annual 6, 8; c-175, 182-202, 254, 256, 259, 261, 262, 272-278, 283, 289, Annual 6.* ***Everett*** *inks-143, 170-175; c-241(w/****Romita****).* ***Kirby*** *a-126-177, 179, 194, 254r; c-126-169, 172-174, (176 w/****Everett****), 177, 178, 249-253, 255, 257, 258, Annual 5, Special 1-4.* ***Simonson*** *a-260p, 271p; c-271.*

THOSE MAGNIFICENT MEN IN THEIR FLYING MACHINES (See Movie Comics)

THREE BEARS, THE (See Surprise Books)

THREE CABALLEROS (See 4-Color No. 71)

THREE CHIPMUNKS, THE (See 4-Color No. 1042)

THREE COMICS (Also see Spiritman)
1944 (10 cents, 48pgs.) (2 different covers exist)
The Penny King Co.

	Good	Fine	Mint
1,3,4-Lady Luck, Mr. Mystic, The Spirit app. (3 Spirit sections bound together)-Lou Fine-a	9.00	25.00	50.00

NOTE: *No. 1 contains Spirit Sections 4/9/44 - 4/23/44, and No. 4 is also from April, 1944.*

3-D (NOTE: *The prices of all the 3-D comics listed include glasses. Deduct 40-50 percent if glasses are missing, and reduce slightly if glasses are loose.)*

3-D ACTION
Jan, 1954 (Oversized) (15 cents)
Atlas Comics (ACI)

	Good	Fine	Mint
1-Battle Brady	8.00	24.00	48.00

3-D ANIMAL FUN (See Animal Fun)

3-D BATMAN
1953, Reprinted in 1966
National Periodical Publications

	Good	Fine	Mint
1953-Reprints Batman No. 48	20.00	50.00	100.00
1966-Tommy Tomorrow app.	5.00	14.00	28.00

3-D CIRCUS
1953 (25 cents)
Fiction House Magazines

	Good	Fine	Mint
1	8.00	24.00	48.00

3-D COMICS (See Tor, 3-D, and Mighty Mouse)

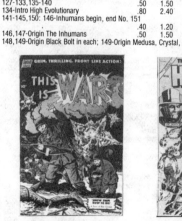

This Is War #5, © STD

This Mag. Is Haunted #16, © CC

Thor #294, © MCG

3-D Circus #1, © FH

3-D Tales Of The West #1, © MCG

Three Stooges #2(3-D), © STJ

3-D DOLLY
December, 1953
Harvey Publications

	Good	Fine	Mint
1-Richie Rich story redrawn from his 1st app. in Little Dot No. 1	15.00	40.00	80.00

3-D-ELL
1953 (3-D comics) (25 cents)
Dell Publishing Co.

1,2-Rootie Kazootie	10.00	28.00	56.00
3-Flukey Luke	8.00	24.00	48.00

3-D FEATURES PRESENT JET PUP
Oct-Dec, 1953
Dimensions Public

1-Irving Spector-a(2)	8.00	24.00	48.00

3-D FUNNY MOVIES
1953 (25 cents)
Comic Media

1	8.00	24.00	48.00

THREE DIMENSION COMICS (See Mighty Mouse)

THREE DIMENSIONAL E. C. CLASSICS (Three Dimensional Tales From the Crypt No. 2)
Spring, 1954 (Prices include glasses)
E. C. Comics

1-Reprints: Wood (Mad No. 3), Krigstein (W.S. No. 7), Evans (F.C. No. 13), & Ingels (CSS No. 5); Kurtzman-c	20.00	50.00	100.00

NOTE: *Stories redrawn to 3-D format. Original stories not necessarily by artists listed. CSS: Crime SuspenStories; F.C.: Frontline Combat; W.S.: Weird Science.*

THREE DIMENSIONAL TALES FROM THE CRYPT (Formerly Three Dimensional E. C. Classics)
Spring, 1954 (Prices include glasses)
E. C. Comics

2-Davis (TFTC No.25), Elder (VOH No.14), Craig (TFTC No.24), & Orlando (TFTC No.22) stories; Feldstein-c	20.00	60.00	120.00

NOTE: *Stories redrawn to 3-D format. Original stories not necessarily by artists listed. TFTC: Tales From the Crypt; VOH: Vault of Horror.*

3-D LOVE
December, 1953 (25 cents)
Steriographic Publ. (Mikeross Publ.)

1	8.00	24.00	48.00

3-D NOODNICK (See Noodnick)

3-D ROMANCE
January, 1954 (25 cents)
Steriographic Publ. (Mikeross Publ.)

1	8.00	24.00	48.00

3-D SHEENA, JUNGLE QUEEN
1953
Fiction House Magazines

1	14.00	40.00	80.00

3-D SUPERMAN
1953 (Large size)
National Periodical Publications

Origin Superman (new art)	30.00	80.00	160.00

3-D TALES OF THE WEST
Jan, 1954 (Oversized) (15 cents)
Atlas Comics (CPS)

1 (3-D)	8.00	24.00	48.00

3-D THREE STOOGES (See Three Stooges)

3-D WHACK (See Whack)

3 FUNMAKERS, THE
1908 (64 pgs.) (10x15'')
Stokes and Company

	Good	Fine	Mint
Maude, Katzenjammer Kids, Happy Hooligan (1904-06 Sunday strip reprints in color)	20.00	50.00	100.00

THREE LITTLE PIGS (See 4-Color No. 218)

3 LITTLE PIGS, THE (See Walt Disney Showcase No. 15,21)
May, 1964 - No. 2, Sept, 1968 (Walt Disney)
Gold Key

1-Reprints 4-Color 218	.40	1.20	2.40
2	.30	.80	1.60

THREE MOUSEKETEERS, THE (1st Series)
Mar-Apr, 1956 - No. 26, Oct-Dec, 1960
National Periodical Publications

1	3.50	10.00	20.00
2-10	2.00	5.00	10.00
11-26	1.20	3.50	7.00

THREE MOUSEKETEERS, THE (2nd Series) (See Super DC Giant)
May-June, 1970 - No. 7, May-June, 1971
National Periodical Publications

1-4	.50	1.50	3.00
5-7 (68 pgs.)	.35	1.00	2.00

THREE NURSES (Formerly Confidential Diary; Career Girl Romances No. 24 on)V3No.18, May, 1963 - V3No.23, Mar, 1964
Charlton Comics

V3No.18-23		.50	1.00

THREE RASCALS
1958; 1963
I. W. Enterprises

I.W. Reprint No. 1 (Says Super Comics on inside)-(M.E.'s Clubhouse Rascals), No. 2('58)	.30	.80	1.60
10('63)-Reprints No. 1	.30	.80	1.60

THREE RING COMICS
March, 1945
Spotlight Publishers

1	1.50	4.00	8.00

THREE ROCKETEERS (See Blast-Off)

THREE STOOGES (See Comic Album No. 18, The Little Stooges, March of Comics No. 232,248,268,280,292,304,316,336,373, & Movie Classics & Comics)

THREE STOOGES
Feb, 1949 - No. 2, May, 1949; Sept, 1953 - No. 7, Oct, 1954
Jubilee No. 1,2/St. John No. 1 (9/53) on

1-(Scarce)-(1949) Kubert-a	17.00	50.00	100.00
2-(Scarce)-Kubert, Maurer-a	14.00	40.00	80.00
1(9/53)-Hollywood Stunt Girl by Kubert, 7 pgs.	14.00	40.00	80.00
2(3-D, 10/53)-Stunt Girl story by Kubert	10.00	30.00	60.00
3(3-D, 11/53)	8.00	24.00	48.00
4(3/54)-7(10/54)	3.50	10.00	20.00

NOTE: *All issues have* ***Kubert-Maurer*** *art.*

THREE STOOGES
Oct-Nov, 1959 - No. 55, June, 1972
Dell Publishing Co./Gold Key No. 10 (10/62) on

4-Color 1043,1078,1127,1170,1187, 6('61)-9(01-827-208)	1.50	4.50	9.00
10-14,16-20	1.25	3.50	7.00
15-Go Around the World in a Daze (movie issue)	1.40	4.00	8.00
21,23-55	.50	1.50	3.00
22-Movie scenes from 'The Outlaws is Coming'	.50	1.50	3.00

THREE STOOGES (continued)
NOTE: *11-14,16-24,26-38 have photo-c.*

3 WORLDS OF GULLIVER (See 4-Color No. 1158)

THRILLING ADVENTURES IN STAMPS COMICS (Formerly Stamp Comics)
Jan, 1953 (25 cents) (100 pages)
Stamp Comics, Inc.

	Good	Fine	Mint
V1No.8-Harrison, Wildey-a	3.50	10.00	20.00

THRILLING ADVENTURE STORIES
Feb, 1975 - No. 2, July-Aug, 1975 (B&W) (68 pgs.)
Atlas/Seaboard Publ.

	Good	Fine	Mint
1-Tigerman, Kromag the Killer begin; Heath, Thorne-a	.40	1.20	2.40
2-Toth, Severin, Simonson-a; Adams-c	.40	1.20	2.40

THRILLING COMICS
Feb, 1940 - No. 80, April, 1951
Nedor/Better/Standard Comics

	Good	Fine	Mint
1-Origin Doc Strange; Nickie Norton begins	30.00	90.00	180.00
2-The Rio Kid & The Woman in Red begin	14.00	40.00	80.00
3-The Ghost & Lone Eagle begin	12.00	35.00	70.00
4-10	9.00	25.00	50.00
11-18,20	6.00	18.00	36.00
19-Origin The American Crusader, ends No. 39,41	10.00	28.00	56.00
21-30: 22-Bondage-c. 24-Intro. Mike, Doc Strange's sidekick. 29-Last Rio Kid	5.00	14.00	28.00
31-40: 36-Commando Cubs begin. 38-Bondage-c	4.00	12.00	24.00
41-52-The Ghost ends. 48-Kinstler-a	3.50	10.00	20.00
53-The Phantom Detective begins; The Cavalier app.; no Commando Cubs	3.50	10.00	20.00
54-The Cavalier app.; no Commando Cubs	3.50	10.00	20.00
55-Lone Eagle ends	3.50	10.00	20.00
56-Princess Pantha begins	7.00	20.00	40.00
57-60	6.00	18.00	36.00
61-65: 61-The Lone Eagle app. 65-Last Phantom Detective & Commando Cubs	6.00	18.00	36.00
66-Frazetta text illo	7.00	20.00	40.00
67,70-73: Frazetta-a(5-7 pgs.) in each. 72-Sea Eagle app.	10.00	30.00	60.00
68,69-Frazetta-a(2), 8 & 6 pgs.; 9 & 7 pgs.	12.00	35.00	70.00
74-Last Princess Pantha; Tara app.	3.50	10.00	20.00
75-78: 75-Western format begins	2.00	6.00	12.00
79-Krigstein-a	3.50	10.00	20.00
80-Severin & Elder, Celardo, Moreira-a	3.50	10.00	20.00

NOTE: ***Schomburg (Xela)** c-No. 38, 40, 46, 54, 57-69 (No.62-71, airbrush),75. Woman in Red not in No. 19,23,31-33,39-45. No. 72 exists as a Canadian reprint with no Frazetta story.*

THRILLING CRIME CASES (Shocking Mystery Cases No. 50 on)
No. 41, June-July, 1950 - No. 49, 1952
Star Publications

	Good	Fine	Mint
41,42	3.50	10.00	20.00
43-Drug mention story	5.00	14.00	28.00
44-Chameleon story-Fox-r	4.00	12.00	24.00
45,46,48	5.00	14.00	28.00
47-Used in **POP**, pg. 84	4.00	12.00	24.00
49-Classic L. B. Cole-c	8.00	24.00	48.00

NOTE: *All have **L. B. Cole**-c; a-43p, 45p, 46p, 49(2pgs.). **Disbrow** a-48. **Hollingsworth** a-48.*

THRILLING ROMANCES
No. 5, Dec, 1949 - No. 26, June, 1954
Standard Comics

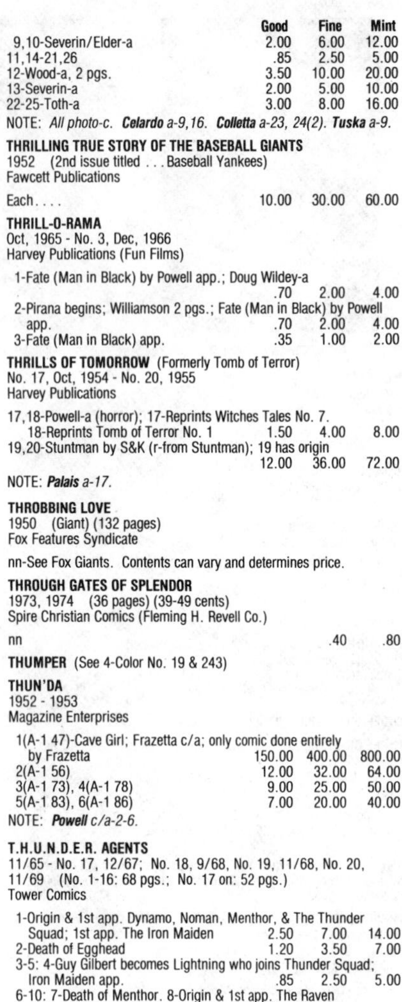

	Good	Fine	Mint
5	2.00	5.00	10.00
6,8	1.50	4.00	8.00
7-Severin/Elder-a, 7 pgs.	3.00	8.00	16.00
9,10-Severin/Elder-a	2.00	6.00	12.00
11,14-21,26	.85	2.50	5.00
12-Wood-a, 2 pgs.	3.50	10.00	20.00
13-Severin-a	2.00	5.00	10.00
22-25-Toth-a	3.00	8.00	16.00

NOTE: *All photo-c. **Celardo** a-9,16. **Colletta** a-23, 24(2). **Tuska** a-9.*

THRILLING TRUE STORY OF THE BASEBALL GIANTS
1952 (2nd issue titled . . . Baseball Yankees)
Fawcett Publications

	Good	Fine	Mint
Each. . . .	10.00	30.00	60.00

THRILL-O-RAMA
Oct, 1965 - No. 3, Dec, 1966
Harvey Publications (Fun Films)

	Good	Fine	Mint
1-Fate (Man in Black) by Powell app.; Doug Wildey-a	.70	2.00	4.00
2-Pirana begins; Williamson 2 pgs.; Fate (Man in Black) by Powell app.	.70	2.00	4.00
3-Fate (Man in Black) app.	.35	1.00	2.00

THRILLS OF TOMORROW (Formerly Tomb of Terror)
No. 17, Oct, 1954 - No. 20, 1955
Harvey Publications

	Good	Fine	Mint
17,18-Powell-a (horror); 17-Reprints Witches Tales No. 7. 18-Reprints Tomb of Terror No. 1	1.50	4.00	8.00
19,20-Stuntman by S&K (r-from Stuntman); 19 has origin	12.00	36.00	72.00

NOTE: ***Palais** a-17.*

THROBBING LOVE
1950 (Giant) (132 pages)
Fox Features Syndicate

nn-See Fox Giants. Contents can vary and determines price.

THROUGH GATES OF SPLENDOR
1973, 1974 (36 pages) (39-49 cents)
Spire Christian Comics (Fleming H. Revell Co.)

	Good	Fine	Mint
nn		.40	.80

THUMPER (See 4-Color No. 19 & 243)

THUN'DA
1952 - 1953
Magazine Enterprises

	Good	Fine	Mint
1(A-1 47)-Cave Girl; Frazetta c/a; only comic done entirely by Frazetta	150.00	400.00	800.00
2(A-1 56)	12.00	32.00	64.00
3(A-1 73), 4(A-1 78)	9.00	25.00	50.00
5(A-1 83), 6(A-1 86)	7.00	20.00	40.00

NOTE: ***Powell** c/a-2-6.*

T.H.U.N.D.E.R. AGENTS
11/65 - No. 17, 12/67; No. 18, 9/68, No. 19, 11/68, No. 20, 11/69 (No. 1-16: 68 pgs.; No. 17 on: 52 pgs.)
Tower Comics

	Good	Fine	Mint
1-Origin & 1st app. Dynamo, Noman, Menthor, & The Thunder Squad; 1st app. The Iron Maiden	2.50	7.00	14.00
2-Death of Egghead	1.20	3.50	7.00
3-5: 4-Guy Gilbert becomes Lightning who joins Thunder Squad; Iron Maiden app.	.85	2.50	5.00
6-10: 7-Death of Menthor. 8-Origin & 1st app. The Raven	.70	2.00	4.00
11-15: 13-Undersea Agent app.; no Raven story	.50	1.50	3.00
16-19	.35	1.00	2.00
20-All reprints	.30	.80	1.60

NOTE: ***Crandall** a-1, 4, 5p, 18; c-18. **Ditko** a-6, 7i, 12p, 14, 16, 18. **Kane** a-1, 5p, 6p, 14, 16; c-14, 15. **Whitney** a-10, 13, 15, 17, 18;*

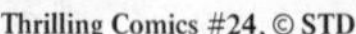

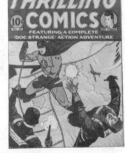

Thrilling Comics #24, © STD

Thrilling Crime Cases #43, © STAR

Thunder Agents #4, © TC

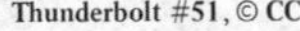
Thunderbolt #51, © CC

Time Warp #1, © DC

Tim Holt #20, © ME

T.H.U.N.D.E.R. AGENTS (continued)
c-17. ***Wood*** *a-1-11,(w/****Ditko****-No. 12,18), (inks-No. 9, 16, 17), 5-17, 19, 20r; c-1-8, 10-13(No. 10 w/****Williamson****).*

THUNDERBOLT (See The Atomic . . .)

THUNDERBOLT (Peter Cannon . . .) (Formerly Son of Vulcan No. 50)
Jan, 1966; No. 51, Mar-Apr, 1966 - No. 60, Nov, 1967
Charlton Comics

	Good	Fine	Mint
1-Origin	.50	1.50	3.00
51	.30	.80	1.60
52-58: 54-Sentinels begin. 58-Last Thunderbolt & Sentinels		.60	1.20
59,60: 60-Prankster app.		.50	1.00
Modern Comics-r. 57,58('77)		.15	.30

THUNDER MOUNTAIN (See 4-Color No. 246)

TICK TOCK TALES
Jan, 1946 - No.34, 1951
Magazine Enterprises

	Good	Fine	Mint
1	2.50	7.00	14.00
2-10	1.20	3.50	7.00
11-34	.70	2.00	4.00

TICKLE COMICS (Also see Gay, Smile, & Whee Comics)
1955 (52 pages) (5x7¼'') (7 cents)
Modern Store Publ.

	Good	Fine	Mint
1	.40	1.20	2.40

TIGER (Also see Comics Reading Libraries)
March, 1970 - No. 6, Jan, 1971 (15 cents)
Charlton Press (King Features)

	Good	Fine	Mint
1	.30	.80	1.60
2-6		.50	1.00

TIGER BOY (See Unearthly Spectaculars)

TIGER GIRL
September, 1968
Gold Key

	Good	Fine	Mint
1 (10227-809)	1.50	4.00	8.00

TIGER-MAN
April, 1975 - No. 3, Sept, 1975
Seaboard Periodicals (Atlas)

	Good	Fine	Mint
1		.50	1.00
2,3-Ditko-a in each		.30	.60

TIGER WALKS, A (See Movie Comics)

TILLIE AND TED-TINKERTOTLAND
1945
W. T. Grant Co.

	Good	Fine	Mint
	1.50	4.00	8.00

TILLIE THE TOILER
1926 - 1933 (52 pgs.) (B&W daily strip reprints)
Cupples & Leon Co.

	Good	Fine	Mint
1	6.00	18.00	36.00
2-8	5.00	14.00	28.00

NOTE: *First strip app. was January, 1921.*

TILLIE THE TOILER (See Comic Monthly)
1941 - 1950
Dell Publishing Co.

	Good	Fine	Mint
4-Color 15(1941)	8.00	24.00	48.00
Large Feature Comic 30(1941)	6.00	18.00	36.00
4-Color 8(1942)	5.50	16.00	32.00
4-Color 22(1943)	5.00	14.00	28.00
4-Color 55(1944)	3.50	10.00	20.00
4-Color 89(1945)	3.00	9.00	18.00
4-Color 106('45),132('46)	2.50	7.00	14.00
4-Color 150,176,184	2.00	6.00	12.00
4-Color 195,213,237	2.00	5.00	10.00

TIME FOR LOVE (Formerly Romantic Secrets)
V2No.52(Exist?), V2No.53, Oct, 1966 - No. 47, May, 1976
Charlton Comics

	Good	Fine	Mint
V2No.52,53(10/66), 1(10/67), 2(12/67)		.40	.80
3-47		.15	.30

TIMELESS TOPIX (See Topix)

TIME MACHINE, THE (See 4-Color No. 1085)

TIME TO RUN
1973 (39, 49 cents)
Spire Christian Comics (Fleming H. Revell Co.)

	Good	Fine	Mint
nn-by Al Hartley (from Billy Graham movie)		.50	1.00

TIME TUNNEL, THE (TV)
Feb, 1967 - No. 2, July, 1967
Gold Key

	Good	Fine	Mint
1,2	1.00	3.00	6.00

TIME WARP
Oct-Nov, 1979 - No. 5, July, 1980 ($1.00)
DC Comics, Inc.

	Good	Fine	Mint
1		.60	1.20
2-5		.60	1.20

NOTE: ***Aparo*** *a-1.* ***Chaykin*** *a-2.* ***Ditko*** *a-1, 3, 4.* ***Kaluta*** *c-1-5.* ***G. Kane*** *a-2.* ***Newton*** *a-1-5.* ***Orlando*** *a-2.* ***Sutton*** *a-3.*

TIM HOLT (Becomes Red Mask No. 42 on)
1948 - No. 41, May, 1954
Magazine Enterprises

	Good	Fine	Mint
1(A-1 14)	15.00	45.00	90.00
2(A-1 17)	10.00	27.00	54.00
3(A-1 19)	6.00	18.00	36.00
4(1-2/49)-10: 6-1st app. Calico Kid	5.00	15.00	30.00
11-Origin & 1st app. Ghost Rider; series begins in Tim Holt	15.00	45.00	90.00
12-16,18,19	3.00	8.00	16.00
17-Frazetta-c	15.00	40.00	80.00
20-Origin Red Mask	5.00	14.00	28.00
21,23-Frazetta-c	12.00	35.00	70.00
22,24,26-30	2.50	7.00	14.00
25-1st app. Black Phantom	3.00	9.00	18.00
31-35,37,38,41: 38-Black Phantom begins	2.00	6.00	12.00
36-Liquid hallucinogenic drug story	3.00	9.00	18.00
39,40-(3-D effect)	4.00	12.00	24.00

NOTE: ***Bolle*** *art in most issues.*

TIM IN SPACE (Formerly Gene Autry Tim)
1950 (½-size giveaway) (B&W)
Tim Stores

	Good	Fine	Mint
	2.00	5.00	10.00

TIM McCOY (Formerly Zoo Funnies; Pictorial Love Stories No. 22)
No. 16, Oct, 1948 - No. 21, Aug-Sept, 1949
Charlton Comics

	Good	Fine	Mint
16-21	6.00	16.00	32.00

TIM McCOY, POLICE CAR 17
1934 (32 pgs.) (11x14¾'') (B&W)
Whitman Publishing Co.

	Good	Fine	Mint
674-1933 movie in pictures	5.00	14.00	28.00

TIMMY (See 4-Color No. 715,823,923,1022)

TIMMY THE TIMID GHOST (See Blue Bird)
1957 - No. 45, Sept, 1966; Oct, 1967 - No. 23, July, 1971
Charlton Comics

	Good	Fine	Mint
1(1957) (1st Series)	1.50	4.00	8.00
2-5	.85	2.50	5.00

TIMMY THE TIMID GHOST (continued)

	Good	Fine	Mint
6-10	.40	1.20	2.40
11,12(4/58,10/58)(100pgs.)	.80	2.40	4.80
13-45('66)		.50	1.00
1(11/67)-Bluebird		.30	.60
2-23		.25	.50
Shoe Store Giveaway		.40	.80

TIM TYLER (See Comics Hits No. 54)

TIM TYLER (Also see Comics Reading Libraries)
1942
Better Publications

	Good	Fine	Mint
1	3.00	8.00	16.00

TIM TYLER COWBOY
No. 11, Nov, 1948 - No. 18, 1950
Standard Comics

	Good	Fine	Mint
11-18	2.00	5.00	10.00

TINKER BELL (See 4-Color No. 896,982, & Walt Disney Showcase No. 37)

TINY FOLKS FUNNIES (See 4-Color No. 60)

TINY TESSIE (Tessie No. 1-23; Real Experiences No. 25)
No. 24, Oct, 1949
Marvel Comics (20CC)

	Good	Fine	Mint
24	.70	2.00	4.00

TINY TIM
1941 - 1949
Dell Publishing Co.

	Good	Fine	Mint
Large Feature Comic 4('41)	12.00	35.00	70.00
4-Color 20(1941)	10.00	30.00	60.00
4-Color 42(1943)	5.50	16.00	32.00
4-Color 235	2.00	6.00	12.00

TINY TOT COMICS
1946 - No. 10, Nov-Dec, 1947
E. C. Comics

	Good	Fine	Mint
1(nn)	8.00	24.00	48.00
2-10	7.00	20.00	40.00

TINY TOT FUNNIES (Becomes Junior Funnies)
June, 1951
Harvey Publ. (King Features Synd.)

	Good	Fine	Mint
9-Flash Gordon, Mandrake	2.50	7.00	14.00

TINY TOTS COMICS
1943 (Not reprints)
Dell Publishing Co.

	Good	Fine	Mint
1-Kelly-a(2)	40.00	90.00	160.00

TIPPY & CAP STUBBS (See 4-Color No. 210,242)

TIPPY'S FRIENDS GO-GO & ANIMAL
July, 1966 - No. 15, Oct, 1969 (25 cents)
Tower Comics

	Good	Fine	Mint
1	.70	2.00	4.00
2-7,9-15: 12-15 titled "Tippy's Friend Go-Go"	.50	1.50	3.00
8-Beatles on front/back-c	.70	2.00	4.00

TIPPY TEEN
Nov, 1965 - No. 27, Feb, 1970 (25 cents)
Tower Comics

	Good	Fine	Mint
1	.50	1.50	3.00
2-27: 5-1pg. Beatle pin-up	.30	.80	1.60
Special Collectors' Editions(1969-nn)(25 cents)	.30	.80	1.60

TIPPY TERRY
1963
Super/I. W. Enterprises

	Good	Fine	Mint
Super Reprint No. 14('63)-Little Grouchy reprints		.60	1.20
I.W. Reprint No. 1 (no date)		.60	1.20

TIP TOP COMICS
April, 1936 - No. 225, May-July, 1961
United Features/St. John/Dell Publishing Co.

	Good	Fine	Mint
1-Tarzan by Hal Foster, Li'l Abner begin; strip-r	60.00	170.00	340.00
2	30.00	85.00	170.00
3	20.00	55.00	110.00
4	15.00	45.00	90.00
5-10: 7-Photo & biography of Edgar Rice Burroughs	10.00	30.00	60.00
11-20	8.50	25.00	50.00
21-40: 36-Kurtzman panel (1st published comic work)	7.00	20.00	40.00
41-50: 41-Has 1st Tarzan Sunday. 43-Mort Walker panel	6.00	18.00	36.00
51-53	5.50	16.00	32.00
54-Origin Mirror Man & Triple Terror, also featured on cover	7.00	20.00	40.00
55,56,58,60	5.00	14.00	28.00
57,59,62-Tarzan by Hogarth	8.00	24.00	48.00
61-Last Tarzan by Foster	5.00	14.00	28.00
63-80: 65,67,68,70,72,73-No Tarzan	4.00	12.00	24.00
81-90	3.50	10.00	20.00
91-100	3.00	8.00	16.00
101-140: 110-Gordo story. 111-Li'l Abner app. 118, 132-no Tarzan	2.00	6.00	12.00
141-170: 151-Gordo story. 157-Last Li'l Abner	1.50	4.00	8.00
171-188-Tarzan reprints by B. Lubbers in all. No. 177?-Peanuts by Shulz begins; no Peanuts in No. 179,181-183	2.00	5.00	10.00
189-225	1.00	3.00	6.00
Bound Volumes (Very Rare) sold at 1939 World's Fair; bound by publ. in pictorial comic boards. (Also see Comics on Parade)			
Bound issues 1-12	110.00	320.00	640.00
Bound issues 13-24	70.00	200.00	400.00
Bound issues 25-36	50.00	140.00	280.00

NOTE: *Tarzan covers-No. 3,9,11,13,16,18,21,24,27,30,32-34,36, 37,39,41,43,45,47,50,52 (all worth 10-20 percent more). Tarzan by* **Foster***-No. 1-40,44-50; by* **Rex Maxon***-No. 41-43; by* **Byrne Hogarth***-No. 57,59,62.*

TIP TOPPER COMICS
1949 - 1954
United Features Syndicate

	Good	Fine	Mint
1-Li'l Abner, Abbie & Slats	1.50	4.50	9.00
2-5	1.25	3.50	7.00
6-25: 21-Peanuts app.	.85	2.50	5.00
26-28-Twin Earths	2.00	6.00	12.00

NOTE: *Many lingerie panels in Fritzi Ritz stories.*

T-MAN
Sept, 1951 - No. 38, Dec, 1956
Quality Comics Group

	Good	Fine	Mint
1-Jack Cole-a	6.00	18.00	36.00
2-Crandall-c?	3.00	9.00	18.00
3,6-8: Drug stories, Crandall-c	5.00	15.00	30.00
4,5-Crandall c/a each; 5-Drug test	4.00	12.00	24.00
9-Crandall-c; drug story	3.00	8.00	16.00
10	2.00	6.00	12.00
11-Used in **POP**, pg. 95 & color illo.	5.00	14.00	28.00
12-Heroin drug mention story	4.00	12.00	24.00
13-18,21-26	2.00	5.00	10.00
19-Drug mention story	2.50	7.00	14.00

Tiny Tot Comics #9, © WMG

Tip Top Comics #3, © UFS

T-Man #4, © QUA

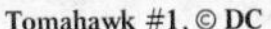
Tomahawk #1, © DC

Tom & Jerry #84, © DELL

Tomb Of Dracula #50, © MCG

T-MAN (continued)

	Good	Fine	Mint
20-Nuclear explosion-c	4.00	12.00	24.00
27-30,32-38	1.50	4.00	8.00
31-Drug story, CCA approved	2.00	6.00	12.00

NOTE: *Anti-communist stories are common.*

TNT COMICS
Feb, 1946
Charles Publishing Co.

	Good	Fine	Mint
1-Yellowjacket app.; drug mention story	3.50	10.00	20.00

TOBY TYLER (See Movie Comics & 4-Color No. 1092)

TODAY'S BRIDES
Nov, 1955 - No. 4, Nov, 1956
Ajax/Farrell Publishing Co.

	Good	Fine	Mint
1	2.00	6.00	12.00
2-4	1.00	3.00	6.00

TODAY'S ROMANCE
No. 5, March, 1952 - No. 8, Sept, 1952
Standard Comics

	Good	Fine	Mint
5,7,8	1.00	3.00	6.00
6-Toth-a	3.00	8.00	16.00

TOKA (Jungle King)
Aug-Oct, 1964 - No. 10, Jan, 1967
Dell Publishing Co.

	Good	Fine	Mint
1	.50	1.50	3.00
2	.35	1.00	2.00
3-10	.25	.70	1.40

TOMAHAWK (Son of . . . No. 131-140 on cover)
Sept-Oct, 1950 - No. 140, May-June, 1972
National Periodical Publications

	Good	Fine	Mint
1	15.00	45.00	90.00
2-Frazetta/Williamson-a, 4 pgs.	12.00	36.00	75.00
3-5	6.00	17.00	34.00
6-10	4.00	12.00	24.00
11-20	2.50	7.00	14.00
21-27,30	1.75	5.00	10.00
28-1st app. Lord Shilling (arch-foe)	2.00	6.00	12.00
29-Frazetta-r/Jimmy Wakely No. 3, 3 pgs.	8.00	24.00	48.00
31-50	1.00	3.00	6.00
51-56,58-70	.70	2.00	4.00
57-Frazetta-r/Jimmy Wakely No. 6, 3 pgs.	5.00	15.00	30.00
71-80		.60	1.20
81-1st app. Miss Liberty	.30	.80	1.60
82,84,85,87-95		.50	1.00
83-Origin Tomahawk's Rangers		.60	1.20
86-Last Lord Shilling; origin King Colosso (Giant Ape)		.50	1.00
96-Origin & 1st app. The Hood, Alias Lady Shilling		.50	1.00
97-106,108,109		.50	1.00
107-Origin & 1st app. Thunder-Man		.50	1.00
110-The Hood & Miss Liberty app.		.50	1.00
111-The Hood & Thunder-Man team-up		.40	.80
112-130		.40	.80
131-Frazetta-r/Jimmy Wakely No. 7, 3 pgs.; origin Firehair retold	.50	1.50	3.00
132,134,136-Six pg. Kubert		.40	.80
133,135,137,138,140		.30	.60
139-Frazetta-r/Star Spangled No. 113		.60	1.20

NOTE: ***Adams*** *c-116-119, 121, 123-130. Firehair by* ***Kubert****-131-134, 136.* ***Maurer*** *a-138.*

TOM AND JERRY (See Comic Album No. 4,8,12, Dell Giant No. 21, Golden Comics Digest No. 1,5,8,13,15,18,22,25,28,35, & March of Comics No. 21,46,61,70,88,103,119,128,145,154,173,190,207, 224,281,295,305,321,333,345,361,365,388,400,480)

TOM AND JERRY (. . Comics, early issues) (M.G.M.)
(Formerly Our Gang No. 1-59)
No. 193, 6/48; No. 60, 7/49 - No. 212, 7-9/62; No. 213, 11/62 - No. 291, 2/75; No. 292, 3/77 - Present
Dell Publishing Co./Gold Key No. 213-327/Whitman No. 328 on

	Good	Fine	Mint
4-Color 193	4.00	12.00	24.00
60-80	1.20	3.50	7.00
81-100	.70	2.00	4.00
101-130	.40	1.20	2.40
131-160	.30	.80	1.60
161-200		.50	1.00
201-212(7-9/62)		.40	.80
213-215-All titled ''. . . Funhouse.'' No. 213,214-(84 pgs.)	.30	.80	1.60
216-230		.40	.80
231-270		.30	.60
271-338: 286-''Tom & Jerry''		.25	.50
Back to School 1(9/56)	1.50	4.00	8.00
Mouse From T.R.A.P. 1(7/66)-Giant, G. K.	.30	.80	1.60
Picnic Time 1(7/58)	1.20	3.50	7.00
Summer Fun 1(7/54)-Droopy written by Carl Barks	4.00	12.00	24.00
Summer Fun 2-4(7/57)	1.20	3.50	7.00
Summer Fun 1('67-G.K.-r)-Reprints Barks' Droopy/Winter Carnival No. 2	.50	1.50	3.00
. . . Tells About Kites(1959, PG&E giveaway)	.85	2.50	5.00
Toy Fair 1('58)-100 pgs.	1.50	4.00	8.00
Winter Carnival 1('52)-Droopy written by Barks	5.00	14.00	28.00
Winter Carnival 2('53)-Droopy written by Barks (Giant)	3.00	9.00	18.00
Winter Fun 3-7('54-'58)	.85	2.50	5.00

NOTE: *No. 60-87,98-121,268,277,289,302 are 52 pages. Reprints-No. 225,241,245,247,252,254,266,268,270,292-327,329,330.*

TOMB OF DARKNESS (Formerly Beware)
No. 9, July, 1974 - No. 23, Nov, 1976
Marvel Comics Group

	Good	Fine	Mint
9-19: 17-Woodbridge-r/Astonishing No. 62		.30	.60
20-Everett Venus r-/Venus No. 19		.30	.60
21-23: 23-Everett-a(r)		.25	.50

NOTE: ***Ditko*** *a-15r, 19r.*

TOMB OF DRACULA (See Giant-Size Dracula & Dracula Lives)
April, 1972 - No. 70, Aug, 1979
Marvel Comics Group

	Good	Fine	Mint
1	1.50	4.00	8.00
2-5: 3-Intro. Dr. Rachel Van Helsing & Inspector Chelm	.50	1.50	3.00
6-9: 6-Adams-c	.40	1.20	2.40
10-1st app. Blade the Vampire Slayer	.40	1.20	2.40
11,12,14-20: 12-Brunner-c(p)	.30	.80	1.60
13-Origin Blade the Vampire Slayer	.30	.80	1.60
21-Origin Dr. Sun		.50	1.00
22-24,26-28,30		.50	1.00
25-Origin & 1st app. Hannibal King		.50	1.00
29-Origin Taj		.50	1.00
31-40: 33-Origin Quincy Harker		.40	.80
41,42,44-49		.40	.80
43-Wrightson-c		.40	.80
50-Silver Surfer app.		.60	1.20
51-53,55-60		.40	.80
54-Birth Dracula's Son		.40	.80
61-69-Last Giant issue		.40	.80
70		.60	1.20

TOMB OF DRACULA (Magazine)
Nov, 1979 - No. 6, Sept, 1980 (B&W)
Marvel Comics Group

	Good	Fine	Mint
1		.60	1.20
2,4-6: 2-Ditko-a (36 pgs.)		.50	1.00
3-Miller-a	.35	1.00	2.00

NOTE: ***Buscema*** *a-4p, 5p.* ***Chaykin*** *c-5, 6.* ***Miller*** *a-3.*

TOMB OF LIGEIA (See Movie Classics)

TOMB OF TERROR (Thrills of Tomorrow No. 17 on)
June, 1952 - No. 16, July, 1954
Harvey Publications

	Good	Fine	Mint
1	6.00	16.00	32.00
2	4.00	12.00	24.00
3-Bondage-c; atomic disaster story	5.00	14.00	28.00
4-7: 4-Heart ripped out	4.00	12.00	24.00
8-12-Nostrand-a	4.00	12.00	24.00
13-Special S/F ish	6.00	16.00	32.00
14-Check-a; special S/F ish.	6.00	16.00	32.00
15-S/F ish.; c-shows head exploding; Nostrand-a(r)	7.00	20.00	40.00
16-Special S/F ish; Nostrand-a	6.00	16.00	32.00

NOTE: ***Palais** a-2, 3, 5-7. **Powell** a-1, 3, 4(1 pg.), 5, 9-16.*

TOMBSTONE TERRITORY (See 4-Color No. 1123)

TOM CAT
July, 1956 - No. 8, July, 1957
Charlton Comics

	Good	Fine	Mint
1-8	.40	1.20	2.40

TOM CORBETT SPACE CADET (TV)
1952 - No. 11, Sept-Nov, 1954
Dell Publishing Co.

	Good	Fine	Mint
4-Color 378,400,421-All by McWilliams	2.50	7.00	14.00
4-11	1.50	4.50	9.00

TOM CORBETT SPACE CADET (See March of Comics No. 102)

TOM CORBETT SPACE CADET
May-June, 1955 - V2No.3, Sept-Oct, 1955
Prize Publications

	Good	Fine	Mint
V2No.1-3	3.00	9.00	18.00

TOM LANDRY & THE DALLAS COWBOYS
1973 (35-49 cents)
Spire Christian Comics/Fleming H. Revell Co.

	Good	Fine	Mint
nn		.50	1.00

TOM MIX (. . . Commando Comics No. 10-12)
Sept, 1940 - No. 12, Nov, 1942 (36 pages)
Given away for two Ralston box tops
Ralston-Purina Co.

	Good	Fine	Mint
1-Origin (life) Tom Mix; Fred Meagher-a	35.00	100.00	225.00
2	25.00	75.00	150.00
3-9	20.00	55.00	120.00
10-12: 10-Origin Tom Mix Commando Unit; Speed O'Dare begins	15.00	40.00	80.00

TOM MIX WESTERN (Also see Master Comics)
Jan, 1948 - No. 61, May, 1953
Fawcett Publications

	Good	Fine	Mint
1	15.00	40.00	90.00
2	10.00	30.00	60.00
3-5	8.00	24.00	48.00
6-8: 8-Kinstler tempera-c	7.00	20.00	40.00
9,10-Used in SOTI, pgs. 323-325	7.00	20.00	40.00
11-20: 11-Kinstler oil-c	5.00	14.00	28.00
21-30	4.00	12.00	24.00
31-40	3.50	10.00	20.00
41-61	2.00	6.00	12.00

TOMMY OF THE BIG TOP
1948 - 1949
King Features Syndicate/Standard Comics

	Good	Fine	Mint
10-12	1.00	3.00	6.00

TOM SAWYER (See Famous Stories & Advs. of. . .)

TOM SAWYER & HUCK FINN
1925 (52 pgs.) (10¾x10'') (stiff covers)
Stoll & Edwards Co.

	Good	Fine	Mint
By Dwiggins; reprints 1923, 1924 Sunday strips in color	7.00	20.00	40.00

TOM SAWYER COMICS
1951? (paper cover)
Giveaway

	Good	Fine	Mint
Contains a coverless Hopalong Cassidy from 1951; other combinations possible.	1.00	3.00	6.00

TOM SKINNER-UP FROM HARLEM
1975 (36 pages) (39 cents)
Spire Christian Comics (Fleming H. Revell Co.)

	Good	Fine	Mint
nn		.40	.80

TOM TERRIFIC! (TV)
Summer, 1957 - No. 6, Fall, 1958
Pines Comics

	Good	Fine	Mint
1	2.00	5.00	10.00
2-6	1.20	3.50	7.00

TOM THUMB (See 4-Color No. 972)

TOM-TOM, THE JUNGLE BOY
1947; Nov, 1957 - No. 3, Mar, 1958
Magazine Enterprises

	Good	Fine	Mint
1	1.25	3.50	7.00
2,3(1947)	.85	2.50	5.00
1(1957)(& Itchi the Monk), 2,3('58)	.35	1.00	2.00
I.W. Reprint No. 1,2,8,10		.40	.80

TONKA (See 4-Color No. 966)

TONTO (See The Lone Ranger's Companion. . .)

TONY TRENT (The Face No. 1,2)
1948 - 1949
Big Shot/Columbia Comics Group

	Good	Fine	Mint
3,4: 3-The Face app.	2.00	6.00	12.00

TOODLE TWINS, THE
1-2/51 - No. 10, 7-8/51; 1956 (Newspaper reprints)
Ziff-Davis (Approved Comics)/Argo

	Good	Fine	Mint
1	2.00	5.00	10.00
2-9	1.50	4.00	8.00
10-Painted-c, some newspaper-r	1.50	4.00	8.00
1(Argo, 3/56)	1.50	4.00	8.00

TOONERVILLE TROLLEY
1921 (Daily strip reprints) (B&W) (52 pgs.)
Cupples & Leon Co.

	Good	Fine	Mint
1-By Fontaine Fox	10.00	30.00	60.00

TOOTS & CASPER (See Large Feature Comic No. 5)

TOP ADVENTURE COMICS
1964 (Reprints)
I. W. Enterprises

	Good	Fine	Mint
1-Reprints/Explorer Joe No. 2; Krigstein-a	.70	2.00	4.00
2-Black Dwarf	.80	2.40	4.80

TOP CAT (TV) (Hanna-Barbera)
12-2/61-62 - No. 3, 6-8/62; No. 4, 10/62 - No. 31, 9/70
Dell Publishing Co./Gold Key No. 4 on

	Good	Fine	Mint
1	1.00	3.00	6.00
2-5	.70	2.00	4.00
6-10	.35	1.00	2.00
11-31: 21,24,25,29-Reprints		.50	1.00

TOP CAT (TV) (Hanna-Barbera)
Nov, 1970 - No. 20, Nov, 1973
Charlton Comics

Tomb Of Terror #12, © HARV

Tom Corbett #10, © DELL

Tom Mix Western #50, © FAW

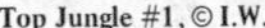
Top Jungle #1, © I.W.

Top Love Stories #13, © STAR

Top-Notch Comics #2, © MLJ

TOP CAT (continued)

	Good	Fine	Mint
1	.50	1.50	3.00
2-20		.50	1.00

NOTE: *No. 8 (1/72) went on sale late in 1972 between No. 14 and No. 15 with the January 1973 issues.*

TOP COMICS
July, 1967 (All rebound issues)
K. K. Publications/Gold Key

	Good	Fine	Mint
1-Beagle Boys (No.7), Bugs Bunny, Chip 'n' Dale, Daffy Duck (No. 50), Flintstones, Flipper, Huckleberry Hound, Huey, Dewey & Louie, Junior Woodchucks, The Jetsons, Lassie, The Little Monsters (No.71), Moby Duck, Porky Pig (has Gold Key label - says Top Comics on inside), Scamp, Super Goof, Tarzan of the Apes (No.169), Three Stooges (No.35), Tom & Jerry, Top Cat (No.21), Tweety & Sylvester (No.7), Walt Disney Comics & Stories (No. 322), Woody Woodpecker, Yogi Bear, Zorro known; each character given own book.	.30	.90	1.80
1-Uncle Scrooge (No.70)	1.00	3.00	6.00
1-Donald Duck (not Barks), Mickey Mouse	.70	2.00	4.00
2-Bugs Bunny, Daffy Duck, Donald Duck (not Barks), Mickey Mouse (No.114), Porky Pig, Super Goof, Three Stooges, Tom & Jerry, Tweety & Sylvester, Uncle Scrooge (No. 71)-Barks-c, Walt Disney's C&S (r-/No.325), Woody Woodpecker, Zorro	.30	.90	1.80
2-Snow White & 7 Dwarfs(6/67)(1944-r)	.80	2.40	4.80
3-Donald Duck	.50	1.50	3.00
3-Uncle Scrooge (No.72)	1.00	3.00	6.00
3-The Flintstones, Mickey Mouse (reprints No.115), Tom & Jerry, Woody Woodpecker, Yogi Bear		.50	1.00
4-The Flintstones, Mickey Mouse, Woody Woodpecker		.50	1.00

NOTE: *Each book in this series is identical to its counterpart except for cover, and came out at same time. The number in parenthesis is the original issue it contains.*

TOP DETECTIVE COMICS
1964 (Reprints)
I. W. Enterprises

	Good	Fine	Mint
9-Young King Cole & Dr. Drew (not Grandenetti)	.40	1.20	2.40

TOP ELIMINATOR (Formerly Teenage Hotrodders; Drag 'n' Wheels No. 30 on)
No. 25, Sept, 1967 - No. 29, July, 1968
Charlton Comics

	Good	Fine	Mint
26-29		.40	.80

TOP FLIGHT COMICS
1947; July, 1949
Four Star Publications/St. John Publishing Co.

	Good	Fine	Mint
1	2.00	6.00	12.00
1(7/49)-Hector the Inspector	1.00	3.00	6.00

TOP GUN (See 4-Color No. 927)

TOP GUNS (See Super DC Giant & Showcase No. 72)

TOPIX (. . .Comics) (Timeless Topix-early issues) (Also see Men of Courage & Treasure Chest)(V1-V5/1,V7/1-20-paper-c)
11/42 - V10No.15, 1/28/52 (Weekly - later issues)
Catechetical Guild Educational Society

	Good	Fine	Mint
V1No.1(8pgs.,8x11")	6.00	16.00	32.00
2,3(8pgs.,8x11")	3.50	8.00	16.00
4-8(16pgs.,8x11")	2.00	6.00	12.00
V2No.1-10(16pgs.,8x11"): V2No.8-Pope Pius XII	2.00	6.00	12.00
V3No.1-10(16pgs.,8x11")	2.00	5.00	10.00
V4No.1-10	2.00	5.00	10.00
V5No.1(10/46,52pgs.)-9,12-15(12/47)-No.13 shows V5No.4	.70	2.00	4.00
10,11-Life of Christ eds.	2.00	6.00	12.00
V6No.1-14	.40	1.20	2.40
V7No.1(9/1/48)-20(6/15/49), 32pgs.	.40	1.20	2.40
V8No.1(9/19/49)-3,5-11,13-30(5/15/50)	.40	1.20	2.40
4-Dagwood Splits the Atom(10/10/49)-Magazine format	1.00	3.00	6.00
12-Ingels-a	3.00	8.00	16.00
V9No.1(9/25/50)-11,13-30(5/14/51)	.40	1.20	2.40
12-Special 36pg. Xmas ish., text illos format	.70	2.00	4.00
V10No.1(10/1/51)-15	.40	1.20	2.40

TOP JUNGLE COMICS
1964 (Reprint)
I. W. Enterprises

	Good	Fine	Mint
1(no date)-Reprints White Princess of the Jungle No. 3, minus cover	.80	2.40	4.80

TOP LOVE STORIES
No. 3, May, 1951 - No. 19, Mar, 1954
Star Publications

	Good	Fine	Mint
3	3.50	10.00	20.00
4,5,7-9	3.00	9.00	18.00
6-Wood-a	6.00	18.00	36.00
10-16,18,19-Disbrow-a	3.50	10.00	20.00
17-Wood art (Fox-r)	5.00	14.00	28.00

NOTE: *All have **L. B. Cole** covers.*

TOP-NOTCH COMICS (. . .Laugh No. 28-45; Laugh No. 46 on)
Dec, 1939 - No. 45, June, 1944
MLJ Magazines

	Good	Fine	Mint
1-Origin The Wizard; Kardak, the Mystic Magician begins; J. Cole-a	45.00	135.00	280.00
2-Jack Cole-a	25.00	70.00	150.00
3-Bob Phantom begins; J. Cole-a	20.00	55.00	115.00
4	15.00	45.00	95.00
5	12.00	35.00	75.00
6	9.00	26.00	56.00
7-Kalthar, the Giant Man x-over in Kardak; The Shield x-over in Wizard; The Wizard dons new costume	20.00	60.00	130.00
8-Origin The Firefly & Roy, the Super Boy	20.00	60.00	130.00
9-Origin & 1st app. The Black Hood	45.00	135.00	280.00
10	20.00	60.00	130.00
11-20: 19-Bondage-c	12.00	36.00	75.00
21-30: 23,24-No Wizard, Roy app. in each. 25-Last Bob Phantom, Roy app. 26-Roy app. 27-Last Firefly. 28-Suzie begins. 29-Last Kardak	11.00	32.00	68.00
31-41,43,44: Black Hood series ends, not in No. 35,36	6.00	18.00	36.00
42,45	3.00	8.00	16.00

TOPPER & NEIL (See 4-Color No. 859)

TOPPS COMICS
1947
Four Star Publications

	Good	Fine	Mint
1-L. B. Cole-c	3.00	9.00	18.00

TOPS
1949 (Large size) (10x13")
Consolidated Book Co. (Lev Gleason)

	Good	Fine	Mint
1,2-(Rare)-Crandall/Lubbers, Biro-a	25.00	70.00	140.00

TOPS COMICS (See Tops in Humor)
1944 (Small size) (7¼x5")
Consolidated Book (Lev Gleason)

	Good	Fine	Mint
2001-The Jack of Spades	5.00	15.00	30.00

TOPS COMICS
1944 (132 pages) (10 cents)
Consolidated Book Publishers

nn(Color-c, inside in red shade & some in full color)-Ace Kelly by Rick Yager, Black Orchid, Don on the Farm, Dinky Dinkerton

TOPS COMICS (continued) — Good / Fine / Mint
(Rare) 8.00 24.00 48.00

NOTE: *This book is printed in such a way that when the staple is removed, the strips on the left side of the book correspond with the same strips on the right side. Therefore, if strips are removed from the book, each strip can be folded into a complete comic section of its own.*

TOP SECRET
January, 1952
Hillman Publ.

1 3.00 8.00 16.00

TOP SECRET ADVENTURES (See Spyman)

TOP SECRETS (. . . of the F.B.I.)
1947 - No. 10, July-Aug, 1949
Street & Smith Publications

1-Powell c/a 4.00 12.00 24.00
2-6,8-10-Powell c/a 3.50 10.00 20.00
7-Used in **SOTI**, pg. 90 & illo.-''How to hurt people;'' used by N. Y. Legis. Comm.; Powell c/a 8.00 24.00 48.00

TOPS IN ADVENTURE
Fall, 1952 (132 pages)
Ziff-Davis Publishing Co.

1-Crusader from Mars & The Hawk; Powell-a 14.00 40.00 80.00

TOPS IN HUMOR (See Tops Comics?)
1944 (Small size) (7¼x5'')
Consolidated Book Publ. (Lev Gleason)

2001(No.1)-Origin The Jack of Spades, Ace Kelly by Rick Yager, Black Orchid (female crime fighter) app. 5.00 15.00 30.00
2 3.50 10.00 20.00

TOP SPOT COMICS
1945
Top Spot Publ. Co.

1-The Menace, Duke of Darkness app. 4.00 12.00 24.00

TOPSY-TURVY
April, 1945
R. B. Leffingwell Publ.

1 1.00 3.00 6.00

TOR (Formerly One Million Years Ago)
No. 3, May, 1954 - No. 5, Oct, 1954 (No No. 2)
St. John Publishing Co.

3-D 2(10/53)-Kubert-a 12.00 36.00 60.00
3-D 2(10/53)-Oversized, otherwise same contents 12.00 36.00 60.00
3-D 2(11/53)-Kubert-a 12.00 36.00 60.00
3-5-Kubert-a; 3-Danny Dreams by Toth 17.00 50.00 80.00

NOTE: *The two October 3-D's have same contents and* **Powell** *art; the Nov. issue is titled 3-D Comics.*

TOR (See Sojourn)
May-June, 1975 - No. 6, Mar-Apr, 1976
National Periodical Publications

1-New origin by Kubert .40 .80
2-Origin-r/St. John No. 1 .30 .60
3,5 .30 .60
4,6-Adams ad, 2 & 1 page .40 .80

NOTE: *All* **Kubert** *c/a; reprints-2-6.*

TORCHY (. . . Blond Bombshell) (See Dollman, Military, & Modern)
Nov, 1949 - No. 6, Sept, 1950
Quality Comics Group

1-Bill Ward-c, Gil Fox-a 120.00 300.00 500.00
2,3-Fox c/a 40.00 100.00 180.00

Good / Fine / Mint
4-Fox c/a(3), Ward-a, 9pgs. 50.00 120.00 220.00
5,6-Ward c/a, 9 pgs; Fox-a(3) each 70.00 180.00 300.00
Super Reprint No. 16('64)-Reprints No. 4 with new cover 5.00 15.00 30.00

TORMENTED, THE (Surprise Adventure No. 3)
July, 1954 - No. 2, Sept, 1954
Sterling Comics

1,2 2.00 6.00 12.00

TORNADO TOM (See Mighty Midget Comics)

TOTAL WAR (M.A.R.S. Patrol No. 3 on)
July, 1965 - No. 2, Oct, 1965
Gold Key

1,2-Wood-a 1.00 3.00 6.00

TOUGH KID SQUAD COMICS
March, 1942
Marvel Comics

1-(Scarce)-Origin The Human Top & The Tough Kid Squad; The Flying Flame app. 130.00 380.00 780.00

TOWER OF SHADOWS (Creatures on the Loose No. 10 on)
Sept, 1969 - No. 9, Jan, 1971
Marvel Comics Group

1-Steranko, Craig-a .50 1.50 3.00
2-Neal Adams-a .40 1.20 2.40
3-Smith, Tuska-a .40 1.20 2.40
4-Kirby/Everett-c .50 1.00
5-Smith, Wood-a (Wood draws himself - 1st pg., 1st panel) .50 1.50 3.00
6,8: Wood-a; 8-Wrightson-c .40 1.20 2.40
7-Barry Smith-a .50 1.50 3.00
9-Wrightson-c; Roy Thomas app. .50 1.00
Special 1(12/71)-Adams-a .50 1.00

NOTE: **Ditko** *a-6, 8, 9r, Special 1.* **Everett** *a-9(i)r; c-5i.* **Kirby** *a-9(p)r.* **Severin** *c-5p, 6. Issues 1-9 contain new stories with some pre-Marvel age reprints in 6-9. H. P. Lovecraft adaptation-9.*

TOWN & COUNTRY
May, 1940

Origin The Falcon 10.00 30.00 60.00

TOWN THAT FORGOT SANTA, THE
1961 (24 pages) (Giveaway)
W. T. Grant Co.

nn 1.25 3.50 7.00

TOYLAND COMICS
Jan, 1947 - 1947
Fiction House Magazines

1 5.00 14.00 28.00
2-4: 3-Tuska-a 3.50 10.00 20.00
148 pg. issue 5.00 14.00 28.00

NOTE: *All above contain strips by* **Al Walker**.

TOY TOWN COMICS
1945 - 1946
Toytown/Orbit Publ./B. Antin/Swapper Quarterly

1-Mertie Mouse; L. B. Cole-a 5.00 14.00 28.00
2-7-L. B. Cole-a 3.00 8.00 16.00

TRAGG & THE SKY GODS (See Mystery Comics Digest No. 3 & Spine Tingling Tales)
June, 1975 - No. 8, Feb, 1977
Gold Key

1-Origin .50 1.00
2-8: 4-Sabre-Fang app. 8-Ostellon app. .30 .60

Tormented #2, © Sterling

Total War #1, © GK

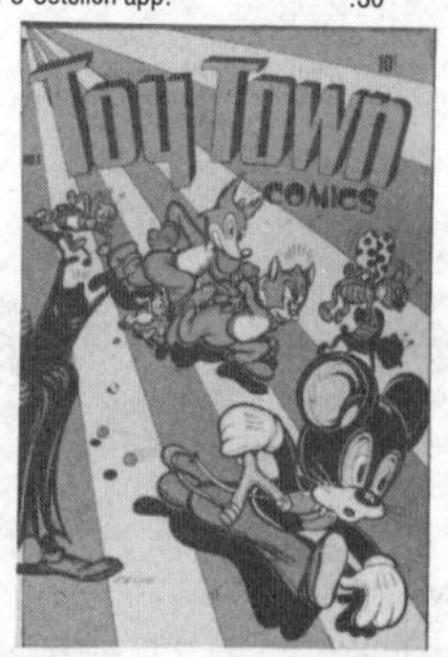

Toy Town #1, © Orbit Publ.

Trail Blazers #1, © S&S

Trapped! #3, © ACE

Treasure Box Of Comics, © News Synd.

TRAGG & THE SKY GODS (continued)
NOTE: ***Santos*** *a-1,2; c-3-7.*

TRAIL BLAZERS (Red Dragon No. 5 on)
1941 - 1942
Street & Smith Publications

	Good	Fine	Mint
1	5.00	14.00	28.00
2-4	3.50	10.00	20.00

TRAIL COLT
1949
Magazine Enterprises

1(A-1 24)-7 pg. Frazetta-a r-in Manhunt No.13; Ingels-c, L.B. Cole-a; (Scarce)	17.00	50.00	100.00
2(A-1 26)-Undercover Girl; Ingels-c; L. B. Cole-a, 6pgs.	10.00	30.00	60.00

TRAPPED
1951 (Giveaway) (16 pages) (soft cover)
Harvey Publications (Columbia University Press)

Drug education comic (30,000 printed?) distributed to schools. Mentioned in **SOTI**, pgs. 256,350 — 2.00 — 6.00 — 12.00

NOTE: *Many copies surfaced in 1979 causing a setback in price; beware of trimmed edges, because many copies have a brittle edge.*

TRAPPED!
Oct, 1954 - No. 4, 1955
Periodical House Magazines (Ace)

1	3.50	7.00	12.00
2,3	1.50	4.00	8.00
4-Krigstein(?)-a	3.00	9.00	18.00

TRAVELS OF JAIMIE McPHEETERS, THE (TV)
December, 1963
Gold Key

1	.85	2.50	5.00

TREASURE BOX OF FAMOUS COMICS
Mid 1930's (36 pgs.) (6-7/8''x8½'') (paper covers)
Cupples & Leon Co.

Box plus 5 titles: Reg'lar Fellers(1928), Little Orphan Annie(1926), Smitty(1928), Harold Teen(1931), Dick Tracy & Dick Tracy Jr. (1933) (These are abbreviated versions of hardcover editions) (Set). . . . — 90.00 — 240.00 — 400.00

NOTE: *Dates shown are copyright dates; all books actually came out in 1934 or later.*

TREASURE CHEST (Catholic Guild; also see Topix)
3/12/46 - V27No.8, July, 1972 (Educational comics)
George A. Pflaum (not publ. during summer)

	Good	Fine	Mint
V1No.1	3.50	10.00	20.00
2-12: 5-Dr. Styx app. by Baily	2.00	5.00	10.00
V2, V3No.1-5,7-20 (1st slick cover)	1.00	3.00	6.00
V3No.6-Jules Verne's ''Voyage to the Moon''	3.00	8.00	16.00
V4No.1-20 (9/9/48-5/31/49)	1.00	3.00	6.00
V5No.1-20 (9/6/49-5/31/50)	.70	2.00	4.00
V6No.1-20 (9/14/50-5/31/51)	.70	2.00	4.00
V7No.1-20 (9/13/51-6/5/52)	.50	1.50	3.00
V8No.1-20 (9/11/52-6/4/53)	.50	1.50	3.00
V9No.1-20 ('53-'54)	.40	1.10	2.20
V10No.1-20 ('54-'55)	.40	1.10	2.20
V11('55-'56), V12('56-'57)	.40	1.10	2.20
V13No.1,3-5,7,9,10,12-V17No.1 ('57-'63)	.30	.80	1.60
V13No.2,6,8,11-Engels-a	1.50	4.00	8.00
V17No.2-'This Godless Communism' series begins (Not in V17No. 3,7,11) Cover shows hammer & cycle over statue of Liberty; 8pg. Crandall-a of family life under communism	7.00	20.00	40.00
V17No.3-7,9-11,13-15,17,19	.30	.80	1.60
V17No.8-Shows red octopus encompassing earth, firing squad; 8pg. Crandall-a	5.00	15.00	30.00
V17No.12-Stalin in WWII, forced labor, death by exhaustion; Crandall-a	5.00	15.00	30.00
V17No.16-Kruschev takes over; de-Stalinization	5.00	15.00	30.00
V17No.18-Kruschev's control; murder of revolters, brainwash, space race by Crandall	5.00	15.00	30.00
V17No.20-End of series; Kruschev-people are puppets, firing squads hammer & cycle over statue of liberty, snake around communist manifesto by Crandall	5.00	15.00	30.00
V18,V19No.1,4,5,11-20,V20('64-'65)		.40	.80
V19No. 2,3,6-10-'Red Victim' anti-communist series in all	3.00	8.00	16.00
V21No.1-9,11-V25('65-'70)-(two V24No.5's 11/7/68 & 11/21/68) (no V24No.6)		.30	.60
V21No.10-Ingels-a	1.50	4.00	8.00
V26, V27No.1-8 (V26,27-68 pgs.)		.30	.60
Summer Edition V1No.1-6('66), V2No.1-6('67)		.20	.40

NOTE: ***Anderson*** *a-V18No. 13.* ***Borth*** *a-V7No. 10-19 (serial), V8No. 8-17 (serial), V9No. 1-10 (serial), V13No. 2, 6, 11.* ***Crandall*** *a-V7No. 20, V16No. 7, 9, 12, 14, 17, 20; V17No. 1, 2, 4, 5, 14, 16, 18, 20; V18No. 1, 7, 9, 10, 17, 19; V19No. 4, 11, 13, 16, 19; V20No. 1, 2, 6, 9, 10, 12, 14-16, 20; V21No. 1-3, 5, 8, 9, 11, 13, 16, 17; V22No. 3, 7, 9-11, 14, 16, 20; V23No. 3, 6, 9, 13, 16; V24No. 8, 10; V25No. 16; V27No. 1,3-5r, 6r, 8(2 pg.); c-V16No. 7, V18No. 10, V19No. 4, V21No. 5, 9, V22No. 7, 11, V23No. 9, 16 at least. V19No. 11, 15, V10No. 13, V13No. 6, 8 all have wraparound covers. All the above Crandall issues should be priced by condition from $4-8.00 unless already priced.*

TREASURE CHEST OF THE WORLD'S BEST COMICS
1945 (500 pgs.) (hardcover)
Superior, Toronto, Canada

Contains Blue Beetle, Captain Combat, John Wayne, Dynamic Man, Nemo, Li'l Abner; contents can vary - represents random binding of extra books — 12.00 — 35.00 — 75.00

TREASURE COMICS
No date (1943) (324 pgs.; cardboard covers) (50 cents)
Prize Publications? (no publisher listed)

nn-(Rare)-Contains Prize Comics No. 7-11 from 1942 (blank inside covers) — 90.00 — 250.00 — 500.00

TREASURE COMICS
June-July, 1945 - No. 12, Fall, 1947
Prize Publications (American Boys' Comics)

1-Paul Bunyan, Marco Polo, Highwayman & Carrot Topp begin Kiefer-a	4.00	12.00	24.00
2-4,9,12	2.00	5.00	10.00
5,6,11-Krigstein-a	4.00	12.00	24.00
7,8-Frazetta, 5 pgs. each	15.00	45.00	90.00
10-Jr. Rangers by Kirby; Kirby-c	5.00	15.00	30.00

TREASURE ISLAND (See 4-Color No. 624, King Classics, & Movie Classics & Comics)

TREASURY OF COMICS
1947; No. 2, July, 1947 - No. 4, Sept, 1947
St. John Publishing Co.

nn(No.1)-Abbie 'n' Slats (nn on cover, No. 1 on inside)	4.00	12.00	24.00
2-Jim Hardy	3.50	10.00	20.00
3-Bill Bumlin	3.00	8.00	16.00
4-Abbie 'n' Slats	3.50	10.00	20.00

TREASURY OF COMICS
Mar, 1948 - No. 5, 1948; 1949, 1950-(Over 500 pgs., $1.00)
St. John Publishing Co.

1	7.00	20.00	40.00
2(No. 2 on cover, No. 1 on inside)	4.00	12.00	24.00
3-5	4.00	12.00	24.00

TREASURY OF COMICS (continued)

	Good	Fine	Mint
1-(1949, 500 pgs., hardcover)-Abbie & Slats, Abbott & Costello, Casper, Little Annie Rooney, Little Audrey, Jim Hardy, Ella Cinders (16 books bound together)	50.00	150.00	300.00
1(1950, 500pgs.)-Same format as above; different-c; (Also see Little Audrey Yearbook)	50.00	150.00	300.00

TREASURY OF DOGS, A
October, 1956 (no month given) (Giant)
Dell Publishing Co.

	Good	Fine	Mint
1	2.00	6.00	12.00

TREASURY OF HORSES, A
1955 (Giant)
Dell Publishing Co.

	Good	Fine	Mint
1	2.00	6.00	12.00

TRIALS OF LULU AND LEANDER, THE
1906 (32 pgs. in color) (10x16")
William A. Stokes Co.

	Good	Fine	Mint
By F. M. Howarth	10.00	30.00	60.00

TRIGGER (See Roy Rogers . . .)

TRIGGER TWINS
Mar-Apr, 1973 (One Shot)
National Periodical Publications

	Good	Fine	Mint
1-Trigger Twins & Pow Wow Smith-r; Infantino-a		.50	1.00

TRIPLE GIANT COMICS (See Archie All-Star Spec. under Archie Comics)

TRIPLE THREAT
Winter, 1945
Special Action/Holyoke/Gerona Publ.

	Good	Fine	Mint
1-Duke of Darkness, King O'Leary	3.50	10.00	20.00

TRIP WITH SANTA ON CHRISTMAS EVE, A
No date (early 50's) (16 pgs.; full color; paper cover)
Rockford Dry Goods Co. (Giveaway)

	Good	Fine	Mint
	2.00	6.00	12.00

TROUBLE SHOOTERS, THE (See 4-Color No. 1108)

TRUE ADVENTURES (Formerly True Western)(Men's Advs. No. 4 on)
No. 3, May, 1950
Marvel Comics (CCC)

	Good	Fine	Mint
3-Powell-a	3.00	8.00	16.00

TRUE ANIMAL PICTURE STORIES
Winter, 1947 - No. 2, Spr-Summer, 1947
True Comics Press

	Good	Fine	Mint
1,2	1.25	3.50	7.00

TRUE AVIATION PICTURE STORIES (Aviation Adventures & Model Building No. 16)
1942 - No. 15, Sept-Oct, 1946
Parents' Magazine Institute

	Good	Fine	Mint
1-(titled . . . Aviation Comics Digest)(not digest size)	2.00	6.00	12.00
2-14	1.00	3.00	6.00
15-(titled "True Aviation Advs. & Model Building")	1.00	3.00	6.00

TRUE BRIDE'S EXPERIENCES (Formerly Teen-Age Brides)
No. 8, Oct, 1954 - No. 16, Feb, 1956
True Love (Harvey Publications)

	Good	Fine	Mint
8-15	1.50	4.00	8.00
16-Spanking issue	4.00	12.00	24.00

NOTE: ***Powell** a-8-10, 12, 13.*

TRUE BRIDE-TO-BE ROMANCES
Aug, 1953 - No. 30, Nov, 1958
Home Comics/True Love (Harvey)

	Good	Fine	Mint
1	3.00	8.00	16.00
2-5	2.00	6.00	12.00
6-15	1.50	4.00	8.00
16,18-22,25-28,30	1.00	3.00	6.00
17-S&K-c, Powell-a	2.00	6.00	12.00
23,24-Powell-a	1.20	3.50	7.00
29-Powell, 1 pg. Baker-a	1.50	4.00	8.00

TRUE COMICS (Also see Outstanding American War Heroes)
April, 1941 - No. 84, Aug, 1950
True Comics/Parents' Magazine Press

	Good	Fine	Mint
1	7.00	20.00	40.00
2-5: 5-Life story of Joe Lewis	4.00	12.00	24.00
6-10	2.50	7.00	14.00
11-30	2.00	5.00	10.00
31-46,48-50	1.20	3.50	7.00
47-Atomic bomb issue	2.00	5.00	10.00
51-81,83,84	.85	2.50	5.00
82-(Rare)-Distr. to subscribers through the mail only; paper cover	15.00	40.00	80.00

NOTE: *No. 80-84 have soft covers and combined with Tex Granger, Jack Armstrong, and Calling All Kids. No. 68-78 featured true FBI adventures.*

TRUE COMICS AND ADVENTURE STORIES
1945 (Giant) (25 cents)
Parents' Magazine Institute

	Good	Fine	Mint
1,2	1.00	3.00	6.00

TRUE COMPLETE MYSTERY (Formerly Complete Mystery)
No. 5, April, 1949 - No. 8, Oct, 1949
Marvel Comics

	Good	Fine	Mint
5	3.50	10.00	20.00
6-8	3.00	8.00	16.00

TRUE CONFESSIONS
1949
Fawcett Publications

	Good	Fine	Mint
1	4.00	12.00	24.00

TRUE CONFIDENCES
Fall, 1949 - No. 4, June, 1950
Fawcett Publications

	Good	Fine	Mint
1	4.00	12.00	24.00
2-4: 4-Bob Powell-a	2.00	5.00	10.00

TRUE CRIME CASES
1944; V1No.6, June-July, 1949 - V2No.1, Aug-Oct, 1949
St. John Publishing Co.

	Good	Fine	Mint
1944-(100 pgs.)	10.00	30.00	60.00
V1No.6, V2No.1	3.00	8.00	16.00

TRUE CRIME COMICS (See Complete Book of . . .)
1942 (132 pages) (25 cents)
Comic House Publications/William H. Wise

	Good	Fine	Mint
1-The War Eagle	15.00	30.00	60.00

TRUE CRIME COMICS
No. 2, May, 1947; No. 3, Jul-Aug, 1948 - No. 6, June-Jul, 1949; V2No.1, Aug-Sept, 1949; V2No.9, Dec, 1949
Magazine Village

	Good	Fine	Mint
2-Jack Cole c/a; used in **SOTI**, pg. 81,82 plus illo.-"A sample of the injury-to-eye motif" & illo.-"Dragging Living people to death;" used in **POP**, pg. 105; "Murder, Morphine and Me" classic drug propaganda story used by N.Y. Legis. Comm.	100.00	250.00	525.00
3-Classic Cole c/a; heroin drug story	60.00	150.00	325.00

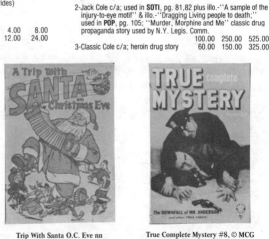

Trigger Twins #1, © DC

Trip With Santa O.C. Eve nn

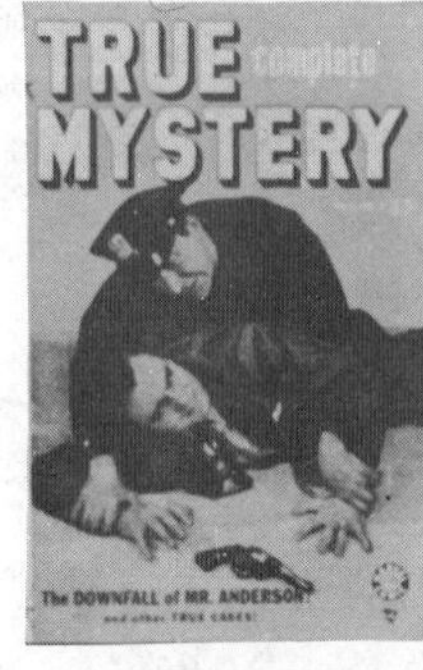

True Complete Mystery #8, © MCG

True Love Pictorial #6, © STJ

True Movie & Television #3, © TOBY

True-To-Life Romances #9(#1), © STAR

TRUE CRIME COMICS (continued) — Good / Fine / Mint

4-Jack Cole-c/a; c-taken from a story panel in No. 3; r-(2) **SOTI** & **POP** stories/No. 2 — 50.00 150.00 300.00
5-Jack Cole-c; Marijuana racket story — 20.00 60.00 135.00
6 — 7.00 20.00 46.00
V2No.1-Used in **SOTI**, pgs. 81,82 & illo.-''Dragging living people to death;'' Toth, Wood (3 pgs.), Roussos-a; Cole-r from No. 2 — 40.00 100.00 210.00
V2No.9-Toth-a — 3.00 9.00 18.00

TRUE GHOST STORIES (See Ripley's . . .)

TRUE LIFE ROMANCES (. . . Romance on cover)
Dec, 1955 - No. 3, 1956
Ajax/Farrell Publications

1 — 2.50 7.00 14.00
2 — 1.50 4.00 8.00
3-Disbrow-a — 3.00 8.00 16.00

TRUE LIFE SECRETS
Mar-April, 1951 - No. 28, Sept, 1955; No. 29, Jan, 1956
Romantic Love Stories/Charlton

1 — 3.00 8.00 16.00
2 — 2.50 7.00 14.00
3-12,15-19 — 2.00 5.00 10.00
13-Headlight-a — 5.00 15.00 30.00
14-Drug mention story(marijuana) — 3.50 10.00 20.00
20-22,24-29 — 1.50 4.00 8.00
23-Suggestive-c — 2.00 6.00 12.00

TRUE LIFE TALES (Formerly Lana?)
No. 8, Oct, 1949 - No. 2, Jan, 1950
Marvel Comics (CCC)

8(10/49), 2(1/50)-Photo-c — 2.00 6.00 12.00

TRUE LOVE CONFESSIONS
May, 1954 - No. 11, Jan, 1956
Premier Magazines

1-Marijuana story — 3.00 9.00 18.00
2-11 — 1.00 3.00 6.00

TRUE LOVE PICTORIAL
1952 - No. 11, Aug, 1954
St. John Publishing Co.

1 — 4.00 12.00 24.00
2 — 2.00 6.00 12.00
3-5(All 100 pgs.): 5-Formerly TeenAge Temptations (4/53); Kubert-a-No. 3,5; Baker-a-No. 3-5 — 8.00 24.00 48.00
6,7-Baker c/a — 5.00 14.00 28.00
8-11-Baker c/a — 4.00 12.00 24.00

TRUE LOVE PROBLEMS & ADVICE ILLUSTRATED (See Love Problems & Advice)

TRUE MOVIE AND TELEVISION (Part magazine)
No. 1, Aug, 1950 - No. 3, Nov, 1950 (52 pgs.) (10 cents)
Toby Press

1-Liz Taylor-c; Gene Autry, Shirley Temple, Li'l Abner app. — 12.00 35.00 70.00
2 — 7.00 20.00 40.00
3-June Allyson-c; lingerie scene; Montgomery Cliff, Esther Williams Andrews Sisters app; Li'l Abner feat. — 7.00 20.00 40.00
NOTE: *16 pages in color, rest movie material in black & white.*

TRUE MYSTERIES (Formerly True Complete Mystery No. 5?)
June, 1949
Marvel Comics

6 — 3.00 9.00 18.00

TRUE MYSTERY (Same as True Complete Mystery?)

TRUE SECRETS (Formerly Love Dramas?)
No. 3, Mar, 1950; No. 4, Feb, 1951 - No. 40, Sept, 1956
Marvel (IPS)/Atlas Comics (MPI)

Good / Fine / Mint

3 — 2.00 6.00 12.00
4-21,23-40: 34-Colletta-a — 1.00 3.00 6.00
22-Everett-a — 2.00 6.00 12.00

TRUE SPORT PICTURE STORIES (Formerly Sport Comics)
Feb, 1942? - V5No.2, July-Aug, 1949
Street & Smith Publications

V1No.5-12 (1941-42) — 3.50 10.00 20.00
V2No.1-12 (1943-44) — 2.50 7.00 14.00
V3No.1-12 (1945-46) — 2.00 5.00 10.00
V4No.1-12 (1947-48), V5No.1,2 — 1.00 3.00 6.00
NOTE: ***Powell** a-V3No.10, V4No.1,2,4,6,10-12, V5No.2; c-V4No.10.*

TRUE STORIES OF ROMANCE
Jan, 1950 - No. 3, May, 1950
Fawcett Publications

1 — 2.50 7.00 14.00
2,3: 2-Photo-c — 2.00 5.00 10.00

TRUE STORY OF JESSE JAMES, THE (See 4-Color No. 757)

TRUE SWEETHEART SECRETS
May, 1950 - No. 11, Jan, 1953
Fawcett Publications

1-Photo-c; Debbie Reynolds? — 2.50 7.00 14.00
2-Wood-a, 11 pgs. — 6.00 18.00 36.00
3-11: 4,5-Powell-a — 2.00 5.00 10.00

TRUE TALES OF LOVE (Formerly Secret Story Romances)
No. 22, April, 1956 - No. 31, Sept, 1957
Atlas Comics (TCI)

22 — .70 2.00 4.00
23-31-Colletta-a in most — .50 1.50 3.00

TRUE TALES OF ROMANCE
No. 4, June, 1950
Fawcett Publications

4 — 2.00 5.00 10.00

TRUE 3-D
Dec, 1953 - No. 2, Feb, 1954
Harvey Publications

1-Nostrand, Powell-a — 8.00 24.00 48.00
2 — 8.00 24.00 48.00

TRUE-TO-LIFE ROMANCES
No. 9, 1-2/50; No. 3, 4/50 - No. 23, 10/54
Star Publications

9(1950) — 5.00 14.00 28.00
3-10 — 5.00 14.00 28.00
11,22,23 — 4.00 12.00 24.00
12-14,17-21-Disbrow-a — 6.00 16.00 32.00
15,16-Wood & Disbrow-a in each — 8.00 24.00 48.00
NOTE: ***Kamen** a-13, **Kamen/Feldstein** a-14. All have **L. B. Cole** covers.*

TRUE WAR EXPERIENCES
Aug, 1952 - No. 4, Dec, 1952
Harvey Publications

1 — 2.50 7.00 14.00
2-4 — 1.50 4.00 8.00

TRUE WAR ROMANCES
Sept, 1952 - No. 21, June, 1955
Quality Comics Group

1-Photo-c — 3.50 10.00 20.00
2-10: 9-Whitney-a — 2.00 5.00 10.00
11-21: 14-Whitney-a — 1.50 4.00 8.00

TRUE WAR STORIES (See Ripley's . . .)

TRUE WESTERN (True Adventures No. 3)
Dec, 1949 - No. 2, March, 1950

TRUE WESTERN (continued)
Marvel Comics (MMC)

	Good	Fine	Mint
1	3.50	10.00	20.00
2: Alan Ladd photo-c	3.00	8.00	16.00

TRUE WEST ROMANCE
1952
Quality Comics Group

21	2.00	6.00	12.00

TRUMP (Magazine format)
Jan, 1957 - No. 2, Mar, 1957
HMH Publishing Co.

1-Harvey Kurtzman satire	8.00	24.00	48.00
2-Harvey Kurtzman satire	5.00	15.00	30.00

NOTE: ***Davis, Elder, Heath, Jaffee** art-No. 1, 2; **Wood**-No. 1. No. 2-article by Mel Brooks.*

TRUMPETS WEST (See 4-Color No. 875)

TRUTH ABOUT CRIME
1949 (132 pages)
Fox Features Syndicate

nn-See Fox Giants. Contents can vary and determines price.

TRUTH ABOUT MOTHER GOOSE (See 4-Color No. 862)

TRUTH BEHIND THE TRIAL OF CARDINAL MINDSZENTY, THE (See Cardinal . . .)

TRUTHFUL LOVE (Formerly Youthful Love)
No. 2, July, 1950
Youthful Magazines

2	2.00	5.00	10.00

TUBBY (Marge's . . .) (Little Lulu)
1952 - No. 49, Dec-Feb, 1961-62
Dell Publishing Co./Gold Key

4-Color 381-Stanley-a	8.00	24.00	48.00
4-Color 430-1st Tubby & Men From Mars story; Stanley-a	4.00	12.00	24.00
4-Color 444,461-All by Stanley	4.00	12.00	24.00
5-Stanley-a	4.00	12.00	24.00
6-10	3.00	9.00	18.00
11-20: 18-Stanley-a	2.75	8.00	16.00
21-30	2.00	6.00	12.00
31-49	1.50	4.00	8.00
. . . & His Clubhouse Pals No. 1(1956)-4 pgs. Stanley art; wrote Gran'pa Feeb stories	3.50	10.00	20.00
. . . & the Little Men From Mars No. 30020-410(10/64-G.K.)-25 cents; 68 pgs.	3.00	8.00	16.00

TUFF GHOSTS (Starring Spooky)
7/62 - No. 39, 11/70; No. 40, 9/71 - No. 43, 10/72
Harvey Publications

1	4.00	12.00	24.00
2-5	2.00	6.00	12.00
6-10	1.50	4.00	8.00
11-20	.70	2.00	4.00
21-30	.50	1.50	3.00
31-43		.50	1.00

TUFFY
1949 - 1950
Standard Comics

1-All by Sid Hoff	2.00	5.00	8.00
2-10	.85	2.50	5.00

TUFFY TURTLE
No date
I. W. Enterprises

	Good	Fine	Mint
1-Reprint	.30	.80	1.60

TUROK, SON OF STONE (See Golden Comics Digest No. 33, March of Comics No. 378,399,408, and Dan Curtis)
Dec, 1954 - No. 125, Jan, 1980
Dell Publishing Co. No. 1-29/Gold Key No. 30(12/62) on

4-Color 596 (12/54)	8.00	24.00	48.00
4-Color 656 (10/55)	6.00	16.00	32.00
3(3-5/56)-5	4.00	12.00	24.00
6-10	3.00	8.00	16.00
11-20	2.00	5.00	10.00
21-30	1.50	4.00	8.00
31-Drug use story	.85	2.25	4.50
32-40	.70	2.00	4.00
41-50	.50	1.50	3.00
51-60	.30	.90	1.80
61-70: 63-Only line drawn-c		.60	1.20
71-83		.50	1.00
84-Origin & 1st app. Hutec		.60	1.20
85-125: 114-(52 pgs.)		.40	.80
Giant 1(30031-611) (11/66)	1.00	3.00	6.00

NOTE: ***Alberto Gioletti** painted-c No. 30-on. Reprints-No. 36, 57, 93, 114, 125.*

TV CASPER & COMPANY
Aug, 1963 - No. 46, April, 1974 (25 cents)
Harvey Publications

1	4.00	12.00	24.00
2-5	2.00	6.00	12.00
6-10	1.50	4.00	8.00
11-20	.70	2.00	4.00
21-30	.50	1.50	3.00
31-46		.50	1.00

TV FUNDAY FUNNIES (See Famous TV . . .)

TV FUNNIES (See New Funnies)

TV FUNTIME (See Little Audrey)

TV LAUGHOUT (See Archie's . . .)

TV SCREEN CARTOONS (Formerly Real Screen)
No. 129, July-Aug, 1959 - No. 138, Jan-Feb, 1961
National Periodical Publications

129-138(Scarce)	1.00	3.00	6.00

TV STARS (Hanna-Barbera)
Aug, 1978 - No. 4, Feb, 1979
Marvel Comics Group

1		.50	1.00
2,4		.40	.80
3-Toth-c/a	.50	1.50	3.00

TV TEENS (Formerly Ozzie & Babs; Rock and Rollo No. 14 on)
Feb, 1954 - V2No.13, July, 1956
Charlton Comics

V1No.14,15: 14-Ozzie & Babs	1.50	4.00	8.00
V2No.3-7-Don Winslow	2.00	5.00	10.00
V2No.8(7/55)-13-Mopsy	1.50	4.00	8.00

TWEETY AND SYLVESTER (1st Series)
June, 1952 - No. 37, June-Aug, 1962
Dell Publishing Co.

4-Color 406,489,524	.70	2.00	4.00
4-20	.70	2.00	4.00
21-37	.40	1.20	2.40

(See March of Comics No. 421,433,445,457,469,481)

TWEETY AND SYLVESTER (2nd Series)
Nov, 1963; No. 2, Nov, 1965 - Present (no No. 109)

True Western #1, © MCG

Tubby #5, © WEST

Turok, Son Of Stone #22, © GK

Twilight Zone #14, © GK

Two-Fisted Tales #41, © WMG

Two-Gun Western #10, © MCG

TWEETY & SYLVESTER (continued)
Gold Key No. 1-102/Whitman No. 103 on

	Good	Fine	Mint
1	.50	1.50	3.00
2-10	.30	.80	1.60
11-30		.50	1.00
31-108,110: 99-Reprints		.25	.50
Mini Comic No. 1(1976)-3¼x6½''		.30	.60

12 O'CLOCK HIGH (TV)
Jan-Mar, 1965 - No. 2, Apr-June, 1965
Dell Publishing Co.

	Good	Fine	Mint
1,2	.85	2.50	5.00

24 PAGES OF COMICS (No title) (Also see Pure Oil Comics, Salerno Carnival of Comics, & Vicks Comics)
Late 1930s
Giveaway by various outlets including Sears

	Good	Fine	Mint
Contains strip reprints-Buck Rogers, Napoleon, Sky Roads, War on Crime	20.00	60.00	120.00

20,000 LEAGUES UNDER THE SEA (See 4-Color No. 614, King Classics, and Movie Comics)

TWICE TOLD TALES (See Movie Classics)

TWILIGHT ZONE, THE (TV) (See Dan Curtis)
1961 - No. 91, April, 1979
Dell Publishing Co./Gold Key

	Good	Fine	Mint
4-Color 1173,1288-Crandall/Evans c/a	3.00	8.00	16.00
01-860-207 (5-7/62-Dell)	1.00	3.00	6.00
12-860-210 on-c; 01-860-210 on inside(8-10/62-Dell)-Evans c/a; Crandall/Frazetta-a(2)	1.50	4.00	8.00
1(11/62-Gold Key)-Evans-a	3.00	8.00	16.00
2,5	.85	2.50	5.00
3,4-Toth-a, 11 & 10 pgs.	1.50	4.50	9.00
6-11,16-20	.70	2.00	4.00
12-Williamson-a	2.00	5.00	9.00
13,15-Crandall-a	1.50	4.00	8.00
14-Williamson/Orlando/Crandall/Torres-a	2.00	6.00	12.00
21-Crandall-a(r)	.30	.80	1.60
22-24		.50	1.00
25-Evans/Crandall-a(r)		.60	1.20
26-Crandall, Evans-a(r)		.60	1.20
27-Evans-a(2)(r)		.60	1.20
28-32: 32-Evans-a(r)		.40	.80
33-50,52-70		.30	.60
51-Williamson-a		.40	.80
71-91: 71-Reprint. 83,84-(52 pgs.)		.25	.50
Mini Comic No. 1(1976-3¼x6½'')		.30	.60

NOTE: ***Bolle** a-13(w/**McWilliams**), 50, 57, 59. **McWilliams** a-59. **Orlando** a-19, 20, 22, 23. **Sekowsky** a-3. (See Mystery Comics Digest 3, 6, 9, 12, 15, 18, 21, 24). Reprints-73, 79, 83, 84, 86.*

TWINKLE COMICS
May, 1945
Spotlight Publishers

	Good	Fine	Mint
1	3.50	10.00	20.00

TWIST, THE
September, 1962
Dell Publishing Co.

	Good	Fine	Mint
01864-209	2.00	6.00	12.00

TWO BIT THE WACKY WOODPECKER (See Wacky. . .)
1953 - No. 3, May, 1953
Toby Press

	Good	Fine	Mint
1-3	.85	2.50	5.00

TWO FACES OF COMMUNISM (Also see Double Talk)
1961 (36 pgs.; paper cover) (Giveaway)
Christian Anti-Communism Crusade, Houston, Texas

	Good	Fine	Mint
	10.00	30.00	60.00

TWO-FISTED TALES (Formerly Haunt of Fear No. 15-17)
No. 18, Nov-Dec, 1950 - No. 41, Feb-Mar, 1955
E. C. Comics

	Good	Fine	Mint
18(No.1)-Kurtzman-c	80.00	200.00	380.00
19-Kurtzman-c	60.00	150.00	280.00
20-Kurtzman-c	40.00	100.00	170.00
21,22-Kurtzman-c	25.00	70.00	130.00
23-25-Kurtzman-c	17.00	50.00	90.00
26-35: 33-''Atom Bomb'' by Wood	12.00	36.00	64.00
36-41	9.00	26.00	40.00
Two-Fisted Annual, 1952	80.00	200.00	390.00
Two-Fisted Annual, 1953	60.00	150.00	280.00

NOTE: ***Berg** a-29. **Craig** a-18, 19, 32. **Crandall** a-35, 36. **Davis** a-20-36, 40; c-30, 34, 35, 41, Annual 2. **Evans** a-34, 40, 41; c-40. **Feldstein** a-18. **Krigstein** a-41. **Kubert** a-32, 33. **Kurtzman** a-18-25; c-18-29, 31, Annual 1. **Severin** a-26, 28, 29, 31, 34-41 (No.37-39 are all-Severin issues); c-36-39. **Severin/Elder** a-19-29, 31, 33, 36. **Wood** a-18-28, 30-35, 41; c-32, 33. Special issues: No. 26 (ChanJin Reservoir), 31 (Civil War), 35 (Civil War). Canadian reprints known; see Table of Contents.*

TWO-GUN KID
3/48(No mo.) - No. 10, 11/49; No. 11, 12/53 - No. 59, 4/61; No. 60, 11/62 - No. 92, 3/68; No. 93, 7/70 - No. 136, 4/77
Marvel/Atlas Comics (MCI No. 1-10/HPC No. 11-59/Marvel No. 60 on)

	Good	Fine	Mint
1	12.00	35.00	70.00
2	6.00	18.00	36.00
3-5	4.00	12.00	24.00
6-10	3.00	9.00	18.00
11-24,26-29	2.00	6.00	12.00
25,30-Williamson-a in both, 5 & 4 pgs.	3.00	9.00	18.00
31-33,35,37-40	1.50	4.00	8.00
34-Crandall-a	2.00	6.00	12.00
36,41,42,48-Origin in all	1.00	3.00	6.00
43,44,47	.85	2.50	5.00
45,46-Davis-a	2.00	6.00	12.00
49,50,52,55,57-Severin-a(3) in each	1.00	3.00	6.00
51-Williamson-a, 5pgs.	3.00	8.00	16.00
53,54,56,59	.50	1.50	3.00
58,60-New origin	.85	2.50	5.00
61-80: 64-Intro. Boom-Boom	.30	.80	1.60
81-100: 85-Rawhide Kid x-over. 89-Kid Colt, Rawhide Kid x-over. 92,98-Last new story. 99-Severin-r(3)		.40	.80
101-Origin retold/No. 58		.30	.60
102-109,111-136		.25	.50
110-Williamson-a(r)		.30	.60

NOTE: ***Davis** c-45-47. **Everett** a-82, 91. **Kirby** a-54, 55, 57-62, 75-77, 90, 95, 101, 119, 120, 129; c-10, 52, 54-65, 67-72, 74-76, 116. **Powell** a-38, 102, 104. **Whitney** a-87, 89-91, 98-113, 124, 129; c-87, 89, 91, 113. Black Rider in No. 11, 12. Kid Colt in No. 13, 14, 16-18, 21.*

TWO-GUN WESTERN (1st Series) (Formerly Casey Crime Photographer)
No. 5, Nov, 1950 - No. 14, June, 1952
Marvel/Atlas Comics (MPC)

	Good	Fine	Mint
5-Intro. & origin Apache Kid by Buscema	3.50	10.00	20.00
6-14	2.00	5.00	10.00

NOTE: ***Crandall** a-8. **Maneely** a-9. **Powell** a-7. **Wildey** a-8.*

2-GUN WESTERN (2nd Series) (Formerly Billy Buckskin; Two-Gun Western No. 5 or Patty Powers No. 5 on?)
No. 4, May, 1956
Atlas Comics (MgPC)

	Good	Fine	Mint
4-Apache Kid; Ditko-a	3.50	10.00	20.00

TWO-GUN WESTERN (Formerly 2-Gun Western)
No. 5, July, 1956 - No. 12, Sept, 1957
Atlas Comics (MgPC)

	Good	Fine	Mint
5-8,12	1.25	3.50	7.00

TWO-GUN WESTERN (continued)

	Good	Fine	Mint
9,11-Williamson-a in both, 5 pgs. each	3.50	10.00	20.00
10-Crandall-a	2.00	6.00	12.00

NOTE: ***Morrow*** *a-9.* ***Powell*** *a-11.*

TWO MOUSEKETEERS, THE (See 4-Color No. 475,603,642) (Becomes Mouse Musketeers)

TWO ON A GUILLOTINE (See Movie Classics)

2001: A SPACE ODYSSEY (Marvel Treasury Special)
Oct, 1976 (One Shot) (Over-sized)
Marvel Comics Group

	Good	Fine	Mint
1-Kirby, Giacoia-a	.50	1.50	3.00

2001: A SPACE ODYSSEY
Dec, 1976 - No. 10, Sept, 1977 (Regular size)
Marvel Comics Group

	Good	Fine	Mint
1-Kirby c/a in all		.60	1.20
2		.40	.80
3-7		.40	.80
8-10-Origin & 1st app. Machine Man		.40	.80
Howard Johnson giveaway(1968, 8pp); 6pg. movie adaptation, 2pg. games, puzzles	.30	.80	1.60

UFO & ALIEN COMIX
1978 (One Shot)
Warren Publishing Co.

	Good	Fine	Mint
Toth, Severin-a(r)	.30	.80	1.60

UFO AND OUTER SPACE (Formerly UFO Flying Saucers)
No. 14, June, 1978 - No. 25, Feb, 1980
Gold Key

	Good	Fine	Mint
14-Reprints UFO Flying Saucers No. 3	.30	.80	1.60
15,16-Reprints		.50	1.00
17-20-New material		.40	.80
21-25: 25-Reprints		.25	.50

UFO ENCOUNTERS
May, 1978 (228 pages) ($1.95)
Western Publishing Co.

	Good	Fine	Mint
11192-Reprints/UFO Flying Saucers	.40	1.20	2.40

UFO FLYING SAUCERS (UFO & Outer Space No. 14 on)
Oct, 1968 - No. 13, Jan, 1977 (No. 2 on, 36 pgs.)
Gold Key

	Good	Fine	Mint
1(30035-810) (68 pgs.)	1.00	3.00	6.00
2(11/70), 3(11/72), 4(11/74)	.85	2.00	4.00
5(2/75)-13: Bolle-a No. 4 on	.50	1.50	3.00

UFO MYSTERIES
1978 (96 pages) ($1.00)
Western Publishing Co.

	Good	Fine	Mint
11400(96 pgs., $1.00)		.60	1.20
11404(Vol.2)		.60	1.20

UNBIRTHDAY PARTY WITH ALICE IN WONDERLAND (See 4-Color No. 341)

UNCANNY TALES
June, 1952 - No. 57, Sept, 1957
Atlas Comics (PrPl)

	Good	Fine	Mint
1-Heath-a	8.00	24.00	48.00
2-5,7,9,10	3.50	10.00	20.00
6-Wolvertonish-a by Matt Fox	5.00	14.00	24.00
8-Tothish-a(Sekowsky?)	5.00	14.00	24.00
11-20	2.50	7.00	14.00
21-27	2.00	6.00	12.00
28-Last pre-code issue; Kubert-a; No. 1-28 contain 2-3 sci/fic stories each	3.00	9.00	18.00
29-41,43-49,52	1.00	3.00	6.00
42,54,56-Krigstein-a	2.50	7.00	14.00
50,53,55-Torres-a	2.50	7.00	14.00
51,57-Williamson-a	3.50	10.00	20.00

NOTE: ***Bailey*** *a-51.* ***Briefer*** *a-20.* ***Colan*** *a-11, 16.* ***Ditko*** *a-4r, 6r, 10r, 12r.* ***Drucker*** *a-37, 42, 45.* ***Everett*** *a-2, 12, 36, 39, 47, 48; c-7, 11, 39, 41, 50, 52, 53.* ***Heath*** *a-14.* ***Krenkel*** *a-19.* ***Krigstein*** *a-42, 54, 56.* ***Lawrence*** *a-27, 28.* ***Maneely*** *a-8, 29; c-33.* ***Moldoff*** *a-7, 11, 23.* ***Morrow*** *a-46, 51.* ***Orlando*** *a-49, 50, 53.* ***Powell*** *a-12, 18, 38, 43, 50, 53, 56.* ***Robinson*** *a-3, 13.* ***Roussos*** *a-8.* ***Sekowsky*** *a-25.* ***Shelly*** *a-23.* ***Wildey*** *a-48.*

UNCANNY TALES
Dec, 1973 - No. 12, Oct, 1975
Marvel Comics Group

	Good	Fine	Mint
1-Crandall-a(r)		.40	.80
2-12		.25	.50

NOTE: ***Ditko*** *reprints-No. 7, 8, 11.*

UNCLE CHARLIE'S FABLES
Jan, 1952 - No. 5, Sept, 1952
Lev Gleason Publications

	Good	Fine	Mint
1-Norman Maurer-a; has Biro's picture	2.50	7.00	14.00
2-5	1.50	4.50	9.00

UNCLE DONALD & HIS NEPHEWS DUDE RANCH (See Dell Giant No. 52)

UNCLE DONALD & HIS NEPHEWS FAMILY FUN (See Dell Giant No. 38)

UNCLE JOE'S FUNNIES
1938
Centaur Publications

	Good	Fine	Mint
1-Games/puzzles, some interior art; Bill Everett-c	10.00	30.00	60.00

UNCLE MILTY
Dec, 1950 - No. 4, June, 1950
Victoria Publications/True Cross

	Good	Fine	Mint
1-Milton Berle	6.00	18.00	36.00
2-4	3.00	9.00	18.00

UNCLE REMUS & HIS TALES OF BRER RABBIT (See 4-Color No. 129,208,693)

UNCLE SAM (Blackhawk No. 9 on)
Autumn, 1941 - No. 8, Fall, 1943
Quality Comics Group

	Good	Fine	Mint
1-Origin Uncle Sam; Fine/Eisner-c, chapter headings, 2 pgs. by Eisner. (2 versions: dark cover, no price; light cover with price); Jack Cole-a	60.00	170.00	340.00
2-Cameos by The Ray, Black Condor, Quicksilver, The Red Bee, Alias the Spider, Hercules & Neon the Unknown; Eisner, Fine c/a	30.00	85.00	170.00
3-Tuska-a	20.00	55.00	115.00
4	15.00	45.00	95.00
5-8	12.00	35.00	75.00

NOTE: ***Kotzky*** *or* ***Tuska*** *a-4-8.*

UNCLE SAM'S CHRISTMAS STORY
1958
Promotional Publ. Co. (Giveaway)

	Good	Fine	Mint
Reprints 1956 Christmas USA	1.00	3.00	6.00

UNCLE SCROOGE (Walt Disney)
Mar, 1952 - No. 39, Aug-Nov, 1962; No. 40, Dec, 1962 - Present
Dell Publishing Co./Gold Key No. 40-173/Whitman No. 174 on

	Good	Fine	Mint
4-Color 386(No.1)-in ''Only a Poor Old Man'' by Carl Barks; reprinted in Uncle Scrooge & Donald Duck No. 1('65) & The Best of Walt Disney Comics('74)	100.00	240.00	400.00

4-Color 456(No.2)-in ''Back to the Klondike'' by Carl Barks; re-

2001: A Space Odyssey #6, MCG

UFO Flying Saucers #2, © GK

Uncanny Tales #27, © MCG

Uncle Scrooge #8, © WDP

Underworld Crime #5, © FAW

Unearthly Spectaculars #1, © HARV

UNCLE SCROOGE (continued) **Good** **Fine** **Mint**
printed in Best of U.S. & D.D. No. 1('66) 50.00 120.00 200.00
4-Color 495(No.3)-Reprinted in Uncle Scrooge No. 105
35.00 90.00 160.00
4(12-2/53-54) 20.00 60.00 100.00
5-Reprinted in W.D. Digest No. 1 17.00 50.00 90.00
6-Reprinted in U.S. No. 106,165 & Best of U.S. & D.D. No. 1('66)
14.00 40.00 80.00
7-Reprinted in Best of D.D. & U.S. No. 2('67)
10.00 30.00 60.00
8-10: 8-Reprinted in No. 111. 9-Reprinted in U.S. No. 104.
10-Reprinted in U.S. No. 67 7.00 20.00 40.00
11-20 6.00 18.00 36.00
21-30 5.00 14.00 28.00
31-40 4.00 12.00 24.00
41-50 3.50 9.00 18.00
51-60 3.00 8.00 16.00
61-66,68-70: 70-Last Barks issue with original story
2.50 7.00 14.00
67,72,73-Barks-r 1.50 4.50 9.00
71-Written by Barks only 2.00 5.00 9.00
74-One pg. Barks-r 1.00 3.00 6.00
75-81,83-Not by Barks 1.00 3.00 6.00
82,84-Barks-r begin 1.00 3.00 6.00
85-100 .85 2.50 5.00
101-110 .70 2.00 4.00
111-120 .50 1.50 3.00
121-141,143-157 .35 1.00 2.00
142-Reprints 4-Color 456 with-c .50 1.50 3.00
158,162-164,166,168-170,178,180-No Barks .30 .60
159-161,165,167,171-177,179,181-190 .40 .80
Uncle Scrooge & Money(G.K.)-Barks reprint from WDC&S No. 130
(3/67) 4.00 12.00 24.00
Uncle Scrooge Goes to Disneyland No. 1(1957-25 cents)-20 pgs.
Barks 5.00 15.00 30.00
Mini Comic No. 1(1976)(3¼x6½'')-Reprint/U.S. No. 115; Barks-c
.60 1.20
NOTE: ***Barks** c-4-Color 386, 456, 495, No. 4-37, 39, 40, 43-71.*
(See Dell Giants No. 33 & 55)

UNCLE SCROOGE & DONALD DUCK
June, 1965 (25 cents) (Paper cover)
Gold Key
1-Reprint of 4-Color 386(No.1) & lead story from 4-Color 29
8.00 24.00 48.00

UNCLE WIGGILY (See 4-Color No. 179,221,276,320,349,391,428, 503,543, & March of Comics No. 19)

UNDERCOVER CRIME (Underground Crime No. 5)
1952
Fawcett Publications
6(Exist?) 3.00 9.00 18.00

UNDERCOVER GIRL (Starr Flagg)
1952 - 1953
Magazine Enterprises
5(No.1)(A-1 62) 10.00 30.00 60.00
6(A-1 98), 7(A-1 118)-All have Starr Flagg 9.00 25.00 50.00
NOTE: *All have **Powell** covers, **Whitney** art.*

UNDERDOG (TV) (See March of Comics 426,438,467,479)
July, 1970 - No. 10, Jan, 1972; Mar, 1975 - No. 23, Feb, 1979
Charlton Comics/Gold Key
1 .85 2.50 5.00
2-10 .50 1.50 3.00
1 (G.K.) .35 1.00 2.00
2-10 .50 1.00
11-23: 13-1st app. Shack of Solitude .30 .60
Kite Fun Book('74)-5x7''; 16 pgs. Sou. Calif. Edison
.30 .80 1.60

UNDERGROUND CRIME (Undercover Crime No. 6)
1952
Fawcett Publications **Good** **Fine** **Mint**
5(Exist?) 3.00 9.00 18.00

UNDERSEA AGENT
Jan, 1966 - No. 6, Mar, 1967 (68 pages)
Tower Comics
1-Davy Jones, Undersea Agent begins .50 1.50 3.00
2-6: 2-Jones gains magnetic powers. 5-Origin & 1st app. of
Merman. 6-Wood-c(r) .40 1.20 2.40
NOTE: ***Gil Kane** a-3-6; c-4, 5.*

UNDERSEA FIGHTING COMMANDOS
May, 1952 - No. 5, Jan, 1953; 1964
Avon Periodicals
1 3.00 9.00 18.00
2-5 2.00 6.00 12.00
I.W. Reprint No. 1,2('64) .85 2.00 4.00

UNDERWATER CITY, THE (See 4-Color No. 1324,1328)

UNDERWORLD (True Crime Stories)
Feb-Mar, 1948 - No. 9, June-July, 1949
D. S. Publishing Co.
1-Sheldon Moldoff-c 7.00 20.00 40.00
2-Moldoff-c; Ma Barker story used in **SOTI**, pg. 95; female electrocution panel; lingerie art 7.00 20.00 40.00
3-McWilliams c/a; extreme violence, mutilation
4.00 12.00 24.00
4-Used in **Love and Death** by Legman; Ingels-a
3.50 10.00 20.00
5-9 2.50 7.00 14.00

UNDERWORLD CRIME
June, 1952 - No. 9, Oct, 1953
Fawcett Publications
1 4.00 12.00 24.00
2-6,8,9 2.50 7.00 14.00
7-Bondage/torture-c 5.00 15.00 30.00

UNDERWORLD STORY, THE
1950 (Movie)
Avon Periodicals
nn-(Scarce) 7.00 20.00 40.00

UNEARTHLY SPECTACULARS
Oct, 1965 - No. 3, Mar, 1967
Harvey Publications
1-Tiger Boy .50 1.50 3.00
2-Jack Q. Frost app.; Wood, Williamson, Adams, Kane art; reprints
Thrill-O-Rama No. 2 2.00 5.00 10.00
3-Jack Q. Frost app.; Williamson/Crandall-a; r-from Alarming Advs.
No. 1, 1962; 2 pgs. Kirby-a 2.00 5.00 10.00

UNEXPECTED, THE (Formerly Tales of the. . .)
No. 105, Feb-Mar, 1968 - Present
National Periodical Publications/DC Comics
105-115,117,118,120,123-127 .40 .80
116,119,121,128-Wrightson-a .50 1.50 3.00
122-Wood-a .50 1.50 3.00
129-132,134-136,139-156: 132-136-(52 pgs.)
.40 .80
133,137,138-Wood-a .60 1.20
157-162-(All 100 pgs.) .40 .80
163-188 .30 .60
189,190,192-195 ($1.00 size) .60 1.20
191-Rogers-a(p) .60 1.20
196-217 .30 .60
NOTE: ***Adams** c-110, 112-118, 121, 124. **Alcala** a-140, 144, 150-153, 156, 157, 168, 169. **Anderson** a-122. **Buckler** a-123. **Ditko** a-189. **Aparo** a-127, 132. **Kaluta** c-200, 203, 212. **Kirby** a-127, 162. **Kubert** c-215, 216. **Moreira** a-133. **Newton** a-204. **Nino** a-162,*

UNEXPECTED (continued)
Special No. 1. ***Orlando*** *a-202; c-191.* ***Perez*** *a-217.* ***Starlin*** *c-198.* ***Toth*** *a-127r.* ***Tuska*** *a-200.* ***Wood*** *a-122i, 137i.* ***Wrightson*** *a-161r(2 pgs.). Johnny Peril in No. 107-117.*

UNEXPECTED ANNUAL, THE (See DC Spec. Series No. 4)

UNITED COMICS
Aug, 1940 - No. 26, Jan-Feb, 1953
United Features Syndicate

	Good	Fine	Mint
1-Fritzi Ritz & Phil Fumble	2.50	7.00	14.00
2-9-Fritzi Ritz, Abbie & Slats	1.50	4.00	8.00
10-26: 25-Peanuts app.	1.00	3.00	6.00

NOTE: *Abbie & Slats reprinted from Tip Top.*

UNITED NATIONS, THE (See Classics Illustrated Special Ed.)

UNITED STATES AIR FORCE PRESENTS: THE HIDDEN CREW
1964 (36 pages) (full color)
U.S. Air Force

Shaffenberger-a	.50	1.50	3.00

UNITED STATES MARINES
1943 - No. 4, 1944; No. 5, 1952 - 1953
Magazine Enterprises/Toby Press

nn-Mart Bailey-a	3.50	10.00	20.00
2-4: 2-Bailey-a	2.50	7.00	14.00
5(A-1 55), 6(A-1 60), 7(A-1 68), 8(A-1 72)	2.00	6.00	12.00
7-11 (Toby)	.85	2.50	5.00

NOTE: ***Powell*** *a-5-7.*

UNIVERSAL PRESENTS DRACULA (See Movie Classics)

UNKEPT PROMISE
1949 (24 pages)
Legion of Truth (Giveaway)

Anti-alcohol	6.00	16.00	32.00

UNKNOWN MAN, THE
1951 (Movie)
Avon Periodicals

nn-Kinstler-c	10.00	30.00	60.00

UNKNOWN SOLDIER (Formerly Star-Spangled War Stories) (See Brave & the Bold No. 146)
No. 205, Apr-May, 1977 - Present
National Periodical Publications/DC Comics

205-218,220-247,250-258		.30	.60
219-Miller-a		.50	1.00
248,249-Origin		.30	.60

NOTE: ***Chaykin*** *a-234.* ***Estrada*** *a-220, 230.* ***Evans*** *c-235.* ***Kubert*** *c-Most.* ***Severin*** *a-252, 253.* ***Simonson*** *a-254-256.*

UNKNOWN WORLD (Strange Stories From Another World No. 2 on)
June, 1952
Fawcett Publications

1-Norman Saunders painted-c	6.00	16.00	32.00

UNKNOWN WORLDS (See Journey Into. . .)

UNKNOWN WORLDS
Aug, 1960 - No. 57, Aug, 1967
American Comics Group/Best Synd. Features

1	3.00	8.00	16.00
2-5	1.50	4.00	8.00
6-19	.85	2.50	5.00
20-Herbie cameo	1.00	3.00	6.00
21-35	.50	1.50	3.00
36-"The People vs. Hendricks" by Craig; most popular ACG story ever; Herbie cameo	.75	2.30	4.60
37-46	.30	.90	1.80
47-Williamson-a r-from Adventures Into the Unknown No. 96, 3 pgs.; Craig-a	.75	2.30	4.60
48-57		.60	1.20

NOTE: ***Ditko*** *a-49, 50p, 54.* ***Everett*** *c-17.* ***Heath*** *a-17.* ***Landau*** *a-56. John Force, Magic Agent app.-No. 35, 36, 48, 50, 52, 54, 56.*

UNKNOWN WORLDS OF SCIENCE FICTION
12/74 - No. 6, 11/75; 12/76 (B&W Magazine) ($1.00)
Marvel Comics Group

1-Williamson/Wood/Torres/Frazetta r-/Witzend No. 1, Adams r-/Phase 1; Brunner & Kaluta-r	.50	1.50	3.00
2	.40	1.20	2.40
3-6	.40	1.20	2.40
Special 1(12/76)-100 pgs.; Newton-c; Nino-a	.40	1.20	2.40

NOTE: ***Brunner*** *a-2, 4; c-4, 6.* ***Chaykin*** *a-5.* ***Corben*** *a-4.* ***Kaluta*** *a-2; c-2.* ***Morrow*** *a-3, 5.* ***Nino*** *a-3, 6.*

UNSANE
June, 1954
Star Publications

15-Disbrow-a(2); L. B. Cole-c	7.00	20.00	40.00

UNSEEN, THE
1952 - No. 15, July, 1954
Visual Editions/Standard Comics

5-Toth-a	3.50	10.00	20.00
6,9,10-Jack Katz-a; 6-1pg. Toth-a	3.00	8.00	16.00
7,8,11,13,14	2.00	6.00	12.00
12,15-Toth-a; Tuska-a, No. 12	3.50	10.00	20.00

NOTE: ***Fawcette*** *a-13.* ***Sekowsky*** *a-8(2), 10, 13.*

UNTAMED LOVE
Jan, 1950 - No. 5, Sept, 1950
Quality Comics Group (Comic Magazines)

1-Ward-c, Gustavson-a	8.00	24.00	48.00
2,4	5.50	16.00	32.00
3,5-Gustavson-a	6.00	18.00	36.00

UNTOLD LEGEND OF THE BATMAN, THE
7/80 - No. 3, 9/80 (No. 1,2: 40¢ issues; No. 3 on: 50¢)
DC Comics

1-Origin		.60	1.20
2,3		.40	.80

NOTE: ***Aparo*** *a-1-3.* ***Byrne*** *a-1.*

UNTOUCHABLES, THE (TV)
1961 - No. 4, Oct, 1962
Dell Publishing Co.

4-Color 1237,1286	1.00	3.00	6.00
01879-207, 12-879-210(01879-210 on inside)	1.00	3.00	6.00
Topps Bubblegum premiums-2½x4½", 8 pgs. (3 different issues) "The Organization," "Jamaica Ginger", "The Otto Frick Story" (drug)	1.00	3.00	6.00

UNUSUAL TALES (Blue Beetle & Shadow From Beyond No. 50 on)
Nov, 1955 - No. 49, Mar-Apr, 1965
Charlton Comics

1	3.50	10.00	20.00
2-5	1.50	4.00	8.00
6-8-Ditko c/a	3.50	10.00	20.00
9-Ditko c/a, 20 pgs.	3.50	10.00	20.00
10-Ditko c/a(4)	4.00	12.00	24.00
11-(68 pgs.); Ditko-a(4)	4.00	12.00	24.00
12-Ditko-a	3.00	8.00	16.00
13,16-20	.85	2.00	4.00
14,15-Ditko c/a	3.00	8.00	16.00
21,24,28,30-49	.50	1.50	3.00
22,23,25-27,29-Ditko-a	.85	2.50	5.00

NOTE: ***Ditko*** *c-22,25,26.*

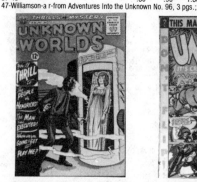

Unknown Worlds #36, © ACG

Unsane #15, © STAR

Untold L.O.T. Batman #1, © DC

USA Comics #17, © MCG

U.S. Paratroops #1, © I.W.

Valor #1, © WMG

UP FROM HARLEM
1973 (35-49 Cents)
Spire Christian Comics (Fleming H. Revell Co.)

	Good	Fine	Mint
		.50	1.00

UP-TO-DATE COMICS
No date (1938) (36 pgs.; B&W cover) (10 cents)
King Features Syndicate

nn-Popeye & Henry cover; The Phantom, Jungle Jim & Flash Gordon by Raymond, The Katzenjammer Kids, Curley Harper & others 15.00 45.00 90.00
(Variations to above contents exist.)

UP YOUR NOSE AND OUT YOUR EAR (Magazine)
April, 1972 - No. 2, June, 1972 (52 pgs.) (Satire)
Klevart Enterprises

V1No.1,2 .30 .90 1.80

USA COMICS (Hedy Devine No. 18 on)
Aug, 1941 - No. 17, Fall, 1945
Timely Comics (USA)

1-Origin Major Liberty, Rockman by Wolverton, & The Whizzer by Avison; The Defender with sidekick Rusty & Jack Frost begin; The Young Avenger only app.; S&K-c plus 1 pg. 250.00 650.00 1350.00
2-Origin Captain Terror & The Vagabond; last Wolverton Rockman 120.00 320.00 650.00
3-No Whizzer 90.00 250.00 500.00
4-Last Rockman, Major Liberty, Defender, Jack Frost, & Capt. Terror; Corporal Dix app. 70.00 180.00 375.00
5-Origin American Avenger & Roko the Amazing; The Black Widow, The Blue Blade & Victory Boys, Gypo the Gypsy Giant & Hills of Horror only app.; Sergeant Dix begins; no Whizzer 60.00 150.00 320.00
6-Captain America, The Destroyer, Jap Buster Johnson, Jeep Jones begin; Terror Squad only app. 65.00 170.00 350.00
7-Captain Daring, Disk-Eyes the Detective by Wolverton app.; origin & only app. Marvel Boy; Secret Stamp begins; no Whizzer, Sergeant Dix 50.00 140.00 300.00
8-10: 9-Last Secret Stamp. 10-The Thunderbird only app. 35.00 100.00 220.00
11,12: 11-No Jeep Jones. 30.00 90.00 180.00
13-16: 13-No Whizzer; Jeep Jones ends. 15-No Destroyer; Jap Buster Johnson ends 20.00 60.00 120.00
17-(Scarce) 25.00 75.00 150.00

U.S. AGENT (See Jeff Jordan . . .)

U.S. AIR FORCE COMICS (Army Attack No. 38 on)
Oct, 1958 - No. 37, Mar-Apr, 1965
Charlton Comics

1 .85 2.50 5.00
2-10 .35 1.00 2.00
11-20 .50 1.00
21-37 .30 .60
NOTE: ***Montes/Bache*** *a-33.*

USA IS READY
1941 (68 pgs.) (One Shot)
Dell Publishing Co.

1-War propaganda; drug mention 8.00 24.00 48.00

U.S. BORDER PATROL COMICS (Sgt. Dick Carter of the . . .) (See Holyoke One Shot)

U.S. FIGHTING AIR FORCE
Sept, 1952 - No. 29, Oct, 1956
Superior Comics Ltd.

1 3.00 8.00 16.00
2 2.00 5.00 10.00
3-10 1.00 3.00 6.00
11-29 .85 2.50 5.00
I.W. Reprint No. 1,9(no date) .40 1.10 2.20

U.S. FIGHTING MEN
1963 - 1964 (Reprints)
Super Comics

	Good	Fine	Mint
10-Avon's With the U.S. Paratroops	.50	1.50	3.00
11,12,15-18	.30	.80	1.60

U.S. JONES
Nov, 1941 - No. 2, Jan, 1942
Fox Features Syndicate

1-U.S. Jones & The Topper begin 25.00 75.00 150.00
2 12.00 35.00 70.00

U.S. MARINES IN ACTION!, THE
1952
Avon Periodicals/Charlton Comics

1-Louis Ravielli c/a 3.00 8.00 16.00
2,3: 3-Kinstler-c 1.50 4.00 8.00
1(Fall '64-Charlton) .30 .80 1.60

U.S. PARATROOPS (See With the . . .)

U.S. PARATROOPS
1964?
I. W. Enterprises

1-Wood-c r-/With the . . . No. 1 .50 1.50 3.00
8-Kinstler-c .50 1.50 3.00

U.S. TANK COMMANDOS
July, 1952 - No. 4, March, 1953
Avon Periodicals

1-Kinstler-c 3.50 10.00 20.00
2-4: 2-Kinstler-c 2.00 6.00 12.00
I.W. Reprint No. 1,8 .40 1.10 2.20
NOTE: ***Kinstler*** *a-3,4,I.W.No.1; c-1,2,4,I.W.No.1,8.*

VACATION COMICS (See A-1 Comics No. 16)

VACATION IN DISNEYLAND
Aug, 1958 - Mar, 1965 (Walt Disney)
Dell Publishing Co./Gold Key (1965)

1(1958-25 cents) 1.00 3.00 6.00
4-Color 1025-Barks-a 6.00 16.00 32.00
1(30024-508)(G.K.)-Reprints Dell Giant No. 30 & cover to No. 1('58) .50 1.50 3.00

VACATION PARADE (Picnic Party No. 6 on)
1950 - 1954 (130 pgs.) (25 cents) (Walt Disney)
Dell Publishing Co.

1-Donald Duck & Mickey Mouse; Carl Barks-a, 55 pgs. 60.00 175.00 350.00
2 7.00 20.00 40.00
3-5 3.00 8.00 16.00

VALLEY OF THE DINOSAURS (TV) (Hanna-Barbera)
April, 1975 - No. 11, Dec, 1976
Charlton Comics

1-Howard inks .40 .80
2-11: 2-Howard inks .30 .60

VALLEY OF GWANGI (See Movie Classics)

VALOR
Mar-Apr, 1955 - No. 5, Nov-Dec, 1955
E. C. Comics

1-Williamson/Torres-a; Wood c/a 17.00 50.00 90.00
2-Williamson c/a; Wood-a 14.00 40.00 76.00
3-Williamson, Crandall-a 10.00 28.00 56.00
4-Wood-c 10.00 28.00 56.00
5-Wood c/a; Williamson/Evans-a 8.00 24.00 48.00
NOTE: ***Crandall*** *a-3, 4.* ***Ingels*** *a-1, 2, 4, 5.* ***Krigstein*** *a-1-5.* ***Orlando*** *a-3, 4; c-3.* ***Wood*** *a-1, 2, 5; c-1, 4, 5.*

VAMPIRELLA (Magazine)
Sept, 1969 - Present

VAMPIRELLA (continued)
Warren Publishing Co.

	Good	Fine	Mint
1-Intro. Vampirella	10.00	27.00	54.00
2	3.50	10.00	20.00
3 (Low distribution)	14.00	38.00	76.00
4-7	2.50	7.00	14.00
8-Vampi begins by Tom Sutton as serious strip (early issues-gag line)	1.75	5.00	10.00
9-Smith-a	2.00	6.00	12.00
10-No Vampi story	2.00	5.00	10.00
11-15: 11-Origin, 1st app. Pendragon. 12-Vampi by Gonzales begins, ends No. 34	1.50	4.00	8.00
16-25	1.00	3.00	6.00
26-40: 28-Intro. Pantha. 31-Origin Luana, the Beast Girl. 32-Pantha ends	.85	2.50	5.00
41-45	.50	1.50	3.00
46-Origin	.70	2.00	4.00
47-50: 50-Spirit cameo	.40	1.20	2.40
51-99: 87,91-Reprints	.35	1.10	2.20
100-Origin retold	.40	1.20	2.40
Annual 1('72)-New origin Vampirella by Gonzales; reprints by Adams(No.1), Wood(No.9)	7.00	21.00	42.00

NOTE: ***Adams** a-1, 10, 17, 19, 51. **Alcala** a-90, 93. **Bode'/Todd** c-3. **Bode'/Jones** c-4. **Brunner** a-10. **Corben** a-30, 31, 33, 54. **Crandall** a-1, 19. **Frazetta** c-1, 5, 7, 11, 31. **Jones** a-5, 9, 12, 27, 32, 33(w/**Wrightson**), 34, 50, 53, 56. **Nino** a-90. **Ploog** a-14. **Smith** a-9. **Sutton** a-11. **Toth** a-92. **Wood** a-8-10, 12, 19, 27, 74r; c-9. **Wrightson** a-33, 63.*

VAMPIRE TALES (Magazine)
Aug, 1973 - No. 11, June, 1975 (B&W) (75 cents)
Marvel Comics Group

	Good	Fine	Mint
1-Morbius, the Living Vampire begins by Pablo Marcos	.40	1.20	2.40
2-Intro. Satana; Steranko-r	.30	.90	1.80
3-Satana app.	.30	.80	1.60
4-6,8-11: 5-Origin Morbius. 6-1st Lilith app. 8-1st Blade app.	.30	.80	1.60
7-Kaluta-a	.30	.90	1.80
Annual 1(10/75)	.30	.90	1.80

NOTE: ***Alcala** a-6, 8, 9. **Boris** c-4, 6. **Chaykin** a-7. **Everett** a-1r. **Heath** a-9. **Infantino** a-3r. **Gil Kane** a-4, 5.*

VARIETY COMICS
1944 - 1945; 1946
Rural Home Publications/Croyden Publ. Co.

	Good	Fine	Mint
1-Origin Captain Valiant	3.50	10.00	20.00
2-Captain Valiant	2.50	7.00	14.00
3(1946-Croyden)-Captain Valiant	2.00	5.00	10.00
4,5	1.50	4.00	8.00

VARIETY COMICS
1946; 1950 (132 pages)
Fox Features Syndicate (Hero Books)

	Good	Fine	Mint
1(1946)-Blue Beetle & Jungle Jo	5.00	14.00	28.00

nn(1950)-See Fox Giants. Contents can vary & determines price.

VARSITY
1945
Parents' Magazine Institute

	Good	Fine	Mint
1	1.00	3.00	6.00

VAUDEVILLE AND OTHER THINGS
1900 (10½x13") (in color) (18+ pgs.)
Isaac H. Blandiard Co.

	Good	Fine	Mint
By Bunny	15.00	40.00	80.00

VAULT OF EVIL
Feb, 1973 - No. 23, Nov, 1975
Marvel Comics Group

	Good	Fine	Mint
1 (Reprints begin)		.50	1.00
2-10: 3,4-Brunner-c		.40	.80
11-23		.25	.50

NOTE: ***Ditko** a-14r, 15r, 20-22r. **Drucker** a-10r(Mystic No. 52), 13r(Uncanny Tales No.42). **Everett** a-11r(Menace No. 2),13r(Menace No.4); c-10. **Krigstein** a-20r(Uncanny Tales No.54).*

VAULT OF HORROR (War Against Crime No. 1-11)
No. 12, Apr-May, 1950 - No. 40, Dec-Jan, 1954-55
E. C. Comics

	Good	Fine	Mint
12	90.00	250.00	500.00
13-Morphine story	60.00	140.00	270.00
14	45.00	120.00	240.00
15	40.00	100.00	200.00
16	25.00	75.00	150.00
17-19	20.00	60.00	120.00
20-22,24,25	17.00	50.00	80.00
23-Used in **POP**, pg. 84	20.00	56.00	90.00
26-B&W & color illos in **POP**	20.00	56.00	90.00
27-35	15.00	40.00	70.00
36-"Pipe Dream"-classic opium addict story by Krigstein; 'Twin Bill' cited in articles by T. E. Murphy & Wertham	15.00	40.00	70.00
37-Williamson-a	15.00	40.00	70.00
38-40: 39-Bondage-c	12.00	32.00	56.00

NOTE: ***Craig** art in all but No. 13 & 33; c-12-40. **Crandall** a-33, 34, 39. **Davis** a-17-38. **Evans** a-27, 28, 30, 32, 33. **Feldstein** a-12-16. **Ingels** a-13-20, 22-40. **Kamen** a-15-22, 25, 29, 35. **Krigstein** a-36, 38-40. **Kurtzman** a-12, 13. **Orlando** a-24, 31, 40. **Wood** a-12-14.*

V. . .-COMICS (Morse code for "V" - 3 dots, 1 dash)
Jan, 1942 - No. 2, Mar-Apr, 1942
Fox Features Syndicate

	Good	Fine	Mint
1-Origin V-Man & the Boys; The Banshee & The Black Fury, The Queen of Evil, & V-Agents begin	25.00	70.00	140.00
2	18.00	50.00	100.00

VENGEANCE SQUAD
July, 1975 - No. 6, May, 1976
Charlton Comics

	Good	Fine	Mint
1-Staton-a		.40	.80
2-6		.25	.50
5,6(Modern Comics-r, 1977)		.15	.30

VENUS
August, 1948 - No. 19, April, 1952
Marvel/Atlas Comics (LMC)

	Good	Fine	Mint
1-Venus begins; Kurtzman's "Hey Look"	20.00	60.00	110.00
2,3,5	10.00	30.00	60.00
4-Kurtzman's "Hey Look"	13.00	40.00	80.00
6-10: 6-Loki app.	10.00	30.00	60.00
11-S/F end of the world(11/50)	13.00	40.00	80.00
12	10.00	30.00	60.00
13-19-Venus by Everett, 2-3 stories each; covers-No. 13,15-19	13.00	40.00	80.00

NOTE: *No. 3,4-content changes to teen-age.*

VERI BEST SURE FIRE COMICS
No date (circa 1945) (Reprints Holyoke One-Shots)
Holyoke Publishing Co.

	Good	Fine	Mint
1-Captain Aero, Alias X, Miss Victory, Commandos of the Devil Dogs, Red Cross, Hammerhead Hawley, Capt. Aero's Sky Scouts, Flagman app.	9.00	25.00	50.00

VERI BEST SURE SHOT COMICS
No date (circa 1945) (Reprints Holyoke One-Shots)
Holyoke Publishing Co.

1-Capt. Aero, Miss Victory by Quinlan, Alias X, The Red Cross, Flagman, Commandos of the Devil Dogs, Hammerhead Hawley,

Vampirella #5, © WP

Vault Of Horror #30, © WMG

Venus #13, © MCG

Vic Verity Magazine #5, © Vic Verity

Voodoo #13, © AJAX

Voyage T.T.B. Of The Sea #2, © GK

VERI BEST SURE SHOT COMICS (continued) Good Fine Mint
Capt. Aero's Sky Scouts 9.00 25.00 50.00

VERY BEST OF DENNIS THE MENACE
July, 1979 - Present (132 pgs.) (Digest) (95 cents)
Fawcett Publications

1-4 .50 1.00

VIC FLINT (Crime Buster. . .)
August, 1948 (Newspaper reprints)
St. John Publishing Co.

1 2.50 7.00 14.00
2-5 2.00 5.00 10.00

VIC FLINT
Feb, 1956 - No. 2, May, 1956 (Newspaper reprints)
Argo Publ.

1,2 1.50 4.00 8.00

VIC JORDAN
April, 1945
Civil Service Publ.

1-1944 daily newspaper-r 2.00 5.00 10.00

VICKI (Humor)
Feb, 1975 - No. 4, July, 1975 (No. 1,2: 68 pgs.)
Atlas/Seaboard Publ.

1-Reprints Tippy Teen .50 1.50 3.00
2-4 .30 .80 1.60

VICKS COMICS (Also see Pure Oil Comics, Salerno Carnival of Comics, & 24 Pages of Comics)
No date (circa 1938) (68 pgs. in color)
Eastern Color Printing Co. (Vicks Chemical Co.)

nn-Reprints from Famous Funnies (before No. 40). Contains 5 pgs. Buck Rogers, 4 pgs. from F.F. No. 15, & 1 pg. from No. 16 30.00 90.00 180.00
nn-16 pg. giveaway; paper-c; no title; r-/Famous Funnies No. 14 20.00 60.00 120.00

VICKY
Oct, 1948 - No. 5, June, 1949
Ace Magazine

nn(10/48), 4(12/48) 1.50 4.00 8.00
nn(2/49), nn(4/49), 5(6/49) 1.50 4.00 8.00

VICTORY COMICS
Aug, 1941 - No. 4, Dec, 1941
Hillman Periodicals

1-The Conqueror by Bill Everett, The Crusader, & Bomber Burns begin; Conqueror's origin in text; Everett-c; No. 1 by Funnies, Inc. 50.00 150.00 300.00
2-Everett-a 25.00 75.00 150.00
3,4 18.00 50.00 100.00

VIC TORRY & HIS FLYING SAUCER
1950 (One Shot)
Fawcett Publications

Powell-a 15.00 40.00 80.00

VIC VERITY MAGAZINE
1945 - 1946 (A comic book)
Vic Verity Publications

1-C. C. Beck-a 2.00 6.00 20.00
2-7: 6-Beck-a 2.50 7.00 14.00

VIGILANTES, THE (See 4-Color No. 839)

VIKINGS, THE (See 4-Color No. 910)

VIRGINIAN, THE (TV)
June, 1963
Gold Key

Good Fine Mint
1(10060-306) .70 2.00 4.00

VOODA (Formerly Voodoo)
No. 20, April, 1955 - No. 22, Aug, 1955
Ajax-Farrell (Four Star Publications)

20-22-Baker-a plus Kamen/Baker story, Kimbo Boy of Jungle, & Baker-c (p) in all 4.00 12.00 24.00
NOTE: *No. 20-**Baker** r-/Seven Seas No. 4.*

VOODOO (Vooda No. 20 on)
May, 1952 - No. 19, Feb, 1955
Ajax-Farrell (Four Star Publ.)

1-South Sea Girl-r by Baker 8.00 24.00 40.00
2-Rulah story-r plus South Sea Girl from Seven Seas No. 2 by Baker (name changed from Alani to El'nee) 7.00 20.00 36.00
3-Bakerish-a 5.50 16.00 28.00
4-Baker-r 5.50 16.00 28.00
5-10: 6,8-Severed head panels 4.00 12.00 24.00
11-14,16-18 3.00 9.00 18.00
15-Opium drug story-r/Ellery Queen No. 3 3.50 10.00 20.00
19-Bondage-c; Baker-a(2)(r) 7.00 20.00 40.00
Annual 1(1952)(25 cents); Baker-a 18.00 50.00 100.00

VOODOO (See Tales of. . .)

VOYAGE TO THE BOTTOM OF THE SEA (TV)
1961 - No. 16, April, 1970
Dell Publishing Co./Gold Key

4-Color 1230(Movie-1961) 2.00 5.00 10.00
10133-412(G.K.-12/64) .70 2.00 4.00
2-5 .40 1.20 2.40
6-14 .30 .90 1.80
15,16-Reprints .50 1.00

VOYAGE TO THE DEEP
Sept-Nov, 1962 - No. 4, Nov-Jan, 1964
Dell Publishing Co.

1 .85 2.50 5.00
2-4 .50 1.50 3.00

WACKY ADVENTURES OF CRACKY (Also see Gold Key Spotlight)
Dec, 1972 - No. 12, Sept, 1975
Gold Key

1 .30 .90 1.80
2-12 .50 1.00
(See March of Comics No. 405)

WACKY DUCK (Formerly Dopey Duck?; Justice No. 7 on)
No. 3, Fall, 1946 - No. 6, Summer, 1947; 8/48 - No. 2, 10/48
Marvel Comics (NPP)

3,5,6('46-47) 3.00 8.00 16.00
4-Infinity-c 3.50 10.00 20.00
1,2(1948) 2.00 6.00 12.00
I.W. Reprint No. 1,2,7('58) .30 .90 1.80
Super Reprint No. 10(I.W. on cover, Super on inside) .30 .90 1.80

WACKY QUACKY (See Wisco)

WACKY RACES (TV)
Feb, 1969 - No. 7, Apr, 1972 (Hanna-Barbera)
Gold Key

1-7 .50 1.50 3.00

WACKY WITCH
March, 1971 - No. 21, Jan, 1976
Gold Key

1 .50 1.50 3.00
2-21 .35 1.00 2.00
(See March of Comics No. 374,398,410,422,434,446,458,470,482)

WACKY WOODPECKER (See Two Bit . . .)
1958; 1963
I. W. Enterprises/Super Comics

	Good	Fine	Mint
I.W. Reprint No. 1,2,7(no date-reprints Two Bit . . .)	.30	.90	1.80
Super Reprint No. 10('63)	.30	.90	1.80

WAGON TRAIN (1st Series) (TV)
1958 - No. 13, Apr-June, 1962
Dell Publishing Co.

4-Color 895,971,1019	1.00	3.00	6.00
4(1-3/60),6-13	1.00	3.00	6.00
5-Toth-a	1.50	4.50	9.00

WAGON TRAIN (2nd Series)
Jan, 1964 - No. 4, Oct, 1964
Gold Key

1	.70	2.00	4.00
2-4	.50	1.50	3.00

WAITING ROOM WILLIE (See Sad Case for . . .)

WALLY
Dec, 1962 - No. 4, Sept, 1963
Gold Key

1	.70	2.00	4.00
2-4	.50	1.50	3.00

WALT DISNEY CHRISTMAS PARADE (Also see Christmas Parade)
Winter, 1977 (224 pgs.) (cardboard covers, $1.95)
Whitman Publishing Co. (Golden Press)

11191-Barks-a r-/Christmas in Disneyland No. 1, Dell Christmas Parade No. 9	.40	1.20	2.40

WALT DISNEY COMICS DIGEST
June, 1968 - No. 57, Feb, 1976 (50 cents) (Digest size)
Gold Key

1-Reprints Uncle Scrooge No. 5	3.00	9.00	18.00
2-4-Barks-r	2.00	5.00	10.00
5-Daisy Duck by Barks (8 pgs.); last published story by Barks (art only) plus 21 pg. Scrooge-r by Barks	2.00	6.00	12.00
6-13-All Barks-r	1.00	3.00	6.00
14,15	.70	2.00	4.00
16-Reprints Donald Duck No. 26 by Barks	1.50	4.00	8.00
17-20-Barks-r	.80	2.40	4.80
21-31,33,35-37-Barks-r; 24-Toth Zorro	.70	2.00	4.00
32	.50	1.50	3.00
34-Reprints 4-Color 318	1.50	4.00	8.00
38-Reprints Christmas in Disneyland No. 1	1.00	3.00	6.00
39-Two Barks-r/WDC&S No. 272, 4-Color 1073 plus Toth Zorro-r	.80	2.40	4.80
40-Mickey Mouse-r by Gottfredson	.50	1.50	3.00
41,45,47-49	.30	.90	1.80
42,43-Barks-r	.50	1.50	3.00
44-(Has Gold Key emblem, 50 cents)-Reprints 1st story of 4-Color 29, 256,275,282	2.00	6.00	12.00
44-Republished in 1976 by Whitman; not identical to original; slightly smaller, blank back cover, 69 cents cover price	.80	2.40	4.80
46,50-Barks-r	.50	1.50	3.00
51-Reprints 4-Color 71	.80	2.40	4.80
52-Barks-r/WDC&S No. 161,132	.50	1.50	3.00
53-Reprint/Dell Giant No. 30	.30	.80	1.60
54-Reprint/Donald Duck Beach Party No. 2	.30	.80	1.60
55-Reprint/Dell Giant No. 49	.30	.80	1.60
56-Reprint/Uncle Scrooge No. 32 (Barks) plus another Barks story	.50	1.50	3.00
57-Reprint/Mickey Mouse Almanac('57) & two Barks stories	.50	1.50	3.00

NOTE: *No. 1-10, 196 pgs.; No. 11-41, 164 pgs.; No. 42 on, 132 pgs. Old issues were being reprinted & distributed by Whitman in 1976.*

WALT DISNEY PRESENTS
June-Aug, 1959 - No. 6, Dec-Feb, 1960-61
Dell Publishing Co.

	Good	Fine	Mint
4-Color 997	.85	2.50	5.00
2(12-2/60)-The Swamp Fox, Elfego Baca, Texas John Slaughter (Disney TV Show)	.70	2.00	4.00
3-6	.70	2.00	4.00

WALT DISNEY'S COMICS & STORIES (Continuation of Mickey Mouse Magazine) (No. 1-30 contain Donald Duck newspaper reprints)
10/40 - No. 263, 8-11/62; No. 264, 10/62 - Present
Dell Publishing Co./Gold Key No. 264-473/Whitman No. 474 on

1(V2No.1)-Donald Duck strip reprints by Al Taliaferro & Gottfredson's Mickey Mouse begin	400.00	1200.00	2600.00
(Prices vary widely on this book)			
2	210.00	625.00	1200.00
3	100.00	300.00	540.00
4	75.00	220.00	400.00
4-Special promotional, complimentary issue; cover same except one corner was blanked out & boxed in to identify the giveaway (not a paste-over). This special pressing was probably sent out to former subscribers to Mickey Mouse Mag. whose subscriptions had expired. (Very Rare - one known copy)	125.00	400.00	750.00
5	70.00	180.00	320.00
6-10	60.00	150.00	250.00
11-14	45.00	120.00	230.00
15-17	40.00	100.00	180.00
18-21: 15-The 3 Little Kittens (17 pgs.). 16-The 3 Little Pigs (29 pgs.). 17-The Ugly Duckling (4 pgs.)	30.00	80.00	150.00
22-30	25.00	60.00	120.00
31-Donald Duck by Carl Barks begins	150.00	450.00	820.00
32-Barks-a	110.00	280.00	575.00
33-Barks-a (infinity-c)	70.00	180.00	360.00
34-Gremlins by Walt Kelly begin, end No. 41; Barks-a	60.00	150.00	300.00
35,36-Barks-a	45.00	130.00	260.00
37-Donald Duck by Jack Hannah	20.00	60.00	120.00
38-40-Barks-a	35.00	90.00	180.00
41-50-Barks-a	25.00	70.00	140.00
51-60-Barks-a; 51-Christmas-c. 52-Li'l Bad Wolf begins, ends No. 203 (not in No. 55)	18.00	52.00	105.00
61-70: Barks-a. 61-Dumbo story. 63,64-Pinocchio stories. 65-Pluto story. 66-Infinity-c. 67,68-Mickey Mouse art (Sunday-r) by Bill Wright	15.00	43.00	86.00
71-80: Barks-a. 75-77-Brer Rabbit stories, no Mickey Mouse	12.00	35.00	70.00
81-87,89,90: Barks-a. 82-84-Bongo stories. 86-90-Goofy & Agnes app. 89-Chip 'n' Dale story	10.00	30.00	60.00
88-1st app. Gladstone Gander by Barks	12.00	35.00	70.00
91-97,99,100: Barks-a. 95-1st WDC&S Barks cover. 96-No Mickey Mouse; Little Toot begins, ends No. 97	8.00	24.00	48.00
98-1st Uncle Scrooge app. in WDC&S	15.00	40.00	80.00
101-106,108-110-Barks-a	7.00	20.00	40.00
107-Barks-a; Taliaferro-c	7.00	20.00	40.00
111,114,117-All Barks	5.00	15.00	30.00
112-Drug (ether) issue (Donald Duck)	6.00	18.00	36.00
113,115,116,118-123: Not by Barks. 116-Dumbo x-over. 121-Grandma Duck begins, ends No. 168; not in No. 135,142, 146,155	2.50	7.50	15.00
124,126-130-All Barks. 124-X-Mas-c	5.00	15.00	30.00
125-Intro. & 1st app. Junior Woodchucks; Barks-a	8.00	22.00	44.00
131,133,135-139-All Barks	5.00	15.00	30.00
132-Barks-a(2) (D. Duck & Grandma Duck)	6.00	18.00	36.00
134-Intro. & 1st app. The Beagle Boys	10.00	28.00	56.00
140-1st app. Gyro Gearloose by Barks	10.00	28.00	56.00

141-150-All Barks. 143-Little Hiawatha begins, ends No. 151,159

Walt Disney's C&S #12, © WDP

Walt Disney's C&S #100, © WDP

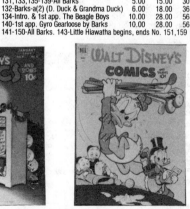

Walt Disney's C&S #140, © WDP

Walt Disney's C&S #161, © WDP

Walt Disney's C&S #261, © WDP

Walt Disney Showcase #30, © WDP

WALT DISNEY'S C & S (continued)

	Good	Fine	Mint
	3.50	10.00	20.00
151-170-All Barks. 164-Has blank inside-c	3.00	9.00	18.00
171-200-All Barks	2.50	7.50	15.00
201-240: All Barks. 204-Chip 'n' Dale & Scamp begin	2.00	6.00	12.00
241-283: Barks-a. 241-Dumbo x-over. 247-Gyro Gearloose begins, ends No. 274. 256-Ludwig Von Drake begins, ends No. 274	1.50	4.50	9.00
284,285,287,290,295,296,309-311-Not by Barks	.80	2.30	4.60
286,288,289,291-294,297,298,308-All Barks stories; 293-Grandma Duck's Farm Friends. 297-Gyro Gearloose. 298-Daisy Duck's Diary-r	1.50	4.50	9.00
299-307-All contain early Barks-r (No.43-117). 305-Gyro Gearloose	2.00	5.00	10.00
312-Last Barks issue with original story	1.50	4.00	8.00
313-315,317-327,329-334,336-341	.50	1.50	3.00
316-Last issue published during life of Walt Disney	.70	2.00	4.00
328,335,342-350-Barks-r	.80	2.40	4.80
351-360-w/posters inside; Barks reprints (2 versions of each with & without posters)	.70	2.00	4.00
361-400-Barks-r	.70	2.00	4.00
401-429-Barks-r	.40	1.10	2.20
430,433,438,441,444,466-No Barks		.30	.60
431,432,434-437,439,440,442,443,445-Barks-r		.50	1.00
446,448-465,467-492-All Barks		.30	.60
447(12/77)(52 pgs.)-Barks		.40	.80

(No. 1-38, 68 pgs.; No. 39-42, 60 pgs.; No. 43-57,61-134,143-168,446,447, 52 pgs.; No. 58-60,135-142,169-Present, 36 pgs.)

NOTE: **Barks** art in all issues No. 31 on, except where noted; c-95, 96, 104, 108, 109, 130-72, 174-78, 183, 198-200, 204, 206-09, 212-16, 218, 220, 226, 228-33, 235-38, 240-43, 247, 250, 253, 256, 260, 261, 276-83, 288-92, 295-98, 301, 303, 304, 306, 307, 309, 310, 313-16, 319, 321, 322, 324, 326, 328, 329, 331, 332, 334, 341, 342, 350, 351. **Kelly** covers(most)-34-94, 97-103, 105, 106, 110-123. The whole number can always be found at bottom of title page in the lower left-hand or right-hand panel. Walt Disney's Comics & Stories featured Mickey Mouse serials which were in practically every issue from No. 1 through No. 392. The titles of the serials, along with the issues they are in, are listed in previous editions. **Floyd Gottfredson** Mickey Mouse serials in issues Nos. 1-61, 63-74, 77-92 plus "Mickey Mouse in a Warplant" (3 pgs.), and "Pluto Catches a Nazi Spy" (4 pgs.) in No. 62; "Mystery Next Door," No. 93; "Sunken Treasure," No. 94; "Aunt Marissa," No. 95; "Gangland," No. 98; "Thanksgiving Dinner," No. 99; and "The Talking Dog," No. 100. Mickey Mouse by Paul Murry No. 152 on. **Al Taliaferro** Silly Symphonies in No. 5-"Three Little Pigs;" No. 13-"Birds of a Feather;" No. 14-"The Boarding School Mystery;" No. 15-"Cookieland" and "Three Little Kittens;" No. 16-"Three Little Pigs;" No. 17-"The Ugly Duckling" and "The Robber Kitten;" No. 19-"Penguin Isle;" and "Bucky Bug" in Nos. 20-23, 25, 26, 28 (one continuous story from 1932-34; first 2 pgs. not Taliaferro).

WALT DISNEY'S COMICS & STORIES
1943 (36 pgs.) (Dept. store Xmas giveaway)
Walt Disney Productions

	Good	Fine	Mint
nn	60.00	150.00	300.00

WALT DISNEY'S COMICS & STORIES
Mid 1940's ('45-48), 1952 (4 pgs. in color) (slick paper)
Dell Publishing Co.(Special Xmas offer)

	Good	Fine	Mint
1940's version - subscription form for WDC&S - (Reprints two different WDC&S covers with subscription forms printed on inside covers)	9.00	25.00	50.00
1952 version	5.00	14.00	28.00

WALT DISNEY SHOWCASE
Oct, 1970 - No. 54, Jan, 1980 (No. 44-49, 68pp, 50-52,54, 52pp)
Gold Key

	Good	Fine	Mint
1-Boatniks (Movie)		.60	1.20
2-Moby Duck		.40	.80
3-Bongo & Lumpjaw-r		.40	.80
4-Pluto-r		.40	.80
5-$1,000,000 Duck (Movie)		.60	1.20
6-Bedknobs & Broomsticks (Movie)		.60	1.20
7-Pluto-r		.30	.60
8-Daisy & Donald		.30	.60
9-101 Dalmatians (cartoon feature); r-4-Color 1183		.50	1.00
10-Napoleon & Samantha (Movie)		.50	1.00
11-Moby Duck-r		.30	.60
12-Dumbo-r/4-Color 668; extra 16pgs. ads		.40	.80
13-Pluto-r		.30	.60
14-World's Greatest Athlete (Movie)		.50	1.00
15-3 Little Pigs-r		.30	.60
16-Aristocats (cartoon feature); r-Aristocats No. 1		.30	.60
17-Mary Poppins; r-M.P. No. 10136-501		.40	.80
18-Gyro Gearloose; Barks-r/4-Color No. 1047,1184	.35	1.00	2.00
19-That Darn Cat; r-T.D.C. No. 10171-602		.50	1.00
20-Pluto-r		.30	.60
21-Li'l Bad Wolf & The Three Little Pigs		.30	.60
22-Unbirthday Party with Alice in Wonderland; r-4-Color No. 341		.50	1.00
23-Pluto-r		.30	.60
24-Herbie Rides Again (Movie); sequel to "The Love Bug"		.50	1.00
25-Old Yeller (Movie); r-4-Color No. 869		.40	.80
26-Lt. Robin Crusoe USN (Movie); r-Lt. Robin Crusoe USN No. 10191-601		.40	.80
27-Island at the Top of the World (Movie)		.50	1.00
28-Brer Rabbit, Bucky Bug-r		.40	.80
29-Escape to Witch Mountain (Movie)	.30	.80	1.60
30-Magica De Spell; Barks-r/Uncle Scrooge No. 36 & WDC&S No. 258	.40	1.20	2.40
31-Bambi (cartoon feature); r-4-Color No. 186		.50	1.00
32-Spin & Marty-r; Mickey Mouse Club		.30	.60
33-Pluto		.30	.60
34-Paul Revere's Ride with Johnny Tremain; 4-Color No. 822-r		.30	.60
35-Goofy		.30	.60
36-Peter Pan; 4-Color-r		.30	.60
37-Tinker Bell & Jiminy Crickett; r-4-Color No. 982,989		.30	.60
38-Mickey & the Sleuth, Part 1		.30	.60
39-Mickey & the Sleuth, Part 2		.30	.60
40-The Rescuers (cartoon feature)		.40	.80
41-Herbie Goes to Monte Carlo (Movie); sequel to "Herbie Rides Again"		.30	.60
42-Mickey & the Sleuth		.30	.60
43-Pete's Dragon (Movie)		.40	.80
44-Return to Witch Mountain (new) & In Search of the Castaways (reprint) (Movies) (68 pgs.)		.40	.80
45-The Jungle Book (Movie); r-No. 30033-803		.40	.80
46-The Cat From Outer Space (Movie)(new), & The Shaggy Dog (Movie)(reprint)		.40	.80
47-Mickey Mouse Surprise Party; reprint; 68 pgs.		.40	.80
48-The Wonderful Advs. of Pinocchio; reprints; 68 pgs.		.40	.80
49-North Avenue Irregulars & Zorro		.40	.80
50-Bedknobs & Broomsticks		.40	.80
51-101 Dalmatians		.40	.80
52-Unidentified Flying Oddball		.40	.80
53-The Scarecrow-r		.40	.80
54(48pgs.)-The Black Hole		.40	.80

WALT DISNEY'S MAGAZINE (Formerly Walt Disney's Mickey Mouse Club Magazine) (50 cents) (Bi-monthly)
V2No.4, June, 1957 - V4No.6, Oct, 1959
Western Publishing Co.

WALT DISNEY'S MAGAZINE (continued)

	Good	Fine	Mint
V2No.4-Stories & articles on the Mouseketeers, Zorro, & Goofy and other Disney characters & people	2.00	6.00	12.00
V2No.5, V2No.6(10/57)	2.00	6.00	12.00
V3No.1(12/57) - V3No.6(10/58)	1.25	3.50	7.00
V4No.1(12/58) - V4No.6(10/59)	1.25	3.50	7.00

NOTE: *V2No.4-V3No.6 were 11½x8½'', 48 pgs.; V4No.1 on were 10x8'', 52 pgs. (Peak circulation of 400,000).*

WALT DISNEY'S MERRY CHRISTMAS (See Dell Giant No. 39)

WALT DISNEY'S MICKEY MOUSE CLUB MAGAZINE (Becomes Walt Disney's Magazine) (Quarterly)
Winter, 1956 - V2No.3, April, 1957 (11½x8½'') (48 pgs.)
Western Publishing Co.

	Good	Fine	Mint
V1No.1	7.00	20.00	40.00
2-4	3.50	10.00	20.00
V2No.1-3	2.50	7.00	14.00
Annual(1956)-Two different issues; ($1.50-Whitman); 120 pgs., cardboard covers, 11¾x8¾''; reprints	6.00	18.00	36.00
Annual(1957)-Same as above	5.00	14.00	28.00

WALT DISNEY'S WHEATIES PREMIUMS (See Wheaties)

WALT SCOTT'S XMAS STORIES (See 4-Color No. 959,1062)

WAMBI, JUNGLE BOY
Spring, 1942 - No. 3, Spring, 1943; No. 4, Fall, 1948 - No. 18, Winter, 1952-53
Fiction House Magazines

	Good	Fine	Mint
1-Wambi, the Jungle Boy begins	14.00	38.00	76.00
2 (1942)	8.00	22.00	44.00
3 (1943)	6.00	18.00	36.00
4(1948)-Origin in text	3.00	9.00	18.00
5-10	2.50	7.50	15.00
11-18	2.00	6.00	12.00
I.W. Reprint No. 8('64)-Reprints Fiction House No. 12 with new cover	1.00	3.00	6.00

WANTED COMICS
No. 9, Sept-Oct, 1947 - No. 53, April, 1953
Toytown Publications/Patches/Orbit Publ.

	Good	Fine	Mint
9-11	2.50	7.50	15.00
12-Used in **SOTI**, pg. 277	5.00	15.00	30.00
13-Heroin drug propaganda story	4.00	12.00	24.00
14-Marijuana drug mention story, 2 pgs.	2.50	7.00	14.00
15-17	2.00	5.00	10.00
18-Marijuana story, 'Satan's Cigarettes'; r-in No. 45 & retitled	9.00	25.00	50.00
19-Drug mention stories (2)	2.50	7.50	15.00
20,23,25-34,36-38,40-44,46-48,53	.85	2.50	5.00
21-Krigstein-a	2.50	7.00	14.00
22-Extreme violence	1.50	4.00	8.00
24-Krigstein-a; marijuana mention story	4.00	12.00	24.00
35-Used in **SOTI**, pg. 160	4.00	12.00	24.00
39-Drug propaganda story ''The Horror Weed''	5.00	14.00	28.00
45-Marijuana story from No. 18	5.00	14.00	28.00
49-Buscema-a	1.50	4.00	8.00
50-Buscema surrealist-c	3.50	10.00	20.00
51-''Holiday of Horror''-junkie story; drug-c	4.00	12.00	24.00
52-Classic ''Cult of Killers'' opium use story; Buscema-a	4.00	12.00	24.00

WANTED: DEAD OR ALIVE (See 4-Color No. 1102,1164)

WANTED, THE WORLD'S MOST DANGEROUS VILLAINS
July-Aug, 1972 - No. 9, Aug-Sept, 1973 (All reprints)
National Periodical Publications (See DC Special)

	Good	Fine	Mint
1-Batman, Green Lantern, & Green Arrow	.25	.75	1.50
2-Batman & The Flash		.50	1.00
3-Dr. Fate, Hawkman, & Vigilante		.50	1.00
4-Green Lantern & Kid Eternity		.50	1.00
5-Dollman/Green Lantern		.40	.80
6-Starman/Wildcat/Sargon		.40	.80
7-Johnny Quick/Hawkman/Hourman; Baily, Meskin		.40	.80
8-Dr. Fate/Flash		.40	.80
9-S&K Sandman/Superman		.40	.80

NOTE: ***Infantino*** *a-2,8.* ***Kubert*** *a-3i, 6, 7.*

WAR
July, 1975 - No. 9, Nov, 1976; No. 10, Sept, 1978 - Present
Charlton Comics

	Good	Fine	Mint
1		.15	.30
2-22		.15	.30
7,9(Modern Comics-r, 1977)		.15	.30

WAR ACTION
April, 1952 - No. 14, June, 1953
Atlas Comics (CPS)

	Good	Fine	Mint
1	2.50	7.00	14.00
2-6,8-10,14	1.50	4.00	8.00
7-Pakula-a	1.50	4.00	8.00
11-13-Krigstein-a	3.00	8.00	16.00

NOTE: ***Heath*** *c-7,14.*

WAR ADVENTURES
Jan, 1952 - No. 13, Mar, 1953
Atlas Comics (HPC)

	Good	Fine	Mint
1-Tuska-a	2.50	7.00	14.00
2-7,9-13: 3-Robinson-a	1.50	4.00	8.00
8-Krigstein-a	3.00	8.00	16.00

NOTE: ***Heath*** *c-13.*

WAR ADVENTURES ON THE BATTLEFIELD (See Battlefield)

WAR AGAINST CRIME! (Vault of Horror No. 12 on)
Spring, 1948 - No. 11, Feb-Mar, 1950
E. C. Comics

	Good	Fine	Mint
1	30.00	80.00	150.00
2,3	17.00	50.00	90.00
4-8	14.00	40.00	76.00
9-Morphine drug use story	16.00	48.00	86.00
10-1st Vault Keeper app.	50.00	140.00	280.00
11-2nd Vault Keeper app.	40.00	120.00	240.00

NOTE: *All have* ***Craig*** *covers.*

WAR AND ATTACK (Also see Special War Series No. 3)
Fall, 1964 - V2No.63, Dec, 1967
Charlton Comics

	Good	Fine	Mint
1-Wood-a	.85	2.50	5.00
V2No.54(6/66)-No. 63 (Formerly Fightin' Air Force)		.40	.80

NOTE: ***Montes/Bache*** *a-55, 56, 60, 63.*

WAR AT SEA
No. 22, Nov, 1957 - No. 42, June, 1961
Charlton Comics

	Good	Fine	Mint
22-42		.50	1.00

WAR BATTLES
Feb, 1952 - No. 9, Dec, 1953
Harvey Publications

	Good	Fine	Mint
1	3.00	8.00	16.00
2-5,7-9	1.50	4.00	8.00
6-Nostrand-a	2.50	7.00	14.00

NOTE: ***Powell*** *a-1-3, 7.*

WAR BIRDS
1952
Fiction House Magazines

Wambi, Jungle Boy #3, © FH

Wanted Comics #29, © Orbit Publ.

War Against Crime #2, © WMG

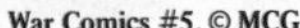
War Comics #5, © MCG

War Heroes #4, © DELL

Warlord #11, © DC

WAR BIRDS (continued)

	Good	Fine	Mint
1	3.50	10.00	20.00
2-7	2.50	7.00	14.00

WAR COMBAT (Combat Casey No. 6 on)
March, 1952 - No. 5, Nov, 1952
Atlas Comics (SAI)

	Good	Fine	Mint
1	2.00	6.00	12.00
2-5: 2-Berg-a	1.00	3.00	6.00

WAR COMICS (See Key Ring Comics)
May, 1940(No mo. given) - No. 8, Feb-Apr, 1943
Dell Publishing Co.

	Good	Fine	Mint
1-Sikandur the Robot Master, Sky Hawk, Scoop Mason, War Correspondent begin	10.00	30.00	60.00
2-Origin Greg Gilday	4.00	12.00	24.00
3-Joan becomes Greg Gilday's aide	4.00	12.00	24.00
4-Origin Night Devils	5.50	16.00	32.00
5-8	3.50	10.00	20.00

WAR COMICS
Dec, 1950 - No. 49, Sept, 1957
Marvel/Atlas (USA No. 1-41/JPI No. 42-49)

	Good	Fine	Mint
1	3.50	10.00	20.00
2-10	2.00	5.00	10.00
11-20	1.00	3.00	6.00
21,23-37,39-42,44,45,47,48	.70	2.00	4.00
22-Krigstein-a	3.00	8.00	16.00
38-Kubert/Moskowitz-a	2.00	6.00	12.00
43,49-Torres-a. 43-Davis E.C. swipe	2.00	6.00	12.00
46-Crandall-a	2.00	6.00	12.00

NOTE: ***Colan** a-49. **Drucker** a-37, 43, 48. **Everett** a-17. **Heath** a-7. **G. Kane** a-19. **Orlando** a-42, 48. **Robinson** a-15.*

WAR DOGS OF THE U.S. ARMY
1952
Avon Periodicals

	Good	Fine	Mint
1-Kinstler c/a	5.00	15.00	30.00

WARFRONT
9/51 - No. 35, 11/58; No. 36, 10/65; No. 37, 9/66 - No. 38, 12/66; No. 39, 12/67
Harvey Publications

	Good	Fine	Mint
1	3.00	8.00	16.00
2-10	1.50	4.00	8.00
11,12,14,16-20	.85	2.50	5.00
13,15,22-Nostrand-a	3.00	8.00	16.00
21,23-27,29,31-33,35	.70	2.00	4.00
28,30,34-Kirby-c	1.50	4.00	8.00
36-Dynamite Joe begins, ends No. 39	.50	1.50	3.00
37-Wood-a, 17pgs.	1.50	4.00	8.00
38,39-Wood-a, 2-3 pgs.; Lone Tiger app.	.85	2.50	5.00

NOTE: ***Kirby** c-28, 29, 34. **Powell** a-(some w/**Nostrand**)-No. 2-6, 9-12, 14, 17, 20, 23, 25, 27, 28, 30, 31, 34.*

WAR FURY
Sept, 1952 - No. 4, March, 1953
Comic Media/Harwell

	Good	Fine	Mint
1	2.00	6.00	12.00
2-4	1.50	4.00	8.00

WAR GODS OF THE DEEP (See Movie Classics)

WAR HEROES (See Marine War Heroes)

WAR HEROES
July-Sept, 1942 (no month); No. 2, Oct-Dec, 1942 - No. 10, Oct-Dec, 1944; No. 11, Mar, 1945
Dell Publishing Co.

	Good	Fine	Mint
1	6.00	16.00	32.00
2,3,5	3.00	8.00	16.00
4-Disney's Gremlins app.	6.00	16.00	32.00
6-11: 6-Cameron-a	2.50	7.00	14.00

NOTE: *No. 1 was to be released in July, but was delayed.*

WAR HEROES
1952 - No. 8, April, 1953
Ace Magazines

	Good	Fine	Mint
1	2.00	6.00	12.00
2-8	1.20	3.50	7.00

WAR HEROES
Feb, 1963 - No. 27, Nov, 1967
Charlton Comics

	Good	Fine	Mint
1	.50	1.50	3.00
2-10	.30	.80	1.60
11-27: 27-1st Devils Brigade by Glanzman		.30	.60

NOTE: ***Montes/Bache** a-3-7, 21, 25, 27; c-3-7.*

WAR IS HELL
Jan, 1973 - No. 15, Oct, 1975
Marvel Comics Group

	Good	Fine	Mint
1-Williamson-a(r)		.40	.80
2-9-All reprints		.30	.60
10-15		.15	.30

NOTE: ***Bolle** a-3r. **Powell, Woodbridge** a-1. Sgt. Fury reprints-7, 8.*

WARLOCK (The Power of. . .) (See Strange Tales)
Aug, 1972 - No. 8, Oct, 1973; No. 9, Oct, 1975 - No. 15, Oct, 1976
Marvel Comics Group

	Good	Fine	Mint
1-Origin by Kane	1.00	3.00	6.00
2,3	.50	1.50	3.00
4-8: 4-Death of Eddie Roberts	.40	1.20	2.40
9-15-Starlin-c/a in all	.35	1.10	2.20

WARLORD, THE (See First Issue Special)
Jan-Feb, 1976; No.2, Mar-Apr, 1976; No.3, Oct-Nov, 1976 - Present
National Periodical Publications/DC Comics

	Good	Fine	Mint
1-Story cont'd. from 1st Issue Special No. 8	2.00	6.00	12.00
2-Intro. Machiste	1.00	3.00	6.00
3-5	.80	2.30	4.60
6-10: 6-Intro Mariah. 7-Origin Machiste	.60	1.80	3.60
11-20: 11-Origin-r. 12-Intro Anton. 15-Tara returns; Warlord has son	.40	1.20	2.40
21-30: 28-1st app. Wizard World	.35	1.00	2.00
31-36,39,40: 32-Intro Shakira. 40-Warlord gets new costume	.30	.80	1.60
37,38-Origin Omac by Starlin	.30	.80	1.60
41-47,49-52		.60	1.20
48-(52pgs.)-1st app. Arak	.30	.90	1.80

NOTE: ***Grell** a-1-51p; c-1-51.*

WARPATH
Nov, 1954 - No. 3, April, 1955
Key Publications/Stanmor

	Good	Fine	Mint
1	2.00	6.00	12.00
2,3	1.50	4.00	8.00

WARREN PRESENTS
Jan, 1979 - Present
Warren Publications

	Good	Fine	Mint
1-9-Eerie, Creepy, & Vampirella-r		.50	1.00

WAR REPORT
Sept, 1952 - No. 5, May, 1953
Ajax/Farrell Publications (Excellent Publ.)

	Good	Fine	Mint
1	2.50	7.00	14.00
2,3,5	1.20	3.50	7.00
4-Used in **POP**, pg. 94	2.00	6.00	12.00

WARRIOR COMICS
1945 (1930's DC reprints)
H. C. Blackerby

	Good	Fine	Mint
1-Wing Brady, The Iron Man, Mark Markon	2.00	6.00	12.00

WAR ROMANCES (See True. . .)

WAR SHIPS
1942 (36 pgs.) (Similar to Large Feature Comics)
Dell Publishing Co.

	Good	Fine	Mint
Cover by McWilliams; contains photos & drawings of U.S. war ships	5.00	14.00	28.00

WAR STORIES
1942 - No. 8, Feb-Apr, 1943
Dell Publishing Co.

1	6.00	16.00	32.00
2-4,6-8: 6-8-Night Devils	3.50	10.00	20.00
5-Origin The Whistler	4.00	12.00	24.00

WAR STORIES (Korea)
Sept, 1952 - No. 5, May, 1953
Ajax/Farrell Publications (Excellent Publ.)

1	3.50	7.00	14.00
2-5	1.20	3.50	7.00

WAR STORIES (See Star Spangled . . .)

WART AND THE WIZARD
Feb, 1964 (Walt Disney)
Gold Key

1 (10102-402)	.85	2.50	5.00

WARTIME ROMANCES
July, 1951 - No. 18, Nov, 1953
St. John Publishing Co.

1-All Baker-a	7.00	20.00	40.00
2-4-All Baker-a	5.00	15.00	30.00
5-8-Baker c/a(2-3) each	4.75	14.00	28.00
9-12,16,18-Baker c/a each	3.50	10.00	20.00
13-15,17-Baker-c only	2.50	7.00	14.00

WAR VICTORY ADVENTURES (No. 1 titled War Victory Comics)
Summer, 1942 - No. 3, Winter, 1943-44 (5 cents)
U.S. Treasury Dept./War Victory/Harvey Publ.

1-(Promotion of Savings Bonds)-Featuring America's greatest comic art by top syndicated cartoonists; Blondie, Joe Palooka, Green Hornet, Dick Tracy, Superman, Gumps, etc.; (36 pgs.)	12.00	35.00	70.00
2	5.00	15.00	30.00
3-Capt. Red Cross (cover & text only); Powell-a	4.50	13.00	26.00

WAR WAGON, THE (See Movie Classics)

WAR WINGS
October, 1968
Charlton Comics

1		.50	1.00

WASHABLE JONES & SHMOO
1953
Harvey Publications

1	5.00	15.00	30.00

WASH TUBBS (See 4-Color No. 11,28,53)

WATCH OUT FOR BIG TALK
1949
Giveaway

Dan Barry-a (about crooked politicians)	2.00	6.00	12.00

WATER BIRDS AND THE OLYMPIC ELK (See 4-Color No. 700)

WEATHER-BIRD (See Comics From . . . & Free Comics to You . . .)
1958 - No. 16, July, 1962 (Giveaway)
International Shoe Co./Western Printing Co.

1	.50	1.50	3.00
2-16	.25	.75	1.50

NOTE: *The numbers are located in the lower bottom panel, pg. 1. All feature a character called Weather-Bird.*

WEATHER BIRD COMICS (See Comics From Weather Bird)
1957 (Giveaway)
Weather Bird Shoes

nn-Contains a comic bound with new cover. Several combinations possible; contents determines price (30 - 50 percent of contents).

WEB OF EVIL
Nov, 1952 - No. 21, Dec, 1954
Comic Magazines/Quality Comics Group

	Good	Fine	Mint
1-Used in **SOTI**, pg. 388. Jack Cole-a; morphine use story	8.00	24.00	48.00
2,3-Jack Cole-a. 2-Bra & slip panels	5.00	14.00	28.00
4-7-Jack Cole c/a	6.00	18.00	36.00
8-11-Jack Cole-a	3.00	9.00	18.00
12-16,19-21: 13-Ravielli-a	2.00	6.00	12.00
17-Opium drug propaganda story	3.00	9.00	18.00
18-Acid-in-face story	2.50	7.00	14.00

NOTE: ***Jack Cole** a(2 each)-2, 6, 8, 9.*

WEB OF HORROR (Magazine)
Dec, 1969 - No. 3, Apr, 1970
Major Magazines

1-Jones-c; Wrightson-a	3.00	9.00	18.00
2-Jones-c; Wrightson-a(2), Kaluta-a	2.00	6.00	12.00
3-Wrightson-c; Brunner, Kaluta, Bruce Jones, Wrightson-a	2.00	6.00	12.00

WEB OF MYSTERY
Feb, 1951 - No. 29, Sept, 1955
Ace Magazines (A. A. Wyn)

1	4.00	12.00	24.00
2-Bakerish-a	3.00	8.00	16.00
3-10: 4-Drug story	2.00	6.00	12.00
11-18,20-26,28,29: 20-r/The Beyond No. 1	1.75	5.00	10.00
19-r-Chall. of Unknown No. 6 used in N.Y. Legis. Comm	2.00	6.00	12.00
27-Bakerish-a(r)/The Beyond No. 2)	2.00	6.00	12.00

NOTE: *This series was to appear as "Creepy Stories," but title was changed before publication. **Cameron** a-1, 17, 18-20, 22, 24, 25, 27; c-17. **Colan** a-4. **Sekowsky** a-1-3, 7, 8, 11, 14, 21, 29. **Tothish** a-by Bill Discount No. 16. No. 29-all-r, 19-28-partial-r.*

WEDDING BELLS
Feb, 1954 - No. 19, 1956
Quality Comics Group

1-Whitney-a	4.00	12.00	24.00
2	2.00	6.00	12.00
3-9	1.50	4.00	8.00
10-Ward-a, 9 pgs.	6.00	18.00	36.00
11-14,17	1.00	3.00	6.00
15-Baker-c	2.00	5.00	10.00
16-Baker-c/a	3.00	8.00	16.00
18,19-Baker-a each	2.50	7.00	14.00

WEEKENDER, THE
1945 - 1946 (52 pages)
Rucker Publ. Co.

V1No.4(1945)	7.00	20.00	40.00
V2No.1-36 pgs. comics, 16 in newspaper format with photos; partial Dynamic Comics reprints; 4 pgs. of cels from the Disney film Pinocchio; Little Nemo story by Winsor McCay, Jr.; Jack Cole-a	5.50	16.00	32.00

WEEKLY COMIC MAGAZINE
May 12, 1940 (16 pgs.) (Full Color)
Fox Publications

(1st Version)-8 pg. Blue Beetle story, 7 pg. Patty O'Day story; two

Wartime Romances #7, © STJ

Web Of Evil #8, © QUA

Web Of Mystery #7, © ACE

Weird Adventures #1, © P.L. Publ.

Weird Comics #10, © FOX

Weird Mysteries #5, © Gillmore Publ.

WEEKLY COMIC MAGAZINE (continued) — Good / Fine / Mint

copies known to exist. Estimated value. . . . $300.00

(2nd Version)-7 two-pg. adventures of Blue Beetle, Patty O'Day, Yarko, Dr. Fung, Green Mask, Spark Stevens, & Rex Dexter; one copy known to exist Estimated value. . . . $250.00

Discovered with business papers, letters and exploitation material promoting **Weekly Comic Magazine** for use by newspapers in the same manner of **The Spirit** weeklies. Interesting note: these are dated three weeks before the first **Spirit** comic. Letters indicate that samples may have been sent to a few newspapers. These sections were actually 15½x22'' pages which will fold down to an approximate 8x10'' comic booklet. Other various comic sections were found with the above, but were more like the Sunday comic sections in format.

WEIRD (Magazine)
Jan, 1966 - V8No.6, Dec, 1974; V9No.2, June, 1976 - Present
(V1-V8, 52 pgs.; V9 on, 68 pgs.)
Eerie Publications

V1No.10(No.1)-Intro. Morris the Caretaker of Weird (ends V2No.10); Burgos-a .40 1.20 2.40
11,12 .60 1.20
V2No.1-4(10/67), V3No.1(1/68), V2No.6(4/68)-V2No.7,9,10(12/68), V3No.1(2/69)-V3No.4 .40 .80
V2No.8-Reprints Ditko's 1st story/Fantastic Fears No. 5 .30 .80 1.60
5(12/69)-Rulah reprint; ''Rulah'' changed to ''Pulah;'' LSD story-reprinted in Horror Tales V4No.4, Tales From the Tomb V2No.4, & Terror Tales V7No.3 .50 1.00
V4No.1-6('70), V5No.1-6('71), V6No.1-7('72), V7No.1-6('73), V8No.1-6('74), V9No.2-4('75-'76)(no V9No.1), V10No.1-3('77) .40 .80

WEIRD ADVENTURES
May-June, 1951 - No. 3, Sept-Oct, 1951
P. L. Publishing Co. (Canada)

1-''The She-Wolf Killer'' by Matt Baker, 6 pgs. 7.00 20.00 40.00
2-Bondage/hypodermic panel; opium den text story 5.00 14.00 28.00
3-Male bondage/torture-c; severed head story 3.50 10.00 20.00

WEIRD ADVENTURES
No. 10, July-Aug, 1951
Ziff-Davis Publishing Co.

10-Painted-c 5.00 14.00 28.00

WEIRD CHILLS
July, 1954 - No. 3, Nov, 1954
Key Publications

1-Wolverton-a r-/Weird Mysteries No. 4 14.00 40.00 76.00
2-Injury to eye-c 12.00 36.00 72.00
3-Bondage E.C. swipe-c 6.00 16.00 32.00

NOTE: ***Bailey*** *c-1.*

WEIRD COMICS
April, 1940 - No. 20, Jan, 1942
Fox Features Syndicate

1-The Birdman, Thor, God of Thunder (ends No. 5), The Sorceress of Zoom, Blast Bennett, Typhon, Voodoo Man, & Dr. Mortal begin; Fine-c 40.00 120.00 260.00
2 30.00 80.00 170.00
3,4: 4-Bondage/torture-c 17.00 50.00 110.00
5-Intro. Dart & sidekick Ace (ends No. 20); bondage/hypo-c 20.00 55.00 120.00
6,7-Dynamite Thor app. in each 15.00 45.00 100.00
8-Dynamo, the Eagle & sidekick Buddy & Marga, the Panther Woman begin 15.00 45.00 100.00
9 14.00 38.00 80.00
10-Navy Jones app. 14.00 38.00 80.00
11-16 12.00 35.00 70.00
17-Origin The Black Rider 12.00 35.00 70.00

Good / Fine / Mint

18-20: 20-Origin The Rapier; Swoop Curtis app. 12.00 35.00 70.00

WEIRD FANTASY (Formerly A Moon, A Girl, Romance; becomes Weird Science-Fantasy No. 23 on)
No. 13, May-June, 1950 - No. 22, Nov-Dec, 1953
E. C. Comics

13(No.1) (1950) 80.00 225.00 450.00
14 50.00 140.00 240.00
15 50.00 120.00 200.00
16-Used in **SOTI**, pg. 144 50.00 120.00 200.00
17 (1951) 35.00 90.00 160.00
6-10 25.00 70.00 120.00
11-13 (1952) 17.00 50.00 90.00
14-Frazetta/Williamson(1st at E.C.)/Krenkel-a, 7 pgs. 40.00 100.00 180.00
15-Williamson/Evans-a(3), 4,3,&7 pgs. 20.00 60.00 110.00
16-19-Williamson/Krenkel-a in all. 18-Williamson/Krenkel-c 17.00 50.00 90.00
20-Frazetta/Williamson-a, 7 pgs. 20.00 60.00 110.00
21-Frazetta/Williamson-c & Williamson/Krenkel-a 40.00 100.00 180.00
22-Bradbury adaptation 15.00 40.00 70.00

NOTE: ***Crandall*** *a-22.* ***Elder*** *a-17.* ***Feldstein*** *a-13(No.1)-8; c-13(No.1)-18 (No.18 w/**Krenkel**), 20.* ***Kamen*** *a-13(No.1)-16, 18-22.* ***Krigstein*** *a-22.* ***Kurtzman*** *a-13(No.1)-17(No.5), 6.* ***Orlando*** *a-9-22 (2 stories in No. 16); c-19, 22.* ***Severin/Elder*** *a-18-21.* ***Wood*** *a-13(No.1)-14, 17(2 stories ea. in No. 10-13). Canadian reprints exist; see Table of Contents.*

WEIRD HORRORS (Nightmare No. 10 on)
Aug, 1952 - No. 9, Oct, 1953
St. John Publishing Co.

1-Tuska-a 6.00 18.00 36.00
2,5 4.00 12.00 24.00
3-Finesque-a; hashish story 5.00 14.00 28.00
4-Finesque-a 4.00 12.00 24.00
6-Ekgren-c 6.00 18.00 36.00
7-Ekgren-c; Kubert, Cameron-a 7.00 20.00 40.00
8,9-Kubert c/a. 8-Bondage-c 7.00 20.00 40.00

NOTE: ***Cameron*** *a-7, 9.* ***Finesque*** *a-1, 2, 4.* ***Morisi*** *a-3.*

WEIRD MYSTERIES
Oct, 1952 - No. 14, Jan, 1955
Gillmore Publications

1-Partial Wolverton-c swiped from splash page ''Flight to the Future'' in Weird Tales of the Future No. 2; ''Eternity'' has an Ingels swipe 12.00 32.00 56.00
2-''Robot Woman'' by Wolverton; Bernard Bailey-c-reprinted in Mister Mystery No. 18; acid in face panel 35.00 100.00 180.00
3-Severed head-c 5.00 15.00 30.00
4-''The Man Who Never Smiled'' (3 pgs.) by Wolverton; B. Bailey skull-c 25.00 70.00 140.00
5-Wolverton story ''Swamp Monster,'' 6 pgs. 25.00 70.00 140.00
6 5.00 15.00 30.00
7-Used in **SOTI**, illo-''Indeed'' & illo-''Sex and blood'' 15.00 45.00 90.00
8-Wolverton-c panel reprint/No. 5; used in a 1954 Readers Digest anti-comics article by T. E. Murphy entitled ''For the Kiddies to Read.'' 6.00 18.00 36.00
9-Excessive violence, gore & torture 5.00 14.00 28.00
10-Silhouetted nudity panel 5.00 14.00 28.00
11-14 4.00 12.00 24.00

NOTE: ***Bailey*** *c-2-8, 10-12.*

WEIRD MYSTERIES (Magazine)
Mar-Apr, 1959 (68 pages) (35 cents) (B&W)
Pastime Publications

1-Torres-a; E. C. swipe from TFTC No. 46 by Tuska-''The Ragman'' 2.00 6.00 12.00

WEIRD MYSTERY TALES (See DC 100 Page Super Spectacular)

WEIRD MYSTERY TALES (See Cancelled Comic Cavalcade)
Jul-Aug, 1972 - No. 24, Nov, 1975
National Periodical Publications

	Good	Fine	Mint
1-Kirby-a	.30	.80	1.60
2,3-Kirby-a; 2-Two pgs. Starlin		.40	.80
4-8,10: 4-2pg. Starlin-a(p)		.40	.80
9-Redondo-a		.40	.80
11-20,22		.20	.40
21-Wrightson-c		.40	.80
23-Wood-a		.40	.80
24-Kaluta-a		.30	.60

NOTE: ***Alcala*** *a-5, 10, 13, 14.* ***Aparo*** *c-4.* ***Bolle*** *a-8.* ***Howard*** *a-4.* ***Kaluta*** *a-4; c-1.* ***Nino*** *a-5, 6, 9, 13, 16, 21.*

WEIRD SCIENCE (Formerly Saddle Romances) (Becomes Weird Science-Fantasy No. 23 on)
No. 12, May-June, 1950 - No. 22, Nov-Dec, 1953
E. C. Comics

	Good	Fine	Mint
12(No.1) (1950)	90.00	250.00	480.00
13	60.00	150.00	250.00
14,15 (1950)	50.00	130.00	230.00
5-10	30.00	80.00	140.00
11-14 (1952)	17.00	50.00	90.00
15-18-Williamson/Krenkel-a in each; 15-Williamson-a. 17-Used in **POP**, pgs. 81,82	20.00	60.00	110.00
19,20-Williamson/Frazetta-a, 7 pgs each. 19-Used in **SOTI**, illo-''A young girl on her wedding night stabs her sleeping husband to death with a hatpin. . .''	30.00	80.00	150.00
21-Williamson/Frazetta-a, 6 pgs.	30.00	80.00	150.00
22-Williamson/Frazetta/Krenkel-a, 8 pgs.; Wood draws himself in his story - last pg. & panel	30.00	80.00	150.00

NOTE: ***Elder*** *a-14, 19.* ***Evans*** *a-22.* ***Feldstein*** *a-12(No.1)-8; c-12(No.1)-8, 11.* ***Ingels*** *a-15.* ***Kamen*** *a-12(No.1)-13, 15-18, 20, 21.* ***Kurtzman*** *a-12(No.1)-7.* ***Orlando*** *a-10-22.* ***Wood*** *a-12(No.1), 13(No.2), 5-22 (No. 9, 10, 12, 13 all have 2* ***Wood*** *stories); c-9, 10, 12-22. Canadian reprints exist; see Table of Contents.*

WEIRD SCIENCE-FANTASY (Formerly Weird Science & Weird Fantasy) (Becomes Incredible Science Fantasy No. 30)
No. 23 Mar, 1954 - No. 29, May-June, 1955
E. C. Comics

	Good	Fine	Mint
23,24-Williamson & Wood-a in both	17.00	50.00	90.00
25-Williamson-c; Williamson/Torres/Krenkel-a plus Wood-a	20.00	60.00	110.00
26-Flying Saucer Report; Wood, Crandall, Orlando-a	14.00	40.00	80.00
27	18.00	50.00	100.00
28-Williamson/Krenkel/Torres-a; Wood-a	20.00	55.00	110.00
29-Frazetta-c; Williamson/Krenkel & Wood-a	50.00	120.00	240.00

NOTE: ***Crandall*** *a-26, 27, 29.* ***Evans*** *a-26.* ***Feldstein*** *c-24, 26, 28.* ***Kamen*** *a-27, 28.* ***Krigstein*** *a-23-25.* ***Orlando*** *a-in all.* ***Wood*** *a-in all; c-23, 27.*

WEIRD SCIENCE-FANTASY ANNUAL
1952, 1953 (Sold thru the E. C. office & on the stands in some major cities)
E. C. Comics

	Good	Fine	Mint
1952	140.00	320.00	600.00
1953	80.00	220.00	400.00

NOTE: *The 1952 annual contains books cover-dated in 1951 & 1952, and the 1953 annual from 1952 & 1953. Contents of each annual may vary in same year.*

WEIRD SUSPENSE STORIES (Canadian reprint of Crime SuspenStories No. 1-3; see Table of Contents)

WEIRD SUSPENSE TALES
Feb, 1975 - No. 3, July, 1975
Atlas/Seaboard Publ.

	Good	Fine	Mint
1-Tarantula begins		.40	.80
2,3		.25	.50

WEIRD TALES OF THE FUTURE
March, 1952 - No. 8, July-Aug, 1953
S.P.M. Publ. No. 1,2/Aragon Publ./Stanmor Publ.

	Good	Fine	Mint
1: Bondage, headlight, hypo needle; Andru-a(2)	17.00	50.00	90.00
2,3-Wolverton-a(3) each. 3 has LSD-like story	50.00	140.00	260.00
4-''Jumpin Jupiter'' satire by Wolverton; partial Wolverton-c	18.00	50.00	100.00
5-Wolverton-c/a(2)	50.00	140.00	260.00
6-Bernard Bailey-c	8.00	24.00	44.00
7-''The Mind Movers'' from the art to Wolverton's ''Brain Bats of Venus'' from Mr. Mystery No. 7 which was cut apart, pasted up, partially redrawn, and rewritten by Harry Kantor, the editor; Bernard Bailey-c	20.00	60.00	110.00
8-Reprints Weird Mysteries No. 1(10/52) minus cover; gory cover showing heart ripped out	7.00	20.00	36.00

WEIRD TALES OF THE MACABRE (Magazine)
Jan, 1975 - No. 2, Mar, 1975 (B&W) (75 cents)
Atlas/Seaboard Publ.

	Good	Fine	Mint
1-Jones-c	.35	1.00	2.00
2-Boris Valejo-c	.30	.80	1.60

WEIRD TERROR (Also see Horrific)
Sept, 1952 - No. 13, Sept, 1954
Allen Hardy Associates (Comic Media)

	Good	Fine	Mint
1	3.50	10.00	20.00
2,3,5,9,10	2.50	7.50	15.00
4,6-Decapitation story	3.50	10.00	20.00
7-Two pg. drug text-story	3.00	8.00	16.00
8-Decapitation story; Ambrose Bierce adapt.	3.00	8.00	16.00
11-End of the world story with atomic blast panels; Tothish-a by Bill Discount	3.50	10.00	20.00
12-Discount-a	2.00	6.00	12.00
13-Severed head panels	2.00	6.00	12.00

NOTE: ***Don Heck*** *a/c-most issues.* ***Landau*** *a-6.* ***Morisi*** *a-2, 3, 5, 7, 12.* ***Palais*** *a-1, 5, 8(2), 12.* ***Powell*** *a-10.* ***Ravielli*** *a-11, 20.*

WEIRD THRILLERS
Sept-Oct, 1951 - No. 5, Oct-Nov, 1952
Ziff-Davis Publ. Co. (Approved Comics)

	Good	Fine	Mint
1-Ron Hatton photo-c	8.00	24.00	48.00
2-Toth, Anderson, Colan-a	7.00	20.00	40.00
3-Two Powell, Tuska-a	6.00	16.00	32.00
4-Kubert, Tuska-a	7.00	20.00	40.00
5-Powell-a	6.00	16.00	32.00

NOTE: ***Anderson*** *a-1-3.* ***Roussos*** *a-4. No. 2, 3 reprinted in Nightmare No. 10 & 13; No. 4, 5 r-/in Amazing Ghost Stories No.? & No. 15.*

WEIRD WAR TALES
Sept-Oct, 1971 - Present
National Periodical Publications/DC Comics

	Good	Fine	Mint
1-Kubert-a	.70	2.00	4.00
2-Kubert (2 pgs.); Crandall-a(r)	.50	1.50	3.00
3,4-Kubert-a	.30	.80	1.60
5,6,10-Toth-a	.30	.80	1.60
7-Kubert-a; Krigstein-a(r)	.30	.80	1.60
8-Adams c/a(i)	.70	2.00	4.00
9,11,12,14-20		.40	.80
13-Redondo-a		.50	1.00
21-35,37-40		.30	.60
36-Crandall, Kubert r-/No. 2		.40	.80
41-50		.30	.60
51,52-Rogers-a		.30	.60
53-63,65-67,70-92,94-106		.25	.50

Weird Mystery Tales #21, © DC

Weird Tales Of The Future #6, © Aragon

Weird Terror #10, © Comic Media

Weird Wonder Tales #1, © MCG

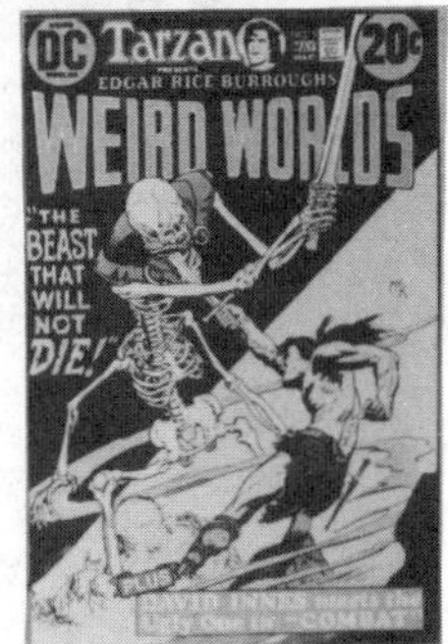

Weird Worlds #5, © DC

Werewolf By Night #3, © MCG

WEIRD WAR TALES (continued)

	Good	Fine	Mint
64,68-Miller-a		.50	1.00
69-Sci-fic issue		.30	.60
93-Origin Creature Commandos		.25	.50

NOTE: ***Alcala*** *a-9, 11, 14-16, 20, 23, 25-29, 35, 42-44, 50, 64, 74.* ***Aparo*** *c-105.* ***Bailey*** *a-21.* ***Chaykin*** *a-40, 61, 62, 67, 69, 76, 82.* ***Ditko*** *a-46, 49, 95, 104, 105.* ***Evans*** *a-17, 22, 35, 46, 74, 82; c-74, 82.* ***Drucker*** *a-2, 3.* ***Heath*** *a-59.* ***Infantino*** *a-5r.* ***Kaluta*** *c-12.* ***Kubert*** *a-68, 69; c-60, 62-69, 75-81, 87, 90, 91, 95, 96, 104, 106.* ***Maurer*** *a-5.* ***Meskin*** *a-4r.* ***Morrow*** *c-54.* ***Newton*** *a-82.* ***Nino*** *a-11, 13, 16, 23-25, 31, 36, 55, 61, 69.* ***Simonson*** *a-10, 72.* ***Staton*** *a-106.* ***Starlin*** *c-88, 89.* ***Tuska*** *a-103.*

WEIRD WESTERN TALES (Formerly All-Star Western)
No. 12, June-July, 1972 - Present (No. 12: 52 pgs.)
National Periodical Publications/DC Comics

	Good	Fine	Mint
12-Bat Lash, Pow Wow Smith reprints; El Diablo by Adams/Wrightson	.50	1.50	3.00
13,15-Adams-a; c-No. 15	.50	1.50	3.00
14-Toth-a		.50	1.00
16-20: 19-Last El Diablo		.30	.60
21-28,30-38		.25	.50
29-Origin Jonah Hex		.60	1.20
39-Origin, 1st app. Scalphunter; Evans inks		.40	.80
40-70: 52,53-Bat Lash app.		.30	.60

NOTE: ***Alcala*** *a-16, 17, 19.* ***Chaykin*** *a-49.* ***Ditko*** *a-99.* ***Evans*** *inks-39-48; c-40.* ***G. Kane*** *a-15.* ***Kubert*** *c-12.* ***Starlin*** *c-44, 45.* ***Wildey*** *a-26.*

WEIRD WONDER TALES
Dec, 1973 - No. 22, May, 1977
Marvel Comics Group

	Good	Fine	Mint
1-Wolverton-a r-from Mystic No. 6	.30	.90	1.80
2-5		.40	.80
6-15		.30	.60
16-18: Venus r-by Everett/Venus No. 19,18 & 17		.40	.80
19-Dr. Druid (Droom)-r		.40	.80
20-22-Dr. Druid		.30	.60

NOTE: All Reprints: ***Check*** *a-1.* ***Ditko*** *a-4, 5, 10-13, 19-21.* ***Drucker*** *a-12, 20.* ***Everett*** *a-3(Spellbound No.16), 6(Astonishing No.10), 9(Adv. Into Mystery No.5).* ***Kirby*** *a-6, 11, 13, 18-22; c-19, 20.* ***Krigstein*** *a-19.* ***Kubert*** *a-22.* ***Torres*** *a-7.* ***Wildey*** *a-2.*

WEIRD WORLDS (See Adventures Into . . .)

WEIRD WORLDS (Magazine)
V1No.10(12/70), V2No.1(2/71) - No. 4, Aug, 1971 (52 pgs.)
Eerie Publications

	Good	Fine	Mint
V1No.10		.60	1.20
V2No.1-4		.50	1.00

WEIRD WORLDS
Aug-Sept, 1972 - No. 9, Jan-Feb, 1974; No. 10, Oct-Nov, 1974
National Periodical Publications

	Good	Fine	Mint
1-Edgar Rice Burrough's John Carter of Mars & David Innes begin; Kubert-c	.40	1.10	2.20
2,3-Adams/Bunkers-a. 2-Wrightson inks	.30	.90	1.80
4-Kaluta-a	.30	.90	1.80
5-7-Last John Carter	.30	.90	1.80
8-Iron Wolf begins by Chaykin	.25	.75	1.50
9,10-Chaykin-a	.25	.75	1.50

NOTE: *John Carter by* ***Anderson****-No. 1-3.* ***Chaykin*** *c-7, 8.* ***Kaluta*** *c-5, 6, 10.* ***Orlando*** *a-4.*

WELCOME BACK, KOTTER (TV) (See Limited Collectors Ed. No. 57)
Nov, 1976 - No. 10, Mar-Apr, 1978
National Periodical Publications/DC Comics

	Good	Fine	Mint
1		.40	.80
2-10		.30	.60

WELCOME SANTA (See March of Comics No. 63,183)

WELLS FARGO (See Tales of . . .)

WENDY PARKER COMICS
July, 1953 - No. 8, July, 1954
Atlas Comics (OMC)

	Good	Fine	Mint
1	1.50	4.00	8.00
2-8	1.00	3.00	6.00

WENDY, THE GOOD LITTLE WITCH
8/60 - No. 82, 11/73; No. 83, 8/74 - No. 93, 4/76
Harvey Publications

	Good	Fine	Mint
1	9.00	25.00	50.00
2	4.00	12.00	24.00
3-5	3.50	10.00	20.00
6-10	2.50	7.50	15.00
11-20	2.00	5.00	10.00
21-30	.85	2.50	5.00
31-50	.50	1.50	3.00
51-70	.40	1.20	2.40
71-93	.25	.75	1.50

(See Casper the Friendly Ghost & Harvey Hits No. 7,16,21,23,27,30, 33)

WENDY WITCH WORLD
Oct, 1961; No. 2, Sept, 1962 - No. 52, Dec, 1973
Harvey Publications

	Good	Fine	Mint
1	6.00	16.00	32.00
2-5	3.00	8.00	16.00
6-10	2.00	5.00	10.00
11-20	1.00	3.00	6.00
21-30	.50	1.50	3.00
31-40	.35	1.00	2.00
41-53		.60	1.20

WEREWOLF (Super Hero)
Dec, 1966 - No. 3, April, 1967
Dell Publishing Co.

	Good	Fine	Mint
1	.25	.75	1.50
2,3		.50	1.00

WEREWOLF BY NIGHT (See Marvel Spotlight)
Sept, 1972 - No. 43, Mar, 1977
Marvel Comics Group

	Good	Fine	Mint
1-Ploog-a-cont'd./Marvel Spotlight No. 4	.70	2.00	4.00
2-7-Ploog-a in all	.30	.90	1.80
8-10		.50	1.00
11,12,17-20		.40	.80
13-16-Ploog-a; 15-New origin Werewolf		.60	1.20
21-30		.40	.80
31		.40	.80
32-Origin & 1st app. Moon Knight	1.00	3.00	6.00
33-Moon Knight app.	.70	2.00	4.00
34,36,38-43		.40	.80
35-Starlin/Wrightson-c		.60	1.20
37-Moon Knight app; part Wrightson-c	.35	1.00	2.00
Giant Size 2(10/74, 68 pgs.)(Formerly G-S Creatures)-Frankenstein app; Ditko-a(r).		.60	1.20
Giant Size 3-5(7/75, 68 pgs.); 4-Morbius the Living Vampire app.		.50	1.00

NOTE: ***Ditko*** *a-Gnt. Size 2r.* ***G. Kane*** *c-21, 22, 24-30, Gnt. Size 3-5.* ***Ploog*** *c-5-8, 13-16.* ***Ploog/Bolle*** *a-6.* ***Sutton*** *a-9, 11, 16, 34, 35.*

WEREWOLVES & VAMPIRES (Magazine)
1962 (One Shot)
Charlton Comics

	Good	Fine	Mint
1	3.00	8.00	16.00

WESTERN ACTION
1964
I. W. Enterprises

	Good	Fine	Mint
7-Reprint	.30	.90	1.80

WESTERN ACTION
February, 1975
Atlas/Seaboard Publ.

WESTERN ACTION (continued) Good Fine Mint

1-Kid Cody by Wildey & The Comanche Kid app.; intro. The Renegade .30 .60

WESTERN ACTION THRILLERS
April, 1937 (100 pages)
Dell Publishers

1-Buffalo Bill & The Texas Kid 7.00 20.00 40.00

WESTERN ADVENTURES COMICS
Oct, 1948 - No. 6, Aug, 1949
Ace Magazines

nn(No.1)-Sheriff Sal begins 6.00 18.00 36.00
nn(No.2)(12/48) 4.00 12.00 24.00
nn(No.3)(2/49)-Used in **SOTI**, pgs. 30,31 5.00 14.00 28.00
4-6 3.50 10.00 20.00

WESTERN BANDITS
1952
Avon Periodicals

1-Butch Cassidy, The Daltons by Larsen; Kinstler-a 6.00 18.00 36.00

WESTERN BANDIT TRAILS (See Approved Comics)
Jan, 1949 - No. 3, July, 1949
St. John Publishing Co.

1-Tuska-a; Baker-c; Blue Monk, Ventrilo app. 5.00 15.00 30.00
2-Baker-c 4.00 12.00 24.00
3-Baker c/a, Tuska-a 6.00 16.00 32.00

WESTERN COMICS (See Super DC Giant)
Jan-Feb, 1948 - No. 85, Jan-Feb, 1961
National Periodical Publications

1-The Vigilante, Wyoming Kid begin 10.00 28.00 56.00
2,3-Last Vigilante 6.00 16.00 32.00
4,5: 5-Nighthawk begins 4.00 12.00 24.00
6-10: 8-Origin Wyoming Kid 3.50 10.00 20.00
11-20 2.50 7.50 15.00
21-40 2.00 6.00 12.00
41-60: 43-Pow Wow Smith begins, ends No. 85 2.00 5.00 10.00
61-85-Last Wyoming Kid. 77-Origin Matt Savage Trail Boss. 82-1st app. Fleetfoot, Pow Wow's girlfriend 1.00 3.00 6.00

NOTE: ***Gil Kane, Infantino*** *art in most.* ***Moreira*** *a-35.*

WESTERN CRIME BUSTERS
Sept, 1950 - No. 10, Mar-Apr, 1952
Trojan Magazines

1 6.00 18.00 36.00
2-5 5.00 14.00 28.00
6-Wood-a 12.00 35.00 70.00
7-Six-Gun Smith by Wood 12.00 35.00 70.00
8 4.00 12.00 24.00
9-Wood-a(2) 14.00 38.00 76.00
10-Wood-a 11.00 33.00 66.00

WESTERN CRIME CASES (The Outlaws No. 10 on?)
No. 9, Dec, 1951
Novelty-Star Publications

9-White Rider & Super Horse; L. B. Cole-c 2.50 7.50 15.00

WESTERN DESPERADO COMICS (Formerly Slam Bang)
1940 (Oct.?)
Fawcett Publications

8-(Rare) 10.00 30.00 60.00

WESTERNER, THE (Wild Bill Pecos)
No. 14, June, 1948 - No. 41, Dec, 1951
"Wanted" Comic Group/Toytown/Patches

14 2.50 7.50 15.00

Good Fine Mint

15-17,20,21,25 1.50 4.00 8.00
18,22-24-Krigstein-a 3.00 8.00 16.00
19-Meskin-a 1.50 4.00 8.00
26(4/50)-Origin & 1st app. Calamity Kate, series ends No. 32; Krigstein-a 3.50 10.00 20.00
27-Krigstein-a(2) 4.00 12.00 24.00
28-41: 33-Quest app. 37-Lobo, the Wolf Boy begins 1.20 3.50 7.00

WESTERNER, THE
1964
Super Comics

Super Reprint No. 15,16(Crack West. No. 65), 17 .25 .75 1.50

WESTERN FIGHTERS
Apr-May, 1948 - V4No.7, Mar-Apr, 1953
Hillman Periodicals/Star Publ.

V1No.1-Simon & Kirby-c 7.00 20.00 40.00
2,3: 2-Kirby-a(p)? 2.50 7.00 14.00
4-Krigstein, Ingels-a 3.00 9.00 18.00
5,6,8-10,12 2.00 5.00 10.00
7-Krigstein-a 3.00 9.00 18.00
11-Williamson/Frazetta-a 12.00 35.00 70.00
V2No.1-Krigstein-a 3.00 9.00 18.00
2-10,12: 4-Berg-a .85 2.50 5.00
11-Frazetta-a? .85 2.50 5.00
V3No.1-11 .70 2.00 4.00
12-Krigstein-a 3.00 8.00 16.00
V4No.1,4-7 .70 2.00 4.00
2,3-Krigstein-a 2.50 7.00 14.00
3-D 1(12/53, Star Publ.)-L. B. Cole-c 7.00 20.00 40.00

NOTE: ***Kinstlerish*** *a-V2No.6, 8, 9, 12; V3 No.2, 5-7, 11, 12; V4No.1(plus cover).* ***McWilliams*** *a-11.* ***Powell*** *a-V2No.2.*

WESTERN FRONTIER
1951
P. L. Publishers

1 2.00 6.00 12.00
2-7 1.00 3.00 6.00

WESTERN GUNFIGHTERS (1st Series) (Apache Kid No. 1-19)
No. 20, June, 1956 - No. 27, Aug, 1957
Atlas Comics (CPS)

20 1.50 4.00 8.00
21,25-27 1.20 3.50 7.00
22-Wood & Powell-a 6.00 18.00 36.00
23-Williamson-a 4.00 12.00 24.00
24-Toth-a 3.00 8.00 16.00

WESTERN GUNFIGHTERS (2nd Series)
Aug, 1970 - No. 33, Nov, 1975 (No. 1-6: 68 pgs.; No. 7: 52 pgs.)
Marvel Comics Group

1-Ghost Rider, Fort Rango, Renegades & Gunhawk app. .25 .75 1.50
2-Williamson, Baker, Kubert-r, 5 pgs.; Ghost Rider app.; Apache Kid-r begin; origin Nightwind (Apache Kid's horse) .60 1.20
3-Black Rider (Black Mask), Western Kid-r begin, end No. 6 .60 1.20
4-Smith-a-1st drawn for Marvel(shelved for two years) .60 1.20
5-9: 6-Gunhawk, Wyatt Earp app.; Ghost Rider dies. 7-Last Gunhawk, Ghost Rider (origin retold); death of Jamie Jacobs. 8-Outlaw Kid-r .40 .80
10-Origin Black Rider by Kirby; sequel to Matt Slade's origin .40 .80
11-17: 12-Matt Slade-r begin (origin), end No. 15. 16-Kid Colt-r begin .30 .60
18-Williamson-r .40 .80

Western Comics #16, © DC

Western Crime Busters #8, © TM

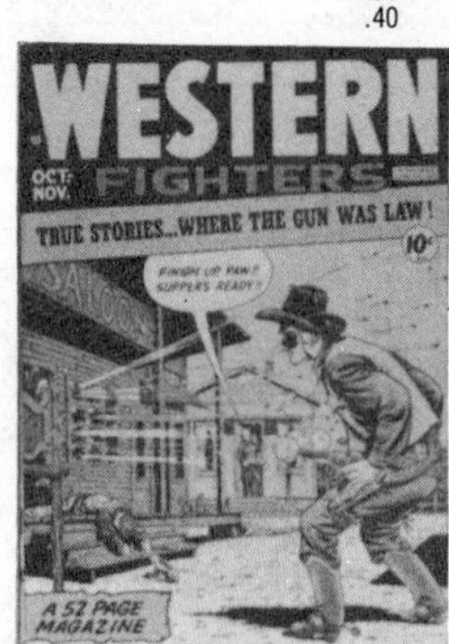

Western Fighters #4, © HILL

Western Hero #91, © FAW

Western Outlaws #20, © FOX

Western Roundup #17, © DELL

WESTERN GUNFIGHTERS (continued)

	Good	Fine	Mint
19-33		.30	.60

NOTE: ***Everett*** *a-6i.* ***Kirby*** *stories-No. 1, 11.* ***Steranko*** *c-14.* ***Torres*** *a-26('57).* ***Wildey*** *a-8r, 9r.* ***Woodbridge*** *a-27('57). Renegades in No. 4, 5; Ghost Rider-No.1-7.*

WESTERN HEARTS
Dec, 1949 - No. 10, Mar, 1952
Standard Comics

1-Severin-a, photo-c	3.50	10.00	20.00
2-Williamson/Frazetta-a, 2 pgs.	9.00	25.00	50.00
3	1.50	4.00	8.00
4-10-Severin & Elder, Al Carreno-a. 5-Photo-c	2.00	5.00	10.00

WESTERN HERO (Wow No. 1-69; Real Western Hero No. 70-75)
May, 1949 - No. 112, Mar, 1952
Fawcett Publications

76-79-Tom Mix, Hopalong Cassidy, & Gabby Hayes begin	5.00	14.00	28.00
80-112	3.50	10.00	20.00

WESTERN KID (1st Series)
Dec, 1954 - No. 17, Aug, 1957
Atlas Comics (CPC)

1-Origin Western Kid	2.50	7.00	14.00
2-8: 7-Romita-a(3)	1.50	4.00	8.00
9,10-Williamson-a in both, 4 pgs. each	3.50	10.00	20.00
11-17: 12-Romita c/a	1.00	3.00	6.00

WESTERN KID, THE (2nd Series)
Dec, 1971 - No. 5, Aug, 1972
Marvel Comics Group

1-Reprints		.30	.60
2,4,5: 4-Everett-r		.25	.50
3-Williamson-r		.30	.60

WESTERN KILLERS
1948 - No. 64, May, 1949; No. 6, July, 1949
Fox Features Syndicate

nn(No date, F&J Trading Co.)-Range Busters	3.50	10.00	20.00
60-Extreme violence; lingerie panel	4.00	12.00	24.00
61-64, 6	3.00	8.00	16.00

WESTERN LIFE ROMANCES (My Friend Irma No. 3?)
Dec, 1949 - No. 2, Mar, 1950
Marvel Comics (IPP)

1-Photo-c	3.00	8.00	16.00
2	1.50	4.00	8.00

WESTERN LOVE
July-Aug, 1949 - No. 5, Mar-Apr, 1950
Prize Publications

1-S&K-a	4.50	13.00	26.00
2,5-S&K-a	3.50	10.00	20.00
3,4	2.50	7.50	15.00

NOTE: ***Meskin & Severin & Elder*** *a-2-5.*

WESTERN LOVE TRAILS
No. 9, March, 1950
Ace Magazines

9	2.00	6.00	12.00

WESTERN MARSHAL (See Steve Donovan. . . & Ernest Haycox's 4-Color 534,591,613,640 [based on Haycox's "Trailtown"])

WESTERN OUTLAWS (My Secret Life No. 22 on)
No. 17, Sept, 1948 - No. 21, May, 1949
Fox Features Syndicate

17-Kamen-a; Baker/Feldstein-a	5.00	15.00	30.00
18,20,21	3.00	8.00	16.00
19-Kamen/Feldstein-a	4.50	13.00	26.00

WESTERN OUTLAWS
Feb, 1954 - No. 21, Aug, 1957
Atlas Comics (ACI No. 1-14/WPI No. 15-21)

	Good	Fine	Mint
1-Heath, Powell-a	3.00	8.00	16.00
2-10: 10-Everett-a	1.50	4.00	8.00
11,14-Williamson-a in both, 6 pgs. each	3.50	10.00	20.00
12,13,18,20,21	1.00	3.00	6.00
15-Torres-a	2.00	6.00	12.00
16-Williamson text illo	1.50	4.00	8.00
17-Crandall-a, Williamson text illo	2.50	7.00	14.00
19-Crandall-a	2.00	5.00	10.00

NOTE: ***Bolle*** *a-21.* ***Colan*** *a-17.* ***Heath*** *c-4, 16.* ***Maneely*** *a-16.* ***Powell*** *a-3, 15, 16.* ***Romita*** *a-7.* ***Severin*** *a-16; c-17.*

WESTERN OUTLAWS & SHERIFFS (Formerly Best Western)
Dec, 1949 - No. 73, June, 1952
Marvel/Atlas Comics (IPC)

60-65	2.50	7.00	14.00
66,68-73: 68-Robinson-a	2.00	5.00	10.00
67-Cannibalism story	2.00	6.00	12.00

WESTERN PICTURE STORIES
Feb, 1937 - No. 4, 1937
Quality Comics Group

1-Will Eisner-a	14.00	40.00	80.00
2-Will Eisner-a	9.00	25.00	50.00
3,4	6.00	18.00	36.00

WESTERN PICTURE STORIES (See Giant Comics Editions No. 6,11)

WESTERN ROMANCES (See Target. . .)

WESTERN ROUGH RIDERS
Nov, 1954 - No. 4, May, 1955
Gillmor Magazines No. 1/Stanmor Publications

1	1.50	4.00	8.00
2-4	.70	2.00	4.00

WESTERN ROUNDUP
June, 1952 - No. 25, Jan-Mar, 1959 (100 pgs.)
Dell Publishing Co.

1-Gene Autry, Roy Rogers, Elliott, Brown, & Rex Allen begin	5.00	14.00	28.00
2	3.50	10.00	20.00
3-5	3.00	8.00	16.00
6-10	2.00	6.00	12.00
11-13,16,17,19-24-Manning-a	2.00	5.00	10.00
14,15,25	1.50	4.00	8.00
18-Toth-a	2.00	6.00	12.00

WESTERN TALES (Formerly Witches. . .)
No. 31, Oct, 1955 - No. 33, July-Sept, 1956
Harvey Publications

31,32-All S&K-a; Davy Crockett app. in ea.	6.00	16.00	32.00
33-S&K-a; Jim Bowie app.	6.00	16.00	32.00

NOTE: *No. 32 & 33 Boy's Ranch-r.*

WESTERN TALES OF BLACK RIDER (Formerly Black Rider; Gunsmoke Western No. 32 on)
No. 28, May, 1955 - No. 31, Nov, 1955
Atlas Comics (CPS)

28-31	2.00	6.00	12.00

WESTERN TEAM-UP
November, 1973
Marvel Comics Group

1-Origin & 1st app. The Dakota Kid; Rawhide Kid-r; Gunsmoke Kid-r by Jack Davis		.30	.60

WESTERN THRILLERS (My Past Confessions No. 8 on)
Aug, 1948 - No. 7, Aug, 1949
Fox Features Syndicate

1-"Velvet Rose" by Kamen/Feldstein; "Two-Gun Sal," "Striker

	Good	Fine	Mint
WESTERN THRILLERS (continued)			
Sisters'' (all women outlaws issue)	8.00	22.00	44.00
2,3,6,7	3.00	9.00	18.00
4,5-Baker/Feldstein-a; Butch Cassidy app. No. 5	4.00	12.00	24.00
52-(Reprint, M.S. Dist.)-1954? No date given (Becomes My Love Secret No. 53)	1.20	3.50	7.00

WESTERN THRILLERS (Cowboy Action No. 5 on)
Nov, 1954 - No. 4, Feb, 1955
Atlas Comics (ACI)

	Good	Fine	Mint
1	2.50	7.00	14.00
2-4	1.50	4.00	8.00

WESTERN TRAILS
May, 1957 - No. 2, July, 1957
Atlas Comics (SAI)

	Good	Fine	Mint
1	2.00	5.00	10.00
2-Severin-c	1.20	3.50	7.00

WESTERN TRUE CRIME (Becomes My Confessions)
No. 15, Aug, 1948 - No. 6, June, 1949
Fox Features Syndicate

	Good	Fine	Mint
15-Kamen/Feldstein-a	5.00	14.00	28.00
16-Kamen/Feldstein-a?	2.50	7.00	14.00
3,5,6	2.00	5.00	10.00
4-Johnny Craig-a	5.00	14.00	28.00

WESTERN WINNERS (Formerly All-West. Winners; Black Rider No.8)
No. 5, June, 1949 - No. 7, Dec, 1949
Marvel Comics (CDS)

	Good	Fine	Mint
5,6-Two-Gun Kid, Kid Colt, Black Rider; 6-Heath Kid Colt story	3.00	9.00	18.00
7-Photo-c w/true stories about the West	3.00	9.00	18.00

WEST OF THE PECOS (See 4-Color No. 222)

WESTWARD HO, THE WAGONS (See 4-Color No. 738)

WHACK (Satire)
Oct, 1953 - No. 3, May, 1954
St. John Publishing Co.

	Good	Fine	Mint
1-(3-D)-Kubert-a	8.00	24.00	48.00
2,3-Kubert-a in each	4.00	12.00	24.00

WHACKY (See Wacky)

WHAM (See Super Spy)
Nov, 1940 - No. 2, Dec, 1940
Centaur Publications

	Good	Fine	Mint
1-The Sparkler, The Phantom Rider, Craig Carter and the Magic Ring, Detector, Copper Slug, Speed Silvers by Gustavson & Speed Centaur begin	20.00	60.00	120.00
2-Origin Blue Fire & Solarman; The Buzzard app.	15.00	45.00	90.00

WHAM-O GIANT COMICS (98 cents)
1967 (Newspaper size) (One Shot) (Full Color)
Wham-O Mfg. Co.

	Good	Fine	Mint
1-Radian & Goody Bumpkin by Wally Wood; 1 pg. Stanley-a	1.00	3.00	6.00

WHAT DO YOU KNOW ABOUT THIS COMICS SEAL OF APPROVAL?
No date (1955) (4pgs.; color; slick paper cover)
No publisher listed (DC Comics Giveaway)

	Good	Fine	Mint
	35.00	100.00	200.00

WHAT IF...?
Feb, 1977 - Present (No. 1: 52 pgs.)
Marvel Comics Group

	Good	Fine	Mint
1	.80	2.30	4.60
2	.50	1.50	3.00
3-5	.40	1.20	2.40
6-8,10	.35	1.00	2.00
9-Origins Venus, Marvel Boy, Human Robot, 3-D Man	.35	1.00	2.00
11,12,14,15	.25	.75	1.50
13-Conan app.	.50	1.50	3.00
16-26,30		.50	1.00
27-X-Men app.	.35	1.00	2.00
28		.40	.80
29-Golden-c		.50	1.00

NOTE: ***J. Buscema** a-13; c-10, 23. **Infantino** a-15, 17. **Gil Kane** a-3, 24; c-2-4, 7, 8. **Kirby** a-11; c-9, 11. **Miller** a-28p; c-27p, 28p.*

WHAT'S BEHIND THESE HEADLINES
1948 (16 pgs.)
William C. Popper Co.

	Good	Fine	Mint
Comic insert-''The Plot to Steal the World''	.85	2.50	5.00

WHEATIES (Premiums) (32 titles)
1950 & 1951 (32 pages) (pocket size)
Walt Disney Productions

(Set A-1 to A-8, 1950)
A-1 Mickey Mouse & the Disappearing Island
A-2 Grandma Duck, Homespun Detective
A-3 Donald Duck & the Haunted Jewels
A-4 Donald Duck & the Giant Ape
A-5 Mickey Mouse, Roving Reporter
A-6 Li'l Bad Wolf, Forest Ranger
A-7 Goofy, Tightrope Acrobat
A-8 Pluto & the Bogus Money

	Good	Fine	Mint
each....	2.00	6.00	12.00

(Set B-1 to B-8, 1950)
B-1 Mickey Mouse & the Pharoah's Curse
B-2 Pluto, Canine Cowpoke
B-3 Donald Duck & the Buccaneers
B-4 Mickey Mouse & the Mystery Sea Monster
B-5 Li'l Bad Wolf in the Hollow Tree Hideout
B-6 Donald Duck, Trail Blazer
B-7 Goofy & the Gangsters
B-8 Donald Duck, Klondike Kid

	Good	Fine	Mint
each....	1.50	4.50	9.00

(Set C-1 to C-8, 1951)
C-1 Donald Duck & the Inca Idol
C-2 Mickey Mouse & the Magic Mountain
C-3 Li'l Bad Wolf, Fire Fighter
C-4 Gus & Jaq Save the Ship
C-5 Donald Duck in the Lost Lakes
C-6 Mickey Mouse & the Stagecoach Bandits
C-7 Goofy, Big Game Hunter
C-8 Donald Duck Deep-Sea Diver

	Good	Fine	Mint
each....	1.50	4.50	9.00

(Set D-1 to D-8, 1951)
D-1 Donald Duck in Indian Country
D-2 Mickey Mouse and the Abandoned Mine
D-3 Pluto & the Mysterious Package
D-4 Bre'r Rabbit's Sunken Treasure
D-5 Donald Duck, Mighty Mystic
D-6 Mickey Mouse & the Medicine Man
D-7 Li'l Bad Wolf and the Secret of the Woods
D-8 Minnie Mouse, Girl Explorer

	Good	Fine	Mint
each....	1.50	4.50	9.00

NOTE: *Some copies lack the Wheaties ad.*

WHEE COMICS (Also see Tickle, Gay, & Smile Comics)
1955 (52 pgs.) (5x7¼'') (7 cents)
Modern Store Publications

	Good	Fine	Mint
1-Funny animal	.40	1.20	2.40

WHEELIE AND THE CHOPPER BUNCH

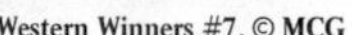
Western Winners #7, © MCG

Wham #2, © CEN

What If...? #13, © MCG

Where Creatures Roam #1, © MCG

Whiz Comics #24, © FAW

Whiz Comics #100, © FAW

WHEELIE & THE CHOPPER BUNCH (cont'd.)
July, 1975 - No. 7, July, 1976 (Hanna-Barbera)
Charlton Comics

	Good	Fine	Mint
1-7-Byrne-a in all	.35	1.00	2.00

WHEN KNIGHTHOOD WAS IN FLOWER (See 4-Color No. 505,682)

WHEN SCHOOL IS OUT (See Wisco)

WHERE CREATURES ROAM
July, 1970 - No. 8, Sept, 1971
Marvel Comics Group

	Good	Fine	Mint
1-Kirby-r		.40	.80
2-8-Kirby-r		.30	.60

NOTE: ***Ditko*** *r-1, 2, 4, 7.*

WHERE MONSTERS DWELL
Jan, 1970 - No. 38, Oct, 1975
Marvel Comics Group

	Good	Fine	Mint
1-Kirby/Ditko-a(r)		.50	1.00
2-10: 4-Crandall-a(r)		.40	.80
11,13-37		.30	.60
12-Giant issue		.50	1.00
38-Williamson-r/World of Suspense No. 3		.40	.80

NOTE: ***Ditko*** *reprints-8, 10, 17, 19, 23, 24, 37.*

WHERE'S HUDDLES? (TV) (See Fun-In No. 9)
Jan, 1971 - No. 3, Dec, 1971 (Hanna-Barbera)
Gold Key

	Good	Fine	Mint
1-3: 3 r-most No. 1	.50	1.50	3.00

WHIP WILSON (Formerly Rex Hart; Gunhawk No. 12 on)
No. 9, April, 1950 - No. 11, Sept, 1950
Marvel Comics

	Good	Fine	Mint
9-11	3.00	9.00	18.00
I.W. Reprint No. 1('64)-Kinstler-c; r-Marvel No. 11	.75	2.20	4.40

WHIRLWIND COMICS
June, 1940 - No. 3, Sept, 1940
Nita Publication

	Good	Fine	Mint
1-Cyclone begins (origin)	15.00	45.00	90.00
2,3	10.00	30.00	60.00

WHIRLYBIRDS (See 4-Color No. 1124,1216)

WHITE CHIEF OF THE PAWNEE INDIANS
1951
Avon Periodicals

	Good	Fine	Mint
nn-Kit West app, Kinstler-c;No. 1, 2	5.00	14.00	28.00

WHITE EAGLE INDIAN CHIEF (See Indian Chief)

WHITE INDIAN
1953 - 1954
Magazine Enterprises

	Good	Fine	Mint
11(A-1 94), 12(A-1 101), 13(A-1 104)-Frazetta-r in all from Durango Kid	17.00	50.00	100.00
14(A-1 117), 15(A-1 135)-Check-a; Torres-a-No. 15	5.00	15.00	30.00

NOTE: *No. 11 reprints from Durango Kid No. 1-4; No. 12 from No. 5, 9, 10, 11; No. 13 from No. 7, 12, 13, 16.*

WHITE PRINCESS OF THE JUNGLE (Also see Top Jungle & Jungle Adventures)
July, 1951 - No. 5, Nov, 1952
Avon Periodicals

	Good	Fine	Mint
1-Origin of White Princess & Capt'n Courage (r); Kinstler-c	12.00	35.00	70.00
2-Reprints origin of Malu, Slave Girl Princess from Avon's Slave Girl Princess No. 1 w/Malu changed to Zora; Kinstler c/a(2)	9.00	25.00	50.00
3-Origin Blue Gorilla; Kinstler c/a	7.00	20.00	40.00
4-Jack Barnum, White Hunter app.; r-/Sheena No. 9	6.00	18.00	36.00
5-Blue Gorilla by Kinstler	6.00	18.00	36.00

WHITE RIDER AND SUPER HORSE (Indian Warriors No. 7 on)
Dec, 1950 - No. 6, Mar, 1951? (Also see Western Crime Cases)
Novelty-Star Publications/Accepted Publ.

	Good	Fine	Mint
1-3	3.00	9.00	18.00
4-6-Adapt. "The Last of the Mohicans"	3.00	9.00	18.00
6-(Accepted reprint)	2.00	5.00	10.00

NOTE: *All have* ***L. B. Cole*** *covers.*

WHITE WILDERNESS (See 4-Color No. 943)

WHITMAN COMIC BOOKS
1962 (136 pgs.; 7¾x5¾"; hardcover) (B&W)
Whitman Publishing Co.

	Good	Fine	Mint
1-Yogi Bear, 2-Huckleberry Hound, 3-Mr. Jinks and Pixie & Dixie, 4-The Flintstones, 5-Augie Doggie & Loopy de Loop, 6-Snooper & Blabber Fearless Detectives/Quick Draw McGraw of the Wild West, 7-Bugs Bunny-reprints from No. 47,51,53,54 & 55 each....	.50	1.50	3.00
8-Donald Duck-reprints most of WDC&S No. 209-213. Includes 5 Barks stories, 1 complete Mickey Mouse serial & 1 Mickey Mouse serial missing the 1st episode	8.00	22.00	44.00

NOTE: *Hanna-Barbera No. 1-6, original stories. Dell reprints-No. 7, 8.*

WHIZ COMICS
No. 2, Feb, 1940 - No. 155, June, 1953
Fawcett Publications

NOTE: *The 1st issue was titled Thrill Comics with "Captain Thunder." Possibly 10 copies were made up and circulated within the office. However, no copies have yet emerged.*

	Good	Fine	Mint
1-(nn on cover, No. 2 inside)-Origin & 1st app. Captain Marvel by C. C. Beck, Spy Smasher, Golden Arrow, Ibis the Invincible, Dan Dare, Scoop Smith & Lance O'Casey begin; No. 1 reprinted in Famous 1st Editions	1000.00	3000.00	7800.00
(Prices vary widely on this book)			
2-(nn on cover, No. 3 inside)	400.00	1000.00	1800.00
3-(No. 3 on cover, No. 4 inside)-Spy Smasher reveals I.D. to Eve	250.00	600.00	1200.00
4-(No. 4 on cover, No. 5 inside)	200.00	500.00	1000.00
5-Captain Marvel wears button-down flap on splash page only	135.00	350.00	700.00
6-10: 7-Dr. Voodoo begins (by Raboy-No. 9-22)	90.00	250.00	500.00
11-14	50.00	150.00	300.00
15-18-Spy Smasher battles Captain Marvel in all; 15-Origin Sivana; Dr. Voodoo by Raboy	65.00	190.00	380.00
19,20	32.00	95.00	190.00
21-Origin & 1st app. Lt. Marvels	40.00	110.00	220.00
22-24: 23-Only Dr. Voodoo by Tuska	25.00	75.00	150.00
25-Origin & 1st app. Captain Marvel Jr., x-over in Capt. Marvel; Capt. Nazi app; origin Old Shazam in text	90.00	240.00	450.00
26-30	17.00	50.00	100.00
31,32: 32-1st app. The Trolls	15.00	45.00	90.00
33-Spy Smasher, Captain Marvel x-over	17.00	50.00	100.00
34-40-The Trolls in No. 37	12.00	35.00	70.00
41-50: 43-Spy Smasher, Ibis, Golden Arrow x-over in Capt. Marvel. 44-Flag-c. 47-Origin recap (1pg.)	8.00	24.00	48.00
51-60: 52-Capt. Marvel x-over in Ibis. 57-Spy Smasher, Golden Arrow, Ibis cameo	5.00	15.00	30.00
61-70	4.50	13.00	26.00
71,74,77-80	3.50	10.00	20.00
72,73,75,76-Two Captain Marvel stories in each; 76-Spy Smasher becomes Crime Smasher	4.00	12.00	24.00
81-99: 86-Captain Marvel battles Sivana Family. 91-Infinity-c	3.50	10.00	20.00
100	4.00	12.00	24.00
101,103-105	2.50	7.50	15.00
102-Commando Yank app.	2.50	7.50	15.00

WHIZ COMICS (continued)	Good	Fine	Mint
106-Bulletman app.	2.50	7.50	15.00
107-141,143-152	2.40	7.00	14.00
142-Used in **POP**, pg. 89; drug mentioned story	3.50	10.00	20.00
153-155-(Scarce)	5.00	15.00	30.00
Wheaties Giveaway(1946, Miniature)-6½x8¼'', 32 pgs.; all copies were taped at each corner to a box of Wheaties and are never found in fine or mint condition; ''Capt. Marvel & the Water Thieves,'' Golden Arrow, Ibis stories	12.00	36.00	72.00

NOTE: ***Krigstein** Golden Arrow-No. 75,78,91,95,96,98,100. **Wolverton** ½ pg. ''Culture Corner''-No. 65-68,70-75,77-85,87-96,98-100, 102-104,106,108,109,115,125,126,128,129,133,134,136,143,146.*

WHODUNIT
Aug-Sept, 1948 - No. 3, Dec-Jan, 1948-49
D. S. Publishing Co.

	Good	Fine	Mint
1-Seven pg. Baker-a	3.50	10.00	20.00
2-Old woman blackmails her doctor for morphine	2.50	7.00	14.00
3	2.00	6.00	12.00

WHO IS NEXT?
January, 1953
Standard Comics

	Good	Fine	Mint
5-Toth, Sekowsky, Andru-a	5.00	14.00	28.00

WHO'S MINDING THE MINT? (See Movie Classics)

WILBUR COMICS
Sum', 1944 - No. 89, 10/64; No. 90, 10/65 (No. 1-46: 52 pgs.)
MLJ Magazines/Archie Publ. No. 8, Spr. '46 on

	Good	Fine	Mint
1	15.00	45.00	90.00
2-4	7.00	20.00	40.00
5-1st app. Katy Keene; Wilbur story same as Archie story in Archie No. 1 except that Wilbur replaces Archie	17.00	50.00	100.00
6-10	5.00	15.00	30.00
11-20	3.50	10.00	20.00
21-30(1949)	2.50	7.00	14.00
31-50	1.20	3.50	7.00
51-90	.85	2.50	5.00

NOTE: *Katy Keene in No. 5-55, 58-61, 63(1 pg.), 64-71.*

WILD
Feb, 1954 - No. 5, Aug, 1954
Atlas Comics (IPC)

	Good	Fine	Mint
1	3.00	9.00	18.00
2-5	2.50	7.00	14.00

WILD (This Magazine Is . . .) (Magazine)
Jan, 1968 - No. 3, 1968 (52 pgs.) (Satire)
Dell Publishing Co.

	Good	Fine	Mint
1-3	.85	2.50	5.00

WILD BILL ELLIOTT
1950 - No. 17, Apr-June, 1955
Dell Publishing Co.

	Good	Fine	Mint
4-Color 278-Titled ''Bill Elliott''	3.00	8.00	16.00
2-17	1.50	4.50	9.00
4-Color 472,520,643	1.50	4.50	9.00

WILD BILL HICKOK
Oct-Nov, 1949 - No. 28, May-June, 1956
Avon Periodicals

	Good	Fine	Mint
1-Ingels-c	8.00	24.00	48.00
2-Painted-c	5.00	14.00	28.00
3,5-Painted-c	2.50	7.00	14.00
4-Painted-c by Howard Winfield, not Frazetta	2.50	7.00	14.00
6-10,12: 8-10-Painted-c; 9-Ingels-a?	2.50	7.00	14.00
11,14-Kinstler c/a	3.00	9.00	18.00
13,15,17,18,20,23: 17-Larsen, plus Reinman-a	2.00	5.00	10.00
16-Kamen-a; r-3 stories/King of the Badmen of Deadwood	2.50	7.00	14.00
19-Meskin-a	2.00	5.00	10.00
21-Reprints 2 stories/Chief Crazy Horse	2.00	5.00	10.00
22-Reprints/Sheriff Bob Dixon's. . ; Kinstler-a	2.00	5.00	10.00
24-27-Kinstler-c/a(r)	2.50	7.00	14.00
28-Kinstler-c/a (new); r-/Last of the Comanches	2.50	7.00	14.00
I.W. Reprint No. 1-Kinstler-c	.50	1.50	3.00
Super Reprint No. 10-12	.50	1.50	3.00

NOTE: *No. 23,25 contains numerous editing deletions in both art and script due to code. **Kinstler** c-6, 7, 11-14, 17, 18, 20-22, 24-28. **Howard Larsen** a-1, 2(3), 4(4), 9(3), 11(4), 12(4), 21(2), 22, 24(3), 26.*

WILD BILL HICKOK & JINGLES (Formerly Cowboy Western)
March, 1958 - 1960 (Also see Blue Bird)
Charlton Comics

	Good	Fine	Mint
68,69-Williamson-a	3.00	8.00	16.00
70-Two pgs. Williamson-a	1.50	4.00	8.00
71-76	.85	2.50	5.00

WILD BILL PECOS (See The Westerner)

WILD BOY OF THE CONGO (Also see Approved Comics)
No. 10, Feb-Mar, 1951 - No. 15, June, 1955
Ziff-Davis No. 10-12,4,5/St. John No. 6 on

	Good	Fine	Mint
10(2-3/51)-Origin; bondage-c by Saunders; used in **SOTI**, pg. 189	4.00	12.00	24.00
11(4-5/51),12(8-9/51)-Norman Saunders-c	3.00	8.00	16.00
4(10-11/51)-Saunders bondage-c	3.00	8.00	16.00
5(Winter,'51)-Saunders-c	2.00	6.00	12.00
6,8,9(10/53),10	2.00	5.00	10.00
7(8-9/52)-Baker-c; Kinstler-a	2.50	7.00	14.00
11-13-Baker-c(St. John)	2.50	7.00	14.00
14(4/55)-Baker-c; r-No. 12('51)	2.50	7.00	14.00
15(6/55)	1.50	4.00	8.00

WILD FRONTIER (Cheyenne Kid No. 8 on)
Oct, 1955 - No. 7, April, 1957
Charlton Comics

	Good	Fine	Mint
1-Davy Crockett	1.50	4.00	8.00
2-6-Davy Crockett in all	.70	2.00	4.00
7-Origin Cheyenne Kid	.70	2.00	4.00

WILD KINGDOM (TV)
1965 (Giveaway) (regular size) (16 pgs.)
Western Printing Co.

	Good	Fine	Mint
Mutual of Omaha's. . .	.85	2.50	5.00

WILD WEST (Wild Western No. 3 on)
Spring, 1948 - No. 2, July, 1948
Marvel Comics (WFP)

	Good	Fine	Mint
1-Two-Gun Kid, Arizona Annie, Tex Taylor	3.50	10.00	20.00
2	2.50	7.00	14.00

WILD WEST (Black Fury No. 1-57)
No. 58, November, 1966
Charlton Comics

	Good	Fine	Mint
V2No.58		.50	1.00

WILD WESTERN (Wild West No. 1,2)
No. 3, Sept, 1948 - No. 57, Sept, 1957
Marvel/Atlas Comics (WFP)

	Good	Fine	Mint
3-Two-Gun Kid	3.50	10.00	20.00
4-10: 10-Charles Starrett photo-c	2.50	7.00	14.00
11-20: 15-Origin Red Larabee, Gunhawk	1.50	4.00	8.00

Wilbur Comics #33, © AP

Wild Bill Elliott #9, © DELL

Wild Bill Hickok #25, © AVON

Willie The Penguin #3, © STD

Wings Comics #41, © FH

Wings Comics #73, © FH

WILD WESTERN (continued)

	Good	Fine	Mint
21-30	1.20	3.50	7.00
31-40	.85	2.50	5.00
41-47,49-51,53,57	.70	2.00	4.00
48-Williamson/Torres-a, 4 pgs; Drucker-a	3.50	10.00	20.00
52-Crandall-a	2.50	7.00	14.00
54,55-Williamson-a in both, 5 & 4 pgs., No. 54 with Mayo plus 2 text illos.	3.00	8.00	16.00
56-Baker-a?	2.00	5.00	10.00

NOTE: *Annie Oakley in No. 46, 47. Arizona Kid in No. 23. Arrowhead in No. 35, 36, 38. Black Rider in No. 5, 12, 14, 30, 33, 35, 38, 41. Blaze Carson in No. 5. Kid Colt in No. 5, 27, 30, 33, 35, 36, 38, 41, 46, 47, 52, 54-56. Ringo Kid in No. 29, 38, 39, 41, 46, 47, 52-56. Texas Kid in No. 23. Two-Gun Kid in No. 5, 30, 33, 35, 36, 41. Wyatt Earp in No.47.* ***Maneely*** *a-10.* ***Powell*** *a-51.* ***Severin*** *a-46, 47.*

WILD WESTERN ACTION (Also see The Bravados)
March, 1971 - No. 3, June, 1971 (52 pgs.)
Skywald Publishing Corp. (Reprints)

	Good	Fine	Mint
1-Durango Kid, Straight Arrow; with all references to "Straight" in the story relettered to "Swift;" Bravados begin		.50	1.00
2-Billy Nevada, Durango Kid		.30	.60
3-Red Mask, Durango Kid		.30	.60

WILD WESTERN ROUNDUP
Oct, 1957; 1964
Red Top/Decker Publications/I. W. Enterprises

	Good	Fine	Mint
1(1957)-Kid Cowboy-r	.50	1.50	3.00
I.W. Reprint No. 1('60-61)	.25	.75	1.50

WILD WEST RODEO
1953 (15 cents)
Star Publications

	Good	Fine	Mint
1-A comic book coloring book with regular full color cover & B&W inside	2.00	6.00	12.00

WILD WILD WEST, THE (TV)
June, 1966 - No. 7, Oct, 1969
Gold Key

	Good	Fine	Mint
1,2-McWilliams-a	1.00	3.00	6.00
3-7	.70	2.00	4.00

WILKIN BOY (See That. . .)

WILLIE COMICS (Formerly Ideal No. 1-4; Crime Cases No. 24 on; Li'l Willie No. 20 & 21) (See Wisco)
No. 5, Fall, 1946 - No. 23, Mar, 1950 (No No. 20 & 21)
Marvel Comics (MgPC)

	Good	Fine	Mint
5(No.1)	1.20	3.50	7.00
6,8,9,12,14-18,22,23	.85	2.50	5.00
7,10,11,13,19-Kurtzman's "Hey Look"	2.00	5.00	10.00

WILLIE MAYS (See The Amazing. . .)

WILLIE THE PENGUIN
April, 1951 - No. 6, April, 1952
Standard Comics

	Good	Fine	Mint
1	.70	2.00	4.00
2-6	.35	1.00	2.00

WILLIE THE WISE-GUY
Sept, 1957
Atlas Comics (NPP)

	Good	Fine	Mint
1	.50	1.50	3.00

WILLIE WESTINGHOUSE EDISON SMITH THE BOY INVENTOR
1906 (36 pgs. in color) (10x16")
William A. Stokes Co.

	Good	Fine	Mint
By Frank Crane	10.00	30.00	60.00

WILL ROGERS WESTERN (Also see Blazing Comics)
No. 5, June, 1950 - No. 2, Aug, 1950
Fox Features Syndicate

	Good	Fine	Mint
5,2: 2-Photo-c	4.00	12.00	24.00

WILL-YUM (See 4-Color No. 676,765,902)

WIN A PRIZE COMICS
Feb, 1955 - No. 2, 1955
Charlton/Simon & Kirby

	Good	Fine	Mint
V1No.1-S&K-a; Poe adapt; E.C. War swipe	10.00	30.00	60.00
2-S&K-a	7.00	20.00	40.00

WINDY & WILLY
May-June, 1969 - No. 4, Nov-Dec, 1969
National Periodical Publications

	Good	Fine	Mint
1-4-Reprints of Dobie Gillis with some art changes		.50	1.00

WINGS COMICS
Sept, 1940 - No. 124, 1954
Fiction House Magazines

	Good	Fine	Mint
1-Skull Squad, Clipper Kirk, Suicide Smith, Jane Martin, War Nurse, Phantom Falcons, Greasemonkey Griffin, Parachute Patrol, & Powder Burns begin	30.00	80.00	160.00
2	14.00	40.00	80.00
3-5	10.00	30.00	60.00
6-10	8.00	24.00	48.00
11-15	6.00	18.00	36.00
16-Origin Captain Wings	8.00	24.00	48.00
17-20	6.00	18.00	36.00
21-30	5.50	16.00	32.00
31-40	5.00	14.00	28.00
41-50	4.00	12.00	24.00
51-60: 60-Last Skull Squad	3.50	10.00	20.00
61-67: 66-Ghost Patrol begins (becomes Ghost Squadron No. 71)	3.50	10.00	20.00
68,69: 68-Clipper Kirk becomes The Phantom Falcon-origin, Part 1; Part 2-No. 69	3.50	10.00	20.00
70-72: 70-1st app. The Phantom Falcon in costume, origin-Part 3; Capt. Wings battles Col. Kamikaze in all	3.00	8.00	16.00
73-80: 73-Bra & slip panels	3.00	8.00	16.00
81-100	3.00	8.00	16.00
101-114,116-124: 111-Last Jane Martin	2.00	6.00	12.00
115-Used in **POP**, pg. 89	3.50	10.00	20.00

NOTE: *Bondage covers are common. Captain Wings battles Sky Hag-No. 75, 76; . . . Mr. Atlantis-No. 85-92; . . . Mr. Pupin(Red Agent)-No. 98-103. Capt. Wings by* ***Elias****-No. 52-64; by* ***Lubbers****-No. 29-32,70-103; by* ***Renee****-No. 33-46.* ***Evans*** *a-85-103, 108(Jane Martin).* ***Larsen*** *a-52, 59, 64, 73-77. Jane Martin by* ***Fran Hopper****-No. 68-84; Suicide Smith by* ***John Celardo****-No. 76-103; by* ***Hollingsworth****-No. 105-109; Ghost Patrol by* ***Maurice Whitman****-No. 83-103; Skull Squad by* ***M. Baker****-No. 52-60; Clipper Kirk by* ***Baker****-No. 60, 61; Ghost Squadron by* ***Whitman****-No. 72-77, 104-110.*

WINGS OF THE EAGLES, THE (See 4-Color No. 790)

WINKY DINK (Adventures of. . .)
No. 75, March, 1957 (One Shot)
Pines Comics

	Good	Fine	Mint
75-Marv Levy c/a	.70	2.00	4.00

WINKY DINK (See 4-Color No. 663)

WINNIE THE POOH
January, 1977 - Present (Walt Disney)
Gold Key No. 1-17/Whitman No. 18 on

	Good	Fine	Mint
1		.40	.80
2-13,15-22		.20	.40
14-New material		.30	.60

WINNIE WINKLE
1930 - 1933 (52 pgs.) (B&W daily strip reprints)
Cupples & Leon Co.

	Good	Fine	Mint
1	5.00	14.00	28.00
2-4	4.00	12.00	24.00

WINNIE WINKLE
1941 - 1949
Dell Publishing Co.

	Good	Fine	Mint
Large Feature Comic 2('41)	6.00	18.00	36.00
4-Color 94('45)	4.00	12.00	24.00
4-Color 174	2.50	7.00	14.00
1(3-5/48)-Contains daily & Sunday newspaper-r from 1939-1941	2.50	7.00	14.00
2-7	1.20	3.50	7.00

WISCO/KLARER COMIC BOOK (Miniature)
1948 - 1964 (24 pgs.) (3½x6¾'')
Given away by Wisco ''99'' Service Stations, Carnation Malted Milk, Klarer Health Wieners, Fleers Dubble Bubble Gum, Rodeo All-Meat Wieners, Perfect Potato Chips, & others
Vital Publications/Fawcett Publications

	Good	Fine	Mint
Blackstone & the Gold Medal Mystery(1948)	1.50	4.00	8.00
Blackstone ''Solves the Sealed Vault Mystery''(1950)	1.50	4.00	8.00
Blaze Carson in ''The Sheriff Shoots It Out''(1950)	1.50	4.00	8.00
Captain Marvel & Billy's Big Game	25.00	70.00	130.00
(Prices vary widely on this book)			
China Boy in ''A Trip to the Zoo'' No. 10	.85	2.50	5.00
Indoors-Outdoors Game Book	.85	2.50	5.00
Jim Solar Space Sheriff in ''Battle for Mars,'' ''Between Two Worlds,'' ''Conquers Outer Space,'' ''The Creatures on the Comet,'' ''Defeats the Moon Missile Men,'' ''Encounter Creatures on Comet,'' ''Meet the Jupiter Jumpers,'' ''Meets the Man From Mars,'' ''On Traffic Duty,'' ''Outlaws of the Spaceways,'' ''Pirates of the Planet X,'' ''Protects Space Lanes,'' ''Raiders From the Sun,'' ''Ring Around Saturn,'' ''Robots of Rhea,'' ''The Sky Ruby,'' ''Spacetts of the Sky,'' ''Spidermen of Venus,'' ''Trouble on Mercury''	1.20	3.50	7.00
Johnny Starboard & the Underseas Pirates('48)	.70	2.00	4.00
Kid Colt in ''He Lived by His Guns''(1950)	2.00	5.00	10.00
Little Aspirin as ''Crook Catcher'' No. 2(1950)	.60	1.80	3.60
Little Aspirin in ''Naughty But Nice'' No. 6(1950)	.60	1.80	3.60
Return of the Black Phantom	1.00	3.00	6.00
Secrets of Magic	1.00	3.00	6.00
Slim Morgan ''Brings Justice to Mesa City'' No. 3	1.00	3.00	6.00
Super Rabbit(1950)-Cuts Red Tape, Stops Crime Wave!	1.00	3.00	6.00
Tex Farnum, Frontiersman(1948)	1.00	3.00	6.00
Tex Taylor in ''Draw or Die, Cowpoke!''('50)	1.50	4.00	8.00
Tex Taylor in ''An Exciting Adventure at the Gold Mine''('50)	1.50	4.00	8.00
Wacky Quacky in ''All-Aboard''	.50	1.50	3.00
When School Is Out	.50	1.50	3.00
Willie in a ''Comic-Comic Book Fall'' No. 1	.50	1.50	3.00
Wonder Duck ''An Adventure at the Rodeo of the Fearless Quack-er!'' (1950)	.50	1.50	3.00

Rare uncut version of three; includes Capt. Marvel, Tex Farnum, Black Phantom Estimated value. . . . $100.00

WISE LITTLE HEN, THE
1934 (48 pgs.); 1935; 1937 (Story book)
David McKay Publ.

	Good	Fine	Mint
1st book app. Donald Duck; Donald app. on cover with Wise Little Hen & Practical Pig; painted cover; same artist as the B&W's from Silly Symphony Cartoon, The Wise Little Hen (1934)	20.00	60.00	120.00
1935 Edition with dust jacket; 40 pgs. with color, 8¾x9¾''	17.00	50.00	100.00
888(1937)-9½x13'', 12 pgs. (Whitman) Donald Duck app.	14.00	40.00	80.00

WITCHCRAFT
Mar-Apr, 1952 - No. 6, Mar, 1953
Avon Periodicals

	Good	Fine	Mint
1-Kubert-a; 1pg. check	10.00	30.00	60.00
2-Kubert & Check-a	8.00	24.00	48.00
3-Kinstler, Lawrence-a	6.00	18.00	36.00
4,6	5.50	16.00	32.00
5-Kelly Freas-c	10.00	30.00	60.00

NOTE: ***Hollingsworth** a-4-6; c-4, 6.*

WITCHES TALES (Witches Western Tales No. 29,30)
Jan, 1951 - No. 27, Oct, 1954; No. 28, April, 1955
Witches Tales/Harvey Publications

	Good	Fine	Mint
1-Bondage-c	8.00	24.00	48.00
2,4,9,10	3.00	8.00	16.00
3,5,6-Bondage-c	4.00	12.00	24.00
7-Rulah-r-name changed to Kohal	4.00	12.00	24.00
8-Bondage-c; injury-to-eye panels	3.50	10.00	20.00
11-13,15,16	3.00	8.00	16.00
14,17-Powell/Nostrand-a	5.00	14.00	28.00
18-Nostrand-a(2)	5.00	14.00	28.00
19-26-Nostrand-a in all; 25-Severed head-c	5.00	14.00	28.00
27,28: 27-Reprints No. 6 with diff.-c. 28-Reprints No. 8 with diff.-c	2.00	6.00	12.00

NOTE: ***Nostrand** a-17-26; 14, 17(w/**Powell**); c-25. **Palais** a-1, 2, 4(2), 5(2), 7-9, 14, 15, 17. **Powell** a-3-7, 10, 11, 19-25, 27. **Woodesque** a-25. No. 28 shows date of December on cover.*

WITCHES TALES (Magazine)
V1No.7, July, 1969 - V7No.1, Feb, 1975 (52 pgs.) (B&W)
Eerie Publications

	Good	Fine	Mint
V1No.7(7/69) - 9(11/69)		.60	1.20
V2No.1-6('70), V3No.1-6('71)		.50	1.00
V4No.1-6('72), V5No.1-6('73), V6No.1-6('74), V7No.1		.40	.80

NOTE: *Ajax/Farrell reprints in early issues.*

WITCHES' WESTERN TALES (Formerly Witches Tales) (Western Tales No. 31 on)
No. 29, Feb, 1955 - No. 30, April, 1955
Harvey Publications

	Good	Fine	Mint
29,30-S&K-r/from Boys' Ranch including-c	6.00	18.00	36.00

WITCHING HOUR, THE
Feb-Mar, 1969 - No. 85, Oct, 1978
National Periodical Publications/DC Comics

	Good	Fine	Mint
1-Toth plus Adams, 3 pgs.	1.00	3.00	6.00
2,6		.50	1.00
3,5-Wrightson, Toth-a	.80	2.40	4.80
4-Toth-a; Cardy-c	.50	1.50	3.00
7-Kaluta, Toth-a	.50	1.50	3.00
8-Adams-a	.80	2.40	4.80
9-11-Toth-a	.50	1.50	3.00
12-Kane/Wood, Toth-a	.50	1.50	3.00
13-Adams c/a, 2pgs.	.80	2.40	4.80
14-Williamson/Garzon, Jones-a; Adams-c	.80	2.40	4.80
15-Wood-a		.60	1.20
16-20		.40	.80
21,22,24-33,35-37		.30	.60
23,34-Redondo-a		.40	.80
38-(100 pgs.); Toth-r		.30	.60
39-64		.30	.60
65-Redondo-a(2)		.30	.60
66-85		.25	.50

NOTE: *Combined with The Unexpected with No. 189. **Adams** c-7-11, 13, 14. **Alcala** a-24, 27, 33, 41, 43. **Anderson** a-9, 38. **Morrow** a-10, 13, 15, 16. **Nino** a-31, 40, 45, 47.*

WITH THE MARINES ON THE BATTLEFRONTS OF THE WORLD
1953 (no month) - No. 2, March, 1954 (photo covers)

Winnie Winkle #4, © DELL

Witches Tales #19, © HARV

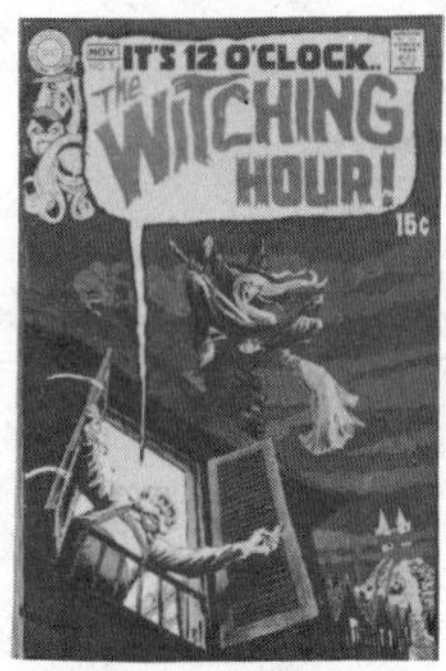

Witching Hour #5, © DC

Woman Outlaws nn, © FOX

Wonder Comics #16, © BP

Wonder Woman #13, © DC

WITH THE MARINES ON THE. . . (cont'd.)
Toby Press

	Good	Fine	Mint
1-John Wayne story	5.00	15.00	30.00
2-Monty Hall in No. 1,2	2.00	5.00	10.00

WITH THE U.S. PARATROOPS BEHIND ENEMY LINES (Also see U.S. Paratroops. .; No. 4 titled U.S. Paratroops. .)
1951 - No. 6, Dec, 1952
Avon Periodicals

1-Wood-c & inside-c	5.00	15.00	30.00
2-6	3.50	10.00	20.00

NOTE: ***Kinstler** a-2, 5, 6; c-2, 4, 5.*

WITNESS, THE (Also see Amazing Mysteries & Marvel Mystery 92)
Sept, 1948
Marvel Comics (MMC)

1(Rare)-Everett-c	20.00	60.00	120.00

WITTY COMICS
1945
Irwin H. Rubin Publ./Chicago Nite Life News No. 2

1,2-The Pioneer, Junior Patrol	2.00	5.00	10.00
3-7-Skyhawk	1.50	4.00	8.00

WIZARD OF OZ (See 4-Color No. 1308, Dell Jr. Treasury No. 5, Marvelous. . ., & Marvel Treasury of Oz)

WOLF GAL (See Al Capp's. . .)

WOLFMAN, THE (See Book & Record Set & Movie Classics)

WOMAN OF THE PROMISE, THE
1950 (General Distr.) (32 pgs.) (paper cover)
Catechetical Guild

	5.00	15.00	30.00

WOMEN IN LOVE (A Feature Presentation No. 5)
Aug, 1949 - No. 4, Feb, 1950
Fox Features Synd./Hero Books

1	8.00	24.00	48.00
2-Kamen/Feldstein-c	6.00	18.00	36.00
3	5.00	14.00	28.00
4-Wood-a	7.00	20.00	40.00

WOMEN IN LOVE
Winter, 1952 (100 pgs.)
Ziff-Davis Publishing Co.

nn-Kinstler-a (Scarce)	10.00	30.00	60.00

WOMEN OUTLAWS (My Love Memories No. 9 on)
July, 1948 - No. 8, Sept, 1949 (Also see Red Circle)
Fox Features Syndicate

1-Used in **SOTI**, illo-''Giving children an image of American womanhood''; negligee panels	14.00	38.00	76.00
2-Spanking panel	10.00	28.00	56.00
3-Kamen-a	10.00	28.00	56.00
4-8	8.00	22.00	44.00
nn(no date)-Contains Cody of the Pony Express	6.00	18.00	36.00

WOMEN TO LOVE
No date (1953)
Realistic

nn-(Scarce)-Reprint/Complete Romance No. 1; c-/Avon paperback 165	15.00	45.00	90.00

WONDER BOY
No. 16, 1955 - No. 18, July, 1955
Ajax/Farrell Publ.

16-Phantom Lady?	6.00	18.00	36.00
17-Phantom Lady app. Bakerish a/c	8.00	24.00	40.00
18-Phantom Lady app.	6.00	18.00	36.00

NOTE: *Phantom Lady not by Matt Baker.*

WONDER COMICS (Wonderworld No. 3 on)
May, 1939 - No. 2, June, 1939
Fox Features Syndicate

	Good	Fine	Mint
1-(Scarce)-Wonder Man only app. by Will Eisner; Bob Kane-a; Eisner-c	100.00	300.00	600.00
2-(Scarce)-Yarko the Great, Master Magician by Eisner begins; Bob Kane, Powell-a; Lou Fine-c (1st)	50.00	150.00	300.00

WONDER COMICS
May, 1944 - No. 20, Oct, 1948
Great/Nedor/Better Publications

1-The Grim Reaper & Spectro, the Mind Reader begin	15.00	45.00	90.00
2-Origin The Grim Reaper; Super Sleuths begin, end No. 8,17	10.00	30.00	60.00
3-5	8.50	25.00	50.00
6-10: 8-Last Spectro. 9-Wonderman begins	7.50	22.00	44.00
11-14-Dick Devens, King of Futuria begins No. 11, ends No. 14	8.50	25.00	50.00
15-Tara begins (origin), ends No. 20	10.00	28.00	56.00
16,18: 16-Spectro app.; last Grim Reaper. 18-The Silver Knight begins	8.00	24.00	48.00
17-Wonderman with Frazetta panels; Jill Trent with all Frazetta inks	11.00	32.00	64.00
19-Frazetta panels	10.00	28.00	56.00
20-Most of Silver Knight by Frazetta	11.00	32.00	64.00

NOTE: ***Ingels** c-8, 11, 12(bondage), 14, 15, 18-20. **Schomburg (Xela)** c-(line)-1-10; (painted)-13-20.*

WONDER DUCK (See Wisco)
1949 - No. 3, Mar, 1950
Marvel Comics (CDS)

1-3	1.50	4.00	8.00

WONDERFUL ADVENTURES OF PINOCCHIO, THE (See Movie Comics)

WONDERFUL WORLD OF DUCKS (See Golden Picture Story Book)
1975
Colgate Palmolive Co.

1-Mostly-r		.30	.60

WONDERFUL WORLD OF THE BROTHERS GRIMM (See Movie Comics)

WONDERLAND COMICS
Summer, 1945 - No. 9, Feb-Mar, 1947
Feature Publications/Prize

1	1.00	3.00	6.00
2-9	.80	2.40	4.80

WONDERS OF ALADDIN, THE (See 4-Color No. 1255)

WONDER WARTHOG MAGAZINE
Winter, 1967 - No. 2, Spring, 1967
Millar Publications

1-Kurtzman, Gilbert Shelton-a begins	4.00	12.00	24.00
2	5.00	15.00	30.00

WONDER WOMAN (See Adventure, All-Star Comics, Brave & the Bold, DC Comics Presents, Giant Comics to Color, Sensation Comics, and World's Finest)

WONDER WOMAN
Summer, 1942 - Present
National Periodical Publications/All-American Publ.

1-Origin Wonder Woman retold (see All-Star No. 8); reprinted in Famous 1st Editions; H. G. Peter-a begins	120.00	350.00	700.00
2-Origin & 1st app. Mars; Duke of Deception app.	60.00	170.00	345.00
3	45.00	130.00	265.00
4,5: 5-1st Dr. Psycho app.	32.00	95.00	200.00
6-10: 6-1st Cheetah app.	24.00	70.00	140.00
11-20	17.00	50.00	100.00

WONDER WOMAN (continued)

	Good	Fine	Mint
21-30	13.00	38.00	76.00
31-40	10.00	28.00	56.00
41-44,46-48	7.00	21.00	42.00
45-Origin retold	12.00	35.00	70.00
49-Used in **SOTI**, pgs. 234,236	8.00	24.00	48.00
50-Used in **POP**, pg. 97	7.00	20.00	40.00
51-60	5.50	16.00	32.00
61-72: 70-1st Angle Man app. 72-Last pre-code	5.00	14.00	28.00
73-90	4.00	12.00	24.00
91-99: 94-Robin Hood x-over. 98-Last H. G. Peter-a	3.50	10.00	20.00
100	4.00	12.00	24.00
101-104,106-110: 107-1st advs. of Wondergirl; 1st Merboy; tells how W.W. won her costume	3.00	8.00	16.00
105-Wonder Woman's secret origin; 1st app. Wonder Girl	4.00	12.00	24.00
111-120	2.00	6.00	12.00
121-130: 122-1st app. Wonder Tot. 128-Origin The Invisible Plane	1.50	4.00	8.00
131-150	1.00	3.00	6.00
151-158,160-170	.85	2.50	5.00
159-Origin retold	1.00	3.00	6.00
171-178	.60	1.80	3.60
179-194: 179-No costume, plain clothes adventures to issue No. 203. 180-Death of Steve Trevor. 193-Drug use	.45	1.40	2.80
195-Wood inks?	.60	1.80	3.60
196 (52 pgs.)-Origin r-/All-Star 8	.70	2.00	4.00
197,198 (52 pgs.)	.60	1.80	3.60
199,200-Jones-c; 52 pgs.	1.30	3.80	7.60
201,204-210: 204-Return to old costume; death of I Ching		.50	1.00
202-Fafhrd & The Grey Mouser debut	.40	1.10	2.20
203-Women's Lib issue	.30	.90	1.80
211(100 pgs.)-Superman x-over		.50	1.00
212,213,215,216: 212-222-Justice League x-overs		.40	.80
214(100 pgs.)		.50	1.00
217-(68 pgs.)		.50	1.00
218-230: 220-Adams assist. 223-Steve Trevor revived as Steve Howard & learns W.W.'s I.D. 228-Both W. Women team up & New World War II stories begin, end No. 243.		.40	.80
231-234,237: 231,232-JSA app. 237-Origin retold		.25	.50
235,236-G.A. Dr. Midnite cameo		.30	.60
238-G.A. Sandman/Sandy cameo		.30	.60
239,240-G.A. Flash cameo		.30	.60
241-G.A. Superman/Spectre x-over; intro Bouncer		.30	.60
242-G.A. Dr. Fate/Spectre x-over		.30	.60
243-247,249,252-260: 243-Both W. Women team-up. 247-Elongated Man x-over. 249-Hawkgirl cameo		.30	.60
248-Death of Steve Trevor Howard		.40	.80
250-Intro & origin Drana, the new Wonder Woman		.30	.60
251-Death of Drana		.30	.60
261-268,270-286: 271-Huntress & 3rd Life of Steve Trevor begin		.30	.60
269-Wood inks		.40	.80
Pizza Hut Giveaway(12/77)-Exact-r of No. 60,62		.40	.80

NOTE: ***Buckler*** *c-237-239.* ***Lopez*** *c-248.* ***Morrow*** *c-233.* ***Nasser*** *a-232; c-232.* ***Perez*** *c-283, 284.* ***Staton*** *a-241, 271-275; c-241, 245, 246, 271-286p.*

WONDER WOMAN SPECTACULAR (See DC Special Series No. 9)

WONDER WORKER OF PERU
No date (16 pgs.) (B&W) (5x7'')
Catechetical Guild (Giveaway)

	Good	Fine	Mint
	2.00	5.00	10.00

WONDERWORLD (Formerly Wonder Comics)
No. 3, July, 1939 - No. 33, Jan, 1942
Fox Features Syndicate

	Good	Fine	Mint
3-The Flame, Dr. Fung by Powell (ends No. 12) begin; Yarko the Great, Master Magician continues by Eisner	35.00	100.00	200.00
4-Lou Fine text illos	30.00	85.00	170.00
5-10	25.00	75.00	150.00
11-Origin The Flame	30.00	85.00	170.00
12-20: 14-Bondage-c	17.00	50.00	100.00
21-Origin The Black Lion & Cub	14.00	40.00	80.00
22-27	10.00	30.00	60.00
28-Lu-Nar, the Moon Man begins; origin U.S. Jones; bondage-c	10.00	28.00	56.00
29,31-33	6.00	18.00	36.00
30-Origin Flame Girl	15.00	45.00	90.00

NOTE: *Yarko by* ***Eisner****-No. 3-10 (at least).* ***Lou Fine*** *c/a-4-11; c-12, 13.* ***Powell*** *a-3, 4.*

WOODSY OWL (See March of Comics No. 395)
Nov, 1973 - No. 10, Feb, 1976
Gold Key

	Good	Fine	Mint
1	.25	.75	1.50
2-10		.50	1.00

WOODY WOODPECKER
1947 - No. 72, 8-9/62; No. 73, 10/62 - Present (no No. 192)
Dell Publishing Co./Gold Key No. 73-187/Whitman No. 188 on

	Good	Fine	Mint
4-Color 169-Drug turns Woody into a Mr. Hyde	3.00	9.00	18.00
4-Color 188	2.50	7.50	15.00
4-Color 202,232,249,264,288	1.50	4.00	8.00
4-Color 305,336,350	1.20	3.50	7.00
4-Color 364,374,390,405,416,431('52)	.85	2.50	5.00
16-30('53-'55)	.70	2.00	4.00
31-72,76-80('55-'63)	.40	1.20	2.40
73-75 (Giants, 84 pgs.)	.30	.90	1.80
81-100		.40	.80
101-120		.30	.60
121-191,193-195		.25	.50
Back to School 1(1952)	2.00	5.00	10.00
Back to School 2-4,6('53-'57)(nn 5)(County Fair No. 5)	1.20	3.50	7.00
Christmas Parade 1(11/68-Giant)(G.K.)	.30	.90	1.80
Clover Stamp-Newspaper Boy Contest('56)-9 pg. story-(Giveaway)	.40	1.20	2.40
County Fair 5('56)-Formerly Back to School No. 2('58)	1.20	3.50	7.00
County Fair 2('58)	.85	2.50	5.00
In Chevrolet Wonderland(1954-Giveaway)(Western Publ.)-20 pgs., full story line; Chilly Willy app.	2.00	6.00	12.00
Meets Scotty McTape(1953-Scotch Tape giveaway)-16 pgs., full size	2.00	5.00	10.00
Summer Fun 1('66-G.K.)(25 cents)		.50	1.00

NOTE: *15 cents editions exist. Reprints-No. 92, 102, 103, 105, 106, 124, 125, 152, 153, 157, 159, 162, 165.*

WOODY WOODPECKER (See Comic Album No. 5,9,13, Dell Giant No. 24, 40, 54, The Funnies, Golden Comics Digest No. 1, 3, 5, 8, 15, 16, 20, 24, 32, 37, 44, March of Comics No. 16, 34, 85, 93, 109, 124, 139, 158, 177, 184, 203, 222, 239, 249, 261, 478, New Funnies & Super Book No. 12, 24)

WOOLWORTH'S CHRISTMAS STORY BOOK (See Jolly Christmas Book & Happy Time Xmas Book)
1952 - 1954 (16 pgs., paper-c)
Promotional Publ. Co.(Western Printing Co.)

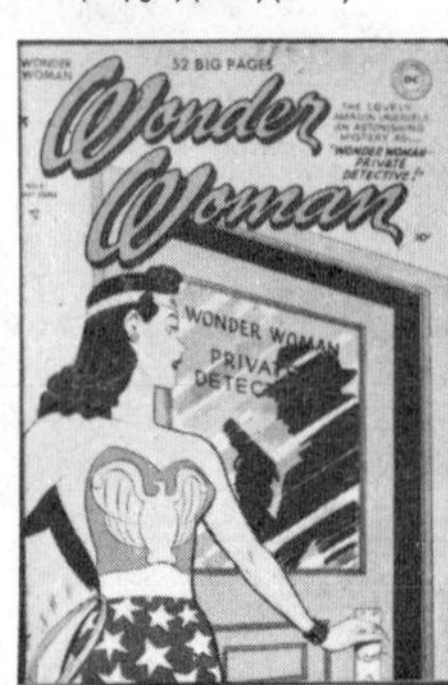

Wonder Woman #41, © DC

Wonder Woman #101, © DC

Wonderworld #15, © FOX

The World Around Us #18, © GIL

World Of Fantasy #8, © MCG

World Of Krypton #1, © DC

WOOLWORTH'S CHRISTMAS. . . (cont'd.)

	Good	Fine	Mint
nn	1.50	4.50	9.00

NOTE: *1952 issue-**Marv Levy** c/a.*

WORLD AROUND US, THE (Ill. Story of. . .)
Sept, 1958 - No. 36, Oct, 1961 (25 cents)
Gilberton Publishers (Classics Illustrated)

	Good	Fine	Mint
1-Dogs	1.50	4.50	9.00
2-Indians-Crandall-a	1.00	3.00	6.00
3-Horses; L. B. Cole-c	1.50	4.00	8.00
4-Railroads	.85	2.50	5.00
5-Space; Ingels-a	2.00	6.00	12.00
6-The F.B.I.; Disbrow, Evans, Ingels-a	2.00	6.00	12.00
7-Pirates; Disbrow, Ingels-a	2.00	6.00	12.00
8-Flight; Evans, Ingels, Crandall-a	2.00	6.00	12.00
9-Army; Disbrow, Ingels, Orlando-a	2.00	6.00	12.00
10-Navy; Disbrow, Kinstler-a	1.00	3.00	6.00
11-Marine Corps.	1.00	3.00	6.00
12-Coast Guard	1.00	3.00	6.00
13-Air Force	1.00	3.00	6.00
14-French Revolution; Crandall, Evans-a	2.00	6.00	12.00
15-Prehistoric Animals; Al Williamson-a, 6 & 10 pgs. plus Morrow-a	3.00	9.00	18.00
16-Crusades	1.00	3.00	6.00
17-Festivals-Evans, Crandall-a	1.00	3.00	6.00
18-Great Scientists; Crandall, Evans, Torres, Williamson, Morrow-a	2.00	6.00	12.00
19-Jungle; Crandall, Williamson, Morrow-a	3.00	9.00	18.00
20-Communications; Crandall, Evans-a	2.00	6.00	12.00
21-Presidents	1.50	4.00	8.00
22-Boating; Morrow-a	.85	2.50	5.00
23-Great Explorers; Crandall, Evans-a	1.50	4.00	8.00
24-Ghosts; Morrow, Evans-a	1.00	3.00	6.00
25-Magic; Evans, Morrow-a	2.00	6.00	12.00
26-The Civil War	1.00	3.00	6.00
27-Mountains (High Advs.); Crandall/Evans, Morrow, Torres-a	1.00	3.00	6.00
28-Whaling; Crandall, Evans, Morrow-a	1.00	3.00	6.00
29-Vikings; Crandall, Evans, Torres, Morrow-a	1.50	4.00	8.00
30-Undersea Adventure; Crandall/Evans, Kirby-a	1.50	4.00	8.00
31-Hunting; Crandall/Evans, Ingels, Kinstler, Kirby-a	1.50	4.00	8.00
32-For Gold & Glory; Morrow, Kirby, Crandall, Evans-a	1.00	3.00	6.00
33-Famous Teens; Torres, Crandall, Evans-a	1.00	3.00	6.00
34-Fishing; Crandall/Evans, Ingels-a	1.00	3.00	6.00
35-Spies; Kirby, Evans, Morrow-a	1.00	3.00	6.00
36-Fight for Life (Medicine); Kirby-a	1.00	3.00	6.00

(See Classics Ill. Special Edition)

WORLD FAMOUS HEROES MAGAZINE
Oct, 1941 - No. 4, Apr, 1942 (a comic book)
Comic Corp. of America (Centaur)

	Good	Fine	Mint
1-Gustavson-c; Lubbers, Glanzman-a; Davy Crockett story; Flag-c	8.00	24.00	48.00
2-4	7.00	20.00	40.00

WORLD FAMOUS STORIES
1945
Croyden Publishers

	Good	Fine	Mint
1-Ali Baba, Hansel & Gretel, Rip Van Winkle, Mid-Summer Night's Dream	3.00	9.00	18.00

WORLD IS HIS PARISH, THE
1953 (15 cents)
George A. Pflaum

	Good	Fine	Mint
The story of Pope Pius XII	3.00	9.00	18.00

WORLD OF ADVENTURE (Walt Disney's. . .)
April, 1963 - Oct, 1963
Gold Key

	Good	Fine	Mint
1-3-Disney TV characters; Savage Sam, Johnny Shiloh, Capt. Nemo, The Mooncussers	.35	1.00	2.00

WORLD OF ARCHIE, THE (See Archie Giant Series Mag. No. 148, 151,156,160,165,171,177,182,188,193,200,208,213,225,232,237, 244,249,456,461,468,473,480,485,492,497,504,509)

WORLD OF FANTASY
May, 1956 - No. 19, Aug, 1959
Atlas Comics (CPC No. 1-15/ZPC No. 16-19)

	Good	Fine	Mint
1	4.00	12.00	24.00
2-Williamson-a, 4 pgs.	5.00	15.00	30.00
3-Sid Check-a	2.50	7.00	14.00
4-7	2.00	6.00	12.00
8-Matt Fox, Orlando, Berg-a	2.50	7.00	14.00
9-Krigstein-a	3.00	8.00	16.00
10,13-15	1.50	4.00	8.00
11-Torres-a	2.50	7.00	14.00
12-Everett-c	1.50	4.00	8.00
16-Williamson-a, 4 pgs.; Ditko, Kirby-a	4.00	12.00	24.00
17-19-Ditko, Kirby-a	3.00	8.00	16.00

NOTE: ***Berg** a-5, 6, 8. **Check** a-3. **Ditko** a-17, 19. **Everett** c-4, 5-7, 9, 13. **Kirby** c-15, 17-19. **Krigstein** a-9. **Morrow** a-7, 8, 14. **Orlando** a-8, 13, 14. **Powell** a-6.*

WORLD OF GIANT COMICS, THE (See Archie All-Star Specials under Archie Comics)

WORLD OF JUGHEAD, THE (See Archie Giant Series Mag. No. 9,14, 19,24,30,136,143,149,152,157,161,166,172,178,183,189,194, 202,209,215,227,233,239,245,251,457,463,469,475,481,487,493, 499,505,511)

WORLD OF KRYPTON
July, 1979 - No. 3, Sept, 1979
DC Comics, Inc.

	Good	Fine	Mint
1-Jor-El marries Lara		.60	1.20
2,3: 3-Baby Superman sent to earth; Krypton explodes; Mon-el app.		.40	.80

NOTE: ***Anderson** a-1, 2i. **Chaykin** a-1-3p.*

WORLD OF MYSTERY
June, 1956 - No. 7, June, 1957
Atlas Comics (GPI)

	Good	Fine	Mint
1-Torres, Orlando-a	4.00	12.00	24.00
2-Woodish-a	1.50	4.00	8.00
3-Torres, Davis, Ditko-a	3.00	8.00	16.00
4-Davis, Pakula, Powell-a; Ditko-c	3.00	8.00	16.00
5,7: 5-Orlando-a	1.50	4.00	8.00
6-Williamson/Mayo-a, 4 pgs.; Ditko-a; Crandall text illo	3.50	10.00	20.00

NOTE: ***Colan** a-7. **Everett** c-3. **Severin** c/a-7.*

WORLD OF SUSPENSE
April, 1956 - No. 8, July, 1957
Atlas News Co.

	Good	Fine	Mint
1-Orlando-a	3.00	8.00	16.00
2,4-6,8: 4-Williamson-a?, 4pgs.	1.50	4.00	8.00
3,7-Williamson-a in both, 4 pgs. each; No. 7-with Mayo	3.50	10.00	20.00

NOTE: ***Berg** a-6. **Ditko** a-2. **Everett** a-1, 5; c-2, 6. **Heck** a-5. **Orlando** a-5. **Powell** a-6. **Roussos** a-6.*

WORLD OF WHEELS (Formerly Dragstrip Hotrodders)
Oct, 1967 - No. 32, June, 1970
Charlton Comics

	Good	Fine	Mint
17-32-Features Ken King		.15	.30

WORLD'S BEST (. . . Finest No. 2 on)
Spring, 1941
National Periodical Publications

1-The Batman, Superman, Crimson Avenger, Johnny Thunder, The

WORLD'S BEST (continued) Good Fine Mint
King, Young Dr. Davis, Zatara, Lando, Man of Magic, & Red, White & Blue begin (inside covers blank)
145.00 425.00 875.00

WORLDS BEYOND (Worlds of Fear No. 2 on)
Nov, 1951
Fawcett Publications

1-Powell, Bailey-a 5.00 14.00 28.00

WORLD'S FAIR COMICS (See N. Y. . . .)

WORLD'S FINEST COMICS (World's Best No. 1)
No. 2, Summer, 1941 - Present (early issues-100 pgs.)
National Periodical Publ./DC Comics (No.1-20 cardboard covers)

2 80.00 240.00 500.00
3-The Sandman begins; last Johnny Thunder; origin & 1st app. The Scarecrow 75.00 220.00 450.00
4-Hop Harrigan app.; last Young Dr. Davis 45.00 130.00 265.00
5-Intro. & only app. TNT & Dan the Dyna-Mite; last King & Crimson Avenger 45.00 130.00 265.00
6-Star Spangled Kid begins; Aquaman app.; S&K Sandman with Sandy in new costume begins, ends No. 7
35.00 100.00 200.00
7-Green Arrow begins; last Lando, King, & Red, White & Blue; S&K art 35.00 100.00 200.00
8-Boy Commandos begin 32.00 95.00 190.00
9-Batman cameo in Star Spangled Kid; S&K-a; last 100pg. ish.
30.00 85.00 170.00
10-S&K-a 30.00 85.00 170.00
11-17-Last cardboard cover issue 25.00 70.00 140.00
18-20: 18-Paper covers begin; last Star Spangled Kid
20.00 60.00 125.00
21-30: 30-Johnny Peril app. 16.00 45.00 95.00
31-40: 33-35-Tomahawk app. 11.00 32.00 65.00
41-50: 41-Boy Commandos end. 42-Wyoming Kid begins, ends No. 63. 43-Full Steam Foley begins, ends No. 48. 48-Last square binding. 49-Tom Sparks, Boy Inventor begins
8.50 25.00 50.00
51-60: 51-Zatara ends. 59-Manhunters Around the World begins, ends No. 62. 7.50 22.00 45.00
61-64,66: 63-Capt. Compass app. 6.00 18.00 36.00
65-Origin Superman; Tomahawk begins, ends No. 101
8.50 25.00 50.00
67-69-(15 Cent issues)(Scarce) 15.00 45.00 90.00
70-73-(10 Cent issues)(Scarce). 70-Last 68pg. issue. 71-Superman & Batman begin as a team 15.00 45.00 90.00
74-80: 74-Last pre-code ish. 5.00 14.00 28.00
81-90: 88-1st Joker/Luthor team-up. 90-Batwoman's 1st app. in World's Finest 3.75 11.00 22.00
91-93,95-99: 96-99-Kirby Green Arrow 2.50 7.50 15.00
94-Origin Superman/Batman team retold 5.00 15.00 30.00
100 6.00 18.00 36.00
101-120: 102-Tommy Tomorrow begins, ends No. 124. 105-Two pgs. Kubert. 113-Intro. Miss Arrowette in Green Arrow; 1st Batmite/Mxyzptlk team-up 2.00 6.00 12.00
121-141,143-150: 125-Aquaman begins, ends No. 139. 140-Last Green Arrow. 143-1st Mailbag. 148-Congorilla-r
1.50 4.00 8.00
142-Origin The Composite Superman(Villain); Legion app.
1.50 4.50 9.00
151-167,169-171,173,174: 154-1st Supersons story. 161-25 cent Giant G-28. 170-25 cent Giant G-40 .70 2.00 4.00
(80 Pg. Giant G-28,G-40) .80 2.40 4.80
168,172-Adult Legion app. .70 2.00 4.00
175,176-Adams-a; both r-Jonn' Jonzz' origin/Det. 225,226
.80 2.40 4.80
177-200: 179-25 cent Giant G-52. 182-Silent Knight-r/Brave & the Bold No. 6. 186-Johnny Quick-r. 187-Green Arrow origin-r/Adv. No. 256. 188-25 cent Giant G-64. 190-193-Robin-r. 197-25 cent Giant G-76; Green Arrow app. 198,199-3rd Superman/Flash race

Good Fine Mint
.25 .75 1.50
(80 Pg. Giant G-52-G-76) .30 .90 1.80
201-Dr. Fate, Green Lantern app. .25 .75 1.50
202-204,206,207: 206-25 cent Giant G-88. 204,207-212, 52 pgs.
.50 1.00
(80 Pg. Giant G-88) .25 .75 1.50
205-6 pgs. Shining Knight by Frazetta/Adv. No. 153 & Tarantula-r; 52 pgs. .50 1.50 3.00
208-Dr. Fate app.; Robotman & Ghost Patrol-r .25 .75 1.50
209-Batman, Hawkman-r .50 1.00
210-214: 210-Green Arrow app.; Black Pirate-r. 211-Atom app.; G.A. Green Lantern-r. 212-Jonn' Jonzz' app.; G.A. Air Wave & Grim Ghost-r. 213-Robin app. 214-Vigilante app.; Two Face begins
.50 1.00
215-Intro. Batman Jr. & Superman Jr. .50 1.00
216-222: 217-Metamorpho begins; Batman/Superman team-up begins. 220-Last Metamorpho .40 .80
223,226-Adams-a(r); 100 pgs.; Deadman origin in 223; 226-S&K, Toth-r; Manhunter part origin-r/Det. 225,226
.30 .90 1.80
224,225,227-(100 pgs.) .25 .75 1.50
228-Toth-a; 100 pgs. .25 .75 1.50
229,231-243: 229-Metamorpho app. .30 .60
230-Adams-a(r); 52 pgs. .40 .80
244-248: 244-Green Arrow, Black Canary, Wonder Woman, Vigilante begin; $1.00 size begins. 245-Not code approved. 246-Death of Stuff in Vigilante; origin Vigilante retold. 248-Last Vigilante .25 .75 1.50
249-The Creeper begins by Ditko, ends No. 255
.25 .75 1.50
250-The Creeper origin retold by Ditko .60 1.20
251-257: 253-Captain Marvel begins. 255-Last Creeper. 256-Hawkman begins. 257-Black Lightning begins .60 1.20
258-Adams-c .60 1.20
259-Rogers-a(p) .60 1.20
260-262: 260-Atom app. .50 1.00
263-274 ($1.00): 268-Capt. Marvel Jr origin retold. 269-Gr. Arrow, Hawkman, Capt. Marvel Jr. app. 272-Gr. Arrow, Mary Marvel app. 273-Plastic Man app. 274-Zatanna begins .50 1.00

NOTE: ***Adams** c-174-176, 178-180, 182, 183, 185, 186, 198-205, 208-211, 244-246i, 258. **Anderson** a-121, 122, 204, 244i, 245, 246, 256. **Aparo** c-249-255, 257, 265, 266. **Buckler** a-257-261; c-243, 259, 260p. **Burnley** a-8, 10; c-7-9, 12. **Ditko** a-249-255. **Giordano** c-260i. **Infantino** a-225. **G. Kane** a-38, 174r. **Kirby** a-187. **Kubert** Zatara-40-44. **Lopez** a-244, 255, 258. **Morrow** a-245-248. **Nasser** a-244-246, 259, 260. **Newton** a-253-274p. **Orlando** a-224. **Perez** c-270. **Robinson** a-2, 9, 13-15; c-2-4, 6. **Schaffenberger** a-246, 249, 253-259i. **Staton** a-262p, 273p. **Tuska** a-230r, 250, 252, 254, 257.*

(Also see 80 Pg. Giant No. 15.)

WORLD'S GREATEST ATHLETE (See Walt Disney Showcase No. 14)

WORLD'S GREATEST SONGS
Sept, 1954
Atlas Comics (Male)

1-(Scarce) Heath & Harry Anderson-a 7.00 20.00 40.00

WORLD'S GREATEST STORIES
Jan, 1949 - No. 2, May, 1949
Jubilee Publications

1-Alice in Wonderland 5.00 14.00 28.00
2-Pinocchio 4.00 12.00 24.00

WORLD'S GREATEST SUPER HEROES
1977 (3¾x3¾'') (24 pgs. in color) (Giveaway)
DC Comics (Nutra Comics) (Child Vitamins, Inc.)

Batman & Robin app.; health tips .25 .75 1.50

WORLDS OF FEAR (World Beyond No. 1)
V1No.2, 1952 - V2No.10, June, 1953

World's Finest Comics #13, © DC

World's Finest Comics #65, © DC

World's Finest Comics #259, © DC

Worlds Unknown #1, © MCG

Wow Comics #58, © FAW

Wulf The Barbarian #1, © ATLAS

WORLDS OF FEAR (continued)
Fawcett Publications

	Good	Fine	Mint
V1No.2,4-6(9/52)	3.50	10.00	20.00
3-Evans-a	4.00	12.00	24.00
V2No.7-9	2.50	7.00	14.00
10-Painted-c; man with no eyes surrounded by eyeballs-c	6.00	18.00	36.00

NOTE: ***Powell*** *a-2, 4, 5.* ***Sekowsky*** *a-4, 5.*

WORLDS UNKNOWN
May, 1973 - No. 8, Aug, 1974
Marvel Comics Group

	Good	Fine	Mint
1-Reprint from Astonishing No. 54; Torres, Reese-a		.40	.80
2-8		.25	.50

NOTE: ***Adkins/Mooney*** *a-5.* ***Buscema*** *a-4.* ***W. Howard*** *inks-3.* ***Kane*** *a-1,2; c-5, 6, 8.* ***Sutton*** *a-2.* ***Tuska*** *a-8. No. 8 has Golden Voyage of Sinbad movie adaptation.*

WORLD WAR STORIES
Apr-June, 1965 - No. 3, Dec, 1965
Dell Publishing Co.

	Good	Fine	Mint
1	.25	.75	1.50
2,3: 1-3-Glanzman-a		.50	1.00

WORLD WAR II (See Classics Special Ed.)

WORLD WAR III
Mar, 1953 - No. 2, May, 1953
Ace Periodicals

	Good	Fine	Mint
1-(Scarce)-Atomic bomb-c	30.00	80.00	165.00
2-Used in **POP**, pg. 78 and B&W & color illos.	20.00	60.00	120.00

WORST FROM MAD, THE (Annual)
1958 - No. 12, 1969 (Each annual cover is reprinted from the cover of the Mad issues being reprinted)
E. C. Comics

	Good	Fine	Mint
nn(1958)-Bonus; record labels & travel stickers; 1st Mad annual; r-/Mad No. 29-34	7.00	20.00	40.00
2(1959)-Bonus is small 33⅓ rpm record entitled "Meet the Staff of Mad;" r-/Mad No. 35-40	10.00	30.00	60.00
3(1960)-20"x30"campaign poster "Alfred E. Neuman for President;" r-/Mad No. 41-46	4.00	12.00	24.00
4(1961)-Sunday comics section; r-/Mad No. 47-54	5.00	14.00	28.00
5(1962)-Small 33⅓ rpm record; r-/Mad No. 55-62	7.00	20.00	40.00
6(1963)-Small 33⅓ rpm record; r-/Mad No. 63-70	7.00	20.00	40.00
7(1964)-Mad protest signs; r-/Mad No. 71-76	3.00	8.00	16.00
8(1965)-Build a Mad Zeppelin	3.50	10.00	20.00
9(1966)-33⅓ rpm record	5.50	16.00	32.00
10(1967)-Mad bumper sticker	2.50	7.00	14.00
11(1968)-Mad cover window stickers	2.50	7.00	14.00
12(1969)-Mad picture postcards; Orlando-a	2.00	6.00	12.00

NOTE: *Covers:* ***Bob Clarke****-No. 8.* ***Mingo****-No. 7, 9-12.*

WOTALIFE COMICS
No. 3, Aug-Sept, 1946 - No. 12, July, 1947; 1959
Fox Features Syndicate/Norlen Mag.

	Good	Fine	Mint
3-12-Cosmo Cat	1.00	3.00	6.00
1(1959-Norlen)-Atomic Rabbit, Atomic Mouse	.85	2.50	5.00

WOTALIFE COMICS
1957 - No. 5, 1957
Green Publications

	Good	Fine	Mint
1-5	.50	1.50	3.00

WOW COMICS
May, 1936 - No. 4, Nov, 1936
David McKay Publications/Henle Publ.

	Good	Fine	Mint
1-Fu Manchu, Eisner-a	40.00	120.00	240.00
2-Ken Maynard, Fu Manchu, Popeye; Eisner-a	30.00	80.00	160.00
3-Eisner-c; Popeye, Fu Manchu	30.00	80.00	160.00
4-Flash Gordon by Raymond, Mandrake, Popeye; Eisner-a	40.00	120.00	240.00

WOW COMICS (Real Western Hero No. 70 on)
Spring, 1941 - No. 69, Fall, 1948
Fawcett Publications

	Good	Fine	Mint
nn(No.1)-Origin Mr. Scarlet by S&K; Atom Blake, Boy Wizard begins; Diamond Jack, The White Rajah, Shipwreck Roberts, Jim Dolan, & Rick O'Shay only app.; the cover of this comic was printed on unstable paper stock and is rarely found in fine or mint condition; bondage-c. (Rare)	600.00	1800.00	3800.00
(Prices vary widely on this book)			
2-The Hunchback begins	40.00	120.00	250.00
3	25.00	70.00	150.00
4-Origin Pinky	30.00	90.00	190.00
5	20.00	60.00	125.00
6-Origin The Phantom Eagle; Commando Yank begins	15.00	45.00	90.00
7,8,10	15.00	45.00	90.00
9-Capt. Marvel, Capt. Marvel Jr., Shazam app.; Scarlet & Pinky x-over; Mary Marvel begins (cameo)	20.00	60.00	120.00
11-17,19,20: 15-Flag-c	8.50	25.00	50.00
18-1st app. Uncle Marvel (10/43); infinity-c	8.50	25.00	50.00
21-30: 28-Pinky x-over in Mary Marvel	5.00	15.00	30.00
31-40	3.50	10.00	20.00
41-50	3.00	8.00	16.00
51-58: Last Mary Marvel	2.50	7.00	14.00
59-69: 59-Ozzie begins	2.00	5.00	10.00

WRECK OF GROSVENOR (See Superior Stories No. 3)

WRINGLE WRANGLE (See 4-Color No. 821)

WULF, THE BARBARIAN
Feb, 1975 - No. 4, Sept, 1975
Atlas/Seaboard Publ.

	Good	Fine	Mint
1-Origin		.60	1.20
2-Intro. Berithe the Swordswoman; Adams, Wood, Reese-a		.50	1.00
3,4: 4-Part Williamson, Milgurm-i		.40	.80

WYATT EARP (See Hugh O'Brian Famous Marshal. . . & Four Color No. 860)

WYATT EARP
11/55 - No. 29, 6/60; No. 30, 10/72 - No. 34, 6/73
Atlas Comics/Marvel No. 23 on (IPC)

	Good	Fine	Mint
1	3.00	8.00	16.00
2-Williamson-a, 4 pgs.	3.50	10.00	20.00
3-6,8-11	1.20	3.50	7.00
7,12-Williamson-a, 4 pgs. each; No. 12 with Mayo	3.00	8.00	16.00
13-19	.85	2.50	5.00
20-Torres-a	1.20	3.50	7.00
21-Davis-c	.85	2.50	5.00
22-24,26-29: 22-Ringo Kid app. 23-Kid From Texas app.	.50	1.50	3.00
25-Davis-a	1.50	4.00	8.00
30-Williamson-r ('72)		.40	.80
31,33,34-Reprints		.30	.60
32-Torres-a(r)		.25	.50

NOTE: ***Kirby*** *c-25, 29.* ***Maurer*** *a-4.* ***Wildey*** *a-24, 28.*

WYATT EARP FRONTIER MARSHAL (Formerly Range Busters; See Blue Bird)
No. 12, Jan, 1956 - No. 72, Dec, 1967
Charlton Comics

	Good	Fine	Mint
12-19 (No. 11 Exist?)	.70	2.00	4.00
20-Williamson-a(4), 8,5,5, & 7 pgs.; 68 pg. issue			

	Good	Fine	Mint
WYATT EARP FRONTIER... (cont'd.)	4.00	12.00	24.00
21-30	.25	.75	1.50
31-72: 31-Crandall-r		.50	1.00

X-MAS COMICS
1941 - No. 2, 1942 (324 pgs.) (50 cents)
No. 3, 1943 - No. 7, 1947 (132 pgs.)
Fawcett Publications

	Good	Fine	Mint
1-Reprints Whiz No. 21, Capt. Marvel No. 3, Bulletman No. 2, Wow No. 3, & Master No. 18; Raboy back-c	90.00	280.00	600.00
2-Captain Marvel, Bulletman, Spy Smasher-r	45.00	135.00	300.00
3-7-Funny animals	8.00	24.00	50.00

X-MAS COMICS
1949 - 1952 (196 pgs.)
Fawcett Publications

	Good	Fine	Mint
4-7-Reprints from Whiz, Master, Tom Mix, Captain Marvel, Nyoka Captain Video, Bob Colt, Monte Hale, Hot Rod Comics, & Battle Stories	14.00	40.00	80.00

XMAS FUNNIES
No date (paper cover) (36 pgs.?)
Kinney Shoes (Giveaway)

	Good	Fine	Mint
Contains 1933 color strip-r; Mutt & Jeff, etc.	10.00	30.00	50.00

X-MEN, THE
Sept, 1963 - Present
Marvel Comics Group

	Good	Fine	Mint
1-Origin X-Men; 1st app. Magneto	40.00	110.00	225.00
2-1st app. The Vanisher	19.00	55.00	110.00
3-1st app. The Blob	10.00	30.00	60.00
4-1st Quick Silver & Scarlet Witch & Brotherhood of the Evil Mutants	8.50	25.00	50.00
5	6.00	18.00	36.00
6-10: 8-1st Unus the Untouchable. 9-Avengers app. 10-1st Silver-Age app. Ka-Zar	3.50	10.00	20.00
11-20: 11-1st app. The Stranger. 12-Origin Prof. X. 14-1st app. Sentinels. 19-1st app. The Mimic	2.00	5.00	10.00
21-27,29,30	1.20	3.50	7.00
28-1st app. The Banshee	1.50	4.00	8.00
31-37	.70	2.00	4.00
38-Origin The X-Men feature begins, ends No. 57	1.00	3.00	6.00
39,40: 39-New costumes	.70	2.00	4.00
41-48: 42-Death of Prof. X (Changeling disguised as). 44-Red Raven app. (G.A.)	.60	1.70	3.40
49-Steranko-c	.70	2.00	4.00
50,51-Steranko c/a	1.50	4.50	9.00
52	.60	1.70	3.40
53-Smith c/a; 1st Smith comic book work	2.00	6.00	12.00
54,55-Smith-c	1.50	4.00	8.00
56-63,65-Adams-a. 65-Return of Prof. X	2.00	6.00	12.00
64-1st Sunfire app.	.70	2.00	4.00
66	.70	2.00	4.00
67-80: 67-All-r. 72-(52 pgs.)	.50	1.50	3.00
81-93	.40	1.20	2.40
94-New X-Men begin; Colossus, Nightcrawler, Thunderbird, Storm, Wolverine, & Banshee join; Angel, Marvel Girl, & Iceman resign	10.00	30.00	60.00
95-Death Thunderbird	5.00	15.00	30.00
96	4.00	12.00	24.00
97-99	3.00	9.00	18.00
100-Old vs. New X-Men; part origin Phoenix	4.00	12.00	24.00
101-Phoenix origin concludes	4.00	12.00	24.00
102-106: 102-Origin Storm. 104-Intro. Star Jammers	2.00	6.00	12.00
107,109,110: 109-1st app. Indicator. 110-Phoenix joins	2.00	5.00	10.00
108-1st Byrne X-Men	2.00	6.00	12.00
111-115	1.50	4.50	9.00
116-119: 117-Origin Prof. X	1.20	3.50	7.00
120,121-1st app. Alpha flight	1.50	4.50	9.00
122,123,125-129: 122-Drug mention. 129-Intro Kitty Pride	.85	2.50	5.00
124-Colossus becomes Proletarian	1.00	3.00	6.00
130-1st app. The Dazzler by Byrne	1.20	3.50	7.00
131,138-Dazzler app; 138-Cyclops leaves; history of X-Men	.60	1.80	3.60
132-136,139,140: 133-Wolverine goes solo. 134-Phoenix becomes Dark Phoenix. 139,140-Alpha Flight app; 139-Sprite (Kitty Pride) joins	.50	1.50	3.00
137-Giant; death of Phoenix	.85	2.50	5.00
141-Intro Future X-Men & The New Brotherhood of Evil Mutants	.25	.75	1.50
142-Deaths of Wolverine, Frank Richards, Storm & Colossus	.30	.90	1.80
143-147,149,151-153	.25	.75	1.50
148-Spider-Woman, Dazzler app.	.25	.75	1.50
150-Double size	.25	.75	1.50
Annual 3(2/80), 4(11/80)	.70	2.00	4.00
Annual 5(10/81)	.35	1.00	2.00
Giant-Size 1(Summer,'75, 50 cents)-1st app. new X-Men; Intro Nightcrawler, Storm, Colossus & Thunderbird; Wolverine app.	10.00	28.00	56.00
Giant-Size 2(11/75)-51 pgs. Adams-a(r)	2.00	6.00	12.00
Special 1(12/70)-Kirby-c/a; origin The Stranger	1.50	4.50	9.00
Special 2(11/71)	1.50	4.50	9.00

NOTE: ***Adams** c-56-63, 65. **Austin** a-108i, 109i, 111-117i, 119-131i, 141i-143i, Annual 3i; c-109i, 111i, 114-122i, 123, 124i-143i. **Byrne** a-108, 109p, 111p-143p; c-110, 113-116, 127, 129-141, 142p. **Cockrum** a-94p-99p, 100, 101p-107p, 145-150; c-97i, 98-108, 110, 111, 117-119, 121, 122, 124-126, 144p-147p, 148, 149p-151p. **Ditko** a-90r. **Everett** c-73 (w/Kane). **Kirby** a-1-17 (No. 12-17-layouts); c-1-22, 25, 26, 30, 31, 35. **Layton** c-112i, 113i. **Perez** c-112p, 128p, Annual 3p. **Toth** a-12. **Wood** c-11i, 34i.*

X, THE MAN WITH THE X-RAY EYES (See Movie Comics)

X-VENTURE
July, 1947 - No. 2, Nov, 1947 (Super heroes)
Victory Magazines Corp.

	Good	Fine	Mint
1-Atom Wizard, Mystery Shadow, Lester Trumble	14.00	40.00	70.00
2	8.00	24.00	40.00

YAK YAK (See 4-Color No. 1186,1348)

YAKKY DOODLE & CHOPPER
Dec, 1962 (Hanna-Barbera)
Gold Key

	Good	Fine	Mint
1	.50	1.50	3.00

YALTA TO KOREA
1952 (8 pgs.) (Giveaway) (paper cover)
M. Philip Corp. (Republican National Committee)

	Good	Fine	Mint
Anti-communist propaganda book	15.00	45.00	90.00

YANG (See House of Yang)
Nov, 1973 - No. 13, May, 1976
Charlton Comics

	Good	Fine	Mint
1-Origin; Opium drug mention		.50	1.00
2-5		.30	.60
6-13		.20	.40
3,10,11(Modern Comics-r, 1977)		.15	.30

YANKEE COMICS
Sept, 1941 - No. 4, Mar?, 1942; No. 7, no date
Harry 'A' Chesler/William H. Wise No. 4-10

1-Origin The Echo, The Enchanted Dagger, Yankee Doodle Jones,

X-Men #28, © MCG

X-Men #130, © MCG

X-Men Special #1, © MCG

The Yardbirds #1, © ZD

Young Allies #14, © MCG

Young Eagle #4, © FAW

YANKEE COMICS (continued)

	Good	Fine	Mint
The Firebrand, & The Scarlet Sentry; Black Satan app.	17.00	50.00	100.00
2-Origin Johnny Rebel; Major Victory app.; Barry Kuda begins	11.00	32.00	65.00
3	10.00	28.00	56.00
4(Exist?)	8.00	23.00	46.00
4-10(small size, 4¾x7¼)-No date; distr. thru Army PX's only; military humor	1.20	3.50	7.00
humor	1.20	3.50	7.00

YANKS IN BATTLE
Sept, 1956 - No. 4, Dec, 1956
Quality Comics Group

	Good	Fine	Mint
1	2.50	7.00	14.00
2-4	1.20	3.50	7.00

YANKS IN BATTLE
1963
I. W. Enterprises

	Good	Fine	Mint
Reprint No. 3	.25	.75	1.50

YARDBIRDS, THE (G. I. Joe's Sidekicks)
Summer, 1952
Ziff-Davis Publishing Co.

	Good	Fine	Mint
1-By Bob Oskner	1.00	3.00	6.00

YARNS OF YELLOWSTONE
1972 (36 pages) (50 cents)
World Color Press

	Good	Fine	Mint
Ill. by Bill Chapman		.50	1.00

YELLOW CLAW
Oct, 1956 - No. 4, April, 1957
Atlas Comics (MjMC)

	Good	Fine	Mint
1-Origin by Joe Maneely; Ditko-a	10.00	30.00	60.00
2-4-Kirby-a in all; 2,4-Severin-c. 3-Everett-c. 4-Kirby/Severin-a	10.00	30.00	60.00

YELLOWJACKET (Jack in the Box No. 11 on)
Sept, 1944 - No. 10, June, 1946
E. Levy/Frank Comunale

	Good	Fine	Mint
1-Origin Yellowjacket; Diana, the Huntress begins	6.00	18.00	36.00
2,3,5	5.00	14.00	28.00
4-Cocaine drug story	5.50	16.00	32.00
6-10: 7,8-Has stories narrated by old witch in 'Tales of Terror'	3.50	10.00	20.00

YELLOWSTONE KELLY (See 4-Color No. 1056)

YELLOW SUBMARINE (See Movie Comics)

YOGI BEAR (TV) (Hanna-Barbera)
12-2/59-60 - No. 9, 7-9/62; No. 10, 10/62 - No. 42, 10/70
Dell Publishing Co./Gold Key No. 10 on

	Good	Fine	Mint
4-Color 1067,1104,1162	.50	1.50	3.00
4(8-9/61)-9(7-9/62)-Dell	.35	1.00	2.00
10(10/62-G.K.),11-titled "Y.B. Jellystone Jollies"-80 pgs.	.30	.90	1.80
12(4/63), 14-42		.50	1.00
13(7/63)-Surprise Party, 68 pgs.		.50	1.00
4-Color 1271,1349	.50	1.50	3.00
. . . Kite Fun Book('62, 8 pgs.)-paper cover; Pacific Gas & Electric giveaway; nn	.80	2.40	4.80

YOGI BEAR (See Dell Giant No. 41, March of Comics No. 253,265, 279,291,309,319,337,344, Whitman Comic Books & Movie Comics under "Hey There It's . . .")

YOGI BEAR
Nov, 1970 - No. 35, Jan, 1976 (Hanna-Barbera)
Charlton Comics

	Good	Fine	Mint
1	.35	1.00	2.00
2-6,8-35: 28-31-partial-r		.50	1.00
7-Summer Fun (Giant); 52 pgs.		.60	1.20

YOGI BEAR (TV)
Nov, 1977 - No. 9, Mar, 1979
Marvel Comics Group

	Good	Fine	Mint
1		.30	.60
2-9		.20	.40

YOGI BEAR'S EASTER PARADE (See The Funtastic World of Hanna-Barbera No. 2)

YOGI BERRA (Baseball hero)
1951 (Yankee catcher)
Fawcett Publications

	Good	Fine	Mint
nn	10.00	30.00	60.00

YOSEMITE SAM (. . . & Bugs Bunny)
Dec, 1970 - Present
Gold Key

	Good	Fine	Mint
1	.35	1.00	2.00
2-10		.50	1.00
11-70		.20	.40

(See March of Comics No. 363,380,392)

YOUNG ALLIES COMICS (All-Winners No. 21)
Summer, 1941 - No. 20, Oct, 1946
Timely Comics (Young Allies, Inc.)

	Good	Fine	Mint
1-Origin The Young Allies; 1st meeting of Captain America & Human Torch; Red Skull app.; S&K-c/splash	145.00	425.00	875.00
2-Captain America & Human Torch app.; Simon & Kirby-c	60.00	180.00	375.00
3-Fathertime, Captain America & Human Torch app.	50.00	150.00	300.00
4-The Vagabond & Red Skull, Capt. America, Human Torch app.	40.00	120.00	240.00
5-Captain America & Human Torch app.	30.00	90.00	180.00
6-10: Origin Tommy Tyme & Clock of Ages; ends No. 19	20.00	60.00	120.00
11-20	15.00	45.00	90.00

YOUNG BRIDES
Sept-Oct, 1952 - No. 32?, 1956
Feature/Prize Publications

	Good	Fine	Mint
V1No.1-Simon & Kirby-a	3.50	10.00	20.00
2-4-S&K-a	2.00	6.00	12.00
V2No.1,3-7-S&K-a	1.75	5.00	10.00
2,8,9-No S&K	.60	1.80	3.60
15-22,24,25,27,29-32	.40	1.20	2.40
23-Meskin-c	.80	2.40	4.80
26-All S&K ish.	2.00	5.00	10.00
28 (V4No.4)-S&K-a	.85	2.50	5.00

YOUNG DR. MASTERS (See Advs. of Young Dr. Masters)

YOUNG DOCTORS, THE
January, 1963 - No. 6, 1963
Charlton Comics

	Good	Fine	Mint
V1No.1-6		.40	.80

YOUNG EAGLE
Dec, 1950 - No. 10, June, 1952; 1957
Fawcett Publications/Charlton

	Good	Fine	Mint
1	3.50	10.00	20.00
2-9	2.50	7.00	14.00
10-Origin Thunder, Young Eagle's horse	2.00	6.00	12.00
4(1/57), 5(4/57) (CC)	.70	2.00	4.00

YOUNG HEARTS
Nov, 1949 - No. 2, Feb, 1950
Marvel Comics (SPC)

	Good	Fine	Mint
1	2.00	6.00	12.00

YOUNG HEARTS (continued)

	Good	Fine	Mint
2	1.20	3.50	7.00

YOUNG HEARTS IN LOVE
1964
Super Comics

	Good	Fine	Mint
17,18: 17-R/Young Love V5No.6, 4-5/62	.25	.75	1.50

YOUNG HEROES (Formerly Forbidden Worlds No. 34)
No. 35, Feb-Mar, 1955 - No. 37, June-July, 1955
American Comics Group (Titan)

	Good	Fine	Mint
35-37-Frontier Scout	.85	2.50	5.00

YOUNG KING COLE (Becomes Criminals on the Run)
Fall, 1945 - V3No.12, July, 1948
Premium Group/Novelty Press

	Good	Fine	Mint
V1No.1-Toni Gayle begins	3.50	10.00	20.00
2-6	3.00	8.00	16.00
V2No.1-3,5-7(7/47)	2.50	7.00	14.00
4-Toni Gayle transvestism story	3.00	8.00	16.00
V3No.1,3-6,12	2.00	5.00	10.00
2-L. B. Cole-a	2.50	7.50	15.00
7-L. B. Cole-c/a	4.00	12.00	24.00
8-11-L. B. Cole-c	3.50	10.00	20.00

YOUNG LAWYERS, THE (TV)
Jan, 1971 - No. 2, April, 1971
Dell Publishing Co.

	Good	Fine	Mint
1,2	.70	2.00	4.00

YOUNG LIFE (Teen Life No. 3 on)
Summer, 1945 - No. 2, Fall, 1945
New Age Publ./Quality Comics Group

	Good	Fine	Mint
1,2: 1-Skip Homier, Louis Prima stories	1.50	4.00	8.00

YOUNG LOVE
2-3/49 - No. 73, 12-1/56-57; V3No.3, 1959 - V7No.1, 6-7/63
Prize (Feature) Publ. (Crestwood)

	Good	Fine	Mint
V1No.1-S&K c/a(2)	6.00	18.00	36.00
2-Photo-c begin; S&K-a; lingerie panel	3.00	9.00	18.00
3-S&K-a	2.50	7.00	14.00
4-6-Minor S&K-a	2.00	5.00	10.00
V2No.1(No.7)-S&K-a(2)	2.50	7.00	14.00
2-5-Minor S&K-a; Severin/Elder-a-No.3	1.50	4.00	8.00
6,8-S&K-c only	2.00	5.00	10.00
7(No.14)-S&K c/a(2)	2.50	7.00	14.00
16-22-S&K c/a	2.00	5.00	10.00
23-25-Photo-c resume; S&K-a in all	1.50	4.00	8.00
26-No S&K	.85	2.50	5.00
27-29,32-35-Minor S&K-a	1.20	3.50	7.00
30,31,36-S&K-a in all	1.50	4.00	8.00
37-73(V8No.1)-Most have S&K-a	1.20	3.50	7.00
V3No.3-6(4-5/60)(Formerly Personal Love)	.35	1.00	2.00
V4No.1(6-7/60)-6(4-5/61)	.35	1.00	2.00
V5No.1(6-7/61)-6(4-5/62)	.35	1.00	2.00
V6No.1(6-7/62)-6(4-5/63), V7No.1	.35	1.00	2.00

NOTE: ***S&K** art not in No. 53, 57, 58, 61, 63-65.*

YOUNG LOVE
No. 39, 9-10/63 - No. 120, Winter/75-76; No. 121, 10/76 - No. 126, 7/77
National Periodical Publ. (Arleigh Publ. Corp. No. 49-60)/DC Comics

	Good	Fine	Mint
39-41,43-63,65-67	.50	1.50	3.00
42-Diary of Mary Robin begins, ends No. 52	.50	1.50	3.00
64-Simon & Kirby-a	.40	1.20	2.40
68-Life & Loves of Lisa St. Claire serial begins, ends No. 78; not in No. 69		.50	1.00
69-(68 pgs.)		.50	1.00
70-72,74-77,81		.40	.80
73-Toth-a	.25	.75	1.50
78,79-"20 Miles to Heartbreak" by Toth & Coletta (Chapter 1 & 4, see Secret Hearts No. 141,142 for Chapter 2 & 3)	.25	.75	1.50
80,82-Morrow-a		.30	.60
83-120: 107-114-(100 pgs.)		.30	.60
121,124-126		.20	.40
122-Toth-a		.30	.60
123-Drug propaganda story		.40	.80

YOUNG LOVER ROMANCES
No. 4, June, 1952 - No. 5, Aug, 1952
Toby Press

	Good	Fine	Mint
4,5	.85	2.50	5.00

YOUNG LOVERS (My Secret Life No. 19 on)
No. 16, 1956 - No. 18, May, 1957
Charlton Comics

	Good	Fine	Mint
16,17('56)	.85	2.50	5.00
18-Elvis Presley picture-c, text story (biography)	17.00	50.00	100.00

YOUNG MARRIAGE
June, 1950
Fawcett Publications

	Good	Fine	Mint
1-Powell-a; photo-c	3.50	10.00	20.00

YOUNG MEN (Formerly Cowboy Romances) (. . . on the Battlefield No. 12-20 (4/53))
No. 4, 6/50 - No. 11, 10/51; No. 12, 12/51 - No. 28, 6/54
Marvel/Atlas Comics (IPC)

	Good	Fine	Mint
4	2.00	6.00	12.00
5-11	1.50	4.00	8.00
12-23: 19-Everett-a	1.50	4.00	8.00
24-Origin Captain America, Human Torch, & Sub-Mariner which are revived thru No. 28	17.00	50.00	100.00
25-28	12.00	35.00	70.00

NOTE: ***Berg** c/a-17. Sub-Mariner by **Everett**-No. 24, 26, 27.*

YOUNG REBELS, THE (TV)
January, 1971
Dell Publishing Co.

	Good	Fine	Mint
1	.70	2.00	4.00

YOUNG ROMANCE COMICS (The 1st romance comic)
Sept-Oct, 1947 - V16No.4, June-July, 1963
Prize/Headline (Feature Publ.)

	Good	Fine	Mint
V1No.1-S&K c/a(2)	9.00	25.00	50.00
2-5-S&K c/a(2-3) each	4.00	12.00	24.00
6-S&K c/a; Robinson/Meskin-a	4.00	12.00	24.00
V2No.1-6(No.7-12)-S&K c/a(2-3) each	3.50	10.00	20.00
V3, V4(No.13-25)-S&K-a in all; all have photo-c	2.00	5.00	10.00
V5, V6(No.26,27,33,34)-S&K-c/a each	2.50	7.00	14.00
V5(No.28-32)-S&K-a each	1.50	4.00	8.00
35,37-48-S&K-a in each	1.20	3.50	7.00
36-S&K, Toth, Ditko-a	2.00	5.00	10.00
49-51-No S&K-a	1.00	3.00	6.00
52-71-S&K-a in most	1.20	3.50	7.00
72-77-No S&K	.70	2.00	4.00
78,79-S&K-a	.85	2.50	5.00
80,81,83,84,86-91-Some S&K-a each	.70	2.00	4.00
82,85-All S&K-a	1.00	3.00	6.00
V11No.1,3,4, V12No.2,4,5-No S&K-a	.50	1.50	3.00
V11No.2,5, V12No.1,3-S&K c/a each	1.00	3.00	6.00
V12No.6-S&K-a	.80	2.40	4.80
V13No.1-S&K c/a(2); Powell-a	1.00	3.00	6.00
V13No.2 - V16No.4	.35	1.00	2.00

NOTE: *Photo-c-55.*

YOUNG ROMANCE COMICS

Young King Cole #1, © PG

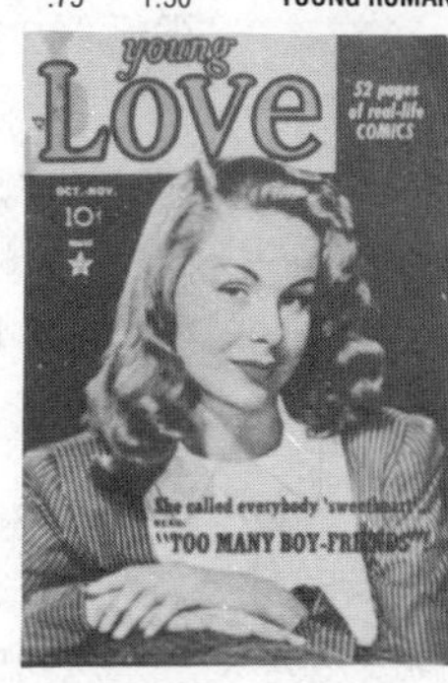

Young Love #5, © PRIZE

Young Romance #10, © PRIZE

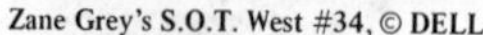
Zane Grey's S.O.T. West #34, © DELL

Zaza The Mystic #10, © CC

Zip Comics #7, © MLJ

YOUNG ROMANCE COMICS (continued)
No. 125, Aug-Sept, 1963 - No. 208, Nov-Dec, 1975
National Periodical Publ. (Arleigh Publ. Corp. No. 127)

	Good	Fine	Mint
125-153,155-162	.40	1.20	2.40
154-Adams-c	.50	1.50	3.00
163,164-Toth-a		.50	1.00
165-196: 170-Michell from Young Love ends; Lily Martin, the Swinger begins		.40	.80
197(100 pgs.)-208		.25	.50

YOUR DREAMS (See Strange World of . . .)

YOUR TRIP TO NEWSPAPERLAND
June, 1955 (12 pgs.; 14x11½")
Philadelphia Evening Bulletin (Printed by Harvey Press)

	Good	Fine	Mint
Joe Palooka takes kids on tour through newspaper	2.00	6.00	12.00

YOUR UNITED STATES
1946
Lloyd Jacquet Studios

	Good	Fine	Mint
Used in **SOTI**, pg. 309,310	7.00	20.00	40.00

YOUTHFUL HEARTS (Daring Confessions No. 4 on)
May, 1952 - No. 3, 1952
Youthful Magazines

	Good	Fine	Mint
1-''Monkey on Her Back'' swipes E.C. drug story from Shock SuspenStories No. 12	7.00	20.00	40.00
2,3	3.50	10.00	20.00

NOTE: ***Doug Wildey** art in all.*

YOUTHFUL LOVE (Truthful Love No. 2)
May, 1950
Youthful Magazines

	Good	Fine	Mint
1	2.00	6.00	12.00

YOUTHFUL ROMANCES (Daring Love No. 15)
Aug-Sept, 1949 - No. 18, July, 1953
Pix-Parade/Ribage

	Good	Fine	Mint
1-Titled Youthful Love-Romances	5.00	15.00	30.00
2-5	3.00	9.00	18.00
6-Drug mention story	2.50	7.00	14.00
7	2.00	6.00	12.00
8-Myron Fess-c(5/54?)	4.00	12.00	24.00
9-18	2.00	5.00	10.00

ZAGO, JUNGLE PRINCE (My Story No. 5 on)
Sept, 1948 - No. 4, March, 1949
Fox Features Syndicate

	Good	Fine	Mint
1-Blue Beetle app.-partial r-/Atomic No. 4 (Toni Luck)	10.00	30.00	50.00
2,3-Kamen-a	8.00	24.00	40.00
4-Baker-c	7.00	20.00	36.00

ZANE GREY'S STORIES OF THE WEST
No. 27, Sept, 1955 - No. 39, Sept, 1958
Dell Publishing Co./Gold Key 11/64

	Good	Fine	Mint
4-Color 197('48),222,230,236('49)	3.00	8.00	16.00
4-Color 246,255,270,301,314,333,346	2.00	6.00	12.00
4-Color 357,372,395,412,433,449,467,484	1.50	4.00	8.00
4-Color 511-Kinstler-a	2.00	5.00	10.00
4-Color 532,555,583,604,616,632,996('59)	1.50	4.00	8.00
27-39	1.20	3.50	7.00
10131-411-(11/64-G.K.)-Nevada; r-4-Color No. 996	.50	1.50	3.00

ZANY (Magazine) (Satire) (See Ratfink & Frantic)
Sept, 1958 - No. 4, May, 1959
Candor Publ. Co.

	Good	Fine	Mint
1-Bill Everett-c	2.00	6.00	12.00
2-4	1.50	4.00	8.00

ZAZA, THE MYSTIC (Formerly Charlie Chan; This Magazine Is Haunted V2No.12 on)
April, 1956 - No. 11, Sept, 1956
Charlton Comics

	Good	Fine	Mint
10,11	2.00	5.00	10.00

ZEGRA JUNGLE EMPRESS (Formerly Tegra) (My Love Life No. 6 on)
No. 2, Oct, 1948 - No. 5, April, 1949
Fox Features Syndicate

	Good	Fine	Mint
2	14.00	40.00	60.00
3-5	10.00	30.00	48.00

ZIGGY PIG AND SILLY SEAL
Fall, 1944 - No. 6, Fall, 1946
Timely Comics (CmPL)

	Good	Fine	Mint
1-Vs. the Japs	4.00	12.00	24.00
2-5	2.00	6.00	12.00
6-Infinity-c	3.00	9.00	18.00
I.W. Reprint No. 1('58)-Reprints/Krazy Komics	.50	1.50	3.00
I.W. Reprint No. 2,7,8	.25	.75	1.50

ZIP COMICS
Feb, 1940 - No. 47, Summer, 1944
MLJ Magazines

	Good	Fine	Mint
1-Origin Kalthar the Giant Man, The Scarlet Avenger, & Steel Sterling; Mr. Satan, Nevada Jones & Zambini, the Miracle Man, War Eagle, Captain Valor begins	60.00	160.00	325.00
2	30.00	80.00	165.00
3	20.00	60.00	125.00
4,5	17.00	50.00	100.00
6-9: 8,9-Bondage-c. 9-Last Kalthar & Mr. Satan	15.00	45.00	90.00
10-Inferno, the Flame Breather begins, ends No. 13	14.00	40.00	80.00
11,12: 11-Inferno without costume	11.00	32.00	64.00
13-19: 17-Last Scarlet Avenger. 18-Wilbur begins	11.00	32.00	64.00
20-Origin Black Jack	15.00	45.00	90.00
21-26: 25-Last Nevada Jones. 26-Black Witch begins; last Captain Valor	11.00	32.00	65.00
27-Intro. Web	15.00	45.00	90.00
28-Origin Web	15.00	45.00	90.00
29,30	8.50	25.00	50.00
31-38: 33,34-Bondage-c. 34-1st Applejack app. 35-Last Zambini, Black Jack. 38-Last Web issue	6.50	19.00	38.00
39-Origin Red Rube	6.50	19.00	38.00
40-47: 45-Wilbur ends	4.00	12.00	24.00

NOTE: ***Meskin** Captain Valor-2, 3, 6, 7, 10, 12, 13, 15, 16 at least.*

ZIP-JET (Hero)
Feb, 1953 - No. 2, Apr-May, 1953
St. John Publishing Co.

	Good	Fine	Mint
1,2-Rocketman-r/Punch Comics	8.00	24.00	48.00

ZIPPY THE CHIMP (CBS TV Presents . . .)
No. 50, March, 1957 - No. 51, Aug, 1957
Pines (Literary Ent.)

	Good	Fine	Mint
50,51	.85	2.50	5.00

ZODY, THE MOD ROB
July, 1970
Gold Key

	Good	Fine	Mint
1	.35	1.00	2.00

ZOO ANIMALS
No. 8, 1954 (36 pages) (15 cents)
Star Publications

	Good	Fine	Mint
8-(B&W for coloring)	1.20	3.50	7.00

ZOO FUNNIES (Tim McCoy No. 16 on)
1945 - No. 15, 1947
Charlton Comics/Children Comics Publ.

Zoo Funnies #8(2nd), © CC

Zoot #15, © FOX

Zorro #1, © GK

ZOO FUNNIES (continued)

	Good	Fine	Mint
101(No.1) (1945)	1.20	3.50	7.00
2(9/45)-5	.70	2.00	4.00
6-15: 8-Diana the Huntress app.	.70	2.00	4.00

ZOO FUNNIES (Also see Nyoka)
July, 1953 - No. 13, Sept.?, 1955
Capitol Stories/Charlton Comics

1	1.50	4.00	8.00
2-7	.85	2.50	5.00
8-13-Nyoka app.	2.50	7.00	14.00

ZOO PARADE (See 4-Color No. 662)

ZOOM COMICS
December, 1945 (One Shot)
Carlton Publishing Co.

nn-Dr. Mercy, Satanas, from Red Band Comics; Capt. Milksop origin retold	8.00	24.00	48.00

ZOOT (Rulah No. 17 on)
1946 - No. 16, July, 1948 (Two No. 13's & 14's)
Fox Features Syndicate

	Good	Fine	Mint
nn-Funny animal only	3.50	10.00	16.00
2-The Jaguar app.	5.50	16.00	28.00
3(Fall,'46)-6-Funny animals & teen-age	3.00	8.00	14.00
7-Rulah, Jungle Goddess begins(6/47); origin	17.00	50.00	90.00
8-10	14.00	40.00	70.00
11-Kamen bondage-c	17.00	50.00	90.00
12	10.00	30.00	50.00
13(2/48), 14(3/48)	10.00	30.00	50.00
13(4/48), 14(5/48)	10.00	30.00	50.00
15,16	10.00	30.00	50.00

NOTE: ***Kamen** c-10-12; art-many issues.*

ZORRO (Walt Disney with No. 882)
May, 1949 - No. 15, Sept-Nov, 1961
Dell Publishing Co.

4-Color 228	6.00	18.00	36.00
4-Color 425,497	3.50	10.00	20.00
4-Color 538-Kinstler-a	4.00	12.00	24.00
4-Color 574,617,732	3.50	10.00	20.00
4-Color 882,920,933,960,976-Toth-a in all	3.00	8.00	16.00
4-Color 1003,1037('59)	2.00	5.00	10.00
8(12-2/60)	1.20	3.50	7.00
9,12-Toth-a	2.00	5.00	10.00
10,11,13-15	1.00	3.00	6.00

ZORRO (Walt Disney)
Oct, 1965 - No. 9, March, 1968
Gold Key

1-Toth-a	1.20	3.50	7.00
2,5,7,8-Toth-a	.85	2.50	5.00
3,4,6,9	.70	2.00	4.00

NOTE: *No. 1-9: reprints from Zorro 4-Color comics.*

Z-2 COMICS (Secret Agent. . .) (See Holyoke One-Shot No. 7)

ZULU (See Movie Classics)

Robert Crestohl

4732 Circle Rd., Montreal, Canada.

(514) 481-2830

Marvel Comics for Sale

Order with confidence; 50-100 copies of each issue available. All comics guaranteed to be in fine or better condition. Add $2.00 for postage & insurance on each order.

Discounts: 5% over $50, 10% over $100.

With alternates: 10% over $50, 15% over $100.

AVENGERS

Issues	Price
23-31	$4.00
32-56, 61-92	3.50
101-118	3.00
119-145	2.50
146-171, 181-191	2.00
172-180, 192-199	1.50
201 up	1.00

CAPTAIN AMERICA

Issues	Price
105-108	$3.00
114-130	2.50
131-160	2.00
161-171, 176-200	1.50
201-246, 256 up	1.00

CONAN

Issues	Price
12-15	$12.00
16-24	10.00
25-37	7.50
26-30	5.00
31-36, 38-40	4.00
41-57, 100	3.00
58-81, 115, 116	2.00
82-99	1.50
101-114, 117 up	1.00

DAREDEVIL

Issues	Price
11-15, 18	$6.00
19-24	5.00
25-40, 81	3.00
41-49, 54-80	2.50
82-99, 101-103	2.00
104-137, 139-157	1.50

DEFENDERS

Issues	Price
6-11	$4.50
12-18	2.50
19-28	2.00
29-55	1.50
56-99, 101 up	1.00

FANTASTIC FOUR

Issues	Price
31-40	$12.00
41-47	8.00
51-60, 66, 67	6.00
61-65, 72-77	5.00
68-71, 78-80	4.00
81-99	3.00

FANTASTIC FOUR (con't)

Issues	Price
101-120	$2.50
124-160, 209-221	2.00
161-199	1.50
201-208, 222-231	1.00

HULK

Issues	Price
104-112	$3.50
113-130, 200	2.50
131-170	2.00
171-175, 183-199	1.50
201 up	1.00

IRON MAN

Issues	Price
6-10	$6.00
11-17	4.00
18-28	3.00
29-46, 48-52	2.50
57-71	2.00
72-99, 101-114	1.50
129 up	1.00

MARVEL TEAM-UP

Issues	Price
2, 3, 4	$7.50
5, 6, 7, 8	6.00
9, 10, 11	5.00
12-22	3.00
23-33	2.50
34-45, 59-70	2.00
46-52, 80-99	1.50
101 up	1.00

SILVER SURFER

Issues	Price
8-14	$10.00
15-18	7.50

SPIDERMAN

Issues	Price
22-25	$15.00
26-30	12.50
31-35	10.00
36-40	8.00
41-50	6.00
51-60	5.00
61-73	4.00
74-95, 99	3.00
103-118	2.50
124-149	2.00
150-160, 163-188	1.50
191-199, 204 up	1.00

STRANGE TALES (old)

Issues	Price
136-168	$3.00

TALES OF SUSPENSE

Issues	Price
59-63	$5.00
64, 65, 66, 99	4.00
67-74	3.50
75-82	3.00
83-98	2.50

TALES TO ASTONISH

Issues	Price
54-58	$6.00
60-64	5.00
65, 66, 67	4.00
68-74	3.50
75-82	3.00
83-92, 94-99	2.50

THOR

Issues	Price
101-112	$10.00
113-118, 193	7.50
119-124, 180, 181	6.00
125-130, 165, 166	4.50
131-140, 200	3.50
141-152	3.00
153-164, 167-179	2.50
182-192, 194-199	2.00
201-246	1.50
247-299, 301 up	1.00

X-MEN (#95 up all mint)

Issues	Price
16-20, 49-51	$8.00
21-27, 54, 55	6.00
29-35, 67-72	5.00
36-48, 52	4.00
53, 56-66	10.00
73-93	3.00
95, 100	35.00
96, 97, 98, 101	25.00
99, 108	20.00
102-107	17.50
109, 110, 111	15.00
112, 113	12.50
114-121, 130	10.00
122-125, 137	7.50
126-129	6.00
131-136, 138	5.00
139, 140, 150	4.00
141-149, 151 up	3.00

Prices expire: April 30, 1983.

I have 20-50 copies of all the earlier issues not listed here. If you want my complete price list, send 25¢.

90%-95% of all books dated after 1975 are nm/mint copies.

SCENE
5075 Stevens Creek Blvd.
Santa Clara, Calif., 95051
authorized appraisals
old & new comics
bought & sold
open 7 days
408-243-5280
The Hulk, the Wasp, Hawkeye, Captain America, Ms. Marvel, Iron Man
Marvel Comics Group ©1981

Master Comics No. 22, 1942. Captain Marvel Jr. x-over in Bulletman. © Faw

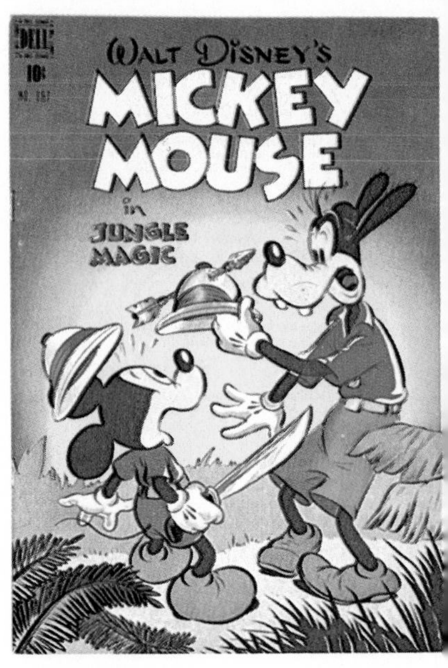

Mickey Mouse Four Color No. 181, 1948. © WDP

Mister Mystery No. 6, 1952. © Argyle Mag.

More Fun Comics No. 65, 1941. © DC

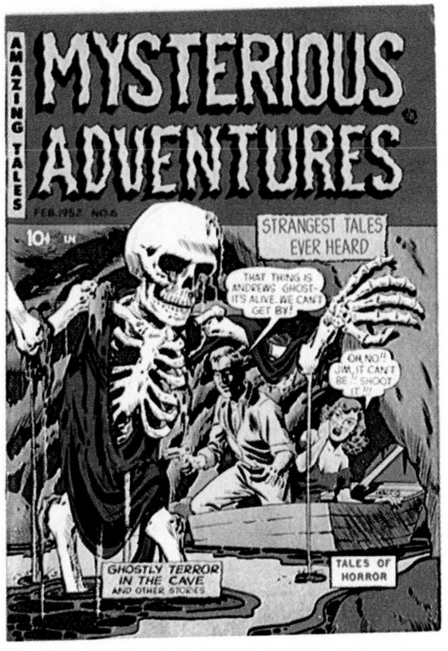

Mysterious Adventures No. 6, 1952. © Story Comics

Mystery Comics No. 3, 1944. Cover by Alex Schomburg. © Best Syndicated Feat.

National Comics No. 18, 1941. Cover by Lou Fine. © Qua

Our Flag Comics No. 1, 1941. © Ace

Our Gang Comics No. 21, 1946. Walt Kelly cover & stories. © Loew's Inc.

Pep Comics No. 16, 1941. © AP

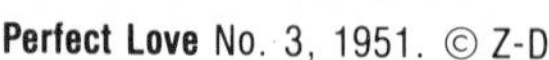

Perfect Love No. 3, 1951. © Z-D

Planet Comics No. 57, 1948. © FH

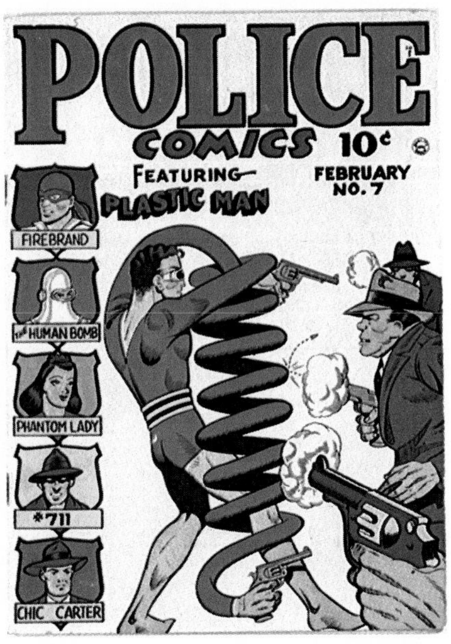

Police Comics No. 7, 1942. Jack Cole cover and story. © Qua

Prize Comics No. 23, 1942. © Prize

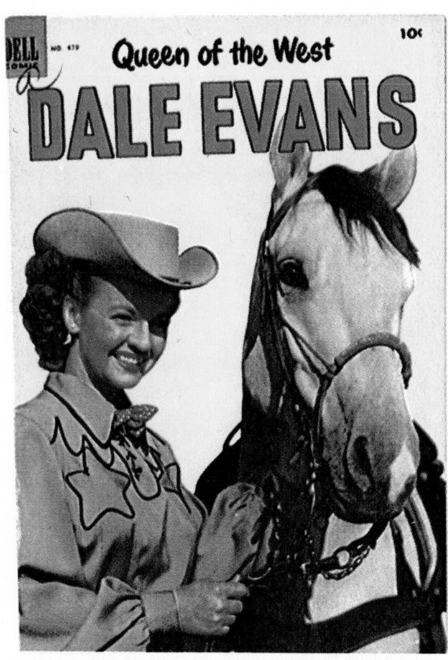

Queen of the West Dale Evans Four Color No. 479, 1953. © Dale Evans

Racket Squad In Action No. 5, 1953. © CC

Raggedy Ann & Andy No. 6, 1946. © Johnny Gruelle Co.

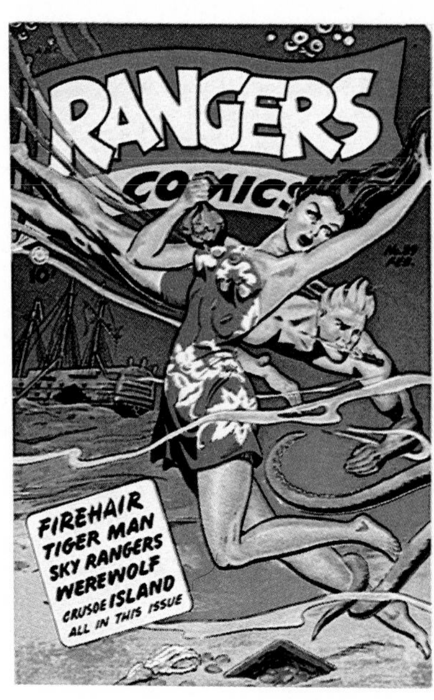

Rangers Comics No. 39, 1948. © FH

Red Ryder Comics No. 38, 1946. © Stephen Slesinger

Romantic Marriage No. 11, 1952. © Z-D

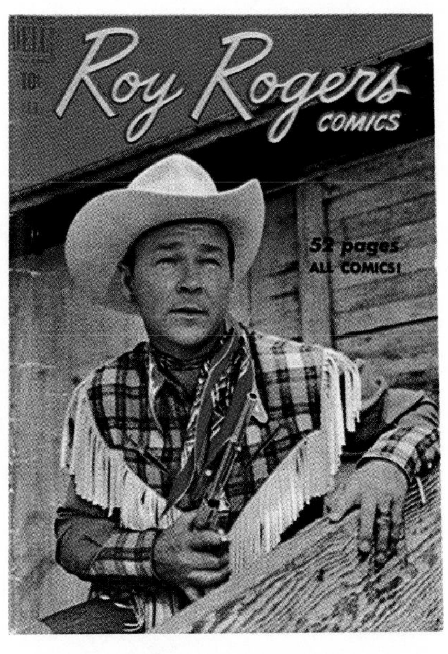

Roy Rogers No. 26, 1950. © Roy Rogers

Sensation Comics No. 28, 1944. © DC

Seven Seas Comics No. 6, 1947. Matt Baker cover art. © Leader Ent.

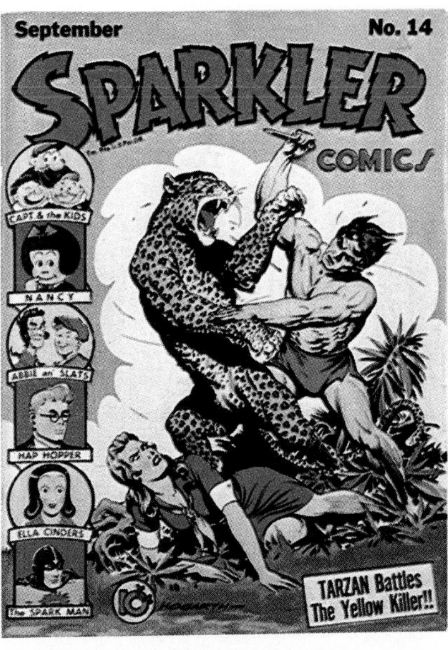

Sparkler Comics No. 14, 1942. © UFS

Speed Comics No. 13, 1941. Intro. Captain Freedom. © Harv

Star Spangled Comics No. 9, 1942. Simon & Kirby cover art. © DC

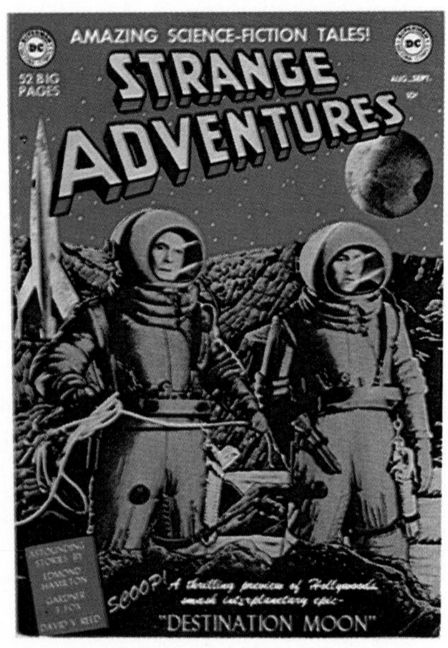

Strange Adventures No. 1, 1950. © DC

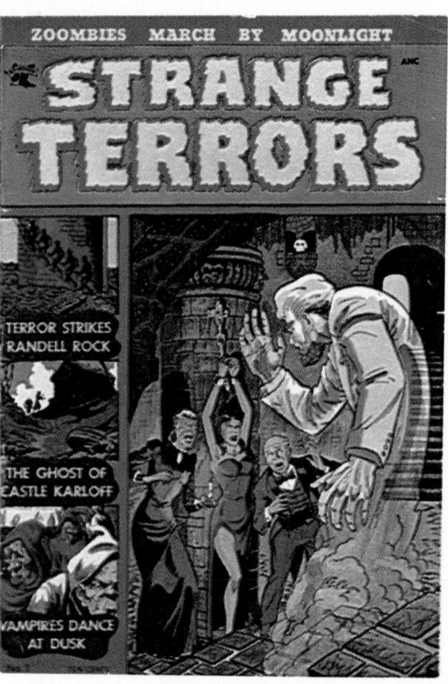

Strange Terrors No. 1, 1952. © Stj

Super Duck No. 1, 1944. © MLJ

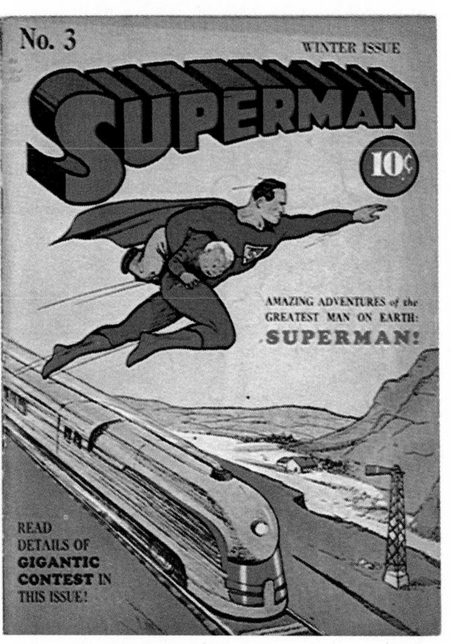

Superman No. 3, 1940. © DC

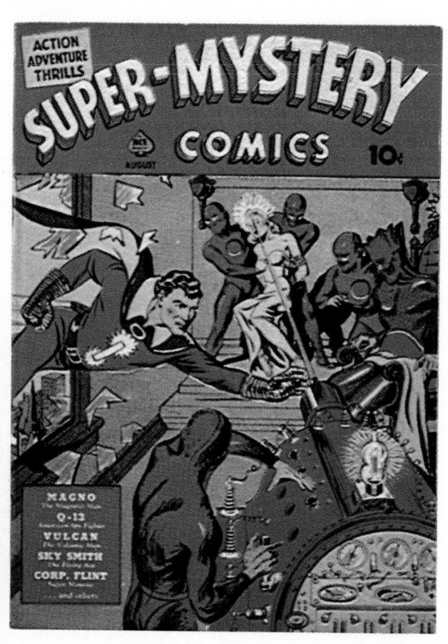

Super-Mystery Comics No. 2, 1940. © Ace

Tarzan No. 27, 1951. © ERB

Tessie The Typist No. 9, 1947. © MCG

This Magazine is Haunted No. 16, 1954; Ditko cover art. © CC

3-D Tales from the Crypt of Terror No. 2, 1954. © WMG

Top Secrets No. 7, 1949. Used in **SOTI**. © S&S

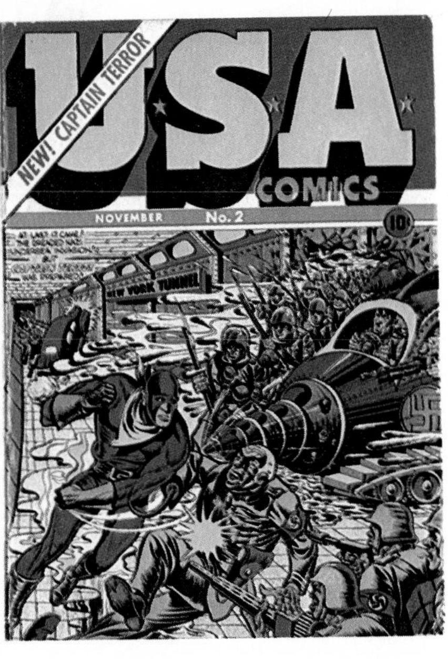

USA Comics No. 2, 1941. © MCG

Vooda No. 22, 1955. © Four Star

Walt Disney's Comics & Stories No. 19, 1942. © WDP

Weird Comics No. 1, 1940. Cover by Lou Fine. © Fox

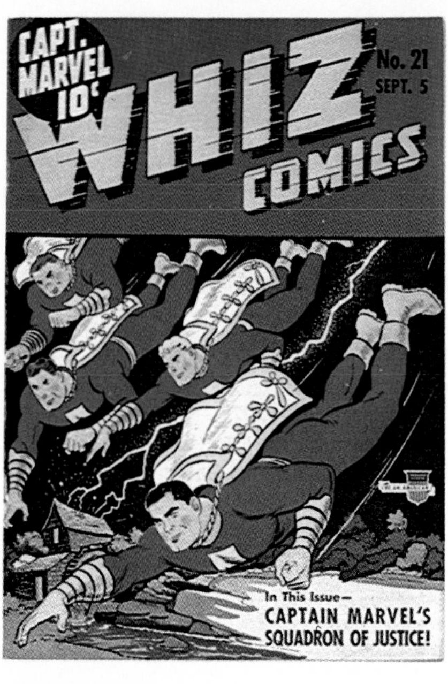

Whiz Comics No. 21, 1941. Origin and 1st app. of Lt. Marvels. © Faw

The Witness No. 1, 1948(Rare). © MCG

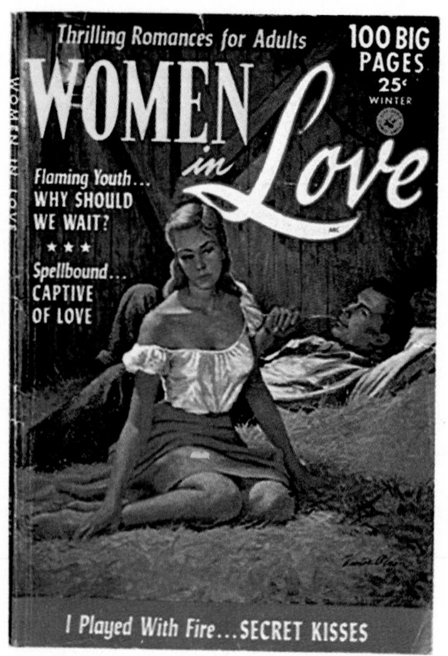

Women In Love, 1952. © Z-D

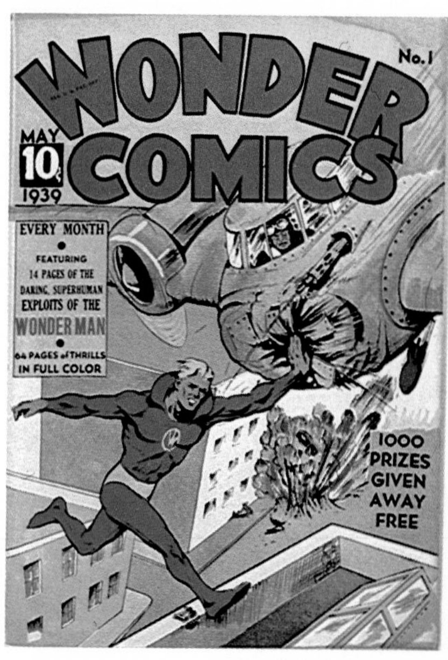

Wonder Comics No. 1, 1939. Cover by Will Eisner. © Fox

VISIT THE MILLION YEAR PICNIC!

We've grown! The Million Year Picnic doubled its retail floor space this year—our customers now enjoy twice the display area to browse through New England's largest collection of comic books! Our total stock has broken the MILLION mark, offering thousands of Golden Age and Silver Age comics—ECs, and 50s esoterica—Arkham House books, Pulp magazines from the 30s and 40s, European imports, rare fanzines, undergrounds, hardback children's and cartoon history books.

W're still growing! In the coming year, look for our grand opening of the new Mega-Picnic! We will be taking over an entire new floor at 99 Mt. Auburn St. here in Cambridge. With over 5 times our present space, we will be able to display not only more comics, but offer a whole spectrum of computer games, movie materials, hardback books, and mysteries.

Collectors from the entire New England area and New York are discovering the trek to Cambridge pays big dividends through our continual sales of our huge stock. We are open 7 days a week so you can fit in a visit to the Picnic during a weekend trip. We are the only store in the country to continually discount our entire back issue stock at sale prices up to 50•

While we DO NOT offer a Picnic catalogue; you can take advantage of these customer services:

1] TEN MOST WANTED LIST: send us up to 10 **3x5** [only] index cards with the book title and number clearly printed or type written in the upper left hand corner. Write the condition that you are looking for and the price you will pay for the book. On EACH card, write your name, address, zip and phone number. We will keep your cards on file, and contact you immediately when we have the books.

2] XEROX PRE-TBG LISTS: The Picnic issues numerous ads yearly in TBG for our important incoming collections. For a $5 annual fee we will send you **first class** a xerox of each ad days before it will be published, assuring you an advantage on prime books and sales.

3] When you sell your collection, remember—we make more money on comics than anyone in New England, and so we have more money to buy collections! We're interested in all areas; Golden Age, Silver Age, Arkham House & rare Science Fiction, Paperbacks, Pulps, Movie material, Disneyana, Records, Cartoon & Humor books and Original Artwork.

FROM BOATNER NORTON PRESS

THE OFFICIAL UNDERGROUND & NEWAVE COMIX PRICE GUIDE
Griffith cover; over 300p, 8 in color, artist cross-index
SC $10.95 + .75 post.
HC $14.95 + .75 post.
Signed by Griffith $24.95 + .75 post.

THE R. CRUMB CHECKLIST
[complete listings, color insert]
SC $9.95 + .75 post.
HC $35.95 + .75 post.

THE CARL BARKS T-SHIRT!
$8.95 + .75 post.

We are accepting advance orders on the following books until October 31, 1982

THE ART OF GEORGE PÉREZ! George will do over 40 pages of new art for this blockbuster of a book! Interior color section; TEEN TITANS cover! Due July/Aug Available in both signed and remarqued editions. Remarqued—autographed to buyer and original Pérez ink sketch.

SC $5.95 + .75
HC $12.95 + .75
Signed $19.95 + .75
REM $44.95 + .75

MADMEN & WISEGUYS by BILL GRIFFITH! Nearly 200 pages with over 40 pages of new UNPUBLISHED Griffy! A collection of this master of the absurd's most creative work. Also available in both Signed and Remarqued editions. Due Fall 1982.

SC $7.95 + .95
HC $15.95 + .95
SG $21.95 + .95
REM $44.95 + .95

THE BEST OF AMERICAN SPLENDOR by HARVEY PEKAR! We feel this will be one of the most important graphic books of the 80s. We hope to have a wraparound cover by R. Crumb [UNCONFIRMED!] In signed and remarqued editions. Due Winter 1982.

SC $7.95 + .95
HC $15.95 + .95
SG $19.95 + .95
REM $39.95 + .95

99 Mt. Auburn Street
Cambridge MA 02138 (617) 492-6763

X-MANIA
MARVEL COMICS GROUP
SPECIAL DOUBLE-SIZED 150TH ISSUE!
X-MEN VS. MAGNETO!
MARVEL COMICS GROUP
KING-SIZE ANNUAL!
X-MEN
OU LA LA BADOON!
WIN A Columbia TEN-SPEED FORMULA 10 RACER!
KING-SIZE ANNUAL!
AVENGERS
CAPTAIN AMERICA TOTALLY DEFEATED!
WITNESS: THE INVINCIBLE IRON MAN KNOCKED OUT OF ACTION!
OBSERVE SPIDER-WOMAN'S DARING MIDNIGHT RESCUE!
BEHOLD: THE DEADLY NEW BROTHERHOOD OF EVIL MUTANTS!
PLUS, A SHOCKING MYSTERY GUEST!
ALL THAT AND A CAMEO APPEARANCE BY THE UNCANNY X-MEN!
AVENGERS ANNUAL #10
Claremont/Golden/Gil
MINIMUM ORDER-100 COPIES
• QUANTITY DISCOUNTS •
100-199 ► 50¢
200-399 ► 45¢
400-999 ► 40¢
1000 or more ► 35¢
X-MEN ANNUAL #5
Claremont/
Anderson/McLeod
MINIMUM ORDER-100 COPIES
• 50¢ Each •
X-MEN #150
Claremont/Cockrum/
Rubenstein & Wiacek
MINIMUM ORDER-100 COPIES
• QUANTITY DISCOUNTS •
100-199 ► 50¢
200-399 ► 45¢
400-999 ► 40¢
1000 or more ► 35¢
Design & Production by
RICHARD BRUNING / ABRAXAS STUDIO
1981 MARVEL COMICS GROUP A Division of Cadence Industries Corp. All Rights Reserved
Capital City Distribution, Inc.

THE BOOKSTOP
★ 3407 Falling Springs Rd. ★
Cahokia, Illinois
618-332-8795
★ HOME OF THE 2 FOR 1 PAPERBACK TRADE ★
TUES. thru SAT.
12 till 6 p.m.
Owners
Pat & Nick Kocurek
FEATURING
COMICS ★ UNLIMITED ★
★ Comics
★ Magazines
★ Posters
★ S. F. Paperbacks
★ S. F. Hardbacks
★ Comic Book Bags
★ 25,000 Back Issues Comics
★ Air Conditioned · Free Parking
★ 3 MINUTES FROM ST. LOUIS · FRIENDLY SERVICE
★ We Buy ★ Sell ★ Trade ★

ARIZONA'S
NUMBER ONE SOURCE FOR ALL
YOUR NEW AND BACK ISSUE
COMICS!
• 100,000 INVENTORY
• RESERVATION SERVICE
• FANZINES • SUPPLIES
• MEDIAZINES • BOXES
• PORTFOLIOS • BAGS
FANTASY GAMES-
complete section
Town's largest
selection of
SF PAPERBACKS
#1
The ONE Book Shop
708 S. Forest Avenue • Tempe, Az. 85281
Just 1/2 block north of the ASU Campus
Open MONDAY · SATURDAY 10 · 5:30 • 967-3551

COMIC CITY
INCORPORATING THE MINNESOTA COLLECTIVE
?
?
POW
!!
BLAM
HEH-HEH-HEH! SEND TWO FIRST-CLASS STAMPS FOR OUR NEW MARVEL-DC PRICE LIST...
... OR ONE DOLLAR FOR OUR UP-TO-DATE GIANT CATALOG FEATURING (HEH-HEH-HEH!) THOUSANDS OF COMICS AND RELATED ITEMS FROM THE GOLDEN AGE TO THE PRESENT! AND YOUR $ IS REFUNDABLE WITH YOUR FIRST ORDER!
... YOUR WANT LIST AND A FIRST-CLASS STAMP WILL GET YOU A SPEEDY REPLY!!
COMIC CITY

30% TO 50% DISCOUNTS FROM OVERSTREET
ALWAYS!
All kinds of comics, from Golden Age to recent. We come out every 5 to 6 weeks with a new catalog crammed with 8 to 12 pages of goodies. Send .50 (NO Canadian coin) for our latest, and if you order you get future catalogs free!
We BUY comics @ 25% to 50% of OVERSTREET. BEFORE shipping anything to us, ask for full details and shipping instructions.
BEA
P. O. Box 811
Temple City, CA 91780

W S A PROGRAM & AFFILIATES

[Fandom's Protective Organization]

WSA PROGRAM ... PLEDGE to the CODE OF ETHICS; Standardizing the methods and procedures for doing business by mail order.

WRB DIVISION ... FRAUD BUREAU dedicated to the prosecution of ALL known mail-fraud in Fandom.

ALL MEMBERS OF **WSA** [and its affiliates] DISPLAY THEIR "WSA" and assigned number. By the display of this Membership Logo, YOU KNOW this Collector, Dealer or Fan has voluntarily subscribed to the CODE OF ETHICS. In turn, the Bureau becomes the **GUARANTOR** as to the honesty, character and integrity of such member. As a result, you can do business with any WSA member with confidence and assurance in buying, selling or trading merchandise. This PLEDGE is available to all eligible fans.

CENTRAL
NATIONAL WSA BUREAU
NO. 000

ACTIVITIES OF THE BUREAU ... Receive and Record Complaints. Investigate, analyze, evaluate, and report on Complaints. Tabulate and maintain permanent files on fraudulent activities. Initiate prosecutive action in fraud cases for and in your behalf. To publish reports to the membership from time to time and otherwise perform such services as necessary and/or requested by members of WSA . SPECIAL SERVICES available consist of National Warning Alert Advisory's ... Monitoring of Transaction(s), etc. Providing of Membership Certificate (suitable for framing), I. D. Wallet Card (excellent for use at Cons), Identification by phone when out of town -- or under emergency situation. ALL SERVICES are provided at a Nominal Cost -- and YOU pay ONLY for those services YOU use.

NOTICE: *The complaint services of the WRB are available to ALL members of Fandom, since WSA membership is NOT a requirement to receiving the Bureau's assistance pursuant to the resolution of unconcluded mail-order transactions. Our 12 YEAR record of service, to those in need of such services, is unsurpassed.*

YOU ARE CORDIALLY INVITED TO BECOME A MEMBER OF WSA TODAY!
Send Large SASE (#10) and 10¢ for handling to receive forms and other material.

WSA

MICHAEL C. WAHL, DIRECTOR
WSA PROGRAM & AFFILIATES
5250 CLEAR LAKE ROAD
GRASS LAKE, MI 49240
(313) 475-2116

WSA

"BEST PRICES FOR BUYING & SELLING" "GENERAL LEE FUN"

For Atlanta's Largest Selection Visit . . .

Now Two Locations To Serve You!

The Paper Chase

- **COMICS** - Golden Age to Recent.
- **MOVIE POSTERS** - large selection of titles to select from.
- **SPORTS COLLECTABLES** - Cards, magazines & supplies.
- **USED BOOKS & MAGAZINES** - Playboy, National Geographic, Life, etc.

Store #1
112 E. Ponce de Leon Ave.
Decatur, Georgia 30030
404/378-6654

Store #2
4763 Buford Hwy., Suite 102
Chamblee, Georgia 30341
404/458-6325

PLAYBOY

COLLECTORS PRICE GUIDE

5th *EDITION* – Over 300 pages

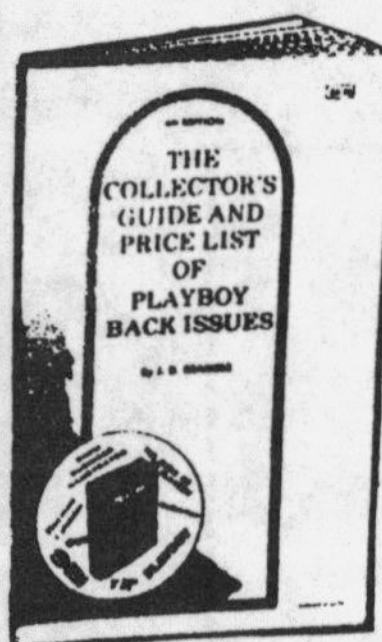

Do You Know...

- The current price of the 1st issue?
- Which issues in the '60s are worth $30, $40, or $50?
- The price of each issue of all Playboy publications?
- How to determine collector grades?

Where to sell your collection; how to protect them for greatest profit?

Send $10.95 plus $1.65 postage, to

BUDGET ENTERPRISES
P.O. Box 592–C, Snowdon Station
Montreal, Quebec, Canada H3X 3T7

– – – – – – – – – –

DEALERS, write for quantity discounts

ALPHA **OMEGA**

2373 E. Shaw • At Maple •• Fresno, CA 93710

BUY • SELL • TRADE

New and Old Comics—Gum Cards—D & D
Sci-Fi & Adult Mags—Video Games
Collector's Accessories
Discount Club—Mail Order

OPEN EVERY DAY **PH: (209) 221-6500** **WSA 1071**

$ $ $ $ $ $ $ $ $ $ $ $ $ $ $

COLLECTABLE INVESTMENTS UNLIMITED

Comics - Original Art - Toys - Memorabilia
- First Edition Books and Magazines -
- Old and Rare Stamps and Coins -
- Specializing in Comic Paintings and Art -

BUY * SELL * TRADE
Consignment and Search Service

Write: Collectable Investments Unlimited
P. O. Box 5064
Pasadena, CA 91107

$ $ $ $ $ $ $ $ $ $ $ $ $ $ $

CHARLESTON SOUTH CAROLINA

BOOK EXCHANGE

All New Comics 10% Off

— WE BUY, SELL & TRADE —

COMICS • SCIENCE FICTION

FANTASY • COLLECTING SUPPLIES

25,000 Science Fiction Paperbacks

Thousands & Thousands of

COMICS

BOOK EXCHANGE
Berkley Sq. Shopping Ctr
Goose Creek, SC 29445
Phone (803) 797-5500

BOOK EXCHANGE
1219 Savannah Hwy.
Charleston, SC 29407
Phone (803) 556-5051

BOOK EXCHANGE
4400 Dorchester Rd.
Brentwood Shopping Ctr.
Charleston, SC 29405
Phone (803) 554-7938

BOOK EXCHANGE
Moultrie Shopping Center
628 Coleman Blvd.
Mt. Pleasant, SC 29464
Phone (803) 884-9479

BOOK EXCHANGE
9 Yeaman's Hall Plaza
Hanahan, North Charleston, SC 29406
Phone (803) 747-4208

SCOTT ROSENBERG

8383 WILSHIRE BLVD.
SUITE 1036
BEVERLY HILLS, CALIF. 90210
(213) 275-1473

B U Y I N G **** B U Y I N G

TOP PRICES PAID
1940-1960 VF-MINT ONLY

DC-NATIONAL DELL-DISNEY EC COMICS FAWCETT

ARCHIE LEV GLEASON & ST. JOHN PUBLISHING CO.

SEND LISTS FOR OUR PRICES

1982 CATALOG

New 24 Page Catalog Now FREE

A COMPLETE AND
COMPREHENSIVE LISTING OF:
MARVEL • E.C.
GOLDEN & SILVER AGE D.C.
DISNEY (BARKS ART)
MISC. GOLDEN AGE

WANTLISTS
Wantlists welcomed, and given close attention.

BUYING
We are also interested in buying comics of any type, particularly large collections. Highest prices paid.

Books offered in all conditions at competitive prices. Top condition is our specialty.

COMICS UNLIMITED Box 3272
Gaithersburg, Md. 20878

WD

WALLY'S BOOK & COMIC EXCHANGE
PROPRIETORS
CARL WALUCONIS
MARY ERLING
128 PARK LANE
KIRKLAND WA 98033
206 822-7333
* OVER ONE HALF MILLION COMICS AND BOOKS
* COMPLETE MARVEL AND DC COLLECTIONS
* EVERYTHING IN COMICS FROM GOLDEN AGE TO PRESENT
* WE PAY TOP PRICES FOR COLLECTIONS
* PAPERBACKS PRICED FROM 10¢ TO 1 DOLLAR
ACROSS THE LAKE FROM SEATTLE
TAKE KIRKLAND EXITS FROM HIGHWAYS 405 AND 520 HEAD DOWNTOWN TOWARD THE WATER
SPEARS

T h e B e s t o f B o t h W o r l d s

Connecticut's Oldest Comic Book Store

New Comics, Fanzines, Sci-Fi Mags, and Collectible Paperbacks.

Comic Inventory Cards, and other Quality Supplies.

One of Connecticut's Longest Mail Order Dealers

SCIENCE FICTION, COMICS FOR COLLECTORS • BUY - SELL - TRADE
HIGHEST BUYING PRICES - SEND LIST OR PARCEL

THE BOOKIE

LARGEST SELECTION SF & COMICS FOR COLLECTORS IN THE AREA

STORE AT:
116 BURNSIDE AVE.
EAST HARTFORD, CONN.
PHONE 289-1208

STORE OPEN AFTERNOONS WEDNESDAY THRU SUNDAY

PLASTIC BAGS • MYLAR SNUGS • ORIGINAL ART
COMIC STORAGE BOXES

COMIC BOOKS

BOUGHT • SOLD • APPRAISED • TRADED

JEFF RUDOLPH
(203) 569-0289

130 NUTMEG LANE - #208
E. HARTFORD, CT 06118

JOHN'S COMIC CLOSET

4610 East 10th Street
Indianapolis, Indiana 46201
(317) 357-6611

NEW COMICS WEEKS EARLY

- ☐ COMICS OLD & RARE
- ☐ PORTFOLIOS
- ☐ PAPERBACKS
- ☐ COLLECTOR SUPPLIES
- ☐ GUM CARDS — SPORTS AND NON-SPORTS

We honor Visa & Mastercard

HOURS
Thur & Fri — 5:30 - 8:00
Sat — 10:00 - 5:30
Sun — 11:00 - 2:00

WE ALSO BUY
Send list of what you have to sell

WANT LIST
accepted with SASE

COLLECTOR'S FEVER
1476 California St., No. 228
San Francisco, CA 94109
415 776 3268

TRADE - SELL - BUY - IN THAT ORDER !

Just about every pulp since 1919, Toys, Games, Comics, - Big New Comics list includes No. 1 SHEENA, JUNGLE, RULAH, PLANET, CRIME DOES NOT PAY, CRIMES BY WOMEN, AIRBOY, LADY LUCK, BRENDA STARR, THE SAINT, RACKET SQUAD, THRILLING, BLUE BEETLE, WONDER, CLAIRE VOYANT, MANHUNT, GANGSTERS AND GUNMOLLS, FAMOUS CRIMES, CRIME SMASHERS, HOUSE OF MYSTERY, MARVEL/DC List - MUCH MORE!

BELOW GUIDE PRICES * ACCURATE GRADING
Please send SASE(large size envelope)for COMPLETE List.

CALIFORNIA COMICS

- Thousands Of New And Rare Comics In Stock
- Magazines And Collector Items
- Search Service Available At Very Low Cost
- Comic Boxes Available
- Comic Bags And Mylars In Stock

For Free List Send S.A.S.E. to:

California Comics
1024 N. Citrus Avenue
Covina, California 91722

Store Hours: Mon. thru Sat. 1-7 (Closed Sun.)

JUST KIDS NOSTALGIA

251 MAIN STREET
HUNTINGTON, N.Y. 11743
(516) 423-8449

BEATLES HOPPY — TOM MIX BUCK ROGERS — POPEYE HOWDY

Non-Sports Cards • Premiums • Toys

Superman, Batman, Wonder Woman, Starfire & Cyborg are trademarks of DC Comics Inc. and are used with permission. ©1981 DC Comics Inc. Spider-Man, Conan, Howard the Duck, Wolverine & The Hulk are ©1982 by Marvel Comics Group - Div. of Cadence Industries. ©1981 Lucasfilm Ltd. Steve Gerber Logotype Inspiration-William Gaines. ©1981 Robert L. Hammer.

BUY - SELL - TRADE
Marvel Comics

For catalog
Send 50 cents to :

Larry Pongratz
651 Gertrude Avenue
Nekoosa Wisconsin 54457

SCIENCE FICTION, FANTASY & COMIC COLLECTIBLES CATALOG

PROMOTIONAL ITEMS
T-SHIRTS
JEWELRY
GUM CARDS
BLUEPRINTS
BUTTONS
PATCHES
BOOKS
MAGAZINES
POSTERS
MODELS

MUCH MUCH MORE

Send 25¢ for our new 32 page illustrated catalog..............

Intergalactic Trading Co., Inc.
P.O. Box 1516
Longwood, FL. 32750

PARK CITY MARKET

LANCASTER, PA

Hours:
Thursday & Friday
2 P.M.-9 P.M.
Saturday
10 A.M.-5 P.M.

Phone For Appointment 717/626/4660

SORRY - NO MAIL ORDERS

WANTED
OVERSTREET COMIC GUIDES 1970-75
Incl. description and price in letter

CORRESPONDENCE ADDRESS
P.O. BOX 2, LANC., PA 17603

COMIC CARNIVAL

The friendliest Comic store in the Midwest, where you'll be in fun company.

FEATURING:

- OLD, NEW AND MIDDLE-AGE COMIC BOOKS
- SCIENCE FICTION AND FANTASY
- ORIGINAL COMIC ART, DON POST MASKS
- POSTERS, PORTFOLIOS & COLLECTORS SUPPLIES

COME SEE US THURSDAY & FRIDAY 12 NOON TO 7, SATURDAY 10 A.M. - 5, SUNDAY 12 NOON - 4.

317 253-8882
6265 N. Carrollton Ave. Indpls., IN 46220

So drop in and join a happy crowd-our customers!

4TH GREAT YEAR!!!

BARBARIANS COMIC SHOP
13755 W. MONTGOMERY
HOUSTON, TEXAS 77086
(713) 999-7240
(LOCATED INSIDE PRINT-A-SHIRT)

WHOLESALE ☆☆ RETAIL
BUY ☆ SELL ☆ TRADE

WE HAVE A FULL LINE OF NEW & OLD COMICS, POSTERS, GUM CARDS, PORTFOLIOS, ORIGINAL ART, MOVIE POSTERS & RELATED ITEMS DUNGON & DRAGONS, FIGURINES NEW & USED PAPERBACKS & MAGIZINES. WE ALSO HAVE ONE OF THE LARGEST SELECTIONS OF T-SHIRTS, TRANSFERS, & RELATED ITEMS ANYWHERE. OVER 750 TRANSFERS TO CHOSE FROM & OVER 30 DIFFERENT STYLES OF SHIRTS TO CHOOSE FROM. WE CAN ALSO MAKE CUSTOM DESIGNS. (MINIMUM OF 24 TRANSFERS ON CUSTOMS). ALL WANT LISTS ACCEPTED. PLEASE INCLUDE AMOUNT TO BE SENT PER WANT LIST. MASTERCARD, VISA, AND AMERICAN EXPRESS ACCEPTED.

☆☆☆☆☆☆☆☆☆☆☆☆☆☆☆☆☆☆☆☆☆☆☆☆☆☆☆

W MONTGOMERY
1960
N HOUSTON ROSSLYN
I-45
N

·COLLECTORS SUPPLIES ·PORTFOLIOS·
·ORIGINAL ART ·CUSTOM T-SHIRTS·
·GAMING·

THE FANDOM ZONE
1708 W. KENNEDY BLVD.
TAMPA, FL. 33606
(813) 254-1390

BOOKIE PARLOR™
posters: complete Frazetta line
comics: new & back issues
sport & non-sports cards
original comic art
used paperbacks
gift certificates
comic boxes
price guides
index cards
magazines
3 mil bags
calendars
fanzines
BP
BOOKIE
PUSHER
©
BOOKIE PARLOR
2920 Wayne Ave.
Dayton, Ohio 45420
1-513-256-6806
Mon. thru Fri. 11am-8pm
Sat. 11am-6pm
MIKE BENNETT '81

CAPTAIN GREEDY SAYS:
FOR L.A. COMIC RELIEF
THE BIGGEST COMIC BOOK STORE IN THE SOUTH BAY AREA!!!!!!
AIR-SHIPPED COMICS ARRIVE ONE WEEK EARLY!!!

CLASSIFIED ADVERTISING

* CLASSIFIED ADVERTISING cont'd. *

COMIC BOOKS WANTED
HIGHEST PRICES PAID FOR COMIC BOOKS BEFORE 1955 PLUS EARLY MARVEL COMICS. I ALSO COLLECT NEWSPAPER COMICS BEFORE 1965. CONTACT ME BEFORE SELLING. I REGULARLY SEND OUT CATALOGUES OF COMICS AND SUNDAY PAGES I HAVE FOR SALE PLUS I HAVE A LARGE SUPPLY OF CONAN ORIGINAL ARTWORK FOR SALE. I AM THE ONLY CANADIAN DISTRIBUTOR OF MYLAR PLASTIC BAGS, CARTONS, CARDBOARD BACKING, ETC. ALL MANUFACTURED BY ERNIE GERBER. ALL THESE ITEMS ARE LISTED FOR SALE IN MY CATALOGUES WHICH YOU CAN RECEIVE BY SENDING ME YOUR NAME AND ADDRESS. CALVIN SLOBODIAN, BOX 550, RIVERS, MANITOBA, CANADA R0K 1X0.

Comics at 50% O.P.G. (G.A. 75% & up). All other items discounted. Send S.A.S.E. & 25¢ per each list. (R.W.F.O.). Ask for the list you want: Comic Book-BLB List • N.P. Comic Strip List • Paperback List • Old Life-Look-Post-Misc. Magazine List.
G. A. Rauch, 3500 Manila Dr., Westerville, Ohio 43081
I also buy the above.

TOP PRICES PAID for old & new comic books, Baseball & non-sport cards . . . . Joe David, 43 Casale Dr. South, Warren, N. J. 07060

North Plains Comics & Books
Send 50¢ For Selling Lists, 25¢ For Buying Lists
P. O. Box 30162, Amarillo, Texas 79120

FREE NON-SPORTS CARD LIST . . . 1950-1982
Bill Kazlausky, 3816 Harland Ct., Columbus, OH 43207

WOOLEY'S AUCTION GALLERY
Each of our deluxe, photo-illustrated catalogs lists hundreds of comics plus original art, pulps, movie items and more. Bid by mail or phone. Current catalog $2, or 1 year subscription just $5. (includes 6 different catalogs with price key). We will also sell items for you on a consignment basis. Wooley's Auction Gallery, Box 651-G, Methuen, MA 01844 Phone (617) 687-6260.

ORIENTALIST COMICS
1: Hindu mythology (Set of 50 different copies of 36 full colour pages 90$). 2: Samaturo, the Samourai. 3: Heroic fantaisy of Hindu Gods in the javanese Shadow Theatre (2 and 3: 160 pages, english text, clothbound, limited edition, 48$ each). Free postage. Send your check in $ to the publisher: TRISMEGISTE 4 rue Frederic-Sauton 75005 PARIS, FRANCE.

T. CRUMM'S COMICS
EC, DC, MARVEL & ARCHIES, TOO
Send SASE Lists
5038 Bowman Rd.
St. Clair, MI 48079

WANTED BY WORLD'S FOREMOST SUPERMAN COLLECTOR, AUTHORITY AND HISTORIAN
All Toys, Memorabilia, Original Art, Games, Premiums. Anything new or old especially of Historical Significance. Superman Collector since 1959. Write: Gary Coddington—P. O. Box 5064—Pasadena, California 91107.

BUYING—SELLING—TRADING: COMIC BOOKS, ORIGINAL COMIC ART, DISNEY ITEMS, EARLY PAPERBACKS etc. Choice E.C.s, Early Marvels, Pulps, Sci-Fic, ERB Items & MORE for trade/sale. Trade my books for your 1964 or earlier U.S. silver coins. Send stamps (2) for my trade/want lists plus free fanzine. As a collector, I pay more. C. A. Hawk, WSA #327, 2622 Oregon St., Racine, WI 53405

COMIC BOOKS BOUGHT AND SOLD. 55,000 in stock. EVERYTHING priced 25%-40% BELOW guide! Virtually no one in comic fandom sells nice material consistently as low as I do! Send want lists. Also, I am paying 30%-50% for your collection. Phone: 607-648-4025. Rick Semowich, Box 94 RD8, Binghamton, N. Y. 13901

Grabbags: 3 comics (good-mint, 1949-1979) for $3. For details, send SASE to D. K. Crawford, 940 N. Franklin St., Manchester, Iowa 52057.

SUPERMAN ITEMS WANTED! OLD OR NEW TOYS, GAMES, FIGURINES, NOVELTIES, PREMIUMS, ANYTHING!!! DANNY FUCHS, 209-80p 18th AVE., BAYSIDE, NY 11360. SINCE 1962, "AMERICA'S FOREMOST SUPERMAN COLLECTOR" (HI DONNA!)

MINT MARVELS 1976-1979
Still some Conan, Howard, Spiderman, Star Wars @35¢. Send Self-Addressed Stamped Envelope to: M. Flannick, 9514 Kentstone Dr., Bethesda, MD 20817

Boys'-Book enthusiasts and collectors: Read the Mystery & Adventure Series Review for articles on the Hardy Boys, Tom Quest, Ken Holt, Rick Brant, and many others. $5.00 yearly from L. M. Wood, Box 3488, Tucson, Ariz. 85722.

The Pinball Collectors' Quarterly: History. Art. Play. Repairs. Parts. Restoration. Written by collectors. Filled with photos! Free 20 word classified with subscription. Send check or money order for $22 payable to Silverball Amusements or $1 for illustrated brochure to: Pinball, P.O. Box 137, Dept. C, LaGrangeville, New York 12540.

COLLECTORS CLASSIFIED, BOX 347G, HOLBROOK, MASS. 02343. MONTHLY SINCE 1975. ADVERTISE COMICS, CARDS, COINS, RECORDS, BOOKS, PAPERBACKS, ALL COLLECTIBLES. 5 ISSUES—$1.00. (OUTSIDE WSA—$3.00). BONUS AD IN MOST ISSUES. SEND 50 WORD AD WITH SUBSCRIPTION. USA SAMPLE: 25¢. CLASSIFIED ADS: 2¢/WORD.

AUCTION: comics, cards, art, etc. Send $1 to: Mindbridge, 1786 Merritt Blvd., Baltimore, MD 21222

Personal new issue service, back issues, undergrounds, art, books, gaming supplies, soundtracks, custom buttons, imports, gum cards, film material. Discounts. Magic City, 1924 Brookfield Dr., Roanoke, VA 24018

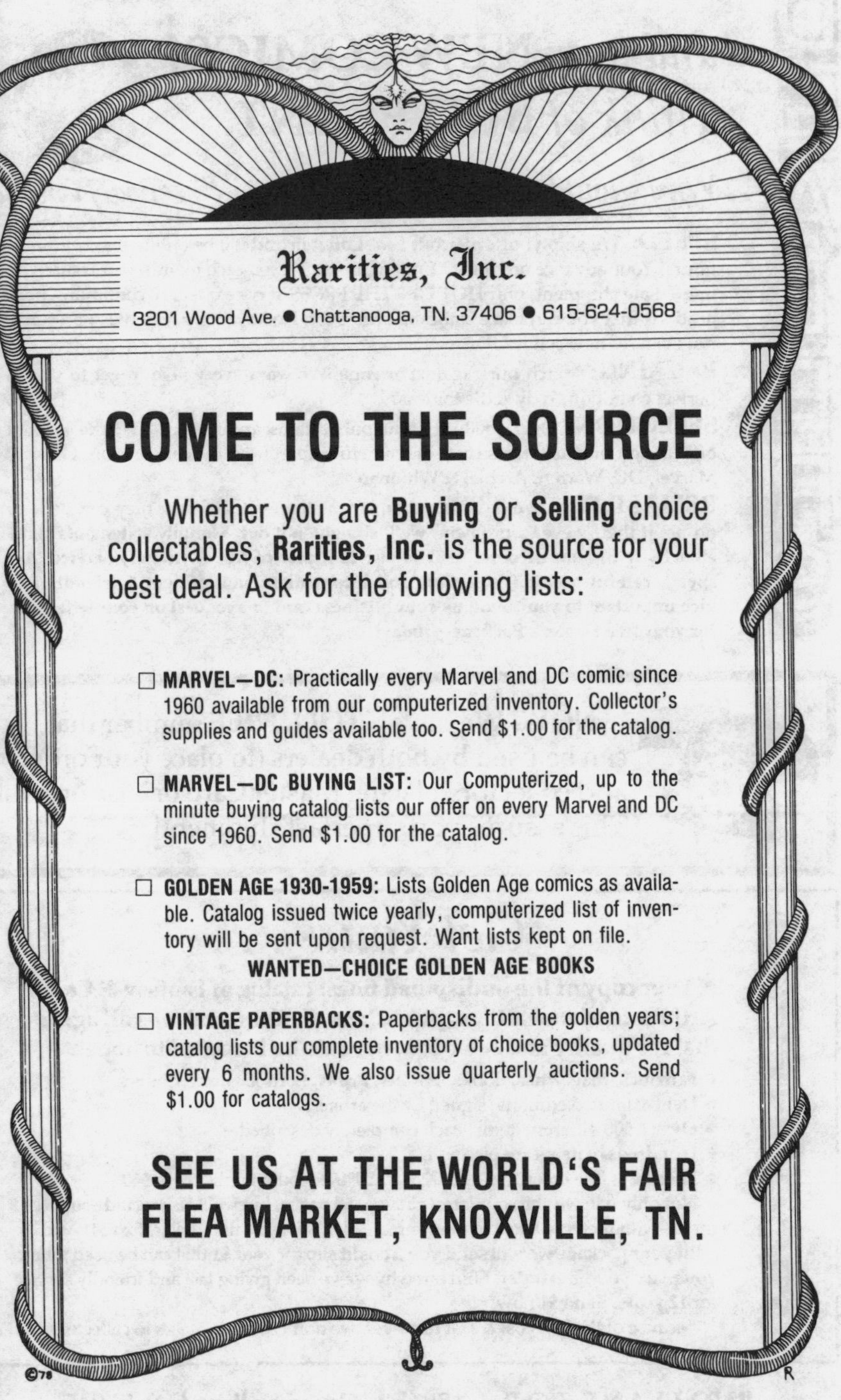
Rarities, Inc.
3201 Wood Ave. • Chattanooga, TN. 37406 • 615-624-0568
COME TO THE SOURCE
Whether you are Buying or Selling choice collectables, Rarities, Inc. is the source for your best deal. Ask for the following lists:
☐ MARVEL—DC: Practically every Marvel and DC comic since 1960 available from our computerized inventory. Collector's supplies and guides available too. Send $1.00 for the catalog.
☐ MARVEL—DC BUYING LIST: Our Computerized, up to the minute buying catalog lists our offer on every Marvel and DC since 1960. Send $1.00 for the catalog.
☐ GOLDEN AGE 1930-1959: Lists Golden Age comics as available. Catalog issued twice yearly, computerized list of inventory will be sent upon request. Want lists kept on file.
WANTED—CHOICE GOLDEN AGE BOOKS
☐ VINTAGE PAPERBACKS: Paperbacks from the golden years; catalog lists our complete inventory of choice books, updated every 6 months. We also issue quarterly auctions. Send $1.00 for catalogs.
SEE US AT THE WORLD'S FAIR
FLEA MARKET, KNOXVILLE, TN.
©78
R